A History of the World

A History of the World

Revised Edition

Marvin Perry

Contributing Area Specialists
Daniel F. Davis
Jeannette G. Harris
Theodore H. Von Laue
Donald Warren, Jr.

Houghton Mifflin Company   ·   Boston

Atlanta · Dallas · Geneva, Illinois · Lawrenceville, New Jersey · Palo Alto · Toronto

THE AUTHORS

Marvin Perry, senior author and general editor, is a member of the history department of the Bernard M. Baruch College of the City University of New York. He has also taught at Walton and Washington Irving High Schools in New York City. Among Dr. Perry's books is *Western Civilization: A Concise History.*

Daniel F. Davis, a specialist in East Asian history, is the Director of Secondary Social Studies for the Stoughton (Mass.) public schools. He was Associate Director of the Service Center for Teachers of Asian Studies, Ohio State University.

Jeannette G. Harris, a specialist in African history, is Educational Specialist for the Department of Education of the Commonwealth of Massachusetts. Dr. Harris chaired the social studies department, Classical High School, Springfield, Massachusetts.

Theodore H. Von Laue, an authority on Russian history, is the Jacob and Francis Hiatt Professor of History at Clark University. Dr. Von Laue is the author of *Sergei Witte and the Industrialization of Russia.*

Donald Warren, Jr., a specialist in Latin American affairs and Brazilian history, is Professor of History at Long Island University in New York.

CONSULTING EDITORS

Dr. Eugene F. Rice, Jr., Department of History, Columbia University.

Larry L. Taylor, Tygarts Valley High School, Mill Creek, West Virginia.

READERS/CLASSROOM CONSULTANTS

Jack A. Gaffney, Program Coordinator, Social Studies, K-12, San Diego Unified School District, San Diego, California.

Shirlie A. Gaskins, North Duplin High School, Calypso, North Carolina.

Claudia Guerrina, Lakewood High School, Lakewood, Colorado.

Bernard Hirshberg, Savannah, Georgia.

Kyle Jeffrey Holcomb, John T. Hoggard High School, Wilmington, North Carolina.

Robert L. Keyes, Renton High School, Renton, Washington.

Christine Naitove, Chapin School, New York, New York.

Mary M. Olinger, Putnam City West High School, Oklahoma City, Oklahoma.

Dr. Allan Scholl, Social Science Specialist, Los Angeles Unified School District, Los Angeles, California.

Connie Williams Sparks, Piedmont High School, Monroe, North Carolina.

Mary Gale Teague, Clyde A. Erwin High School, Asheville, North Carolina.

Karl Valois, St. Joseph High School, Trumbull, Connecticut.

Robert A. Weaver, Snider High School, Fort Wayne, Indiana.

David W. Weinstock, Rio Americano High School, Sacramento, California.

Front cover: Red jasper head of an Egyptian pharaoh, actual height less than two inches, made about 1380 B.C. From the collection of Norbert Schimmel.

Back cover: Sardonyx cameo, possibly of Alexander the Great, from the Hellenistic or early Greco-Roman period.

Frontispiece: Frieze from the Parthenon, Athens, Greece.

Printed in the U.S.A.

ISBN: 0-395-42710-X

BCDEFGHIJ-D-96543210/898

Contents

Features

PICTURE GROUPINGS

Maps, Graphs, Charts, Tables

MAPS

GRAPHS, CHARTS, TABLES

TO THE STUDENT

Why study history?

To learn about the past.

As you study world history you will learn about the challenges and achievements of people throughout the world in different periods of time. The pleasure and satisfaction you will gain from examining this amazing record is the initial reason for studying world history.

To understand the present.

The more knowledge you gain of the past, the more insight you will have into the present. Links between the past and the present are all around you. History will help you understand yourself and the world in which you live.

To appreciate your heritage.

Knowledge of world history will give you an even greater appreciation of your heritage. Among your legacies are democracy from ancient Athens, written

law from Mesopotamia, arabic numerals from India. You will come to value these contributions from the past that are the foundation of your culture and tradition.

To broaden your perspective.

World history introduces you to places and societies all over the world. Knowledge of other peoples and other cultures will give you a better perspective of the times in which you live.

To acquire background for critical thinking.

Problems and their solutions are central to any survey of world history. You will have many opportunities to uncover the roots of present-day issues. Your understanding of the past will enhance your ability to evaluate and deal effectively with concerns of your own times.

How this book helps you learn.

Many features of <u>A History of the World</u> will help you learn and enjoy world history.

Unit and Chapter Introductions

Dramatic illustrations, time lines, overviews, and brief outlines prepare you for the content that follows and help you read with purpose, locate information, and review for exams.

Section Organization

The title of each chapter section, combined with the headings printed in bold type, form an outline of the chapter narrative and help you organize information.

Chapter Check-ups and Reviews

Each chapter section ends with check-up questions to help you review new vocabulary and recall important information. At the end of the chapter, a summary and review exercises help you recall and apply what you have learned.

Enrichment and Skill-building

Each Unit Review provides discussion questions, special projects, and a list of books to expand your knowledge of the topics taught in the unit. Following each Unit Review, there is practice in using a specific study skill that will help you read and understand world history.

Documents and Primary Sources

Throughout the narrative firsthand accounts of the people and events of the past help give you a true sense of history in the making. Excerpts from documents that have shaped the thoughts and actions of people are included. Each Chapter Review contains an exercise that teaches you how to interpret primary sources.

Links to the Past

An understanding of how the past relates to the present is one of the most valuable lessons to be learned from world history. "Linking Past and Present" appears in each chapter and features evidence of the past that is present in our everyday lives.

Paintings, Prints, Photographs

The art in this book has been chosen to broaden your understanding of people, places, and events. Captions provide background information and relate the illustrations to the text narrative.

Maps, Graphs, Charts

Numerous maps appear throughout the book to help you locate places and to increase your knowledge of the relationships between history and geography. Graphs and charts help you interpret historical developments. Special suggestions for using maps are found on pages 417 and 865.

Reference Section

At the back of the book a special reference section provides useful aids to learning—atlas maps, a time chart of world history, a table of nations, a glossary of special terms, and an index.

The Rise of Western Civilization

Long before there were written records, people were making achievements that were very important in the history of the world. Prehistoric men and women learned to fashion tools and weapons, to control fire, and to use spoken language. Gradually they also learned to grow food and tame animals. In some places, people began to live in villages, create art, trade with one another, and learn new crafts and skills. These accomplishments were part of the foundation of present-day civilization.

About 5,000 years ago, civilization began in four great river valleys in Africa and Asia. The earliest civilizations were in Mesopotamia and Egypt. People in those lands built cities, developed organized religion and government, and learned specialized skills and jobs. Most important, in terms of history, they began to write and keep records. Other peoples of the ancient Near East made important new contributions in government, religion, and technology.

Civilization soon appeared in other parts of the Mediterranean world. The people of some Greek city-states developed the ideas of democratic government and political freedom, along with brilliant traditions in the arts, science, and philosophy. The Romans adopted much from Greek culture. With a talent for law and political organization, Rome built a vast empire uniting many peoples of the ancient world.

The achievements of ancient peoples became the basis for Western civilization — the civilization shared by Europeans, Americans, and other peoples they have influenced. The following chapters describe the achievements of prehistoric peoples and the growth of early civilizations in the Near East and Mediterranean world.

The Persians ruled all the Near East by 500 B.C. People from the lands in their empire traveled to Persepolis, bearing gifts for the Persian ruler. The gold plaque in the background comes from Phoenicia. Inscribed on it are letters of the Phoenician alphabet, from which our writing system developed.

In prehistoric times people in Britain formed ceremonial
circles of huge stones, each weighing several tons. The most
awesome is Stonehenge (below). Its double circle of
''standing stones'' — up to thirteen feet tall — looms over the
plain where the center was erected.

The Beginnings of Civilization

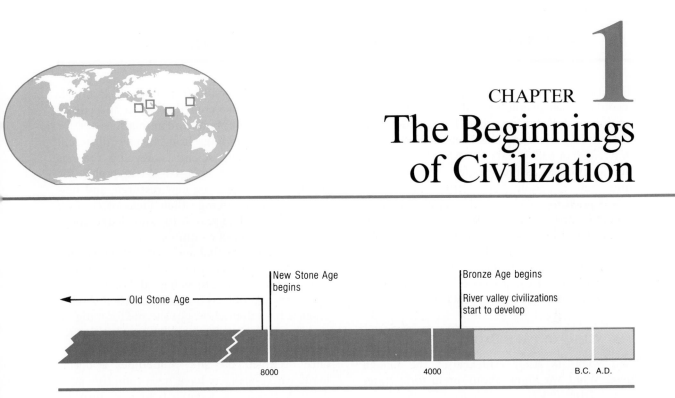

Old Stone Age

New Stone Age begins

Bronze Age begins

River valley civilizations start to develop

8000

4000

B.C. A.D.

Some of the most impressive achievements in human history were made in the period before people kept written records. Because there are no records of names, dates, or events from prehistoric times, scholars and scientists have devoted much time and research to finding unwritten clues and trying to tell the story of the people of those times. They have traced human progress in many areas — making tools, using fire, developing language. They have concluded that people changed from hunting and gathering their food to farming, herding, and building settlements. They have looked for evidence of people's religious beliefs and artistic creativity.

About 5,000 or 6,000 years ago, people in river valleys in Asia and Africa began to build cities, organize governments, and keep written records. The civilizations they built were based on the achievements made during the immense stretch of prehistoric time.

This chapter examines how scientists study prehistory and the conclusions they have drawn about the human achievements that led to the first civilizations.

CHAPTER OUTLINE

1 Achievements Are Made in the Old Stone Age

2 The New Stone Age Brings Change

3 Civilizations Emerge in Asia and Africa

1 Achievements Are Made in the Old Stone Age

The study of history depends greatly on written records, which people over the centuries have set down on clay, stone, wood, bone, and paper. Yet systems of writing and keeping records are only 5,000 or 6,000 years old, while the story of human progress is much older. The period of time before people kept written records is called *prehistory.* Some of the most significant events in history took place during prehistoric times. The exact dates of those achievements are not known, nor are the names of the men and women who made them. Still, they are part of our history. How do we learn about those achievements of the distant past?

THE STUDY OF PREHISTORY

Scientists study evidence of the human past. What we know about prehistoric times comes from unwritten evidence — tools, drawings, pottery, weapons, jewelry, and other objects made by prehistoric people. Because many of the objects left from the earliest part of prehistory are simple stone tools and weapons, the period as a whole has been named the Stone Age.

Scientists in several fields carry on research about the way Stone Age people lived and what they accomplished. Some of the evidence they find is in the form of *artifacts,* objects shaped by human beings. Other evidence is provided by *fossils,* human or animal bones and teeth and other traces left in rocks by plants and animals.

Scientists examine this evidence in different ways. Archeologists often study places where prehistoric people lived, looking for the remains of homes, graves, and towns and examining the artifacts found there. In the related field of anthropology, scientists study artifacts, bones, and other clues and try to determine what people looked like, what they ate, how long they lived, and other characteristics. Geologists analyze fossils and the rocks in which they are found, while chemists and physicists use special methods to estimate the ages of artifacts and other remains from the past. Botanists and zoologists also contribute their specialized knowledge about plants and animals.

With the findings from all these different kinds of research, scientists develop theories about how human beings lived in prehistoric times. New discoveries, new research, and new techniques may change their ideas or confirm their theories. The search for knowledge about the human past is a continuing process.

Archeologists find and study artifacts. One of the richest sources of clues to the prehistoric way of life is an archeological "dig," a site where ancient objects are deeply buried. Archeologists base their choice of the site for a dig on clues such as the shape of the ground surface and stories or traditions that indicate people once occupied the site. Sometimes a dig is made where artifacts have been found by accident. A farmer plowing a field may turn up stone arrowheads, or a bulldozer operator may uncover the foundations of an ancient building.

Even before starting to dig, or excavate, archeologists make a map of the site. The map is blocked off in numbered squares so that workers can later identify exactly where an artifact was found. Next, the soil is carefully removed layer by layer. If a worker comes upon an artifact — perhaps a piece of pottery — he or she uses a small, soft brush to remove the soil without damaging the object. The loosened soil may be sifted through a fine screen so that even tiny objects are not lost.

The artifacts are photographed, labeled, cleaned, and then studied carefully to classify and identify them. Experts spend hours putting together fragments of bone, pottery, or other artifacts. They make drawings to show what an object may have looked like unbroken. Samples of soil, clay, paint, and the like may be sent to chemical laboratories to be analyzed.

Scientific techniques are used to find the age of artifacts. One important question that archeologists try to answer is how old an object is. A major discovery in scientific methods of dating was made in 1948 by an American chemist, Willard Libby. For his technique of carbon-14 dating, Libby was later given the Nobel Prize. The method depends on the fact that all living organisms, plant or animal, contain a certain amount of radioactive carbon, called carbon-14. When the organism dies, the carbon-14 begins to decrease at a fixed rate. By analyzing how much carbon-14 is left in a piece of wood or bone or other once-living material, scientists can tell its approximate age. Other radioactive elements, such as potassium-40, uranium, and thorium, are also used in methods for dating rocks and minerals. Several other methods using chemical and physical analysis have been devised to date the remains of living things.

STONE AGE HUNTERS AND GATHERERS

Many years of study and research have produced a picture of what most scientists believe life was like in prehistoric times. The longest part of this period is called the Old Stone Age, or Paleolithic (pay-lee-oh-LITH-ik) Age.[1]

Old Stone Age people hunt and gather food. The men and women of the Paleolithic Age were *nomads,* people who have no permanent homes but wander from place to place. Small groups, usually twenty to thirty people, traveled together following herds of wild animals, which they killed for meat. They also gathered wild fruit, nuts, seeds, honey, roots, and grains, and caught fish in streams and rivers.

Scientists have uncovered evidence of the achievements of Paleolithic people. For example, about fifty years ago, Chinese villagers directed archeologists to a cave said to be "full of dragon bones." The scientists who excavated the cave think it may have been first inhabited some 460,000 years ago. They found over 100,000 stone artifacts and evidence that the cave dwellers used fire.

Paleolithic people did not build permanent dwellings or settle in villages. They made temporary homes in caves or in tents constructed of branches and animal skins.

---

[1]This term comes from two Greek words: *lithos,* which means "stone," and *palaios,* "ancient."

One way scientists learn about the past is by studying artifacts. These Chinese archeologists are uncovering some of the 7,000 large pottery figures of horses and warriors that were buried in a Chinese emperor's grave about 210 B.C.

When the animals left the area or the food supply ran short, the people moved on.

Stone Age people make impressive achievements. In modern terms, human progress in the Stone Age seems extremely slow. Yet the achievements of the Paleolithic people were remarkable. Early in this period, human beings made a variety of tools that had specific uses. They learned to control and use fire, and they used spoken language.

Most of the Paleolithic tools found by archeologists are of stone, which is longer lasting than wood or bone. There are many different types of tools — daggers and spearpoints for hunting, hand axes and choppers to cut up meat, and scrapers for cleaning animal hides. Some tools were used to dig up roots, to peel the bark off wood, and to remove the skin from animals. Not all tools were of stone. Sharpened wooden sticks, hardened in a fire, were used as spears. Later in the period, splinters of bone were used as needles and fishhooks.

Learning how to control fire brought changes in the lives of Paleolithic people. Fire provided warmth and light in the cave or shelter and kept wild animals away at night. Fire was useful in hunting, too. A band of hunters with torches could drive a herd of large animals

OLD STONE AGE
ACHIEVEMENTS
Paleolithic toolmakers often
used flint, a hard but brittle
stone that breaks into curved
shapes. This skillfully flaked
spear (below) may have been
made about 19,000 B.C. The
lifelike horse (left) is from the
cave of Lascaux.

over the edge of a cliff rather than trying to kill them with their clumsy short spears. People also used fire to cook their food. Smoke from a fire helped preserve food and make animal skins more waterproof.

Using spoken language was a great advance for Paleolithic people. Anthropologists believe that speech contributed much to human progress and achievements. Knowledge, skills, and information could be passed from parents to children. People could discuss ideas and share experiences.

Neanderthal people develop beliefs. One widespread group of Paleolithic hunting people was the Neanderthal (nee-AN-dur-thahl). Scientists estimate that these people lived from 100,000 to 40,000 years ago. They were named for the valley in Germany where their remains were first found. Artifacts and living sites of Neanderthal people have been found in many other places in Europe, Asia, and North Africa. Some Neanderthal people apparently had rituals they hoped would guarantee them success in the hunt. These Stone Age people also carefully buried their dead, placing tools, ornaments, food, and bunches of wildflowers in the graves. From this evidence, many scholars have concluded that Paleolithic people had religious beliefs, including the idea of a life after death.

Cro-Magnon people develop art. Religious beliefs may also have been the inspiration for some of the earliest prehistoric art. This was created by people who have been named Cro-Magnon (kroh-MAG-nun), from the place in southern France where a road-building crew found a grave filled with artifacts. Most of the Cro-Magnon art found so far has been in Europe and Asia. It includes beads, necklaces, and bracelets carved from ivory, pebbles painted with colorful designs, and small female figurines cut from stone. Cro-Magnon people also made small ivory and bone sculptures depicting animals, birds, and fish. A flute carved from bone suggests that they played music. Their most famous works of art, however, are the paintings found on the walls of caves in many parts of Europe.

The first cave art was discovered almost by accident. In 1875 a Spanish nobleman, Don Marcelino de Sautuola, learned that an ancient cave had been found on his estate by a hunting dog and its master. An amateur archeologist, Don Marcelino began to look for fossils and artifacts in the cave. One day in 1879 his young daughter Maria came to the cave with him, took her lantern, and began to explore a part of the cave in which her father could not stand upright. Looking up, Maria could see that the ceiling was covered with paintings of animals. She called Don Marcelino, and together they found pictures of more than twenty-five animals. There were bison, deer, horses, and other animals, some life-size or larger, painted in red, brown, yellow, and black.

The cave, named Altamira, soon became widely known. Since then, several other caves with paintings have been found in northern Spain and southwestern France. The most famous was found in 1940, when four young boys in Lascaux (lahs-KOH), France, went looking for their lost dog, which had fallen down a hole. The Lascaux cave contains dozens of paintings of animals in an even wider range of colors than those of Altamira.

In all, over a hundred decorated caves and shelters have been found in this part of Europe. Scholars believe that the cave paintings were made between 12,000 and 30,000 years ago. It has been suggested that the Cro-Magnon cave artists drew these animals as part of a ritual they hoped would bring success in hunting.

The environment undergoes changes. Late in the Old Stone Age, the earth's weather and climate changed and grew cooler. Scientists think that variations in temperature have produced at least four long cold periods, or Ice Ages, over several million years. Each Ice Age probably lasted tens of thousands of years.

The most recent Ice Age is thought to have reached its height about 20,000 years ago. As the weather steadily cooled, the Arctic ice cap thickened and spread. Huge, slow-moving rivers of ice called glaciers formed in mountain ranges. The sheets of ice spread to cover much of the Northern Hemisphere. In North America they reached southward to the present-day Ohio Valley. Northerly parts of Europe and Asia also were ice-covered.

Because so much of the earth's water was frozen in the ice sheets, the water level in the oceans dropped by several hundred feet. Land that today is far under water was exposed, sometimes forming land bridges between islands and continents. Even where the land was not covered by ice, the weather tended to be cool and rainy. About 10,000 years ago, at the end of the Old Stone Age, the weather grew warmer, the glaciers melted, and climates in many places became hotter and drier. About this same time prehistoric people began to make significant advances, developing many new skills and ways of living.

CHECK-UP

1. Vocabulary: *prehistory, artifact, fossil, nomad.*
2. (a) What kinds of evidence do archeologists and anthropologists look for to find out how people lived before written records were kept? (b) What other types of scientists contribute to the study of prehistory?
3. Explain why the Stone Age was given that name.
4. Describe how men and women lived during the Paleolithic Age in terms of (a) food, (b) shelter, (c) tools, (d) the use of fire.
5. What evidence is there that Paleolithic people held some kind of religious beliefs?
6. (a) Who were the first prehistoric artists? (b) Where did they live? (c) Give some examples of the art they created.

2 The New Stone Age Brings Change

The period of prehistory that began about 10,000 years ago was a time of important changes for humankind. Although people still made tools of stone, they learned to shape and polish them more carefully. For this reason, the period is called the Neolithic Age, or New Stone Age. (*Neo-* means "new.") Changes other than the new way of making tools had an even greater impact on how people lived. In this period, people first developed farming, tamed wild animals, and established villages. They also learned to make pottery, weave cloth, and work with metals. The change to the Neolithic way of life did not occur quickly or everywhere at once. Neolithic achievements were probably made first by people in the Near East, the area from Egypt to Mesopotamia (map, page 33).

Farming and herding begin in the Near East. A change in the way people obtained their food was one important development that

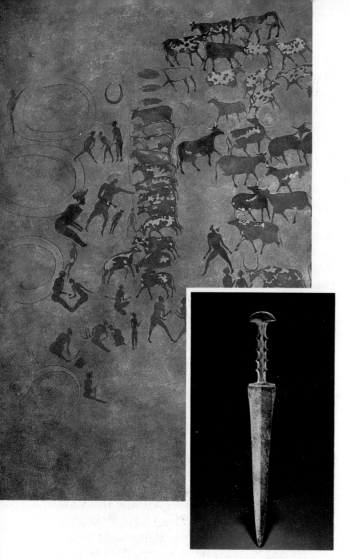

NEW STONE AGE ADVANCES
On a cliff in the Sahara, Neolithic artists painted scenes of cattle near corrals (above left). The presence of herds in what is now desert suggests that the Sahara once received more rainfall. The bronze dagger (above right) came from what is now Iran.

marked the Neolithic Age. This change most likely occurred first in the Near East, where wheat and barley grew wild as grasses, and wild sheep and goats roamed the hills. Some groups of people tamed, or domesticated, the wild animals and became herders. At about the same time, other people in the Near East began to gather seeds from the wild grasses and to plant and cultivate grain crops.

Over the next few thousand years, people in other parts of the world also began to raise crops from wild plants and to domesticate the animals that lived in their area. People in the Americas began to grow corn, and herders in southwestern Asia tamed wild horses for riding. Farming became a way of life throughout much of Europe, while people in southeastern Asia learned to grow rice in wetlands called paddies.

The cultivation of food-producing plants and the domestication of animals gave people more dependable sources of food. Instead of spending their time searching for wild grains, roots, and berries, people grew crops near their homes. In some farming societies, men continued to hunt animals for meat, while women and children tended the crops. Herders still lived a nomadic life, moving to find pasture for their animals. But instead of tracking animals over great distances, they could kill goats or sheep from their own herds. Domesticated animals provided milk and cheese as well as meat and hides for both farmers and herders.

Farmers settle in villages. To be near their growing crops and to store the extra food they grew, farming peoples began to build permanent settlements or villages. Even in late Paleolithic times, before the development of farming, some hunter-gatherers had built such villages. They spent part or all of a year in areas where food was abundant — near a river or lake well-stocked with fish or in a valley with plenty of wild wheat and barley and herds of gazelles or goats. The development of farming greatly speeded up the shift to village living.

In the Near East, where farming began, villages were becoming common by 8,000 years ago. One of the earliest known towns was the walled city of Jericho, built about 7000 B.C.[2] near the eastern end of the Mediterranean. Çatal Hüyük (chuh-TUL hoo-YOOK) in Asia Minor was built about a thousand years later (map, page 33). As many as several thousand people lived in some Neolithic farming villages.

Villagers develop special skills. Village living allowed people to learn new skills. Not

---

[2]The calendar used today in most countries of the Western world divides time into two periods: before the birth of Christ (B.C.) and since then (A.D.). The letters A.D. stand for the words *anno Domini,* a Latin phrase meaning "in the year of our Lord."

everyone in the Neolithic farming villages had to work all day in the fields in order to raise enough food for the group. People could devote part of their time to nonfarming tasks. Some people had time to make tools and weapons; some made shelters or clothing from animal skins. Some learned to weave reeds into baskets; some made pottery containers for cooking and for storing food and water. These workers became *artisans,* people with skills in specialized crafts.

Ideas of trade and private property develop. The demand for the products of expert artisans, such as toolmakers, potters, and weavers, led to trade. A toolmaker might trade with a farmer, exchanging a stone hoe and ax for grain or a sheep. A potter might trade clay pots for animal skins to make boots or clothing. This kind of trade, in which one good is exchanged for another, is known as *barter.*

Increased trade and village living allowed people to acquire more possessions. Hunters and herders, who moved from place to place, accumulated few goods. Farmers and artisans who lived in permanent settlements were different. People began to be concerned about protecting what they owned from other villagers and from outsiders who might raid the village.

Çatal Hüyük provides information about Neolithic life. In recent years archeologists have unearthed several Neolithic settlements. What they have found at these sites is the basis for their ideas about the life of Neolithic people. One site is the ancient town of Çatal Hüyük, which had between 3,000 and 6,000 inhabitants. There the villagers built rectangular, flat-roofed houses made of oak and bricks of dried mud. Probably to provide protection and make construction easier, they built the walls of the houses against each other. The only entrance to any house was through the roof and down a ladder. The main room of each house had sleeping platforms and a cooking area.

The people of Çatal Hüyük decorated their buildings. Benches and pillars were decorated with cattle horns; walls were painted with colorful flowers, geometric designs, playful leopards, dancers, and hunting scenes. Archeologists have concluded that much of the art

had religious significance. Some buildings were probably shrines, decorated with plaster carvings and statues of clay, marble, or limestone. The main deity was a mother goddess who was believed to control the harvest and therefore the life of the village.

By examining skeletal remains, anthropologists estimate that the average person in Çatal Hüyük lived about thirty years. The dead were buried in their homes and food was put into the graves. This suggests that people believed in some kind of life after death. Graves also contained tools, jewelry, mirrors, and weapons.

Çatal Hüyük was a farming village whose people grew crops of wheat and barley and raised herds of sheep and cattle. The villagers also hunted wild animals. Among the people of Çatal Hüyük were skilled artisans who made finely woven clothing of wool and linen. Traders from other regions brought alabaster and marble to exchange for obsidian, a volcanic rock resembling glass. Artisans used obsidian for making jewelry, mirrors, and knives.

Artisans develop new skills. As Neolithic people specialized in certain crafts, they developed new *technology.* That is, they learned to use new methods and materials and to create new tools for their work. They learned to bake clay pottery and bricks to make them more long-lasting. By turning clay on a flat disk, or potter's wheel, they could shape plates or bowls quickly and precisely. Neolithic toolmakers sharpened stone tools by grinding them on rocks rather than chipping off flakes. Their finely polished tools were sharper and more durable than earlier ones.

Another important advance was the plow, which was pulled by oxen. This invention enabled Neolithic farmers to bring more land under cultivation. People also learned how to spin wool into thread and made looms for weaving thread into cloth. Other Neolithic inventions were the wheel and the sail, both of which improved transportation and encouraged trade.

Artisans learn to work with metals. In late Neolithic times artisans in the Near East learned to work with metal to make tools and weapons. The knowledge of metalworking spread from the Near East and was also

LINKING PAST AND PRESENT
The Potter's Craft

Today's potters practice a craft that was developed in Neolithic times. No one knows how people discovered pottery making. Perhaps it developed when someone realized that a clay-coated basket would hold liquid. Baked at a high temperature, the clay hardened and turned into pottery.

Pottery met many needs of Neolithic people. It provided containers for carrying water and storing oil. Pottery vessels were used for cooking food and for storing grain and dried vegetables and fruits. Seeds to be used in planting were stored in pottery containers to keep them dry and protect them from insects, chickens, and mice.

The first pottery was made entirely by hand. In late Neolithic times, the invention of the potter's wheel made it easier to shape pottery in a variety of forms. The jar at right, from the Yellow River valley in China, shows one of the ways in which early people decorated pottery.

learned independently by artisans in other parts of the world.

Copper was probably the first metal used, for it is easily worked and easy to extract from the rock where it is found. Copper tools and weapons could be sharpened more easily than those made of stone, and they could be recast and reshaped if broken. Soon toolmakers discovered how to make bronze by combining copper with a small amount of tin. Bronze was harder and more durable than copper. It made weapons and tools with a sharper cutting edge. The demand for bronze objects and for tin led to a great increase in trade.

The term *Bronze Age* is used to describe the period when bronze replaced copper and stone as the main material used in tools and weapons. This period began in different parts of Asia and Europe at widely separated times and lasted for thousands of years in some regions. The knowledge of bronze-working was discovered first in southwestern Asia about 5,000 years ago. In this same region, at about the same time, the first civilizations also arose.

CHECK-UP
1. Vocabulary: *artisan, barter, technology.*
2. (a) Where did farming and the domestication of animals begin? (b) What advantages did farming and herding have over hunting and gathering as a way of life?
3. In what way did farming encourage the development of (a) village life, (b) specialization, (c) trade?
4. What do the discoveries made at Çatal Hüyük reveal about Neolithic life?
5. (a) Name four important inventions or technological changes of the Neolithic Age. (b) How did each of these affect people's lives?
6. (a) To what does the term *Bronze Age* refer? (b) Where and when was this metal first used?

3 Civilizations Emerge in Asia and Africa

Because of the achievements made during the Neolithic Age, people's food supply became more reliable, the population increased, and trade expanded. Settlements became larger, and some grew into cities. Along with the growth of cities came the beginnings of organized government and religion, the development of specialized occupations and advanced technology, and the use of written symbols to keep records. These developments — cities, organized government and religion, specialized occupations and advanced technology, and writing — characterize early civilization.

The first civilizations are in river valleys. The first civilizations emerged in four great river valleys in Asia and Africa. The earliest of all, Mesopotamian civilization, appeared about 5,000 years ago in the region between the Tigris (TY-gris) and Euphrates (yoo-FRAY-teez) rivers. Egyptian civilization developed on the banks of the Nile River in northern Africa. Civilization in India emerged in the valley of the Indus River, and Chinese civilization took shape along the Yellow River.

Historians have looked for reasons why civilizations developed first in river valleys. Several connections have been suggested. People may have settled along rivers because they were a source of food and fresh water for both human beings and a variety of wild animals. As agriculture developed, the rivers supplied water for growing crops and raising livestock. In addition, some rivers flooded each year and deposited fertile soil on the fields. Because travel by water was easier than travel on foot, rivers encouraged trade. These factors made river valleys attractive places to live. Population increased, and villages grew into cities.

Birthplaces of Civilization

Find the four river valley civilizations on the map. Name the rivers where these civilizations developed. On what continent was each civilization located?

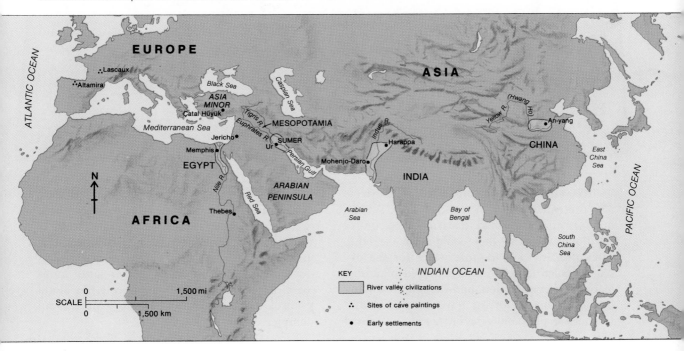

FEATURES OF EARLY CIVILIZATION

Among the earliest cities in the world was Mohenjo-Daro (top), which was built to a carefully planned pattern. As centers of civilization, early cities depended on people to keep records (center, record-keepers in Egypt). Cities also needed a reliable source of food. The picture below shows an Egyptian husband and wife planting crops in a field watered by irrigation.

Governments are organized. The rivers also presented a challenge to Neolithic settlers and farmers. People had to learn how to control the flood waters so they could farm the land. They needed ways to store water for the dry season. Such large projects required planning, leadership, cooperation, and the labor of many people. Many historians have concluded that the need to plan and direct irrigation and flood control was one reason why governments were organized. In Neolithic farming villages, there were leaders and families who had more power and prestige than others. In the first cities, such leaders became rulers. They organized armies for defense and brought together large numbers of people to work on projects like flood control and the building of walls, palaces, and temples.

The larger populations in cities also made organized government necessary. Laws were issued to keep order among the people. Government officials were chosen to oversee large projects, to judge those who broke laws, and to collect taxes to pay for the protection and upkeep of the city. Rulers governed a clearly defined area — sometimes a single city and the land around it, sometimes a larger territory with several cities and many small villages.

Government and religion are closely connected. Evidence found by archeologists indicates that even in Paleolithic times people had beliefs involving nature and animal spirits and some form of life after death. Similarly, Neolithic farming peoples believed that there were gods who controlled the sun, the rain, the winds, and other natural forces. People sought ways to win the gods' help and approval. By the time of the first civilizations, religious rituals and the priests who performed them held an important place in daily life.

Beliefs and rituals helped shape the governments that developed in the river valley civilizations. Rulers were seen either as gods or as the chosen representatives of the gods. In this role, the ruler served as chief priest and led religious observances. Laws were seen as the ruler's way of carrying out commands from the gods. In the ancient river civilization of China, for example, rulers were thought to have a "mandate from heaven" — the gods' approval to rule as long as they ruled well. Cruel or weak rulers would lose this approval, it was thought, and fall from power.

Priests held great power in the government. People labored and paid taxes for the building of huge temples. In special areas of the temple, the priests lived, studied, and taught younger priests. From the offerings of people who wanted the gods' help, the temples became wealthy as well as powerful.

People in cities follow specialized occupations. The members of the priesthood were not the only special class of people living in early cities. Cities could develop only where farmers grew enough food for both themselves and the city dwellers. This allowed city dwellers to follow many specialized occupations. The population of an ancient city included artisans, merchants, and government officials, as well as a large number of ordinary laborers, farmers, and fishermen.

Working full-time at specialized jobs encouraged the growth of new skills and new knowledge. People who spent all their time weaving cloth, for example, became very skillful. Living in the city, they could share ideas with other weavers. They could try new methods that further improved their skills and products. Traders from other cities and towns brought new ideas, materials, crafts, and methods. Such inventions as the loom and the potter's wheel may have been spread through the ancient world by traders.

Systems of writing and record-keeping develop. As systems of government, religion, and trade became more complex and organized, some kind of record-keeping was necessary. Government officials, for example, needed to write down what taxes were owed or how much grain was stored in a warehouse. Laws also had to be written down. Priests needed to keep track of the passage of time or the positions of the sun or moon, which were important in religious rituals. Merchants wanted to identify their goods and keep records of what they bought and sold. Almost every ancient civilization devised some form of writing, and this is why the beginning of civilization also marked the beginning of written history.

CHECK-UP

1. What were the characteristics of early civilizations?
2. (a) Name the four river valleys in which civilization first emerged. (b) In what ways might river valleys have encouraged the development of civilization? (c) Why was organized government needed in river valleys?
3. In the early civilizations, what effect did religion have on (a) the role of the ruler? (b) the formation of laws?
4. What factors allowed city dwellers to develop more specialized skills?
5. In what ways were writing systems useful and necessary (a) to government officials? (b) to priests? (c) to merchants?

Chapter 1 Review

Summary

Human beings made important achievements in the period of *prehistory,* before there were written records. Our knowledge of this period comes from the unwritten evidence found by archeologists and other scientists. Because the tools, weapons, and other artifacts remaining from prehistoric times are mainly of stone, the period usually is called the Stone Age.

The longest part of the Stone Age is called the Old Stone Age, or Paleolithic Age. People in this period lived by hunting and gathering their food. They also made some important advances—making tools for specific uses, controlling and using fire, developing spoken language. The Cro-Magnon people in Europe and Asia created decorative paintings, sculpture, and jewelry. Some Paleolithic peoples evidently developed religious beliefs.

The New Stone Age, or Neolithic Age, began about 10,000 years ago, at about the same time as the end of the last Ice Age. Changes occurred in some parts of the world, where people began to plant crops, domesticate animals, and establish villages. Neolithic artisans made pottery, wove cloth, and improved their tools and weapons. People invented new tools such as the plow, the wheel, and the sail. Late in the Neolithic Age, artisans in the Near East learned to work with metals, making tools, weapons, and ornaments of copper and then of bronze.

Some Neolithic farming villages gradually grew into cities. As cities developed, so did organized government and religion, specialized skills and technology, and systems for writing. All these were important parts of the first civilizations, which emerged about 5,000 years ago in four river valleys in Asia and Africa.

Vocabulary Review

1. Match the following words with the listed definitions: *artifact, artisan, barter, fossil, nomad, prehistory, technology.*
(a) The hardened, preserved remains of plants or animals.
(b) Someone skilled in a specialized craft.
(c) A person who has no permanent home.
(d) The use of methods, materials, and tools to accomplish work.
(e) The period of time before systems of writing and record-keeping were developed.
(f) Trade in which people exchange goods without using money.
(g) An object, shaped or made by an ancient human being, that has survived to our times.

2. Distinguish between the terms in each of the following pairs:
(a) archeology; geology.
(b) Old Stone Age; Bronze Age.
(c) Paleolithic Age; Neolithic Age.
(d) Neanderthal; Cro-Magnon.

Relating Geography and History

1. **Locating places.** Locate each of the following on a map in this chapter:
(a) Asia
(b) Africa
(c) Euphrates River
(d) Nile River
(e) Tigris River
(f) Yellow River
(g) Indus River

2. **Interpretation.** (a) Name the four river valleys in which early civilizations emerged. (b) What advantages and challenges did river valleys offer to early peoples? (c) What developments have made these factors less important today than they were in ancient times?

Discussion Questions

1. Although prehistoric peoples left no written records, experts have learned much about life in the Stone Age. Explain why this is so.
2. Explain how the use of spoken language and the development of writing were important steps forward in the preservation of knowledge.
3. How were the lives of Paleolithic people affected by the use of (a) tools? (b) fire? (c) language?
4. (a) What skills did Neolithic people develop? (b) How did these skills make possible the growth of civilization?
5. (a) What are the main characteristics of civilization? (b) Explain how the development of

each characteristic affected people's lives in ancient times.

Reading Sources

Excavations have led to discoveries that give archeologists insight into the cultures of Paleolithic peoples. The following passage describes a site inhabited by Cro-Magnon people and suggests what their life may have been like. Read the passage. Then answer the questions that follow.

Nelson Bay Cave lies about 300 miles east of Capetown, South Africa, along the Indian Ocean. It is carved into a 200-foot-high sandstone bluff about 65 feet up from the present beach, and it was inhabited continuously during Cro-Magnon times by a succession of peoples beginning about 18,000 years ago. The cave opening faces south and is 100 feet wide; inside there is a spacious chamber roughly 30 feet high and 100 to 150 feet deep; a spring rises at the very back and has done so for more than 35,000 years, so the cave has always had a convenient supply of fresh water. As a dwelling place it offered . . . many natural advantages. . . .

The cave overlooked an open grassland studded with low-growing trees. . . . The sea lay as much as 50 miles away, and the Nelson Bay peoples rarely, if ever, went there: . . . the cave contains no fossil marine life of any kind. Instead, the early residents lived on what was close at hand. While the women collected seeds and berries and dug up roots and bulbs, the men hunted the game that roamed in abundance over the wide plain—antelopes, ostriches, baboons, and . . . the giant buffalo, weighing 3,500 pounds. . . .

To make the cave more homelike, its occupants added certain refinements. They encircled their hearths with stones and may have built a semi-circular windbreak between the hearths and the mouth of the cave—the postholes for a somewhat later windbreak are still there. . . . In winter, and especially at night this windbreak would have been comforting, for the climate of South Africa was cooler then than now.

(a) What advantages did the Nelson Bay Cave offer the Cro-Magnon people as a place to live? (b) How did archeologists conclude that the Nelson Bay Cave dwellers rarely went to the sea? (c) What kinds of food did the Nelson Bay people eat? (d) How do you think archeologists discovered what was in these people's diet? (e) What did the occupants do to make the Nelson Bay Cave more comfortable? (f) How did archeologists determine that there may have been a windbreak erected between the hearths and the mouth of the cave? (g) Why would such a windbreak have been important?

Skill Activities

1. **Word research.** *Neolithic* means "new stone." The prefix *neo-* comes from the Greek word *neos,* meaning "new." Use a dictionary to find and define five words that have the prefix *neo-.* Explain how each is related to the idea of newness.

2. **Reports.** Find information about one of the following topics and prepare a report: (a) Stonehenge (in England); (b) Neanderthal people; (c) prehistoric lake-dwellers in Europe; (d) Cro-Magnon people; (e) Peking Man; (f) Java Man.

3. **Classifying.** Listed below are inventions and other advances made by ancient people. Classify these achievements under one of three headings: *Paleolithic Age, Neolithic Age,* and *Civilization.* Base your classifications on your knowledge of when the invention or advance first occurred.

(a) Development of organized religion.
(b) Cultivation of crops.
(c) Control of fire.
(d) Establishment of villages.
(e) Knowledge of hunting.
(f) Development of writing.
(g) Knowledge of toolmaking.
(h) Establishment of cities.
(i) Domestication of animals.
(j) Development of metalworking.

The splendor of Egyptian civilization and its god-king is suggested by this gold-covered throne inlaid with silver, colored glass, and semiprecious stones. Found in the tomb of the pharaoh Tutankhamen, the throne shows the young ruler and his wife Ankhesenamun.

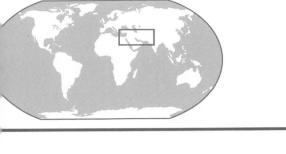

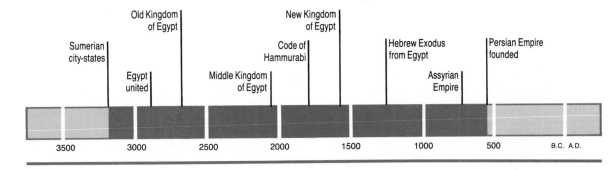

		Old Kingdom of Egypt		New Kingdom of Egypt				Persian Empire founded	
Sumerian city-states				Code of Hammurabi		Hebrew Exodus from Egypt			
	Egypt united		Middle Kingdom of Egypt				Assyrian Empire		

| 3500 | 3000 | 2500 | 2000 | 1500 | 1000 | 500 | B.C. A.D. |

The first of the river valley civilizations developed among the Sumerians, a people of Mesopotamia. In the city-states of Sumer, government and religion were organized, a writing system was used, and advances were made in architecture and technology. The Sumerians' achievements in many fields were passed on to the later peoples of Mesopotamia.

Another great civilization grew up in Egypt along the Nile River. More stable than the civilizations in Mesopotamia, Egyptian civilization endured for thousands of years. Eventually both Egypt and Mesopotamia fell under the rule of conquerors who established great empires.

Contributions to civilization were also made by many other peoples of the Near East. In this region new religious beliefs developed, and advances were made in writing, technology, and trade.

This chapter describes the civilizations and empires that developed in the ancient Near East.

CHAPTER OUTLINE

1 Civilization Begins in Mesopotamia

2 Egyptian Civilization Lasts 3,000 Years

3 Other Near Eastern Peoples Make Contributions

4 Later Empires Dominate the Near East

1   Civilization Begins in Mesopotamia

The earliest of the river valley civilizations developed in Mesopotamia, the region between the Tigris and the Euphrates rivers. The Greeks gave this land the name *Mesopotamia*, which means "between rivers." Today it is the country of Iraq. Mesopotamia was part of the Fertile Crescent, a great arc of fertile land stretching from the Persian Gulf to the eastern shore of the Mediterranean Sea.

SUMERIAN CIVILIZATION

City-states develop in Sumer. In late Neolithic times, about 6,000 years ago, nomadic herders settled in the southern part of Mesopotamia and gradually changed to the farming way of life. Near the mouths of the two rivers, they found a marshy area that provided grazing for their herds and plentiful fish and bird life. The people drained the swamps so that they could farm the rich land. They built dams and dikes to keep the rivers from flooding their

Mesopotamia

Find the Fertile Crescent on the map. What rivers flowed through it? Into what body of water did they flow? Name the cities that grew up along these rivers.

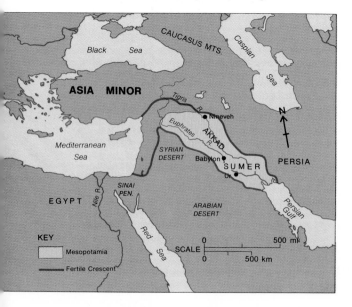

fields. In the drier northern areas they built irrigation canals. These were used to carry water from the rivers to the fields when there was little rain.

Most of Mesopotamia was a dry plain that stretched as far as the eye could see. In summer the ground baked hard under the scorching heat and the hot, dust-filled wind. The only desirable area was the fertile river valley, crisscrossed with canals.

Into this farming area came Sumerian (soo-MEHR-ee-un) nomads from the mountains to the northeast. The Sumerians mixed with the farming people, and southern Mesopotamia became known as Sumer (soo-mer). Gradually the farming villages along the river grew into twelve *city-states*. Each city-state included a city and the farmlands around it. Each had its own government and was independent of the other city-states.

The Sumerians, like other ancient peoples, believed in many gods. This belief is called *polytheism*. Each city-state considered itself the property of one of the gods, who chose the city's ruler and protected the city. Rulers were therefore thought to be responsible to the gods for keeping the irrigation system working, storing food for emergencies, and overseeing building projects.

Sumerian artisans use new methods. There was little stone or timber in Mesopotamia, so Sumerian artisans worked with clay from the rivers. To construct homes, palaces, and temples, the Sumerians shaped clay into bricks and dried it in the sun. Bricks for important buildings were baked, which made them last much longer. Most houses and temples were windowless, with rooms built around a central court.

In each city, people built a large brick temple called a ziggurat (ZIG-uh-rat), to provide a home for their gods. Shaped like a pyramid, the ziggurat had several levels, each smaller than the one below it. Stairways connected the different levels and led to a shrine at the top of the ziggurat, which towered over the plain around it.

Around the base of the ziggurat were homes for the priests and shops for artisans. Most potters, weavers, metalworkers, and other artisans worked either for the temple or for the royal court. By the time of the Sumerian city-states, the artisans of Sumer knew how to make tools and weapons of bronze. The first known use of the wheel was in Sumer, about 6,000 years ago. The potter's wheel was also used.

The Sumerians keep records on clay tablets. The Sumerians also devised a system of record-keeping that used baked clay. With a sharp-pointed stick, a Sumerian scribe, or record-keeper, pressed wedge-shaped symbols into a square tablet of damp clay. This form of writing is called *cuneiform* (KYOO-nee-uh-form). If scribes made mistakes, they could smooth out the clay and make corrections. The completed tablet was dried or baked and then stored in a library.

Cuneiform tablets are an invaluable record of the history of the Sumerians and of later peoples in Mesopotamia. Each tablet ended with the complete date (day, month, and year) and the name of the city where the record was made. The tablets recording business transactions were also marked with the signature seals of buyers, sellers, and witnesses. Made in the shape of hollow cylinders, signature seals were carved in stone and worn on a cord around the owner's neck. The pictures on seals often were miniature scenes of life in Mesopotamia — a farmer plowing, a priest receiving offerings, a woman weaving. When the seal was rolled across the damp clay of a tablet, it left the owner's distinctive personal symbol. So that no one could tamper with a contract, the tablet was wrapped in a thin layer of clay. The words of the contract were inscribed again on the outside of the "envelope."

The Sumerians establish schools. Only a few people were trained to write in cuneiform. The Sumerians established schools that trained boys in this art. Students were mostly the sons of upper-class professionals — priests, temple and palace officials, army officers, sea captains, and other scribes. The poor could not afford the schools' fees, and girls were not enrolled.

The work was demanding. Hundreds of clay tablets on which Sumerian students prac-

TIMETABLE

The Ancient Near East

B.C.

3200–2350*	The Sumerians develop civilization in Mesopotamia.
3100*	Upper and Lower Egypt are united.
2686–2181	Old Kingdom: the Egyptians build pyramids.
2040–1786	Middle Kingdom: the pharaohs regain power.
1792–1750	Hammurabi rules Mesopotamia.
1570–1090	New Kingdom: the Egyptians build an empire.
1450*	The Hittites rule an empire in Asia Minor.
1379–1360	Akhenaton tries to change traditional Egyptian beliefs.
1290*	Moses leads the Hebrews out of Egypt.
660*	The Assyrian Empire reaches its height.
547–500	The Persian Empire unites all Near Eastern peoples.

*APPROXIMATE DATES

ticed their lessons have been discovered. They show that many years of disciplined work were needed to master cuneiform writing. To help their pupils practice, teachers prepared "textbooks" of word lists and mathematical problems. Students who learned the art could work as scribes for the temple, the royal court, or wealthy merchants.

Sumer falls to conquerors. The Sumerians did not form a strong or united government. Wars over land and water rights were common among the city-states. About 2350 B.C. Sargon the Great, the ruler of the neighboring kingdom of Akkad, conquered the city-states. He brought them under his control as part of the world's first *empire,* a state in which one ruler controls other kingdoms or territories that are included within the empire's boundaries. Sargon's empire stretched from the Persian Gulf to the Mediterranean Sea.

The empire established by Sargon lasted only about a hundred years. Other neighboring peoples invaded and conquered the Tigris-Euphrates valley. One of the Sumerian city-states, Ur, regained power about 2100 B.C. and

MESOPOTAMIAN ACHIEVEMENTS

The exceptional skill of Mesopotamian artisans is apparent in the bronze head (below) from Nineveh, believed to be a portrait of Sargon of Akkad. From the tomb of Queen Shubad of Ur came the magnificent gold head of a bull (left), made to decorate a harp. The boundary marker (bottom right) reflects not only the Mesopotamians' concern with property but also their advances in law. (The symbols represent Mesopotamian gods, who were believed to serve as witnesses in legal transactions.) The Mesopotamians recognized that even daily tasks were worthy of record — such as the woman spinning as she is fanned by a slave (bottom left).

ruled both Sumer and Akkad. Invasions and warfare continued, however. Another city, Babylon, became powerful. About 1792 B.C. a Babylonian ruler named Hammurabi conquered and united Mesopotamia.

All the conquerors of Mesopotamia adopted the Sumerians' achievements. The Akkadians and the Babylonians both spoke Semitic (seh-MIT-ik) languages, which were unlike the Sumerian language. They borrowed cuneiform writing, however, and used it for their own languages. Sumerian religious beliefs, technology, art, written laws, and literature became the foundation for later civilizations in Mesopotamia.

MESOPOTAMIAN SOCIETY AND CULTURE

The people of Mesopotamia worship many gods. The belief in many gods continued among later Mesopotamians. These people believed in many major gods and goddesses and in thousands of lesser spirits and demons. They believed these were found everywhere — in the sky, in rivers, in wind and fire and storms. Prayers and rituals written on clay tablets indicate that the Mesopotamians greatly feared these gods and demons. They were thought to cause natural disasters such as floods, famines, and sandstorms — all of which occurred frequently in Mesopotamia. To protect themselves, the Mesopotamians wore charms and performed rituals. Rulers and priests consulted the gods before making decisions. Priests studied dreams and the stars and looked for signs that would show what the gods wanted.

The Mesopotamians believed that the dead descended to a gloomy underworld. In the *Epic of Gilgamesh,* one of the world's earliest literary works, an unknown Babylonian poet described the underworld: a huge dark cave "where they sit in darkness, where dust is their food and clay their meat; they are clothed like birds with wings for garments; over bolt and door lie dust and silence."

Mesopotamians have written laws. Rulers in Mesopotamia were expected to carry out the gods' wishes in making and enforcing laws. Laws, like business contracts and religious records, began to be written down in cuneiform. Probably the first written laws came from Ur-Nammu, who ruled Ur about 2100 B.C. Hammurabi, the ruler of Babylon, had the laws of the kingdom collected and organized. He then had the code of laws recorded on a block of stone eight feet high. This made the laws visible to all the people and provided a lasting record. Copies of the laws were made on clay tablets and sent to all the lands ruled by Babylon. (Some of these laws appear on page 44.)

Hammurabi's laws seem harsh today. They show many inequalities in Babylonian society. Nobles and priests were punished less severely than common people. Crimes involving property were treated very seriously.

Women had fewer legal rights than men, but some ran shops and inns, owned property, and were allowed to testify in court even if they were slaves. Laws protected Mesopotamian wives from abuse and neglect and made sure they received some payment if they were divorced. On the other hand, a wife might be forced into slavery for three years to pay back a debt her husband owed.

The Mesopotamians make advances in mathematics and astronomy. Written laws were one advance made possible by having a system of writing. The Mesopotamians also made important advances in practical mathematics and astronomy. In mathematics, they drew up multiplication and division tables and made calculations using geometry. The Mesopotamians' number system used a base of 60. From this came the system of dividing a circle into 360 degrees and an hour into 60 minutes.

The first written records in astronomy were made by the Mesopotamians. The clear dry air made it possible to observe the stars regularly and record the changing positions of the planets and the different phases of the moon. From the information in these records, the Mesopotamians developed a twelve-month calendar based on the cycles of the moon.

The Mesopotamians develop widespread trade. Because Mesopotamia lacked a number of resources — among them stone, timber, and metal — trade was important to the economy from earliest times. The two rivers provided a

The Code of Hammurabi

Hammurabi's laws dealt with everything that affected the community: religion, irrigation, military service, crime, business and property dealings, and marriage and family relations. Portions of Hammurabi's laws follow.

> If a [free man] accused another [free man] and brought a charge of murder against him, but has not proved it, [the] accuser shall be put to death. . . .
>
> If a [man] stole either an ox or a sheep . . . or a pig or a goat, if it belonged to the [temple] or if it belonged to the state, he shall make thirtyfold restitution [repayment]. If it belonged to a private citizen, he shall make good tenfold. If the thief does not have sufficient to make restitution, he shall be put to death. . . .
>
> If a robber has not been caught, the robbed [man] shall set forth the particulars regarding his lost property in the presence of [the city's] god, and the city and governor in whose territory and district the robbery was committed shall make good to him his lost property. . . .
>
> If a [man] was too lazy to make the dike of his field strong . . . and a break has opened up in his dike and he has accordingly let the water ravage the farmland, the [man] in whose dike the break was opened shall make good the grain that he let get destroyed. . . .
>
> If a son has struck his father, they shall cut off his hand.
>
> If a [man] has destroyed the eye of a member of the aristocracy, they shall destroy his eye. . . .
>
> If a [man] has knocked out a tooth of a [man] of his own rank, they shall knock out his tooth.

Which was punished more severely — theft from a private citizen or theft from the state? How did the law make sure that irrigation works would be kept in good repair? How were personal injuries to be punished?

---

way to ship goods. The wheel and the sail improved transportation by both land and water.

Each Mesopotamian city had a bazaar or marketplace, and merchants also set up trading posts in foreign lands. Copper came from lands around the Persian Gulf, precious metals from central Asia, and ivory from Africa and the west coast of India. Cedar and cypress woods and oils were shipped from lands around the Mediterranean Sea. In exchange, Mesopotamian merchants exported wool and woven cloth, fine handicrafts, grain, and hides.

Clay tablets reveal Mesopotamian history. Thousands of cuneiform tablets have been found in the Near East, dating back to the time of the Sumerian city-states. They include trade contracts, lists of rulers, maps, poems, legends, prayers to the gods, and laws. Until the nineteenth century, however, they could not be read.

In the 1840's a British officer named Henry Rawlinson found the key to cuneiform writing. He identified three types of writing on a huge cliff, known as the Behistun (bay-hihs-TOON) rock, located on the old caravan route between Babylon and Ecbatana (map, page 59). Rawlinson scaled the sheer face of the cliff and made copies of the writings. One inscription was in Babylonian cuneiform; the others were in a Semitic language and Old Persian, which scholars knew how to read. Rawlinson guessed that the three inscriptions said the same thing. After many years of labor and comparing the scripts, he succeeded in translating most of the message.

The Behistun rock was the key to the cuneiform tablets. It enabled scholars to translate the Mesopotamians' own records of their history, thoughts, and achievements, the oldest written records in the world.

1. Vocabulary: *city-state, polytheism, cuneiform, empire.*
2. (a) Where was Mesopotamia? (b) What was the Fertile Crescent? (c) What skills did the Mesopotamians develop in controlling the waters of the Tigris and Euphrates rivers?
3. (a) What was a Sumerian city like? (b) What achievements did the people of Sumer make in architecture and technology? (c) How did the Sumerians keep written records?
4. What did later Mesopotamians take from Sumerian civilization?
5. (a) Describe Mesopotamian religious beliefs. (b) What part did they play in government and law?
6. What advances did the Mesopotamians make (a) in mathematics and science? (b) in trade?
7. How did scholars decipher cuneiform writing?

2 Egyptian Civilization Lasts 3,000 Years

Southwest of Mesopotamia, in the valley of the Nile River in Egypt, another civilization emerged. Although Egyptian civilization began somewhat later than that of Sumer, it was more stable and endured for several thousand years.

THE GROWTH OF EGYPTIAN CIVILIZATION

The Egyptians depend on the Nile River. Since ancient times, Egypt has been called "the gift of the Nile." Without this mighty river, all Egypt would be desert, for it receives little rainfall. From its source in central Africa, the Nile flows north for more than 4,000 miles, emptying into the Mediterranean Sea. Heavy spring and summer rains at the source of the Nile once caused the river to overflow regularly each July.[1]

The yearly flooding of the Nile made it possible for Neolithic farmers to grow crops in the valley. The floodwaters brought moisture to the dry land and also left behind a layer of rich black soil that was excellent for crops. Farmers planted their crops as soon as the floodwaters receded. Silt carried by the river gradually built up a marshy, triangular *delta* at its mouth. This rich land was the home of many wild birds and animals and could be drained to create more farmland.

[1] The annual Nile floods continued from ancient times to 1970, when the Aswan Dam was built to provide hydroelectric power and control the water supply.

To increase the number of crops they could grow each year, the ancient Egyptians built reservoirs to store water and dug canals to

Ancient Egypt

Into what sea does the Nile River flow? What bodies of water did Egyptian traders use? With which islands did they trade?

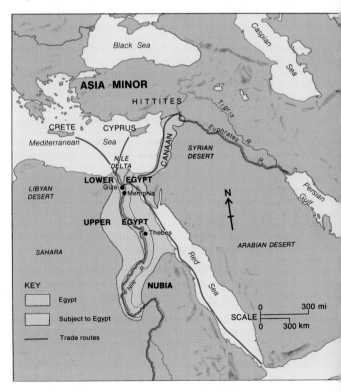

carry it to the fields. Building canals and reservoirs required the labor of large numbers of workers. People had to invent new technology and carefully plan and organize large irrigation projects. They also devised methods of keeping track of the time when floods would occur.

Besides encouraging farming, the Nile was an excellent transportation route. It helped unite the villages along the river. Vast deserts to the east and west of the river protected Egypt from attack, allowing people of the Nile villages to enjoy long periods of peace and prosperity.

The Egyptians believe in many gods. Like other farming peoples in ancient times, the Egyptians believed that many gods controlled nature, sent the yearly floods, and made the crops grow. The sun, the stars, and the Nile itself were seen as gods or as the dwelling places of gods. People in different parts of Egypt developed rituals to honor the god they saw as most important.

Egyptian polytheism included the worship of animals such as cats or crocodiles. The Egyptians believed the gods could change their shape at will and appear as birds or animals or in human form. Thoth, the scribe of the gods, for example, was often shown as a man with the head of a bird.

An important feature of Egyptian religion was the belief in life after death. The Egyptians connected their beliefs about birth and death with the rising and setting sun and with the yearly floods of the Nile. The god Osiris (oh-SY-ris) was seen as the ruler of the Nile and rich harvests, who died each year and was brought back to life by his wife Isis (EYE-sis). Egyptians believed that, when they died, their souls would be weighed against a feather symbolizing the law. Those who had lived good lives would journey to the Other World, ruled by Osiris.

Egypt is united under one ruler. The farming villages along the Nile gradually were united into two kingdoms — Upper Egypt and Lower Egypt. About 3100 B.C. a ruler of Upper Egypt known as Menes (MEE-neez) conquered Lower Egypt and brought all of Egypt under his rule. Where the two kingdoms met, he built the city of Memphis as his capital. A double crown became his symbol.

Menes' rule established the first *dynasty,* or family of rulers, in Egypt. There were at least thirty dynasties in Egypt's history. Each of these dynasties ruled until it was overthrown or there were no heirs to rule. Some ruling families were foreigners who had gained control of Egypt, but most were Egyptian. Strong dynasties kept the country united as one kingdom. Other dynasties ruled in times of unrest and controlled only part of Egypt.

Scholars divide the early history of Egypt according to the three periods when strong dynasties united the country. They call these the Old Kingdom (2686–2181 B.C.), the Middle Kingdom (about 2040–1786 B.C.), and the New Kingdom (about 1570–1090 B.C.)[2]

Powerful rulers govern Egypt. The strong rule set up by Menes became the basis of the Old Kingdom. During this period the rulers of Egypt established a strong central government in which they held supreme power.

To the people of Egypt, the ruler, later called *pharaoh* (FAIR-oh), was more than a king. He was also considered one of Egypt's many gods. As a god, the pharaoh was believed to possess the secrets of heaven and earth. One Egyptian praised the pharaoh's power in these words:

> What is there that thou dost not know? Who is there that is as wise as thou? What place is there which thou hast not seen? There is no land which thou hast not trodden. . . . All is done according to thy will, and whatever thou sayest is obeyed.

Most pharaohs thought of themselves as the protectors of the people and so tried to rule justly. One pharaoh advised his son, "Do right so long as thou abidest on the earth. Calm the weeper, oppress no widow, expel no man from the possessions of his father. . . . Take heed lest thou punish wrongfully. . . . "

The pharaoh and many officials control Egyptian life. The pharaoh was responsible for all aspects of life in Egypt — keeping the irriga-

---

[2]It is impossible to give exact dates for ancient Egypt because records refer only to the dynasty in power — for instance, "in the ninth year of the Sixteenth Dynasty." Modern historians use several different methods to calculate the dates in terms of the modern calendar.

Most famous of the Egyptian pyramids are the three at Giza, including Khufu's tomb, seen at the right in this picture. One of the "Seven Wonders" of the ancient world, Khufu's pyramid was the largest ever built, with a base covering 13 acres. Over the centuries its outer layer of smooth white stone was removed by builders from the nearby city of Cairo.

tion works in order, directing the army, keeping peace, and issuing laws. He also controlled trade and the economy. Egyptian peasants paid most of their taxes in grain, which was stored in the royal warehouses. If there was a famine, feeding the people was the pharaoh's responsibility. Taxes and payments from other countries were used to maintain public buildings, irrigation works, and port facilities. The pharaoh owned Egypt's mines and quarries and the trading fleets that sailed to foreign lands. Foreign merchants had to deal with royal officials, not with the merchants of Egypt.

Many officials were appointed to supervise the details of government. The most important official was the chief overseer. Acting in the name of the pharaoh, he presided over the royal court, acted as a diplomat, and was in charge of tax collection and public works. Lesser officials helped the chief overseer carry out the many details of running the Egyptian government and economy. Gradually, powerful officials became an upper class of nobles.

Pyramids are built during the Old Kingdom. As lasting monuments to their power, pharaohs of the Old Kingdom had immense pyramids built to serve as their tombs. These demanded not only the greatest skills of Egypt's architects and engineers, but also the labor of thousands of workers. Except for passages leading to burial chambers, the pyramids were built of solid stone. Huge limestone blocks were built up in layers and then covered with a smooth facing of white limestone. Because so many of these tombs were built during the Old King-

dom, this period is often called the Pyramid Age.

The Great Pyramid was one of three that still stand in the desert on the west bank of the Nile near Giza. It was built about 2600 B.C. for the Pharaoh Khufu. Standing 450 feet high, the Great Pyramid is made of more than two million stone blocks, each weighing about two and a half tons. It took years to build such a tomb. Using logs as rollers and levers, teams of Egyptian workers dragged huge blocks of stone up ramps. The blocks were fitted in place with such precision that a knife blade could not be slipped between them.

The Old Kingdom declines. Royal power reached its height with the age of pyramid-building. Then the nobles gained more authority in the government. Some who governed in distant parts of Egypt challenged the supreme rule of the pharaoh, and Egypt was torn by civil war for nearly 200 years. An ancient Egyptian poet described the hardships of wartime:

> The wrongdoer is everywhere....
> Plunderers are everywhere....
> Nile is in flood, yet none ploweth....
> Laughter hath perished and is no longer made.
> It is grief that walketh through the land....
> The storehouse is bare.

The Middle Kingdom restores Egypt's prosperity. About 2040 B.C. Egypt again came under the control of a strong dynasty, which ruled from Thebes. Culture and trade flourished for 250 years during the Middle Kingdom.

47

The pharaohs sent expeditions into Nubia to bring back gold, while trading expeditions traveled to Palestine, Syria, and the island of Crete in the Mediterranean. Eventually the power of nobles and priests grew again and weakened the pharaoh's rule. As the Middle Kingdom's power declined in the late 1700's B.C., invaders from Asia moved into the delta region.

A foreign dynasty rules Egypt. The newcomers were called Hyksos, meaning "Princes from Foreign Lands." They had horses and war chariots, bronze swords and daggers, and heavy bows. These superior weapons helped the Hyksos gain power and establish a ruling dynasty by about 1670 B.C. Egypt remained under foreign rule for about 100 years. Then the Egyptians learned to use the Hyksos' weapons and regained their independence.

Egypt expands during the New Kingdom. After overthrowing the Hyksos about 1570 B.C., a new dynasty established the New Kingdom and began a time of expansion for Egypt. Aggressive pharaohs built an empire, conquering land eastward to the Euphrates River in Mesopotamia and southward in Africa. The period is sometimes also called the Empire Age.

The pharaohs demanded that the conquered peoples of the empire pay *tribute* to Egypt. This tribute included slaves, food products, and treasure such as gold, jewels, or ivory. Besides providing Egypt with goods, the payment of tribute was a way of showing that the conquered people recognized the supremacy of Egypt.

Outstanding pharaohs rule the New Kingdom. Several strong pharaohs ruled Egypt during the 500 years of the New Kingdom. Among them was Thutmose (thoot-MOH-suh) II, who became pharaoh about 1512 B.C. Thutmose added Nubia to the empire and conquered Syria and Palestine (map, page 59). Thutmose's wife, Hatshepsut (hat-SHEP-soot), was the daughter of an earlier pharaoh. When Thutmose died, she seized power and ruled for more than twenty years. Hatshepsut was the first great woman ruler in history. She did not seek military victories but built temples and sent large trading expeditions to other lands. The temples she ordered built at Thebes are among the outstanding achievements of Egyptian architecture. Thutmose's son, Thutmose III, regained the throne when Hatshepsut died. A strong warrior-king, Thutmose III ruled for nearly thirty years more and expanded the empire along the Euphrates. The tribute he demanded from his conquests was used to decorate temples in Egypt.

Akhenaton tries to change Egyptian religious beliefs. Even strong pharaohs were sometimes challenged by powerful priests and nobles. In the 1300's B.C. the pharaoh Amenhotep IV tried to reduce the power of the priests in Egyptian government. He sought to change the Egyptians' worship of many gods to the worship of a single supreme god, Aton, who was represented by the sun.

Amenhotep took the name Akhenaton (ah-kuh-NAH-tun), which means "It is well with Aton." He spoke of Aton as the creator of the universe and the god of love, justice, and peace. While Akhenaton tried to give a new direction to Egyptian religious thought, his religion is usually not considered a true belief in one God. Akhenaton's religion recognized two gods — Aton and the pharaoh himself, who was still worshiped as a god.

The Egyptian priests strongly opposed Akhenaton's attempt to change Egyptian religion, and the worship of Aton gained few followers. Shortly after Akhenaton died, about 1360 B.C., his nine-year-old son-in-law Tutankhamen (too-tahng-KAH-mun) became pharaoh. The monuments to Aton were destroyed, and the new religion soon died.

Rameses maintains the empire. Rameses (RAM-uh-seez) II, who ruled from 1304 B.C. to 1237 B.C., was one of the last effective rulers of the New Kingdom. When he came to the throne, Hittite warriors from Asia Minor (page 53) were making inroads into the eastern parts of Egypt's empire. Rameses fought nearly twenty years against the Hittites before peace was made. His marriage to the daughter of the Hittite king helped to keep peace for the rest of his long reign. In this period, Rameses had many temples built and colossal statues made of himself and his family. The statues of Rameses at the temples of Abu Simbel, carved in a rock cliff, were 65 feet high.

Egyptian civilization declines. The pharaohs' power at home again began to weaken. This time outside invasions also threatened the existence of the empire. By about 1200 B.C. Egyptian civilization had passed its time of greatness. Libyans from the desert to the west invaded the fertile valley of the Nile. The "Sea Peoples" — raiders from Asia Minor and islands in the Mediterranean and Aegean (ih-JEE-un) seas — attacked the coast. Egypt had to abandon its empire. In succeeding centuries Egypt came under the rule of many different peoples, among them Kushites from the south, Assyrians, and Persians. Egyptian dynasties often came back into power, however. Not until the conquests of Alexander the Great (page 77) in the fourth century B.C. did native rule in Egypt finally end.

Over 3,000 years, Egyptian civilization had remained stable. Dynasties changed, but the way of life continued.

EGYPTIAN SOCIETY AND CULTURE

The Egyptians leave written records. Early in the Old Kingdom the pharaohs began to keep written records of their reigns. As in Mesopotamia, these records provide much of our knowledge of ancient Egypt. The Egyptian writing system was a form of picture writing called *hieroglyphics* (hy-ruh-GLIF-iks). The term *hieroglyphic* comes from Greek and means "sacred carving." Greek travelers in Egypt probably used this term because they first saw the writing carved on the walls of Egyptian temples. The Egyptians also wrote on paper scrolls, which they made from a reedlike plant called papyrus (puh-PY-rus).

In the simplest form of hieroglyphics, a picture stood for one idea. For instance, a picture of a woman was used to indicate the *idea* of a woman; a picture of a bird indicated the idea of a bird. In time, the system changed so that pictures stood for sounds as well as ideas. The owl, for example, stood for an *m* sound. Hieroglyphics could be used almost like letters of the alphabet.

Scholars decipher Egyptian hieroglyphics. As Egypt declined, most of the knowledge of reading hieroglyphics disappeared. For centuries scholars puzzled over their meaning. Then, in A.D. 1799, French engineers working in the Nile delta dug up a stone tablet. The tablet, now known as the Rosetta stone, had been carved in 196 B.C. It contained inscriptions in three languages — hieroglyphics, a more recent Egyptian script, and Greek. Like the Behistun rock (page 44), the Rosetta stone provided a key to deciphering ancient writing. A French scholar named Jean François Champollion (shahm-poh-lee-OHN) guessed correctly that all the inscriptions said the same thing. By comparing them, he deciphered the hieroglyphics.

Scribes have important skills. The scribes who wrote hieroglyphics were a special class in Egyptian society. Scribes kept the records that made government orderly and efficient. They recorded lists of imports and exports, taxes, tribute payments, materials for building temples, calculations for surveying land, workers available for the irrigation works, and supplies needed for the army. Scribes also worked in the temples. They wrote down hymns and poems to the gods and instructions for religious ceremonies. Some wrote poems, stories, and folk tales.

It took years of training to become a scribe. Schooling began at about age five and lasted for some twelve years. Students spent their days from sunrise to sunset copying lists for practice. Trained scribes were in great demand, for there were always records to be kept. Scribes often lived in the households of high officials and shared in their comfortable lives. Some became officials themselves. One Egyptian father advised his son, "Learn to write, for this will be of greater advantage to you than all the other trades. . . . School is useful for you, and the work done there will [last forever], like mountains."

Egypt has skilled artisans. Artisans also held a special place in Egyptian society. They produced a great variety of finely made goods — furniture, cloth, glassware, baskets, and jewelry. Some of these products were used in trade. Others went to decorate the homes and the tombs of the wealthy. The more skilled the artisans were, the more they were paid.

Priests and nobles have wealth and power. The families of those who held high government positions made up the upper class of nobles in ancient Egypt. Paintings and small clay models of their homes show that they lived in spacious houses built around a central courtyard with beautiful gardens. Many servants waited on them. Priests were the nobles' equals in high Egyptian society. They advised the pharaoh and planned and directed the religious ceremonies.

Most people in Egypt are peasants. Life in Egypt depended on the labor of thousands of peasants. Peasant men and women worked in the fields from dawn to dark. They grew wheat, barley, and fruit and raised herds of cattle, sheep, and goats. They also grew cotton and flax, which was used to make linen cloth. The peasants produced the food for Egypt's cities and the surplus on which the pharaoh's trade depended.

The pharaohs were considered the owners of the land, although they might give some large holdings to nobles or temples. Peasant farmers had to turn over part of their crops and livestock to the pharaoh as rent or taxes. Often peasants were also obliged to work on the irrigation system or to build temples and tombs for the pharaohs.

Prisoners become slaves. The labor of slaves helped to maintain Egyptian society. Most slaves were prisoners captured in war. Enslaving conquered peoples was a common practice throughout the ancient world. The number of slaves increased greatly during the New Kingdom while the Egyptians were building an empire.

Slaves performed a variety of tasks. Some became the household servants of nobles and priests. A few who showed special ability were appointed to important government positions. Many slaves, however, were forced to work in the pharaoh's mines or to pull the oars on the pharaoh's ships. Their lives were short and miserable.

Women are respected in Egypt. Although the upper-class Egyptian woman was expected to obey her father and her husband, she had a number of rights. She could inherit and own property and sell it without asking any man's permission. She could also run a business and testify in court. An Egyptian wife and mother was shown great respect. While divorce was permitted, it was not common. Marriage usually lasted for the lifetime of the couple.

Sometimes the wives and mothers of pharaohs became the real power in government, though they usually ruled from behind the scenes. Only one woman, Hatshepsut (page 48), ruled as pharaoh in her own right.

The Egyptians develop knowledge of medicine and astronomy. Papyrus scrolls provide evidence of the Egyptians' knowledge of medicine. One of the first medical textbooks was an Egyptian work written on the diagnosis and treatment of injuries. The scroll shows that the Egyptians understood the structure of the body, set broken bones, and treated wounds. They also classified diseases and used a variety of medicines to cure sickness. Egyptian doctors were highly regarded in the ancient world. Rulers in other lands often called for their services as court physicians.

The Egyptians also studied astronomy. Their observations of the sun and stars were important both in farming and in conducting religious rituals. Noting that the Nile flooded each year soon after the star Sirius was seen in the sky, the Egyptians developed a calendar to predict the time of the flood. This calendar was based on the sun and had 365 days. It was more accurate than the Sumerians' moon-based calendar and was the best calendar created in ancient times.

Architects and engineers develop new techniques. Egyptian engineers and architects used their skills in building the massive temples, palaces, and tombs of the pharaohs. Engineers used geometry to survey and map the land, to plan buildings, and to develop irrigation works. Egyptian architects were the first to use stone columns in building homes and such public buildings as temples and palaces.

Tombs provide a "home" for the dead. The Egyptians saw death as a continuation of life. They believed that in the Other World, people would do all the things they enjoyed in life. They would hunt, fish, picnic, and enjoy the company of family and friends. Musicians and dancers would entertain them, and servants would care for their needs.

Funerals took elaborate preparations. The bodies of people who had died were carefully

EGYPTIAN OCCUPATIONS

The ancient Egyptians worked at a variety of tasks. Artisans wove clothing, made jewelry, carved sculptures, forged metals, built cabinets, and worked with leather (right, a sandalmaker and his tools). Peasants planted, cultivated, and harvested crops. (In the center picture a woman gathers the wheat her husband has cut with a sickle). Wealthy Egyptians were entertained by dancers, acrobats, and musicians who played such instruments as the flute and harp (bottom left). The high priest (bottom right) not only directed religious ceremonies but also advised Egypt's pharaoh.

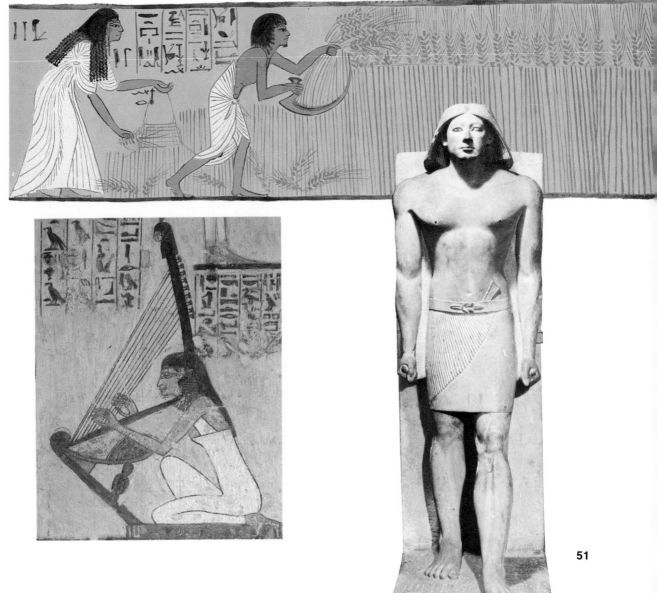

Much Egyptian art was hidden in tombs. This portrait of an overseer and his wife was found in a tomb cut from solid rock at Thebes. The carving is part of a scene that shows high-ranking officials at a feast.

preserved before their burial. Chemicals were used to dry out, or mummify, the body. The mummy was then painted, wrapped in fine linen, and adorned with jewelry. Egyptian embalmers were so skillful that modern archeologists have found mummies that still have hair, skin, and teeth after thousands of years of burial. Many of the burial customs and rituals of the Egyptians are recorded in a collection of illustrated scrolls known as the Book of the Dead.

In the tombs, Egyptians placed whatever they felt the person would need in the afterlife. The tomb was considered the "home" of the dead person. Only some handfuls of food and a few tools were buried with a poor person. The tombs of the wealthy, however, were filled with clothing, food, furniture, games, perfumes, cosmetics, jewels — everything that might be needed for a pleasant life in the Other World.

Many Egyptians worked to supply fine objects for the tombs. Artists carved sculptures and painted scenes for the walls. Artisans carved furniture of fine wood inlaid with gold and ivory. Jewelers fashioned gold and enamel into ornaments and masks. Weavers made fine linen as wrappings for the dead. Many of the luxury goods obtained from other lands were destined to be buried in Egyptian tombs.

The tomb of Tutankhamen displays Egypt's wealth. Pyramids were commonly built as tombs during the Old Kingdom. Later, other kinds of tombs were built or carved from rock for the pharaohs and nobles. Because the tombs were filled with valuable objects, they were often broken into and robbed. In A.D. 1922, a British archeologist named Howard Carter discovered the unrobbed tomb of Tutankhamen, who came to the throne about 1358 B.C. and died at the age of eighteen (page 48).

Carter's first impression in the dim light was of "strange animals, statues, and gold." Excavations revealed an immense treasure of thousands of objects: golden furniture, stone boxes and vases, carved and painted chests, statues of gold, and jewelry made of precious stones. The mummy of Tutankhamen was found in a separate chamber, lying in a coffin of solid gold. His face was covered with a gold mask studded with jewels.

The treasure of "King Tut's" tomb was the greatest single archeological find from ancient Egypt. It provided good evidence of the enduring wealth and power of this civilization.

CHECK-UP

1. Vocabulary: *delta, dynasty, pharaoh, tribute, hieroglyphics.*
2. (a) How was the Nile River important to early peoples in Egypt? (b) What part did religion play in their lives?
3. (a) What kind of government developed in ancient Egypt? (b) When was the country united? (c) What are the three main divisions of ancient Egyptian history?
4. (a) For what is the Old Kingdom particularly remembered? (b) In which period did rulers build an empire? (c) What lands did the empire include? (d) What happened to the empire?
5. (a) What were the different classes in Egyptian society? (b) What was the position of scribes and artisans?
6. Describe the advances the Egyptians made (a) in medicine, (b) in astronomy, and (c) in engineering.
7. What evidence do we have of the Egyptian belief in life after death?

3 Other Near Eastern Peoples Make Contributions

Where Europe and Asia meet, at the eastern end of the Mediterranean Sea, is the peninsula of Asia Minor (map, page 59). Since ancient times this peninsula and the coast south of it have been a crossroads for traders, nomadic herders, and invading armies. Many different peoples migrated to this region, and some settled there. In ancient times, the peoples of this area included Hittites, Lydians, Phoenicians, and Hebrews. Each of these peoples made important contributions to civilization.

Indo-Europeans migrate to the Near East. About 2000 B.C. people known as Aryans[3] (AIR-ee-unz) began to migrate from their homeland, somewhere northeast of the Black Sea. They traveled in several directions, mostly to the south and west. As they migrated, the Aryans took with them a distinctive language. Today this language is usually called Indo-European, because it became the ancestor of nearly all the languages now spoken in Europe and India. One group of Aryans settled in the mountains of western Asia Minor and mixed with the people living there. They became known as the Hittites.

Hoping to gain control of the trade routes in northern Mesopotamia, the Hittites invaded this area about 1600 B.C. They raided Babylon, Syria, and Palestine and challenged Egypt's power. By about 1450 B.C. the Hittite empire included Asia Minor and northern Syria.

The Hittites learn to use iron. While other Near Eastern peoples were still using bronze, Hittite artisans had discovered how to work iron ore into iron. Ironworking was more difficult than working with bronze. It required much higher temperatures and new techniques. At first iron was rare and was used mainly for religious objects or for swords and statues presented as royal gifts.

The peoples of the Near East soon realized that iron tools and weapons were stronger and sharper than those made of bronze. According to many historians, the Hittites kept the secret of ironworking until the fall of their empire, about 1200 B.C. Within the next 200 years, however, knowledge of ironworking spread throughout the region.

The Lydians introduce the use of coins. For centuries Near Eastern merchants had carried on trade by bartering one kind of goods for another. In exchange for stone, timber, and metals, for example, the Sumerians traded clothing, grain, and handicrafts.

The Lydians of northern Asia Minor began the use of coins in trade. Gold, silver, or a mixture of both metals was formed into disks of equal weight. Stamped into the metal of the coin were its value and a symbol that showed government authority and approval. Official Lydian government coinage was in use by about 560 B.C. during the reign of Croesus (KREE-sus).[4]

The newly invented coins made trade much easier. Suppose, for example, a shepherd wanted some pottery, and his only wealth was sheep. In a barter system, he would have to find a potter who wanted some wool or a sheep. When coins became the medium for exchange, the shepherd could sell a sheep to anyone who had the coins to buy it. With the coins, he could buy the pottery he wanted. Peoples in all parts of the Near East soon recognized the usefulness of coins, and they became accepted as payment throughout the Mediterranean world.

Phoenician seafarers spread ideas. Southeast of Asia Minor, along the eastern shore of the Mediterranean Sea, was the land of Phoenicia (fih-NISH-uh). The land is dry and hilly, and the Phoenicians turned to the sea, becoming sailors, shipbuilders, and merchants. The ports of Tyre and Sidon were busy centers of trade. Phoenicia was famous for its tall cedar trees, used in shipbuilding. Timber was exported to Egypt as early as the Old Kingdom. The Phoenicians were also the first to make

---

[3]Other Aryans (AIR-ee-unz), also called Indo-Europeans, migrated into Persia and India.

[4]People still use the phrase "rich as Croesus" to refer to someone with immense wealth.

objects of clear glass. Another famous product was cloth dyed a deep purple. The dye was obtained from seashells and cost so much to produce that only the wealthy could afford garments dyed with "royal purple."

Adventurous Phoenician sailors explored the Mediterranean. They established colonies as far away as northern Africa and southern Spain (map, page 68), as well as on several Mediterranean islands. The colony at Carthage (KAR-thidj) was founded in 814 B.C. by the Phoenician city-state of Tyre. Sailing out into the Atlantic Ocean, the Phoenician traders may even have reached Britain and southern Africa. Because they spread the ideas of the Near East as well as its products, the Phoenicians are called carriers of civilization.

The Phoenicians use a new writing system. The Phoenicians used a writing system based on an early alphabet. Each letter-symbol stood for a sound, and so any word could be written by using combinations of letters. The letter-symbols were far easier to learn than the thousands of picture symbols needed to write hieroglyphics. Phoenician traders carried the alphabet wherever they traded. About 800 B.C. the Greeks adopted this system, and created the alphabet on which our own is based.

Migrating peoples occupy the eastern Mediterranean coast. A group of people related to the Phoenicians settled south of Phoenicia on the coast and in the fertile inland valley. They gave their name to the land, calling it Canaan (KAY-nun). About 1200 B.C., migrating peoples called Philistines occupied part of Canaan. From their name, the land became known as Palestine. Another part of this region became the home of the Israelites, or Hebrews. The Hebrews were a small group of people, yet their influence in world history was great.

Early Hebrew history is recorded in the Bible. The first books of the Bible are the source for much of early Hebrew history.[5] Orig-

---

[5]These books are the section called the Old Testament in the Christian Bible; they also comprise the Hebrew Scriptures, the Bible accepted by modern Jews. Christians also accept the New Testament as holy Scripture.

LINKING PAST AND PRESENT

Portraits from the Past

When you look at the front or "face" of a coin, you assume that it will show someone's head or face. The tradition of showing portraits on coins is a very old one. The earliest coins often pictured the rulers who issued them. This assured people that royal authority backed up the value of the coin. Portraits on coins sometimes give us our only idea of what ancient rulers looked like (though the artist may tactfully have shown them as better looking than they really were).

Besides portraits, ancient coins frequently used symbols, and modern coins continue that tradition. Many ancient coins showed a god or goddess who was considered a special protector of the city or country. Similarly, modern coins have portrayed "Liberty." This silver coin is from the fifth century B.C., when the use of coins had

spread from Lydia throughout the Mediterranean. The coin pictures a helmeted goddess who is probably the wise Athena (page 66). The lively dolphins were a symbol of sea power, appropriate for the island kingdom of Sicily where the coin was made.

Ships loaded with lumber appear in this rock carving showing a Phoenician harbor. Cedar was especially prized in the ancient Near East. Solomon built his temple in Jerusalem of Phoenician cedar, and the wood was also used in Assyrian palaces. The Egyptians imported cedar for the pharaohs' funeral boats.

inally herders from Mesopotamia, the Hebrews traveled into Canaan with their leader, Abraham. Because of a famine, some Hebrews then moved to Egypt, and many settled there as farmers and herders. Later, however, the pharaohs began to persecute the Hebrews in Egypt. They were made to pay heavy taxes and were forced to work on the building of Egyptian temples, palaces, and tombs. About 1290 B.C., during the rule of Rameses II (page 48), the Hebrews of Egypt fled to the Sinai (SY-ny) Peninsula. Their flight, known as the Exodus, was led by Moses, a Hebrew who had been raised at the pharaoh's court.

Moses came to be regarded as the Hebrew people's chief law-giver. While they were in the Sinai desert, according to the Bible, Moses gave them the set of moral laws known as the Ten Commandments. The Hebrews believed these laws came from their God, whom they called Yahweh. A strong leader, Moses kept the people united during their travels, and eventually they returned to the land of Canaan, which they believed God had promised them.

A Hebrew kingdom is established. The Hebrews warred with the Canaanites and the Philistines. About 1020 B.C. they established a kingdom under the first Israelite king, Saul. Saul's successor, David, was a poet-king who defeated the Philistines and made Jerusalem the royal capital. His trade treaty with King Hiram of Tyre gave the Hebrews a share in the rich Phoenician trade. The Hebrew kingdom reached its height of power and prosperity under the rule of David's son Solomon, who ruled about 972–922 B.C. A large army protected the kingdom. Hebrew-Phoenician trading expeditions were sent into the Red Sea and possibly the Indian Ocean. In Jerusalem, Solomon built a palace and a magnificent temple for Yahweh. Many skilled artisans from Phoenicia helped to build the Temple with cedar wood, gold, and silver.

After Solomon died, the Hebrew kingdom broke in two. The northern part was conquered in 722 B.C. by the Assyrians, and many Hebrews were taken away as slaves. The southern part was conquered in 586 B.C. by Nebuchadnezzar (neb-uh-kud-NEZ-er), who destroyed Solomon's Temple. Several thousand Hebrews were captured and sent to Babylon. When the Persians conquered Babylon in 538 B.C., they allowed the exiles, now called Jews, to return home. Palestine was under Persian rule at that time and continued to be held by other conquerors for centuries.

The Hebrews contribute a new religious outlook. The Hebrews had a lasting influence

The symbols on this oil lamp have their origins in the ancient Hebrew faith. The ram's horn (left) is blown during the Jewish New Year as a call for repentance. In the Feast of Lights candles in the menorah (center) are lit one by one during an eight-day period.

on world religions. They believed in one God, a belief called **monotheism.** This made the Hebrew religion profoundly different from the Mesopotamian and Egyptian belief in a great number of gods.

Other Near Eastern peoples believed that their gods had human characteristics and weaknesses. The gods needed food, drink, and sleep; they misbehaved and were punished; they could grow old and die. To the Hebrews, God (or Yahweh) was eternal, ageless, and supreme. He had created the universe and all within it; he had total power. The Hebrews were not permitted to make any statues or paintings of Yahweh, for they believed that God was simply too awesome to be represented.

Hebrew law emphasizes moral behavior. The Hebrews believed that God set forth standards of right and wrong behavior, but they held each individual responsible for observing those standards. Hebrew law was based mainly on the laws handed down by Moses and was recorded in the first five books of the Bible, also called the Torah. Hebrew law stressed fairness and justice and set up strict rules for be-

havior and religious observances. These are some examples of Hebrew law:

> Honor thy father and thy mother: that thy days may be long upon the land which the Lord thy God giveth thee.
> Thou shalt not kill.
> Thou shalt not bear false witness against thy neighbor. (Exodus 20:12, 13, 16)

> Thou shalt neither vex a stranger, nor oppress him: for ye were strangers in the land of Egypt.
> Ye shall not afflict any widow, or fatherless child. (Exodus 22:21–22)

> Thou shalt not curse the deaf, nor put a stumblingblock before the blind, but shalt fear thy God . . .
> . . . thou shalt love thy neighbor as thyself. (Leviticus 19:14, 18)

Prophets express Hebrew beliefs. Throughout Hebrew history, many men and several women were inspired to act as prophets — that is, messengers of God. The prophets preached obedience to God's law, warned of the dangers of breaking this law, and urged the Hebrews to remain firm in their faith. The wise sayings and teachings of such prophets as Elijah, Isaiah, Deborah, Micah, and many others are recorded in the early books of the Bible along with the laws, history, and literature of the Hebrews.

CHECK-UP

1. Vocabulary: *monotheism.*
2. (a) Who were the Aryans? (b) Why was the spread of their language significant? (c) What advances did the Hittites make in technology?
3. (a) How did the Lydians and the Phoenicians contribute to trade? (b) What other contributions did the Phoenicians make?
4. (a) Describe the early migrations of the Hebrews. (b) When and why did they flee from Egypt?
5. (a) What part did Moses play in Hebrew history? (b) What are the Ten Commandments?
6. (a) When was the Hebrew kingdom established? (b) Who were its early kings? (c) What happened to it after Solomon died?
7. What kind of religious belief originated with the Hebrews?

4 Later Empires Dominate the Near East

Both Mesopotamian and Egyptian rulers had built empires by conquering other lands and bringing different peoples under one rule. By about the ninth century B.C., powerful rulers in the Near East again began to build empires. These included the lands of the ancient empires as well as many smaller kingdoms. Eventually the entire Near East came under one rule.

The Assyrians are ruthless conquerors. The Assyrians lived in the upper Tigris valley, a region frequently invaded by people from the nearby mountains. The Assyrians became skilled and ruthless warriors. Their well-trained army used iron weapons, horse-drawn war chariots, and battering rams that could knock down the walls of enemy cities.

Early Assyrian rulers invaded other lands mainly for plunder. They deliberately used terror in the lands they invaded. The conqueror Tiglath-Pileser (py-LEE-zur), who defeated people in northern Mesopotamia, boasted:

> Like the Thunderer (the storm-god Adad) I crushed the corpses of their warriors . . . in battle. . . . I made their blood to flow over all the ravines and high places of mountains. I cut off their heads and piled them up at the walls of their cities like heaps of grain. I carried off . . . their goods and their property beyond reckoning. . . . Their troops who had fled before my weapons and had thrown themselves at my feet, I took away as prisoners and added to the people of my country.

The Assyrian Empire is well organized. By about the eighth century B.C. the Assyrians had developed efficient methods to govern the people they conquered. Officials were appointed to collect taxes and tribute, keep law and order, and build public works. Roads were built to tie together the parts of the empire, and messengers carried news from place to place. Assyrian rulers, however, still used terror to control their subjects in conquered lands.

The Assyrian Empire reached its height about 660 B.C., during the reign of Assurbanipal (ah-shur-BAH-nih-pal). By this time the lands from Egypt to the Persian Gulf were under Assyrian control. The Assyrians adopted the religion, art, and literature of Mesopotamia. During a brief period of peace, Assurbanipal undertook a building program. In the capital city of Nineveh (NIN-uh-vuh) he built a library that contained thousands of cuneiform tablets written in Babylonian, Assyrian, and Sumerian.

A new Babylonian empire arises. The Assyrians never had complete control of their empire. The conquered peoples frequently rebelled against harsh Assyrian rule. In 612 B.C. an alliance of Chaldeans (kal-DEE-unz) from Babylon and Medes (MEEDZ) from Persia overthrew the Assyrians and destroyed the city of Nineveh.

The Chaldeans remained powerful for several decades. The greatest Chaldean king was Nebuchadnezzar, who ruled from 605 B.C. to

In this rock carving an Assyrian sculptor captured the excitement of a hunt. Chariots like the one shown were used both in hunting and combat, where they gave warriors greater mobility.

562 B.C. Nebuchadnezzar conquered much of the Fertile Crescent, capturing Jerusalem and the Phoenician city of Tyre. Nebuchadnezzar also rebuilt Babylon into a magnificent city. Huge gates in the city walls were decorated with colorful glazed bricks in animal designs. The ziggurat of the Babylonian god Marduk was rebuilt. The city of Babylon became most famous for a series of terraces planted with trees and flowers and watered by streams. Supposedly built for Nebuchadnezzar's wife, these became famous as the "hanging gardens" of Babylon.

Persian rulers conquer a vast territory. The Chaldean lands were soon threatened by the Persians, one of several Aryan peoples who had settled in the area east of Mesopotamia. About 547 B.C., led by Cyrus the Great, the Persians began to build the largest empire that had yet existed in the ancient Near East. Cyrus conquered his neighbors, the Medes and the Chaldeans, and released the Hebrews from their captivity in Babylon (page 55). He then took over the rest of the Fertile Crescent and Asia Minor; his son brought Egypt into the empire.

The next ruler, Darius (duh-RY-us) the Great, extended the Persian conquests into northern India. Darius's only failure was his invasion of Greece in 490 B.C. His son Xerxes (ZERK-seez) also failed to conquer Greece. Although stopped in their move westward, the Persians united all the Near Eastern peoples — Egyptians, Babylonians, Assyrians, Hebrews, Phoenicians, Hittites, and Lydians — under one rule and blended together the many different cultures.

Persian kings organize and unite their empire. Persian rulers sought ways to tie the vast empire together. They improved and extended the Assyrians' roads to link distant cities and speed travel by soldiers, merchants, and messengers. Cyrus the Great set up the first efficient postal system, using relays of mounted messengers. The 1,200-mile-long Royal Road from Sardis to Susa had more than eighty stations where couriers could change horses (like the Pony Express of the American West, 2,400 years later). Everywhere in the empire the same coins and same system of weights and measures were used. Government officials and merchants throughout the empire commonly used the same language, Aramaic (air-uh-MAY-ik), in official business.

To govern the empire, Darius divided it into twenty provinces and appointed governors

Persepolis, the capital of the Persian Empire, was famous throughout the ancient Near East for its grandeur. The palace of Darius had broad stairways flanked by carvings of warriors on guard, nobles in stately procession, and people bearing tribute from all parts of the empire (see page 22).

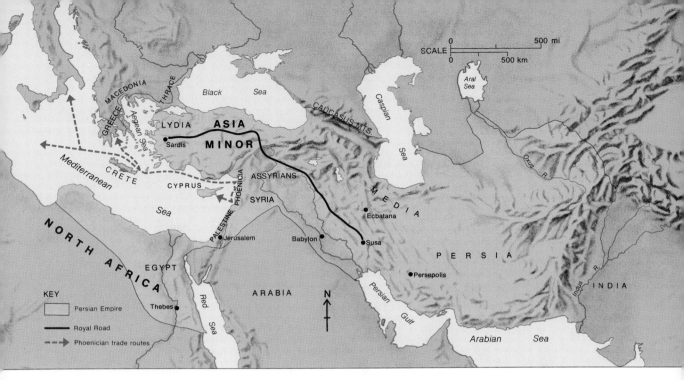

The Persian Empire

What lands did the Persian Empire include? Messengers traveled through the empire on the Royal Road. Which cities did this route link?

to supervise them. Through inspector-spies, known as "Eyes and Ears of the King," the ruler kept track of these governors. Officials were often chosen from the local people, another practice that helped hold the empire together. The Persians allowed the different peoples in their empire to keep their local customs, beliefs, and traditions. They had only to pay their taxes and provide recruits for the army.

A new religion emerges among the Persians. Most Near Eastern peoples believed in many gods who helped or rewarded people in exchange for sacrifices. About the sixth century B.C. a Persian religious teacher named Zoroaster (zor-oh-AS-tur) began to teach that human beings had a choice between doing good and doing evil. He saw the world as a struggle between these forces. Ahura Mazda (AH-hoo-ruh MAZ-duh), the Wise Lord, was seen as the supreme god, standing for truth, goodness, and light. Ahriman (AH-rih-mun) was the Evil Spirit, representing darkness.

According to Zoroaster, Ahura Mazda and the forces of good would triumph at the end of the world, when the earth would be destroyed by fire. Those who had chosen to follow the way of truth and goodness would, he said, enter a realm of eternal light and goodness, while others would be punished.

Zoroaster's followers considered him the first of several great prophets and the author of their sacred book, the Zend-Avesta. The Persian kings made Zoroastrianism the official religion of the empire, and it spread widely in the Near East. The religion has endured through the centuries and is still followed in present-day Iran and India.

CHECK-UP

1. (a) What methods did the Assyrians use to govern their empire? (b) When and how were the Assyrians overthrown? (c) What empire succeeded them?
2. (a) Where did the Persians live when they began to build an empire? (b) What lands and peoples were included in the Persian Empire? (c) Where did Persian expansion fail?
3. (a) What factors helped to unite the Persian Empire? (b) How was the empire governed?
4. Describe the religion introduced by Zoroaster.

Chapter 2 Review

Summary

The world's first civilization arose in Sumer, along the Tigris and Euphrates rivers in southern Mesopotamia. The Sumerians developed irrigation systems and devised building techniques using baked clay bricks. They kept records written in cuneiform, made advances in technology, mathematics, and astronomy, and drew up written codes of law. Sumerian traditions of law, religion, art, and government were adopted by later peoples of Mesopotamia.

The civilization that developed along the Nile River endured 3,000 years because of its strong traditions. The Egyptians were ruled by a pharaoh, who was considered one of many gods. Pharaohs of the Old Kingdom built pyramids as tombs. Trade flourished during the Middle Kingdom, and New Kingdom pharaohs built an empire. Numerous high-ranking officials ran Egypt's complex government and economy. Along with the priests, these nobles were the upper class in Egyptian society. Scribes, artisans, and other skilled workers held an important place in Egypt, but the majority of Egyptians were peasants. Egyptians made advances in medicine, created a sun-based calendar, and showed a talent for engineering. Their belief in a life after death influenced many customs.

Other Near Eastern peoples also made significant contributions. The Phoenicians spread the use of an alphabet; the Lydians introduced the use of coins; and the Hittites discovered how to work with iron. The religion of the Hebrews introduced laws for moral behavior and the belief in one God.

Later Near Eastern rulers built empires. The Assyrians' efficient methods of governing were later adopted by the Persians. By about the fifth century B.C. the Persian Empire had united all the different peoples and cultures of the ancient Near East.

Vocabulary Review

1. Match the following words with the listed definitions at the top of the next column: *city-state, cuneiform, delta, dynasty, empire, hieroglyphics, monotheism, pharaoh, polytheism, tribute.*

(a) The belief in many gods.
(b) An area formed by soil deposited at the mouth of a river.
(c) An independent state consisting of a city and surrounding territory.
(d) Wedge-shaped writing that was inscribed on clay tablets.
(e) Payment demanded from a conquered people.
(f) A ruler of ancient Egypt.
(g) The belief in one God.
(h) The Egyptian system of writing.
(i) A state and the conquered lands it rules.
(j) A family of rulers.

2. Explain the importance of each of the following in the Persian Empire: (a) Aramaic, (b) the Eyes and Ears of the King, (c) Ahura Mazda.

People to Identify

Identify the following people. Name the civilization with which each was connected and tell why he or she was important.

1. Moses
2. Menes
3. Akhenaton
4. Hatshepsut
5. Nebuchadnezzar
6. Solomon
7. Cyrus the Great
8. Zoroaster
9. Sargon the Great
10. Assurbanipal

Relating Geography and History

1. Locating places. Locate each of the following on a map in this chapter:

(a) Tigris River
(b) Thebes
(c) Canaan
(d) Asia Minor
(e) Babylon
(f) Nile River
(g) Euphrates River
(h) Black Sea
(i) Mediterranean Sea
(j) Persian Gulf

2. Comparing maps. Compare a modern map with the map on page 40. What nations now exist in what was once known as the Fertile Crescent?

3. Interpretation. Historians have called Egypt "the gift of the Nile." (a) How did the annual flooding of the Nile affect agriculture in ancient

Egypt? (b) For what other reasons was the Nile important?

Discussion Questions

1. Describe how each of the following characteristics of civilization developed in Mesopotamia: (a) cities, (b) organized government, (c) specialized occupations, and (d) written records.
2. Egyptian civilization lasted for almost 3,000 years. Why? What factors helped to make Egyptian society stable?
3. (a) What were the teachings of Zoroastrianism? (b) How did that religion differ from the Mesopotamian and Egyptian religions?
4. What contributions to civilization were made by each of the following: (a) Hittites, (b) Lydians, (c) Phoenicians, (d) Hebrews?

Reading Primary Sources

A primary source is an original account written by someone who witnessed at first hand the event or activity described. When primary sources are quoted, special kinds of punctuation are sometimes used. A set of dots like this . . . means that words have been left out. Words enclosed in brackets [ ] are not part of the primary source. They have been added to replace difficult words or to give extra information.

The following primary source is from an account written by a Greek historian who traveled to Egypt in the 400's B.C. and observed Egyptian embalmers at work. Read the account. Then answer the questions that follow.

> There are a set of men in Egypt who practice the art of embalming. . . . These persons, when a body is brought to them, show the bearers various models of corpses, made in wood, and painted so as to [be lifelike]. . . . The embalmers . . . then ask in which way it is wished that the corpse should be prepared. The bearers tell them, and having concluded their bargain, take their departure, while the embalmers . . . proceed to their task. The mode of embalming . . . is the following.
> They make a cut along the flank with a sharp Ethiopian stone and take out the whole contents of the abdomen, which they then cleanse . . . with palm wine. . . . After this they fill the cavity with . . . every sort of spicery . . . and sew up the opening.

Then the body is placed in [a chemical preservative] for seventy days and covered. . . . [At the end of that] time, which must not be exceeded, the body is washed and wrapped round, from head to foot, with bandages of fine linen cloth, smeared over with gum . . . and in this state it is given back to the relations, who enclose it in a wooden case . . . shaped into the figure of a man. Then, fastening the case, they place it in a [special] chamber, upright against the wall. Such is the most costly way of embalming the dead.

(a) List the tools and materials used in the embalming process. (b) Which passages in the account suggest that the embalmers were paid for their services? (c) Do you think everyone in Egypt was embalmed in this way? Explain your answer. (d) Using the information on pages 50 and 52, explain how the embalming process was connected with Egyptian religious beliefs.

Skill Activities

1. **Reports.** Find information about one of the following topics (all connected with ancient Egypt) and prepare a report: (a) how the pyramids were built; (b) the Sphinx; (c) the treasures found in Tutankhamen's tomb; (d) the rock temples of Abu Simbel; (e) the temple of Amon-Re at Karnak; (f) the pharaoh Rameses II; (g) Nefertiti (the wife of Akhenaton).
2. **Bulletin boards.** Make a bulletin-board display featuring ancient coins. Find pictures of coins from ancient Near Eastern countries in encyclopedias, library books, or magazines. Draw or trace pictures of the coins, and print information about them under the pictures.
3. **Making time lines.** Draw a time line that shows the three major periods in ancient Egyptian history — the Old Kingdom, the Middle Kingdom, and the New Kingdom. Place specific events in the correct time period.
4. **Making charts.** Make a chart to show basic information about the Hittites, Assyrians, Lydians, and Phoenicians. Use these headings: *People, Location, Period, Achievements.*
5. **Paraphrasing.** To paraphrase is to rewrite something in your own words. Turn to page 44 and reread Hammurabi's code. Paraphrase two or three of those laws by rewriting them in your own words.

The ancient Greeks excelled at making and painting fine pottery. Note how the artist has balanced the clusters of grapes above the ship with the leaping dolphins below it.

CHAPTER 3

The Greek City-States

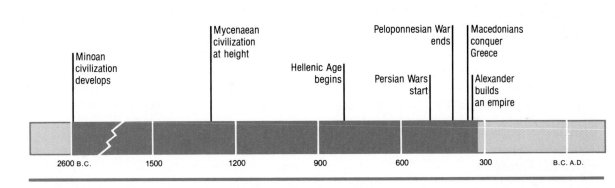

| Minoan civilization develops | Mycenaean civilization at height | Hellenic Age begins | Peloponnesian War ends | Macedonians conquer Greece | | Persian Wars start | | Alexander builds an empire |

2600 B.C.   1500   1200   900   600   300   B.C. A.D.

The early civilizations of the Near East and Egypt took shape in river valleys. The civilization of the Greek peninsula and nearby Aegean islands was centered on the sea. The Greeks lived in small, independent city-states. At first these city-states were ruled by kings. Later they were governed by nobles. Gradually, however, the Greeks of some city-states came to govern themselves and choose their own leaders. In developing the idea of government by the people, the Greeks had a lasting influence on Western civilization.

The Greek city-states were often at war with one another. They joined forces to defeat the Persian Empire, but were seriously weakened by a war between Sparta and Athens, the leading city-states. In 338 B.C. the city-states were conquered by Philip of Macedonia. His son Alexander built an empire that included many peoples and promoted the spread of Greek ideas to other lands.

This chapter describes how Greek civilization developed and spread in the Mediterranean world.

CHAPTER OUTLINE

1   Greek Civilization Begins in the Aegean
2   Greek City-States Develop
3   The City-States Fall to Conquerors

1 Greek Civilization Begins in the Aegean

Between Asia Minor and the Greek peninsula lies the Aegean (ih-JEE-un) Sea, a part of the eastern Mediterranean Sea. The Aegean islands and the Greek mainland are regarded as the cradle of Western civilization. There many ideas developed that influenced the politics, art, and thought of Western civilization.

Minoan civilization develops on Crete. Centuries before civilization developed in Greece itself, an early civilization grew up on the island of Crete to the southeast (map, page 67). It is usually called Minoan (mih-NOH-un) civilization after a legendary king named Minos (MY-nus). As early as 2600 B.C., people on Crete were working with bronze and gold and developing a system of writing. Their civilization was at its height between 1700 B.C. and 1450 B.C., when Crete dominated the lands around the Aegean Sea.

The Minoans built magnificent palaces that housed royal families, priests, and government officials. The palace at Knossos (NAW-suhs) was like a small city, with more than 800 rooms. Its walls were brightly painted with lively scenes showing men and women athletes, fanciful animals, and scenes from daily life. In the palace workshops, artisans made and decorated fine pottery, bronze daggers, tools, and other objects. The Minoans were seafaring traders, exporting wine, honey, and olive oil to Egypt, Asia Minor, Syria, and Greece.

Minoan civilization began to decline about 1450 B.C., perhaps because of a disastrous earthquake or volcanic eruption. Soon afterward, Greeks from the mainland invaded Crete. The palace at Knossos was destroyed about 1400 B.C., either by the invaders or by another earthquake.

The Mycenaeans rule Crete and mainland Greece. The invaders of Crete were Greek-speaking Indo-European tribes who had moved into the mountainous Greek peninsula about 1900 B.C. They mixed with the local population and settled throughout the peninsula. Warrior-kings ruled walled cities built around their palaces at Mycenae (my-SEE-nee), Thebes, and other places in southern Greece. Their civilization is usually called Mycenaean (my-suh-NEE-un), after the palace at Mycenae. This was the first palace investigated by archeologists, who believe Mycenae was the richest and most important town.

The Mycenaeans borrowed much from the Minoan civilization. Mycenaean pottery and jewelry were decorated with designs in the Minoan style, and Mycenaean kings probably employed Minoan artisans. Mycenaean scribes kept their records in a kind of writing that had been borrowed from Crete. The Mycenaeans took over the Minoans' sea trade, sending their ships to Egypt, Phoenicia, Sicily, and southern Italy.

Rival Mycenaean kingdoms were often at war with one another. About 1300 B.C., the ruler of Mycenae may have brought several kingdoms together in an empire that controlled the Aegean region. Writers of the time refer to the people of these kingdoms as the Achaeans (uh-KEE-unz).

Greece enters a dark age. Frequent warfare among the kingdoms caused a decline in Mycenaean civilization after 1200 B.C. Mycenaean palaces were destroyed, and many Mycenaeans moved to other areas. With the collapse of this civilization (about 1100 B.C.), Greece entered a dark age that lasted until about 800 B.C. Wars were common, and trade, farming, and the arts were disrupted. During the early part of the dark age, a tribe of Greeks called Dorians moved into the southern part of the peninsula. Though the Dorians spoke Greek, they were illiterate, and the art of writing was forgotten. There are few written records from this time.

Hellenic civilization develops. Not all the accomplishments of Aegean civilization were forgotten during the dark age, particularly among the Greeks who had moved to Asia Minor and central Greece. By about 800 B.C., the great age of Greek civilization began to take shape. It is known as the Hellenic (huh-LEN-ik) Age, from Hellas, the Greeks' name for their

MINOAN AND MYCENAEAN ART

Minoan wall paintings, like the picture of the woman with a lamp (above right), give insight into life on Crete. In the palace of Knossos, according to legend, was a maze—like that on the Minoan coin above—where a mythical beast called the minotaur roamed. The octopus vase (left) suggests how important the sea was to Crete and Mycenae. Although the hunters on the dagger (top) are dressed in Minoan style, the gold and silver inlay work was a Mycenaean specialty.

country. From their Mycenaean ancestors the Hellenic Greeks inherited skills such as pottery making and metalworking. They followed some of the same religious practices and told many of the same myths and legends.

Most Greeks were farmers who grew wheat, barley, olive trees, and grapevines. On the dry slopes of the mountainous land they raised sheep and goats. Greek artisans worked in small workshops with simple hand tools. They produced fine woolen textiles, pottery, and metal tools and weapons.

Because the coastline had excellent harbors, the Greeks became fishermen and traders. They shipped wool, wine, olive oil, marble, and pottery all over the Mediterranean. In exchange, they imported goods from other lands: grain from Egypt and Italy, fruit from Phoenicia and Sicily, copper from the island of Cyprus, tin from England, glass from Egypt, dyes from Phoenicia, and ivory from Africa. Trade also brought new ideas. The Greeks adopted the Phoenician alphabet for writing their own language. They also learned the

Lydian practice of using coins and gained knowledge of geometry from the Egyptians.

Greek myths tell stories of many gods. In this period, the basic ideas of the ancient Greek religion developed. Like farming peoples in the Near East, the Greeks turned to religion for an explanation of changes in nature and as a means of gaining good fortune or a rich harvest. For advice they sometimes consulted oracles, special temples whose priestesses and priests gave vaguely worded hints about the future. The most famous of these oracles was the one at Delphi (DEL-fy).

In another way, the religion of the Greeks was very different from those of the Near East and Egypt. The Greeks believed in many gods, who were said to live on Mount Olympus in northern Greece. The Greeks did not view these deities as terrifying or all-powerful, however, but thought of the gods as if they were a family whose members experienced joy and sorrow just as human beings did. Myths showed the gods as living very much the way wealthy Greeks lived and often taking part in the everyday lives of the Greek people. These myths were told and retold in poems and plays.

The most important Greek god was Zeus (ZOOS). His wife was Hera (HEER-uh), the goddess of marriage. Other important gods were:

Poseidon (poh-SY-dun), god of the sea.
Ares (AIR-eez), god of war.
Apollo (uh-PAHL-oh), god of music, prophecy, medicine, and rational thinking.
Athena (uh-THEE-nuh), goddess of wisdom and handicrafts.
Aphrodite (af-ruh-DY-tee), goddess of love and beauty.
Demeter (dih-MEE-tur), goddess of farmland and grain.
Hades (HAY-deez), god of the underworld.

The Greeks hold festivals to honor the gods. The Greeks built temples to the gods and honored them with many festivals. Musicians and poets presented their best songs, and athletes tried to give their best performances.

The most famous athletic games were held every four years at Olympia to honor Zeus, whose temple was there. The Olympic stadium held 40,000 spectators. The best athletes from all Greece competed in foot racing, jumping, throwing the discus and javelin, wrestling, boxing, and other contests. The winners were honored with a dignified ceremony and given a wreath of olive leaves.[1]

Homer's epics tell the story of legendary heroes. One of the most important influences on Greek religion and thought was the poet Homer, who probably lived during the eighth century B.C. Nothing is known of Homer's life. According to tradition, he was a blind poet who lived in Asia Minor. His two great epics,[2] the *Iliad* and the *Odyssey* (OD-uh-see), helped to shape the Greek outlook and character. For centuries Greek children grew up reciting Homer's works and learning about the deeds of legendary heroes.

The stories told in Homer's epics take place near the end of the Trojan War, a struggle between the Mycenaean Greeks and warriors from the city of Troy in Asia Minor. The war is believed to have actually been fought by warriors allied with the king of Mycenae about 1300 B.C. According to Homer, the war broke out when a Trojan prince named Paris kidnapped the Greek king's wife Helen, who was famous for her beauty. The war was finally won by the Greeks, who captured Troy by trickery. The heroes of the *Iliad* are the Greek warrior Achilles (uh-KILL-eez) and the Trojan prince Hector. The *Odyssey* describes the adventures of the hero Odysseus (oh-DIS-syoos) on his way home to Greece after the Trojan War.

The *Iliad* and the *Odyssey* are works of poetry, not history. Yet both works provide insight into the ways of life, outlooks, and values of the early Greeks. In the *Iliad*, Homer spoke of the deeds of noble warriors who were not only brave and skillful in battle, but also concerned about their honor and pride. In the following passage from the *Iliad*, Andromache

---

[1]The stadium at Olympia was buried by an earthquake in A.D. 500. When the ruins were discovered in 1875, they gave a French educator the idea for the modern Olympic games, which began in 1896.

[2]An epic is a long poem that relates the adventures of a hero or several heroes.

(an-DROM-uh-kee), the wife of the hero Hector, begs him not to leave home for battle. Hector's reply to his wife shows the spirit of the Homeric hero:

"Hector," she said, "you are possessed. This bravery of yours will be your end. You do not think of your little boy or your unhappy wife, whom you will make a widow soon. . . . And when I lose you I might as well be dead. There will be no comfort left, when you have met your doom — nothing but grief."

"All that, my dear," said the great Hector, . . . "is surely my concern. But if I hid myself like a coward and refused to fight, I could never face [my people]. . . . Besides, it would go against [my nature], for I have trained myself always, like a good soldier, to take my place in the front line and win glory."

To Homer, a hero was more than just a brave warrior. He was "a speaker of words and a doer of deeds"; that is, he combined courage with intelligence. Developing these characteristics became the ideal goal of Greek education.

The Ancient Greek World

Along the shores of what seas did the Greeks settle? Find each of the following places on the map: Knossos, Mycenae, Troy, Olympia, Delphi, Sparta, Athens.

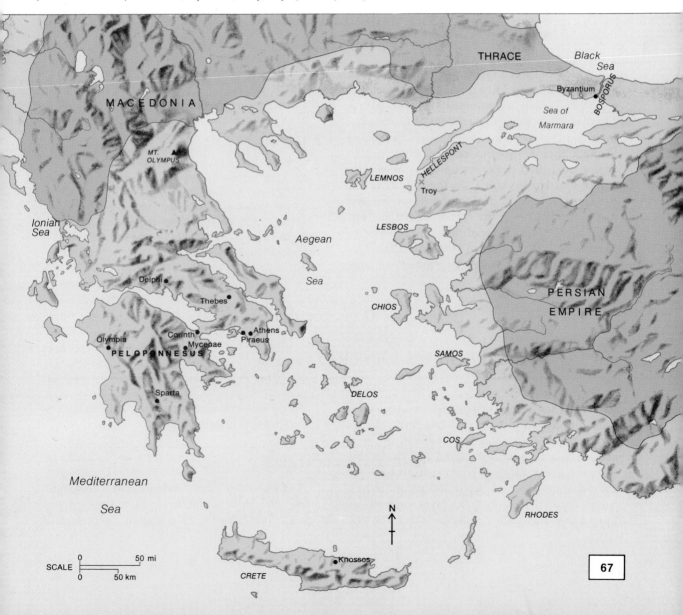

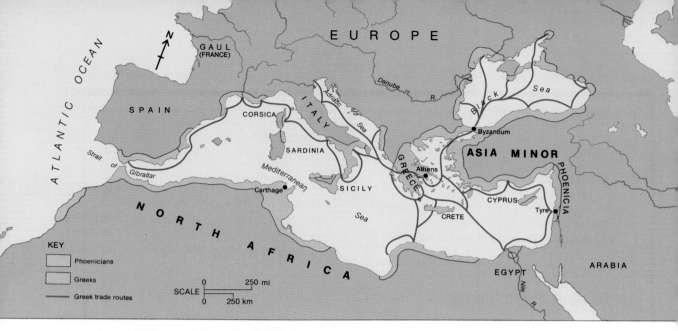

Greek and Phoenician Colonies

In what parts of the Mediterranean world did the Greeks start colonies? Where were colonies established by the Phoenicians?

Colonies spread Hellenic culture. Between about 800 B.C. and 750 B.C. the Greeks began to establish *colonies* — settlements in other lands. These colonies were independent of Greece but maintained close ties with the Greek homeland through their trade and culture. Over a 200-year period the Greeks set up colonies in Asia Minor and North Africa, on the islands of the Aegean Sea, in Sicily and southern Europe, and along the coast of the Black Sea. The settlers carried Greek traditions and ways of living to their new homes, spreading Hellenic culture to many areas of the Mediterranean world.

CHECK-UP

1. Vocabulary: *colony.*
2. (a) Where did Minoan civilization develop? (b) What caused its decline?
3. (a) Who were the Mycenaeans? (b) What did the Hellenic Greeks inherit from them?
4. What did the Greeks borrow from (a) the Phoenicians? (b) the Lydians? (c) the Egyptians?
5. (a) When did Hellenic culture begin to develop? (b) What part did religion play in it?
6. (a) Who was Homer? (b) How did his epics influence Greek education?
7. To what areas did Greek settlers spread Hellenic culture?

2 Greek City-States Develop

As the Hellenic Age began, independent city-states developed in Greece. These grew out of earlier villages that had been built in the rugged mountains and on scattered islands. In this way, the geography of Greece encouraged the development of small, separated communities. Their citizens were fiercely loyal and determined to preserve their independence. The two leading city-states, Sparta and Athens, developed in very different ways.

ATHENS AND SPARTA

City-states are independent communities. The Hellenic period was a time of frequent wars, and the Greeks built forts on hills

68

or mountaintops for their protection. A city-state, or **polis** (POH-lis),[3] often grew up around such a fort. The Greek city-states were small; the largest, Sparta, covered about 3,200 square miles (smaller than the state of Connecticut). The "ideal" size for a polis was a population of about 5,000 male citizens, who were the only people counted in official records. Many city-states were smaller, and a few were larger. Athens, the largest in population, had about 35,000 male citizens in the middle of the fifth century B.C. The rest of the population of 350,000 consisted of women, children, foreign residents, and slaves.

The polis was the center of Greek community life. People gathered in an open marketplace to conduct business and discuss politics. Shrines or temples usually were built on a hilltop along with the fortress. The polis was small enough for all citizens to become actively involved in the community. Besides its independence, each polis also cherished its self-sufficiency and its own way of life.

Sparta trains its men to be fearless warriors. The polis of Sparta (map, page 67) was settled by Dorians who occupied part of the southern peninsula of Greece, the Peloponnesus (pel-oh-puh-NEE-sus). In the eighth century B.C., the Spartans conquered nearby regions and forced many of the people to work as farm laborers, or helots (HEL-uhts). The helots worked for the polis (not for individual owners) on the farms of Sparta. They outnumbered the Spartans by as much as ten to one. The Spartans lived in constant fear of a revolt and established a strong military government to maintain order.

The Spartan aim was to produce strong-bodied, fearless people, both men and women. Every stage of a Spartan's life was planned. Sickly babies were left to die. At the age of seven a Spartan boy moved into a military barracks. There he lived until he became a full-fledged citizen at age thirty, toughening his body, learning discipline, and training for war. Winter and summer he went barefoot and wore

only a short tunic. He learned to be brave and cunning and to endure pain. Spartan women also were trained in gymnastics and physical endurance.

Spartans were expected to marry, but the family was regarded as less important than the polis. The polis gave each family land and helots to farm it. The women of Sparta had the responsibilities of managing their farms and households. The men of Sparta spent most of their time fighting or practicing military skills. They spent leisure time at a soldiers' club. Even after retiring at age 60, Spartan men served the government or military schools of the polis.

In all of Greece there were no braver warriors than the men trained in Sparta. Yet while other Greeks admired the Spartans' courage and obedience to authority, they also criticized the one-sidedness of Spartan training. They felt that the really excellent man did not neglect his mind or ignore art, music, poetry, and literature. Northeast of Sparta, in the city-state of Athens, people followed a very different ideal.

The Athenians value the development of many abilities. Athens became the commercial and cultural center of Greece. The Athenians came to look upon themselves as the teachers of all Greece. They were proud of their political

---

[3]The word *polis* referred to the city-state, to the fortress, and to the people as a whole. It is related to the English words *politics* and *metropolitan*.

TIMETABLE

Ancient Greece

B.C.

2600*	Minoan civilization develops on Crete.
1400–1230*	Mycenaean civilization reaches its height.
800*	The Hellenic Age begins.
621–510	Political reforms lead to the establishment of democratic government in Athens.
490–479	The Greek city-states fight the Persian Empire.
431–404	The Peloponnesian War weakens the city-states.
338	Philip of Macedonia conquers Greece.
336–323	Alexander the Great builds an empire.

*APPROXIMATE DATES

freedom; they boasted of their artists, playwrights, poets, and thinkers. Unlike the Spartans, the Athenians believed that a man's life was empty if he failed to use his mind and develop all his talents. This ideal did not extend to Athenian women, however, who were educated only in the skills needed to run a household.

The Athenians develop new ideas of government. In Egypt and Mesopotamia, people were ruled by kings who were regarded as gods or as the chosen representatives of the gods. The Greeks were the first people in history to establish a government in which free citizens ruled themselves. Athens was not the only polis where this change occurred. The people of Athens, however, took the lead in the creation of *democracy,* which comes from a Greek word meaning "rule by the people."

It took several centuries for Athens to develop into a democracy. Like the other city-states, it was at first ruled by a king. About 800 B.C. the wealthiest landowners, or nobles, became increasingly powerful. They chose a group of officials known as archons (AR-konz) to rule the city-state. The archons, who were nobles, tended to favor the upper class. The merchants, artisans, and farmers of Athens began to protest against their rule.

Athenian laws are written. In 621 B.C. an aristocrat named Draco (DRAY-koh) drew up the first written code of laws for Athens. Greek laws were harsh, and Draco's code did not change them.[4] Nevertheless, once the laws were put in writing, people could know clearly what they said. Previously the archons who served as judges could interpret the laws as they pleased.

Solon makes political reforms. Discontent in Athens continued, particularly among the farmers. The nobles owned most of the farmland, and many peasant farmers were deeply in debt to them. Those who could not pay what they owed lost their land to the nobles, and some even became slaves as a way of paying their debts. The growing number of slaves made it hard for free peasants to find work. The archons encouraged the unemployed to establish settlements in other lands, but this solution was not popular.

In about 594 B.C. the aristocrats turned the problem over to a statesman, poet, and merchant named Solon (SOH-lon), who was regarded as very wise and just. Given full power to deal with the unrest in Athens, Solon made many changes. He canceled the debts of the poor, freed those who had been enslaved for debt, and made slavery for debt illegal. He repealed many of Draco's laws. Solon then made political reforms that decreased the power of the nobles. Athenian citizens were divided into four classes based on wealth, not on noble birth. This gave the merchants a voice in government, for citizens in the three highest classes could hold public office. Moreover, all male citizens could become members of the Assembly, the lawmaking body, and could serve on juries.

To improve the farmers' prosperity, Solon encouraged them to grow new crops — olives for oil and grapes for wine. Both oil and wine were exported, and Athens' trade grew quickly. Solon also ordered all citizens to teach their sons a skill or trade and granted Athenian citizenship to artisans from other cities. Athens' prosperity and trade grew still more as beautiful pottery and other handicrafts were traded throughout the Mediterranean.

Solon's reforms did not completely satisfy either the nobles or the lower classes, but the Assembly pledged to abide by them. Solon himself resigned his office and traveled abroad.

Pisistratus promotes cultural life. About 560 B.C. a politician named Pisistratus (py-SIS-trah-tus) gained the support of the poor and by 546 was in firm control as the ruler of Athens. In ancient Greece, the sole ruler of a polis was known as a *tyrant*. Most came to power by force. As some tyrants used oppressive measures, the word later came to mean "a person who rules harshly." Though Pisistratus was a tyrant, his rule generally benefited Athens.

Many nobles, including the aged Solon, objected to rule by a tyrant. But Pisistratus had support among both city dwellers and farmers. He gave more land to the farmers and granted them loans to grow more grapes and olives for trade. In the city of Athens, Pisistratus improved the water supply and built temples and fountains.

---

[4]Even today, harsh laws are called Draconian laws.

The Olive Tree

For about 5,000 years the silver-leaved olive tree has been an important part of life in the countries around the Mediterranean Sea. People prize the olive tree for its beauty and hardiness. Of even more value is the tree's small oval fruit (being harvested in this picture) and the sweet oil pressed from the fruit.

A Greek family's typical evening meal was bread spread with olive oil, cheese, olives, and figs. Olive oil was used not only for cooking but also as a soap, a cosmetic, and a body rub for warriors and athletes. The rich oil is still used in some of these ways today. The beautifully grained wood of the tree makes fine carvings.

According to Greek legend, the olive tree was created by the goddess Athena as part of a competition to see which Olympic deity could give human beings the most useful gift. Athena won, and received the city of Athens in return for her gift.

Pisistratus also promoted Athenian cultural life. He encouraged sculptors and painters and sponsored drama festivals. He had Homer's epics collected and gave prizes for public readings of them. His promotion of the arts laid the foundation for Athens to become the cultural center of Greece.

Cleisthenes establishes more democratic practices. Since the time of Solon, Athens had been moving toward a more democratic government. About 510 B.C. Cleisthenes (KLYS-thuh-neez) became head of a political party opposed to tyrants. After consulting with the Assembly, he reformed the political system. Cleisthenes divided Athens into ten areas called *demes* (DEEMZ). Fifty men from each deme served on an advisory council. All male citizens could vote in the Assembly, whether they owned land or not.

To safeguard the new democratic government, Cleisthenes started a new practice. Once a year the Athenians were given the opportunity to point out anyone they believed was a threat to Athens — for instance, a person who might wish to become tyrant. If 6,000 votes were cast against a particular person, he was forced to leave Athens for ten years. Because votes were written on a piece of broken pottery called an *ostrakon,* this practice became known as ostracism. Few people actually were ostracized, but the custom gave citizens more power.

THE PERSIAN WARS

A threat by Persia unites the Greeks. Although democratic Athens and military Sparta had developed in very different ways, the people of the Greek city-states had many things in common. They spoke the same language, believed in the same gods, read and recited the Homeric epics, and competed in the same athletic contests. The Greeks considered themselves superior to all non-Greeks, whom they called "barbarians."

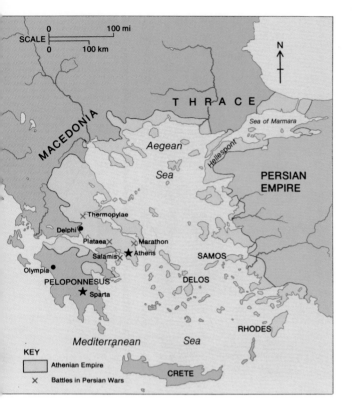

The Empire of Athens

This map shows battles of the Persian Wars. Locate Marathon, Thermopylae, and Salamis. Why was control of the Hellespont important to both Persians and Greeks? What sea did Athens dominate when it formed an empire after the Persian Wars?

Yet the Greeks had never been politically united. They were intensely loyal to their own polis, and the many city-states were often at war with one another. Only the threat of conquest by the Persian Empire made the Greeks set aside their quarrels and unite.

There were a number of Greek settlements in Asia Minor, which the Persians had occupied about 546 B.C. (page 58). In 499 B.C. some of the Greek colonists in Asia Minor rebelled against the rule of the Persian king, Darius. Athens sent twenty ships to help the rebels, but they were defeated. To punish Athens, Darius invaded Greece.

In 490 B.C., the Persians landed at Marathon, about 25 miles from Athens, and were met by a small Athenian citizen-army. In the battle, the Persians were thoroughly defeated.

Wanting the news of their victory to reach Athens as quickly as possible, the Greeks sent a messenger. Their swiftest runner, Phidippides (fy-DIP-ih-deez), had just returned from a trip to Sparta, 150 miles away. According to legend, he set off immediately for Athens. Reaching the city, Phidippides cried out the message, "Rejoice, we are victorious!", then collapsed and died. The modern marathon, a race of about 26 miles, is named in memory of the Greek victory at Marathon and honors the runner who carried the message.

The Persians invade Greece again. The Persians were unwilling to accept defeat. Ten years after the battle at Marathon, Darius' son Xerxes (ZERK-seez) set out with a large army to conquer all of Greece. The invading Persians crossed the waters of the Hellespont[5] and made their way through mountainous northern Greece. At the narrow mountain pass of Thermopylae (thur-MOP-uh-lee), they clashed with the Greek army. Led by Leonidas (lee-ON-uh-dus), the king of Sparta, 300 Spartans and about 700 other Greeks refused to retreat. The small Greek force held off the much larger Persian army for three days. Then a traitor showed the Persians a path around the pass. The Greek historian Herodotus (hih-ROD-uh-tus) described how bravely the Greeks met their death:

> Here they resisted to the last, with their swords if they had them, and if not, with their hands and teeth, until the Persians, coming on from the front over the ruins of the wall and closing in from behind, finally overwhelmed them.

The Greeks defeat the Persians at sea. Once Thermopylae fell, the Persians had an open route to Athens. The terrified Athenians fled to the nearby island of Salamis (SAL-ah-mis) and watched as the Persians burned the city. The Athenians, however, had built a strong new navy on the advice of their leader Themistocles (thuh-MIS-tuh-kleez). The Greek ships now gathered around Salamis.

Themistocles tricked the Persians into sailing their fleet into a narrow passage between

---

[5]The Hellespont is a narrow channel between the Sea of Marmara and the Aegean Sea. Today it is called the Dardanelles.

the island and the mainland. Crowded together and getting in each other's way, the Persian ships were easily rammed and sunk by the Greek vessels. Xerxes watched in horror as his hopes for conquest sank to the bottom of the sea. The following year (479 B.C.) the Spartans defeated the Persians at Plataea (pluh-TEE-uh), forcing the invaders to withdraw from Greece.

Victory brings a "golden age" to Athens. The Persian Wars were a crucial period in history. The defeat of the Persians stopped their attempts to expand their empire into Europe. It therefore gave the Greeks the freedom to develop political and artistic ideas that still influence Western civilization. The center of these developments was Athens. There Greek democracy and culture reached their height in a "golden age" during the half century after Persia's defeat.

THE GOLDEN AGE OF ATHENIAN DEMOCRACY

Athens builds an empire. Even after the defeat of Persia, the Greeks did not feel safe. The Persian Empire was still a mighty power. Furthermore, old rivalries among the city-states broke out again after the Persian Wars. To protect themselves, both Sparta and Athens made agreements called *alliances* with other city-states. The city-states in an alliance agreed to join forces to protect themselves against enemies.

In 478 B.C. the Athenians formed an alliance with more than 150 other city-states of Asia Minor and the Aegean islands. It was called the Delian (DEE-lee-un) League, for it met on the island of Delos. Each city-state contributed ships, soldiers, and money. As Athens had a more powerful fleet and greater wealth, it soon came to dominate the league. When some city-states tried to leave the alliance, Athens forced them to remain. The Delian League had turned into an Athenian empire.

Athenian democracy reaches its height. Athens now became the political and cultural center of the eastern Mediterranean. This was partly due to the leadership of Pericles (PEHR-uh-kleez), who led the Athenians from about 460 B.C. to 429 B.C. This great statesman had the city of Athens rebuilt, strengthened its defenses, and promoted democracy. His leadership of Athens was so remarkable that the period is often called the Age of Pericles.

Pericles was a firm believer in people's participation in government. Government jobs

---

PRIMARY SOURCES IN WORLD HISTORY
Pericles' Funeral Oration

During the golden age, Athens benefited from the leadership of Pericles (495–429 B.C.), a statesman who held the democratic ideal in the highest regard. After war broke out with Sparta, Pericles gave a speech honoring the Athenian soldiers who had died in the fighting. Below is part of what he said about the government of Athens.

Our [form of government] is called a democracy because power is in the hands not of a minority but of the whole people. When it is a question of settling private disputes, everyone is equal before the law. When it is a question of putting one person before another in positions of public responsibility, what counts is not membership in a particular class, but the actual ability which the man possesses.

Here each individual is interested not only in his own affairs but in the affairs of the state as well. . . . We do not say that a man who takes no interest in politics is a man who minds his own business; we say that he has no business here at all.

Why did Pericles think of Athens as a democracy? Which counted more in Athens — nobility or ability? What did Pericles say about the responsibilities of citizens?

YOUNG PEOPLE IN ANCIENT GREECE

Greek girls spent most of their lives at home occupied with household tasks. At left, a young woman works with wool. Boys, on the other hand, attended school. Above, one student is reciting — perhaps some lines from Homer — while another writes with a sharp-pointed instrument called a stylus.

were open to all classes, and government officials were paid salaries, so that even poor citizens could serve as officials. The government of Athens, said Pericles, "is in the hands of the many and not of the few."

The Athenians cherished freedom of speech and thought. Citizens could criticize leading generals or statesmen without being punished. In the Assembly every citizen was free to say what he thought. The poorest shoemaker had as much right to speak and vote as the richest landowner. The Greek philosopher Plato said that Athens was "full of liberty and free speech."

Athenians govern themselves directly. The number of Athenian citizens was small enough for them to govern themselves in a direct democracy. There was no need to elect representatives as most modern democracies do. About forty times a year all citizens met in the Assembly. There they debated, voted, and made the laws. They themselves decided whether to sign a trade treaty, build a navy, or make peace. It was assumed that each Athenian citizen could think intelligently about community affairs.

Athens had no professional government officials or judges and no professional soldiers.

The duties of government were performed by ordinary citizens. They took care of the public buildings, kept the waterfront safe for ships, and watched over the city's food supply. They served in the army and rowed ships in the navy. Rather than being elected, officials were chosen by lot (a process similar to having one's name picked out of a hat). They held office for one year and could not hold the same position again. This gave every male citizen a chance to serve the community. The Athenians believed every citizen should take part in government. A man who would not vote, hold government office, or serve on juries was seen as useless.

For practical reasons, the most active politicians and military leaders came from noble families. These men felt a responsibility to serve their city, and they also had the time and education to do so. In time, wealthy merchants began to take a greater role in government.

The Athenians value education. The Athenians considered education necessary for good citizenship. Boys were enrolled in private schools or taught at home by tutors, often educated slaves. They learned reading, arithmetic, and the works of Homer and other great poets. They wrote their lessons on wax-covered wooden tablets, using a pointed stick. Young men studied public speaking, geometry, astronomy, and poetry. They were encouraged to discuss their ideas about art, politics, and questions of right and wrong.

The Greeks cherished learning, but they also valued physical strength and health. They encouraged athletics, including running, wrestling, and gymnastics. To round out their education, young Greeks studied singing, dancing, and playing a harplike instrument called a lyre. The Greeks felt it was important for citizens to understand and appreciate beauty and artistry.

At eighteen, young Athenian men began two years of military training and service. They then became citizens and could take part in the government of their city.

Many people in Athens are excluded from public life. Although Athenian democracy was a remarkable advance, it had limitations. Only adult men — about ten percent of the population — were full citizens. Greek women did not have the same rights as men. Most Greeks agreed with the thinker Aristotle, who said: "The male is by nature superior, and the female inferior, and . . . the one rules and the other is ruled." Athenian women took no part in the public or political life of the city. They could not hold political office, compete in sports, or take part in drama festivals. Greek women received no formal education, although some young women learned to read and write at home. Training in household skills was considered the only education a woman needed.

Most foreigners living in Athens were also barred from citizenship. Because of Athens' extensive trade, there were many foreigners in the city-state. At first none of them had any political rights. Solon's reforms gave citizenship to some foreign artisans, in hopes of attracting skilled workers to Athens.

Slaves also could not be citizens. In Athens, as in other parts of the ancient world, slavery was accepted as part of life. Perhaps a quarter of the population were slaves. Some were Greeks who had been captured in wars with other city-states. Most were foreign prisoners of war. Household slaves worked as tutors and servants and were often looked upon as trusted members of the family. Slaves who worked for Greek artisans might in time learn a skill and earn enough to buy their freedom. Even when a male slave became free, however, he could not become a citizen.

CHECK-UP

1. Vocabulary: *polis, democracy, tyrant, alliance.*
2. (a) Describe a polis. (b) In what ways was it the center of Greek life?
3. (a) What was the aim of education in Sparta? (b) How did the Spartans achieve this aim? (c) How did the Greeks of other city-states view Spartan education?
4. How did each of the following contribute to the development of democracy in Athens: (a) Draco, (b) Solon, (c) Cleisthenes?
5. (a) Why did Persia invade Greece? (b) What important consequences did the Persian Wars have?
6. (a) Why was the Delian League formed? (b) How did Athens become dominant in the league? (c) What did Pericles accomplish as the leader of Athens?
7. (a) What part were citizens expected to play in the government of Athens? (b) What kind of education did Athenians think a citizen should have? (c) What groups of people could not take part in the government of Athens?

3 The City-States Fall to Conquerors

In the 50 years after the defeat of the Persians, the Greek city-states reached the height of their civilization. This period of glory and prosperity did not last, however. The city-states began to quarrel among themselves. They were so weakened as a result that they could not resist a threat from an enemy to the north of Greece.

Athens and Sparta fight the Peloponnesian War. To resist the might of Athens and its allies, Sparta found allies among the other city-

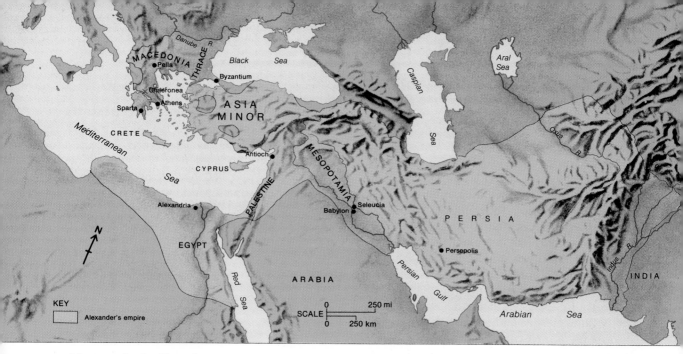

Alexander's Empire

What lands were included in Alexander's empire? Use the scale to estimate the distance of the eastern boundary of the empire from the farthest western point.

states in the Peloponnesus. In the year 431 B.C. the Peloponnesian (pel-uh-puh-NEE-zhun) War broke out between the two city-states.

Sparta invaded the countryside near Athens. Knowing the Spartans were better fighters on land, Pericles brought the Athenians inside the walls of the city. He sent the Athenian navy to attack Sparta by sea. Disaster struck Athens as disease swept through the crowded city, claiming thousands of lives. One of the victims was Pericles himself, who died in 429 B.C. His successors, Athens' new leaders, made a number of unwise decisions. Sparta continued to win both land and sea battles and finally forced Athens to make peace in 404 B.C.

War weakens the Greek city-states. The 27-year Peloponnesian War involved many city-states besides Sparta and Athens. It was a great tragedy for all of Greece, causing widespread destruction and loss of life. The war also brought political unrest. Fighting broke out in many city-states between those who wanted democratic government and those who wanted aristocrats to rule. Democracy declined even in Athens, and a small group of nobles ran the city.

Those Greeks who worried about foreign invasion thought that the danger was still the

Persian Empire. A new kingdom, however, was arising in Macedonia (mass-uh-DOH-nyah), the northern part of the Greek peninsula. In 359 B.C., a young ruler named Philip became king of Macedonia. Philip built a strong army and won the support of some city-states that opposed Athens. In Athens, a great statesman and orator, Demosthenes (dih-MOSS-thuh-neez), warned citizens of this new danger, but the quarrelsome city-states could not unite soon enough to stop the invaders. In 338 B.C., at Chaeronea (ker-oh-NEE-uh), Philip's forces crushed the Greek alliance. The Greek city-states had lost what they loved most — their independence.

Alexander of Macedonia establishes an empire. Philip was assassinated in 336 B.C., and his twenty-year-old son Alexander became ruler. He is known to history as Alexander the Great. From his father, Alexander acquired military skill, leadership ability, and a deep desire to conquer the Persian Empire. Alexander's tutor had been the great Greek thinker Aristotle (page 89). From him Alexander had learned scientific curiosity, a love for Greek culture, and the heroic tales of Homer's epics. Alexander dreamed of matching the deeds of the heroes of the *Iliad* and *Odyssey*.

Daring and intelligent, Alexander became one of the greatest military leaders in history. In 334 B.C. he crossed the Hellespont and freed the Greek colonies in Asia Minor. Phoenicia was next to fall, and then Egypt, where Alexander founded the city of Alexandria. In 331 Mesopotamia came under Alexander's rule. After the king of Persia was defeated in battle, Alexander pushed on to northwestern India. Between 334 B.C. and 326 B.C. Alexander's armies conquered the lands from Egypt to India without losing a single battle.

Alexander's empire breaks apart. In 323 B.C. Alexander died in Babylon of a fever. He was not quite 33 years old. His death ended the brief period of unity that had brought together Greece and the Near East. None of Alexander's generals was able to control the vast empire, and it broke into three separate kingdoms. One general, Ptolemy (TOL-uh-mee), ruled Egypt. Others ruled in Asia and Macedonia.

Greek civilization spreads through the empire. Although Alexander's empire broke apart, his conquests had a lasting effect. He encouraged Greek soldiers, merchants, and government officials to settle in the conquered lands. The increased contacts between the Greeks and the peoples of the Near East helped to spread Greek culture. The Greek language became widely used in the cities of the Mediterranean world. Upper-class people throughout the Near East became educated in Greek literature, ideas, and customs.

The spread of Greek culture through the lands Alexander had conquered marked the opening of a new stage of civilization called the Hellenistic Age. In the Hellenic Age (page 64), the Greeks had divided people into "Greek" and "barbarian," a word they applied to all non-Greeks. The Greeks felt themselves to be unquestionably superior to the non-Greeks. In the Hellenistic Age, the distinction between Greek and non-Greek lessened. Some influences from the Near East came into Greece. More importantly, Greek culture spread throughout the entire Mediterranean world.

CHECK-UP

1. (a) What led to the Peloponnesian War? (b) What were its consequences?
2. Why was Philip of Macedonia able to conquer Greece?
3. (a) What factors contributed to Alexander's greatness? (b) What lands did he conquer? (c) What became of Alexander's empire?
4. How did Greek civilization spread to the Near East?

Chapter 3 Review

Summary

About 2600 B.C. the Minoans on the island of Crete developed a civilization that had close ties to the sea. Mycenaeans from the Greek peninsula invaded Crete about 1400 B.C. and took control of the trade the Minoans had once dominated. With the fall of Mycenae about 1100 B.C., the Greeks entered a dark age. In the Hellenic Age that followed, the Greeks developed ideas about the gods and became familiar with the Homeric epics, whose heroes possessed qualities — intelligence, bravery, and a sense of beauty — that became the Greek ideal.

About 800 B.C. city-states developed in Greece. Two of these — Sparta and Athens — stood out in the Hellenic Age. The military city-state of Sparta had the bravest warriors in Greece. Athens, where the idea of democracy was born, was famous for its statesmen, thinkers, writers, and artists. Athens was a direct democracy in which the male citizens made the laws, voted, and held office. The Athenians took great pride in their city and expected all citizens to perform their civic duties.

Proud of their independence, the city-states often quarreled with one another. When the mighty Persian Empire threatened to conquer Greece in the early fifth century B.C., however, the city-states united to preserve their freedom. Their victory over Persia led to a golden age in Athens. When Athens built an empire, Sparta challenged its rival and brought on the Peloponnesian War. The weakened Greek city-states were easily conquered by Philip of Macedonia in 338 B.C.

Philip's son, Alexander the Great, made Greece part of an empire that stretched from Egypt to India. Alexander encouraged contacts between Greeks and non-Greeks. During the Hellenic Age, the period after Alexander's death, Greek ideas of culture spread to the lands of the Near East.

Vocabulary Review

1. Match the following words with the listed definitions: *alliance, colony, democracy, polis, tyrant.*

(a) The Greek word for city-state.
(b) A ruler who held sole power in a Greek city-state.
(c) A form of government based on rule by the people.
(d) A group of people who settle in a territory outside their homeland.
(e) An agreement between two or more states for their mutual benefit.

2. Distinguish between the terms in each of the following pairs:
(a) Minoan civilization; Mycenaean civilization.
(b) Trojan War; Peloponnesian War.
(c) Battle of Marathon; Battle of Chaeronea.
(d) Hellenic Age; Hellenistic Age.
(e) helots; archons.
(f) Delian League; Athenian empire.

People to Identify

Identify the following people and tell why each was important:

1. Alexander
2. Cleisthenes
3. Homer
4. Pisistratus
5. Philip of Macedonia
6. Pericles
7. Solon
8. Xerxes

Relating Geography and History

1. **Locating places.** Locate each of the following on a map in this chapter:
(a) Persia
(b) Mycenae
(c) Macedonia
(d) Athens
(e) Sparta
(f) Crete
(g) Peloponnesus
(h) Mediterranean Sea
(i) Aegean Sea
(j) Marathon
(k) Salamis

2. **Interpretation.** (a) How did the geography of Greece differ from that of Egypt? (b) How did geography affect the way the ancient Greeks lived? Discuss their agricultural methods, trade patterns, and form of government.

3. **Comparing maps.** Using the world map in the Atlas at the back of this book and the map on page 76, determine what nations now exist in the lands once conquered by Alexander the Great.

Discussion Questions

1. (a) What has Western civilization inherited from ancient Athens? (b) How did Athenian ideals encourage the full development of an individual's abilities?

2. Despite their shared language and religion, Athens and Sparta were very different. Describe what the people of each of these cities might have found to admire and to criticize about each other.

3. Trace the development of democracy in Athens through the contributions of (a) Draco, (b) Solon, (c) Cleisthenes, (d) Pericles.

4. (a) Compare the education of Athenian boys and girls. (b) In what ways were women excluded from participation in Athenian life?

5. (a) What was the importance of the outcome of the Persian Wars for the ancient Greeks? (b) Why were the Persian Wars a crucial turning point in the history of Western civilization?

6. What role did Alexander the Great play in spreading Greek culture throughout the Mediterranean?

Reading Primary Sources

The passage below is part of an oath taken by young Athenian men when they began military training. Read the passage. Then answer the questions that follow.

> I will not disgrace the sacred arms, nor will I desert my comrades in the ranks. I, alone or with many others, will defend the sacred and holy places. My fatherland I will [leave] . . . greater and better than I found it. I will obey those in authority, and I will observe wholeheartedly the laws now in force and whatever others the people may pass. And if anyone seeks to annul [cancel] the laws or refuses to obey them, I will not heed him; but alone, or with many others, I will defend them; and I will honor the religion of my fathers.

(a) Name five things that the young men of Athens promised to do in taking this oath. (b) What evidence can you find in the oath that Athenian laws were passed by the citizens of that city and not handed down by powerful rulers? (c) Compare this oath to the American Pledge of Allegiance. What promises in the Athenian oath are not found in the Pledge of Allegiance?

Skill Activities

1. **Word research.** The word *democracy* comes from the Greek word *demokratia*, which has two parts, *demos*, meaning "the people," and *-kratia*, meaning "government." Listed below are six words ending in the English suffix *-cracy*, "government." Look up each word in a dictionary to find out who would run the government in each case.

(a) aristocracy
(b) theocracy
(c) autocracy
(d) plutocracy
(e) gerontocracy
(f) ochlocracy

2. **Placing events in time.** In each of the following groups, arrange the three events or developments in the correct time sequence.

(a) Solon comes to power.
   The Macedonians conquer Greece.
   The Hellenic Age begins.
(b) The Golden Age of Greece begins.
   Cleisthenes comes to power.
   Mycenaean civilization reaches its height.
(c) Philip of Macedonia is assassinated.
   The Peloponnesian War begins.
   Pisistratus comes to power.

3. **Reports.** Write a report on one of the following: (a) the discovery of the ruins of Troy; (b) the Delphic oracle; (c) the route of Odysseus; (d) the Athenian jury system; (e) the story of Helen of Troy in the *Iliad;* (f) the life of Alexander the Great; (g) family life in ancient Greece; (h) triremes (Greek warships).

4. **Making charts.** Make a chart representing the major Greek gods and goddesses. In the first column write the name of each god or goddess. In the second column briefly describe the parts of nature or areas of life each was believed to control. In the third column list the symbol that represents each deity. (For example, Athena is represented by an olive tree.)

5. **Relating past and present.** The modern Olympic Games trace their origin to ancient Greece. Greek athletes from many city-states came together in a spirit of friendship to compete at the stadium in Olympia. Find out what traditions and events from the ancient games have been retained in the modern Olympics.

Three columns in the Temple of Athena at Delphi frame a dramatic landscape. Even though the columns are all that remain of the temple, they give an idea of the beauty of Greek architecture.

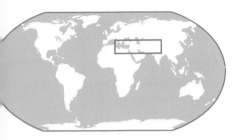

Greek Culture

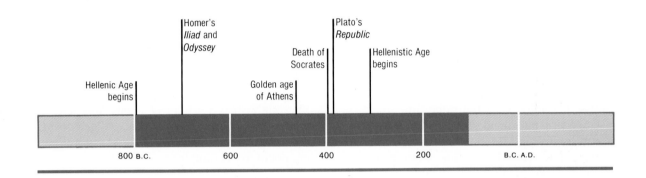

| Hellenic Age begins | Homer's *Iliad* and *Odyssey* | Golden age of Athens | Death of Socrates | Plato's *Republic* | Hellenistic Age begins |

800 B.C.   600   400   200   B.C. A.D.

Western civilization owes much to ancient Greece. The Greeks were the first people to develop the ideas of political liberty and democratic government. They also made extraordinary achievements in art, literature, science, and philosophy. In these fields, they set standards for later Western civilization.

The Greeks placed a high value on individual excellence. Greek poets, playwrights, and historians wrote enduring masterpieces. Artists and architects created simple and beautiful styles that continue to serve as models. Greek thinkers possessed a tremendous curiosity about their world and people's place in it. They questioned and analyzed everything from nature to government to the meaning of life. In examining these questions, Greek thinkers searched for answers based on reason, facts, and logic. They developed methods and ways of thinking that are the foundation of modern science and philosophy.

This chapter discusses the achievements the ancient Greeks made in art and literature and their development of philosophy and scientific thought.

CHAPTER OUTLINE

1   Art and Literature Flourish in Greece

2   Scientific Thought and Philosophy Develop

3   Learning Continues in the Hellenistic Age

1 Art and Literature Flourish in Greece

The ideas of democratic government that developed in Athens are one important part of our heritage from ancient Greece. Western traditions in art, architecture, and literature also began with the brilliant achievements made in Greece in the golden age. What Pericles said of Athens 2,400 years ago was in fact true: "Future ages will wonder at us as the present age wonders now."

The Greeks value excellence. The Greeks admired and encouraged the development of many different talents. To lead a full life, they said, a person should be able to discuss philosophy, understand mathematics, appreciate art, participate in civic affairs, and stay in good physical condition. At the same time, they expected each person to strive to do everything according to high standards of excellence. The Greeks had confidence that human beings could achieve great things. One of the great Greek playwrights wrote:

Wonders are there many — none more wonderful than man. His the might that crosses seas swept white by storm winds. . . . His is speech and wind-swift thought.

The Greeks value moderation. The Greek ideal of excellence demanded intelligence, effort, and self-discipline. This was true for a statesman, a soldier, an artisan, or any other citizen. The Greeks felt that people should use their reason to control their emotions. They admired a life of moderation — of balance between extremes. Those who followed the principle of moderation had self-control. They did not eat, drink, or even sleep too much. They did not devote their lives entirely to one thing, such as enjoying themselves or acquiring wealth. They tried to avoid being too angry or boastful or proud. The ideal of moderation was sometimes called the "golden mean." It was reflected in many aspects of Greek life, from art to government. Greek education emphasized a balanced and well-rounded life. "Moderation," said a Greek playwright, is "the noblest gift of heaven."

Poets express Greek ideals. Poetry played an important part in expressing the Greek view of life. Homer's epics were a basic part of a Greek's upbringing (page 66). These poems vividly showed people striving to live up to standards of courage and honor.

Poems also were written to honor victors in athletic games and heroes killed in battle. One of the most famous writers of such poems was Pindar, who lived in the fifth century B.C. In one of his poems for a winning athlete, Pindar wrote, "Success, for the striver, washes away the effort of striving."

Another outstanding early Greek poet was Sappho (SAF-foh), who was born about 600 B.C. She established a school of music and singing for wealthy young women. Many of her poems are about friendship and love, like the following poem to her daughter.

I have a child; so fair
As golden flowers is she,
My Cleis, all my care.
I'd not give her away
For the kingdom of Lydia;
Nor lands men long to see.

Poetry develops into drama. Greek poetry was an important part of religious festivals. Dancers and singers took part, and poems were chanted by a group of performers called the chorus. These performances gradually developed into plays. In the last part of the sixth century B.C., an actor named Thespis stepped away from the chorus and spoke lines as an individual. Soon a second and then a third actor began to take major roles and spoke back and forth with the chorus.

In time the new form of drama became the central feature of important festivals. The Athenian ruler Pisistratus (page 70) sponsored the first drama festival in 534 B.C. The best actor, the best chorus, and the best poet-playwright were honored at the end of a festival.

Plays were popular entertainment for all Athenians. Because Greece has a mild climate,

GREEK DRAMA

The idea of having an audience sit around the stage originated in ancient Greece. At the theater in Athens (left) comedies and tragedies were performed. The pottery statues below show how comic actors dressed.

the dramas were performed outdoors, in a large theater built into the side of a hill. The theater held as many as 20,000 people. Opening day was a public holiday. The poor were given money to buy seats, and prisoners were even released from jail to watch the performances. Many people brought food, for performances often lasted from sunrise to sunset.

Early Greek dramatists write tragedies. The early Greek dramas were based on old stories of gods and heroes. Playwrights used these stories to explore human problems. They showed the dignity of heroes in the face of trouble and demonstrated how noble men and women could be. The plays that they wrote were called tragedies.

Greek dramatists saw the universe as governed by fate or destiny. Many plays dealt with the idea that destiny would somehow punish men and women who were too stubborn or too proud. The dramatists believed that people had freedom to make decisions, which might bring them greatness. If they chose unwisely or rashly, however, they would bring disaster upon themselves and others. If they were too proud of their success, they would be punished.

This theme was used by the three greatest writers of Greek tragedy: Aeschylus (ESS-kih-lus), Sophocles (SOF-uh-kleez), and Euripides (yoo-RIP-ih-deez). All lived in Athens in the fifth century B.C. during what was called the "golden age" (page 73). The following passage from a play by Sophocles (496–406 B.C.) expresses a warning against arrogance:

The man who goes his way
Overbearing in word and deed,
Who fears no justice,
Honors no temples of the gods.
May an evil destiny seize him
And punish his ill-starred pride.

The dramatist Euripides (480–406 B.C.) wrote during the Peloponnesian War. His play *The Trojan Women* is set in the ancient time of the Trojan War, but laments the destructiveness of war in general. This speech by Hecuba, wife of the king of Troy, shows how timeless the themes of Greek tragedies are.

I mourn for my dead world, my burning town,
My sons, my husband, gone, all gone! . . .

Come, you widowed brides of Trojan
    fighting-men,
Weeping mothers, trembling daughters,
Come weep with me while the smoke goes up
    from Troy!

The Greek Theater

When modern playwrights and theater designers look for new ideas, they often go back to the oldest drama of all — the Greek theater. As in some modern theaters, audiences in ancient Greece sat in a half-circle around a circular area where the actors, dancers, and musicians performed. Actors changed their masks and costumes behind a wall called the "scene."

The actor Thespis, who introduced spoken dialogue, also began the tradition of wearing masks onstage. Distinct styles of masks let the audience know immediately whether a character was good or evil, happy or grief-stricken, male or female. (No women acted in Greek plays.) The mask fitted over the actor's head like a large helmet, making him taller. To look even more impressive, actors playing gods or heroes also wore thick-soled boots and padded costumes. Members of the chorus, which commented on the action, were barefoot so that they could

move and dance easily. The chorus wore identical masks showing the characters they represented — for instance, old men or maidens in a tragedy, birds or animals in a comedy. The mask above is the mask of tragedy.

Playwrights also write comedies. Greek playwrights could also be lighthearted and witty. Greek comedies were mostly about politics and current events. The comic dramatist Aristophanes (air-iss-TOF-uh-neez) made fun of Athenian politicians, generals, philosophers, and other playwrights. Some of the best-known of Aristophanes' plays are *The Birds, The Wasps,* and *Lysistrata.*

The Greeks develop a new approach to history. Another important form of Greek literature was the writing of history. Greek historians were the first to examine the past with a critical eye. They carefully investigated events, checked facts, and tried to understand people's actions and motives.

Herodotus, traditionally called the "father of history," was born about 484 B.C. His vivid account of the Persian Wars set a new standard for reporting (page 72). Herodotus often included ancient stories and legends in his accounts, but he also made his own investigations of recent events. He traveled widely in the Near East and Egypt, writing colorful descriptions of people and places. (Herodotus' account of the embalming process used by the ancient Egyptians appears on page 61.)

Thucydides emphasizes factual reporting. Thucydides (thoo-SID-uh-deez) lived during the Peloponnesian War (page 76). He began his history in 431 B.C. when the war broke out between Athens and Sparta and made a special effort to provide an accurate record of events as they happened. Thucydides' history, unlike Herodotus' work, contained no myths, legends, or supernatural explanations for events. Thucydides believed that the historian must search for human motives and natural causes. The great skill with which he analyzed and reported on politics and events made his work a model for later historical writers. (See page 93 for a passage from Thucydides' history.)

The Greeks are outstanding artists and architects. Like Greek literature, Greek art and architecture provided models that are still followed today. Greek painters and sculptors

GREEK ART

Greek sculptors portrayed the gods in human form. From the Parthenon comes the carving of Artemis, goddess of hunting (below). The bronze head of Aphrodite, goddess of love (above), is enhanced by the colors of a fine patina, the film that gradually forms on bronze and copper over the centuries. At right is a sculpture of a Greek boxer.

85

showed human beings as ideally beautiful. Statues of athletes had well-developed and well-proportioned bodies, while the faces of men and women were shown with perfect features. Even the Olympian gods and goddesses were pictured in the form of beautiful human beings, for that was the way the Greeks imagined them.

Greek architects strove for harmony and balance. They applied mathematical laws of proportion to their temples and theaters and tried to make structures fit in with the natural surroundings. One remarkable example of this harmony is the group of pillared temples on the Acropolis (uh-CROP-uh-liss), a hill in the center of Athens. They were part of the great rebuilding program that Pericles (page 73) began about 460 B.C. The largest is the Parthenon, the temple to Athena, patron goddess of Athens. Begun in 447 B.C., the temple took fifteen years to finish. The Parthenon seems to have grown out of the rocky hillside in the center of the city. It is simple, but perfectly proportioned, built of white marble. Parts of the carved sculptures on the building were once painted in bright colors. The columns are neither too tall nor too thick, and just the right amount of space separates them. Nothing breaks the artistic unity of the temple.

The Parthenon originally held a 40-foot-tall ivory and gold statue of Athena. It was made by the sculptor Phidias (FID-ee-us), who also created a large statue of Zeus for the temple at Olympia.

The Greeks set lasting standards of beauty. The Greeks set artistic standards that are still followed in the Western world. The style of Greek architecture has been used in thousands of public buildings in the United States and Europe.

"Beauty of style . . . and grace and good rhythm depend on simplicity," wrote the philosopher Plato. Pericles similarly noted, "We are lovers of the beautiful, yet simple in our tastes." Simple but beautiful, balanced and graceful — these are the characteristics of ancient Greek art, the style that is now called "classical."

CHECK-UP

1. Explain what the Greeks meant by "moderation" in living.
2. (a) What part did poetry play in Greek life? (b) How did it evolve into drama?
3. (a) What was the usual subject of Greek tragedy? (b) What did Greek dramatists say about pride? (c) Who were the greatest writers of Greek tragedy?
4. (a) Why is Herodotus considered the "father of history"? (b) What was different about Thucydides' approach to writing history?
5. What were the characteristics of Greek art and architecture?

2 Scientific Thought and Philosophy Develop

The Mesopotamians and Egyptians took the first steps toward the creation of science. They observed events in nature and recorded them, improved their tools and technology, and used mathematics in business and engineering. They were not true scientific thinkers, however, because they assumed that the actions of gods and demons caused all natural events. The Greeks of the Hellenic Age began to search for different ways to explain the natural world.

Greek thinkers are curious about the natural world. Our word *philosophy* comes from a Greek word meaning "love of wisdom." For the ancient Greeks, the love of wisdom meant a search for knowledge about the universe and human beings' place in it. Philosophers tried to understand events by finding out what caused them. They did not accept explanations that said the gods were responsible for whatever happened. The philosophers tried to analyze nature in an orderly way. They believed that nature follows general rules called *natural laws,* and they set out to find those laws. They felt this could be done by using their ability to reason.

Probably the earliest scientist and philosopher was Thales (THAY-leez), who came from one of the Greek city-states in Asia Minor. Born about 640 B.C., Thales lived at the same time as Solon (page 70). Thales observed the world curiously and carefully, looking for natural explanations. Noting that living things required water, he concluded that water was the basic element of nature. Thales also looked for a natural cause for earthquakes, which myths blamed on the actions of Poseidon, the god of the sea. Thales suggested instead that the earth floated on water and was sometimes rocked by great waves.

Thales was widely respected in his time, and other natural philosophers followed his way of thinking and reasoning. By looking for natural laws and causes, they laid the foundations for modern thinking about science and philosophy.

Greek scientific thinkers explore many fields. Other Greek thinkers applied Thales' approach in several areas of study. Some of them had ideas that contributed to modern knowledge and scientific thinking. Pythagoras (pih-THAG-ur-us), who lived in the sixth century B.C., believed that the universe was arranged according to mathematical laws. He studied music, astronomy, and mathematics to find these laws or principles. Students today still learn Pythagoras' theorem about the relationship between the sides of a right triangle. In the late fifth century B.C., Democritus (dih-MOK-ruh-tus) taught that nature was made up of tiny atoms, particles that could not be divided. Although modern science has found even smaller particles, Democritus' idea was the first atomic theory.

Some Greek doctors used a scientific approach in treating illness. Hippocrates (hih-POK-ruh-teez) is supposed to have founded a medical school on the island of Cos about 430 B.C. He taught physicians to find the causes of disease by using their reason, not by blaming illness on the anger or ill will of the gods. The doctors trained by Hippocrates took notes on the appearance and behavior of their patients and carefully recorded the medicines and methods they used in treating sick people. In this way, Greek doctors began to separate medicine from magic. Hippocrates' ideas about doctors' responsibilities were put in the form of the "Hippocratic Oath," which is still a guide for physicians today.

The Greeks influence modern scientific study. The modern scientific approach had its beginnings in the thinking of the Greek philosophers and scientists. This way of thinking is based on observing nature, making logical deductions, and looking for proof and evidence. The growth of scientific thinking did not end traditional Greek religious practices. Many Greeks, however, came to believe that physical events and human behavior could be explained by natural causes, without referring to the actions of the gods.

The Sophists consider problems of society. The earliest Greek philosophers used reason in studying nature and the physical world. Later philosophers tried to answer questions about society and the individual. In the decades after the Persian Wars, teachers known as Sophists traveled from city to city teaching speech, grammar, poetry, gymnastics, mathematics, and music. The Sophists were interested not in nature but in issues of citizenship, politics, and law. They felt these were practical questions that were important to individuals and to the community.

The Sophists claimed they could teach people how to make good laws, speak well, and win debates in the Assembly. Their teaching attracted ambitious young men who were eager to succeed in politics.

In Athens, the Sophists angered many citizens by arguing that the gods did not exist. Clever leaders, the Sophists said, used fear of the gods to force people to follow customs and obey laws. They also argued that Athenian laws were not based on principles of justice but represented only the wishes of the most powerful group in the city. Some Sophists attacked traditional ideals of moderation and self-discipline. These attacks on age-old Athenian beliefs convinced many Athenians that the Sophists were a bad influence on young people, encouraging them to disobey the law and neglect their duties as citizens.

Socrates stresses use of reason. Another criticism of the Sophists was made by Socrates (SOK-ruh-teez), who is considered one of the most extraordinary thinkers in history. Socrates was born in Athens probably in 469 B.C., about ten years after the end of the Persian Wars, and died in 399 B.C., five years after the end of the Peloponnesian War. His life thus spanned both the golden age of Athenian culture and the terrible years of the war with Sparta. Socrates worked as a stonecutter but became famous for his thoughtful conversations with other men of Athens. He never wrote down his teachings, so that most of what we know about Socrates comes from the writings of his student Plato (PLAY-toh).

Socrates agreed with the Sophists that it was more important to gain knowledge of human beings than to investigate nature. He also agreed that knowledge was acquired through reason and that the individual could be improved through education. However, said Socrates, the Sophists had not looked into the questions that really mattered: What is the purpose of life? What are the values by which people should live? He criticized the Sophists for teaching young Athenians only the methods for success in politics.

Socrates emphasizes careful thinking and questioning. According to Socrates, an individual should rely on reason, not emotions, to govern his or her behavior. Socrates wanted his fellow Athenians to think critically about how they lived their lives. "The unexamined life," he said, "is not worth living." To help people think in this careful way, Socrates carried on conversations, or dialogues, with his students. In these dialogues the speakers were led to question the truth of every statement and examine critically their own thoughts and the views of others. This question-and-answer approach taught them to reject views that they could not logically defend. To Socrates, such a discussion between people who were genuinely searching for understanding was the key to knowledge of life.

Socrates is executed for his views. Many leading Athenians disapproved of Socrates'

teachings. His insistence on critical thinking and his criticisms of democracy appeared to threaten the city's traditions. He was officially accused of corrupting Athenian youth and of undermining belief in the city's gods. The Athenian leaders probably hoped that Socrates would leave Athens and go into exile. He chose to stand trial, however, and was condemned to death for teaching dangerous ideas. Throughout this ordeal, Socrates refused to go against his conscience. A man of worth, said Socrates, cares only about "acting justly or unjustly." To carry out the death sentence, Socrates calmly drank poison and talked with his students until it took effect.

Plato questions ideas about government and democracy. Socrates' teachings were recorded by his most famous student, Plato (427–347 B.C.). Like his teacher, Plato stressed the importance of knowledge and character. While Socrates was most concerned about the individual, Plato felt that society as a whole should be regulated by reason. He said that laws must serve the best interests of everyone, not just the strongest or the richest people.

The years during and after the Peloponnesian War were difficult for Greece. Plato was critical of the leaders of Athens in this period, particularly after the trial and death of Socrates. He left the city for many years but returned in 387 B.C. to set up his own school, called the Academy.

Plato blamed democracy for the troubles of Athens. He expressed his ideas in the *Republic*, a description of an ideal state. According to Plato, few ordinary Athenian citizens had enough knowledge or experience to govern wisely. He felt that the average citizen could not be trusted to think clearly or vote intelligently. Therefore, he said, democracy produced poor leaders and poor government. In the *Republic*, Plato suggested that men trained as philosophers would make the wisest and best leaders. He wrote:

> . . . there will be no end to the troubles of states, or indeed, . . . of humanity itself, till philosophers become kings in this world, or till those we now call kings and rulers really and truly become philosophers. . . . There is no other road to happiness, either for society or the individual.

According to Plato, these "philosopher-kings" would not be interested in money or power. Rather, they would spend many years getting the education and experience needed to become wise and just rulers. In Plato's ideal city-state, the common people would lose their right to take part in the government but would have able rulers. Although he was critical of Athenian democracy, Plato was the first thinker to analyze political systems.

Aristotle studies all fields of knowledge. Probably the most brilliant student at Plato's Academy was Aristotle (384–322 B.C.). He explored every field of knowledge known to the ancient Greeks. The son of a physician, Aristotle studied plants, animals, astronomy, and physics, keeping careful records of his observations. In science, Aristotle taught that a theory should be accepted only if it agreed with the facts that could be observed. Many later scientists followed his methods, and he is considered the founder of the science of biology. When Aristotle set up his own school, the Lyceum, it emphasized the study of nature.

Aristotle tried to discover and organize the basic ideas in many other fields of knowledge. In his *Poetics,* he examined what made plays good or bad. Aristotle's *Rhetoric* (RET-ur-ik) outlined the ways in which a speaker should organize an effective speech. Aristotle also wrote on logical thinking, ethics, and government.

In his book *Politics,* Aristotle looked at different forms of government in terms of how they were run and what benefits and responsibilities their citizens had. He emphasized the importance of able leaders and respect for the law. "Political society," he wrote, "exists for the sake of noble actions."

With Aristotle, Greek philosophy reached its height. He influenced not only his own students but also philosophers and scientists centuries later. In 343 B.C. he became the tutor of Alexander the Great, giving the prince a respect and love for Greek culture and learning.

This sculpture of Aristotle shows the philosopher wearing a simple tunic and sandals, the style of dress common throughout ancient Greece. Notice how the artist has used blocks of stone to balance the feet of the statue.

CHECK-UP

1. Vocabulary: *philosophy, natural law.*
2. What contributions to the development of science were made by (a) Thales, (b) Pythagoras, (c) Democritus, (d) Hippocrates?
3. (a) Who were the Sophists? (b) What did Socrates have in common with the Sophists? (c) Why did he criticize them?
4. Describe Socrates' method of teaching.
5. (a) What were Plato's criticisms of Athenian democracy? (b) What kind of rulers did he suggest in his *Republic?*
6. (a) What fields of knowledge did Aristotle study? (b) What was his approach to science?

3 Learning Continues in the Hellenistic Age

The knowledge and culture of the Hellenic Age were preserved during the second stage of Greek civilization, the Hellenistic Age. This period began in 323 B.C. with the death of Alexander the Great. As Greek learning spread throughout Alexander's empire, Greek scientists made important findings, and new ideas developed in philosophy.

Alexander's conquests inspire new learning. Many scientists and philosophers had accompanied Alexander's expeditions to the Near East. Their travels gave them a vast amount of new knowledge about plants, animals, geography, and astronomy. The Greeks also acquired new skills and ideas from the different peoples of the empire — mathematics and astronomy from the Near East, medical knowledge from Egypt.

Many scientists at Alexandria studied astronomy. The scientist who drew the diagrams on this piece of papyrus may have been illustrating ideas on planetary motion and distances from the earth to the sun.

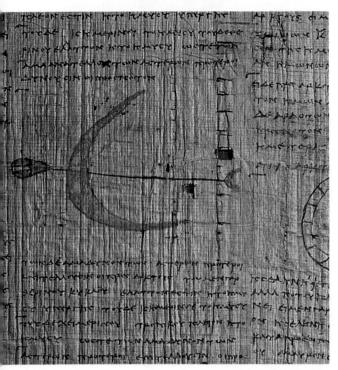

Alexandria is the center of Hellenistic culture. The city of Alexandria in Egypt (map, page 76) had been founded by Alexander in 332 B.C. After his death, Egypt came under the rule of one of his generals, Ptolemy. By 304 B.C. Ptolemy established a new dynasty, whose rulers encouraged scholarship in Alexandria. They set up the greatest library and research center the ancient world had known. The museum had botanical gardens, a zoo, and an observatory for studying stars. The library had about 500,000 books written on papyrus scrolls.

Outstanding scholars and scientists were invited to work in the library at Alexandria. The rulers of Egypt supported them and their research. The scholars at the library collected important writings from all over the Greek world. The library had, for instance, copies of the works of Homer, the plays of the Athenian dramatists, and the medical books from Hippocrates' school. The sacred writings of the Hebrews were translated into Greek there.

Hellenistic scientists discover important principles. Besides gathering knowledge, the scientists at Alexandria also made new and important discoveries. Many still influence modern science. A mathematician named Euclid (YOO-klid) organized earlier knowledge of geometry into a logical system. He also worked out hundreds of geometrical proofs, writing a textbook that became the basic work in geometry. Students in geometry courses today still study Euclid's proofs.

Eratosthenes (er-uh-TOS-thuh-neez) was both a scholar and head librarian at Alexandria about 230 B.C. From earlier Greek scientists, Eratosthenes knew that the earth was round. Using geometry, he estimated its circumference with remarkable accuracy. He also correctly declared that the oceans of the earth were connected, and he made accurate maps of the world he knew.

Aristarchus (air-iss-TAR-kus) was a mathematician and astronomer from the island of Samos. He argued that the sun was the center of the universe, but this idea was too startling for other Greek scientists to accept. Their observations seemed to prove that the sun revolved around the earth. People continued to believe in an earth-centered universe for another 1,700 years.

Archimedes (ahr-kuh-MEE-deez) studied at Alexandria but spent most of his life on the island of Sicily. His work in mathematics and physics led him to discover the principles of the lever and the pulley as well as the natural laws for calculating the weight of an object in water. In his own time Archimedes was famous for his inventions, especially weapons such as the catapult. Greek philosophers and scientists, however, generally were not interested in applying science to practical matters. Archimedes preferred to be recognized for his work in pure mathematics.

Philosophers consider new problems. Both Hellenic and Hellenistic philosophers believed they could use reason to discover rules to explain and direct human conduct. There was an important difference, however. In the Hellenic Age philosophers had been concerned particularly with the individual as a citizen of the polis. In the Hellenistic Age, the Greek city-states were no longer the center of political life. The Greek world grew larger and more complex as Greeks settled in other lands and exchanged ideas with other peoples. In this changing world, Hellenistic philosophers gave more thought to the individual as an individual rather than as a member of a community.

Philosophers seek rules for living. Two important Hellenistic schools of philosophy developed in Athens about the third century B.C. One was Epicureanism, named after Epicurus (ep-ih-KYOOR-us), a writer and teacher. Epicurus tried to define the ways in which people could live untroubled lives. He advised against trying to gain wealth, political power, or fame, since such attempts increase anxiety. For the same reason, he said, wise people should not give in to strong emotions. They should try to keep their bodies "free from pain" and their minds "released from worry and fear." He recommended the enjoyment of simple pleasures such as intelligent conversation with good friends or lying "on the soft grass by a running stream under the branches of a tall tree."

Some later followers of Epicurus chose to indulge in pleasures such as luxurious living and rich food and drink. This was contrary to Epicurus' aim, but gave the word *epicurean* its modern meaning: someone whose main interest is in pleasure, especially in eating.

Stoicism (STOH-ih-siz-um), the other Hellenistic philosophy, had the most enduring influence. It was founded about 300 B.C. by Zeno, who met with his followers in an open walkway, or *stoa*, in the marketplace of Athens. The Stoics, like Socrates, emphasized dignity, self-control, and reason. Zeno stated that the essential part of a person was reason. The individual, said Zeno, should accept what life brings and remain indifferent to pain, pleasure, and unhappiness.

Stoicism endured for several hundred years. Its ideas influenced both the Romans and the early Christians. Later Stoics said that all human beings are by nature equal because they all have the power to use reason. This ability, they said, gives individuals dignity and enables them to recognize the dignity of others. "Our [lives] should not be based on cities or peoples, each with its own view of right and wrong," declared a Stoic philosopher, "but we should regard all men as our fellow countrymen and fellow citizens." This Stoic belief in the equality of human beings throughout the world showed how the Greeks' outlook was changing in the Hellenistic Age.

CHECK-UP

1. (a) Why did learning grow in the Hellenistic Age? (b) What city was the center of learning in this period? (c) What encouraged learning in that city?
2. What contributions to science were made by (a) Euclid, (b) Eratosthenes, (c) Aristarchus, and (d) Archimedes?
3. (a) In what ways did Hellenistic philosophers follow the traditions of Hellenic philosophers? (b) How did Hellenistic philosophy differ from earlier philosophies?
4. (a) What was the main goal of Epicurus' philosophy? (b) How did he recommend that people achieve this goal?
5. (a) Why did Zeno consider emotions unimportant? (b) What did the Stoics emphasize?

Chapter 4 Review

Summary

As well as making a contribution to Western ideals of democratic government and political freedom, the Greeks greatly influenced art, architecture, science, and philosophy. The Greek ideal was a balanced life in which both excellence and moderation were goals to be attained.

Early Greek poetry gradually evolved into Greek drama. The three great writers of tragedy during the golden age of Athens were Aeschylus, Sophocles, and Euripides. In the same period the writers Herodotus and Thucydides set new standards for writing history. In Greek art and architecture, the ideals were beauty, simplicity, and perfect proportion. Classical Greek architecture influenced the design of later Western buildings.

Philosophy and science developed together in the Hellenic Age (800–323 B.C.) as thinkers looked for ways to explain the physical world and human behavior according to reason and logic. Socrates urged people to examine their own lives. Aristotle organized and analyzed many fields of knowledge.

The conquests of Alexander the Great spread Greek culture and learning over a wide area. In the period known as the Hellenistic Age, science and philosophy continued to develop. The ideas of the Stoic philosophers were influential for hundreds of years.

Vocabulary Review

1. Write the sentences listed below on a sheet of paper. In each sentence fill in the blank with one of these words: *city-state, natural law, philosophy, technology.*
(a) The Greek word for "love of wisdom" is __?__ .
(b) To improve the methods, materials, and tools used in a specific craft is to improve its __?__ .
(c) An independent state consisting of a city and its surrounding territory is a __?__ .
(d) Greek philosophers named the rules by which nature operates __?__ .

2. Explain the relationship between the two items in each of the following pairs:

(a) dialogue; Socrates.
(b) the *Republic;* Plato.
(c) observation; Aristotle.

People to Identify

Tell whether each of the following people lived in the Hellenic Age (800–323 B.C.) or the Hellenistic Age (after 323 B.C.). Also tell why he or she was important.
1. Thespis
2. Sappho
3. Thales
4. Sophocles
5. Aristotle
6. Euclid
7. Euripides
8. Democritus
9. Archimedes
10. Aristarchus
11. Eratosthenes
12. Hippocrates

Relating Geography and History

1. **Map interpretation.** A *strait* is a narrow passage of water joining two larger bodies of water. The Hellespont and Bosporus are examples. Study the map on page 67. What two bodies of water are joined by (a) the Hellespont? (b) the Bosporus? (c) Using the map on page 68, explain why these straits were important for Greek trade.

2. **Reports.** Through their maps, written observations, and mathematical calculations, the following ancient Greeks advanced the early study of geography: (a) Strabo, (b) Eratosthenes, (c) Ptolemy. Choose one of these geographers. Find information about his accomplishments and prepare a brief report.

Discussion Questions

1. Describe the interests and qualities that the Greeks thought essential to the development of a full life.
2. It has been said that Greek drama deals with timeless themes. What does this statement mean? Name some of those themes.

3. Why was the development of the scientific outlook an important advance in the history of Western civilization?

4. (a) Socrates shared some of the Sophists' beliefs, but he said that their philosophy had failed. Why? (b) What solution did he offer? (c) Why did his approach anger Athenians?

5. (a) Why is it said that Greek philosophy reached its height with Aristotle? (b) What subjects did he discuss in his writings?

6. (a) What were the major differences in the teachings of Epicurus and those of the Stoics? (b) How did later followers of each philosophy change it?

7. (a) Why did Alexandria become a center of learning during the Hellenistic Age? (b) What advances in mathematics and science came from Alexandria during that time?

Reading Primary Sources

In the following passage Thucydides describes his efforts to discover the truth about the events of the Peloponnesian War. Read the passage. Then answer the questions below.

> And with regard to my factual reporting of the events of the war, I have made it a principle not to write down the first story that came my way, and not even to be guided by my own general impressions. Either I was present myself at the events which I have described or else I heard of them from eyewitnesses whose reports I have checked with as much thoroughness as possible. . . . Even so, the truth was [not] easy to discover; different eyewitnesses give different accounts of the same events, speak out of partiality [favor] for one side or the other or else from imperfect memories. And it may well be that my history will seem less easy to read because of the absence in it of a romantic element.

(a) In what two ways did Thucydides get his information? (b) What problems did he experience with the testimony of eyewitnesses? (c) Why, do you think, did he decide not to use either his own general impressions or the first information that came to him? (d) What do you think he meant when he said that his story might seem hard to read because it lacked "a romantic element"? (Think about the difference between his work and that of Herodotus.) (e) Would a modern historian who wanted to write about the Peloponnesian War have the problems Thucydides described? Explain.

Skill Activities

1. Paraphrasing. Paraphrase (rewrite in your own words) each of the following statements made by Greek thinkers. You may use more than one sentence.
(a) "The unexamined life is not worth living" (page 88).
(b) "Wonders are there many—none more wonderful than man" (page 82).
(c) "Moderation is the noblest gift of heaven" (page 82).
(d) "Our [lives] should not be based on cities or peoples, each with its own view of right and wrong, but we should regard all men as our fellow countrymen and fellow citizens" (page 91).
(e) "Success, for the striver, washes away the effort of striving" (page 82).

2. Stating both sides of an issue. Plato argued that the people of Athens would be happier under the rule of a philosopher-king than they were under democratic government. Write a script for a debate on his idea. Make clear the arguments on both sides of the issue. Be sure that *your* point of view is not obvious.

3. Reports. Find information about one of the following topics and prepare a report: (a) the Acropolis; (b) the trial of Socrates; (c) the Hippocratic oath; (d) the life of Aristotle; (e) the Elgin Marbles (Greek sculptures now in the British Museum); (f) Aesop's fables; (g) the Sword of Damocles; (h) the library at Alexandria; (i) Greek poetry that has survived to our times.

4. Interpreting pictures. Look in library books or an encyclopedia to find a picture of the Parthenon as it looked during the period of this chapter. Draw a picture or make a model of the Parthenon. Then write a paragraph telling how the Parthenon is an example of the Greek ideal of beauty. (Refer to page 86 of this book as a source of information for your paragraph.)

5. Making charts. Make a chart of the accomplishments of ten ancient Greek dramatists, scientists, and philosophers. In three separate columns, write (1) the name of each; (2) the accomplishments of each; and (3) whether each lived during the Hellenic or Hellenistic Age.

The army played an important part in Roman history. Legions helped to build an empire and keep peace throughout the Roman lands. The soldiers below are from the Praetorian Guard, formed to protect the emperor. In time the Guard grew powerful enough to influence the choice of ruler.

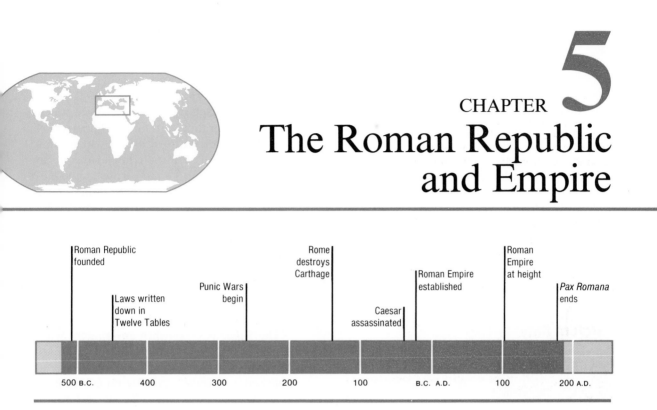

CHAPTER

The Roman Republic and Empire

5

Roman Republic founded

Laws written down in Twelve Tables

Punic Wars begin

Rome destroys Carthage

Caesar assassinated

Roman Empire established

Roman Empire at height

Pax Romana ends

| 500 B.C. | 400 | 300 | 200 | 100 | B.C. A.D. | 100 | 200 A.D. |

In the fifth century B.C., when the Greek city-states were defending their way of life against the invading Persians, Rome was only a small town in Italy. In the centuries that followed, Rome created the largest and most powerful empire of the ancient world. At its height the Roman Empire stretched from the island of Britain to the sands of Arabia. Roman rule brought peace, order, and civilized life to the Mediterranean world. It united many different peoples in a common civilization under one set of laws. People throughout the Empire were proud to say, *"Civis Romanus sum"* — "I am a citizen of Rome."

The Greeks had developed ideas of democratic government and explored new forms in literature, architecture, science, and philosophy. The Romans adopted much from Greece and added their own talents in engineering, government, and above all, law.

This chapter describes how Rome grew from a republic into an empire.

CHAPTER OUTLINE

1   The Romans Build a Strong Republic
2   The Republic Comes to an End
3   Rome Unites a Vast Empire
4   Roman Society Changes
5   The Romans Build on Greek Culture

95

1 The Romans Build a Strong Republic

Early in its history, Rome was a small town on the Tiber River in the central part of the Italian peninsula. This location gave Rome several advantages. The fertile plains could support a large population. The Tiber provided a route to the sea, giving Rome the opportunity for foreign trade. Rome was located in the heart of Italy and could expand in many directions.

The Greeks and Etruscans influence Roman culture. The early settlers of Rome were a people called the Latins, who were one of many different peoples living in the Italian peninsula. Greek colonists had established city-states in

Ancient Italy

The city of Rome was located in the central part of Italy, a peninsula of southern Europe. What mountains stretched for much of the length of Italy? What island lay south of the peninsula?

Sicily and southern Italy, and the Romans adopted their alphabet, military techniques, and styles of literature, art, and architecture. A people called the Etruscans (ee-TRUS-kunz) lived in prosperous trading cities to the north and west of Rome. From the Etruscans the Romans learned practical skills in sanitation, road building, architecture, and pottery making. By about the seventh century B.C., the Etruscans controlled Rome and much of the land nearby. Etruscan kings ruled Rome for over a hundred years. During their reign, Rome grew into a great city built on seven hills along the Tiber. The Forum — a central public square — was built between two of the hills.

The Romans establish a government without a king. In 509 B.C., according to tradition, the Romans drove out their Etruscan ruler and established a *republic* — a government without a king. While the Roman Republic had no king, it was not a democracy like Athens. Its leaders all came from the class of wealthy landowners, who were called patricians (puh-TRISH-uns). Two officials called consuls directed the daily affairs of governing and also led the army. Consuls held office for only a year; there was little risk that they would gain too much power or make themselves king.[1]

A 300-member council of patricians, the Senate, was the most powerful part of the government of the Republic. The Senate controlled Rome's finances and foreign affairs. In the Senate, Rome's most influential citizens debated vital issues and made the important decisions affecting the state. Most senators had held other high government positions. They believed that they honored themselves and their families by serving Rome well. The military banners carried by the Roman armies bore the letters *SPQR*. These letters stood for Latin words that meant "the Senate and the people of Rome."

The people gain a voice in government. Assemblies of Roman citizens made up

---

[1] The consuls could cancel each other's decisions by using the power to *veto*, the Latin word meaning "I forbid."

another part of the Roman government. The membership and the powers of these assemblies changed over the years. In the early years of the Republic, an assembly of soldier-citizens made laws and approved the election of government officials.

The common people, or plebeians (plih-BEE-unz), had little say in the government. They took part in an assembly, but it had much less power than the Senate. Roman laws worked against the plebeians, even though they were citizens. They could not hold high government positions or marry patricians. The plebeians' struggle to gain equality with the patricians went on for 200 years.

Early in the Republic, plebeians threatened to stop serving in the army and paying taxes. Since Rome was constantly at war with its neighbors in Italy, this was a serious threat to the Republic. To avoid civil war between the different groups within the country, the plebeians were given the right to form their own assembly. It could pass laws affecting only the common people. It also elected officials called tribunes, who protected the plebeians' rights. In 451 B.C. the plebeians succeeded in having Roman laws collected and written down for the first time. Known as the Twelve Tables, these laws gave the common people some protection against unfair decisions by patrician judges.

The plebeians' position continued to improve, especially that of wealthy plebeian merchants. Plebeians could no longer be enslaved for debt. They also gained the right to marry patricians and hold the office of consul. Eventually they won the right to become members of the Senate.

By 287 B.C., plebeians and patricians had equal legal rights. Nevertheless, real political power remained in the hands of the patricians and wealthy plebeians, who made up the nobility. These nobles still held the highest offices in the Republic and dominated the Senate.

Rome becomes a military power. Despite the long struggle between patricians and plebeians, Rome continued to expand. The Romans showed a devotion to their city, a toughness of character, and a genius for warfare and diplomacy. They knew how to wage war successfully, how to gain allies, and how to treat a defeated enemy. By the middle of the third century B.C., Rome ruled most of Italy.

The army had been important throughout Rome's history. In 390 B.C., after an attack by people called Gauls from north of Italy, the Senate required plebeians as well as patricians to serve as soldiers. The sturdy Roman farmer made an excellent soldier. He was loyal to his city and strong enough to march thirty miles a day carrying sixty pounds of armor, weapons, and supplies.

The strength of the Roman army was its superior discipline and organization. Roman troops used the same weapons as their enemies — swords, spears, daggers, bows and arrows, and stones. While their opponents often fought like an unorganized mob, the Romans adopted and improved upon the tight battle formation used by Greek foot soldiers. The basic army unit was the legion. It was made up of 3,000 to 6,000 infantry soldiers and 100 or more troops on horseback. Fighting as part of such a unit strengthened the determination and confidence of the Roman soldier.

TIMETABLE

Rome: From Republic to Empire

B.C.

509*	The Romans establish a republic.
490–287*	Plebeians gain civil rights and written laws.
264–241	First Punic War: Rome acquires provinces.
218–202	Second Punic War: Hannibal is defeated.
149–146	Third Punic War: Carthage is destroyed.
60	The First Triumvirate is formed.
49	Caesar marches on Rome.
44	Caesar is assassinated.
31	Octavian becomes ruler of Rome.
27	Rome becomes an empire under Augustus; the Pax Romana begins.

A.D.

117	The Empire reaches its greatest extent.
180	The Pax Romana ends.

*APPROXIMATE DATES

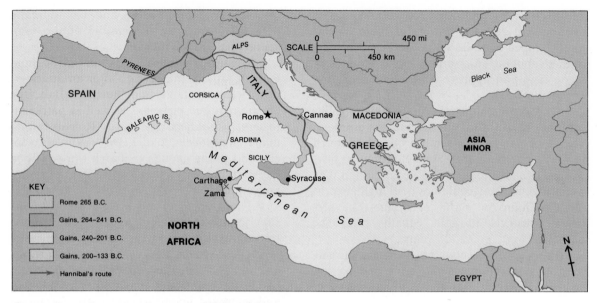

Growth of Roman Power, 264–133 B.C.

During the Punic Wars, Rome gained land outside Italy. What gains had Rome made by
201 B.C.? After that date, what lands did Rome take over?

Rome gains allies in Italy. Despite the strength of its army, Rome could not have conquered Italy without the help of other peoples of the peninsula. Through wise diplomacy, Rome made allies of some former enemies. Some defeated cities and peoples were granted Roman citizenship; others were permitted to keep their local self-government. Rome gave the conquered peoples protection and maintained order throughout the Italian peninsula.

Its conquests in Italy gave Rome the additional soldiers it needed to expand further. Besides nearly 300,000 male Roman citizens, there were some 700,000 allies in Italy. Some Roman statesmen opposed involvement in wars outside Italy. Rome's growing power, however, brought it into conflict with the other states of the Mediterranean world.

Rome and Carthage go to war. In 264 B.C. Rome went to war with the North African city-state of Carthage (KAR-thidj). Founded by the Phoenicians (page 53), Carthage had become a strong sea power. It controlled large areas in the western Mediterranean, including parts of Spain, North Africa, and many islands. Rome considered Carthage a threat to its allies in southern Italy and to the supply of grain from the island of Sicily. The series of wars that Rome fought with Carthage are called the Punic (PYOO-nik)[2] Wars.

Rome began the war with a stronger army, for it could call on its Italian allies for extra soldiers. The Carthaginians, on the other hand, had a superior navy. The Romans quickly built their own fleet and won victories both at sea and in Sicily. Carthage eventually was forced to make peace in 241 B.C. Rome's victory in the First Punic War gave it Sicily as its first *province,* territory that was outside the Italian peninsula (see map).

Hannibal invades Roman territory. As the Carthaginians continued to expand in Spain, Rome planned to attack them there. In 218 B.C., however, the Carthaginian general Hannibal decided to strike at Rome by invading Italy from the north. This marked the start of the Second Punic War. With his entire army and a number of war elephants, Hannibal traveled northeast through Spain, crossed what is now southern France, and reached the Alps in

---

[2]*Punic* is derived from the Latin word for "Phoenician."

northern Italy. The Carthaginians struggled across the steep and icy mountain passes into Italy. The Gauls who lived there joined the Carthaginians against Rome, and even some Roman allies helped the invaders.

Moving southward through Italy, Hannibal showed his military genius at the Battle of Cannae (KAN-ee) in 216 B.C. When the Romans attacked, Hannibal pulled back the forces in the middle of his battle line. To the Romans, it looked like the start of a retreat. Falling for the trick, the whole Roman army surged forward in pursuit. Hannibal's cavalry, which was waiting on both ends of the line, swung around behind the Romans. Trapped in a pocket, four legions of Roman soldiers were killed or captured.

The people of Rome were shocked by the costly defeat. "The streets were loud with the wailing and weeping of women," wrote the historian Livy. Even worse, the Romans feared that Hannibal would now march on Rome itself. These were the Republic's worst days.

Hannibal is defeated. Though Hannibal continued to win battles in Italy, he lacked the military strength to capture the city of Rome. Moreover, the Roman allies near the city remained loyal. To relieve the pressure on the city of Rome, an army led by the Roman general Scipio (SKIP-ee-oh) attacked the Carthaginians in Spain, preventing help from being sent to Hannibal. In 204 B.C. the Romans also invaded North Africa. To protect his homeland, Hannibal returned to Carthage. He was defeated by Scipio in the Battle of Zama in 202 B.C. This was Hannibal's first defeat, and it ended the war. This second victory over Carthage gave Rome even more land (map, page 98).

The Romans destroy Carthage. In 146 B.C. Rome defeated Carthage in a third war. Although Carthage had become too weak to be a threat, many Romans wanted to crush it permanently. Driven by old hatreds and the memory of Hannibal's victories, the Romans burned Carthage to the ground and sold its survivors into slavery. The region became a Roman province.

The Romans gain control of the Greek world. The defeat of Carthage in the Second

ROMAN MILITARY MIGHT

The statue at right shows one of Rome's famed citizen-soldiers who helped to build an empire. In battle Roman soldiers protected themselves by positioning their shields in a formation called the tortoise (below). The sculpture is part of a column built to honor the emperor Trajan (page 106).

Punic War had given Rome control of the western Mediterranean Sea. The lands of the eastern Mediterranean still belonged to cities and Hellenistic kingdoms that had arisen after the breakup of Alexander's empire. Shortly after Hannibal's defeat, Rome went to war against his ally, the kingdom of Macedonia. By 196 B.C. Rome had defeated the Macedonians and taken over as the "protector" of the Greek city-states in Asia Minor. Other victories followed in Greece and Asia Minor. By 133 B.C. Rome had extended its rule over the entire Mediterranean, including all the Greek world.

CHECK-UP

1. Vocabulary: *republic, province.*
2. (a) What advantages did Rome's location offer? (b) What did the early Romans borrow from the Greeks? (c) from the Etruscans?
3. (a) Why did plebeians and patricians come into conflict? (b) What rights did plebeians gain? (c) How did written law benefit them?
4. What factors helped Rome become a military power?
5. (a) What were the causes of the Punic Wars? (b) What were the results?
6. What territory did Rome control by 133 B.C.?

2 The Republic Comes to an End

While Rome's wars brought it new lands and power, critical social and political problems developed at home. Some leaders attempted to solve these problems, but the Republic began to decline.

Rome faces a crisis in agriculture. The decline of the Republic began with a crisis in agriculture that brought ruin to thousands of small farmers. Hannibal's invasion had destroyed farms and farmland; other farms had been neglected while their owners had been away fighting. Since grain and other farm products were being sent to Rome from conquered lands, prices in Italy fell and so did the farmers' incomes. Lacking the money to rebuild, many farmers sold out to landowners who had grown wealthy during the war. The newly rich owners created large estates known as *latifundia*. They found workers for their farms among the thousands of slaves taken as prisoners during the Punic Wars.

Many of the small farmers who had neither land nor jobs moved to the Roman cities to look for work, but few were able to find jobs there. Although many of them had been soldiers for Rome, they now became part of a huge class of unemployed and resentful city poor people.

The Gracchus brothers work for reform. The Gracchus (GRAH-kus) family of Rome were wealthy plebeians who were active in politics. Tiberius Gracchus, elected tribune in 133 B.C., promised to help the farmers. He called for taking public land and distributing it among the landless farmers. Tiberius also wanted to enforce an ancient law that limited the size of farms on public land. To many landholding senators, however, both these proposals appeared as threats. They also feared that Tiberius was seeking to stir up the poor people in order to gain political power for himself. When Tiberius sought re-election as tribune, violence broke out. Tiberius and 300 of his followers were killed in the rioting. Tiberius' death was blamed on a group of senators.

Gaius Gracchus, a younger brother of Tiberius, became tribune ten years later and urged even more reforms. He had grain given to the poor, opened up more land for the farmers, and secured more rights for the middle class. In 121 B.C. fighting broke out between the Romans who supported Gaius and those who opposed his policies. Gaius and several thousand people were killed.

Roman politics become corrupt and violent. The Roman Republic in the second century B.C. was very different from the Rome that had defeated Carthage. Fear of Carthage had kept the Romans united and loyal. Now they were often bitterly divided by domestic issues

ROMAN DAILY LIFE

Most Romans in the Republic led simple lives. The sculpture at right shows a farmer on his way to market. In the background is a shrine to the Roman gods. Farmers took their goods — olive oil, grain, vegetables, fruit, meat, and herbs — to shops in nearby towns. Women ran a number of these businesses, such as the poultry market (below). Many Romans along the coast fished for a living (below right). The family was highly respected in Rome, and its members — unlike Greek families — usually dined together (bottom).

Roman sculptors were skilled at portraying people. This carving is of Caesar, whose name became a title used in Germany (*kaiser*) and Russia (*czar*).

and conflicts between rich and poor. As long as there were thousands of land-hungry farmers and unemployed city poor, there was danger of riots and violence. The Senate attacks on the Gracchus brothers introduced violence as a means of dealing with political opponents.

The Senate could not provide leadership in these years of turmoil. Many patricians became more concerned with keeping their power and wealth than with promoting the welfare of Rome. The common people were ready to follow leaders who promised them food and entertainment. The Republic had passed the peak of its greatness.

Roman slaves revolt. Another cause of unrest in the Republic was fear of the thousands of slaves in the population. Most were war captives transported from their homes to Italy. While slave uprisings were not common, the ferocity of those that did break out terrified the Romans. In 135 B.C., slaves on the island of Sicily revolted and captured several towns before being subdued. In 73 B.C. the slave Spartacus proclaimed a war to free slaves in Italy. Some 90,000 slaves ran away to join his revolt. For two years the slave army defeated Roman forces and devastated southern Italy. The revolt ended when Spartacus was killed in battle. The victorious general, Marcus Licinius Crassus, had 6,000 slaves put to death by crucifixion.

Ambitious generals gain power. During this period of unrest, it was easy for powerful and ambitious military leaders to gain popular support. In 105 B.C. Gaius Marius, a popular general, began to recruit soldiers from the jobless poor of the cities. Before this time, only men who owned property could be Roman soldiers. They had served in the army out of loyalty to Rome. The landless Romans of the cities, on the other hand, volunteered for service because Marius had promised them money, loot from conquered peoples, and land when the fighting was over. These soldiers' loyalty was to Marius rather than to the government of Rome.

Other ambitious commanders followed Marius' example in building up private armies. A general who had the confidence and support of his soldiers could intimidate the Senate and influence lawmaking. Marius' greatest rival was another commander, Lucius Cornelius Sulla. The bloody wars between the supporters of these two rival generals finally came to an end with Sulla's capture of Rome. Sulla used his victory to restore the authority of the Senate, though he kept the real power for himself. In 82 B.C. Sulla was given the title of *dictator.* This position, granted only in times of crisis, carried absolute power but was supposed to be limited to a term of six months. Actually Sulla remained dictator for two years, using his power to have many opponents murdered.

The First Triumvirate is formed. The ambitions of military commanders continued to menace the Republic. Using their troops for their own political advantage, generals sought to run the state. In 60 B.C. three ambitious and wealthy military heroes banded together in what was known as the First Triumvirate (try-UM-vih-rut). The three were Gnaeus Pompey, known as Pompey the Great for his victories in the east; Crassus, the victor over Spartacus and one of the richest men in Rome; and Julius Caesar (SEE-zur). The three had few aims in common except their opposition to the Senate. Each was jealous of the other's power, but they at first cooperated to gain the post of consul for Caesar.

Knowing he also needed the backing of an army to succeed in politics, Caesar then took command of the Roman legions in Gaul. Over the next ten years Caesar showed a genius for leadership and military strategy. He brought all of Gaul (roughly the area now called France) under Rome's control and briefly invaded Britain. Caesar described his successes in his book *The Gallic Wars*.

Caesar takes control of Rome. In Rome, Pompey was gaining political power and the support of the Senate. In 49 B.C. he persuaded the Senate to order Caesar to return home without his army. To obey would have left Caesar without power. Instead, Caesar deliberately led his troops into Italy. Civil war began again. Caesar defeated Pompey's armies in Italy and in Greece and went on to more victories in Egypt, Asia Minor, Africa, and Spain. Returning to Rome in 46 B.C. as its greatest hero, he

easily took over the government and was named both dictator and consul.

Caesar made many worthwhile reforms that won him popular support in both the provinces and the cities. He reorganized the government in the provinces, lowering taxes and making the governors responsible to him. To aid the poor in Rome, he resettled 100,000 army veterans and others in new colonies and gave them land to farm. He granted citizenship to more people outside Italy. Caesar also put into effect a new and accurate calendar, the Julian calendar. In 44 B.C., along with many other honors, he was named dictator for life.

Caesar is assassinated. Caesar's power, success, and popularity alarmed many nobles and senators. They feared that he would destroy the Senate and become a king, thereby ending the Republic. To prevent this, on March 15, 44 B.C., a group of nobles led by Marcus

Growth of Roman Power by 44 B.C.

By 44 B.C. the Mediterranean Sea could be called a "Roman lake." Use the information on this map to explain why that description was accurate.

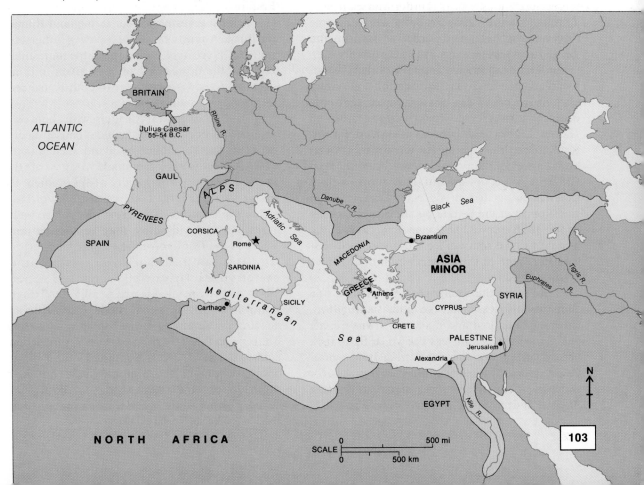

Brutus and Gaius Cassius stabbed Caesar to death in the Senate.

Octavian's victory brings the Republic to an end. The death of Caesar ended the danger of one-man rule, but it plunged Rome back into civil war. A second triumvirate was formed by three of Caesar's supporters — Mark Antony, Lepidus, and Octavian (Caesar's adopted son). They defeated the armies of Brutus and Cassius, but Antony and Octavian then became rivals. In 31 B.C., in a naval battle off the coast of Greece, Octavian's fleet crushed the combined navies of Antony and Cleopatra, Queen of Egypt. This victory made Octavian the unchallenged leader of Rome. The Roman Republic had come to an end.

CHECK-UP

1. Vocabulary: *latifundia, dictator.*
2. (a) What problems did Roman farmers face after the Punic Wars? (b) What did the Gracchus brothers offer as a solution for these problems? (c) Why did the Senate oppose these reforms?
3. How did changes in the following contribute to the decline of the Republic: (a) the Senate? (b) the Roman army?
4. (a) How did Caesar become head of the Roman government? (b) What reforms did he make?
5. (a) How did Caesar's rule come to an end? (b) What happened to the Republic after Caesar's death?

3 Rome Unites a Vast Empire

Octavian's triumph in 31 B.C. marked the end of the Roman Republic. It also brought an end to a century of political murder and civil war. Throughout the Mediterranean world, people hoped for peace and orderly government. These became the goals of the new Empire.

Octavian becomes emperor. Like Caesar, Octavian believed that the republican system no longer worked. He was convinced that only a single strong ruler could restore order in Rome. Caesar had been assassinated for his ambition to rule alone. By the time of Octavian, however, many nobles had been killed in the struggle for power, and others now realized that Rome needed strong rule. Octavian won the support of the Senate by allowing it to keep some of its power. Octavian encouraged the Senate to give him advice, permitted it to administer some of the provinces, and let it have its own treasury.

In 27 B.C. the Senate gave Octavian a title that was also used for the gods — *Augustus,* meaning "honored and majestic." This became the name by which he was known. He also took the honorary title "caesar," which most later rulers added to their own names. Augustus (or Augustus Caesar) was also referred to as "first citizen," which implied that Rome was still a republic. In reality, however, Augustus' rise to power marked the beginning of the Roman Empire.

Augustus restores order throughout Roman territory. Augustus was not a power-hungry tyrant but a creative and responsible statesman. He used the power he had been given to bring order and good government to both Rome and its far-flung provinces.

Ambitious military leaders with their own armies had been one of the chief causes of disorder in the Republic. To avoid such disruption, Augustus took complete control of the army. He gained the loyalty of his soldiers by giving veterans large bonuses and land in Italy or the provinces. This gave Rome a well-trained and loyal army that kept order and guarded the frontiers of the Empire.

Augustus tried to improve government in the provinces. He carefully supervised the actions of provincial governors and took direct control of provinces that might cause trouble, leaving the Senate to oversee the provinces that were peaceful. To encourage loyalty to Rome and to himself, Augustus granted citizenship to more people in the Empire, including men from the provinces who served in the Roman army. Former soldiers and their families gained

ROMAN EMPERORS

Roman artists portrayed the emperors in many forms of art. Augustus, honored as one of the gods, is shown in armor decorated with scenes from Roman myths (right). The portrait of Tiberius (top right) is made of carved glass. Roman emperors were also honored with equestrian statues — statues that showed them on horseback. The only equestrian statue that remains from ancient Rome is one of Marcus Aurelius (above).

many benefits as well as the feeling that Augustus was interested in their welfare.

Augustus also tried to restore those qualities that had made the Romans a great people — devotion to the Roman state, close family ties, hard work, discipline, and simple living. Laws were passed to encourage people to marry and raise families. Augustus sponsored the building of roads, water systems, and other projects that both improved people's lives and provided jobs for some of the poor in the cities. While unemployment and poverty still existed in Rome, the government gave free or low-cost grain to the poor.

The Roman Peace begins. Augustus died in A.D. 14. His rule had brought Rome peace and a large measure of prosperity. It introduced a period known as *Pax Romana* (PAKS roh-MAH-nuh) — "the Roman Peace." For 200 years, from 27 B.C. to A.D. 180, the vast Roman

Empire enjoyed just and orderly government. The ancient world had never before experienced such a long period of stability.

Augustus' successors lack his abilities. The Empire had no law of succession; that is, there was no rule stating how the next emperor would be chosen. Most rulers chose their heirs from members of their family. The first four emperors after Augustus were related to him or to his second wife, Livia. They are known as the Julio-Claudian dynasty. None of these rulers was equal to Augustus in statesmanship, although they maintained many of his policies that kept the empire strong.

With the rule of Augustus' stepson Tiberius (A.D. 14–37), plots and violence again became common in Roman politics. Tiberius ran the Empire well, however, unlike the next emperor, Caligula (kah-LIG-yoo-lah). Caligula was both cruel and insane and after four years of rule was assassinated by members of the imperial guard. These soldiers then chose a peaceful scholar named Claudius to be emperor. Claudius restored order during his reign (A.D. 41–54) and backed the military expedition that made Britain part of the Empire.

The last of the Julio-Claudian line was the emperor Nero, Claudius' stepson. Nero began his reign well but soon turned to bloodthirsty violence. When Rome was devastated by fire in A.D. 64, Nero blamed it on the Christians and began to persecute them. Four years later the army rebelled against him, and Nero committed suicide.

Military leaders become emperors. In the year following Nero's death, lawlessness swept Rome as military commanders competed for the throne. After the execution of two emperors and the suicide of another within a year, the army chose Vespasian as emperor. In his ten-year reign (A.D. 69–79), Vespasian restored discipline in the army and in the administration of the Empire. He also put down uprisings in the provinces of Gaul and Judaea (joo-DEE-uh).

The Jews revolt against Rome. Roman rule in Judaea clashed with Jewish loyalties and with the desire of the Jews to re-establish their ancient kingdom. In A.D. 66, they had begun a full-scale revolt, and the emperor Nero had sent Vespasian to Judaea to put down the rebellion. When Vespasian's soldiers declared him emperor, he returned to Rome, leaving his son Titus to carry on the war. In A.D. 70, Roman soldiers captured Jerusalem and destroyed the Temple. About a thousand Jews took refuge in the mountaintop fortress of Masada (muh-SAH-dah) and for nearly two years resisted the Roman siege. The fortress finally fell to the Romans in A.D. 73. Rather than surrender their last outpost, nearly all the defenders of Masada committed suicide.

The "good emperors" bring stable rule. Titus and his younger brother Domitian followed their father as emperor. After Domitian's assassination in A.D. 96, the Senate chose a respected senator, Nerva. To avoid the violence that usually accompanied the choice of an emperor, Nerva introduced a wise new policy. He adopted as his son and named as his successor a man with proven ability — Trajan (TRAY-jun), the Spanish-born military governor of the region north of Italy. The adoptive system introduced by Nerva was followed by later emperors until A.D. 180. It ensured a succession of competent rulers who are sometimes called the "Good Emperors."

The Roman Empire reached its greatest size under Trajan's rule (A.D. 98–117). He brought Mesopotamia under Roman rule and added new lands north of the Danube and east of the Black Sea. A wise and popular ruler, he also eased taxes in the provinces, provided aid for the poor, and had many buildings constructed in Rome.

Trajan's successor, Hadrian (A.D. 117–138), devoted his reign to making the empire secure rather than adding more territory. He encouraged people in the provinces to join the armies that guarded their borders. In the province of Britain, he had a defensive wall built along the frontier. Hadrian admired Greek culture and was a poet and amateur architect.

In A.D. 132–133 Hadrian suppressed a second Jewish revolt in Judaea and imposed harsh punishments on the rebels. The Romans renamed the province Syria Palestina (or Palestine), forbade Jews to enter Jerusalem except once a year, and encouraged non-Jews to settle there. Most of the Jews who survived were sold into slavery or sought refuge in other lands.

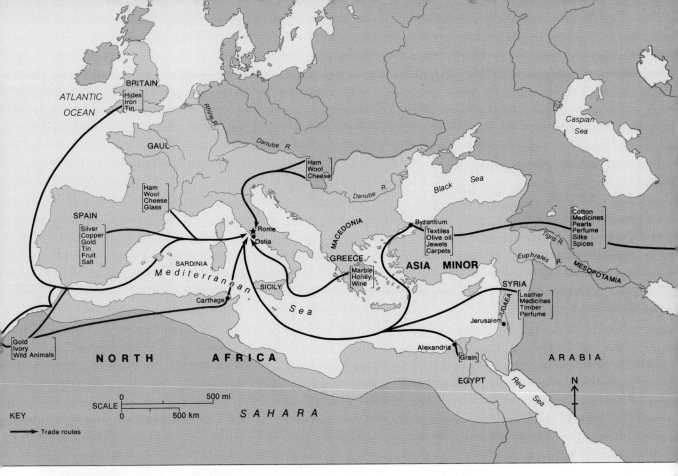

Trade in the Roman Empire

People in the Roman Empire traded extensively with each other and with other lands. Which country grew grain for Rome's bakeries? Where were the mines that supplied Rome with metals? What products came from North Africa? from Asia?

The Pax Romana comes to an end. The last of the emperors chosen by the adoptive system was Marcus Aurelius (uh-REE-lee-us), who began his rule in A.D. 161. He was a scholarly man who followed the ideas of the Stoic philosophers (page 91), but he was forced to concentrate on border wars with the Germanic tribes. Marcus Aurelius abandoned the adoptive system, which had worked so effectively, and chose his son, Commodus, as his successor. Commodus was not fit to rule. His succession to the throne in A.D. 180 marked the end of the Pax Romana.

Peace and order bring prosperity. During the 200 years of the Pax Romana, Roman armies extended the borders of the Empire in Asia Minor, secured the frontiers in Europe at the Rhine and Danube rivers, and conquered most of Britain. These troops guarded against civil wars within the cities and prevented warfare between cities.

The Pax Romana was generally a time of order and good government. The Romans demonstrated a great talent for organizing and governing. Roman governors, assisted by capable officials, enforced Roman law and settled disputes in the provinces. At first, almost all government officials were upper-class Romans, but in time many talented people in the provinces became administrators.

Roman rule brought prosperity. The Romans built roads, improved harbors, cleared forests, drained swamps, irrigated deserts, and turned undeveloped land into prosperous farms. Trade flourished as goods were carried over roads built by Roman engineers and made safe by Roman soldiers. Products from all over the Roman Empire flowed into Rome.

Landmarks in Technology

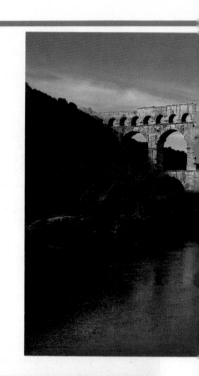

ROMAN ENGINEERING

Roman engineers and architects made outstanding technological achievements. Their buildings and public works helped make people's lives more comfortable. They built aqueducts to carry water to more than 200 cities. Elaborate plumbing systems provided hot and cold water and steam for the public baths.

Engineers made travel within the Empire easier by building a network of paved roads that covered over 50,000 miles. They provided for drainage by laying the pavement of stone slabs over crushed stone, brick, and pottery. Ditches alongside the roads carried away run-off water.

Architects found ways to design buildings with large interiors where many people could gather. The Romans were thus the first to emphasize the space inside buildings as well as the overall appearance.

Among the tools Roman carpenters used were hammers, cutting tools, and mason's squares (below). Using such simple instruments, Roman architects constructed a variety of buildings. The temple known as the Pantheon (right) is considered a triumph of engineering. Its dome forms a nearly perfect hemisphere. Arches within the concrete walls redistribute the weight of this dome and allow a large open interior.

The structures shown on these pages indicate how extensively the Romans used the arch, both for decoration and for practical purposes. The aqueduct in France (top left) has three levels of arches supporting a roadway (still in use) and a channel for water. Most of the arches in the Colosseum (above) served as entryways. This stadium seated 50,000 people on concrete tiers around an oval arena where gladiatorial contests were held. While the Romans used concrete for most of their buildings, their roads — like this road in Turkey (top right) — were paved with large blocks of stone.

Rome also imported goods from foreign lands as far away as China.

Hundreds of new cities were built in the Empire, particularly in southern Gaul. Old cities grew larger and wealthier. The cities enjoyed much self-government and served as centers of education and culture.

Rome unites many peoples. From Britain to Arabia and from the Danube River to the sands of the Sahara, some 70 million people, speaking different languages and following different customs, were united under Roman rule and Roman law. Citizenship was granted generously, and in A.D. 212 virtually all free people in the Empire became Roman citizens. Peoples from different lands learned to speak Latin, the Roman language. They used the same system of weights and measures, obeyed the same laws, and swore allegiance to one emperor. Almost all felt proud and honored to be called citizens of Rome.

CHECK-UP
1. (a) How did Augustus become emperor? (b) What measures did Augustus take to restore order in the Empire?
2. (a) How were Roman emperors chosen in the time of Augustus? (b) How were they chosen after the reign of Nero? (c) after the election of Nerva?
3. (a) Why did Jews in Judaea rebel against Roman rule? (b) What were the results?
4. (a) Name three of the "Good Emperors." (b) About when did each rule? (c) What brought this period of good rule to an end?
5. How did Roman rule (a) improve transportation, (b) encourage agriculture, (c) expand trade, (d) promote city life?

4 Roman Society Changes

Roman society underwent many changes from the early days of the Republic to the period of the Pax Romana. The wealth of the upper class increased, cities flourished, and education came increasingly under the influence of Greek ways. Family life changed, and women gained greater freedom.

Roman cities are centers of culture. The prosperity of the Roman Empire rested on the flourishing cities in Italy and the provinces. Roman engineers built a network of stone-paved roads linking cities and making trade and travel easy within the Empire. Provincial cities tended to copy the city of Rome. With schools, libraries, theaters, and public baths, they too became centers of culture and entertainment.

Class divisions separate the citizens of Rome. There were great contrasts between rich and poor in Rome and, to a lesser extent, in the provinces. In the Roman Republic, the distinction between plebeians and patricians had been mainly one of birth. Gradually the plebeians had gained legal equality. By the time of the Empire, class divisions between the Romans were based mainly on wealth.

Prominent among upper-class Romans were wealthy landowners whose fields were in the nearby countryside. Merchants, doctors, lawyers, and government officials were also members of the upper class, as were some scholars, writers, and artists. The most distinguished Romans belonged to the old senatorial families. They had wealth, social position, and political power.

Wealthy Romans lived in luxurious town houses or large country villas with swimming pools, courtyards, and winter and summer dining rooms. They dressed in fine silk and wore gold ornaments and jewels. At a traditional Roman banquet, guests reclined on couches and were waited on by slaves and entertained by dancers, acrobats, and musicians. Roman nobles dined far into the night on such unusual dishes as ostrich boiled with sweet sauce, roast parrot, flamingo boiled with dates, and larks' tongues.

The poor people in the cities and the Roman countryside had little share in politics or culture. Unemployment was widespread, because slaves did much of the work and there

EXTENT OF THE ROMAN EMPIRE

The vast extent of Rome's empire is suggested by these pictures. Right, the 23-foot-high wall built by the emperor Hadrian stretches nearly 75 miles across northern England. Above is a wall painting from the Nile delta of Egypt, at the southern boundary of the Empire.

was little industry. Public building projects provided some jobs for the poor, but probably half of Rome's one million people depended on the free food given them by the government. The city poor lived in wooden houses crowded closely together.

Rome depended heavily on agriculture. Farmers formed the bulk of the Empire's population. They toiled long hours to provide cheap food for the people in the cities.

Roman society includes slaves. As in other ancient civilizations, slavery was common in Rome. In the early days of the Republic, most slaves were poor Italian farmers who had lost their freedom because of inability to repay their debts. Once Rome began to expand, the number of foreign slaves increased enormously. In the first war with Carthage, the Romans enslaved 75,000 prisoners of war. Caesar's conquest of Gaul brought thousands of other captives into the Roman slave markets. By the time of Augustus, slaves may have accounted for a quarter of the population of Italy.

Under the Republic, slaves were often badly treated. During the Empire, the lot of household slaves improved greatly. Educated Greeks often became respected teachers in Roman families. Other slaves were skilled artisans. Life was still harsh and brutal for most slaves, who rowed the galleys of the Roman navy, worked on latifundia, or cut stone in the quarries.

Several emperors passed laws protecting slaves from cruel masters. Seneca, a Stoic philosopher, urged humane treatment: "Kindly remember that he whom you call your slave sprang from the same [human] stock, is smiled upon by the same skies, and on equal terms with yourself breathes, lives, and dies." In time Roman law provided for the freeing of slaves under certain conditions. Freed slaves became citizens with most of the rights and privileges of other Roman citizens.

Family life changes. In the early days of the Republic the father, or *paterfamilias* (pah-tur-fah-MIL-ee-us), had absolute authority over every person in his household, including slaves and distant relatives. By the second century A.D., however, family discipline was much less harsh. Some parents became overindulgent,

This portrait of a Roman mother and child comes from the city of Alexandria. It is made of sapphire-blue glass painted with gold.

and old-fashioned Romans complained that children were spoiled and poorly disciplined.

The change in family authority brought Roman women more freedom. In the early days of the Republic, a Roman woman went from the absolute authority of her father's household to the absolute rule of her husband. By the time of the Empire, however, a father could no longer force his daughter to marry against her will. A woman could own property and keep her own money or property if divorced. She could also make business arrangements and draw up a will without her husband's approval.

Roman women enjoyed greater freedom and respect than did upper-class women in Greece. Roman women went out visiting or shopping as they pleased. Girls from noble Roman families had opportunities for education that were denied the daughters of Greek nobles. Roman girls might be taught Greek and Latin literature as well as skills in music and dance. Some upper-class Roman women formed groups that read and discussed poetry.

The mothers, daughters, and wives in prominent senatorial families often acquired great political influence. These women were self-assured and powerful. Cornelia, the mother of Tiberius and Gaius Gracchus, influenced Roman politics through her sons. Livia, the dynamic wife of Augustus, often advised him

on decisions. She ensured the succession of her son Tiberius as emperor. From about A.D. 211 to 235, several influential women from the same family held great power in Rome. The empress Julia Domna was in charge of the government while her son, the emperor Caracalla, was fighting abroad. She also was active in Roman cultural life and supported writers and philosophers. Her niece Julia Mamaea was the mother of the emperor Alexander Severus (A.D. 222–235) and made many of the decisions of her son's reign.

Schools educate young Romans. Many of the important Roman values and attitudes were learned at home. A formal system of schooling for Roman boys developed, however, during the Republic. (Girls were generally taught at home.) A teacher called a *litterator* taught young boys reading and writing, and they learned arithmetic from a teacher called a *calculator*. Older boys attended grammar school, where they studied music, geometry, astronomy, literature, and oratory. As in Greece, public speaking and debating were essential skills in Roman political life, and some students continued their studies in the school of rhetoric.

Rome's conquest of the Hellenistic world had a great influence on Roman education. Thousands of educated Greeks came to Rome, often as slaves. Many of them became private tutors for the children of the wealthy. They introduced young Romans to Greek art, science, philosophy, and literature.

Roman cities provide popular entertainment. The Roman people, both rich and poor, loved violent sports and games. The most popular forms of entertainment in both the Republic and the Empire were chariot races, displays of armed combat, and acts with wild animals. The rich staked fortunes on the outcome of the competition, and the poor bet their last coin. Roman politicians sponsored games and parades to win the voters' approval. Some of Rome's greatest public buildings, such as the Colosseum and the Circus Maximus, were erected to house these events.

The drivers in chariot races might be trained slaves or daring Roman nobles. They drove teams of swift horses in thrilling and dangerous races. Roman crowds also loved contests between trained gladiators. Usually slaves or condemned criminals, gladiators fought each other with swords or spears. Most fights were to the death. If not, the crowd might demand either death or freedom for the loser. Even more brutal were the contests between animals or between people and animals. In some events tigers were set against elephants, or people were sent into the arena with lions or wild bulls. In one spectacle during the reign of the emperor Titus, 5,000 wild animals were killed. Much of Rome's trade with Africa was devoted to securing animals for these contests.

CHECK-UP

1. (a) What role did cities play in the Roman Empire? (b) Who made up the upper class in Rome? (c) How did the poor live in Rome?
2. (a) How were slaves treated in the Roman Republic? (b) in the Roman Empire? (c) What kind of work did they do?
3. How did the status of Roman women differ from that of Greek women?
4. Describe the education of Roman boys.
5. What kinds of entertainment did the Romans enjoy?

5 The Romans Build on Greek Culture

From the Greek cities in southern Italy and Sicily, the Roman Republic had absorbed some elements of Greek civilization. After the lands of the eastern Mediterranean came under Roman control, the Greek influence on Rome increased greatly. This culture, which blended Greek and Roman influences, is called Greco-Roman culture.

Greek culture is brought to Rome. Rome's eastern conquests in the second century B.C. brought thousands of Greek intellectuals, businessmen, and slaves to Italy. Roman generals shipped libraries and works of art from Greek cities to Rome. Wealthy Romans hired (or bought as slaves) Greek teachers, poets, and philosophers to live in their households. Some Romans even sent their sons to Athens to study. Increasingly Rome came under the influence of Greek culture.

Expansion also brought Rome into contact with the laws and legal traditions of other peoples, particularly the Greeks. Roman lawyers selected elements of the different legal codes and incorporated them into Roman law. Gradually there evolved a code of law that applied throughout the Empire.

Roman philosophy, literature, science, art, and architecture had roots in ancient Greece. Roman intellectuals preserved and spread the Greek stress on excellence and the use of reason. The Romans added their own practical skills and abilities — organizational ability, skill in engineering, and a talent for government and law. Greco-Roman culture spread throughout the Empire during the Pax Romana, and people in the Roman cities enjoyed its benefits. Many Roman emperors gave their help and support to Roman writers and artists.

Poets express Roman ideals. One of the greatest works of Greco-Roman literature was written at the request of the emperor Augustus. The poet Virgil (70–19 B.C.) glorified the Roman talent for governing in the *Aeneid* (ih-NEE-id), an epic poem like those of Homer (page 66). The *Aeneid* tells the legend of Aeneas, whose descendants supposedly founded Rome. Virgil's poetry expressed his optimism that Rome's destiny was to bring the blessings of peace and stability to the Mediterranean world. The Greeks might be better sculptors, orators, or thinkers, said Virgil, but only the Romans knew how to govern an empire.

Another great poet of Augustus' time was Horace (65–8 B.C.). The son of a freed slave, he became a friend of Virgil and later of Augustus. Like them, he had grown up under the Republic and remembered the agony of its civil wars. Horace felt human greed had caused these conflicts, and he criticized the luxurious lives of many wealthy Romans. He asked, "Why do we strive so hard in our brief lives for great possessions?" It would be better, he said, if the

Romans would follow the Greek ideal of moderation.

While Horace and Virgil preferred the country and wrote poems praising the Roman countryside, the poet Ovid (AW-vid) was a city dweller. Ovid lived from 43 B.C. to A.D. 18. He spoke for the upper-class people of the Empire, who had given up the simple life of the Republic. Ovid wrote of wealth, fashion, romance, and the enjoyment of life. He retold Greek and Roman myths in the *Metamorphoses*.

Juvenal criticizes Roman society. The last great Roman writer was Juvenal (A.D. 60–140). A keen observer of the Roman world, he found much to criticize with his biting wit. Juvenal's description of a crowded city still sounds fresh today:

> Though we hurry, we merely crawl;
> We're blocked by a surging mass ahead, a
>   pushing wall
> Of people behind. A man jabs me, elbowing
>   through, one socks

> A chair pole against me, one cracks my skull
>   with a beam, one knocks
> A wine cask against my ear. My legs are caked
>   with splashing
> Mud, from all sides the weight of enormous
>   feet comes smashing
> On mine, and a soldier stamps his hobnails
>   through to my sole.

The Romans add realism to art. Just as Roman poets were keen observers of everyday life, Roman sculptors sought to show the unique qualities of an individual. Greek artists had tried to portray perfect human beauty, but the Romans carved every detail realistically. They showed unruly hair, a prominent nose, and age lines and wrinkles. Another popular form of art in Rome was the wall painting. Wealthy Romans had portraits, ocean views, or scenes from mythology painted on the walls of their homes. Roman artisans were skilled in working with bronze and terra cotta and in carving jewels.

LINKING PAST AND PRESENT

Discovering the Past in Pompeii

On a hot August day in A.D. 79, the volcano Vesuvius in southwestern Italy erupted almost without warning. Deadly fumes and tons of poisonous ash filled the air, quickly burying the prosperous town of Pompeii (pom-PAY). Time stopped for Pompeii; for about 1,800 years it lay under twelve feet of ash and mud that protected it from age and weather. When archeologists began to explore Pompeii in the late 1800's, they found a perfectly preserved picture of first-century Roman life.

Though many Pompeiians escaped, the searchers found tragic evidence of those who had not. Loaves of bread sat on the shelves of a bakery; cups lay on tables in an inn. Excavations revealed wealthy private homes, with walls colorfully painted with landscapes, scenes from myths, and delightful designs of animals, fruits, and flowers. The painting at right shows Primavera, who symbolized spring. Signs on

Pompeii's walls advertised shops and praised political candidates. Modern observers could only marvel at the private life of Pompeii — tragically stopped in a few hours of terror.

Roman architecture is practical. Roman architects were skilled engineers. They discovered the principle of the arch and used arches in their buildings, bridges, monuments, and aqueducts. The Romans also combined series of arches to make vaulted roofs.

Roman architects often followed Greek models for public buildings, but they developed techniques to save on costs. It was expensive to import marble from Greece or ship Italian marble to other parts of the Empire, so Roman architects built with brick, concrete, and common stone, and then covered these materials with thin slabs of fine marble.

Roman theaters, amphitheaters, public baths, and temples were built to last. Many Roman rulers are remembered for the great building projects they sponsored. The remains of Roman buildings, bridges, and aqueducts can be seen today in the lands once ruled by the Empire. Some are still in use.

The Romans take a practical approach to science. As in architecture, the Romans' achievements in science were practical. They used science to build roads, bridges, tunnels, and reservoirs. Roman engineers planned roads that were used for centuries. They developed efficient sewer systems and built aqueducts to carry water to the cities of the Empire.

Ptolemy and Galen dominate Roman science. The two most prominent scientists of the Greco-Roman age were Ptolemy (TAHL-uh-mee) and Galen (GAY-lun), who both lived during the second century A.D. Ptolemy was a mathematician, geographer, and astronomer who worked in Alexandria (page 90) about A.D. 300. His *Almagest* (a Greek-Arabic word meaning "the greatest") summed up the ancient world's knowledge of astronomy and geography. Ptolemy proposed a model of the universe in which the earth stood in the center of the universe while the sun, moon, and planets moved about it in circles or combinations of circles. Although Ptolemy based his system on a mistaken belief, it seemed to account for most of the changes that could be observed in the skies. The system seemed so logical that it was accepted until the sixteenth century.

Galen was a Greek, but his theories dominated Roman medicine. To study the workings of the body, Galen dissected animals. Although Galen's work contained many errors, it was the basis for Western medical knowledge until modern times.

Roman thinkers follow the Stoic tradition. The leading philosophy of the Roman world during the Pax Romana was Stoicism (page 91). Roman Stoics carried on the traditions begun by Greek philosophers.

Most famous of the Roman Stoics was the emperor Marcus Aurelius (page 107). In his book of *Meditations,* he expressed the Stoic belief that people should live simple lives, control their emotions, and be self-sufficient.

The Romans have a talent for law. A system of law and justice was perhaps Rome's greatest contribution to Western civilization. The law codes of present-day Italy, Spain, France, and the nations of Latin America — particularly those provisions dealing with the family, private property, and business contracts — are based on Roman law. The Romans believed law should reflect principles of reason and justice and should protect the citizen's person and property. The Roman writer and orator Cicero (SIS-er-oh) said that the law should not be "bent by influence or broken by power or spoiled by money." Cicero considered obedience to law to be one of the requirements of civilized life: "We are servants of the law in order that we may be free," he said.

One branch of Roman law, the Law of Nations, was applied to citizens in all parts of the Empire. Under this law a citizen was not a Briton, a Spaniard, an Italian, or a Greek, but a Roman. The idea that law could be based on just and rational principles and could apply to all peoples regardless of nationality was a major contribution to civilization.

CHECK-UP

1. (a) What was Greco-Roman culture? (b) How did it develop?
2. (a) According to Virgil, what quality set the Romans apart from other people? (b) On what did Horace blame the fall of the Republic?
3. Describe Roman achievements in art, architecture, and science.
4. What ideas did Roman Stoics teach?
5. (a) What were the basic principles of Roman law? (b) What was the Law of Nations?

Chapter 5 Review

Summary

Starting as a small town in central Italy, Rome built the greatest empire of the ancient world. Ruled at first by Etruscan kings, the Romans in 509 B.C. set up a republic led by members of the Senate and by assemblies representing the people. Over several hundred years, the common people, or plebeians, gained more power, but Roman government continued to be dominated by the upper class, or patricians, and by wealthy plebeians.

The Roman Republic became a great military power, conquering the rest of the Italian peninsula. Rome gained control in the western Mediterranean by defeating Carthage in the Punic Wars, and expanded to the east by conquering the Hellenistic states. This conquest brought widespread Greek influences into Roman culture. Ambitious military leaders seeking power eventually brought the Republic to an end. In 27 B.C. Octavian, later called Augustus, became in effect the first Roman emperor.

Augustus' rule marked the beginning of the Pax Romana, two hundred years of peace and stability in the Mediterranean world. The Roman Empire united peoples with different customs and traditions under a common ruler and a common system of laws and justice. Trade expanded, cities thrived, and Greco-Roman culture spread in Europe and North Africa.

Vocabulary Review

1. Match the following words with the listed definitions: *dictator, latifundia, province, republic*.
   (a) A form of government that is not a monarchy.
   (b) A territory outside the Italian peninsula that was conquered and governed by Rome.
   (c) The great landed estates of ancient Rome.
   (d) A Roman ruler with absolute power.
2. Distinguish between the terms in each of the following pairs:
   (a) patricians; plebeians.
   (b) *Aeneid; Almagest.*
   (c) Battle of Cannae; Battle of Zama.
   (d) Law of Nations; Twelve Tables.

People to Identify

Identify the following people. Tell whether each lived during the period of the Republic or the Empire and why he was important.

1.	Ptolemy	7.	Antony
2.	Ovid	8.	Spartacus
3.	Galen	9.	Vespasian
4.	Virgil	10.	Marcus Aurelius
5.	Hannibal	11.	Trajan
6.	Augustus	12.	Julius Caesar

Relating Geography and History

1. **Locating places.** Locate each of the following on a map in this chapter:
   (a) Carthage   (e) Spain
   (b) Greece   (f) Tiber River
   (c) Rome (city)   (g) Judaea
   (d) Gaul   (h) Mediterranean Sea
2. **Making maps.** In A.D. 79 the volcano Vesuvius erupted and buried the towns of Herculaneum and Pompeii (page 114). Use an atlas or encyclopedia to locate these towns. (The modern town of Resina has been built on the site of ancient Herculaneum.) Draw a map showing the towns and the distance of each from Vesuvius. Include a scale and direction indicator.

Discussion Questions

1. (a) How did the Punic Wars expand Rome's power? (b) What new provinces were acquired by 133 B.C.?
2. (a) What were the political reforms desired by Tiberius and Gaius Gracchus? (b) Why were these reforms opposed by the Senate? (c) How did the conflict between the Senate and the Gracchus brothers eventually weaken the Roman Republic?
3. (a) Why did the Senate accept Octavian (Augustus) as emperor when it had opposed Julius Caesar? (b) In what ways was Augustus an effective ruler?
4. (a) How did the Romans' policies toward conquered peoples enable them to administer their large empire peacefully? (b) What were the benefits of the Roman Empire to the people of the provinces? (c) Give an example of the harsh side of Roman rule.

5. (a) What did Cicero mean by saying, "We are servants of the law in order that we may be free" (page 115)? (b) Why is law considered to be one of the Romans' greatest contributions to Western civilization?

6. Discuss differences in Roman society under the Republic and under the Empire. In answering, include references to the treatment of slaves, the authority of Roman fathers over their families, and the status of women.

Reading Primary Sources

During the early Republic, Roman officials began to publish lists of laws they planned to enforce. From these simple beginnings Roman law evolved into legal principles that applied to peoples throughout the Empire. Read the Roman legal principles quoted below. Then answer the questions that follow the quoted material.

> In the case of major offenses, it makes a difference whether something is committed purposely or accidentally.
>
> In inflicting penalties, the age and inexperience of the guilty party must be taken into account.
>
> The principles of law are these: to live uprightly, not to injure another man, to give every man his due.
>
> No one is compelled to defend a cause against his will.
>
> No one suffers a penalty for what he thinks.
>
> Every individual is subjected to treatment in accordance with his own action and no one . . . [inherits] the guilt of another.
>
> The burden of proof is upon the party [accusing], not on the party denying.
>
> The credibility of witnesses should be carefully weighed [in judging their testimony]. . . . [One should take into account whether a witness's] life is honorable and blameless or on the contrary he is a man branded with public disgrace, . . . whether he is hostile to the party against whom he bears testimony or friendly.

(a) How did the law protect persons accused of crimes? (b) Which of these principles protect the liberties of individuals? (c) Which of them places the interests of society above those of the individual? (d) The United States Constitution guarantees citizens freedom of religion and of speech. Do any of the Roman legal principles you have just read indicate that the citizens of Rome enjoyed these freedoms? Explain.

Skill Activities

1. Word research. (a) Use a large dictionary to find three terms that begin with the word *Roman.* Define each term and explain how it is related to Roman civilization. (b) The names of the months of the year are derived from Latin words or names. Use a dictionary to find out the original meaning of the name of each month.

2. Writing a summary. A summary is a restatement, in brief form, of the main ideas of a speech or a piece of writing. Reread Section 2 of this chapter, "The Republic Comes to an End," and write a one-page summary of the reasons given there for the decline of the Republic.

3. Reports. Find information about one of the following topics and prepare a report: (a) the life of Hannibal; (b) augurs (Roman religious officials who foretold the future); (c) the aqueducts built by the Romans to supply their cities with water; (d) the legend of Aeneas; (e) gladiatorial combat; (f) the excavation of the buried city of Pompeii; (g) Etruscan art.

4. Bulletin boards. Make a bulletin-board display to illustrate Roman influence on present-day Western culture. Include examples from art, literature, government, law, architecture, language, and engineering.

5. Making charts. Make a chart of the major Roman gods and goddesses. In the first column write the name of the god or goddess. In the second column briefly describe what parts of nature or areas of life each was believed to control. In the third column list the Greek name for each deity.

6. Exploring the arts. Choose one or two scenes from William Shakespeare's play *Julius Caesar* and, with some classmates, prepare to present them to your class. Before your presentation, explain what the scenes are about and where they fit in the history that you have studied in this chapter.

Rome's administrative heart was the area known as the Roman Forum (below). In its government buildings the Senate met, records were kept, and Augustus was named emperor. Although the Forum fell into ruin after the decline of Rome, its remains suggest the skill of Roman architects.

The Decline of the Roman World

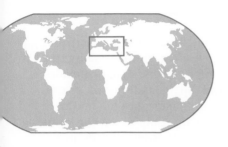

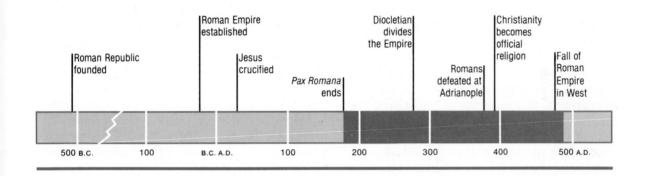

Roman Republic founded

Roman Empire established

Jesus crucified

Pax Romana ends

Diocletian divides the Empire

Romans defeated at Adrianople

Christianity becomes official religion

Fall of Roman Empire in West

500 B.C.   100   B.C. A.D.   100   200   300   400   500 A.D.

The 200 years of the Pax Romana were the high point of Greco-Roman civilization. During this time the Mediterranean world enjoyed peace and good government. Trade expanded, city life flourished, and Greco-Roman culture spread to many places. A series of crises in the third century A.D. ended this orderly world. Invasions and civil wars disrupted transportation and trade and contributed to the decline of city life. Strong emperors increased taxes and introduced other measures to deal with the crises. By the fifth century, however, the weakened Roman Empire was overrun by Germanic tribes. The Empire split into two parts, and power shifted away from Rome. This marked a new stage in the history of Western civilization.

In this time of change, a new religion, Christianity, began to spread in the Roman world. Like the fall of the Roman Empire, the growth of Christianity brought great changes. The ancient world was drawing to a close.

This chapter describes the decline of Rome and the rise and spread of Christianity.

CHAPTER OUTLINE

1 The Roman Empire Declines

2 Many Factors Cause the Decline of Rome

3 Christianity Spreads Throughout the Empire

1 The Roman Empire Declines

The Pax Romana had brought the ancient world 200 years of peace, rule by law, and civilized life. The Roman system of government endured during the reigns of both able and incompetent rulers. When the emperor Commodus began his reign late in the second century A.D., however, the Empire was facing serious problems in many areas. The stability brought by the Pax Romana came suddenly to an end.

War and unrest weaken the Empire. The third century A.D. found the Roman Empire facing serious crises and without strong leadership to overcome them. The discipline and loyalty of the army broke down, as men enlisted simply to gain weapons and spoils. Soldiers were loyal to their commanders rather than to Rome, and military leaders fought one another for the throne. One general after another became emperor, but none ruled for more than a few years. Nearly all these emperors were assassinated.

As troops were called back from the frontier to fight in the clashes between rival military leaders, the Empire's border defenses were weakened. Germanic tribes from northern Europe crossed the Roman frontier along the Rhine and Danube rivers. They invaded Greece, Italy, and Spain and raided coastal cities in Asia Minor. Some tribes in Gaul tried to break away from the Empire. At the same time, the Persians seized Roman lands in the Near East.

The civil wars and invasions hurt Rome's economy. Transportation and trade were disrupted, cities plundered, and crops destroyed. To pay the expenses of the army, emperors increased taxes, seized goods from citizens, and forced people to work for the state. Resentment grew among both peasants and townspeople.

The cities of the Mediterranean world, which were the centers of Greco-Roman civilization, began to decay. Food supplies were short and prices high. Many urban dwellers fled to the countryside.

Strong emperors make reforms. In A.D. 284 the army elected Diocletian (dy-uh-KLEE-shun) emperor. He and his successor Constantine (reigned 306–337) tried to save the empire by imposing strong one-man rule. They made drastic changes, which resulted in Rome's becoming a tightly controlled state. The changes worsened the plight of farmers and townspeople alike. To ensure a supply of food, the imperial government forced farmers to stay on their land. Government agents hunted down those who tried to leave their farms. Government workers and artisans also had to keep their jobs for life and pass them on to their children. To support the army, his luxurious court, and the officials of the imperial government, Diocletian imposed high taxes. Town officials had to serve as tax collectors for life, paying the difference between the taxes the state demanded and the amount they could collect. Artisans and merchants, as well as the city officials, were ruined financially, and city life declined even more.

The Empire is divided. To make the Empire easier to govern, Diocletian appointed a loyal general as co-ruler in the western regions.

TIMETABLE

The Late Roman Empire

A.D.

180	The Pax Romana ends when Commodus takes the throne.
285	Diocletian divides the Empire.
312	Constantine grants Christians religious toleration in the Roman Empire.
330	Constantine builds Constantinople as the capital of the Empire.
376	The Visigoths cross the Danube and settle in the Empire.
378	The Visigoths defeat the Romans at Adrianople.
392	Christianity becomes the official religion of the Empire.
410, 455	Barbarians attack and loot the city of Rome.
476	The Western Roman Empire collapses.

GERMANIC ART

The Germanic peoples carved stones to mark graves or important places (above right).
From one grave in England came the Swedish helmet with Roman-style designs (above
left), weapons, jewelry, and a silver dish from Constantinople.

He moved the imperial court to Asia Minor and ruled from there. Rome was no longer the center of the Empire. The split between the two parts of the Empire grew wider and rival rulers fought for power. In 330, the emperor Constantine built a new imperial capital at Constantinople, overlooking the waterway where Europe and Asia meet (map, page 122). The division of the Empire soon became accepted fact.

The shift of power to the East had serious consequences. The Western Empire was already weak economically. Yet it had to pay for the troops and border defenses to keep out the Germanic tribes. With the split of the Empire, the West could no longer depend on financial and military help from the wealthier eastern regions.

The reforms of Diocletian and Constantine restored order, but the cost to Roman citizens was heavy. These emperors, moreover, did not solve Rome's problems but merely delayed the collapse of the Empire.

Germanic tribes move into the Empire. The Germanic peoples who lived in the forests and marshes of northern Europe were a continuing problem for the Romans. The Germanic peoples were organized in tribes rather than states. They had no written laws, written literature, or philosophy, and so the Romans looked on them as uncivilized barbarians. The warmer climate, rich farmlands, and wealth of the Roman lands attracted the Germanic tribes. They settled along the Rhine and Danube rivers, and only the troops along the frontier kept them from crossing into Roman territory.

Late in the fourth century, the Danube plain was invaded by Huns, a fierce nomadic people from Central Asia. Terrified of the

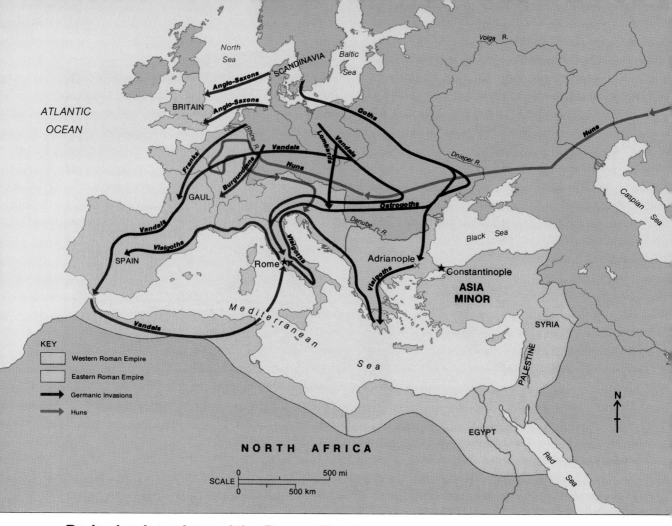

Barbarian Invasions of the Roman Empire

Diocletian divided the Empire to make it easier to govern. What were its two capitals? What two rivers formed the boundary of the Western Roman Empire? Which barbarian tribes crossed this boundary?

Huns, a Germanic tribe called Visigoths (West Goths) asked for refuge within the Roman Empire. In A.D. 376 the Roman emperor reluctantly allowed the Visigoths to cross the Danube River into what is now Rumania.

Two years later Rome was at war with its unwelcome guests. In the Battle of Adrianople (ay-dree-uh-NOH-pul), the Visigoth cavalry defeated the Roman army. This was a clear sign that Rome could no longer defend its borders. As more soldiers were called home to defend Italy, the border defenses soon collapsed. Germanic tribes began pouring into the Empire. Some moved into Gaul, others into Spain. The Visigoth leader Alaric led his troops into Italy, demanding land and a generalship in the Roman army. When his demands were refused,

the Visigoths attacked and looted the city of Rome in 410. To make peace, Rome allowed them to set up a kingdom in Spain and Gaul.

The Huns now threatened the Western Roman Empire. In 451 their king, Attila (AHT-uh-luh),[1] led his forces into Gaul. An alliance of Germanic tribes and the remnants of the Roman army defeated Attila. A year later, the Huns invaded northern Italy, but hunger and disease forced them to withdraw. The death of Attila in 453 ended the Hun threat, but the Germanic invasions continued.

---

[1] Known as the "Scourge (whip) of God," Attila conquered lands from the northeastern shore of the Black Sea west to the Rhine River.

Rome falls to barbarian rulers. One Roman province after another fell to invading Germanic tribes. In 455 the city of Rome was again looted, this time by the Vandals, a Germanic tribe that had established a kingdom in North Africa. The Vandals, less civilized than the Goths, caused such destruction that we now have the word *vandalism* as a reminder of the reputation they gained.

By this time, the Romans had hired many Germanic soldiers to fight in the Roman army. In A.D. 476 some of these Germanic officers overthrew the Western Roman emperor, Romulus Augustulus, who was only a child. They declared a fellow German, Odoacer (oh-doh-AY-sur), king of Italy. This event is traditionally regarded as the end of the Roman Empire in the West.

Some Roman traditions continued in the Western Empire after 476, but it was ruled by Germanic kings. Odoacer was killed in 493 by Theodoric (thee-AH-dur-ik), king of the Ostrogoths, or East Goths. Supported by the Eastern Roman emperor, Theodoric restored peace and prosperity in Italy, reigning until 526.

CHECK-UP

1. (a) What crises did the Roman Empire face in the third century A.D.? (b) How was Rome's economy affected by these crises?
2. (a) What steps did Diocletian take to save the Empire from collapsing? (b) What were the consequences of dividing the Roman Empire? (c) Where was the capital moved?
3. (a) Why did Germanic tribes want to move into the Roman Empire? (b) What was the significance of the Battle of Adrianople?
4. (a) Where did the Huns come from? (b) How did they speed up the decline of Rome?
5. What event is traditionally considered the end of the Western Roman Empire?

2 Many Factors Cause the Decline of Rome

In the second century A.D. the Roman Empire spanned the Mediterranean world and seemed indestructible. Yet by the end of the fifth century it had collapsed. Rome did not collapse suddenly. The Empire went through a long slow decline. The conditions that brought about this decline came from both inside and outside the Empire.

Rome loses its citizens' confidence and loyalty. In the third and fourth centuries many Romans lost confidence in the values of their civilization and in the Empire itself. Little creative or original work was done in art and literature. The upper classes in the cities no longer felt a responsibility to serve the Empire or preserve their civilization and its values. Seeking only their own security, nobles fled to their country estates, the latifundia, and fortified them against the threat of invasion. Secluded behind the walls of their estates, nobles made little effort to help the struggling Empire.

The government itself contributed to this decline of spirit. The threat of Germanic invasion forced emperors to spend more and more money on defense. To pay for the food, weapons, and armor needed by soldiers, the state increased taxes, seized grain and property from citizens, and forced people to repair roads and bridges and do other work. These demands ruined both the prosperous townspeople and the small farmers. Many of them came to hate and fear the imperial officials more than they did the Germanic invaders. Overburdened by taxes and forced labor, townspeople avoided public service and did little to organize resistance against the Germanic invaders. The majority of Roman citizens became indifferent to the fate of Rome.

The army deteriorates. The strength of Rome had always depended on its soldier-citizens. By the fourth century, the quality of the army had declined. Roman soldiers were no longer dedicated to the Empire. Increasingly the army came to consist of men from the less civilized parts of the Empire or from the lower classes in the cities. These soldiers were hostile to the well-to-do city dwellers and had little understanding of Rome's goal of preserving order and spreading peace.

As conditions grew worse, many Roman citizens avoided military service, and the government recruited men from the Germanic tribes. In time, most of the soldiers and officers of the Roman army were Germanic.

The population declines. As the Empire declined, its population grew smaller. From 70 million people during the Pax Romana, the Empire's population fell to 50 million by the late fourth century. This loss was due to warfare, famine, a declining birthrate, and plagues (that is, widespread outbreaks of disease). Population loss hurt the Empire in several ways. First, a smaller number of taxpayers had to bear the increasing costs of running the Empire. Second, fewer people were available to farm the land, and there were famines and food shortages. Third, the smaller population added

to the problems of finding soldiers for the army.

The Empire is weak economically. Although Roman towns were centers of commercial and cultural life, they did not develop enough industries to provide jobs for the common people. Wealthy city dwellers depended on the incomes from their country estates. They had no interest in starting businesses. Since most people had little money to spend, there was little reason to produce goods for sale.

The widespread use of slave labor discouraged both economic growth and new developments in technology. The Romans were skilled engineers and architects, but they seldom invented new ways of producing goods. With so much slave labor available, it seemed pointless to find more efficient methods of production. The slaves themselves had no interest in increasing production. Consequently, few new industries developed, and older ones did

LINKING PAST AND PRESENT

Cities from the Roman World

Many of Europe's great cities began as frontier outposts of the Roman Empire. Roman officials and merchants made their homes there, and Roman soldiers were stationed nearby. The settlement of *Vindobona* — modern Vienna — was an important Roman center on the Danube River, one of the Empire's boundaries. On the Rhine River, the emperor Claudius founded a colony about A.D. 50 and named it *Colonia Agrippina* after his wife. From that colony grew modern Cologne, Germany.

After Julius Caesar conquered Gaul, a fishing village on the Seine River became the Roman town of *Lutetia Parisiorum,* named for the Parisii, a Gallic tribe. Today the city of Paris exists in the same location. In Britain, Roman life centered on the fort of *Londinium,* some of whose walls still stand in modern London. (At right is the Roman amphitheater at Nimes, France.) As the Empire weakened, the frontier towns declined. Centuries later, however, cities developed on the sites of many of the old Roman outposts.

The Romans often made pictures by arranging small colored stones in a pattern. This picture shows some of the activities on the Roman country estates. Towers on the building indicate that it was used as a fortress as well as a residence.

not grow. Moreover, the use of slaves reduced the number of jobs available for the common people.

Roman cities decline. These economic and social problems had the most serious effects in the cities. Romans who had fled to the latifundia produced their own food and goods. They no longer looked to the cities for any of their needs. Moreover, the power of the government did not extend to these country estates. Political power passed, therefore, from the central government to the landowning nobles. The agricultural workers on the latifundia were no longer independent farmers. They had to remain on the land they farmed but did not own. A new society was taking shape in which the center of life was no longer the city but the fortified latifundia. These developments pointed to the end of ancient civilization and the beginning of a new stage in Western history — the Middle Ages.

CHECK-UP

1. (a) What were the signs that many Romans had lost confidence in the Empire? (b) How did the government itself make this situation worse?
2. What changes in the army contributed to the decline of Rome?
3. (a) What factors brought about a drop in population? (b) What were the effects of the decline in population?
4. How was the Roman economy weakened (a) by the lack of industries? (b) by the use of slave labor?
5. How did the movement to the latifundia affect (a) the cities? (b) the central government?

3 Christianity Spreads Throughout the Empire

At the same time that the Roman Empire began to decline, a new religion, Christianity, was gaining followers in the Mediterranean world. By the time the Empire came to an end, the new teachings had become the official religion throughout the vast territories that had been ruled by Rome.

The Empire allows different religious beliefs. While the Romans brought their laws and government authority to all parts of the Empire, they allowed local peoples to keep many of their own religious customs. Romans themselves followed a number of different religions and tolerated and respected local beliefs in the provinces.

Many Jews hope for a Messiah. In the Roman province of Judaea (Palestine) and elsewhere in the Empire, the Jews had considerable religious freedom. Because of their belief in one God, Jews were not required to take part in the worship of the emperor.[2] The Romans established a line of Jewish kings named Herod on the throne of Judaea, though Roman officials and soldiers also occupied the country.

Many Jews hoped to regain their independence. Some hoped for the coming of the Messiah[3] (muh-SY-ah), or savior, that had been promised by Old Testament prophets. The Messiah, they believed, would, like King David, restore their kingdom's ancient greatness and would bring an age of prosperity and peace.

Jesus lives and teaches in Palestine. Early in the first century A.D. a teacher named Jesus gained a following among the people of Judaea. The account of Jesus' preaching appears in the Gospels, the first four books of the New Testament in the Christian Bible. Jesus himself left no writings. His teachings and the events of his life were preserved by word of mouth and then recorded by four writers — Matthew, Mark, Luke, and John. The earliest account is that written by Mark.

According to the Gospels, Jesus was born in Bethlehem during the rule of the emperor Augustus. The Gospel of Luke says that even as a young boy, he had a great interest in religious questions and astounded Jewish scholars and teachers with his knowledge. Some years later, according to all the Gospels, Jesus began to preach and teach and to gather followers around him.

The accounts in the Gospels indicate that Jesus accepted the Jewish laws and traditions set down in the Old Testament but put a new emphasis on love, compassion, and a personal relationship with God. The Gospel writers report that he attracted enthusiastic crowds, as well as devoted individual followers, and worked miracles of healing. In about A.D. 30, Jesus traveled to Jerusalem to celebrate the Jewish holiday of Passover. Crowds that gathered there welcomed him as "king of the Jews" and "Messiah."

Jesus' popularity appeared threatening to both the traditional Jewish leaders and the Roman authorities. He was arrested and brought before the Roman governor, Pontius Pilate, who ordered his death by crucifixion, the usual Roman form of execution.

Christianity attracts new followers. At the time of the Crucifixion, the followers of Jesus made up only a small Jewish sect. They believed Jesus was the Son of God and that he had risen from the dead and later been taken to heaven. The disciples believed they had the responsibility to spread Jesus' teachings to other people. At first the disciples taught and preached mainly to other Jews in the Near East, but as the new beliefs attracted more followers, Christianity — the religion based on Jesus' teachings — spread throughout the Mediterranean world.

---

[2]From about the time of Augustus, the Roman emperor began to be regarded as a god. Formal rituals honoring him were part of official ceremonies wherever Rome ruled. They were considered acts of loyalty to Rome.

[3]*Messiah* in Hebrew meant "the anointed one," referring to the ancient custom of using holy oil in religious ceremonies. The Greek word for "the anointed one" was *Christos,* or Christ.

EARLY CHRISTIAN ART

The pictures here reflect the extent of early Christianity. The carving showing saints (left) comes from Turkey. Above, a picture of loaves of bread and fish was found in Palestine. It illustrates a familiar Bible story. From Italy comes the picture of Jesus as the Good Shepherd (below). Lambs were often used as symbols of Jesus' followers.

Paul travels as a Christian missionary. One reason for the spread of Christianity outside the Near East was the work of a Greek-speaking Jew named Saul, from the city of Tarsus in Asia Minor. According to the Bible, Saul was working actively against the disciples and their followers when he was suddenly converted to a belief in Jesus and in Christianity. Taking the new name of Paul, he became a *missionary* and traveled to many parts of the

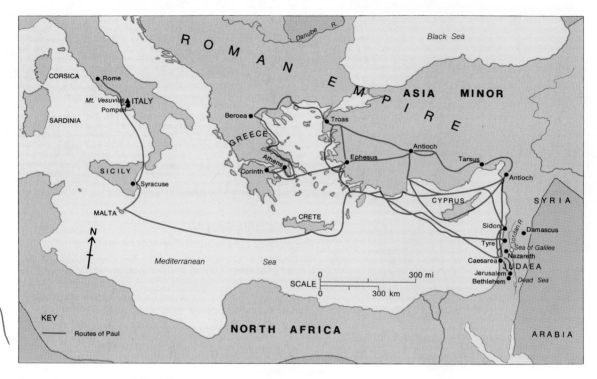

The Journeys of Paul

In his missionary effort, Paul traveled to many parts of the Empire. What cities did he visit in Judaea? in Asia Minor? in Greece?

Roman Empire to spread the teachings of Jesus among both Jews and non-Jews. For twenty years, from about A.D. 45 to 65, he set up Christian communities in Greece and Asia Minor, writing letters to them to reinforce their faith. Many of these letters, or Epistles (ee-PIHS-ulz), appear in the New Testament.

Paul also set forth doctrines that are the basis of Christianity. He taught that all human beings are born sinful because Adam and Eve disobeyed God, but that Jesus was sent by God to redeem humanity from their sins. By dying on the cross, said Paul, Jesus had made it possible for human beings to gain salvation and enter the kingdom of heaven. Therefore, he taught, any man or woman, rich or poor, Jew or non-Jew, could gain salvation through faith in Christ and belief in his teachings and his mission.

Christianity spreads within the Empire. The peace and unity of the Pax Romana made it easier for Paul and other missionaries to carry the message of Christianity throughout

the Roman Empire. As a Roman citizen, Paul had certain privileges and protection anywhere in the Empire. Moreover, travel was easy between cities, and a common language, Greek, was spoken in most countries in the eastern Mediterranean.

By about A.D. 57 there was a group of Christians in Rome itself led by Peter, bishop of Rome and one of the original disciples of Jesus. Paul wrote to this congregation expressing his hopes to travel as far as Spain. In about A.D. 59, Paul was arrested in Jerusalem by Roman authorities and, as a Roman citizen, was sent to Rome for trial. Traditions differ as to whether he was released or executed there by the emperor Nero.

Key figures like Paul and other missionaries — both men and women — helped maintain contacts among the scattered early Christian communities. As the new religion grew, the Christian Church emerged as a strong organization. Calling its members brothers and sisters, the Church gave people a sense of community and fellowship. It welcomed people of all classes and nationalities. The development of an organized church structure strengthened the new religion.

Christians are persecuted. Generally tolerant of different religions, Roman authorities did not at first interfere with Christianity. As more and more people turned to Christianity, however, Roman officials began to see it as a threat to their rule. The Christians did not accept the Roman gods or celebrate their festivals. Although they obeyed Roman law, they refused to worship the emperor as a god, which was seen as an act of disloyalty to Rome. The Romans found some Christian ways strange. Christians stayed away from the gladiatorial contests and at times refused to serve in the army.

When fire swept through Rome in A.D. 64, the emperor Nero blamed it on the Christians and began the first official persecutions. Property belonging to Christians was seized, and they were imprisoned, executed, or sent to face wild beasts in the arena. Several later emperors, particularly Diocletian and Marcus Aurelius, ordered widespread persecutions. Although some Christians abandoned their religion or practiced it secretly, persecution failed to stop the spread of Christianity. Many Romans were impressed by the heroism and devotion of those who became martyrs by dying for their faith. The dedication of these martyrs inspired many people to convert to Christianity.

Christianity is accepted in the Empire. The invasions and unrest of the third century A.D. (page 120) brought more converts and new strength to the Christian Church. The persecutions ceased, and Christianity became one of the many religions allowed in the Empire. In A.D. 312 the Roman Emperor Constantine converted to Christianity, becoming the first Christian emperor. He issued a law allowing Christians to practice their religion freely and became a strong supporter of the church. In 380, during the reign of Theodosius I (thee-uh-DOH-shus), worship of the old gods was declared illegal, and Christianity soon became the official religion of the Roman Empire.

Christian thinkers describe their goals and beliefs. As the Christian Church grew, many writers and thinkers explained its doctrines and set forth principles for following Christianity. These early Christian thinkers are usually called "Fathers of the Church." One of the earliest and greatest Church Fathers was Augustine (A.D. 354–430). Born in North Africa, Augustine studied Latin literature and Greek philosophy in Carthage. After converting to Christianity, he became a bishop in Roman Africa.

The barbarian invasions of Rome in the early 400's brought terror to Italy. Some non-Christians blamed the disaster on Christianity, claiming that the ancient gods were punishing Rome. Christians, on the other hand, wondered why good people should have to suffer. In response, Augustine wrote a book called *The City of God.*

The true Christian, said Augustine, was a citizen of a heavenly city that could never be destroyed by ungodly barbarians. The cities and empires of earth did not matter, he said, only the individual's salvation. Nonetheless, Augustine declared, Christians should try to run their earthly city according to Christian principles and teachings. Augustine believed that the aim of life was the fulfillment of God's will. His contrast of the earthly sinful city and the perfect City of God remained an important idea for later Christian thinkers.

CHECK-UP

1. Vocabulary: *missionary.*
2. (a) What was Roman policy toward religion in the Empire? (b) Why was the prediction of a Messiah important to the Jews under Roman rule?
3. (a) Where are Jesus' life and teachings described? (b) Why did Roman and Jewish authorities consider Jesus' popularity a threat?
4. (a) How did Paul influence the growth of Christianity? (b) How did the political unity of the Empire affect the spread of Christianity?
5. (a) What kinds of opposition did early Christians encounter? (b) Why did the Roman government begin to tolerate Christianity? (c) How did Christianity come to be accepted in the Empire?
6. (a) Who was Augustine? (b) What did he believe should be the aims of a Christian's life?

Chapter 6 Review

Summary

In the third century A.D., when the Pax Romana had ended, a series of crises severely weakened the Roman Empire. Civil wars raged as rival military leaders fought for the imperial throne. Germanic tribesmen crossed the Rhine-Danube frontier and invaded several areas in the Empire. The civil wars and Germanic attacks disrupted the economy and caused people to flee from cities and take refuge on fortified country estates.

To cope with the crises that faced Rome, the emperors Diocletian and Constantine increased taxes and tightened state control over the daily lives of citizens. Burdened by high taxes, many Romans lost confidence in the Empire. Population fell, the economy failed, and the army lost its loyalty to Roman ideals.

The Empire was divided, and the weakened frontier defenses in the western regions could no longer keep out barbarian invaders. Overrun by the Visigoths and other Germanic tribes, the Western Roman Empire collapsed in A.D. 476. Its fall marked the end of the ancient world and the start of a new stage in the history of Western civilization.

As the Roman Empire declined, a new religion, Christianity, attracted growing numbers of followers in the Mediterranean world. By the end of the fourth century it had become the official religion of the Empire.

Vocabulary Review

1. Write the sentences listed below on a sheet of paper. In each sentence, fill in the blank with one of these words: *latifundia, missionary, monotheism, nomad, province.*
(a) Someone who travels and attempts to convert people to a particular religion is a __?__ .
(b) A member of a tribe that moves from place to place, tending its herds, is a __?__ .
(c) The great landed estates of ancient Rome were called __?__ .
(d) __?__ is a territory that is governed by another country.
(e) The belief in one God is __?__ .

2. Choose the term that best completes each of the following sentences:
(a) The accounts of the life of Jesus written by Matthew, Mark, Luke, and John are known as (1) the Pax Romana, (2) the Gospels, (3) *The City of God.*
(b) Augustine is known as one of the (1) Roman emperors, (2) prophets, (3) Church Fathers.
(c) The Germanic tribe that looted Rome in A.D. 455 was the (1) Visigoths, (2) Huns, (3) Vandals.

People to Identify

Match the following people with the numbered phrases that describe them: *Attila, Pontius Pilate, Romulus Augustulus, Paul, Diocletian.*
1. The emperor whose replacement by Odoacer marked the fall of the Roman Empire in the West.
2. One of the two strong emperors who restored order to the Empire after the crises of the third century.
3. The Roman governor of Judaea who ordered the execution of Jesus.
4. A missionary who brought Jesus' teachings to much of the Roman Empire.
5. The king who led the Huns to battle in Gaul and northern Italy.

Relating Geography and History

1. **Locating places.** Locate each of the following on a map in this chapter:
(a) Rhine River   (e) Judaea
(b) Danube River   (f) Jerusalem
(c) Constantinople   (g) Bethlehem
(d) Adrianople

2. **Comparing maps.** Using the world map in the Atlas in the back of this book and the map on page 122, determine what nations now exist in· what was once (a) the Western Roman Empire and (b) the Eastern Roman Empire.

3. **Using maps to make a chart.** You have now read about several battles that were decisive events in ancient history. Use the maps on pages 72, 76, 98, and 122 to locate the following battle sites: Marathon, Thermopylae, Salamis, Plataea, Chaeronea, Cannae, Zama, and Adrianople.

Mark each battle on an outline map. Then make a chart with information about the battles. For each battle give the date, the location, the forces involved, and the outcome. Write a sentence explaining why each battle was important.

Discussion Questions

1. (a) What problems arose in the Roman army during the third century A.D.? (b) How was the fall of the Roman Empire directly related to these problems?

2. How did efforts to halt Rome's decline affect Roman citizens?

3. How did the barbarian invasions contribute to the decline of Rome?

4. (a) What was the significance of the growth of the latifundia in the third century A.D.? (b) What other factors weakened the Roman economy?

5. (a) Why did the early Christians come into conflict with the Roman state? (b) Why and how did Christianity spread throughout the Roman Empire?

Reading Primary Sources

In A.D. 98 the historian Tacitus wrote a description of the early Germanic tribes with whom the Roman troops had been fighting along the Rhine and Danube rivers. This passage from his record describes the Germanic soldiers. Read the passage. Then answer the questions that follow.

> Only a few of them use swords or large lances: they carry spears . . . with short and narrow blades, but so sharp and easy to handle that they can be used, as required, either at close quarters or in long-range fighting. Their horsemen are content with a shield and a spear; but the foot-soldiers also rain javelins on their foes: each of them carries several, and they hurl them to immense distances. . . . Their horses are not remarkable for either beauty or speed, and are not trained to execute various [turns] as ours are. . . . [The Germans'] strength lies in infantry rather than cavalry. So foot-soldiers accompany the cavalry into action, their speed of foot being such that they can easily keep up with the charging horsemen. . . .

(a) What was the Germanic soldier's most important weapon? (b) Why was it particularly useful?

(c) Which did Tacitus believe to be superior, the Germanic horsemen or the Roman horsemen? Why? (d) What was the strongest part of the Germanic army?

Skill Activities

1. **Word research.** Many English words and terms come from the Latin *civis,* meaning "citizen." Under the Republic a citizen was an inhabitant of Rome who was entitled to the rights and privileges of a freeman. Look up the following terms in a dictionary and tell how each is related to citizenship:

(a) civics
(b) civil
(c) civilian
(d) civil war
(e) civil servant
(f) civil rights
(g) civil liberties
(h) civil defense

2. **Reports.** Find information about one of the following topics and prepare a report: (a) the Baths of Caracalla in Rome; (b) Christian paintings in the catacombs of Rome; (c) the Battle of Chalons; (d) the development of Romance languages; (e) Hadrian's Wall (in Britain); (f) the life of Constantine the Great.

3. **Reading timetables.** Timetables show you when important events took place. They help you keep important events in the right order and estimate the number of years in a given period. Using the Timetables on pages 97 and 120, answer the following questions: (a) When did Christianity become the official religion of Rome? (b) When did the Third Punic War end? (c) Which happened first, the Visigoths' settling in the Roman Empire or their victory at Adrianople? (d) How many years did the Pax Romana last? (e) Approximately how many years did the Roman Republic last? (f) How many years did the Roman Empire last?

4. **Ranking causes.** Read the following list of causes of the fall of the Roman Empire. On a separate sheet of paper, rank these causes, beginning with the one you think was most important. Tell why you ranked them as you did.

(a) Rome's defenses were weakened when troops left the frontier to fight in the civil wars.
(b) Many Romans lost confidence in the values of their civilization.
(c) Rome's economy was weak and stagnant.
(d) The latifundia became centers of political power.

Unit One Review

Review Questions

1. What are the characteristics of civilization?

2. (a) Why were writing systems developed in ancient civilization? (b) Compare the writing systems of the ancient Sumerians and Egyptians, including the way the writing was done and how it looked. (c) Why were the Behistun rock and the Rosetta stone important to our knowledge of ancient civilizations? (d) What was the advantage of the Phoenicians' writing system?

3. (a) Explain the similarities between Hammurabi's code, Draco's code, and the Twelve Tables. (b) Why were they especially beneficial to the common people? (c) How was the Athenian view of law different from that of the Mesopotamians and Egyptians? (d) What was the greatest contribution of Roman law to Western civilization?

4. (a) How did the Greeks differ from the Mesopotamians and Egyptians in their view of the natural world? (b) How did the beliefs of each of those peoples affect their accomplishments in mathematics and science?

5. How did geographic conditions influence the development of political life in (a) Mesopotamia, (b) Egypt, and (c) Greece?

6. Choose three empires from the ancient world and answer the following questions about each: (a) How was the empire created? (b) What methods were used to govern conquered peoples? (c) What advantages did the ruling people offer their subjects? (d) Why did each empire decline?

7. What were the most important contributions to Western civilization of (a) the Hebrews, (b) the Greeks, and (c) the Romans?

Projects

1. **Making time lines.** Prepare a time line of events in the ancient world. Begin with the emergence of Sumerian civilization in the Tigris and Euphrates river valley and end with the fall of the Roman Empire in the West. For information refer to the time lines in the chapters in this unit.

2. **Evaluating historical figures.** Create a Hall of Fame of the Ancient World. Make a list of the men and women you think should be included and write a brief paragraph explaining why each person deserves this honor.

3. **Research and report.** The Greeks and Romans were the first to provide travel guides about scenic and historic places. The most famous guide listed the Seven Wonders of the World. Using an encyclopedia, prepare a report that tells what the Seven Wonders were and where they were located. Illustrate your report.

4. **Making maps.** Draw or trace an outline map of the Near East and the lands that border on the Mediterranean Sea. On the map, show the Nile, Tigris, and Euphrates rivers and the ancient cities.

5. **Exploring the arts.** Many of the civilizations of the ancient world had distinctive styles of architecture. Prepare a model or a drawing of an example of one of the following: (a) Mesopotamian ziggurats; (b) Egyptian pyramids; (c) the columns used in Greek temples; (d) Roman aqueducts, outdoor arenas, or public baths.

Books to Read

Casson, Lionel. *Ancient Egypt*. Time-Life.

Coolidge, Olivia. *Greek Myths*. Houghton Mifflin.

Coolidge, Olivia. *Roman People*. Houghton Mifflin.

Edey, Maitland. *The Sea-Traders*. Time-Life. The Phoenicians and their civilization.

Hadas, Moses. *Imperial Rome*. Time-Life.

Hamblin, Dora Jane. *The First Cities*. Time-Life. Jericho, Çatal Hüyük, and other ancient cities.

Kramer, Samuel Noah. *Cradle of Civilization*. Time-Life. Archeology and the history of Sumer.

Macaulay, David. *City*. Houghton Mifflin. Construction of an ancient Roman city.

Macaulay, David. *Pyramid*. Houghton Mifflin.

Purdy, Susan and Cass Sandak. *Ancient Greece*. Franklin Watts.

Purdy, Susan and Cass Sandak. *Ancient Rome*. Franklin Watts.

Thwaite, Anthony. *Beyond the Inhabited World*. Clarion. A brief, heavily illustrated history of Britain under the Romans.

How to Study World History

Improving Your Reading

The ability to understand and remember what you have read is a useful study skill. A simple, five-step method called SQRRR will help you improve your reading. SQRRR stands for *Survey, Question, Read, Recite, Review.* The SQRRR method is explained below, and examples are provided to help you apply it to your reading of this book.

Survey. Begin any new reading assignment by getting a general idea of what the material is about. This can be done by reading the section titles and the headings. Look, for example, at the title of Section 1 of Chapter 6 (page 120). That title — "The Roman Empire Declines" — tells you the general topic of the section. Within that section you will find headings printed in dark type. They will tell you the main points that will be discussed:

War and unrest weaken the Empire.
Strong emperors make reforms.
The Empire is divided.
Germanic tribes move into the Empire.
Rome falls to barbarian rulers.

Surveying the title and headings of any section will prepare you for your study of that section.

Question. Step two is to turn each title and heading you have located into a question. Most of the questions you form will begin with one of the following words: *who, what, when, where, why,* or *how.* Below, the title and headings from Section 1 of Chapter 6 have been turned into questions.

Why did the Roman Empire decline?
How did war and unrest weaken the Empire?
What reforms did the emperors make to halt Rome's decline?
When and why was the Empire divided?
Who were the Germanic tribes that moved into the Empire?
How and when did Rome fall?

If you read to find the answers to these questions, you are more likely to look for and remember important information.

Read. The next step is to read the assignment carefully and, while you read, to look for answers to the questions you asked.

Recite. The last two steps in the SQRRR method will help you remember what you have read. After you have read the material carefully, recite to yourself — in your own words — the answers to the questions you have asked. This will help you to organize the information and fix it in your memory.

Review. The final step is to look again at the headings you have surveyed and repeat your answers to each of the questions you asked in step two. If you are preparing for a test, review the material quickly each day until it is time to take the test.

Check Your Skill

Use the following questions to check your understanding of SQRRR:

1. To get a general impression or overview of a reading selection, you should (a) recite, (b) read carefully, (c) survey.

2. On page 125 of Chapter 6, "Roman cities decline" is (a) a section title, (b) a heading, (c) a footnote.

3. The way to find answers to the questions you make up using the SQRRR method is to (a) skim, (b) read carefully, (c) review headings.

4. If you survey Section 2 of Chapter 6 (pages 123–125), you will learn that (a) small farmers were ruined by high taxes, (b) slaveowners did not like to work with their hands, (c) a population drop contributed to Rome's decline.

5. In the SQRRR method, reciting helps you to (a) give oral reports, (b) remember what you have read, (c) build your vocabulary.

6. The method suggested for reviewing an assignment is to (a) make up new questions, (b) reread the selection and take notes, (c) reread the headings and again answer your questions.

Apply Your Skill

For practice in improving your reading, apply the SQRRR method to Section 1 of Chapter 7 (pages 138–143). Turn the section title and the headings into questions. Write the questions on a sheet of paper. In your own words, write brief answers.

Hm que nobles faitz darmes et honourable aduemies par les guerres de france et dangleterre soient notablement et moult honourablement enre giftrees et mis en memoire per petuele p quoy les preudommes et vaillantz aient exemple deulx vigoureusement encouragiet en bien faisant. Je vueil recorder et traictier histoire et matiere de grant seante. Mais auant que ie la commence ie requier au sauueur de tout le monde qui de neant crea toutes choses quil

vueille creer et mettre en moy sens et entendemet si vertueux q̃ ce liure que iay encommencie ie puisse continuer et perseuerer en tele maniere que tous ceulx qui se liront verront et orront y puissent prendre bonne con solacion esbatement deduit z plaisance et moy enclxoir en se grace. On dit et vray est q̃ toutes edifices sont maconnees z ou ures lune pierre apres laultre. Et toutes grosses riuieres sont faictes et rassemblees de diuers lieux z de plus ruysseaulx et sources. Tout pareillemet les

UNIT TWO

The West in the Middle Ages

The centuries following the fall of the Roman Empire in the West span the period between the ancient world and modern times. In the history of Western civilization, they are called the Middle Ages. During this time, new civilizations developed in lands once ruled by Rome. In the Near East, North Africa, and Spain, the followers of the new religion of Islam built an empire. In the eastern Mediterranean, the rich eastern provinces of Rome became the Byzantine Empire.

In Western and Central Europe, the end of Roman rule brought great changes during the early Middle Ages (500–1050). City life almost disappeared, the economy was disrupted, and arts and learning declined. Yet this was also a formative period, for medieval civilization was taking shape. This new civilization was a combination of Christian influences, Germanic traditions, and the Greco-Roman heritage.

The Christian Church was the most stable institution in the Middle Ages after the decline of Roman authority, providing unity and leadership. While a few strong rulers established kingdoms in parts of Europe, most political power lay in the hands of landowning nobles. The small worlds of the village, the castle, and the lord's manor were the basis of medieval life (that is, life during the Middle Ages). Gradually peace and prosperity returned to Europe. Agriculture and trade thrived, and towns bustled with activity. Interest in learning revived, and arts and literature flourished. Strong rulers began to create national states in England and France, and some monarchs challenged the Church's authority in political life. By the High Middle Ages (1050–1270), medieval civilization was at its height in Western Europe. The following chapters describe how medieval civilization developed and what it achieved.

Medieval books were laboriously printed by hand and were often richly illustrated. This manuscript page is from a famous French history of medieval England, France, and Spain. The picture shows Queen Isabella of England entering Paris in 1328.

Some medieval manuscripts were "books of hours," which contained prayers and religious instruction for different hours of the day. This painting from a late medieval book of hours shows peasants working near a castle, a scene that was typical of the period as a whole.

The Early Middle Ages

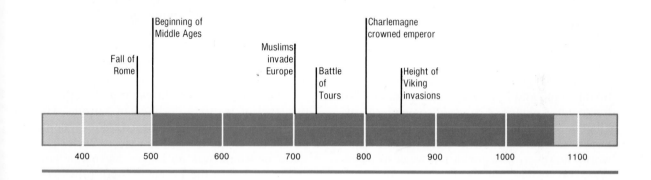

| 400 | 500 | 600 | 700 | 800 | 900 | 1000 | 1100 |

Fall of Rome

Beginning of Middle Ages

Muslims invade Europe

Battle of Tours

Charlemagne crowned emperor

Height of Viking invasions

The fall of Rome and the rise of Germanic kingdoms marked the end of ancient times and the beginning of the Middle Ages. During the Middle Ages the center of European culture shifted from the lands around the Mediterranean Sea to regions that had barely been touched by Greco-Roman civilization.

A new civilization — medieval civilization — took shape during the early Middle Ages (A.D. 500–1050). There were few strong rulers or governments in this period, and a political system grew up in which power was divided among many local lords. Economic and social life also changed, centering on the lands held by these lords. The Christian Church influenced both politics and society in medieval civilization. The traditions of Rome — and of the Germanic tribes as well — played a part in creating the new way of life in medieval Europe.

This chapter tells about the rise of medieval civilization in Western and Central Europe and describes the new social and economic systems that developed during this period.

CHAPTER OUTLINE

1 Medieval Civilization Develops in Europe

2 A Feudal System Takes Shape

3 Life Centers on the Manor

1 Medieval Civilization Develops in Europe

The gradual decline of the Roman Empire in the West left Western and Central Europe in confusion. Strong government had vanished, and economic life was in turmoil. Although Germanic kingdoms were established, it was mainly the strength and organization of the Christian Church that provided a feeling of unity in Europe.

A TIME OF CHANGE

Germanic customs replace Roman ways. By the fifth century, Germanic peoples had established kingdoms in North Africa, Italy, Spain, Gaul, and England — lands formerly belonging to Rome. The rulers of some Germanic kingdoms admired Roman civilization and hoped to share its advantages. The Roman world, however, had grown too weak to be revived. Moreover, the traditions of the Germanic peoples were very different from those of the Romans.

At its height the Roman Empire had been a world of cities with a rich culture. By the end of the Empire, many towns were abandoned as people fled to country estates. The center of social, economic, and political life shifted from city to countryside. Since the Germanic invaders were rural people, they did not try to revive the old cultural centers or build new ones of their own.

Germanic political life was also very different from that of the Roman Empire. The Germanic peoples were divided into tribes, and their loyalties were to their own tribe and its chieftain. There was no idea of loyalty to a state that included many different peoples. A Germanic kingdom was viewed as the personal property of its ruler. By custom Germanic kings divided up their lands and willed them to their sons, a practice that resulted in frequent civil wars.

Another area of difference between Germanic peoples and Romans was law. Roman law was written law. It applied to each citizen of the Empire, regardless of place of birth. At the time of the invasions, Germanic law consisted of the unwritten laws of each tribe. No one law applied to all the tribes. Eventually some Germanic rulers had the tribal laws put into written form.

The Germanic system of justice was also less advanced than the Roman court system. In Roman courts, judges had investigated evidence and demanded proof. Germanic judges used trial by ordeal to determine guilt. In a typical ordeal, a defendant was tied up and thrown into a river. A defendant who sank was considered innocent; floating was interpreted as proof of guilt.

Learning declines. After the fall of Rome, the level of learning declined in Europe. The old Roman schools disappeared. Few people except the clergy learned to read or write. The Latin of Rome was no longer the major language spoken in the former Roman provinces. Knowledge of Greek was almost lost, so that few people could read Greek works of literature, science, or philosophy.

Among the Germanic tribes, there was a rich oral tradition of songs and legends, but there was no written literature. The Germanic alphabet, called runes, was used mainly for inscriptions on monuments.

Some scholars preserve learning. Compared with the time of the Pax Romana (page 107), the sixth to eighth centuries seemed to be a "dark age." Yet learning did not completely disappear in Europe. Some scholars preserved Greco-Roman knowledge.

The Ostrogoth king Theodoric, who ruled Italy from 493 to 526, admired Roman culture and encouraged scholarship at his court. Boethius (boh-EE-thee-us), a Roman in Theodoric's service, translated some of Aristotle's writings from Greek into Latin and wrote commentaries on Greek works in music and mathematics. Cassiodorus (kas-ee-uh-DOR-us), another Roman in Theodoric's court, collected, copied, and translated ancient manuscripts, which might otherwise have been lost. He did much of this work after retiring to a monastery, setting an example that other monks would follow.

Churchmen in other parts of Europe also helped to preserve learning. In Spain in the early seventh century, Bishop Isidore of Seville wrote an encyclopedia covering many topics — mathematics, music, astronomy, medicine, religion, zoology. In 731, the Venerable Bede, a scholarly English monk, completed a history of the Church in England. Written in Latin, Bede's work is generally regarded as the finest history written in the Middle Ages.

THE MEDIEVAL CHURCH

The Church has a strong influence on medieval civilization. The early part of the Middle Ages, when people in Europe were struggling to recover from the destruction and chaos caused by the breakup of the Roman Empire, was also a formative time. Germanic, Christian, and Roman traditions were being woven together into a new civilization.

A guiding force in this new civilization was Christianity. As contacts between Romans and the Germanic tribes increased during the Empire's decline, many Germans had been converted to Christianity. Christian missionaries carried on the process of conversion after the fall of Rome.

The Christian Church gave form and unity to the new civilization arising in Europe. Centered in Rome, the Church was the leading institution in medieval society. Government and society were fragmented, but the Church was a bond that united Christian peoples.

Nearly everyone in medieval Europe saw the Church as the guardian and interpreter of religious truth. Medieval people believed that the way to heaven was through the Church. Only by obeying the Church, they believed, could they gain salvation.

The Church develops a strong organization. The Christian Church had begun as small communities of people who met to worship together. By the late years of the Roman Empire, the Church had developed a strong organization. The leading Church officials were the bishops. The most influential bishops were those in major cities or the oldest and largest

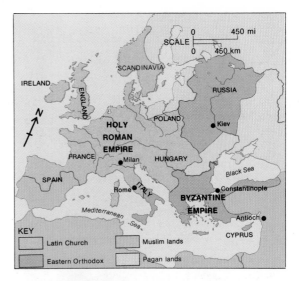

Christianity in Europe, About A.D. 1000

The map shows the parts of Europe where people had become Christian by the year 1000. What two forms of Christianity were found in Europe at this time?

Christian communities — Rome, Constantinople, Jerusalem, Milan, and Antioch. Bishops supervised the priests in their districts and settled disputes over Church teachings and religious practices. The bishop of Rome, later called the Pope, came to be considered head of the Church. Popes believed they inherited from Peter, the first bishop of Rome (page 128), the responsibility for the souls of all Christians. They felt it was their duty to lead Christians on the path marked out by God. An important early Pope was Gregory I (also called Gregory the Great), who held that position from 590 to 604. Under Gregory, the Church not only watched over Christians' spiritual lives. It also took over powers and duties that were usually the responsibility of governments. For centuries to come, the Church played a part in European political affairs.

For most people, the local priest was their connection with the Church and with God. The priest administered the sacraments, which were special religious ceremonies such as baptism, communion, and marriage. The priest also gave advice, taught people the rules of right and wrong, and tried to help the sick and needy. As

ILLUMINATED MANUSCRIPTS

The illustrated books prepared by monks are known as illuminated manuscripts. Below, an illustration from a medieval Bible shows monks preparing such a manuscript. In the tinted drawing at left the artist used a picture of Saint George killing a dragon to decorate the letter "R." Notice how a small figure was added to give height to the drawing of the saint. Below left is a picture of a monk harvesting wheat, a typical scene in a monastery, where work was combined with prayer. Other pictures from illuminated manuscripts appear on pages 134 and 136 of this book.

few people could read, the priest was their source of Church teachings. The local churches were centers of village life. There men, women, and children gathered for worship and to celebrate Church festivals.

Monks and nuns also do the work of the Church. Some men and women chose to serve the Church in other ways. They took vows as monks or nuns, living apart from society and devoting their lives to prayer and good works. Monks lived in monasteries and nuns in convents. Many followed the rules and guidelines set forth by Saint Benedict, who founded a monastery at Monte Cassino in Italy in 529.

Other men and women who founded religious orders developed similar sets of rules.

Monks and nuns made valuable contributions to medieval society. They taught better methods of farming and skills such as carpentry and weaving to the peasants who worked on the monastery's lands. Convents and monasteries also established hospitals, provided shelter for travelers, and were centers of learning. Monks kept classical learning alive by reading and writing Latin, studying ancient manuscripts, and copying them by hand. Many of the copies they made were works of art, beautifully decorated and illustrated.

The monasteries of England and Ireland played a particularly important role in preserving learning. Saint Patrick had converted the Irish to Christianity in the early fourth century. In Ireland, Latin became the language of both the Church and of scholars at a time when it was in danger of disappearing. Some Irish scholars could read Greek long after such knowledge had almost completely disappeared elsewhere in Western Europe.

Monks and nuns, particularly in Ireland and England, also served as missionaries and spread Christianity. During the early Middle Ages, they converted many Germanic pagans to Christianity. In this way they helped to shape a common Christian civilization for most of Europe. To the people of the Middle Ages, monks and nuns were selfless people who devoted their lives to God. They were viewed as providing the finest example of the Christian way of life.

FRANKISH KINGDOMS

Frankish rulers form kingdoms. The decline of Roman rule left Western and Central Europe disorganized. A new medieval style of government appeared in the kingdom of the Franks. A Germanic people, the Franks had migrated westward from their homeland in the valley of the Rhine River. As Rome's border defenses weakened in the fourth and fifth centuries, Frankish tribes settled in Roman territory (map, page 122). About 481 a Frankish ruler named Clovis united the various Frankish tribes and conquered the Romans and other Germans in northern Gaul. Clovis married a Christian, Clotilda, and after a successful battle

---

PRIMARY SOURCES IN WORLD HISTORY
The Rules of Saint Benedict

The rules drawn up by Saint Benedict required monks to obey the head of the monastery and to live for hard work and prayer. They could own nothing and could not marry. Benedict provided the following guidelines to a Christian life:

In the first place, to love the Lord God with all one's heart, all one's soul, and all one's strength.
Then, [to love] one's neighbor as oneself.
Then not to kill.
Not to steal. . . .
To honor all men.
Not to do to another what one would not have done to oneself.
Not to seek soft living.
To relieve the poor.
To love one's enemies.
Not to be proud.
To visit the sick.
To bury the dead. . . .
To console the sorrowing.
To prefer nothing [above] the love of Christ.
Not to yield to anger. . . .
Not to forsake charity.
Not to swear. . . .

To utter truth from heart and mouth.
To do no wrong to anyone, and to bear patiently wrongs done to oneself.
To put one's hope in God.

What guideline did Benedict put above all others? What kinds of behavior did he advise against? What qualities did he recommend? What did he mean by the phrase "to honor all men"?

about 496, he and his warriors converted to Christianity. A few years later he captured part of the Visigoths' kingdom in southern Gaul. Only a defeat by the Ostrogoth king Theodoric (page 138) kept Clovis from taking all of Gaul.

After Clovis died in 511, however, the Frankish lands were divided among his sons. The rulers gradually lost much of their power to nobles who held large estates. In each Frankish kingdom real power fell into the hands of the king's chief officer, who was known as the Mayor of the Palace and was closely allied with the landowning nobles.

Frankish lands are reunited. One Mayor of the Palace, Pepin II, triumphed over the mayors of rival kingdoms and reunited the

Charlemagne's Empire

This map shows the lands ruled by Charlemagne and the division of his kingdom after his death. Describe the location of the lands that were conquered by Charlemagne.

KEY
☐ Frankish lands in 768
☐ Conquests of Charlemagne (768–814)
--- Division of empire in 843

SCALE
0 — 300 mi
0 — 300 km

Frankish lands. From 687 to 714, Pepin ruled all the Franks. Pepin's son, Charles Martel (which means "Charles the Hammer"), inherited the title and the lands. From 717 to 741 he ruled as Mayor of the Palace over most of Gaul. In 732, Charles's Frankish forces defeated an invading Muslim army at the Battle of Tours. This important victory halted the Muslim advance into Western Europe.[1]

A Mayor of the Palace becomes king. In 751, Pepin the Short, son of Charles Martel, was given the title "king of the Franks" instead of "Mayor of the Palace." The Pope in Rome and the Frankish nobles approved the change. Establishing a custom for later rulers, the Pope crowned Pepin as king "by the grace of God."

The Pope supported Pepin because he wanted the Franks to protect the Church from the Lombards, another Germanic people. Having conquered much of northern Italy in the sixth century, the Lombards were threatening the papal lands around Rome. Pepin invaded Italy, defeated the Lombards, and gave the Pope the territory between Rome and Ravenna. This region became known as the Papal States.

Charlemagne promotes learning and expands his kingdom. In 768 Pepin's son Charlemagne (SHAR-luh-main), or Charles the Great,[2] became king of the Franks. Charlemagne was an extraordinary figure in medieval history. Well over six feet tall, he was described by the monk Einhard as "large and strong, and of lofty stature" with a "stately and dignified" appearance. Charlemagne, said Einhard, was devoted to his children: "He was so careful of the training of his sons and daughters that he never took his meals without them when he was at home, and never made a journey without them." A devout Christian, Charlemagne had a beautiful church built at Aachen (AH-kun), his capital, and attended services there regularly.

---

[1]The Muslims, followers of the new religion of Islam, conquered much of the Near East, North Africa, and Spain in the seventh and early eighth centuries. The rise of Islam is discussed in Chapter 10.
[2]His name combines the French form of the Latin *Carolus* ("Charles") and *Magnus* ("great"). This dynasty that started with Pepin is called the Carolingian (kehr-oh-LIN-jee-un).

Einhard described how this warrior-king of the Franks was attracted to the cultures of ancient Greece and Rome:

> He was not satisfied with command of his native language merely, but gave attention to the study of foreign ones, and in particular was such a master of Latin that he could speak it as well as his native tongue. . . . He could understand Greek better than he could speak it. . . . Alcuin, . . . who was the greatest scholar of the day, was his teacher. . . . The King spent much time and labor with him studying rhetoric, dialectics, and especially astronomy. . . . He also tried to write, . . . but [because he began] late in life, [his efforts] met with ill success.

Hoping to improve the training of his officials and the clergy, Charlemagne brought some of the finest scholars in Europe to his palace school. Directed by the English monk Alcuin (who had taught the king), they collected books and read the works of ancient Roman authors. These scholars wrote poems, histories, and religious works, in which they imitated the style of Roman literature. While they produced no great works of philosophy or science, they did help to keep interest in ancient writings alive.

Charlemagne expanded his kingdom by conquering the Lombard kingdom in Italy and taking part of northern Spain from the Muslims. He added Bavaria (in what is now Germany) to his kingdom and after terrible wars forced the Germanic Saxons to submit to his rule and convert to Christianity.

Charlemagne is crowned Emperor of the Romans. On Christmas Day in the year 800, Pope Leo III crowned Charlemagne "Emperor of the Romans." This indicated that the Roman idea of a strong centralized government had not died. Doubtless some believed that Charlemagne was reviving the Roman Empire. Charlemagne's empire did not, however, have Roman law or political organization. Moreover, it had no great cities that could serve as centers of trade and learning.

Charlemagne's empire, in fact, was the sign of something new. Charlemagne was a German whose government grew out of Germanic customs. He was also a Christian who

In this sculpture Charlemagne is shown holding the orb and scepter that symbolize his authority. The cross stands for his role as defender of the Church.

spread the faith, protected the Church against its enemies, and was crowned emperor by the Pope. Scholars in his kingdom preserved the learning of the Greco-Roman past. This blending of Germanic, Christian, and Roman elements came to characterize the civilization of the Middle Ages.

CHECK-UP

1. In what ways did Germanic political, legal, and cultural traditions differ from those of the Roman world?
2. (a) How did the Christian Church help to unify the people of Europe? (b) What was the organization of the Church?
3. What contributions did monks and nuns make to medieval civilization?
4. (a) What was the relationship between Pepin II, Charles Martel, and Pepin the Short? (b) How did each strengthen the Frankish kingdom?
5. (a) What lands did Charlemagne take over? (b) In what way was his empire the sign of something new?

2 A Feudal System Takes Shape

Charlemagne's great empire in Western and Central Europe was held together primarily by the strong personality of its ruler. It was not strong enough to survive Charlemagne's death in 814, and the great landowners and nobles once again came into power. A political system developed in which there was no strong central ruler or government.

Charlemagne's empire breaks apart. Charlemagne's son Louis the Pious inherited the throne and tried to preserve his father's empire. His efforts were resisted by the Frankish nobles, who sought to increase their own power at the expense of the emperor. After Louis died in 840, his three surviving sons agreed in the Treaty of Verdun (843) to divide the empire (map, page 142). The settlement did not bring stability, however. Charles the Bald, in the west, and Louis the German, in the east, fought over the middle section held by their brother Lothair. Eventually that section was also divided into different domains.

With the breakup of the empire, the Carolingian kings lost their authority over the nobles who held large estates. Once again, Europe was politically divided. It was also beset by invasions.

Viking raiders terrorize Europe. In the ninth century Europe was invaded from several directions. The most fearsome invaders were the Vikings or Northmen — the ancestors of the Norwegians, Swedes, and Danes of today. The Vikings came from the forests of Scandinavia. They were excellent shipbuilders, adventurous seamen, and ferocious warriors. They were feared all along the European coast, from the North Sea to the Mediterranean. Sailing in open boats powered by sails and oars, some Vikings traveled to Iceland and Greenland. They established settlements there between 850 and 1000. It is likely that these Vikings explored the northeast coast of North America, which they called Vinland, 500 years before Columbus reached the Americas.

During the ninth century Viking bands raided coastal settlements in Western Europe and pushed inland along the rivers. Wherever they landed, the Vikings looted settlements, enslaved or killed the local people, and burned homes and villages. As time passed, most Vikings became Christians and turned from raiding to trade. Some settled on the coasts in Britain, France, and southern Europe. In the 800's and 900's, however, they were so feared that people prayed: "God deliver us from the fury of the Northmen."

Europe faces other invaders. The Vikings were not the only invaders to disrupt early medieval Europe. The Magyars were originally nomads from Central Asia. Superb horsemen, they swept across the broad Danube plain in the late ninth century and invaded northern Italy and southern Germany. Along the Mediterranean, people faced raids by still other invaders. From their bases in Spain and North Africa, Muslim pirates attacked coastal regions and captured Mediterranean islands.

This Viking helmet, combining plates of iron with flexible chain mail, was intended to terrify enemies as well as protect the wearer.

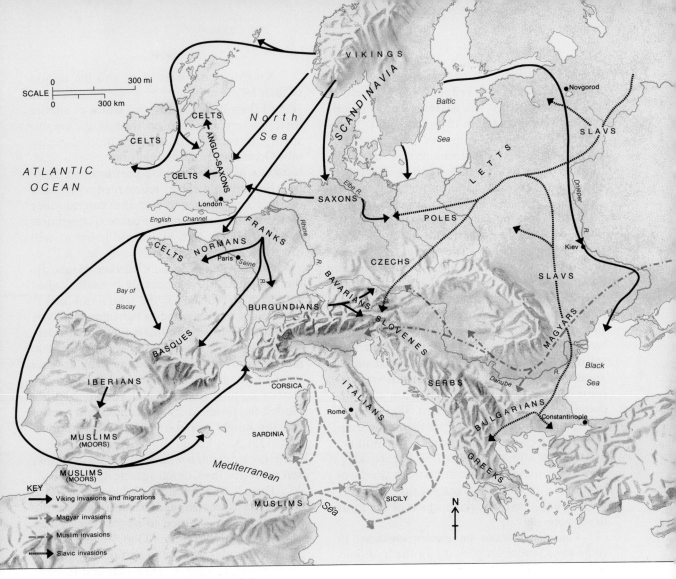

Peoples of Europe, 800–1000

The period after 800 was marked by invasions and migrations throughout Europe. What groups invaded Europe? Which of these groups swept over the largest area?

The invasions went on until early in the tenth century and had terrible consequences for Western Europe. Like the earlier Germanic invasions, they weakened central authority, disrupted trade, hurt agriculture, and left settlements and monasteries in ruins. People no longer looked to a central ruler for security. They turned instead to the local lords, who had their own armies. Western Europe had entered an age in which lords, not kings, held political power.

Feudalism develops in Western Europe. Living in an age of warfare and disorder, lords sought allies among their fellow nobles. The basis for these alliances was the lords' land. In exchange for military assistance and other services, one lord granted land, called a *fief* (FEEF), to another noble. The noble who received the land was called a *vassal.* The lord-vassal relationship was cemented by a solemn ceremony in which the vassal pledged loyalty to the lord. The system of relationships that grew out of this granting of fiefs was called *feudalism.* It became the main political arrangement in Europe after the breakup of Charlemagne's empire in the ninth century.

The feudal system sets up new relationships. Feudalism affected all classes of people in medieval society. In return for his pledge of loyalty, the vassal received the lord's protection and a grant of land. The peasants who lived on the fief were included in the lord's grant. They raised the crops that supported the vassal and they, too, expected protection in time of trouble. The vassal owed the lord several other obligations. Vassals had to aid the lord in war and were supposed to raise ransom money if the lord was captured by an enemy. Vassals provided lodgings when the lord traveled through their territory. They gave a gift when the lord's son was knighted and when his eldest daughter married. Each vassal sat in the lord's court and helped to judge cases involving disputes between the lord and other vassals.

Relationships between lords and vassals were complex. The same noble might be a vassal to several lords. Moreover, a vassal might grant land to other nobles and in this way become a lord. For example, William of Normandy, holder of a fief from the king of France, conquered England in 1066. The English nobles became his vassals. Yet William himself was still a vassal of the French king. Sometimes there was a clash between two lords to whom a vassal had sworn loyalty. Then the vassal would have to decide which of the lords to support.

Feudalism draws on earlier customs. In some ways feudalism grew out of the traditions of the Germanic tribes. The Germanic warriors had pledged their loyalty to heads of war bands. The vassal's oath of loyalty to a feudal lord grew out of that practice. Feudal law included many elements of Germanic law, and feudal attitudes reflected the Germanic respect for the warrior. Feudalism also drew on the pattern set by the fortified latifundia of the late Roman Empire.

Lords are warriors. In an age when warfare was common, the feudal lord had to be primarily a warrior. Through combat, lords protected their lands, enlarged their estates, and added to their wealth. A young noble was trained to be a knight. He learned how to wear armor, ride a war-horse, and fight with sword and lance. When the youth had proved his ability and courage, he was knighted in an impressive ceremony.

Knights yearned for glory and the respect of their fellow nobles. They wanted minstrels to sing of their heroic deeds and ladies to admire their bravery. To keep up their skills, knights spent time each day practicing with their weapons. Occasionally, lords held tournaments, contests in which knights took part in mock combat. For the audiences, tournaments provided exciting entertainment. For the knights, they were a challenge in times of peace. The winners in a tournament won praise and honor as well as valuable prizes.

Knighthood reflects Christian ideals. By the twelfth century a code of behavior called *chivalry* had evolved for the feudal nobility. A true knight was expected to fight bravely, to be loyal to his lord, and to treat other knights with respect and courtesy. He was also expected to protect women, children, and the weak. In time the Church added a religious element to the warrior culture of the feudal knight. A priest blessed the future knight's weapons and prayed that the knight would always "defend the just and right." A knight was expected to be a Christian gentleman who honored Church laws and defended the Church against its enemies.

The Church recognized that the warfare among lords contributed to disorder. In the eleventh century it tried to impose the "Peace of God" and the "Truce of God." These rulings restricted feudal warfare to certain days of the week and certain times of the year and forbade fighting in places such as churches. Although only partially effective, the restrictions did offer people some protection from constant fighting.

Castles are fortified against attack. Because they lived in violent times, feudal lords built homes designed to serve as fortresses. The first castles were built in the ninth century, at the time of the Viking raids, and were made of timber and earth. In the eleventh century lords began to build castles of stone.

Encircled by massive walls and strong guard towers, the lord's castle stood high on a rocky hill or by the bend of a river. There were no buildings near it. Trees and bushes were cut down so that lookouts could easily see an approaching enemy. Around the castle was a moat, a wide ditch filled with water. When an enemy force approached, the drawbridge across the moat was raised, and the knights defending the castle took positions high on the castle walls.

Attacking forces laid careful plans to capture a castle. First, they filled part of the moat with logs and earth so they could cross it. Once they had a road across the moat, the attackers tried to go under, over, or through the castle walls. As the attackers raised ladders against the castle walls, its defenders hurled boiling water, hot oil, melted lead, and huge stones at the climbing soldiers. Some attackers tried to scale the wall; others tried to break it down with battering rams. Other soldiers manned machines that hurled huge stones against the wall until a section crumbled.

Sometimes the attackers used a movable tower, the top of which was as high as the castle wall. Built of heavy timber, the tower was pushed on wheels or rollers close to the castle. After a drawbridge was lowered from the tower to the castle wall, the attacking soldiers rushed across the bridge and fought hand-to-hand with the castle's defenders.

Another method of attack was to tunnel under the castle walls. The attackers used timbers to support the roof of their tunnel. After the tunnel reached a point well under the castle wall, the timbers were set on fire. When the wood burned through, the castle wall above it collapsed.

Feudal life centers on the castle. The castle was a home as well as a fortress. In it lived the lord and lady, members of their family, knights and other men-at-arms, household officials, and servants. The most important official was the steward, who kept records of the lord's lands and revenues. Because the lord's

---

LINKING PAST AND PRESENT

Coats of Arms

In the confusion of a medieval battle or tournament, it was very important to know who your allies were and where your leader was. Because helmets and suits of armor concealed the knights' identity, warriors had to identify each other by the symbols, or *arms,* painted on their shields. Later these symbols also were embroidered on sleeveless coats worn over the armor.

Early coats of arms had fairly simple designs, like those on the shields in this scene of a tournament. As time went on and designs grew more complicated, an art called heraldry grew up to create coats of arms. Colors used in heraldic designs have special names: *azur* (blue), *gules* (red), *sable* (black), *vert* (green), and *purpure* (purple). Two ''metals'' are used — *argent* and *or* (silver and gold). Other special terms describe the designs and the heraldic beasts that often are shown on coats of arms. Among the many designs from heraldry that still appear in the flags and coats of arms of modern nations are the English lion, the red dragon of Wales, and the German black eagle.

LIFE OF THE FEUDAL NOBILITY

Lords spent their time in activities connected with battle (above right), yet they also enjoyed social events. The painting above shows the clothing worn at a banquet. Men dressed in tights and jackets, and women wore headdresses to add to their height. Pointed toes became fashionable, even on armor.

wealth came from his lands, he was careful to choose a competent steward. The wise lord often discussed the management of the estate with the steward. The steward listed the livestock and produce in each village on the lord's lands and kept records of the taxes and rents owed by the peasants. He recorded daily expenses and made certain that the cook and baker did not waste or steal food.

The castle had bedrooms, a kitchen, storerooms, and a chapel where the lord and his family attended religious services. The most important room in the castle was the great hall. Here the lord and lady ate, gave orders to servants, and received guests. After dinner, which was often a feast, traveling entertainers amused the family and guests. These performers wandered from castle to castle in search of an audience. They knew that a good performance would bring them food, a place to sleep, and a few coins. Clowns called jesters amused the diners with clever remarks and foolish actions.

Jugglers, acrobats, magicians, and animal trainers also performed. Minstrels played harps, guitars, or flutes and sang about the deeds of brave knights.

Noblewomen have many duties. The lady of the castle supervised the household. She looked after the preparation of food and kept a garden where she grew herbs to use in cooking and for medicine. She also taught young girls in her household how to sew, spin, and weave, and she tended the sick and wounded. When the lord was away from the castle, the lady took charge. She supervised the household officials and made financial decisions. If the lord was taken prisoner in war, she raised the ransom to pay for his release. Sometimes she put on armor and went to war.

For amusement the noblewomen enjoyed chess and other board games or played a musical instrument. They embroidered tapestries to cover the bare castle walls and keep the rooms warmer. A lady might also join her husband on the hunt, a favorite recreation of the medieval nobility.

A noble's daughter was usually married by the age of fourteen, often to a man who was much older. The marriage was arranged by her father. A noble's daughter who did not marry might become a nun. People in the Middle Ages believed that women should be subordinate to men. Nevertheless, the Church taught that both men and women were children of God, and it regarded marriage as a sacred rite.

Noblewomen have some political power. In some parts of Europe, women could inherit lands and the power that went with them. In England, Matilda, the daughter of King Henry I, raised an army and went to war in 1135, trying to establish her claim to the English throne. In the early 1200's, Blanche of Castile ruled France while her son King Louis was away and did much to bring peace and unity among the various regions.

Eleanor of Aquitaine, another twelfth-century noblewoman, inherited her father's rich lands in southern France. A brilliant ruler in her own right, Eleanor married, first, King Louis VII of France and, later, Henry II of England. She played an important role in the politics of both countries.

CHECK-UP

1. Vocabulary: *fief, vassal, feudalism, chivalry.*
2. (a) What happened to Charlemagne's empire after his death? (b) Why was there great disorder in Europe in the ninth century?
3. (a) What were the obligations of the feudal lord to his vassal? (b) What duties did vassals owe to their lord?
4. (a) What training did young nobles receive? (b) What qualities did the code of chivalry demand of knights? (c) What did the Church do to limit warfare?
5. (a) What skills did women of noble families learn? (b) What was the position of noblewomen in medieval society?

3   Life Centers on the Manor

The wealth of feudal lords came from the labor of the peasants who lived on their land. In the last years of the Roman Empire, many peasants had begun to work for landowners instead of owning their own land. Some peasants gave their land to nobles in return for protection. Other peasants lost their lands because of debt. By the early Middle Ages few peasants owned the land they farmed.

Peasants become serfs. The overwhelming majority of people in medieval Europe were peasants. Most peasants were *serfs* who did not have the freedom to leave the land where they were born. When a new lord acquired a fief, he acquired the serfs as well. Serfs lived in a small village on the lord's estate or *manor.* From the lord the serfs received housing and land to farm. In return, they farmed the lord's land, looked after his animals, and did other tasks on the estate.

Feudalism was the basic political arrangement during the Middle Ages; *manorialism* was the basic economic system. Only the toil of peasants made this way of life possible, for neither the nobility nor the clergy did work that produced goods.

The manor is a self-sufficient world. Each lord owned at least one manor; great lords owned many. The Church also held many manors. Fifteen to thirty families usually lived in the village on a manor. Besides the serfs' cottages, the village included the lord's castle or manor house, a church, and workshops. Surrounding the village were fields, pastureland, and forests. In the forest were wild animals that the lord hunted; in the pastures cattle, sheep, and horses grazed. If the soldiers of another lord attacked a manor, the peasants found protection inside the walls around the manor house.

Almost everything needed for daily life was produced on the manor. The people of the manor raised grain and other crops in its fields and orchards. Carpenters and stonemasons did the building and repairing, and blacksmiths made weapons for knights and tools for household use. Women spun wool into thread and wove the thread into fabric for clothing. A priest tended to the religious needs of the people. While goods such as salt and iron had to be obtained from the outside, the manor was largely self-sufficient, able to produce almost everything it needed.

Medieval farmers share land and labor. Medieval farmers understood that soil loses its fertility if the same crops are planted year after year. They used compost and manure to enrich the soil, but there was never enough fertilizer. To keep the soil from losing its fertility, farmers used a two-field system. One field was kept idle, or fallow, while the other was planted half with spring wheat and other crops and half with winter wheat and rye. The following year the field that had been planted was left fallow, and the fallow field was farmed.

Each field was divided into strips. Many of these strips belonged to the lord, but some were set aside for the serfs. Because the fields were not all equally fertile, each serf was given strips in several different fields.

A single farmer could not plow and harvest without help. The plow was heavy, the oxen small, and the harness poor. As many as eight oxen might be needed to pull a plow.

THE MEDIEVAL MANOR

This diagram shows a manor where the two-field system of farming was used. What land did the serfs farm? How did the lord get a share of the crops? What was done to help the land regain its fertility?

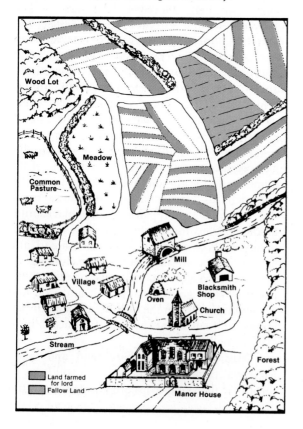

Serfs thus shared their oxen and worked together to get the land plowed and the crops harvested. Each family received the produce from its own strips, but all the plowing and harvesting were done cooperatively.

The serf has rights as well as duties. Serfs owed many obligations to their lords. They farmed the land set aside for the lord — his domain — and turned over all its crops to him. They had to bake their bread in the lord's oven, grind their wheat in the lord's mill, and press their grapes in his winepress. They paid for these services by giving the lord of the manor part of the crops they grew on their own strips of land. Serfs also dug ditches, gathered firewood, built fences, and repaired roads and buildings. Besides helping in the fields, women made clothing for the lord's family. Each serf worked about three days a week for the lord.

Serfs could not leave the manor without the lord's permission. The lord could even decide whom a serf would marry. (Serfs who did not wish to marry the person the lord chose for them could pay a fine instead.)

Although serfs were not free, neither were they slaves. Their rights were protected by custom. Their children could not be taken from them and sold. As long as serfs carried out their duties to their lord, they could live in their cottages and farm their strips of land. If a lord tried to take away these rights, serfs might resist by refusing to work.

Serfdom is a harsh way of life. Serfs lived in crowded one- or two-room cottages. The roofs were made of thatch, and the walls were mud-plastered logs. The floors were often hard-pounded dirt. In winter the open windows were closed with wooden shutters or stuffed with straw. There was no chimney. Smoke from the hearth seeped out through the thatched roof. Rough benches, a table, beds, and perhaps a storage chest were the only furniture. The serfs might share their homes with chickens and pigs.

Unlike the lord, serfs almost never sat down to a feast. They ate a simple diet — vegetables, coarse brown bread, grain, cheese, and soup. Honey from their beehives sweetened their food. Fresh meat, milk, and butter were luxuries. The wild animals in the forests belonged to the lord, and serfs were forbidden to

MANOR LIFE

Peasants performed numerous tasks on the manor. The picture at left shows serfs beating flax to loosen its fibers and a woman spinning fibers into linen thread from which clothing will be made. Above, serfs are shown working in a bakery. They also labored in the fields (picture, page 136).

hunt them. When crops failed, peasants faced starvation.

The life of a serf was hard and tiring. Men and women worked in the fields from sunrise to sunset. This backbreaking labor left them exhausted and made them age quickly. Disease often crippled and killed their children. Warring lords might destroy their homes, steal their animals, and ruin their crops. The serfs' way of life was passed on to their children. They, too, were born into a life of serfdom.

Although serfs had hard lives, they did have some simple pleasures. Traveling minstrels and entertainers — acrobats, bear-trainers, and actors — visited the manors. Wrestling and football were other forms of amusement. On holidays, serfs gathered in front of the village church to sing and dance.

Serfs rarely left the manor where they lived. Dense forests separated one manor from another. Poor roads and few bridges made travel difficult for everyone; thieves and warring knights made it dangerous. Peasants lived, worked, and died on the lord's estate and were buried in the village churchyard. They knew almost nothing of the outside world.

Most serfs accept their position in life. Open rebellion by serfs was rare until the fourteenth century. Lords simply had too much military and legal power for serfs to oppose them effectively. Moreover, the serfs — like everyone else in medieval times — believed that God determined a person's place in society and that some people were meant to be nobles and others, serfs. Men of lowly birth sometimes joined the clergy and a few even became abbots or bishops. Sometimes a lord conferred knighthood upon a peasant who distinguished himself in battle. Nevertheless, most serfs simply accepted their position and hoped for a better life in the world to come.

CHECK-UP

1. Vocabulary: *serf, manor, manorialism.*
2. (a) Why did most people live on manors during the early Middle Ages? (b) What did a manor include?
3. (a) What was the two-field system of farming? (b) Why was it used? (c) Why were fields divided into strips?
4. (a) What kinds of obligations did serfs have? (b) What rights did they have? (c) How were those rights protected?
5. (a) Describe the housing and food of a serf. (b) Why did serfs tend to accept their lot in life?

Chapter 7 Review

Summary

After the fall of Rome, there was a decline in trade, town life, and learning in Western and Central Europe. During the early Middle Ages (500–1050), the Church emerged as the institution that unified the people and influenced their lives and beliefs.

Medieval civilization gradually developed as Germanic, Christian, and Greco-Roman elements began to blend together in the Kingdom of the Franks. In 800 the Frankish ruler, Charlemagne, was crowned Emperor of the Romans by the Pope, a sign that the Roman ideal of unity and organization had not died.

Charlemagne's heirs could not hold the empire together. Raids by Vikings, Magyars, and Muslims caused widespread disorder. Unable to provide protection, monarchs lost their power to lords who owned great manors and had their own armies. Feudalism, which was based on relationships between lords and their vassals, developed as central authority declined.

The lord's land was worked by serfs—peasants who could not leave the manor, the lord's estate. They lived in a small village on the manor and performed many tasks for the lord in exchange for protection. Largely self-sufficient, the manor was the basic economic unit of the Middle Ages.

Vocabulary Review

1. Write the sentences listed below on a sheet of paper. Fill in the blank in each sentence with one of these words: *chivalry, feudalism, fief, manor, manorialism, serf, vassal.*

(a) The main political arrangement in Europe after the break-up of Charlemagne's empire was ___?___, a system based on the relationship between lords and vassals.

(b) A ___?___ was land granted to one noble by another in exchange for military assistance and other services.

(c) ___?___ was the code of behavior followed by feudal nobles.

(d) A peasant who was legally bound to the estate of a lord was a ___?___ .

(e) The estate of a medieval lord was called his ___?___ .

(f) A noble who pledged his services to another noble in exchange for a grant of land and serfs was a ___?___ .

(g) The economic system of Europe during the Middle Ages was ___?___ .

2. Explain the importance of each of the following to the history of the Middle Ages: (a) Battle of Tours, (b) Magyars, (c) Vikings, (d) two-field system, (e) Mayor of the Palace.

People to Identify

Match the following people with the numbered phrases that describe them: *Saint Patrick, Theodoric, Pepin the Short, Clovis, Venerable Bede, Charlemagne.*

1. United the Frankish tribes and conquered most of Gaul in the late 400's.
2. Wrote the history of the Church in England.
3. Supported the scholarly work of Boethius.
4. The Frankish king who became "Emperor of the Romans."
5. Converted the Irish to Christianity in the early 300's.
6. The first Mayor of the Palace to be crowned Frankish king.

Relating Geography and History

1. **Locating places.** Locate each of the following on a map in this chapter:

(a) Gaul   (d) Monte Cassino
(b) Italy   (e) Tours
(c) Aachen   (f) Scandinavia

2. **Review.** The term *terrain* (ter-RAYN) refers to land features. (a) What type of terrain did feudal lords prefer for building castles and fortresses? (b) What changes did they make in the surrounding land to further strengthen their defenses?

3. **Comparing maps.** Using the map of Europe in the Atlas at the back of this book and the map on page 142, determine what nations now exist in the area ruled by Charlemagne (a) in 768 and (b) in 814.

Discussion Questions

1. Central authority declined during the early Middle Ages. (a) What does this statement

mean? (b) Suggest factors that may have contributed to this decline.

2. (a) Distinguish between the feudal system and the manorial system. (b) How did each system develop? (c) What was the relationship between the two systems?

3. The Germanic rulers of territories that had formerly belonged to Rome admired Roman civilization and wanted to keep it alive, yet they were unable to do so. Why?

4. Explain the relationship between each of the following: (a) lord and vassal; (b) lord and serf; (c) lord and Church.

5. What differences were there between serfdom and slavery?

6. In the ninth century Western Europe was invaded by peoples from the north and from Central Asia. How did these invasions affect civilization in Western Europe?

Reading Primary Sources

As you have seen in earlier chapters, historians can gain valuable insights into a society by examining its laws. Read this excerpt from the laws of a medieval English manor called Dernale. Then answer the questions that follow.

Here began the customs of the bond-tenants [serfs] of the manor of Dernale. . . .
. . . when any one of them dieth, the lord shall have all the pigs of the deceased, all his goats, all his mares at grass, and his horse also, if he had one for his personal use, all his bees, . . . all his cloth of wool and flax, and whatsoever can be found of gold and silver. The lord also shall have all his brass pots. . . .

Also the lord shall have the best ox . . . and [the] Holy Church [shall have] another. After this, the rest of the animals ought to be divided thus, if the deceased has children . . . — one for the lord, one for the wife, one for the children; and if he leaves no children, [the animals] shall be divided into two parts — one for the lord and one for the wife of the deceased equally.

Also it is not lawful for a bond-tenant to make a will . . . without [the permission] of the lord of the manor. . . .

And as to the sheep, let them be divided like all the other goods of the deceased which ought to be divided. . . . This is inserted in this place by itself, because . . . the bond-tenants said that . . . all the sheep

ought to remain wholly to the wife of the deceased. Which is quite false. . . .

Also, if the lord wishes to buy corn or oats, or anything else, and [the tenants] have such things to sell, it shall not be lawful [for] them to sell anything elsewhere, except with the lord's [permission], if the lord is willing to pay them a reasonable price.

(a) Which of a serf's possessions automatically became the property of the lord when the serf died? (b) Which possessions did the lord have to divide with the serf's family? (c) How were they divided? (d) Which of these laws protect the interests of the lord? (e) Which protect the interests of the serfs? (f) What evidence is there of a disagreement between the lord and the serfs? (g) Who do you think decided how this disagreement should be settled? Explain your answer.

Skill Activities

1. Reports. Find information about one of the following topics and prepare a report: (a) medieval castles; (b) Viking longboats; (c) medieval monasteries; (d) the life of Saint Patrick; (e) the training of knights; (f) medieval armor; (g) typical events of a medieval tournament; (h) the origin of Saint Bernard dogs.

2. Word research. The word *medieval* refers to the period between ancient times and modern times. *Medieval* comes from the Latin *medius,* meaning "middle," and *aevum,* meaning "age." Below are some other terms with the root *medi-*. Find each term in the dictionary and explain how it indicates a middle position.
(a) mediate
(b) mediocre
(c) medium of exchange
(d) Mediterranean Sea

3. Exploring the arts. Illuminated manuscripts were books illustrated with drawings, paintings, and designs around the borders. Often the pictures were scenes of medieval life. For some examples of the art found in such manuscripts, look at pages 134, 136, and 140. Study about illuminated manuscripts in the library and then create your own version. Copy several sayings onto a large sheet of paper. Enlarge and decorate the first letter of each saying. Add colorful borders, scenes, and designs to make your manuscript look like a page from a medieval book.

In the painting below the citizens of a town in Flanders have gathered to receive a document freeing them from obligations to a feudal lord. The growth of self-governing towns marked a new stage in medieval civilization.

CHAPTER

8

Medieval Europe at Its Height

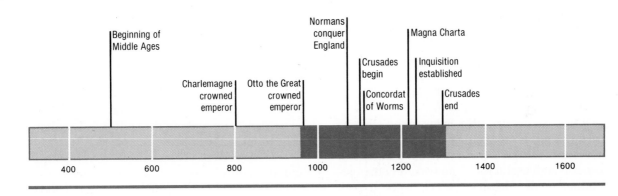

Beginning of Middle Ages

Charlemagne crowned emperor

Otto the Great crowned emperor

Normans conquer England

Crusades begin

Concordat of Worms

Magna Charta

Inquisition established

Crusades end

400   600   800   1000   1200   1400   1600

During the High Middle Ages (1050–1270), Western Europe entered a period of growth and vitality. Technological improvements and the cultivation of new lands increased farm production. The population grew, trade revived, town life was reborn, and serfdom declined. In England and France, kings began to create strong central governments that provided greater security. Struggles between the Holy Roman Emperors and the Popes, however, prevented unity in Germany and Italy.

Another important development of the High Middle Ages was a surge of interest in opposing Muslim power. As a result, Europeans took the offensive against Muslims in Spain and in the Near East. Another sign of growing strength was the German expansion into lands along the Baltic Sea in Eastern Europe.

This chapter describes the economic growth of Western Europe, the rise of states, and the clash that took place between medieval monarchs and Popes.

CHAPTER OUTLINE

1   The European Economy Expands

2   European Nations Take Shape

3   The Church's Authority Grows

4   Christian Europe Expands

1 The European Economy Expands

By the middle of the eleventh century, Western Europe had entered a period of growing prosperity. The High Middle Ages (1050–1270) witnessed an agricultural revolution, an increase in trade and commerce, the rebirth of towns, and the rise of an enterprising middle class.

Advances are made in agriculture. During the Middle Ages new kinds of agricultural equipment greatly increased farm production. An improved plow made it possible to cultivate more land. The old plows were light and could not cut deeply into the soil. With the new heavier plows, farmers could cultivate moist, rich land that the older kinds of plow could not break up.

New inventions also made it possible to use farm horses more efficiently. Horses moved faster and had greater stamina than oxen and so were more useful for farm work. Yet the old-fashioned yoke harness, which worked well with oxen, tended to choke horses. The new collar harness shifted the strain of pulling from the horse's neck to its shoulders. Horses could be used both for plowing and for pulling loads. The horseshoe was another important new idea. The metal shoes protected horses' hoofs and made it easier for horses to work on rocky land. Some of these advances are shown on pages 158–159.

A new method of using land also increased food production. A three-field system gradually replaced the widely used two-field system (page 150), particularly in northern Europe. Under the new system, a third of the land was planted in autumn with winter wheat. Another third was planted the following spring with oats and vegetables, and the last third was left unplanted. With the three-field system, more land was under cultivation than with the older method. The water mill and the windmill, two inventions that made it easier to grind grain, allowed the farmers to take advantage of the larger harvests.

New lands are cleared. In the eleventh and twelfth centuries, large tracts of land in many parts of Europe were cleared and settled. Peasants drained swamps, cut down forests, and established new villages. Vast areas of the continent were brought under cultivation for the first time. Lords encouraged the farming of new lands because the new crops increased their income.

The settlement of new lands helped bring about a decline in serfdom. Most serfs were reluctant to leave their homes and move to the new lands. To give them an incentive to move, lords promised them freedom from most or all personal services. Serfs who did settle on the new lands often were allowed to pay the lord rent instead of working his lands. In time they came to regard the land they farmed as their own. They were making the shift from serfdom to freedom.

Trade revives. The changes in agriculture and the cultivation of new lands altered the conditions of life in Europe. With greater food production, the number of deaths from starvation and dietary disease decreased, and population increased. Surplus food meant that a greater number of people were free to work at nonfarming tasks such as crafts.

The rapid growth of population also increased the demand for goods, which brought an expansion of trade. During the early Middle Ages, Italian towns had maintained a weak trade link with the Byzantine lands in the eastern Mediterranean. In the eleventh century, the Italians defeated the Muslim pirates who had been raiding the coasts. Once they were able to protect their lands and ships from Muslim raiders, the Italians could increase their trade with the Byzantine Empire and North Africa. The growing population in Western Europe provided a market for silks, sugar, spices, and dyes from the East. Italian merchants were quick to fill this demand. By the High Middle Ages the Italian city-states of Venice, Genoa, Milan, and Pisa controlled the Mediterranean trade.

Other avenues of trade opened up between Scandinavia and the Atlantic coast; between northern France, Flanders, and England; and along the rivers between the Baltic

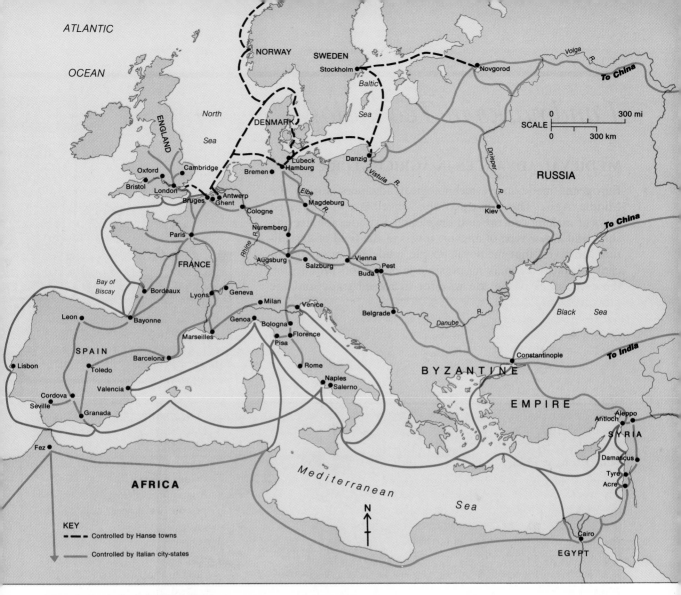

Medieval Trade Routes

The revival of trade encouraged contacts among people all over Europe. What trading towns were found along the following rivers: Rhine, Elbe, Vistula, Danube?

Sea in the north and the Black Sea and Constantinople to the south. The demand for the fine woolen cloth manufactured in Flanders was so large that it accounted for much of the trade along the Atlantic coast. In exchange for this cloth, Scandinavian merchants offered hunting hawks and fur; the English, raw wool; the Germans, iron and timber.

Trade fairs are held. With the revival of trade, fairs began to be held regularly at major trading sites. At these fairs merchants and artisans from many places set up stalls and booths to display their wares. Swords, leather saddles, household utensils, rugs, shoes, silks, spices, furs, metalwork, and fine furniture were among the many goods sold. Each fair lasted about three to six weeks. Then the merchants would move on to another site. To protect traders from robbers, lords provided guards for merchants traveling to and from the fairs.

Merchants share the risk in business ventures. The increase in trade also led to changes in ways of doing business. Individual merchants had limited funds to carry on business.

Landmarks in Technology

MEDIEVAL ADVANCES IN AGRICULTURE

Europeans made many technological advances during the Middle Ages. They invented the wheelbarrow, improved ways of making cement, and developed a rudder for steering ships and a new type of anchor. It was in the field of agriculture, however, that medieval people made the most significant advances. By making possible greater food production, these advances paved the way for increased trade and the growth of cities.

Among medieval inventions in agriculture were the horseshoe (right) and a heavy plow and the horse collar (left). The new plow had two blades — one cut the soil and the other turned it over. The horse collar and horseshoe made it possible to use horses more efficiently.

One of the first inventions to use energy other than the muscles of people or animals was the water wheel. Since ancient times the water wheel had been used to grind grain (above). In the Middle Ages the water wheel — along with the windmill — was adapted for use in preparing cloth, tanning leather, and working metal.

Some windmills were used to pump water from mines. The medieval Dutch used the windmill (above) to drain marshes for farmland, a practice that continued well into modern times.

In a large-scale business, two or more merchants pooled their money to finance long-distance trading expeditions. This arrangement reduced the risk, because no one merchant had to provide all the money. The development of insurance to cover loss or damage to shipments of goods also helped to reduce the merchants' risk.

Banking practices are developed. Moneychangers developed another new business technique. Moneychangers were people who exchanged coins from one region for those of another, much as banks today exchange money from one country for money from another. Moneychangers kept their coins in strongboxes, and people found it convenient to leave money with them for safekeeping. After the moneychangers set aside the funds needed for each day's business, they could lend the rest and charge interest. This practice was the origin of modern banking.

Moneychangers also made it possible for people to do business without coins changing hands. A merchant buying goods could simply tell a moneychanger to transfer funds to the account of the person who was selling the merchandise. The moneychanger subtracted the amount from the buyer's account and credited that amount to the seller. A merchant traveling to another city could carry a moneychanger's "letter of credit" which other moneychangers would accept as cash. Because of these services, merchants could do business without having to carry heavy gold and silver coins that might be lost or stolen.

The moneychangers eventually came to be called bankers. Their services encouraged the growth of business, and they used their profits to finance ventures in trade and industry. They also lent money to kings and to the Church. Some northern Italian bankers established banks in cities in other parts of Europe.

Guilds regulate business. Still another commercial development of the Middle Ages was the appearance of *guilds.* These were organizations formed by merchants and master artisans. At first guilds were simply a form of fellowship among artisans, but soon they began to set regulations and protect their members. Merchant guilds prevented outside traders from doing business in a town. Craft guilds were made up of master artisans who practiced the same trade — for example, shoemaking, glassblowing, carpentry, or weaving. An artisan who opened a shop without having been accepted by the guild would not stay in business long. The guild would close the shop, burn the goods, and lock the artisan in the town pillory. (The pillory was a wooden board in which a prisoner's head and hands were clamped. It was set up in an open place in the middle of town, so that prisoners had to endure the jeers of the townspeople as well as the discomfort of the pillory.)

The guilds also discouraged competition among their members. They set strict rules to prevent any member from making much more money than the others. All members of the shoemakers' guild, for example, had to keep their shops open the same number of hours, pay their employees the same wages, produce shoes of equal quality, and charge customers a so-called "just price." Guild rules were strictly enforced. Violators could be fined, thrown out of the guild, or punished in some other way. Medieval records tell of an English herring merchant who sold his fish below the established price and was therefore beaten.

Young artisans serve an apprenticeship. To become a member of a craft guild, a young person first had to serve as an *apprentice* to a master artisan. An apprenticeship lasted from two to seven years, depending upon the craft. The young apprentice lived in the master's house, helped in the shop, and learned the trade. During this time the apprentice received little or no pay.

After completing the apprenticeship, the youth became a *journeyman*[1] — a day laborer who worked for a master for a daily wage. Most journeymen aspired to become masters, but this demanded great skill. The test for a master was to prove one's skill by presenting a well-executed piece of work — called a masterpiece — to the guild's governors. For example, a journeyman wishing to become a master baker

[1]The "journey" in *journeyman* does not mean that this person was a traveling worker. It refers to a day's work, from the French word for "day."

Come to the Fair!

The trade fairs of the Middle Ages gave people a rare and exciting opportunity to look at goods from faraway places — foods, furs, cloth, metalwork, and gems. Although goods imported from other countries can be bought in any store today, people still enjoy the atmosphere of an international fair. As in the Middle Ages, part of the excitement of a fair is seeing visitors from faraway places.

The greatest fairs in medieval Europe were those at Troyes and nearby towns in northern France. They became annual events. Other great fairs were held wherever trade routes crossed. In Russia, trading caravans carrying tea, cotton, furs, and other rare goods traveled hundreds of miles to the fair at Novgorod. Some medieval fairs featured one kind of product, such as cloth. Others, like the one shown below, displayed a variety of goods. Today, international fairs are more likely to feature automobiles or computers, but they still draw crowds of interested people from all over the world.

might bake a cake for the guild. If the masterpiece was judged to be worthy, the new master was admitted to the guild and was free to open a shop and take on apprentices.

Towns grow and become self-governing. During the early Middle Ages, towns had virtually disappeared except in Italy. Even the Italian towns suffered a decline in trade and population. In the eleventh century towns reappeared throughout Europe. In the next century they became active centers of commercial and intellectual life.

Expanded trade and an increased food supply encouraged the growth of towns. Towns often grew up at locations that were natural places for merchants to gather — on seacoasts and riverbanks, at crossroads, and near castles and monasteries. Greater farm production provided food for the urban population of artisans, merchants, students, and laborers.

Many of the new towns were on lands held by a feudal lord. While a lord might try to treat the townspeople like serfs, the townspeople resisted. They wanted to make their own laws and to settle disputes in their own courts. They expected to marry whom they pleased and to do as they wished with their property. By paying feudal lords money — and sometimes by fighting them — townspeople gained *charters.* A charter was a document in which a lord gave the people of a town the right to set up their own laws and establish their own system of

MEDIEVAL GUILDS

In the Middle Ages, guilds of spinners, weavers, dyers, and tailors were all involved in garment-making. Above left is a picture of a master watching apprentices dye cloth. In the tailor's shop (above right) the master serves a customer while apprentices sew garments and stock the shelves.

taxes. Through their charters, European towns became self-governing city-states, the first since Greco-Roman times.

Medieval towns are small and crowded. Most medieval towns had small populations. The largest towns — Florence, Ghent, Bruges (BROOZH), and Paris — had between 50,000 and 100,000 inhabitants. High thick walls, towers, and drawbridges protected the towns from outside attack. The towns were usually crowded, and garbage cluttered the narrow, crooked streets. At street level were the shops of merchants and artisans, many of whom lived above their businesses. During the day the streets were crowded with merchants, peddlers, beggars, women shopping and selling goods, men carting produce and other merchandise, and children playing. Religious processions and executions of criminals attracted large crowds. Townspeople also gathered to watch street musicians and traveling entertainers. At night, however, few people ventured into the unlighted streets. The elderly watchmen were no

match for the thieves who lay in wait for passers-by.

Opportunities expand for women and serfs. Women had many more opportunities in the towns than in the country. On the manor, women worked in the fields, made clothing, and did household chores. In towns, women spun, wove, and dyed cloth; and some worked as shoemakers, tailors, bakers, glovemakers, or barbers. Women also brewed beer and ale, made charcoal, sold fish and poultry, and operated inns and restaurants. In Paris and London, women dominated the silk-making industry. In many towns the wives and widows of masters were admitted to guilds. These guildswomen had all the privileges of a master, including the right to train apprentices.

Towns also contributed to the decline of serfdom. "City air makes a man free," went a medieval proverb. Many serfs fled from the manors with the hope of hiding safely in a crowded town. After remaining in the town for a year and a day, serfs became entitled to freedom. Their lord could not force them to return to the manor. Towns even benefited the serfs who remained on the manor, for they could sell their surplus produce to townspeople. In this way some serfs raised enough money to buy their freedom.

The middle class develops. Towns brought about the rise of a new social class — the *middle class,*[2] made up of master artisans, merchants, and their families. The life of people in the middle class was very different from that of clergy and nobles. Their world was the market rather than the church or the manor. Members of the middle class had no obligations to a lord. Their prosperity came from industry and trade. They believed people could use their skills to improve their position in life. The members of the middle class were active in town government, and their business activities brought wealth to the town. In the centuries to come, the middle class would bring about great economic, political, and intellectual changes in European life.

2 European Nations Take Shape

The revival of trade and the reappearance of towns were signs of growth in Western Europe. Another sign of vitality was the development of national states. England and France achieved a large measure of unity during the Middle Ages. Conflicts within Germany and Italy, however, kept those regions divided into numerous independent territories.

THE CHANGING ROLE OF KINGS

Kings have limited authority. Numerous Germanic kingdoms had been established in Europe in the early Middle Ages. Charlemagne had built a large empire, but Europe returned to political disunity when that empire was divided in 843 (page 144). As the feudal system developed, power came into the hands of noble lords who owned vast lands and maintained their own armies. In some parts of Europe, kings still held court, but they had little power. Often a king was simply regarded as the chief feudal lord, to whom the nobles of the region owed loyalty as vassals. Some kings in early medieval Europe were actually less wealthy and powerful than many nobles who were their vassals.

Changing times bring greater royal power. The feudal lords did not want kings to grow stronger, for they feared that a strong monarch would reduce their power and take away their land. Late in the Middle Ages, this began to happen in France and England. Kings expanded their territories and created strong central governments. They appointed officials who enforced royal law and tried people in royal courts. In return for the protection that a strong central government could provide,

---

[2]These townspeople were known by similar names in different countries, all derived from the word *burg,* which meant a fortified town. In England they were burgesses; in France, the *bourgeoisie* (boor-zhwah-ZEE); in Germany, burghers.

The British Isles About 870

In the ninth century the British Isles were inhabited mainly by Anglo-Saxons and Celts. In what part of the islands did the Celts live? What Anglo-Saxon kingdoms existed by 870?

people were willing to pay taxes to royal officials. Gradually people transferred their loyalty from the local lord to the monarch.

The growth of towns helped to strengthen royal power. By taxing the townspeople, kings raised money to hire soldiers. This meant that kings no longer had to depend on the lords to supply them with fighting men. Because the professional soldiers were loyal to the ruler who hired them, the king could depend on them to fight lords who resisted royal rule. The king could also hire educated townspeople to serve as tax collectors, judges, secretaries, and administrators. These loyal and trained government officials contributed to the growth of royal power.

ENGLISH KINGS ESTABLISH THEIR AUTHORITY

Invaders settle in England. The story of early England is one of many invasions. In the year A.D. 43, armies of the Roman emperor Claudius had conquered much of the island of Britain (map, page 107), then inhabited by Celtic (KEL-tik) peoples. The Romans built roads and towns. Areas under Roman rule prospered. Many Roman soldiers and merchants settled there. When Rome began to collapse in the fifth century, however, the Roman legions abandoned Britain. The island was soon invaded by three Germanic tribes — Jutes, Angles, and Saxons — who crossed from the continent. Roman culture died out. Eventually the invaders set up seven kingdoms in England, the southern part of the island of Britain. Since the Angles and Saxons dominated these kingdoms, historians use the term *Anglo-Saxon England* in speaking of this period of English history.

Early in the ninth century, Danish Vikings invaded England. Alfred the Great, the ruler of the kingdom of Wessex (the West Saxons), took the lead in resisting the Danes. He strengthened the army of the combined kingdoms and built a fleet of ships to fight off the invaders. Alfred's forces defeated the Danes in 886 and forced them to agree to a peace. The Danes withdrew to the eastern third of England, which became known as the Danelaw. The rest of England accepted Alfred's rule.

Alfred rules England. Ruler of England from 871 to 899, Alfred was a cultural leader as well as a warrior. He established a school at his court and translated Latin works into the Anglo-Saxon language. He also had his scholars begin the writing of *The Anglo-Saxon Chronicle*, a record of events in England. This record was continued by English scholar-monks for many years after Alfred's death.

Alfred's son and grandson regained the lands held by the Danes. For a short time Anglo-Saxon monarchs ruled most of England. Yet it was not the Anglo-Saxons who made England a unified national state.

The Norman conquest increases royal power. In 1066, Normans from northern France invaded England near the seacoast vil-

The Norman conquest of England is commemorated by the Bayeux (bah-YUH) Tapestry. According to tradition, it was embroidered by Matilda, wife of William the Conqueror. The section above shows Saxons defending a hill against the Normans.

lage of Hastings. Though French-speaking, they were descendants of the Vikings who had first raided France and then settled there. Led by William, the duke of Normandy, the Normans defeated Harold, the Saxon king, and quickly conquered England.

While armed resistance to Norman rule soon ended in England, it took much longer for the defeated Saxons to accept the language and culture of their conquerors. For some time, the ruling class spoke Norman French and followed French customs, while the common people and the old Saxon nobles kept their own traditions. Gradually, however, Norman and Anglo-Saxon speech blended together into what became the English language.

William establishes strong central control. William the Conqueror (as he came to be called) was determined to establish effective control over his new kingdom. He kept a sixth of the land for himself and divided the rest among the Norman lords, or barons. These Norman barons pledged their loyalty to William and promised to provide him with soldiers when needed. None of the barons had enough soldiers to threaten William's power.

William strengthened royal authority in England by setting up an efficient administration. The Anglo-Saxon rulers had divided their kingdoms into shires, or counties, which were administered by royal officials. William continued this practice, which gave him control over local government.

To find out what he could collect in taxes from the English, William had his officials make a detailed list of people and their property. Royal officials traveled around England and counted the number of people on every farm and in every village. The list also recorded cattle, sheep, pigs, farm equipment, and other property. This record became known as the *Domesday* (DOOMZ-day) *Book* and was used as a basis for assessing taxes for many years.

The king's courts create a common law. The kings who followed William strengthened unity in England by making changes in the legal system. Several confusingly different legal systems had existed previously. There had been the old Anglo-Saxon law, the French feudal law introduced by the Normans, the Church law, and business laws that had developed in the new towns. William's youngest son, Henry I, who ruled from 1100 to 1135, began the process of establishing a common legal system for all England. He sent royal judges to different parts of the kingdom to try cases.

This system was expanded by Henry II, who was the son of Henry's daughter Matilda, and the first of a line of kings known as the Plantagenets (plan-TADJ-uh-nitz). During his reign (1154–1189), Henry tried to bring as much legal business as possible into the royal courts instead of the courts of the feudal lords. In the royal courts, judges appointed by the king heard cases. The decisions of the royal judges were written down and used as guides

165

for future decisions, replacing older, unwritten laws. In time these decisions became what is called the ***common law*** in England. The common law helped to unite the people, provided a fairer system of justice, and became the foundation of the English legal system.

A jury system also began to take shape during the reign of Henry II. In each district a number of citizens were called together to report to visiting royal judges. Taking an oath to tell the truth, these people gave the judges the names of persons suspected of wrongdoing. This practice became the foundation of the grand jury system, which is still used in English-speaking countries today. Juries were also used to settle disputes over the ownership of land. Eventually the custom of having a jury (that is, a group of citizens) make the final decision in such cases led to trial by jury.

The Magna Charta limits royal power. The power of the English monarch grew steadily after the Norman conquest in 1066. It began to weaken late in the reign of Henry II, whose sons quarreled with him and with each other over the throne. The first to inherit, Richard I ("the Lion-hearted"), was a hero but spent little of his reign in England. The English were taxed heavily to support his foreign wars.

Richard's brother John (who ruled from 1199 to 1216) was a much-disliked king whose demands for high taxes and other oppressive actions led the angry barons to rebel. In 1215 the barons forced John to set his seal to the Magna Charta (MAG-nuh KAHR-tuh), which means "Great Charter." In this famous document the king agreed to recognize the barons' rights and privileges, including that of fair trial. He also agreed that taxes could not be collected without the consent of the council of advisers.

Historians regard the agreement between the feudal barons and King John as one of the foundations on which British and American liberties rest. Originally meant to assure the nobles' rights, three principles stated in the Magna Charta came to be applied widely.

1. Taxation only with representation. The Magna Charta stated that no unusual taxes "shall be imposed in our kingdom except by the common council of our kingdom." Over the

Edward I's support of Parliament is indicated by this painting, which shows him presiding over a session of the assembly. The presence of clergy suggests the Church's importance in medieval politics.

centuries this came to mean that the English monarch had to have the consent of the people's representatives to levy taxes.

2. Right to trial. The Magna Charta provided that "no freeman [can] be taken or imprisoned or dispossessed or banished or in any way destroyed . . . except by the lawful judgment of his peers [social equals] or by the law of the land." The barons who drew up the document had intended this to mean that they must be tried by their fellow barons. In time this idea was expanded into the principle that any accused person had a right to trial by jury and could not be imprisoned unless tried and convicted.

3. Limits to power. Implied in the Magna Charta was the notion that monarchs had no right to rule in any way they pleased but rather had to govern according to law.

Parliament grows in power. The Magna Charta placed some limits on the power of the English monarch. Other limits grew out of the development of the English Parliament. Parliament had its roots in Anglo-Saxon traditions.

Before making decisions, the Anglo-Saxon rulers had sought the advice of important men in the kingdom. William the Conqueror continued this tradition by seeking the advice of important churchmen, landowners, and nobles. These advisers to the monarch met in a body called the Great Council. During the late 1200's the council came to include lesser landowners and townsmen. It developed into a *parliament,* an official group of representatives.

In 1261 a noble named Simon de Montfort led a rebellion of the English barons to win more rights from the king. Seizing power, de Montfort tried to win the support of the townspeople by inviting them to attend a parliamentary meeting in 1265. Two knights came from each shire. Two townsmen represented each important town.

The barons' rebellion was suppressed by Prince Edward, who came to the throne in 1272 as Edward I. During his reign (1272–1307), Edward regularly called meetings of Parliament and sometimes invited knights and townsmen to attend. The Parliament that Edward called in 1295 is sometimes known as the "model Parliament" because it set the pattern for later assemblies. In time the members of Parliament split into two groups, each called a "house." The House of Lords was made up of bishops and great nobles. In the House of Commons were lesser landowners (the knights) and townsmen.

Gradually the point of view developed that the monarch should consult Parliament before deciding major issues. Over the years the power of Parliament grew, mainly because it had control of money matters. Monarchs had to have the approval of Parliament before they could raise money through taxes. They could not build roads, raise the salaries of their officials, or pay the expenses of keeping an army without the funds collected through taxes. Frequently in need of money, the English rulers had to turn to Parliament for help. On such occasions Parliament was in a position to demand additional powers from the monarch.

The foundations are laid for limited monarchy. Thus there emerged in England during the Middle Ages a strong king, a centralized government, and a unified state. The rights of the people were protected by basic principles made clear in the common law, the Magna Charta, and the rise of Parliament. These principles were: (1) English subjects had certain liberties; (2) the king could not violate those liberties; and (3) the power to govern rested not with the king alone but with king and Parliament together. The foundations had been laid for *limited monarchy* — a government in which limits are set on the monarch's powers.

FRENCH KINGS BUILD A UNIFIED STATE

Early French kings lack power. William of Normandy had conquered England in one stroke and had firmly established royal power. The road to national unity in France was more difficult.

France had been the western part of Charlemagne's empire. By the end of the tenth century it was a patchwork of territories ruled by feudal lords. In 987 the Count of Paris, Hugh Capet, was named king by a group of his fellow nobles, but he had little power beyond his own lands. He was unable to control the other lords, all of whom had their own armies and ruled in their own regions. Some of these lords ruled over a larger area than the king did.

TIMETABLE

Europe in the High Middle Ages

1066	The Normans conquer England.
1077	Pope Gregory VII and Henry IV meet at Canossa.
1095	Pope Urban calls for the Crusades.
1122	The Holy Roman Emperor and the Church reach an agreement at Worms.
1202–1204	Philip II regains French lands from England.
1215	King John is forced to accept the Magna Charta.
1233	The Inquisition is created.
1291	The last Christian outpost in the Holy Land is taken by the Muslims.

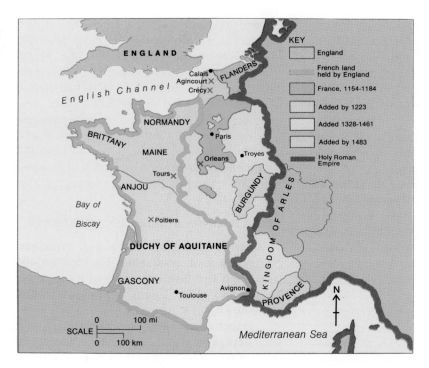

KEY

England

French land held by England

France, 1154-1184

Added by 1223

Added 1328-1461

Added by 1483

Holy Roman Empire

Medieval France

The Capetian kings gradually added to their holdings around Paris. Why was England an obstacle to state-building in France? During what period did the French kings gain control of the largest amount of territory?

The French kings seek territory. The descendants of Hugh Capet, who are known as the Capetian (kah-PEESH-un) kings, held the throne of France until 1328. It took centuries for them to create a unified state. Their first objective was to add to their territory. The French kings used every means they could to get more land. When a lord died without heirs, the king might take over his estate. Kings made alliances with landholding families and sometimes married the daughters of great lords. They gained the support of townspeople, who provided them with soldiers and skilled administrators — and also with tax revenues. When all else failed, French kings went to war and took the nobles' lands by force.

The French regain land from English rulers. England, across the English Channel, was a major obstacle to French unity. The English monarch controlled much of France. This situation developed after William of Normandy's conquest in 1066, which made him ruler of both England and his native Normandy. Henry I inherited other French territories from his father, the count of Anjou. Henry II married Eleanor, duchess of Aquitaine (page 149), who ruled much of southern France. With this marriage, the ruler of Eng-

land came to control more land in France than the French king did. To regain these English holdings became an overriding goal of the kings of France.

The French monarch who laid the basis for a unified state was Philip II, known as Philip Augustus. In 1202 Philip went to war with King John of England and stripped the English ruler of most of his territories in northern France. This tripled the size of Philip's kingdom and made him stronger than any French lord.

French monarchs strengthen royal power. Philip's successors continued to add to the royal lands. Louis IX, whose reign lasted from 1226 to 1270, made changes in legal matters to strengthen royal power. He drew up the first laws that applied throughout the kingdom and outlawed private warfare. Louis also established royal courts to replace the courts of feudal lords. Later French kings also found new ways of raising money, including taxing the clergy and sending out royal officials to collect revenues. By the end of the Middle Ages, France was a unified state, although regional and local loyalties remained strong.

The government of France differs from that of England. Government in France differed from the English government in several respects. In England, where Parliament served as a check on the ruler, the basis for limited monarchy had been laid. In France, there were no such checks on the king's power. French kings sometimes called meetings of nobles and clergy in various parts of the country. Eventually these meetings developed into the Estates-General, an assembly for all of France. This assembly, however, never became an important political body. French kings tended to ignore it since they did not need to ask for help in raising money. The Estates-General therefore had little chance to restrict royal power. In contrast to the limited monarchy in England, France was moving toward *absolute monarchy* — a government in which the monarch has complete power.

GERMANY AND ITALY REMAIN DIVIDED

German lords resist central authority. The German lands had formed the eastern part of Charlemagne's empire (page 143). When the empire collapsed, the German lands were broken into large duchies (DUCH-eez), lands ruled by dukes. Following an ancient Germanic practice, the dukes elected a fellow noble as king. The German king, however, had little authority outside his own lands; the other duchies were largely independent of his rule.

Otto the Great, who became the German king in 936, was determined to establish and expand his power as king. He defeated some dukes in war and made alliances with others. To gain more support against his fellow nobles, Otto granted fiefs to German bishops, making them vassals of the crown. By this action, Otto set the stage for a long struggle for power between the German kings and the Pope.[3]

The German king tries to re-establish Rome's empire. In 962 Otto convinced the Pope to crown him "Emperor of the Romans." Like Charlemagne, Otto wanted this title to indicate that he had inherited the power of ancient Rome as well as the backing of the Church. Later German kings all claimed the title, and the lands they ruled came to be called the Holy Roman Empire.

Otto and his successors as emperor wanted to dominate Italy and the papacy. The Pope, however, sided with the German dukes and with the northern Italian cities, which feared the Holy Roman Emperor. The struggle with the papacy weakened the German rulers' authority and was the main reason the German territories did not become united during the Middle Ages.

Italy remains divided. Like the German lands, Italy remained divided during the Middle Ages. By the fourteenth century Italy was broken into several regions. In the south were the kingdoms of Naples and Sicily, sometimes known as the Kingdom of the Two Sicilies. Northern Italy was divided into many rich and independent city-states that were often at war with each other. In central Italy, the Pope ruled the Papal States (page 142).

CHECK-UP

1. Vocabulary: *common law, parliament, limited monarchy, absolute monarchy.*
2. (a) Why had kings held little power early in the Middle Ages? (b) What developments caused that to change?
3. (a) What peoples invaded Britain starting in A.D. 43? (b) Describe Alfred's achievements.
4. (a) What steps did William the Conqueror take to set up a strong monarchy in England? (b) What changes in England's system of laws strengthened the power of the monarch?
5. (a) Why did the English barons force King John to accept the Magna Charta? (b) What three basic principles were established by this document?
6. (a) What were the origins of the English Parliament? (b) How was Parliament able to limit the monarch's authority?
7. (a) What steps did French monarchs take to unify their state? (b) In what way was England an obstacle to French unity? (c) How did Philip II overcome this obstacle?
8. How did the power of the English and French monarchs differ?
9. Why did neither Germany nor Italy become united during the Middle Ages?

---

[3]Medieval bishops were both clergymen and feudal lords. They therefore had obligations to both the Pope and to the lord whose vassals they were. As feudal lords, they had fighting men who could aid the king. Because bishops were educated, they also were useful as government officials.

3 The Church's Authority Grows

In the High Middle Ages the European economy prospered, and governments provided greater order and stability. The period was also marked by a growing religious vitality. There was a call for greater spiritual devotion among the clergy. Popes sought to prevent lords and kings from interfering with Church affairs; they also tried to ensure that Christians lived in accordance with Church teachings.

The Church's political involvements bring calls for reform. Early in the tenth century the Church faced many problems. For some leading families in Italy, the papacy had become a political prize. They plotted and even committed murder to get relatives named as Pope. People who were aware of this plotting had little respect for the papacy. The authority of the papacy was further weakened by lords who

Matilda, Countess of Tuscany, was a strong ally of the Pope. This picture shows her mediating between Henry IV and Gregory VII at their famous meeting at Canossa (page 171).

collected income from Church taxes and appointed the bishops and abbots in their own regions. This gave the lords control over the churches and monasteries in their territories. Bishops and abbots who were chosen for political reasons often lacked religious devotion. Still another problem for the Church was a decline in spiritual values among the clergy. Many priests and monks seemed more concerned with possessions and pleasures than with the Church's work.

Many serious-minded clergy called for reform. The Benedictine monks of the French abbey of Cluny, founded in 910, demanded that clergymen live strict and holy lives. The Cluniac monks also demanded that the clergy not be allowed to buy their positions in the Church, and they tried to free their monasteries from the control of lords.

In the middle of the eleventh century a Church council ended political interference in the appointment of Popes. The council named a group of leading clergymen, called cardinals, to be responsible for choosing the Pope.

The Pope and the Holy Roman Emperor clash. The most zealous supporter of reform was a Benedictine monk named Hildebrand, who became Pope Gregory VII in 1073. Gregory believed that the Pope's mission was to establish a Christian society on earth. To fulfill this mission, Gregory demanded that the Holy Roman Emperor submit to papal authority. According to Church theory, both emperor and Pope were chosen by God. Emperors, therefore, were expected to rule in accordance with Christian principles and to follow the Pope's advice in the proper use of their power. Gregory maintained that emperors had a solemn duty to obey the Pope, the spiritual leader of the Christian world. This led to a bitter struggle between Gregory and Henry IV, the Holy Roman Emperor from 1056 to 1106.

The quarrel began over the appointment of bishops. Pope Gregory insisted that only the Church had the power to appoint bishops. Henry resisted such an idea. The German bishops were his most important allies. If he could not appoint them, he would lose their allegiance, military support, and financial aid.

The disagreement becomes a struggle over authority. Gregory claimed that, as Pope, he could depose the emperor — remove him from the throne. Henry would not accept such control. He persuaded the German bishops who were his vassals to declare Gregory deposed. Pope Gregory, in turn, decided in 1076 to *excommunicate* Henry — in other words, to expel him from the Church. The decree of excommunication read, "I declare Henry deprived of his kingdom in Germany and Italy because he has rebelled against the Church." This decree in effect also freed the German nobles from their feudal loyalty to Henry. The conflict over the appointment of bishops had grown into a struggle over who was the supreme authority — emperor or Pope — in Europe.

Henry seeks forgiveness. The German bishops hesitated to support Henry, fearing they might also be excommunicated. The German nobles seized the opportunity to strike at Henry's power, and civil war swept through Germany. Matters grew worse when the nobles invited Pope Gregory to travel to Germany to crown a new emperor.

To stop the Pope, Henry journeyed to Italy in January, 1077. He hoped to persuade Gregory to lift the ban of excommunication. This would deprive the German lords of their legal justification for rebellion. Henry arrived at Canossa, where Gregory was a guest of Matilda of Tuscany, who ruled much of central Italy and was one of the Pope's strongest supporters. For three days the German emperor stood barefoot in the snow outside the castle walls until Pope Gregory accepted his plea for forgiveness. The image of the emperor pleading for forgiveness increased the prestige of the papacy. The journey to Canossa was also a victory for Henry, because Gregory abandoned his plan to support the rebellious German lords and crown a new emperor.

Church and state reach a compromise. Years later, in 1122, the Church and a new Holy Roman Emperor, Henry V, reached a compromise at the city of Worms (VORMZ) in Germany. The compromise, called the Concordat (agreement) of Worms, ruled that monarchs had no authority over the Church. (The

The Holy Roman Empire About 1200

The Holy Roman Empire included many small states. How did its boundaries compare with those of Charlemagne's empire (map, page 142)?

Church reached similar agreements with the rulers of France and England.) Bishops were to be chosen only by the Church. The archbishop, the highest-ranking bishop in an area, gave the bishop a staff and a ring as symbols of spiritual power. This signified that the bishop's role as spiritual leader came from the Church alone. From the monarch, the bishop received a scepter, the symbol of political power. This act indicated that the bishop was also the monarch's vassal. The Concordat of Worms thus recognized that bishops were both spiritual leaders *and* feudal landholders.

Conflict weakens the Holy Roman Emperor's authority. The Concordat did not end the conflict between the papacy and the Holy Roman Emperor. Popes continued to claim that kings and emperors were subordinate to the papacy. The Holy Roman Emperors, on the other hand, claimed supremacy over the papacy and also tried to get control of the prosperous northern Italian city-states. Between 1154 and 1186, Holy Roman Emperor Frederick I (known as Frederick Barbarossa, or "Red Beard") made six military expeditions to Italy trying to assert his authority over these cities. Aided by the Pope, the cities managed to resist Frederick's army. These expeditions, like Henry IV's conflict with Pope Gregory VII, weakened the emperor's authority.

The papacy reaches the height of its power. The high point of papal power was reached under Innocent III (1198–1216), who stated that the Pope, "lower than God but higher than man, . . . judges all and is judged by no one." Innocent made the papacy the center of European political life. He claimed that the Pope had the right to intervene in the internal affairs of any kingdom. For example, when King John of England ignored the Pope's wishes, Innocent excommunicated John and issued an order that in effect closed the churches in England. Eventually John was forced to back down, and he became a vassal of the Pope. During Innocent's papacy, a Church council ruled that no state could tax the clergy and declared that laws harmful to the Church need not be obeyed.

Crimes against the Church are punished. Popes believed that they had a sacred mission to show people the way to salvation. For this reason, they fought monarchs who challenged papal authority. For the same reason, they opposed *heresy* (HEHR-uh-see) — that is, the holding of beliefs that the Church considered wrong.

Freedom of religion is a modern idea that had no place in the medieval outlook. The clergy taught that people had to obey God's rules exactly as taught by the Church. Heresy was the greatest crime in the Middle Ages. The Church held that heretics (people declared guilty of heresy) had committed treason against God.

The Church tried to persuade heretics to give up their beliefs. If that failed, it threatened them with excommunication. An excommunicated person was expelled from the Church and denied the sacraments. This unfortunate person lived without the fellowship of friends, died without the comfort of a priest, and was denied hope of salvation.

The Church's authority is challenged. In the twelfth and thirteenth centuries several groups challenged the teachings of the Church. One of these groups was the Waldenses, followers of Peter Waldo, a rich French merchant who gave away his property to the poor in 1170. The Waldenses preached the Gospel in the language of the people rather than in Latin. They also accused the clergy of leading immoral lives. Church authorities condemned the movement as heretical and excommunicated Waldo.

A more extreme break with the beliefs of the Church was that of the Albigensians, who were particularly strong in southern France. They taught that anything physical or material was evil and refused to believe that Jesus could have taken a human form. When the Albigensians refused to give up their beliefs, Pope Innocent III in 1209 called on kings and lords to exterminate them. A merciless war to destroy the Albigensians went on for more than twenty years.

The Inquisition punishes heresy. In 1232 Pope Gregory IX set up the Inquisition, a Church court that sought out and tried people suspected of being heretics. The accused people were urged to confess their heresy and to ask forgiveness. Sometimes torture was used to make people admit to heresy. If they confessed, they were given minor punishment and welcomed back into the Church. If they did not confess, or if they held to their beliefs, they were turned over to the government authorities for punishment. Heretics might lose their property, be exiled or imprisoned, or be executed by burning at the stake.

Religious orders are formed. Zeal for reform also led to the establishment of two orders of friars, the Franciscans and the Dominicans. (Friars were monks who did not live in monasteries but wandered among the people, preaching and doing good works.)

The Dominican order was founded by Saint Dominic (1170–1221), a Spanish nobleman, as a reaction against the Albigensians. Known as the Preaching Friars, the Dominicans included some of the leading teachers of religion in medieval universities. They also served as missionaries and worked actively in the Inquisition and other efforts to suppress heresy.

The Franciscans were named after their founder, Saint Francis of Assisi (1182–1226). Born into a wealthy Italian merchant family, Francis had an intense religious experience when he was in his mid-twenties. It caused him to give up his possessions and devote his life to trying to live as Jesus had. Francis went into villages and towns preaching, healing, and befriending people. He soon gathered a band of followers who adopted his way of life. The Franciscans grew from a movement of inspired laymen, or nonclergy, into an organized religious order that carried out papal policy. They came to serve the Church as teachers and missionaries in Eastern Europe, North Africa, the Near East, and China.

CHECK-UP

1. Vocabulary: *excommunicate, heresy.*
2. From what abuses did the Church suffer in the tenth century?
3. (a) According to Church theory, why did Popes have authority over emperors? (b) How did Pope Gregory VII and Henry IV test the Church's theory? (c) What compromise was reached in 1122?
4. (a) Why did the Church seek to end heresy? (b) Why did the Church declare the Waldenses and Albigensians to be heretics?
5. What was the purpose of the Inquisition?
6. (a) What two religious orders were formed late in the twelfth century? (b) How did each serve the Church?

4 Christian Europe Expands

In the early Middle Ages, Christian Europe had been threatened by invading Muslims, followers of the new religion of Islam. The Muslims took over the islands of Sicily and Sardinia, conquered most of Spain, and raided France and Italy. By the eleventh century, however, the kings and great lords of Western and Central Europe had grown strong enough to take the offensive against the Muslims. Encouraged by the Popes, Christians waged holy wars against the Muslims in Spain and in the Holy Land (which is what the Christians called Palestine). The Germans expanded Christian lands by colonizing regions in Eastern Europe.

European lands are recaptured from the Muslims. In the eleventh century the Italian city-states of Genoa and Pisa drove the Muslims from the island of Sardinia. By the end of the century Norman knights had retaken Sicily from the Muslims. Italian and Norman ships began to patrol the western Mediterranean, preventing the Muslims from attacking Christian ships. This gave the Italian city-states an open route to the rich markets of the eastern Mediterranean.

Christians also took the offensive against the Muslims in Spain. By the middle of the eighth century, Muslims controlled most of the Iberian peninsula (present-day Spain and Portugal). Only some small kingdoms in the northern part of that peninsula remained in Christian hands. These Christian kingdoms, determined to recover the rest of Spain, began a 500-year struggle known as the Reconquest. From the eleventh century on, the Christian rulers of Castile led the war against the Muslims in Spain, regaining considerable territory (map, page 174). By the thirteenth century, only the kingdom of Granada was still held by the Muslims.

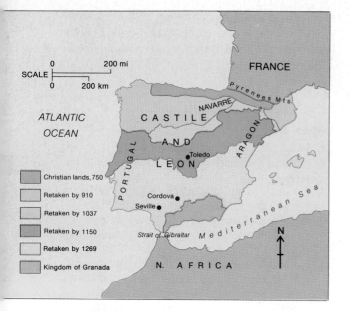

The Christian Reconquest of Spain

After Muslims conquered most of the Iberian peninsula, the remaining Christian kingdoms began the struggle to regain control. By what date was most of the peninsula again under Christian rule?

The Pope calls for a crusade. Meanwhile, at the end of the eleventh century, Europeans decided to carry the struggle against Islam into the eastern Mediterranean. Turkish Muslims had gained control of the Holy Land. In 1095 Pope Urban II appealed to the lords and knights of Europe to liberate the Holy Land from the Muslims. The Pope wanted Jerusalem to be in Christian hands. Moreover, he hoped that the knights and lords would stop warring among themselves and fight for a Christian cause — the recovery of the Holy Land.

Pope Urban's appeal created great excitement. Lords and knights, eager for glory, adventure, and wealth, began to organize armies. They saw themselves as armed pilgrims who would rescue Christian holy places from the Muslims. Thus, the holy wars that became known as the Crusades began.[4]

---

[4]The word *crusade* comes from the Latin word *crux*, meaning "cross." The crusaders — those who "took the cross" — sewed the symbol of the cross on their outer garments.

Crusades by the common people fail. The spirit of the Crusades spread in Western Europe. Some preachers wandered through the villages, urging the common people to take part in the Crusades. The most remarkable of these preachers was Peter the Hermit. Small and thin, with a long gray beard, Peter rode a donkey through the French countryside, calling the peasants to become crusaders. Thousands of poor people abandoned their villages and joined Peter's march. The simple peasants, who knew little of the world outside their villages, expected to find Jerusalem just beyond the horizon. Some thought that Peter was leading them straight to heaven.

Few of the peasant crusaders ever reached Jerusalem. Peter's army made its way to Constantinople, only to be destroyed by the Turks in Asia Minor.

Another army of common people formed in Germany. Regarding all non-Christians as enemies of the faith, these people began their crusade by massacring Jews, despite the efforts of bishops to protect them. The German crusaders were slaughtered after they began looting in Hungary.

Christian forces capture Jerusalem. The first major crusade was more carefully planned than the peasant undertakings. Lords and knights gathered to form an army. In the spring of 1097 the army assembled in Constantinople. From the capital of the Byzantine Empire the knights crossed to Asia Minor. A crusader described the hardships they encountered in that peninsula:

> [In the desert] hunger and thirst [attacked] us everywhere and we had hardly anything left to eat except thorns. . . . Such was the food on which we wretchedly lived. Most of our horses died there, so that many of our knights had to go on foot; because of our lack of mounts we used . . . goats, sheep, and dogs to carry our baggage.

The Christian army arrived at Antioch and captured it from the Turks after a long siege. In June, 1099, three years after leaving their homes, the crusaders stood outside the walls of Jerusalem. Five weeks later the Christians captured the city.

The Muslims regain some lands. In what became known as the First Crusade, the knights of Europe had won a victory. They had captured Jerusalem and carved out four Christian states in the Near East (map, page 176). Yet these Christian states were like islands in a Muslim sea. Their chance of surviving was small.

When the Muslims retook Edessa, one of the Christian states, in 1144, Pope Eugenius III called for the Second Crusade. King Louis VII of France and the Holy Roman Emperor, Conrad III, raised large forces. These armies suffered terrible losses to the Turks; only a small number of the crusaders even reached the Holy Land.

Under Saladin (SAL-uh-din), the brilliant sultan of Egypt, the Muslims fought back against the Christian invaders. Famous for his bravery and honor, Saladin was admired even by the Christian knights. Saladin united both Egyptian and Syrian Muslims under his command. In 1187 he invaded Palestine and recaptured several cities, including Jerusalem.

The Third and Fourth Crusades fail. Shocked by the loss of Jerusalem, the leading

The Four Major Crusades

Christian knights gathered at Constantinople for the First Crusade. Which Crusades passed through Vienna? Which Crusade ended at Constantinople?

KEY

→ First Crusade (1096–1099)

--▶ Second Crusade (1147–1149)

→ Third Crusade (1189–1192)

--▶ Fourth Crusade (1202–1204)

☐ States founded by Crusaders

rulers in Europe took up the cross in the Third Crusade (1189–1192). These rulers were Richard I of England, Philip Augustus of France, and Emperor Frederick I. Rivalry between the English and French kings doomed this crusade. Furthermore, the crusaders were no match for Saladin's able command.

Pope Innocent III called the Fourth Crusade (1202–1204) to demonstrate anew that the papacy was the leader of Christian Europe. In 1202, 10,000 crusaders gathered in Venice, Italy, ready to depart for the Holy Land. Only a few ever reached the Near East to fight the Muslims. Instead, the bulk of the crusading army attacked Constantinople in 1204. They looted and defiled churches and massacred the

Byzantine defenders. The Pope was enraged, for the Fourth Crusade did much to tarnish the image of the crusading movement.

The Muslims continued to retake the lands that had been conquered by the Christian crusaders. In 1291, almost 200 years after Pope Urban's speech, the last Christian outpost in Palestine fell to the Muslims.

The Crusades lead to change. In the beginning, the Crusades had strengthened the power of the papacy. It was the Pope who had inspired the crusading armies and acted as their spiritual leader. Later Popes, however, called for crusades against heretics and rulers who resisted papal commands. Many Christians came to feel that the papacy was using religious zeal to increase the Church's political power. As their criticisms grew, the prestige of the papacy declined.

The Crusades also contributed to the decline of feudalism. Many noblemen lost their fortunes paying for weapons and transportation to the Holy Land. Some nobles lost their lives. Monarchs took advantage of their weakened opponents to strengthen royal power.

European trade grew as a result of the Crusades. Europeans who went on the Crusades came to know and value the products of the East — sugar, rice, fruits, spices, silk, cotton, cosmetics, pistachio nuts, mirrors, dyes, perfumes, and many other goods. The increased demand for these goods led to greater trade between East and West, and the Italian cities benefited. These cities had furnished transportation for the crusaders. They invested their profits from that endeavor in products of the East and carried the goods back to eager buyers in Western Europe.

Germans expand eastward. The reconquest of Spain and the Crusades were signs of the growing strength of Christian Europe in the High Middle Ages. A third sign was the German conquest and colonization of areas south of the Baltic Sea. Several factors led to this expansion. Lords hoped to carve out new estates, while peasants wanted land of their own and freedom from the burden of manorial obligations. Missionaries sought to convert the inhabitants of these new lands, non-Christian Slavs and Prussians,[5] to Christianity. Merchants were looking for new opportunities for trade.

The Germans did succeed in conquering some Slavic peoples and converting them to Christianity. They also won victories over the Prussians. The German drive against the Prussians was spearheaded by the Teutonic Knights, an order of military monks. Founded during the Crusades to run a hospital in Jerusalem, the Knights were all noblemen. In the early 1200's the Teutonic Knights carried on a crusade to convert the Prussians and conquer their lands.

The German expansion brings change to Eastern Europe. The German expansion eastward had important consequences. Thousands of German settlers, merchants, and missionaries moved into the Baltic Sea region. Towns were established in places where urban life had been virtually unknown. Using the new heavy plows (page 156), the German colonists cleared vast tracts of land for agriculture. This expansion increased German territory by a third, and spread Christianity and the German language and culture into a large area.

Colonization of the new lands also encouraged the spread of trade. In the late 1200's cities along the Baltic Sea joined with the older German cities in a trade league. Through this alliance the cities sought to expand their trade with foreign lands, to protect shipping from pirates, and to combat competition, particularly from Denmark. In the middle 1300's the trade union became known as the Hanseatic League.[6] The member cities controlled much of the trade of northern Europe, from the eastern end of the Baltic Sea to the western end of the North Sea (map, page 157).

CHECK-UP

1. (a) How did the Muslims threaten Christian Europe? (b) How did Christians in Italy and Spain react to this threat?

2. (a) Why did Pope Urban II command Christians to win the Holy Land from the Muslims? (b) Why were crusaders eager to enlist in this cause?

3. Briefly describe the results of the four major Crusades.

4. How did the Crusades affect (a) the power of the papacy, (b) feudalism, (c) Italian cities?

5. (a) What were the results of German expansion along the Baltic coast? (b) What were the goals of the Hanseatic League?

---

[5]The Slavs were the main inhabitants of the part of Europe that is east of the Elbe River (map, page 157) and north of the Greek peninsula. The Prussians were a people living along the Baltic Sea. The Germans who conquered them took the name *Prussian* as their own. (The history of Eastern European peoples is discussed in Chapter 17.)

---

[6]*Hanseatic* (han-see-AT-ik) is derived from *hanse*, the German word for merchant guild.

Chapter 8 Review

Summary

The High Middle Ages (1050–1270) was a period of vitality for Western Europe. Improvements in agricultural technology and the cultivation of new lands increased food production and led to population growth. Trade revived, banking practices developed, and merchants and artisans formed guilds. The growth of towns contributed to the decline of serfdom and led to the rise of the middle class.

Powerful rulers laid the foundations of modern European states. England was unified soon after the Norman conquest in 1066, but it took French kings centuries to create a unified state. The development of Parliament and the Magna Charta limited the power of the English monarch. There were no similar checks on the French king.

The Church often claimed a role in European politics, which led to quarrels with the Holy Roman Emperor and other monarchs. These quarrels prevented the development of unified states in Germany and Italy. Reform movements, the subduing of heresy, and the emergence of religious orders revealed the vitality of the Church in this period. Additional signs of European strength were the conquest of Muslim lands and the German conquest and colonization of lands along the Baltic coast.

The Crusades were an attempt by Europeans to take control of the Holy Land from the Muslim Turks. While ending in failure, the Crusades led to important changes. They contributed to the decline of feudalism in Europe and stimulated trade between Europe and the East.

Vocabulary Review

1. Look up each of the following terms in the Glossary at the back of this book. On a separate sheet of paper, write a sentence for each term. Be sure your sentences show that you understand the meaning of these terms: *absolute monarchy, apprentice, charter, common law, excommunicate, guild, heresy, journeyman, limited monarchy, middle class, parliament.*

2. Distinguish between the terms in each of the following pairs:

(a) House of Lords; House of Commons.
(b) *Anglo-Saxon Chronicle; Domesday Book.*
(c) Plantagenet kings; Capetian kings.
(d) Teutonic Knights; Hanseatic League.
(e) Reconquest; Crusades.

People to Identify

Match the following people with the numbered phrases that describe them: *Saint Dominic, William the Conqueror, Frederick Barbarossa, Gregory VII, Peter the Hermit, John, Gregory IX.*

1. The Norman ruler who led the invasion of England in 1066 and laid the foundations for a strong central government.
2. The English king who was forced to accept the Magna Charta.
3. The religious leader who recruited an army of French peasants to fight in the Crusades.
4. The Pope who set up the Inquisition in 1233.
5. The Spanish nobleman who founded a teaching and missionary order in reaction to the Albigensian heresy.
6. The Pope who clashed with Henry IV, the Holy Roman Emperor, over which of them would have supremacy.
7. The Holy Roman Emperor who attempted to conquer northern Italy and gain control of the papacy.

Relating Geography and History

1. **Locating places.** Locate each of the following on a map in this chapter:

(a) Hastings   (f) Canossa
(b) Jerusalem   (g) Worms
(c) Constantinople   (h) Ghent
(d) Aquitaine   (i) Venice
(e) Poitiers   (j) Florence

2. **Finding evidence.** For trading purposes, where were towns in medieval Europe most likely to develop? Consider access to land and water trade routes, the number of potential customers at any one site, and the merchants' need for protection. Support your conclusions with specific examples from the chapter.

Discussion Questions

1. What factors helped the European economy to expand in the High Middle Ages?

2. What was the significance of the development of the middle class in European society?

3. (a) Contrast the ways in which England and France achieved unity. (b) Why was the development of unified states a sign of vitality in Western Europe?

4. How did the struggle for supremacy between the Pope and the Holy Roman Emperor affect the development of unity in Germany and Italy?

5. How did the Magna Charta (a) strengthen Parliament, (b) limit the power of the monarch, and (c) protect the rights of English subjects?

Reading Primary Sources

Along with the growth of towns in the eleventh and twelfth centuries came the formation of merchant and craft guilds. Merchant guilds were organized by townspeople who sold goods that had been made by others. The following passage, taken from the regulations of a merchant guild in Southampton, England, shows that guilds did not limit themselves to setting business policies. Read the passage. Then answer the questions that follow.

> And if any guildsman strikes another with his fist and is convicted thereof, he shall lose [membership in] the guild until he shall have bought it back for ten shillings and taken the oath of the guild again like a new member. . . .
>
> And no one of the city of Southampton shall buy anything to sell again in the same city, unless he is of the guild. . . .
>
> No one of the guild ought to be partner . . . in any . . . merchandise . . . with anyone who is not of the guild. . . .
>
> If any guildsman falls into poverty and has not the wherewithal to live and is not able to work or to provide for himself, he shall [receive aid] from the guild.

(a) What was the punishment for a person who struck another guild member? (b) What rules of the guild concerned people who were not members of the guild? (c) What was the purpose of the rules that did not have to do with regulating business? (d) Today, who would perform the kind of function mentioned in the last paragraph?

Skill Activities

1. Identifying cause and effect. You will find the study of history more interesting if you think, as you read, about why things happened the way they did, or about cause and effect. Each of the following sentences describes an *effect.* Read each sentence. Then reread the page or pages indicated in parentheses and decide what you think were the most important *causes* of each effect. On a separate sheet of paper, list these causes in your own words and explain why you chose them. (You may select causes other than those discussed on the pages indicated.)

(a) *Effect:* By the eleventh century, European farmers were able to produce more food than they needed (page 156).

(b) *Effect:* In the twelfth century, town populations grew and towns became active commercial and cultural centers (page 161).

(c) *Effect:* The Holy Roman Emperor stood barefoot in the snow for three days in January, 1077 (page 171).

(d) *Effect:* In the late 1200's and 1300's trade increased within Europe and between East and West (page 177).

2. Research. Many rulers are known by their nicknames. William of Normandy, for example, is known as William the Conqueror. Use a biographical dictionary or an encyclopedia to find out how the following rulers got their nicknames: (a) John Lackland, (b) Frederick Barbarossa, (c) Richard the Lion-Hearted, (d) Philip the Bold, (e) Louis the Lion. Include in your answer the dates and important events of each ruler's reign and the country he governed.

3. Reports. Find information about one of the following topics and prepare a report: (a) the *Domesday Book;* (b) the history of Vatican City; (c) the legend of King Arthur; (d) the life of Saladin; (e) the Swiss Guards; (f) the Children's Crusade; (g) the Battle of Hastings; (h) medieval illuminated manuscripts; (i) the Bayeux Tapestry; (j) Thomas à Becket.

4. Word research. The common law in England is the law that applies to all citizens. *Common* comes from the Latin *communis.* Find *common* in a dictionary and explain what it means in your own words. Then tell how the following terms relate to *common:*

(a) commons
(b) communicate
(c) community
(d) commonwealth
(e) commoner
(f) commune

In 1271 a family of merchants named Polo set out for China from the harbor of Venice (below), one of the Italian cities that was prospering from the revival in trade. The painting suggests how European contacts with other lands were growing by the late Middle Ages.

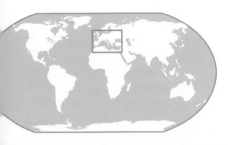

The Culture of Medieval Europe

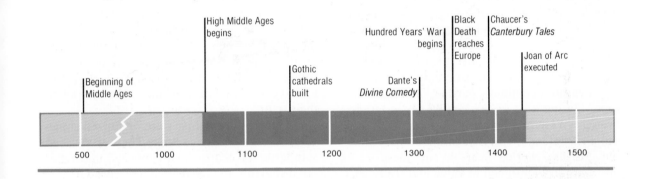

High Middle Ages begins

Beginning of Middle Ages

Gothic cathedrals built

Hundred Years' War begins

Dante's *Divine Comedy*

Black Death reaches Europe

Chaucer's *Canterbury Tales*

Joan of Arc executed

500 1000 1100 1200 1300 1400 1500

The High Middle Ages marked the peak of medieval civilization in Western Europe. Agricultural production increased, towns grew, trade prospered, and states began to form. With the growth of towns, there was a revival of interest in learning and the arts. The first universities were organized, and European scholars rediscovered classical works in philosophy and science. A varied literature and a distinctive form of architecture, the Gothic, developed. Most work in literature and the arts was an expression of Christian beliefs and devotion to the Church.

In the fourteenth century, however, a number of crises occurred in Western Europe. These included a decline in population, peasant rebellions, war between England and France, and challenges to papal authority. The changes that resulted from these crises brought an end to the medieval period.

This chapter describes the cultural achievements of the High Middle Ages and the crises that led to great changes in medieval civilization in the fourteenth century.

CHAPTER OUTLINE

1 Interest in Learning Revives

2 New Styles Develop in Medieval Art

3 The Middle Ages Draws to a Close

1 Interest in Learning Revives

During the early Middle Ages (A.D. 500–1050), the breakdown of urban life and the general disorder following the Germanic invasions caused a serious decline in the level of learning in Europe. Greco-Roman learning did not die out altogether, however. In European monasteries, monks studied and copied ancient manuscripts (page 140). Scholars outside Europe also collected and studied works from Greece and Rome. In the High Middle Ages (1050–1270), a renewed interest in learning accompanied prosperity and the growth of towns. Signs of this interest included the rise of universities and a rebirth of scientific studies.

Learning continues outside Christian Europe. During the High Middle Ages, trade brought Western Europeans into contact with the civilizations of the Byzantine Empire and the Muslim world. Scholars in these civilizations had continued to value and study ancient Greek works of literature, philosophy, and science. Many of these texts had been translated into Arabic and studied by Muslim scholars.

As interest in learning revived in medieval Europe, Spain and Sicily became the principal centers where ancient works were translated into Latin, the language of European scholars. A famous school of translation grew up at the university of Toledo in Muslim Spain. There Christian, Jewish, and Muslim scholars collected and translated Greek and Arabic manuscripts into Latin. The court of the Norman rulers of Sicily also attracted scholars from the Byzantine Empire and the Muslim lands in the Mediterranean.

Medieval universities develop. In Europe, the rise of towns and the middle class encouraged the revival of learning. Townspeople had the money to support schools. Moreover, as a town's population grew, so did the need for trained bankers, lawyers, doctors, and city officials. Schooling was needed to prepare young people for careers in these professions.

To gain an education, young people were sent to study with scholars (often monks or priests) who were famous for their learning. These meetings of students and teachers eventually developed into universities. By about 1200 there were universities at Paris, at Oxford in England, and at Bologna (boh-LOH-nyah) and Salerno in Italy.

In France and England, universities were organized and run by the teachers. In Italy, however, the students hired and paid the professors. To get their money's worth, the students set strict rules. Professors were fined or dismissed for being absent, for giving boring lectures, or for not dealing adequately with a subject. If teachers wanted to travel, they had to leave behind a sum of money to guarantee their return.

Universities at first were organized somewhat like guilds (page 160). They established standards for courses and protected and regulated students and teachers. To receive a degree of "master" and enter the teachers' guild, students had to pass examinations and write a scholarly paper. The basic curriculum included the seven liberal arts: grammar (Latin language and literature), rhetoric (composition and speech), logic (the art of reasoning), arithmetic, geometry, astronomy, and music. More advanced courses included theology (the study of religious thought and Church teachings), mathematics, physics, ethics, law, and medicine. Lectures and examinations were given in Latin. The curriculum relied heavily on Latin translations of ancient texts, principally the works of Aristotle (page 89). In mathematics and astronomy, students read Latin translations of Euclid and Ptolemy, two Greek scholars. Students of medicine studied the works of the two great medical men of the ancient world, Hippocrates and Galen.

University life is demanding. The medieval student's day was long and hard. Students rose before five o'clock in the morning, went to church until six, and attended class until ten o'clock. After a simple midday meal of soup or stew, they returned to classes until five in the afternoon.

Living conditions were often uncomfortable. Students sat on hard benches or on straw scattered on the floor. In winter, classrooms might be cold and damp. Candles were the only light for studying at night. Books were costly and rare, for they had to be copied by hand on parchment or sheepskin. Usually the teacher read aloud from a book while the students took notes on slates. Not until the 1400's did printed books come into use. Students relied on their memories to learn their assignments.

Medieval students have familiar interests and problems. In some ways, medieval students were much like modern ones. Letters to students from their parents still sound familiar. One father wrote his son, "I have learned . . . that you do not study in your room or act in the schools as a good student should, but play and wander about, disobedient to your master and indulging in sport." Another father complained that he had sent his son to college to study, but the youth preferred "play to work and strumming a guitar while the others are at their studies."

Students' letters home also brought up familiar problems:

> Well-beloved father, I have not a penny, nor can I get any save through you, for all things at the University are so dear [expensive]; nor can I study in my [lawbooks], for they are all tattered. Moreover, I owe ten crowns in dues to the Provost [head of school], and can find no man to lend them to me. . . .
>
> Well-beloved father, to ease my debts . . . at the baker's, with the doctor, . . . and to pay . . . the laundress and the barber, I send you word of greetings and of money.

Religion guides medieval thinking. The best minds of the Middle Ages studied the Bible and the writings of important clergy. When scholars wanted an answer to a question, they turned to the Bible and to Church authorities. They saw Christian teachings as a guide to life and as the basis of knowledge. Medieval thinkers held that politics, economic life, law, and views of nature must be based on the Bible. To understand nature and society, they argued, one first needed to understand God's intentions for humanity.

As the writings of ancient Greek philosophers and scientists began to circulate in Western Europe, medieval thinkers faced a problem. Greek philosophy seemed to conflict with Christian teachings. Some Christian thinkers distrusted scholars who studied Greek philosophy. They thought that the logic of the Greeks would lead people away from God. Medieval philosophers called Scholastics disagreed. They argued that reason could be used to explain Christian teachings. The Scholastics did not challenge or reject Christian beliefs. They never doubted the existence of God or the teachings of the Bible. "I would not be a philosopher if this were to separate me from Christ," wrote one Scholastic.

Probably the most brilliant Scholastic was Thomas Aquinas (uh-KWY-nus), a member of the Dominican order of monks in the thirteenth century. According to Aquinas, both reason and Christian teachings came from God. Therefore, he taught, both reason and faith pointed to the same truths. Aquinas's book, the *Summa Theologica* (1267–1273), used Aristotle's methods of logic to examine and explain certain points in Church teachings. The *Summa* had an important influence on later Christian thinkers.

Religion influences the medieval view of the universe. In the Middle Ages people believed that God had created the world especially for human beings and had placed the earth in the center of the universe. Medieval thinkers were certain that the moon, sun, and stars were pure and unchanging — superior to anything found on the earth — and that they followed different laws of motion from those that applied on the earth.

Interest in science grows. Aquinas and many other medieval thinkers, however, developed an interest in studying the natural world. Many ancient scientific works were translated into Latin in the High Middle Ages. They were brought into Western Europe along with translations of the works of Muslim scholars. These writings, which had been unknown in Europe during the early Middle Ages, stimulated a new interest in observing nature.

The greatest naturalist among medieval scholars was Albertus Magnus (Albert the

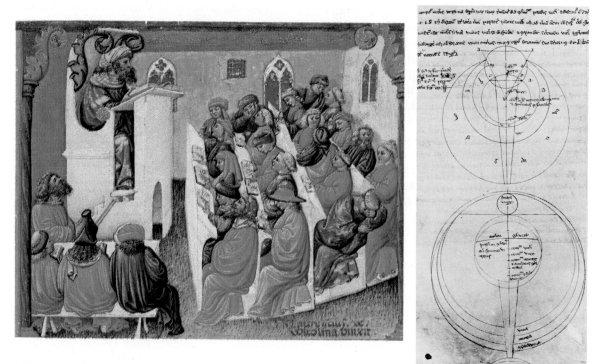

MEDIEVAL SCHOLARS

Some medieval students had small hand-printed books to use in class, while the professor lectured from a large volume (above). The curiosity of medieval scholars is indicated by Roger Bacon's diagram of the human eye (above right).

Great), who was the teacher of Thomas Aquinas at the universities in Paris and Cologne (kuh-LOHN). Albert wrote about geology, chemistry, botany, and zoology. His interest in the world of nature is shown in the following passage:

> I have examined the anatomy of different species of bees. In the rear part, that is, behind the waist, I discovered a transparent, shining bladder. If you test this with your tongue, you find that it has a slight taste of honey. In the body there is only an insignificant spiral-shaped intestine and nerve fibers which are connected with the sting. All this is surrounded with a sticky fluid.

Another medieval scholar who experimented in science was Roger Bacon (1214–1294). An English Franciscan monk and philosopher, Bacon criticized professors for neglecting science. Bacon studied Muslim writings on light rays, performed experiments in optics,

and observed that light traveled faster than sound. In his writings he gave a good description of the eye and discussed the causes of tides and the appearance of rainbows. He is often credited with inventing gunpowder. Bacon felt sure that science would bring great changes in people's lives. He predicted that one day ships would move

> without rowers, . . . cars . . . without animals [to pull them]. Also flying machines can be constructed so that a man sits in the midst of the machine [turning] some engine by which artificial wings are made to beat the air like a flying bird. . . . Also machines can be made for walking in the sea and rivers, even to the bottom without danger.

Medieval science is limited. Although medieval scholars made important experiments and observations of nature, their investigations frequently were mixed with ideas based on magic, superstition, and folk legends. Their experiments and equipment were so mystifying to other people that scholars such as Roger Bacon often were thought to be using sorcery. Some medieval scholars studied astrology and alchemy (AL-kuh-mee), an ancient study that eventually grew into modern chemistry. In medieval times, however, alchemists still were looking for magic formulas or substances that would, for instance, turn lead into gold. Medieval scholars also continued to believe many of the mistaken theories of earlier Greek and Muslim scientific thinkers.

CHECK-UP

1. How was the revival of learning in Western Europe aided (a) by contact with Muslim and Byzantine civilizations? (b) by the rise of towns?
2. (a) What courses did medieval students study at universities? (b) Describe the conditions under which students learned.
3. (a) Who were the Scholastics? (b) How did Aquinas use logic in his *Summa Theologica*?
4. (a) In what areas did medieval scholars advance scientific knowledge? (b) What limited their achievements?

2 New Styles Develop in Medieval Art

With the growth of towns in the High Middle Ages, intellectual life revived, as shown by the rise of universities and the new interest in classical learning. Developments in literature, the arts, and architecture were other signs of the flourishing culture of the times.

MEDIEVAL LITERATURE

Religious themes are used in medieval drama. Despite the revival of learning, most people in the Middle Ages still could not read or write. The spoken word — in hymns, songs, and dramas — was important in bringing Church teachings to a wide audience. Stories from the Bible and the lives of the saints were told in religious pageants and dramas in verse. These mystery plays, or miracle plays, were at first presented inside the church. Later the performers moved outside to the courtyard or the town square. A later development in religious drama was the morality play. Characters representing human virtues and vices such as Good Deeds or Greed acted out the conflicts between good and evil, often in a comic way. The most famous morality play was *Everyman*.

Local languages are used in literature. Since Roman times Latin had been the language of the Church and of scholars. By the Middle Ages, Latin was no longer used in everyday speech even in Italy. French, Spanish, Italian, and Rumanian were local languages that grew out of Latin. In northern Europe, several languages developed from the languages of the Germanic tribes. These common, or *vernacular* (vur-NAK-yoo-lur), languages gradually began to be used in both written and spoken literature.

Old legends that had been told or sung by bards were now written down in the vernacular. Some took the form of epic poetry (page 66) that told about the heroic deeds of knights and warriors. Most of the medieval epics came from northern Europe. The oldest great literary work in a vernacular language is *Beowulf*. Based on Danish legend, it was first written down in the early eighth century in Anglo-Saxon, one of the languages of England. This poem tells the story of the hero Beowulf, who stalked and killed the monster Grendel before becoming king of his people. A Scandinavian epic, the *Volsunga Saga*, tells of the destruction brought by greed to possess a magic gold ring. The German epic called the *Song of the Nibelung* describes the rivalry between early medieval kingdoms.

Epics also retold the stories that had grown up around heroes of the early Middle Ages. In France, the *Song of Roland* was based on tales of the warriors of Charlemagne's court. The *Poem of the Cid* tells the story of an eleventh-century Spanish hero who fought the Muslims in Spain. In England, the tales were of King

CHIVALRY

The literature and music of the High Middle Ages reflected the growth of chivalry (page 146). This ideal was exemplified by the knights at the court of King Arthur, shown in the tapestry above. An outgrowth of the chivalric ideal was courtly love. The picture on the right shows a troubadour being bound by a golden thread symbolizing love.

Arthur, his court at Camelot, and the knights of the Round Table. Arthur and his knights became symbols of the highest medieval ideals of courage, faith, and chivalry.

Court troubadours write of love. Vernacular languages were also used by medieval poets who wrote short verses and songs on non-religious themes. At the courts of noble families in southern France, poets wrote and sang about courtly love. Their poems were addressed to noblewomen, praising their beauty and pledging to them the singer's devotion and loyalty. Unlike minstrels, who were professional entertainers, the poet-musicians, or troubadours, were usually nobles. The troubadour pledged to honor and serve his lady as loyally as he would his lord. Love songs praised ladies for their beauty and charm and expressed the joys and pains of love.

> I would tell her I loved her, did I know but the way.
> Could my lips but discover what a lover should say.

> Though I swear to adore her every morning I rise,
> Yet, when once I'm before her, all my eloquence flies.

Poets and other artists found support and hospitality in the nobles' courts and castles. Eleanor of Aquitaine, her daughter the countess of Champagne, and other noblewomen encouraged troubadours in their courts in France. Many noblewomen wrote poetry themselves. A famous woman writer of the late 1100's was Marie de France. She wrote poems, fables, and a long courtly romance. Some of these works were based on legends about King Arthur.

Courtly love sets new standards. The poetry of courtly love reflected a changing attitude toward women, at least in the upper classes. Knights were expected to treat women with respect, gentleness, and consideration. The idea of romantic love developed. It was believed that love would improve a man's character and inspire him to noble deeds. To prove worthy of his lady's love, a knight had to demonstrate bravery, loyalty, and charm. The rough warrior therefore acquired manners, skill in using words to express himself, and taste in music and poetry.

While courtly love led knights to treat noblewomen with greater respect, it also created an idealized, artificial image of women. The women whom poets praised were seen only as helpless, beautiful, and pure.

Dante creates a masterpiece in the vernacular. The greatest poet of the Middle Ages was Dante Alighieri (DAHN-tay ah-lee-GYAY-ree), of Florence, Italy. In the tradition of the troubadours, Dante (1265–1321) wrote love poems to his beloved Beatrice. His masterpiece, however, was the *Divine Comedy,* a description of the poet's journey through hell, purgatory, and paradise, guided by the Roman poet Virgil. Within this framework, Dante gave a vivid description of the people and places of medieval Italy. The poem was written in medieval Italian and helped establish the vernacular as a literary language.

In the *Divine Comedy,* Dante's journey represents the progress of the soul toward God. Dante first pictures the torments of hell, or the Inferno. In Dante's Inferno, sinners endure burning sand, violent storms, total darkness, and fearful monsters. The lowest level of the Inferno is set aside for Lucifer (the devil). Dante portrays him tormenting the men the poet thought were the greatest traitors in history — Judas, who betrayed Jesus; and Brutus and Cassius, who assassinated Caesar.

Dante and his guide travel to purgatory and then to paradise, a place of light, music, and gentleness. In paradise, the poet's beloved Beatrice introduces him to the saints and the Virgin Mary, and for an instant he has a dazzling vision of God.

Chaucer describes medieval society. Late in the fourteenth century an English poet, Geoffrey Chaucer, wrote a long narrative poem called *The Canterbury Tales.* In this masterpiece of English literature, Chaucer painted a vivid picture of everyday life in medieval England.

LINKING PAST AND PRESENT
Musicians of the Middle Ages

Every instrument in a modern band or orchestra has at least one ancestor in the musical instruments of the Middle Ages. While few musicians today are equally skillful on guitar, violin, trumpet, flute, bagpipes, and drums, the medieval jongleur (JONG-glur) was expected to play at least nine or ten of the hundreds of different instruments available. Unlike the troubadours, who were knightly poets and composers, the jongleurs were professional traveling entertainers.

Most of the instruments the jongleurs played originated in the Near East. There were wind instruments played by blowing — pipes, flutes, recorders (still played today), and shawms, which were like the modern clarinet. The ancestor of the trombone was the sackbut, and there were many kinds of horns and trumpets.

There were also many stringed instruments; some were played with a bow, while others were strummed like the modern guitar.

The "plot" of *The Canterbury Tales* is the journey of a group of pilgrims to the cathedral at Canterbury. Chaucer's descriptions of the pilgrims show humor, charm, and an unfailing understanding of human nature. Like Dante, Chaucer encouraged the use of the vernacular in literature. He wrote in the dialect spoken by the people of medieval London. *The Canterbury Tales* was so widely read that this dialect had a strong influence on the development of modern English.

The following passages from the Prologue to *The Canterbury Tales* introduce the reader to some of Chaucer's pilgrims:

> A Monk there was, one of the finest sort
> Who rode the country; hunting was his
>   sport. . . .
> This Monk was therefore a good man to
>   horse;
> Greyhounds he had, as swift as birds, to
>   course. . . .
> His head was bald and shone like looking-
>   glass;
> So did his face, as if it had been greased.
> He was a fat and [well-conditioned] priest.

A "worthy woman" from the city of Bath was a cloth-maker who was fashionably dressed:

> Her kerchiefs were of finely woven ground
>   [cloth];
> I dared have sworn they weighed a good ten
>   pound,
> The ones she wore on Sunday, on her head.
> Her hose were of the finest scarlet red
> And gartered tight; her shoes were soft and
>   new.
> Bold was her face, handsome, and red in hue.

MEDIEVAL ART AND ARCHITECTURE

Medieval artists express religious devotion. Like literature, art and architecture reveal much about the outlook of an age. Nearly all the artists of the Middle Ages — painters, sculptors, woodcarvers, architects — created works intended to show their faith and devotion to the Church. The people of a medieval town took great pride in the beauty of their church. To decorate it, artists and artisans created paintings, carvings, tapestries, and stained-glass windows. These depicted scenes in the lives of Jesus and of the saints. Since many people

MEDIEVAL ARCHITECTURE AND CHURCH ART

The Church of Saint Paul in Pisa, Italy (above), is an example of Romanesque architecture, the style common in the earlier part of the Middle Ages. In the twelfth century medieval architects began to experiment with new styles. Compare the rounded Romanesque arches with the arches in the Gothic cathedral of Notre Dame in Bayeux, France (next page, left). The Gothic arches, as this picture shows, allowed a church to have much larger windows. Note the flying buttresses on the upper level of the cathedral. The Gothic-style arch is also used in the painting of Saint Clare, from an Italian altarpiece (next page, right). The order of nuns she founded, the Poor Clares, were dedicated to a way of life similar to that followed by the Franciscans (page 173).

could not read, these works of art helped them become familiar with Bible stories and Church teachings.

Medieval architecture shows Roman influence. Two styles of architecture developed during the Middle Ages. The earlier style, Romanesque (roh-mun-ESK), was used most commonly from about the ninth through the twelfth centuries. The most typical feature of Romanesque buildings was the rounded arch or several rounded arches forming a vault. This style of building was adapted from Roman architecture. Romanesque structures usually had massive walls and small windows, making the interiors dark and somber. There was little

color or use of ornament, though doorways and walls were decorated with religious sculptures. Churches, castles, and monasteries in Romanesque style were built throughout Europe, with distinctive variations in different countries.

Gothic architecture evolves. The walls of Romanesque buildings were massive because they had to support the weight of the roof. Late in the twelfth century, stonemasons began to construct buildings that were higher and more graceful. Instead of using rounded arches to support the roofs, they designed pointed arches. To take care of the weight of the roof, the walls were supported from the outside by leaning arches called flying buttresses. The walls could, therefore, be made taller and less massive, and much of the wall space could be used for beautiful stained-glass windows.

The new style of architecture came to be called Gothic. The high arched ceilings and tall windows made Gothic buildings lighter and more spacious than Romanesque structures. Gothic architecture came to be used for castles, college buildings, and town halls. Its first and most impressive use, however, was the soaring, graceful Gothic cathedral.

The building of a great Gothic cathedral might take many years. Its construction was an act of religious devotion in which an entire town took part. The wealthy gave their money, the poor their labor, and the artisans their skills to make these buildings beautiful works of art. The Gothic cathedrals were a profound expression of medieval religious feeling.

CHECK-UP

1. Vocabulary: *vernacular.*
2. (a) How did people of medieval Europe learn the teachings of the Church? (b) What were morality plays?
3. (a) What were the earliest forms of medieval literature to be written in the vernacular? (b) Name two of these works and the countries in which they were written.
4. (a) What were the subjects of the troubadours' poetry? (b) How did Eleanor of Aquitaine and other noblewomen help to set the standards of courtly love?
5. (a) How did Dante's *Divine Comedy* express the medieval outlook? (b) What effect did Chaucer's *The Canterbury Tales* have on the English language?
6. (a) What were the two major styles of architecture in medieval Europe? (b) How did they differ?

3 The Middle Ages Draws to a Close

The twelfth and thirteenth centuries were the high point of medieval civilization. In the fourteenth century, medieval civilization underwent great upheavals. Economic distress, a decreasing population, devastating warfare, and a weakening of the power of the Church were signs of these difficult times. They were also signs that the medieval period was coming to an end.

Famine and disease bring a drop in population. In the late Middle Ages, Western Europe was burdened with economic problems. The earlier increases in agricultural production did not continue. Not much was known about methods of keeping soil fertile. As a result, the soil in heavily farmed areas became worn out and unproductive. In the late Middle Ages there were periods of severe famine, and starvation was a frequent threat.

The greatest blow to fourteenth-century Europe was the bubonic plague, perhaps the worst natural disaster in human history. Known as the Black Death, the bubonic plague was carried by fleas on rats. It probably first struck in Asia in 1331–1332 and moved west across Russia. Italian ships returning from Black Sea ports carried the plague to Sicily. In 1348 it began to spread throughout Europe with incredible speed. Perhaps twenty million people — between a third and a half of the European population — died from the plague.

The terrified survivors were seized by mass hysteria. Believing the plague to be a punishment from God, some people wandered from place to place beating themselves and each other with sticks and whips. Others turned to magic and witchcraft. Frightened mobs slaughtered Jews in the belief that they had caused the plague.

Peasant rebellions break out. The millions of deaths among farm workers and artisans left farmlands and workshops idle. Fewer crops and goods were produced, and both wages and prices rose. Badly in need of money, nobles demanded more taxes from peasants. In 1381 John Ball and Wat Tyler led English peasants in a revolt against new taxes. Ball aroused the peasants in a speech attacking the inequality between them and the rich:

> For what reason do they thus hold us in bondage? Are we not all descended from the same parents, Adam and Eve? and what can they show, or what reasons give, why they should be more the masters than ourselves? except, perhaps, in making us labor and work, for them to spend. They are clothed in velvets and rich stuffs, ornamented with ermine and other furs, while we are forced to wear poor cloth. They have wines, spices, and fine bread, when we have only rye [bread]. . . . They have handsome [houses] and manors, when we must brave the wind and rain in our labors in the field; but it is from our labor they have wherewith to support their pomp.

The peasants' revolt in England, like similar revolts in France and Flanders, was put down by the king's soldiers.

Social unrest occurred in the towns as well as the countryside. The wage earners of Flor-

When John Ball and his "army" marched on London (below), they were met by the troops of Richard II. The king persuaded them to disband and then used harsh measures to prevent future revolt.

ence (1378), the weavers of Ghent in Flanders (1382), and the poor of Paris (1382) rose up against the upper class in those cities. Like the peasant uprisings, the rebellions of the urban poor were put down by force.

England and France fight the Hundred Years' War. The long-standing dispute between the kings of France and England (page 168) brought on a series of destructive conflicts known as the Hundred Years' War (1337–1453). The English king, Edward III, held land as a vassal of the French king. He was also the French king's nephew and so tried to claim the French throne and acquire still more land in France. In the opening phase of the war, English archers armed with powerful Welsh longbows inflicted terrible casualties on mounted French knights at the battles of Crécy (kray-SEE) in 1346 and Poitiers (pwah-TYAY) in 1356.

The longbow brought changes in medieval warfare. It allowed archers to shoot arrows farther and faster than did the traditional crossbow. Using their longbows, English foot soldiers cut down wave after wave of charging French cavalry. The French knights were formidable only on horseback. A knight whose horse was killed or who was knocked to the ground could barely move because of the heavy armor he wore. The longbow also allowed less wealthy men to become soldiers, for they did not have to bear the expenses of keeping a horse and buying weapons and armor.

The Hundred Years' War continued on and off throughout the fourteenth century. Fought entirely on French land, it caused great suffering for the French peasants and townspeople. Many were killed, and much valuable farmland was destroyed by marauding bands of soldiers. At the battle of Agincourt (ah-zhan-KOOR) in 1415, the archers and knights of the English king, Henry V, again dealt the French a resounding defeat. This victory gave England control of most of northern France. By a treaty signed in 1420, Henry married the French king's daughter Catherine and was named heir to the throne. It appeared that England would soon join the two lands under one crown.

Joan of Arc inspires the French. At this critical point a seventeen-year-old peasant named Joan of Arc came to the rescue of

No actual portraits of Joan of Arc exist. This miniature was published in a book written by a poet from Orleans, scene of one of her victories.

France. The French king's son, the Dauphin (DAW-fin), had been denied the throne by the peace treaty. Believing that God had commanded her to drive the English out of France, Joan gave the Dauphin courage and persuaded him to let her lead the troops. Dressed in armor and carrying a religious banner, Joan rallied the French troops and led them to victory at Orleans in 1429. The Dauphin was then crowned king of France as Charles VII. Other victories followed, but in 1430 Joan was captured by opponents of the French king and turned over to the English. A church court condemned her as a heretic and a witch, and Joan was burned at the stake.[1]

Joan had set an example that inspired the French people and strengthened their devotion to France. They fought the English with new courage. By 1453 the English had lost all their lands in France except the northern port city of Calais (KAH-lay).

---

[1] In 1920 the Catholic Church proclaimed Joan of Arc a saint.

In this picture of the Battle of Poitiers, taken from a fourteenth-century account of the Hundred Years' War, English archers confront French knights grouped under the lily banner of the kings of France. The archers are shown using the longbow, an invention that originated in Wales.

French kings gain strength after the Hundred Years' War. Besides giving the French people a sense of unity, the Hundred Years' War increased the power of the French monarch. During the war French kings introduced new taxes that added greatly to the royal income. This enabled them to hire soldiers who were loyal to the monarchy. The French ruler no longer had to rely on the uncertain loyalty of troops supplied by feudal vassals. Having the service of well-paid and loyal troops gave the king considerable control over the country.

The successor of Charles VII was Louis XI (1461–1483). Louis was a shrewd ruler who took advantage of every opportunity to strengthen royal power. In fact, his enemies called him "the Spider" because of his clever scheming. With the English no longer in France, the greatest feudal lord was Charles the Bold, the duke of Burgundy. To weaken Burgundy's power, Louis supported Swiss troops who fought against the duke. After the duke was killed in battle in 1477, the king managed to acquire much of Burgundy's rich land. When other feudal lords died with no heirs, Louis acquired still more land for the crown. Although high taxes made him unpopular, the king still had the support of townspeople and the artisans of the guilds. Louis' success contributed to the development of absolute monarchy in France.

English nobles go to war over the throne. The aftermath of the Hundred Years' War in England was at first very different from the war's results in France. Henry VI had been an infant when he inherited the throne in 1422. Several powerful families had taken advantage of that to acquire great influence in England, and Henry never fully controlled the kingdom. The loss of French lands and the unpopular peace settlement with France added to the widespread discontent.

The English royal family, the Plantagenets, was split into two rival branches — the houses of York and Lancaster. In 1455 the duke of York challenged Henry's right to the throne. Civil war began between those who supported York and those who backed Henry, a Lancaster. This struggle later came to be called the Wars of the Roses because of the two houses' symbols — a red rose for Lancaster, a white rose for York.

In thirty years of intermittent fighting, four kings came to the English throne and were deposed, murdered, or killed in battle. Hundreds of noblemen from England's most prominent and powerful families were killed in the Wars of the Roses, seriously weakening the English nobility. In 1485 Henry Tudor, a Lancastrian, defeated and killed King Richard III, son of the duke of York. He became king as Henry VII and devoted his reign (1485–1509) to unifying England. Henry married Elizabeth of York and was the founder of the Tudor dynasty of monarchs. Members of this family ruled England until 1603.

Papal authority declines. As the power of monarchs grew in the late Middle Ages, the authority and political power of the Pope declined. This change in papal authority became evident when Pope Boniface VIII came into conflict with Philip IV of France in 1296. To raise revenue, Philip demanded taxes from the French churches, disregarding the Church decree against the taxing of its property. Though threatened with excommunication, Philip refused to back down.

Next, Philip put on trial and then imprisoned a French bishop, another violation of Church law. In 1302 Boniface issued a decree asserting the Pope's supreme authority over all rulers, but Philip sent soldiers to arrest him. Although he was soon released, the elderly Pope died a month later.

Clement V, a French archbishop and a friend of Philip IV, was elected Pope in 1305. Not wanting to leave his native country for Rome, Clement set up the papal court in Avignon (ah-vee-NYON) in southeastern France. From 1309 to 1377, all the Popes were French and ruled from Avignon, not Rome. Under the influence of the French king, they often had to pursue policies favorable to France. To the people of Rome, this period of the papacy was known as the Babylonian Captivity, a comparison to the time when the Hebrews had been in exile in Babylon (page 55). Clearly the Pope's power had declined greatly since the days of Innocent III.

The papacy returned to Rome in 1377, but conflicts continued. In 1378, the Romans insisted on the election of an Italian Pope, Urban VI. Urban, however, clashed with the cardinals, the clergymen who elected the Pope. The cardinals, most of them French, left Rome and elected Clement VII to be Pope at Avignon. Urban refused to step down and excommunicated Clement, who in turn excommunicated Urban. To the anguish of pious Christians, there were now two Popes. This period, known as the Great Schism (SIZ-um), ended in 1417. (*Schism* means division.) The Great Schism further undermined the prestige of the papacy and the unity of the Church.

Christians call for reforms in the Church. The reputation of the papacy also was undermined by the involvement of Popes in politics. Many Christians felt that certain Popes behaved more like princes concerned with political power than like spiritual leaders. They believed that the Church should confine itself to religious matters and not interfere with monarchs. Reformers also attacked the Church for its wealth and argued that the clergy should be subject to the laws of the state. They urged the clergy to return to the simple piety of the early followers of Jesus. These pleas for reform, however, went unheeded. Eventually they led to a division within the Christian Church (described in Chapter 15).

The Middle Ages leave an important legacy. It was once common to view the Middle Ages as the "dark ages," a period of cultural darkness that followed the fall of Greco-Roman civilization. People later began to appreciate the richness and creativity of medieval civilization and the important changes that occurred in the Middle Ages. By the fifteenth century, England and France were strong, unified states. Monarchs had great power, but people had begun to gain a voice in government through representative parliaments. The new middle class in the towns had wealth and influence. Christianity and the Church remained important forces in people's lives and in cultural developments, but the political power of the Church was lessening. These changes were all signs that the medieval period was gradually coming to an end.

CHECK-UP

1. (a) What caused a decline in Europe's population in the late Middle Ages? (b) Why was there a rapid rise in prices? (c) Why did peasant revolts break out?
2. (a) What was the basic cause of the Hundred Years' War? (b) How did the war affect royal power in France?
3. What effect did the Wars of the Roses have on the English nobility?
4. (a) How did the controversy between Pope Boniface VIII and Philip IV show that papal authority had diminished? (b) What other events weakened the authority of the Church?
5. What Church reforms did Christians call for in the fourteenth century?

Chapter 9 Review

Summary

Medieval civilization reached its height in the twelfth and thirteenth centuries. Prosperity increased, towns grew, and an interest in learning revived. The first universities developed, and contacts with Muslim and Byzantine cultures made the knowledge of ancient Greece and Rome available in Western Europe. One group of thinkers, the Scholastics, used Greek methods of reasoning to support the teachings of the Church.

Most artists and writers in the Middle Ages expressed their Christian beliefs and devotion to the Church. A rich literature began to be written in the vernacular languages. Epics recounted legends of national heroes. Dante's *Divine Comedy* and Chaucer's *Canterbury Tales,* two masterpieces of medieval writing, gave a vivid picture of the times. The troubadours, writing mainly about love, began a tradition of non-religious writing and helped to establish a new attitude toward women. Architecture moved from the massive Romanesque style to the graceful Gothic.

During the fourteenth century, devastating warfare, severe famine, and epidemic disease brought significant changes to Europe, increasing the power of kings and reducing the political power of the Popes. These changes would bring the Middle Ages to an end.

Vocabulary Review

1. Match the following words with the listed definitions: *excommunicate, middle class, parliament, vassal, vernacular.*
   (a) A social class that emerged in medieval towns, made up of artisans and merchants and their families.
   (b) A noble granted land by a feudal lord in exchange for military assistance and other services.
   (c) To expel a person from the Roman Catholic Church.
   (d) The language commonly spoken in a region or country.
   (e) A representative assembly that makes the laws of a nation.

2. Distinguish between the terms in each of the following pairs:
   (a) Battle of Agincourt; Battle of Orleans.
   (b) Gothic architecture; Romanesque architecture.
   (c) *Beowulf; Song of Roland.*
   (d) *Canterbury Tales; Divine Comedy.*

People to Identify

In each of the following sentences fill in the blank with a name from this list: *Thomas Aquinas, Henry VII, Urban VI, Joan of Arc, Clement V, Albertus Magnus, John Ball.*

1. The English king who defeated Richard III to end the War of the Roses and start the Tudor dynasty was __?__ .
2. __?__ was a medieval scholar who studied geology, chemistry, botany, and zoology.
3. __?__, a peasant, led the French troops to victory at the Battle of Orleans in 1429.
4. In 1378 __?__ excommunicated Clement VII, after which Clement excommunicated him.
5. __?__ led a peasant revolt in England against new taxes.
6. __?__ set up the papal court at Avignon, France in 1309.
7. The greatest of the Scholastics was __?__ , who was greatly influenced by the writings of Aristotle.

Relating Geography and History

1. **Locating places.** Locate each of the following on a map in Chapter 8:
   (a) Paris   (d) Agincourt
   (b) Calais   (e) Orleans
   (c) Crécy   (f) Avignon

2. **Map study and review.** Study the map on page 168 showing French territorial changes resulting from the Hundred Years' War (1337–1453). (a) How does the map show the French lands held so long by the English? (b) What happened to those lands as a result of the Hundred Years' War? (c) By what date was Burgundy taken over by the French king? (d) Reread page 191. In what part of Europe was the war fought? Describe the damage that resulted. (e) What territory did England retain in France?

Discussion Questions

1. (a) What concerns were there among Christian thinkers about the relationship between faith and reason? (b) Why did the revival of learning in the late Middle Ages *not* lead to the development of modern science?

2. Tell how each of the following began to take form during the Middle Ages: (a) strong, unified states, (b) universities, (c) modern European languages.

3. (a) In what ways was epic poetry different from the earlier literature of the Middle Ages? (b) List several great epic poems, the subjects they explored, and the languages in which they were written. (c) What are Dante's *Divine Comedy* and Chaucer's *Canterbury Tales* about, and why are they important?

4. What events were evidence of the decline of the political power of the Church during the thirteenth and fourteenth centuries?

5. (a) The Middle Ages were once thought of as "the Dark Ages." Why? (b) What arguments could be used to disprove this view?

6. Medieval civilization entered a period of crisis and change during the fourteenth century. (a) Give examples of events and developments that caused upheavals in Western Europe. (b) What were the results of these changes?

Reading Primary Sources

The Black Death is the worst epidemic ever to have struck Europe. Giovanni Boccaccio (boh-KAH-chee-oh) was in Florence when the plague broke out. Read his account of the destruction it caused. Then answer the questions that follow.

> In the year 1348 . . . that most beautiful of Italian cities, noble Florence, was attacked by deadly plague. It started in the East either through the influence of the heavenly bodies or because God's just anger with our wicked deeds sent it as a punishment to mortal men; and in a few years [it] killed [about two-thirds of the population of the city]. . . . Against this plague all human wisdom and foresight were [in] vain. Orders had been given to cleanse the city of filth; the entry of any sick person [into the city] was forbidden; much advice was given for keeping healthy. At the same time humble [prayers] were made to God by pious persons. . . .
>
> The violence of this disease was such that the sick communicated it to the healthy who came near them. . . . To speak to or go near the sick brought infection and . . . death. . . . To touch the clothes or anything else the sick had touched or worn gave the disease to the person touching.
>
> One citizen avoided another. . . . Such terror was struck into the hearts of men and women by this calamity that brother abandoned brother . . . and very often the wife [abandoned] her husband. . . . What is worse and nearly incredible is that fathers and mothers refused to see and tend their children, as if they had not been theirs.

(a) What possible explanations did Boccaccio give for the plague's origins? (b) What steps did the Florentines take to keep the plague from striking their city? (c) How was the disease spread? (d) What effect did the plague have on relationships between people?

Skill Activities

1. Placing events in time. On a separate sheet of paper, list the following events in sequence, giving the correct date for each entry.
(a) The Black Death reaches Europe.
(b) The Hundred Years' War ends.
(c) The quarrel between Boniface VIII and Philip IV begins.
(d) The Battle of Orleans is fought.
(e) John Ball leads the English peasant revolt.
(f) The Hundred Years' War begins.
(g) Joan of Arc is burned at the stake.
(h) Dante Alighieri is born.
(i) Thomas Aquinas completes his *Summa Theologica.*
(j) Henry VI inherits the throne of England.
(k) The weavers of Ghent rebel against the upper class.
(l) The Battle of Crécy is fought.

2. Reports. Find information on one of the following and prepare a report: (a) the Peasants' Revolt in England in 1381; (b) the life of Joan of Arc; (c) the Wars of the Roses; (d) medieval clothing; (e) a Gothic cathedral in England or France; (f) the Dance of Death (a reaction to the plague); (g) the method of electing Popes.

3. Making models. After studying about medieval suits of armor and the Welsh longbow, make models to display in your classroom. Be prepared to explain (a) why the longbow could shoot arrows farther than earlier bows and (b) why soldiers using the longbow could defeat knights mounted on horseback.

Unit Two Review

Review Questions

1. (a) Explain the terms *manorialism* and *feudalism*. (b) What conditions led to the rise of these institutions? (c) What factors led to their decline during the High Middle Ages?

2. (a) Why did the Church become powerful during the Middle Ages? (b) Describe the power of the papacy under Innocent III. (c) Why did the Church's power decline near the end of the Middle Ages?

3. (a) What factors led to the disappearance of towns after the fall of Rome? (b) How did agricultural improvements result in the re-emergence of towns during the High Middle Ages?

4. How did the growth of towns in the High Middle Ages affect (a) the class system? (b) interest in learning? (c) trade throughout Europe?

5. During the Middle Ages, England and France became unified but Germany and Italy did not. Why?

6. (a) What factors limited the power of the English kings during the Middle Ages? (b) Why were the French kings able to establish an absolute monarchy?

7. (a) Which of the Crusades was the most successful? Why? (b) In what ways did the Crusades fail? (c) How did the Crusades contribute to the development of modern Europe?

8. (a) Name and describe the two important styles of architecture that developed during the Middle Ages. (b) Using several examples, describe the ways in which literature changed during the Middle Ages.

Projects

1. Making time lines. Make a time line covering the period from 500 to 1430. Include not only events that can be marked by one date but also those (like the Hundred Years' War) that took place over a longer period of time.

2. Evaluating historical figures. Create a Hall of Fame of Medieval Europe. Make a list of the men and women you think should be included, and write a brief paragraph explaining why each of them deserves this honor.

3. Research and report. Medieval nobles enjoyed a variety of indoor and outdoor amusements. Find information about the origins and the rules of (a) falconry, (b) backgammon, (c) jousting, (d) chess.

4. Making maps. Draw a map of Western Europe in 1400. Use a different color for each unified state. Choose another color to show areas that had not yet been unified. Indicate the locations of major cities and label them.

Books to Read

Asimov, Isaac. *The Shaping of England.* Houghton Mifflin.

Asimov, Isaac. *The Shaping of France.* Houghton Mifflin.

Barber, Richard. *A Strong Land and Sturdy.* Clarion. Heavily illustrated account of England in the Middle Ages.

Brochard, Phillippe. *The Days of Knights and Castles.* Silver Burdett.

Coolidge, Olivia. *Tales of the Crusades.* Houghton Mifflin.

Fremantle, Anne. *Age of Faith.* Time-Life.

Gibson, Michael, and Harry Strongman. *The Vikings.* Silver Burdett.

Gies, Joseph. *Life in a Medieval City.* Crowell.

Gies, Joseph, and Frances Gies. *Life in a Medieval Castle.* Harper.

Gies, Joseph, and Frances Gies. *Women in the Middle Ages.* Barnes and Noble.

Macaulay, David. *Castle.* Houghton Mifflin. The construction of a medieval castle.

Macaulay, David. *Cathedral.* Houghton Mifflin. How medieval builders constructed cathedrals.

Morgan, Gwyneth. *Life in a Medieval Village.* Lerner. Thirteenth-century England.

Simons, Gerald. *Barbarian Europe.* Time-Life.

Unstead, R. J. *Kings, Barons, and Serfs* (*A Pictorial History,* Volume 2). Silver Burdett. History of the period from 1086 to 1300.

Unstead, R. J. *Years of the Sword* (*A Pictorial History,* Volume 3). Silver Burdett. History of the years 1300 to 1485.

How to Study World History

Building Your Vocabulary

Strong vocabulary skills can help you in all of your studies. There are many ways to increase your vocabulary.

Strategies. The following strategies can help you learn new words:

1. As you are reading, be aware of words that you do not understand.

2. In a notebook, make a list of the words that you want to learn.

3. Look up the definitions of the words on your list and write them in your notebook.

4. Study these words from time to time.

5. Look for these new words in your reading and try to use them in your writing.

Using context. When, in your reading, you come across a word that you do not understand, you can often figure out the word's meaning from the context — the setting in which it is used. There are several kinds of context clues:

Sense of the passage. Although a particular word may be unfamiliar, you will usually understand the general meaning of the passage. Look for clues in the passage to the meaning of the word. Use your own knowledge and experience to help you understand what the word must mean. For example, turn to page 182 and read the second paragraph that follows the heading **Medieval universities develop.** Notice the word *scholars.* There are several clues in the passage to the meaning of that word. The passage is about universities, places where people study. Another clue is the phrase that follows *scholars:* "who were famous for their learning." These clues indicate that scholars are people of learning.

Examples. An example can explain an unfamiliar word by showing you what kinds of things the word refers to. For example, *curriculum* is used in the fourth paragraph under the heading **Medieval universities develop** (page 182). An example of the curriculum of a medieval university is given: grammar, rhetoric, logic, arithmetic, geometry, astronomy, and music. You can probably figure out from the list of subjects that *curriculum* means "the course of study."

Synonyms. Sometimes an unfamiliar word will be restated or defined. If you know the meaning of the second word, you can figure out the meaning of the unknown word. For instance, in this section look at the word *context* in the paragraph that opens with the heading, "Using Context." You can understand what *context* means because it is defined in the same sentence as "setting."

Check Your Skill

Use the following questions to check your understanding of vocabulary-building skills:

1. Which of the following is *not* a strategy to help you learn new words? (a) As you read, skip over words that you don't understand. (b) Make a list of words that you want to learn. (c) Use new words in your writing.

2. The context of a word is (a) the definition, (b) a synonym or example, (c) the setting in which the word is used.

3. In Section 3 of Chapter 9, in the third paragraph under the heading **Famine and disease bring a drop in population** (page 190), you will find the word *hysteria.* Using context clues, choose the meaning of the word *hysteria:* (a) great boredom, (b) despair, (c) uncontrollable fear.

4. The context clue that helps you understand the meaning of *hysteria* is (a) the passage in which it appears, (b) a footnote, (c) a synonym.

5. The word *schism* is used on page 193. You know that *schism* means division because of which context clue: (a) the passage in which it appears, (b) an example, (c) a synonym.

Apply Your Skill

For practice in building your vocabulary, apply the following skills as you study Section 1 of Chapter 10 (pages 202–208):

1. Choose five to ten words that you find unfamiliar or difficult and list them in a notebook.

2. Try to determine the meaning of the words from the context in which they are used. Write those definitions next to the words you have listed.

3. Look up the words in a dictionary to check their meanings and correct any that you missed.

4. Write a paragraph in which you use the new words that you have learned.

二 亍 寸 矛 永

Civilizations Beyond Europe

Like medieval civilization in Europe, two empires in neighboring lands were greatly influenced by religion. In the eastern Mediterranean, the Byzantine Empire grew out of the surviving provinces of the Roman Empire. Its Greek culture and Eastern Christian beliefs separated it from Western Europe. The religion of Islam began in Arabia, and its dedicated followers quickly spread the new faith, building a vast empire in Asia, Africa, and Europe. Great civilizations with different beliefs and traditions also had grown up in other parts of the world. Several of these were as ancient as those from which the Western tradition arose. In both India and China, river valley civilizations emerged early in recorded history.

The Indus Valley people in South Asia built great cities as early as 2500 B.C. Their conquest by Aryan invaders from Asia produced a distinctive culture in India. In China, civilization spread from the Yellow River valley throughout the vast country. By the time of the Middle Ages in Europe, Chinese culture was perhaps the most advanced in the world. Nearby, the island country of Japan combined native traditions with Chinese influences to create another unique culture.

The diversity of peoples in Africa and the Americas resulted in many different cultural traditions. Wealthy trading empires grew up along the Nile River and in the Sudan of Africa. Much of southern Africa was settled by migrating Bantu-speaking peoples. Mesoamerican civilization developed in what is now Mexico and influenced a wide area in the Americas. In South America the Incas established an extensive empire.

The following chapters describe the development of civilizations in the non-Western world.

Many civilizations developed beyond Europe. One of the oldest of these civilizations emerged in China. The painting (left) shows a Chinese emperor crossing a river in the mountains. To the left of the painting are the basic brush strokes used in Chinese writing. The bottom character spells out the word *yung,* meaning "eternity."

The Dome of the Rock reflects Jerusalem's character as a meeting place for religions. An Islamic shrine built about 690, it is believed to stand on the site of the Hebrew temple of Solomon. Inscriptions on its walls come from the holy writings of Islam; the dome is Byzantine in style.

Byzantine and Islamic Civilizations

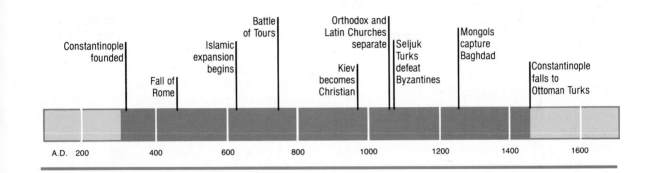

Constantinople founded | Fall of Rome | Islamic expansion begins | Battle of Tours | Kiev becomes Christian | Orthodox and Latin Churches separate | Seljuk Turks defeat Byzantines | Mongols capture Baghdad | Constantinople falls to Ottoman Turks

A.D. 200   400   600   800   1000   1200   1400   1600

As Europe faced the disorder of the early Middle Ages, two empires to the east were becoming prosperous and powerful. The Byzantine Empire, centered at Constantinople, grew up in the eastern regions of the Roman Empire after the fall of Rome. Despite continual invasions, the Byzantines developed a rich culture deeply influenced by Eastern Orthodox Christianity. The Islamic empire was based on a new religion, which began in Arabia in the seventh century and quickly spread to other parts of Asia and to Africa and Europe.

Both Byzantine and Islamic civilizations had widespread and lasting influences. Their scholars valued the knowledge of ancient Greece and Rome and used it as a basis for their own achievements. Trade made these civilizations prosperous and encouraged the spread of ideas. Both empires, however, eventually fell to invaders from Asia who established new empires.

This chapter describes the rise of the Byzantine and Islamic empires and their eventual defeat by Asian conquerors.

CHAPTER OUTLINE

1   The Byzantines Develop a Rich Civilization

2   Islam Spreads in Asia and Africa

3   Islamic Culture Reaches Its Height

4   New Empires Dominate the Muslim World

1 The Byzantines Develop a Rich Civilization

Late in the third century A.D. the Roman Empire was divided into eastern and western regions. The eastern provinces thrived while the western regions were weakened by attacks of Germanic tribes. Gradually the center of power in the Empire shifted from Rome to the eastern Mediterranean. Even before the West fell to invaders in A.D. 476 (page 123), there were, in effect, two empires. The new civilization that took shape in the east was called Byzantine (BIZ-un-teen) civilization. It endured for a thousand years.

A NEW EASTERN EMPIRE

A new capital is built for the Roman Empire. When the emperor Diocletian divided the Roman Empire, he moved his imperial court to Asia Minor. A co-emperor continued to rule in Italy, but Rome was no longer the center of the Empire. In A.D. 330 the emperor Constantine founded a new capital city for the Empire. Called Constantinople, it was built on the site of the ancient Greek city of Byzantium (bih-ZAN-shee-um), on a peninsula in the straits of the Bosporus. This waterway is regarded as the traditional dividing line between Europe and Asia.

The new capital was a fortress city, perfectly situated to resist attack from land or sea. The three seaward sides of the peninsula were protected by the sea and a single wall. On the land side were a wide moat and three massive walls. For centuries, invaders tried in vain to break through Constantinople's defenses.

Byzantine civilization develops in a new empire. Constantinople became the center of the new Byzantine Empire that developed out of the Eastern Roman Empire. The Byzantine culture was a blending of several influences. Its language and traditions were Greek, and its system of law and administration was Roman. Its religion followed the beliefs and practices of the early Christian communities in the eastern Mediterranean. Byzantine artists were influenced by Greek, Asian, and early Christian sources.

Byzantine emperors considered themselves the successors of the Roman emperors and so claimed to rule all the lands that had once been part of the Roman Empire. There was no established line of rulers in Constantinople, however. Political intrigue and struggles for power were frequent, and many emperors died violently.

Byzantine emperors were absolute rulers who held that God had chosen them to rule. The emperors made and unmade the laws, took charge of foreign affairs, commanded the army and navy, and supervised trade and industry. By claiming the right to appoint the patriarch (PAY-tree-ark), the head of the Church in Constantinople, the emperors also influenced Church policy.

Justinian and Theodora lead the empire. The first great Byzantine ruler was Justinian, who reigned nearly forty years, from 527 to 565. Justinian's most lasting achievement was in the field of law. With the decline of Rome, the Roman laws and legal system were in danger of being lost. Justinian appointed a commission of scholars to collect and organize the ancient laws and legal principles of Rome along with major Roman writings on law. The law codes of many countries in Europe and Latin America today trace their roots to Justinian's Code.

Justinian often relied on the advice of his wife Theodora. Theodora's background was unusual for an empress, for she was not from the nobility but was the daughter of a bear trainer in the circus. She had been an actress, a profession most people looked on as degrading. When Theodora became Justinian's wife, she showed great political skill. Until her death in 548, she was influential in lawmaking and choosing officials. In a number of crises, this strong-willed and intelligent woman gave Justinian the courage to act decisively. In 532, rioting crowds burned parts of Constantinople and tried to place another emperor on the throne. Though some officials urged Justinian to flee, Theodora persuaded him to face the crowds, restore order, and reassert his power.

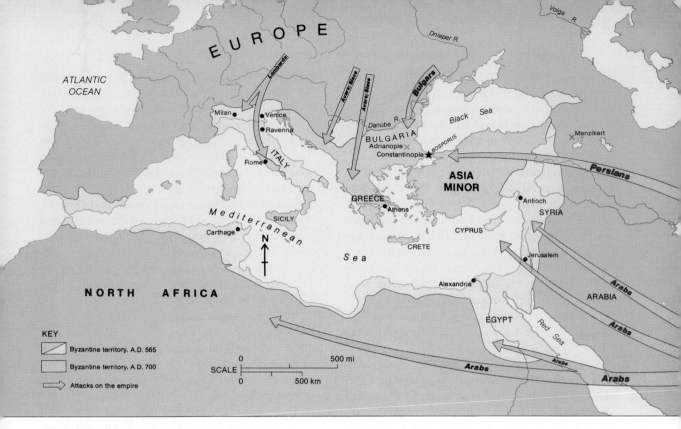

The Byzantine Empire, 565–700

The map above shows how the Byzantine Empire decreased in size. What lands were included in the empire in 565? Which of these had been lost by 700? Name the different peoples who carried out attacks against the Byzantines.

Justinian tries to restore the grandeur of Rome. Justinian dreamed of regaining the Roman lands in the western Mediterranean that the Germanic tribes had conquered. Early in his reign, Byzantine forces retook North Africa, Sicily, and southern Spain from the Goths and Vandals. Later they recaptured all of Italy, establishing a western capital at Ravenna in about 585.

The Byzantine military victories were due to the superb organization of the army, which followed the Roman tradition. Byzantine generals were skilled in military strategy and understood the importance of efficient supply lines and well-built roads and bridges. The backbone of the Byzantine army was its cavalry. Cavalry soldiers wore steel helmets and suits of armor and were armed with sword, dagger, lance, and bow and arrow. The stirrup, first used by the Byzantines in the sixth century, increased the horseman's effectiveness in battle, letting him wield his lance or sword without falling from his horse.

Invaders threaten Byzantine lands. Although Justinian's conquests regained much Roman territory, the Byzantine Empire paid a high price for these victories. The long and costly wars drained the treasury. Short of funds, the government neglected the defenses of its territories in the Near East and the Balkan Peninsula. Less able rulers succeeded Justinian and could not control the army.

Early in the 600's, the Balkans were invaded from the north, first by Slavic tribes from lands around the Black Sea, then by Avars, a people originally from Central Asia. The Avars and Slavs besieged Constantinople in 626 but could not break through the city's thick walls. From the east, the Persians attacked Syria, Palestine, and Egypt, all of which were part of the empire.

Threatened on every side, the Byzantine Empire steadily lost territory throughout the seventh century. The Germanic Lombards conquered much of the Byzantine lands in Italy, and by 631 the Visigoths recaptured all of

Spain. The Bulgars from Central Asia conquered the Slavic tribes in the Balkans and became a constant threat to Byzantine territory.

A new power threatens the Byzantine Empire. The greatest threat to the Byzantines, however, came from the Arabs who followed the new religion of Islam (page 209). By 642, Muslim Arabs had taken Egypt, Syria, and Palestine from Byzantium. Beginning in 673, they regularly attacked Constantinople by land and sea. By this time, however, the Byzantine defenders were aided by a new invention called "Greek fire." A fiery explosive liquid shot from tubes, it set enemy ships afire and made blazing pools of flame on the surface of the water. Armed with this frightening weapon, the light Byzantine ships held off the better-built Arab ships.

Byzantium protects Christian Europe. In 717–718, a massive Arab naval attack on Constantinople failed. This defeat ended for a time the Muslim advances in the eastern Mediterranean and was crucial for the history of Europe. If Constantinople had fallen, the Muslims would have been able to overrun the Balkans and sail up the Danube River into the heart of Europe. After this defeat and the defeat by the Franks at Tours in 732 (page 142), however, the Muslim invaders made no more conquests in Europe.

The Byzantine and Roman churches grow apart. Even as the Muslim threat was being halted, the Christian world was beginning to lose its unity. Over the years, important differences developed between Church teachings and practices in the Byzantine Empire and those in Western Europe. The two churches differed over ceremonies, holy days, the display of religious images, and the rights of the clergy.

Western European Christians came to accept the Pope at Rome as head of all Christians, but the Byzantines regarded the patriarch of Constantinople as leader of the Eastern, or Orthodox, Church. Christians in Western Europe also refused to recognize the Byzantine emperors' claim to be the successors to the Roman emperors. Byzantine emperors objected when, in 800, the Pope crowned Charlemagne as Holy Roman Emperor (page 143).

The final break between East and West came in 1054. The Christian Church split into the Latin Church in the West, ruled from Rome (and later called Roman Catholic), and the Orthodox Church in the East, ruled from Constantinople.

The Byzantine Empire prospers. There were other contrasts between Byzantium and medieval Western Europe. In the West trade, town life, and learning declined after the fall of Rome. The Byzantine Empire, on the other hand, remained a center of wealth and culture. Constantinople grew into a magnificent city of over half a million people. The city's location at the crossroads of Asia and Europe helped make it a bustling center of trade and industry as well as the heart of the empire. Into its markets came carpets from Persia, jewels from India and Southeast Asia, and slaves, ivory, and gold from Africa. Down the rivers of Eastern Europe came Scandinavian merchants with furs, fish, and Slavic slaves.

Byzantine artisans contributed to the empire's prosperity. After traders smuggled silkworms out of China, the Byzantines developed a thriving silk industry. From captive Arabs brought to Constantinople, the Byzantines learned the carefully guarded secret of making

---

TIMETABLE

Byzantine Civilization

330	Constantinople becomes the capital of the Roman Empire.
476	The Western Roman Empire falls to invaders.
527–565	Justinian rules the Byzantine Empire.
718	The Muslim siege of Constantinople fails.
988	Kievan Russia is converted to Eastern Christianity.
1054	The Orthodox Church and the Catholic Church are split.
1071	The Seljuk Turks defeat the Byzantines at Manzikert in Asia Minor.
1204	The crusaders capture Constantinople.
1453	Constantinople falls to the Ottoman Turks.

paper from rags. Taxes on the prospering industries and trade provided the money needed to run the government and pay for the defense of the Byzantine Empire.

THE DECLINE OF BYZANTIUM

New enemies weaken the empire. The Byzantine Empire remained fairly stable and prosperous for several hundred years despite continuing invasions. To protect their lands, Byzantine emperors relied on shrewd diplomacy in addition to well-trained military forces. Emperors were experts at making alliances, arranging political marriages, and using bribes to gain friends. They kept their enemies divided by stirring up hatreds among them. Nevertheless, continuing attacks from various directions nibbled away at Byzantine territory.

In the early eleventh century a formidable new enemy appeared in the east. The Seljuk Turks, originally from Central Asia, had converted to Islam. Moving steadily westward, in 1071 they destroyed the Byzantine army at the town of Manzikert on the empire's eastern frontier (map, page 203). The Seljuks were now in a position to overrun Asia Minor.

The Byzantines appealed to European Christians for military help in resisting the Turks. Western Europeans did want to drive the Turks from Christian holy places in the Near East, but they had little interest in restoring lands to the Byzantines. Crusading knights set up their own kingdoms in territories they captured in the Near East. In 1204, during the Fourth Crusade, the Western European knights and Venetian merchants decided to capture the rich city of Constantinople for themselves rather than fight the Muslims. The knights wanted the city's wealth, while the Venetians sought control over the rich Byzantine trade.

The crusaders devastated Constantinople. They destroyed sacred books, vandalized churches, and carried gold, jewels, and works of art back to Western Europe. The Venetians seized islands along Constantinople's major trade routes. Not until 1261 was Constantinople restored to the Byzantines.

Constantinople falls to the Turks. The Byzantine Empire had been disastrously weakened. It also faced problems of crushing taxes, decreasing agricultural production, declining trade, and loss of territory.

The deathblow to the empire was dealt by another group of Turks. The Ottoman Turks (page 221) had accepted Islam and begun to build an empire in Asia Minor. They drove the Byzantines and the earlier Turkish conquerors from Asia Minor and occupied much of the Balkans. By the beginning of the fifteenth century, the Byzantine "empire" consisted of only the city of Constantinople and two small territories in Greece.

In 1453 the Turks attacked Constantinople itself, outnumbering the Byzantines sixteen to one. Aided by a huge cannon that fired thousand-pound iron balls, the Turks broke down Constantinople's great walls. The invaders looted the city and slaughtered thousands of people. After more than a thousand years, the Byzantine Empire had come to an end.

THE INFLUENCE OF BYZANTIUM

The Byzantines influence history. The Byzantine Empire played an important role in world history. While learning declined in Europe in the early Middle Ages, Byzantine scholars were studying the literature, philosophy, science, mathematics, law, and arts of ancient Greece and Rome. Although they made few original contributions, the Byzantines kept much ancient knowledge from being lost. Their work stimulated scholarship in the Muslim world and helped bring about the revival of learning in Western Europe.

Byzantium was the eastern stronghold of Christianity, protecting Europe from invading Islamic armies for centuries. In addition, Orthodox missionaries carried Eastern Christianity and Byzantine culture to many Slavic peoples in southern and eastern Europe. So that the Slavs could read the Bible, two Byzantine missionaries, Cyril and Methodius, invented an alphabet for writing the Slavic language. A form of this Cyrillic (suh-RILL-ik) alphabet is still used in Russian and other Slavic languages.

Byzantine art blends several traditions. The Byzantine artists were influenced by both the

BYZANTINE ART

The Byzantines excelled in making mosaic pictures and icons, and their distinctive style influenced artists in other lands. The mosaic (right) shows the emperor Justinian holding a model of the Hagia Sophia. Another Byzantine mosaic is the picture of Jesus on page 127. The icon above, showing Mary and the infant Jesus, is from Russia.

classical Greco-Roman style and the arts of the Near East. They combined vivid colors and elaborate designs, often using religious themes or symbols. Byzantine artists were especially noted for their skill in making mosaics (moh-ZAY-iks), designs formed from thousands of small pieces of colored stone and glass. Both Greeks and Romans had used mosaics on walls, pavements, and other flat surfaces. The mosaics that decorated Byzantine churches were the most brilliant use of this art form.

Another typical form of Byzantine art was the *icon* (EYE-kon), a small religious image usually painted on wood. Icons, regarded as holy, were kept both in homes and Orthodox churches. Byzantine artisans also were famous for their cut gems, metalwork, and illuminated manuscripts.

Byzantine architecture was also distinctive. After riots and fire destroyed much of Con-

stantinople in 532 (page 202), Justinian undertook a vast program to build fortresses, monasteries, and churches. The city's new cathedral, finished in five years, was Hagia Sophia (HAH-jah soh-FEE-ah), the "Church of Holy Wisdom." It was the most magnificent church in the Mediterranean world at the time. In designing it, Byzantine architects developed a new way of placing a rounded dome over a rectangular building. Light from the forty arched windows in the lofty central dome brilliantly lit the interior of Hagia Sophia. Worshippers were awed by the splendid marble pillars and walls, the mosaics set in gold, and the objects in gold, silver, and ivory decorating the interior.

Later Eastern Orthodox churches usually had the same high central dome and mosaic decorations on the walls, floor, and ceiling. The buildings were in the shape of a squared, or

Greek, cross. Byzantine styles in art and architecture spread to many parts of the empire, particularly the parts of Eastern Europe where missionaries carried the teachings of the Orthodox Church. Richly decorated Greek-cross churches became most common in Greece, the Balkans, and Russia.

EARLY RUSSIA

Russia has ties with Constantinople. Byzantine culture and religion had a great influence on the Russian state that took shape in the tenth century in the easternmost part of Europe. During the ninth century, a band of Vikings called Rus (RUSS) moved into this area of Slavic peoples and set up a string of fortified towns along major rivers. One of these forts was at Kiev (kee-EV); another was at Novgorod (map, page 219).

Viking raiders at first attacked Constantinople, but later became traders. They demanded and got trading rights from the Byzantine emperor and opened new trade routes between the Baltic and Black seas. Furs, amber, and slaves were the basis of the Rus trade with the Byzantines. Rus traders also brought beeswax for candles and honey for sweetening food, exchanging these for Byzantine gold, silver, and silk.

The Russian state forms around Kiev. Located on a high bluff overlooking the Dnieper (NEE-pur) River, the fortified town of Kiev became the center of the first Russian state. It brought together the lands ruled by several princes. Its ties with the Byzantine Empire were strengthened in 957 when the princess Olga visited Constantinople and became a Christian. In about 988 her grandson Vladimir I converted to Eastern Orthodox Christianity, and all the Kievans became Christians. Vladimir then married the sister of the Byzantine emperor. Kiev soon became a resplendent outpost of Byzantine culture.

In Kiev, landownership counted less than control of trade; feudalism as practiced in Western Europe was unknown. The rulers of Kiev, who had the title "grand prince," were merchant-warriors. With their aristocratic followers, called boyars, they collected tribute from their subjects and profited from the trade that linked Constantinople with the Baltic Sea. The rulers of Kiev conferred with the important boyars and the people before making decisions. This made their government flexible, but the influence of powerful boyars often made it unstable.

Invaders attack Kiev and Novgorod. The grand princes of Kiev were often at war with the rulers of lesser towns and with the nomads of the steppes — high plains — of Central Asia. Disaster struck Kiev when nomadic Mongols from Central Asia invaded in 1237. The princes of Kiev, caught in a power struggle among themselves, were no match for the Mongol horsemen. By 1240 the city was devastated, and all Kievan Russia had fallen under Mongol rule (map, page 219). A Catholic monk passing through Kiev in 1245 wrote, "We found an innumerable multitude of dead men's skulls and bones lying upon the earth. It was once a very large and prosperous city, but it is now in a manner brought to nothing; for there do scarce remain two hundred houses, and the inhabitants of these are kept in extreme bondage."

The other early Russian river town, Novgorod, lay farther north. It escaped the Mongols' destruction, although it had to send tribute payments to the Mongol rulers. Led politically by wealthy merchants, Novgorod had close trade ties with the towns of the Hanseatic League (page 177). Protected by wide marshes, Novgorod also was able to resist the attempts of the Swedes and the Teutonic Knights to expand into Russia. In 1240 Prince Alexander of Novgorod defeated invading Swedes at the Neva River (map, page 394). In memory of the victory at the Neva, he became known as Alexander Nevsky, one of the great heroes of Russian history. Two years later Alexander also defeated the invading Teutonic Knights.

Mongols rule Russia. Though some cities remained independent, Russia was under Mongol domination for more than two centuries. During this period of isolation from both Byzantium and Western Europe, there was little political, economic, or cultural development. The wealth and influence of the Orthodox Church grew, for the Mongols did not interfere with the Church or demand tribute from it.

Russian princes, competing for the favors of the Mongol rulers, could not effectively unite against them. In addition, small states grew weaker because their rulers divided the lands among several heirs. Not until the late fourteenth century did the princes of Moscow, leaders in the northeast, become strong enough to bring the Russians together to resist Mongol rule (Chapter 17).

CHECK-UP

1. (a) Why was the Eastern Empire able to survive after the fall of Rome? (b) What different cultural traditions contributed to Byzantine civilization?
2. What was Justinian's greatest achievement as emperor?
3. (a) What groups of people threatened the Byzantine Empire in the seventh and eighth centuries? (b) How did the Byzantines defend Constantinople against the Arabs? (c) Why was the defeat of the Arabs important?
4. (a) What issues divided Eastern and Western Christianity? (b) How did religious differences cause political differences?
5. (a) How did the Crusades affect the Byzantine Empire? (b) When and how did the final collapse of the empire come about?
6. (a) Describe the Byzantines' contributions to scholarship and the arts. (b) How and where has Byzantine influence survived?
7. (a) How were Russia's ties with the Byzantine Empire established? (b) Why and how did the trade ties of Kiev and Novgorod differ? (c) How did the Mongol invasion affect the trading towns of Kiev and Novgorod?

2 Islam Spreads in Asia and Africa

The Muslim invaders who weakened and finally conquered the Byzantine Empire were followers of a new religion that began in the seventh century among the Arabs of the Arabian Peninsula. Inspired by the teachings of a remarkable leader, the armies of the new faith built an empire that stretched from Spain to India. A new civilization centered on the Muslim faith developed in these lands.

Most Arabs are nomads. The Arabian Peninsula (map, page 211) is mainly a dry, rocky plateau. Farming and village life developed only in scattered oases, where there was water from springs or wells. Most of the peoples of Arabia were nomads called bedouin (BED-oo-in), who spoke a Semitic language, Arabic. They lived in tribal groups, moving their tents from one oasis to another to find pasture and water for their herds of camels, goats, and sheep. The bedouin traded with the agricultural communities of the oases. They provided camels and served as guides for the caravan trade across the peninsula.

Living in a harsh desert environment led the bedouin to prize loyalty to the tribe, valor in combat, hospitality to guests, and personal honor. One bedouin tribe occasionally raided another tribe. Bedouin tribes also made raids on merchant caravans, or the villages in the oases. Individuals depended on the tribe for protection; there was no written law.

Not all Arabs were nomads, however. Towns grew up around oases and on the coast, where ocean winds brought moisture to the land. Linked by sea routes and caravan trails, some towns became centers of trade.

Arabs follow different religions. The trading town of Mecca was also a holy city. Many Arabs traveled to Mecca to worship at an ancient holy well and at a shrine called the Kaaba (KAH-ah-bah). The shrine contained statues of many deities as well as a black stone (probably a meteorite) that Arabs believed was sacred.

Most desert Arabs worshiped tribal gods that they believed were found in stones, the desert sand, and the sun and stars. In the towns and trading centers, however, many Arabs had acquired some beliefs and traditions of Judaism and Christianity. Some Arabs had converted to these faiths.

ISLAMIC RELIGIOUS ART

Most Islamic religious art consists of decorative writing made up of passages from the Koran. Among the few pictures of Mohammed is this miniature, which shows the prophet with a halo of flame, his features hidden by a veil. The tile (right) is a picture of the Kaaba at Mecca, the holiest shrine of Islam.

Mohammed establishes a new faith. Mohammed was an Arab born in Mecca about the year 570. As a young man, he took part in the caravan trade, becoming known for his honesty and good business sense. Mohammed married Khadija, a widow who ran her own prosperous business, and became a successful trader.

According to tradition, Mohammed often went to meditate in a cave in the hills outside Mecca. When he was about 40, he believed he had a vision of the angel Gabriel, who ordered him, "Recite in the name of thy Lord!" Mohammed was convinced that he had been chosen to serve as a prophet and bring the Arabs a new faith.

Mohammed rejected the many deities of the tribal religions. The new faith he offered the Arabs was monotheistic, like Judaism and Christianity. It is called Islam (iss-lahm), which in Arabic means surrender to Allah, or God. The followers of Islam are called Muslims, "those who submit to Allah's will."

The Koran outlines Muslim beliefs. The Koran is the holy book of Islam. Muslims believe it contains the word of Allah as it was revealed to Mohammed. They believe the Koran should not be questioned or changed. Even translations from Arabic are discouraged.

Muslims view Allah as the creator and ruler of heaven and earth, an all-powerful God who is merciful, compassionate, and just. According to the Koran, on the Day of Judgment, unbelievers and the wicked will be dragged into a fearful place of "scorching winds and seething water. . . . Sinners shall eat bitter fruit and drink boiling water. . . ." Faithful Muslims who have led virtuous lives are promised a garden of pleasure called Paradise.

Muslims believe that Islam is the completion of the beliefs of Judaism and Christianity. They regard Jesus and the Hebrew prophets as messengers of God, but they believe that Mohammed was the last and greatest of the prophets. Muslims view Mohammed as entirely human, not divine; they worship only Allah.

Muslims have religious obligations. Mohammed insisted that men and women follow the way of Allah. Individual Muslims have five religious duties, called the "Five Pillars of Islam." (1) A Muslim must accept and repeat the statement of faith: "There is no God but Allah, and Mohammed is his Prophet." (2) At least five times a day, the believer faces the holy city of Mecca and prays. (3) Muslims have a religious duty to be generous to the poor. (4) During the holy month of Ramadan (the ninth month in the Muslim calendar), believers do not eat or drink between sunrise and sunset. (5) Muslims are expected to make at least one pilgrimage to the holy city of Mecca if they can afford to do so.

Mohammed flees from Mecca. Mohammed's teachings aroused great hostility in Mecca. Islam's belief in one God upset those who believed in the tribal gods. Mohammed also spoke out against rich merchants and against moneylenders who charged high interest on borrowed money. To escape persecution, Mohammed and a small band of followers left Mecca in 622 for Medina, a town about 280 miles away. Their flight is known as the Hegira (hih-JY-ruh), or "breaking of former ties." An important event in Muslim history, it is commemorated by yearly pilgrimages. The date of the Hegira became Year One of the Muslim calendar.

Many people in Medina welcomed Mohammed as a community leader. He met with people of all classes and races, for all believers in Islam, rich or poor, were considered equal. He gained political power and respect as a judge, making decisions on family relations, inheritance of property, and punishment for crimes. Mohammed rejected traditional tribal law as a way of settling disputes. The law of Islam was to be the final authority.

Not all the people of Medina accepted Mohammed's leadership. The Jews of Medina in particular would not accept Mohammed as a prophet. Although Mohammed had adopted some Jewish customs, he now began to persecute Arabian Jews, seizing the farmlands they held around Medina.

Islam makes converts by force. Mohammed began to preach a holy war against pagans and nonbelievers. Making alliances with other bedouin tribes, he ordered his followers to raid the trading caravans from Mecca and to subdue unfriendly tribes.

In 630 Mecca surrendered to a Muslim army without a fight. Bedouin tribes all over Arabia began to accept Islam and recognize the authority of the Prophet, as Mohammed came to be called. By the time of his death in 632, Mohammed had united the often feuding Arabian tribes into a powerful force dedicated to Allah and Islam.

Mohammed's successors extend Islamic power. After Mohammed's death his friend Abu Bakr became his successor and was given the title of *caliph* (KAY-lif). The caliph was regarded as the Defender of the Faith, who was given his authority by Allah. As the political leader of a religious state, he governed in accordance with the law set forth in the Koran.

Islam gave the many Arab tribes the unity, discipline, and dedication to succeed in wars of conquest. Weakened by warfare and internal problems, the Persian and Byzantine empires could not withstand the armies of Islam. Under the first four caliphs, who ruled from 632 to 661, Muslim armies conquered Palestine, Syria, Egypt, and most of Persia. Arab warriors went into battle with a sword and a militant faith. They believed they were engaged in a holy war to spread Islam to nonbelievers, or infidels (IN-fih-delz). According to the Koran, those who died in a holy war, or *jihad* (jih-HAHD), were assured of a place in Paradise.

New rulers cause a division in Islam. The fourth caliph, Ali, was married to Mohammed's daughter Fatima (FAH-tih-mah). When Ali was murdered in 661, a member of the powerful Umayyad (oo-MY-yad) family claimed the caliphate. Rivalry broke out between the Umayyad supporters and the Shi'a (SHEE-ah),[1] those who thought that only direct descendants of the Prophet should rule. The Shi'a refused to accept the Umayyads and broke away from the main group of Muslims. For hundreds of years

---

[1] About ten percent of modern Muslims belong to Shi'ite sects. They are the majority in present-day Iran and Iraq.

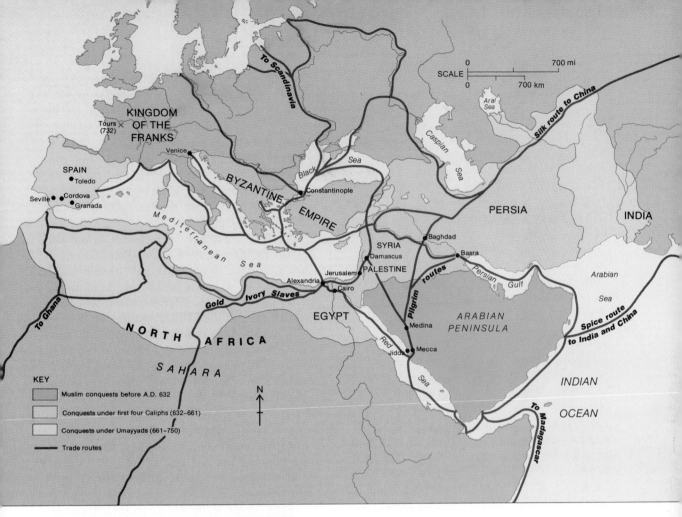

The Expansion of Islam, 632–750

This map shows the lands ruled by the Muslims in 632 and the territory that was added to them. What additions were made by the first four caliphs? by the Umayyads?

the Shi'a made attempts to regain the caliphate. Over time Shi'ite Muslims developed some beliefs and traditions different from those of traditional Muslims, known as the Sunni.

The Umayyads create an empire. With the support of the Muslim majority, the Umayyads ruled from 661 to 750 and made widespread conquests. Islam's territory in the east extended into India and to the borders of China. The Muslim advance into southeastern Europe was stopped in 718 by the Byzantine defenders of Constantinople. To the west, Arabs and Moors took North Africa from the Byzantines and most of Spain from the Visigoths. The Muslims began to move farther northward in Europe but were stopped by the Franks at the Battle of Tours in 732.

The Umayyad rulers moved the Muslim capital to Damascus, Syria. Arab Muslims, however, still held the most important positions in the government, the army, and society. This was resented by Persians, Syrians, Egyptians, and other non-Arabs who had become Muslims. In 750, several discontented groups, both Arabs and non-Arabs, rebelled against the Umayyad rulers and put a new dynasty in power.

The Muslim Empire flourishes. The new ruling family was the Abbasids (uh-BAS-idz), who remained the rulers of Islam for 500 years. Though they also were Arabs, the Abbasids had a wider outlook than the Umayyads. They chose their officials from many peoples, not just Arabs. Moving the capital to Baghdad in 763,

As a sign of hospitality Muslims offered guests water for washing, often in a fine ewer or vase (above). Items such as this and the rug on page 218 were among the goods traded by Muslim merchants.

conquest. Their attempts to reconquer Spain continued for 500 years (page 173). Despite this conflict, Muslim and Christian cultures in Spain existed side by side for centuries and greatly influenced one another.

The Muslims expand trade. Muslim conquests greatly stimulated trade and travel. By the tenth century Arabic was spoken by many different peoples from Spain to lands east of Persia, making communication easier. Adventurous Arab merchants reached Ceylon and Malaya by sea and even established a colony in Canton, China. Merchants and travelers also journeyed by caravan on the overland routes across Central Asia. Pilgrims came to Mecca from all parts of the Muslim world.

The Muslims dominated trade with eastern Asia until the fifteenth century. Arab traders brought spices from Asia and sold them to Venetian merchants for their customers in Europe. Through Baghdad, at the heart of the Muslim world, passed Chinese porcelain, African gold, and Egyptian grain.

Islam continues to expand. During the long reign of the Abbasid caliphs (750–1258), Islam continued to gain converts. Its cultural influence was felt from Spain to India. From northern Africa, traders and conquerors carried Islam south and west to other parts of Africa (Chapter 13). Still another Islamic empire was established in India (Chapter 11).

they established a brilliant court where science, art, and learning flourished. Under Abbasid rule, Persian, Arab, and other influences combined to create a distinctive Muslim culture.

Umayyad rule continues in Moorish Spain. When the Umayyad rulers were overthrown, one surviving member of the family fled to Muslim Spain. By 756, he ruled most of the Iberian peninsula. Moorish Spain,[2] like other centers of Islamic culture, flourished while the rest of Europe was struggling with the hardships of the early Middle Ages. By the tenth century Cordova, the Moorish capital, was a center of learning, arts, and scholarship, rivaling the court at Baghdad. Toledo, Seville, and Granada were also rich, thriving cities. Agriculture, industry, and trade prospered in Spain.

The Christian kingdoms in the northern Iberian peninsula never accepted the Muslim

---

[2]Muslim Spain was often called "Moorish Spain" after the Moors, the North Africans who had first conquered it for Islam in 711.

CHECK-UP

1. Vocabulary: *caliph.*
2. (a) How did the geography of Arabia affect the growth of towns? (b) What qualities did the bedouin tribes prize?
3. (a) Who was Mohammed? (b) What five religious duties must Muslims perform? (c) What was the Hegira?
4. (a) Why did Islam spread so rapidly? (b) How far east and west did the Umayyads extend their empire?
5. (a) What city became the Abbasid capital? (b) How did Abbasid rule differ from Umayyad? (c) Where did Umayyad rule continue after the empire came under Abbasid control?
6. What part did the Muslims play in trade between Asia and Europe?

3 Islamic Culture Reaches Its Height

Islamic civilization reached its greatest glory at the end of the eighth century, under the Abbasid rulers at Baghdad. Mohammed had established not only a new religion but also a new kind of society. Islamic beliefs were expressed in government, the arts, social customs, and business dealings. The Islamic faith and the Arabic language united people from different backgrounds.

Islam allows other customs and beliefs. Muslim rulers defended, enforced, and spread the faith through laws laid down in the Koran. Islamic belief held that all Muslims were equals, regardless of their social class or race. In the lands they conquered, Muslims allowed other believers in one God to practice their religions and customs and have their own communities. Jews and Christians, called "People of the Book," had to obey Muslim laws and pay a special tax. People who followed pagan religions, however, were forced to convert.

Islam improves the lot of slaves. Slavery was common in most cultures of the time. In Muslim lands the lives of slaves improved, for the Koran called for humane treatment and permitted slaves to own property. Most slaves in the Muslim world were household servants and helpers in workshops. Some were well educated and became government officials, entertainers, or soldiers.

The Koran defines women's roles. The Koran also gave women more protection than traditional Arab law, although they did not have equality with men. The Koran forbade the bedouin custom of killing unwanted infant girls. It also gave women a certain share in family inheritances and let them own property. A divorced wife could keep part of her dowry, the property her family gave her when she married. She was entitled to support from her former husband and also could marry again. A number of Muslim women, particularly in the caliphs' court and the upper classes, were well educated and became known as artists, writers, and supporters of the arts.

Nonetheless, the Koran also stated that "men have authority over women because Allah has made the one superior to the other." A Muslim man could have as many as four wives if he could provide well for all of them, but a woman could have only one husband. It was nearly impossible for an unhappy wife to get a divorce, but a man could divorce his wife simply by saying three times, "Thou art dismissed."

The lives of Muslim women gradually became more restricted, particularly in towns and among the upper classes. It became customary for a woman to wear a heavy veil, covering all but her eyes, when she went out of her home. At home — whether in a palace or a tent — women lived in special separate quarters (called the harem). No men except family members could enter this area.

Muslim civilization makes notable advances. When Islamic civilization was at its height, people in the cities and royal courts of the Muslim world lived more comfortably than people in medieval Europe. Cordova in Moorish Spain had paved streets that were lighted at night. In many cities, pipes carried water to the

TIMETABLE

Islamic Civilization

622	Mohammed and his followers leave Mecca (the Hegira)
632	The caliphs begin to extend Islamic power.
661	The assassination of Ali divides the Muslims into Shi'ites and Sunni.
732	The Muslim advance in Western Europe is halted at Tours.
763	The Abbasid court moves to Baghdad.
1220	Genghis Khan leads the Mongol invasion of the Muslim world.
1258	The Mongols take Baghdad, ending Abbasid rule.
1453	The Ottoman Turks capture Constantinople.
1526	Suleiman leads Ottoman forces into southeastern Europe.

This panel of tiles from Persia gives an idea of the luxury that surrounded an upper-class Muslim woman. It shows a servant waiting upon a noblewoman in her private garden. While women wore heavy veils in public, they went unveiled in their own quarters. Their clothes were made of fabrics from many places — muslin from Iraq, damask from Damascus, and Chinese silk.

baths and courtyard fountains of private homes. Muslim agriculture and irrigation were far more efficient than the farming methods used in Western Europe. The Muslims had already learned how to keep the soil fertile by planting different crops in different years. They introduced Arabian horses to Europe, as well as a variety of new foods, including oranges, lemons, and melons.

Muslim artisans developed great skill. Persian carpets (page 218) decorated the floors and walls of both palaces and tents. Syria and Spain produced such fine swords that "Damascus blades" and "Toledo steel" were prized throughout the world. Artisans in Cordova became famous for gold, silver, and leatherwork.

Muslim rulers encourage scholarship. Learning in the Muslim world was also more advanced than in medieval Europe. Mohammed encouraged education, saying that "the seeking of knowledge is a duty of every Muslim, man or woman." The Muslim world therefore valued scholarship, and some caliphs established libraries and study rooms in their palaces where scholars could hold classes. Great universities developed in many parts of the Muslim world, from Cordova in Spain to Timbuktu in Africa. The university at Cordova attracted brilliant scholars, Christian and Jew-

ish as well as Muslim. Ancient works in Greek were translated into Arabic, which became the language of learning and literature for many Spanish and Portuguese Christians.

The caliphs who ruled in Baghdad at the height of the golden age were Harun al-Rashid (786–809) and his son al-Mamun (813–833). They established a college and sponsored the collection and translation into Arabic of Greek, Latin, Hebrew, Sanskrit, and Persian works. Interested in different cultures, Harun al-Rashid corresponded with other rulers, among them Charlemagne and the emperor of China.

Muslim scholars study mathematics and science. The spread of Islam gave Muslim mathematicians and scientists access to the works of earlier thinkers in many lands. From India they acquired the concept of the zero and "Arabic" numerals, passing these ideas on to the West. A ninth-century Arab mathematician wrote the first work on algebra; others worked out new ideas in geometry and trigonometry. Arab scientists discovered some basic chemical processes and formulas and made new compounds. (*Algebra, alcohol,* and *alkali* are all derived from Arabic words.)

Muslim astronomers tested and corrected the observations made by ancient astronomers, particularly the Greek scientist Ptolemy (page

115). Observatories were built in the great Muslim centers at Cordova, Toledo, Baghdad, and Cairo. There astronomers worked out new ways of calculating the movements of stars and planets. They made accurate star maps, naming such stars as Betelgeuse, Rigel, and Aldebaran. The Persian poet Omar Khayyám (ky-YAHM), who is best known for the collection of poems called the *Rubáiyát,* was also a mathematician and astronomer.

The Muslims make advances in medicine. Using the medical knowledge of the ancient Greeks, physicians in Muslim lands became the best-trained and most skillful doctors of the time. Surgeons performed amputations and removed cancerous tissue. Muslim advances in chemistry created new medicines and anesthetics that were used in performing operations. Hospitals were efficient; the best had separate wards for fevers, surgical cases, and eye diseases.

The Persian al-Razi, or Rhazes (RAY-zeez), headed the hospital in Baghdad in the ninth century. He wrote a medical encyclopedia in which he discussed measles, kidney stones, poisons, skin diseases, and ways of maintaining one's health. He carefully noted the symptoms of various illnesses. The works of Rhazes, translated into Latin, were widely consulted by doctors in medieval Europe.

Muslim thinkers study classical philosophy. Muslim scholars translated and studied the works of Greek philosophers. These scholars played an important role in the revival of learning in medieval Western Europe.

The most eminent Muslim thinker was Avicenna (ah-vih-SEN-ah), whose name in Arabic was ibn-Sina. Born in Afghanistan in 980, Avicenna was a poet, doctor, scientist, and philosopher who wrote about every field of knowledge, relying heavily on Aristotle (page 89). Avicenna's *Canon of Medicine,* based on Greek knowledge, was widely used by physicians in both Muslim and Christian lands.

Another giant of Muslim learning was Averroës (ah-VEHR-oh-eez), or ibn-Rushd. Born in Spain in 1126 into a family of religious scholars and judges, Averroës became chief judge in Cordova. His commentaries on Aristotle's writings were read by medieval Christian philosophers. Averroës' attempts to reconcile Greek methods of logic with Islamic doctrine had a great influence on the Scholastics (page 183).

Ibn-Khaldun (1332–1406), a North African historian, judge, and politician, developed a new approach to writing history. He studied geographic and economic conditions, trying to find a pattern that would explain why civilizations develop, flourish, and decline. "The essentials of historical science," he wrote, "are the examination and verification of facts, the careful investigation of the causes which brought about those facts, and a sound knowledge of the manner in which events have taken place."

Classic Muslim literature develops. Because the Koran was not allowed to be translated, educated people throughout the Muslim world learned Arabic. The Koran set the style for other Islamic literature, which included histories, geographies, philosophical and scientific works, and, above all, poetry. The caliphs, many of whom were skilled poets, encouraged writers.

Folk tales, fantasies, and legends were popular forms of Muslim literature. Once the court moved to Baghdad, much literature came to be written in the Persian language, using Arabic script. The world-famous *Thousand and One Nights* (sometimes called *The Arabian Nights*) is set in Harun al-Rashid's Baghdad, but it is a collection of stories from India, Persia, Arabia, and other lands. Among the well-known tales are those about Aladdin and his wonderful lamp and Sinbad the Sailor.

Religion inspires art and architecture. In any Muslim city or village the mosque (MOSK), the Muslim place of worship, stood out from all the other buildings. The mosque was a constant reminder of the Islamic faith. Its slender minaret, or tower, was the tallest structure in a town. From it, a muezzin (myoo-EZ-in), or prayer leader, called the faithful to prayer five times a day.

In building mosques, tombs, palaces, and private homes, Muslim architects adapted features from other styles. They transformed the solid rounded arch of the Romans to a delicate "horseshoe" arch held up by slender columns.

Landmarks in Technology

MUSLIM ACHIEVEMENTS

While the Muslims emphasized scientific theory rather than practical use, they nevertheless made advances in technology. Astronomers used lenses to improve telescopic observations, and engineers applied knowledge of geometry to building. Using new techniques of iron-making, Muslim craftsmen produced exceptionally fine swords. The Muslims also invented the first mechanical clock.

In agricultural technology, the Muslims improved on Persian irrigation methods, built aqueducts, and spread the use of the Persian windmill. To ventilate homes, Muslim architects constructed towers to catch the wind. The Muslims served as channels for the preservation and spread of knowledge from ancient Persia, Greece, and India. They laid the groundwork for the technological achievements of many later peoples.

To get accurate information for his map (left), geographer Al-Idrisi sent men to different parts of the Muslim world to do research and make drawings. The map is designed so that one looks upward from northern Europe at the bottom of the map toward Arabia and the Indian Ocean. The proof in Arabic of one of Euclid's theorems in geometry (above) reflects Muslim interest in mathematics. The Muslims used geometry to design mosques and palaces. To decorate these buildings, they developed complex designs using geometric figures.

Muslim observatories brought scientists from many fields together. This scene (left) shows some of the tools they used: compass, quadrant, astrolabe, globe, builder's square, and plumb. Architects used the builder's square and plumb to build walls and floors that were straight. Some astronomical instruments were used to map the skies (above, a painting of the constellations called the Great Bear and Little Bear). Other tools helped scientists make more accurate maps, measure the depth of wells and the height of mountains, tell time, and study the motions of planets (left, a diagram of an eclipse of the moon). Muslim work in astronomy provided the foundation for later advances in navigation.

Magic Carpets

In Arabian folk tales, heroes used a flying carpet to travel magically from place to place. Outside the world of the storyteller's imagination, Muslims found many practical uses for beautiful handmade carpets. The floors and walls of mosques, palaces, houses, and tents were covered with rugs in glowing colors. Even today, many faithful Muslims carry a small rug to use in their daily prayers.

The ancient skills of making carpets are still carried on in Iran (Persia), Arabia, Turkey, and other Muslim countries. Carpets are made by knotting thousands of small pieces of wool yarn onto a background fabric. Some very fine Indian rugs have as many as 2,400 knots in a square inch.

Many carpets have intricately interwoven geometric designs (right). Other patterns show fruit, flowers, blossoming trees, and animals. In one huge carpet in a Persian palace, pearls and jewels supposedly were used in fruit and flower designs, while a border of emeralds represented a green meadow.

Domed roofs in Byzantine style made building interiors airy and open. Mosaics of light and dark stone or glazed tiles were formed into graceful geometric patterns on walls, roofs, and courtyards. There were no statues or paintings of religious figures in mosques, because the Koran forbade representing living creatures. Passages from the Koran were written in decorative Arabic script on both the inside and outside walls.

Persian artists excelled in delicate miniature paintings, which were influenced by Chinese art. Scenes showing historical figures, lovers, hunters, or warriors often were used as book illustrations or painted on pottery. Some details in these miniatures were so small that they were painted with a single hair. Like other aspects of Islamic culture, styles in art and architecture had a widespread influence throughout the Muslim world.

CHECK-UP

1. (a) In what ways did religious ideas influence the Muslim state? (b) How did the Muslims treat believers of other faiths?
2. (a) What attitude did Islam take toward slavery? (b) How did the status of women change under Islamic law?
3. (a) How did life in Muslim lands compare with life in medieval Europe? (b) How did Muslim rulers encourage learning?
4. (a) In what fields of science were the Muslims particularly advanced? (b) What were some specific accomplishments in each of these fields?
5. How did each of the following contribute to both Muslim and European learning: (a) Rhazes, (b) Avicenna, (c) Averroës?
6. (a) Why did educated Muslims in other countries learn Arabic? (b) How did religious beliefs influence Muslim art and architecture?

4 New Empires Dominate the Muslim World

The Arab Muslims had built a vast empire stretching from India to Spain. The empire was unified by a common language (Arabic), a common faith, and a common culture. By the eleventh century, however, the empire founded by the Arabs was losing its position of dominance in the Islamic world.

Invaders threaten the Muslim world. In the late tenth century, the Seljuk Turks, originally from Central Asia, entered Muslim lands and converted to Islam. The Seljuks soon conquered much of Persia, Syria, and Palestine and took control of Asia Minor from the Byzantines. While the Abbasid caliphs in Baghdad remained the religious and cultural leaders of Islam, Seljuk sultans had the political power. The Seljuk empire, however, lasted only until the end of the eleventh century, when it broke up into smaller states.

In the eleventh and twelfth centuries, the Muslims lost Sicily to Norman knights and large parts of Spain to the Christian kingdoms (map, page 174). Taking advantage of Seljuk weakness in the Near East, European crusaders carved out their own kingdoms from Muslim lands.

Genghis Khan unites Mongol herders. In the thirteenth century a new wave of invaders burst out of Central Asia. They were Mongols, nomadic tribes who for centuries had wandered the highlands and plains of Mongolia, fighting one another and seeking pasture for their herds. Early in the thirteenth century, a remarkable leader united the Mongol tribes. His name was

The Mongol Empire, 1294

The Mongols built one of the world's largest empires. What Muslim lands (map, page 211) came under Mongol rule? What lands did the Mongols attack but fail to conquer?

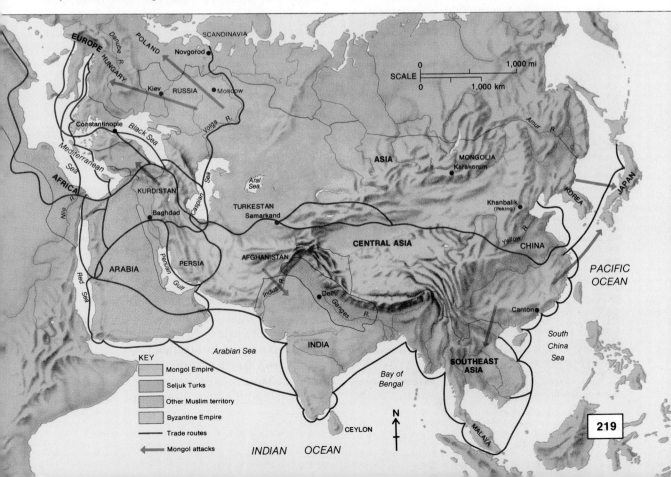

Temujin, but he was known by the title Genghis Khan, which means "ruler of the world."

Genghis Khan demonstrated extraordinary skill as a military strategist. In a short time he molded the Mongol horsemen into a well-disciplined, fast-moving military force and became one of the greatest conquerors in world history. Eager for plunder and glory, Genghis Khan first turned to the rich civilization of China. By the year 1215 his forces had destroyed its capital city and gained enormous wealth.

The Mongols extend their conquests. With China under their control, the Mongols turned westward. The superb Mongol archers, mounted on fast-moving ponies, poured across Asia into Persia. Killing and burning to terror-

Ranks of Ottoman soldiers moving through the hills suggest the military power that made the Turks feared in Asia and Europe. This scene comes from a history of Suleiman (page 221).

ize the peoples whose lands they invaded, the Mongols destroyed schools, libraries, mosques, and palaces and slaughtered thousands of Muslims. By 1227, when Genghis Khan died, the eastern part of the Muslim world had fallen to the Mongols.

The Mongol advance did not stop with the death of Genghis Khan. In less than a century the Mongols built the largest empire the world had ever known (map, page 219). Some Mongol forces swept across Russia and threatened central Europe. Others continued the advance on Muslim lands in the Near East. Genghis's grandson, Hulagu (hoo-LAH-goo), invaded Persia. Storming Baghdad in 1258, the Mongols burned, plundered, and killed with savage fury. They devastated the palaces, libraries, and schools that had made Baghdad the cultural capital and glory of the Islamic world. Among the 50,000 people slaughtered in the city was the last Abbasid caliph. A year later the Mongols marched into Syria, again killing and looting. The Mongols' brutal advance westward was finally stopped in 1260 in Palestine by the army of the Mamluks, the Turkish rulers of Egypt. In the same year, the Mongol Empire was divided among several princes. The most powerful was Kublai Khan, ruler of China (page 259).

Tamerlane leads new Mongol invasions. By the beginning of the fourteenth century, the Muslim world seemed more secure. In the Near East, the Muslims had recaptured the last Christian state founded by crusaders. The Mongols had by this time converted to Islam. They remained in Persia but could advance no farther westward.

In the late 1300's the Mongols once again menaced the Near East. Tamerlane (Timur the Lame) was the son of a Central Asian chieftain who claimed descent from Genghis Khan. His armies swept through Afghanistan, Kurdistan, Persia, and Syria. They destroyed Delhi in India and occupied Moscow in Russia for a year. To discourage resistance, Tamerlane built huge pyramids from the heads of thousands of slaughtered victims. After Tamerlane's death in 1404, his empire disintegrated.

The Ottoman Turks build a new empire. The collapse of Tamerlane's empire left the way open for another group of empire-builders

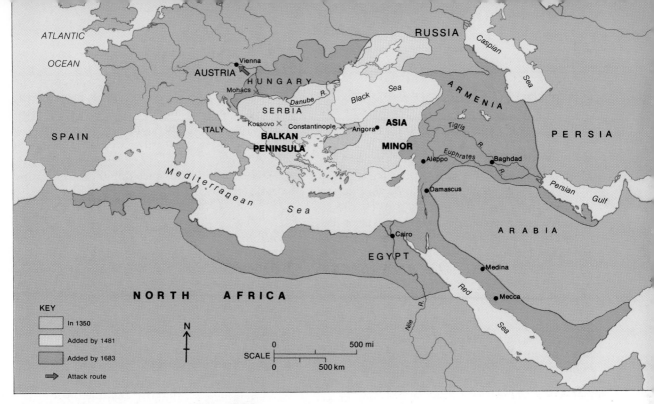

The Ottoman Empire, 1350–1683

The Ottoman Empire included land on three continents. Compare this empire with that ruled by the Muslims (map, page 211). What lands were included in both empires? Which Ottoman lands had not been ruled by the Muslims?

— the Ottoman Turks. In the last part of the thirteenth century, the leaders of several Turkish tribes had been granted land in Asia Minor by the Seljuks. One warrior, Osman, established a small but strong state. In the late 1300's, the Ottoman Turks (whose name came from Osman) overran Asia Minor and much of the Balkan Peninsula. They lost Asia Minor to Tamerlane but resumed their conquests after his death. In 1453 the Ottoman Turks took Constantinople, ending the Byzantine Empire (page 205). They now ruled an empire that stretched from the Danube River along the entire Black Sea.

The Ottoman Empire reached its height in the sixteenth century, with the conquest of Egypt, North Africa, Syria, and the Arabian coast (including the Muslim centers at Mecca and Medina). Suleiman "the Magnificent," who ruled as Ottoman sultan from 1520 to 1566, invaded southeastern Europe. His armies crushed Hungarian forces at Mohács (MOH-hahch) in 1526 and moved westward. The Turkish siege of Vienna in 1529 failed, but the Ottomans gained control of parts of present-

day Austria, Hungary, Poland, and Russia. They developed an effective system of administration that kept part of their empire in existence into the twentieth century.

Although there was once again a unified Islamic empire, it lacked the vitality that had kept the Muslim world more advanced than Europe during the Middle Ages. The Ottomans did not restore the cultural brilliance, the thriving trade, or the prosperity that the Muslim world had known under the Abbasid caliphs of Baghdad.

CHECK-UP

1. How was the Muslim world weakened (a) by the Seljuk Turks? (b) by Christian crusaders from Western Europe?
2. (a) Who were the Mongols? (b) What territories did the Mongol Empire include? (c) How did the rise of the Mongols affect various parts of the Muslim world?
3. (a) Who were the Ottoman Turks? (b) Why was their capture of Constantinople important? (c) What lands came under Ottoman control?

Chapter 10 Review

Chapter Summary

Byzantine civilization took shape in the eastern half of the divided Roman Empire and was based on Greek language and culture. The Orthodox Church of Constantinople grew apart from the Latin Church in Rome, reaching a final break in 1054. The Byzantine Empire retook much of the territory of the Romans and for a time protected Christian Europe from Muslim invasion. It gradually lost territory to a series of invaders and finally fell to the Ottoman Turks in 1453. The Byzantines preserved many elements of Greco-Roman civilization. Byzantine religion and culture spread to Eastern Europe, particularly influencing Kievan Russia.

The religion of Islam was founded by Mohammed in Arabia in the seventh century. Muslim armies spread the new faith in the Near East, Africa, and Asia. At its height, the Muslim Empire spread from Spain to India. Muslim scholars studied classical works and made advances in science and medicine.

Invaders from Central Asia weakened the Byzantine and Islamic empires. Much of the Muslim world fell to the Mongols led by Genghis Khan. Finally, the Ottoman Turks took both Byzantine and Muslim lands into their growing empire.

Vocabulary Review

1. Look up each of the following terms in the Glossary at the back of this book. On a separate sheet of paper, write a sentence for each term, showing that you understand its meaning: *caliph, empire, monotheism, nomad.*
2. Explain the relationship between the terms in each of the following pairs:
(a) mosque; mosaic.
(b) *jihad;* infidel.
(c) Umayyads; Abbasids.
(d) patriarch; Pope.
(e) Muslims; Moorish Spain.
(f) Allah; Koran.

People to Identify

Identify the following people and tell why each was important:

1. Justinian	7. Omar Khayyám
2. Fatima	8. Genghis Khan
3. Suleiman	9. Theodora
4. Mohammed	10. Tamerlane
5. Ibn-Khaldun	11. Averroës
6. Alexander Nevsky	

Relating Geography and History

1. **Locating places.** Locate each of the following on a map in this chapter:
(a) Mecca   (g) Baghdad
(b) Medina   (h) Constantinople
(c) Kiev   (i) Vienna
(d) Mohács   (j) Black Sea
(e) Cordova   (k) Balkan Peninsula
(f) Damascus   (l) Danube River
2. **Reports.** The city of Constantinople, now over 2,500 years old, has been known by three different names over the centuries. Write a report on this great city and include the following information: (a) its present name; (b) the name of the country of which it is now a part; (c) reminders of the city's Byzantine past that are still in existence. Include a map showing the city's location and tell what is unique about this location.
3. **Comparing maps.** Compare the map of the Mongol Empire on page 219 with the map of the Ottoman Empire on page 221. (a) On each map, locate the following places of interest: Constantinople, Baghdad, the Mediterranean Sea, the Black Sea, the Nile River, Arabia, and Persia. (b) Which empire included land on three continents? Name those continents. (c) What lands did the Ottomans control that had not been part of the earlier Mongol Empire?

Discussion Questions

1. (a) Describe the powers that were held by Byzantine rulers. (b) Why were there frequent power struggles within the empire?
2. (a) How did foreign trade enrich Byzantine civilization? (b) What contributions did the Byzantines themselves make in scholarship, art, and architecture?
3. (a) Describe the influence of the following peoples on early Russia: (a) Rus, (b) Byzantines, (c) Mongols.

4. (a) What contributions did the Muslims make to science, medicine, and mathematics? (b) What Muslim achievements were passed on to Western civilization?

5. (a) How did religious faith help the Muslims build an empire? (b) How were government and religion related in Muslim society?

6. (a) What groups invaded parts of the Muslim Empire between the eleventh and the fourteenth centuries? (b) What effect did each of these invasions have on the Empire?

Reading Primary Sources

Alexius I was the Byzantine emperor from 1081 to 1118. Soon after his coronation, he left the capital at Constantinople to fight invading Franks. The following passage is from the decree by which he designated his mother the head of the government during his absence. Read the passage. Then answer the questions below.

> Now I, your sovereign, am preparing . . . for a campaign against the enemies of Rome, and with great care am collecting and organizing an army, yet I deem the administration of financial and political affairs a matter of supreme importance. And certainly I have found [a way to continue] . . . good government, that is, that the whole administration should be entrusted to my . . . most deeply honored mother [Anna Dalassena]. I, your sovereign, therefore decree . . . that . . . whatever orders . . . she shall give, provided they bear her seal, . . . these shall be accounted as coming from my sovereign hand. . . . With regard to promotions and successions to the judgeships of the higher and lower courts, . . . my holy mother shall have sovereign power to do whatsoever shall seem good to her. . . . And again with regard to increase of salaries and . . . [exemption from] taxes, these my mother shall settle absolutely. For her words and her commands shall be considered as given by me, your sovereign, and not one of them shall be annulled, but shall remain valid and in force for the coming years.

(a) What was the major concern of Alexius at the time the decree was made? (b) When Anna Dalassena put her seal on a written document, what was to be the effect? (c) What appointments did Alexius specify that his mother might make?

(d) What kind of power did Alexius's mother have over salaries and taxes? (e) What evidence is there in the decree that the acts of Anna Dalassena during her son's absence would remain in force upon his return?

Skill Activities

1. Reports. Find information about one of the following topics and prepare a report: (a) the Islamic calendar; (b) Damascus steel; (c) dervishes (members of certain Muslim religious orders); (d) Byzantine mosaics; (e) the position of women in a present-day Muslim country; (f) the Hagia Sophia; (g) the Alhambra (the castle of the Moorish rulers in Spain); (h) Arabian horses.

2. Bulletin boards. Make a bulletin-board display featuring Byzantine and Islamic architecture. Label each illustration with the following information: (a) the location and purpose of the building; (b) the approximate date of its construction; (c) its special features; (d) whether it is an example of Islamic or Byzantine architecture.

3. Writing a summary. Reread Section 1 of this chapter, "The Byzantines Develop a Rich Civilization," and write a one-page summary of the reasons given there for the rise and fall of Byzantine civilization.

4. Comparing timetables. This chapter covers two great medieval civilizations, the Byzantine and the Islamic. Refer to the Timetables on pages 204 and 213 and answer the following questions: (a) When did the Seljuk Turks defeat the Byzantines? (b) Which happened first, the Hegira or the fall of the Roman Empire in the West? (c) Which happened first, the final break between the Orthodox and the Catholic churches or the division of the Muslims into Shi'ites and Sunni? (d) How many years passed between the time the crusaders captured Constantinople and the time Constantinople fell to the Ottoman Turks? (e) How many years after the Ottomans captured Constantinople did they enter southeastern Europe?

5. Word research. Many English words have Arabic origins and have come to us through Spanish or French and Latin. Look up each of the following words in a dictionary. Then, on a separate sheet of paper, write the meaning of each word.

(a) almanac   (d) zenith
(b) cipher   (e) nadir
(c) algebra   (f) albatross

This picture from a Hindu epic shows the god Krishna and his wife Radha. They represent some of the characteristics — bravery, loyalty, and devotion — important to Indian civilization, and legends about them are very popular.

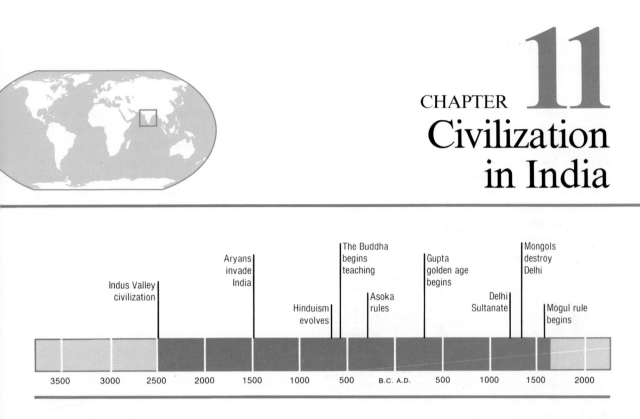

Civilization in India

One of the early river valley civilizations developed in the Indus Valley of South Asia, the peninsula that is often called India. About 1500 B.C., Aryan invaders from the northwest overran South Asia. Their culture blended with Indus Valley traditions to create a distinctive civilization. The religion of Hinduism was the most important influence in that civilization. Many centuries of Hindu dominance gave South Asia cultural unity. Although many kingdoms were established in India, no ruler succeeded in uniting the area politically.

The cultures of later invaders were eventually absorbed into Indian civilization. The arrival of the Muslims, however, introduced ideas and customs so different that the two civilizations remained somewhat separate from each other.

This chapter describes the development of ancient Indian civilization and the outside forces that influenced it socially and politically over many centuries.

CHAPTER OUTLINE

1 Indian Civilization Develops
2 Religious Thought Shapes Indian Society
3 Indian Empires Are Established
4 India Comes Under Muslim Rule

1 Indian Civilization Develops

The huge triangular peninsula of South Asia is so geographically and culturally distinct from the rest of Asia that it can be thought of as the Indian *subcontinent.* Although cut off from eastern Asia by the Himalayas, the subcontinent experienced many waves of invasion and migration through the mountain passes on the northwest frontier. Many different peoples came with their own languages and cultures, but most eventually became part of Indian culture.

Today India is only one of several political divisions in South Asia. Historically, however, the entire peninsula was the home of a distinctively Indian civilization whose roots lie deep in the past.

Great cities are built in the Indus Valley. The cities of the Indus Valley are the most recently discovered of all the early centers of civilization. In the 1920's, archeologists found the remains of two great cities on the Indus River and one of its tributaries. They named the cities Mohenjo-Daro and Harappa. These cities, and the society they ruled, developed at about the same time as civilization arose in Sumer (page 40), flourishing about 2500 B.C. The territory of the Indus Valley civilization was much larger than ancient Egypt or Mesopotamia. It included much of the northwest corner of the subcontinent, where Pakistan is located today.

Harappa and Mohenjo-Daro were carefully planned cities, each about a square mile in area. Wide streets were laid out in an orderly pattern. Buildings were square, with windowless brick walls facing the street. (See picture on page 34.) A huge central fortress contained rooms for storing grain, an assembly hall, and public baths. Most homes were spacious; some were two stories high. They had indoor bathrooms, with the earliest known sewer systems for drainage.

Archeological excavations have yielded much information about the life of the Harappans, as the ancient Indus Valley people are now called. The Harappans grew grain and fruit on irrigated farmlands and domesticated many animals, including elephants, sheep, goats, cats, and dogs. They seem to have been one of the earliest peoples to grow cotton and make cotton cloth. The Harappans devised a standardized system of weights and measures for weighing grain and gold. Harappan artisans worked with copper, bronze, and gold. They baked building bricks and pottery in large ovens on the edge of the city.

Statues found in the two Harappan cities show women and men with long hair and men with beards. Patterned or embroidered robes, probably of cotton cloth, left one shoulder bare. Harappan jewelry included necklaces, earrings, and bracelets of gold and semiprecious stones. Children played with toys of baked clay — whistles, small carts, and animals.

The Harappans engage in trade. As in many early civilizations, merchants used stone or clay seals to mark goods and sign contracts. Those from the Indus Valley were flat seals, used like modern rubber stamps. They com-

---

TIMETABLE

Civilization in South Asia

B.C.

2500*	Great cities flourish in the Indus Valley.
1500*	Aryans invade the Indus Valley.
530*	The Buddha begins his teaching.
321*	The Mauryan Empire is established.
269–232	Asoka reigns.

A.D.

320–500*	The Gupta Empire brings about a golden age in India.
712	The Rajputs halt a Muslim invasion.
1206	The Delhi sultanate is established by Muslim invaders.
1398	Tamerlane destroys the city of Delhi.
1526	Baber establishes the Mogul Empire.
1556–1605	Mogul culture flourishes during the reign of Akbar.

*APPROXIMATE DATES

bined carved animal designs and a few pictographs (picture-like symbols) that probably represented the merchant's name. These are the only surviving examples of Indus Valley writing. So far, no one has deciphered their meaning.

The Harappans built seaports on the Arabian Sea. Traders sailed along the coast and into the Persian Gulf, trading in cotton cloth, grain, turquoise, and probably timber and ivory. Some of the distinctive Harappan seals have been found in Sumer, showing that trade was going on between the two centers of civilization as early as 2300 B.C.

Invaders end the Indus Valley civilization. After about a thousand years of prosperity, the Indus Valley civilization began to decline. Mohenjo-Daro was abandoned, perhaps because its people feared roving tribes who were attacking border territories. Harappa, 350 miles to the north, was destroyed in a sudden massive attack by invading Aryans.

The Indian Subcontinent

Lofty mountain ranges seem to cut the Indian subcontinent off from the rest of Asia. How were Aryan invaders able to enter the subcontinent? What rivers are shown on the map? Along which river did an early civilization develop?

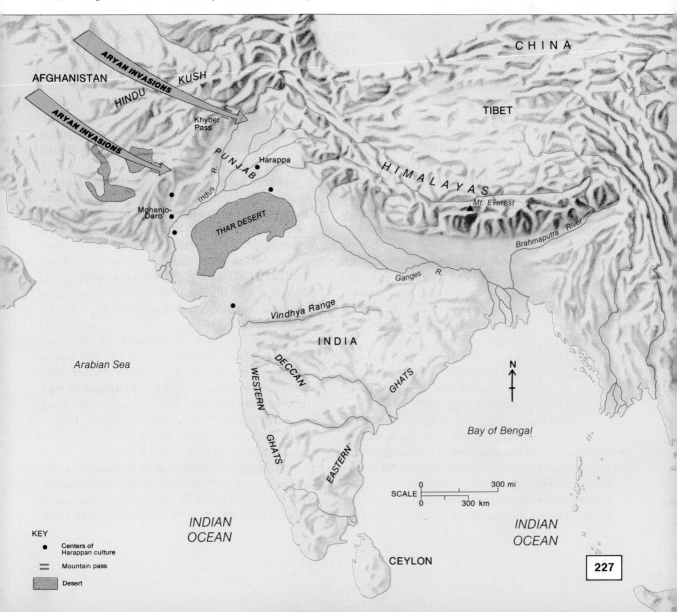

KEY
• Centers of Harappan culture
= Mountain pass
▨ Desert

INDUS VALLEY CRAFTS

Among the items made by artisans of the Indus Valley were pottery jars used for storing grain (left) and stamp seals. Many of these seals show animals common to the valley — sheep, water buffalo, elephants, and oxen (above).

The Aryans probably came from the steppes of Asia, west of the Hindu Kush, and entered South Asia by way of the mountain passes. They were taller and lighter-skinned than the Indus Valley people. The Aryans built no cities and had no art, architecture, or written language. They were nomadic herders who measured their wealth in livestock. Even their word for war meant "a desire for more cattle." The peaceful city-dwelling Harappans could not withstand the fierce Aryans, who wielded bronze axes and attacked swiftly in horse-drawn war chariots. Many Harappans fled south to the region called the Deccan (map, page 227) or to southern India. The rest became slaves of the conquerors. Yet many elements of their civilization survived and were absorbed into the Aryan way of life.

The Aryans bring a new language to India. Aryans migrated west to Europe as well as southeast to Persia and India. To all these regions they took their language, now known as Indo-European (page 53). The Indo-European language that the Aryans brought to India became Sanskrit, the language of classical Indian literature. Modern Hindi, Bengali, and other languages of India are also Indo-European in origin.

Early Indian history is unwritten. History as a series of dates and events did not become as important in India as it did in Western civilization. One reason for this was the Indian concept of a constant cycle of death and rebirth. Since the Indians believed everything had happened before and would happen again, they did not find it important to record the reigns of monarchs, the dates of battles, and the like.

From the fall of the Indus Valley civilization, about 1500 B.C., until the third century B.C., no written records or inscriptions were kept in India. The great literature of that time was passed down orally. The information we have comes from archeological studies or from reports written by foreign travelers, mainly Greek, Persian, and Chinese.

Religious literature gives a picture of the Vedic Age. Nearly all that is known about the first thousand years of the Aryans' dominance in northern and northwest India comes from

228

the four religious books known as the Vedas (VAY-duz). Composed in rhythmic poetry, the Vedas are a huge collection of battle hymns, religious rituals, wise sayings, chants, and tales. The Vedas show how Aryan life changed between 1500 and 500 B.C., the period that is called the Vedic Age.

The Vedas were carefully memorized and passed from generation to generation by telling and retelling. Learning the Vedas became part of the education of every upper-class boy and a few upper-class girls. The Aryan priests were responsible for transmitting these holy books word-for-word. Nothing was to be changed in their recital — not even an accent or syllable.

Oldest and most important of the Vedas is the Rig-Veda. It contains more than a thousand hymns, prayers, and songs. These portray the early Aryans as a proud people who enjoyed fighting, singing, and chariot racing. They also reveal that the Aryans worshiped natural forces, such as the sun, moon, rain, and fire. They thought of these forces as divine beings who had human qualities. Indra, the leading god in the Rig-Veda, ruled the skies, rain, and thunder. The Aryans pictured him as a military leader who liked fighting and feasting. They made offerings of food and drink to Indra and to other deities.

Aryan society changes. The early Aryans had a simple three-level class system: warrior-nobles, priests, and commoners who tended the herds of cattle. One of the warriors was chosen to be the chief, or rajah. He and an assembly of nobles ran the tribe's affairs. The class system was fairly flexible, and people could move between classes. Male and female roles were clearly defined: men made war and tended cattle; women raised crops, wove cloth, ground grain, and looked after households and children. Although women took no part in the tribal assemblies, they still had some freedom, including a say in choosing their husbands.

The Aryans' conquest of the Indus Valley changed their simple way of life. Aryan society gradually grew more rigid and more complex as tribes claimed land and settled down. Small kingdoms were established, and the rajah became a hereditary king, not simply a chosen leader.

Class divisions become stricter. In Aryan belief, both human beings and gods were part of a universal order. The priests taught that each detail of a ritual or sacrifice had to be perfect so that this order would not be upset and destroyed. By late in the Vedic Age, therefore, priests known as *Brahmins* had replaced warriors as the most influential class. Next came the warrior-nobles, the *Kshatriya* (SHAT-ree-uh). The *Vaisya* (VY-shuh), the common people, were merchants, traders, and artisans as well as landowning farmers and herders.

There was a great social gap between these three classes and the laboring class, the *Sudra* (SHOO-drah). The Sudra included the conquered Indian peoples as well as the descendants of Aryans who had married non-Aryans. They were looked down upon and were not even considered Aryan.

The Vedic Age sets the pattern for Indian thought and society. Gradually the Aryans came to regard class distinctions as an important and unchangeable part of the universal order. The members of each class had their own *dharma* (DAR-muh) — certain rights and duties, a certain place in society. An ancient book of laws summed these up: "The best occupations are: teaching the Veda for a Brahmin, protecting the people for a Kshatriya, and trade for a Vaisya.... The Lord [Brahman] gave only one occupation to the Sudra: to serve these others with meekness." This rigid class structure persisted as Indian society became even more complex.

CHECK-UP

1. Vocabulary: *subcontinent.*
2. (a) Where did the first civilization in South Asia develop? (b) How did the people of this civilization live? (c) What brought the civilization to an end?
3. How did the Aryan way of life differ from the Indus Valley civilization?
4. (a) What sources have historians used to draw conclusions about Indian history? (b) What kinds of information do these sources give?
5. (a) What social classes existed in early Aryan society? (b) How did conquest change this arrangement? (c) How had the class system changed by late in the Vedic Age?

2 Religious Thought Shapes Indian Society

Religious beliefs and customs were the major force in everyday Indian life and society. The simple tribal religion of the Aryans developed gradually into the complex beliefs of Hinduism. Hinduism drew on many traditions as it evolved, but stayed flexible enough to be the dominant faith of most of the people of India.

HINDUISM AND HINDU SOCIETY

The Upanishads set forth the basic ideas of Hinduism. For hundreds of years, priests memorized and passed on the hymns and poems of the Vedas. Religious thinkers commented on these hymns and speculated on the ideas in them. One famous collection of these writings is the Upanishads (oo-PAN-ih-shahdz), which date from about 800 B.C. to 600 B.C. They discuss basic ideas about right and wrong, the universal order, and human destiny.

The Upanishads describe a "world spirit" or "supreme principle," called Brahman. Hindus believe that this spirit is present in every living creature and that, at the same time, everything is a *part* of the world spirit. The goal of a Hindu is to return to Brahman and be absorbed back into the universal spirit. Hindus believe that, to achieve this goal, the human soul must progress and become purer. They do not expect to accomplish this in one lifetime; they believe the soul is reborn over and over in different bodies until it is purified. How quickly or slowly this purification happens depends on one's *karma.*

Karma can be understood most simply as the accumulated good and bad acts of all one's previous lives. Hindus believe that good karma assures a person of being reborn into a better life. A person with bad karma may not be reborn in a human body, but perhaps as a snake or insect.

Hindu ideas about class, dharma (duty), and karma are closely related. Performing the correct dharma for one's class and status is essential to achieving good karma.

Hindus recognize many deities. Hindus believe in many different gods and goddesses, but all are considered to be symbols and expressions of Brahman. Each deity can appear in many forms, or incarnations, but each form is still part of the universal spirit. The most important gods are Brahma the creator, Shiva the destroyer, and Vishnu the preserver.

Within the basic beliefs of Hinduism, its followers can worship in many different ways. People in different regions, villages, or families may honor separate gods or goddesses and may follow different rituals and customs. All are worshiping Brahman, the world spirit, however.

Hindu epics tell stories of heroes. Other important sources of Hindu tradition are two great epics from the Vedic Age. These tales of war, love, and adventure, which are still well known in India, illustrate the virtues and ideals that are important in Hindu life.

The leading characters in the *Ramayana* (rah-MAH-yuh-nuh), Prince Rama and Princess Sita, represent the ideal Hindu couple — the perfect hero and his devoted wife. Through exciting and heroic stories, the epic teaches moral lessons. The *Mahabharata* (muh-HAH-buh-RAH-tuh) brings together hundreds of ancient myths and legends in the story of a great war in which mortals and gods fight side by side to control a kingdom. It is thought to be based on a real war fought about 1000 B.C. These Hindu epics have been compared to Homer's epics (page 66), which were probably composed about the same time.

Many castes develop within Hindu society. In Aryan and early Hindu society, the division of people into four classes was considered part of the divine order. Most modern historians think that the *caste system* — a system of rigid social groupings — grew up alongside this class structure. The word *caste* was first used by Portuguese traders who reached India in the sixteenth century. They used their word for "clan" *(casta)* to describe the hundreds of social groups they observed.

HINDU ART

Hindu gods take many forms. Shiva, often shown as a fierce warrior, appears as lord of the dance (right). The bronze statue is surrounded by a halo representing the cycle of creation, death, and rebirth — ideas basic to Hinduism. Above is the bull Nandi, who carries Shiva and provides the music.

Castes were based in part on people's work. Even in late Aryan times, people with the same occupation — hunters or weavers or blacksmiths, for instance — commonly lived together in their own village or in one part of a town. People of different nationalities who moved into India also chose to live by themselves and to keep their own customs. Each of these groups formed a distinct caste.

Over thousands of years, the caste system grew more rigid. Subcastes formed within castes, and each had tiny differences in customs — different ways of preparing food, for instance. The most important caste rules concerned sharing meals, marrying within one's caste, and choosing appropriate occupations.

Caste distinctions were also linked with Hindu beliefs. Each higher group feared that contact with someone of a lower caste would bring spiritual "pollution" or uncleanliness. The safest way to avoid breaking caste rules was simply to have as little as possible to do with members of other castes. In effect, this made each caste a self-contained community.

Outcastes are cut off from Hindu society. One large group of people was excluded from being a real part of society. These people were the *outcastes,* also known as Untouchables. These casteless, classless persons were regarded as the lowest of all human beings. All the Hindu castes avoided contact with them. Untouchables therefore led a very segregated life, doing menial tasks that caste members would not perform, such as street-sweeping, the cremation of corpses, and the execution of criminals. Outcastes were often not allowed to live in a village with caste Hindus and could not even take water from the village well.

Hindu women have few freedoms. As Hindu society grew more complex, women's lives became more restricted. Hindu law and tradition set up certain expectations for both men and women. The ideal couple were Rama and Sita, the hero and heroine of the *Ramayana.* Sita was unquestioningly loyal, obedient, and devoted to Rama. These were the qualities expected of married Hindu women. They were supposed to run their households smoothly, look after their children, and obey their husbands without question. In return, upper-class women were honored and respected. A husband was supposed to give his wife as many luxuries — jewelry, rich foods, fine clothing — as he could afford.

Although women in early Hindu society had little real independence, they did have some rights. They could own property, such as their jewelry, which their daughters could inherit. A few women owned business property, though they were restricted in business dealings with men. Most upper-class women received some education, especially in the arts, music, and dance. Some of these women wrote poetry and drama.

A few women take part in public life. Some women were exceptions to the general pattern. In a few small kingdoms, a daughter could inherit the throne and rule as rani (RAH-nee), or queen; some women ruled until their infant sons grew up. Occasionally women of the nobility gained political power and ruled provinces within a kingdom. A thirteenth-century queen named Rudramma ruled in her own right, although she referred to herself as "he" in official documents. In Hindu history there are even a number of women who were warriors. Several ranis became famous because they led the defense of their castles after the rajahs had been killed in battle.

Widows are excluded from society. In families that followed strict Hindu custom, a woman faced a bleak future after her husband died. A widowed woman, particularly in an upper-class family, could not remarry or return to her own family. As her only hope was to be reunited with her husband in her next life, she lived with his family and was held responsible for the welfare of his soul. She had to live plainly and frugally, spending her time in prayer. She could not wear bright clothes or perfume, attend festivals, or enjoy such foods as honey and meat.

In several ancient cultures it was the custom for the wives of a king or warrior (and sometimes his servants) to commit suicide and be cremated with him. This custom later was practiced in Hindu society. Rather than live under the grim circumstances that faced most widows, some women chose death by burning. This ritual was followed as late as the nineteenth century.

BUDDHISM

Buddhism appeals to those unhappy with the caste system. The caste system was part of the most basic Hindu beliefs, not merely a social custom that could be changed. Understandably, many Sudras and outcastes were discontented with the misery of their lives. In Hinduism their only hope of change lay in the next life, not this one. Buddhism (BOO-diz'm), which emerged in the sixth century B.C., marked a profound break with some Hindu beliefs. It appealed to many who suffered from the inequality of the caste system.

Gautama becomes "the Enlightened One." Siddhartha Gautama (GAW-tuh-muh), born about 563 B.C., was the son of a Kshatriya noble. His wealthy father tried to protect him from the realities of the world. Gautama grew up in luxury, married, and had a son. According to legend, when he was nearly thirty years old, Gautama was given four "signs." As he walked in the palace grounds, he saw three men, one very old, one painfully ill, and one dead. Gautama was deeply troubled by his first encounters with age, pain, and death. Then he saw a fourth man — a wandering religious beggar — and realized that this was the way of life he must follow.

Gautama first tried the traditional Hindu ways of finding understanding. He studied with a teacher and lived a solitary life in the forest. He tried fasting, but found that it made him too weak to think clearly. Then he turned to meditation, sitting under a fig tree. After 49 days, the answers to his questions suddenly came to him clearly. He became the Buddha, "the Enlightened One."

The Buddha taught the way to enlightenment. Many of the important ideas of Buddhism were presented in a sermon that the Buddha gave shortly after this experience. He pointed out Four Noble Truths. First, sorrow (or suffering) is part of all life. Second, people suffer because they are constantly wanting and trying to get things they cannot have. Third, the way to escape suffering is to overcome these frustrating desires and reach a stage of "not wanting." Finally, the Buddha pointed out the steps on the path to enlightenment, or *nirvana.* He advised people to follow a "middle way," one that avoided the extremes of too much pleasure and too much self-denial.

The teachings of the Buddha challenged some Hindu beliefs. Buddhism placed more importance on how one lived than on one's caste. The Brahmins' ceremonies and rituals were not important in Buddhism. The Buddha also taught that it was possible for a person to gain enlightenment in one lifetime (as the Buddha had) and so escape Hinduism's cycle of rebirth.

For the next forty years, the Buddha and his followers traveled widely, preaching gentleness and compassion. Buddhist teachings had a wide appeal, for people from any caste could,

BUDDHIST SHRINES

As Buddhism spread from India, shrines and statues of the Buddha became common in many lands. The porcelain figure of the Buddha (below) was made in China. The temples (left) are known as stupas. They evolved from mounds of stones placed on the graves of chiefs. To Buddhists, the stupa's base represents earth and the dome stands for heaven.

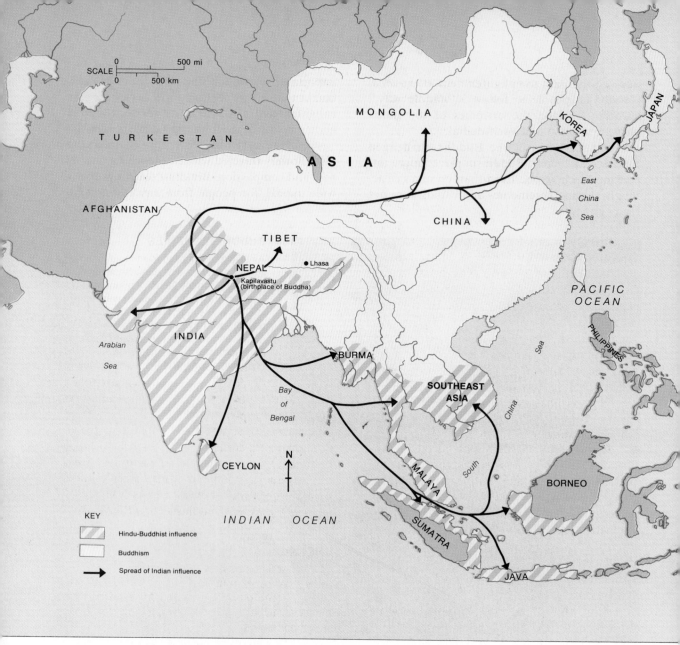

Spread of Hinduism and Buddhism By About A.D. 750

The religions of Hinduism and Buddhism both spread from India to other lands. Where outside of India were followers of both religions found? In what lands did Buddhism become the major religion?

and did, join Buddhist communities. The Buddha himself died at age eighty, in about the year 483 B.C.

Buddhist monasteries are established. The Buddha established a community of monks and, at the request of his aunt, a community of nuns. Buddhist monks and nuns followed a careful discipline when they joined the religious orders. They wore yellow robes, lived simply, owned little, and usually begged their food from followers. Sometimes pilgrims and scholars joined a community for a short time.

Like Christian monasteries in medieval Europe, Buddhist monasteries became centers of learning and education. Monks and nuns also studied medicine and looked after the sick and aged in their communities. Rulers and nobles donated land and money to Buddhist communities, which sometimes grew into large complexes that included shrines, teaching halls, the monastery or convent itself, and resthouses for pilgrims. Several monasteries eventually became much like medieval universities. They taught not only Buddhist doctrine but also logic, grammar, medicine, and the Vedas. Students of all faiths were welcomed.

Buddhist beliefs change as Buddhism spreads. As Buddhism spread, disagreements grew up about some of its teachings and beliefs. Originally the Buddha had presented a system of ethics and guidelines for living. His followers considered him only a teacher. The Hinayana school of Buddhism remained close to these original teachings. Another group of Buddhists, however, came to look upon the Buddha as a god ruling over lesser gods. They developed a ritualized religion with temples, saints, and statues of the Buddha. This was the Mahayana school of Buddhism.

In the centuries after the death of the Buddha, Buddhism became widespread in India. Buddhists and Hindus had many things in common, however, and Hinduism gradually absorbed a number of important Buddhist teachings and attitudes. Some Hindus accepted the Buddha as another incarnation of the god Vishnu. Beginning in about the first century A.D., Buddhism began to disappear as a separate faith in India.

While Buddhism was declining in India, however, missionaries and travelers were carrying its message into other parts of Asia, where it eventually became the dominant religion. Mahayana Buddhism in particular spread into China, Japan, and Korea. Hinayana Buddhism became well established in Ceylon (present-day Sri Lanka), Burma, and Southeast Asia.

JAINISM

The Jains devote themselves to self-denial. Many small groups with differing beliefs sprang up within Hinduism. None gained the worldwide importance of Buddhism, and most lasted only a short time. One that endured into modern times as an independent group was Jainism.

The founder of the Jains (JYNES) was given the name Mahavira ("Great Hero") by his followers. He lived at the same time as the Buddha. Mahavira described karma (page 230) as an actual substance that clung to the soul and diminished its original purity and brightness. Unlike the Buddha, he thought that strict self-denial and life in a monastery were the only way to purify the soul and rid it of karma.

The Jains practice nonviolence. Jains did not pray or worship gods. They took vows not to steal, lie, or desire anything, and they would not kill any living being. *Ahimsa*, or nonviolence, was their central belief. Interpreting this idea in its fullest sense, Jains did not go to war or fight back if attacked. They would not eat meat or even do farm work, because working the soil would kill plant and animal life. To avoid stepping on insects as they walked, strict Jains hired people to sweep the ground in front of them. They strained the water they drank, and some even wore masks to filter the air they breathed. Jainism attracted only a limited number of followers and never spread outside India. Its ideal of *ahimsa*, however, was adopted in varying degrees by Buddhists and others.

CHECK-UP

1. Vocabulary: *caste system, outcaste.*
2. (a) What was the main religious goal of Hindus? (b) How did karma and dharma affect this goal? (c) How are the Indian epics related to Hindu beliefs?
3. (a) To what three areas of life did the rules of caste specifically apply? (b) How did the caste rules make each caste, in effect, a self-contained community?
4. (a) What qualities were Indian women expected to possess? (b) What rights did they have? (c) What limitations did society impose on them?
5. (a) Who was the Buddha? (b) What Hindu beliefs did the Buddha's teachings challenge?
6. (a) Why did Buddhism gain followers in India? (b) To what parts of Asia did Buddhism spread? (c) What happened to Buddhism in India?
7. Describe how the Jains applied their belief in nonviolence.

3 Indian Empires Are Established

By about the sixth century B.C. — the time of the Buddha — several kingdoms existed in northeast India, on the great plain of the Ganges River. This was also the part of India in which both the Buddha and Mahavira lived and taught. It was the center of Indian culture at the time.

Magadha takes control of northeast India. The kingdom of Magadha on the Ganges River, though not the largest in the region, was the most stable and prosperous. It had iron mines, rich soil, abundant forests for timber, and elephants, which were valuable in war and as beasts of burden. Magadha also had a thriving trade up and down the Ganges River.

Magadha's ruler Bimbisara (who ruled about 545–494 B.C.) was a good administrator who built roads, coordinated village governments, and made the kingdom stronger than its neighbors. A friend and follower of the Buddha, Bimbisara was generally a peaceful ruler. He conquered one small kingdom and gained control of trade in the Ganges delta. Through marriage, he acquired land to the north.

Succeeding kings of Magadha secured still more territory. By the following century, Magadha controlled the entire plain of the Ganges and all of northern India as far as the Punjab.

It was the largest single kingdom established in India up until that time, with its capital at Pataliputra (modern Patna).

The Persian Empire claims northwest India. About the same time that Magadha was growing stronger, an invading army led by Cyrus the Great of Persia (page 58) crossed the mountains into northwest India. This army brought a new wave of foreign influence. By about 518 B.C., Darius I, Cyrus's successor, had conquered the Indus Valley and the Punjab. This part of India remained under Persian rule for about 200 years. The courts and cities of the Persians became centers of learning and culture, where young men from Magadha and other kingdoms were sent for an education.

Alexander conquers Persia but loses India. Persian power in India ended as Alexander the Great moved steadily across the Near East, extending his vast empire (map, page 76). He defeated the Persians in several great battles, then moved into India in 327 B.C. Though the Persians and Indians fought fiercely, Alexander's army crossed the Indus River. By then, however, his troops felt they had gone too far into unknown hostile territory, and they threatened to mutiny. Alexander moved his army out of India, but some forts

Buddhist art in India was influenced by the Hellenistic style introduced to the subcontinent by the conquests of Alexander the Great. At right is a scene from the life of the Buddha. Although the theme is Indian, the style of the sculpture has much in common with the art of ancient Greece.

and settlements of Greek colonists remained near the northwest frontier. Alexander's sudden death in 323 B.C. left northwest India without an effective ruler.

Chandragupta Maurya establishes a new empire. Soon after the death of Alexander, a young adventurer named Chandragupta Maurya (MAH-oor-yah) took over the kingdom of Magadha. Taking advantage of the confusion in northwest India, he then moved into the territory Alexander had abandoned. This gave him an empire that included all of northern India and part of what is now Afghanistan.

The Mauryan Empire, with its capital at Pataliputra, had a strong central government in which the emperor was the supreme authority. To make administration easier, the empire was divided into districts and provinces. Chandragupta depended on a powerful army and a wide-ranging network of spies to control the many local governments and officials in his huge empire. Historians give credit for his successful administration to a royal adviser named Kautilya, who wrote a guidebook on practical, ruthless politics. His book is one of the earliest historical documents that survives from ancient India.

The ambassador to Chandragupta's court from one of the Greek states wrote a work describing the Mauryan Empire. It gives the impression that, while Chandragupta's reign may have been harsh in some ways, he worked hard for his people. The empire prospered as roads were built between different regions. Irrigation systems brought good harvests.

According to legend, Chandragupta gave up the throne after twenty-four years and adopted the strict life of a Jain monk. His son added territory in the south to the empire. About 269 B.C. the Mauryan Empire passed to Chandragupta's grandson Asoka (ah-SHOH-kuh).

Asoka's reign brings a golden age to India. Asoka began his career with the fierce conquest of the coastal province of Kalinga in 261 B.C. Some 100,000 people were killed in battle, thousands of others died from hunger and disease, and 150,000 were taken prisoner. Overwhelmed by this slaughter, Asoka was converted to Buddhism and renounced war and violence.

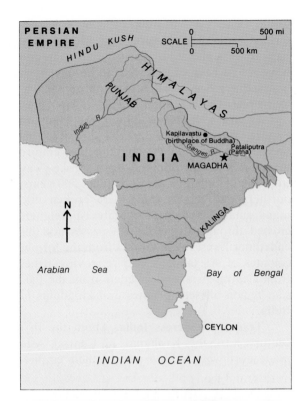

Asoka's Empire About 260 B.C.

Asoka's empire included most of the subcontinent of India. What part of the subcontinent was not under his rule?

Asoka has been judged one of the great rulers in world history. Modern historians base this view partly on the many rulings and edicts that he placed in public places for his subjects to read. The inscriptions appear throughout the empire engraved on rocks, in caves, and on columns. They reveal a ruler who preferred gentleness and persuasion to force and war.

The teachings and ethics of Buddhism set the tone for the remaining thirty years of Asoka's reign. One of his most famous edicts states that he "desires security, self-control, justice, and happiness for all beings." Asoka supported the ideal of *ahimsa* (page 235), urging respect for both human and animal life and encouraging vegetarianism. Though several members of his family became Buddhist missionaries in other countries, he strongly supported tolerance for all beliefs. On a practical level, Asoka's government set up programs that would benefit all his subjects. One edict described some of these programs: "I have had banyan trees planted to give shade to man and beast. . . . I have caused wells to be dug; resthouses have been erected; and numerous watering places have been provided."

An age of invasions follows the Mauryan Empire. After Asoka's death in 232 B.C., his successors were unable to hold the huge empire together. States far from the capital broke away from the empire. For about the next 500 years, northern and central India were broken into many small kingdoms and states. Foreigners crossed through the mountain passes and invaded northwest India. Greeks from the former colonies of Alexander's empire, roving tribes from Central Asia, and invaders from the Persian region all set up states and kingdoms in India.

Trade routes cross India. About the first century A.D., the Kushanas of Central Asia made northwest India a part of their empire.

By the time of Kanishka, the most famous Kushana king, their territory extended through Central Asia to the borders of the Chinese Empire. It lay astride many of the great overland trade routes from the Near East to China, including the silk route (map, page 254). Along these routes traveled not only merchants but also Buddhist missionaries encouraged by Kanishka.

India was rapidly becoming a center for east-west trade. Overland trade also flourished between the Greek states in India and the Mediterranean. Sea trade was established between the Arabs and the kingdoms in the southern part of the Indian peninsula.

Tamil culture is dominant in the south. The cultures of south India developed quite separately from those in the north. Not even the huge Mauryan Empire included all the south, and none of the invaders of India reached the land south of the Deccan (map, page 227). This southern region was settled by

---

LINKING PAST AND PRESENT
Asoka's Legacy

The official seal, or emblem, of the modern nation of India shows three curly-maned lions standing back-to-back. In choosing this symbol, the people of India called on a tradition nearly 2,300 years old, from the reign of the great emperor Asoka. Along many roads in northern India, Asoka had tall stone columns built, with carved inscriptions that carried his thoughts to the people of the huge Mauryan Empire. The lion symbol (right) comes from the sculptured design that topped one of these pillars.

Asoka's stately pillars, cut from single blocks of sandstone polished to a shiny luster, stood about forty feet high. Some weighed as much as fifty tons. Workers used ox-drawn carts to haul the pillars to their roadside sites. Many different designs were carved on the tops of the columns, but the lions have become the best known. They also appear on modern India's stamps and coins.

people from the Indus Valley who had fled southward from the Aryan invaders. Called Dravidians (drah-VID-ee-unz), they established a distinctive culture in south India.

The Dravidians differed from the Aryans in both appearance and language. The Dravidian languages, still spoken today in India and Sri Lanka, are not Indo-European. They are unrelated to any other language in the world. The main Dravidian language is Tamil (TAM-ul). Over time, Tamil culture was influenced somewhat by the cultures of northern India, particularly by Hinduism. Yet it retained many distinctive characteristics.

Trade by sea flourishes in south India. The Tamils were seafarers who traded with Southeast Asia and conquered and occupied much of the island of Ceylon. Tamil kings built harbor facilities and encouraged trade. By about the first century A.D. there was a thriving trade from southern Indian ports to China and Egypt, then part of the Roman Empire. Taking advantage of the monsoon winds, Arab traders crossed the sea to India in summer and returned to Arabia in winter when the winds reversed direction. They carried cargoes of spices, jewels, perfumes, textiles, and exotic animals to trade with the Roman world. The Indian traders in turn sailed to islands in the Indian Ocean for spices to sell to the Arabs. India took mostly gold in trade from the West, but it bought textiles and porcelain from China. India's trade spread its culture and religion throughout much of Southeast Asia.

The Gupta Empire brings prosperity to northern India. About A.D. 320, after several hundred years of invasions and turmoil, northern India was again united under one ruler. Like the earlier Mauryan Empire, this new empire was centered at Magadha on the Ganges plain. The first emperor united several kingdoms through marriage, took the name Chandra Gupta (after the earlier emperor), and established a new line of rulers. Under the Gupta rulers, northern India became the center of a brilliant and creative culture. Government rule was benevolent, and literature, art, science, and technology all flourished. The Gupta Empire lasted for about 200 years and eventually included most of northern India except the mountainous northwest frontier. It was the last great Hindu empire in India.

Hinduism influences Gupta writers. Gupta literature showed the importance of Hinduism in everyday Indian life. Many fables and folktales from this period (such as the tale of Sinbad the Sailor) were translated and became known in Persia and then in Europe. Gupta writers produced memorable plays and lyric poetry in classical Sanskrit. India's greatest poet and playwright, often compared with Shakespeare, was Kalidasa (kah-lih-DAH-suh). His play *Shakuntala,* based on an idea from one of the Hindu epics, is still performed in India today.

Advances are made in science and mathematics. The Gupta rulers were Hindu, but Buddhism was still influential. Some monasteries had developed into universities with large libraries. Buddhist scholars came there from China and other countries to which Buddhism had spread. Astronomy, mathematics, and surgery in Gupta India were far ahead of the rest of the world at the time. Probably the most impressive contributions were made by Gupta mathematicians. They established the decimal system, the idea of zero, and the beginnings of algebra. Although Arab mathematicians later were given credit for so-called Arabic numerals, the Arabs themselves called mathematics "the Indian art."

Invasions end the Gupta Empire. About the middle of the fifth century, invaders from Central Asia began to raid the borders of the Gupta Empire. By about A.D. 500 the empire had fallen, and northern India again was fragmented into separate states and kingdoms.

One strong kingdom did arise in the Ganges valley after the fall of the Guptas. A young prince named Harsha united two kingdoms in 606 and began a rule of more than forty years. His empire was really a loosely organized group of feudal states, which Harsha controlled by keeping in constant contact with their rulers. The emperor encouraged literature and the arts (he was himself a playwright), and followed Buddhist principles of tolerance and gentleness. On his death, however, the empire broke up, and for the next few hundred years northern India remained disunited.

1. How did the Magadha rulers gain control of the land along the Ganges River?
2. How did Persian rule of northwest India come to an end?
3. (a) What empire replaced both Magadha and Persia in northern India? (b) What factors made it possible for this empire to be ruled with efficiency?
4. (a) Why has Asoka been called one of the great rulers of the world? (b) What happened to the empire after Asoka's death?
5. (a) Who were the Dravidians? (b) How did their culture differ from cultures in northern India?
6. (a) Why did India become a center for east-west trade? (b) With what other places did India trade by land? (c) By sea?
7. What achievements were made in literature and mathematics under Gupta rule?

4 India Comes Under Muslim Rule

Soon after the rise of Islam, its militant followers set about conquering and converting neighboring peoples (Chapter 10). Between 712 and 1526 four different groups of Muslims invaded India. Eventually most of the Indian peninsula was united under Muslim rule. The majority of Indian people remained Hindu, but the Muslim rulers exerted a lasting influence on their society and culture.

Muslim and Hindu beliefs conflict. All of India's earlier invaders had gradually been absorbed into Hindu culture and society. The beliefs of Islam and Hinduism, however, differed in their most basic principles. The Muslims believed strongly in one god and in equality among all people. The Hindus were equally firm in accepting many deities as part of the world spirit and in seeing class divisions as divinely ordered. The two faiths could exist side by side, but they could not blend.

The Rajputs hold back an Arab invasion. In 712, the first Muslim invaders crossed the mountains from Persia and moved into the Indus Valley. Their advance was stopped by the barren Thar Desert (map, page 227) and by the Rajputs (RAHJ-poots), the warrior clans of the northwest. The Hindu Rajputs claimed to be the direct heirs of the Kshatriya class of Aryans. Proud and warlike, they held to a strict code of honor and chivalry. Although the many independent Rajput kingdoms fought constantly among themselves, they united to stop the Muslim invaders. The Muslims could not advance beyond the Indus Valley and the mountains on the northwest frontier, but they claimed that region for the Islamic empire.

Mahmud of Ghazni terrorizes India. The next invasion of India was launched by Turkish Muslims from one of the mountain kingdoms, Ghazni (in present-day Afghanistan). Its ruler, Mahmud, was rapidly expanding his empire. He did not want Indian land but did want the gold and treasure of the cities, temples, and monasteries. Beginning about A.D. 1000, Mahmud led seventeen quick, merciless raids on India — about one a year — killing Buddhist and Hindu monks and priests, and carrying off slaves and plunder. Since Hindus were "infidels" to the Muslim invaders, the raids were encouraged by the caliph of Baghdad as a holy war. Mahmud's raids so devastated northern India that all resistance stopped. He eventually took the Punjab region into his empire, along with the Muslim frontier kingdoms.

The Rajputs fail to stop another Muslim invasion. About 1175 the empire of Ghazni was taken over by a group of Turks led by a chieftain named Muhammad Ghori. The Rajput confederacy, which depended on elephants, could not hold off the fast-moving Turkish archers mounted on horseback. Muhammad Ghori's victorious armies occupied India as far south as the Deccan. On Muhammad's death in 1206, his generals found themselves far from home in the Indian provinces. One general, a freed slave named Aybek, declared the Indian territories a separate Muslim kingdom or sultanate, with its capital at Delhi.

The Delhi sultanate establishes Muslim control of India. The rulers of Delhi were proclaimed sultans of India by the caliph of Baghdad, and they remained in power for more than 300 years. At its greatest extent, the sultanate included the entire northern plain, much of the Deccan, and even parts of the south. The sultanate was never stable, however. Palace intrigues, revolts, and assassinations brought about the downfall of many sultans. The sultans also found it hard to rule the distant provinces. Local princes and governors frequently rebelled and declared their independence.

Mongol invasions set the stage for conquest. In the early 1200's, Genghis Khan led his fierce Mongol warriors across Asia, conquering and destroying as he established a huge empire. The Mongols then turned west and attacked many of the great cultural centers of the Muslim empire, destroying Baghdad in 1258 (page 220). The Mongols also raided northern India, seeking treasure, not territory. For Muslims in the cities besieged by the Mongols, the Delhi sultanate seemed like an island of safety. Scholars, scientists, artists, and thousands of others fled into India from Baghdad and other Near Eastern cities. The sultanate became a center of Muslim learning and culture.

Mongol raids on northern India continued throughout the next century. In the late 1300's, the conqueror Tamerlane led his Mongol armies through Central and Western Asia, looting and destroying. Although he was a zealous Muslim himself, Tamerlane devastated the great Muslim cities in Asia. In 1398, Delhi was destroyed and thousands of people killed. The sultanate survived for a hundred years more but steadily lost power.

The Mogul dynasty begins. In the early 1500's, Baber, a descendant of Genghis Khan and Tamerlane, led his army into India. In 1526 the Delhi sultanate fell. Though Baber died shortly after the conquest, he succeeded in establishing a new empire in India, called the Mogul Empire (from the Persian word for Mongol).

Akbar introduces an era of toleration. Baber's grandson Akbar was only thirteen years old when he inherited the throne in 1556. He soon gained absolute power and became a wise and skillful ruler. Akbar was an excellent general. During his 49-year reign, the Mogul Empire expanded to include all the north of India and much of the Deccan. Akbar was also a wise statesman. He understood how important compromise was in uniting the many different peoples and religions within the empire.

The Rajput kings in particular had always been a problem for Muslim rulers. Their strong fortresses controlled the routes southward to the Deccan. Akbar shrewdly made the Rajputs his allies, gave them important positions in the court and the army, and married Rajput women (so that his heirs were part Hindu). He allowed all Hindus religious freedom and canceled the special taxes that non-Muslims had to pay in nearly every other Muslim land.

The Mogul Empire

By 1700 the Moguls controlled more of India than had Asoka (map, page 237). What lands did the Moguls add after 1605? Locate the following cities on the map: Ghazni, Delhi, Agra, Patna, Surat. Which of these cities had been part of the Delhi sultanate in 1525? What had happened to the sultanate by 1605?

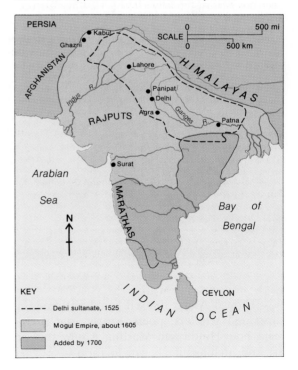

MOGUL ART AND ARCHITECTURE

Close ties with the Muslim world influenced Indian art during the Mogul period. The painting of an Indian woman with a musical instrument (right) is in the Indian tradition, but the background resembles Persian art. The spirited picture of a noble riding an elephant (below) comes from an album of paintings made during the reign of Akbar. The Taj Mahal (above), which has been described as "poetry in stone," is a masterpiece of Mogul architecture.

Though Akbar himself could not read, he supported scholars, poets, artists, and architects, both Hindu and Muslim. A new style in art and architecture began to form — neither Hindu nor Persian, but distinctively Mogul.

The Mogul Empire expands under Akbar's successors. Jahangir (juh-HAHN-geer) and Shah Jahan, the two rulers who succeeded Akbar, never achieved his greatness or wisdom. However, they continued his policies of fairness, tolerance, thrift, and compromise between Muslim and Hindu attitudes. They expanded the empire still more and carefully maintained good relations with their Hindu allies.

Akbar's son and grandson both supported the arts, and the brilliant Mogul style flourished in art, music, poetry, and architecture. Akbar's son Jahangir (1605–1628) married a clever and beautiful Persian woman, Nur Jahan. She and her family influenced both politics and ways of living in the empire. Persian influence increased at court and among the upper classes, both Hindu and Muslim. Nobles spoke Persian, while a new mixed language, Urdu, gradually formed from a blend of Indian languages and the Persian spoken by soldiers.

Jahangir's son, Shah Jahan, led a rebellion against his father and had his brothers murdered to secure the Mogul throne in 1628. He too maintained a luxurious court and spent enormous amounts of money constructing mosques, forts, and other public buildings. Although he made many conquests, Shah Jahan is best remembered for the tomb he had built for his wife, Mumtaz Mahal (Nur Jahan's niece). The Taj Mahal, in the Mogul city of Agra, is one of the architectural wonders of the world.

Aurangzeb attempts to conquer all India. Though their reigns were marked by cruelty as well as brilliance, the first three Mogul emperors held together an empire of very unlike parts. Shah Jahan's son Aurangzeb (OR-ung-zeb), who imprisoned his father and seized the throne in 1658, reversed the policies of compromise and tolerance that had made this possible.

A stricter Muslim than the earlier emperors, Aurangzeb tried to force the Hindu population to follow the laws and practices of Islam. He reintroduced the special tax on non-Muslims and took away the rights of many Hindu nobles. These practices, and a general attitude of noncompromise, also led to disagreements with important allies of the Mogul Empire.

Aurangzeb — nicknamed the "World Shaker" — withdrew his support for the arts and poured all the empire's treasure into an attempt to conquer the Deccan and the south. As he concentrated on war, however, he neglected the government, which became weak and corrupt. By the time of Aurangzeb's death in 1707, the Mogul Empire had lost its cultural brilliance and political strength, though it had gained vast amounts of territory.

New forces rebel against the Moguls. The Hindu Rajputs were among the important allies offended by Aurangzeb's intolerant policies. Always dangerous, the warlike Rajputs again became a constant source of rebellion in the north.

Another people who held firm against Mogul power were the Sikhs (SEEKS), followers of a new religion established about the time of the first Muslim conquest. The Sikhs, neither Hindu nor Muslim, adopted distinctive names and customs and formed a small, self-sufficient society. Their center of power lay in the Punjab.

Aurangzeb's tactics also created a new, powerful enemy in the Deccan. The Marathas (mah-RAH-tahz), a Hindu people living along the western coast, established a small independent empire within the Mogul Empire. Though badly organized, the Marathas remained a threat to unity in India for more than a hundred years. European traders, who began to establish outposts in India in the seventeenth century, took advantage of this disunity to gain control of the country (Chapter 25).

CHECK-UP

1. (a) Why were Muslim invaders unable to penetrate past the Indus Valley in 712? (b) What enabled Muslims to gain control of the Punjab about the year 1000? (c) What military advantage did the Muslims have over the Rajputs?

2. (a) How did Delhi become the center of a separate Muslim kingdom? (b) What groups of invaders weakened the Delhi sultanate? (c) What caused the fall of the sultanate in 1526?

3. (a) How did Akbar successfully unite different peoples within the Mogul Empire? (b) What new style of art and architecture emerged during his reign? (c) How did Persian culture influence Mogul culture?

4. (a) Compare the reign of Aurangzeb with that of Akbar. (b) How did Aurangzeb's reign weaken the Mogul Empire? (c) What three powerful groups in India became enemies of the Moguls?

Chapter 11 Review

Summary

The Indian subcontinent (South Asia) was the site of one of the great early river valley cultures, at Harappa and Mohenjo-Daro in the Indus Valley. About 1500 B.C. the highly organized Harappan culture declined and was overrun by nomadic Aryans from Central Asia. Many of the original Dravidian settlers fled to the southern part of the Indian peninsula, where they developed the distinctive Tamil culture. Those who remained became part of Aryan culture, which was the basis for India's traditional Hindu society.

Hinduism developed in India over several thousand years. Its ideas of universal order, a world spirit, and class divisions in society became basic parts of Indian culture. The second great religion to develop in India was Buddhism, founded in the sixth century B.C. Though Buddhism gained many followers, it became more important in other parts of Asia than in India.

India was never united politically. The Mauryan Empire included about two thirds of the peninsula, reaching its height under the emperor Asoka in the third century B.C. No other great state existed until the Gupta Empire in the fourth century A.D. After the rise of Islam, a series of invasions from Central Asia eventually established Muslim rule over much of India. The Mogul Empire reached its height in the 1500's and 1600's under the emperors Akbar, Jahangir, and Shah Jahan. It began to decline in the reign of Aurangzeb.

Vocabulary Review

1. Write the sentences listed below on a sheet of paper. In each sentence, fill in the blank with one of these words: *caliph, caste system, outcaste, subcontinent.*
(a) India is such a distinct geographical area that it is often called a __?__ .
(b) A __?__ is the political and religious head of a Muslim state.
(c) The hereditary social groupings into which Hindu society was divided formed its __?__ .
(d) __?__ was the term applied to a person excluded from Indian society.

2. Distinguish between the terms in each of the following pairs:

(a) Gupta Empire; Mauryan Empire.
(b) Hinayana; Mahayana.
(c) Vedas; Upanishads.
(d) *ahimsa; nirvana.*
(e) *rani;* rajah.
(f) Rajputs; Aryans.
(g) Sanskrit; Tamil.

People to Identify

Identify the following people. Name the country or empire with which each was connected and tell why he or she was important.
1. Mahavira
2. Kalidasa
3. Shah Jahan
4. Rudramma
5. Bimbisara
6. Genghis Khan
7. Mahmud of Ghazni
8. Aurangzeb

Relating Geography and History

1. **Locating places.** Locate each of the following on a map in this chapter:
(a) Himalayas
(b) Harappa
(c) Magadha
(d) Delhi
(e) Mohenjo-Daro
(f) Ganges River
(g) Indus River
(h) Pataliputra
(i) Brahmaputra

2. **Research.** The three great river systems of India are the Indus, Ganges, and Brahmaputra. Do research in atlases and encyclopedias to find (a) the source of each river; (b) its length; (c) where the mouth of the river is located; and (d) into what body of water the river flows. Trace the route of each river on the map on page 227.

Discussion Questions

1. The Himalayas cut South Asia off from the rest of Asia and yet did not prevent foreign cultural influences from reaching the Indian subcontinent. Explain.
2. How and why did the Aryans' way of life change after they invaded the Indus Valley?
3. Compare Hinduism and Buddhism. (a) What doctrines do these religions share? (b) In what way did Buddhism challenge Hindu beliefs about caste and class? (c) Why did Buddhism become less important in India after about the first century B.C.?

4. India's empires produced outstanding leaders. Explain why historians regard each of the following as a great ruler: (a) Chandragupta Maurya, (b) Asoka, (c) Akbar.

5. Until the arrival of the Muslims, India had successfully absorbed the cultures of all invaders. How did each of the following help to make this possible: (a) Hinduism? (b) the caste system?

6. Why did the Muslims, unlike all previous invaders of India, remain a distinct religious and cultural group that was not absorbed into Hindu society?

Reading Primary Sources

Each Hindu caste followed its own rules of *dharma.* About 2,000 years ago many of these rules were written down in a work known as the *Laws of Manu.* The following passage describes the duties of the Kshatriyas (warrior-nobles). Read the passage. Then answer the questions that follow.

> A Kshatriya king who, while protecting his people, is defied by enemies, should not shrink from battle but should remember the duty of a Kshatriya not to turn back in battle, to protect his people, and to honor the Brahmins.
>
> Those who fight with all their strength and do not turn back go to heaven.
>
> But the Kshatriya who [has agreed to fight for another and] is killed while fleeing from battle takes upon himself all the sins of his master, and whatever merit he may have gained for the next world is taken by his master. . . .
>
> As the weeder pulls up weeds and leaves the corn to grow, even so must the king protect his kingdom and destroy his enemies.

(a) What were the duties of Kshatriyas? (b) What punishment was said to await a Kshatriya who was killed while running away from battle? (c) According to the *Laws of Manu,* how did a Kshatriya win a place in heaven? (d) Which part of this passage has to do with the Hindu belief in *karma?* (e) The fourth paragraph uses figurative language to make a point. Explain that point.

Skill Activities

1. Placing events in time. This chapter deals with Indian civilization over a long period of time. The Timetable on page 226 will help you to place the events about which you have just read in the proper sequence. To see how these events fit in with other developments in world history, copy that Timetable on a separate piece of paper, expanding it to include the following events:

(a) 3200 B.C. — Sumerians in Mesopotamia develop the earliest civilization.
(b) 2600 B.C. — The Great Pyramid is built in Egypt.
(c) 399 B.C. — Socrates is put on trial in Athens.
(d) A.D. 45 — Paul begins Christian missionary work.
(e) 476 — The Roman Empire falls.
(f) 1066 — The Normans conquer England.
(g) 1215 — The Magna Charta becomes law in England.
(h) 1348 — The Black Death reaches Europe.
(i) 1492 — Columbus reaches America.

2. Reports. Find information about one of the following topics and prepare a report: (a) the life of Asoka; (b) the life of Siddhartha Gautama (the Buddha); (c) the origins of the caste system; (d) the *Ramayana;* (e) the life of Cyrus the Great; (f) the status of Untouchables in present-day India; (g) Jainism; (h) the story of Sinbad the Sailor; (i) the life of Tamerlane; (j) the *Bhagavad-Gita* (a sacred Hindu text in the form of a philosophical dialogue).

3. Making charts. Use a dictionary or an encyclopedia to prepare a chart of Indo-European languages. Show the main branches and the languages within each branch.

4. Research. Several types of religious structure are found in India. Use an encyclopedia to find information on the stupa, the pagoda, and the mosque. Describe the appearance of each structure. Where did it originate? For what purposes is it used?

5. Bulletin boards. Prepare a bulletin-board display on ancient India. Include information on natural features such as rivers, historical places, famous people, art, and architecture. Use pictures and drawings to illustrate your display.

The five-clawed dragon on this Chinese silk embroidery was the symbol of a rain spirit. While dragons were evil creatures in the mythologies of many other lands, in China they symbolized imperial authority and were even believed to have the power to protect the emperor.

Civilization in China and Japan

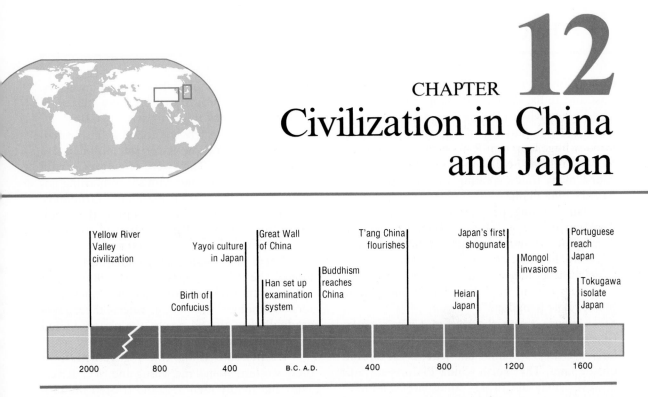

Yellow River Valley civilization · Yayoi culture in Japan · Great Wall of China · T'ang China flourishes · Japan's first shogunate · Portuguese reach Japan · Birth of Confucius · Han set up examination system · Buddhism reaches China · Heian Japan · Mongol invasions · Tokugawa isolate Japan

2000 — 800 — 400 — B.C. A.D. — 400 — 800 — 1200 — 1600

The civilization of China is one of the oldest in the world, dating back for nearly 4,000 years. Since early times the Chinese were deeply concerned with achieving good government. Following the ideals and ethics of the philosopher Confucius, they developed a system in which government officials were chosen by merit. It endured for hundreds of years, surviving the rise and fall of many ruling houses and the constant threat of invasion. The brilliant culture of the Chinese Empire was a model for all Asia.

Japan borrowed many ideas from Chinese culture but developed them in a distinctive way. A feudal society grew up, and military leaders centralized the country's government. Both Japan and China preserved their traditional cultures well into the nineteenth century by deliberately isolating themselves from foreign influences.

This chapter describes the growth of the civilizations of China and Japan.

CHAPTER OUTLINE

1 The Chinese Establish Lasting Traditions

2 China's Rulers Create an Empire

3 Imperial China Dominates Asia

4 Japan Develops a Feudal Society

5 Tokugawa Shoguns Unify Japan

1 The Chinese Establish Lasting Traditions

China's first civilization, like those in the Near East and India, developed along a great river. The Yellow River (*Hwang Ho* in Chinese) begins in the mountains of western China and forms a huge loop as it flows nearly 3,000 miles to the Yellow Sea. The river has changed course many times, creating a broad valley, the North China Plain.

The farming people of the river valley were cut off geographically from the rest of Asia by desert and mountains. Believing themselves to be the only civilized people in the midst of tribes they considered "barbarian," the Chinese came to call their land *Chung-Kuo,* "the Middle Kingdom."

Legends relate the rise of China's early rulers. Like the Nile, the Yellow River regularly overflows its banks and leaves rich topsoil on the land. The North China Plain is so flat, however, that disastrous floods are common. According to legend, the Hsia (SHEE-ah), China's first ruling house, or dynasty, was started about 2000 B.C. by Yu, a great hero. Yu supposedly found a way to control the floodwaters of the Yellow River so that farmers could live in the valley.

The Shang dynasty rules in North China. Early Chinese rulers were thought to be "sons of heaven" who were given the "mandate of heaven" — the approval of the gods to rule as long as they ruled well. According to tradition, the later Hsia rulers were so cruel that they lost the mandate of heaven to the Shang (SHAHNG) dynasty about 1600 or 1500 B.C.

For many years, the Shang people were thought to have existed only in legend. In the 1920's, however, archeologists found the ruins of a great Shang city at An-yang, on the North China Plain (map, page 253). The excavations at An-yang produced much information about the Bronze Age culture of the Shang. Unlike other Bronze Age peoples, the Chinese continued to make most tools and weapons of stone, bone, and wood. Bronze was made into objects used by the rulers and priests in religious rituals. Shang metalworkers made beautiful cups and cauldrons to hold the food or drink offered to the gods and to the spirits of royal ancestors. Some of these bronze articles were buried in the tombs of kings and nobles.

The Shang rulers controlled a fairly small state near the Yellow River but influenced a much larger area. They were often at war with neighboring people and with sheep-herding nomads who trespassed on the Shang farmlands. One of these neighboring peoples, the Chou (JOH) from the Wei River region to the west, overthrew the Shang about 1100 B.C.

Local rulers gain power under early Chou kings. The Chou reigned nearly 900 years, longer than any other dynasty in Chinese history. Although the Chou rulers themselves gradually lost all real power, the period named after them was an important one.

At first the Chou rulers governed from their western homeland along the Wei River. They put family members and trusted military leaders in charge of the eastern lands taken from the Shang. Each local lord lived in a walled town protected by an army of warrior-nobles. The lord also ruled the local population of peasants and slaves. In time these lords grew quite independent of the Chou kings and, in 771 B.C., rebelled against them. The Chou rulers fled 300 miles east along the Wei River to a new capital at Loyang.

Chinese culture and technology advance. The Eastern Chou rulers had little power and less land than many of the great local lords. Their long reign (770–256 B.C.) was a time of war, lawlessness, and disunity, but also of important developments in Chinese society. Agriculture, technology, trade, and transportation all were undergoing changes. Metalworkers of the Chou period learned to work with iron, making sturdy plows and sharp weapons. Canals for shipping grain were built, and irrigation systems were developed. Towns grew up as trading centers, and a class of merchants and traders formed. Merchants became wealthy and influential, although they were considered the lowest social class.

Some new ideas, such as the knowledge of ironworking, had probably come into north

A Shang artist created this bronze rhinoceros, used to hold ceremonial foods.

China from western and Central Asia. The nomadic herding peoples there also had learned to domesticate and ride horses. These mounted horsemen raided border areas and were a danger to farmers there, but they introduced horseback riding to the Chinese. This skill brought many changes. Soldiers learned to ride horseback rather than drive war chariots. Mounted messengers could carry news much faster than runners, and better communication helped rulers control their distant territories. Many Chinese also adopted the nomads' clothing style of wearing trousers rather than the traditional long robe.

Individual states develop systems of government. New states grew up in a ring around the old central states of the North China Plain. Chinese culture now spread over an area from the borders of Mongolia in the north to the Yangtze River in the south (map, page 253). This area included many people whom the inhabitants of the Middle Kingdom considered uncivilized barbarians.

The rulers in the almost-independent outlying states began to centralize their rule. They established tax systems, military organizations, and codes of law. Some took control of the trade in salt and iron, which brought their states a good income. States in north China began to build walls along their frontiers to keep out nomadic invaders. To organize such large projects as irrigation, flood control, and defense, the rulers needed efficient government.

To run the government, there grew up a new class of trained public officials and admin-istrators, or **bureaucrats** (BYOO-ruh-kratz). Most of these men were not high-ranking nobles but scholars and teachers. Some were philosophers who were interested in theories of politics and government. The bureaucrats traveled from state to state working for different rulers as tutors, consultants on correct behavior, and political advisers. Some attracted students and set up schools.

The writings of some of these teachers became guides for later Chinese society. Their books came to be known as "the classics," and the period when the teachers lived has been called China's Classical Age.

Confucius considers the roles of people in society. One of the traveling bureaucrats was Kung Fu-tzu ("Master Kung"), whom we know by his Latinized name, Confucius. He is regarded as China's greatest philosopher and teacher. Confucius (551–479 B.C.) lived at about the same time as the Buddha in India. Confucius was not a religious teacher, however. He was not concerned with the soul, an afterlife, or the worship of gods. He was most interested in questions of ethics and of morality in politics. He tried to define ways in which individuals should live and behave in their everyday relationships with others.

Confucius outlined five basic social relationships: between ruler and subjects, father and son, husband and wife, older and younger brothers, and friends or members of a community. In the first four relationships, one person was viewed as superior and worthy of respect and obedience. In turn, this superior person was expected to set a good example of moral behavior. According to Confucius, evil rulers were responsible for the evil actions of their officials and subjects. Similarly, a father was responsible for his children's good or bad behavior.

Confucius tried to teach his followers to develop the qualities that would make them virtuous public officials. The Confucian virtues included inner qualities such as integrity, loyalty, and generosity, but they also included good manners, culture, and politeness.

Mencius teaches that the individual is good. The philosopher Meng-tzu, who is known to the West as Mencius, lived about 200 years after Confucius (372–289 B.C.). He taught the ideas of Confucius and also made significant new contributions to Chinese thought. Mencius argued that individuals are naturally good and that this goodness can be developed into the Confucian virtues. He also defended the people's right to overthrow a ruler who did not live up to high principles and so lost the mandate of heaven.

Taoism urges harmony with nature. While Confucian philosophers set up strict rules for people's behavior within society, the Taoists rejected these as artificial. Their aim was to discover the *Tao* (DOW) or "way" of the natural universe and live in harmony with nature. The first great teacher of Taoist thought was supposedly the wise man Lao-tse (LAO-DZUH), who may have been only a mythical figure.

In about the third century B.C., the principles of Taoist thought were collected in a book called the *Tao Te Ching*. Taoist thinkers agreed, though, that the Tao could not really be explained in words. It had to be sensed or felt. Typical Taoist symbols were raw silk, an uncarved block of wood, and a newborn child. All of these were in their natural state, unchanged by society. To find the way of the natural universe, some Taoists became hermits and went to live in the mountains and forests. Their mystical philosophy served as a balance to the practical rules of Confucianism. Both ways of thinking endured in China until modern times.

The Legalists place the state above the people's welfare. Another important philosophy was developed by Hsun-tzu (SHUN-DZOO), who lived about the same time as Mencius. In contrast to Mencius, Hsun-tzu felt that people were basically evil and selfish but could be improved by education, great teachers, and strict laws. In the third century B.C., two of his followers evolved the philosophy known as Legalism. Legalists felt that a ruler must have absolute power so that he could turn all his people's efforts toward making the state wealthy and powerful. Rulers and statesmen in the state of Ch'in (page 253) adopted many Legalist ideas. By 256 B.C., the Ch'in leaders had defeated other Chinese states and destroyed the last Chou rulers. They put Legalism into practice in organizing an empire.

Chinese philosophies stress the importance of the family. The family was always the most important part of Chinese society. It was considered more important than the individual or the government. One of the most important virtues was filial piety — respect and obedience to one's parents. This respect extended to the family's ancestors. The early rulers of China worshiped not only various deities, but also the spirits of their "honored ancestors."

The importance of the family is reflected in Chinese philosophies. In three of the relationships described by Confucius, older male

---

PRIMARY SOURCES IN WORLD HISTORY
Classic of Filial Piety

A major theme in Confucianism was filial piety. Fulfilling filial duties, Confucius said, was the foundation on which good character was built. In this passage, he describes a son's duties to his parents.

Filiality is the foundation of virtue and the root of civilization. . . .

In serving his parents a filial son renders utmost respect to them at home; he supports them with joy; he gives them tender care in sickness; he grieves at their death; he sacrifices to them with solemnity. . . .

He who really loves his parents will not be proud in high station. He will not be insubordinate in an inferior position. Among his equals he will not be [quarrelsome]. . . . As long as these three evils are not uprooted, a son cannot be called filial even though he feast his parents daily with three kinds of choice meat.

What duties, according to Confucius, does a son owe his parents? How does filial love affect his relationships outside the family?

members of a family — the father, the husband, and the eldest son — were given positions of respect and superiority. Most political thinkers believed this same relationship existed between rulers or high officials and their subjects. That is, the king had the same authority over his subjects as a father over his family.

Women are given a lesser role. These same attitudes affected the status of women in Chinese society. Because maintaining the family name was considered so important, the birth of a son or grandson was a joyous event. Daughters might be loved, but only through marriage could a woman bring "honor" to her family. From obedience to her father, a woman moved on to obedience to her husband and then to her sons. She could own nothing except her dowry and even in her own household might have to be obedient to her mother-in-law or her husband's other wives. Only in old age might a woman acquire some authority of her own as a mother-in-law.

On the other hand, women were shown respect in various ways. In addition to maintaining the household, peasant women worked in the fields with men and were valued by their husbands. Merchants and officials had high regard for the advice and common sense of their wives. Moreover, a woman's prestige increased when her son brought back a wife, who would obey her and assume many of the homemaking responsibilities.

Age brings respect. The Chinese, both men and women, looked forward to old age, for it brought them wisdom, respect, and leisure. Filial piety required the eldest son to provide a good life for his aging parents. There were few sins in ancient China greater than showing disrespect for a parent, living or dead.

Women's work in China included silk-making. Even women of the emperor's court helped prepare the silken strands by pounding them, as shown in this scene from an ancient scroll.

CHECK-UP

1. Vocabulary: *bureaucrat.*
2. (a) Where did civilization first develop in China? (b) How was the Shang dynasty proved to be real, not legendary?
3. (a) Why was war within China common during the Chou period? (b) What technological advances did the Chinese make in Chou times?
4. (a) Why did scholars become important in Chinese society? (b) What five basic relationships did Confucius identify? (c) What qualities did he urge his followers to develop?
5. What were the basic teachings (a) of Mencius? (b) of the Legalists?
6. How was Taoism different from other Chinese philosophies?
7. Describe traditional Chinese attitudes toward (a) the family, (b) women, and (c) old age.

2 China's Rulers Create an Empire

Although the last Chou rulers had little real power, the fall of this dynasty in 256 B.C., after 900 years, was a turning point in Chinese history. The dynasties that followed the Chou established, extended, and maintained the Chinese Empire.

Chinese dynasties rise and fall. Throughout Chinese history, ruling houses faced the same basic problems: rebellions by local lords and peasants, barbarian invasions, and natural disasters. These problems caused the rise and fall of dynasties in a regular pattern. Many historians discuss Chinese history in terms of this dynastic cycle.

The dynastic cycle followed a pattern generally like this: A new dynasty begins with a period of peace, prosperity, and loyalty to the ruler. Population increases. The government spends money on public works — walls, canals, and roads. As the dynasty continues, less able rulers come to power. Court officials and bureaucrats become corrupt and used to luxury, which causes them to spend more of the government's money. More money also may have to be spent on defending newly won lands or holding off invaders. The peasants are taxed more heavily, but the government still does not have enough money to keep things in repair. Peasant rebellions break out. During the uprisings, dams and walls are weakened by neglect, allowing floods or invasions. Crops are destroyed, and famine may result. These weaken the government still more, and nobles begin to seize power from the ruling dynasty. The population decreases, and tax revenues are smaller. Finally the old dynasty falls. The new dynasty starts by establishing a period of peace and prosperity, and the cycle begins again.

The Ch'in dynasty unites China. The ruler of the powerful state of Ch'in overthrew the last of the Chou rulers in 256 B.C. By 221 the Ch'in had brought together the other states under a strong central government. The Ch'in dynasty lasted less than fifteen years, but it established the basis for the Chinese Empire, which endured into the twentieth century.

The Ch'in ruler took the name *Shih Huang Ti* (SHER HWAHNG DEE), "First Emperor." His most trusted adviser was Li Ssu (LEE SOO), one of the originators of Legalism. They began to apply Legalist thinking to all of China, strengthening defenses and crushing the local lords. To protect the empire from nomadic tribes, the First Emperor extended the walls built by the rulers of states on the northwest border. About one million laborers were forced to work on the Great Wall (map, next page). When completed, it stretched from the Yellow Sea to China's western frontier, a distance of about 1,500 miles (about the distance between Denver and Boston). Soldiers were stationed on the wall to defend China's frontier.

To help unify the country, the government built roads and canals, making communication between provinces quicker and safer. Li Ssu simplified the written language so that more people could learn to read and write. Weights and measures were standardized throughout the country, making it simpler for government officials to collect taxes and for merchants to transact business. Ch'in armies also extended the emperor's rule by making conquests in southern China.

The Ch'in suppress freedom of thought. As followers of Legalism, the Ch'in officials felt that other ways of thinking were dangerous to

The Great Wall winds its way for almost 1,800 miles in mountainous northern China. Made of earth and brick, the wall varies in height from 20 to 50 feet. From its towers, guards watched for attacking raiders. In peaceful times, gates in the wall were left open, permitting merchants to enter China.

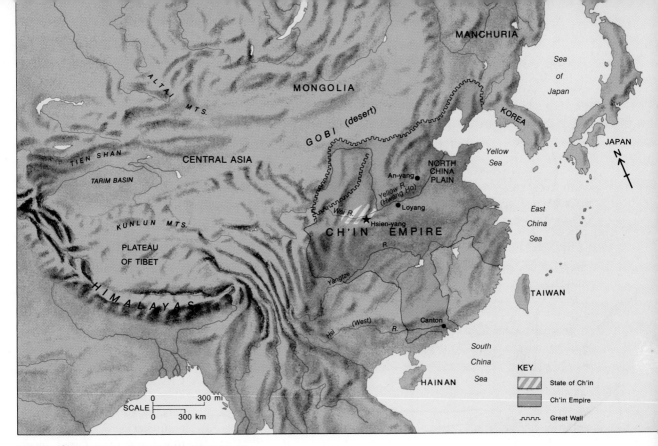

The Ch'in Empire, 221-206 B.C.

Chinese civilization developed on the North China Plain. What river flows through that plain? What protected the northern boundary of the Ch'in Empire?

the state. In 213 B.C., Li Ssu began a widespread program of book burning. The court library kept copies of early histories and the classics, but privately owned books were ordered destroyed. Scholars who discussed earlier times, criticized the government, or objected to the control of ideas were executed or banished, along with their families.

These actions by the Ch'in authorities abruptly ended the creativity of China's Classical Age. They also weakened the dynasty. The banished Confucian scholars had been the best-trained public officials. Without them, the government was not run well. In addition, many educated and influential people could not wholeheartedly support the rigid Legalist policies. Soldiers and peasants rebelled, and the dynasty fell only a few years after the death of the First Emperor.

Han rule lasts for four centuries. For several years rival leaders competed for power. In 202 B.C., a military leader declared himself emperor and established the Han (HAHN) dynasty.

This leader came from a peasant family and had been a bandit in the mountains before becoming a soldier. He took the title *Kao Tsu* (KOW DZOO), which means "Great Ancestral Father."

Kao Tsu and his successors drew on Ch'in patterns of governing but avoided the extremes of that rigid rule. This enabled the Han dynasty to endure until A.D. 220 with only a few years out of power. The 400 years of Han rule were so remarkable that the Chinese still call themselves "the Han people." The Han capital at Ch'ang-an[1] in the Wei River valley became a model city, with great parks, palaces, and public buildings.

Wu Ti expands the Han empire. The Han's greatest growth in land and power came about during the long reign of Wu Ti (141-87 B.C.). To the south, Han armies conquered many non-Chinese peoples along the southern

---

[1]Many cities have occupied the site of Ch'ang-an. The modern city is called Sian or Xian (SHEE-ahn).

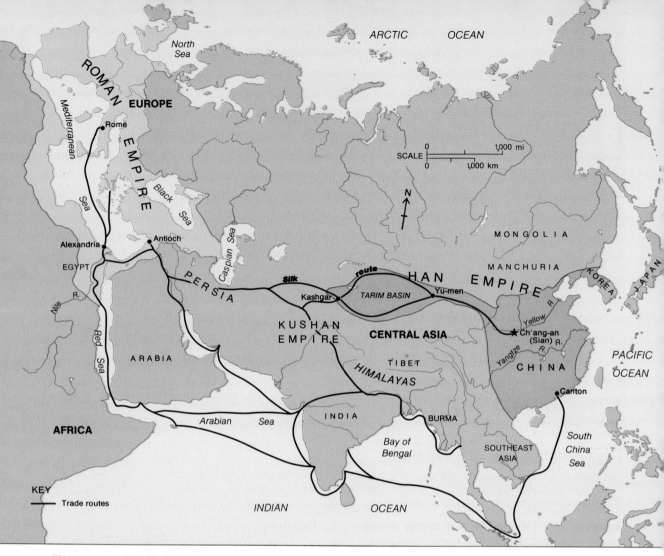

The Han Empire About A.D. 100

Under Han rule, the Chinese Empire stretched from the Pacific coast far to the west. Describe the routes followed by merchants who carried goods between Canton and Rome.

coast and in Southeast Asia. To the north and east, the empire expanded far beyond the Great Wall to include large parts of Korea and Manchuria.

Wu Ti also launched a campaign against the nomadic Huns of Central Asia. After his death, the Chinese conquered most of the barren mountains and steppes of Central Asia, including the Tarim Basin. By about the first century B.C., the borders of China reached as far west as the Kushan empire in Central Asia and northern India (page 238).

Trade develops between China and the West. Since ancient times the Chinese had known how to raise silkworms and weave silk cloth from the fibers spun by the worms. As no

other people knew this secret, Chinese silk was valuable for trade. Merchant caravans on the silk route traveled from oasis to oasis around the desert of the Tarim Basin. They carried silk and jade from China to India, Persia, and the eastern provinces of the Roman Empire.

Trade provided a way for ideas as well as goods to travel between cultures. In trading with Rome, the Chinese, for the first time in their history, encountered a civilization they considered as rich and varied as their own. They called the Roman Empire "Great Ch'in," while the Romans referred to China as *Serica*, "the silk country."

Confucian ideas return to government. Han rulers realized that the growing empire needed well-educated officials to run it properly. Scholars who followed the Confucian ideas of ethical government became influential at court. Written examinations were used to find enough educated and competent men to fill government jobs. Soon these scholar-officials replaced men of noble birth as the leading class in Han society. Scholar-officials were most likely to be the sons of landowners, who were wealthy enough to afford a good education. Merchants, no matter how well educated, were barred from government posts because moneymaking was despised by the Han rulers. In theory, farmers or peasants had a chance to rise in society through their skills or talents, but this rarely happened. The examination system, set up as a way to find efficient bureaucrats, later developed into the first real civil service system.

Science and technology develop. Important advances in science were made in the Han period. The Chinese had been recording information about the stars and planets since ancient times. Comets, sunspots, and eclipses were thought to be messages from heaven. By Han times, Chinese astronomers had devised an accurate calendar, star maps, and several astronomical instruments. Chinese scientists also had discovered the principle of the magnetic compass used to determine direction and had made an instrument to record earthquakes. Other scientists experimented in chemistry and made discoveries in medicine.

About the first century A.D., the Chinese learned to make paper. Like silk weaving, this remained a uniquely Chinese skill for centuries. China's other most famous craft — the making of fine porcelain or "china" — also began during the Han dynasty. Han potters invented glazes that gave plates and bowls a smooth, clean surface.

The Age of Disunity begins. By early in the second century A.D., the later Han rulers were facing economic ruin. There were rivalries among powerful families at court and between generals in the provinces, as well as widespread peasant rebellions. Even the examination system had become corrupt. Officials were more likely to be chosen through political influence than on the basis of their knowledge. In 220 A.D., the Han empire split into three kingdoms. Nomads crossed the frontier and swept into north China. Constant warfare caused great hardship for the peasants throughout China. This time of trouble came to be called the Age of Disunity. It continued for more than 300 years, until the year 589.

CHECK-UP

1. (a) Under what conditions did a new dynasty generally begin? (b) What frequently happened when less able rulers came to power? (c) What usually brought about the end of a dynasty?
2. (a) What dynasty established the Chinese Empire? (b) How did this dynasty try to protect and unify the empire?
3. (a) What areas did the Han rulers add to China? (b) With what foreign lands did Han merchants trade?
4. (a) Why did Han rulers set up an examination system? (b) How did this affect the social class system?
5. What advances had Chinese scientists and astronomers made by Han times?
6. What brought about the Age of Disunity?

3 Imperial China Dominates Asia

The Chinese Empire was reunited in the sixth century by the Sui dynasty. For a time it was the greatest empire in the world. Under later dynasties, imperial China surpassed Europe in culture and technology, and Chinese civilization became a model for all eastern Asia.

The Sui reunite the empire. Near the end of the Age of Disunity, a military leader in northern China conquered the south and declared himself first emperor of the Sui (SWIH) dynasty. There were just two Sui emperors, and their dynasty lasted from 589 to 618, less than thirty years, but they accomplished much in rebuilding the empire.

The two Sui emperors rebuilt the Great Wall, reconquered part of Central Asia, and reclaimed part of Southeast Asia. They began an ambitious program of canal-building, which included the Grand Canal linking the Yellow River and the Yangtze (map, page 257). Because China's great rivers all flow west to east, canals were important for north-south transportation and for trade between the rice-producing provinces of the Yangtze delta and the cities of the north.

The T'ang build a stronger empire. Tired of being sent to war and forced to labor on the canals and the Great Wall, the people soon rebelled against Sui rule. In a struggle for power, a former Sui official and his son took control of the throne in 618. The T'ang (TAHNG) dynasty which they established lasted until 907. It created another "golden age" in China.

The second T'ang emperor, T'ai-tsung (TYE-DZOONG), was a warrior, a scholar, and a good administrator. During his reign (626–649), he strengthened the government without

imposing too heavy a tax burden on the people. Chinese armies extended the empire by making conquests in Central Asia and Tibet.

In 655 all of Korea was brought under Chinese control. The leader of this campaign was the empress Wu Hou (WOO HOH). From about 660 on, she held the real power at court while weak emperors were on the throne. She became emperor in her own right in 690 (and was the only woman ever to hold that title in China). Because she was a woman and an outsider at court, Wu Hou depended on the help of the scholar-officials. Court officials forced her from the throne in 705, when she was eighty years old, but her reign had greatly increased the influence of the bureaucrats in government.

The examination system gains new importance. The examination system first used in Han times was based on the Confucian ideal of choosing officials for ability, not on the basis of noble birth. All the rulers after the Han made some changes or improvements aimed at reaching this ideal. In fact, only the sons of aristocrats and high officials were likely to have the classical education and the influence to become examination candidates. Peasants could rarely afford years of education and study. Nevertheless, it was the dream of every person in China to become — or have a son become — a member of the educated class known as gentry. By the middle of the T'ang dynasty, the system provided enough trained scholars to fill most high government positions.

T'ang culture becomes a model for Asia. China's central position encouraged trade and communication with other Asian nations. There was great demand in both Europe and Asia for Chinese silk and porcelain. The exchange of goods and ideas was two-way. Tea was introduced into China from Southeast Asia, and new ideas in mathematics and astronomy developed from contact with India. Foreign religions, including Buddhism, Islam, and some Eastern sects of Christianity, were also brought into China and won converts there.

As the center of the greatest empire in the world at that time, the T'ang capital at Ch'ang-an drew both Chinese and foreign visitors. They admired its broad streets, elegant houses, temples, palaces, and landscaped parks. The

TIMETABLE

Chinese Civilization

B.C.

2000*	Chinese civilization develops in the Yellow River valley.
1100*	Chou rulers begin a 900-year reign.
551	Confucius is born.
256–221	Ch'in rulers unify China.
202	Han rulers begin to expand the empire.

A.D.

220	The Han dynasty falls, bringing on the Age of Disunity.
589–618	Sui rulers rebuild the Great Wall and build the Grand Canal.
618–907	The Chinese Empire reaches its height under the T'ang dynasty.
1260–1294	Kublai Khan makes China a part of the Mongol Empire.
1368	Rebellion ends Mongol rule, and the Ming dynasty begins.
1644	The Ming dynasty comes to an end.

*APPROXIMATE DATES

Namibia transforms ethnic strife to unity

WINDHOEK, Namibia (AP) — Less than a year after Namibia was ablaze with a war and wracked by seemingly insurmountable ethnic differences, the territory is ready for a peaceful transition to independence from South Africa this week.

The diverse people of this vast, arid land have set aside their weapons and begun working together to transform Africa's last colony into one of the continent's few democracies. Independence officially begins Wednesday.

"We confounded the doubters," said Sam Nujoma, the territory's designated president, who led the South-West Africa People's Organization during its 23-year guerrilla war against South African rule.

Black nationalist guerrillas and right-wing whites who once fought each other have been preaching reconciliation in what has been a remarkably smooth approach to independence for Namibia, formerly known as South-West Africa.

"We have accepted that South-West Africa as we knew it will be replaced by an independent Namibia," said Jan de Wet, leader of the right-wing National Party. "We are glad to offer our skills and resources to this country if we are welcome."

SWAPO OFTEN was depicted by whites as a "Marxist-terrorist" organization during the war. But since winning U.N.-supervised elections in November, the leftist organization has made numerous compromises in an attempt to accommodate the 11 distinct ethnic groups that make up Namibia's 1.3 million people.

SWAPO's support comes predominantly from the northern Ovambo tribe, but Nujoma also has named blacks who are not Ovambos to key positions to allay fears that SWAPO will be a tribal-based government. He also has appointed whites and businessmen from opposition parties to his Cabinet.

"The future government wants to ensure that ... policies and laws will be supported by the widest possible cross-section of the population," said Otto Herrigel, a German-descended Namibian who will serve as Nujoma's finance secretary.

Seven parties won seats in the elections, and they have sharp ideological differences. But within weeks, the 72-member constitutional assembly unanimously agreed on a democratic constitution that guarantees fundamental rights and regular elections.

T'ang culture was copied by other countries in Asia, notably Japan, Korea, and Tibet.

Buddhism is influential in Chinese culture. Buddhism had first reached China from India in about the first century A.D., encouraged by King Kanishka of the Kushan empire in Central Asia (page 238). Some Buddhist ideas seemed to violate the Confucian rules for proper conduct and family responsibility, but Buddhism appealed to those who looked for peace and spiritual comfort. Traders, missionaries from India, and Chinese converts carried Buddhist ideas and knowledge between India, China, and Korea.

Buddhist monasteries in China, like those in India, became centers of learning, places of pilgrimage, hospitals, and schools. As they ac-

quired gifts of land and money, the Buddhist monasteries also gained political power. Buddhism was encouraged and protected by early T'ang rulers, particularly the empress Wu Hou.

In time, however, Confucian scholars and T'ang rulers began to fear the monasteries' influence. About the middle of the ninth century, a T'ang ruler ordered the destruction of thousands of Buddhist monasteries and temples and forced many monks and nuns to give up their religious life. This ended the period of Buddhism's greatest influence in China.

The T'ang dynasty ends in political confusion. From the eighth century on, the imperial government was steadily weakened by enemy attacks on its borders. At the same time,

The T'ang Empire About 750

The T'ang dynasty remained in power for about three hundred years. What important empires existed in other lands in Asia and Europe at the time of this map?

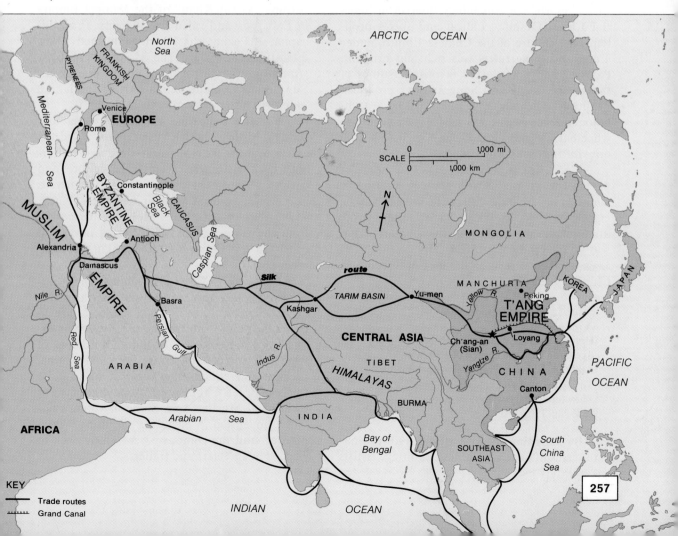

KEY
— Trade routes
⊢⊣⊢⊣ Grand Canal

257

military leaders in the provinces rebelled and drove the last T'ang emperor from the throne in 907. More than fifty years of disorder passed before a new dynasty, the Sung, reunited the country under one ruler.

The Sung prosper in southern China. When the Sung dynasty was established in 960, nomadic peoples controlled much land in northern China. Repeated invasions finally forced the Sung to leave the north in 1126. The period that followed, called the Southern Sung (1127–1279), was one of growth and prosperity.

Goods from the south were traded with the Chinese population in the north, with the nomads of Central Asia, and with markets in Asia and Europe. Ocean-going trade became important, for the Chinese had learned to build large ships and to navigate by using the compass. Population shifted to the cities, which grew into busy urban centers. The rich farmlands of the Yangtze Valley produced rice, tea, and silk for export, increasing Sung prosperity.

The arts and technology flourish in imperial China. Despite political and social problems, the culture of the Chinese Empire under T'ang and Sung rulers was rich and brilliant. Painting and poetry were favorite pastimes of the gentry. T'ang and Sung artisans produced beautiful porcelain and silks. Chinese technology developed such useful items as the wheelbarrow and gunpowder, which was used only for fireworks, not weapons.

T'ang China was, above all, a time for poets. The greatest T'ang poets — Li Po, Po Chu-i, and Tu Fu — all were writing in the eighth century. Li Po, a Taoist, often wrote about nature. Po Chu-i, who lived slightly later, was a government official. His poem "Red Cockatoo" comments on the lack of freedom in Chinese society:

> Sent as a present from Annam —
> A red cockatoo.
> Colored like the peach-tree blossom,
> Speaking with the speech of men.
> And they did to it what is always done
> To the learned and eloquent.
> They took a cage with stout bars
> And shut it up inside.

By Sung times, Taoist attitudes toward nature were influencing Chinese painting. Artists emphasized the beauty and serenity of natural landscapes and objects such as a single branch or flower. With only a few brush strokes and quiet colors, these paintings gave a quick impression of a scene.

The Chinese had invented paper about the first century A.D., and they later developed a method of printing an entire sheet from a carved wooden block. Folded, these sheets became the pages in a Chinese book. By about the eleventh century, classics from Taoism, Buddhism, and Confucianism were printed by this method.

China comes under Mongol rule. In the early 1200's, the Mongol leader Genghis Khan (page 220) began his conquest of Asia with the invasion of northern China. By 1215, the Mongol archers and horsemen had defeated the northern rulers and gone on to conquests in Central Asia. After Genghis Khan's death in 1227, his grandson Kublai Khan completed the conquest of the Southern Sung. In 1260 Kublai became "Great Khan" of the Mongol Empire in East Asia and ruled for 34 years. From his capital at Peking, the Khan established a new dynasty called Yüan. The Mongols gradually wiped out the ships and soldiers of the last Sung rulers, making China part of the largest empire in history (map, page 219).

For the first time in China's long and brilliant history, foreign "barbarians" ruled the entire country. The Mongols were very different from the Chinese in language, culture, and customs. They kept their separate identity as one way of controlling their Chinese subjects, whom they did not trust. Mongols lived apart from the Chinese, obeyed different laws, and restricted the Chinese to low-ranking government posts.

European travelers visit China. The Mongol Empire's control of the vast central plains of Asia and Eastern Europe made it safe to travel overland from Europe to China. Numerous European travelers, including a number of Christian missionary friars, reached China. Ideas and inventions also began to move more freely between China and Europe and between China and Muslim Asia. Some of China's notable inventions, including printing, gunpowder, and the compass, were taken back to Europe by travelers and traders.

SUNG AND MING ART

Artists of the Sung and Ming dynasties produced objects that are still treasured today. Sung artists, influenced by Taoist ideas about nature, often painted animals and birds (top, right). The fine porcelain jar above, frcm the Ming period, also shows the Chinese interest in nature. The Ming water buffalo (above, right) is carved from jade, a stone for which the Chinese felt a special reverence.

The most famous of the European travelers was a young Venetian trader, Marco Polo. With his father and uncle, he traveled by caravan on the silk route across Central Asia, arriving in China in 1275. Marco had learned several Asian languages in his travels, and the Khan sent him to various Chinese cities on government missions. The Polos returned to Venice in 1292 with a large fortune. Marco Polo's colorful account of his travels in China was widely read in medieval Europe. Europeans were amazed that a society so rich and advanced as China had never before come to their attention.

The Ming dynasty emphasizes classical scholarship. The death of Kublai Khan in 1294 weakened Mongol rule, and rebellions broke out in many parts of China. In 1368 the peasant leader of one rebel army seized Peking and declared himself emperor and founder of a new dynasty — the Ming.

After years of Mongol rule, the Ming emperors wanted to return to a purely Chinese state, modeled after the earlier T'ang and Sung dynasties. Once again the examination system became very important. The version of the system introduced under the Ming lasted into the twentieth century. Stressing traditional ideas, the Ming rulers limited the examinations to knowledge of the Confucian classics. Scholars restored the classics and collected China's ancient knowledge in an encyclopedia.

Not all the works of Ming literature were scholarly versions of the classics. Popular novels were read by ordinary people as well as scholars. The most famous was *All Men Are*

Brothers, an adventure story about a band of outlaws led by a hero like Robin Hood. The novel remained popular into modern times.

China becomes a sea power. Trade by sea with other parts of Asia had grown under the Mongols, and the Chinese became skilled navigators and shipbuilders. Between 1405 and 1433, the Ming rulers sent a great admiral named Cheng Ho (JUNG HOH) on seven expeditions to India, Arabia, and the east coast of Africa, the most ambitious sea voyages of the time. Cheng Ho's visits helped bring most of Asia into the Chinese tributary system. To acknowledge the superiority of the Chinese emperor, the rulers of "inferior" countries had to send him gifts, or tribute.

The Chinese look inward to their traditions. About the middle of the fifteenth century, the Ming rulers stopped sponsoring expeditions and encouraging trade. China became more cut off from the rest of the world. In the 1590's the Ming rulers were seriously weakened in fighting off a Japanese invasion of Korea (page 266). Internal disorder and rebellion brought the dynasty to an end in 1644. By this time, however, the traditional Chinese culture was so well-established that it endured through the reign of another foreign dynasty, the Manchu (1644–1912). China's stability depended on maintaining traditional values and deliberately remaining apart from the changes taking place in the rest of the world.

CHECK-UP

1. What steps did the Sui take to rebuild the empire after the Age of Disunity?
2. Explain what happened to each of the following under the T'ang dynasty: (a) the examination system, (b) trade, (c) Buddhism.
3. In what ways did China prosper under the Southern Sung?
4. (a) How did China come under foreign control in the thirteenth century? (b) What was the relationship between the Chinese people and the Mongol rulers? (c) How did Mongol rule encourage the spread of ideas?
5. (a) How did the Ming attitude toward trade change? (b) What were the results of this change?

4 Japan Develops a Feudal Society

Japan includes four large islands and thousands of smaller ones. It lies near enough the continent of Asia to have acquired ideas, institutions, and culture from the more ancient culture of China. Over many centuries, the Japanese shaped these borrowed elements into a unique culture of their own.

Mainland Asia influences Japanese culture. By about the second or third century B.C. — the early years of the Han dynasty in China — the Japanese people of the Yayoi culture were growing rice in irrigated fields and working with both bronze and iron. Their technology and agricultural methods had probably come from China and Korea.

A class system developed among these farming people. By about the third century A.D., they began to build huge mounds of earth as tombs for their rulers. The way of life of these mound-builders has been called the *Kofun,* or "tomb culture." The burial mounds were often surrounded by thousands of *haniwa,* clay statues of horses and other animals, boats, houses, and people, including knights in armor.

Chinese travelers to prehistoric Japan reported that people lived in many small tribal communities or clans, which were often at war with one another. The clans' rulers were also religious leaders. A number of clans had powerful women rulers during this period, and until about the ninth century A.D., women frequently ruled in Japan as queens or empresses.

Nature worship is part of early Japanese culture. The most ancient beliefs of the Japanese were based on reverence and awe for the forces of nature, which were seen as spirits, called *kami.* Out of these beliefs evolved the religion called Shinto. This religion had no complex rituals or philosophy but found beauty and wonder in all nature. *Kami* were thought to be present in such awesome forces as storms and lightning, as well as in other natural objects such as rocks, rivers, or trees. The influence of Shinto beliefs can be seen in Japanese art, literature, and architecture, which show sensitivity to natural forms and design.

Legends surround the Japanese imperial family. According to myth and tradition, in about the seventh century B.C., the grandson of Amaterasu, the sun goddess, descended to earth with three sacred objects: a bronze mirror representing Amaterasu, the iron sword of her brother the storm god, and a jewel naturally curved in the shape of a comma. (A mirror, a sword, and a curved jewel are still the symbols of Japanese imperial authority.) A later descendant of Amaterasu, known as Jimmu, is traditionally regarded as the first emperor of Japan and the founder of the imperial family, the Yamato.

The story is part legend, part history. Historical records do indicate that by the fifth century A.D. the Yamato kings ruled over a sizable territory in central and southern Honshu, in Kyushu, and even in the Korean peninsula. Because of their claim to descent from the sun goddess, the Yamato line of rulers acquired a special authority that even powerful nobles did not question. Although many of its later rulers had little real power, the imperial family in Japan was never overthrown. It has reigned uninterruptedly into the twentieth century and is the most ancient ruling house in the world.

Japan borrows institutions from mainland Asia. Chinese technology and culture had influenced Japan for hundreds of years. In about the sixth century A.D., however, the Japanese began deliberately to choose things to borrow from the Chinese culture and the culture of Korea, which had been greatly influenced by China. About the middle of the sixth century, the Japanese imperial court officially admitted Buddhism to Japan over the objections of some powerful clans who were strong Shintoists.

In 592 Prince Shotoku became chief adviser to his aunt, the empress Suiko. Shotoku began to reorganize the Japanese government to strengthen the central government and weaken the clans. In 604 he made his ideas offi-

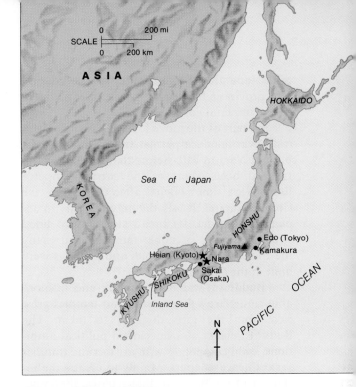

Japan About 1200

The islands that make up Japan form an arc stretching about 1,800 miles along the coast of Asia. Name the four main islands. On which island were most cities located?

cial in the Seventeen-Article Constitution. It declared the supremacy of the emperor and took away the inherited offices held by members of clans. Instead, government officials were to be appointed by merit, following the Confucian principles used in China.

Shotoku also began the custom of sending diplomatic missions to China. With the missions went many students who studied the culture and technology of China. They learned about Chinese art, architecture, music, government methods, and the Buddhist religion and brought their knowledge home to Japan. For the next 200 years, the Japanese imported Chinese learning through such missions.

The Taika Reforms establish a Chinese-style system. Prince Shotoku's policy was continued in the mid-600's by the Taika (TY-kah) Reforms. The purpose of these reforms was to establish a stronger central government modeled after that of T'ang China. All land in Japan was declared the property of the imperial government, which would allot land to the peasants who farmed it. The Taika Reforms also included a new tax system, a network of roads, and the reorganization of the country into provinces headed by governors appointed by the imperial government.

As part of the move toward a stronger central government, a permanent capital city was built at Nara in 710. Before that time, the capital had been wherever the current emperor lived. Nara was modeled after Ch'ang-an, the Chinese capital. It was the only real city in Japan at the time. Its broad streets were lined with the homes of noble families, and many tile-roofed Buddhist temples and pagodas were built in the Chinese style.

Buddhism was both popular and fashionable, and Nara's monasteries and temples grew rich from the gifts donated to them. The Buddhist clergy also developed political ambitions, even competing with aristocratic families for influence at court. Mainly to escape the influence of the Buddhist monasteries, the imperial court moved to a new capital in 784.

Japanese culture flourishes at the Heian court. The new capital was given the name Heian (HAY-AHN), "the capital of peace and tranquility." The city itself had broad tree-lined parkways. Houses were set in large gardens, beautifully landscaped with lakes and waterfalls. Later renamed Kyoto, the city remained the Japanese capital until the nineteenth century.

TIMETABLE

Japanese Civilization

A.D.

400*	Yamato kings gain power.
604	Prince Shotoku strengthens imperial rule.
646	The Taika Reforms strengthen the central government.
784	The imperial court moves to Heian, where arts and literature flourish.
1185	Minamoto Yoritomo becomes the first shogun.
1281	The Mongol invasion of Japan fails.
1338	The Ashikaga shogunate begins.
1467–1567	Feudal lords grow powerful as the central government collapses.
1600	Japan is unified under the Tokugawa shogunate.

*APPROXIMATE DATES

For about 300 years (until the 1100's), the aristocratic families at the imperial court in Heian lived in peace and developed a luxurious way of life. Only a few thousand people took part in this society, for most of the Japanese people were still peasants. The Heian court, however, greatly influenced what came to be Japan's characteristic culture.

Chinese traditions influence language and literature. A common spoken language had helped to unify Japan, but this language was not written. The Japanese therefore borrowed the Chinese writing system, although the two languages are totally unrelated. Since writing Japanese words with Chinese characters was difficult, some educated Japanese chose to write in the Chinese language. Monks wrote Buddhist and Confucian religious texts in Chinese characters, and the first histories of Japan were also written in Chinese about the seventh century.

Although most educated Japanese men continued to be proud of their ability to write scholarly Chinese, two new scripts were devised for writing Japanese according to its sounds. The women of the Heian court did all their writing in these Japanese scripts. They wrote diaries, poems, letters, and novels describing the elegant life and intrigues of the court. These writings by the court ladies mark the beginning of Japan's national literature.

The most famous of the court novels, still read today, is *The Tale of Genji.* Often called the first novel in world literature, it was written about A.D. 1000 by the Lady Murasaki Shikibu, lady-in-waiting to a wife of the emperor. The book is a long romance about Prince Genji, a hero who appears as the perfect Japanese court gentleman. Its vivid descriptions and style have made it a world classic.

Nobles challenge the imperial court's power. For most of the Heian period, the rich Fujiwara family held the real power in Japan. Members of this family married into the imperial family and held many influential posts. By about the middle of the eleventh century, however, the power of the central government (and the Fujiwaras) began to decline. Court families grew more interested in luxury and their personal fortunes than in governing. Many noble families and religious groups (both Shinto and

The Japanese Kimono

In Japan today many people still wear robes called kimonos, a style of dress that dates back to feudal times. The design of each kimono tells a great deal about its wearer. On the sleeves or back are small circular emblems. These are family crests similar to the coats-of-arms used in medieval Europe. The crest shown here is a stylized design of three cloves. Each noble family had a crest, which was worn by the family and the samurai who served it.

In addition to crests, kimonos often have designs representing different ideas. The pine tree stands for endurance; the shellfish (shown here) represents long life. A glance at the kimono's sleeves tells the marital status of the wearer. Only a young unmarried woman would wear a kimono with extremely long sleeves (called "swinging sleeves") and a bold design. The kimono of a married woman would have a subdued design and much shorter sleeves.

Buddhist) owned land on which they paid no taxes; this caused government income to drop.

Large landowners living away from the capital set up private armies, and the countryside became lawless and dangerous. Farmers and small landowners traded parts of their land to strong warlords in exchange for protection. With more land, the lords gained more power. This marked the beginning of a feudal system somewhat like that in medieval Europe.

Military leaders assume political authority. Two powerful warrior families, the Taira and the Minamoto, struggled for power for about thirty years. In 1180 full-scale war broke out between them. Five years later the Minamoto family and its army defeated the Taira in an epic naval battle on the Inland Sea. The young Emperor Antoku was drowned, and the imperial sword (one of the symbols of imperial power) was lost.

The victorious Minamoto leader, Yoritomo, established his government in the town of Kamakura, where it would be independent of the imperial court. Yoritomo soon gained the title of *shogun,* which means "barbarian-subduing general." In theory, the shogun ruled over military matters in the name of the emperor. In practice, the shogun was the real ruler, and his descendants inherited his title.

To secure the loyalty of the provincial warrior nobles, Minamoto Yoritomo appointed a noble as the "protector" of each province. In so doing, he strengthened the feudal structure throughout the country.

With the establishment of the Kamakura shogunate (that is, government by the shogun), Japan had, in effect, become a military dictatorship. While the imperial line continued unbroken, military leaders and their families remained in control of Japan's government into modern times. The Kamakura shogunate was the first of three to rule Japan between 1185 and 1868.

Honor and loyalty are "the way of the warrior." A class of warriors called *samurai* (SAH-MOO-RYE) dominated society in feudal

Japan. The chief symbols of every samurai's honor were his two swords — one long, one short. A samurai's life was devoted mostly to developing and perfecting skills in swordsmanship and archery. His ideals were personal bravery and loyalty to his lord, which was considered more important than loyalty to friends, family, or the emperor. The samurai code came to be called *Bushido* (BOO-SHEE-DOH), or "the way of the warrior." It called for a life of discipline, duty, and self-control, on and off the battlefield.

Honor was supremely important to a samurai. If he felt dishonored in any way, he considered himself obliged to commit *seppuku*, or ritual suicide. This also was true for women of the samurai class. (*Seppuku* is popularly called *hara-kiri*, which means "belly-slitting.")

The samurai had the right to inherit land, and a lord often rewarded loyal warriors by giving them the land of defeated enemies. In early feudal Japan, women of the samurai class also could inherit both land and an honored position. They, too, were expected to be honorable, brave, and loyal. As samurai were often away fighting, samurai women managed the estates. Some women, such as Masako, the wife of Yoritomo, were active politically.

Different forms of Buddhism become popular. Buddhism had at first appealed mainly to the court aristocrats in Japan. During the feudal period, however, new Buddhist sects became popular among the common people. Traveling preachers and Buddhist priests carried their messages to villagers and rural people, and Buddhist scriptures were translated into Japanese.

A very different form of Buddhism, known as Zen Buddhism, was brought from China by Japanese monks around the year 1200. Zen emphasized enlightenment through meditation and included some elements of Taoism (page 250). It stressed simplicity and discipline. Zen Buddhism had an immediate appeal for the samurai. Its discipline helped them develop qualities they needed to follow their strict code of bravery and loyalty. Even though Buddhism is a religion of nonviolence, the samurai applied Zen attitudes to the martial arts, particularly swordsmanship and archery.

A "divine wind" saves Japan from Mongol conquest. By the late 1200's, China had become part of the growing Mongol Empire. The Mongol ruler, Kublai Khan (page 258), demanded that Japan also accept his rule. When his demand was refused, he send a fleet to invade Japan in 1274. The samurai fought off the invading Mongol horsemen, helped by a fierce storm that forced the fleet to withdraw. Seven years later, a Mongol invasion force of about 140,000 men again attacked Japan. Again, a storm swept out of the Pacific. The raging winds and towering waves of the typhoon wrecked many Mongol ships and left thousands of soldiers stranded in Japan. Believing that the

The samurai were a favorite subject of Japanese artists. This mounted warrior is shown wearing plate armor over his kimono.

typhoon had been sent by the *kami* to protect them, the Japanese named the storm *kamikaze*, which means "divine wind."

The victory over the Mongols proved to be expensive for the Kamakura shogunate and for the samurai. Some samurai had spent so much in the war that they could no longer afford to maintain their horses and weapons. The shogun had no new lands to give them. Discontented samurai and nobles deserted the shogun to support an ambitious emperor who wanted more political power. Civil war broke out, and the Kamakura shogunate ended in 1333 with the suicide of the last shogun and his entire family and staff.

Local lords take power away from the central government. The nobles who joined with the emperor did not in fact give power back to the imperial family, but claimed it themselves. One warlord, Ashikaga Tokauji, had himself made shogun in 1338, establishing his family as Japan's second line of military rulers. From the start, however, the Ashikaga leaders lacked the support of most samurai.

The last hundred years of the Ashikaga shogunate (1467–1567) are sometimes called the Age of the Country at War. The central government had almost collapsed, and neither shogun nor emperor was in control. The local lords, now called daimyo (DYE-MYOH), had the loyalty of the samurai and held absolute rule over the people of their territories. Their samurai were almost constantly at war with each other.

Class lines break down. War destroyed old distinctions between classes. The lower classes became more important in Japanese society. The samurai, however, lost prestige because the daimyo recruited peasants and commoners to serve in the armies. Many old noble families of the court lost their estates to the daimyo and so had no income. For a time in the early 1500's, an emperor could not be officially enthroned because the court was too poor to pay for the ceremony. One emperor had to earn a living by writing poems and selling them on the street.

Zen Buddhism inspires artistic brilliance. The Ashikaga shoguns and most samurai followed Zen Buddhism, and the great Zen monasteries influenced politics, trade, and the arts. A brilliant period of Zen-inspired art began in the fifteenth century. Certain arts are typical of this Zen style: the tea ceremony, the simple arrangements of Japanese gardens, and landscape paintings done with a few brush strokes. Each uses the ideas of simplicity and attention to detail that are a part of the Zen approach.

Artists at the shoguns' court also developed the Noh style of drama, which became the classic theater of Japan. Noh is presented on a bare stage with stylized movements and elaborate masks and costumes.

Towns and trade flourish amid disorder. The changes taking place in Japanese society encouraged trade and crafts despite the disorder and warfare. Some merchants prospered by supplying food and equipment to the armies. Peasants also became more prosperous because of new farming techniques. Farmers, artisans, and merchants met on market day to trade goods, crafts, and food. Some merchants and artisans formed groups that were somewhat like the guilds of medieval Europe (page 160).

As in medieval Europe, the increase in trade and the rise of markets led to the growth of towns. People settled near market places, monasteries, seaports, or around the fortified castles of the daimyo. Although the old feudal system was breaking down, the Japanese economy and arts continued to thrive.

CHECK-UP

1. Vocabulary: *shogun, samurai.*
2. (a) On what were ancient Japanese religious beliefs based? (b) What were *kami?*
3. On what did the Japanese imperial family base its claim to power?
4. (a) What things did the Japanese borrow from Chinese culture? (b) What were the Taika Reforms?
5. (a) How did a shogun replace the emperor as the actual ruler of Japan? (b) What were the characteristics of the samurai way of life?
6. (a) What saved Japan from the Mongol invasion? (b) How did victory against the Mongols affect the Kamakura shogunate?
7. (a) How did power shift to the daimyo during the Ashikaga shogunate? (b) What caused the power of the samurai to decline? (c) Why did towns begin to grow during the Ashikaga shogunate?

5 Tokugawa Shoguns Unify Japan

Japan's central government broke down during the last years of the war-torn Ashikaga shogunate (1467–1567). Feudal lords fought for power. Finally strong military leaders emerged, reorganized the country, and unified it as a nation. In the early 1600's, a new shogunate was established by the Tokugawa family.

The Portuguese introduce European ideas. The arrival of European traders and missionaries influenced events in Japan in several ways. About 1542 a Portuguese ship landed near Kyushu, and soon many Portuguese traders were visiting Japan regularly. In 1549 the Jesuit missionary Francis Xavier began his mission to make Japan the first Christian country in Asia. His descriptions of Japan were so enthusiastic that other Jesuits soon followed. The Jesuits at first made many converts to Christianity. By 1582, it was estimated that there were about 150,000 Christians in Japan (in a population of about twenty million). By 1600 there were about 300,000.

The Portuguese and Japanese found each other's customs and manners strange but often admirable and interesting. Both Japan and Portugal had feudal societies that stressed pride and honor. The Europeans were impressed by the Japanese culture, with its politeness and sense of restraint. The Japanese respected the discipline of the Jesuit order, regarding the missionaries as aristocrats and men of learning. Both countries were eager for the profits that trade would bring, since trade with China had been stopped because of piracy.

European weapons also had a great effect on the Japanese. Daimyo whose soldiers had guns had an advantage over archers, swordsmen, and cavalry. The superior Portuguese weapons (including their armed ships) may have provided one motivation for Japan to move toward national unity.

Nobunaga begins to unite Japan. Oda Nobunaga, an ambitious local lord, took advantage of European weaponry and missionary support. He began his conquests in about 1551, at the age of nineteen. By 1568, through almost constant warfare, he had captured the capital at Kyoto as well as the lands of other daimyo. The last Ashikaga shogun was forced out of office. Nobunaga's armies included more peasants than samurai, but they were equipped with the newly introduced guns, which gave them an advantage even over trained warriors.

Nobunaga was determined also to destroy the military power of the warrior-monks in Buddhist monasteries, and he ordered several brutal massacres. Because of his hatred for Buddhism, Nobunaga welcomed the Jesuits to Kyoto and allowed them to live and preach there.

Hideyoshi unites the country. Nobunaga's best general, Hideyoshi, claimed leadership after Nobunaga's assassination in 1582. Within ten years he had brought all of Japan under his control. Hideyoshi's ambition was to unite all Asia in a great empire. The conquest of China was his main goal, but two unsuccessful invasions of Korea in the 1590's ended this dream.

Hideyoshi then sought to restore peace and stability in Japan by eliminating anything he feared might cause unrest. He ruled with absolute control but gained the support of the imperial court by rebuilding the palace and giving the emperor an income. The daimyo in theory continued to rule their own territories. To lessen their influence, however, Hideyoshi sometimes moved powerful daimyo into areas far from the capital or gave them territory near daimyo he trusted.

Though born a commoner, Hideyoshi tried to stop rapid social change by re-establishing old class distinctions. New laws forbade samurai to leave their lords, peasants to leave their farms, or artisans to move away from their villages. Hideyoshi once again made swords the exclusive possession of the samurai, ordering all commoners to give up their weapons.

The power of the Buddhist monasteries had been broken. Hideyoshi now began to worry about the Jesuits' influence and the loyalty of Japanese Christians. In 1587 he banished the missionaries, although the Church continued to operate secretly.

Japan's last shogunate begins. A power struggle among the daimyo began when Hideyoshi died in 1598, leaving his five-year-old son as his heir. Another of Nobunaga's generals, Tokugawa Ieyasu (EE-eh-YAH-soo), settled the conflict by winning a decisive victory at the town of Sekigahara in 1600. The Tokugawa family established Japan's last shogunate, which remained in power until 1868.

As shogun, Ieyasu began to reorganize the daimyo's lands to make his rule more secure. His own headquarters were at the village of Edo (which grew into the modern city of Tokyo), where he built a huge fortress-castle. Near Edo were the Tokugawa family's "house lands" and the lands of the most loyal lords. Those daimyo whom Ieyasu trusted less were sent away to domains in remote parts of the country. Ieyasu gave his son the title of shogun in 1603 but continued to rule until his death in 1616, at the age of 73.

Christianity is suppressed in Japan. Ieyasu and his successors were convinced that foreign missionaries and Japanese Christians were a threat to the country's stability. News of Spanish and Portuguese conquests in other parts of the world added to Japanese fears of outside influences. In 1614 Ieyasu ordered the missionaries and some Japanese converts to leave the country. His successors increased the persecutions, and by the 1630's Christianity was openly practiced only around the trading town of Nagasaki. In 1637 the peasants near Nagasaki, many of whom were Christians, rebelled against the local lord's heavy taxes. The incident turned into the final defense of Christianity in feudal Japan. More than 20,000 people — the last large group of Japanese Christians — were massacred when the shogun's army attacked a castle where they had taken refuge.

The shoguns choose isolation. Fearful of foreign influence, later shoguns strictly limited all foreign contacts. Laws issued in the 1630's forbade Japanese to travel abroad or to return home if they had already left the country. The Dutch, who made no attempt to introduce missionaries, were the only European traders allowed in Japan. Along with the Chinese trad-

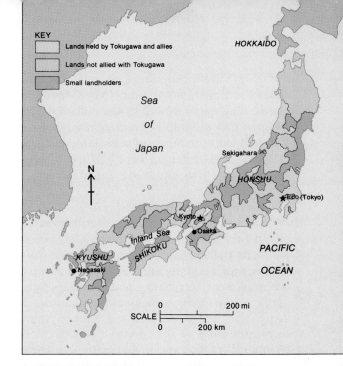

Tokugawa Japan

The Tokugawa rulers strengthened their power by awarding land near Edo to lords who were loyal allies. How is the landholding pattern shown on the map?

ers, they were restricted to the area around Nagasaki.

Once a year the Dutch traders traveled to Edo to give gifts to the shogun. For about the next 200 years, these visits were almost the only occasion for an exchange of news between Japan and Europe. Later in the period, a few educated samurai were allowed to study the Dutch language and "Dutch learning," mainly science, medicine, and military technology. For the most part, however, Japan was isolated from the rest of the world.

The daimyo's freedoms are limited. In dealing with the daimyo, the Tokugawa shoguns followed a policy of "divide and conquer." For various reasons they might change, take away, or reduce the size of a lord's landholdings. Fearing rebellion, the shoguns kept the daimyo from forming alliances. Marriages between daimyo families or visits to another lord's lands or to the emperor had to be approved by the shogun. The emperor himself never left the imperial capital at Kyoto.

The most effective method for weakening the daimyo was the system of "alternate attendance." Roughly half the daimyo and their households were required to live in Edo, the shogun's capital, for a year. When the year ended, they were replaced by the other daimyo. Daimyo had to build permanent residences in Edo and leave members of their families there as hostages. The system kept half the daimyo and their samurai under the watchful eyes of the shogun.

Tokugawa policies bring prosperity. The system of alternate attendance had unexpected results for Japan's economy. A network of major roads linked the daimyo's lands with Edo. Towns, inns, and busy markets grew up to serve the travelers. Merchants and artisans prospered. Some family businesses grew into large companies, and merchants and bankers came to control much of the country's wealth. Merchants still ranked very low socially, but some used their wealth to improve their status. A merchant might, for example, pay a poor samurai family to adopt his son and raise him as a samurai.

Some peasant farmers became poorer because of heavy taxes on rice, but many prospered by growing cash crops to sell to the townspeople. Commerce was becoming more important and more profitable than agriculture. Edo soon became Japan's largest and wealthiest city. By 1800 it had about a million people. Osaka was the financial capital, where daimyo and samurai sold the rice crops from their estates to obtain cash.

Changes affect the samurai and daimyo. Although many merchants and peasants prospered under the Tokugawa, the daimyo and samurai rapidly fell into financial trouble. Their incomes came mostly from agriculture, especially rice, which was heavily taxed. They did not benefit from the increased trade and prosperity in the towns, though they had to pay the resulting higher prices. The daimyo's expenses for "alternate attendance" in Edo were very high. Keeping up several luxurious houses and traveling back and forth to Edo often took more than half their income.

Trained only as professional soldiers, the samurai found themselves unemployed during the peace of the Tokugawa period. They shared the financial troubles of the daimyo because their only income was a salary (paid in rice) from the feudal lord. If a lord went into debt or lost his land, his samurai suffered too. Their income might be cut or they might become *ronin* (ROH-NIN) — samurai who had no lord to serve. Although it was against the law and also meant giving up their social rank, some samurai became farmers or merchants. Most preferred to remain proud but poor. Like the daimyo, they went deeply into debt.

In an effort to help the samurai find a new place in society, the shoguns encouraged education. Some samurai turned to teaching martial arts; others took government posts.

Popular arts flourish in the cities. Life in the fast-growing cities was busy and exciting for the merchants, business people, and samurai who had adopted city living. Literacy in Japan was high, and books of fiction and poetry were widely read. Two popular new forms of theater emerged. In the *bunraku*, or puppet theater, large puppets acted out exciting historical dramas or realistic plays. The live actors of the *kabuki* theater portrayed exciting stories against a background of colorful costumes and scenery.

A new type of poetry, the *haiku* (HYE-KOO), also became popular with all classes of people. A haiku is very short — three lines totaling seventeen syllables — and gives the reader an instant image or picture. The following is the work of a haiku poet named Onitsura:

THE WORLD UPSIDE DOWN
A trout leaps high —
below him, in the river bottom,
clouds flow by.

A new school of artists began to produce pictures that showed the bustling life of the city — scenes of actors backstage at the theater, crowded streets, and busy main highways. The technique of woodblock printing, which produced books inexpensively, also gave ordinary people a chance to own colorful prints by these artists. From an artist's original drawing, a woodcarver made many printing blocks — one for each shade or color. Each color was printed in turn on the paper. Many copies of an original drawing could be produced in this way. Prints by great artists such as Hiroshige, Uta-

JAPANESE STREET SCENES

Japanese artists depicted city life in Tokugawa Japan. The carving at left shows an actor and a musician typical of the performers who played to enthusiastic audiences. Booksellers like the one above sold their wares on city streets.

maro, and Hokusai later become popular in Europe and influenced Western art styles.

New ways of thinking develop. The Tokugawa policies of isolation cut off the people of Japan from Western ideas for about 200 years. The strict class structure of centralized feudalism kept peace and brought prosperity. Yet Japan did not stand still during its isolation. Social change continued. People of the merchant and peasant classes gained the education, freedom, and respect that only the samurai class had once enjoyed. Although Japan did not become industrialized at this time, its artisans developed and perfected their skills. Banking and commerce continued to grow. Unlike China, which resisted change, Japan moved forward during its isolation, though it moved in different ways than did the West.

CHECK-UP

1. Why did the Japanese at first welcome contact with Portuguese missionaries and traders?
2. (a) How did Oda Nobunaga use European technology to begin the unification of Japan? (b) What did Hideyoshi do to strengthen central control?
3. What steps did the Tokugawa shoguns take (a) to end Christian influence? (b) to put a policy of isolation into effect? (c) to limit the power of the daimyo?
4. How did the Tokugawa period affect (a) merchants and artisans, (b) daimyo and samurai, and (c) the growth of popular arts?

Chapter 12 Review

Summary

The first Chinese cultures grew up about 2000 B.C. along the Yellow River in north China. During China's Bronze Age, individual lords began to govern their own states and develop systems of centralized government. These became the basis for the Chinese Empire, which was established in the third century B.C. and became great during the 400 years of Han dynasty rule. The empire reached its height during the T'ang and Sung periods. It became a model for the rest of Asia. The philosophies of Confucianism, Taoism, and Legalism influenced Chinese thought and government. An examination system based on Confucian ideals established a class of scholar-officials.

China was conquered by the Mongols in the 1100's. After 200 years, Chinese rule was restored by the Ming dynasty. Ming rulers adopted a policy of isolation that endured until modern times.

The Japanese borrowed many elements of culture from China, but the two Asian civilizations developed in different ways. By about the twelfth century, real governing power passed from the Japanese imperial family to hereditary military leaders called shoguns. Feudalism developed, dominated by landowning lords (daimyo) and warriors (samurai). In the sixteenth century a strong national state was created. Contacts and trade with Europe flourished for a time, but in the mid-1600's the Tokugawa shoguns adopted a policy of isolation from the rest of the world.

Vocabulary Review

1. Match the following terms with the listed definitions: *bureaucrat, dynasty, samurai, shogun.*
(a) A series of rulers from the same family.
(b) A trained public official who is appointed rather than elected.
(c) One of the military leaders who ruled Japan from the twelfth century to the nineteenth century.
(d) A noble trained as a warrior in feudal Japan.
2. Distinguish between the terms in each of the following pairs:

(a) Han dynasty; T'ang dynasty.
(b) Classical Age; Age of Disunity.
(c) Middle Kingdom; Mongol Empire.
(d) haniwa; kami.
(e) Shinto; Zen Buddhism.
(f) Bushido; ronin.

People to Identify

Match the following people with the numbered phrases that describe them: *Kublai Khan, Lao-tse, Shih Huang Ti, Confucius, Li Po, Hsun-tzu, Marco Polo.*
1. A traveling bureaucrat who became China's greatest philosopher and teacher.
2. The first (and possibly mythical) teacher of Taoism.
3. The Mongol ruler who conquered the Southern Sung.
4. The Venetian trader who wrote of his travels in China in the thirteenth century.
5. The founder of Chinese Legalist philosophy.
6. The author of *The Tale of Genji.*
7. A great Taoist poet of the T'ang dynasty.
8. The Ch'in ruler who unified China.

Relating Geography and History

1. **Locating places.** Locate each of the following on a map in this chapter:
(a) Edo
(b) Nara
(c) Peking
(d) Ch'ang-an
(e) An-yang
(f) Wei River
(g) Yellow River
(h) Heian (Kyoto)
(i) North China Plain
(j) Inland Sea
(k) Yangtze River
2. **Reading maps.** (a) On the map of China on page 253, follow the routes of the Yellow, Yangtze, Wei, and Hsi rivers. In what direction do all of these rivers flow? (b) Find the Grand Canal on the map on page 257. (Use the map key.) What rivers does it connect? (c) Why were canals so important for trade between the different regions of China?
3. **Interpretation.** Though close to the rest of Asia, the island nation of Japan was somewhat isolated from mainland influences. How did Japan's location affect the spread of cultural influences from the mainland?

Discussion Questions

1. (a) Describe the teachings of Confucius. (b) How did his teachings differ from those of the Taoists?

2. (a) How did the Ch'in unify China? (b) How did the Han rulers use Confucian ideas to strengthen their government?

3. (a) What was the examination system? (b) Was this system democratic? Explain.

4. Describe the influence of Chinese culture on Japanese (a) religious beliefs, (b) government, (c) writing.

5. What achievements did the Japanese themselves make in (a) literature, (b) drama, and (c) art?

6. (a) Why did a feudal society develop in Japan? (b) What were the roles in this society of the emperor, the samurai, and the shogun? (c) How did the rise of the daimyo affect these roles?

7. (a) What did Nobunaga, Hideyoshi, and Tokugawa Ieyasu each do to break the power of the daimyo? (b) Compare and contrast the attitudes of Nobunaga and Tokugawa Ieyasu toward the Jesuits and Japanese Christians.

Reading Primary Sources

In A.D. 604 Japan's Prince Shotoku completed his Seventeen-Article Constitution. This document was not a constitution in the modern sense but a set of rules of behavior that the prince wanted people to follow. Read the following excerpts from the constitution. Then answer the questions that follow.

> Harmony should be valued and quarrels should be avoided. Everyone has his [opinions], and few men are far-sighted. . . .
>
> Do not be envious! For if we envy others, then they in turn will envy us. The evils of envy know no limit. If others surpass us in intelligence, we are not pleased; if they are more able, we are envious. But if we do not find wise men and sages, how shall the realm be governed? . . .
>
> Employ the people in forced labor at seasonable times. . . . Employ them in the winter months when they are at leisure, but not from spring to autumn, when they are busy with agriculture or with the mulberry trees [the leaves of which are fed to silk-worms]. For if they do not attend to the mulberry trees, what will there be for clothing?
>
> Decisions on important matters should not be made by one person alone. They should be discussed with many people. . . . One should consult with others so as to arrive at the right conclusion.

(a) Why did Shotoku say that people should be employed in forced labor only during the winter months? (b) How did Shotoku advise people to go about making important decisions? (c) What did he mean when he said that "the evils of envy know no limit"? (d) To what group in society was this constitution probably addressed?

Skill Activities

1. Placing events in time. In each of the following items, arrange the three events or developments in the order in which they happened.
(a) China conquers all of Korea.
The Great Wall is built.
Marco Polo visits China.
(b) The Chinese learn to make paper.
China enters the Age of Disunity.
Confucius dies.
(c) Minamoto Yoritomo becomes the first shogun.
The Tale of Genji is written.
Francis Xavier arrives in Japan.
(d) A "divine wind" saves Japan from Mongol conquest.
The Taika Reforms are introduced.
A mound-building culture develops in Japan.

2. Making diagrams. Using the information on page 252, draw a diagram that shows the typical stages of the Chinese dynastic cycle. Be sure to label each part of your diagram. Then write a paragraph explaining how the Ch'in or Han dynasty fits the pattern you have shown.

3. Reports. Find information about one of the following topics and prepare a report: (a) Japanese Noh drama; (b) the Japanese tea ceremony; (c) similarities and differences between the code of chivalry followed by medieval European knights and the samurai code known as *Bushido;* (d) the Great Wall of China; (e) the history of Shintoism; (f) Japanese ancestor worship; (g) the Chinese writing system.

People outside of Africa were unaware of the continent's long history of metalworking until bronze sculptures were shipped to Europe in the late 1800's. This plaque from the wealthy kingdom of Benin shows a king and his attendants. It may have decorated the king's house.

CHAPTER **13**

Civilization in Africa

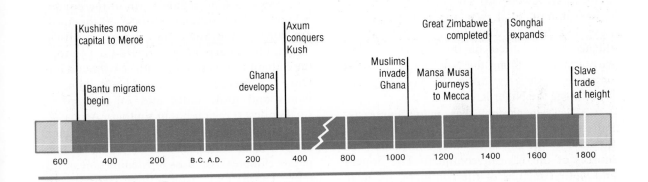

Kushites move capital to Meroë

Bantu migrations begin

Ghana develops

Axum conquers Kush

Muslims invade Ghana

Mansa Musa journeys to Mecca

Great Zimbabwe completed

Songhai expands

Slave trade at height

600   400   200   B.C. A.D.   200   400   800   1000   1200   1400   1600   1800

Africa is a vast continent inhabited by many groups of people, each with its own identity and history. The oldest African civilization developed in the Nile Valley of Egypt. South of Egypt, ancient kingdoms grew up along the Nile River as early as 2000 B.C. In western Africa, the great trading empires of Ghana, Mali, and Songhai later arose along the Niger River. The history of central, southern, and eastern Africa was affected greatly by the mass migrations of Bantu-speaking peoples. Traders from Arabia and northern Africa brought the influence of Islam, which spread widely in Africa south of the Sahara.

Slavery had long existed in Africa, but the arrival of European traders and the demand for labor in European colonies expanded the slave trade into a brutal profit-making business. The slave trade had a devastating effect on the peoples and societies of Africa.

This chapter describes the historical development of the major African kingdoms and empires and the disruptive effects of the slave trade on the continent.

CHAPTER OUTLINE

1 Trading Empires Develop in Africa

2 Bantu Peoples Migrate

3 The Slave Trade Damages African Life

273

1 Trading Empires Develop in Africa

The civilizations that developed in Africa reflected the variety and contrasts found on the continent. The peoples of Africa differ greatly in language, customs, and appearance. The geography of this huge continent also shows sharp contrasts. Along the Nile River, which flows from the tropical forests of central Africa through the deserts of the north, several early civilizations developed. The first, and perhaps the most influential, was Egypt (Chapter 2). Egypt's political, economic, and cultural influence had an effect on the history of other early kingdoms along the Nile. Later, empires based on trade grew up in the western grasslands along the Niger River.

Africa's geography has many contrasts. Patterns of settlement and trade were influenced by the varied climates and natural resources of the African continent. The hottest and wettest regions of the continent are near the equator, in the basin of the Congo River. Heavy rainfall and warm humid air encourage the growth of lush rain forest. Near the edge of the rain forest is the *savanna,* an open grassland dotted with shrubs and scattered clumps of trees. The savannas provide land for farming and herding. These grasslands are also the home of Africa's great herds of wild animals — gazelles, giraffes, wildebeests, zebras, lions, and elephants.

The grassland region north of the equator is known as the Sudan (soo-DAN). At the northern edge of the Sudan lies the great African desert, the Sahara. Larger in size than Europe, the Sahara is a wasteland with few inhabitants. Only in scattered oases can people build settlements and grow dates and other crops. A smaller desert region lies in southern Africa.

At opposite ends of the African continent are two narrow strips of coastal land with temperate climates like those of Mediterranean Europe. Throughout history, these coastal strips have attracted both African and European settlers.

Kush inherits the power of ancient Egypt. Near the great bend of the middle Nile River is the region called Nubia. It was settled in ancient times by the people of Kush (map, page 277), who were darker-skinned than the Egyptians living to the north. From about 2000 B.C., Egypt dominated Kush politically, but the Kushites developed their own cultural traditions. Trade along the Nile and riches from emerald and gold mines made the kingdom prosperous. Between about 800 and 750 B.C., as Egypt went into a period of decline, the Kushites proclaimed their independence and began conquering Egyptian lands. By 730 B.C. a Kushite king ruled as pharaoh of all Egypt.

The Kushites set up a new capital at Meroë. Kushite rule in Egypt did not last long.

TIMETABLE

Traditional Africa

B.C.

730	A Kushite king becomes pharoah of Egypt.
540	The Kushite capital is moved to Meroe.
500*	The Bantu-speaking peoples begin migrations.

A.D.

300*	The Soninke lay the foundations for Ghana by entering the gold-salt trade.
350*	Axum conquers Kush.
1054	Muslims from North Africa invade Ghana.
1230	Mali begins to expand.
1468	The Songhai begin their conquests.
1518	The first slaves from Africa are shipped to the West Indies.
1590	The Moroccans defeat Songhai.
1600*	The Ashanti clans unite in a confederation.
1807	Britain declares the slave trade illegal.

*APPROXIMATE DATES

African Landforms and Vegetation

The maps on the next page show the major landforms and vegetation of Africa. Using the landforms map, locate the Sudan, Sahara, Congo Basin, and Great Rift Valley. What kinds of vegetation are found in each of these regions?

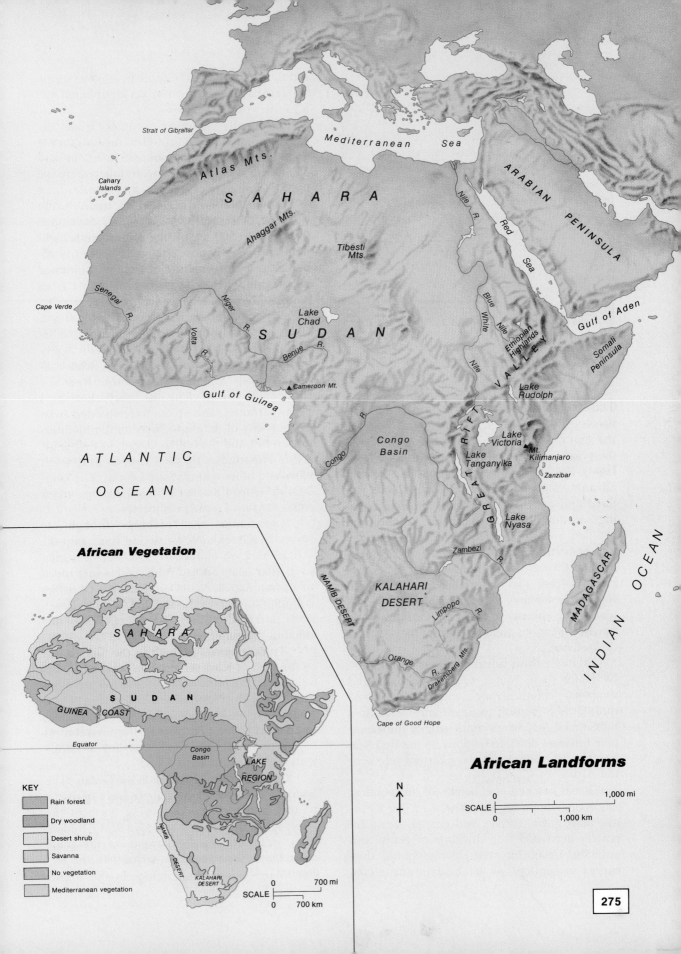

Strait of Gibraltar

Canary
Islands

Cape Verde

Mediterranean Sea

Atlas Mts.

S A H A R A

Ahaggar Mts.

Tibesti
Mts.

Senegal R.

Niger
R.

Lake
Chad

S U D A N

Volta
R.

Benue   R.

Cameroon Mt.

Gulf of Guinea

A R A B I A N

P E N I N S U L A

Nile R.

Red
Sea

Gulf of Aden

Blue

White

Nile

Nile

Ethiopian
Highlands

Somali
Peninsula

Lake
Rudolph

V A L L E Y

A T L A N T I C

O C E A N

Congo

Congo
Basin

Lake
Victoria

Lake
Tanganyika

G R E A T   R I F T

Mt.
Kilimanjaro

Zanzibar

Lake
Nyasa

Zambezi   R.

MADAGASCAR

I N D I A N   O C E A N

NAMIB DESERT

KALAHARI
DESERT

Limpopo   R.

Orange   R.

Drakensberg Mts.

Cape of Good Hope

African Vegetation

SAHARA

S U D A N

GUINEA   COAST

Equator

Congo
Basin

LAKE
REGION

NAMIB
DESERT

KALAHARI
DESERT

KEY

Rain forest

Dry woodland

Desert shrub

Savanna

No vegetation

Mediterranean vegetation

0   700 mi

SCALE

0   700 km

African Landforms

N

0   1,000 mi

SCALE

0   1,000 km

This carving on the wall of a 2,000-year-old temple shows a god worshiped in ancient Kush. Note that the figure has the head of a ram.

The Assyrians invaded Egypt in 671 B.C. and drove the Kushites back to their own lands to the south. About 540 B.C., the Kushites moved their capital south along the Nile to Meroë (MEHR-oh-ee). This new location had several advantages. First, the river's yearly floods watered and enriched more land, allowing farming and cattle herding to expand. Second, iron ore had been discovered in Meroë about 650 B.C. The Kushites had learned the art of smelting and forging iron, probably from the Assyrians. As Kush also had timber for fuel, Meroë soon became one of the major ironworking centers of the ancient world. The Kushites made fine iron weapons and agricultural tools such as the iron hoe.

Meroë's third advantage was its location on major trade routes. Gold, iron tools and weapons, ebony, ivory, and cattle flowed through Meroë north to Egypt and west across the Sahara. An eastern route led into the Ethiopian hills and down to seaports on the Red Sea. Southward, trade goods were carried into central Africa.

Kush reached the height of its political and economic power about 200 B.C. The Kushites built great temples and created beautiful pottery decorated with drawings of plants and animals. Using Egyptian hieroglyphics, they carved inscriptions on tombstones and altars,

but they kept records of trade in another script. Modern scholars have not yet deciphered the Kushite writing.

Gradually nomadic peoples from the desert began to raid Kush. The kingdom's trade and farm production declined. In about A.D. 350, Kush was invaded and conquered by the rival trading state of Axum (AHK-soom).

Axum becomes a center of trade. Axum was one of several city-states that developed from 600 to 500 B.C. in the southeastern highlands of what is now Ethiopia. The early inhabitants were a mixture of local dark-skinned peoples and lighter-skinned immigrants from Arabia. Their language and culture blended African and Arabian influences. By about A.D. 50, Axum controlled a sizable territory (map, page 277) and a far-flung trade. Trade agreements were made with the Greeks, who controlled much of the Mediterranean-Red Sea commerce. African elephants, ivory, rhinoceros horn, perfumes, and spices were shipped from the port city of Adulis to ports on the Mediterranean Sea and the Indian Ocean. In exchange, Axum imported cloth, glass, copper, iron, small tools, and other manufactured goods. The kingdom developed its own written language and a style of massive stone architecture.

Christianity was probably brought to Axum by Greek merchants, and it became the official religion about A.D. 395. For centuries, even after Islam spread from Arabia into much of eastern Africa, Axum survived as a Christian stronghold. Relatively isolated, Axum developed into modern Ethiopia, where Christianity remains the major religion.

Trade empires are built in the Sudan. Far to the west of Kush and Axum, other states developed in the huge savanna of the western Sudan. Three empires rose and fell in turn. These Sudanic states overlapped in time and space (map, next page), as each in turn gained control of the trans-Saharan trade that linked Africa with the Near East and Europe.

Gold and salt are traded in the Sudan. The Soninke (soh-NEEN-kay) people were farmers, traders, and metalworkers living north of the Niger River at the northern edge of the Sudan. They were strategically located on the trade route that linked northern Africa with the forests to the south. From mines in the forests came gold. From the Sahara came salt, an equally valuable product. The salt was traded throughout the western Sudan and the forest regions. The gold was eagerly sought in northern Africa and in Europe.

Gold and salt were traded by silent barter. Desert traders from the north brought their salt and other goods to a prearranged place, beat out a signal on the drums, and then went some distance away. The gold miners came with their gold, placed what they considered an equal value of gold beside the salt, and then left. The salt traders returned and, if they agreed to the bargain, took the gold and beat the drum again. If they were not satisfied with the amount of gold, however, they went away again and waited for the miners to offer more.

The traders' caravans had to pass through the land of the Soninke. By about A.D. 300 the Soninke began to act as agents for traders in both gold and salt, and eventually they gained control of the valuable trade. Their ruler, or *ghana* (GAH-nuh), became known as "king of the gold," and the kingdom was called Ghana.[1] To keep the price of gold high, the ghana carefully controlled how much of the metal was mined and sold.

Trade wealth supports a growing empire. The state taxed the trade in salt and gold. It also taxed the jewelry, metalwork, and other goods produced in Ghana. These tax funds were used to support government officials, maintain an army, and provide a lavish lifestyle for Ghana's royalty. By about A.D. 1000, Ghana

---

[1]The modern nation of Ghana lies southeast of the lands of the ancient kingdom. Modern Ghana is thought to have been settled by migrating people from ancient Ghana.

Sudanic States

This map shows kingdoms and empires that developed in the Sudan, the grassland region south of the Sahara. What states developed in the western part of the Sudan?

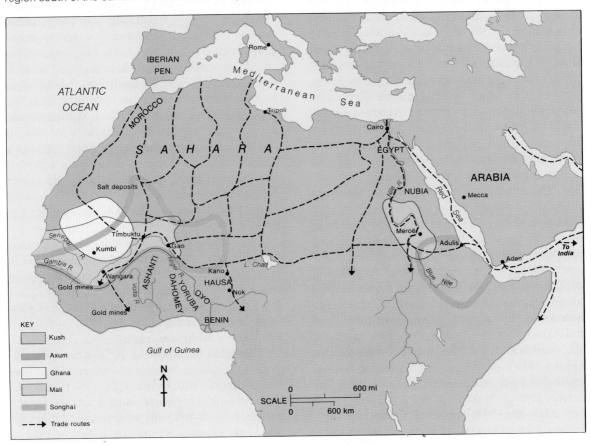

KEY
- Kush
- Axum
- Ghana
- Mali
- Songhai
- - - → Trade routes

was at the height of its power. The rulers of a number of smaller states paid tribute to the king in taxes and in goods.

Two capitals reflect two ways of life. Ghana's capital city, Kumbi, was in fact "twin" towns situated only a few miles apart and linked by road. The business capital was mainly a Muslim town, where traders brought fruit, wheat, and textiles from northern Africa and Spain. The Muslims also brought their religion with them, and the influence of Islam spread quickly.

The second town, where the king resided, was a center of traditional Soninke culture. The kings of Ghana recognized that the Muslims were necessary to the kingdom's trade and government, but the kings did not accept Islam and did not want Muslim ways to influence their subjects. In traditional Soninke belief, the king was considered a god and the people's spiritual guide.

Ghana provides the model for other empires. The great empires in western Africa all followed a similar pattern of development and decline. Their wealth came from gold and from the control of trade. They also conquered neighboring states and demanded tribute from these conquered peoples. Kings had absolute power and were assisted in their rule by members of the royal family and by appointed officials. Islam was a growing religious and political influence in the Sudan, and some rulers adopted the new religion. Most Africans, however, kept their traditional beliefs, honoring family ancestors and spirits of nature.

The empires of the western Sudan were large and diverse, held together by tribute and strong personal rule rather than by any sense of loyalty to the state. The causes of their decline also were similar. Rival members of the nobility challenged the king's control, weakening central authority. Subject states began to pull away, making the empire vulnerable to foreign attack. In the case of Ghana, Muslims from northern Africa invaded in 1054; they captured the capital in 1076. The invaders remained in Ghana only a short time, but warfare disrupted trade and agriculture. Ghana never regained its former glory.

Mali inherits the power of Ghana. Ghana's place at the crossroads of the north-south cara-

van route was taken by the Mandingo (man-DING-go) people of Mali (MAH-lee). Mali began as a small state about the end of the eighth century. In the eleventh century its rulers converted to Islam. Sundiata (soon-dee-AH-tuh), who became king about 1230, greatly expanded the kingdom and built a new capital city. Mali soon gained control of the caravan routes and the revenues from trade.

Mali reaches toward the sea. Abu Bakari II, ruler of Mali in the early 1300's, dreamed of reaching the sea and exploring the world beyond it. He ordered 200 ships and 200 supply boats to be built and outfitted for a voyage of two years. The ships were constructed on a plain along the coast between the Senegal and Gambia rivers (map, page 277).

The fleet set sail with orders not to return until they had reached the end of the ocean or had run out of food. Only one ship eventually returned, and its captain reported that all the other ships had been lost. Abu Bakari then prepared for a second expedition, this time leading the fleet himself. In 1311 the expedition sailed down the Senegal River and into the Atlantic Ocean. It headed west and was never heard from again.

Mali attains its greatest size and wealth. Abu Bakari II was succeeded by his brother, Mansa Musa, one of Mali's most famous kings. In 1324 Mansa Musa, a devout Muslim, made a pilgrimage across the Sahara to Mecca in Arabia and along the way displayed Mali's dazzling wealth. Amazed chroniclers reported that Mansa Musa traveled with 12,000 slaves dressed in silk. He took with him 50,000 ounces of gold to give as presents and as alms for the poor.

The Mali empire reached the peak of its power during Mansa Musa's reign (1312–1332). It stretched from the Atlantic coast inland to the cities of Timbuktu and Gao (map, page 277). Timbuktu was renowned for its great mosque and royal palace. Its university was a center of Muslim scholarship.

Songhai becomes the largest Sudanic empire. Like Ghana, Mali was weakened by internal rivalries, raids by nomadic desert peoples, and rebellion by vassal states, including the Songhai (SONG-hye) city of Gao. As Mali weakened, the Songhai grew stronger. Led by a

This map of northern Africa, made in Spain in 1375, suggests the importance of trade in African life. Mansa Musa, the ruler of Mali, is shown holding a gold nugget to barter with an Arab merchant on a camel. Trade routes linked the peoples of Africa and tied the continent to Europe and Asia. Agricultural goods, ivory, and especially gold were among the products that Africans supplied to other lands.

powerful king named Sunni Ali, the Songhai captured Timbuktu in 1468 and went on to conquer much of the middle and upper Niger River valley.

After the death of Sunni Ali in 1492, the throne was seized by one of his generals, who ruled from 1493 to 1528 under the name of Askia Mohammed. A devout Muslim, he tried to unite his territories in an Islamic empire by launching a series of wars. His religious zeal also drew scholars back to Timbuktu, which once again became famous as a center of Muslim studies and culture. Greater in extent than either Ghana or Mali, Songhai at the height of its power covered an area about the size of Western Europe.

Songhai is the last great empire in the Sudan. Internal rivalries and disorder gradually weakened Songhai. In 1590 the sultan of Morocco sent an invasion force against the Sudanic state. Five months of desert travel to Songhai cost the Moroccans many soldiers. Nevertheless, with the advantage of firearms, the Moroccans were able to defeat a much larger army. The Songhai empire never recovered, and no new power replaced it. The Moroccans remained in the Sudan, but they never established a new empire.

African trade routes begin to change. As the Sudanic empires declined, the whole pattern of trade in western Africa was changing. When Mali was growing weak, its traders had sought new routes to avoid the Songhai, who dominated the routes through the western Sudan. Mali's traders moved west, east, and south and developed new coastal trade routes. These linked the savanna, the forest, and the newly established Portuguese trading posts on the Atlantic coast (map, page 347).

With the decline of Songhai, the trade routes across the Sahara collapsed. The new coastal trade routes became more important economically. For the first time, African traders looked west and south toward the Atlantic Ocean instead of north toward the Mediterranean Sea. This shift was critical in the later history of western Africa. The western Sudan declined in importance. Coastal communities from the Senegal River to the Niger delta became the center of economic and political power.

CHECK-UP

1. Vocabulary: *savanna.*
2. (a) How do the climate and vegetation in Africa's rain forest differ from the savanna? (b) Where is the large desert region of Africa? (c) What parts of Africa have a climate like that of Mediterranean Europe?
3. (a) What was the relationship between Kush and ancient Egypt? (b) In what three ways did the move to Meroë benefit Kush?
4. How did Axum's ties with Greece affect (a) its trade? (b) its religion?
5. (a) How was the gold-salt trade carried on? (b) How did Ghana use this trade to build an empire?
6. (a) What was notable about the Mali empire under the reign of Mansa Musa? (b) How did Songhai become the largest Sudanic state? (c) What caused its decline?
7. What caused a shift in the pattern of trade in western Africa?

2 Bantu Peoples Migrate

The early growth of states and kingdoms in the rest of Africa was more complex than it was along the Nile and Niger rivers. Climate and landforms in many parts of the continent made settlement and farming difficult. Massive migrations of people also changed patterns of settlement in this vast region.

Bantu-speaking peoples migrate east and south. In the history of almost every continent there have been great migrations of peoples that lasted over many generations. The movement of Bantu-speaking peoples out of western Africa into the lands to the east and south is believed to have begun almost 2,500 years ago. It continued in a series of waves until the nineteenth century.

The Bantu peoples probably originated in the highlands region of present-day Nigeria, not far from the town of Nok (map, page 277). In their homeland, at the edge of forest and savanna, they lived by farming, fishing, and some herding of sheep and goats. The Bantu peoples differed in appearance and ways of living, but they spoke related languages. While the reasons for their migrations are not clear, the Bantu eventually occupied about a third of the African continent.

Bantu migrants interact with other peoples. As they moved to new areas, the Bantu peoples came in contact with other African groups and learned to live in a variety of environments. Some of the Bantu-speaking peoples moved east across the savanna. In the open grasslands they learned to cultivate grains. Others moved southward along rivers to the tropical forests near the equator. Some local peoples were conquered and absorbed into the dominant Bantu culture, while others fled deeper into the forest. Farther south, local hunters and gatherers sought refuge from the migrants by moving into desert regions.

Migrating Bantu peoples also moved eastward into the Great Rift Valley (map, page 275). There they came into contact with cattle herders from the northeast, who also were migrating southward. Some Bantu learned a new way of life from the herders. Others settled as farmers. For generations, farmers and herders lived side by side, competing for land and for dominance over one another.

Iron technology increases productivity. The earliest Bantu pioneers had no knowledge of ironworking. After about 500 B.C., iron smelting techniques spread from Meroë (page 276) into western and southern Africa. By 300 B.C., iron technology may have also developed independently at Nok. In any case, later waves of Bantu migrants carried this knowledge with them. Iron tools made the cultivation of savanna and forest areas easier and more productive. Iron weapons were more effective against enemies. Metalworkers also created works of art using bronze, gold, and other metals.

New food crops are also spread by Bantu migrants. The migrating Bantu farmers also benefited from new food crops that grew well in warm, moist climates. The banana and a starchy root called taro were introduced from Southeast Asia into eastern Africa, probably by Asian sailors or traders. They became basic

Masks have long been an important form of art in Africa. This wooden mask was worn by Luba kings when they first came to power.

foods for the people of eastern Africa, spreading inland to the lake region and beyond.

The Luba build a network of Bantu states. By the eighth or ninth century A.D., the Luba, a Bantu-speaking people in central Africa, had established a strong agricultural economy. Copper mining in the Katanga region and long-distance trade increased the wealth of the Luba. In the sixteenth century, a series of powerful warrior kings organized a Luba state. The Luba king was always a descendant of the kingdom's founder. Authority was passed down to provinces, then to chiefdoms, and finally to villages made up of family groups. Such a political organization became common in Africa.

Around 1600, a son of the Luba king conquered the neighboring state of Lunda, married its queen, and then broke off his allegiance to the Luba. Other members of the royal family also founded separate states, and the Lunda empire developed as a series of loosely associated kingdoms. In this way, the Luba royal family influenced the formation of states throughout central Africa.

The Kongo empire rises along the coast. Near the mouth of the Congo River lay the kingdom of Kongo, founded in the fourteenth century. The Kongo empire grew and prospered, extending south along the Atlantic coast. Its people were known for their skill in pottery making, weaving, ironworking, and sculpture. They traded extensively with neighboring states and, in the 1400's, with the Portuguese.

Other Bantu people create Great Zimbabwe. By A.D. 1000, settlements of Bantu farmers and herders were well established on the fertile plateau between the Zambezi and Limpopo rivers in southeast Africa. The area also became a major producer of gold, which was mined locally and exported out of Sofala on the coast. Imports included cotton, brass, porcelain, and spices.

A wealthy Bantu kingdom, whose origins are something of a mystery, arose in this region. By the fifteenth century, it was at the height of its wealth and power. All that remains of this civilization today are massive stone ruins (picture, page 282). The most extensive are known as Great Zimbabwe (zim-BAH-bway), meaning "the dwelling of the chief." The stonework still standing at Great Zimbabwe includes a fort, a

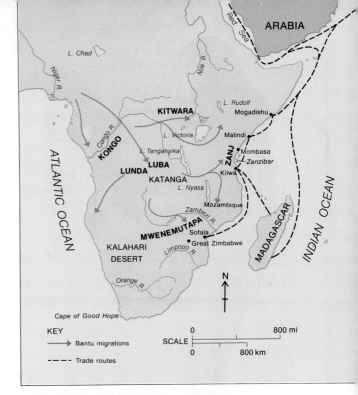

Migration in Southern Africa

About 2,500 years ago, Bantu-speaking peoples began to migrate across Africa. What was the general direction of their migrations?

temple, and other buildings. They were constructed of huge granite blocks shaped with iron tools and skillfully fitted together without mortar.

Trade links Africa and Arabia. The people of Great Zimbabwe were one part of an extensive trade network that linked the African interior with ports on the Indian Ocean. Since the first century A.D., merchants had been moving back and forth between Arabia and Africa's eastern coast. African gold, iron, ivory, and slaves were transported great distances from the interior to the sea. Foreign goods such as cloth, beads, and porcelain were carried inland along the same routes.

Arab merchants began to settle eastern Africa as early as the seventh century. In the tenth century, unrest in the Muslim world forced many more Arabs to flee to Africa. By this time, Bantu-speaking migrants had also reached the coast. Bantu and Arabs intermarried, and a distinct culture evolved. Except in Ethiopia (page 276), Islam spread along the coast. A new language, Swahili (swah-HEE-lee), developed. Combining basic Bantu grammar and many Arabic words, Swahili became the

GREAT ZIMBABWE

This aerial view shows the stone ruins of Great Zimbabwe, which was built in a wooded valley. Many objects found here came from other regions, suggesting that the site was an important trade center. The soapstone carving (left) was found at the ruins but may have been made by later peoples who lived in the area.

language of trade all along the coast and soon spread inland. Today it is spoken as a first or second language in much of eastern and central Africa.

Trade supports city-states in eastern Africa. From the thirteenth to the fifteenth century, many independent Muslim city-states flourished along the east African coast from Kilwa north to Mogadishu (map, page 281). Their wealth was shown by their great mosques, palaces, and other buildings of stone. The most powerful of these city-states was Kilwa, which controlled the coast as far south as Sofala. The merchants of Kilwa dominated the trade in gold that was brought from the interior.

Ships from Arabia, India, and China docked at the coastal cities to unload and take on cargo. Ivory, gold, iron, rhinoceros horn, palm oil, and cinnamon were among the principal exports. Silks, jewels, and porcelain, imported from East Asia, adorned the homes of the wealthy. Glass beads from India and fine porcelain from China, found among the ruins at Great Zimbabwe, show how rich and far-flung was this trade.

East African city-states lose their independence. In 1497 a Portuguese fleet led by Vasco da Gama (page 350) arrived on the east coast of Africa. Determined to take over trade in the Indian Ocean, the Portuguese demanded tribute in gold, then attacked and destroyed the coastal cities. Within ten years, Portuguese traders, armed with guns and cannon, had captured all of the towns. Although Portuguese control did not last, it ruined the prospering trade and the rich culture of the city-states of eastern Africa. Early in the nineteenth century, they were taken over by the Arab sultan of Zanzibar.

CHECK-UP

1. (a) Where did the Bantu-speaking peoples originate? (b) Into what parts of Africa did they migrate?
2. (a) What different ways of life did migrating Bantu peoples follow? (b) How did they benefit from the introduction of ironworking and new food crops?
3. How did the Luba influence the formation and organization of states in central Africa?
4. What was Great Zimbabwe?
5. (a) How did African and Arab influences mix on the east coast? (b) How did this affect language? (c) What caused the decline of the coastal city-states?

3 The Slave Trade Damages African Life

Trade provided the economic basis for the growth of African states and empires. It brought new religions, new weapons, and new political relationships to Africa. At first, trade was mainly in Africa's mineral and food resources. Increasingly, however, trade involved a very different type of resource — the African people themselves.

Slavery is a part of African society. In Africa, as in the rest of the world, slavery had been common since ancient times. War captives, criminals, debtors, or the very poor were likely to become slaves. Slaves were not necessarily treated as inferiors, but might be looked on as part of a family or as trusted servants. Nor was slavery limited to any particular class or group. Kings or scholars, as well as criminals and the poor, could become slaves.

Slaves are sold in international trade. Along with gold, ivory, and other exports, small numbers of slaves were commonly traded in Africa. In the western Sudan, captives taken in warfare might be enslaved and sent north across the Sahara. Along the east coast, slaves used to transport ivory from the interior might then be sold and shipped to Arabia or India. This early trade in slaves was generally limited to people who, for one reason or another, were already slaves in their own land. As more Arabs settled in Africa, however, the slave trade increased. To meet the demand for slaves in Muslim lands, Africans were captured by "slave raiding" in the interior. Even more drastic changes in the nature of slavery began with the arrival of Europeans in Africa.

European traders reach the west coast of Africa. In the mid-fifteenth century, Portuguese explorers sailed along the Guinea Coast of western Africa seeking a sea route to India. They also sought gold, which they found in the area west of the Volta River (map, page 277). The coastal peoples acted as middlemen, selling gold from the forest region in exchange for cloth, beads, and a variety of other European goods. Some African slaves were also bought by the Portuguese to serve as house servants in Portugal.

Plantations demand large numbers of workers. In the 1490's and early 1500's, the Portuguese began growing sugar cane on islands off the African coast. To plant and harvest the crop, they used African slaves imported from the mainland. At first the slave traffic was small. It was a part of the trading system that had been going on between the Portuguese and the Africans since the mid-1400's.

Because sugar imported from Asia was very expensive, the demand for African sugar was great, and profits were high. To meet the demand, the Portuguese set up sugar *plantations.* This type of agriculture required large tracts of open land and much hard human labor. Plantation field work was so harsh that few laborers would do it willingly. Moreover, because the plantations occupied great areas of land, there were usually not many workers living nearby. Laborers had to be brought to the plantation and be fed, clothed, and housed and somehow persuaded (or forced) to stay. As the Portuguese demand for plantation workers grew, the Kongo kingdom and the region to the south began to supply slaves for this purpose.

African slaves are sent to the Americas. The profits from plantation agriculture encouraged other Europeans to follow this method in their new colonies. After Europeans reached the Americas, vast sugar plantations were set up in the Spanish, French, and Portuguese colonies of Brazil and the West Indies. The demand for workers increased, but recruiting plantation workers from the Indian population proved impractical, and the Spanish rulers forbade enslaving the Indians. The plantation owners turned to western Africa, therefore, for their labor supply.

The first shipload of black African slaves sailed from western Africa to the West Indies in 1518. Over the next 350 years, the traffic in human beings steadily grew. African slaves were sent to mine gold and silver and grow sugar cane and coffee in Latin America. Later they grew tobacco and cotton in England's North American colonies. By the 1750's, slaves had replaced gold as the major cargo leaving Africa.

When the trade finally ended in the mid-nineteenth century, many millions of Africa's people had been carried across the Atlantic.

The vast majority of slaves sent to the Americas came from western Africa, from the region between the Senegal River and the area south of the Congo River. Many of these people were captured and brought to the west coast from the interior of the continent.

The slave trade in eastern Africa also grows. While most of the European slave trade came from West Africa, the Portuguese also shipped slaves from Mozambique in eastern Africa to colonies in the Americas. The French took slaves from eastern Africa to work on sugar plantations on islands in the Indian Ocean. The Arab slave trade along the eastern coast was growing as well.

When the transatlantic slave trade declined in the nineteenth century, the trade from eastern Africa increased dramatically. Arab caravans from Zanzibar, whose sultan controlled the coast, raided far into the interior. Many of the slaves were brought to Zanzibar to work the island's clove plantations. The rest were sent to Arabia, the Ottoman Empire, Persia, and India. Though this trade involved fewer people than the Atlantic slave trade, the totals still reached into the millions.

The nature of slavery changes. In traditional African and Arab cultures, slaves were not necessarily enslaved for life. In most early societies, slaves could buy their freedom or gain it through military service. Slavery was not rare, nor was it considered wrong. When it was found that enormous profits could be made from the slave trade and from plantations using African slave labor, traditional attitudes toward slavery began to change. Because most slaves in Europe and its colonies were black Africans, Europeans came to associate bondage with African birth or descent. Moreover, children inherited their parents' status as slaves.

African states are drawn into the slave trade. European slave traders depended mainly on African and Arab traders to supply them with slaves. At first, there were enough locally owned slaves (often captives taken in wars) to satisfy the Europeans' demands. Increasingly, wars were waged for the purpose of capturing people to sell as slaves. The slaves were traded for firearms, which the Africans used to wage war and to protect themselves from enslavement. Yet to buy more guns, they had to capture and sell more people. In this way the Europeans played Africans against each other, offering guns in exchange for slaves.

Many African rulers began to take part in the slave trade. Once involved, they found it difficult to stop. Local rulers who tried to halt the trade met with little success. In the kingdom of Kongo, for instance, King Affonso (who ruled about 1506–1545) welcomed Catholic missionaries, converted to Christianity, and encouraged Portuguese ways. In trying to maintain good relations with Portugal, Affonso wrote to the Portuguese king to protest slave raiding:

> We cannot reckon how great the damage is, since [the slave traders] are taking every day our natives, sons of the land and the sons of our noblemen and vassals and our relatives, because the thieves and men of bad conscience grab them . . . and get them to be sold. . . . Our country is being completely depopulated. . . . That is why we beg Your Highness to help and assist us in this matter . . . because it is our will that in these kingdoms there should not be any trade of slaves nor outlet for them.

Neither Affonso's protests nor those of other African rulers brought any action from European officials.

Inland states lose control of the slave trade. The effects of the slave trade on African states varied widely. While some states became strong enough to challenge the Europeans, others were weakened or destroyed. The slave trade in western Africa particularly affected several important kingdoms of the Yoruba (YOH-ruh-bah) people on the Gulf of Guinea (map, page 277).

The Yoruba kingdom of Oyo lay inland on the Niger River. It reached the height of its power in the seventeenth century, mainly through wars using European firearms. As long as Oyo kept up a steady flow of slaves to European-controlled ports on the coast, it received fresh supplies of weapons. In time, however, states along the slave route between Oyo and the coast challenged Oyo's power. Seeking to share in the riches of the slave trade, these states made their own trade agreements with the Europeans. As Oyo's control over the slave trade diminished in the late eighteenth century, its wealth decreased and its power weakened.

South of Oyo, near the mouth of the Niger River, was the kingdom of Benin (beh-NEEN).[2] It was a wealthy trading kingdom known particularly for its artisans' skills in working bronze. The Portuguese first visited Benin in 1485 and soon developed a trade in ivory, pepper, palm oil, and slaves. In exchange, Benin imported European luxury goods and weapons. With the help of firearms, Benin took over neighboring territory and provided a steady supply of slaves to the slave traders. Benin's subject states, however, sought to share directly in the profits from the slave trade. Gradually the city-states along the coast and in the Niger

River delta took control of the trade. By the end of the seventeenth century, the Benin empire was beginning to fall apart.

Dahomey pushes to the sea. Gaining control of the coast was important for the kingdom of Dahomey (dah-HOH-mee), which emerged in the 1600's. To defend itself against Oyo to the east and the slave-trading states along the coast, Dahomey was organized as a military state. About a third of its soldiers were women. In the early 1700's, Dahomey conquered the coastal states to the south but still had to pay tribute to Oyo. To maintain its defenses and pay tribute, Dahomey needed guns. The need for firearms involved it in the European slave trade. At first concerned with stopping the trade, Dahomey soon became a major slave-trading power.

Ashanti unites and expands. To the west, the gold center of Ashanti (map, page 277) had grown prosperous through trade with peoples to the north and with the Portuguese along the coast. In the 1600's, slave raids from the east and south caused the Ashanti clans to unite for

---

[2]The territory of the kingdom of Benin is part of the modern nation of Nigeria. The modern nation of Benin was once the kingdom of Dahomey. (The nations of modern Africa are shown in the Atlas at the back of this book.)

AFRICAN ART

Among Africa's finest carvings is this ivory head from Benin (below left). The ornaments on the headdress represent Portuguese diplomats. Brass weights used by the Ashanti for weighing gold dust often depicted scenes of daily life. In the one shown here (below right) a family prepares a meal.

protection. They formed a confederation called the Ashanti Union and pledged allegiance to a single ruler whose symbol was a sacred throne called the "Golden Stool." The Ashanti Union grew powerful enough to expand its territory and gain control of the coastal slave trade. In time, the Ashanti became strong enough to challenge the growing British presence on the coast (Chapter 27).

The slave trade undermines African economies. For about 300 years, the slave trade robbed Africa of its most valuable resource —its people. Population declined as millions of Africans — the young and the strong — were taken from their villages and towns. Millions more were killed in the constant raids and warfare to capture slaves. Crops, farms, and whole villages were destroyed. Few workers were left to rebuild or replant.

In exchange for African slaves, the Europeans brought guns and luxury goods to trade with local rulers. Yet the slave trade did not enrich most Africans, nor did it supply real wealth in money terms. Local industries did not develop; traditional crafts vanished. European traders were interested only in buying slaves. The economies of many states were so dependent on the slave trade that stopping it was very hard.

The slave trade undermines African culture. African societies lost many of their strongest and most productive members to the slave trade. They lost generations of potential leaders and many of the people who had been educated to carry on Africa's historical and cultural heritage.

The enslaved Africans who survived were in strange lands, far from their families and their villages. They learned new languages, adopted new religions, and found new ways of surviving. Totally cut off from their African homeland, they lost touch with their cultural roots. Their heritage became a fast-fading memory, passed along in fragments to their children — never totally forgotten, but never fully known.

The transatlantic slave trade causes great human suffering. The cost of the slave trade in human suffering was tremendous. People were kidnapped or captured in bloody slave raids, then marched in chains for hundreds of miles to the coast. There captives might be imprisoned for weeks in damp, dark dungeons, waiting for a slave ship to arrive.

LINKING PAST AND PRESENT

The Family Compound

In traditional African villages, family members lived in neighboring households within a living space called a compound, which was like a family village within the larger village. Even in present-day Africa, the family compound is an important part of many people's lives. Village compounds held not only the separate small houses of different family members but also huts for animals, storage rooms for grain, cooking areas, and an open space for community living. Most compounds, like this one in Nigeria, were at least partly enclosed by a wall of woven grass, timber, or mud.

Africans who grew up in village compounds were used to being constantly with members of their families, sharing work and free time. In

modern African cities, people of related families often choose to live close together, creating a city version of the family compound.

This drawing, done by a British seaman in 1846, records the conditions that existed below deck on a slave ship. Africans from all walks of life were taken as slaves, marched to the coast of Africa, and shipped to the Americas where they were forced to work on plantations.

Conditions on board a slave ship were notorious for their brutality. The chained men and women were "stacked" on narrow shelves in the hold of the ship. The air was foul, the food was often spoiled, and disease was widespread. Many people died at sea; others jumped overboard. Finally, after five weeks, the ship docked in the Americas, where the Africans were sold. From then on, their fate was hard work and often cruel treatment.

The slave trade comes to an end. African rulers such as King Affonso (page 284) had protested against the slave trade. Many Europeans also recognized the horrors of the trade. They wrote books and pamphlets protesting against slavery, made speeches, and tried to influence their governments. The profits of the slave trade were enormous, however, and for many years these pleas were ignored.

Finally, in 1807, the government of Great Britain declared the slave trade illegal. Other European nations soon followed. Yet the demand for slaves was so great that even laws and naval patrols could not stop the trade. The dependence of some African rulers on slave trading also made them reluctant to halt it. Not until the mid-nineteenth century did the transatlantic slave trade finally come to an end. The trade in eastern Africa, centered at Zanzibar, continued until late in the nineteenth century and possibly into the twentieth.

With the end of the slave trade, African trading relations with other countries collapsed. Other kinds of commerce and industry had not been developed. Wide areas had been devastated by the slave trade and the constant warfare that went with it. The slave trade left much of Africa weak politically and economically. It was unable to resist takeover by European colonial powers.

CHECK-UP

1. Vocabulary: *plantation*.
2. How did the introduction of plantation agriculture (a) increase the demand for slaves? (b) change the nature of slavery?
3. (a) How were African states drawn into the slave trade? (b) How did the slave trade affect the kingdoms of Oyo and Benin?
4. How did the slave trade (a) undermine the economies of African states? (b) destroy the cultural heritage of Africans? (c) cause the loss of future leaders?
5. (a) Describe the conditions on slave ships. (b) Why were European nations reluctant to stop the slave trade? (c) When did the slave trade come to an end in western Africa? (d) in eastern Africa?

Chapter 13 Review

Summary

Africa is a continent with many different peoples and civilizations, as well as a variety of sharply contrasting regions. These include rain forests, savannas (grasslands), deserts, and temperate coastal areas. Soon after Egyptian civilization began along the Nile, other early African states and kingdoms grew up to the south along the river. Kush was influenced by neighboring Egypt but developed independently. Axum established a culture that continues in modern Ethiopia. Later, in western Africa, the empires of Ghana, Mali, and Songhai in turn rose to power by controlling the prosperous gold-salt trade. Islam was introduced in western Africa by Arab traders and became influential there.

Vast migrations of Bantu-speaking peoples began about 2,500 years ago, influencing the rise of states in eastern, southern, and central Africa. In East Africa, trade with Arabia and Asia brought both prosperity and Muslim influence.

Both Africans and Arabs traded in slaves. European traders, however, brought a new demand for plantation slave labor. The nature of slavery changed drastically. Over several hundred years, the slave trade brought suffering to millions and caused lasting damage to African society and culture.

Vocabulary Review

1. Write the sentences listed below on a sheet of paper. In each sentence, fill in the blank with one of these terms: *plantation, savanna, tribute.*
   (a) The Sudan is a ___?___ , a dry, flat grassland.
   (b) Payment made by one ruler or nation to another as a sign of submission or as the price of military protection is called ___?___ .
   (c) A ___?___ was a large tract of land on which slaves grew crops such as sugar cane.
2. Distinguish between the terms in each of the following pairs:
   (a) Luba; Lunda.
   (b) Ashanti Union; Dahomey.
   (c) Swahili; Bantu.
   (d) Kushites; Songhai.
   (e) Soninke; Mandingo.

People to Identify

Match the following people with the numbered phrases that describe them: *Sundiata, Abu Bakari II, Vasco da Gama, Mansa Musa, Sunni Ali.*
1. Fourteenth-century ruler of Mali whose daring attempts at Atlantic exploration met with disaster.
2. Fifteenth-century Songhai king who conquered much of the Niger River valley and captured Timbuktu.
3. Thirteenth-century king who greatly expanded the kingdom of Mali and built a new capital city.
4. Portuguese explorer whose fleet reached the east coast of Africa in 1497.
5. Fabulously wealthy Muslim king under whose rule the Mali empire reached its peak.

Relating Geography and History

1. **Locating places.** Locate each of the following on a map in this chapter:
   (a) Ghana   (g) Congo Basin
   (b) Meroë   (h) Guinea Coast
   (c) Sudan   (i) Timbuktu
   (d) Sahara   (j) Zambezi River
   (e) Kush   (k) Great Zimbabwe
   (f) Kilwa   (l) Niger River
2. **Comparing maps.** Using the maps on pages 277 and 281 and the map of Africa in the Atlas at the back of this book (page 864), determine what present-day nations exist in the Sudan and in the lands once settled by the Bantu.
3. **Reports.** Use your school or public library to find out more about the important African city of Timbuktu. You may want to emphasize the university, the architecture, or the history of Timbuktu as a center for African trade. Prepare a report summarizing the information you find.

Discussion Questions

1. Describe the ways in which trade was influential in the development of the kingdoms of (a) Kush, (b) Axum, (c) Ghana.

2. (a) How did the economy of Ghana provide a model for other Sudanic states? (b) What were the three Sudanic empires and how did each fall from power?

3. (a) Describe Muslim influence in the Mali empire. (b) What part did Arabian traders have in the development of wealthy city-states in eastern Africa from 1300 to 1500?

4. (a) Why did the European demand for slaves increase between 1500 and 1750? (b) Compare and contrast traditional African patterns of slavery with those that developed under plantation agriculture.

5. Why was the slave trade, once under way, hard to stop (a) in European colonies? (b) in Africa? (c) How was it finally stopped?

6. How did the slave trade undermine African society and culture?

Reading Primary Sources

The Muslim conquests during the Middle Ages brought a common religion, law, and language to an area extending from the Atlantic Ocean to India. These elements of a common culture encouraged travel and trade within the empire. The most famous Muslim traveler was Ibn Battuta (1304–1377), whose writings are a major source of our knowledge of fourteenth-century Africa. Read the following passage from Ibn Battuta's account of his visit to the kingdom of Mali. Then answer the questions that follow it.

> Their women are of surpassing beauty and are shown more respect than the men. The state of affairs among these people is indeed extraordinary. Their men show no signs of jealousy whatever . . . [and a] person's heirs are his sister's sons, not his own sons. This is a thing which I have seen nowhere in the world except among the [people] of Malabar [on the west coast of India]. But those are heathens; *these* are Muslims, [careful] in observing the hours of prayer, studying books of law, and memorizing the Koran. Yet their women show no bashfulness before men and do not veil themselves, though they are [faithful] in attending the prayers. Any man who wishes to marry one of them may do so, but [Mali women] do not travel with their husbands, and even if one desired to do so, her family would not allow her to go. . . .

(a) From which of his relatives, according to Ibn Battuta, did a boy in Mali inherit property? (b) Among what other people did he say he had seen customs similar to those he described in Mali? (c) What distinction did he make between those people and the people of Mali? Why? (d) Which do you think was considered more important by the people of Mali, a woman's relationship with her husband or her relationship with the family into which she was born? Give evidence to support your answer.

Skill Activities

1. Word research. You will recall that one of the commodities traded by Africans was salt. Salt is cheap and plentiful today, but was once a precious substance. Use the library and reference books to find the following information, all connected with salt: (a) the origin of the word *salary;* (b) the meanings and origins of the following phrases: "not worth one's salt"; "the salt of the earth"; "take with a grain of salt"; "salt something away."

2. Reports. Find information on one of the following topics and prepare a report: (a) the rock paintings of the Sahara; (b) the bronze sculptures of Benin and the "lost wax" process used to make them; (c) the Tuareg people of the Sahara; (d) Mount Kilimanjaro; (e) traditional African religions; (f) the ruins of Zimbabwe; (g) African masks.

3. Paraphrasing. Reread the letter on page 284 written by King Affonso of Kongo to the king of Portugal. Then paraphrase it. (To review what paraphrasing means, see the definition given on page 61.)

4. Making models. In a typical African village, family members lived in huts near one another to form a compound. Using the picture on page 286 and illustrations from encyclopedias, make a model of a traditional family compound to display in your class.

5. Bulletin boards. Make a bulletin-board display of African art for your classroom. Use pictures from magazines or copy illustrations from books. Try to find examples of African art from the period covered in this chapter (before 1800) and of modern-day African art. Attach a label to each picture telling when the work was completed and what area of Africa it is from.

As civilizations developed in the Americas, some customs spread from group to group. The ceremonial ball game of the Olmecs, who lived in what is now Mexico, came to be played over a wide area. The pottery figure of a ballplayer below was created by an artisan of the Mayan people.

14

Civilization in the Americas

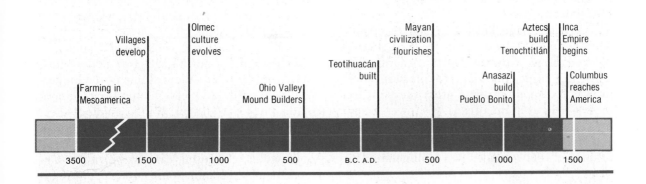

Farming in Mesoamerica

Villages develop

Olmec culture evolves

Ohio Valley Mound Builders

Teotihuacán built

Mayan civilization flourishes

Anasazi build Pueblo Bonito

Aztecs build Tenochtitlán

Inca Empire begins

Columbus reaches America

| 3500 | 1500 | 1000 | 500 | B.C. A.D. | 500 | 1000 | 1500 |

The early civilizations in Asia, Africa, and Europe were able to exchange ideas and influences as they developed. The cultures of the Americas, however, grew up in almost complete isolation from the rest of the world. Over many thousands of years, the peoples of the Americas gradually settled in many different environments and developed a variety of distinctive cultures and languages.

Like the peoples of other continents, the first Americans developed techniques of farming and metalworking and brilliant traditions in arts and crafts. Religion played an important part in American cultures, inspiring the building of temples and cities. Trading networks were established, and some powerful states gained immense wealth. A complex civilization developed in what is now Mexico. In the Andes of South America a great empire emerged. People to the north of Mexico developed a wide variety of societies.

This chapter describes the early civilizations that developed among the Indian peoples of the Americas.

CHAPTER OUTLINE

1 Civilization Develops in Mesoamerica

2 The Aztecs and Incas Establish Empires

3 Many Cultures Arise North of Mexico

1 Civilization Develops in Mesoamerica

Scientists believe that thousands of years ago many bands of hunting peoples migrated from Asia to settle in North America. They gradually moved south and east until scattered groups were living throughout North and South America. About 1200 B.C. the earliest civilization in the Americas developed among the Olmec people in what is now Mexico. Other early American peoples followed the pattern set by the Olmecs.

A land bridge links Asia and the Americas. During the most recent Ice Age, glaciers covered large areas of North America and northern Europe. Since much of the earth's water was locked up in these great sheets of ice, the water level in the oceans was lower. Scientists think that the Bering Strait between Asia and North America was then dry land, forming a "bridge" between the two continents. This bridge may have formed twice, about 30,000 years ago and 12,000 years ago.

The first human beings who lived in the Americas were probably hunters who wandered across the land bridge following herds of animals. These people probably came from different parts of Asia. They did not come in large groups, nor did they all come at one time. One theory is that people migrated from Asia over a period of several thousand years, whenever the land bridge existed.

Though glaciers covered all of what is now Canada and the northern United States, there were ice-free river valleys. Some of the hunters traveled south and east along these natural paths (map, next page). South of the ice sheet they found vast forests, lakes and rivers, and an abundance of wild animals to hunt. Huge mammoths, elk, bison, camels, wolves, and tigers roamed the land. Some hunters moved farther and farther south. After many centuries, they reached the southern tip of South America, 11,000 miles from the Bering Strait.

A variety of languages develops. As these migrant hunters found widely scattered new homes in the Americas, they became very different from one another. Each group developed its own language and distinctive habits and customs. Eventually hundreds of different languages were spoken by the Indians of North and South America.

American Indians develop distinctive technology. After the glaciers melted and the land bridge from Asia disappeared, the people of the Americas were cut off from the civilizations developing in other parts of the world. This helps to explain why the technology developed by early peoples in the Americas was different from that of other early civilizations. Although some American Indians worked with metals such as gold, silver, and copper, they did not learn to make bronze or work with iron. Metals were used mainly for ornaments. People continued to make their tools and weapons of stone, wood, or bone. Though they knew about the wheel, they did not use it for transportation.

TIMETABLE

Civilization in America

B.C.

1200*	The Olmec begin to lay the foundations of Mesoamerican civilization.
500–400*	The Mound Builders develop a farming society in the Ohio River valley.

A.D.

100*	The first Mesoamerican city is built at Teotihuacán.
300–700*	Mesoamerican civilization reaches its height among the Maya.
850–950*	Maya civilization collapses.
1085*	The Anasazi complete Pueblo Bonito.
1200*	The Mississippian culture reaches its height.
1325*	The Aztecs build Tenochtitlán.
1438	The Incas begin to build an empire in South America.
1580*	The Iroquois League is formed.

*APPROXIMATE DATES

Hunters become farmers. The climate in North America changed as the glaciers melted. Some areas became hotter and drier. Many of the great herds of animals vanished, and food became scarcer. Gradually some of the hunters learned to cultivate grains and other plants that they found growing wild. These farming peoples settled down in villages and tended their crops.

The first farming settlements were located in Mesoamerica, the area that stretches from central Mexico into Central America (*meso* means "middle"). In the fertile Valley of Mexico, people were growing corn and other crops as early as 3500 B.C. By 1500 B.C. many Mesoamericans were living in villages and growing squash, beans, and cotton as well as corn. They added to their food supply by hunting wild animals and fishing. From these small farm settlements, several cultures developed.

The Olmecs lay the foundation for Mesoamerican civilization. By about 1200 B.C., when the Shang people in China were farming along the Yellow River, a people we call the Olmecs had settled on the coast of the Gulf of Mexico (map, page 295). We do not know what these people called themselves or whether they were newcomers to this region. The name we use means "rubber people," because the Olmecs were the first people to tap rubber trees for sap. Most archeologists believe that Olmec culture set the pattern for civilization in Mesoamerica.

The Olmecs had a hieroglyphic form of writing. While Egyptian hieroglyphics were deciphered with the Rosetta stone (page 49), no one has yet found a way to read either the Olmec writing or the similar writing systems of later Mesoamerican peoples. Since archeologists cannot read the Olmec writing, most of our knowledge of the Olmecs and other early American peoples depends on other kinds of remains.

The Olmecs also worked with mathematical ideas. Their number system was based on combinations of only three symbols — a dot (standing for "one"), a bar (for "five"), and zero. Centuries before mathematicians in India discovered the idea of the zero (page 239), Mesoamerican priests were using it to make remarkably precise calculations. The Mesoameri-

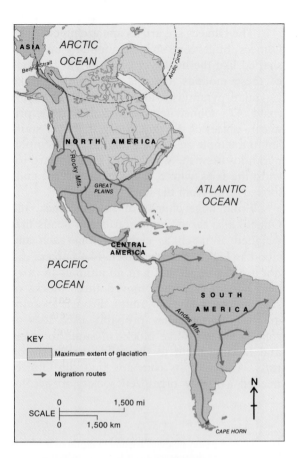

Migrations in the Americas

This map shows the routes that scientists believe migrating hunters followed in the Americas. Where did the hunters probably cross from Asia to America? How far south did migrating people travel?

cans observed, recorded, and accurately predicted eclipses and the orbits of planets. They developed two calendars — one for everyday use and one used by the priests.

Religious ritual was important in Olmec life. The Olmecs had a ceremonial ball game (later called *pok-a-tok*) that was something like basketball. The players could not touch the hard rubber ball with their hands. Instead they had to use their elbows and hips in trying to send the ball through a small stone ring set sideways in a high wall. Archeologists believe that some players were sacrificed to the gods at the end of the game. In time, the ceremonial ball game was played in centers throughout Mesoamerica.

The Olmecs are artists and architects. The Olmecs built cone-shaped mounds of earth shaped like the nearby volcanoes. On the tops of these mounds, temples were built. Unlike Egyptian pyramids, which were built as tombs (page 47), Olmec temple-pyramids were primarily places of worship. Steep flights of stairs led to a temple on the flat summit. The temple-pyramids drew the worshipers' eyes upward toward the skies, where, it was believed, the gods looked down from the stars.

From huge chunks of volcanic rock, the Olmecs also carved enormous stone heads that weighed as much as eighteen tons each and stood as high as fourteen feet. The Olmecs did not use the wheel and had no animals to carry heavy loads. Yet they moved these blocks of stone more than sixty miles through swamps and rain forest. They probably used logs as rollers, moving huge blocks of stone to rivers and floating them to the religious centers on rafts. Archeologists conclude that the Olmecs needed a highly organized society to accom-

The Olmec carving below is a copy in stone of the hand and knee protectors worn by players in the ceremonial ball games.

plish this labor and to maintain the religious centers. Priests probably directed the hundreds of workers who carried out the work.

Olmec influence spreads. By about the first century B.C., Olmec culture had vanished. Olmec sculptures were broken and buried, and the religious centers were swallowed up by the fast-growing vines and trees of the rain forest. They were not rediscovered until the twentieth century.

Yet archeologists have found much evidence that the Olmecs influenced other peoples. Small Olmec carvings, many made from highly prized jade, have been found all over Mesoamerica. Sculptures that show Olmec influence appear in places as far apart as western Mexico and southern Guatemala (map, next page). Later Mesoamerican peoples adopted or improved on the Olmec system of writing, number system, calendar, style of architecture, and ritual ball game. Because of this, Olmec culture is considered the "parent culture" in Mesoamerica.

A city is built in the Valley of Mexico. The Olmec religious centers were places of pilgrimage and worship rather than cities where all classes of people lived and worked. Mesoamerica's first city was built about A.D. 100 in the fertile Valley of Mexico. The building of Teotihuacán (TAY-oh-tee-wah-KAHN) marked the beginning of a brilliant cultural period that lasted some 700 years. The farming population in the Valley of Mexico had grown large enough to support large numbers of artisans and artists, architects, musicians, and poets. Most of their creative work was devoted to religion, for the people of this city apparently worshiped hundreds of gods. The name Teotihuacán, in fact, means "where the gods live."

The Teotihuacanos' most important god was Quetzalcóatl (ket-sahl-KOH-atl), the Feathered Serpent god. They believed that he had given them all the good things of civilization: knowledge of farming, writing, the calendar, arts, crafts, and laws. Quetzalcóatl was thought of as a gentle god of peace and humility. The people of Teotihuacán appear to have followed his code, living peacefully as farmers and traders.

The Teotihuacanos also were skilled in arts and crafts. Artisans used molds to make figures

Mesoamerican Civilization

The Olmecs are believed to have laid the foundations for Mesoamerican civilization.
What cultures were probably influenced by the Olmecs? by Teotihuacán? Aztec culture
developed in much the same area as Teotihuacán. Identify that area.

with movable arms and legs and produced life-size masks of highly polished stone. The walls of homes in Teotihuacán were covered with joyful scenes of dancing gods, singing jaguars, prancing birds, and chanting priests. Beautifully painted pottery reproduced the wall paintings in miniature. Many of these objects were valued by people of other cultures. Traders from Teotihuacán carried products hundreds of miles to other parts of Mesoamerica. In time the Teotihuacanos built the largest trade empire in Mesoamerica.

About A.D. 600, wandering tribes from the north attacked and burned Teotihuacán. Its people fled, but their skills and learning were adopted by people of other Mesoamerican cultures.

The Mayas build city-states connected by trade. At about the same time that Teotihuacán was expanding, people known as the Mayas (MY-uhz) were building religious centers in the Yucatan Peninsula, where modern Mexico and Guatemala meet. Two other early centers were built at Uaxactún (wah-shak-TUN) and Tikal (tee-KAHL). Between about A.D. 300 and 700, Mesoamerican civilization reached its height at the Maya centers.

In Maya society, priests shared control with ambitious rulers who expanded the religious centers into city-states. At the head of each city-state was the *halach uinic* (hah-LAHCH oo-ee-NEEK), the "true man." These leaders were absolute rulers. Maya paintings show that they often went to war, probably to add to their territory or to take prisoners who were made slaves or were sacrificed to the gods.

Wide, paved roads and sea routes linked the Maya city-states. Merchants carried on an active trade in corn, salt, smoked meat, dried fish, honey, wood products, and animal skins. They also traded in luxury items, including jade, carved shells, fine pottery, and textiles.

Maya priests play an important role in society. Although priests were not the sole

MESOAMERICAN ART
AND ARCHITECTURE

The feathered headdress of the god Quetzalcóatl was a symbol of authority in Mesoamerica. In the wall painting from Teotihuacán (right) it is worn by a priest. The Mayan carving (above right) shows a woman presenting a jaguar mask to an important leader wearing a feather headdress. Similar scenes were carved on the wooden beams inside Mayan temple-pyramids such as that at Tikal (above).

rulers in the city-states, they played an important role in the everyday lives of the Mayas. The priests' chief concern was time, for apparently it was believed that the gods would destroy the world if ceremonies were not held on exactly the right day. The priests also taught that the day on which a person was born influenced his or her future. They decided which days were lucky or unlucky for couples to marry, for crops to be planted, for trading ventures to begin, for wars to be fought, or for new temples to be built.

To obtain accurate measurements of time, Maya priests observed the stars and planets, kept records of the seasons, and accurately predicted eclipses. Their calendar was one of the most accurate ever developed. The Maya year had 365 days, the last five of which were considered unlucky.

The Maya priests were also the record-keepers. They taught the sons of nobles how to read the written language. They also taught young men who were training to be priests how to interpret the calendar.

Ordinary people support a rich state.
Priests, nobles, and warriors were the upper classes of Maya society. Warriors fought the frequent wars between city-states. Maya nobles helped run the government. They collected taxes, kept records of work that was done, and oversaw the road system. In their leisure time they wrote poetry, collected art objects, and enjoyed music.

Vast resources were needed to keep the Maya upper classes in comfort, but none of these people paid taxes. Neither did the many artisans or merchants. Taxes came from the Maya peasants. Each peasant family had to set aside part of its corn crop for taxes. Men also had to work on building projects and serve as soldiers. To meet their tax bills, farmers spent their spare time gathering forest products and making tools, ornaments, and household goods for sale.

Farm women gathered honey, wove cloth, and made pottery. Their fine weaving and pottery were much in demand, since nobles used these objects as gifts. Maya women also cared for their households and worked in the fields. They shared the responsibility of paying taxes but could not hold public office. In fact, Maya women were not allowed to enter the temples.

Maya society declines. The emphasis in Maya society was on respect for tradition, and the civilization apparently changed little for about 600 years. Then, between about A.D. 850 and 950, the great Maya centers were abandoned one by one. The Mayas did not move away, for their descendants still live in the same area; yet their civilization collapsed. No one is sure why. Mesoamerican civilization never again reached the heights it had attained under the Mayas.

CHECK-UP

1. (a) According to scientists, how were the Americas first settled? (b) How were the people of the Americas cut off from civilizations in other parts of the world?
2. (a) In what ways was the Olmec culture the "parent culture" of Mesoamerica? (b) What achievements did the Olmecs make in mathematics and astronomy?
3. (a) How did Teotihuacán differ from the Olmec centers? (b) What gifts did the Teotihuacanos believe they had received from Quetzalcóatl? (c) How did their way of life reflect this belief?
4. (a) Who ruled Maya society? (b) What was the role in society of the priests? (c) of the common people?

2 The Aztecs and Incas Establish Empires

In the fifteenth century, a new kind of state developed in both Mesoamerica and South America. Through conquest, small tribes gained control of great amounts of land and wealth. Two major warrior-states were formed — one by the Aztecs in Mesoamerica and the other by the Incas in South America. Although there were many similarities in their cultures, the Aztecs and Incas governed their huge states differently.

THE AZTECS

A nomadic tribe grows powerful. As Maya civilization was dying out, other states came to power in Mesoamerica. One nomadic tribe from the dry lands to the north had slowly migrated southward to the Valley of Mexico. The people of this tribe called themselves Aztecs. About 1325 the Aztecs built the village of Tenochtitlán (teh-NOHCH-tee-TLAHN) on an island in a lake, where Mexico City is today. By the 1400's their city-state had conquered other tribal groups in central Mexico and was rapidly expanding.

The chief priests and warriors of the Aztecs elected the ruler, though some rulers took control by force. The ruler had absolute power; he was head of state, military commander, and chief priest. His word was law, and he expected his commands to be obeyed without question. The greatest nobles and priests fell on their

In Mesoamerica, carvings were often covered with mosaic work. The people of Teotihuacán made mosaic masks, and the Aztecs adopted the practice and applied it to other objects. This double-headed serpent made of turquoise and shell is an ornament believed to represent the Aztec idea of time. Compare this type of mosaic work with that used in Byzantium (picture, page 206).

faces when the Aztec ruler appeared. Even to look on his face might be punished by death.

The Aztecs excel as builders. The Aztecs borrowed ideas and skills from other peoples in Mesoamerica. Aztec architecture had its roots in Teotihuacán. From the Olmecs' successors came the Aztec calendar and writing system. The Aztecs' social system, their religion, and many of their arts and crafts also came from earlier cultures in Mesoamerica.

As engineers and builders, however, the Aztecs had no equal in Mesoamerica. Broad causeways linked the island city of Tenochtitlán with the mainland. Aztec engineers built aqueducts to carry fresh water from the mainland to the city and sewers to carry away waste. Dams protected the city from floods, and irrigation systems carried water to crops during the dry season.

Tenochtitlán grew into a great city with broad open plazas and large marketplaces. The homes of the wealthy were built around courtyards with fountains, and many had colorful roof gardens. By the mid-1400's Tenochtitlán had an estimated population of about 300,000, greater than that of any city in Europe at the time.

The Aztecs found an unusual way to increase the amount of land available for growing food for the people of Tenochtitlán. Along the shores of the shallow lake that surrounded the city, Aztec farmers floated large mats made of reeds woven together. Covered with soil and planted with seeds, the mats became floating gardens. The floating gardens were a tremen-

dous success. Today, although the lake is gone, the gardens still supply some of Mexico City's food.

A trade empire develops. The Aztec state did not rule directly over conquered peoples. Instead of appointing governors to rule conquered lands, the Aztecs demanded tribute. Tribute payments included food, clothing, woven blankets, precious stones, furs, feathers, fine woods, and slaves or captives. Trade and tribute, not political organization, held the Aztec state together. Products from across Mesoamerica poured into the great marketplace of Tenochtitlán.

Human beings are sacrificed. As the population grew, the Aztecs sought new sources of tribute. They particularly wanted more human prisoners. While some captives became slaves, most were destined to be sacrificed. Like other Mesoamerican peoples, the Aztecs apparently believed that the sun would stop shining if they did not make offerings to the sun-god. Usually they offered flowers and food. On special occasions, however, and in times of crisis, it was believed that the sun must be given human hearts. Other gods and goddesses were also given human sacrifices.

In earlier Mesoamerican cultures, human sacrifice had been rare; to be chosen for sacrifice to the gods was considered an honor. Under the Aztecs sacrifices were made frequently. Aztec priests encouraged warfare solely to gain prisoners for sacrifice. In one incident, 20,000 captives were sacrificed at the dedication of a single temple in Tenochtitlán. The practice of sacrificing people in such numbers caused the Aztecs to be hated and feared by the other peoples of Mesoamerica.

The Aztec practice of human sacrifice gives a one-sided picture of their religious life. The Aztecs continued to worship some gentle deities, including Quetzalcóatl. Moreover, some Aztecs rejected the practice of human sacrifice and urged that it be replaced by offerings of songs and flowers to the gods.

Education is important in Aztec society. Aztec society was organized much like that of the Mayas, but it was less rigid. Education gave the Aztecs the opportunity to advance socially. All Aztec children were required to go to school, where they learned Aztec history and religion. Girls were taught weaving, while boys learned their duties as subjects and warriors.

Even greater opportunities existed in the schools where young people were trained to be priests. There both boys and girls could learn how to read and write, interpret the calendar, use medicines, make prophecies, compose poetry, and debate. Education made it possible for a young man from any class to become a high-ranking government official, a battle commander, or a priest. Women, regardless of their education, were expected to devote themselves to their homes and families.

The Aztec system of education produced people with great awareness and curiosity. The Aztecs studied their environment, describing and naming hundreds of plants and animals. Educated Aztec men and women discussed the meaning of life and the importance of self-knowledge. Some said that life was only a dream, an interruption within a higher life that would resume after death. One Aztec poet-king wrote:

> Is life really lived in the form world?
> We are not always on earth —
> Only a little while here.
> Though it be jade, it is shattered.
> Though it be gold, it is broken.
> Quetzal feather[1] is torn.
> We are not always on earth —
> Only a little while here.

---

[1]The emerald-green feathers of the quetzal (ket-SAHL), a tropical bird found only in remote areas, have been highly prized since ancient times in Mesoamerica.

The Aztecs were the last Indian kingdom in Mesoamerica. In 1519, Spanish conquerors arrived and abruptly brought to an end the Aztecs' rule (Chapter 16).

THE INCA EMPIRE

Early cultures develop in the Andes. In the valleys of the rugged Andes, which form the mountainous backbone of South America, many different cultures developed. The South American cultures had some similarities to those in Mesoamerica. Andean farmers used

The Inca Empire

At its height, the Inca Empire covered much of what are now Ecuador, Peru, Bolivia, and Chile. What linked the parts of the empire together?

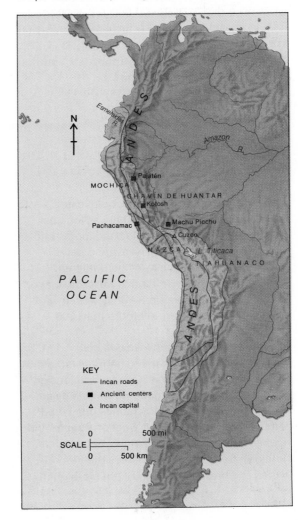

similar farming methods, though they were later in starting to grow corn — the staple food in Mesoamerica. So that they could use the steep slopes of mountains for crops, they built terraces — wide, step-like banks of soil. On these terraces they grew potatoes, squash, beans, peanuts, and cotton. In dry regions they learned how to irrigate the land. The Andeans at an early date also learned to work with metals and to weave fine textiles. They raised llamas and alpacas for their wool and meat.

As early as 1000 B.C. some villages in the central Andes became religious centers. Several fairly large states developed and conquered their neighbors, but none dominated the area until the fifteenth century A.D. By 1438 a people called the Incas had come to control a large area around Cuzco (coos-koh). They gradually expanded their lands until they ruled an empire that stretched 2,000 miles along the Pacific coast. The empire included lands that are now part of Peru, Ecuador, Bolivia, Chile, and Argentina. Probably about six million people lived in the Inca empire.

Inca engineers conquer the mountains. The Incas had some things in common with the Aztecs. They too had been a small tribe that had grown powerful through conquest. Like the Aztecs, the Incas worshiped the sun. They also had adopted the achievements of earlier cultures. From coastal peoples they learned techniques of weaving and pottery-making. From peoples to the north they learned to work with gold and silver. The "gold of the sun" covered the walls of the great temple in Cuzco, and gold and silver jewelry glittered on Inca nobles.

Like the Aztecs, the Incas were superb engineers. The different parts of the empire's rugged terrain were linked by an excellent system of roads, which ran across coastal deserts and over the highest mountains in the Western Hemisphere. Swinging bridges woven of reeds and vines crossed rivers and canyons. Sometimes tunnels were dug through mountains. The Incas' major roads were so well built that traces of paving remain today. The roads were traveled by merchants, officials, and messengers carrying royal orders. Inca travelers went

LINKING PAST AND PRESENT
Peruvian Weaving

Modern weavers marvel at the complicated fabrics made by Peruvian weavers as long as 2,500 years ago. Using simple hand looms and tightly spun yarns, women weavers created beautiful textiles that have lasted until the present. Some Peruvian fabrics were loose and open, like lace. Others were tightly woven with thread so fine that there are more than 200 strands in an inch.

The Peruvian weavers followed bold geometric designs or made patterns of fantastic human and animal figures. One favorite design was a cat-like creature, once worshiped by an ancient religious cult. Many fabrics combined cotton threads with the soft wool of alpacas and vicuñas (still prized today in fine woolen clothing). Colors were sometimes the natural beiges and browns of the wool but more often

were bright shades made with paint or natural dyes. Ponchos, shirts, skirts, turbans, and belts were all made from uncut woven panels. The Peruvians used some of their most beautiful woven cloths to wrap the dead for burial. The design shown here is a fragment from such a wrapping.

PERUVIAN ART AND ARCHITECTURE

Like the Aztecs, the Incas adopted techniques and practices that had been developed by earlier cultures. The Inca people dressed in much the same way as the pottery flute player (left), a figure made centuries before the Incas built their empire. Communication within the empire depended on messengers, whose speed was indicated by a bird's head and wings as shown on the pre-Inca ear spool (below). In the Inca city of Machu Picchu, built on top of a mountain at an altitude of nearly 8,000 feet, crops were grown on terraces, another practice the Incas adopted.

on foot, for they had no wheeled vehicles and used their animals only to carry loads. Inns along the roads provided shelter and comfort for travelers.

Inca rule is centralized. The Inca empire had a stronger political organization than the Aztec state. The Incas ruled directly over the peoples they conquered, forcing them to accept the Inca religion, language, and style of clothing. To keep rebellious peoples under control, the Incas resettled them in the midst of loyal groups. Every village had a leader who was closely supervised by government officials. These officials enforced royal laws and punished wrongdoers. They kept detailed records of the size of the population and the food supply. Lacking a written language, they used the *quipu* (KEE-POO) to keep records. *Quipus* were made of colored cords of various lengths and were knotted at intervals to indicate different sums.

Inca society was more rigid than Aztec society. People in the "empire of the sun" remained in the social class in which they were born. There were the common people, and there were Inca nobles. At the head of Inca society was the emperor. The Incas believed that the emperor was descended from the sun. The emperor's rule was absolute. His wife might rule for him when he was away from the capital at Cuzco, but she was expected to be completely obedient when he was home. Criticism of the emperor or of his policies brought death.

Though the people of the Inca empire lived under strict laws, they had a great deal of security. The needy could draw upon the food and wool in the royal storehouses at any time. Nevertheless, ordinary people lived bleak lives. They had to work hard to produce enough extra crops to fill the storehouses. Rigid laws limited their freedom, and detailed official records kept them from having much privacy. They might be told whom to marry and were rarely permitted to travel. Rule by the Incas had created much discontent within the empire by the beginning of the sixteenth century.

CHECK-UP

1. Where did the Aztecs come from and where did they settle?
2. (a) What achievements did the Aztecs borrow from other Mesoamericans? (b) In what ways was Tenochtitlán a remarkable city? (c) What educational opportunities did Aztec society offer?
3. How did the Aztec state control the peoples it conquered?
4. (a) Describe the system of roads built by the Incas. (b) How did the Incas control the peoples they had conquered?
5. How did Inca and Aztec societies differ?

3 Many Cultures Arise North of Mexico

Hundreds of different cultures and languages developed among the Indians who settled the North American continent north of Mexico. These different peoples are often grouped by geographical regions where people had similar ways of life (map, page 305). As in Mesoamerica, archeologists have found evidence that several distinctive cultures emerged as early as 1000 B.C. Some were influenced by the Mesoamerican civilization to the south. Trade, agriculture, and arts flourished, and different forms of political organization developed.

The Anasazi build cities in cliffs and canyons. By the first century A.D., a people known as the Anasazi (ah-nah-SAH-zee) had created a farming culture in the dry lands of the Southwest — present-day Arizona, New Mexico, Colorado, and Utah. The name Anasazi was given them by the Navajo Indians, who much later discovered the ruins of their huge, many-storied homes. In the Navajo language *Anasazi* means "strange ancient ones."

The early Anasazi probably learned farming techniques about 1500 B.C. from the peoples of Mesoamerica. Corn, beans, and squash became their staple foods.

The Anasazi at first lived in dugout houses roofed with logs. About A.D. 700, as the population increased, they began to build houses of stone or sun-baked clay called adobe (uh-DOH-bee). Communities grew more crowded, and society became more complex. Houses were built close together and on top of each other. Hundreds of people in the community worked together to build huge "apartment houses," which were several stories high and had many rooms (picture, page 306). People hauled logs long distances to make the framework and roof; they cut blocks of sandstone for the walls. The Spaniards who arrived several hundred years later called these huge buildings *pueblos* (PWEB-lohz), which means "towns" in Spanish.[2]

Many pueblos were built in canyons or high on steep cliffs. One of the largest, Pueblo Bonito (in present-day New Mexico), took more than a hundred years to build and was completed about A.D. 1085. It had 650 rooms and could house well over a thousand people. Nearby pueblos in the same canyon were almost as large. Every great pueblo had a central room or *kiva* (KEE-vah) used for community ceremonies and religious rituals. Colorful murals decorated the walls of the kiva.

As farmers in a dry land, the Anasazi were dependent on natural forces, and these were the center of their religion. The Anasazi devised a kind of "sun clock" to track the seasons and the cycles of the sun. Men oversaw the rituals that people hoped would bring good hunting, enough rain, and successful crops. Women in Anasazi society owned all the houses and property and headed family clans.

The Anasazi culture stretched over a huge area in the Southwest. Networks of wide roads linked central pueblos with outlying villages and other centers. The people traded with Mexican Indians for copper and feathers and with Indians of the Great Plains for buffalo meat. Their only farm animals were turkeys, but they kept dogs as pets.

About 1150, a very long drought struck the central area of Anasazi culture. Gradually all the great pueblos were abandoned. The Anasazi moved away to join neighboring groups, and the first great culture of the Southwest vanished.

The Hopewell people carry on widespread trade. About the fifth or fourth century B.C., a highly organized farming society developed in the Ohio River valley. Living in villages along the river, these people became known as "Mound Builders" because of the large earthen mounds they constructed. Some of these structures were burial mounds, and others were ceremonial mounds in the shape of animals such as snakes, turtles, or birds. The Mound Builders traded widely along the rivers and lakes, acquiring copper from the northern Great Lakes region, seashells from the Gulf of Mexico, and mica (a shiny mineral) from people to the east. Their artists worked with wood, stone, and copper to make ornaments and household objects (picture, page 306). The Mound Builders' way of life, called the "Hopewell culture,"[3] spread over the central part of the continent from what is now Wisconsin to the Gulf Coast and as far west as present-day Kansas. The Hopewell way of life lasted for about a thousand years, until A.D. 400 or 500.

The Mississippian culture borrows from Mesoamerica. Both ideas and goods were exchanged in the trade among the Indian peoples of the Americas. By about A.D. 1200, people along the lower Mississippi River had built the most advanced culture north of Mexico. Their culture, which archeologists call the Mississippian, was influenced by ideas from Mesoamerica. Mississippian society was divided into strict classes under a ruler known as the Great Sun. In the center of the walled villages stood steep-sided earth pyramids with wooden temples on the flat summits. High-ranking nobles built their homes on smaller mounds, and other mounds were used for burials. Religion included the Mesoamerican idea of a feathered serpent god.

---

[2]This term is now used both for the buildings and for the present-day Indians, such as the Zuñi and Hopi, who are the Anasazi's descendants.

[3]The culture was named for a farmer in southern Ohio, on whose land archeologists discovered mounds and objects from this culture.

The Mississippian culture prospered from both trade and farming, and its influence spread throughout the southeast. Fortified villages, located mainly along rivers, grew into city-states with populations of up to 20,000. Artisans worked in metal and stone, making knives and hoe blades for trade. A trade in salt also developed. The largest town of this culture was located near the site of present-day St. Louis. Its central temple mound was 100 feet high and covered fifteen acres.

The Mississippian way of life lasted among the Natchez people (map, next page) until French explorers arrived in the Mississippi Valley in the 1600's.

Wealth is important in the Northwest Coast culture. Along the Pacific coast, from present-day northern California to Alaska, a very different culture was established by about 1000 B.C. The people of the Northwest Coast culture area included the Nootka, Haida, Tlingit, Kwakiutl, and Chinook. Unlike other Indian peoples who lived to the north of Mexico, the Northwest Coast people did not depend on farming and apparently had no ties with Mesoamerica. They lived well by fishing the rivers and the ocean, gathering berries, and hunting wild animals for food and furs. The abundant forests provided cedar wood for making canoes, large houses, ceremonial masks, and finely carved boxes (picture, page 306). In front of the houses or carved into the doorposts were tall wooden totem poles.[4]

The Northwest Coast peoples were also unusual among North American Indians because they greatly valued wealth and possessions. Their communities were divided into strict social classes, with a large population of slaves captured in raids. As a way of showing off their wealth, chiefs and other prominent villagers occasionally held a gigantic giveaway celebration. It was called the potlatch, from a Nootka word that means "giving." Food, furs, blankets, engraved pieces of copper, and even slaves were given to the guests who gathered to

celebrate a special occasion. The prestige of an entire clan or village might depend on how much was given away. In return, the guests had to give a potlatch where they tried to make an even more impressive showing of wealth.

The Eskimos create a unique way of life. The Eskimos, or Inuit, who settled the northernmost parts of North America, shared some land and some customs with the Indians of the Northwest Coast. Because the Eskimos were probably the last migrants from Asia, however, they had little in common with the American Indians to the south. They created a way of life uniquely adapted to the Arctic environment. The Eskimos hunted walrus, whale, fish, seal, and caribou for food. From these animals they made practically everything they needed — harpoons, fishing hooks, knives, needles, warm weatherproof clothing, sleds, kayaks, tents for summer use, and oil for lamps. In their leisure time they carved bone and ivory, making maps of their fishing grounds and pictures of their daily life. They made use of their forbidding surroundings by storing food in its natural "freezer." Some even used snow and ice to build homes. This way of life met the Eskimos' needs so well that it remained virtually unchanged until modern times.

Indians develop strong communities. Like most farming peoples, Indians throughout North America were generally peaceful and hard-working. Their local villages and tribal groups were organized fairly democratically. The rigid class divisions of the Mississippians and the Northwest Coast peoples were unusual. More commonly, respected elders and warriors formed a governing council. The council might name one person to lead a war party or hunting band, but there was no king or absolute ruler.

American Indians
North of the Rio Grande

The map on the next page shows where Indian peoples lived when Europeans first reached the Americas. Into what regions is the map divided? Using the Atlas map of North America at the back of this book as a guide to present state boundaries, identify the Indians who once lived in different parts of the United States.

---

[4]The totem was a clan or family symbol, usually an animal such as an owl or a bear. A totem pole showed a series of totems and might be several feet tall.

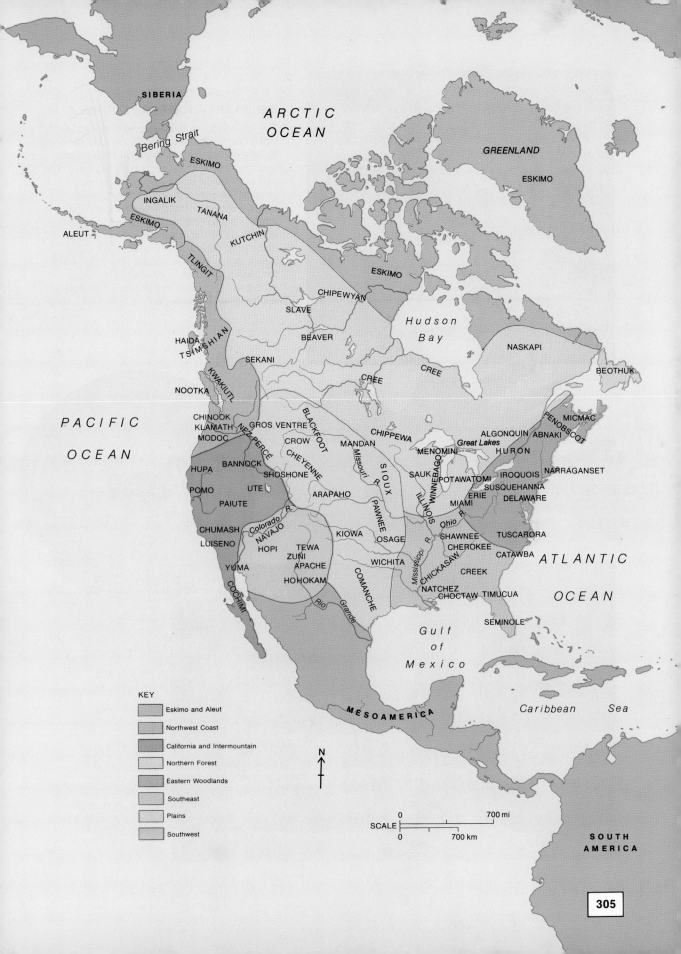

SIBERIA

ARCTIC
OCEAN

Bering Strait

GREENLAND

ESKIMO

ESKIMO

INGALIK

TANANA

ESKIMO

ALEUT

KUTCHIN

TLINGIT

ESKIMO

CHIPEWYAN

SLAVE

*Hudson
Bay*

NASKAPI

HAIDA

BEAVER

TSIMSHIAN

SEKANI

CREE

CREE

BEOTHUK

KWAKIUTL

NOOTKA

PACIFIC

OCEAN

CHINOOK

BLACKFOOT

CHIPPEWA

MICMAC

PENOBSCOT

KLAMATH

GROS VENTRE

NEZ PERCE

CROW

MODOC

CHEYENNE

MANDAN

Great Lakes

ALGONQUIN

ABNAKI

MENOMINI

HURON

HUPA

BANNOCK

SHOSHONE

Missouri

SIOUX

SAUK

WINNEBAGO

POTAWATOMI

IROQUOIS

NARRAGANSET

POMO

UTE

R.

ERIE

SUSQUEHANNA

PAIUTE

ARAPAHO

PAWNEE

R.

ILLINOIS

MIAMI

DELAWARE

CHUMASH

Colorado R.

NAVAJO

KIOWA

OSAGE

Ohio R.

SHAWNEE

TUSCARORA

LUISENO

HOPI

TEWA

SHAWNEE

CHEROKEE

CATAWBA

ATLANTIC

YUMA

ZUÑI

APACHE

WICHITA

CHICKASAW

CREEK

OCEAN

HOHOKAM

COMANCHE

NATCHEZ

COCHIMI

Rio

Grande

CHOCTAW

TIMUCUA

SEMINOLE

*Gulf
of
Mexico*

Caribbean   Sea

KEY

Eskimo and Aleut

Northwest Coast

California and Intermountain

Northern Forest

Eastern Woodlands

Southeast

Plains

Southwest

MESOAMERICA

N

Mississippi R.

SCALE

0   700 mi

0   700 km

SOUTH
AMERICA

INDIAN ART AND ARCHITECTURE

The Indians north of Mexico were skilled in many crafts. The Anasazi constructed elaborate apartment houses like Mesa Verde (bottom), which was protected by the cliffs around it. The clay bowl below was made by later Pueblo peoples. Its design indicates the Indians' awareness of the world around them. This interest is also reflected by the eagle (center left), made by the Hopewell Indians, who hammered copper obtained from the Great Lakes region into thin sheets. The Indians along the heavily forested Northwest Coast became skilled woodworkers and produced objects such as the sun mask (left).

Most Indian peoples had a strong sense of community and did not believe in private ownership of land. A farming village might allot fields to different families, but there was no change in ownership involved. Most Indians shared a deep respect for the land and a feeling of harmony with the natural environment, as revealed in this Tewa Indian song.

SONG OF THE SKY LOOM
O our Mother the Earth, O our Father the
   Sky,
Your children are we, and with tired backs
We bring you the gifts you love.
Then weave for us a garment of brightness;
May the warp be the white light of morning,
May the weft be the red light of evening,
May the fringes be the falling rain,
May the border be the standing rainbow,
Thus weave for us a garment of brightness,
That we may walk fittingly where birds sing,
That we may walk fittingly where grass is
   green,
O our Mother the Earth, O our Father the
   Sky.

Communities often welcomed new members who came from a different tribe, spoke a different language, or had new skills and ideas. Strangers or captives taken in war were likely to be adopted into the community.

Children were brought up to feel a part of community life. Those who were the same age learned the same skills and entered adulthood together. Girls in their teens were initiated into the women's societies and learned the skills they would need as adults and the rituals of their people, such as ceremonial dances. Boys similarly underwent training in skills as well as learning their parts for rituals and dances.

Towns and villages form alliances. Large kingdoms or empires did not grow up among the Indian peoples north of Mexico. Different Indian peoples, however, often joined together in loose alliances or confederacies. Villages in an alliance sometimes sent tribute to a central leader, but they continued to govern themselves independently.

At the time the English settlers arrived in America in the early 1600's, a leader known as Powhatan had brought together one of the largest of these confederacies. It included about 200 villages in what is now Virginia. At the same time, about fifty settlements in the southeast were allied in what the English called the Creek Confederacy. In addition to the Creek Indians, this confederacy included the Choctaw, Chickasaw, and Cherokee. When the English arrived, these southeastern Indians were prosperous, peaceful farmers and traders living in walled villages.

The best-known alliance, and perhaps the longest-lived, was the Iroquois (IHR-uh-kwoy) League in what is now New York State. It included the "Five Nations," the Seneca, Cayuga, Onondaga, Oneida, and Mohawk. Each of these peoples spoke an Iroquois language. (In 1722, they were joined by the Tuscarora, who had moved from the south.)

The Iroquois League was probably formed about 1580 to keep peace among the Five Nations. Though its members never cooperated fully, they did keep peace among themselves. The leading women in each family clan in the Five Nations chose a man to be a member of the League council, which met yearly. Respected warriors, known as the "solitary pine trees," served as advisers. At the time the Europeans arrived in this part of North America, the Iroquois League was dominant in the northeast.

CHECK-UP

1. (a) From where did the early Anasazi probably learn their farming techniques? (b) What was noteworthy about Anasazi architecture? (c) What role did women play in Anasazi culture?

2. What was the purpose of the mounds built by the people of the Hopewell culture?

3. (a) What Mesoamerican influences can be seen in the Mississippian culture? (b) What brought an end to the Mississippian way of life?

4. How was the culture of the Northwest Coast different from other Indian cultures north of Mexico?

5. In what ways did the Eskimos adapt to their Arctic environment?

6. (a) How were most Indian communities governed? (b) What larger groupings did villages sometimes form? (c) What was the purpose of the Iroquois League?

Chapter 14 Review

Chapter Summary

The first people to live in the Americas were wandering hunters from Asia who are believed to have crossed into North America between about 30,000 and 12,000 years ago. These peoples gradually settled throughout the two American continents. Some of the nomadic hunters began to farm and by about 3500 B.C. had settled in villages in Mesoamerica. By about 1200 B.C., the Olmec had established patterns that became the "parent culture" for Mesoamerican civilization. This civilization reached its height with the Mayas, whose culture flourished between A.D. 300 and 700. Worship of the sun, the ceremonial ball game, and temple-pyramids were typical of Mesoamerican religion.

In the fifteenth century, warrior-states became the dominant culture in Mesoamerica and South America. The Aztecs in Mesoamerica built an empire based on conquest and trade from their capital city Tenochtitlán. In South America Inca conquests created an empire in the Andes.

North of Mexico, farming began about 1500 B.C. The earliest distinctive cultures in what is now the United States were developed by the Anasazi in the Southwest, the Hopewell and Mississippians farther east, and the people of the Northwest Pacific Coast. Trading and political alliances linked many of the different North American peoples, most of whom were peaceful farmers and town dwellers.

Vocabulary Review

1. Match the following words with the listed definitions. Then, on a separate sheet of paper, write a sentence for each word. Be sure your sentences show you understand the meaning of each term: *artifact, city-state, hieroglyphics, polytheism.*
(a) The belief in many gods.
(b) A tool, weapon, or other object that has survived from ancient times.
(c) An independent state consisting of a city and its surrounding territory.
(d) A system of writing that uses pictures to stand for words or sounds.

2. Write the sentences listed below on a sheet of paper. In each sentence, fill in the blank with one of the following terms: *Olmecs, Aztecs, totem, Mayas, Incas, Iroquois League, Powhatan Confederacy, pueblo.*
(a) Mesoamerican civilization reached its height in the culture of the ___?___ .
(b) The ___?___, in what is now Virginia, was one of the largest Indian alliances in North America.
(c) The culture of the ___?___ set the pattern for Mesoamerican civilization.
(d) A ___?___ was a symbol that represented a family or clan among the peoples of the Pacific Northwest.
(e) The ___?___, in what is now New York State, was an alliance that included the Seneca, Cayuga, Onondaga, Oneida, and Mohawk.
(f) The ___?___ were hated and feared by their neighbors because of their use of war prisoners as human sacrifices.
(g) The Spanish word for town, given to the buildings of the Anasazi, is ___?___ .
(h) By the fifteenth century, the ___?___ had built an enormous empire in South America.

Relating Geography and History

1. Locating places. Locate each of the following on a map in this chapter:
(a) Bering Strait
(b) Mesoamerica
(c) Teotihuacán
(d) Tenochtitlán
(e) Yucatan Peninsula
(f) Cuzco
(g) Ohio River
(h) Mississippi River

2. Reading maps. On the map on page 299, study the physical features of the Inca Empire. (a) Use the map scale to estimate the length of the empire in miles. (b) What physical features made it difficult to maintain communication and trade between the different regions of the empire? (c) How did the Incas solve this problem?

Discussion Questions

1. Why do we depend on archeologists' findings for most of our information about American Indian civilizations?

2. Explain the part trade played in each of the following societies: (a) Maya, (b) Aztec, (c) Anasazi, (d) Mississippian.

3. (a) What were the benefits of Inca rule for the people who were conquered by the Incas? (b) What were some disadvantages of Inca rule? (c) In what ways did the Incas and the Aztecs differ in their methods of maintaining control over their empires?

4. Why were a number system and calendar important in Mesoamerican cultures?

5. In general, what attitudes did the North American Indians have toward (a) land ownership and use, (b) political organization, (c) strangers or captives, (d) nature?

Reading Primary Sources

After the Spanish conquest of Mexico, some Maya priests had Spanish scribes write down the myths, ceremonies, and prophecies of their ancestors. The following passage from these writings suggests problems that may have led to the decline of Maya civilization. Read the passage. Then answer the questions that follow.

> The vegetation was fast disappearing. . . . Too many mouths in our houses; too many mouths for the number of calabashes [squash].
>
> The strength of many great warriors ebbs away. . . . There is no one left on whom to lean. . . . There is no one left with sufficient understanding to set in order the days [to adjust the calendar]. . . . And so there will be no great abundance of water.
>
> [There came enemies from the north and west.] In great distress we were scattered among the forests and in the mountains. . . .
>
> We mourn the scattering abroad of the books of hieroglyphic writing. . . . For months there was discord among the [chiefs], and all . . . men suffered deeply. . . .
>
> The lords [the gods] bind up their faces in pain because . . . men swelter in toil and hunger is their burden, and because of their bad conscience about protecting the people. . . .
>
> One by one the stars fall.

(a) According to the passage, why did the Mayas not have enough food? (b) What could have been a factor in the decline of education among the Mayas? (c) In your own words, list two more of the Mayas' problems described by the priest and write a sentence or two telling how each might have contributed to the collapse of Maya civilization. (d) What did the priest say about the attitude of the gods toward the Mayas' plight? (e) What do you think the priest meant by saying "One by one the stars fall"?

Skill Activities

1. Word research. We still use a word derived from an Indian name for the god of wind, *Hurakan,* to describe the great wind storms that sometimes devastate coastal regions of North America. Use a dictionary to find out the origins of the words listed below. Make a chart showing from which Indian language each word came and what it means. What other Indian words can you add to the list?

(a) tepee   (g) succotash
(b) canoe   (h) raccoon
(c) chili   (i) wampum
(d) chinook   (j) coyote
(e) moccasin   (k) tomato
(f) potato

2. Making charts. Make a chart comparing the civilizations of Mesoamerica and South America. Use the following categories: (a) location, (b) religious beliefs and practices, (c) government, (d) art and architecture, (e) cultural or scientific achievements.

3. Writing a summary. Write a one-page summary of the account of Aztec civilization given on pages 297–299. (To review what is included in a summary, see page 117.)

4. Reports. Find information about one of the following topics and prepare a report: (a) Indian games; (b) varieties of housing among North American Indian tribes; (c) the uses of feathers by Plains Indians; (d) potlatches; (e) family life among the Indians; (f) the Great Serpent Mound (in Ohio); (g) the origin of the term *Indian;* (h) the ruins of Machu Picchu; (i) varieties of Indian dress; (j) shamans; (k) the Inca city of Cuzco; (l) Aztec *chinampas* (floating gardens); (m) the Maya calendar; (n) legends of Quetzalcóatl; (o) Nazca designs; (p) totem poles.

5. Exploring world literature. Reread the poem on page 307. Explain how the poet used imaginative language to reflect the closeness many Indians felt to the natural environment.

Unit Three Review

Review Questions

1. Compare the Islamic and Hindu religions. (a) How was each religion begun and how did it spread? (b) How did each religion affect the development of the society where it was practiced?

2. Buddhism played a role in Indian, Chinese, and Japanese society. (a) Describe its influence on each society. (b) In which country did its influence last the longest?

3. How did Mongol invasions affect the history of (a) the Islamic Empire, (b) India, (c) China?

4. The Tokugawa shoguns in Japan and the rulers of Western African societies took different approaches to trade with European nations. (a) Describe differences in their attitudes toward Europeans. (b) For which group was contact with Europeans most disruptive? Why?

5. Describe and compare the cities of Constantinople and Tenochtitlán at the height of their power.

6. (a) Describe the achievements in science and mathematics of the Arabs and the Mayas. (b) What achievements did the Arabs borrow from India? (c) Why did Mesoamerican cultures not borrow ideas and practices from European and Asian cultures?

7. What was the reason for an extensive slave trade among (a) the Aztecs? (b) the kingdoms of western Africa? (c) What were the eventual results of the slave trade for the African peoples?

Projects

1. Research and report. The peoples studied in this unit all produced distinctive forms of architecture. Prepare an illustrated report on the architecture of (a) China, (b) Japan, (c) Islamic peoples, (d) India, or (e) the Aztecs, Mayas, and Incas. Focus on unique features of each architectural style and on the way religion influenced the type of buildings created.

2. Relating past and present. Use a current almanac to prepare a map showing present-day countries where Islam, Buddhism, and Hinduism are the major religions. Information on the major religion of each country can be found in the short articles about the nations.

Books to Read

Chu, Daniel. and E.P. Skinner. *A Glorious Age in Africa*. Doubleday.

Davidson, Basil. *African Kingdoms*. Time-Life.

Dickey, Thomas, John Man, and Henry Wiencek. *The Kings of Eldorado*. Stonehenge Press. Heavily illustrated account of Inca, Maya, and Aztec civilizations.

Dickinson, Peter, *The Dancing Bear*. Little, Brown. A novel set in the city of Byzantium around the year 588.

Duncan, David D. *The World of Allah*. Houghton Mifflin.

Garlake, P.S. *The Kingdoms of Africa*. Phaidon.

Gibney, Frank. *The Lords of Japan*. Stonehenge Press. History of Japan from the first emperors to the last shoguns.

Hibbert, Christopher. *The Emperors of China*. Time-Life.

Josephy, Alvin M., Jr. *The Indian Heritage of America*. Knopf.

July, Robert W. *A History of the African People*. Scribner.

Leonard, Jonathan Norton. *Ancient America*. Time-Life.

Leonard, Jonathan Norton. *Early Japan*. Time-Life.

McIntrye, Loren. *The Incredible Incas and Their Timeless Land*. National Geographic.

McKern, Sharon S. *Exploring the Unknown*. Praeger. Archeological investigation of ancient American cultures.

Paton Walsh, Jill. *The Emperor's Winding Sheet*. Farrar, Straus and Giroux. Exciting novel about the fall of Byzantium.

Robinson, Gail. *Raven the Trickster: Legends of the North American Indians*. Atheneum.

Rogers, Michael. *The Spread of Islam*. Phaidon. Study of Islamic history and art.

Schafer, Edward H. *Ancient China*. Time-Life.

Sherrard, Philip. *Byzantium*. Time-Life.

Shulberg, Lucille. *Historic India*. Time-Life.

How to Study World History

Skimming and Scanning

Skimming and scanning are two study skills you have probably used many times. When you *skim* a reading selection, you read through it rapidly to get a general idea of its content. When you *scan* a reading selection, you also read rapidly, but you are looking for specific rather than general information. Below are some guidelines for using skimming and scanning to help you study more efficiently.

Skimming. In skimming a selection, take the following five steps: (1) Read the title of the selection. (2) Read the first two or three paragraphs. Introductory paragraphs usually preview the content of a selection. (3) Read the first and last sentences of all other paragraphs. (4) Read headings, and notice words in **boldface type (darker letters such as these).** (5) Read the summary at the end of the selection. In this book, there is a summary in each chapter review. In other reading, the final paragraph often summarizes the content.

Because reading material is organized in different ways, you will have to adjust your skimming techniques to what you are reading. For instance, some selections may begin with an introductory paragraph that gives a summary of the content. An example of this is found in the first paragraph of the subsection "The Olmecs lay the foundation for Mesoamerican civilization" on page 293 of Chapter 14.

Scanning. As noted earlier, the purpose of scanning a selection is somewhat different from the purpose of skimming. Scanning is a technique for locating specific information. This technique is often used for finding answers to review questions or assignments. Keep in mind key words or phrases related to the information you are seeking. For example, suppose you want to answer Check-up Question 2a on page 297: "In what ways was the Olmec culture the 'parent culture' of Mesoamerica?" The phrases *Olmec* and *parent culture* are key words to keep in mind as you scan the section.

With the words or phrases in mind, glance down the page or columns of the reading selection. Use such clues as section titles, headings, words in boldface type, first and last sentences of paragraphs, and illustrations to help you find the key words you are looking for. In answering Check-up Question 2a, the heading on page 293, "The Olmecs lay the foundation for Mesoamerican civilization" and the phrase *parent culture* can be used to locate the information you need to answer the question.

Check Your Skill

Use the following questions to check your understanding of what you have read.

1. When you want to locate specific information, such as a place name, you should (a) skim, (b) scan, (c) summarize.

2. Which of the following is *not* a step in skimming? (a) Read the title. (b) Ask yourself questions about the selection. (c) Read the summary.

3. Scanning is a technique for (a) getting a general idea of a reading selection, (b) reading thoroughly, (c) locating specific information.

4. Check-up Question 1 on page 302 asks: "Where did the Aztecs come from and where did they settle?" To answer that question, a key word to scan for might be (a) Inca, (b) Mesoamerican, (c) Aztec.

5. Using the steps you have been given, skim Section 3 of Chapter 14, "Many Cultures Arise North of Mexico." Which of the following facts should you pick up? (a) The Eskimos carved bone and ivory. (b) The Mississippian ruler was known as the Great Sun. (c) The Anasazi first lived in dugout houses with log roofs.

Apply Your Skill

Scan Section 2 for the answer to Check-up Question 2a on page 302: "What achievements did the Aztecs borrow from other Mesoamericans?" Use these questions to help you check your mastery of the technique: (a) What key words or phrases did you keep in mind as you scanned? (b) What clues such as headings or boldfaced words did you glance at as you looked for the key words? (c) Did using the scanning techniques save you time in finding your answer? Why or why not?

The Foundations of Western Civilization

A Short Survey of Ancient and Medieval History

THE ANCIENT WORLD

The Prehistoric Period

Some of the most impressive achievements in human history took place before people kept written records. This span of time is called prehistory. Our knowledge of the prehistoric period comes from unwritten evidence, such as fossils and artifacts, that scientists have studied.

Achievements are made in the Old Stone Age. Most of the objects remaining from the early part of the prehistoric period are stone tools and weapons. For this reason, the period as a whole has been named the Stone Age. The longest part of this period is called the Old Stone Age, or Paleolithic Age.

Paleolithic men and women were nomads who moved from place to place hunting wild animals, catching fish, and gathering foods that grew wild. They made a variety of tools and weapons with specific uses — spearpoints, hand axes, choppers, and scrapers. Paleolithic people eventually also learned to control fire. They developed spoken language and could pass on knowledge and skills. There is evidence that some Paleolithic people held religious beliefs. Some also created works of art.

Farming leads to a new way of life. The later stage of prehistory began about 10,000 years ago. Because people of this time shaped their stone tools more carefully, the period is called the Neolithic Age, or New Stone Age.

A number of significant advances made in this period had far-reaching effects on the way people lived. In some areas people learned to plant food crops and to tame wild animals. Farming peoples began to build permanent settlements or villages near their growing crops. Because their food supply was more dependable, some Neolithic people could devote time to nonfarming skills and crafts — making tools, building shelters, or producing pottery. The demand for such products led to trade. In time trade brought contacts between villages.

New methods and materials are used. Neolithic craftsworkers, or artisans, created more advanced technology — the use of new tools, methods, and materials. Among their inventions were the plow, the potter's wheel, and the weaver's loom. The wheel and the sail made transportation easier and also encouraged trade. In late Neolithic times some artisans in the Near East learned to work with the metal copper, and metal tools and weapons began to take the place of stone. The knowledge of metalworking spread, and improvements were made. Gradually people began to work with bronze, a mixture of metals that is harder than copper. The term *Bronze Age* is used to describe the period when bronze became the main material used in tools and weapons.

The first civilizations develop. Because of the achievements made during the Neolithic

Age, people's food supply became more reliable, the population increased, and trade expanded. Settlements became larger, and some villages grew into cities. The first civilizations emerged in four great river valleys in Mesopotamia, Egypt, China, and India (map, page 33). The rivers provided food and water for humans and animals, as well as a means of trade and travel.

The people of the river valley civilizations built cities, leading to the beginnings of organized government and religion, the development of specialized occupations and advanced technology, and the use of written symbols to keep records. These developments are all characteristics of early civilization. As almost every ancient civilization devised some form of writing, the beginning of civilization also marked the beginning of written history.

The Ancient Near East

Several of the earliest civilizations developed in the region called the Near East. Farming and metalworking probably began in this area, and there people also made advances in religion, trade, writing, engineering, mathematics, and astronomy. Some Near Eastern peoples built empires and developed methods of governing.

Mesopotamian civilization begins in Sumer. Sumer, the home of the earliest civilization, lay between the Tigris and Euphrates rivers in the region called Mesopotamia. It was at one end of the Fertile Crescent, an arc of fertile land between the Persian Gulf and the Mediterranean Sea (map, page 40). Farming villages along the rivers in time grew into twelve city-states, each of which included a city and the farmlands around it.

The Sumerians believed in many gods, who were thought to protect the cities and choose their rulers. Rulers were therefore considered to be responsible to the gods for making and enforcing laws, storing food for emergencies, overseeing building projects, and looking after the irrigation system that provided water for farming.

The records that were essential to these tasks were kept on clay tablets in a form of writing called cuneiform. These Sumerian tablets are the oldest written records in the world.

Many of the Sumerian tablets concern trade, which was important to the economy because Mesopotamia lacked a number of resources.

The Mesopotamians make achievements in many fields. Sumer was conquered about 2350 B.C. by Sargon, the ruler of Akkad, who built the world's first empire. After this empire fell, other city-states in the region rose to power. These later civilizations in Mesopotamia all built on the knowledge, skills, and beliefs of the Sumerians. The Mesopotamians kept written records of their observations in astronomy, drew up multiplication and division tables, made calculations using geometry, and had the first written laws. About 1700 B.C., Mesopotamia was united under the rulers of Babylon. One of these, Hammurabi, had the laws of Babylon collected and recorded in cuneiform.

Egyptian civilization develops along the Nile River. Another early center of civilization was in the valley of the Nile River, southwest of Mesopotamia. Farming villages thrived there because of the rich soil brought by the Nile's yearly floods. These villages gradually were united into two kingdoms — Upper Egypt and Lower Egypt (map, page 45). About 3100 B.C. a ruler known as Menes brought all of Egypt under his control and established Egypt's first dynasty, or family of rulers.

Egyptian civilization continued during the reigns of at least thirty dynasties. After Menes, there were three periods when strong dynasties united Egypt. The Old Kingdom (2686–2181 B.C.) is often called the Pyramid Age because of the great tombs built for its rulers. The Middle Kingdom (about 2040–1786 B.C.) brought flourishing trade with Palestine, Syria, and the island of Crete. The New Kingdom (about 1570–1090 B.C.) saw the establishment of an empire, as Egyptian rulers conquered land eastward to the Euphrates River in Mesopotamia and southward in Africa.

Egyptian traditions last for thousands of years. While rulers changed, society and culture in Egypt remained stable for over 3,000 years. Religious beliefs influenced much of life in Egypt. Egypt's ruler, the pharaoh, was looked on as one of many gods who controlled natural forces. Because Egyptians viewed death as a continuation of life, many burial rituals developed. Egyptian tombs, especially those of the pharaohs and wealthy nobles, were furnished with objects to assure a comfortable life in the Other World.

The Egyptians made many practical advances. They devised a writing system called hieroglyphics to record religious rituals as well as government records, medical texts, and observations in science. Both scribes and artisans held important positions in Egyptian society. Engineers used geometry to survey and map the land and to develop irrigation works. Architects built massive temples, palaces, and tombs. The remains of these structures show the wealth and power of Egyptian civilization.

Other Near Eastern peoples contribute to civilization. Late in the New Kingdom, Egypt declined and other peoples gained power. Among those who challenged Egypt were the Hittites, who built an empire that included Asia Minor and northern Syria. Hittite artisans discovered how to work iron ore into iron, which was stronger and sharper than bronze. Knowledge of ironworking gradually spread throughout the ancient Near East.

While the Hittites built an empire by conquest, the kingdom of Lydia in northern Asia Minor developed a trade empire. To make trade easier, the Lydians began to use coins. Soon coins were accepted as payment throughout the Mediterranean world.

Another trading kingdom was the land of Phoenicia, whose merchants kept records with a writing system that used an early alphabet. The Phoenicians carried this writing system wherever they traded. About 800 B.C. it was adopted by the Greeks, who created the alphabet on which our own is based.

The Hebrews contribute a new religious outlook. Another significant contribution was made by the Hebrews, or Israelites, a nomadic people who settled in Canaan, south of Phoenicia. They were the first monotheists, people who believe in only one God. The Hebrews considered their God eternal and all-powerful. They believed that God set standards of right and wrong behavior for human beings but that each person was responsible for observing those standards. Hebrew history, law, and literature were recorded in the first part of the Bible.

Empires dominate the Near East. Beginning about the ninth century B.C., the Hebrews

and other Near Eastern peoples came under the rule of a succession of powerful empires. The Assyrians were skilled and ruthless warriors who built an empire stretching from Egypt to the Persian Gulf. Assyrian rulers developed harsh but efficient methods of government, building roads to link the different parts of the empire. They were eventually overthrown by a rebellion in 612 B.C.

About fifty years after the fall of the Assyrians, the Persians began to build what became the largest empire in the ancient Near East (map, page 59). They united all the Near Eastern peoples under one rule with a common official language. The Persian rulers Cyrus and Darius divided the empire into provinces ruled by governors. Local traditions were respected, but the empire was given unity by an extended road system, a postal service, and a standard system of coinage. A new religion, Zoroastrianism, also spread widely in the Persian Empire.

Ancient Greece

Civilizations also began to develop in the nearby eastern Mediterranean, particularly the Greek peninsula and neighboring islands. The people of the small, independent Greek city-states developed new political ideas. The idea of government by the people arose for the first time. The Greeks also made lasting achievements in art, literature, science, and philosophy.

Hellenic civilization develops. Greek civilization developed out of two earlier civilizations in the Aegean region. Minoan civilization reached its height on the island of Crete by 1700 B.C., while Mycenaean civilization spread throughout southern Greece about 1400 B.C. Skills in crafts, styles of art, and legends from Crete and Mycenae became part of the Hellenic civilization that developed about 800 B.C.

One of the most important influences on Hellenic civilization was the poet Homer. His epic poems, the *Iliad* and the *Odyssey,* described heroes who were brave, intelligent, and proud. Developing these qualities became the goal of Greek education. Hellenic ideas spread throughout the Greek peninsula and to the colonies the Greeks established in neighboring lands along the Mediterranean and Black seas.

Different ways of life develop in Sparta and Athens. City-states developed in Greece as in the Near East, but they remained independent, self-sufficient communities. A city-state, or polis, usually grew up around a hilltop fort. The polis was the center of Greek life, and all citizens took part in the community. Eventually two city-states, Sparta and Athens, became leaders in Greece.

The polis of Sparta in southern Greece emphasized military skills, discipline, and service to the Spartan state. Men spent most of their time fighting or practicing military skills. Women also were trained to be strong physically, and managed the farms of Sparta.

Northeast of Sparta, in the city-state of Athens, people followed a very different ideal. Athens became the commercial and cultural center of Greece, and the Athenians gradually developed the idea of giving people a voice in their government. Reforms made by Solon about 594 B.C. enabled all male citizens to become members of the Assembly that made laws. About 510 B.C., Cleisthenes made it possible for all citizens to vote in the Assembly.

The Greeks unite to defeat Persia. About 500 B.C. the independence of the Greek city-states was threatened by the growing Persian Empire under Darius. Although the Greeks shared the same language, religious beliefs, and Homeric traditions, they had never been politically united. They were intensely loyal to their own polis, and the many city-states were often at war with one another. The threat of conquest, however, made the Greeks set aside their quarrels and unite. In battles at Marathon in 490 B.C. and at Salamis in 480 B.C., they defeated the Persian forces.

Athenian democracy reaches its height. The victory over Persia gave the Greeks the freedom to develop political and artistic ideas that still influence Western civilization. After the Persian Wars, democracy flourished in Athens under the leadership of Pericles.

The government of Athens was a direct democracy. All the citizens — adult free men — met in the Assembly to debate, vote, and make the laws. Instead of electing professional officeholders, ordinary citizens performed the duties of government. The Athenians believed that every citizen should be active in the polis. Women, slaves, and most foreigners in Athens were barred from citizenship, however.

Art and literature flourish in Athens. Democratic Athens also became the center of Greek culture, following an ideal that encouraged the development of many different talents. Each person was expected to strive to do everything according to high standards of excellence. These Greek ideals were expressed in plays, poetry, and other arts.

Greek playwrights wrote tragedies using ancient themes to explore human problems. The three greatest writers of Greek tragedy — Aeschylus, Sophocles, and Euripides — all lived in Athens in the fifth century B.C. History was another form of Greek literature. Herodotus, called the "father of history," wrote a vivid account of the Persian Wars. Thucydides emphasized accuracy in writing history.

Like Greek literature, Greek art and architecture provided models that are still followed today. Greek painters and sculptors showed human beings as ideally beautiful. Architects strove for proportion and balance in designing temples and theaters.

The Greeks develop science and philosophy. The Greeks influenced modern thinking in areas other than politics and the arts. Greek scientists and philosophers observed nature, made logical deductions, and tried to discover natural laws. They studied mathematics, the structure of matter, and medical science.

Philosophers used reason to learn more about people and society. Our word *philosophy* comes from a Greek word meaning "love of wisdom." For the ancient Greeks, this meant a search for knowledge. The three major philosophers were Socrates, his student Plato, and Aristotle, who studied in Plato's Academy.

Socrates (who died in 399 B.C.) used a question-and-answer approach, or dialogue, to make his students think critically and logically. Plato, who recorded Socrates' ideas, also was the first thinker to analyze political systems. He expressed his ideas in the *Republic,* a description of an ideal state. Aristotle tried to discover and organize the basic ideas in many fields of knowledge — biology, physics, drama, public speaking, government. In science, he taught that a theory should be accepted only if it agreed with facts that could be observed.

The Greek city-states are conquered. Even during the golden age of Athens, the Greek city-states could not remain at peace. Old rivalries continued to cause friction among the city-states, and Persia remained a threat. In 431 B.C. the city-states of the Peloponnesus, led by Sparta, went to war against Athens, which had built an empire in the lands around the Aegean Sea. Pericles' death early in the war deprived Athens of wise leadership. Sparta won one battle after another, both on land and at sea, and forced Athens to make peace in 404 B.C.

The 27-year Peloponnesian War caused widespread destruction and loss of life in Greece. Democratic government declined in this period of unrest. When invaders from the north, led by Philip of Macedonia, attacked Greece, the weakened city-states were unable to stop them. The Macedonians crushed the Greek forces in 338 B.C., and the city-states lost their independence.

Alexander builds an empire. After Philip was assassinated, his twenty-year-old son Alexander became ruler. Alexander was one of the greatest military leaders in history. Between 334 B.C. and 326 B.C. his armies conquered the lands from Egypt to India without losing a single battle (map, page 76).

After Alexander's death in 323 B.C., his empire broke apart. Alexander's conquests, however, marked the opening of a new stage of civilization — the Hellenistic Age — when Greek language and culture spread throughout the entire Mediterranean world.

New approaches develop in science and philosophy. Studies in science and philosophy continued during the Hellenistic period, centering on the great library in Alexandria, Egypt. Outstanding Hellenistic scholars included Euclid, whose work in geometry is still studied, and Archimedes, an inventor and scientist.

Two schools of philosophy — Epicureanism and Stoicism — developed in Athens during the Hellenistic period. Epicureanism, named after Epicurus, urged people to live untroubled lives and not seek wealth, political power, or fame. Stoicism, founded about 300 B.C. by Zeno, emphasized dignity, self-control, and reason. This philosophy remained important for several hundred years, influencing both the Romans and early Christianity.

Ancient Rome

While Hellenic civilization was at its height, a small town in Italy was growing into a major center of Western civilization. By the first century B.C., Rome created the largest and most powerful empire of the ancient world. For 200 years, under Roman rule, people throughout the Empire prospered. Crises in the third century, however, led to the downfall of Rome.

The Romans establish a republic. In 509 B.C., according to tradition, the Romans established a republic — a government without a king. This government was led by wealthy landowners called patricians, and the common people, or plebeians, had little political influence. A 300-member council of patricians, the Senate, was the most powerful part of the government. Gradually the plebeians succeeded in gaining equal legal rights, but the patricians and wealthy plebeians kept the real political power in the Republic.

Rome gains control of the Mediterranean world. The Roman Republic continued to expand and by the middle of the third century B.C., it ruled most of the Italian peninsula. In 264 B.C. Rome went to war with the North African city-state of Carthage, which had been founded by the Phoenicians. In three wars, called the Punic Wars, Rome defeated Carthage and gained provinces outside Italy. By 146 B.C. Rome controlled the lands around the western Mediterranean Sea. The eastern Mediterranean — the center of Hellenistic culture — was brought under Roman rule by 133 B.C.

Rome faces an economic crisis. The destruction of the Punic Wars caused critical problems in Italy. Many farmers whose farms had been ruined sold out to wealthy landowners. For farm workers, the landowners used prisoners of war who had been made slaves. As a result, many farmers lost both their lands and their livelihoods. They joined the huge class of unemployed poor in the cities.

Military leaders gain power. During this postwar period of crisis, the leadership of the Roman Senate failed. Many patricians became more concerned with keeping their own power and wealth than with promoting Rome's welfare. Ambitious military leaders took advantage of the unrest by recruiting soldiers from the many jobless poor in the cities. Promising their soldiers wealth and land, these generals built private armies whose loyalty was to their leader rather than to Rome.

The Republic comes to an end. In 46 B.C. the government of Rome came under the control of Julius Caesar, a general who had conquered Gaul (modern France) for Rome. Caesar reorganized the government in the provinces, aided the poor, and granted citizenship to more people. Immensely popular, Caesar was named dictator for life, which many nobles saw as a threat to the Republic. On March 15, 44 B.C., a group of nobles stabbed Caesar to death in the Senate. This action did not save the Republic but plunged Rome back into civil war. Eventually Caesar's adopted son Octavian defeated his opponents and became the unchallenged leader of Rome in 31 B.C., bringing the Roman Republic to an end.

Octavian won the Senate's support, and in 27 B.C. he was given the title *Augustus,* meaning "honored and majestic." He also took the name "Caesar," which later rulers used. Augustus' rise to power marked the beginning of the Roman Empire. He used his authority to bring order and good government to both Rome and its provinces.

The Empire prospers during the Roman Peace. Augustus' rule introduced a 200-year period known as the *Pax Romana,* the Roman Peace. Throughout Rome's vast empire (map, page 103), Roman governors and officials enforced Roman law. Roman armies extended the borders of the Empire in Asia, secured the frontiers in Europe at the Rhine and Danube rivers, and conquered most of Britain.

Roman rule brought prosperity to the many peoples in the Empire. The Romans built roads, improved harbors, cleared forests, drained swamps, irrigated deserts, and turned undeveloped land into prosperous farms. Hundreds of new cities were built in the Empire, and old cities grew larger and wealthier. These Roman cities had considerable self-government and became centers of education and culture. Trade flourished as goods from the Empire and from foreign lands flowed into Rome.

Greco-Roman culture develops. Ideas also reached Rome from other parts of the Empire. The strongest influence came from Greece, cre-

ating a culture that is often called Greco-Roman. One of the greatest literary works of this period was the *Aeneid,* written in Augustus' reign by the poet Virgil to glorify the Roman talent for governing.

New styles developed in art and architecture. Whereas Greek artists had tried to portray perfect human beauty, Roman sculptors carved every detail realistically. Romans also were skilled and practical architects and engineers. They discovered the principle of the arch, planned roads that were used for centuries, developed efficient sewer systems, and built aqueducts to carry water to the cities.

The two most prominent scientists of the Greco-Roman age were Ptolemy and Galen. Ptolemy described an earth-centered universe, a system that seemed so logical it was accepted until the sixteenth century. Similarly, Galen's study of the human body remained the basis of Western medical knowledge for centuries.

The Romans have a talent for law. The people within the Roman Empire were united under one law that applied to all citizens, regardless of nationality. This system of law and justice was perhaps Rome's greatest contribution to Western civilization. The Romans believed law should reflect principles of reason and protect citizens and their property.

War and unrest weaken the Empire. The order and good government of the Roman Peace came to an end in A.D. 180, and the next century found the Roman Empire facing serious crises. The discipline and loyalty of the army broke down, and military leaders fought one another for the throne. As troops were called back from the frontier to fight in the clashes between these leaders, the Empire's border defenses were weakened. Germanic tribes crossed the frontier and invaded the Empire. Transportation and trade were disrupted, crops destroyed, and cities plundered. Many urban dwellers fled to the countryside.

Reforms fail to solve Rome's problems. The emperors Diocletian and Constantine imposed strong control in an attempt to end the unrest. To ensure a supply of food, peasant farmers were forced to stay on their land. Government workers and artisans also had to keep their jobs for life and pass them on to their children. Artisans, merchants, and city officials were ruined financially by high taxes, and city life declined even more.

To make the Empire easier to govern, Diocletian appointed a loyal general as co-ruler in the western regions. He moved the imperial court to Asia Minor. In 330, the emperor Constantine built a new imperial capital at Constantinople in Asia Minor. Diocletian and Constantine's reforms restored order but did not solve Rome's problems. They merely delayed the collapse of the Empire.

Rome falls to barbarian tribes. The Germanic invasions increased late in the fourth century. In A.D. 378 a Germanic tribe called Visigoths defeated the Roman army at the Battle of Adrianople, and it became clear that Rome could no longer defend its frontiers. As the border defenses collapsed, Germanic tribes began pouring into the Empire.

One Roman province after another fell to invading tribes. In A.D. 476 Germanic officers who had been hired to fight in the Roman army overthrew the Western Roman emperor, Romulus Augustulus. They declared a fellow German, Odoacer, king of Italy. This event is traditionally regarded as the end of the Roman Empire in the West.

Christianity spreads in the Roman Empire. At about the time the Empire began to decline, a new religion, Christianity, was gaining followers. The new faith had its beginnings early in the first century A.D., when a teacher named Jesus gained a following among the people of the Roman province of Judaea. Many believed he was the Messiah, or savior, whom the Jewish people expected. By about A.D. 30, Jesus' popularity began to appear threatening to the authorities. He was arrested and crucified, the usual Roman form of execution.

After the Crucifixion, the followers of Jesus spread Christianity throughout the Mediterranean world (map, page 128). As more and more people turned to the new religion, Roman officials began to see it as a threat. Christians were persecuted, but the spread of Christianity continued. In 312 the Roman Emperor Constantine converted to Christianity. Worship of the old gods was declared illegal in 380, and Christianity became the official religion of the Roman Empire soon after.

EUROPE IN THE MIDDLE AGES

The Early Middle Ages

In the history of Western civilization, the centuries following the fall of the Roman Empire in the West are called the Middle Ages. During this time, new civilizations developed in lands once ruled by Rome. In Arabia, the new religion of Islam arose in the seventh century. Its followers, called Muslims, built an empire that stretched from Spain to India. In the eastern Mediterranean, the rich eastern provinces of Rome became the Byzantine Empire.

In Western and Central Europe, great changes occurred during the early Middle Ages (500–1050). City life almost disappeared, the economy was disrupted, and learning declined. A new civilization — medieval civilization — was taking shape, blending Christian, Germanic, and Greco-Roman influences.

An organized Church develops. By the late years of the Roman Empire, the Christian Church had developed a strong organization. The leading Church officials were bishops. Of these clergy, the bishop of Rome, later to be called the Pope, came to be considered the head of the Church. For most people, the local priest was their connection with the Church. Priests administered the sacraments, gave advice, and tried to help the sick and needy.

Other men and women served the church by becoming monks and nuns. They lived apart from society, devoting their lives to prayer, good works, and scholarship. Convents and monasteries served as hospitals, provided shelter for travelers, and became centers of learning.

Medieval kingdoms develop in Western Europe. In the eighth century, a unified kingdom was established by the Franks, a Germanic people living in what is now France. Their greatest ruler was Charlemagne, or Charles the Great, who became king in 768. Charlemagne built an empire by conquering lands in Italy, Spain, and what is now Germany (map, page 142). On Christmas Day, 800, Pope Leo III crowned him "Emperor of the Romans."

Charlemagne's empire was not like the Roman Empire, however, but the sign of something new. The form of government and the laws he established were derived from Germanic customs. As a Christian, he defended the Church against its enemies and was crowned emperor by the Pope. Charlemagne also encouraged scholars to preserve the learning of the Greco-Roman past. This blending of Germanic, Christian, and Roman elements came to characterize medieval civilization.

Raiders terrorize Europe. The breakup of Charlemagne's empire after his death left Europe once again with little centralized government. To add to the disorder, Europe suffered frequent invasions in the ninth century. The most fearsome raiders came by sea from Scandinavia and were known as Vikings or Northmen. In the 800's and 900's they spread terror all along the European coast.

Other invaders, the Magyars, came from the broad Danube plain in eastern Europe and swept across Italy and Germany. Along the Mediterranean, people faced raids by Muslim pirates based in Spain and North Africa.

Feudalism develops to provide protection. The invasions disrupted European life, hindering trade, hurting agriculture, and leaving settlements and monasteries in ruins. As there was no central authority to offer protection, people turned to local lords who owned large estates and had their own armies.

The system of protective alliances and relationships that developed is called feudalism. In exchange for military assistance and other services, one lord granted land to another noble, who became his vassal. The lord-vassal relationship was cemented by a solemn ceremony in which the vassal pledged loyalty to the lord. In return for his pledge, the vassal received the feudal lord's protection as well as the grant of land. The peasants who lived on the land also were included in the lord's grant. They raised the crops that supported the vassal

and they, too, expected protection in time of trouble. Feudalism became the main political arrangement in Europe after the breakup of Charlemagne's empire.

Frequent warfare shapes medieval life. Because they lived in violent times, feudal lords were primarily warriors who fought to protect and extend their lands. They built castles that were encircled by massive walls and guarded by watchtowers. Young nobles were trained to be knights. Gradually a code of behavior called chivalry grew up for knights and lords. It demanded loyalty, bravery, respect for women, and devotion to the Church.

In some parts of medieval Europe, women could inherit land and the power that went with it. The world of most women, however, was limited to the castle. Noblewomen supervised their households, tended the sick and wounded, and ran the estate when the lord was away.

Life centers on the manor. The wealth of feudal lords came from the labor of the peasants who lived on their land. Most of these peasants were serfs who owned no land and were not free to leave the lord's estate. They lived in cottages in a small village on the lord's estate, or manor. From the lord the serfs received housing and land to farm. In return, they worked together to farm the lord's land and perform other tasks on the manor.

Almost everything needed for daily life was produced by the farmlands, mills, and workshops on the manor. Serfs rarely left the lord's lands, for travel was difficult and dangerous. Peasants lived, worked, and died on the lord's estate and were buried in the village churchyard. They knew almost nothing of the outside world.

Medieval Europe at Its Height

By the middle of the eleventh century, medieval civilization was at its height. The High Middle Ages (1050–1270) witnessed an agricultural revolution, an increase in trade and commerce, the rebirth of towns, and the rise of an enterprising middle class. Kings began to create strong central governments that provided greater security.

Advances in agriculture bring population growth. During the Middle Ages, the food supply increased greatly because of new inventions and more efficient ways of farming. In some parts of Europe a new, heavier plow made it possible to bring large tracts of land under cultivation for the first time. The water wheel and the windmill made it easier to grind grain. As food production rose, the number of deaths from starvation and malnutrition decreased, and the population grew.

Trade and commerce revive. Because the growing population needed more products, trade expanded. By the High Middle Ages, several city-states in Italy controlled the profitable Mediterranean trade. Other trade routes opened up in northern Europe and along the rivers between the Baltic Sea in the north and the Black Sea and Constantinople to the south.

The increase in trade led to changes in ways of doing business. Merchants pooled their money to raise money for large-scale trading expeditions. Banking practices developed when moneychangers began to lend money and provide letters of credit and other services for merchants. Still another commercial development was the appearance of merchant and craft guilds. The guilds protected their members from outside competition and regulated business in a town. Through the apprentice system, young workers learned a craft or trade.

Towns grow and a middle class develops. Expanded trade and an increased food supply encouraged the growth of towns. Townspeople gained the right to set up their own laws and establish their own system of taxes. Many European towns became self-governing city-states, the first since Greco-Roman times.

A new social class grew up in the towns. Master artisans, merchants, and their families made up this growing and prosperous middle class, who had no obligations to a lord.

Medieval universities are founded. As towns grew and prospered, there was a revival of learning. To gain an education in fields such as law or medicine, young men were sent to study with scholars who were famous for their learning. These meetings of students and teachers eventually developed into universities. The curriculum of these schools was based on Latin translations of ancient Greek works.

England becomes a strong unified state. As towns grew and trade expanded in the High Middle Ages, kings became stronger and more able to establish central authority. The first state to become unified was England, after its conquest by William of Normandy in 1066. William (often called William the Conqueror) set up a strong and efficient central government. He kept a sixth of the land for himself and divided the rest among the Norman feudal lords, who became his vassals.

William's successors made changes that strengthened royal rule. Under Henry II, in the twelfth century, a common law for the whole kingdom was established by the royal courts. The system of trial by jury also was begun.

The Magna Charta and Parliament limit royal power. The power of the monarch grew steadily until it was challenged by the English barons. In 1215 they forced King John to grant them certain rights in the Magna Charta. Some of these rights became a basic part of the British system of government. They were (1) the consent of the people's representatives to levy taxes; (2) right to trial by jury; and (3) the monarch's duty to govern according to law.

The power of the English monarch also came to be limited by a Parliament made up of representatives of the people. The restraints that the common law, the Magna Charta, and Parliament placed on the English ruler laid the foundations for limited monarchy.

French monarchs strengthen royal power. Rulers in France also created a unified state by adding to the territory they held as feudal lords. In 1204 Philip II (Philip Augustus) became stronger than any French lord by taking over most of the territories held by the English in northern France.

Louis IX strengthened royal power by drawing up laws that applied throughout the kingdom, outlawing private warfare, and establishing royal courts. By the end of the Middle Ages, French kings had created a state in which the monarch had nearly absolute power.

Italy and Germany remain divided. The power of the Pope, of the rich city-states, and of local rulers kept Italy divided during the Middle Ages. As was the Germanic custom, German dukes elected one noble as king, but this ruler had little authority over them.

In 962 the German king Otto the Great convinced the Pope to crown him "Emperor of the Romans." German kings who followed him all claimed this title, and the lands they ruled came to be called the Holy Roman Empire (map, page 171). Later Holy Roman Emperors frequently became engaged in power struggles with the Popes, for the Church claimed considerable political authority in Europe.

The Crusades contribute to change. Early in the Middle Ages, the Muslim empire included lands in Spain, North Africa, and the Near East. With Church support, medieval lords in the eleventh century began to war against the Muslims. In a series of wars known as the Crusades, Europeans tried to take control of the Holy Land (Palestine) from the Muslim Turks. In the First Crusade, the Christian forces captured Jerusalem (1099) and set up Christian states in the Holy Land. Despite later Crusades, the Muslims gradually regained these lands over the next century.

The Crusades marked a period of change for Western Europe. They encouraged the growth of trade, contributed to the decline of feudalism, and weakened the authority of the papacy. The Crusades also brought Western Europeans into contact with Muslim culture and the civilization of the Byzantine Empire. Scholars in these civilizations had preserved much ancient Greek and Roman knowledge, inspiring a revival of learning in the West.

Art and literature flourish in the High Middle Ages. Medieval art and literature often reflected people's religious beliefs. The most dramatic expression of devotion to the Church was the soaring Gothic cathedral, which used the pointed arch and flying buttresses to achieve great height and a feeling of spaciousness. Gothic architecture replaced the earlier, more massive, Romanesque style.

Important developments in medieval literature included the recording of ancient legends and epics and the beginning of the use of the vernacular (people's everyday languages) rather than Latin. The greatest poet of the Middle Ages was Dante Alighieri of Florence, Italy, who wrote the *Divine Comedy* in medieval Italian. An English poet, Geoffrey Chaucer, wrote *The Canterbury Tales*, which painted a vivid picture of everyday medieval life.

The End of the Middle Ages

The twelfth and thirteenth centuries were the high point of medieval civilization. In the fourteenth century, medieval civilization underwent great upheavals.

Famine and disease cause a drop in population. In the late Middle Ages, the population of Western Europe declined. As the soil in heavily farmed areas was worn out, famine and starvation became frequent threats. The bubonic plague, known as the Black Death, spread through Europe in 1348, killing between a third and a half of the population.

England and France are involved in constant war. The suffering caused by natural disasters was increased by a series of conflicts between France and England known as the Hundred Years' War (1337–1453). Fought entirely on French land, the war caused great hardship. France's eventual victory was due in part to a young peasant, Joan of Arc, who led French troops to victory at Orleans in 1429. Joan's example inspired the French people, and by 1453 they had driven the English from all of France except the city of Calais. The victory helped strengthen the French kings' power.

Almost immediately after their defeat, the English found themselves in civil war at home. Disputes over the throne led to the Wars of the Roses (1455–1485) between the rival houses of York and Lancaster. The Tudor dynasty was established at the end of the war.

Church authority declines. As the power of monarchs grew in the late Middle Ages, the authority of the Pope declined. A conflict between the French king and the Pope led eventually to a situation in which there were two rival Popes. Such disputes undermined the Pope's prestige and the unity of the Church.

During this period many Christians questioned the Church's active role in political affairs and criticized its accumulation of wealth. Although Christianity and the Church remained important forces in people's lives and in cultural developments, the political power of the Church was diminishing by the fifteenth century. The Church's decreased authority, along with the growth of towns and the rise of unified states, were signs that the medieval period was gradually coming to an end.

Sonate Premiere
Par moi W. A. Mozart pour ma chère Epouse
Violino
Cembalo
All° moderato

UNIT FOUR

Transition to Modern Times

In the three centuries following the end of the Middle Ages, European society, politics, and intellectual life underwent many changes. The ways of thinking and living that developed during this period were much more like those of today than like those of the medieval period. These developments did not mark an abrupt departure from medieval views but a gradual change, or transition, to attitudes that are a part of modern civilization.

Europe began to move closer to the modern era during the period called the Renaissance. People turned their attention to human beings and their achievements; the medieval emphasis on the Church lessened. The spirit of the Renaissance inspired artistic creativity and encouraged European explorers to make long voyages to distant parts of the globe. Their discoveries led to the establishment of vast empires, and trade and new wealth brought sweeping changes in the European economy.

Another step away from medieval attitudes was taken as reformers challenged some Church teachings and questioned the actions of the clergy. As a result of these protests, people in many parts of Europe left the Catholic Church to follow new branches of Christianity.

Political changes that had begun in the Middle Ages continued as European rulers unified their countries and created strong, centralized governments. At the same time, the people of some states found ways to secure their rights and limit their rulers' powers.

Still another step toward modern times was the growth of a spirit of scientific curiosity. Seventeenth-century thinkers no longer accepted older explanations of nature but used observation and experiment to find natural laws. Similarly, in the Enlightenment of the eighteenth century, philosophers tried to use reason to understand people, politics, and society.

The following chapters describe the movements that marked the transition from medieval to modern times.

Marseilles, subject of the painting on the facing page, was one of many port cities that prospered as European merchants found world-wide markets in the 1700's. Other important changes affected styles of art and music. The score of a Mozart sonata, seen in the background, symbolizes the notable achievements of European composers of the Classical period.

Inspired by classical Greece, the Renaissance artist Raphael portrayed ancient philosophers in his *School of Athens,* part of which appears below. His use of natural poses and differing expressions reflects the Renaissance interest in people as individuals.

Renaissance and Reformation

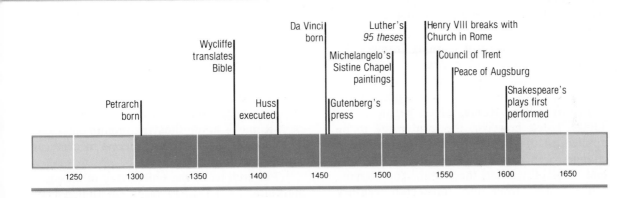

The end of the medieval period in Europe was marked by changes in attitudes toward politics, religion, and learning. These changes became more widespread and sweeping during the fourteenth and fifteenth centuries, bringing about the cultural movement called the Renaissance and the religious movement known as the Reformation.

The Renaissance began as a revival of interest in the literature and culture of ancient Greece and Rome. Its emphasis was on the richness of earthly life and on human achievements. One result of the Renaissance spirit was a brilliant period of creativity in the arts.

The Reformation also marked a breaking away from the attitudes of the Middle Ages. It began with attempts to make reforms in the Church and led eventually to the end of religious unity in Western and Central Europe.

This chapter describes the achievements of the Renaissance and explains how the Reformation came about.

CHAPTER OUTLINE

1   The Renaissance Brings Change
2   The Renaissance Spirit Is Reflected in Literature and Art
3   The Reformation Ends Religious Unity in Western and Central Europe

1 The Renaissance Brings Change

Late in the Middle Ages, European rulers gained new authority, while the absolute authority of the Church began to be questioned. At the same time, a long period of wars, epidemics, and economic upheaval in Europe came to an end. A new spirit of optimism, confidence, and creativity emerged. In the fourteenth century, these developments led to the start of a remarkable period that is known as the Renaissance.

Interest in classical learning inspires the Renaissance. The word *renaissance* (reh-nuh-SAHNS) is French for "rebirth." It originally referred to a new interest in the learning of ancient Greece and Rome, which began in the 1300's. Later, however, the term came to be applied to the period in which far-reaching changes occurred in the arts, intellectual life, and ways of viewing the world. The Renaissance lasted from the fourteenth century through the sixteenth century, and its influence continued even longer.

The Renaissance differed from the Middle Ages in several ways. One was a renewed appreciation for the arts and learning of ancient Greece and Rome. Another was a new interest in worldly matters, accompanied by a growing emphasis on human life and accomplishments. While the ideas and institutions of the Middle Ages did not completely disappear, the Renaissance outlook became much more like that of modern times.

Scholars study the humanities. Renaissance scholars' interest in Greek and Roman learning developed into the study of the humanities — Latin and Greek language and literature, composition, rhetoric, history, and philosophy. Music and mathematics were sometimes studied also. Renaissance scholars believed that the ancient Greeks and Romans had excelled in these subjects and that classical ideas were good models to follow. They searched in monasteries and libraries for manuscripts to read, restore, and share with other scholars.

Renaissance scholars found the literature of the ancients exciting to read and beautiful to hear. They wanted to write as gracefully and speak as eloquently as the Greeks and Romans. The scholars who took part in the intellectual movement that grew out of the study of the humanities were called *humanists*.[1]

The Renaissance begins in Italy. The Renaissance began about 1350 in the northern Italian city-states, which had grown prosperous from the revival of trade in the Middle Ages. Italian merchants and bankers had the wealth to acquire libraries and fine works of art. They admired and encouraged art, literature, and scholarship. Surrounded by reminders of ancient Rome — amphitheaters, monuments, and sculptures — they took an interest in classical culture and thought.

Petrarch leads the rediscovery of classical literature. Francesco Petrarch, an Italian poet born in 1304, led the early development of Renaissance humanism. Regarding ancient Roman times as a much grander period than his own day, he studied Roman literature and philosophy and encouraged others to become interested. In the process of collecting ancient manuscripts, Petrarch rediscovered a number of Roman authors whose work had been forgotten during the Middle Ages. He saw books as "welcome . . . companions . . . [that] encourage you, comfort you, advise you, . . . take care of you, . . . [and] teach you the world's secrets."

In his scholarly writings in Latin, Petrarch discussed the ideas of Roman writers and imitated their style. He also wrote hundreds of love poems in Italian. These poems were more realistic in feeling than the courtly love poems of the troubadours. Petrarch loved writing so much that he often worked all night long at his desk. When a worried friend urged him to relax, he replied, "nothing weighs less than a pen,

---

[1] *Humanist* is derived from the Italian word *umanista,* which means a teacher of the humanities, particularly the Latin language.

LINKING PAST AND PRESENT

Venice, "Queen of the Adriatic"

When the Renaissance began in Italy, a unique and varied culture was already flourishing in the rich city of Venice on the Adriatic coast. Built on more than a hundred islands linked by canals and bridges, Venice drew thousands of travelers and tourists, just as it does today. It was the center of trade and finance between Europe and the East. Spices, gold, and other prized goods from Asia passed through the offices of Venetian merchants and bankers. Crusaders had sailed to the Holy Land in Venetian ships. All marveled at the city's elaborate palaces and churches and at the thousands of sleek black boats, or gondolas, that traveled the canals (right).

The "Most Serene Republic of Venice," independent since the ninth century, was ruled by a duke, or *doge* (DOHZH), elected by the merchant-nobles. Venice's powerful fleet brought it an empire in the Mediterranean and made it the leading sea power of the time.

and nothing gives more pleasure; it is useful not only to the writer but to others far away, perhaps even to those who will be born a thousand years from now." On July 19, 1374, Petrarch was found dead in his library, his head resting on an open book, his pen fallen from his hand.

The Renaissance emphasizes life on earth. In his studies of Latin language and literature, Petrarch sought to understand the thoughts and feelings of the ancient Romans. This approach to classical literature was different from that of thinkers in the Middle Ages. The Scholastics (page 183) had tried to fit the ideas of ancient writers into a medieval framework, using Greek philosophy to support and clarify Church teachings. Renaissance humanists tried to understand the entire civilization of the ancient world, not just selected ideas. They looked on the literature of the ancient Greeks and Romans as a guide to a joyous, successful way of life. Medieval thinkers had regarded earthly

existence as a preparation for an afterlife; the people of the Renaissance emphasized living life on earth as fully as possible. They took ancient literature as their guide to understanding human nature, the conduct of statesmen, the duty of citizens, and the meaning of beauty.

Renaissance thinkers study history critically. The study of history was important for Renaissance humanists. They believed that history, like classical literature and philosophy, would help them understand their own times. In their efforts to learn more about ancient Greece and Rome, they carefully examined and compared copies of ancient manuscripts. Often they discovered mistakes that medieval scribes had made in copying the texts. Occasionally they found that certain documents were forgeries. This led them to question the works of long-established authorities. Medieval thinkers had tended to accept Aristotle's writings as unquestioned truth. Renaissance humanists, however, said that Aristotle's works should be seen as a product of the time in which he wrote.

Politics are important in the Renaissance. Many Renaissance humanists were leaders of society and were active in the politics of their cities. Like the ancient Greeks and Romans, they valued public service and praised those who were useful to society. They felt that an education in the humanities was a sound preparation for a rewarding life. The skills the humanists sought to cultivate — eloquence in communicating ideas, effective public speaking, polished manners, an elegant writing style — were valuable ones for social and political leaders.

Machiavelli takes a practical view of politics. Political rivalry was intense among the Italian city-states and their rulers. The Pope, the Holy Roman Emperor, and the rulers of France and Spain all were involved in struggles for power in Italy. Renaissance political thinkers were ambitious for fame and power. As a guide, they looked back to Roman history rather than to medieval ideals. They also turned to the advice given in guidebooks on how rulers could become more successful and skillful in politics.

The most famous of these guidebooks was written by Niccolo Machiavelli (mah-kyah-VEL-ee) of Florence, a diplomat and student of politics. Machiavelli (1469–1527) drew on Roman history to set up guidelines for rulers of his time. Machiavelli was cynical about human behavior and believed that a ruler should do whatever was necessary to gain and keep power. In his book *The Prince* (written about 1513), Machiavelli pointed out that successful rulers often lied, broke treaties, and killed in order to gain and keep power. In politics, Machiavelli said, policies must be judged only by their results.

Wealthy patrons support the Renaissance. Renaissance life centered on the society, commerce, and politics of the bustling, prosperous cities. In wealthy cities such as Florence, Milan, and Venice, the rulers, noble families, and high-ranking clergy became patrons, or supporters, of the arts. Most Renaissance artists came to depend for their livelihoods on wealthy patrons.

The cultural center of Renaissance Italy was Florence, which was dominated by the Medici (MEH-dih-chee) family. The Medici were bankers who had branch offices in cities throughout Western Europe. They became active in the politics of Florence in the 1400's and controlled the city for most of the next 300 years. In 1450, Cosimo de' Medici founded the Platonic Academy in Florence, and it became a center of studies in Greek philosophy.

The best-known member of the Medici family was Cosimo's grandson Lorenzo (1449–1492), known as "the Magnificent." Lorenzo was a classical scholar, a skilled architect, and a talented poet who wrote in the style of Petrarch. A leading patron of the arts, he hired painters and sculptors to create works of art for his palace, and invited artists, painters, and philosophers to his court. He expanded the university at Florence to give the city's young people an opportunity to study classical literature. His agents searched Greece for ancient manuscripts to add to his library.

Women of the wealthy and noble Italian families also played important roles as patrons of the arts. Many upper-class women were well educated in classical languages and literature, and some took an active behind-the-scenes role in politics.

One of the most remarkable women in Renaissance Italy was Isabella d'Este (DES-tay), who lived from 1474 to 1539. As a child she and her sister Beatrice studied the humanities and learned to read and speak Latin and Greek. At the family estate, their father translated plays by Roman dramatists and had them staged. Their mother was an art collector.

Isabella married Francesco Gonzaga, ruler of a small state in northern Italy. As the patron of many distinguished writers and artists, she made her court famous. A special room was built to display the paintings she commissioned. Isabella collected many of the books just beginning to come from Italian printers. Her own learning and her encouragement of the arts made Isabella known in her time as "the first woman of the world."

The Renaissance encourages the development of talents. The Renaissance was characterized by an intense appreciation of individ-

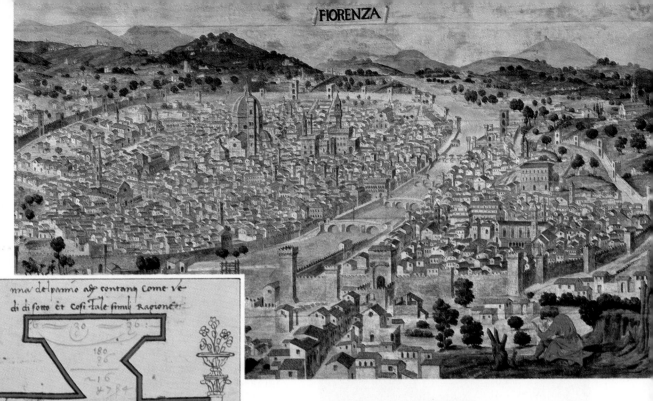

RENAISSANCE FLORENCE

From the hills above Florence a Renaissance artist painted this view of the city (above). Still present today are the domed cathedral and the bridges. At left is a page from an arithmetic textbook used in Florence in the 1400's. The illustration shows merchants trading wool and cloth, products that contributed to the city's prosperity.

ualism. The people of this time were interested in the unique qualities that made one person stand out from others. Like the Romans, they were ambitious for fame and worldly success. Like the Greeks, they believed human beings could achieve great things. These attitudes encouraged a spirit of curiosity and adventure.

The men and women of the upper classes benefited most from the new spirit of the times. They had the wealth and leisure to develop the many talents expected in the ideal Renaissance individual. This ideal was a person who not only was educated in the humanities but also could talk with wit and charm, create paintings and sculpture, perform music, write poetry and essays, and be fluent in several languages, including Latin. Men were expected to be good swordsmen, and both men and women took part in sports, including an early form of tennis.

Printing spreads Renaissance ideas. The Renaissance was a time of change in tech-nology as well as in culture. One of the new developments was the printing press. In the 1450's Europeans first used movable metal type to print a book. A German, Johann Gutenberg, is usually credited with printing the first book, a copy of the Bible. Most of the early printed books were religious works, but printing was soon used for other kinds of books as well. By 1500 there were hundreds of printers, in nearly every country in Europe.

The invention of printing made books and new ideas available to a much larger audience. It was many times faster to print a book than to make a copy by hand. Before printing, there were probably fewer than 100,000 books in all of Europe. By 1500 there were more than nine million. As printed books were also much less expensive than handwritten ones, more people could afford them. Moreover, many of the new books were written in the vernacular (page 185) rather than in Latin, the language used by

This portrait of Erasmus was painted by the German painter Hans Holbein the Younger (page 335). Holbein formed a close friendship with Erasmus when he illustrated *The Praise of Folly*.

A great admirer of classical literature, Erasmus wrote with both wit and elegance. He felt that the study of the humanities was more valuable than the study of science. In *The Praise of Folly* (1509), Erasmus criticized scholars, scientists, philosophers, and clergy of his own time for being narrow-minded. This work had a wide influence, as did Erasmus's Latin translation of the New Testament (1516), which was admired for its style and scholarship. The new craft of printing made Erasmus's books available throughout Europe; he was one of the first authors whose books were read by thousands of people.

Another important scholar of the northern Renaissance was Sir Thomas More, an English statesman. More and Erasmus were close friends. The Dutch scholar wrote *The Praise of Folly* while staying in England, and More encouraged Erasmus to begin his study of Greek. More was a devout Catholic and a student of both Church doctrine and the humanities. His book *Utopia*, published in Latin in 1516, described an ideal, peaceful society,[2] and so conveyed More's criticism of the politics, society, and religion of his time.

scholars and the clergy. Many more people thus were able to read the books that printing made available.

Renaissance ideas spread to northern Europe. Printing helped spread the spirit and ideas of the Renaissance northward from Italy to France, England, Germany, and the Netherlands (Holland and Belgium). The most respected and influential humanist of the northern Renaissance was Desiderius Erasmus (ih-RAZ-mus), who was born about 1466 in Rotterdam, Holland. Erasmus traveled widely, meeting with other scholars and encouraging the new interest in the humanities in Holland and Belgium, the German states, and England. Ordained a Catholic priest, Erasmus carefully studied both the humanities and Christian doctrines. He sought peace and unity as well as reforms within the Church. He wanted the Church to return to the simple religious devotion of early Christianity, but did not agree with the leaders of the Reformation (page 338) who were breaking away from the Church.

CHECK-UP

1. Vocabulary: *humanist.*
2. In what ways was the Renaissance period different from the Middle Ages?
3. (a) Explain why the Renaissance began in Italy. (b) What was Petrarch's view of the ancient Romans?
4. (a) Why was politics important to people of the Renaissance? (b) What was Machiavelli's approach to politics?
5. (a) What family made Florence the cultural center of the Renaissance? (b) What part did patrons of the arts play in the Renaissance? (c) How did Isabella d'Este and other women take part in the Renaissance?
6. (a) How did the invention of printing help to spread Renaissance ideas throughout Europe? (b) Who were two important northern Renaissance scholars and what books did they write?

---

[2]More's book, like *The Praise of Folly,* was widely read, and the word *utopia* came to mean an ideal place or society.

2 The Renaissance Spirit Is Reflected in Literature and Art

The Renaissance spirit and the renewed interest in ancient Greece and Rome were the inspiration for a brilliant creative period in literature and art. Writers and artists used stories from ancient history and classical mythology as their subjects. They also adapted styles used by Greek and Roman authors, artists, and architects. Most important, they portrayed people with great realism, bringing out the subject's individuality. Human beings were the focus of the arts of the Renaissance.

RENAISSANCE LITERATURE

Rabelais and Montaigne express the Renaissance spirit in France. The emphasis on individuality was reflected in very different ways in the works of two great French Renaissance writers. François Rabelais (RAHB-uh-lay), who was born in France about 1494, encouraged the Renaissance ideal of living a full, busy life. He himself was a monk, a scholar, and a physician, who also studied plants and Roman archeological sites. Rabelais wrote, "Let nothing in the world be unknown to you." Over a period of about twenty years, Rabelais wrote a five-volume work, *Gargantua and Pantagruel,* that made fun of those who did not take the humanist point of view. The books combined humor, lively imagination, and exciting adventures with scholarship.

In contrast to Rabelais, the other great French Renaissance writer lived quietly and wrote short, thoughtful essays that reflected his personal thoughts and interests. Michel de Montaigne (mon-TAYN) drew on his own observations, experience, and travels. He wrote in a conversational style, exploring ideas about friendship, education, and many other subjects that interested him. Montaigne's *Essays* were first published in 1580 and influenced European literature into modern times.

Cervantes mocks medieval ideals. In Spain the greatest writer of the Renaissance was Miguel de Cervantes Saavedra, usually known as Cervantes (sur-VAN-teez). Cervantes (1547–1616) served as a soldier against the Turks and was imprisoned for five years by pirates in North Africa. He later became a Spanish tax collector. Cervantes' eventful life gave him a wealth of material for his masterpiece, *Don Quixote* (kee-HOH-tee), published first in 1605. In this book Cervantes mocked the way medieval codes of chivalry distorted reality. Don Quixote is a kind, elderly gentleman who spends so much time reading medieval tales that he loses his sense of reality. He decides to become a knight and sets out to do heroic deeds. Blind to the real world, Don Quixote sees a herd of sheep as an army and thinks windmills are giants. He idealizes a servant on a nearby farm, describing her in the terms of courtly love (page 186) rather than seeing her as the sturdy peasant she really is.

Shakespeare provides insight into human behavior. In England the Renaissance spirit reached its height in the work of the poet and playwright William Shakespeare (1564–1616). Many people regard Shakespeare as the world's finest dramatist and the greatest writer in the English language. Shakespeare was an actor and playwright, not a classical scholar; a fellow writer said that he had "small Latin and less Greek." However, he shared the humanists' interest in other times and places, particularly the ancient world. Several plays — such as *Julius Caesar* and *Antony and Cleopatra* — drew on Greek and Roman history. Others take place in Renaissance Italy and in medieval England, Scotland, and Denmark.

Shakespeare also shared the Renaissance spirit of admiration for humanity. In the play *Hamlet,* he wrote: "What a piece of work is man! How noble in reason! . . . in action how like an angel!" Shakespeare's plays portrayed the whole range of human feelings — joy, love, greed, jealousy, ambition, rage, sorrow. His characters were complex, believable people. Few writers in any age have explored human behavior and feelings with such insight.

RENAISSANCE ART AND ARCHITECTURE

Renaissance artists portray individuals. Like the writers of the Renaissance, the artists of the time looked back to the ancient Greeks and Romans for their themes and ideas. They used ancient works of art as their models in depicting a variety of subjects — stories from Greek mythology, scenes from Roman history, incidents in the Bible and Church history. They also portrayed Renaissance politicians and patrons of art and ordinary people busy with their daily activities. Artists, like writers, were fascinated with the uniqueness of each person they portrayed.

Medieval artists had used their creativity mainly to serve the Church and express their religious feelings. Their paintings generally showed people whose faces had little individuality and who were stiffly posed. Renaissance art, like classical art, emphasized the uniqueness of each human face and figure. In portraits, Renaissance artists tried to capture each individual's character and to show that person's feelings and personality in a lifelike way.

Artists strive for balance and proportion. Renaissance artists and architects saw nature as beautiful because it was balanced and well proportioned. They hoped to achieve these same qualities in their own work so that it would appear more realistic. Medieval painters often drew people larger than buildings. Renaissance artists, however, tried to show people, trees, buildings, and mountains in the proper sizes relative to each other.

Renaissance architects admired Greek and Roman buildings and strove for the same kind of balance and proportion in the buildings they designed. They scorned the Gothic cathedral, the symbol of the Middle Ages, which soared upward toward heaven and seemed to defy laws of balance. Renaissance architects turned back to the Romanesque style (page 188), adding domes, windows, and balconies to let in light and air. They tried to make all the parts of a building appear perfectly balanced in size and shape.

The use of perspective adds realism to painting. Another step toward realism was the discovery of how to achieve perspective — the impression of depth and distance on the flat surface of a painting. The Florentine painter Giotto (JOT-toh) first used this technique in about 1300. Giotto's realistic style seemed odd to medieval eyes, however, and his advances were ignored until the Renaissance.

In the fifteenth century, the Florentine architect Filippo Brunelleschi (broo-nuh-LES-kee) discovered that painters could use mathematical laws in planning their pictures and thus show perspective accurately. His friend Masaccio (mah-ZAT-choh) applied these laws in his paintings. By making it seem that a system of lines met at a certain focal point in the painting, Masaccio created an illusion of space and distance.

Renaissance artists use new materials. Many medieval paintings were frescoes, paintings on freshly plastered walls. This technique had been used since ancient times, but it had a serious drawback. Frescoes had to be painted quickly while the plaster on the wall was still wet. Medieval painters also commonly used a kind of paint called tempera. It too dried so quickly that painters could not change or correct what they had painted.

A new technique, oil painting, was developed by the Flemish painter Jan van Eyck (IKE), who lived from about 1380 to about 1440. ("Flemish" refers to the language or people of Flanders, a part of the Netherlands.) Oil painting let artists work more slowly and allowed them to obtain more lifelike effects. They could create a much wider range of colors and impressions. They could show realistically the look and texture of different fabrics — the smoothness of silk, the intricacy of lace, the coarseness of wool, the softness of fur.

The use of oil-based paints quickly spread from Flanders to other parts of Europe. In Italy, Renaissance artists soon began to use both perspective and oil painting to produce works now considered masterpieces.

Raphael is a master of design. While the Renaissance produced many outstanding artists, three of the greatest were Raphael, Michelangelo, and Leonardo da Vinci. All were Italians born in the last part of the fifteenth century. Raphael Santi combined religious art with a Renaissance spirit. He became famous for his paintings of madonnas, pictures of Mary the mother of Jesus. Rather than depicting the angelic, otherworldly Mary shown in medieval paintings, Raphael painted a human, loving woman. Raphael was also a master of design and a skilled architect. He grouped figures effectively and used perspective skillfully to create a sense of balance in his paintings.

Michelangelo creates lasting masterpieces. Most Renaissance artists possessed several talents — painting, sculpture, architecture. Many were poets as well. Michelangelo Buonarroti, commonly called Michelangelo (my-kul-AN-juh-loh), was the greatest sculptor of the Renaissance. Though he was also immensely skilled as a painter, poet, and architect, Michelangelo called sculpture "the first of arts." He greatly admired the sculptures of ancient Greece and Rome. In sculpture, he said, "each act, each limb, each bone is given life and, lo, man's body is raised breathing, alive, in wax or clay or stone."

When he was 23, Michelangelo made the statue called the *Pietà* (pyay-TAH), which shows Mary holding the body of Jesus after the Crucifixion. This work won the artist instant fame. One of Michelangelo's contemporaries wrote, "It would be impossible for any craftsman or sculptor, no matter how brilliant, ever to surpass the grace or design of this work or to try to cut and polish the marble with the skill that Michelangelo displayed."

In 1508 Pope Julius II, a leading patron of the arts, called Michelangelo to Rome to paint religious scenes on the ceiling of the Sistine Chapel. The paintings were to show Biblical events from the Creation to the great flood of Noah's time. For four years Michelangelo worked on the ceiling, stretched out on his back atop a high platform. The sun's heat beat down on him through the roof of the chapel, and paint dripped into his eyes. When darkness came, he worked by candlelight. He suffered from cramps in his legs; his eyesight began to fail. "I have been here a thousand years," Michelangelo wrote to his father. "I am more exhausted than man ever was." Despite his agony, Michelangelo created a masterpiece. The Sistine Chapel paintings made his reputation as Rome's greatest artist.

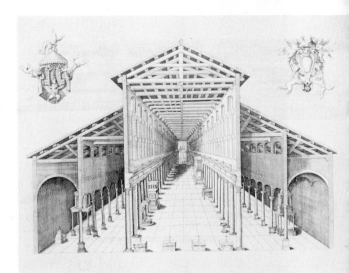

The use of perspective is shown in this Renaissance drawing of a cross section of a church in Rome. The artist drew lines meeting at a central point, thus giving the impression of distance.

Michelangelo lived to be nearly 90 and remained active as a painter, sculptor, and architect. When he was in his 70's, he began to complete the plans for building St. Peter's Church in Rome. He worked at designing the interior and the huge dome until his death in 1564.

Leonardo fulfills the Renaissance ideal. Less famous in his time than Michelangelo, Leonardo da Vinci (dah-VIN-chee) is now regarded as a universal genius, the ideal admired by the people of the Renaissance. Leonardo, who lived from 1452 to 1519, had great curiosity and energy. He left few completed paintings, but they include such famous works as *The Last Supper* and the *Mona Lisa*. Like other artists of the time, Leonardo depended on his patrons. They included Duke Ludovico Sforza of Milan, the duke's wife Beatrice d'Este, and King Francis I of France. Leonardo's work at the court of the French king helped spread Renaissance ideas from Italy to France.

The proof of Leonardo's genius is found in the many notebooks he left. He drew objects and people as he saw them with his own eyes. To find out more about the human body, he dissected corpses and made careful drawings of the structure of muscles and bones. Leonardo

examined natural objects — a bird's wing, the vein of a leaf, the leg of a horse — with close attention to detail. He tried to find general rules that would apply to the information he gained from his observations. This approach to the study of nature reflected views that eventually became important in the shaping of modern scientific investigation.

Leonardo was also an engineer, scientist, and inventor who was far ahead of his time. Leonardo's notebooks recorded designs for inventions such as flying machines, submarines, and machine guns. These drawings are so precise that modern engineers have used them to build working models.

Northern Renaissance artists emphasize realistic detail. Although many painters from northern Europe traveled to Italy to study, they did not all share the Italians' interest in classical themes and styles. In their landscapes, portraits, and other works, the northern painters emphasized precise, realistic detail and the use of light and shadow. Many artists used reli-

gious themes and symbols. Many also vividly showed contemporary life in the Dutch towns and countryside. The center of the northern Renaissance in art was the Netherlands, especially the region of Flanders. It was a Flemish artist, van Eyck (page 332), who was the first master of oil painting.

The greatest painter of realistic contemporary scenes was Pieter Brueghel (BROY-gul) the Elder (1525–1569). Using a wealth of detail and often sly humor, he created large, dramatic paintings of farm workers and crowds of townspeople at work and play. Later, Dutch painters such as Jan Vermeer and Jacob van Ruisdael (ROYS-dahl) continued the tradition of painting carefully detailed landscapes and interior scenes. Dutch art reached its height in the 1600's with the paintings of Rembrandt. Remarkable for their use of light and color, his paintings dramatically showed both the people and places of his time.

The leading German artist of the Renaissance was Albrecht Dürer, who was equally

RENAISSANCE ART

The masterpieces created by Renaissance artists have seldom been equaled. Michelangelo drew upon the ancient Greek ideal of beauty for his statue called *David* (facing page, far left). Pieter Brueghel painted richly detailed scenes of everyday life, as in *The Peasants' Wedding* (left). The work of an unknown Italian artist, *The Judgment of Paris* (below, left) portrays characters from a Greek legend. Instead of Greek robes, they wear clothes made of the rich fabrics of Renaissance Italy. Leonardo da Vinci's painting *Ginevra de' Benci* (below, right) captures the likeness of a young woman of Florence.

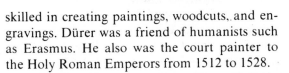

skilled in creating paintings, woodcuts, and engravings. Dürer was a friend of humanists such as Erasmus. He also was the court painter to the Holy Roman Emperors from 1512 to 1528.

Another German painter, Hans Holbein the Younger (1497–1543), was the most famous portrait painter of his time. Holbein created portraits that vividly show his subjects' personalities as well as the realistic details of their clothing and the objects around them. Two of Holbein's most famous portraits are of his friends Erasmus and Sir Thomas More. Holbein also worked with publishers in the new and growing printing industry. He illustrated numerous books, including Erasmus's *Praise of Folly*. To escape the religious wars in Europe, Holbein moved to England, where he became court painter to King Henry VIII in 1536.

CHECK-UP

1. Identify the European country in which each of the following Renaissance writers worked, and name one work by each: (a) Rabelais, (b) Montaigne, (c) Cervantes, (d) Shakespeare.

2. (a) What subjects were painted by Renaissance artists? (b) Compare portraits done in the Middle Ages with those done in the Renaissance.

3. (a) How did perspective add to realism in painting? (b) How did the use of oil paints make paintings more lifelike?

4. For what sort of works is each of these artists famous? (a) Raphael, (b) Michelangelo, (c) Leonardo da Vinci.

5. (a) Where was the center of northern Renaissance art? (b) What techniques and subjects did northern painters emphasize?

3 The Reformation Ends Religious Unity in Western and Central Europe

The Renaissance brought to Europe a spirit and a way of thinking quite different from that of the Middle Ages. Another kind of break with medieval times came as reformers challenged the authority of the Church, whose political influence had weakened in the late Middle Ages. By the fourteenth century, reforms within the Church were being demanded in many countries of Europe.

Wycliffe calls for changes in Church doctrine. In the late 1300's John Wycliffe (WIK-lif), a scholar at Oxford University in England, questioned the teaching that a person could gain salvation only through the Church. Wycliffe said that the Bible, not the Church, should be regarded as the supreme source of authority for Christians. In 1378, when the Great Schism (page 193) caused the naming of two rival Popes, Wycliffe wrote a severe criticism of the papacy. He also denounced bishops and other clergy for amassing wealth and neglecting their religious duties.

So that people could read the Bible for themselves, Wycliffe and his followers made the first complete translation of the Bible in English. His followers, known as the Poor Preachers, were trained to teach in the language of the people instead of the Latin of the Church. The Church condemned Wycliffe's teachings as heresy, but his movement for Church reform continued to have an influence long after his death in 1384.

Huss criticizes the Church. One of those influenced by Wycliffe was John Huss, head of the University of Prague in Bohemia (boh-HEE-mee-uh), a state in the Holy Roman Empire. Like Wycliffe, Huss challenged the authority of the Pope and criticized the Church's wealth. His ideas appealed to many people but angered Church and university officials. In 1410 he was excommunicated. Nevertheless, he traveled to Germany to attend a Church council that was trying to end the Great Schism. Although the Holy Roman Emperor had promised that Huss would be safe at the council, he was arrested, found guilty of heresy, and burned at the stake

in 1415. His execution and the emperor's broken promise enraged the Czech (CHEK) people of Bohemia.

In 1420 some of Huss's followers, called Hussites, began a rebellion against the Church and the emperor. The Pope called together an army for a crusade against the rebels. The Hussites resisted strongly, and years of bitter fighting followed. Peace was finally made in 1434, but many Hussites went on with their efforts to secure Church reform.

Martin Luther adopts new beliefs. Dissatisfaction with the Church was particularly strong in the German states of the Holy Roman Empire. Devout Germans denounced the practice of letting bishops buy their positions. Many Germans resented the worldliness, lack of piety, and greed of some members of the clergy.

The man who became the leader of the protest against the Church was a German monk, Martin Luther (1483–1546). Luther taught Biblical studies at the University of Wittenberg. He led a strict and pious life but was troubled by a feeling of sin and feared that he would never enter heaven. After an intense emotional struggle, Luther came to believe that men and women could be saved only by the grace of God, which would grant them faith in Christ. He believed that, while a true Christian would perform good works, these did not bring salvation. Christians, Luther thought, gained salvation through grace and faith.

Luther challenges the Church. Luther's beliefs brought him into direct conflict with the Church over the question of how people could be pardoned for sins. The Church taught that most sins would be forgiven if a person confessed to a priest, regretted the action and asked forgiveness, and did penance, such as fasting or prayer. Still another way of being pardoned for sins, however, was to be given an indulgence. An indulgence, it was believed, reduced the time that one's soul would have to spend in suffering or punishment before the soul reached heaven. Indulgences were at first

LUTHERANISM AND THE PRINTED WORD

The invention of the printing press in the 1450's played a part in the spread of the ideas of Martin Luther (shown at left in a portrait by his friend Lucas Cranach). Luther translated the Bible, which in printed form became available to many more readers in Europe.

given for special service to the Church, such as going on a crusade. By Luther's time, they could be obtained in return for a money contribution to the Church. Some clergy sold indulgences primarily as a way of raising funds for the Church or for the bishops. Some allowed people to believe that an indulgence guaranteed their entry to heaven.

The sale of indulgences was widely criticized, and on October 31, 1517, Luther challenged this practice publicly. On a church door in Wittenberg he nailed 95 theses, or arguments, attacking the sale of indulgences and inviting a debate. News of Luther's challenge spread quickly. Although Church officials opposed Luther, many people agreed with his ideas, and he began to question other Church teachings. Like earlier reformers, Luther said that the Bible provided all the guidance a person needed to live a Christian life. Luther believed that people should read the Bible to find the path to faith. He did not think they had to rely on the interpretations given by the Pope or the clergy. He urged changes in church services and said that members of the clergy should be allowed to marry.

Luther defies the Pope and the emperor. Luther's speeches and writing won more followers, including several German princes who protected him. The Pope ordered Luther to give up his beliefs, but Luther burned the papal order before a crowd of cheering students, professors, and townspeople. Early in 1521 the Pope excommunicated him.

In May, 1521, Charles V, the Holy Roman Emperor, summoned Luther to appear before the imperial assembly, which met in the city of Worms. Luther refused to go against his own conscience and change his views, reportedly saying, "Here I stand. I cannot do otherwise." Declared an outlaw by the emperor, Luther took refuge in the castle of Frederick of Saxony, a German prince. While Luther was in hiding, he translated the New Testament into German, making it possible for more people to read the Bible.

The Protestant movement spreads. Neither Church officials nor the Holy Roman Emperor could keep the reform movement from spreading among those who were dissatisfied with Church practices. Many Germans agreed with those reformers who called for a return to the piety of the early Christians. Many also were attracted by Luther's belief that each person could communicate directly with God.

Luther's teachings were not the only reason why many Germans became Lutherans, as his followers were called. Many townspeople resented the fact that their money flowed from Germany to Rome to pay Church taxes and buy Church offices. They thought the money should remain in Germany and be used to expand German trade and industry. Other Germans were annoyed that Italians controlled the most important offices in the Church. Some German princes backed Luther because they saw a chance to acquire property owned by the Church. The princes' support for Luther was a way of demonstrating their independence from the Holy Roman Emperor.

The emperor tried to suppress the growing strength of the Lutheran movement. In 1529 several Lutheran princes met and issued a formal protest against these efforts. Because of this, they became known as Protestants (PROT-iss-tunts). The support of the German Lutheran princes made possible the survival of the reform movement, which split the Western Church into Roman Catholics, who accepted the Pope's authority, and Protestants, who did not. The movement itself came to be called the Reformation.

TIMETABLE

The Reformation and Counter-Reformation

1517	Luther's 95 theses question practices of the Church.
1530	German princes sign the Augsburg Confession.
1534	The Act of Supremacy establishes the English monarch as head of the church in England.
1536	Calvin becomes a Protestant pastor in Geneva.
1540	Ignatius Loyola establishes the Jesuit order.
1545–1563	The Council of Trent reaffirms Roman Catholic doctrine.
1555	The Peace of Augsburg ends religious wars in Germany.

Religious wars break out. The Lutheran princes continued their open rebellion against the Church and the Holy Roman Emperor. In 1530 many of them signed the Augsburg Confession, a written statement of their beliefs. The rebellion eventually led to a series of wars. Emperor Charles V could not effectively control the Lutheran princes, for his lands in Austria and Hungary were being invaded by the Ottoman Turks (page 221), who occupied much of southeastern Europe. Charles was also hampered by France, which sided with the rebellious Protestant princes in order to limit the emperor's power.

Charles's brother Ferdinand of Austria, who had been chosen to be the next emperor, reached a compromise with the princes. In 1555 a treaty called the Peace of Augsburg ended the religious wars in Germany. The treaty allowed the German princes to decide which religion would be followed in their lands. Most of the southern German rulers remained Catholic; most of those in the north chose to become Lutheran. The division into Protestant and Catholic states (map, next page) became a major barrier to German unity.

Calvinism develops in Geneva. The Reformation spread to other lands where opposition to the Church had been mounting for years. Lutheranism was adopted in Denmark, Sweden, Norway, and Finland. Various forms of Protestantism developed elsewhere in Europe.

The Swiss city of Geneva was an important center for Protestant thinking. The earliest Swiss reformer, Ulrich Zwingli, had taught at the same time as Luther. In 1536 a French scholar and theologian, John Calvin, joined the reformers in Geneva and developed the form of Protestant belief called Calvinism. Calvin, like Luther, regarded the Bible as the supreme authority in matters of faith, attacked abuses by the clergy, and emphasized the importance of faith in salvation. A central idea of Calvin's philosophy, however, was predestination, the belief that certain people were chosen by God for salvation. According to Calvin, those who had not been chosen could never enter heaven, no matter how good a life they lived on earth. Calvinists considered it likely that strict obedience to God's laws was a sign that a person had been predestined for salvation. Calvin ex-

Christian Europe About 1600

The Reformation ended religious unity in Western and Central Europe. What Protestant groups are shown on the map?

plained his teachings in a book called *Institutes of the Christian Religion.*

Calvin and his followers tried to make Geneva a holy city. The Calvinists supervised people's lives to make certain they lived strictly and solemnly. Laws punished those who gambled, made noise during church services, drank at certain hours, sang "outrageous songs," and did not know their prayers. While those who challenged Calvinist teachings faced persecution or exile from Geneva, the city at the same time became a refuge for Protestants persecuted in other countries.

Calvinism spreads in Europe. Calvinist teachings were carried to other countries by dedicated missionaries. Although the French rulers remained Catholic, Calvinism appealed to many French people, some of whom were already Protestants. The French Calvinists became known as Huguenots (HYOO-guh-nots). A Scottish Protestant, John Knox, carried many Calvinist ideas to Scotland in the 1550's, laying the foundations for the Presbyterian Church. Calvinism also influenced "reformed" churches in other parts of Europe, including Holland, Hungary, and Bohemia.

The English king breaks with the Pope. Some of the earliest demands for Church reform had been made in England (page 336). The Reformation in England, however, became closely connected with a struggle for political power. In 1527 the Tudor king Henry VIII, who ruled England from 1509 to 1547, sought to divorce his wife, the Spanish princess Catherine of Aragon. Henry feared that their only surviving child, Mary, would not be accepted as heir to the English throne. Moreover, Henry wanted to marry Anne Boleyn (BUL-in), a lady-in-waiting at his court.

Because the Church prohibited divorce, Henry asked the Pope to annul (set aside) his marriage. Catherine bitterly objected and called for aid from her nephew Charles V, the Holy Roman Emperor. A decision on the annulment was delayed as the emperor tried to use his influence on the Pope.

Henry and his advisers began to take steps to remove England from the authority of the

Henry VIII broke away from the Pope's authority, and England later became Protestant. This portrait was done by Hans Holbein, his court painter.

Pope. Henry named Thomas Cranmer, a churchman who agreed with some Protestant ideas, to be archbishop of Canterbury, the highest church office in England. Cranmer approved the annulment of the marriage with Catherine, and Henry married Anne Boleyn early in 1533.

The English Parliament next was persuaded to approve a break with the Church in Rome. In 1534 Parliament passed the Act of Supremacy, making the monarch head of what was now called the Church of England. Two years later Henry closed the English monasteries and convents, seizing their rich lands and properties and selling them to loyal subjects.

Although he wanted to be free of the Pope's authority, Henry VIII himself remained a Catholic. The Reformation in England was carried forward by Cranmer and others. They urged a new English translation of the Bible and began to prepare the Book of Common Prayer for use in the Church of England.

Henry did insist on exerting the power given him by the Act of Supremacy. Some English Catholics who supported reform felt unable to give up their loyalty to the Pope. The most prominent was Sir Thomas More (page 330), a valued adviser to the king. Henry had More executed for not accepting the Act of Supremacy.

England becomes a Protestant nation. Henry VIII married six times, but he had only one son. Edward VI, who was nine years old when Henry died in 1547, had been taught by Protestant tutors, including Cranmer. Protestantism became more established in England during his reign. Edward was in poor health, however, and ruled England for only six years. After his death in 1553, the crown went to his half-sister Mary I, the daughter of Catherine of Aragon. A devout Roman Catholic, Mary ordered the persecution of English Protestants who refused to become Catholics again. She married Philip II, the Catholic king of Spain.

When Mary died in 1558, she was succeeded by her half-sister Elizabeth I, the daughter of Anne Boleyn. With a shrewd understanding of the English people's attitudes, Elizabeth turned England back to Protestantism. In 1571 Parliament gave official approval to the Thirty-Nine Articles, a statement setting forth the doctrines of the Church of England.

The Counter-Reformation makes changes within the Church. Roman Catholic officials and clergy were alarmed by the spread of Protestantism in many parts of Europe. The Church undertook a number of reforms and other actions that were intended to strengthen and spread Catholicism. These efforts are called the Counter-Reformation or Catholic Reformation.

In 1545 Pope Paul III called leading churchmen to gather at Trent in northern Italy to deal with problems facing the Church. The Council of Trent (1545–1563) did not change basic teachings. Catholics were to continue to accept the principles that (1) only the Church could explain the Bible, (2) both faith and good works were necessary for salvation, and (3) the Pope was the highest and final authority in the Church. Church ritual was to remain an essential part of the Catholic faith, and the clergy were not allowed to marry.

The Council of Trent did, however, recommend important reforms. It banned the sale of indulgences and tightened discipline for the clergy. It insisted that only worthy people should enter the clergy, ordered the establishment of seminaries to train the clergy, and encouraged reform of monasteries and convents. These actions corrected abuses that had long disturbed many Church members.

The Catholic Church takes action against Protestantism. The Church took other steps as part of the Counter-Reformation. In Catholic countries the Inquisition (page 172) expanded its activities, threatening Protestants in those countries with imprisonment or death. The Church also drew up a list of books, called the Index, that Catholics were forbidden to read, own, or sell. In this way the Church hoped to prevent the spread of ideas it regarded as heresy.

New religious orders were set up to serve the Church and spread Catholic teachings. The most important of them was the Society of Jesus, commonly known as the Jesuits (JEZH-oo-its), founded by a young Spanish nobleman named Ignatius Loyola. Approved by Pope Paul III in 1540, the order sought to keep Catholics from leaving the Church, to persuade Protestants to return to the Church, and to win converts to Catholicism. To achieve these aims, the Jesuits founded colleges and seminaries and sent missionaries to many lands.

The Reformation has lasting effects. The Reformation had a profound influence on later history. The religious unity that had characterized Western and Central Europe in the Middle Ages vanished as Christians were divided into Catholics and Protestants. Protestants themselves were divided into a number of different groups.

In both Catholic and Protestant countries, the Reformation strengthened the state at the expense of the churches. Protestant rulers rejected the authority of the Pope, while Catholic rulers allowed the Church fewer privileges and less say in political matters.

The Reformation and Counter-Reformation both encouraged the spread of education. Because the Protestant reformers insisted that individuals should read the Bible themselves, it became important for men and women to be able to read. This led to an increase in the amount of education that both men and women received and encouraged new translations of the Bible into vernacular languages

An anonymous Renaissance artist painted this scene showing Ignatius Loyola, founder of the Jesuit order, kneeling before Paul III, the Pope who gave permission for Loyola to establish the order.

that more people could understand. As part of the Counter-Reformation, the Jesuits played an important role in education by establishing Catholic schools and universities.

CHECK-UP

1. How did Wycliffe and Huss each challenge the teachings of the Church?
2. (a) What teachings and practices of the Church did Luther challenge? (b) Why did people support Luther?
3. (a) What part did Calvin play in the Reformation? (b) What did he mean by predestination? (c) How were his ideas put into practice in Geneva?
4. (a) How did the Act of Supremacy mark a break between the English monarch and the Catholic Church? (b) How did Henry's successors encourage or discourage the establishment of Protestantism?
5. (a) What steps did the Roman Catholic Church take to try to stop the spread of Protestantism? (b) What are these efforts called?

Chapter 15 Review

Summary

The fourteenth century saw the beginning of the Renaissance, a rebirth of interest in ancient Greece and Rome. The Renaissance began in Italy, where wealthy merchants and bankers encouraged the arts and the study of the humanities—Greek and Latin language and culture. It marked a breaking away from the Middle Ages and the beginning of modern times. Renaissance people placed a high value on varied achievements and individuality. Wealthy people began to support the arts, thus encouraging a period of great creativity in painting, sculpture, and literature. Meanwhile, emphasizing the importance of understanding life on earth, scholars studied history and politics. The Renaissance spread from Italy and flourished in other parts of Europe in the fifteenth and sixteenth centuries.

As early as the fourteenth century, there were calls for reform in the Church. Major changes did not occur, however, until the early sixteenth century when Martin Luther challenged basic Church teachings. Those who protested against Church teachings and practices became known as Protestants; the overall movement for change was called the Reformation. Lutheranism and other forms of Protestantism spread in northern Europe. The Catholic Church instituted the Counter-Reformation to make reforms and strengthen its position. Important results of the Reformation were the end of religious unity in Western and Central Europe and the strengthening of government authority.

Vocabulary Review

1. Write the sentences listed below on a sheet of paper. In each sentence, fill in the blank with one of the following words: *excommunicate, humanist, vernacular.*
(a) A ___?___ was a Renaissance scholar who studied ancient Greek and Roman literature and philosophy.
(b) The ___?___ is the language commonly spoken in a given country.
(c) The Pope had the power to ___?___, or expel, a Christian from the Church.
2. Distinguish between the terms in each of the following pairs:

(a) Lutheran; Calvinist.
(b) *Utopia; Don Quixote.*
(c) Peace of Augsburg; Council of Trent.
(d) Reformation; Counter-Reformation.

People to Identify

Match the following people with the numbered phrases that describe them: *Machiavelli, Mary I, Erasmus, Luther, Leonardo da Vinci, Loyola, Calvin, Michelangelo.*
1. Founded the religious order known as the Jesuits.
2. Protestant theologian who taught the doctrine of predestination.
3. English ruler who attempted to restore Catholicism.
4. Painted the ceiling of the Sistine Chapel.
5. Wrote *The Prince.*
6. Dutch humanist who wrote *The Praise of Folly.*
7. A genius of the Renaissance, whose notebooks contain many sketches of imaginative inventions.
8. German monk whose 95 theses challenged the sale of indulgences by the Church.

Relating Geography and History

1. **Locating places.** Locate each of the following on a map in this chapter:
(a) Florence
(b) Geneva
(c) Oxford
(d) Prague
(e) Wittenberg
(f) Augsburg
(g) Trent
(h) Swiss Confederation
2. **Making charts.** Using the map on page 339, make a chart of religious groups in Europe about 1600. For each nation or territory shown on the map, list its principal religion in one column and minority religions in another column.

Discussion Questions

1. Why did Renaissance thinkers consider the study of the humanities important?

2. (a) What were the effects of the invention of printing? (b) How did the availability of books printed in vernacular languages help to spread new ideas?

3. How did the work of each of the following writers reflect the Renaissance outlook: (a) Petrarch, (b) Erasmus, (c) Rabelais, (d) Cervantes, (e) Shakespeare?

4. How did Luther and Catholic Church leaders disagree on the following matters: (a) the authority of the Pope; (b) the Bible as the sole guide for a Christian life?

5. What role did each of the following rulers play in England's break with the Catholic Church and the establishment of the Church of England: (a) Henry VIII, (b) Mary I, (c) Elizabeth I?

6. How did the Reformation affect (a) religious unity in Europe? (b) the influence of the Church in European political affairs?

Reading Primary Sources

Baldassare Castiglione (kahs-teel-YOH-nay), a Renaissance writer and diplomat, spent much of his life in the courts of Italian princes and nobles. He is famous for his description of the qualities needed by those who wished to be successful in court life. The book in which this description appeared, *The Book of the Courtier* (1528), was accepted throughout Western Europe as a guide to civilized behavior. Read the following excerpts from the book. Then answer the questions that follow.

> Besides his noble birth . . . I would have the Courtier . . . endowed by nature not only with talent and beauty of person and feature, but with a certain grace and . . . air that shall make him at first sight pleasing and agreeable to all. . . .
>
> I am of [the] opinion that the principal and true profession of the Courtier ought to be that of [military service]. . . .
>
> Above all things [he must avoid showiness] and that [shameless] self-praise by which men . . . excite hatred and disgust in all who hear them. . . .
>
> It is fitting also to know how to swim, to leap, to run, [and] to throw stones, for besides the use that may be made of this in war, a man often has occasion to show what he can do in such matters [from which a good name is to be won]. . . .
>
> I would have him . . . accomplished in letters, at least in those studies that are called the humanities. . . . Let him be well

versed in the poets, and not less in the orators and historians, and also [skilled] in writing verse and prose, especially in this [Italian] tongue of ours. . . .

> Our Courtier ought not to [be] a great eater or drinker, or given to excess in any habit. . . .

(a) What words show that Castiglione thought good looks were important? (b) What, according to Castiglione, should be the courtier's profession? (c) What two qualities, according to Castiglione, should the courtier be certain to avoid? Why? (d) Compare and contrast the Renaissance ideal of the courtier with the Athenian ideal of the well-rounded citizen.

Skill Activities

1. Scanning. Scan pages 332–333 for the answers to the following questions. On a separate sheet of paper, write down your answers. (To review the *scanning* technique, turn to page 311.) (a) About when did Raphael live? (b) Who called sculpture "the first of arts"? (c) What was the subject of Michelangelo's *Pietà*? (d) Which artist worked for Pope Julius II?

2. Skimming. Skim the material under RENAISSANCE ART AND ARCHITECTURE on pages 332–335. (To review the *skimming* technique, turn to page 311.) Then answer the following questions on a separate sheet of paper. (a) What general topic is discussed on these pages? (b) What new materials did Renaissance artists use? (c) Name three Italian artists discussed in this section. Now, from your skimming, write three questions that you would ask yourself in preparing to read this material carefully.

3. Reports. Find information on one of the following topics and prepare a report: (a) the method of printing developed by Gutenberg; (b) the Tudor rulers of England (from Henry VII through Elizabeth I); (c) the Medici family; (d) the Peasants' War (in Germany); (e) the life of Isabella d'Este; (f) the inventions of Leonardo da Vinci; (g) the history of Saint Peter's Church (in Rome).

4. Word research. Some words change in meaning when they are capitalized. Look up the following words in a large dictionary and find out how their meanings differ depending on whether or not they are capitalized: (a) *catholic,* (b) *protestant,* (c) *reformation.* Then tell how the two meanings of each word are related.

India, shown here in a map drawn by a Portuguese mapmaker in 1578, was one of the Asian lands sought by European adventurers who sailed into unknown seas during the Age of Exploration. Portuguese ships had reached India in 1498.

Exploration and Economic Change

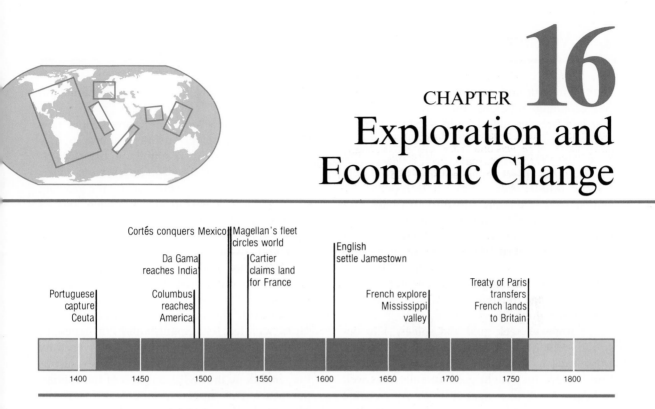

At the same time that the Renaissance and Reformation were altering European society and culture, daring seafarers were making discoveries that transformed economic life. During the great Age of Exploration (1415–1620), European sea captains found a water route to India, sailed around the world for the first time, and brought the knowledge of two new continents to Europe.

The Age of Exploration marked the beginning of Western expansion, which by 1900 enabled Europeans to control much of the globe. The discovery, conquest, and colonization of distant lands led to an extraordinary increase in trade and in the supply of money. During the Age of Exploration a world economy was emerging. New wealth, new resources, and a new economic outlook started the growth of a capitalist economy in the West.

This chapter describes the discoveries of the Age of Exploration and the changes that brought about a revolution in the world's economic life.

CHAPTER OUTLINE

1 Western Europe Expands

2 Voyages of Exploration Bring Change

3 The Spanish and Portuguese Settle the Americas

4 The Dutch, English, and French Gain Colonies

5 Changes Bring a Revolution in Economic Life

1 Western Europe Expands

In the fifteenth and sixteenth centuries, the social, economic, religious, and scientific changes that had been taking place in Western Europe all came together to bring about an era of worldwide expansion and exploration. There had been European expansion movements during the Middle Ages. Western Europeans regained lands from the Muslims in Spain and the eastern Mediterranean. Crusaders carved out feudal states in the Near East. Germans expanded eastward at the expense of Slavs and Prussians. Now, however, a combination of causes brought a far greater movement of expansion. It had far-reaching effects in distant parts of the globe.

Europeans seek gold and spices. The desire for wealth was the first motive that pushed Europeans to make long voyages of exploration. Europeans sought gold and silver as well as luxury goods like sugar and silk, which came from Asia. They also coveted spices from Asia, which were needed to preserve food, particularly meat. All the essential spices, such as cloves and pepper, grew in the East.

For centuries, Muslim traders had controlled the rich land and sea trade routes to Asia, from the Indian Ocean to the Mediterranean Sea (Chapter 10). On the European end, the Italian city-state of Venice (page 156) had a virtual *monopoly* — exclusive control — on trade with the Muslims. Spices and other goods from Asia flowed through Venice to the rest of Europe. Scarce European gold poured into the pockets of Venetian merchant-bankers and Muslim traders. Other European merchants — especially the Portuguese — hoped to break the Venetian-Arab monopoly by finding an all-water route to the East, thus avoiding lands held by the Muslims.

Merchants acquire power and influence. Europe's hard-working, wealthy, and ambitious merchant class was a vital factor in bringing about the Age of Exploration. European merchants organized expeditions that traveled over land and sea in search of markets and profits. In Renaissance times, some merchants also held considerable political power. Many rulers were deeply in debt to wealthy merchants and bankers.

To gain new lands, new power, and new wealth for themselves and their countries, European rulers gave their support to overseas expeditions. Joining these ventures were many young noblemen who were hurt by the growing scarcity of land in Europe. Younger sons of landowners knew they would not inherit family estates. They looked beyond Europe for land, gold, and adventure.

Religious zeal encourages expansion. A desire to spread Christianity was another reason for the European voyages to distant parts of the world. The anti-Muslim spirit of the Crusades persisted. The Spanish and Portuguese in particular felt that they had a God-given duty to drive the Muslims out of other lands, just as they had done in the Reconquest of the Iberian peninsula. They hoped to take Africa from the Muslims and to convert the peoples of Asia.

The Renaissance fosters a spirit of adventure. The restless, individualistic spirit of the Renaissance helped launch the Age of Exploration. Sea captains who ventured into uncharted oceans, explorers who penetrated unknown lands, soldiers who conquered vast overseas territories — all were driven by curiosity, the desire for glory, and the hope of fame. This spirit of adventure helps to explain why Europeans took the lead in discovery and exploration in the fifteenth century.

Improvements in ships and navigation make long voyages possible. The motives for the Age of Exploration are often summed up as a search for "glory, God, and gold." Another important influence, however, was technological progress that made long voyages practical and possible. More seaworthy ships and improved skills in navigation allowed sea captains to venture far from the sight of land. Sailing ships could carry smaller crews and undertake longer voyages than galleys propelled by rowers. Ships began to carry new kinds of weaponry — cannon and guns.

Navigational instruments also were improving. Sea captains used the astrolabe to find their latitude by observing the position of the sun, moon, and stars. The mariner's compass was made more accurate.

Prince Henry of Portugal encourages exploration. In the twelfth century, the small, seafaring country of Portugal had been established in territory recaptured from Moorish Spain. In the 1400's, the Portuguese still had strong anti-Muslim feelings. Prince Henry, a younger son of King John I, tried to begin a new crusade in 1415 by capturing the Muslim city of Ceuta (SYOO-tah) in North Africa. Historians consider this event the opening date of the Age of Exploration.

In the capture of Ceuta, Prince Henry's men liberated more than a thousand Christian slaves, and the prince vowed to devote his life to conquering the Muslims in Africa. The Portuguese also learned that Africa was the source of the gold the Arabs traded. They had believed that Arab traders brought gold by ship from India. Now they learned that camel caravans brought gold dust across the Sahara from Timbuktu in West Africa (page 278). In search of African gold, Henry sent Portuguese sea captains farther and farther south along the West African coast. They traded in gold, ivory, and fish, but their most important goal was to find a sea route to the East.

Portugal leads in knowledge about the seas. Prince Henry's interest in ships and sailing helped Portugal move ahead of wealthier European states in the search for a sea route to India. The Portuguese adopted the innovations in shipbuilding and navigation. Their shipyards began to build seaworthy caravels (CAIR-uh-velz), ships capable of surviving the fierce gales of the Atlantic Ocean. These ships also could maneuver quickly in naval battles.

Prince Henry spent his own fortune to establish a naval station at Sagres on the southwestern tip of Portugal. For forty years he directed the gathering of geographical information. To Sagres came ship's pilots from Italy, Jewish astronomers from the eastern Mediterranean lands, and experienced seamen from Spain. From Arab scholars and Portuguese sailors, Prince Henry collected information about the stars, tides, winds, and currents. His mapmakers used this information to draw maps of African coastal waters. With these

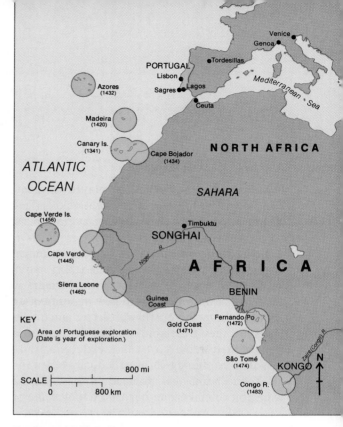

Portugal Explores the West African Coast

Portuguese explorers steadily advanced southward along the West African coast. When did they reach the Gold Coast?

maps, which were kept secret by the Portuguese, sea captains could sail with confidence into unfamiliar waters. Prince Henry himself made no voyages, but his success in advancing knowledge of the sea caused English writers to call him "the Navigator."

Trading posts and plantations are a basis for empire. The Portuguese established two profitable institutions in West Africa — the fortified trading post and the plantation. These became the economic base for Portugal's overseas empire. Both were later introduced in Asia, the Americas, and other parts of Africa.

Trading posts, guarded by armed soldiers, were built where rivers emptied into the sea. The posts provided a central point where traders stored goods to sell or barter for slaves or African products. The soldiers and their weapons were also used to "persuade" local rulers to give the Portuguese a trade monopoly. The Portuguese trading posts set the pattern for other European outposts for centuries to come.

Landmarks in Technology

ACHIEVEMENTS IN NAVIGATION

Developments in technology played a great part in bringing about the Age of Exploration. Navigational instruments and new ship designs helped to make long ocean voyages possible.

Navigation was one of the biggest challenges explorers faced. Away from land, earlier sailors had no way of knowing where their ships were, so voyages were confined to coastal waters. With new instruments, explorers could sail into the ocean with less chance of becoming lost since they were able to track the courses and positions of their ships.

New ocean-going ships called caravels were another kind of technological advance. In these ships explorers were able to make long-distance voyages.

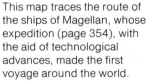

One of the first instruments that helped navigators at sea find the position of their ships was the astrolabe. This brass astrolabe (above, right) was made by Muslim craftsmen in Egypt in 1236. The three figures shown on these pages (left to right) are using the cross-staff, the astrolabe, and the back-staff. These instruments were used to measure the distance of the sun or of certain stars above the horizon. Navigators used the measurements to determine the ship's latitude — that is, its distance north or south of the equator.

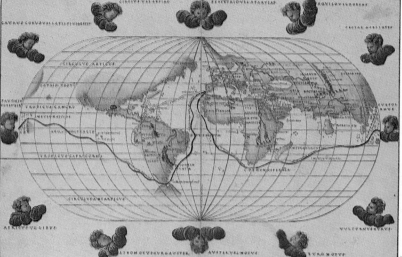

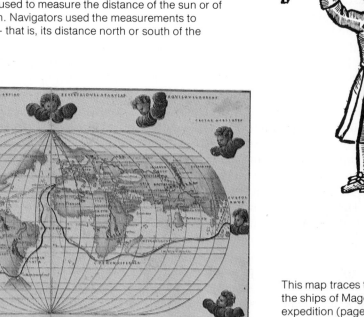

This map traces the route of the ships of Magellan, whose expedition (page 354), with the aid of technological advances, made the first voyage around the world.

348

Ocean-going caravels, like this German one (left), were larger than caravels used on inland seas. Three or four masts, square and triangular sails, and sternpost rudders made these ships fit for ocean travel. The compass (below) was the most important instrument of navigation. Because it always showed the direction of magnetic north, it could be used to set a ship's course at night or in cloudy weather. Other early navigational instruments worked only when the sun or stars were visible.

The Portuguese did not invent the plantation system of agriculture. The success of their sugar plantations in West Africa, however, made this type of agriculture common in colonial settlements throughout the world. Plantation agriculture was an important factor in the expansion of the slave trade (page 283).

CHECK-UP

1. Vocabulary: *monopoly*.
2. (a) What part did Venice play in the trade between Asia and Europe? (b) Why were European merchants interested in developing new trade routes?
3. How was European expansion affected (a) by the growth of a wealthy merchant class? (b) by religious zeal? (c) by the Renaissance?
4. What improvements in ships and navigation made long voyages possible?
5. (a) What factors allowed Portugal to take the lead in collecting sailing knowledge and making voyages of exploration? (b) What two institutions were the economic base for Portugal's overseas empire?

2 Voyages of Exploration Bring Change

Late in the fifteenth century, European adventurers began to make daring voyages that, in only about thirty years, changed forever what people knew and thought about the rest of the world. The Portuguese took the lead, and other Western European nations soon followed them in seeking new lands and riches. (See the map on pages 352–353 for explorers' routes.)

THE PORTUGUESE IN ASIA

Dias sails around the tip of Africa. Portuguese sailors spent nearly seventy years exploring the coast of West Africa before they found the passage to India. In 1488 a South Atlantic gale blew the ships of Bartholomeu Dias (DEE-ahs) around the southern tip of the African continent. Days later, the exhausted crew saw land again, but the sun was rising on their right rather than on their left, and they realized they were now sailing north along the east coast of Africa. Dias called the tip of the continent "Cape of Storms." The Portuguese king, however, was so jubilant at the news Dias brought that he gave the area its present-day name, the Cape of Good Hope.

Vasco da Gama reaches India. Dias's discovery of a sea route into the Indian Ocean encouraged Portugal to send Vasco da Gama on a diplomatic mission to the Indies. Da Gama's fleet, however, was armed with cannon and carried goods to trade.

Da Gama's voyage to South Africa was the greatest navigational feat of the fifteenth century. Following the pattern of the winds in the South Atlantic, he sailed westward, then circled back toward the west coast of Africa. The fleet was out of sight of land for fourteen weeks. When the ships reached land in November, 1497, they were within 100 miles of the Cape of Good Hope (map, pages 352–353).

Da Gama rounded the Cape of Good Hope and sailed up the coast of East Africa. Soon he saw the minarets and white plaster houses of the rich Muslim city of Mozambique. Arab merchants regularly traded with India, and an Arab pilot guided da Gama's fleet across the Indian Ocean to Calicut, on the west coast of India. Da Gama landed there, saying, "We come in search of Christians and spices." He brought the ruler of Calicut gifts from the Portuguese king. These included "twelve pieces of striped cloth, four scarlet hoods, six hats, four strings of coral, a case containing six washstand basins, a case of sugar, two casks of oil, and two of honey."

Portugal takes over the Asian trade. With da Gama's voyage, Portugal was in a position to dominate the spice trade. The Indians were not impressed by European trade goods, and the Muslim traders resented the Portuguese as competitors. Nevertheless, the Portuguese in India acquired a fortune in spices, drugs, and dyes to take back to Europe. Some Indian merchants and rulers welcomed the new opportunity for trade. In other cases, the Portuguese resorted to terrorism, using the ship's cannon to make Indian rulers grant trading rights.

Goods transported from Calicut to Europe by sea cost the Portuguese only a fifth of what they cost when brought over land and water by the Arabs and Venetians. Prices for Asian goods were now within the reach of many more Europeans. Trade in both Asian and European cities increased greatly. Europe, however, produced few goods that wealthy Asians wanted to buy. To pay for the expensive Asian goods, therefore, Europeans had to use gold and silver, or **bullion** (BULL-yun).

The Portuguese also acquired Asian goods by taking part in the local trading that flourished from the Indian Ocean to the South China Sea. Portuguese merchant captains traded East Indian sandalwood and spices for cargoes of Chinese silk and porcelain. The Portuguese could sell these luxury goods for high prices in the bazaars of India or trade them for spices. Portuguese fleets carrying ivory, pepper, cinnamon, cloves, and nutmeg then sailed the Indian and Atlantic oceans in the long and dangerous voyage back to Portugal.

The overwhelming superiority of their cannons and guns gave the Portuguese an advantage in the Asian trade. By 1511 the Portuguese had captured the port of Goa on the coast of India, as well as several islands strategically located along the sea routes.

SPAIN IN THE WESTERN HEMISPHERE

Columbus reaches the Americas. Portugal's main interest lay in finding an eastward passage to India around Africa. In 1484 an Italian mariner, Christopher Columbus, proposed to sail westward to India, but King John II of Portugal rejected the idea. Columbus had seriously underestimated the circumference of the globe and thought that his proposed voyage would cover about 2,500 miles. The Portuguese naval advisers were skeptical of his figures, for they had calculated the westward distance to Asia as about 10,000 miles.

Columbus then took his proposal to the rulers of Spain. Having conquered the last Moorish stronghold on Spanish soil, Ferdinand

Christopher Columbus for many years lived in Lisbon, where he heard the reports of Portuguese discoveries along the coast of Africa. By the 1480's Columbus had formed his plan to sail west across the Atlantic.

and Isabella were ready to consider overseas ventures. Queen Isabella provided Columbus with funds to outfit a small fleet — the caravels *Niña* and *Pinta* and the flagship *Santa María*. The fleet sailed first from Spain to the Canary Islands. Leaving the Canary Islands on September 6, 1492, Columbus sailed west with the trade winds. Although the weather and winds were good, some of the crew were nervous at being out of sight of land, and Columbus offered a prize to the sailor who first saw land. On the early morning watch of October 12, the lookout on the *Pinta* saw white sand gleaming in the moonlight and shouted that they had found land: *"Tierra, tierra!"*

Columbus was convinced that he had found Japan. Believing that he had a mission to bring Christianity to Asia, he named the coral island San Salvador ("Holy Saviour" in Spanish). From the friendly Arawaks on the island, Columbus learned of a richer land to the south (probably present-day Cuba). He sailed there

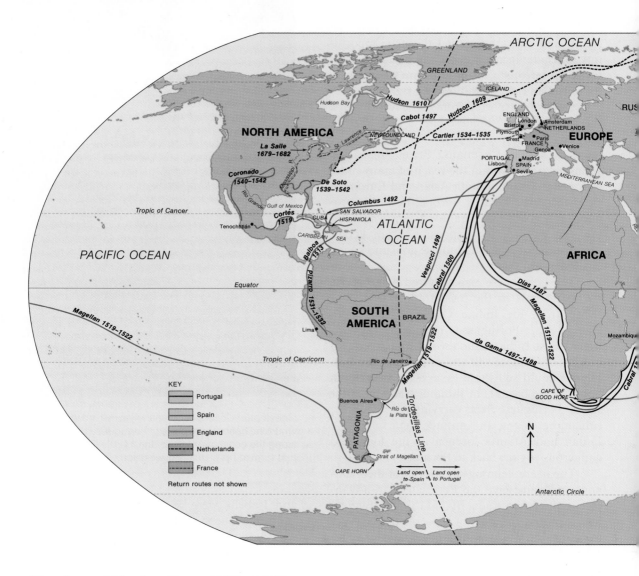

The routes of great explorers are shown here. What explorer led an expedition that sailed around the world? What country sponsored that expedition? What part of South America lay west of the line drawn by the Treaty of Tordesillas?

The Age of Exploration, 1492–1682

The routes of great explorers are shown here. What explorer led an expedition that sailed around the world? What country sponsored that expedition? What part of South America lay west of the line drawn by the Treaty of Tordesillas?

expecting to meet the Grand Khan of China, for whom he had a letter from Queen Isabella. After visiting the island of Hispaniola,[1] where the *Santa María* was wrecked, Columbus set

[1]There are now two countries — Haiti and the Dominican Republic — on the island of Hispaniola.

sail for Spain in the *Niña*. He took some of the Arawaks with him to prove that he had reached Asia. He called them "Indians." Delighted by the voyage, the queen gave Columbus the title "Admiral of the Ocean Sea."

Columbus makes later voyages. Still convinced that he had found Asia, Columbus returned to the Caribbean in 1493 and 1498. On the voyage in 1493, he and his two brothers brought seventeen shiploads of settlers to Hispaniola and established the first European colony in the Americas. Columbus and his brothers proved to be such poor administrators of the Hispaniola colony that in 1500 they were all arrested by a royal investigator and sent back

Arctic Circle

ASIA

JAPAN

CHINA

INDIA

Canton
Macao

Goa
Calicut
CEYLON

PHILIPPINE
ISLANDS

SOUTH
CHINA
SEA

PACIFIC
OCEAN

SPICE ISLANDS
(MOLUCCAS)

EAST INDIES

INDIAN
OCEAN

Magellan 1519–1522

AUSTRALIA

Tordesillas Line

0   2,000 mi
ALE
0   2,000 km

Land open
to Portugal

Land open
to Spain

to Spain. Ferdinand and Isabella pardoned Columbus and financed one more voyage in 1502. During his later travels in the Caribbean islands, Columbus realized that the nearby mainland must be a continent, but he still believed it was Asia.

Spain and Portugal agree to divide the world. The rulers of Spain immediately sent the news of Columbus's first voyage to Pope Alexander VI. Trying to prevent disputes between Spain and Portugal, the Pope established an imaginary "line of demarcation" in the Atlantic Ocean. It gave Spain possession of all lands already "discovered and to be discovered" west of Europe. Portugal was to have the

lands to the east of the line. King John of Portugal, however, threatened war against Spain, claiming the Spanish monarchs had been given too great an advantage.

In 1494, diplomats from the two countries met at Tordesillas (tor-day-SEE-yahs), Spain. They agreed to another dividing line, 370 leagues (about 1,100 miles) west of the Azores. The Treaty of Tordesillas, like the Pope's order, presumed that Spain and Portugal had the right to divide the entire non-Christian world between themselves. It recognized both Spain's interest in westward exploration and Portugal's accomplishments in eastward voyages. (The revised treaty line allowed Portugal to claim what is now Brazil; Spain was given the rest of the Americas.)

A mapmaker names the new continents. To follow up Spain's claim, more and more Spanish-sponsored expeditions set out seeking westward routes to the Indies. An Italian sailor, Amerigo Vespucci, made voyages for both Spain and Portugal and wrote a vague but colorful account of his travels. In 1507 a German geographer and mapmaker labeled the new southern continent with the Latin form of Vespucci's first name. *America* eventually became the name for both continents in the Western Hemisphere.

The Spaniards explore the Caribbean. Columbus had established a base for further Spanish exploration of the Caribbean area. In 1508 Juan Ponce de León, who had sailed with Columbus, explored the island of Puerto Rico and founded a colony. Searching for the legendary "fountain of youth," Ponce de León discovered and named the Florida peninsula on Easter Sunday, 1513.

Vasco Núñez de Balboa, a settler in Hispaniola, went to look for gold on the mainland and established a settlement in what is now Panama. In 1513, he crossed the narrow isthmus of Panama and became the first European to see the "Great South Sea" — what is now called the Pacific Ocean.

Magellan's fleet circumnavigates the globe. A Portuguese navigator, Ferdinand Magellan, persuaded Spain's ruler, Charles I (who became Charles V as Holy Roman Emperor in

1519), to finance an expedition to explore the Pacific Ocean and its islands. This voyage was by far the boldest undertaking of the Age of Exploration.

In September, 1519, Magellan's five ships, with 265 men on board, set sail from Spain. After the Atlantic crossing, they explored the Río de la Plata (REE-oh day lah PLAH-tuh), the huge estuary between present-day Argentina and Uruguay (map, pages 352–353). Magellan sailed south until faced with mutiny from a crew who were cold and weary from Atlantic gales. His fleet wintered about 200 miles north of the tip of South America.

When spring at last came, three of Magellan's ships continued southward, reaching a point where the nights lasted only three hours. With enormous skill and luck they navigated the raging tides and the tortuous passages of the strait that now bears Magellan's name. Emerging into the "Great South Sea," Magellan found it so calm that he called it *Mar Pacífico* — the "peaceful sea." At latitude 32° south he turned northwest and headed for the "Isles of the Moluccas where the cloves grow." Antonio Pigafetta, an Italian on the voyage, wrote a journal for the Spanish king, describing the horrors of the Pacific crossing:

> We were three months and twenty days without getting any kind of fresh food. We ate biscuit, which was no longer biscuit, but powder of biscuits swarming with worms, for they had eaten the good. We drank yellow water that had been putrid for many days. We also ate some ox hides that covered the top of the mainyard. . . . We left them in the sea for four or five days, and then placed them for a few moments on top of the embers, and so ate them. . . . Rats were sold for one-half ducado [a gold coin] apiece, and even then we could not get them. But above all other misfortunes the following was the worst. The gums of both the lower and upper teeth of some of our men swelled, so that they could not eat under any circumstances and therefore died. . . . However, I, by the grace of God, suffered no sickness. We sailed about four thousand *leguas* [12,000 miles] during those three months and twenty days through an open stretch in that Pacific Sea. In truth it is very pacific, for during that time we did not suffer any storm. . . .

> Had not God and His blessed mother given us so good weather we would have all died of hunger in that exceeding vast sea. Of a verity I believe no such voyage will ever be made [again].

Though many sailors died, two ships at last reached the Philippine Islands, southeast of the Asian mainland. Magellan, like Columbus and da Gama, proved less able as a diplomat than as a sea captain. He died in a fight with the Filipinos.

The prevailing easterly winds made it impossible for Magellan's ships to sail back into Spanish waters. They continued west through Portuguese territory, where one was captured. The *Victoria* alone rounded the Cape of Good Hope in 1522 and sailed back to Spain with a rich cargo of cloves. Of the 265 men who had left Seville three years before, only 18 sailors completed the voyage.

This first circumnavigation of the globe showed that the Pacific Ocean separated Asia and the Americas and that this ocean was much larger than suspected. In addition, the voyage demonstrated that all the oceans on earth are connected and that the trade winds follow a consistent pattern, affecting weather and navigation. Their new knowledge enabled Western Europeans to sail almost anywhere on the face of the planet.

CHECK-UP

1. Vocabulary: *bullion.*
2. How did the voyages of Dias and da Gama help Portugal establish trade with Asia?
3. (a) What happened to the Arab-Venetian monopoly of Asian trade? (b) What advantages did the Portuguese have in Asia?
4. (a) What voyage did Columbus propose to King John of Portugal? (b) Why did the king turn him down? (c) Why were the Spanish rulers interested? (d) What was the result of the voyage?
5. (a) What was the purpose of the Treaty of Tordesillas? (b) How did the treaty divide the world?
6. (a) What achievements were made by Balboa and Ponce de León? (b) Why was the voyage of Magellan's fleet important?

3 The Spanish and Portuguese Settle the Americas

At the time of the European discovery of the Americas, some 25 to 100 million people were living in the lands that stretched from Hudson Bay to Cape Horn. In language, culture, and technology, the peoples of the Americas differed far more than the peoples of Europe at the time.

By the early 1500's, when the Spaniards arrived on the mainland, two native American peoples had built strong states that controlled large territories. The warlike Aztec state, with its capital at Tenochtitlán (teh-NOHCH-tee-TLAHN), dominated most of the Valley of Mexico. On the west coast of South America, the Incas' skill in organization and government administration had created a huge empire. Neither of these civilizations was able to withstand conquest by the Spanish.

SPANISH CONQUESTS

Spaniards seek gold in the Americas. The first settlers from Spain stayed mainly on the

---

TIMETABLE
Exploration and Colonization

1488	Dias sails around the tip of Africa.
1492	Columbus reaches the Americas.
1494	The Treaty of Tordesillas divides the known world between Spain and Portugal.
1498	Da Gama reaches India.
1521	Cortés conquers Mexico.
1519–1522	Magellan's fleet sails around the world.
1532	Pizarro conquers the Inca empire.
1534	Cartier claims the St. Lawrence Valley for France.
1607	The first English colony in America is started at Jamestown.
1609	Hudson's explorations give the Dutch a claim to land along the Hudson River.
1763	The Treaty of Paris turns France's North American empire over to Britain.

Caribbean islands. Soon, however, the Spaniards' desire for gold led them to the mainland, where they encountered and soon overthrew the rich, powerful Aztec and Inca states. Many of the Spanish conquerors, or *conquistadores* (kon-kee-stah-DOH-rehs), were sons of aristocratic families. They were seeking fame, gold, land, and adventure. Some were motivated by religious reasons as well. Many were exceptionally brave, determined, and daring; they were also ruthless.

Cortés is welcomed by the Aztecs. Hernán Cortés was a typical conquistador — courageous, charming, and ruthless. He sailed from Cuba to the Gulf Coast of Mexico in 1519, with a fleet of eleven vessels carrying 508 soldiers, two priests, sixteen horses, and several small cannon. (See map, pages 352–353.)

The Aztec ruler Moctezuma believed that the unfamiliar-looking Europeans might be gods or at least messengers from the god Quetzalcóatl (ket-sahl-KOH-atl).[2] Although his warriors could have easily overcome Cortés's small army, Moctezuma sent ambassadors with gifts of gold and intricate featherwork. Unsure of the Spaniards' intentions, Moctezuma hoped the intruders would take the gifts and leave. But the gifts of gold only made the Spaniards want to find its source.

Cortés gains Indian allies. To prevent his outnumbered soldiers from leaving, Cortés ordered the ships sunk and began to march inland. He persuaded the Tlaxcalans, who hated Aztec rule, to join him against the Aztecs.

Malinche, an Aztec noblewoman who had been sold into slavery, aided Cortés in dealing with the local leaders. Fluent in several Indian languages and quick to learn Spanish, she acted as both interpreter and informer. Her knowledge and influence helped Cortés make allies of other Indians and keep track of Aztec spies.

---

[2]According to Aztec legend, Quetzalcóatl had sailed toward the east and would someday return from there. The Spaniards arrived in one of the years predicted for Quetzalcóatl's return.

Tenochtitlán falls to the Spaniards. Cortés's army and allies crossed the mountains to the lake-city of Tenochtitlán. Moctezuma offered no resistance, but some of the Aztec nobles recognized the threat the Spaniards posed. In a fierce battle, they drove the Spaniards out of the city. More than half the conquistadores were wounded or killed, and most of the treasure they had seized was lost.

Undiscouraged by the heavy losses, Cortés gathered his Indian allies and began a siege of Tenochtitlán. Moctezuma had died mysteriously. His successor Cuauhtémoc (kwow-TAY-mok) and a small loyal army resisted until most of the Aztec warriors had been killed or captured or had fallen ill with smallpox. After a three-month siege, Tenochtitlán fell to Cortés in 1521.

Pizarro conquers the empire of the Incas. The great Inca empire lay south of the Aztec lands, in the mountains of what is now Peru. The Spaniards' conquest of the Incas was quicker than the defeat of the Aztecs but equally dramatic. Francisco Pizarro had gained permission from Spain's ruler, Emperor Charles V (page 353), to attempt the conquest of the South American coast. When Pizarro arrived in 1532, the Inca ruler, Atahualpa (at-ah-WAHL-puh), met him cordially and was immediately taken prisoner. In the fighting that followed, the Inca foot soldiers, armed with spears, war clubs, and bows and arrows, were no match for Spanish cannon, steel swords, or mounted soldiers. Not one Spaniard died in the fierce fighting that killed hundreds of the Inca people.

Pizarro promised to set Atahualpa free on the payment of a great ransom — a room full of gold. Once the gold had been collected from throughout the empire, Pizarro ordered Atahualpa strangled. One fifth of the ransom was sent to the king of Spain. The rest was divided among some 150 conquistadores, who began to fight among themselves in their greed for gold. Pizarro himself was assassinated. Unrest continued until the viceroy (VYS-roy), the king's representative, arrived from Spain in 1551.

Legends of gold encourage further exploration. The Spanish conquests of the Aztec and Inca empires gave Spain control of territory stretching from modern Mexico to Chile. Other Spanish adventurers explored the lands around the great South American rivers, claiming still more of the continent. Rumors of treasure and legends of cities whose streets were paved with gold lured men to explore the unknown lands north of Mexico.

Hernando de Soto, who had been with Pizarro, led an expedition to Florida. He and his men traveled north as far as the present-day Carolinas and then turned westward, reaching the Mississippi River in 1541 and exploring the lands nearby. Francisco de Coronado set out northward from Mexico (New Spain) in 1540 and conquered the Zuñi pueblos. His expedition then split up. Some followed the course of the Colorado River inland from the coast. Others traveled to the north and became the first Europeans to see the Grand Canyon of the Colorado River. Another group traveled as far east as modern Kansas. (See de Soto's and Coronado's routes on the map on pages 352–353.)

Although neither de Soto nor Coronado found gold or rich empires, their travels extended Spain's American territories across the entire southern edge of what is now the United States. In 1560, Spain claimed these lands as the province of "New Mexico."

Atahualpa was the Inca ruler who lost his life to the Spanish conquerors.

An Indian artist of the 1500's may have drawn these rock pictures of Spaniards who rode into the Canyon de Chelly in what is now the state of Arizona.

COLONIZATION AFTER CONQUEST

The Spanish empire spreads. Spain's empire in the Americas grew rapidly after Cortés conquered Mexico in 1519. With the conquest of Peru, it spread down the west coast of South America. The viceroyalties of New Spain (Mexico) and Peru became the centers of Spanish colonial settlement. The southernmost limit of Spanish lands lay in what is now Chile. To the north the Spanish empire continued to grow in what is now the American West.

Settlers bring Spanish culture to the Americas. The rulers of Spain gave large tracts of land to the conquistadores and certain favored colonists. A class of colonial landowners grew up, who had great wealth but no political power in the colony. Spanish colonies were ruled by viceroys appointed by the monarch to carry out royal policies established in Spain by a council. In addition to forms of government and patterns of landowning, the Spaniards also brought their language and the Catholic religion to the Indians of the lands they conquered.

The Spaniards demand labor and tribute from the Indians. The Spanish aristocrats who held most of the land in the colonies felt it was degrading to work the soil, handle tools, or deal in commerce. To do the hard work on the plantations and in the mines, the settlers and their descendants, called *creoles*, used the Indian peasants. Forced labor, particularly in the silver mines of what are now Peru, Bolivia, and Mexico, cost the lives of thousands of Indians.

Because the Indians had been converted to Christianity, the Spanish rulers issued policies designed to protect them. Indians could not be bought or sold as slaves, and colonists had to be granted a royal license to use Indian labor. Despite the royal policies, Indian men and women still could be assigned to a colonist and forced to work.

Life for the peasants, called peons, changed little. Before the conquest, landless peasants had worked for the Aztec and Inca nobles. After it, they labored for the Spanish creoles. Indian peons dug out the silver shipped to Europe, harvested the wheat that creoles ate, and wove the cloth worn in the colonies. They labored to build the cathedrals, universities, and spacious palaces where viceroys governed and bishops preached. The peons were often harshly treated, poorly fed, exhausted, and sick.

Spanish missionaries work in the Americas. Catholic priests and friars accompanied the earliest Spanish expeditions. One of the first missionaries to the Indians was Bartolomé de Las Casas, who settled in Hispaniola in 1502. About ten years later, Las Casas became a priest and then a Dominican friar. He began a lifelong campaign to protect Indians from colonists who were interested only in the profits to be made from their labor. King Ferdinand supported the work of Las Casas and named him "Protector of the Indians." Las Casas wrote one of the first histories of Spanish colonial America.

In the late 1500's, as part of the missionary effort of the Counter-Reformation, the Catholic Church sent many of Spain's best-trained friars to the Americas to convert the Indians. In order to preach the Gospel, the friars learned Indian languages. They wrote accounts of the Indians' traditions and customs and set up schools to teach them new skills.

The most successful schools were the mission villages set up by the Jesuits (page 341) in what is now Paraguay. Here Indians learned European crafts and farming methods. The

Wealthy colonists in New Spain owned estates that spread over many miles. Here a landowner rides out with his daughter to inspect his holdings.
Courtesy Time-Life Books Inc.

mission villages achieved great economic success. Eventually the Spanish rulers felt threatened by the Jesuits' economic power and expelled them from the Americas. With their departure, the mission villages collapsed.

The Church tried to protect its Indian converts and lessen the shock of cultural change. Catholic churches were built on the sites of Indian temples, and Indians were allowed to perform traditional dances on Christian holy days.

At the same time, Church policies tended to cut Indians off from Spanish colonial culture and society. The Indians lived separately in their own villages. Few spoke Spanish. Indians ate corn and went barefoot or wore sandals; creoles ate wheat and wore boots. Even the Church, which championed the Indians' cause, regarded them as childlike and in need of special protection.

The Portuguese colonize Brazil slowly. Missionary efforts by the Jesuits also played an important part in the settlement of Brazil by the Portuguese. In 1500, following the same sailing pattern as da Gama (page 350), the fleet of Pedro Cabral had made a wide arc into the western Atlantic and chanced upon the coast of Brazil. This territory was immediately claimed by Cabral for Portugal. Eventually the Portuguese claimed the east coast of South America as far south as present-day Uruguay.

Most of the settlements in Brazil were founded by wealthy nobles to whom the Portuguese king gave large grants of land. Unlike the Spanish colonies, however, the Portuguese colonies drew settlers from all classes of society. By the mid-1500's there were some fifteen fortified towns on the Brazilian coast. Jesuit missionaries were the pioneers in exploring the territories inland, where they established schools and mission churches for the Indians. Portuguese settlers followed the missionaries inland. Some of these people were farmers looking for good grazing land. Others were adventurers looking for gold or for Indians to capture and sell as slaves.

The Indian population declines drastically. Although forced labor and conquest killed many Indians, particularly in the Spanish colonies, the Indians' worst enemies were the new diseases brought to the Americas from Europe, Asia, and Africa. In the span of a generation, smallpox, measles, flu, and the common cold killed hundreds of thousands. The Arawaks of the Caribbean islands were wiped out altogether. In some areas of the Mexican mainland, the population fell to about a third of what it had been before the Europeans arrived. It was several generations before the Indian population began to grow again.

African slaves are brought to the Americas. The tragic deaths of so many Indians caused a severe labor shortage in the Spanish colonies. By the mid-1500's the Portuguese settlers in Brazil also needed laborers for their newly established sugar plantations. The result was the importing of slave labor from Africa. In 1518 Spain licensed Portuguese slavers to ship captured black Africans directly to the Americas. The Crown justified its policy by two arguments: (1) Blacks (unlike the Indians in the Americas) were not Christians and had already been enslaved in Africa. Being sent to America would not change their status as slaves but, in the Church's view, would give them the chance to convert to Christianity. (2) Africans were supposed to be accustomed to heavy field work in a tropical climate, while Indians were not. African slaves eventually provided most of the heavy labor for plantations throughout tropical and semitropical America.

LINKING PAST AND PRESENT

The Countess and the Cinchona Tree

European settlers in tropical countries were often troubled by strange illnesses. In 1638 Francisca de Ribera, countess of Chinchon, was living in Peru with her husband, the Spanish viceroy. She fell ill, but her fever was cured by the powdered bark of an evergreen plant (shown here in an old print). The Peruvian Indians used this *quinaquina* bark to cure many fevers.

'Cinchona officinalis'

The countess ordered some of the powdered bark shipped back to Spain. Widely used, quinine (KWY-nine) was popularly called ''Countess powders'' or ''Jesuits' bark,'' since Jesuit missionaries took it to other colonies. When Linnaeus (page 407) classified the Peruvian trees, he named them *cinchona* after the Spanish countess.

Quinine became an even more effective medicine after scientists isolated it from the tree bark in 1820. Quinine is still used to flavor tonic water. It was the only remedy for malaria until chemists developed synthetic forms during World War II.

Blacks adapt to colonial life. African slaves and their descendants in the Spanish and Portuguese colonies differed from the native Indian peons in significant ways. The blacks had been forcibly transported from their homelands and cut off from their traditions. Slaves living on the same plantation might come from different African societies and speak very different languages. With their ties to Africa cut, black people in the Americas adopted Christianity and European speech, clothing, and customs. The American Indians, on the other hand, tended to remain isolated in their scattered villages and to cling to their centuries-old, traditional ways.

New groups enter the colonial population. Intermarriage was common between European or African men and Indian women in the colonies. Their children made up new population groups in the Americas. Those whose parents were European and Indian were called mestizos. The descendants of Europeans and black Africans were called mulattos.

This "mixed" population grew more quickly than the Indian population. Children who survived infancy tended to be more immune to disease than their parents. Moreover, these people felt at home in Latin America;[3] they had no memory of a homeland abroad, and they had not been conquered. Most spoke Spanish or Portuguese, were baptized Christians, and followed other European ways. In Brazil, where social class lines were not rigid, people from all groups mingled freely, particularly in the towns. Throughout Latin America, people with mixed ancestry came to make up most of the urban population. From their ranks would come many of modern Latin America's leaders.

Colonization brings cultural exchange. The encounter between the Europeans and the American Indians has been compared to a steel

---

[3]The countries of the Americas where Spanish and Portuguese — both Latin-based languages — are spoken came to be known as Latin America.

container smashing against a clay pot. The Europeans' technology gave them enormous military and economic advantages over the Indians. The Mesoamerican and Inca civilizations perished in the conquest, and millions of Indians died as a result of forced labor and disease. Yet cultural exchange did take place. American potatoes, corn, tomatoes, and chocolate were added to the European diet. Europeans in tropical America slept in Indian hammocks, and explorers to the north used canoes and tepees.

To the Americas the Spanish conquerors brought the horse, firearms, and the use of the wheel. The first European settlers introduced the metal fishhook, the potter's wheel, the plow, new techniques of weaving, and new farming methods. They brought many new foods — wheat, chicken, beef, pork, and fruits such as apples, pears, plums, peaches, lemons, limes, and oranges. The breeding of cattle, sheep, goats, pigs, mules, and donkeys affected both diet and transportation.

Settlers in Latin America brought their style of architecture, their languages, and their Roman Catholic religion. Royal governors laid down the European code of law as well as the idea of private ownership of land. From Florida south to Chile and Brazil, European ways took root in the lands that were ruled by Spain and Portugal.

CHECK-UP

1. Vocabulary: *creole.*
2. (a) In the early 1500's what powerful states ruled large parts of what are now Mexico and Peru? (b) How were Cortés and Pizarro able to conquer these empires? (c) How did de Soto and Coronado add to Spain's lands in the Americas?
3. (a) Why did the landowning Spaniards force Indians to labor for them? (b) What steps did the Spanish rulers take to protect the Indians? (c) How were the Indians cut off from colonial society?
4. How did the Portuguese gain territory in South America?
5. (a) Why did the Indian population diminish after the Spanish conquest? (b) Where did the Spanish and Portuguese setttlers get the workers they needed?
6. (a) How did blacks and Indians differ in their reactions to colonial life? (b) How did the mixed population differ from the native Indians?
7. In what ways did cultural exchange take place between Europeans and American Indians?

4 The Dutch, English, and French Gain Colonies

England, France, and the Netherlands took only a small part in the early voyages of exploration, for religious dissent and civil wars focused their interests at home. In addition, their ships had to sail farther to go around either Africa or South America. By the time these countries were ready to join in the explorations, both Spain and Portugal had already claimed colonial empires.

Northern Europeans seek a new passage to India. The Dutch and English looked first for a route northeast to Asia and the Spice Islands. Their seafarers sailed north of Scandinavia and into the Arctic Ocean along the coast of Russia. Ice made this route impassable for much of the year, however. The Dutch and English next set out across the Atlantic, hoping to find a northwest passage through North America.

In 1497 King Henry VII sent an Italian navigator, John Cabot (Giovanni Caboto), westward to the Americas. Cabot reached Newfoundland and explored its coast (map, pages 352–353). He reported rich fishing grounds but also described a cold land quite different from the tropical islands found by Columbus.

Henry Hudson, an English explorer, made four voyages in search of a northwest passage. In 1609, sailing for Dutch merchants, Hudson took his ship *Half Moon* up the Hudson River, giving the Netherlands claim to land along the river. Dutch settlers established the colony of New Netherland, including what is now New

York City (originally called New Amsterdam). Other Dutch holdings in the Western Hemisphere were some islands in the Caribbean, the colony of Dutch Guiana (now Suriname), and parts of Brazil.

The Netherlands becomes a leading center of trade. When the Dutch revolted against their Spanish rulers in 1568, their ships could no longer enter either Spanish or Portuguese ports. Undiscouraged, the Dutch decided to take over the Portuguese trade routes and set up their own trade with India and the East Indies. In 1602 the Dutch East India Company was formed and soon gained control of nearly all the Portuguese ports in Asia. The Netherlands also became the only European country allowed to trade with Japan. By the mid-1600's the Dutch had a near-monopoly on the Asian trade.

Similarly, the Dutch West India Company, founded in 1621, soon controlled much of the slave trade and other shipping in the Atlantic and the Caribbean. One major goal of the Spaniards and Portuguese was the spread of Christianity, but the Protestant Dutch sent no missionaries. Their main interest was successful and profitable trade.

In the Americas, the Dutch were an important power for only a brief period, but their control of islands in the East Indies lasted for nearly three centuries. The forts and fleets of the Dutch East India Company protected its monopoly in pepper and spices. Later, cotton, silk, tea, and coffee made up the bulk of the Dutch trade.

England challenges Spain on the seas. Like the Netherlands, England concentrated on developing its trade and sea power. To trade in Africa, India, or the Americas, however, the English had to fight both rival traders and pirates from other countries. Traders of the English East India Company, chartered by Queen Elizabeth I in 1600, fought both the Portuguese and the French to gain trading posts in India (Chapter 25). English privateers, sailing with royal approval, captured Spanish treasure ships and attacked ports in South America.

English colonists settle in North America. The territories chosen for the first English settlements in the Americas were in areas unclaimed by Spain or Portugal. In the early 1600's, many people migrated from England to the West Indies, Bermuda, and the Virginia settlement founded at Jamestown in 1607. Meanwhile, English ships were exploring the coastline of what came to be called New England. The first colony there was founded at Plymouth in 1620, followed a few years later by the Massachusetts Bay Colony. (The development of the English colonies is discussed in Chapter 19.)

France begins overseas expansion. The French, too, sought territory in the Americas. In the early 1500's, French fishing boats regularly sailed the ocean off Newfoundland. The French king hoped the northwest passage would be found there and sent out several expeditions. In 1534 Jacques Cartier (car-TYAY) reached the St. Lawrence River and claimed for France the land that is now eastern Canada. The first permanent French colony in North America was Quebec, founded as a trading post in 1608 by Samuel de Champlain (sham-PLAYN). Considered the "father of New France," Champlain charted the coast of what is now Maine and established other settlements at Montreal and in Nova Scotia. He explored much of northeastern North America in his efforts to build up the fur trade to support New France.

French traders, trappers, and missionaries were the first Europeans to explore large areas of eastern and central North America. Louis Joliet (joh-lee-ET), a fur trapper, and Jacques Marquette (mar-KET), a priest, traveled by boat in the Great Lakes and down the Wisconsin and Mississippi rivers (1672). The Sieur de la Salle, a French nobleman who had emigrated to New France to become a fur trader, sailed the lower Mississippi River in 1682, starting north of the Ohio River and traveling down to the Gulf of Mexico. La Salle claimed the entire Mississippi valley for France and named it Louisiana for King Louis XIV.

The North American lands claimed by France covered a vast area but were sparsely settled. At scattered trading posts around the Great Lakes and in the Mississippi and Ohio river valleys, French traders bought the valuable furs collected in the wilderness by French and Indian trappers. In the valley of the St. Lawrence River, the king granted large tracts of farmland to French lords. Because the local

Indians, who were mainly hunters, could not be recruited as farm laborers. French peasants were encouraged to migrate to New France. As tenant farmers, they worked on the lands owned by the lords, much as they had done in France.

France finds colonial wealth in Africa and the Caribbean. Except for the trade in furs, France's possessions in North America yielded little wealth. The islands France acquired in the West Indies were far more profitable. Large sugar plantations, worked by slaves imported from Africa through France's trading posts in Senegal, brought in great wealth. France's colony of St. Domingue (doh-MANG), on the island of Hispaniola, was at one time regarded as the richest colonial possession in the world.

Britain destroys France's colonial empire. By the mid-1700's, a general conflict among European nations brought Britain and France into competition not only in Europe but also over their colonial territories in North America, India, and the Caribbean. For the North American colonists, the most significant war was the Seven Years' War (1756–1763), known in American history as the French and Indian War.

In 1757 the British won their first colonial victory over the French in India (Chapter 25). Then British naval and land forces in North America captured the fort that guarded the St. Lawrence River. The city of Quebec, the stronghold of New France, fell in 1759. Britain's superiority at sea decided the outcome of the war. France's island colonies in the Carib-

Colonies in the Americas, Around 1700

By 1700 seven European nations had claimed lands in the Western Hemisphere. What were those nations? Which ones had colonized areas near the English settlements along the Atlantic coast? (See inset map.)

bean and its slave-trading posts in Africa fell to the British. In the Treaty of Paris (1763), France lost nearly all its North American colonial possessions but was given back its rich sugar colonies in the Caribbean. French lands in Canada went to Britain, while the Louisiana territory from the Mississippi River westward went to Spain.

CHECK-UP

1. (a) Why did northern Europeans search for a northwest passage? (b) What were the results of the voyages of Cabot and Hudson?
2. (a) How did the Netherlands become an important commercial power? (b) How did the goals of the Dutch differ from those of Spain and Portugal? (c) Where were the Dutch most influential?
3. (a) What problems did the English face in establishing overseas trade? (b) Where did English colonists first settle in North America?
4. (a) What explorations did the French make in North America? (b) Which of France's colonies were the most profitable?
5. (a) In what parts of the world were France and Britain at war in the mid-1700's? (b) What lands in North America did Britain gain from France?

5 Changes Bring a Revolution in Economic Life

The voyages of exploration brought European nations vast new lands and new resources. The resulting changes in economic life were so great that the years 1450–1700 are often called the Commercial Revolution. Important changes occurred in ways of carrying on business and trade, but even greater changes took place in the basic ways that people thought about money and all the economic aspects of life.

MERCANTILISM

Mercantilist policies strengthen the power of European states. The manor-centered economy of the early Middle Ages had given way to a town-centered economy in the High Middle Ages. This, in turn, gave way to a state-centered economy in early modern times. During the Age of Exploration, European rulers

European Colonies About 1700

KEY

	English
	French
	Dutch
	Portuguese
	Spanish
	Swedish
	Danish

GREENLAND

ICELAND

Hudson Bay

NEWFOUNDLAND

NEW FRANCE

CAPE BRETON I.
Louisbourg

Quebec

Montreal

NOVA SCOTIA

St. Lawrence R.

Great Lakes

Wisconsin R.

NEW ENGLAND

Plymouth

LOUISIANA

Ohio R.

VIRGINIA

Jamestown

Colorado R.

Mississippi R.

NEW SPAIN
(MEXICO)

Gulf of Mexico

BERMUDA

Mexico City
(Tenochtitlán)

Veracruz

BAHAMAS

CUBA

ST. DOMINGUE

SANTO DOMINGO

PUERTO RICO

WEST INDIES

JAMAICA

Caribbean Sea

PACIFIC OCEAN

NEW ANDALUSIA
(VENEZUELA)

TRINIDAD

ATLANTIC OCEAN

DARIEN
(PANAMA)

Orinoco R.

GUIANA

N

NEW GRANADA
(COLOMBIA)

Amazon R.

to Portugal,
1654

NEW CASTILE
(PERU)

Bahia

Lima

Cuzco

BRAZIL

São Vicente

NEW ESTREMADURA
(CHILE)

LA PLATA

Buenos Aires

SCALE

0   1,000 mi

0   1,000 km

Swedish and Dutch Colonies About 1650

Fort Orange
(Albany)

NEW NETHERLAND

NEW ENGLAND

Hudson River

Delaware R.

N

New Amsterdam
(New York)

Fort Christina
(Wilmington)

MARYLAND

NEW SWEDEN

ATLANTIC OCEAN

Delaware Bay

VIRGINIA

SCALE

0   100 mi

0   100 km

increased their power enormously. The combination of economic growth and expanding royal power gave rise to the theory called **mercantilism.** Mercantilists believed that the power of the state could be greatly enlarged by directing economic activities according to certain basic principles.

One mercantilist principle was that the state should accumulate wealth in the form of bullion (gold and silver). In the 1600's a ruler's power was judged by the luxury of the royal court and the size of the armed forces. As armies were made up mostly of hired soldiers called mercenaries, a ruler short of cash could not afford to build a large navy or recruit a large army. Royal power therefore depended on a plentiful supply of bullion. To increase the country's supply of bullion, rulers encouraged exports, which brought money into the country. To stop precious metals from leaving the country, they discouraged or forbade buying foreign goods.

Colonies played an important part in mercantilist thinking. Mercantilists sought colonies that would be profitable for the home country. The colony was expected to supply wealth, either gold or silver from its mines (which added to the bullion supply) or valuable products. These might be spices from the East Indies, sugar from the Americas, or slaves from Africa. Mercantilists naturally insisted that colonies buy goods from the home country, not from other lands or even other colonies. For instance, for Mexican chocolate to reach Peru, it first had to be shipped to Seville in Spain, then sent back to the colonies. Merchants and shipowners in Spain, not the colonies, made most of the profits.

Joint-stock companies are formed. It took large amounts of money to send ships on the long voyages to Asia or the Americas. Moreover, while profits could be great, so were the risks. Many ships never completed the long and dangerous ocean voyage. Few individual merchants could afford the high costs of an Asian voyage or the loss of a ship at sea. To finance trading voyages, a new type of business arrangement, the joint-stock company, developed. It operated in much the same way as a modern corporation: Investors purchased shares of stock that gave them part ownership in the business. This arrangement attracted large amounts of money and at the same time reduced the risk to individual investors.

Two of the most successful joint-stock companies were the English East India Company and the Dutch East India Company. In one very profitable voyage, the English company returned 220 percent to its investors. For centuries the Dutch East India Company paid its stockholders annual dividends averaging 18 percent.

Rulers encouraged the formation of such joint-stock companies by granting these enterprises certain privileges in return for a fixed share of the companies' profits. For example, Queen Elizabeth I was a shareholder in the voyage Francis Drake made around the world in the *Golden Hind* in 1577–1580. With her share of the profits from this venture, Elizabeth paid off all of England's foreign debts, balanced the national budget, and had a large sum left over to invest.

A new outlook emphasizes hard work and thrift. To the new class of rich traders, wealth was money and goods, whereas under feudalism, wealth had meant land. The wealthy middle-class merchants believed that money should be used to make more money. Instead of leaving their savings idle or spending money on luxuries, they wanted to put it to work. For the middle class, hard work and thrift were virtues. This outlook was very different from that of most rulers and aristocrats, who looked down on money-making and those who took part in it.

The Dutch burghers were typical of the new class of wealthy merchants — tough-minded, hardworking individuals out to make money. They found efficient ways to lower costs, drove hard bargains to get the maximum profits, and tried to capture more and more of the market from competitors. The Dutch fought to sail their ships everywhere on the globe — to fish off all coasts, to exchange goods with all peoples, and to deal in every type of economic good.

Mercantilism leads to rivalries at sea. European rulers and states competed fiercely for the new wealth of the colonies throughout the world. In the sixteenth century the Portuguese grew rich by monopolizing the trade in African slaves and Asian spices. Spain also prospered from the share of treasure its rulers received from the Americas. Rulers in other European nations realized that one way to weaken Spain was to cut off the flow of bullion from the Americas.

Both patriotism and the hope of a fortune brought pirates and buccaneers to the Caribbean to prey on Spanish treasure ships. Merchant privateers smuggled goods into Spanish colonies, plundered towns along the Caribbean coast, and captured ships loaded with silver, gold, and gems from Spanish colonial mines. Dutch, English, and, later, French joint-stock companies, with royal approval, waged naval war against Spain.

The Spanish monopoly in the Americas began to crack in 1562. A daring English merchant, John Hawkins, defied Spanish trade laws and brought European goods and African slaves to the Spanish settlements in the Caribbean. The colonists welcomed him, and he sold his cargo at a good profit. In 1577 Hawkins's cousin, Francis Drake, sailed his ship *Golden Hind* into the Pacific, captured Spanish ships, and seized a year's output of Peruvian silver in Panama. Unwilling to run the risk of capture by returning to England across the Atlantic, Drake sailed westward across the Pacific. Three years later he completed the second circumnavigation of the globe.

Before long, the French and the Dutch also began to prey on Spanish shipping, particularly the ships carrying gold and silver. In 1628, Admiral Piet Heyn (PEET HINE) of the Dutch West India Company captured the Spanish silver fleet in the Caribbean. The treasure included four million gold and silver ducats, which helped the Dutch finance their war against Spanish rule and made Heyn a Dutch national hero.

UPHEAVALS IN THE EUROPEAN ECONOMY

Inflation damages Europe's economy. The Americas had been a new and unexpected source of great wealth for Spain and Portugal — gold from the Inca treasure and the mines of Brazil, silver from the rich mines of Mexico and Peru (including what is now Bolivia). This huge new supply of precious metals was desirable from a mercantilist point of view, but it created problems. Wealthy Europeans bought more and more goods and food. As these products became scarce, prices began to rise. At the same time, population throughout Europe was growing, and more people needed more food and other goods. This too made prices rise — particularly for basic foods like bread and cereal grains.

The increasing prices, or *inflation,* affected different groups of people in different ways. Landowning nobles, who received fixed rents from peasants, could buy less with the same income. City workers could buy less food with their wages as prices continued to rise. Merchants, on the other hand, often profited by charging higher and higher prices for the goods they sold. Because people were demanding more goods than Europe could produce, foreign trade boomed.

The profit motive brings changes in agriculture. The demand for more food led some English landlords to change the traditional ways of using farmland. They took away the common lands[4] from the peasants or raised rents on farmlands so that poorer peasants could no longer afford them. Thousands of peasants had to leave the land their families had always farmed.

The landlords then hired peasants as laborers at low wages or rented the land to the prosperous yeoman farmers. Both the landowners and the yeomen profited from this change in agriculture. The peasants who had lost their land, however, made up a whole new group of homeless poor, who had to find work. Like trade, agriculture had become commercial — farm land and farm labor had become things that were bought and sold. This marked a great change from farming in the Middle Ages, when farm workers were bound to the land on the lords' estates.

Trade lays the foundations for capitalism. The origins of modern capitalism can be seen

---

[4]In most villages a plot of land, the commons, was set aside for community use as pasture land or farm plots.

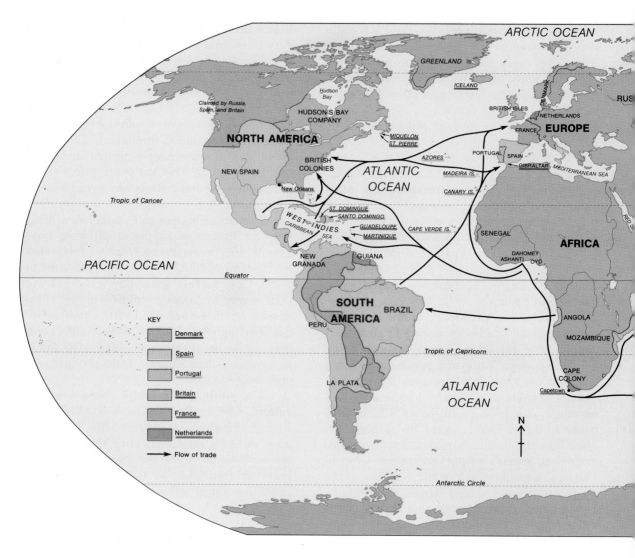

World Trade, 1763

European merchant ships followed the routes shown here as they carried on trade around the world in the late eighteenth century. What country had colonies in the East Indies? Describe the extent of the British colonial empire during this time.

first in the busy town life and prosperous trade that developed in the late Middle Ages. *Capital* includes money and goods — such as land and plantations, ships and shops — that are used to make more money. *Capitalism* is the economic system that rests on the private ownership and use (or investment) of capital. During the late Middle Ages, new business practices in Italy stimulated the development of capitalism in a number of ways.

Profits from trade and interest on loans enabled Italian merchants and bankers to accumulate large amounts of capital, which they reinvested in their own businesses or in other enterprises. Merchants also entered into agreements that allowed them to pool their money and expand their businesses. As business activity increased, merchants devised bookkeeping systems, which were necessary to run banks and businesses on a large scale. The development of banking and the extending of credit (page 160) also made business dealings easier.

The Commercial Revolution promotes a capitalist economy. The capitalist practices of the Middle Ages became more widespread and well established during the Age of Exploration. The mercantile capitalism of the 1600's and

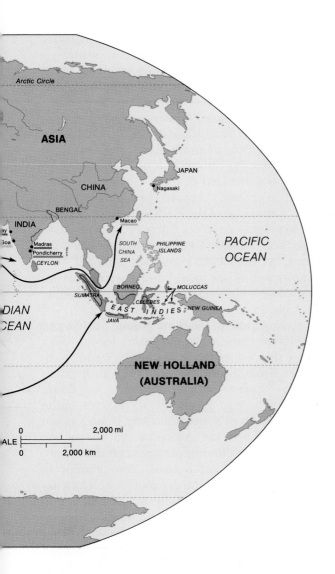

Arctic Circle

ASIA

JAPAN

CHINA

Nagasaki

BENGAL

INDIA

Macao

Madras
Pondicherry

Goa

CEYLON

SOUTH
CHINA
SEA

PHILIPPINE
ISLANDS

PACIFIC
OCEAN

BORNEO

MOLUCCAS

SUMATRA

CELEBES

NEW GUINEA

EAST INDIES

JAVA

INDIAN
OCEAN

NEW HOLLAND
(AUSTRALIA)

0   2,000 mi

SCALE

0   2,000 km

1700's differed from modern capitalism but established the basis for its development.

Capitalism can be regarded as having three major characteristics:

1. Private ownership. In a capitalistic system, capital (money and property) belongs to individuals, who are free to decide what to do with it. They may bank money to draw a fixed rate of interest, risk their capital in business, or buy shares (or stock) in a company of their choosing.

2. Profit motive. Capitalists believe that when enough people want a particular product, there will be producers who will supply it because they want to make a profit. The demand for sugar, for example, led to the development of plantations to supply it. A company produces goods and services to make profits for those who have invested in it — that is, its owners. The profit motive — the wish to make a profit — is an essential part of capitalism.

3. Market economy. In capitalism a money value is placed on all forms of property. That is, just about everything — land, goods, people's time and labor — can be bought and sold. Buyers and sellers of goods and services meet to exchange these things in what economists call the market. The prices of goods or services depend, therefore, on how much people want and how much is available for them to buy.

By the end of the Commercial Revolution, urban Europeans thought in terms of a **market economy,** a way of living that depended on buying and selling goods and services. This way of thinking was perhaps the major change of the Commercial Revolution. Markets and trade had flourished in medieval times, and people owned great wealth. But people generally did not think of their wealth as something to invest at a profit. When royal governments invested in the voyages of exploration, and when nobles and merchants invested in joint-stock companies, it was a new way to use wealth.

Similarly, in medieval society people did not think of their land or their labor as things that could be bought and sold. Monarchs and the feudal nobility, in a sense, "owned" the land that they inherited or took by force. The idea of selling that land to make a profit was simply not part of medieval thinking. Most common people were not free to sell their labor to an employer. Peasants or serfs owed their labor to the lord or landowner who owned the land they farmed. They had no choice as to where or for whom they would work. Apprentices and indentured servants owed their labor to a master. No one bargained for wages or better working conditions. When landlords took over the common lands, the homeless peasants were the beginning of a real labor force.

Land, labor, capital, and management are the basic factors in producing goods that people want. In traditional society, people did not think in terms of buying and selling their land and labor or of making a profit from their capital. Neither did they think of themselves as managers of these resources. The Commercial Revolution brought a change in this thinking. While modern industrial capitalism did not develop until late in the eighteenth century, it had its beginnings in the mercantile capitalism of the Commercial Revolution.

A CHANGED AND CHANGING WORLD

The Age of Exploration and the Commercial Revolution caused great and lasting changes. For the first time people could think of the world in global terms. Also for the first time, people began to look at their lives in economic terms — buying and selling, making a profit. Huge regions of the world began to come under European influence and control. Vast changes occurred as people were exposed to one another's ideas, beliefs, and customs.

Europe becomes the center of world trade. Europe experienced an enormous expansion of business activity. The supply of money increased, trade expanded, and people invested in large-scale business enterprises (joint-stock companies). All of these developments stimulated the growth of capitalism.

The Commercial Revolution put Europe at the center of worldwide trade. In the expanding economy Europeans were investors, bankers, and profit-takers. Whatever took place in the banking and marketing centers of Europe affected people all over the world. For example, when European capitalists invested in Brazilian dyewood, Bolivian silver mines, or the hides of Argentine cattle, they changed the lives of American Indians in countless ways. In Africa the slave traffic had a devastating effect on culture and society (Chapter 13).

Europeans drank Asian tea sweetened with sugar grown in America by African slaves. They paid for spices and silk from Asia with African and Brazilian gold or Mexican and Peruvian silver. Rich Europeans hung Chinese wallpaper in their homes, collected jade carvings, and wore the long Muslim garment called "pyjamas." The demand for "india" ink, for calico (from Calicut), and for Chinese porcelain ("china") grew so great that industries were set up in Europe to produce similar goods.

The center of business shifts to northern Europe. The new trade routes that opened up during the Age of Exploration broke the Arab-Venetian monopoly on trade with Asia. The Italian city-states lost their position as Europe's leading commercial centers to the European states on the Atlantic coast. Portugal and Spain were the first to profit from the new trade routes, but the Netherlands and England gradually took the lead in trade. London and Amsterdam became the centers of commercial life.

Knowledge of the earth increases. The Age of Exploration and the Commercial Revolution produced a flood of new information about geography, animal life, plants, and minerals. New knowledge of the world and its resources inspired a revolution in science (described further in Chapter 18).

New kinds of foods are grown. Settlers and explorers found new and exotic foods, which were shipped from one part of the world to another. From the tropical Indies — both East and West — Europe brought ever-increasing quantities of colonial goods: sugar, rice, tea, cacao (the bean from which chocolate is made), and tobacco. From the Americas the rest of the world received four important vegetables — potatoes, corn, sweet potatoes, and manioc (a plant with a large starchy root from which tapioca is made). The potato and corn thrived in Europe, manioc in Africa, and the sweet potato in Asia, increasing the food supply on all three continents. The Asian orange and banana flourished in the Americas. So did the sheep, chickens, pigs, horses, and cattle brought to the Americas by European settlers.

Shifts occur in the world's population. The balance of world population also began to shift once Europeans began to settle among Africans, American Indians, and Asians. The increase in the white population was greater than that in any other group. This was true in part because disease and other hardships decimated other populations. Between 1493 and 1700, epidemics wiped out millions, particularly among the Indians of the Americas. The slave trade claimed the lives of millions of Africans.

Although plagues struck the port cities of Europe, the European population kept growing because of an improved food supply. People

NEW KNOWLEDGE OF THE WORLD

A new awareness of the world was revealed in the work of artists who lived during the Age of Exploration. A parrot taken to Venice from the West Indies was a subject for the Venetian artist Vittore Carpaccio in 1507 (above). *The Geographer* (right) was painted by the Dutchman Jan Vermeer in the mid-1600's.

from Europe could emigrate to colonies around the world. The Europeans' descendants came to occupy most of North America and parts of South America, southern Africa, and Australia. Perhaps the most significant consequence of the Age of Exploration was the settlement of the lands in the Western Hemisphere by peoples of diverse races and nationalities. All the way from Argentina to Canada, new nations with multicultural societies began to emerge.

CHECK-UP

1. Vocabulary: *mercantilism, inflation, capital, capitalism, market economy.*
2. (a) As mercantilism was practiced in Europe, why was the accumulation of gold and silver bullion important? (b) What part did colonies play in mercantilist goals?
3. What were the advantages of joint-stock companies in sponsoring ships on long voyages?
4. (a) What were the chief sources of Spain's and Portugal's colonial wealth? (b) What did the Dutch and English do to challenge Spain?
5. (a) What brought about increases in prices in Europe? (b) What groups benefited?
6. (a) What changes occurred in European agriculture? (b) How did these create a supply of labor?
7. (a) What capitalist practices grew up in medieval Italy? (b) What are three characteristics of capitalism?
8. What lasting changes did the Age of Exploration and the Commercial Revolution bring about in (a) trade, (b) diet, (c) population?

Chapter 16 Review

Summary

The great social changes that occurred in Europe during the Renaissance and Reformation paved the way for European exploration and expansion in all parts of the world. As a result of the voyages of the Age of Exploration (1415–1620), Europeans found a water route to India, made contact with the American continents and the Pacific Ocean, and, for the first time, circumnavigated the globe. Merchants competed for trade in Asia, Africa, and the Americas.

The Portuguese took the lead in these voyages and were the first to establish colonies overseas. Spain conquered the Aztecs and Incas and gained an empire that included southwestern North America and much of South America. The Netherlands, Britain, and France established colonies farther north in North America.

Mercantilist policies led European states to build foreign trade, accumulate wealth in the form of gold and silver, and establish colonies whose resources could be exploited. The social and economic changes that took place in Europe and in the areas it influenced changed the nature of the European and world economies. This new economic outlook emphasized the money value of land and labor, and the investment of capital to make a profit. The period known as the Commercial Revolution saw the beginning of the modern market economy.

Vocabulary Review

1. Write the sentences listed below on a sheet of paper. In each sentence, fill in the blank with one of the following words: *bullion, capital, capitalism, creole, inflation, market economy, mercantilism, monopoly.*
(a) __?__ is the economic system that is based on a free market and open competition.
(b) A large quantity of gold or silver is called __?__ .
(c) __?__ is an economic system that depends on the buying and selling of goods and services.
(d) __?__ was an economic policy that stressed the accumulation of gold and silver, the founding of colonies, and profit from foreign trade.
(e) A person descended from one of the Spanish or Portuguese colonists in the Americas was known as a __?__ .
(f) Wealth or property that is used to produce more wealth is called __?__ .
(g) A scarcity of goods may cause rising prices, or __?__ .
(h) __?__ is the control of all trade in a certain product.

2. Distinguish between the terms in each of the following pairs:
(a) Treaty of Paris; Treaty of Tordesillas.
(b) Commercial Revolution; Age of Exploration.
(c) trading post; plantation.
(d) caravel; astrolabe.

People to Identify

Identify the following people. Name the country with which each was connected and tell why he or she was important.
1. Vasco da Gama
2. Henry the Navigator
3. Atahualpa
4. Jacques Cartier
5. Moctezuma
6. Samuel de Champlain
7. Vasco Núñez de Balboa
8. Francisco de Coronado
9. Bartolomé de Las Casas
10. Henry Hudson
11. Queen Isabella
12. Ferdinand Magellan

Relating Geography and History

1. **Locating places.** Locate each of the following on a map in this chapter:
(a) Calicut
(b) Ceuta
(c) Brazil
(d) Peru
(e) Mexico
(f) Cape of Good Hope
(g) New France
(h) Louisiana
2. **Making maps.** On an outline map of the world, show and label the voyages of the Spanish, Portuguese, French, English, and Dutch explorers discussed in this chapter. Use the map

on pages 352–353 as a model. Also label the seven continents, equator, oceans, and major seas.

Discussion Questions

1. What factors brought about the Age of Exploration in fifteenth-century Europe?

2. (a) Why was Portugal the first European country to make long voyages and establish overseas colonies? (b) What role did Prince Henry have in making Portugal a leading sea power?

3. Explain how Spanish conquest and colonization affected the American Indians.

4. Compare French, Dutch, and English exploration of North America. (a) Name the early explorers. (b) Explain each country's motives for exploration. (c) List the areas claimed by each.

5. The Age of Exploration and the Commercial Revolution together resulted in a world that had a Europe-centered economy. Explain.

Reading Primary Sources

Cortés and his soldiers were surprised at the wealth of the Aztec civilization. The following description of the marketplace of Tenochtitlán was written by Bernal Díaz, one of the men who accompanied Cortés. Read the passage. Then answer the questions that follow.

When we arrived at the great square, we were struck by the throngs of people and the amount of merchandise they displayed. . . . Each kind of merchandise . . . had its place marked out. Let us start with the dealers in gold, silver, and precious stones, feathers, cloth, and embroidered goods, and . . . men and women to be sold as slaves. . . . Then there were merchants who sold homespun clothing, cotton, and thread, and others who sold cacao. . . . In another section they had skins of tigers, lions, deer, and other animals. . . .

We will go on and tell of those who sold beans and other vegetables, of those who sold fowls, turkeys, rabbits, deer, ducks, young dogs, and other things of that sort. . . . Let us talk of the sellers of fruit and of those who sold cooked food, and all the kinds of pottery . . . from huge jars to tiny jugs. . . . And there were those who sold honey and honey cakes and other sweets that they made from nuts, and sellers of lumber, and sellers of firewood. . . .

There were soldiers among us who had been in many parts of the world, . . . who said that they had never before seen a marketplace so large and so well laid out, and so filled with people.

(a) What merchandise from the Tenochtitlán marketplace would you be likely to find in a shopping mall today? (b) List some of the foods of the Aztecs' diet, as shown by the products displayed in the marketplace. (c) According to the Spanish soldiers, how did the Tenochtitlán marketplace compare with others they had seen?

Skill Activities

1. Finding cause and effect. Read each pair of sentences listed below. Decide which of the two statements is the cause and which is the effect. Write a sentence for each pair explaining why you answered as you did.

(a) Europeans needed spices to preserve food. Portuguese merchants sought a sea route to the Spice Islands.

(b) European rulers of the 1600's needed gold and silver to build up the power of their states. European states were rivals in establishing overseas colonies.

(c) Moctezuma believed that Cortés and his men might be gods or messengers from Quetzalcóatl. Aztec legend told that Quetzalcóatl had sailed away to the east and would one day return.

(d) Voyages to America and Asia were risky and expensive. Joint-stock companies were formed to attract investors and reduce their financial risks.

2. Reports. Find information about one of the following topics and prepare a report: (a) the legend of El Dorado; (b) the practice of privateering; (c) advances in navigation; (d) how joint-stock companies worked; (e) the legend of the Seven Cities of Cibola; (f) advantages and disadvantages of the mercantile system.

Elizabeth I used her power with wisdom and courage. During her reign England enjoyed prosperity and order and successfully challenged the Spanish empire. Many portraits of Elizabeth exist; one of the finest, seen below, was the work of an unknown artist.

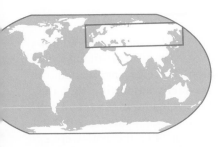

The Growth of European States

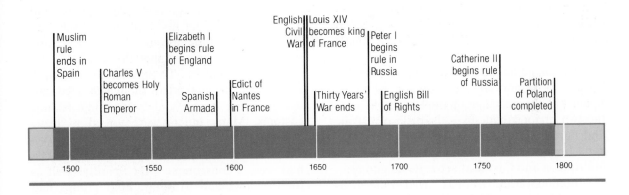

| Muslim rule ends in Spain | Charles V becomes Holy Roman Emperor | Elizabeth I begins rule of England | Spanish Armada | Edict of Nantes in France | English Civil War | Louis XIV becomes king of France | Thirty Years' War ends | Peter I begins rule in Russia | English Bill of Rights | Catherine II begins rule of Russia | Partition of Poland completed |

1500   1550   1600   1650   1700   1750   1800

During the period of the Renaissance, the Reformation, and the Commercial Revolution, the political life of Europe underwent great changes. Feudalism was disappearing, and the foundations of modern states were being laid.

Monarchs in the sixteenth and seventeenth centuries exercised greater authority than had medieval rulers. Many rulers gained control over the clergy and the nobility in their lands. By the eighteenth century, monarchs were concerned mainly with securing power and territory. While not all medieval attitudes, practices, or institutions had disappeared, several European states were stronger and more unified than the feudal monarchies of the Middle Ages.

This chapter describes the development of early modern states in Europe.

CHAPTER OUTLINE

1 Spain Dominates Europe for a Century

2 The Bourbons Come to Power in France

3 The Thirty Years' War Disrupts Europe

4 Absolute Monarchy Triumphs in France

5 Parliament Gains Power in England

6 States Develop in Eastern Europe

1 Spain Dominates Europe for a Century

During the Middle Ages, Spain had prospered under Muslim rule. The Christian kingdoms in the north, however, were determined to regain the rest of the peninsula, and gradually their Reconquest succeeded (page 173). By the late 1400's, only Granada was still under Muslim control. The Christian kingdoms in Spain were Castile (including Leon), Aragon, and Navarre (map, page 174). In the sixteenth century these Christian kingdoms were unified, and Spain became the leading state in Europe. Within a century, however, Spanish power declined.

Ferdinand and Isabella centralize power in Spain. An important step toward a united Spain was the marriage in 1469 of the heirs to the two major kingdoms — Isabella of Castile and Ferdinand of Aragon. Ferdinand and Isabella became skillful, strong co-rulers, governing Aragon and Castile as separate kingdoms.

Ferdinand and Isabella faced some difficult problems in building a unified state. Spanish nobles had become very independent during the centuries of the Reconquest. To reduce this power, the monarchs removed prominent nobles from important government positions, destroyed castles built without royal permission, and forbade private warfare. The rulers won the support of other nobles by allowing them to marry members of the royal family and by giving them honorary, though unimportant, offices.

Isabella and Ferdinand were known as "the Catholic kings," and Isabella in particular used the Church to strengthen her rule in Castile. The Church in Spain, over which the Pope had little authority, came under royal control, and Ferdinand and Isabella appointed high church officials. With royal support, the Inquisition (page 341) in Spain used harsh methods against heretics and Jews. Ferdinand and Isabella also waged war against the Muslims in Granada, and in 1492 it fell to Christian forces, completing the Reconquest.

Muslims and Jews are persecuted in Spain. The long struggle to drive out the Muslims had tended to make the Spaniards intolerant of other religions. Wishing Spain to be wholly Catholic, Ferdinand and Isabella ordered Jews and Muslims to convert to Christianity. The Spanish Inquisition, however, persecuted the Jewish converts severely, suspecting that they still practiced their religion in secret. Thousands of Jews were tortured; some were burned at the stake. Finally, in 1492, the Jews were expelled from Spain.

The Muslims who remained after the fall of Granada were at first told they could keep their religion and customs, but in 1502 the Catholic rulers insisted that the Muslims convert to Christianity. To stay in their homes, many Muslims converted, though they continued to speak Arabic and follow some Islamic customs. Many others were forced to leave Spain.

The policies of Ferdinand and Isabella had serious consequences for Spain as well as for the Jews and Muslims. Both groups had contributed substantially to Spanish arts, culture, and intellectual life. The Jews also had played an important role as business leaders

Charles V became king of Spain at the age of nineteen (in 1516) and Holy Roman Emperor in 1519. No European monarch had ever ruled so much land. This portrait was painted by the artist Titian.

and merchants. The Muslims had developed advanced farming methods, which had improved Spanish agriculture. The policies of Spain's rulers thus weakened the economy at a critical point in Spanish history.

The Hapsburgs come to power in Spain. Charles, the grandson of Isabella and Ferdinand, became king of Spain in 1516 (page 353). This brought the influential Hapsburg family of Austria into power in Spain. The Hapsburgs traced their roots back to the thirteenth century when Rudolf I of Hapsburg gained control over Austria. Hapsburg princes gradually took over the lands of weaker lords. Skillfully arranged marriages connected the family with several royal families in Europe and added to Hapsburg territory. In 1477 Maximilian I of Hapsburg married Mary of Burgundy, whose lands included the rich provinces of the Netherlands. Their son Philip married Juana, the daughter of Ferdinand and Isabella; Charles, the new Spanish king, was their son.

Charles's inheritance of the Spanish throne gave the Hapsburgs control of Spain and its growing overseas empire. When his grandfather Maximilian died in 1519, Charles also inherited the Hapsburgs' Austrian territories. That same year he was elected Holy Roman Emperor.[1] Not even Charlemagne had ruled so vast an empire.

Charles V has overwhelming responsibilities. The Spanish at first regarded Charles as a foreigner, but he gradually won their loyalty and continued his grandparents' efforts to unify and strengthen Spain. As king of Spain, Charles V ruled a country brimming with vitality. During his reign, Spanish adventurers in the Americas conquered Mexico and Peru and explored much of what is now the southern United States. Treasure taken from the Aztecs and Incas and silver and gold from American mines began to pour into Spain.

In Europe, however, Charles faced problems that he could not solve. The German princes who had become Lutherans (page 338) refused to acknowledge the emperor's authority. Spain attempted to expand in Italy, bringing on war with France. Charles had also become involved in protecting Hapsburg lands in Austria from the Ottoman Turks, who invaded central Europe and besieged Vienna during the 1500's (page 221). As Holy Roman Emperor, Charles V felt he had the responsibility of defending Christian Europe from the Muslims. The struggle between the Ottoman Empire and the Hapsburgs continued to drain Hapsburg energies and wealth for more than a century.

Eventually, exhausted by these many challenges, Charles gave up his throne in 1556 and retired to a Spanish monastery. His brother Ferdinand I inherited the eastern Hapsburg lands — Austria, Hungary,[2] and Bohemia — and the crown of the Holy Roman Emperor. Spain, the Netherlands, and Spain's lands in America and in Italy went to Charles's son, Philip II. (See map, page 377.)

Philip II strengthens royal authority. Philip was king from 1556 to 1598, ruling as an absolute monarch. His goals were to strengthen both Spanish power and the power of the Roman Catholic Church. In Madrid, the new capital, Philip set up councils to deal with Spain's overseas possessions, with the country's finances and defense, and with the Inquisition. Both at home and in dealing with other nations, Philip was dedicated to increasing the authority of the Church.

The Inquisition continues in Spain. Like earlier rulers, Philip wanted Spain to be entirely Catholic. Protestants were ordered to convert to Catholicism or leave Spain. Many were tried before the Inquisition and were urged to renounce their beliefs. Those who refused were imprisoned; some were tortured and executed. As Protestantism had not taken deep roots in Spain, it soon disappeared.

Philip also lashed out at the descendants of the Muslims of Granada, called Moriscos. These converted Muslims still retained much of their ancient culture. Some continued to practice Islam in secret. When Philip banned the use of Arabic and imposed other restrictions in

---

[1] As king of Spain, Charles was Charles I. He was the fifth Holy Roman Emperor named Charles, however, and "Charles V" is the title by which he is most commonly known.

[2] Much of Hungary had come under Ottoman rule after the Battle of Mohács (1526), but its throne was claimed by the Hapsburgs.

1569, the Moriscos of Granada rebelled. After a cruel struggle, the Moriscos were subdued and sent to other parts of Spain. Their children were taken from them and put in Christian homes. In 1609 Philip's son (Philip III) expelled the 300,000 remaining Moriscos.

Christian forces war against the Turks. Philip was also in conflict with the Muslims because of the Turkish pirates who were attacking ships in the Mediterranean Sea. Fearing that the Ottoman Turks would expand into the western Mediterranean, Philip joined forces with the Pope and the Republic of Venice against the Ottoman Empire. In 1571 the combined Christian fleets fought the Ottomans in a great naval battle near the seaport of Lepanto (lih-PAHN-toh) in Greece. The Christian forces decisively defeated the Turks and freed some 10,000 Christians held as slaves on the Turkish ships. The Christians failed to follow up on the victory, however, and the Ottoman Empire remained a power in the Mediterranean for another 300 years.

Portugal is united with Spain. Philip successfully united the entire Iberian peninsula by adding Portugal to the lands ruled by Spain. On the death of the Portuguese king in 1580, Philip was next in line to the throne. The Portuguese had no wish to be ruled by Spain, but Philip sent troops into Portugal and easily overcame all resistance. Portugal came under the Spanish crown, and Philip acquired Portugal's vast overseas empire.

Dutch Protestants rebel against Spanish rule. Philip's empire in Europe included the Netherlands (the present-day Netherlands and Belgium). His religious and economic policies there, however, made Spanish rule hated by many. Believing that Spain should profit from its holdings in the Netherlands, Philip increased taxes and restricted Dutch trade to give an advantage to Spanish merchants. He also established the Inquisition there in an attempt to impose Catholicism on the growing number of Calvinists in the northern provinces.

In 1566 the Dutch began a rebellion that lasted many years. Its leader was William, Prince of Orange, known as "William the Silent." Eventually the seven northern provinces, which were Protestant and Dutch-speaking, became the United Netherlands. They declared themselves a republic in 1581, but it was many years before Spain recognized their independence. The ten southern provinces, whose inhabitants were mostly Catholic, joined in the rebellion but later returned to Spanish rule as the Spanish Netherlands.

Spain clashes with England. The war in the Netherlands brought Spain into open conflict with England. Philip had long wanted to restore Catholicism in England, and in 1554 he married Mary I, England's Catholic queen. They had no children, however, and Mary's Protestant half-sister Elizabeth inherited the English throne on Mary's death in 1558. Philip proposed marriage to Elizabeth several times but was never accepted.

When the Dutch revolt broke out, Queen Elizabeth sent troops to aid the Protestant rebels. Philip was enraged by this action, as well as by the English attacks on Spanish treasure ships and by the execution of Mary, Queen of Scots (page 387).

In 1588 Philip sent a fleet, which he called the Invincible Armada, to invade England (map, next page). About 130 ships, carrying more than 3,000 cannon, set sail for England. Instead of the glorious victory Philip expected, however, the Spanish fleet met with disaster. Poor planning and storms prevented the ships from picking up troops and supplies in the Netherlands. Moreover, the English ships were smaller and quicker, and their captains and crews were more skillful sailors. In a sea battle in the English Channel, the Armada was soundly defeated, and several ships were sunk. Storms blew many of the remaining Spanish ships into the North Sea. To return home, the commander of the Armada took his crippled fleet around Scotland and Ireland. More ships were wrecked, and only about half of the original Armada returned to Spain. The defeat of the Armada was a terrible blow to Spanish prestige and to Philip's power.

Spain's power declines. In the middle of the sixteenth century, Spain had been regarded as the foremost power in Europe. Wealth from the Americas poured into Spain's treasury and financed its wars. Within a century, however, Spain lost most of its power, and in 1700 the Spanish Hapsburg line came to an end. What caused the decline?

Europe About 1560

In 1556, Emperor Charles V divided his vast empire between his brother Ferdinand, ruler of Austria, and his son Philip, the king of Spain. Find the lands that each ruler received. Why did France fear Hapsburg power? Note that the map shows the route taken by the Spanish Armada. How did the surviving Spanish ships make their way back to their homeland?

1. The cost of war. The wars fought by Charles V and Philip II were a terrible drain on Spain's resources. Spain itself did not have a strong enough economy to support these wars.

2. The neglect of trade and industry. Unlike other Western European states, Spain lacked an enterprising middle class of merchants and business leaders. The persecution and expulsion of Jews and Muslims had deprived Spain of many of its most industrious and productive citizens. Furthermore, Spanish society placed a low value on commerce and industry. Young men were encouraged to become soldiers or to enter the clergy or government service — occupations that contributed little to production or trade. Many ambitious young men left Spain to seek wealth and adventure in the Americas.

3. Changes in agriculture. Because trade in wool was profitable, the Spanish government granted special privileges to sheep raisers. Land that could have been used for farming was set aside for grazing sheep. As herds grew larger, overgrazing destroyed shrubs and grasses on hillsides, resulting in erosion. Farmers grew discouraged and gave up farming. Moreover, the Muslims' advanced farming and irrigation methods were abandoned when they were forced to leave the country. Food shortages developed, and eventually Spain had to use some of its wealth to pay for food imports.

4. The dependence on temporary wealth. Much of Spain's wealth in the sixteenth century was short-term, consisting of Aztec and Inca treasure and gold and silver from the newly discovered American mines. The Spanish did not invest this wealth but used it to pay for wars and to import food and manufactured goods. Gold and silver pouring into Europe caused inflation (page 365), forcing Spain to pay more and more for the products it had to purchase.

Successful raids by English and Dutch pirates and smuggling in the Americas soon reduced Spain's income from its colonies. Moreover, the amount of silver mined in Spain's colonies gradually decreased. By the middle of the seventeenth century, Hapsburg Spain was poor and weak. It never again threatened to dominate Europe.

CHECK-UP

1. (a) What steps did Ferdinand and Isabella take to strengthen central authority in Spain? (b) What were their policies toward Muslims and Jews? (c) What effects did these policies have on Spain?
2. (a) Who were the Hapsburgs? (b) How did they gain control of Spain?
3. (a) What lands were ruled by Charles V? (b) What problems did he face? (c) When Charles gave up the throne, how were the Hapsburg lands divided?
4. (a) What were the main goals of Philip II? (b) What two events during his reign brought increased power to Spain?
5. How did Philip meet with failure in (a) the Netherlands? (b) England?
6. What were the causes of Spain's loss of power in the seventeenth century?

2 The Bourbons Come to Power in France

Since the late Middle Ages, French rulers had tended to be absolute monarchs. Royal authority was unchecked by a parliament or even by powerful nobles. French rulers imposed royal law and taxes throughout their realm and promoted trade to make the kingdom stronger. They developed a professional army and used it to uphold their authority. From the sixteenth century on, the Bourbon family of kings strengthened absolute monarchy in France. At the same time, the Bourbons laid the foundations of a modern centralized state.

Religious wars rage in France. France was one of the states in which the Reformation caused conflict and upheaval. The French monarchs remained Catholic, but many French nobles became Protestants. They did so partly for religious reasons and partly to weaken the French monarchy. Rival Protestant and Catholic nobles competed for control in France. Catherine de Médicis,[3] mother of three kings

who ruled France between 1559 and 1589, used her political skill to try to maintain a balance between them. In 1562, however, a full-scale civil war erupted between Huguenots (French Protestants) and Catholics. For more than thirty years, France was swept by bloody struggles.

On August 24, 1572, many Protestant nobles were gathered in Paris for the wedding of Henry of Navarre, one of their leaders. Perhaps encouraged by Catherine, mobs of Parisians began a massacre of the Huguenots. The riots and killings spread, and thousands of Huguenots were killed in what came to be called the St. Bartholomew's Day Massacre.

Henry IV's rule brings toleration and prosperity. In 1589 Henry of Navarre inherited the throne as Henry IV and tried to restore peace after the years of violence. Since the French would not accept a Huguenot king, Henry converted to Catholicism. Henry was the first king from the Bourbon family. He was courageous and intelligent and became one of the best-loved monarchs in French history. To protect the Huguenots and end religious conflict in France, Henry issued the Edict of Nantes

---

[3]Catherine was a member of the Medici family (page 328). She married King Henry II of France, who died in 1559. Three of her sons ruled as kings of France. Henry III, her youngest son, ruled from 1574 to 1589.

(NAHNT) in 1598. This edict (or order) granted the Huguenots a large measure of religious freedom, equal treatment under the law, and equal opportunity to hold positions in the government. Such a policy of religious toleration was unusual for the time. The Edict of Nantes helped bring order to France after decades of civil war.

Henry's policies also brought prosperity to his kingdom. His superintendent of finances, the Duc de Sully, increased the amount of money raised for the royal treasury. He reduced waste and dishonesty in the government and encouraged trade by building roads and canals and by improving ports.

Richelieu strengthens royal authority. In 1610 Henry was murdered by a religious fanatic, and the throne went to his nine-year-old son, Louis XIII. Henry's second wife, Marie de Médicis, ruled France until the young king came of age, but many French nobles objected to the Italian advisers she chose. After Louis assumed responsibility as king in 1615, the Huguenots again revolted against the crown. In 1624, however, a remarkable statesman, Cardinal Richelieu (ree-shuh-LYOO), became Louis' chief minister and brought the monarchy new strength.

Cool-headed and clear-sighted, Richelieu is regarded as one of the great statesmen in French history. His main goals were to strengthen the king's absolute authority at home and to block Hapsburg expansion elsewhere in Europe. Richelieu was willing to use ruthless measures to achieve these goals. He imprisoned and executed nobles who threatened royal authority. While he did not revoke the Edict of Nantes protecting the Huguenots, he sent troops to capture the main Protestant towns and destroy the Huguenots' armies.

Royal power was more important to Richelieu than religion. To prevent the Hapsburgs from dominating Europe, Richelieu took France into the Thirty Years' War on the side of the Protestant states (page 381). France also went to war against Catholic Spain. By the time of Richelieu's death in 1642, France was a major power in Europe.

CHECK-UP
1. (a) What kind of rule did French kings exercise from the Middle Ages on? (b) Why did some French nobles become Protestants?
2. (a) What caused the civil wars in France in the last part of the sixteenth century? (b) What did Henry IV do to end religious conflict? (c) To what family did Henry IV belong?
3. What steps did Richelieu take to strengthen the French monarchy?

3 The Thirty Years' War Disrupts Europe

While Spain under the Hapsburgs had declined by the seventeenth century, the Hapsburg rulers of Austria remained the leading family in Europe. Through their ties to Spain and as Holy Roman Emperors, the Austrian Hapsburgs dominated much of the continent. Only Bourbon France was a serious rival for political dominance, but religious conflicts were a challenge to Hapsburg authority. These conflicts led to the long and destructive Thirty Years' War.

European states try to maintain a balance of power. Starting in the sixteenth century, the states of Europe became concerned with maintaining a *balance of power.* That is, they tried to prevent any one state from becoming so strong that it could dominate the others. In the sixteenth and early seventeenth centuries, the balance of power was threatened by both Spanish and Austrian Hapsburgs.

Hapsburg rulers claim Bohemia. In the sixteenth century, Bohemia was a prosperous state with a population made up of Czechs and Germans. Complex political and family ties linked Bohemia with neighboring Austria, Hungary, Poland, and the German states. In 1516 Louis II, the grandson of Poland's ruler, became king of both Bohemia and Hungary. Louis was killed resisting the Ottoman Turks at the Battle of Mohács in 1526. Hoping for Austria's help against the Turks, the nobles gave the crowns of Bohemia and Hungary to Ferdinand I, the Hapsburg ruler of Austria (who was married to Louis' sister). This made Bohemia part of the Hapsburg domains.

Religious differences in Bohemia lead to war. The question of Hapsburg power in Bohemia involved religious differences as well as politics. After the Reformation, Bohemia became a battleground between the Catholic Hapsburgs and the Czech and German Protestants. The Protestant Czechs treasured the memory of John Huss (page 336), the religious reformer who had been executed for heresy in 1415. In 1618 the Czech nobles rebelled against their Hapsburg ruler, Ferdinand II, and killed several officials. The following year, Ferdinand became Holy Roman Emperor and ended the religious toleration that the Bohemian Protestants had been promised earlier. In response, the Bohemians deposed him and chose Frederick V, a German Protestant prince, as their king. They hoped this would bring them support from the Protestant rulers of England and the Netherlands, who were related to King Frederick.

The war involves many states. The Czech uprising marked the beginning of the Thirty Years' War (1618–1648), a conflict that eventually engulfed most of the major European states. Emperor Ferdinand II soon sought support from other Catholic rulers. A Spanish army was sent by his Hapsburg cousin, Philip III of Spain, and by another cousin, Maximilian, the Catholic ruler of the German state of Bavaria. In 1620 this allied army quickly defeated the Bohemians at the Battle of White Mountain and deposed Frederick. The emperor gave Frederick's German territories to Maximilian.

The war began to spread when the Bavarian army attacked Protestant regions in northern Germany and threatened territory held by Denmark. King Christian IV of Denmark entered the conflict in order to protect the Protestants, prevent the restoration of Catholic rule in Germany, and increase his own holdings. In 1626, however, he was defeated by the brilliant Austrian general Albrecht Wallenstein, and Denmark soon left the war.

Other states try to maintain the balance of power. The Hapsburg victories allowed Emperor Ferdinand II to take over the estates of the rebellious Protestant nobles in Bohemia as well as the lands of several Lutheran princes in Germany. He ordered the return of property taken from the Catholic Church since the Reformation. He also expelled Protestant clergy and teachers from Bohemia and imposed Hapsburg rule on the embittered Czechs.

The increasing power of the Hapsburg Holy Roman Emperor alarmed other European

Towns and cities were devastated in the fighting of the Thirty Years' War. More than 20,000 people lost their lives when Bavarian forces besieged the German Protestant city of Magdeburg in 1631. Notice the fort (at right) in this old engraving of the attack.

rulers. The religious differences that had begun the war were overshadowed by the struggle to maintain the balance of power. To prevent Hapsburg domination, both Catholic France and Protestant Sweden entered the conflict on the side of the German Protestants.

Swedish forces invaded Germany in 1630, led by King Gustavus Adolphus, one of the great generals in modern history. Under the leadership of this "Lion of the North," the Swedes turned back the Hapsburg advance. Although Gustavus Adolphus was killed in battle in 1632, he had kept the Protestant German states from falling to Hapsburg rule.

In 1635, Cardinal Richelieu and Louis XIII brought France into the war, allied with the Protestant forces of Sweden, the Netherlands, and the German princes. From 1635 to 1648 the forces of the French and Swedish armies hammered away at the forces of the Span-

ish and Austrian Hapsburgs. The armies of both sides slaughtered innocent civilians and destroyed towns and farms. Probably over a third of the German population died during the conflict. Flight from war and oppression may have reduced the Bohemian population from three million to 800,000.

The Thirty Years' War has lasting results. Five years of peace talks eventually brought about the Peace of Westphalia in 1648. Although the Thirty Years' War caused few territorial changes, it affected the European balance of power in several ways.

The Hapsburgs, as Holy Roman Emperors, had failed in their attempts to impose Catholicism throughout the empire and to unite the German states. The war thus ended the medieval dream of a Europe fully united under the Holy Roman Emperor and faithful to the Roman Catholic Church. The treaty left the

Europe About 1648

The Thirty Years' War brought important changes to Europe. Compare this map with the map on page 377. Identify changes that affected the Netherlands, Switzerland, and Brandenburg.

German princes free to rule their own states and choose their own religion. Though the German people did not have this choice, the treaties promised them the right to emigrate if they wished. With the loss of Hapsburg power, France was the leading state in Western Europe, while Sweden dominated the area around the Baltic Sea. Spain finally recognized the independence of the United Netherlands (page 376), while Switzerland, also Protestant, became independent of the control of the Holy Roman Empire.

The Thirty Years' War was the last of the religious wars brought about by the Reformation. Monarchs no longer went to war or made alliances purely for religious reasons. After the middle of the seventeenth century, the politics of states were determined more by threats to their security and by desire for land and economic power.

CHECK-UP

1. Vocabulary: *balance of power.*
2. (a) How did Bohemia come under Hapsburg rule? (b) How did religious differences in Bohemia lead to the Thirty Years' War?
3. During the Thirty Years' War, what goal was sought by each of the following: (a) the Holy Roman Emperor, (b) the German Protestant princes, (c) Denmark, (d) Sweden, (e) France?
4. (a) How did the Thirty Years' War change the balance of power in Europe? (b) What states gained their independence?

4   Absolute Monarchy Triumphs in France

At the end of the Thirty Years' War, Bourbon France had become the dominant power in Western Europe. The long reign of Louis XIV (1643–1715) was devoted to increasing French power and prestige. It marked the triumph of absolute monarchy in France.

Cardinal Mazarin strengthens central authority. When Louis XIII died in 1643, the new king, Louis XIV, was not quite five years old. His mother, Anne of Austria (a Spanish Hapsburg), ruled for her son along with the new chief minister, Cardinal Mazarin (MAZ-uh-rin), who had been trained by Richelieu.

After Richelieu's death in 1642, Mazarin became extremely powerful and was hated and feared by many. In the late 1640's some nobles, with the backing of peasants and city-dwellers, led a series of unsuccessful rebellions against strong central rule. The nobles' attempt to regain power convinced the king and others that only rule by a monarch with absolute power could prevent civil war and the destruction of the French state.

Louis claims the "divine right" of kings. Like other monarchs of the day, Louis believed that kings "are born to possess all and command all." Louis claimed that the ruler's power came from God and that no subject dared question it. This theory is known as the *divine right* of kings. A French bishop, Jacques Bénigne Bossuet (boh-SWEH), expressed the theory in the following words.

> It is God Who establishes kings. . . . Princes thus act as ministers of God and [are] His lieutenants on earth. It is through them that He rules. . . . That is why . . . the royal throne is not the throne of a man but the throne of God Himself. . . .
>
> It appears from this that the person of kings is sacred, and to move against them is sacrilege. . . .

After Mazarin's death in 1661, Louis XIV ruled personally as an absolute monarch, concentrating the governing power of the state in his own hands. His famous statement of this power was "*L'état, c'est moi*" ("The state — it is I"). No minister, however capable and loyal, determined policy for the king.

Louis XIV rules in a magnificent setting. Louis worked tirelessly and carefully to increase the glory of France and the monarchy. Because of the splendor of his reign he was called the "Sun King." The early years of Louis' personal rule gave France greater unity and a stronger central government than it had ever had. The old noble military families lost much of their independence and power, for Louis selected many of his chief ministers and administrators from the newer nobles and the middle class.

Louis and his chief ministers spent lavishly on palaces and public buildings. The most magnificent was at Versailles (vehr-SYE), near Paris. Thousands of laborers took more than twenty years to complete it. The palace was half a mile long and contained hundreds of rooms, including a 240-foot-long hall with walls paneled in mirrors. Other rooms were decorated with tapestries, marble statues, and elaborate ceiling paintings depicting Louis' achievements. The palace was surrounded by acres of formal gardens with statues and fountains. The splendor of Versailles was the talk of Europe.

The royal court moved to Versailles in 1682, and social life revolved around the "Sun King." Louis required many nobles to live in the palace, where an elaborate system of ceremonies and code of manners kept them busy. Nobles who otherwise might have been plotting against the king became concerned with giving Louis his shirt in the morning, holding his candle at night, or watching him dine. It was important to know the latest gossip and to be noticed by the king at court. The nobles were eager to please Louis in hopes that he would grant them pensions or appointments as bishops, ambassadors, or generals.

Louis XIV was king for 72 years. During his long reign, art, literature, drama, music, and ballet flourished in France, for Louis was the patron of many artists and writers. In architecture, furniture, and dress, France set the style for Europe. French replaced Latin as the international language of diplomacy. Other monarchs sought to imitate the elaborate fashions, etiquette, and pageantry of Louis' court.

France follows mercantilist policies. Realizing that a strong monarchy depended on a healthy economy, Louis XIV in 1665 named Jean Baptiste Colbert (kohl-BAIR) his minister of finance. Colbert was a strong advocate of mercantilism (page 364). He urged the establishment of French colonies and trading companies to compete with the Dutch and English. He also improved methods of taxation, supported shipbuilding and a new navy, and had canals and roads built. The government encouraged new industries by inviting foreign artisans to teach their skills to French workers. The French silk, tapestry, and furniture industries prospered with this help.

The prosperity resulting from Colbert's policies did not last, however. Although Louis wished to strengthen the state, his luxurious court life, elaborate building programs, and frequent wars drained the French treasury. Unlike England, where the power of the monarch was limited by Parliament, France had no legislative body that could call a halt to the king's spending. The French assembly, the Estates-General (page 169), had not met since 1614.

Persecution of Huguenots hurts the French economy. Louis XIV was convinced that a large religious minority weakened the nation and might bring on civil war. Hoping for a France with "one king, one law, and one faith," he opposed the religious toleration that had been granted the French Protestants, the Huguenots.

Huguenots had served France well in the armed forces and as government officials. They were also important to France's business and industry. Louis XIV nevertheless demanded that the Huguenots convert to Catholicism. When persuasion failed, he turned to persecution. Finally, in 1685, he simply repealed the Edict of Nantes (page 378) and prohibited the Huguenots from practicing their religion. Tens of thousands of Huguenots fled to Protestant lands — England, the Netherlands, Switzerland — and some made their way to English colonies in North America. France lost many of its ablest business leaders and artisans as well as their wealth.

LOUIS XIV AND VERSAILLES

Louis XIV, the "Sun King," became the symbol of royal splendor in Europe. This full-length likeness was painted by Hyacinth Rigaud, an artist who won fame for his portraits of royal figures during Louis' reign. Below is Louis' palace at Versailles, as it looks today.

Europe About 1721

Major territorial changes came about in Europe between the end of the Thirty Years' War (map, page 382) and 1721. What lands on the Baltic Sea did Russia gain from Sweden? What royal family had come to power in both France and Spain? How had the boundaries of the Holy Roman Empire changed?

Louis XIV's policies threaten the balance of power. The Thirty Years' War had not only ended Hapsburg dominance in Europe, but also had given Bourbon France the chance to control the continent. Following Richelieu's ambitious policies, Louis wanted to extend French lands to the north and east to give France a border that was easier to defend. Louis also planned to put a Bourbon prince on the Spanish throne, thereby gaining control of Spain and its huge overseas empire.

Fearful of Louis' ambitions, other European states formed alliances to resist him. Between 1667 and 1714 France went to war four times. The most destructive of these wars was

the War of the Spanish Succession (1701–1713). It is often called the first of the world wars because most of the leading states of Europe were involved.

A Bourbon prince claims the Spanish throne. The succession to the Spanish throne was in doubt because the Hapsburg king of Spain had no heirs. In 1700 he named as his successor Philip of Anjou, the grandson of Louis XIV. The naming of a Bourbon prince to the Spanish throne was a great diplomatic victory for France. It was unacceptable to the other major European powers, for a Bourbon-controlled Spain would have disrupted the balance of power in Europe. England, Hapsburg

Austria, the German state of Brandenburg-Prussia,[4] and the United Netherlands joined forces to oppose Philip's succession.

The balance of power is restored. The war went badly for France, but disagreements among the allies ended the fighting before France suffered great losses. The Peace of Utrecht (YOO-trekt), composed of several treaties signed in 1713 and 1714, again attempted to restore a balance of power in Europe. Philip of Anjou kept the Spanish throne and Spain's colonial empire, on condition that the same king would never rule both Spain and France. The Spanish Netherlands and Spanish land in Italy, however, went to the Austrian Hapsburgs. Britain took Gibraltar[5] from Spain and gained some French possessions in North America and the West Indies. Like Hapsburg Austria and Hapsburg Spain before it, Bourbon France had failed in its attempt to dominate Europe.

Louis leaves an empty treasury. At the time of Louis XIV's death in 1715, France faced a terrible economic problem. Wars and extravagant spending had emptied the royal treasury and left the country in debt. The system of taxation placed the burden of taxes on the peasants, who could least afford to pay them. These financial problems were made worse by wars during the reign (1715–1774) of Louis XV, Louis' great-grandson and successor, and by the nobles' attempts to regain power. Financial problems helped to weaken the monarch and bring on the French Revolution in 1789 (Chapter 20).

CHECK-UP

1. Vocabulary: *divine right.*
2. (a) How did Louis XIV expand the personal power of the French monarch? (b) How did Colbert strengthen the French economy? (c) How did Louis' religious policies hurt the economy?
3. (a) What caused the War of the Spanish Succession? (b) What were the results of the war for Spain and its territories? (c) How did the war affect the balance of power in Europe?
4. How did the reign of Louis XIV harm France financially?

5 Parliament Gains Power in England

Although absolute monarchy continued to develop in France, England's Parliament was successful in limiting the English monarch's power. The expansion of Parliament's control and the passage of laws protecting the rights of English citizens were crucial developments.

England flourishes under Elizabeth I. The Tudor dynasty, established in 1485 at the end of the Wars of the Roses (page 192), ruled England until 1603. The second Tudor ruler, Henry VIII, strengthened the authority of the Crown by breaking with the Pope and becoming head of the English church (page 340). Henry's daughter Elizabeth I came to the throne in 1558. Intelligent, self-confident, and respected by all, Elizabeth was one of the great monarchs of European history.

Elizabeth's 45-year reign was one of England's greatest ages. Despite challenges to her rule, Elizabeth succeeded in keeping peace within her kingdom. She showed respect for English traditions, chose excellent advisers, and was able to persuade Parliament to approve her policies. The spirit of the Renaissance also made Elizabethan England a time of remarkable artistic creativity.

England prospered under Elizabeth. English merchants, searching for new markets and raw materials, traded around the world. England gained its first trading post in India, and London became a busy center of commerce. By increasing overseas trade, expanding the English navy, and sponsoring voyages of discovery, Elizabeth laid the foundations of an empire.

---

[4]Brandenburg and Prussia were ruled by the king of Prussia.

[5]Gibraltar is the small peninsula on the coast of Spain that controls the passage from the Atlantic Ocean to the Mediterranean Sea (map, page 385).

Britain's Crown Jewels

A nation's crown jewels — priceless gems and gold ornaments — are one symbol of the monarch's power. Britain's crown jewels have a long and colorful history — some were used to finance wars; others were damaged when kings wore their jeweled crowns into battle. The gravest threat to the crown jewels was Oliver Cromwell, who had them sold. New ones had to be made for the coronation of Charles II in 1660. The coronation symbols, or regalia, include a crown of gold encrusted with gems; a golden globe called the Orb; and the royal scepter, which holds the huge *Star of Africa* diamond.

Some historic gems were rescued from Cromwell and later set in a crown made for Queen Victoria. Today Queen Elizabeth II (right) wears this crown for such events as the opening of Parliament. Jewels in the crown include a huge sapphire, an uncut ruby, four great pearls from earrings worn by Elizabeth I, and a second *Star of Africa* — as well as 2,782 smaller diamonds, 17 sapphires, 11 emeralds, 5 rubies, and 273 pearls.

The Church of England became solidly established during Elizabeth's reign. A moderate Protestant, Queen Elizabeth generally favored religious toleration. England's aid to the Protestant Dutch in their successful revolt against Spain, as well as the stunning defeat of the Spanish Armada (page 376), made it clear that England had become the leading Protestant nation in Europe.

Several groups of Roman Catholics challenged the queen's right to the throne, however. They supported the claim of Mary, Queen of Scots (Mary Stuart), Elizabeth's cousin and a Roman Catholic. Mary was forced to give up the throne of Scotland in 1567 and took refuge in England, where she was kept virtually a prisoner for nearly twenty years. Backed by agents of France and Spain, she continued to be the center of plots against Elizabeth. Elizabeth eventually was convinced by her advisers that the Scottish queen was a danger, and so she reluctantly ordered Mary's execution (by beheading) in 1587 (page 376).

Parliament clashes with Stuart kings. Mary Stuart's son, James I,[6] succeeded Elizabeth in 1603. James, however, lacked the queen's abilities either to persuade officials and politicians or to win the English people's support. James claimed to rule by divine right and so was involved in an almost constant struggle with Parliament, which was determined to take a greater role in governing England.

During the reign of Charles I (1625–1649), the son of James I, tensions between Parliament and the monarch intensified. The conflict centered on two issues — taxes and religion.

---

[6]Elizabeth never married and had no heir. James became King James VI of Scotland in 1567 when Mary, Queen of Scots, was forced to abdicate, or give up the throne. As king of England, he was called James I. Stuart rule united England and Scotland under one monarch in 1603, but they remained separate countries.

Because of extravagant spending and foreign wars with France and Spain, both James I and Charles I were constantly short of funds. When Charles asked Parliament for more money in 1628, Parliament refused until the king would agree to sign the Petition of Right. Like the Magna Charta, the Petition of Right is one of the foundations of English liberty. It limited the power of the king and set forth specific rights: (1) The monarch could not collect taxes without Parliament's consent. (2) Civilians could not be forced to provide food and shelter for soldiers. (3) Military law could not be imposed in time of peace. (4) No person could be imprisoned except upon a specific charge.

Although Charles agreed to the Petition of Right, he continued to levy taxes in a manner that Parliament considered illegal. When Parliament protested, Charles dismissed it. For the next eleven years, until 1640, the king ruled without Parliament. This heavy-handed tactic aroused bitter opposition.

Religious divisions bring unrest in England and Scotland. Charles's troubles with Parliament were made worse by his religious policies. While the Church of England had become the established church in Elizabeth's reign, some people remained Roman Catholic and a growing number followed other Protestant faiths. The English Protestants called Puritans wanted to "purify" the Church of England by eliminating what they considered to be Roman Catholic practices. Puritans criticized the wearing of rich robes by the clergy, the ornamentation in churches, elaborate rituals, and kneeling at communion.

James I turned down the Puritans' requests for changes in church practices. He did sponsor a new English translation of the Bible. Published in 1611, it is commonly called the "King James Version."

In the reign of Charles I, the archbishop of Canterbury, William Laud, encouraged harsh persecutions of Puritans. Many were imprisoned or fined. They continued to gain supporters, however, particularly among middle-class townspeople, and they were well represented in Parliament.

In 1637 Charles I tried to impose Anglican (Church of England) forms of worship in Scotland. The Lowland Scots, who were Calvinist Presbyterians (page 339), rose in revolt. Needing funds to fight in Scotland, Charles was forced to call a meeting of Parliament in 1640. As Parliament refused to vote Charles money unless its complaints were settled, the king dissolved it after three weeks. It is thus known as the Short Parliament.

Parliament places more limits on the monarch's powers. Desperate for funds, Charles called for new elections to Parliament in November 1640. The new Parliament was not officially dissolved until 1653 and is known as the Long Parliament.

This Parliament also was determined to reduce the monarch's powers. It passed laws calling for regular sessions of Parliament and abolishing the special court called the Star Chamber, where royal officials had held secret trials. Laws also made it illegal for the monarch to raise taxes without Parliament's consent. The laws passed by the Long Parliament were landmarks in the growth of liberty in England.

Oliver Cromwell, leader of Parliament's forces in the English Civil War, took the title "Lord Protector." Parliament offered in 1657 to make Cromwell king of England, but he refused.

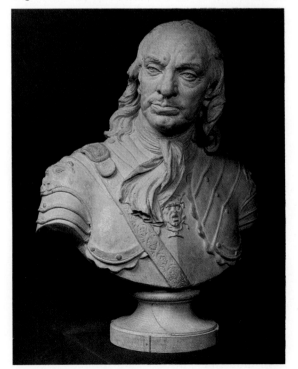

Soon after the end of the Civil War, much of London was destroyed in a great fire (1666). During the time of rebuilding, the city gained many fine churches designed by the famous architect Sir Christopher Wren.

Civil war breaks out between king and Parliament. In June, 1642, Parliament moved to weaken the king's command over the army. Many Puritan members also called for reforms in the Church of England. Charles rejected Parliament's proposals and brought in troops to arrest its leaders. Outraged, the people of London rioted and, in August, a civil war began. The king's supporters, called Cavaliers or royalists, included Anglicans (members of the Church of England) and Catholics, most members of the nobility, and royalist members of the House of Commons. Parliament had the support of both Puritans and other middle-class townspeople, who resented the king's arrogance and high expenses. They were known as Roundheads because many Puritans cropped their hair short instead of wearing the long, curly wigs fashionable at the royal court. The struggle became known as the English Civil War but was in fact several wars fought throughout England and southern Scotland between 1642 and 1651.

The parliamentary forces were organized into the New Model Army, which was well disciplined and dedicated. After early royalist victories, the parliamentary army won important battles in 1644 and 1645 and took King Charles prisoner. Though the king escaped to Scotland and raised an army to invade England, his troops were again defeated in 1648. A Puritan general named Oliver Cromwell emerged as leader of the parliamentary forces.

Cromwell establishes a republic. Cromwell used his control of the army to seize power from moderate Puritans who wanted to negotiate with the king. In 1648 Cromwell expelled his opponents from Parliament. The remaining members abolished the House of Lords and brought the king to trial for treason. Charles I was beheaded early in 1649. Most English people were shocked by the execution and uncertain about what appeared to be the end of monarchy in England.

Still backed by the army, Cromwell then formed a new government, a republic known as the Commonwealth. The Puritan leader, however, was unable to set up a smoothly working government that had the support of the English people, and so he took more and more power for himself. When Parliament tried to resist him, he dismissed it. In 1653 Cromwell took the title "Lord Protector" and ruled England, Scotland, and Ireland until his death in 1658.

The civil war continued during the Commonwealth, for the king's son Charles gathered royalist supporters who fought in Ireland and Scotland. With great ruthlessness, Cromwell put down the rebellion in Ireland and forced Irish Catholic landholders to turn over their estates to Protestant English settlers. The massacre of the Irish rebels in 1649 and the loss of property created great bitterness. The Irish said the "curse of Cromwell" had doomed their land.

The Stuart Restoration returns a monarch to the throne. After the death of Cromwell in 1658, the English were ready to return to monarchy. In 1660 Parliament invited Charles II, son of the executed king, to return to the

The English Bill of Rights

In 1689 Parliament drew up "an act for declaring the rights and liberties of the subject." Known as the English Bill of Rights, the document describes how James II attempted to suppress Protestantism. It then includes a list of rights aimed at preventing future abuses of royal power. Among those rights are the following:

1. That the pretended power of suspending of laws, or the execution of laws, by regal authority, without consent of Parliament, is illegal. . . .

4. That levying money for or to the use of the crown . . . without grant of Parliament . . . is illegal.

5. That it is the right of the subjects to petition the king, and all commitments [arrests] and prosecutions for such petitioning are illegal.

6. That the raising or keeping a standing army within the kingdom in time of peace, unless it be with consent of Parliament, is against law.

7. That the subjects which are Protestants may have arms for their defense . . . as allowed by law.

8. That election of members of Parliament ought to be free.

9. That freedom of speech, and debates or proceedings in Parliament, ought not to be . . . questioned in any court or place out of Parliament.

How does the English Bill of Rights limit the monarch's power to (a) make or revoke laws and (b) tax subjects? How does the Bill of Rights protect freedom of speech?

throne. His reign (1660–1685) is called the Restoration period. Known as the "Merry Monarch," Charles II was popular with his subjects but often at odds with Parliament. England was still troubled by serious religious divisions between Catholics, Anglicans, and other Protestants (including Puritans), who were called nonconformists. Charles urged more tolerant policies for Catholics and nonconformists than Parliament was willing to grant. He particularly wanted to be sure that his brother James, a Roman Catholic, would inherit the throne. For the last four years of his reign, therefore, Charles did not call a meeting of Parliament.

Parliament chooses new rulers. James II inherited the crown in 1685. Lacking his brother's charm, he lost still more public support by his policies. The English assumed, however, that James's Protestant daughter Mary would succeed him. When a son was born, they feared a return to absolute rule and Catholicism. In 1688, therefore, Parliament offered the crown jointly to Mary and her husband, William of Orange, leader of the Dutch Republic (page 376). The English people acclaimed this change of monarchs and called it the Glorious Revolution. James fled the country; in Scotland he found supporters who for many years afterward tried to reclaim the throne for members of the Stuart family.

The Glorious Revolution was a major step in establishing Parliament's supremacy over the English monarch. In 1689 Parliament presented the new rulers, Mary and William III, with a Bill of Rights, to which they were expected to agree. This declaration made it illegal for the monarch to make or suspend laws, levy taxes, or raise a standing army during peacetime without Parliament's approval. Subjects had the right to petition the monarch, and the ruler could not interfere with freedom of speech within Parliament.

English parliamentary government becomes a model for other states. The English revolutions of the seventeenth century had a great impact on government in the Western world. Parliamentary government, the rule of law, limited monarchy, and the protection of individual liberties became firmly established in Britain. They brought Britain centuries of stable government that was able to meet political crises in an orderly way.

1. (a) In what ways did England benefit from Elizabeth's rule? (b) Why did she order the execution of Mary, Queen of Scots?
2. (a) How did the attitudes of James I and Charles I lead to clashes between the monarchy and Parliament? (b) What were the main points of the Petition of Right?
3. (a) What events led up to dismissal of the Short Parliament? (b) What actions did the Long Parliament take? (c) What action caused civil war to break out in England?
4. Who were (a) the Cavaliers? (b) the Roundheads? (c) the New Model Army?
5. (a) How did Oliver Cromwell gain power in England? (b) What form of government did he introduce?
6. (a) What was the Restoration? (b) In what way was the Glorious Revolution a victory for Parliament? (c) How did the Bill of Rights limit the English monarch's power?

6 States Develop in Eastern Europe

By the sixteenth century most of Western Europe had been settled for centuries. The frontier lay in the region east of the Elbe River, which was thickly forested, with many rivers and extensive marshlands. Farther east, broad grassy plains, the steppes, stretched from the Carpathian Mountains into Asia. Since ancient times it had been easy for Asian nomads to cross the steppes and invade Europe. Frequent invasions slowed the formation of states in Eastern Europe. The variety of languages, peoples, and religions also made state-building difficult. Despite these obstacles, several strong states grew up.

Many Eastern Europeans are Slavs. The majority of the people living in Eastern Europe were Slavs, who came originally from the dense woods and vast swampy area near the Pripyat River (map, page 394). After the Germanic tribes moved west and south into Roman territory (page 121), Slavic peoples began to move westward into the lands the Germans had left. By the time of Charlemagne, the Slavs had split into three major groups, divided by geography and religion. The Western Slavs — mainly Poles, Czechs, and Slovaks — became Roman Catholics and had ties with states in Western Europe. The Eastern Slavs, mostly Russians and Ukrainians, joined the Eastern Orthodox Church, linked wih the Byzantine Empire. The South Slavs, who included Croatians, Serbians, and Bulgarians, were divided between the two Christian churches.

Late in the ninth century, the South Slavs were cut off from the rest of the Slavic peoples as Magyars from Asia invaded the Danube River plain. The Magyars were not Slavic; moreover, their language was not related to the Indo-European languages spoken by almost everyone else in Europe.

Magyars establish the Hungarian state. The Magyars were horseback-riding nomads originally from lands near the Volga River. Led by a chief named Arpád, they migrated into Europe at the end of the ninth century. Their raids westward were stopped by Otto I of Germany (page 169), and they settled down on the Danube River plain. Arpád's descendants continued to rule the Magyars until 1301, drawing on their organization and fighting spirit to build the Hungarian state. About the year 1000 Stephen, a descendant of Arpád, was crowned king with the Pope's approval.[7] During Stephen's long reign, the Hungarians were converted to Christianity. Stephen unified Hungary and established a feudal system that gave power to a few landowning nobles.

A number of strong rulers acquired territory for Hungary and made it powerful. In the early 1200's, however, the king weakened his rule by giving even more land to the major landowning nobles in return for their support of a crusade. In 1222 the smaller landowners forced this king to sign a document that guaranteed them the right to their lands, freed them from paying taxes, and granted the right to hold a yearly assembly. The document also said

---

[7] Stephen was declared a saint in 1083. The "crown of St. Stephen" became an important national symbol.

that no land or offices could be held by foreigners or Jews. All later kings of Hungary had to sign this guarantee of the nobles' rights.

Foreign rulers strengthen the Hungarian kingdom. In 1241 Hungary, like the rest of Eastern Europe, was overrun by Mongol invaders (page 220). Half the population was killed, and the country was devastated. The Arpád line of rulers died out, and in 1308 the Hungarian nobles gave the crown of Saint Stephen to Charles Robert of Anjou. A descendant of Norman knights, he was one of several distant members of the Arpád family who were claiming the throne. Charles introduced Western feudal practices and the ideals of chivalry. He also encouraged trade and the growth of towns.

Charles married the daughter of the Polish king. Their son Louis I ruled Hungary for forty years (1342–1382) and became known as Louis the Great. A patron of learning, Louis continued his father's feudal policies in an attempt to limit the nobles' power. The rulers of territories to the east became vassals of the Hungarian king. To the south, however, Hungary had to defend itself against the Ottoman Turks, who were moving into Eastern Europe. The Ottomans continued to threaten Hungary throughout the fourteenth and fifteenth centuries. Nevertheless, Hungary remained powerful in Central Europe.

In 1526, at the Battle of Mohács (page 380), the Turks defeated the Hungarians, and the Hungarian king was killed. Although the Hapsburgs claimed the crown of Hungary, the Ottomans continued to advance. By 1540 most of Hungary was under Ottoman rule. Only the province of Transylvania preserved its independence, for its rulers resisted control by either the Turks or the Hapsburgs.

Poland emerges as a power in Central Europe. To the north of Hungary, the foundations of a Polish state were laid late in the tenth century. Like other medieval rulers, the early Polish kings found it difficult to gain control over the nobles. A further obstacle to centralized rule was the system of inheritance. When a ruler died, the land was divided among his sons instead of going to just one son. This made it difficult for any one person to become more powerful than the others. Not until the 1300's

did a strong ruler emerge. He was Casimir III, who ruled Poland from 1333 to 1370.

Casimir introduced a long period of peace, encouraging trade, industry, and agriculture. Because of his concern for the Polish peasants, he was called the "Peasants' King." Casimir encouraged immigrants from Western Europe to settle in areas where many people had been killed in the Mongol invasions. The university he established in Krakow, then the Polish capital, became a famous center of learning. At a time when Jews were being driven out of other European countries, Casimir granted them the right to settle in Poland, maintain their own schools, and practice their religion freely.

Casimir appointed his nephew Louis the Great of Hungary as his successor in 1370, but Louis took little interest in governing Poland. Louis' daughter Jadwiga (yad-VEE-guh), however, was one of Poland's best-loved rulers. In 1386 she married Jagello (yah-GEL-oh), grand duke of Lithuania. Under the Jagello line of rulers, the Lithuanians (a non-Slavic people) were converted to Christianity. At the height of its power in the sixteenth century, the united Polish-Lithuanian state was the largest kingdom in Eastern Europe. It reached from the Baltic Sea to the Black Sea and stretched eastward deep into Russia (map, page 377).

Polish nobles have great power. During the sixteenth century Poland enjoyed a golden

The Polish patriot Thaddeus Kosciusko (page 393) led a valiant but unsuccessful effort to save Poland from the forces of Russia and Prussia.

age of culture and prosperity. The kingdom was a major source of grain for Europe. The University at Krakow became famous, and Poland shared in the learning of the Renaissance. The brilliant astronomer Copernicus (page 402) studied at Krakow. Poland's economy, however, was based on the labor of serfs and the power of feudal nobles. While serfdom was vanishing in Western Europe, it became more common in the East. Unlike the countries of Western Europe, where strong central rule was developing, Poland remained little more than a loose union of feudal estates.

When the Jagello dynasty ended in 1572, Polish nobles began the practice of electing their monarch. To gain support, each new ruler added to the nobles' feudal privileges. Polish nobles prided themselves on their many rights and their control over the parliament. Each had the right to halt proceedings by a veto and even to dissolve the parliament. This prevented effective government, kept central rule weak, and blocked the development of a national army that could protect the state.

Poland is partitioned by stronger states. Poland was unable to avoid being involved in Europe's wars, and other states interfered in the country's affairs. Invasions by Sweden, the Ottoman Empire, and Russia created nearly continuous disorder. By 1772 Russian influence was strong, particularly in eastern Poland. To maintain the balance of power, Poland's neighbors — Russia, Prussia, and Austria — all agreed to take areas of Polish land. The 1772 partition took about a third of Poland's land and half its population.

The humiliation of the partition sparked a reform movement in Poland. The Polish parliament tried to correct the flaws in the government and in 1791 proclaimed a new constitution with a hereditary monarch and reforms in feudal practices. Empress Catherine the Great of Russia, however, sent troops into Poland to stop this movement. More Polish territory went to Russia and Prussia in 1793.

In 1794 Polish patriots raised a volunteer army. Although they were brilliantly led by Thaddeus Kosciusko (kos-ee-US-koh), they could not stop the combined forces of Prussia and Russia. What was left of Poland was divided between Russia, Prussia, and Austria in

Partitions of Poland

Poland, weakened by wars and lack of strong central rule, fell prey to three powerful neighbors. Which country gained the largest share of Poland? Which gained the city of Danzig?

1795. With this third partition, Poland ceased to exist as a nation.

The Russian state develops. Farther east in Europe, much of Russia had been under Mongol rule from 1240 onward (page 207). By the fourteenth century, however, the forest town of Moscow was the center of a state known as Muscovy. Strategically located near the headwaters of four rivers, Muscovy had the advantage of able leaders who worked to unify their lands. The grand dukes of Moscow were clever, miserly (one was called Ivan Moneybags), and eager to gain more land.

In the fifteenth century Ivan III, who is known as Ivan the Great, laid the foundation for a centralized state. Ruling from 1462 to 1505, Ivan asserted Moscow's independence from the Mongols. He gained control over Novgorod, ended the influence of the Hanseatic League (page 177), and took over border lands

Building the Russian State

Russia's expansion from the region around Moscow to the area shown here made it the dominant state in Eastern Europe. By what year had Russia gained access to the Baltic Sea?

from Lithuania. Ivan set a pattern of expansion that has continued throughout Russian history.

When Ivan married Sophia, niece of the last Byzantine emperor, he proclaimed himself heir to Constantinople, which had fallen to the Turks in 1453. As a symbol of his new authority, Ivan adopted the title *czar* (a word derived from "Caesar") and insisted on the same absolute power the Byzantine emperors had held. He strengthened central rule by ending the self-government of towns, ignoring the council of boyars (nobles), and taking over the boyars' estates to give to his supporters. Ivan's rule was less restricted by church, nobles, or town privileges than that of any Western European monarch. Ivan III thus made the czar an *autocrat,* a ruler with unlimited power over his subjects.

Ivan IV adds to Russia's lands but terrorizes the people. The first ruler to be crowned with the title "czar" was Ivan IV (Ivan III's grandson), who is known as Ivan the Terrible. Ivan's father died when Ivan was three, and his mother when he was eight. While the boyars

fought over control of Russia, Ivan was often left hungry and in rags. This neglect made him hostile to the boyars for the rest of his life.

Ivan became czar in 1547, at the age of seventeen, and married Anastasia Romanov (roh-MAH-nuf) in the same year. Despite a spinal disease that kept him in constant pain, Ivan was an able and energetic man. He established a national assembly, had a new law code drawn up, and created a strong landowning class loyal to himself. He reorganized the army and conquered Mongol strongholds on the Caspian Sea, giving Russia control of the Volga River and the sea trade. Ivan also expanded Russia's holdings into Siberia. Trying to gain land and a port city on the Baltic Sea, he warred unsuccessfully for 25 years against Sweden and the Polish-Lithuanian state.

Ivan's policies underwent a sharp change after Anastasia died suddenly in 1560. Suspecting the boyars of murdering her, Ivan threatened to abandon Moscow unless its people gave him full power to punish the boyars. As revenge, Ivan took personal control of the boyars' territories, which included most of Russia's wealthy towns, trade centers, and cultivated farmlands. The czar then organized a

Boyars bearing gifts of black-tailed ermine furs were sent by Ivan IV as ambassadors to the court of the Holy Roman Emperor in 1576.

special army to destroy the boyar families. Dressed in black and riding black horses, his troops murdered thousands and spread terror.

Russia enters the Time of Troubles. While Ivan's policies gave the czar absolute power, the murder of thousands of boyars left Russia with few trained officials. Following Ivan's death in 1584, Russia was in turmoil. Attempts to restore order resulted in new limits on the freedom of the peasants. Landowners needed the peasants' labor, while the government depended on their taxes. Gradually, the peasants became serfs, completely under the control of the landowners.

Contributing to the unrest of the time were the rebellious Cossacks. These independent groups of runaway serfs, farmers, and adventurers were organized as military communities. One Cossack group led by the hero Yermak began Russia's expansion eastward into Siberia in 1581. Other Cossacks, however, were frequently in revolt against the czars. Disorder was so widespread that the period from about 1598 to 1613 is known as the Time of Troubles. Moscow was threatened by civil war, peasant revolts, and invasion by Swedish and Polish armies. Several groups tried to seize power. In 1613, an assembly of townspeople and landholders elected a new czar, Michael Romanov, who began a new dynasty. The Romanov family ruled Russia until 1917 and transformed the state into the Russian Empire.

Peter strengthens czarist autocracy. The changes that made Russia an empire and established the modern state came in the reign of Peter I, called Peter the Great. He ruled from 1682 to 1725, becoming sole czar in 1696.[8]

Among the monarchs of that age, Peter stood out as a giant. Nearly seven feet tall, he had immense physical strength, vitality, and curiosity. As a boy, he began to admire the Western customs of the foreign traders he knew in Moscow. He also learned military skills, shipbuilding, and sailing. As czar, he tirelessly promoted change, with the goal of helping Russia catch up with Western Europe.

---

[8]Peter was only ten years old in 1682 and ruled for a time with his half-brother and half-sister. By 1689 he was effectively in control of the government; his half-brother died in 1696.

Ivan IV celebrated a Russian victory over the Mongols with the construction of St. Basil's Cathedral (now a museum) in Moscow.

The countries of northern Europe were constantly at war with each other during Peter's reign. Allied with the kings of Poland and Denmark, Peter began the Great Northern War against Sweden (1700–1721). King Charles XII of Sweden, a brilliant military leader, was victorious at first. Peter, however, retrained and reorganized Russia's army and navy with Western technical help and turned back the Swedish invasion. Victory gave Russia territory along the Baltic Sea and made it an empire. Peter took the title of emperor, or "czar of all the Russias." Russia was now the major power in northern Europe.

In addition to reforming Russia's army and navy, Peter brought other institutions under his centralized rule. The council of boyars was replaced by appointed officials, and all landowners were required to serve the state either in the civil service or in military service. New industries were begun and supported with

Catherine the Great ruled Russia from 1762 to 1796. Her policies encouraged Russian nobles to adopt Western ways.

social life (an idea inherited from the Mongols) and tried to train his bureaucrats in the Western European manner.

As a symbol of Russia's turn toward the West, Peter in 1703 founded a new capital, St. Petersburg, on the bleak marshes near the Baltic coast. The new city was far removed, in outlook and geography, from the old capital in Moscow. Peter's efforts to change Russia, however, created a deep cultural and social gulf between the westernized nobles and the rest of the people, who continued to follow traditional ways. The state, moreover, tended to be unstable because it depended on strong personal rule.

Catherine extends Western influence in Russia. The outstanding rulers among Peter's successors were Czarina (empress) Elizabeth, who ruled from 1741 to 1762, and her successor, Catherine II, known as Catherine the Great. Catherine, a German princess, was sent to Russia at age fifteen to marry the Grand Duke Peter, Elizabeth's heir. Catherine converted to the Russian Orthodox Church, educated herself by reading Western literature, and gained self-confidence and charm. Soon she had won the favor of the czarina and the court.

Peter III, an unpopular ruler, came to the throne early in 1762, but within a few months he was deposed and murdered. Catherine spoke Russian with a German accent and had a dubious claim to the throne, yet her reign (1762–1796) was the most illustrious in the history of Russia. The famous French writers of the day hailed her as the most forward-looking of European monarchs.

Although she also wished to westernize Russia, Catherine's style of rule was different from that of Peter the Great. She freed the nobles from having to follow careers in the civil or military service, and she encouraged them to develop their estates and administer their own affairs. She also gave merchants and townspeople more freedom and encouraged trade, education, and the arts and sciences. Catherine's rule, however, brought benefits only to the educated upper classes. She did virtually nothing for the serfs. A rebellion by serfs and Cossacks in 1773 led to even more repression by the czarist officials.

state funds. Even the Russian Orthodox Church came under state control. The Russian peasants fared worst of all during Peter's reign. They were forced to work on state building projects or serve in the army. The status of serfs came close to slavery.

Peter introduces Western European ways. Peter's intention was to transform completely the old Russian, or Muscovite, way of life. In 1697 and 1698, disguised as an ordinary traveler, he became the first czar to visit Western Europe. What he learned in France, England, and the Netherlands convinced him that Russia must westernize if it wanted to compete with other countries. Peter proclaimed that the Russian nobles must adopt Western styles of clothing and shave off their long beards. He also started schools for the children of the nobility, modernized the Russian calendar, simplified the alphabet, and edited Russia's first newspaper. He ended the exclusion of women from

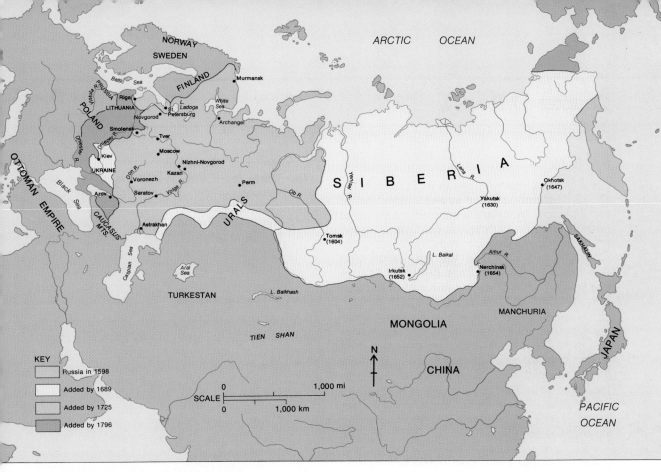

Imperial Russia, 1598–1796

The Russian czars continued their territorial expansion through the 1600's and 1700's. What was the largest addition to Russian territory between 1598 and 1689? On what inland sea had Russia gained an outlet by 1796?

Catherine expands the Russian empire. Since the time of Ivan IV the Russian czars had sought a port that would allow Russia to trade easily with the West. Ports on the Baltic Sea were closed by ice each winter. In two wars with the Ottoman Turks, Catherine finally succeeded in gaining control of the northern shore of the Black Sea. Russia also gained rich farmlands in the west and considerable territory from the partitions of Poland (page 393). By the end of Catherine's reign, Russian society and culture were more stable, and Russia was a major power in world politics.

CHECK-UP

1. Vocabulary: *czar, autocrat.*
2. (a) What was the major ethnic group in Eastern Europe? (b) What other groups of people lived there?
3. (a) What people settled in Hungary? (b) What prevented Hungary from developing into a centralized state?
4. (a) How did the Polish state become the largest state in Eastern Europe? (b) How did Polish nobles weaken the central government? (c) What caused Poland to disappear as a nation in the 1700's?
5. (a) Where did a new Russian state develop during Mongol rule? (b) On what did Ivan III base his claim that Russia was the heir of the Byzantine Empire? (c) What measures did Ivan IV take to strengthen Russia? (d) What was the Time of Troubles?
6. (a) How did Peter the Great make Russia the major power in northern Europe? (b) What were his policies toward the boyars and the Church? (c) Name five steps Peter took to westernize Russia.
7. (a) How did Catherine II become czarina of Russia? (b) What long-sought Russian goal did she achieve?

Chapter 17 Review

Summary

Great political changes began in Europe in the 1500's. Monarchs created strong, unified states, and it became important to maintain a balance of power among them. Religious conflicts following the Reformation also led to wars.

Spain was united in the late 1400's and dominated Europe for a century. Under Charles V, Spain and its empire became part of the vast domain of the Hapsburgs of Austria.

Another powerful ruling family, the Bourbons, came to rule France at the end of religious civil wars. French rulers, with no check on their power, became absolute monarchs. In the Austrian Hapsburg lands, religious conflicts led to the destructive Thirty Years' War (1618–1648), which involved much of Europe. The war established France, under Louis XIV, as the leading state in Western Europe.

England prospered in the reign of Elizabeth I, but the Stuart kings tried to assert absolute power. The English Parliament rebelled and set up a short-lived republic. Monarchy was restored, but Parliament continued to limit royal power.

Many factors slowed the growth of states in Eastern Europe, though strong kingdoms existed in Hungary and Poland. The rulers of Moscow unified Russia in the 1500's, and by 1700 it had become a major European power.

Vocabulary Review

1. Match the following words with the listed definitions: *autocrat, balance of power, czar, divine right.*
(a) A ruler who has unlimited power over his subjects.
(b) The theory that monarchs receive their power from God and consequently should not be questioned or disobeyed.
(c) The distribution of power among the nations of a region so that no one state can dominate the others.
(d) The title of the emperors of Russia from the late 1400's to 1918.
2. Distinguish between the terms in each of the following pairs:

(a) Moriscos; Huguenots.
(b) Thirty Years' War; War of the Spanish Succession.
(c) Tudors; Stuarts.
(d) Restoration Period; Glorious Revolution.
(e) Magyars; Slavs.
(f) boyars; Cossacks.

People to Identify

Identify the following people and the country where each lived. Also tell why each was important:

1. Charles V	8. Arpád
2. Philip II	9. Stephen
3. Elizabeth I	10. Casimir III
4. Richelieu	11. Jadwiga
5. Ferdinand II	12. Ivan IV
6. Louis XIV	13. Peter I
7. Oliver Cromwell	14. Catherine the Great

Relating Geography and History

1. **Locating places.** Locate each of the following on a map in this chapter:

(a) Spain	(i) Ottoman Empire
(b) Netherlands	(j) Lepanto
(c) Austria	(k) Gibraltar
(d) Bohemia	(l) Moscow
(e) Hungary	(m) St. Petersburg
(f) Poland	(n) Brandenburg-
(g) Russia	Prussia
(h) Sweden	

2. **Map study and interpretation.** Study the map of imperial Russia on page 397. Note river routes and the location of early port cities. (a) Use this information and your knowledge of the climates of northern Europe to explain why Russian czars had long wanted a southern water route for trade with Europe. (b) How did Russia finally gain an ice-free port?

3. **Making maps.** Make a map that shows changes in the borders of Poland between 1560 and 1795. Use the maps on pages 377, 382, 385, and 393 for reference. Include with your map a key explaining the colors or patterns you use to show each change.

Discussion Questions

1. Why was Spain unable to remain the leading nation of Europe after the sixteenth century?

2. (a) How did the Thirty Years' War change from a religious conflict to a struggle to maintain the balance of power in Europe? (b) What were the results of the war for those nations involved?

3. (a) Compare the religious policies of Ferdinand and Isabella in Spain with those of Henry IV in France. (b) How did policies of these rulers affect conditions within their respective countries? (c) How was France affected when Louis XIV reversed the religious policies of Henry IV?

4. Louis XIV of France believed in the theory of divine right. (a) How did this theory support his becoming an absolute ruler? (b) What were the results of his reign (both positive and negative) for France?

5. How was the balance of power in Europe threatened by (a) Hapsburg Austria and (b) Bourbon France? (c) In each case, how was the balance of power maintained?

6. Why is the Petition of Right regarded as a landmark in the history of liberty in England?

7. Explain how the English Civil War was a conflict over (a) religion, (b) royal authority, and (c) the power of Parliament.

8. (a) What features of government became firmly established in Britain by the end of the seventeenth century? (b) How did these features establish limits on royal authority?

9. Why was central government weak in Poland but strong in Russia?

Reading Primary Sources

Louis XIV believed that kings should rule by divine right, as he ruled France. The following statements are taken from the advice Louis gave to his seventeen-year-old grandson Philip when Philip became king of Spain. Read the passage. Then answer the questions below.

> 1. Never omit any of your duties, especially toward God.
> 4. On every occasion declare yourself on the side of virtue and against vice.
> 5. Have no attachment ever to anyone.
> 7. Love the Spaniards . . . ; do not give preference to those who flatter you most; esteem those who for a good cause venture to displease you; these are your real friends.
> 9. Endeavor to keep your finances in good order; . . . keep your commerce in mind; live in close union with France, since there is nothing so advantageous to our two powers as this union which nothing can withstand.
> 16. Do all in your power to get to know well the most important people, in order that you may make suitable use of them.
> 18. Treat everyone well; never say anything vexing to anyone, but do honor to people of quality and merit.
> 33. I will end with one of the most important pieces of advice that I can give you: Never allow yourself to be ruled; be the master; have no favorites or prime minister; listen to, and consult your Council, but . . . you decide yourself.

(a) What advice did Louis give Philip that would have led the other European monarchs to be concerned about the balance of power? (b) Which advisers does Louis say are the real friends of the king? (c) Why, according to Louis, should a monarch become well acquainted with the most important people? (d) Which of the suggestions would help Philip maintain absolute power as a ruler?

Skill Activities

1. Making timetables. Use an encyclopedia to find information about one of the following military commanders: (a) Gustavus Adolphus, (b) Oliver Cromwell, (c) Thaddeus Kosciusko. Put your information in a timetable. Show important events (birth date, battles, political achievements) in the life of the person chosen.

2. Making charts. Among the rulers discussed in this chapter are Isabella of Spain, Elizabeth I of England, and Catherine II of Russia. Make a chart about these rulers, using the following headings: *Dates of Rule, How Throne Was Gained, Outstanding Achievements of Reign.*

3. Organizing information. Among the families that dominated European history after the Renaissance were the Hapsburgs, the Tudors, the Stuarts, the Bourbons, and the Romanovs. Make a family tree for one of these families. Use the following dates as a guide for the period of your research: Hapsburgs, 1493–1780; Tudors, 1485–1603; Stuarts, 1603–1714; Bourbons, 1589–1715; Romanovs, 1613–1796. Include important dates and marriages and a few words about the outstanding figures in the family.

The graceful yet powerful music of Wolfgang Amadeus Mozart reflected the artistic achievements of the Enlightenment. Mozart began his career at an early age and gave concerts with his sister and father at many European royal courts.

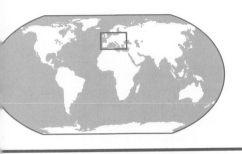

CHAPTER 18

Scientific Revolution and Enlightenment

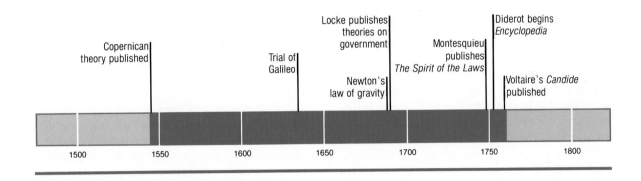

Copernican theory published

Trial of Galileo

Locke publishes theories on government

Newton's law of gravity

Montesquieu publishes *The Spirit of the Laws*

Diderot begins *Encyclopedia*

Voltaire's *Candide* published

1500   1550   1600   1650   1700   1750   1800

The way in which people live and think today has been shaped to a great extent by important developments that took place in Western Europe from the sixteenth to the eighteenth centuries. In science, scholars were developing totally new ways of looking at the natural world. Instead of relying on accepted theories or Church teachings, these scholars made careful observations and carried out a variety of experiments. They posed problems and looked for answers that could be stated precisely and in mathematical terms. Their results brought such sweeping changes in the way people of the Western world viewed the universe that the period became known as the Scientific Revolution.

After the Scientific Revolution began, other thinkers tried to look at government and society in the same systematic way. They believed that by using reason, they could solve society's problems and improve people's lives. This period became known as the Age of Reason or the Enlightenment.

This chapter discusses how ideas and new attitudes became widespread in the Western world during the periods of the Scientific Revolution and the Enlightenment.

CHAPTER OUTLINE

1 Scientists Develop a New View of Nature

2 Enlightenment Thinkers Seek Reforms

1   Scientists Develop a New View of Nature

The Renaissance inspired a spirit of curiosity in many fields. Artists and writers produced enduring masterpieces; explorers traveled to distant parts of the globe. Scientists began to question ideas that had been accepted for centuries. Their new theories and discoveries led to changes so great that historians speak of a Scientific Revolution. During this period the medieval view of the universe was rejected, and the foundations of modern science were laid.

A NEW VIEW OF THE UNIVERSE

Medieval thinkers see the earth as the center of the universe. The medieval view of the universe was a combination of Church teachings and the theories of Aristotle and Ptolemy. In the second century A.D., Ptolemy had pictured a universe with the earth at the center, and medieval thinkers countinued to accept this view. Around the earth revolved seven "planets" — the moon, the sun, Mercury, Venus, Mars, Jupiter, and Saturn. These were the heavenly bodies that medieval astronomers believed they could see moving across the sky.[1] People in the Middle Ages believed that the stars lay beyond the planets, and beyond that was the dwelling place of God. This earth-centered view of the universe is called the geocentric theory. It reflected the Christian view that God had designed the universe especially for human beings.

Medieval thinkers accept Aristotle's views. People in the Middle Ages thought of objects on earth and in the skies as being made of very different materials. The moon, the sun, and other heavenly bodies were believed to be made of ether, an unchanging substance that was too pure and spiritual to be found on Earth. Earthly objects, on the other hand, clearly changed: ice melted and became water; burning logs turned into ashes; rocks slowly wore down.

According to Aristotle, everything in the world was made of four elements — earth, water, fire, and air. Medieval thinkers accepted Aristotle's ideas about these four elements and their behavior. For instance, earthly objects made mainly of the lighter elements — air and fire — were supposed naturally to rise upwards. A flame leaped upward, they pointed out, whereas a stone fell to the ground. Medieval thinkers also followed Aristotle's belief that heavenly bodies obeyed different laws of motion than did earthly objects. Planets, for example, were thought by medieval scholars to move in circles, for the circle was considered a sign of perfection.

Copernicus proposes a sun-centered universe. The geocentric view of the universe was challenged by Nicolaus Copernicus (koh-PUR-nih-kus), a Polish churchman, doctor, and astronomer who worked in the early sixteenth century. Copernicus was convinced that the sun was at the center of the universe and that the earth was one of the planets moving around it. This theory, he believed, was a better explanation of the movements astronomers observed in the sky than was Ptolemy's idea. It was the movement of the earth, Copernicus said, that made the sun seem to move.

The heliocentric, or sun-centered, theory that Copernicus proposed marked the beginnings of modern astronomy and modern scientific thinking. Copernicus realized, however, that most scholars and clergy of the time would reject his theory because it conflicted with the geocentric view of the universe. Though he spent more than thirty years working on the theory, his book, *On the Revolutions of the Heavenly Spheres,* was not published until 1543, the last year of his life. Not until the next century did Copernicus's theory become widely accepted.

Galileo proves his observations by experiment. Early in the seventeenth century, an Italian scientist and mathematician, Galileo Galilei, made observations of the skies that convinced him of the truth of Copernicus's theory. From 1592 to 1610 Galileo taught math-

---

[1] The word *planet* came from a Greek word meaning "wanderer." The other planets in the solar system could not be seen until powerful telescopes were invented.

Galileo's discoveries led to significant advances in physics and astronomy.

ematics at the University of Padua in Italy. As part of his work, he studied the physical laws affecting motion. Realizing that the laws of physics could be expressed in mathematical equations, he worked with careful measurements and observations.

Galileo's emphasis on mathematics, measurement, and experiment was crucial for modern science. He insisted that knowledge of nature came from making "sensible experiments and necessary demonstrations." For example, Galileo experimented with falling objects by dropping them from different heights and by rolling objects down slopes of different lengths. By measuring distances that objects traveled within a given time, Galileo concluded that the speed of a falling object follows a mathematical law.

These experiments were one of the earliest attempts to use what is now called the *scientific method.* The scientific, or experimental, method consists of five steps: (1) stating the problem, (2) forming a hypothesis or a tentative theory, (3) making observations and experiments, (4) interpreting data, and (5) drawing conclusions. This method, championed by Galileo, became the basis for modern scientific research.

Galileo studies the stars and planets. Galileo's studies of the skies led him to disagree with Church doctrines as well as with the teachings of Aristotle. Soon after the telescope was invented in the Netherlands early in the 1600's, Galileo began to build a telescope he could use to observe the skies. Using his telescope, he was able to see individual stars in the Milky Way and the craters on the moon. He described his discoveries enthusiastically:

> . . . it is a most beautiful and delightful sight to behold the body of the moon . . . so that the diameter of this same moon appears about 30 times larger, its surface about 900 times, and its solid mass nearly 27,000 times larger than when it is viewed only with the naked eye: and consequently anyone may know, with the certainty that is due to the use of our senses, that the moon certainly does not possess a smooth and polished surface, but one rough and uneven, and, just like the face of the earth itself, it is everywhere full of vast [bulges and] deep chasms. . . .
> After the moon, I frequently observed other heavenly bodies, both fixed stars and planets, with incredible delight. . . .

Galileo also noted how sunspots constantly changed shape. His observations seemed to contradict the medieval belief that objects in the heavens were perfect, fixed, and unchanging. The papers he published telling about his discoveries were challenged, but soon other scientists used their own telescopes and agreed with his reports. Galileo felt his observations proved that objects in the skies were not any purer or more nearly perfect than those found on earth. He thus concluded that objects throughout the universe are subject to the same natural laws.

Galileo supports Copernicus's theory. Searching the skies with his telescope, Galileo soon was convinced that the Copernican theory was right. He discovered, for instance, that Jupiter has satellites revolving about it in the same manner that the moon revolves about the earth. This discovery challenged the view that all heavenly bodies moved around the earth. Many Church scholars, however, interpreted some passages in the Bible as meaning that the earth was stationary. In 1616, the Church forbade the teaching of Copernicus's theory.

Early in the 1620's Galileo was given the Pope's permission to write a book comparing the Ptolemaic and Copernican systems. Soon after the book was published in 1632, however, Galileo was brought to trial before the Inquisition and was accused in these words:

> . . . you, Galileo, . . . aged seventy years, were in the year 1615 denounced to this Holy Office for holding as true the false doctrine taught by some that the sun is the center of the world and immovable and that the earth moves, . . . and for following the position of Copernicus. . . .

Although the elderly scientist promised not to teach the heliocentric theory, he was condemned to remain under arrest in his own country house. His book was banned, and printers were forbidden to print anything Galileo wrote. His ideas could not be stopped, however, for scientists outside Italy continued to read his writings.

Kepler discovers laws of planetary motion. Galileo was not alone in looking for new theories to explain what he observed in the skies. Among his contemporaries were the astronomers Tycho Brahe (BRAH-eh) in Denmark and Johannes Kepler in Germany.

Like Renaissance artists, scientists of this time often depended on royal or wealthy patrons. Brahe worked first for the Danish king. With royal support, he built one of the earliest modern observatories, Uraniborg, which means "castle of the skies." Brahe agreed with part of the Copernican theory — that planets move around the sun — but still believed the sun circled the earth once a year. About 1600 Brahe began to work at the court of the Holy Roman Emperor in Prague. Kepler moved there to assist the older astronomer and published Brahe's work after the Danish scientist's death in 1601. A few years later, Kepler published his own three laws of planetary motion. These laws made sense only if one first accepted the Copernican view that planets revolve about the sun.

Kepler's theories differed in an important way from those of Copernicus, however. Copernicus had accepted the ancient Greek belief that planets move in perfect circles. Kepler's first law was in disagreement with that idea; it stated that the path of a planet is an ellipse (oval in shape) rather than a circle.

Kepler's second law also stated a new idea — that planets do not always move at the same speed but travel more quickly as they move closer to the sun. Kepler's third law showed that there is a mathematical relationship between a planet's distance from the sun and the time it takes to complete one orbit around the sun. All these laws indicated that there was a mathematical order in the planetary system.

Newton describes an orderly universe. The ideas of Copernicus, Galileo, Brahe, and Kepler had introduced a new way of studying and thinking about the universe. Isaac Newton (1642–1727), an English mathematician and scientist, used these and other new ideas to revolutionize scientific thinking. A scientific genius, Newton made significant discoveries in physics, astronomy, and mathematics.

Newton showed that all objects in the universe — things on earth, as well as moons, stars, galaxies, and planets — obey the same laws of motion. He explained this by demonstrating the actions of two forces: gravity and inertia (in-ER-shuh). According to the law of inertia, a body at rest will remain at rest unless a force causes it to move. Similarly, a moving object will continue to move in a straight line unless another force causes it to halt or to change its direction.

Gravity is the attraction that masses of matter exert on each other. Every body in the universe exercises a gravitational force on every other body. This force, Newton found, increases in proportion to the mass of the object. The greater the mass, the stronger its gravitational pull. In addition, the closer together objects are, the greater the pull of gravity.

Newton's discoveries made it possible to explain the movements of planets. According to the law of inertia, the planets would move in a straight line endlessly into space. What prevents this from happening is the gravitational pull from the mass of the sun. The sun's gravity forces the planets into elliptical orbits (as Kepler had observed).

Newton's achievement was remarkable. Building on the discoveries of Copernicus, Galileo, and Kepler, he had uncovered essential laws that operate everywhere in the universe. The same forces that cause planets to move about the sun make apples fall to the ground;

The First Scientific Organizations

The scientific curiosity and creativity of the seventeenth century encouraged scientists in several countries to organize clubs where they could meet and discuss ideas. The first of these, the Royal Society in London, was given its charter in 1662 by King Charles II, who took a lively interest in science and experimented in his own laboratory. Many important discoveries were first presented in papers read to the members, or fellows, of the Royal Society. Newton, for instance, presented his reflecting telescope to the Society in 1672 and was its president from 1703 to 1727.

In 1675 Charles II also chartered the Royal Observatory at Greenwich (GRIN-idj) near London, hoping that its research in astronomy would produce practical aids to navigation. One of the many famous scientists who directed the observatory was Edmond Halley, who predicted the path of what we now call Halley's comet (right). Because of the Royal Observatory's prestige, the meridian line passing through Greenwich was chosen in 1884 to be the *prime meridian,* from which longitude and time zones throughout the world are measured.

orbiting planets and falling apples follow the same laws of motion. Newton's laws, moreover, could be expressed mathematically. In 1687 he published his *Mathematical Principles of Natural Philosophy,* which is usually called the *Principia* (prin-SIP-ee-ah), from its Latin title. The universe he described was like a giant clock, all of whose parts followed strict mechanical and mathematical principles and worked together with perfect precision. A religious man, Newton believed God to be the creator and architect of the orderly universe, the clockmaker who set everything in motion.

ADVANCES IN THE NATURAL SCIENCES

Careful observation and use of the scientific method were also becoming important in other areas of science. Renaissance artists such as Leonardo and Michelangelo (page 333) made careful drawings of the structures of plants, animals, and the human body. At the same time, physicians began to study the human body in a scientific way.

Vesalius studies the human body. A Flemish doctor named Andreas Vesalius (vuh-SAY-lee-us) became the leader in studying human anatomy, the structure of the body. As a student, Vesalius was not satisfied with learning only from the writings of Galen, the leading physician of the Greco-Roman world (page 115). Neither did he accept many of the long-accepted ideas that were based on studies of animals. Defying the ban placed by religious authorities on dissecting human bodies, Vesalius studied corpses and skeletons.

William Harvey, an English doctor, worked out bold new ideas about the function of the human heart and blood vessels. In this painting Harvey demonstrates his theories to King Charles I.

These studies caused great controversy, but Vesalius soon became the leading physician in Europe. (He was the court physician for both Emperor Charles V and Philip II of Spain.) As a medical lecturer at the University of Padua, Vesalius urged his students to learn by investigating for themselves, as he had done. In 1543 (the year Copernicus's theory was published) Vesalius published a magnificently illustrated textbook on anatomy. His work corrected many errors that had been taught for hundreds of years. It marked the beginning of the modern study of anatomy.

Harvey describes the circulation of the blood. Because of Vesalius and his students, Padua became a center for medical studies. William Harvey, an English doctor, studied anatomy there in about 1600 and then returned to London. He practiced medicine and became the court physician for James I and Charles I. Conducting his own experiments, Harvey examined the hearts of many animals. "I found the task so . . . full of difficulties," he wrote, "that I was almost tempted to think . . . that the motion of the heart was only to be comprehended by God." Harvey's careful work enabled him to discover and explain the circulation of the blood and the workings of the heart. His book on this subject was published in 1628.

Leeuwenhoek discovers the world of microscopic animals. Scientists' investigations in many fields were made easier by the skills of Dutch artisans who learned to grind fine glass lenses that magnified objects many times. This discovery was made about 1600. Galileo used it in building his telescopes (page 403); other scientists used one or more lenses to make microscopes.

Anton van Leeuwenhoek (LAY-vun-hook) was a Dutch shopkeeper and amateur scientist who ground fine glass lenses to help him in studying nature. He soon learned to make lenses that showed objects hundreds of times larger than they really were. Leeuwenhoek used his microscope to study the eye of an ox, the brain of a fly, wool fibers, and the seeds of plants. He even watched the blood racing through a tadpole's body.

One day Leeuwenhoek put some water under the lens of his microscope and saw "living creatures, . . . little animals," swimming rapidly about. Soon he was looking with "wonder [at] a thousand living creatures in one drop of water." Leeuwenhoek had uncovered a mysterious new world — the world of one-celled living things, too small to be seen with the naked eye. He immediately shared this discovery with other scientists. In 1683 the Royal Society of London (page 405) published some of Leeuwenhoek's reports and drawings.

Both Newton and Leeuwenhoek had opened up new worlds for scientists to explore.

Newton had explained the workings of the universe; Leeuwenhoek had discovered the world of the infinitely small.

Scientists develop a classification system. One of the aims of early scientists was to find laws or systems that would reveal a logical order in nature. In the eighteenth century a Swedish naturalist, Carolus Linnaeus (lih-NEE-us), studied plants and animals and wrote careful descriptions of them. To collect plants, he traveled through the arctic regions of Europe, covering nearly a thousand miles on foot. From his observations Linnaeus developed a system for naming and classifying plants, which he published in 1753. Five years later, he published a system classifying more than 4,000 animals. A French naturalist, the Comte de Buffon, made similar detailed studies of animals.

It was Linnaeus's system that first assigned a two-word Latin name to each kind of living thing — for instance, *Canis familiaris* for domestic dogs. This was the basis for the classification system that scientists still use today.

Philosophers encourage scientific study. A number of thinkers who were not actually working scientists played important roles in the Scientific Revolution. They suggested methods for organizing scientific thought and research. Sir Francis Bacon, an English statesman and writer, wanted science to help people live more comfortable lives and be better informed about the world around them. In his book *Novum Organum* (1620) Bacon urged scientists to use careful observation and experiments as the basis for working out theories. His work pro-

vided a guide for later scientists and scholars who sought to organize and classify knowledge.

In France at about the same time, René Descartes (day-KART) took a different approach. A genius in mathematics, Descartes sought a way to explain problems in both science and philosophy in terms of a mathematical method. His *Discourse on Method* was published in 1637. For Descartes, the only clear truth was his own mind and ability to reason. He expressed this in the famous statement, "I think, therefore I am."

CHECK-UP

1. Vocabulary: *scientific method.*
2. (a) Describe the medieval view of the universe. (b) How did earthly and heavenly objects differ, according to medieval thinkers? (c) How did Copernicus's explanation of the universe conflict with the medieval view?
3. (a) What new approach did Galileo take to the study of nature? (b) What advance in technology helped him? (c) Why was Galileo's support of the Copernican theory attacked?
4. What contributions did Brahe and Kepler make to astronomy?
5. (a) What two forces were important in Newton's explanation of the motion of planets? (b) What was new about his description of the universe?
6. What contributions to modern science were made by each of the following? (a) Vesalius, (b) Harvey, (c) Leeuwenhoek, (d) Linnaeus.
7. What part did Bacon and Descartes play in the Scientific Revolution?

2 Enlightenment Thinkers Seek Reforms

The influence of the scientific approach and of scientists' search for order and method soon spread beyond the world of science. Philosophers greatly admired Newton because he had successfully used reason to explain the laws governing the universe. They hoped to apply the scientific method to studying and improving human society. They urged applying reason to all aspects of social and political life — gov-

ernment, law, economics, religion, and education. This period therefore came to be called the Age of Reason or the Enlightenment. It began with some key ideas that were put forth in the seventeenth century by English political thinkers.

Hobbes tries to find a science of government. Thomas Hobbes, an English political theorist, sought to create a science of politics.

Influenced by meeting Galileo and Descartes, Hobbes said that there are basic laws governing human behavior and that these laws are as precise as those in the physical world. If these laws were correctly understood, he said, it would be possible to create a government that works according to scientific principles.

Hobbes believed that people act out of self-interest. Because they want power, possessions, security, honor, and fame, they compete violently with each other. Without government to make and enforce laws, Hobbes felt there would be a war "of every man against every man." To maintain civilized life, said Hobbes, a strong government must set rules that control human nature.

Hobbes lived at the time of the English Civil War (page 389) and considered that conflict an example of the dangerous capacities of human nature. He maintained that a strong ruler was necessary to avoid total disorder. His book *Leviathan* (1651) compared the state to a whale, arguing that each must be controlled by a single mind. He did not believe that rulers derived their power from God, however. Rather he introduced the idea that people made a "social contract," trading their liberties for order and good government. Few people agreed with Hobbes's thinking, but later philosophers examined the questions he raised.

Locke proposes the idea of natural rights. The most influential ideas on government in the Age of Reason were those of John Locke. Locke became deeply involved in the politics of the Glorious Revolution in England (page 390). In his *Two Treatises of Government* (1689) he justified Parliament's actions in replacing the English monarch.

According to Locke, the purpose of government is to protect what he called the "natural rights" of its citizens. All people, said Locke, are born free and equal, with a right to life, liberty, and property. Another natural right, he believed, was "the pursuit of happiness," the individual's private rights and choices. If a government fails to protect the rights of its citizens, said Locke, the leaders of the government have "put themselves into a state of war with the people." The people have the right (or duty), he declared, to overthrow that government and establish a better one.

Locke's theory of government was immensely influential in modern political thinking. His principle that government derives its power from the consent of the people is the foundation of modern democracy. Since the purpose of government is "the good of mankind," said Locke, people are justified in rebelling against governments that persistently and unjustly repress them. These ideas were later used in struggles for liberty both in Europe and the Americas. The American Declaration of Independence (page 431) echoed Locke's theory of natural rights and his view of a society based on freedom.

Locke influences ideas on education. Locke's ideas on knowledge and education were closely related to his political ideas. He was also influenced by Newton's discoveries in science. An individual, Locke said, is not born good or evil, wise or ignorant. Rather, people's characters and knowledge are shaped by their experiences and the thoughts they have about those experiences. Locke compared the mind of a newborn child to a tablet on which no one has written. The child's experiences in growing up, he said, determined what that child would be like as an adult. Nine of every ten people, wrote Locke, "are good or evil, useful or not, [because of] their education."

Enlightenment philosophers question religious authority. The Enlightenment thinkers believed that human thought ought to be independent of any authority, religious or governmental. Knowledge, they thought, was gained only through a careful and rational analysis of nature and human experience. Most of them therefore rejected many of the traditional beliefs of religion. Some were atheists, people who deny the existence of God. Most, however, were deists. That is, they believed in God but rejected the authority of the clergy and many Christian teachings. They tried to make religion fit with their understanding of nature. Deists accepted only those principles of religion they considered reasonable, such as the existence of God. The deists looked upon Jesus as a great moral teacher rather than as the son of God.

The Enlightenment is centered in France. The social critics and philosophers of this period in France were known as *philosophes* (FIL-oh-sofs). Many of the reforms the philosophes proposed were a reaction against the French traditions of absolute monarchy and the divine right of kings. They also challenged the traditional view that the nobility and clergy were entitled to special privileges. The Church in France paid no taxes. Religious authorities exercised *censorship* — that is, they stopped the publication of works considered a threat to accepted teachings. French nobles were largely free of taxation and held the highest positions in the government, the army, and the Church by right of birth. Many of the philosophes looked to England as an example of a country where reforms had brought religious liberty, political rights, and a monarchy that was limited by law.

Enlightenment thinkers call for freedom of thought. The philosophes considered wars and persecutions in the name of religion to be unreasonable. They could find no rational justification for religious fanaticism or intolerance. They wanted individuals to be able to choose their own religious beliefs freely and not be persecuted for them.

Enlightenment thinkers also believed people should be free to express their ideas on other subjects. They opposed censorship by either the Church or the government. A number of philosophes spent time in prison or in exile for writings to which the authorities objected.

Probably the most brilliant and influential of the philosophes was the writer Voltaire (vohl-TAIR), whose real name was François Marie Arouet. Voltaire wrote political essays and clever stories in which he attacked or made fun of intolerance and superstition. His most famous work was *Candide* (1759). Voltaire vowed to fight for tolerance: "I shall not cease . . . to preach tolerance from the rooftops as long as persecution does not cease."

Voltaire, like many philosophes, admired England for the reforms already made there. He wrote:

> English law . . . has restored each man to all the rights of nature of which he has been deprived in most monarchies. These rights are: full liberty of his person [and] of his goods; freedom to speak to the nation by the pen; freedom not to be tried under any criminal charge except by a jury formed of independent men; freedom not to be tried in any case

except according to the precise terms of the law; freedom to profess peacefully any religion he wishes.

Montesquieu urges the separation of powers in government. The Baron de Montesquieu (MON-tus-kyew), a French lawyer and aristocrat, also admired the English system of government and the freedoms that English people were guaranteed. Like John Locke and others, he tried to set down ideas or principles that would lead to good government and preserve people's rights. "Liberty [is not] an unlimited freedom," he said. "Liberty is a right of doing whatever the laws permit."

In a book called *The Spirit of the Laws* (1748), Montesquieu put forth the principle of *separation of powers,* the division of authority among three branches of government. One branch, the legislature, would make the laws. A second branch, the executive, would see that the laws were carried out. The third branch, the judiciary, would interpret the laws, judge lawbreakers, and handle disputes between individuals. Separation of powers, Montesquieu believed, would prevent any individual or group from gaining absolute control of the government. In this way, he maintained, the liberty of the people would be safeguarded. Montesquieu's principle of separation of powers greatly influenced the authors of the United States Constitution (page 437).

Many philosophes write for the *Encyclopedia*. In their admiration for science and other fields of human knowledge, a number of philosophes in France cooperated in publishing the *Encyclopedia.* This multi-volume work aimed to collect information on many topics, with emphasis on science and technology. Its complete title, in fact, was *Classified Dictionary of the Sciences, Arts, and Skills.* The *Encyclopedia* expressed the spirit of the Enlightenment, and many philosophes, including Voltaire and Montesquieu, wrote articles for it. The chief editor was the French writer Denis Diderot (dee-DROH). The mathematician and physicist Jean d'Alembert (dah-lahm-BAIR) edited the scientific articles.

Diderot began publication of the first volumes in 1751. Censors of both the French government and the Church banned the work for

French philosophes often gathered at the homes of aristocrats to debate their ideas. Above, a famous actor reads to a group of philosophes and aristocrats.

undermining royal authority, encouraging a spirit of revolt, and fostering "moral corruption, . . . irreligion, and . . . unbelief." Diderot finally convinced the government to permit publication of some volumes of the *Encyclopedia,* but the articles had to be carefully worded to avoid criticism by the censors. The *Encyclopedia* was widely read in other parts of Europe, however, and new volumes were brought out regularly until 1777.

Enlightenment thinkers seek reforms in society. The *Encyclopedia* was one way in which the philosophes attacked injustices they saw in eighteenth-century society. Articles in the *Encyclopedia* often presented writers' opinions as well as factual information. For instance, one article described war as a "violent sickness," a madness unworthy of civilized people. If humans would act according to reason, it said, they would never "surrender themselves to the fury of war." Another article condemned slavery, insisting that no one has the right to deprive people of their freedom: "Men and their liberty are not objects of commerce;

they can be neither sold nor bought nor paid for at any price. . . . There is not, therefore, a single one of these unfortunate people regarded only as slaves, who does not have the right to be declared free."

Calls for social reform were not limited to France. Writers in other countries also sought ways to eliminate abuses and injustices. Again, they hoped that science and reason would improve conditions. For example, the eighteenth-century prison system was frequently brutal and unjust. Physical punishment, such as beating or branding, was common; a person might be hanged for stealing.

In his treatise *Of Crimes and Punishments* (1764), Cesare Beccaria (bek-uh-REE-uh), an Italian economist and law professor, condemned severe punishments, particularly capital punishment (the death penalty). Beccaria also criticized the use of torture, which was then a common method of obtaining confessions. He pointed out that under torture, an innocent person might confess to crimes. Unconvinced that the system then in use discouraged crime, Beccaria urged a scientific investigation into the effectiveness of punishment and called for crime prevention through education.

John Howard, an English reformer, called attention to the mistreatment of convicts in a tract called *State of the Prisons in England and Wales* (1777). "Many prisons are scantily supplied, and some are almost totally unprovided with the necessaries of life," said Howard. As a result, he concluded, prisons often changed convicts from healthy individuals to starving, sickly people.

Enlightenment thinkers value education. The philosophes believed that knowledge and education were essential if people were to become better and happier. Their views on learning were largely based on the ideas of John Locke (page 408). The philosophes interpreted Locke's theory to mean that human beings were born good but might become wicked if they were improperly brought up, badly educated, and poorly governed. The philosophes thought the cause of crime and evil was a poor environment rather than corrupt human nature. They argued that evil exists not because of human nature but because of society. If the conditions of life were improved, these reformers reasoned, people would behave better. A proper education, they said, could mold children into intelligent and responsible citizens.

Locke's ideas on natural rights and on the importance of education had revolutionary implications. If, as he said, people are born fundamentally equal, then all children, rich or poor, could become educated under proper conditions. This was a difficult idea for most philosophes, who were well-educated people from middle-class or aristocratic families. They generally distrusted the common people, whom they considered too superstitious and ignorant to be enlightened. The view that all children can benefit from education, however, gradually gained support. It became the basis of the movement for public schooling in the nineteenth and twentieth centuries.

Rousseau proposes new approaches to education and social change. The philosophe who most influenced educational theory was Jean Jacques Rousseau (roo-SOH). Born in Switzerland, Rousseau spent much of his adult life in France. He met with other philosophes and wrote for the *Encyclopedia* but violently disagreed with them on many issues. Most Enlightenment thinkers admired progress in the arts and sciences. Rousseau, however, thought that arts and sciences were a part of the way of life that corrupted people's natural goodness.

Rousseau drew a sharp distinction between "civilized people" and what he called "natural man," or the "noble savage." People who live in a civilized society, said Rousseau, are unhappy, insecure, and selfish. He argued that people who lived outdoors, in harmony with nature, were happier, less selfish, and less greedy for possessions. He gave a romantic, idealized picture of their lives.

Rousseau believed more in people's intuitions about goodness than in a rational scientific approach. He did feel, however, that social and political reforms could create a society that allowed people to realize their natural goodness. He applied his theories to education in a book titled *Émile* (1762). Rousseau felt that children should grow up in the country and be allowed to enjoy their youth. They should learn from books, he said, only when they become interested in learning. He recommended this plan for "Nature's pupil":

> Give his body constant exercise, make it strong and healthy in order to make him good and wise; let him work, let him do things, let him run and shout, let him be always on the go; make a man of him in strength, and he will soon be a man in reason.

Rousseau published his political philosophy in the same year he wrote *Émile*. Both Hobbes and Locke had used the idea of a "social contract" that people make with their ruler or government. For Rousseau, however, a society was formed by people making a social contract with the others in the community, agreeing to work for the good of all.

Enlightenment thinkers disagree on democracy. Rousseau believed that people, acting together, were capable of making wise decisions about government. This belief also set him apart from most other philosophes. While they supported political liberty, few philosophes favored democracy. They agreed with Voltaire that the common people were incapable of governing themselves. "Once the [common people]

Frederick II, Prussia's "enlightened despot," greatly admired French philosophes and artists. He even invited Voltaire to live at his court.

begin to reason," Voltaire wrote, "then everything is lost. I [hate] the idea of government by the masses." According to Voltaire, the best form of government was a monarchy in which the ruler was familiar with the teachings of the philosophes and respected the people's rights. Such an "enlightened" monarch would rule justly and would introduce reforms.

European monarchs adopt Enlightenment ideas. Although the philosophes were a small group, they had great influence. Enlightenment ideas were spread not only by their books but also by their visits and letters to European rulers and political leaders. In the last part of the eighteenth century several monarchs —Holy Roman Emperor Joseph II of Austria, Frederick II of Prussia, and Catherine the Great of Russia — introduced reforms that seemed to reflect the spirit of the Enlightenment. They became known as *enlightened despots.* (A despot is an autocratic ruler.)

At times these enlightened despots allowed religious toleration, ended censorship, stopped the use of torture, and widened opportunities for education. Some tried to improve conditions for serfs. Behind these reforms, however,

lay the realization that the struggle for power in Europe called for efficient government administration, a growing economy, and the loyalty of subjects. These monarchs made few real changes in the social structure of their states.

Enlightenment ideas spread to a wider audience. There were many ways in which new ideas could spread in eighteenth-century Europe. Organizations like the Royal Society (page 405) gave those interested in science or other fields a chance to meet, hear lectures about one another's discoveries, and discuss ideas. Lively discussions took place in the newly popular coffeehouses. Although the Enlightenment began among the educated upper classes, its ideas eventually were spread to ordinary people by journals, newspapers, inexpensive pamphlets, and even political songs.

In Paris, wealthy and intelligent French women held salons (sah-LONZ), where writers, philosophers, and artists met regularly. They played music, read poetry, and discussed ideas. Salons were noted for witty, intelligent conversation. Contributors to the *Encyclopedia* often met at the salon of Marie-Thérèse Geoffrin (juh-FRAHN), a wealthy widow who corresponded with the king of Sweden and Catherine the Great of Russia (page 396). Madame Geoffrin also gave financial backing to the *Encyclopedia.* A rival salon was that at the home of Julie de Lespinasse (les-pih-NAHS). One philosophe wrote this description of her salon:

> She could unite the different types [of visitors], even the most antagonistic, sustaining the conversation by a well-aimed phrase, animating and guiding it at will. . . . Politics, religion, philosophy, news: nothing was excluded. Her circle met daily from five to nine. There one found men of all ranks in the state, the Church, and the court, soldiers and foreigners, and the leading writers of the day.

Women's role in the Enlightenment (as in the Renaissance) was mainly a supporting one. Some took part in the correspondence among the philosophes and wrote lively descriptions of eighteenth-century life and society. Only a few, however, could gain the education to participate actively in science and the arts. One of these was Emilie du Châtelet (shah-tuh-LAY), a noblewoman trained as a mathematician and physicist. She translated Newton's work from Latin into French.

Only a few philosophes extended their ideals for society to include women as equals. Most claimed that women were intellectually inferior to men. Rousseau, for example, said that women lacked the intellectual ability to make significant contributions to the arts and sciences. The mathematician Jean d'Alembert (page 409), however, argued that education would improve women's minds and urged the philosophes to set an example by giving their daughters and sons the same education.

Eighteenth-century artists emphasize balance and gracefulness. The Enlightenment's admiration for order and reason also affected all the arts — music, literature, painting, and architecture. In the 1500's and 1600's, wealthy and powerful European monarchs had built elaborate palaces such as Versailles (page 383) to display the richness of their state. The musicians, painters, and writers of the time had also used elaborate, complicated styles in their work. This period, which lasted into the early 1700's, is known as the Baroque (bah-ROHK). Probably the outstanding figure in the Baroque period was the composer Johann Sebastian Bach in Germany.

Under the influence of the Enlightenment, styles in the arts began to change. Artists worked in a simple and elegant style that borrowed ideas from classical Greece and Rome. The period after about 1750 is therefore called the Classical.

The philosophes and other writers of this time tried to write in a clear, logical way. They admired the scientific approach, which emphasized form and order. Two well-known English writers in this style were Joseph Addison and Richard Steele. They published several magazines that made the ideas of John Locke and other philosophers known to the English public. French classical writing emphasized drama. The tragedies of Racine (rah-SEEN) and the witty, satirical comedies of Molière (mohl-YAIR), though written in the previous century, are considered classical works.

Three composers in Vienna, Austria, were the most important figures of the Classical period in music. They were Franz Josef Haydn (HY-dun), Wolfgang Amadeus Mozart (MOHT-sart), and Ludwig van Beethoven (BAY-toh-vun). Haydn was particularly important in developing several modern musical forms, such as the sonata and the symphony. Mozart wrote hundreds of works, although he only lived to be 35 years old. His operas, such as *Don Giovanni* and *The Marriage of Figaro*, set a new style. The compositions of both Haydn and Mozart are still loved for their simple, beautiful elegance, while those of Beethoven are known for their power and grandeur.

Mozart and Beethoven, who lived near the end of the Classical period, took part in an important change that was occurring in music. Before this time, most composers had worked at the courts of nobles and monarchs or held church positions. Except in church, the audiences who heard their music were mainly members of the nobility and the upper classes. In the late 1700's, however, musicians began to give public performances. People from all classes flocked to concert halls and theaters and eagerly awaited new compositions by their favorite musicians.

CHECK-UP

1. Vocabulary: *philosophe, censorship, separation of powers, enlightened despot.*
2. Why was the eighteenth century called the Age of Reason?
3. (a) How did Hobbes view human nature? (b) Why did he favor strong government?
4. Describe Locke's views on (a) natural rights, (b) the purpose of government, and (c) education.
5. (a) How did their belief in science and reason influence the religious attitudes of Enlightenment thinkers? (b) What traditional attitudes about monarchs, nobles, and clergy did the philosophes challenge?
6. (a) What did Voltaire admire about the British government? (b) Why did Montesquieu call for the separation of powers in government?
7. (a) How did Rousseau's views differ from those of other philosophes? (b) What were Rousseau's views on education?
8. (a) In what ways did Enlightenment ideas influence other parts of society? (b) What part did women play in the Enlightenment?

Chapter 18 Review

Summary

The Scientific Revolution and the Enlightenment were important in shaping modern ways of thinking about both the physical universe and human society. During the Scientific Revolution, the medieval earth-centered view of the universe was rejected, and scientists used observation, experimentation, and mathematics to develop new theories. Building on earlier work of Copernicus, Galileo, Brahe, and Kepler, the English scientist Isaac Newton described a universe governed by mathematical laws of motion. In the natural sciences, Vesalius, Harvey, Leeuwenhoek, and Linnaeus used the scientific method to find a system and order in living things.

The Enlightenment, or Age of Reason, built on the achievements of the Scientific Revolution. Enlightenment thinkers in England and France (the philosophes) tried to understand and improve society, government, and humanity through the use of reason. They maintained that individuals had natural rights that should be protected from oppressive government. The philosophes attacked religious persecution and limits on freedom of thought. The Enlightenment emphasis on rational thought, political rights, and personal freedom would bring great changes in politics and society.

Vocabulary Review

1. Write the sentences listed below on a sheet of paper. Fill in the blank in each sentence with one of these words or phrases: *censorship, enlightened despot, philosophe, scientific method, separation of powers:*

(a) Someone like Rousseau, who was a leading social critic of the Enlightenment, was known as a __?__ .

(b) An __?__ was a ruler of Europe who introduced reforms that seemed to reflect the spirit of the Enlightenment.

(c) __?__ is the practice of stopping the publication or distribution of works that may seem to threaten established institutions.

(d) __?__ is a method of ensuring that no one branch of government will be dominant.

(e) The __?__ uses experimentation and observation to study the natural world.

2. Distinguish between the terms in each of the following pairs:

(a) Enlightenment; Scientific Revolution.
(b) gravity; inertia.
(c) *Candide; Émile.*
(d) executive; legislature.
(e) *Principia; Encyclopedia.*

People to Identify

Match the following people with the numbered phrases that describe them: *Johann Sebastian Bach, Denis Diderot, Marie-Thérèse Geoffrin, Franz Josef Haydn, Johannes Kepler, John Locke, Isaac Newton, Jean Jacques Rousseau.*

1. Set forth three laws of planetary motion.

2. Chief editor of the *Encyclopedia.*

3. Claimed that citizens have the right to overthrow their government when it fails to protect their rights.

4. German composer of the Baroque period.

5. Wealthy Parisian who gave financial backing to the *Encyclopedia* and held the salon where many of its contributors met.

6. Argued that people who live in harmony with nature are happier than those who live in civilized societies.

7. Used gravity and inertia to explain laws of motion in operation throughout the universe.

8. Classical composer who developed the sonata and the symphony.

Relating Geography and History

1. Comparing maps. During the eighteenth century, European cartographers (mapmakers) were able to correct many of the errors made on earlier maps by using (1) telescopes to make more accurate projections of distance and (2) information from explorers and travelers. Compare the map on page 216 of this book with the map on page 856. Which do you think was drawn later? Explain your answer.

2. Research. Because of the detailed records he kept of his voyage to Australia and New Guinea (1699–1701), William Dampier (DAM-pih-ur) has been called the "pioneer of scientific exploration." (a) Use a geographical dictionary, atlas, or gazetteer to locate several places named for him — Dampier Strait, Dampier Archipelago, and Dampier Land. In what present-day nation or region is each located? (b) How did Dampier's desire to explore and map foreign lands reflect the scientific curiosity of the Enlightenment?

Discussion Questions

1. Why did the advances in science made during the seventeenth century become known as the "Scientific Revolution"?

2. (a) How did the geocentric and the heliocentric theories differ? (b) Why did many scholars and the clergy reject the heliocentric theory?

3. How did the discoveries of (a) Galileo, (b) Kepler, and (c) Newton support or help to explain the heliocentric theory?

4. How was the scientific method used by (a) Harvey and (b) Vesalius?

5. In what ways did the Enlightenment grow out of the Scientific Revolution?

6. What were the ideas of Enlightenment thinkers on (a) religious authority, (b) religious wars or persecutions, (c) censorship?

7. (a) What did the philosophes criticize about France? (b) What did they praise about the British government?

8. (a) Why did Hobbes support absolute monarchy? (b) How did Locke's views challenge the concept of absolute monarchy?

9. What ideas of (a) Locke and (b) Rousseau influenced education?

10. In what ways did the *Encyclopedia* reflect the ideas of the philosophes?

11. What proposals to prevent a government's abuse of power were made by (a) Locke and (b) Montesquieu? (c) How did Rousseau's ideas promote democracy?

Reading Primary Sources

In the following passage, Leeuwenhoek describes some of the tiny animals he saw through his microscope. Read the passage. Then answer the questions that follow.

> In the year 1675, about half-way through September, . . . I discovered living creatures in rain, which had stood but a few days in a new tub. . . . This observation provoked me to investigate this water . . .

because these little animals were to my eye more than 10,000 times smaller than the . . . water-flea or water-louse, which you can see alive and moving in water with the bare eye.

> I saw . . . that the bodies consisted of five, six, seven, or eight very clear globules, but . . . [I was not] able to . . . [see] any membrane or skin that held these globules together, or in which they were enclosed. When these animalcules [little animals] bestirred themselves, they sometimes stuck out two little horns, which . . . continually moved, after the fashion of horses' ears. The part between these little horns was flat, their body . . . [otherwise] being roundish, save only that it ran somewhat to a point at the end; at which pointed end it had a tail . . . [almost] four times as long as the whole body, and looking as thick, when viewed through my microscope, as a spider's web. At the end of the tail there was a pellet . . . [as big as] one of the globules of the body; and this tail I could not perceive to be used by them for their movements in very clear water. These little animals were the most wretched creatures that I have ever seen. . . .

(a) In what kind of water did Leeuwenhoek discover the animalcules? (b) What was their size in comparison to the smallest animals visible to the human eye? (c) How did the animalcules change when they moved? (d) Describe their tails. (e) Using Leeuwenhoek's description, draw an enlarged picture of what he apparently saw, labeling the parts of the animal he described.

Skill Activities

1. Biographies. Write a biographical sketch of one of the following scientists: (a) Copernicus, (b) Tycho Brahe, (c) Galileo, (d) Linnaeus, (e) Vesalius. Include information about the scientist's early life and education, reasons for his interest in science, his contribution to the Scientific Revolution, and the reaction to his work when it was first reported or published.

2. Word research. Leeuwenhoek's *microscope* introduced the world to microorganisms, living things too small to be seen with the naked eye. *Micro-* comes from the Greek word *mikros,* meaning "little." How does each of the following words reflect a similar idea: (a) microbe, (b) microfilm, (c) micron, (d) microbiology, (e) microwave?

Unit Four Review

Review Questions

1. In what ways did the views of the Renaissance thinkers represent a break with traditional views?

2. (a) What influence did Machiavelli's writing have on ways of thinking about politics? (b) How did Thomas Hobbes' theories expand on Machiavelli's views?

3. (a) Which ideas and developments of the Renaissance contributed to the Age of Exploration? (b) How did the discoveries of the Age of Exploration help to bring about the great economic changes of the Commercial Revolution? (c) How was Europe's position in world trade affected by the Commercial Revolution?

4. (a) Describe the religious conflicts that brought about the Thirty Years' War. (b) How did that war affect the states of Europe?

5. (a) What events led to Spain's becoming the most powerful state in Europe in the sixteenth century? (b) What developments caused Spain's decline in the seventeenth century?

6. (a) Explain what is meant by balance of power. (b) How did concern over the balance of power play a part in the wars of Louis XIV?

7. (a) Why did rulers in Eastern Europe find it difficult to develop strong centralized states? (b) How did the czars build a powerful Russian state?

8. What were the major contributions to science of (a) Copernicus, (b) Kepler, (c) Newton, (d) Vesalius, and (e) Linnaeus?

9. Voltaire said, "English law . . . has restored each man to all the rights of nature of which he has been deprived in most monarchies." What political changes in England between 1628 and 1689 might have led Voltaire to make this remark?

10. What did each of the following contribute to the modern outlook: (a) the Reformation, (b) the Scientific Revolution, (c) the Enlightenment?

Projects

1. Making charts. Make a chart comparing the monarchs of England, France, Spain, and Russia that you have studied in this unit. Include in your chart (a) names, (b) dates of birth and death, (c) countries ruled, (d) dates of rule, and (e) notable events of the monarchs' reigns. When you have completed your chart, choose one ruler and write a one-page biography of that person.

2. Evaluating historical figures. Create a Hall of Fame for 1300–1700. Choose one of the following groups: (a) explorers, (b) religious reformers, (c) philosophers, (d) scientists, (e) writers and artists. Make a list of the men and women you think should be included and write a brief paragraph explaining why each person deserves this honor.

Books to Read

Asimov, Isaac. *Great Ideas of Science.* Houghton Mifflin. Includes biographical sketches.

Blitzer, Charles. *The Age of Kings.* Time-Life. The seventeenth century in Europe.

Chamberlin, Eric Russell. *Everyday Life in Renaissance Times.* Putnam.

Elliott, John H. *Imperial Spain, 1469–1716.* New American Library.

Gilbert, Creighton, ed. *Renaissance Art.* Harper.

Hale, John R. *The Age of Exploration.* Time-Life.

Hale, John R. *The Renaissance.* Time-Life.

Mattingly, Garrett. *The Armada.* Houghton Mifflin.

Miquel, Pierre. *The Age of Discovery.* Silver Burdett.

Morison, Samuel Eliot. *Admiral of the Ocean Sea.* Little, Brown. A biography of Columbus.

O'Dell, Scott. *The Amethyst Ring.* Houghton Mifflin. An easy-to-read novel about the Spanish conquest of the Aztecs and the Incas.

Rahn, Joan Elma. *Plants That Changed History.* Atheneum. About the impact of cereals, spices, sugarcane, and potatoes on history and ways of living.

Sanderlin, George. *Eastward to India: Vasco da Gama's Voyage.* Harper.

Simon, Edith. *The Reformation.* Time-Life.

Sootin, Harry. *Isaac Newton.* Julian Messner.

How to Study World History

Building Map Skills

The ability to read maps has lifelong usefulness. Maps are especially important in studying history. *Political maps* — that is, maps showing countries and their boundaries — are essential in a world history textbook. In Chapter 17 there are several political maps showing the same area at different periods of time. They illustrate how European national boundaries changed from the sixteenth century to the eighteenth century. Learning to use such political maps will help you read history with better understanding. Below are some guidelines for studying political maps.

Identify the topic of the map. Begin your study of any map by making sure that you understand the map's purpose. The title of the map is a good starting point. The map on page 377 is entitled "Europe About 1560." This tells you that it shows the political boundaries of European nations and empires about the year 1560. The map on page 393, "Partitions of Poland," describes the divisions of Poland made by other European nations.

Also consider the time period covered by a map. The map's title may include this information, as does "Europe About 1560." On other maps, the time period may be indicated in the map key. On the map "Partitions of Poland," dates on the colored areas indicate the period covered by the map.

Study the symbols on the map. Once you have determined the purpose of a map, examine the map key. The key explains the meaning of the colors and symbols. On the map on page 377, "Europe About 1560," one color shows the areas belonging to the Spanish Hapsburgs in 1560 and another color shows the areas belonging to the Austrian Hapsburgs. What color shows the holdings of the Spanish Hapsburgs? the Austrian Hapsburgs? There are two symbols in the key. The line with an arrow traces the route of the Spanish Armada to England and back to Spain. The heavy black line outlines the territory that was part of the Holy Roman Empire in 1560.

Many of the maps in this book have a number of frequently used symbols that are not listed in every map key. The directional symbol helps you find north on the map. The "Europe About 1560" map uses broken lines to show national boundaries and dots for cities.

Examine the map scale. The scale of a map helps you to determine the distance, in miles or kilometers, between points shown on a map. On the map on page 377, the scale shows that 3/4 inch on the map equals 300 miles or 480 kilometers.

Analyze and draw conclusions from the map. Use the symbols on the map to help you understand and analyze information. For example, by examining the map "Europe About 1560" on page 377, you can learn which countries were included in the Holy Roman Empire and which countries were held by the Spanish and Austrian Hapsburgs. Using this information, you can draw conclusions about the reasons for the lack of unity within the Holy Roman Empire and for France's fear of Hapsburg power.

Check Your Skill

Use the following questions to check your understanding of what you have read:

1. A major purpose of a political map is to show (a) rivers and lakes, (b) trade routes, (c) national boundaries.

2. The map on page 397 indicates that (a) Russia was smaller in 1796 than it was in 1598, (b) Russia's territory doubled in size between 1598 and 1689, (c) Poland took over parts of Russia by 1796.

3. From the information on the map on page 385, you can learn (a) reasons for the decline of the Spanish Hapsburgs, (b) the countries under Bourbon control in 1721, (c) the extent of territory conquered by Russia during the 1600's.

Apply Your Skill

Look at the map of the Age of Exploration in Chapter 16 (pages 352–353). Write a paragraph explaining the purpose of the map and the meaning of the various colors and route lines used. List three conclusions that can be drawn from studying the information on the map.

We the People

Revolution and Nationalism in the Western World

Advances in science, technology, industry, and the arts were featured at London's Great Exhibition, opened by Queen Victoria in 1851. Of equal importance with changes displayed at the Exhibition were new ideas of liberty and equality, symbolized by the words "We the people" from the Constitution of the United States.

New ways of thinking about government, science, economics, and religion had brought many changes to the Western world by the eighteenth century. The Enlightenment had raised questions about the rights of men and women, the duties of government, and the structure of society. Concern for individual freedoms became so strong that it led to revolution in many lands.

In Britain's American colonies, revolution brought the establishment of a new nation, the United States. Americans, nevertheless, retained many British political institutions and ideas. The revolution in France, however, sought not only changes in government but also reforms in France's feudal social structure. The French Revolution later turned to violence, paving the way for the rise of a strong ruler, Napoleon Bonaparte.

European monarchs allied to defeat Napoleon and then attempted to restore traditional forms of government. The spirit of revolution persisted, however. Throughout Europe, people rebelled against repressive rule and demanded a greater voice in their own governments. Although most of these revolutions failed, the demands and hopes continued. Gradually more people won a measure of liberty and equality. New nations were established both in Europe and in Latin America. In North America, the United States expanded, while another great nation, Canada, developed to the north.

A revolution in technology occurred at about the same time as these political revolutions. The Industrial Revolution led to sweeping social and economic changes in the Western nations.

The following chapters describe the revolutionary changes in the West during the eighteenth and nineteenth centuries.

George Washington led the army of citizen soldiers that won the struggle to establish the independence of the United States. This painting by the American artist John Trumbull shows Washington after the surrender of the British army at the Battle of Yorktown.

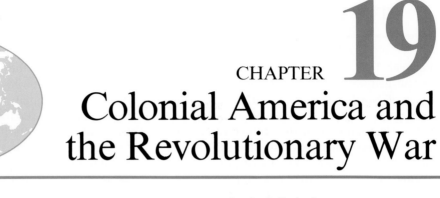

CHAPTER **19**

Colonial America and the Revolutionary War

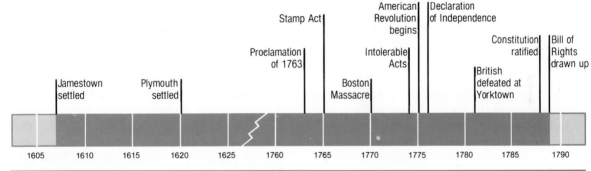

American Revolution begins | Declaration of Independence

Stamp Act

Proclamation of 1763 | Intolerable Acts | Constitution ratified | Bill of Rights drawn up

Jamestown settled | Plymouth settled | Boston Massacre | British defeated at Yorktown

1605 1610 1615 1620 1625 1760 1765 1770 1775 1780 1785 1790

In the seventeenth and eighteenth centuries, thirteen colonies were established in the land that Britain claimed in North America. These colonies offered settlers economic opportunities as well as more personal freedom and self-government than they had in Europe. Eventually conflicts developed between the colonies and Britain when Parliament tried to establish tighter control over colonial trade and industry. Other actions by Parliament increased the colonists' resentment. They argued that Parliament was attempting to strip them of their rights as British subjects. Many Americans defied British laws, and in 1775 the conflicts exploded into war.

In the following year the colonies proclaimed their independence, and in 1783 they achieved it. After a period of weak and unstable government, the United States adopted a constitution that set the new nation on a solid foundation.

This chapter discusses the founding of the English colonies in America, the breaking away of the colonies from England, and the events that led to the establishment of the United States.

CHAPTER OUTLINE

1 The English Colonies Are Founded
2 The Colonists Object to British Policies
3 Revolution Brings Independence

421

1 The English Colonies Are Founded

Between 1607 and 1733, settlers from England established thirteen colonies on the Atlantic coast of North America. From England, they brought with them ideas of political freedom that took root and flourished in these colonies.

The first colony is established in Virginia. In 1607 a joint-stock company of London merchants financed a settlement of English colonists at Jamestown in what is now Virginia (map, page 363). (The colony was named after King James I.) England's first permanent settlement in North America nearly failed, however. Knowing of the wealth in Spain's colonies, the Virginia colonists hoped to make their fortunes by discovering gold or silver or finding a water route to the Pacific. They were not prepared for the hardships they found nor did they expect to do farm work. More than half of the original 104 colonists died of starvation or disease during the first winter. Only the discipline imposed by a strong-willed leader, Captain John Smith, kept the Jamestown settlement from disaster.

The settlers' relations with the nearby Indians varied during the first decades of Jamestown's existence. Indians of the Powhatan confederacy (page 307) gave the settlers food during the first hard years. Indian farmers also taught the English how to grow corn, yams, and the tobacco that eventually made the colony prosperous. There were conflicts, however, and many Indians and settlers were killed. As the English settlements grew, the Indians were forced to leave their farms and villages and move farther inland.

The Plymouth colony is started. As the colonists at Jamestown gave up their dreams of finding wealth and settled down to farming, two new groups of English colonists arrived in the region that came to be called New England (map, next page). These settlers were not seeking fortunes but rather hoped to build communities where they would be free to practice their religious beliefs.

The first to arrive were a group of Puritans (page 388). Like other nonconforming Protes-tants in England, they thought that the Church of England followed practices too much like those of the Roman Catholic Church. Declaring themselves separate from the Church of England, some Puritans formed their own "Separatist" churches. When King James I came to the throne (page 387), he began severe persecutions of nonconformists, and in 1607 many left England for the Protestant Netherlands. The Separatists found it hard to make a living in the Netherlands, however, and they began to fear that their children would forget English ways.

In 1619 the Separatists received permission to settle on land owned by the London Company, the same company that had sponsored the colony at Jamestown. Because they did not have the money to finance the voyage, they formed a joint-stock company with non-Separatists who wanted either to settle in North America or to invest in the venture. The following year about 100 people set sail from Plymouth (PLIM-uth), England, aboard the small ship *Mayflower*. About one third of the company were Separatists, who now called themselves "Pilgrims." Blown off course, they landed on the coast of what is now Massachusetts late in November. A month later the *Mayflower* passengers found a good harbor and established a settlement, which they named Plymouth.

Like the first settlers in Virginia, the Plymouth colonists suffered from disease and malnutrition, and many died during the first winter. They, too, were given food, help, and farming advice by the local Indians. Unlike the Virginia adventurers, however, who had hoped to make their fortunes and return to England, the Pilgrims were seeking a permanent home. The colonists included entire families, men and women with skills as farmers and artisans.

Another colony is founded in New England. The second group of settlers in the northern colonies had much in common with the Plymouth colonists. The founders of Massachusetts Bay Colony also were Puritans who had

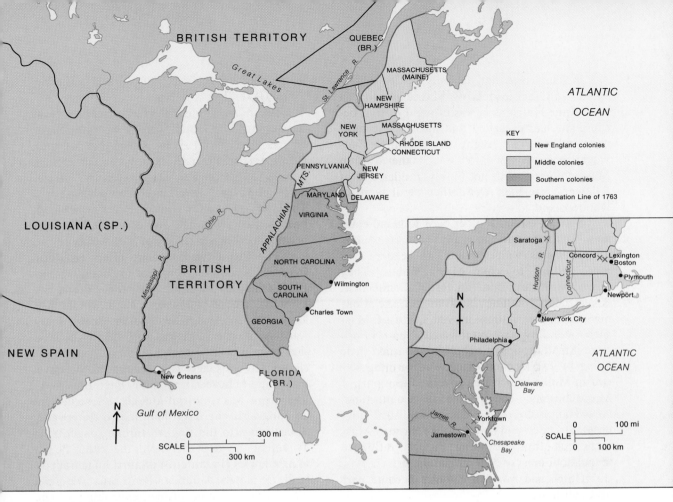

The Thirteen Colonies

England established thirteen colonies along the Atlantic seaboard. Which were the New England colonies? the middle colonies? the southern colonies?

been persecuted in England for both political activities and religious practices. In America, the Puritans hoped to set up communities and churches that, they believed, would be more pleasing to God than the ones they left behind.

In 1630, the year the colony was founded, more than 1,000 settlers arrived in Massachusetts Bay. Over the next twelve years, 19,000 more arrived. Better organized, better educated, and wealthier than the Plymouth colonists, the people of Massachusetts Bay fared better than the earlier settlers. In 1691 Massachusetts Bay absorbed the Plymouth colony.

Exiles from Massachusetts settle in Rhode Island. While the settlers in New England sought a place to follow their own religious beliefs, they did not welcome people with other views. The leaders of Massachusetts Bay insisted that all people in the colony conform to Puritan ways and beliefs. Some settlers disagreed. One minister, Roger Williams, preached that the government had no authority in religious matters and that the colonists had no right to land unless they had bought it from the Indians.

In 1635 the Puritan leaders banished Williams from Massachusetts but gave him until spring to leave the colony. Early in 1636 Williams and other discontented settlers moved south, establishing a colony in what is now the state of Rhode Island. This settlement was the first in America to separate the authority of church and state and to allow its people religious freedom. Because of these policies, the first Jews to settle in English America made their homes in Rhode Island.

Williams was not the only settler to disagree with the leaders of Massachusetts. In 1637 Anne Hutchinson was brought to trial because she had preached that most of the ministers in the colony taught false doctrines. Convicted of heresy, she too was banished from Massachusetts. With her family and a band of followers, she started another settlement in Rhode Island.

Settlers establish other New England colonies. The search for good farmland, as well as disagreements with the Puritan leaders, led more settlers to leave Massachusetts. They moved westward into the fertile Connecticut River valley, settling in what became Connecticut. Other settlers moved north of Massachusetts Bay and established New Hampshire. Small groups of people who earned their living by fishing, lumbering, and farming settled in Maine, which was governed as a part of Massachusetts. The people in Connecticut, New Hampshire, and Maine established governments, laws, and churches like those of Massachusetts, thus spreading Puritan influence throughout most of New England.

Dutch and Swedish colonies become part of English America. In the early seventeenth century, Dutch and Swedish colonists settled in parts of what are now the states of New York, New Jersey, and Delaware. One of Henry Hudson's voyages (page 360) had given the Dutch a claim to the Hudson River valley, which they called New Netherland. Settlement of New Netherland was slow because the Dutch West India Company was more interested in trade than in colonization. The company established a fur-trading post at Fort Orange and a settlement named New Amsterdam along what is now New York harbor. Farther south along the coast, Swedish settlers established the colony of New Sweden in 1638. New Sweden was captured by the Dutch in 1655 and became part of New Netherland.

The English were trade rivals of the Dutch and viewed them as intruders in North America. They also envied the Dutch monopoly of the inland fur trade and wanted control of the excellent harbor at New Amsterdam. In 1664 Charles II of England granted the territory between the Connecticut River and Delaware Bay

to his brother, the duke of York (later King James II).

When an English fleet was sent to New Amsterdam, the Dutch were in no position to defend their colony. New Amsterdam's population was small, and its government lacked popular support. The Dutch quickly surrendered, and New Netherland became New York. The land south of the Hudson River, which had been settled by Dutch and Swedish colonists, became the English colony of New Jersey.

The Pennsylvania colony offers religious freedom. Another group of nonconforming Protestants in England was the Society of Friends, whose members were commonly known as Quakers. The Quakers stressed inward spiritual experiences and did not believe that people needed the guidance of church or clergy. They rejected war, denounced the slave trade, and believed in religious toleration. William Penn was a devout Quaker whose father, an admiral in the navy, had helped restore the Stuart kings to the English throne (page 389). To repay the debt he owed the elder Penn, King Charles II granted William a huge tract of land in North America. Penn was the sole owner, or proprietor, of the new colony, which he called Pennsylvania, or "Penn's Woods." Another tract of land, given to William Penn by the duke of York, later became the colony of Delaware.

Penn had been persecuted and imprisoned in England for his beliefs. In his colony he established policies of religious toleration and political liberty, as well as giving generous land grants. In 1682, Penn signed a treaty with neighboring Indians, paying them for most of the land the king had granted him. Penn also barred the sale of alcohol to Indians and tried to keep white traders from cheating them.

Penn's policies attracted settlers not only from England but also from many European countries where there were religious conflicts. Among the settlers were Presbyterians, Anglicans, and Quakers from the British Isles, Lutherans and Calvinists from Germany, and Huguenots from France. Despite their differing backgrounds, these settlers built a thriving colony of farmers, trappers, merchants, and artisans. William Penn's "city of brotherly love,"

EARLY COLONISTS

The people who settled the early colonies had a variety of reasons for breaking old ties and coming to an unfamiliar land. At Plymouth the Pilgrims sought freedom to worship in their own way (above, Pilgrims on their way to church). William Penn (left) had a similar goal in establishing Pennsylvania as a haven for Quakers, but his colony attracted people of various faiths. Jamestown (below, as it looked in 1607) was settled by Englishmen hoping to establish a successful commercial venture.

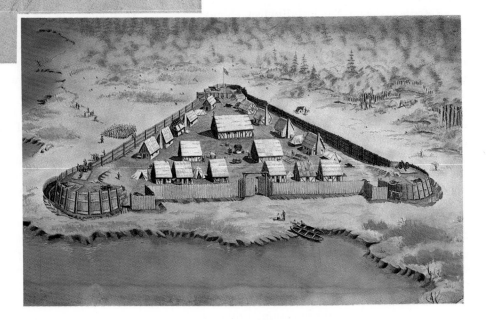

Philadelphia, became the richest and largest city in the Thirteen Colonies.

Maryland and the Carolinas grow out of royal grants. Like Pennsylvania, Maryland and the Carolinas began as proprietary colonies. Maryland was given by Charles I to the family of George Calvert, the first Lord Baltimore, in 1632. Lord Baltimore, a royal adviser, had converted to Roman Catholicism and wanted Maryland to be a refuge for Catholics who were persecuted in England. The first settlers reached Maryland in 1634. The fertile land and pleasant climate attracted more settlers, and Protestants soon outnumbered Catholics. In 1649 Maryland's colonial assembly passed the Toleration Act, which granted religious freedom to all Christians in the colony.

In 1663 Charles II granted a large area of land south of Virginia to a group of enterprising noblemen. It was named Carolina after the Latin form of the king's name (*Carolus*). The first settlement in Carolina was started in 1670 at Charles Town (later called Charleston). Like Virginia, Carolina prospered by growing tobacco and, later, rice. Eventually conflicts arose between the small farmers in the north and the plantation owners in the south. In 1712 the northern and southern parts of the colony were placed under separate governments. In 1729 both North Carolina and South Carolina became royal colonies.

Reformers begin the last English colony. King George II granted the land between South Carolina and Spanish Florida to a group of English reformers led by James Oglethorpe. The king hoped that the colony would keep Spanish settlements from expanding northward. The reformers wanted to start a colony in which people who had been imprisoned for debt in England could make a new beginning. The first settlers came to Georgia (named for the king) in 1733. Oglethorpe eventually gave up his charter, and Georgia became a royal colony.

The colonies provide economic and political opportunities. Following the settlement of Georgia, the British had an unbroken line of thirteen colonies stretching along the Atlantic coast of North America between Spanish Florida and French territory to the north (map, page 423). Different as these colonies were, they had a number of traits in common that set them off from Britain and other European nations as well as from the other colonies in the Americas.

Settlers in the American colonies had the chance to own their own land, an opportunity many could never have hoped for in Europe. The average farm in New England and the middle colonies (those between New England and the South) was large by European standards, though still small enough to be worked by the family that owned it. South of Delaware Bay were many large plantations, whose owners grew cash crops that were exported to Europe. Even in the southern colonies, however, the majority of white settlers were not plantation owners but small farmers who worked their own land.

The colonists also had greater freedom and more political rights than people in many European nations. Some traditional English liberties, such as trial by jury and protection from unlawful imprisonment, had been transplanted to America. In addition, each colony had its own elected assembly. In Britain, only men who owned a substantial amount of property could vote for representatives to the House of Commons; few small farmers or artisans could vote. Each of the colonies in America also had property requirements for voting, but a larger percentage of the male colonists were able to fulfill them.

Most blacks in the colonies are slaves. One group of people in the colonies did not benefit from these opportunities. The experience of people of African ancestry was very different from that of the white European settlers. The first black settlers in the colonies were twenty Africans who arrived in Virginia in 1619. They had been brought by a Dutch ship and were sold as *indentured servants.* An indenture was an agreement to work a certain number of years (usually four to seven) for the person who paid one's passage to America. The servant learned a skill, worked on a farm, or helped in a household. When the term of the indenture was completed, he or she was free.

In the early years of the colonies, indentured servants included both black and white workers. Black indentured servants — like white indentured servants — gained their freedom at the end of their indentures and could become farmers or laborers. The terms of service for black indentured servants gradually became longer, however. Eventually black workers were required to give lifelong service, and their children were, by law, the property of the people who owned the parents. By the end of the seventeenth century, the enslavement of blacks was legal in all the colonies.

The black population increases as plantations spread. The plantation agriculture that developed in the southern colonies encouraged the growth of slavery. By 1715, plantation crops grown for export were important in the economies of the southern colonies. Most of the work on the plantations was done by black slaves brought to America from Africa (page 358).

Blacks — nearly all of them slaves — made up a large percentage of the southern colonies' populations. In 1715, for example, blacks made up about 24 percent of the population of Virginia and 62 percent of the population of South Carolina. North of Maryland, the percentage of blacks in the colonial populations was much smaller, ranging from less than 2 percent in New Hampshire to almost 13 percent in New York.

The Virginia colony became a success when it found a cash crop — tobacco that could be exported to England. Slaves tended the crop and packed the leaves in barrels for shipment.

CHECK-UP

1. Vocabulary: *indentured servant.*
2. (a) What did the colonists who settled Jamestown hope to find in America? (b) In what ways were the founders of the Plymouth and Massachusetts Bay colonies different from the Virginia settlers?
3. (a) What attitudes of the Puritan leaders led to the founding of Rhode Island? (b) What other colonies were started by settlers from Massachusetts? (c) Who were the first settlers in the Hudson River valley?
4. What were the attitudes toward religious freedom (a) in Rhode Island? (b) in Pennsylvania? (c) in Maryland?
5. (a) What crops made Virginia and the Carolinas prosperous? (b) For what reasons was Georgia established?
6. (a) How did most early colonists make their living? (b) What attracted colonists to the North American colonies?
7. (a) Describe the system of indentured service. (b) How did the system eventually result in slavery for blacks?

2 The Colonists Object to British Policies

The bonds between Britain[1] and its American colonies grew weaker over time. An ocean separated the colonies from Britain, and the colonists had developed their own social, political,

and economic institutions. When Parliament enacted laws that the colonists felt interfered with their freedom, the tensions between Britain and the colonies increased and led eventually to revolution.

Parliament restricts colonial trade and industry. Following its mercantilist economic

[1]The Act of Union in 1707 united England and Scotland as Great Britain.

policies (page 364), Britain expected the colonies to provide it with raw materials at low prices and to buy back British manufactured goods. Parliament passed laws to regulate colonial trade to Britain's advantage. The Navigation Acts of 1660 and 1663, for example, required colonists to sell certain products, such as tobacco, sugar, and indigo, only to England and its possessions. Colonial merchants, who wanted to sell their goods at the highest possible prices, resented these restrictions.

In the early eighteenth century, Parliament took steps to prevent the colonists from developing industries that would compete with British manufacturers. In the Hat Act (1732), for example, the export of hats made in the colonies was forbidden. The Iron Act (1750) removed taxes on Britain's imports of iron ore from the colonies, but it outlawed the colonial manufacture of iron goods. The purpose of the law was to force colonists to buy British-made iron products rather than manufacturing their own.

The colonists evade British laws. Parliament's restrictions on the colonial economy were difficult to enforce. The colonists resented the restrictions, and many of them smuggled in goods to avoid paying British taxes. The many harbors along the Atlantic coast made it easy for smugglers' boats to evade the British customs officials. The British also found that colonial officials tended to favor the colonists and did not always strictly enforce the laws. Moreover, distance made enforcement difficult. These circumstances caused resentment on both sides of the Atlantic.

France challenges Britain over colonies. Difficulties with the colonists were not the only problem Britain faced in North America. Since 1689, France and Britain had been on opposite sides in a series of wars in Europe. The two countries also were rivals for colonies and trade in several parts of the world. With each war in Europe, British and French forces had also clashed in North America. In addition, as French settlements expanded, disagreements arose over boundaries, especially in the Ohio Valley.

The French and Indian War[2] was the last British–French conflict in North America. This war, fought in Canada and on the American frontier, ended in 1763 with a victory for Britain. As a result, British rule was extended over most of eastern North America.

Colonists and Indians clash on the frontier. Because of France's colonial policies, many Indians had fought with the French in the conflicts with Britain and the colonists. Now that the war was over, the Indians had other reasons to oppose the colonists. As settlers began to move west away from the coastal areas, they took over lands where Indians lived, farmed, and hunted. Angered by the loss of their land and by British policies in the region, many widely scattered groups of Indians united under Pontiac, an Ottawa leader. In May, 1763, they raided frontier settlements and captured British forts in the region between the Great Lakes and the Ohio River. After months of fierce fighting, the British forced Pontiac to give up the rebellion in August, 1764.

---

[2]This is the name given to the American phase of the Seven Years' War, which also was fought in Europe and in India between 1756 and 1763 (page 362). The earliest battles in North America were in 1754, before the official declaration of war.

TIMETABLE

From Colonies to Nation

1607   English settlers establish a colony at Jamestown in Virginia.

1733   The first settlement in Georgia is started.

1763   Britain defeats France in the French and Indian War.

1765   The Stamp Act Congress challenges Parliament's right to tax the colonists.

1770   The Boston Massacre heightens tensions.

1774   The First Continental Congress protests the Intolerable Acts.

1775   Colonial militia rout British troops at Lexington and Concord.

1776   The colonies declare their independence.

1781   Cornwallis surrenders at Yorktown.

1783   The Treaty of Paris ends the Revolutionary War.

1788   The Constitution is ratified.

1791   The Bill of Rights is adopted.

Britain's prime minister, Lord Grenville, claimed that Pontiac's War showed it was necessary to keep British troops stationed in the colonies. Many Americans, however, feared that a British army on American soil would be used mainly to control the colonists. Grenville further angered Americans when he issued the Proclamation of 1763, which barred settlement west of the Appalachian Mountains. He hoped this measure would prevent more clashes between the colonists and the Indians and, at the same time, keep the colonists more firmly under British rule by keeping them nearer the coast. The colonists simply viewed the Proclamation as interference in their affairs.

Britain seeks revenue from the colonies. The French and Indian War had another effect on the colonists. The wars with France had been costly for the British. Grenville now decided that, as the American colonies had benefited from the wars, they should pay a large part of the cost.

Grenville's first step was to clamp down on smuggling, which kept Britain from collecting many tax revenues. He called for strict measures to enforce the laws. For example, British naval vessels were assigned to patrol American waters to catch smugglers. Dishonest officials who did not enforce the laws were replaced by men who would not ignore smuggling. Finally, colonists accused of smuggling were to be tried by British judges, not by juries made up of their fellow colonists.

Parliament took several other steps to increase revenues and help pay the cost of running the colonies. In 1764 it passed the Sugar Act, which lowered the tax on imported molasses in hopes that fewer colonists would smuggle it in to avoid paying the tax. The act also imposed new taxes on "luxury" goods like sugar, coffee, and wine, which the colonies imported. To reduce the cost of stationing troops in North America, Parliament passed the Quartering Act of 1765. This required colonists to provide living quarters and certain supplies for British troops. Finally, in 1765 Parliament passed the Stamp Act, which placed a tax on printed matter — newspapers and pamphlets, playing cards, licenses, deeds and other legal documents, and advertisements.

The colonists protest Grenville's plan. The colonists were outraged by Grenville's program. They believed that it violated long-standing rights of British subjects. They were particularly angered by the Stamp Act. While the other laws regulated imports and exports, the Stamp Act was simply an effort to increase British revenues. The colonists admitted that Parliament had the right to regulate their trade, but they argued that only their own representative assemblies had the right to tax them. "Taxation without representation," they declared, was against the principles of English law.

Protests against the tax were widespread in the colonies. Colonists wrote newspaper articles and pamphlets denouncing it, and colonial assemblies adopted resolutions denying Parliament the right to tax the colonies. In 1765 delegates from nine colonies met in New York to discuss the situation. At this meeting, called the Stamp Act Congress, the delegates challenged Parliament's right to tax the colonies for revenue. They sent petitions to the king and to Parliament, asking for repeal of the Stamp Act. The delegates also called on colonial merchants to stop buying or selling British goods. Groups of patriots known as the Sons and Daughters of Liberty sprang up throughout the colonies. Their members pressured merchants — sometimes by force — to stop dealing in British goods. Merchants in Britain complained about the business they were losing, and in 1766 Parliament reluctantly repealed the Stamp Act.

The Townshend Acts increase colonial resentment. Parliament continued to maintain that it had every right to tax the colonists. In 1767 it passed the Townshend (TOWN-zend) Acts, which imposed new taxes. The new taxes raised the prices of many everyday items —particularly paint, glass, paper, and tea.

The colonists claimed that the new law was another case of "taxation without representation." Samuel Adams, a Bostonian, expressed their feeling: "If our trade may be taxed, why not our lands? Why not the produce of our lands, and everything we possess or make use of?" Merchants and shopkeepers again refused to carry British goods.

Resentment leads to violence. Anger over British policies was particularly great in Boston.

Before 1774 the colonists blamed Parliament more than the king for the government actions that they felt violated their rights. After the passage of the Intolerable Acts, the colonists turned against George III and even pulled down statues of the king.

Bostonians hated seeing British soldiers in their streets and resented being questioned by British sentries. There were fights between the soldiers and the people of Boston. In March, 1770, a squad of British soldiers fired into a crowd that had been taunting them and pelting them with sticks and snowballs. Five colonists were killed, and several more were wounded. This incident, which American patriots called the Boston Massacre, deepened tensions.

Parliament soon repealed the Townshend Acts, except for the tax on tea, and the situation grew calmer. The basic disagreements between Britain and the colonies, however, remained unresolved.

The Tea Act renews colonial resistance. The East India Company, which had made a fortune in colonial India (page 364), had bought a large supply of tea to expand its trade with China. In 1773 Parliament tried to help the Company's expansion by granting it special rights to sell tea in America. American tea merchants were angered by this new competition, while other colonists saw the Tea Act as another attempt by Parliament to impose a tax on them. When the tea ships of the East India Company docked in American ports, the colo-

nists refused to unload them. Certain colonists in Boston decided to go even further. Disguised as Indians, they climbed aboard the ships and dumped several hundred chests filled with tea into Boston harbor. Some colonists applauded this form of protest. Others viewed the "Boston Tea Party" as a criminal act, since the colonists had destroyed valuable property and defied British law.

Parliament passes the Intolerable Acts. To punish the Bostonians, an angry Parliament passed a series of laws that colonists called the Intolerable Acts (1774). One law closed the port of Boston to all ships until Massachusetts paid the East India Company for the tea. Another law put an end to self-government in Massachusetts. A third allowed royal officials charged with certain crimes to be tried in Britain or in another colony to avoid hostile colonial juries. Finally, a new Quartering Act allowed troops to be housed in homes (instead of in their usual barracks) whenever the commanding officer thought it was necessary.

Colonists meet in a Continental Congress. Upset at the harshness of the Intolerable Acts, leaders throughout the colonies decided to meet and discuss how they could settle their differences with Britain. The meeting, called the Continental Congress, was held in Philadelphia in 1774, with delegates from twelve colonies. They protested the Intolerable Acts and organized committees to prevent the sale of British goods. This time the British government refused to give in to the colonists. As tension mounted, men in the colonies began to drill and collect military supplies.

The colonists fight at Lexington and Concord. By the following spring, the disagreements between Britain and the Thirteen Colonies brought violence. In April, 1775, British troops were sent from Boston to the nearby towns of Concord and Lexington to destroy weapons and gunpowder that the *militia,* or citizen soldiers, had stored there. The British soldiers also had orders to seize two leaders of the colonial resistance, Samuel Adams and John Hancock. Warned that the British soldiers were on their way, the militia gathered at Lexington and Concord to stop them. Although the colonists could not stop the soldiers from destroying their store of weapons, they took cover behind trees and stone walls to attack the British troops returning to Boston. In all, about 350 people were killed or wounded.

The fighting at Lexington and Concord was a turning point in the relationship between Britain and the colonies. When the Second Continental Congress met in Philadelphia, its members knew that there would be further trouble with Britain. They created an army; named George Washington, a Virginia planter, as its commander; and assumed some of the responsibilities of a central government for the colonies.

In England, King George III was enraged by the colonists' actions. He ignored petitions sent by the Continental Congress. He also approved the ending of all trade with the colonies and sent more troops to America to crush the rebellion.

The colonies move toward independence. In the spring of 1775 few Americans, angry as they were, favored separation from Britain. Support for independence grew over the next six months as fighting continued and the colonists debated the issue. This debate was greatly influenced by a pamphlet titled *Common Sense,*

which was published in January, 1776. Thomas Paine, its author, called upon Americans to give up their "agreeable dream" of reconciliation and declare their independence from Britain. *Common Sense* was widely read in every colony, and public opinion veered sharply toward independence.

During the spring and summer of 1776, the colonists moved to break their ties with Britain. First, the Congress broke economic ties by declaring American ports open to all ships except those of Britain. Next, it appointed a committee to prepare a document that would explain Americans' reasons for separating from Britain.

On July 4, 1776, the Second Continental Congress adopted the Declaration of Independence, written largely by Thomas Jefferson, a Virginia planter. This document reflected John Locke's theory of natural rights (page 408), which had been so influential in the ideas of the Enlightenment. The Declaration stated that

Chief author of the Declaration of Independence, Thomas Jefferson put basic ideas of freedom into memorable words. Jefferson continued to be a forceful leader after American independence was won.

the people have the right to abolish a government that does not support their interests and to establish a new one. The American people, said the Declaration, had been forced by the unreasonable tyranny of King George III to end their ties and loyalty to the British government. In signing the Declaration, the members of the Second Continental Congress formally made a break with Britain, proclaiming that "these United Colonies are, and of Right ought to be, Free and Independent States."

CHECK-UP

1. Vocabulary: *militia*.
2. (a) How did Parliament apply mercantilist policies to colonial trade? (b) What was the reaction of the American colonists to the Navigation Acts?
3. (a) What was the outcome of the French and Indian War? (b) How did Pontiac's War affect relations between Britain and the American colonies?
4. (a) What steps did Grenville take to improve Britain's financial situation? (b) How did the colonists react to Grenville's program?
5. (a) What were the Townshend Acts? (b) Why did the colonists object to them? (c) What were the Intolerable Acts?
6. (a) What caused the outbreak of fighting in Massachusetts in 1775? (b) What convinced many Americans that independence was the best solution to their problems with Britain? (c) What were the main points of the Declaration of Independence?

3 Revolution Brings Independence

The Americans had declared their independence but still had to win it. They began the Revolution with forces that were poorly trained, badly supplied, and few in number compared with the British troops. They had capable leaders, however, and were strengthened by their dedication to the cause of liberty. The Americans emerged victorious from the Revolutionary War and adopted a plan of government that became a model for other nations.

The colonists' loyalties are divided. Not all American colonists wanted independence as much as the leaders who signed the Declaration of Independence. A large number, probably about 20 percent of the population, remained loyal to the king. Some of these Loyalists, as they were called, emigrated to Canada or worked with the British army in America. Another substantial portion of the colonial population did not support either side in the war. About a third of the colonists, called Patriots, actively supported the movement for independence. These people were numerous and enthusiastic enough to gain control of the governments in all the colonies (which now were called states). Americans' divided allegiances, however, made it difficult to recruit enough soldiers to form an army.

The Continental Army faces financial problems. When the leaders of the Revolution decided to form a "Continental Army," they also faced difficulties in raising money and obtaining supplies. Because the Continental Congress had no power to levy taxes, it asked the new states to contribute the money and supplies needed to fight the war. This method of raising money was a failure. Of the $100 million it requested from the states, the Congress received less than $5 million. The Congress turned to printing paper money as its major source of income, but with disastrous results. The money became worthless and caused inflation.

As a result of the financial problem, the Continental Army seldom had adequate supplies to feed, clothe, and equip its troops. Soldiers were never sure when they would be paid. Their pay, when it came, did not buy much because of inflation. By 1781 a pair of shoes cost $100; a barrel of flour, $1,575. These hardships made it even more difficult to recruit soldiers.

Many men joined and later deserted, especially during the winter months.

Because of the difficulty of keeping men in the Continental Army, its commander — General Washington — was forced to rely on the state militias. The militiamen, however, were willing to fight only within their own states. When the scene of the fighting shifted across state lines, they went home, considering that they had carried out their responsibilities. Washington never knew how large his army would be from one month to the next.

Despite these problems, the colonial forces had certain advantages over the British. First, Washington was a leader who inspired great loyalty. Second, the Patriot soldiers were fighting on their own territory and so could use their knowledge of the land in planning and fighting battles. Finally, many American soldiers were deeply committed to winning independence from British rule.

The British face disadvantages. The Americans were not alone in having serious military problems. The British, too, faced supply problems, for 3,000 miles lay between the troops and the source of their supplies. In addition, the American colonies covered so large an area that the British could only bring scattered areas under control. Although the British forces were more numerous and better trained in traditional warfare than the Continental Army, they were unaccustomed to the strike-and-run fighting style of the American sharpshooters, and they were often surprised by American tactics. The British government frequently appointed new commanders for the troops in America, making a consistent strategy difficult. Moreover, Britain was not fully committed to the war. Many members of Parliament thought that India and other British colonies were more important than the American lands. A number of British politicians even sympathized with the American cause.

Victory at Saratoga is the turning point of the war. In March, 1776, the colonial forces finally drove the British out of Boston. The following summer the British moved southward to New York, planning to capture New York harbor, seize control of the Hudson River valley,

Benjamin Franklin served his country in many ways — in the Continental Congress, as the Thirteen Colonies' representative in France, and at the convention that later wrote the Constitution.

and isolate New England from the rest of the colonies. In September they succeeded in capturing New York City. Fighting continued for a year without important gains for either side. Then, in the fall of 1777, the turning point of the war came near Saratoga, New York. There an American general, Horatio Gates, surrounded a British force of nearly 5,000 men commanded by General Sir John Burgoyne. This force had moved south from Canada to seize the Hudson River valley. Unable to obtain relief or supplies, Burgoyne was forced to surrender.

The American victory impressed Britain's enemies in Europe. The American writer and scientist Benjamin Franklin had been in Paris negotiating for French help since the outbreak of war. In 1778 France decided to aid the Americans in their struggle against Britain. Later, Spain and the Netherlands also backed the American cause. The foreign help provided much-needed weapons, money, and troops. A

The Continental Army spent the winter of 1777–1778 at Valley Forge in Pennsylvania. Though cold and hungry, the soldiers prepared for the battles that would come in the spring by drilling under the direction of the Prussian officer Baron von Steuben.

number of experienced European military men volunteered their services in training and leading the American soldiers. A French noble, the Marquis de Lafayette, closely assisted Washington. Others who joined the Americans were Casimir Pulaski and Thaddeus Kosciusko of Poland, Baron de Kalb (a German friend of Lafayette's), and Baron von Steuben of Prussia.

The British surrender at Yorktown. Despite foreign aid, the Americans were unable to win a decisive victory until 1781. In the spring of that year Lord Cornwallis, commander of the British army, abandoned his campaign to subdue the southern colonies. He moved 7,000 troops into Yorktown, Virginia, on a peninsula in Chesapeake Bay, and began to fortify it. This move was a serious mistake. A French fleet blocked the mouth of the bay and prevented help from reaching Cornwallis by sea. Washington's troops and a large French force surrounded Cornwallis, who surrendered in October, 1781. For all practical purposes, the war was over.

The Treaty of Paris ends the war. Peace negotiations among the United States, Britain, France, the Netherlands, and Spain took almost two years. The Treaty of Paris, signed in September, 1783, officially ended the war. By that treaty Britain recognized the independence of its former colonies. The territory of the United States stretched from the Atlantic Ocean to the Mississippi River, and from the Great Lakes to Spanish Florida (which Britain had returned to Spain in a separate treaty).

The new states organize their governments. Having won their independence, the thirteen states had to decide what form of government they would adopt. All the states chose republican forms of government and all adopted written constitutions, or plans of government. The unwritten British constitution, they reasoned, had failed to protect them from the tyranny of George III. Many of the state constitutions included bills of rights, which listed certain freedoms guaranteed to citizens.

Drawing on their experience with the colonial governments, the planners of the state constitutions limited the powers of government officials. The greatest powers were given to the lower houses of the state assemblies, or legislatures, whose members were directly elected by voters. In most states, the governors were elected by the members of the assembly.

The new states were not democratic in the modern sense. Although they extended voting rights to more free white males, they did not abolish property requirements altogether. Women could not vote, nor could black slaves or American Indians, either male or female.

The idea of religious freedom, which had been important in several colonies, influenced the states. The Virginia Statute of Religious Liberty, drafted by Thomas Jefferson and adopted in 1786, was the first state law to ensure freedom of religion. It allowed citizens to follow the religion of their choice and declared that people's beliefs would not affect their rights as citizens. (At the time, other states had religious tests for voting, officeholding, and jury duty.) It also declared that no Virginian could be compelled to attend or support any church.

A weak central government is established under the Articles of Confederation. To bring the states together, the Second Continental Congress submitted a plan of union for their approval in 1777. This plan, the Articles of Confederation, called for a "league of friendship" among the states.

The Articles of Confederation (approved by all the states in 1781) set up a Congress in which each state had one vote. Its duties were to conduct foreign relations, settle disputes between states, and rule in certain matters of common concern, such as relations with the Indians and the fixing of weights and measures.

The Congress, however, could not impose taxes to raise money, nor did it have any way to

The Eagles of North America

The eagle is an ancient symbol of freedom, strength, and courage, used as an emblem by many nations in different parts of the world. The bald eagle, a native North American bird, was chosen in 1782 to appear on the Great Seal of the United States. (You see the Great Seal most often on the back of the dollar bill. The wooden carving shown in the illustration below is a horizontal version of the Seal.) The eagle also has appeared on many coins. When the United States government issued $10 and $20 gold coins, they were known as "eagles" and "double eagles."

The bald eagle today is endangered in North America but, as the national bird, is protected by law.

Mexico, too, uses an eagle as its symbol. According to an ancient Aztec legend, the Aztecs were supposed to settle and build a city wherever they found an island in a lake and saw an eagle perched on a cactus and holding a snake in its beak. This place turned out to be the site of Tenochtitlán (page 297), where present-day Mexico City stands. The Aztec eagle and cactus have appeared on Mexico's flag since the country became a republic in 1824.

The Constitution of the United States

The opening passage — or preamble — of the United States Constitution presents the reasons of the American people for adopting a new form of government.

> We the people of the United States, in order to form a more perfect union, establish justice, insure domestic tranquillity, provide for the common defense, promote the general welfare, and secure the blessings of liberty to ourselves and our posterity, do ordain and establish this Constitution for the United States of America.

What does each of the following phrases in the Constitution mean: (a) "form a more perfect union," (b) "insure domestic tranquillity," (c) "promote the general welfare"?

enforce its decisions. These weaknesses caused problems for the new nation, but many Americans feared the power that a strong central government would have.

The United States faces problems with Europe. The weak government set up by the Articles of Confederation encountered severe difficulties in its dealings with other nations, both in North America and abroad. Hoping that the former colonies would not succeed in forming a lasting nation, Britain refused to withdraw from frontier forts on American soil, as was required by the Treaty of Paris. The British claimed that Americans had already broken the treaty, since some states had passed laws delaying the payment of debts owed to British subjects. Congress advised the states that these laws violated the peace treaty, but it had no power to take action to change state laws.

The new nation also was in serious economic trouble. In winning independence, Americans had lost the privilege of selling their goods to Britain and its possessions. Americans still needed to buy British manufactured goods

and, by the late 1780's, American merchants were deeply in debt to Britain. Spain, meanwhile, closed the Mississippi River to American trade in an attempt to limit American settlement along the river.

Finally, in the Mediterranean, North African pirates interfered with American shipping and captured American seamen to sell as slaves. The Congress was unable to make the Mediterranean safe for American ships. It was too poor to bribe the pirates (a policy followed by other nations) and too weak to fight them.

The government lacks authority at home. The most severe problems faced by the Congress were due to its lack of authority over the individual states. Because it could not levy taxes, it asked the states to provide funds but could do nothing if they did not. Lacking the power to regulate commerce, the Congress could not prevent the trade wars that strained relations among various states. Finally, the Confederation government was not organized to provide leadership or enforce its decisions. Many thoughtful Americans came to believe that the Articles of Confederation had to be revised.

America's leaders decide to write a constitution. In May, 1787, fifty-five delegates, including some of the ablest men in the country, assembled at Philadelphia to consider possible amendments to the Articles of Confederation. The delegates were practical men — farmers, merchants, lawyers, and bankers. Many had political experience as members of the Congress and as governors or state legislators.

The delegates soon recognized that revision of the Articles would not solve the nation's problems. They decided, instead, to write an entirely new constitution. Working in secret sessions through the summer of 1787, the delegates completed their work by September. The Constitution they presented to the people set up a *federal system* of government — one in which power would be shared between the central government and state governments. The powers of the central, or federal, government were carefully spelled out in the Constitution. The states were to retain control of their own internal affairs.

Leaders set up safeguards to balance government power. Although the writers of the Constitution wanted to set up a central government with power enough to manage the nation's problems, they also remembered their experiences with royal authority. They wanted to make certain that no one person or group of people would be able to gain too much power.

The federal system, which divided power between the federal and state governments, was one safeguard against tyranny. Some of the writers of the Constitution followed the ideas of Enlightenment thinkers such as Montesquieu (page 409). Adopting his principle of the separation of powers, the founders created three separate branches of government: executive, legislative, and judicial. To prevent the concentration of power in any one of the three branches, they set up a system of "checks and balances." (See the chart on page 502.)

The Constitution is ratified. Before the new Constitution could take effect, it had to be approved by at least nine of the states. The men who had drafted the Constitution knew that they would face strong opposition and that ratification was not at all certain. Not even all the members of the Philadelphia convention agreed on the Constitution's provisions.

Many Americans thought that the Constitution gave too much power to the federal government. These people, called anti-federalists, warned that the proposed federal government would dominate the states and deprive citizens of their liberties. They especially objected to the absence of a bill of rights.

Those who favored the Constitution, called federalists, campaigned vigorously for its adoption. Many believed that the nation was in such a state of crisis that if the Constitution were not adopted, the United States would break up. Federalists throughout the country worked tirelessly for their cause. Three leading federalists — James Madison, Alexander Hamilton, and John Jay — published a series of brilliant essays explaining how the new Constitution would remedy the defects of the Articles of Confederation. The essays, called *The Federalist*, along with the promise of a bill of rights, helped to win support for the new plan of government. In June, 1788, New Hampshire became the ninth state to ratify, or vote its approval. This guaranteed that the Constitution would go into effect. By 1790 all thirteen states had ratified the Constitution.

The Bill of Rights is adopted. The newly elected Congress met in 1789, and one of its first acts was to draw up ten amendments to the Constitution. These were to be a Bill of Rights, guaranteeing Americans freedom of religion, of speech, of assembly, and of the press. It also assured them of trial by jury, protection from cruel and unusual punishments, and other basic liberties. The tenth amendment answered the fears of many Americans about federal power. It stated that the powers not given to the federal government by the Constitution were retained by the states or by the people.

American political freedom becomes a model for other nations. With the ratification of the Constitution and the adoption of the Bill of Rights, the success of the American nation was assured. Americans had won their independence and, equally important, they had created a lasting government of their own. The founders of the nation constructed a government that has met the test of time and upheld high standards of individual liberty. Their success inspired people around the world to work toward the establishment of liberty in their own countries.

CHECK-UP

1. Vocabulary: *federal system.*
2. (a) What problems did the American Patriots face at the beginning of the Revolution? (b) What advantages did they have over the British?
3. (a) Why was the Battle of Saratoga a turning point in the Revolutionary War? (b) What were the terms of the Treaty of Paris (1783)?
4. (a) What plan of government was set up by the Second Continental Congress? (b) What problems did the new nation face during the 1780's?
5. (a) What kind of government was created in the Constitution? (b) Why did the anti-federalists oppose the Constitution? (c) How were their fears put to rest?

Chapter 19 Review

Summary

Between 1607 and 1733, settlers from England established thirteen colonies along the eastern coast of North America. The first permanent English colony was started at Jamestown, Virginia, by colonists who hoped to make their fortunes. Other English settlements were founded by people seeking a place to practice their religion as they wished. Still other settlers emigrated to have farms of their own and greater political freedom. The Dutch and the Swedish also established North American colonies, but these were taken over by the English.

In an attempt to make the colonies profitable for the home country, the British Parliament passed a number of laws restricting colonial industry and regulating colonial trade. The colonists' protests and resistance against these measures led to conflicts that ended in war. In 1776, the colonies issued the Declaration of Independence; it formally broke their ties with Britain and British rule.

The course of the American Revolution turned in favor of the colonists after the Battle of Saratoga in 1777. With aid from other European nations, the Patriot forces led by George Washington won the final battle of the war at Yorktown, Virginia, in 1781. The Treaty of Paris (1783) recognized American independence. The new nation was governed at first by a weak alliance, the Articles of Confederation. By 1787 a new plan of government seemed necessary, and a Constitution was drafted for the United States. Later a Bill of Rights was added to guarantee Americans certain freedoms.

Vocabulary Review

1. Write the sentences listed below on a sheet of paper. In each sentence, fill in the blank with one of these words or phrases: *militia, indentured servant, federal system.*
(a) In a __?__ of government, the national government provides central authority, while individual states retain control of local affairs.
(b) An __?__ signed an agreement to work a certain number of years in exchange for passage by ship to America.
(c) To protect themselves, the colonists of Massachusetts formed a citizen army or __?__ .
2. Distinguish between the terms in each of the following pairs:
(a) French and Indian War; Pontiac's War.
(b) Separatists; Puritans.
(c) Townshend Acts; Intolerable Acts.
(d) Battle of Yorktown; Battle of Saratoga.
(e) *Common Sense; The Federalist.*

People to Identify

Identify the following people and tell why each was important:
1. John Smith
2. Roger Williams
3. Anne Hutchinson
4. William Penn
5. Lord Baltimore
6. James Oglethorpe
7. Thomas Paine
8. Thomas Jefferson
9. George Washington
10. James Madison

Relating Geography and History

1. **Locating places.** Locate each of the following on a map in this chapter:
(a) Jamestown
(b) Plymouth
(c) Boston
(d) New York
(e) Philadelphia
(f) Charleston
(g) Saratoga
(h) Yorktown
2. **Interpretation.** How did the distance between the British colonies and Great Britain contribute to the colonists' spirit of independence?

Discussion Questions

1. What were the reasons for the founding of each of the following colonies: (a) Virginia, (b) Massachusetts Bay, (c) Rhode Island, (d) Georgia?
2. (a) How did the beliefs of the Puritans and the Quakers differ? (b) What effect did these differences have on attitudes toward religious freedom in each colony?
3. (a) How did farming in the New England and middle colonies differ from farming in the southern colonies? (b) What effect did the growth of plantation agriculture have on the slave trade?

4. (a) How did the Navigation Acts of the 1660's reflect Britain's mercantilist policies? (b) How did the colonists react to these laws?

5. (a) What was Lord Grenville's reason for issuing the Proclamation of 1763? (b) Why did Parliament pass the Sugar Act? (c) the Quartering Act of 1765? (d) the Stamp Act? (e) Why did the colonists oppose these laws?

6. What was the purpose of (a) the First Continental Congress? (b) the Second Continental Congress?

7. (a) How were the ideas of John Locke reflected in the Declaration of Independence? (b) What ideas of Montesquieu's influenced the men who wrote the Constitution?

8. How was each of the following concerns dealt with in the state governments that were established after independence was won: (a) limiting the power of government officials, (b) voting rights, (c) religious freedom?

9. (a) Describe the plan of government outlined in the Articles of Confederation. (b) What were the weaknesses of that government? (c) How did the plan of government embodied in the Constitution remedy those weaknesses?

Reading Primary Sources

In the following passage Benjamin Franklin gave his opinion on British colonial rule. Read the passage. Then answer the questions that follow.

When I consider the extreme corruption [that exists] . . . among all . . . men in this old rotten state, and the glorious public virtue so predominant in our rising country, I cannot but [believe that] . . . more mischief than benefit [will come] from a closer union. I fear they will drag us after them in all the plundering wars which their desperate circumstances, injustice, and [greed] . . . may prompt them to undertake; and their . . . [wastefulness] . . . is a gulf that will swallow up every aid we may . . . afford them. Here numberless and needless places, enormous salaries, pensions, bribes, groundless quarrels, foolish expeditions, false accounts, contracts, and jobs, devour all revenue and produce continual necessity in the midst of natural plenty. I [believe], . . . therefore, that to unite us intimately will only be to corrupt and poison us also.

(a) What country does Franklin call "this old rotten state"? (b) What phrase does he use to refer to the American colonies? (c) What reasons does he give for opposing a closer union with Britain? (d) According to Franklin, what are some of the wasteful practices that use up the government's money? (e) What does Franklin think would be the effect on the colonies of continued union with England?

Skill Activities

1. Recreating history. Prepare three newspaper accounts of the Boston Tea Party. In one account, portray the event through the eyes of a British loyalist. In the second, describe the incident from the viewpoint of an American Patriot. Make the third account a balanced objective report focusing on the facts and giving an impartial description of what occurred.

2. Placing events in time. On a separate sheet of paper, list the following events in sequence, giving the correct date for each.
(a) Britain issues the Proclamation of 1763.
(b) The First Continental Congress meets in Philadelphia.
(c) A colony is started at Jamestown.
(d) Minutemen fight British troops at Lexington and Concord.
(e) Maryland passes the Toleration Act.
(f) The Declaration of Independence is signed.
(g) The French and Indian War begins.
(h) Colonists hold the Stamp Act Congress.
(i) Cornwallis surrenders at Yorktown.
(j) The United States Constitution is written.
(k) Parliament passes the Intolerable Acts.
(l) North and South Carolina become separate royal colonies.

3. Stating both sides of an issue. George Grenville, British prime minister from 1763 to 1765, believed the American colonists should contribute to their own defense and help Britain reduce the cost of running the colonies. With this purpose in mind, he established policies that the colonists opposed. Write a script for a debate between the British supporters of Grenville's policies and the American colonists who opposed them. In writing your script, try not to favor one side over the other.

4. Bulletin boards. The colonial militias and the first thirteen states had their own flags, each with its special symbol and motto. Make a display or series of drawings for the classroom bulletin board showing some of these flags.

Napoleon Bonaparte became the subject of many romanticized paintings by French artists of the revolutionary period. Below, this portrait of Napoleon on horseback, painted by the artist Jacques-Louis David, showed the French emperor against a background in the Alps.

CHAPTER 20

The French Revolution and Napoleon

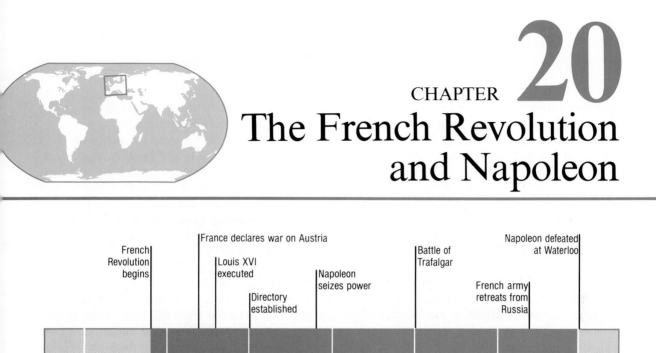

French Revolution begins

France declares war on Austria

Louis XVI executed

Directory established

Napoleon seizes power

Battle of Trafalgar

French army retreats from Russia

Napoleon defeated at Waterloo

1785   1790   1795   1800   1805   1810   1815

The ideals of Enlightenment thinkers, which had influenced the Americans' war for independence, also played a part in the outbreak of the French Revolution in 1789. French society was based on feudal ideas, economic inequality, special class privileges, and the absolute rule of kings. The French Revolution overthrew long-established customs and institutions and proclaimed the ideals of liberty and equality. Individual rights were recognized and representative government was established, bringing lasting reforms to French society and government.

Napoleon Bonaparte, who became emperor of the French, carried the ideas of the Revolution to other nations but was stopped in his attempts to dominate Europe. The French Revolution and Napoleon's conquests changed the course of European history.

This chapter describes the events of the French Revolution and the Napoleonic era that followed and spread revolutionary ideas throughout the continent of Europe.

CHAPTER OUTLINE

1   Many Problems Lead to Revolution in France

2   The French Revolution Achieves Reforms

3   The Revolution Turns to Violence

4   Napoleon Tries to Conquer Europe

1 Many Problems Lead to Revolution in France

In America, revolutionaries had sought independence from Britain but had retained many British political ideas and institutions. The revolutionaries in France had far more ambitious goals. They wanted to overthrow traditions that were centuries old and to reshape French society completely. These goals were a result of the conditions in France in the Old Regime (ray-ZHEEM), the period just before the French Revolution. Discontent in all levels of society finally erupted in violence that ended this way of life.

French society has three classes. The social structure in eighteenth-century France was a legacy of the feudalism of the Middle Ages. French society was divided into three classes, called estates (page 169). The First Estate consisted of the clergy; the Second Estate, the nobility. Everyone else belonged to the Third Estate. The First and Second Estates together included only 500,000 people, out of a total population of 24 million. Both the nobility and the clergy enjoyed special privileges. The privileged status of the first two estates aroused growing resentment among the less privileged.

Many of the clergy live in luxury. The First Estate, the clergy, played a prominent role in French life. In addition to providing religious services, village priests operated schools and helped the poor. The Church collected a large tax from the peasants and owned perhaps 10 percent of the land in France. Although these landholdings brought in a huge income, the Church did not pay taxes to the government on its property. Instead, it made a yearly gift to the government. The Church itself determined how large that gift would be.

The First Estate was divided into two groups, higher clergy and lower clergy. The higher clergy held the important posts in the Church — archbishops, bishops, and abbots (the heads of monasteries). By the late eighteenth century only nobles were named to these high Church positions. Like other aristocrats, the higher clergy usually lived in luxury, spending huge sums on hunting dogs, horses, carriages, entertainment, fine furniture, and works of art. Some members of the clergy (such as Cardinal Richelieu and Cardinal Mazarin) had also acquired great political power.

The lower clergy were parish priests who came from the middle and lower classes. Many parish priests lived in poverty. They resented the luxurious lives of the higher clergy and were sympathetic to the concerns of the people.

Many nobles seek more power. Members of the Second Estate also were highly privileged. The nobility owned about a quarter of the land in France. They held the highest offices in the Church, the government, and the army, and many of them received generous gifts and pensions from the king. Some nobles owned large estates but paid almost no taxes. As in feudal times, nobles continued to receive produce, labor, and fees for various services from the peasants on their estates. Not all nobles were wealthy or powerful, however. Many lived on run-down country estates, which brought in such small incomes that the nobles could barely afford to maintain them.

The French nobility had often sought to undermine the king's absolute rule. In the last part of the seventeenth century, Louis XIV had established nearly unchallenged personal rule (page 383). Under the weaker kings who succeeded him in the eighteenth century — Louis XV and Louis XVI — the nobles again tried to regain their power. They insisted on keeping and expanding their privileges at the expense of the peasants.

Most of the Third Estate live in poverty. The three groups that made up the Third Estate — peasants, city workers, and the middle class — included both rich and poor. The majority, the peasants, were poor. Even though peasants owned about half the land in France, often their farms were too small to support a family. Many peasants owned no land at all and worked as day laborers.

Old-fashioned ways of farming were one reason for the poverty of the French peasant. Agricultural methods in France had changed little since the Middle Ages, and the crop yield per acre of land was low. Another reason for rural poverty was taxation. Because the clergy and the nobles paid almost no taxes, the heaviest tax burden fell on the peasants. The peasants paid taxes to both the Church and the king. In some regions, taxes took almost 60 percent of a peasant family's income. Every time the government needed more money, it raised the peasants' taxes. An army of government tax collectors terrorized peasants into paying by threatening them with loss of their homes, whipping, imprisonment, or forced labor.

French peasants were better off than the peasants in most Central and Eastern European countries, where serfdom was still common. Nevertheless, even though most French peasants were no longer serfs, they still had to grind their grain in the lord's mill, bake their bread in the lord's oven, and press their grapes in the lord's winepress. As in the Middle Ages, their labor and part of the crops they raised were owed to the lord as payment for using these facilities.

By 1789, French peasants were in an angry mood. They wanted a fairer tax system and an end to the payment of fees to the lords of the manors. A poor harvest in 1788, followed by a hard winter, added to their distress and anger.

City workers also live in poverty. In the cities the working class consisted of laborers in small-scale industries and artisans who worked for masters in their craft. The bad harvest of 1788 caused a grain shortage that drove up food prices in the city markets. A worker's family might have to spend half its income just to buy bread. Unrest quickly spread among the hungry people of the cities.

The middle class is well-to-do and ambitious. The middle class, or bourgeoisie (boorzhwah-ZEE), consisted of merchants, bankers, lawyers, doctors, intellectuals, and government officials below the top ranks. Unlike the rest of the Third Estate, the bourgeoisie had money, education, and the chance to achieve many of their ambitions. They did not, however, have the prestige or influence that came with membership in the nobility. This meant they could not hope to hold the highest positions in the government, the army, or the Church.

Wealthy bourgeoisie had once been able to buy some government positions (such as judgeships) that gave them titles of nobility. In

Marie Antoinette, queen of France and the wife of Louis XVI, became a target for those who criticized the extravagance of the French court.

the late 1700's, the old nobility tried to stop this practice. It became almost impossible for the bourgeoisie to move into the nobility.

Many of the bourgeoisie were attracted by the Enlightenment ideas of the philosophes (page 408). The philosophes (most of whom were members of the middle class) challenged the basic idea of the Old Regime — that monarchs, clergy, and nobility were the natural leaders of society. From Locke onwards, Enlightenment thinkers had stressed ideas of equality and liberty. Such ideas soon became a powerful force in France.

France faces financial ruin. In addition to the different discontents of the members of the three estates, France in the 1700's was virtually bankrupt. Louis XIV, who died in 1715, had left enormous debts created by wars and luxurious living. France's debts continued to grow. Further European wars, as well as aid to the colonists during the American Revolution (page 433), emptied the royal treasury. Both Louis XV and Louis XVI borrowed heavily from bankers. They still spent lavishly on luxuries and on gifts for favorite nobles.

France's inefficient and unfair system of taxation made it impossible for the government to raise enough money to cover these expenses or repay its debts. Few of the wealthy, including the bourgeoisie, paid a fair share of taxes. The tax burden fell most heavily on the peasants, who were least able to pay. France was in a peculiar position — it was a prosperous nation with an empty treasury. The only answer seemed to be to tax the nobility and clergy. Louis XVI appealed to the First and Second Estates to agree to a tax on their lands, but they refused. The financial crisis that followed was the final cause leading to revolution.

CHECK-UP

1. (a) Into what three classes was French society divided in the eighteenth century? (b) What people belonged to each class?
2. (a) What special privileges did the clergy and nobility in France enjoy? (b) What attitude did the nobles take toward the monarchy?
3. (a) Why were most of the French peasants so poor? (b) What led to unrest among the city workers? (c) What were the complaints of the bourgeoisie?
4. (a) Why was the French treasury bankrupt by the late 1700's? (b) What made the problem difficult to solve?

2 The French Revolution Achieves Reforms

The revolution that began in France in 1789 was supported by groups with very different motives. The bourgeoisie revolted because the social system kept them from having power in the state, while the political system suppressed liberty. The peasants rebelled to escape oppressively high taxation and their feudal obligations to the nobles. The poor people of the cities were driven to rebellion by poverty, resentment of the wealthy minority, and the hope of reform. Although all these groups resented the nobility's wealth and influence, it was the actions of the nobles themselves that set off the French Revolution.

The financial crisis causes a meeting of the Estates-General. By July, 1788, France faced a serious financial crisis. As the nobles refused to be taxed, Louis XVI had to call a meeting of the Estates-General to obtain additional taxes. This assembly of delegates from the three Estates (page 442) had not met since 1614. The king hoped for approval of a plan to tax the First and Second Estates. The nobles, however, intended to use the Estates-General to protect their privileges, weaken the king's power, and give them control of the government.

The Estates-General met at Versailles in May, 1789, but was unable to act because the delegates could not agree on voting procedures. Traditionally, each of the three Estates had met separately and cast its vote as a body. For an issue to be decided, two of the three Estates had to agree. Because the nobility and clergy could be expected to vote together, the Third Estate was likely always to be outvoted two to one.

At this meeting, the delegates of the Third Estate were mostly from the bourgeoisie. They demanded that the three estates meet together, with each delegate having one vote. Because about half of the 1,200 delegates were from the Third Estate, they would then have a greater opportunity to bring about reform. Moreover, the Third Estate could also count on the support of some reform-minded delegates of the lower clergy and nobility. One clergyman, the Abbé Sieyès (syay-ES), had written a famous pamphlet called "What Is the Third Estate?" In it he voiced his demands in these words:

> We have three questions to ask:
> *First:* What is the Third Estate? Everything.
> *Second:* What has it been heretofore in the political order? Nothing.
> *Third:* What does it demand? To become something. . . .

The bourgeoisie establish the National Assembly. The Third Estate's delegates decided to force the Estates to meet as one body. At Sieyès's suggestion, on June 17, 1789, they declared themselves the National Assembly and invited the First and Second Estates to meet with them.

Urged on by the nobles, Louis XVI ordered the three estates to continue to meet separately. Locked out of their meeting place at Versailles, the delegates of the Third Estate moved to the palace's indoor tennis court. Many of the clergy and some nobles joined them. Defying the king, they demanded a constitution for France and swore not to disband the National Assembly until they had achieved this goal. The spokesman for the assembly was the Comte de Mirabeau (mee-rah-BOH), a nobleman representing the Third Estate. Mirabeau told the king's messenger that the delegates would leave only "at the point of bayonets."

Faced with this solidarity, Louis gave in and, after a week, ordered all nobility and clergy to join the Third Estate in the National Assembly. The king's recognition of the National Assembly was the first victory for the bourgeoisie.

The Parisians storm the Bastille. The bourgeoisie had the upper hand in the National Assembly but, to enact reforms, they still had to overcome the resistance of the king and many of the nobility. The king was persuaded by court nobles to send troops into Paris and Versailles. This move, however, simply spread the rebellion and brought the first violence of the revolution.

Food shortages, unemployment, and high prices had increased the resentment of the people of Paris. The calling of the Estates-General had raised their hopes for reform, but now they feared that the king's soldiers would crush the National Assembly. Afraid also that royal troops would attack the city, the people of Paris armed themselves.

On July 14, 1789, the Parisians massed outside the Bastille (bas-TEEL). This fortress had long been used as a prison and had become a hated symbol of oppression to the Parisians. Seeking guns and gunpowder, the crowds charged into the courtyard of the prison. Its guards fired into the crowd, killing nearly a hundred people. When soldiers who sided with the Parisians threatened to bombard the Bastille, its defenders surrendered. The angry crowd stormed into the fortress and killed the commander and some of his men.

Opposed by the citizens and the city militia of Paris, the frightened king withdrew his troops. The National Assembly continued to meet, but many nobles fled the country. Living abroad, they were known as émigrés (ay-mih-GRAY). Many tried to get outside help to halt the reforms and revolution.

French peasants revolt. The spirit of rebellion spread among the poor people of France, and uprisings soon broke out in the French countryside. Rumors circulated that the nobles were organizing armed bands to kill peasants and seize their property. Desperate with fear, the peasants let loose centuries of stored-up hatred against the nobles. They burned the lords' manors and destroyed records of feudal obligations. Without these written records, the lords could not demand payments from the peasants. Middle-class landowners and prosperous farmers also lost their homes and property to the rebelling peasants.

TIMETABLE

The French Revolution and Napoleon

1789	The Estates-General meets; the Third Estate declares itself a National Assembly and abolishes feudal privileges.
1791	The Constitution of 1791 establishes the Legislative Assembly.
1792	France declares war on Austria. The National Convention abolishes the monarchy, and France becomes a republic.
1793	Louis XVI is executed. The Jacobins take control of the republic.
1795	A new constitution establishes the Directory.
1799	Napoleon overthrows the Directory.
1804	Napoleon declares himself emperor.
1805	The British defeat Napoleon at Trafalgar.
1812	The Grand Army reaches Moscow and begins its retreat from Russia.
1813	Napoleon is defeated in the Battle of the Nations at Leipzig.
1814	Napoleon is exiled to Elba.
1815	Napoleon returns to France, is defeated at Waterloo, and is exiled to St. Helena.

Both soldiers and citizens attacked the Bastille in July, 1789, thus setting off the violence that led to the overthrow of the French monarchy.

The August Decrees end feudalism in France. This peasant upheaval, known as the Great Fear, made some aristocrats realize that they could no longer protect the Old Regime. One after another the nobles rose in the National Assembly to give up their feudal rights. In a decree issued on August 4, 1789, the National Assembly announced the end of feudalism in France. Serfdom was ended, along with the Church's right to demand taxes and the nobility's right to take fees, taxes, and labor from the peasants.

The National Assembly continued to make reforms, issuing decrees to put the August 4 resolutions into action. Inspired by the ideals of the American Revolution, the National Assembly also decided to issue a declaration of rights, as a way of preparing for a constitution. On August 27, it issued a statement called the Declaration of the Rights of Man and Citizen (next page). This Declaration, along with the August Decrees, marked the end of feudalism and the Old Regime in France.

The constitution that the National Assembly intended to write would limit the king's power and make France a constitutional monarchy. Cool to these reforms, Louis XVI delayed his approval.

Parisian women force Louis XVI to approve reforms. The peasants had been granted their demands, but unrest continued among the city poor. Unemployment had grown worse, for many Parisian women made their living by making hats and dresses for noblewomen. As more aristocratic families fled France, there was less and less work for the women. On October 5, 1789, Parisian women rallied to protest the shortage of bread and the soaring food prices. Soon the cry was raised "To Versailles!" Both the king and the National Assembly were at Versailles, twelve miles outside Paris. Thousands of women and a crowd of supporters marched the distance in the rain, armed with sticks, pikes, and farm tools. They stormed the palace and forced the king and queen, along with the Assembly, to return to Paris to deal with the food crisis.

The National Assembly makes reforms. Over the next two years, the National Assembly, controlled by the bourgeoisie, continued the work of reform. There were five main areas of change.

1. Equality and individual rights. The Declaration of the Rights of Man proclaimed a society based upon the "natural rights" of liberty and equality. The slogan of the Revolution became "Liberty, equality, fraternity." The bourgeoisie gained the equality they had demanded, while the nobility and clergy lost their special privileges. All offices in Church, government, and army were open to all citizens regardless of birth.

The Declaration followed the ideas of the Enlightenment, affirming the dignity of the in-

446

dividual and stating that government belonged to the people as a whole. The reformers saw the Declaration as a statement of ideals that, if realized, would end long-standing abuses and usher in a new society.

2. *Government administration.* France had been divided into provinces, most of which had once been feudal kingdoms or duchies. The reformers divided the country into departments, which were all about the same size and had elected officials.

The Assembly also made changes in land ownership. The government took land from the Church and seized the estates of nobles who had fled. Much of this land was then sold to peasants.

3. *Church influence.* The National Assembly not only seized Church lands but attempted to bring the Church and the clergy under state control. Bishops and priests were to be elected by popular vote and paid by the French government. The Pope, members of the clergy, and many French Catholics violently opposed this move, however, and it lost the reformers much support.

4. *Aid to business.* The National Assembly aided business by abolishing taxes on goods transported within France. It approved the use of the metric system as the standard system of weights and measures throughout France.

5. *Constitutional government.* In 1791 the National Assembly achieved the goal that it had sworn to achieve in June, 1789. The Constitution of 1791 limited the power of the king and set up a new law-making body, the Legislative Assembly. To vote for representatives to the assembly, a male citizen had to pay a certain amount of taxes. (This qualification barred about 30 percent of adult men.) Only property owners could sit in the assembly. Women could neither vote nor hold office. For its time, the Constitution of 1791 was generous in granting

---

PRIMARY SOURCES IN WORLD HISTORY

Declaration of the Rights of Man

The Declaration of the Rights of Man and Citizen, issued on August 27, 1789, set forth the ideals of the French Revolution. Like the English Bill of Rights and the American Declaration of Independence, it reflected people's hopes for individual rights and freedom.

1. Men are born and remain free and equal in rights. . . .

2. The aim of every [government] is the preservation of the natural . . . rights of man. These rights are liberty, property, security, and resistance to oppression.

3. The source of all sovereignty [authority] is essentially in [the people of] the nation. . . .

5. The law has the right to forbid only such actions as are injurious to society. Nothing can be forbidden that is not [prohibited] by the law, and no one can be [forced] to do that which it does not order.

6. Law is the expression of the general will [of the people]. All citizens have the right to take part personally, or by their representatives, in its formation. It must be the same for all, whether it protects or punishes. . . .

7. No man can be accused, arrested, or detained, except in the cases determined by the law and according to the forms that it has prescribed. . . .

9. Every man [is] presumed innocent until he has been pronounced guilty. . . .

11. The free communication of ideas and opinions is one of the most precious of the rights of man; every citizen, then, can freely speak, write, and print, subject to responsibility for the abuse of this freedom in the cases determined by law. . . .

17. Property being a sacred and inviolable right, no one can be deprived of it, unless a legally established public necessity evidently demands it, under condition of a just and prior [payment].

What does the Declaration list as natural rights? How does it define law? How does the Declaration seek to protect equality, freedom of expression, and ownership of property?

the vote. The greatest gains, however, were made by the well-to-do bourgeoisie.

The Revolution causes reactions in other countries. The sweeping reforms of the revolutionary government brought both sympathetic and hostile reactions in other countries. In England, the statesman Edmund Burke wrote the most famous attack on the ideas and principles of the Revolution. Burke, a brilliant Irish-born writer and speaker, had been sympathetic to the American colonists. In his *Reflections on the Revolution in France* (1790), however, he denounced the French revolutionaries. Burke feared that the violent changes in France would cause total disorder and bring about tyranny.

In reply to Burke, the American writer Thomas Paine (page 431) defended the new French republic. In his pamphlet *The Rights of Man,* Paine claimed that hereditary governments, such as a monarchy, produced incompetent and tyrannical rulers. Another response to Burke was that of the English political writer Mary Wollstonecraft. A friend of Paine and other supporters of the Republic, Wollstonecraft wrote *A Vindication of the Rights of Man.*

Women seek to share in the new equality. The Constitution of 1791 gave women no political rights. Many women had taken part in the events of the Revolution, and some hoped for a share in the "equality" promised in the Declaration of the Rights of Man. These women urged better education for girls, marriage and divorce laws that were fair to women, and the inclusion of women on juries. In Paris, Rose Lacombe founded a women's political group supporting the principles of the Revolution. Olympe de Gouges (GOOZH), a playwright, responded to the Declaration by writing her own *Declaration of the Rights of Woman and of Women Citizens* (1791). For speaking out against extreme revolutionary leaders and defending the king, de Gouges was later executed.

Hopes for reform were not limited to women in France. Mary Wollstonecraft, the English writer who had defended the Revolution, expanded her ideas two years later in another book, *A Vindication of the Rights of Women.* Replying to both Burke and Rousseau (page 411), she stated that it was natural for the "rights of man" to be extended to include women. She urged better education for women as a way of working toward this goal.

CHECK-UP

1. (a) What forced the king of France to call a meeting of the Estates-General? (b) What changes in the voting procedure of the Estates-General did the bourgeoisie demand? (c) How did they achieve this goal?
2. (a) What revolutionary actions did the people of Paris take in 1789? (b) What caused these actions? (c) What were the results?
3. (a) What caused the Great Fear? (b) What was the result?
4. Between 1789 and 1791, what reforms did the National Assembly make (a) in government? (b) in individual rights?
5. (a) How did foreign political thinkers react to the Revolution? (b) How did women support the revolutionary effort?

3 The Revolution Turns to Violence

The Constitution of 1791 marked the end of the first stage of the French Revolution. The bourgeoisie had made many gains — an end to the special privileges of the nobility, a limitation on the king's powers, and a chance to participate in government. Most of the middle class was satisfied with the changes brought by the Revolution. The peasants, too, had benefited from reforms. Some people in France, however, believed that more drastic and sweeping changes were necessary. The Revolution entered a second stage marked by violent upheavals that involved much of Europe.

Radicals seek to end the monarchy. The most extreme, or radical, of the revolutionaries wanted no king, not even one with limited power. They wanted France to become a republic. Among the radicals were many wage earners and small shopkeepers of Paris, who were known as the *sans-culottes* (SANZ kyoo-LOT).[1] Though they had played a significant role in the Revolution by storming the Bastille and marching on Versailles, the Parisian working class had gained fewer benefits than the bourgeoisie and the peasants. The people of Paris thought they should have a greater voice in the government. They wanted the government to raise wages, to lower food prices, and to find a way of preventing food shortages. Their ideal was a nation of small shopkeepers and no millionaires. "Let no one have more than one workshop, more than one store," read a sans-culotte petition.

Some of the bourgeoisie viewed the demands of the sans-culottes as a threat to private property and to bourgeois control of the government. Others, however, became leaders of the radicals and gained control of the Revolution. The violence of the second stage of the Revolution was destructive to many of the gains of the first stage.

The king loses the loyalty of his subjects. A number of events helped the radicals take control of the French Revolution. One was the royal family's attempt to flee France. While the French people liked Louis XVI, his queen — Marie Antoinette (an-twah-NET) — was not popular. (See her picture on page 443.) Married to Louis since 1770, she was an Austrian. Her parents had been Maria Theresa, the Hapsburg ruler of Austria, and Holy Roman Emperor Francis I. Her brothers Joseph I and Leopold II were Holy Roman Emperors during much of the period of the Revolution. The queen was disliked by the French people both for her Austrian birth and her extravagant, frivolous court life.

Since 1789, the royal family had been virtually prisoners in their palace in Paris. Marie Antoinette and some of the royal advisers began planning an escape to the Austrian-held Netherlands. On the night of June 20, 1791,

Louis XVI, Marie Antoinette, and their four-year-old son Louis slipped out of the palace and headed northeast toward the frontier. Although the royal family were dressed as middle-class citizens and traveling in a plain coach, the king was recognized, arrested by guards, and forced to return to Paris. When the royal family reached the city, they were greeted by stony silence. Parisians refused to remove their hats, and soldiers refused to salute the king.

The attempted flight of the royal family cost Louis his subjects' support. Many now suspected both the king and queen of plotting with Austria and with the *émigré* nobles who had taken refuge there and appealed for Austrian aid. In public meetings, the people of Paris called for the end of monarchy and the establishment of a republic. When the king agreed to the new constitution, however, the National Assembly allowed him to keep the throne.

France goes to war with Austria and Prussia. The events of the early years of the Revolution caused tension between France and other countries that were its traditional rivals. At first the remaining monarchs of Europe saw the Revolution as a weakening of France's power. The arrest of Louis XVI, however, made them fear revolution in their own lands.

The French revolutionaries, for their part, feared that Austria was preparing to support the *émigré* nobles in a *counterrevolution* — a movement to restore the old way of government. Some revolutionaries also saw themselves as crusaders in the struggle for liberty. They began to talk of spreading "a war of the people against kings."

On April 20, 1792, France declared war on Austria. Prussia supported Austria, and the two countries invaded France. They threatened to destroy Paris if the king or queen were harmed. Enraged by this threat, the Parisians rioted. A mob attacked the palace on August 10, killing hundreds of guards and servants. A temporary radical government, the Commune, seized control and imprisoned the king. The Commune ordered elections to choose representatives for a new assembly. For the first time, all adult males were allowed to vote, though only a small percentage did so.

---

[1] The literal meaning of *sans-culotte* is "without knee breeches." Instead of the knee breeches ("culottes") worn by upper-class men, the workers wore long trousers. Middle-class revolutionaries also adopted the style and the name.

France becomes a republic. The newly elected National Convention met for the first time in September, 1792. Its first act was to end the monarchy and declare France a republic. The radical members then decided that the royal family was a threat to the republic. Louis was accused of working with the nobles and foreign agents. The Convention, by one vote, sentenced him to death, and he was sent to the guillotine (GEE-yuh-teen)[2] on January 21, 1793. Marie Antoinette was executed on similar charges later that year. Their son, who had title to the throne as Louis XVII, died in prison in 1795 at the age of ten.

The establishment of a republic and the execution of the king and queen showed that the French Revolution had moved into a radical stage. Some historians call this the Second French Revolution.

Republican leaders in France now sought to spread their revolutionary reforms, offering to help "liberate" people in other countries. The army of republican France had already forced the invading Austrians and Prussians to retreat and had conquered the Austrian Netherlands. European monarchs and aristocrats were alarmed by these developments. In response to the growing threat posed by republican France, other nations — Britain, the Netherlands, Spain, and Sardinia — became allies of Austria and Prussia. This alliance inflicted several defeats upon the republican army.

The French republic faces a crisis. By the spring of 1793, conditions throughout the new French republic were desperate. As food prices soared, hungry Parisians looted stores. In western France clergy and nobles led a counter-revolutionary movement, with the aid of peasants who objected to the changes forced on the Catholic Church.

Violent disagreements also developed among the revolutionaries themselves. The most radical groups were centered in Paris, and included the political club called the Jacobins.[3] With other radicals, the Jacobins formed a strong minority in the National Convention. This radical minority was known as "the Mountain" because its members occupied seats in the highest part of the assembly hall. Two of the most prominent Jacobins were Georges Danton and Maximilien Robespierre (ROHBZ-pih-air), both lawyers. Even more extreme in his beliefs was Jean-Paul Marat (mah-RAH), the editor of a revolutionary newspaper. The more moderate members of the Convention were the Girondists, whose supporters were mainly from other parts of France.

The Committee of Public Safety mobilizes France for war. The radical leaders of "the Mountain" came from the bourgeoisie, but they realized that the support of the common people was essential. To keep popular support and help France survive the crisis, the Jacobins in the National Convention established the Committee of Public Safety. This group of about a dozen men had nearly unlimited power. To help the poor, they regulated the prices and supply of bread and other essential goods. They also set up plans that regulated small industries producing weapons and equipment for the army.

In August, 1793, the Committee called on the whole nation to take part in the war effort. For the first time in European history, a national draft called all able-bodied men for army service. Everyone in the nation had a duty: Women were to work in hospitals or sew tents and uniforms. Children collected old clothing to make bandages. The elderly were expected to give speeches that would arouse patriotism.

The new French army had one million men and was the largest army assembled up till that time. It was united by loyalty to the republic and led by ambitious young generals. Soldiers marched off to war singing the "Marseillaise" (mar-say-YEZ), the anthem of the French Revolution.

Reforms are made at home. The Jacobins also proposed more reforms for France. They drew up a new constitution that declared the purpose of government to be the protection of the welfare and rights of all citizens. It gave all men the right to vote and the right to work. (The Constitution of 1793, like that of 1791, did not grant political rights to women.) The National Convention also outlawed slavery in the

---

[2]The guillotine was a machine used to behead people given the death penalty. It was named after its inventor, Joseph Guillotin.

[3]The Jacobins were a political club organized in 1789. They met in the Convent of Saint-Jacques, built by the Jacobin, or Dominican, friars, from which their name came.

French colonies, eliminated imprisonment for debt, and made plans to provide public education for boys and girls. Because of the emergency caused by the war, the Constitution of 1793 was never put into effect.

The Jacobins introduce the Reign of Terror. The leading member of the Committee of Public Safety, Robespierre, was certain that everything he did was for the good of France, the republic, and the Revolution. He hated the Old Regime and wanted to create a new and better society in which all people would be free, equal, and educated. Nothing, he felt, could stand in the way of this ideal. In an attempt to make the republic safe and secure, the Jacobins began what was called the Reign of Terror. A "tribunal," or court, was set up to arrest, try, and execute anyone judged to be an enemy of the republic. Between September 1793 and July 1794, at least 20,000 people (perhaps as many as 40,000) were executed during the Reign of Terror. Many others were imprisoned. The victims included clergy, aristocrats, and common people — anyone who disagreed politically with the Jacobins. Those taken before the tribunal had no chance to defend themselves, and most trials were a mockery of justice. In the countryside, there were mass executions. In Paris, carts filled with the condemned rolled through the streets to the public square where the guillotine was set up.

Huge crowds watched these executions, shouting insults at the victims. When a famous person was to be guillotined, men and women left their jobs to be present at the spectacle. Women wore silver and gold guillotines as jewelry; children even played with toy guillotines.

Robespierre dominated the Committee of Public Safety and soon became the symbol of the Reign of Terror. As the Terror claimed more and more victims, not even Robespierre's fellow leaders felt safe. Danton and other politicians were executed early in 1794 for attempting to stop the Terror. French victories on the battlefield had lessened fears that the republic was threatened by enemies. Feeling the cold chill of the guillotine blade at their necks, several members of the National Convention arranged for Robespierre's arrest on July 27, 1794. The next day he and his followers were sent to the guillotine.

A Jacobin poster called for the "unity and indivisibility of the republic" and for "liberty, equality, and fraternity" — or death.

Moderates regain control of France. The fall of Robespierre ended the Terror and restored control of the government to more moderate leaders. Although their desires for reform had helped bring on the Revolution in 1789, these moderate leaders wanted no more of the Jacobins. Mostly members of the bourgeoisie, they did not want the common people to have political power, nor did they want the monarchy restored.

A new constitution, adopted in 1795, set up a republic headed by a committee of five men, called the Directory. Once again, only property owners were allowed to vote, and the five directors suppressed uprisings by both the radical *sans-culottes* and the supporters of monarchy. Nonetheless, the Directory proved to be a weak government. It made no attempt to halt the growing inflation, and discontent with the Directory grew rapidly among the French people.

451

The French Revolution brings lasting changes. The French Revolution had transformed French society. It ended feudalism, absolute monarchy, and the special privileges of the nobles and clergy. A written constitution guaranteed individual rights — trial by jury, and freedom of religion, of speech, and of the press (although these were lost during the Terror). The bourgeoisie gained political power to become the most important class in France.

Two forces that the reformers of 1789 had not anticipated also developed during the revolutionary period. Whereas wars had once been fought solely by professional soldiers, the Revolution involved all the people of France. The human and material resources of the entire state were mobilized to defeat the enemy. Increasingly, as time went on, wars would be fought in this way.

The other idea that had its beginnings in the Revolution was **nationalism** — a feeling of devotion to one's country, rather than a feeling of loyalty to a ruler or a small group. Threatened by outside forces, the French people fought to preserve their new republic. In the next two centuries, ideas of nationalism spread throughout the globe.

CHECK-UP

1. Vocabulary: *counterrevolution, nationalism.*
2. (a) What were the aims of the radical revolutionaries? (b) How did they gain control of the revolution? (c) What led to the executions of Louix XVI and Marie Antoinette?
3. (a) How did European monarchs react to the Revolution? (b) What caused France to declare war on Austria? (c) What other nations joined the war against France? (d) What problems within France threatened the republic by 1793?
4. (a) What group became dominant in the National Convention? (b) How did the Committee of Public Safety mobilize France for war?
5. (a) What was the Reign of Terror? (b) How did the government of France change after Robespierre's death?

4 Napoleon Tries to Conquer Europe

The government of the Directory was weak and unpopular, and the people of France were tired of war, revolution, and violence. In November, 1799, a group of politicians easily carried out a coup (KOO),[4] overthrowing the Directory and installing a popular general as the head of the French government. Over the next fifteen years, this leader, Napoleon Bonaparte, conquered much of Europe. Many of the reforms of the French Revolution spread to other lands.

Napoleon is a hero in France. By 1799, Napoleon Bonaparte was a well-known military hero. Born on the island of Corsica in 1769, he had gone to military school in France and become an officer. In 1793, he joined the French revolutionary forces and showed great talent for planning and leadership.

In 1796 Napoleon was given command of the French forces fighting the Sardinians and Austrians in Italy. His brilliant organization of the French troops won several crucial battles, forcing the Austrians to seek peace and making Napoleon a hero. Napoleon next led an expedition to Egypt, where France hoped to establish a base for striking at Britain in both Africa and India. The expedition was a military failure, but it had several important results. Napoleon established French influence in Egypt, setting up a reorganized system of government. He also took with him some French scholars who began to study the arts and history of ancient Egypt. It was the engineers in Napoleon's army who found the Rosetta stone that made it possible to read Egyptian hieroglyphics (page 49).

The Consulate is established to rule France. On his return to France, Napoleon became part of the plot to replace the Directory. With the Abbé Sieyès (page 444) and others, he forced the Directory to resign (November, 1799). Napoleon's soldiers then surrounded the legislative assembly, and it quickly disbanded.

---

[4]A coup, or *coup d'état* (koo-day-TAH), is the sudden overthrow of a government, often by military leaders.

Collecting the World's Treasures

Early travelers from Europe were often enthusiastic collectors of souvenirs from their journeys. Kings, generals, and ordinary soldiers brought home works of art, which they kept in their private homes and palaces. Today many great private collections can be seen in public art museums.

The first of these great public museums was the Louvre (LOO-vruh) in Paris, once a royal palace housing the art treasures of the French royal family. The French revolutionary government opened the Louvre to the public in 1793. When Napoleon became emperor, he ordered new rooms built to hold the treasures his armies had taken from Egypt and from other parts of Europe. Napoleon brought so much ancient Egyptian art back to France that a new section was built on the Louvre simply to display the collection. At right is pictured one of Napoleon's captured treasures — an Egyptian sculpture of many centuries ago.

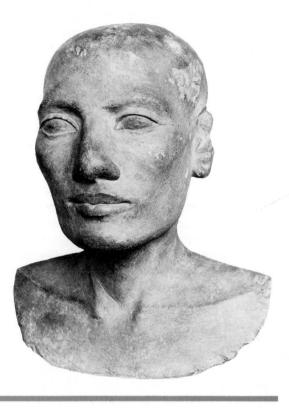

France was to remain a republic under the new government, the Consulate. Its real leaders, however, were three officials called consuls (who took their title from ancient Rome). Sieyès had intended to run the Consulate, but Napoleon became First Consul and quickly concentrated power in his own hands. In 1802 he was made First Consul for life.

Napoleon rules France as a dictator. Napoleon was a remarkable organizer and politician as well as an outstanding military leader. He had great powers of concentration and could work for eighteen or twenty hours at a stretch without getting tired. He knew how to win and keep the support of all the different groups of people in France. He was also ambitious and proud and once said that he loved "power as a musician loves his violin." He was determined to have both power and glory.

Napoleon won the support of the bourgeoisie by re-establishing order and assuring them of positions in government and the army.

He also won middle-class support by promoting trade and industry and establishing taxes on imports, which protected French businesses from foreign competition. A national bank (the Bank of France) was started to provide credit for businesses and assure France's economic stability. Napoleon also pleased business owners by forbidding workers to strike.

At the same time, Napoleon won the support of workers and peasants. Because business was prospering, there were jobs repairing roads, clearing harbors, and building canals. To please the poor, Napoleon made food available at low prices. He allowed the French peasants to keep the land that they had gained during the Revolution.

Napoleon's policies won him the support of the great majority of the French people. Even most of the nobles who had fled during the Revolution returned to France, promising their loyalty to Napoleon. Many soon held high government posts.

Napoleon's law code reflects reforms of the Revolution. As part of his reorganization of the government, Napoleon in 1800 appointed a staff of lawyers to draw up a clear, written code of laws for all of France. This was the first attempt in modern times to make such a code. Still in use in France today, the Napoleonic Code[5] reflected some of the ideals of the Enlightenment and the Revolution. Under the code all French men were regarded as equals, no matter what their birth or wealth. Feudalism and class privileges were abolished. The code allowed people to practice the religion of their choice and protected their property rights.

On the other hand, some of the code's provisions worked against equality. Workers were treated as inferior to employers. Men received almost total control over their families and family property, while women lost some rights.

Napoleon reaches an agreement with the Church. Religious toleration, promised in the code, was one result of the Revolution. Napoleon at the same time sought to make peace with the Catholic Church, because many clergy and other French Catholics resented the changes of the Revolution (page 447). In 1801 Napoleon reached an agreement with the Pope. Although the French government continued to appoint members of the French clergy and to pay their salaries, the Church had the right to confirm or refuse these appointments. For its part, the Church gave up its claims to land seized during the Revolution.

Napoleon promotes government-supported education. Napoleon's centralized government needed trained military officers and educated public officials. To provide them, Napoleon established a national military academy and created an administrative body, called the University of France, to take full charge of schools and colleges. In time, this institution became the central board of education for all of France. It set up a standard course of study for all teachers and schoolchildren and supervised the educational system.

Political liberties are lost. While Napoleon preserved many of the social reforms of the French Revolution, he ignored some of the individual freedoms the French had won. Napoleon did not favor political liberty or free elections. He believed that France should be governed by an absolute but enlightened ruler. Freedom of speech and freedom of the press came to an end. Newspapers printed what the government wanted people to read; those that did not were closed down. Critics of the government were reported by Napoleon's spies and punished.

Napoleon becomes an emperor. While making administrative reforms in France, Napoleon was also trying to deal with the country's foreign enemies. Using both diplomacy and military skill, he broke up the alliance between Russia, Austria, and Britain and signed peace treaties with these nations. Following these victories at home and abroad, Napoleon's power seemed secure. In 1804, with popular approval, France became an empire and Napoleon took the title Napoleon I, Emperor of the French.

Napoleon's ambitions went beyond being emperor of the French — he aimed to rule Europe. The peace treaty with Britain in 1802 had left Napoleon in control of much of Italy and western Europe. Peace could not last long, for French expansion threatened British trade and sea power. By 1803 Britain and France were again at war. In 1805 other European nations — Russia, Austria, Sweden — formed an alliance against Napoleon. Prussia also joined the war to halt Napoleon's advance in the German states. The period of warfare that followed is called the Napoleonic Wars.

Napoleon's armies overrun Europe. Between 1805 and 1807 Napoleon's armies won stunning victories over Austria, Prussia, and Russia. Prussia and Russia lost territory, and Austria withdrew from the alliance after a defeat at Austerlitz in 1805. Napoleon became the virtual master of Europe (map, next page). Some lands he annexed to France. In others Napoleon placed his relatives or loyal generals on the throne.

In some ways, Napoleon extended the reforms of the Revolution to other lands. His administrators in conquered lands reduced the privileges of the aristocracy and the clergy. They set up the Napoleonic Code and fairer

---

[5]The Napoleonic Code also became the basis of laws in many areas where France was influential, including the state of Louisiana and the province of Quebec in Canada.

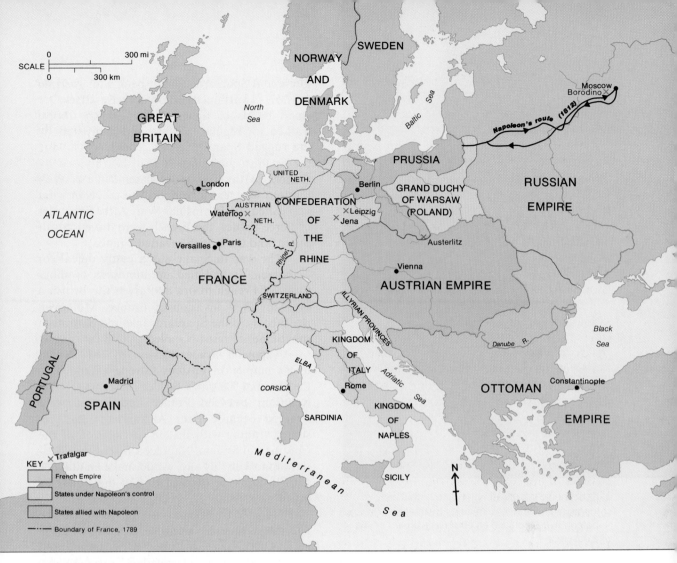

Napoleon's Empire

Napoleon extended his power over almost the entire continent of Europe. Which states did he directly control? Which states became his allies?

systems of taxation. They abolished serfdom, promoted public education, opened high positions to talented men, and supported religious toleration. These reforms speeded up the social and political modernization of Europe.

There was another side to Napoleon's rule. Conquered lands were forced to provide soldiers for his army, taxes to support it, and raw materials for French industries. Opposition to Napoleonic rule was ruthlessly suppressed. Soon those who had at first welcomed Napoleon as a "liberator" grew to hate his rule.

Napoleon fails to defeat Britain. Napoleon's most determined enemy was Britain. Britain supported Napoleon's enemies, seized French ships, and kept neutral ships from reaching French ports. In 1805 the combined French and Spanish fleets left the Mediterranean Sea on their way to invade England. At Trafalgar (truh-FAL-gur), off the southwest coast of Spain, they were intercepted by the British fleet, led by Horatio, Lord Nelson. Though Nelson was killed in the battle, half of Napoleon's ships were destroyed, and the British remained supreme at sea.

After Trafalgar, Napoleon gave up his dream of invading England. He decided to defeat Britain by striking at its trade, the heart of British prosperity. Napoleon's plan, called the Continental System, forbade France's allies

Napoleon took the title of emperor in 1804. At his coronation (shown in this painting by the artist David) Napoleon himself placed an empress's crown on his wife Josephine.

and all countries under French control to import British products. Napoleon hoped the Continental System would ruin Britain. The plan failed. British merchants simply increased their trade with the United States and began smuggling goods into Europe.

The Continental System also hurt European businesses by cutting them off from goods they needed. This turned the middle-class merchants in Europe against Napoleon.

Napoleon's campaign fails in Spain. When Portugal refused to abide by the Continental System, Napoleon occupied that country and then determined to take Spain, the other nation of the Iberian peninsula. In 1808 Napoleon sent a large army into Spain, forced the Spanish king to abdicate, and made his own brother, Joseph Bonaparte, king of that country. Bitterly resenting the French occupation, the Portu-

guese and Spaniards fought back with *guerrilla warfare* — warfare based on surprise attacks by small bands of fighters. The French troops, trained for regular warfare and hampered by the rugged Spanish terrain, could not subdue the Spanish guerrillas. A British army, led by General Arthur Wellesley (later Duke of Wellington) was sent to support the rebels in what was called the Peninsular War. After five years of fierce battles, the French were driven out of Spain, and the British invaded France.

The war in Spain was a costly defeat for Napoleon. It had tied up hundreds of thousands of French troops and given the British a base for their invasion of France. Moreover, the success of the Spaniards inspired patriots in other lands to resist Napoleon.

Napoleon invades Russia. By 1812 Napoleon's empire in Eastern Europe extended to the Russian Empire's border (map, page 455). Relations between France and Russia were strained because Czar Alexander I had resumed trading with Britain in violation of the Continental System. Napoleon feared that Russia, supposedly his ally, would make an alliance with Britain. He decided to end the threat by invading Russia.

Napoleon gathered troops from France and the conquered countries, creating an army of 614,000 men. In June, 1812, the Grand Army, as it was called, invaded Russia. Realizing they could not beat the French in battle, the Russians slowly retreated eastward. The huge French army depended for food on the farms and villages it conquered, but the Russians deliberately set fire to farms and crops as they retreated. Lured deeper into the vast Russian steppes, the Grand Army ran short of supplies. Disease, hunger, exhaustion, desertion, and battle losses reduced its numbers. In September the Russians made a stand at Borodino, some seventy miles west of Moscow, but were again forced to retreat.

The Russian retreat allowed Napoleon to reach Moscow, but the victory was useless. The city was deserted, and the Russians had set fires that eventually destroyed nearly all of it.

The French retreat becomes a disaster. Realizing that his army could not survive a Russian winter in the devastated city, Napoleon ordered a retreat. Only about 100,000 soldiers remained in France's Grand Army. On October 19, 1812, they began the long march westward.

The retreat became one of the worst disasters in history. The soldiers had little food and not enough warm clothing. Russian peasants and horsemen attacked soldiers who fell behind. The temperature fell to 30 degrees below zero. "The road is littered with men frozen to death," wrote one of Napoleon's generals. "The soldiers throw away their guns because they cannot hold them; both officers and soldiers think only of protecting themselves from the terrible cold." Fewer than 40,000 soldiers survived the retreat from Moscow.

European nations join to defeat Napoleon. Meanwhile, in the German state of Prussia, anti-French leaders took steps to arouse people's feelings of nationalism and patriotism. They introduced reforms to make the citizens feel closer to their country and king. These reforms encouraged the Prussians to stand together in defense of their country. Elsewhere in Europe, other patriots urged rebellion against Napoleon.

In 1813, after Napoleon's retreat from Russia, Prussia declared war on France. Other states soon joined Prussia. In October, 1813, allied forces from Prussia, Austria, Russia, and Sweden defeated Napoleon in the "Battle of the Nations" at Leipzig (LYP-sig), Germany.

The victorious allies then invaded France. When they reached Paris in March, 1814, Napoleon abdicated. Louis XVIII, younger brother of the executed Louis XVI, was crowned king of France. The allies exiled Napoleon to the small island of Elba, off the western coast of Italy.

Napoleon returns for the "Hundred Days." Napoleon was only forty-four years old. He still longed for the excitement of battle, the cheers of his soldiers, and the glory of victory. Moreover, he knew many French people were dissatisfied with their new king.

Escaping from Elba, Napoleon landed on the southern French coast on March 1, 1815, with a thousand soldiers. King Louis XVIII sent his troops to arrest Napoleon. Sure of his ability to win back the soldiers' loyalty, Napoleon walked up to the royal troops. "If there is one soldier among you who wishes to kill his emperor," he said, "here I am." The king's troops shouted, "Long live the emperor!" and joined Napoleon. On March 20, 1815, Napoleon entered Paris and received a hero's welcome. This began the period known as the Hundred Days.

Napoleon's return renewed the war against France. The European allies were meeting at the Congress of Vienna (page 462), and once again they united against the French. In June, 1815, the opposing forces met at Waterloo in the Austrian Netherlands. Napoleon's army was decisively defeated by troops led by the British Duke of Wellington and the Prussian field marshal, Gebhard von Blücher (BLOO-kur).

Napoleon surrendered to the British, who sent him to St. Helena, a lonely island in the South Atlantic, a thousand miles from the coast of southern Africa. On this rocky island Napoleon Bonaparte, emperor of the French and would-be master of Europe, spent the last six years of his life.

The Napoleonic era spreads revolutionary ideas. Napoleon's conquests radically changed Europe by spreading many of the French Revolution's reforms and ideals. Governments were organized more efficiently, feudal ideas were rejected, and ideas of freedom and equality took root. In reaction to Napoleon, ideas of nationalism grew. As a result, many European peoples sought to create independent nations.

CHECK-UP

1. Vocabulary: *guerrilla warfare.*
2. (a) What kind of government did Napoleon establish in 1799? (b) How did he gain the support of the bourgeoisie? (c) of workers and peasants?
3. (a) What was the Napoleonic Code? (b) What agreement did Napoleon reach with the Church? (c) How did he promote education? (d) What freedoms did Napoleon suppress?
4. (a) What were Napoleon's plans for the rest of Europe? (b) What reforms of the French Revolution spread to conquered lands? (c) What led to opposition to Napoleon's rule?
5. What actions did Napoleon take against (a) Britain, (b) Spain, and (c) Russia? (d) How did each of these actions contribute to Napoleon's defeat?

Chapter 20 Review

Summary

The Old Regime in France was based on absolute monarchy and a nobility and clergy with special privileges. Unfair taxation and unequal opportunities caused widespread discontent among the Third Estate—the middle class, the peasants, and the city workers. In 1789 a financial crisis forced Louis XVI to call a meeting of the Estates-General. The bourgeoisie took over the meeting. Aided by uprisings of peasants and Parisian workers, they ended feudal privileges and limited the king's power.

In the early stage of the French Revolution, France became a limited monarchy with a constitution and guarantees of individual rights. In 1792, radicals who wanted to end monarchy altogether took control of the revolution. A republic was established, the king was executed, and thousands of French people were killed in a Reign of Terror. Other European monarchs went to war against the French republic.

A moderate, but weak, government came to power in 1794. It was easily overthrown in 1799 by a popular general, Napoleon Bonaparte. By 1804 he had made himself emperor. Napoleon's military genius enabled him to overrun much of Europe, bringing some of the reforms and ideas of the Revolution to other countries. His absolute rule, combined with growing feelings of nationalism, aroused opposition to French occupation in many places. An alliance of European nations finally defeated Napoleon in 1815.

Vocabulary Review

1. Write the sentences listed below on a sheet of paper. Fill in the blank in each sentence with one of these words: *counterrevolution, guerrilla warfare, nationalism.*
(a) Citizens' devotion to and pride in their country is called ___?___ .
(b) The movement to restore the government of France as it had been before the revolution was a ___?___ .
(c) The Spaniards and Portuguese fought Napoleon's forces with ___?___ , in which small bands of soldiers made sudden surprise attacks.

2. Explain the importance of each of the following to the French Revolution: (a) Third Estate, (b) National Assembly, (c) Bastille, (d) *émigrés,* (e) Declaration of the Rights of Man and Citizen, (f) Constitution of 1791, (g) *sansculottes,* (h) Jacobins, (i) Committee of Public Safety, (j) Reign of Terror, (k) Constitution of 1795, (l) Directory.

3. Explain the importance of each of the following to the reign of Napoleon: (a) Consulate, (b) Napoleonic Code, (c) University of France, (d) Continental System, (e) Peninsular War, (f) the Grand Army, (g) the Hundred Days, (h) Battle of Waterloo.

People to Identify

Match the following people with the numbered phrases that describe them: *Louis XVI, Abbé Sieyès, Marie Antoinette, Louis XVII, Maximilien Robespierre, Lord Nelson, Duke of Wellington, Gebhard von Blücher.*

1. The leader of the Prussian forces that defeated Napoleon at Waterloo.
2. The son of the executed French monarchs.
3. In 1788, called the first meeting of the Estates-General since 1614.
4. A prominent Jacobin who became the leading member of the Committee of Public Safety and led the Reign of Terror.
5. The leader of the British fleet that defeated Napoleon at Trafalgar.
6. A member of the First Estate who wrote a pamphlet demanding political power for the Third Estate.
7. The French queen beheaded in 1793.
8. The leader of the British forces that defeated Napoleon at Waterloo.

Relating Geography and History

1. **Locating places.** Locate each of the following on a map in this chapter:
(a) Paris   (e) Moscow
(b) Versailles   (f) Leipzig
(c) Corsica   (g) Elba
(d) Trafalgar   (h) Waterloo

2. **Map study and interpretation.** Napoleon's drive to power led to some of history's most ex-

citing land and sea battles. On the map on page 455, locate the following battle sites: Austerlitz, Trafalgar, Leipzig, and Waterloo. Then make a chart with information about the battles. For each battle, give the date, the location, the forces that were involved, and the outcome. Also write a sentence explaining how each battle affected Napoleon's plans for his empire.

Discussion Questions

1. For what reasons was each of the following groups in France dissatisfied with conditions in the Old Regime: (a) the nobility, (b) the peasants, (c) the bourgeoisie?

2. (a) Compare what Louis XVI wanted with what the nobility wanted from the 1789 meeting of the Estates-General. (b) Why was Louis' recognition of the National Assembly a victory for the bourgeoisie?

3. (a) How did the reforms of the National Assembly weaken the power of the clergy? (b) How did the National Assembly's reforms and the 1791 Constitution benefit the bourgeoisie?

4. (a) Why were the *sans-culottes* dissatisfied with the results of the Constitution of 1791? (b) Why did the bourgeoisie resist the demands of the *sans-culottes*?

5. (a) How did the Jacobins gain the support of the common people? (b) What changes were made by the moderates who took control of the government after the fall of Robespierre?

6. (a) What problems was France facing when Napoleon overthrew the Directory? (b) What policies of Napoleon won him the support of the French people? (c) List several of his reforms that improved conditions in France. (d) Which of his policies limited political liberties?

7. (a) Why did the Continental System fail? (b) What strategy did the Russians use to defeat Napoleon's army?

Reading Primary Sources

John Frederick Sackville, the Duke of Dorset, was the English ambassador to France from 1783 to 1789. The following passages are excerpts from letters in which he describes some of the events leading up to the French Revolution. Read the passages. Then answer the questions that follow.

November 27, 1788. The price of bread has again been raised a French sol [a coin]. . . . At Pontamouson in Lorraine . . . the public . . . [wheat warehouses] have been broken into and pillaged by the . . . [peasants].

December 11, 1788. Bread has again been raised one sol and is . . . now at fourteen sols per pound. I understand that it is to be gradually raised to sixteen sols and no higher. The distress of the poor is already very great . . .

April 30, 1789. This city has for some days . . . been alarmed by a very serious tumult, which began about six o'clock on Monday evening when a number of workmen employed by a . . . [large] manufacturer . . . assembled in a riotous manner . . . [to demonstrate against] their master, . . . of whom they had demanded an increase of wages on account of the . . . [high] price of bread, and who . . . had declared in a public . . . [meeting] that fifteen sols a day were wages sufficient for workmen to . . . [live] on. . . . On the following morning, . . . the rioters assembled again in much greater force, . . . [many] having furnished themselves with . . . [weapons]. . . . It happened that on that day there were races . . . that drew together a large company of persons of rank and fashion, many of whom . . . were prevented [from] passing . . . by the . . . people . . . who insisted on their declaring themselves in favor of the Third Estate. . . . The military was called out. . . .

(a) Why did the peasants break into the wheat warehouses? (b) What was the price of bread on December 11, 1788? (c) If the manufacturer paid his laborers fifteen sols per day, about how long would each laborer have to work to pay for one pound of bread? (d) What other evidence do the letters contain of unrest among the people?

Skill Activities

1. Evaluating historical figures. Prepare a "Who's Who" of the French Revolution. People that might be included are (a) Louis XVI, (b) Marie Antoinette, (c) Maximilien Robespierre, (d) Georges Danton, (e) Charlotte Corday, (f) Jean Paul Marat. Write a few sentences describing each one's part in the Revolution.

2. Evaluating sources. Write a short essay comparing the American Declaration of Independence with the Declaration of the Rights of Man (page 447). Note the ways the American Declaration influenced the French document.

After Napoleon's defeat, the statesmen of Europe held a peace conference in Vienna to discuss the dismantling of the French conqueror's empire. While officials of many countries attended, most decisions were made by the representatives of Austria, Britain, Prussia, and Russia.

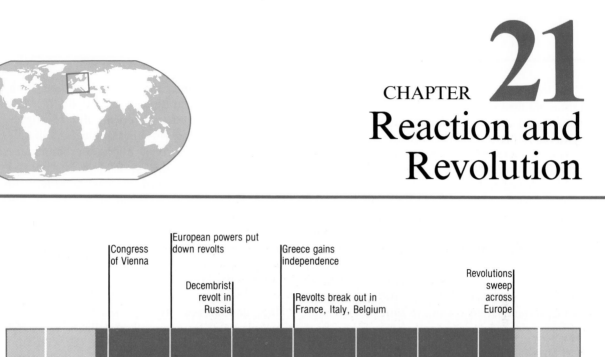

CHAPTER **21**

Reaction and Revolution

Congress
of Vienna

European powers put
down revolts

Decembrist
revolt in
Russia

Greece gains
independence

Revolts break out in
France, Italy, Belgium

Revolutions
sweep
across
Europe

1810 1815 1820 1825 1830 1835 1840 1845 1850

By 1815, after 25 years of turmoil, Napoleon had been defeated, and Europe was once again at peace. Reacting against the disorder caused by the French Revolution, many of Europe's rulers and diplomats met and attempted to restore stability by taking away many of the freedoms that people had gained. They also tried to restore the balance of power by dividing up Napoleon's conquests and restoring former ruling families to their thrones.

The ideas unleashed by the French Revolution continued to inspire the reformers who were seeking freedom in many countries. At the same time, popular movements for unity and independence arose among nationality groups. Waves of revolution swept across Europe between 1820 and 1830 and again in 1848. Although most of these revolutions failed, they indicated the strength of nationalist feeling and the growing political power of the working class.

This chapter identifies the ideas and events that influenced European life between 1815 and 1848.

CHAPTER OUTLINE

1 Europe Reacts to Napoleon's Downfall

2 Romanticism Influences Art and Politics

3 1848 Is a Year of Revolutions

461

1   Europe Reacts to Napoleon's Downfall

Napoleon's conquests had made great changes in the political map of Europe, upsetting ruling houses and threatening the balance of power. Between September, 1814, and June, 1815, following Napoleon's abdication, monarchs and diplomats from many European countries met in Vienna, Austria. The great powers — Britain, France, Austria, Prussia, and Russia — were represented, as well as smaller states. The purpose of the Congress of Vienna was to work out a peace settlement. European leaders hoped to undo the changes brought by the French Revolution and restore former rulers to their thrones. Their plans reflected the conflicting political trends then at work in Europe.

TRENDS IN EUROPEAN POLITICS

The Congress of Vienna seeks to restore traditional ways. The mood of the delegates to the Congress of Vienna was one of *conservatism* — a political philosophy based on the desire to preserve traditions and long-established institutions. Nineteenth-century conservatism was a reaction against the ideas of the Enlightenment and the radical changes of the French Revolution. Conservatives such as Edmund Burke in England (page 448) felt that traditional ways of doing things were basic and valuable to society. They were horrified by radical social change and the revolutionary principle of equality. Nineteenth-century conservatives believed that institutions such as the monarchy and the nobility were necessary for a well-run society. Many also believed that organized religion was basic for a stable society. They viewed the French revolutionaries as fanatics who had come close to destroying civilization.

Liberals call for equality and change. While the conservatives tried to restore past traditions, other movements that grew out of the Enlightenment and the French Revolution persisted. These movements, liberalism and nationalism, called for basic reforms and sought independence from the rule of monarchs. *Liberalism* was a political philosophy based on a belief in individual freedom, equality under law, and freedom of thought and religion. Both the French Declaration of the Rights of Man (page 447) and the American Bill of Rights (page 437) expressed liberal ideals. Liberals called for written constitutions, parliamentary government, and the protection of "natural rights." They believed it was necessary to change institutions and traditions that did not promote such ideas.

There were disagreements among the nineteenth-century liberals, who were mainly members of the rising middle class — bankers, merchants, lawyers, journalists, university students, and intellectuals. Some liberals feared the uneducated and propertyless common people, who far outnumbered them. They felt that giving political power to the common people might threaten both liberty and property. Other liberals, particularly in France, favored a republic in which all citizens, rich and poor, would be able to vote and to hold office.

Nationalist feelings emerge in the French Revolution. Ideas of nationalism developed among the people of France during the Revolution (page 452). When foreign monarchs threatened to conquer France, the French people — men and women, young and old — united to defend *la patrie* (pah-TREE), their homeland. There had never been such an army before in European history. The soldiers of the Revolution did not fight for money or for an individual leader, but for the nation. Similar feelings developed later among the people of some of the countries conquered and occupied by the armies of Napoleon.

Nationalism had wide appeal in nineteenth-century Europe. It developed among people who had strong ties to a particular land and shared a common language, history, and traditions. They took great pride in their own culture and felt distinct from other people. In many parts of Europe, people who shared such feelings did not live in a united or independent country. Nationalist movements became common in these regions. Often they combined with liberal ideals to bring about revolutions for independence and reform.

THE CONGRESS OF VIENNA

Metternich dominates the Congress. All the delegates to the Congress of Vienna had a stake in re-establishing conservatism and discouraging liberal and nationalist ideas. There were nine ruling monarchs at the meeting, including Czar Alexander I of Russia, King Frederick William III of Prussia, and Emperor Francis I of Austria. The other delegates and diplomats were nearly all aristocrats. As the host, the Austrian emperor lavishly entertained the rulers, princes, nobles, and diplomats.

The leading figure at the Congress was the Austrian diplomat Prince Klemens von Metternich (MET-ur-nik), a handsome and intelligent aristocrat. Metternich hated the liberal ideas proclaimed by the French Revolution. The belief that society could be reshaped according to the ideals of liberty and equality, said Metternich, had brought 25 years of revolution, terror, and war.

Metternich also despised nationalism, fearing it would cause war in Europe. Nationalism was particularly threatening in the Austrian Empire, where many different peoples lived under Austrian rule. The spirit of nationalism, Metternich feared, could lead to the break-up of the Austrian Empire.

Prussia and Russia threaten the balance of power. The question of what to do with the territories that had been part of Napoleon's empire caused serious disagreements among the delegates at the Congress of Vienna. One dispute threatened to involve Europe in another war. Both Prussia and Russia hoped to gain new lands and agreed to work together to accomplish their goals. Prussia wanted to take over the German kingdom of Saxony. Czar Alexander wanted to create a new Polish kingdom by combining the Polish lands that Russia held with those taken by Austria and Prussia in the partitions (page 393). The new Polish kingdom would be placed under Russian control.

Britain and Austria, however, saw the westward extension of Russia as a threat to the balance of power in Europe. Metternich declared that he had not fought Napoleon only to give way to the czar.

France gains a voice in the Congress. The dispute gave Prince Talleyrand of France the

Prince Klemens von Metternich, Austria's foreign minister, was that nation's representative at the Congress of Vienna. Metternich led the efforts of those who wanted Europe to return to past ways.

chance to regain some influence for his defeated country. He joined with Metternich and the British delegate, Viscount Castlereagh, in an alliance to oppose Prussia and Russia. Faced with this threat, Russia and Prussia backed down and reduced their demands for land.

The Congress of Vienna changes European borders. After months of diplomatic bargaining, the delegates at Vienna finished their work. The peace settlement changed many borders in Europe, with the intent of restoring a balance of power (map, page 464). The allies did not punish France severely, because they wanted to keep the restored Bourbon monarchy strong. Although France had to give up lands gained by Napoleon, it kept border territories conquered during the Revolution. France, therefore, possessed more land after 1815 than it had before the French Revolution.

The lands that Napoleon had taken were divided in several ways. The Netherlands

463

Europe in 1815

Hoping to restore the balance of power upset by Napoleon, the Congress of Vienna changed national borders in Europe and restored former monarchs. Which two leading powers had territories within the boundaries of the German Confederation?

became a kingdom that included Belgium (the former Austrian Netherlands). Switzerland regained its independence. Austria received the northern Italian states of Lombardy and Venetia, as well as other territory on the Adriatic Sea. Prussia received the Rhineland and part of Saxony, although not as much as it had wanted. Russia was granted Finland and a large part of the Polish territories, though less than the czar had wanted. Sweden received Norway. Britain obtained the Dutch Cape Colony in South Africa (map, pages 366–367) and naval bases in the North Sea, the Mediterranean, and the Indian Ocean.

German states form an alliance. In 1805 Napoleon had officially ended the Holy Ro-

man Empire, making its Hapsburg ruler, Francis I, simply emperor of Austria. One of the acts of the Congress of Vienna was the establishment of a new German Confederation to replace the former empire. The Confederation was a loose alliance of 39 states dominated by Austria.[1]

European monarchies are restored. One guiding principle of the Congress was "legitimacy" — the restoration of ruling families who had been displaced by the French Revolution and the Napoleonic Wars. The Congress con-

---

[1] Only the predominantly German territories of the Austrian Empire (the western half) were part of the German Confederation.

sidered these families the only rightful, or legitimate, rulers of their lands. Monarchy was restored in France, Spain, Portugal, Sardinia (which regained Piedmont), and the Kingdom of the Two Sicilies (Naples). The Church regained the Papal States.

The restoration of the Bourbon kings in France was briefly interrupted by Napoleon's return and the "Hundred Days," from March to June, 1815 (page 457). The delegates at Vienna had already agreed on a settlement, but Napoleon's action cost France more land.

The Concert of Europe maintains European stability. In 1815 Russia, Austria, Prussia, and Great Britain agreed to act together in the future to preserve peace in Europe and to maintain the territorial settlement of the Congress of Vienna. Crises that might lead to war were to be settled by conferences among diplomats. Their agreement was called the Quadruple Alliance. After France joined the alliance, it became known as the Concert of Europe.

Another agreement among European monarchs about this time was called the Holy Alliance. Proposed by Czar Alexander, it was not truly an alliance but rather a pledge that monarchs would follow moral principles in ruling their subjects and in dealing with each other. The king of Prussia and the Austrian emperor joined the czar in the Holy Alliance. Britain, however, doubting the sincerity of those three rulers, refused to take part in the agreement, and the Holy Alliance played little part in European diplomacy.

The peace settlement arranged at the Congress of Vienna succeeded in maintaining European peace for many years. No one country emerged from the Congress of Vienna strong enough to dominate the continent, nor was any power so unhappy that it turned to war to undo the settlement.

Metternich tries to suppress liberalism and nationalism. One of Metternich's aims at the Congress of Vienna had been the preservation of peace in Europe. Another was the suppression of liberalism and nationalism. Metternich turned the Concert of Europe into an agreement to protect absolute monarchy by checking liberal ideas and nationalist movements. Encouraged by Metternich, the monarchs of Europe joined in a common effort to resist any threats to the established order. This effort came to be called "Metternich's system."

In accordance with Metternich's system, conservative rulers set up spy systems, censored books and newspapers, and imprisoned liberals. In 1819, student political clubs in German universities called for German unity and liberal reforms. Using his influence over the states in the German Confederation, Metternich had them issue the Carlsbad Decrees. These set up a spy system to report on liberal and radical organizations and established censorship over newspapers and university lectures.

Britain strongly opposed the repressions of the Metternich system. The British viewed the Concert of Europe solely as a means of maintaining the balance of power. Having no desire to interfere in the politics of other nations, Britain left the Quadruple Alliance but still took part in European conferences.

REVOLUTIONS FROM 1820 TO 1830

Movements for liberal reform persist. The ideas and spirit of revolution were not destroyed by the actions of the Congress of Vienna. Liberals and nationalists in many countries continued to organize secret societies, print revolutionary newspapers, collect weapons, and plan revolts.

The first challenge to the Metternich system occurred in Spain. King Ferdinand VII, restored to the throne in 1815, ruled harshly and persecuted liberal reformers. In 1820, Spanish army officers revolted and forced the king to restore the constitution of 1812. Fearful of revolution, the members of the Quadruple Alliance sent a French army in 1823 to crush the rebellion. The leaders of the revolt were brutally punished, and Ferdinand's repressive rule continued.

Italian reformers seek independence and unity. Revolts also broke out in 1820 in Italy, where reformers hoped to unify the many Italian states under one constitutional government. They also hoped for freedom from the various foreign powers that controlled the Italian states. Hapsburg Austria, the dominant power in Italy, ruled Lombardy and Venetia in the north; and other members of the Hapsburg family ruled Tuscany and Parma. In the south, a Spanish

Greece won its independence from Ottoman rule in 1829. In this picture the artist showed Greek patriot fighters in traditional clothing.

Bourbon king ruled the Kingdom of the Two Sicilies, which included Sicily and the state of Naples. The Papal States in central Italy (including Rome) were governed by the Pope. Only the Kingdom of Sardinia — the island of Sardinia and the state of Piedmont — were ruled by an Italian family, the House of Savoy.

Austrian armies quickly put down the revolts, first in Naples, and then in Piedmont. Rulers in other Italian states jailed and executed leaders of the reform movements, and several thousand Italians fled to other lands. The Pope joined other conservative European rulers and denounced the uprisings.

A revolt in Russia fails. Secret revolutionary societies also formed in Russia, led by young army officers who had learned liberal ideas from the French. They hoped to westernize Russia and establish a constitution. Because the officers represented only a fraction of the nobility and had no popular support, they had no chance of success. Their uprising in December, 1825 — the Decembrist uprising — was easily smashed by the new czar, Nicholas I, and the leaders of the revolt were executed or exiled. To prevent the spread of liberal ideas, Nicholas imposed rigid censorship and estab-

lished a secret police force to spy on potential troublemakers.

Greece gains independence. Despite the Metternich system, rebellions continued to break out in Europe and in European colonies in Latin America (Chapter 23). The first successful national revolution was in Greece. In 1821, Greek patriots revolted against rule by the Ottoman Empire. Sympathy for the Greeks was strong. Educated Europeans and Americans admired the heritage of classical Greek culture; the Russians considered the struggle as a holy war of Orthodox Greeks against Muslim Turks. Though their governments at first refused to aid the Greek patriots, many individuals volunteered their help. One was the English poet Lord Byron, who was killed in the fighting in 1824. In 1827, Britain, France, and Russia finally entered the war, and Greek independence was declared in 1829.

The people of Paris again rebel. The spirit of liberalism also lived on in France. When Louis XVIII had become king in 1814, he recognized that the French people would not accept a return to absolute monarchy. He issued a so-called "constitutional charter" that protected many of the rights gained by the peasants and bourgeoisie in the French Revolution. It provided for an elected legislature, although only wealthy property owners could vote. Freedom of speech, of the press, and of religion were guaranteed. Many conservative nobles, led by the king's brother, found the charter far too liberal. They hoped for a return to the Old Regime.

When Louis died in 1824, his brother succeeded him as Charles X. Ignoring the charter and the legislature, Charles tried to bring back special privileges for the nobility and the clergy. In July, 1830, he ordered censorship of newspapers and put restrictions on voting that took this right from many wealthy bourgeoisie. Led by students and middle-class liberals, the people of Paris rose in revolt. Workers and students stormed into the streets. To hamper the movement of government troops, they built barricades, using paving stones, furniture, tree trunks, and wagons. Behind these barricades, guns in hand, they defiantly sang the "Marseillaise," the anthem of the French Revolution. The king fled to Britain.

Many of the revolutionaries had hoped to set up another republic and make radical reforms, but the middle-class liberals took control. Instead of setting up a republic, they named a new king, Louis Philippe (LOO-ee fih-LEEP), a member of the Bourbon family.

Louis Philippe was known as the "citizen king," for he dressed and acted like a wealthy member of the bourgeoisie. His policies generally favored those well-to-do businessmen and bankers who had put him on the throne, and so they satisfied neither the conservative nobility nor the liberals and radicals who had fought the July Revolution. The right to vote was still limited to the wealthy, less than three percent of the adult male population.

Revolts break out in Italy and Belgium. Metternich's fear that any revolution would create unrest in Europe was justified. The 1830 revolution in France touched off revolts in Italy and Belgium. In Italy, Austrian troops again crushed the rebels. In predominantly Catholic Belgium, religious and cultural differences inspired a revolt. Stirred by the events in Paris, Belgian patriots proclaimed their independence from the Protestant, Dutch-speaking Netherlands. The Concert of Europe, at the urging of France and Britain, arranged a peace settlement that established a constitutional monarchy in Belgium. The Belgians elected a German prince, Leopold I, as their king.

Polish rebels are crushed. Russia took little part in solving the Belgian crisis because a rebellion in Poland broke out at the same time. The Congress of Vienna had set up a new kingdom of Poland ruled by the czar, but Poles had not abandoned their hopes for independence.

Patriotic Polish students and army officers were inspired by the revolutions in France and Belgium. When the czar proposed sending Polish troops to suppress those revolutions, the Poles rebelled against Russian rule. The rebels were not united, however, and they lacked the support of the peasants, who wanted land. Russian armies defeated the rebels, and Czar Nicholas I imposed even stricter rule on Poland. Polish nationalist rebellions continued throughout the later 1800's, but none succeeded.

CHECK-UP

1. Vocabulary: *conservatism, liberalism.*
2. (a) According to conservatives of the nineteenth century, what institutions were necessary for a well-run society? (b) What was their view of the revolutionaries in France?
3. (a) What were the main principles of liberal political philosophy in the nineteenth century? (b) From what social class were liberals mostly drawn? (c) What differences were there among liberals?
4. Why did liberals tend to support nationalist movements in the early nineteenth century?
5. (a) What were the aims of the Congress of Vienna? (b) Who was the dominant person in the Congress? (c) What was the German Confederation?
6. Which nations formed (a) the Concert of Europe? (b) the Holy Alliance? (c) What were the purposes of these alliances?
7. (a) What countries won their independence in the 1820's? (b) What was the outcome of the French Revolution of 1830? (c) What other countries were inspired to revolt by the French uprising of 1830?

2 Romanticism Influences Art and Politics

Along with liberalism and nationalism, another important new movement — romanticism — swept Europe during the nineteenth century. The changes caused by romanticism were greatest in the arts, but its ideas and attitudes also influenced social and political reforms of the time. Romanticism particularly influenced the nationalist movements that arose after the

Napoleonic Wars. The territorial settlements made by the Congress of Vienna intensified nationalist movements for independence.

Romanticism stresses emotion over reason. Arts and literature in the Classical period (page 413) had followed Enlightenment ideals of balance, order, and reason. Toward the end of the eighteenth century, European writers, painters,

ROMANTICISM AND NATIONALISM IN ART

Moonrise Over the Sea (above) by the German painter Caspar David Friedrich reflects the Romantic view of nature, while Ludwig Emil Grimm's painting of a peasant woman (right) shows nationalist interest in the traditions of the German people. Romantic composers, such as Franz Liszt (below, at the piano), often used nationalist themes in their music.

and musicians reacted against these ideals. The Romantic movement stressed the expression of intense individual emotions and imagination. Romanticism, which began in Germany and Italy, also was a reaction against the great influence that French culture had had throughout Europe.

To the Romantics, an individual's feelings were the source of creativity. Enlightenment ideas, they felt, hindered the imagination by imposing strict rules on creative works.

Romantic writers take a new view of nature. The Romantics followed some of the ideas of Rousseau (page 411) and saw nature as beautiful and mysterious, a source of in-spiration and emotion. Romantic poets sought to paint memorable images with their words, to create a sense of wonder and delight.

The first important book of the Romantic movement was *Lyrical Ballads* (1798), by the English poets William Wordsworth and Samuel Taylor Coleridge. The Romantics' feeling for nature is shown in the following lines by Wordsworth:

> My heart leaps up when I behold
>   A rainbow in the sky:
> So was it when my life began;
> So is it now I am a man;
> So be it when I grow old,
>   Or let me die!

Romantic writers emphasize imagination.
Besides their lyrical descriptions of nature, many writers of the Romantic movement used their imaginations to create stories and poems based on fantasy and the supernatural. One typical Romantic poem was Coleridge's fanciful description of the summer palace of Kublai Khan (page 258):

In Xanadu did Kubla Khan
A stately pleasure-dome decree:
Where Alph, the sacred river, ran
Through caverns measureless to man
   Down to a sunless sea.

Some Romantic writers created a form of fiction called "gothic." This style of writing emphasized tales of terror and mystery set in picturesque ruined buildings. One master of the gothic short story was the American author Edgar Allan Poe. Mary Shelley, the daughter of Mary Wollstonecraft (page 448) and the wife of the Romantic poet Percy Bysshe Shelley, wrote the gothic novel *Frankenstein* in 1818. Gothic ideas influenced other Romantic novelists, such as Charlotte and Emily Brontë (BRON-tee), sisters who wrote *Jane Eyre* and *Wuthering Heights* (1847).

Romanticism influences the development of nationalism. The German writer and philosopher J. G. von Herder believed that each people has a unique national character, which is expressed in folk traditions, language, and historic institutions. Writers such as Madame de Staël in France examined the histories and cultures of their countries in an attempt to understand and express this "national character." Some Romantic scholars, such as the Grimm brothers in Germany, collected folktales and songs. Elias Lonnrot composed Finland's national epic, the *Kalevala*, out of folk legends.

Romantic novelists and dramatists tried to recapture the colorful legends and atmosphere of their countries' past. One of the first and most influential historical novelists was Sir Walter Scott, who retold English and Scottish history in such books as *Ivanhoe* and *Rob Roy*. Scott was inspired by the earlier German poet and playwright Johann Wolfgang von Goethe. In France, Victor Hugo and Alexandre Dumas wrote exciting novels such as *The Hunchback of Notre Dame* and *The Three Musketeers,* set in earlier times.

Many musicians of the Romantic period also emphasized nationalist ideas and themes. For instance, Frédéric Chopin (sho-PAN) of Poland and Franz Liszt (LIST) of Hungary expressed national pride by using folk rhythms and melodies in their musical compositions. Many great Austrian and German composers, such as Ludwig van Beethoven, Franz Schubert, and Robert Schumann, wrote music imitating folk songs and reflecting the Romantic interest in nature. In Italy, the music of Giuseppe Verdi helped bring together those who wanted a united Italy. Richard Wagner (VAHG-nur) in Germany based his operas, such as *The Ring of the Nibelung*, on Germanic myths and legends. Romanticism encouraged national pride, which brought demands for statehood and freedom from foreign rule.

CHECK-UP

1. How were Romantic ideas a reaction against the Enlightenment?
2. (a) What two English writers set the style for Romantic poetry? (b) Name some writers who used the gothic style.
3. How did Romantic writers and musicians contribute to nationalist movements?

3   1848 Is a Year of Revolutions

The revolutions of the 1820's and 1830's had challenged the conservatism of the Congress of Vienna. Movements for reform and for independence continued in a number of countries. Economic problems combined with people's discontent to set the stage for another wave of revolutions in 1848.

Economic problems trouble Europe. Between 1846 and 1848 Europe suffered an economic crisis. Disease ruined the potato crop, and drought reduced the grain harvest. These shortages caused high prices, food riots, and widespread suffering, particularly in Ireland, where potatoes were the basic food. At the same time, many businesses throughout Europe failed, which led to severe unemployment. Blaming their governments for their misery, the common people sought reforms.

Discontent increases in France. As in 1830, rebellion in France was the spark that set off other revolutions. Louis Philippe's rule (page 467) had never satisfied a large section of the people of France. Many people looked back to the First Republic (page 450) and again wanted to do away with monarchy altogether. The outcome of the 1830 revolt was still resented by French radicals, especially in the working class, which suffered from unemployment and low wages. Laws prevented workers from striking, and few of them could meet the property requirements for voting. Noting their angry mood, the political writer Alexis de Tocqueville

(TOHK-vil) warned, "I believe that we are at this moment sleeping on a volcano."

A new reform movement called *socialism* attracted many working-class men and women. Some socialist thinkers believed that the government, not private individuals, should own factories, banks, and other businesses and run them for the whole society. Others called for cooperative enterprises in which the workers would also be the owners.

A workers' revolt follows a moderate revolution. Two revolutions broke out in France in 1848 — one in February, the other in June. In February, tired of delays in reforms, the Parisians rioted and once again set up barricades for street fighting. Louis Philippe abdicated, and the Second Republic was established.

The leaders of the new government were divided in their aims. Some of these Frenchmen favored political liberty but not social reform. They were willing only to give all men the right to vote. Others, led by the socialist

REBELLION IN FRANCE

Again in 1848, rebellion broke out in France as resentment built up against Louis Philippe, the target of the satirical cartoon above. Parisians took their struggle into the streets (left) and set up barricades to defend themselves from government troops.

Gathering the News

The name ''UPI'' or ''AP'' or ''Reuters'' at the beginning of a newspaper story identifies the news service that sent the information to your local paper. United Press International (UPI), Associated Press (AP), and Reuters (ROY-terz) are the most famous of the international news-gathering sources. The first such agency was Reuters.

Julius Reuter began his business in France in the 1840's, using carrier pigeons and the newly invented telegraph. (There were not yet any telephones or radio.) Flying between cities that had no telegraph link, the pigeons carried news in a capsule strapped to one leg. When London and Paris were linked by telegraph, Reuter began to send financial reports between those cities. By 1855, newspapers realized the usefulness of this service, and the London *Times*

printed a speech by Napoleon III that had been telegraphed from Reuters' Paris office (shown in this picture). Soon other news services were formed, providing newspaper readers with more up-to-date news than ever before.

Louis Blanc (BLAHNK), urged the new government to make changes that would benefit the workers. As a result of Blanc's demands, the government set up a "national workshop" program to provide jobs. Desperate for work, nearly 200,000 people traveled to Paris to sign up; 120,000 found jobs.

The cost of the workshop program upset many taxpayers, both peasants and bourgeoisie. When elections were held, these voters chose more conservative delegates to the assembly. In June of 1848 the government closed the workshops, and the Parisian workers rose in revolt over the loss of jobs. Men, women, and children again set up barricades in the streets of Paris.

The workers' revolt split France in two. Opposing the working class were all those who owned property — peasants, bourgeoisie, and aristocrats. The middle class no longer supported the aims of the working class. They feared the effects of a socialist society. Three days of desperate, violent street fighting followed as the workers stood alone against government troops. More than 10,000 were killed or injured. Thousands more were thrown into prison.

The workers' revolution of 1848 left deep divisions in French society. In reaction to the uprising, the assembly changed the constitution to ensure strong government control, though it also gave voting rights to all adult males. Looking for security and order, French voters then elected Louis Napoleon president of France. Nephew of the emperor Napoleon, Louis Napoleon's conservative rule made him very popular. In 1852 the voters overwhelmingly approved his becoming Emperor Napoleon III. The Second Empire replaced the republic created in 1848.

Nationalism leads to revolt in Austrian lands. With the overthrow of Louis Philippe, revolutionary movements again spread from France throughout Europe. In the Austrian Empire, these rebellions included several nationalist uprisings among the different peoples of the empire. Germans were the dominant nationality in the Austrian Empire, making up about 25 percent of the population. In Hungary, the eastern part of the empire, Magyars

(Hungarians) were the largest nationality group. Some of the Slavic peoples, such as the Croats, felt oppressed by both the Germans and the Magyars. Still other nationalities in the Austrian Empire — Serbs, Czechs, Italians, Rumanians — also wanted self-government.

Austria's Hapsburg rulers used the army and the bureaucracy (which was controlled mainly by Germans) to hold their empire together. Unity became increasingly difficult, however, as the spirit of nationalism grew. With new pride in their national histories and traditions, Czechs and Hungarians in particular protested against German domination of the Austrian Empire. Writers began to write in their own language instead of the Latin, German, and French they had been taught to use in school.

Rebellions break out in Austria, Bohemia, and Hungary. Less than a month after the February, 1848, revolution in France, German students and workers in the Austrian capital of Vienna revolted. They demanded a constitution and an end to feudal practices. Students and workers took control of parts of the city, and peasants rebelled in the countryside. In response to the rebels' demands, the emperor dismissed Metternich, who had become a symbol of repression. (Metternich, now 75 years old, fled the country.) The government also abolished serfdom and promised a constitution. Having gained these demands, the peasants no longer were interested in revolution, though unrest continued in the cities.

A few weeks after the revolt in Vienna, Czech nationalists in Bohemia revolted against German dominance. They called for a constitution for Bohemia and demanded that the Czech language be used on an equal basis with German in the schools and government.

The most serious threat to Austrian rule occurred in Hungary. In March, 1848, Louis Kossuth, a Hungarian patriot, led the Hungarians in demanding a greater degree of self-government. Two weeks later, Hungary adopted a constitution that left it within the Austrian Empire but otherwise in control of its own affairs. The constitution ended feudal privileges, guaranteed freedom of religion and of the press, and gave all adult male property owners the right to vote.

The plans of the Hungarian revolutionaries, however, concentrated on forming a Hungarian state based on the Magyar language and culture. The Croats, Serbs, and Rumanians — about half the population in Hungary — opposed Magyar domination.

The Austrian government suppresses the rebellions. Hapsburg Austria cleverly took advantage of both its military strength and the differences among the various nationality groups. In June, 1848, the imperial troops bombarded Prague, the capital of Bohemia. With the help of the Bohemian Germans, the Czechs were suppressed. In October, Austrian soldiers, mostly peasants, attacked students and workers in Vienna. Thousands were killed as the imperial army retook the city.

The Hungarian rebels resisted longer. In September, 1848, when the Austrians led a Croatian army against the Hungarians, Kossuth's troops pushed them back. In April, 1849, the Hungarians proclaimed Hungary an independent republic. The new Austrian emperor, Francis Joseph, called for help from Czar Nicholas I of Russia. In June, a Russian army of 130,000 attacked Hungary from the east, and by August the rebels had been defeated.

TIMETABLE

Reaction and Revolution

1814–1815	The Congress of Vienna restores a balance of power in Europe.
1824	Charles X succeeds to the throne of France.
1825	Nicholas I of Russia crushes the Decembrist uprising.
1829	Greece wins independence from Turkey.
1830	Charles X is ousted by a revolution and is succeeded by Louis Philippe. Belgium wins independence from the Netherlands. Russia crushes a Polish nationalist revolt.
1848	Revolutions in France lead to the establishment of the Second Republic. Revolutions sweep across Europe.
1852	France again becomes an empire under Napoleon III.

German liberals seek a unified state. The news of revolution in France and in the Austrian Empire heartened many German liberals and nationalists, whose main aim was a unified Germany. Unification was opposed, however, by the princes who ruled the many German states. These rulers, members of the German Confederation, were still influenced by the conservative ideas and laws of Metternich. Liberal ideas were suppressed in the German states.

The February revolution in France inspired the middle-class German liberals and workers to stage demonstrations in Berlin and other cities in March, 1848. Terrified by the bloodshed, the king of Prussia, Frederick William IV, granted his subjects a constitution and an assembly. Other German rulers followed his example. This encouraged German middle-class liberals to elect delegates to a national assembly, the Frankfurt Parliament. The meeting drew up plans for a united Germany that would include all the German states except Austria. They asked Frederick William to be emperor of a unified Germany, but he refused. He would not accept a crown from commoners. Prussia's refusal weakened the Frankfurt Parliament, and it was disbanded.

Revolts break out in Italy. The desire for a united Italy free from foreign rule had been growing since the Congress of Vienna. Resentment was especially strong in the Austrian-held states of northern Italy. Patriots such as Giuseppe Mazzini (maht-TSEE-nee) led a movement that came to be called the Risorgimento (ree-sohr-jee-MEN-toh), or "resurgence." In 1831 Mazzini had founded a secret society called Young Italy. Its aim was the establishment of a republic, with Rome as its capital. Another secret revolutionary society was known as the Carbonari (kar-boh-NAH-ree).

In 1848, there were revolts in many parts of Italy. Even before the February revolution in Paris, Italians in the Kingdom of the Two Sicilies had taken up arms against their Spanish Bourbon king, who then granted a liberal constitution. Several other rulers of Italian states also made liberal reforms, but the revolution quickly spread to the Austrian-held lands. In March, 1848, republics were proclaimed in Venice and Milan. The king of Sardinia, the only state under Italian rule, declared war on Austria. Near the end of the year, the Pope fled Rome, and in February, 1849, the Roman Republic was proclaimed.

By mid-1849, however, the Austrians had regained control. They defeated the Sardinians, reoccupied Milan, and bombarded Venice into submission. In the south, the Bourbon king had crushed the Sicilian revolutionaries. France sent an army that defeated the Roman Republic and restored the Pope to power.

Although Italian revolutionaries everywhere were defeated, the aims of the Risorgimento persisted. Sardinia was a monarchy, but the new ruler who came to the throne in 1849 kept the liberal constitution won in the revolution. As the only state in Italy with an Italian ruling family[2] as well as a constitution, Sardinia became the focus of revolutionary hopes.

The revolutions of 1848 began with great promise, but in country after country they were suppressed by the military strength and unity of the ruling powers. Nevertheless, some of the reforms won by the revolutionaries were retained — the right to vote, the end of serfdom, representative assemblies. The end of this year of revolutions was, therefore, not the end of people's hopes for freedom and national unity.

CHECK-UP

1. Vocabulary: *socialism.*
2. (a) What sources of dissatisfaction led to revolutions in 1848? (b) How did the February and June revolutions in France differ? (c) What new political philosophy gained strength among French workers? (d) How did Louis Napoleon come to power?
3. Why was Austria faced with revolts in 1848 (a) by the Czechs? (b) by the Magyars? (c) How did Austria suppress the uprisings?
4. (a) What was the main aim of the revolutions in Germany? (b) How successful were they?
5. (a) What was the Risorgimento? (b) What were its aims?

---

[2]The ruling family, the House of Savoy, had for centuries held a large territory in northwestern Italy, including Piedmont. The Savoys gained the island of Sardinia early in the 1700's; it was the only territory they managed to keep during the French conquests of the 1790's. The mainland territories were restored at the Congress of Vienna.

Chapter 21 Review

Summary

After the fall of Napoleon, the Congress of Vienna in 1815 returned conservatives to power throughout Europe. Conservatives fought to restore the traditional authority of monarch, aristocracy, and clergy. They were challenged by liberals, who sought to extend individual rights and continue the reforms made during the French Revolution. Other opposition to the conservatives came from nationalists, who wanted independence and unity for nationality groups. Between 1820 and 1848, liberals and nationalists organized a number of revolutions that threatened conservative rule.

In both 1830 and 1848, it was a revolution in France that triggered those in other countries. Greek and Belgian patriots won independence. Liberal and nationalist revolutions also broke out in the German states, the Austrian Empire, and Italy. After some early successes, however, the revolutions were suppressed. One reason for their failure was the split between middle-class liberals and more radical workers. Another was rivalry between different nationalist groups. Although some liberal reforms were made, conservative rulers continued to dominate the countries of Europe.

Vocabulary Review

1. Match the following words with the listed definitions. Then, on a separate sheet of paper, write a sentence for each word. Be sure that your use of the word shows that you understand its meaning: *conservatism, liberalism, socialism.*

(a) A political philosophy that emphasizes progress and reform; in the early 1800's those who supported this philosophy favored individual freedom, equality under the law, and freedom of thought and religion.

(b) A political philosophy that calls for government, rather than private individuals, to own factories, banks, and businesses and to run them for the whole society.

(c) A political philosophy that emphasizes the preservation of traditions and established institutions.

2. Explain the relationship between the two terms in each of the following pairs:

(a) Quadruple Alliance; Concert of Europe.
(b) House of Savoy; Kingdom of Sardinia.
(c) Romanticism; *Lyrical Ballads.*
(d) Second Republic; Second Empire.
(e) Risorgimento; Young Italy.

People to Identify

In each sentence, fill in the blank with a name from this list: *Klemens von Metternich, Ferdinand VII, Charles X, Leopold I, Emily Brontë, Frédéric Chopin, Richard Wagner, Louis Napoleon, Louis Kossuth, Frederick William IV.*

1. A Polish composer, __?__ used folk rhythms and melodies in his compositions.
2. __?__, a German prince, was chosen to be the first king of newly independent Belgium.
3. __?__ led the Hungarians in a prolonged revolt against Austrian rule.
4. The Frankfurt Parliament asked __?__ to be the emperor of a unified German state.
5. The Austrian noble and diplomat who dominated the Congress of Vienna was __?__ .
6. All of the liberal reforms instituted by Louis XVIII were ignored by __?__, the next king of France and Louis' brother.
7. __?__ wrote the Romantic novel *Wuthering Heights.*
8. __?__ was restored to the Spanish throne in 1815.
9. The president of France who became emperor in 1852 was __?__ .
10. __?__ based his opera, *The Ring of the Nibelung,* on German myths and legends.

Relating Geography and History

1. Locating places. Locate each of the following on a map in this chapter:

(a) Belgium	(g) Naples
(b) Milan	(h) Poland
(c) Greece	(i) Papal States
(d) Venetia	(j) Hungary
(e) Lombardy	(k) Prague
(f) Vienna	(l) Berlin

2. Comparing maps. Compare maps that show Europe before the Congress of Vienna and after the boundary settlements agreed to at that conference (maps, pages 455 and 464). List the countries that gained territory and also the countries that lost territory.

Discussion Questions

1. Compare the attitudes of nineteenth-century European conservatives and liberals regarding (a) government, (b) organized religion, and (c) individual rights and freedoms.

2. (a) How had feelings of nationalism been shown during the French Revolution? (b) How did French nationalism influence other peoples of Europe?

3. (a) What were the main concerns of the delegates at the Congress of Vienna? (b) What did the delegates decide to do about the lands Napoleon had conquered? Why?

4. (a) What was the Metternich system? (b) Give two examples of how it was used to suppress liberal movements.

5. (a) Why was the czar of Russia able to suppress the Decembrist revolt? (b) What conditions enabled Greece and Belgium to become independent states?

6. Explain the major characteristics of romanticism, and name examples of Romantic literature or music.

7. What were the aims of the people who rebelled in 1848 in (a) France? (b) the Austrian Empire?

Reading Primary Sources

The February, 1848, rebellion in France influenced people throughout Europe. In the passage below, Carl Schurz, who was a student in Germany at that time, described students' reactions to news of the French rebellion. Read the passage. Then answer the questions that follow.

One morning, toward the end of February, 1848, I sat quietly in my attic chamber, working, ... when suddenly a friend rushed breathlessly into the room, exclaiming: "What, you sitting here! Do you not know what has happened? ... The French have driven away Louis Philippe and proclaimed the republic."

I threw down my pen. ... We tore ... to the market-square, the accustomed meeting place for all the student[s]. ... The market was already crowded with young men talking excitedly. There was no shouting, ... only agitated conversation. What did we want there? This probably no one knew. But, since the French had driven away Louis Philippe and proclaimed the republic, something of course must happen here, too. ...

The next morning there were the usual lectures to be attended. But how profitless! ... What [the professor] had to say did not seem to concern us. ... We ... [were] impelled by a feeling that now we had something more important to do. ... Now had arrived in Germany the day for the establishment of "German unity." ... The word *democracy* was soon on all tongues. We were profoundly, solemnly in earnest. ...

On the 18th of March we too had our mass demonstration. ... At the head of the procession Professor Kinkel bore the tricolor — black, red, and gold — which so long had been prohibited as the revolutionary flag. ... He spoke with wonderful eloquence ... as he depicted ... the liberties and rights of the German people, which now must be conceded by the princes or won by force by the people.

(a) What were the events that so excited the German students? (b) Why were the students no longer interested in the lectures they attended? (c) What parts of the passage reveal the liberal views of the students? (d) What parts show their nationalist views?

Skill Activities

1. Reports. Several men played important parts in the Congress of Vienna — Austria's Metternich, Talleyrand of France, Viscount Castlereagh of Britain, and Czar Alexander I of Russia. Find out more about these historical figures and prepare a report presenting the position each might have taken on one of the following issues: (a) nationalist and liberal movements in Europe, (b) Russia's proposal to create a Polish kingdom under Russian control, (c) the Concert of Europe, or (d) the territorial changes decided on by the Congress.

2. Bulletin boards. Make a bulletin-board display of the national flags of Europe. Under each flag, list the country it represents and provide information about the history of the flag and its design.

This painting of the triumphant procession of a patriot leader
into the city of Turin reflects the nationalist fervor inspired by
the movement to unify smaller Italian states with the Kingdom
of Sardinia in the late 1850's.

The Impact of Nationalism in Europe

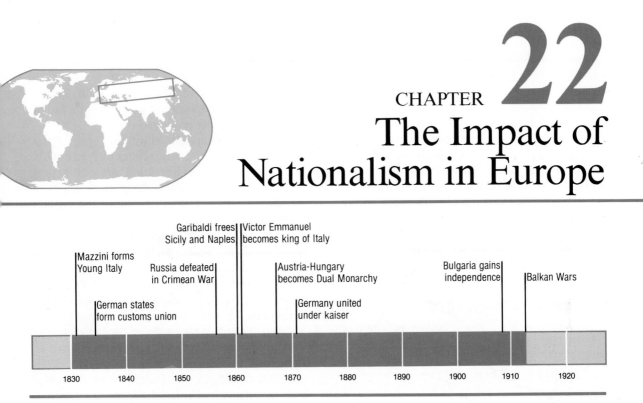

Mazzini forms Young Italy

German states form customs union

Russia defeated in Crimean War

Garibaldi frees Sicily and Naples

Victor Emmanuel becomes king of Italy

Austria-Hungary becomes Dual Monarchy

Germany united under kaiser

Bulgaria gains independence

Balkan Wars

1830 1840 1850 1860 1870 1880 1890 1900 1910 1920

In the last part of the nineteenth century, the struggle for unification, self-rule, and independence continued in Europe. Italy and Germany both became unified countries in 1870–1871, and nationalist feelings of pride and loyalty played a major role in their unification. Those who fought to realize their nationalist goals felt they had a noble cause.

For the Eastern European empires, each of which included many peoples, nationalism brought problems. The Austrian Empire of the Hapsburgs faced unrest from Slavic nationalities and was forced to grant equal status in the empire to Hungary. Revolts by different national groups had nearly destroyed the Ottoman Empire by 1900. In imperial Russia, expansionist ambitions added more territory. Discontent among the empire's minorities created unrest, however, and led the czars to tighten their control over Russia.

This chapter tells the story of how nationalist movements during the nineteenth century led to the establishment of new states in Europe but weakened three vast empires.

CHAPTER OUTLINE

1 Italy Becomes a Unified Nation

2 Bismarck Leads German Unification

3 Nationalism Weakens Empires in Eastern Europe

1 Italy Becomes a Unified Nation

In 1815, after Napoleon's defeat at Waterloo, the Congress of Vienna had re-established a number of kingdoms, states, and duchies in Italy. Many Italians, however, sought to unify their nation. During the Napoleonic Era, Italy had been dominated by the French. Napoleon had allowed some states to have representative assemblies. The French had built roads and introduced a single system of laws.

When Napoleon's defeat ended French rule, many Italians wanted to create a strong, unified Italy. A united country, free of foreign rule, could promote economic growth for the benefit of its people. A series of revolts failed, however, and Italy remained divided.

Mazzini demands unity for Italy. After 1815, leaders of the Risorgimento (page 473), Italy's movement for liberation and unification, formed secret societies to keep alive hopes of freedom from foreign rule. One of the earliest of these societies was the Carbonari, a revolutionary group that led a number of revolts throughout the 1820's and 1830's. None of the revolts had any lasting success.

Around this time a new leader, Giuseppe Mazzini, became prominent among Italian nationalists. In the early 1830's Mazzini had formed Young Italy, a secret organization of revolutionaries dedicated to seeking the independence and unification of Italy (page 473). Mazzini reminded the Italians that their Roman ancestors had ruled the greatest empire of the ancient world. In the Middle Ages the Church of Rome had carried its beliefs to all of Western Europe. During the Renaissance, Italian artists, writers, and artisans were the envy of all Europe. But "all is now changed," said Mazzini; "we have no flag of our own, . . . [we have] no voice among the nations of Europe."

In 1848 a series of revolts broke out, and nationalists took control of many parts of Italy. By 1849, however, these revolutionary governments were overthrown and Austria again dominated much of Italy.

Cavour makes practical plans for unification. The unsuccessful revolutions of 1848 had shown that fiery words, noble thoughts, and brave patriots were not enough to bring independence. Italy needed trained soldiers and powerful allies to drive out the Austrians and become unified. The man who best understood this was Count Camillo di Cavour (kuh-VOOR), prime minister of the Kingdom of Sardinia.

Unlike the emotional Mazzini, Cavour was cautious and practical. Mazzini had called for a mass uprising, but Cavour knew that Young Italy and other nationalist groups were no match for Austrian troops. He wanted the

Unification of Italy, 1870

Important steps in the unification of Italy are shown on this map. The dates show when various Italian states were united with the Kingdom of Sardinia.

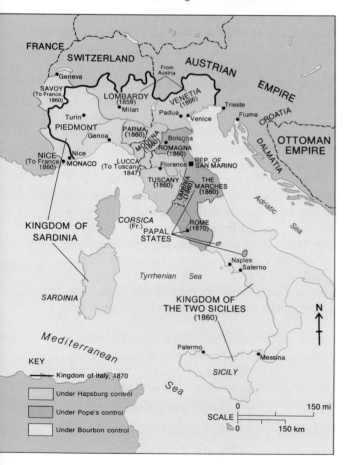

ITALIAN LEADERS

Different strategies were followed by the two extraordinary Italian leaders pictured here. Cavour (left) was a shrewd and careful diplomat. The flamboyant Garibaldi (above) inspired Italian patriots with his exciting speeches and daring actions.

Kingdom of Sardinia to take the lead in driving Austria out of northern Italy.

With the approval of Victor Emmanuel II, Sardinia's king, Cavour worked to modernize the kingdom's economy and build up its army. He constructed railways, improved agriculture, developed industry, and strengthened the state's finances. These policies gave Sardinia the strong economic base it needed to lead the movement for unification.

Sardinia gains allies. Cavour next sought allies for Sardinia. In the middle 1850's Sardinia became an ally of Britain and France, who were fighting Russia in the Crimea (page 486). Cavour had no quarrel with Russia, but he felt the friendship of Britain and France might prove useful. Furthermore, it increased Sardinia's prestige to fight beside the great powers and take part in the peacemaking.

In 1858 Cavour signed a treaty with Napoleon III of France. By the terms of this treaty, if Austria threatened Sardinia, France would help to drive Austria from Lombardy and Venetia. In return, Sardinia would give two small border territories, Nice (NEES) and Savoy, to France.

Other states join Sardinia. With France as an ally, Cavour was ready for trouble with Austria. The Austrians, fearing Sardinia's growing power, declared war in 1859. Napoleon kept his promise, and French troops sided with Sardinia. The French and Sardinian forces won quick victories. Then, to Cavour's surprise and anger, the French emperor signed a truce with Austria that gave Lombardy, but not Venetia, to Sardinia. Napoleon III had broken his promise to Cavour because he feared that Sardinia would take over the Papal States. French Catholics would have blamed their emperor for any territory the Pope lost.

Cavour tried to persuade Victor Emmanuel II to continue the war until all of northern

The Red Cross — Symbol of Help

The tradition of help from the Red Cross began in 1859 on a battlefield in Italy, where more than 40,000 Italian and Austrian soldiers lay dead or wounded. Horrified by the slaughter, a young Swiss observer named Henri Dunant (du-NAHN) vowed to find a way of providing better care for victims of war. Dunant persuaded the European powers to sign an agreement in 1864 establishing the International Red Cross. The countries agreed not to interfere with medical rescue work in wartime and to respect the symbol of a red cross on a white background. Years later Dunant was given the Nobel Peace Prize for his work.

At about the same time, Clara Barton, an American teacher, was organizing efficient nursing care for soldiers injured during the American Civil War and the Franco-Prussian

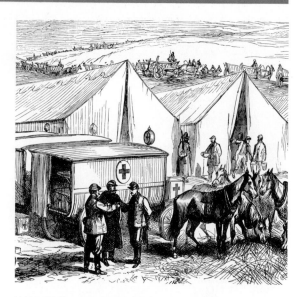

War. At the request of European officials, Barton persuaded the United States government to sign the international agreement in 1882. She headed the American Red Cross until 1904.

Italy was liberated, but the king accepted the peace terms. Besides gaining Lombardy, Sardinia received an unexpected bonus; the people of Parma, Modena, and Tuscany ousted their ruling princes, and voted to join Sardinia. Romagna (roh-MAHN-yah), one of the regions of the Papal States, also voted to join Sardinia. France approved this enlargement of Sardinia and obtained Nice and Savoy in exchange for its approval.

Garibaldi liberates the south. While northern Italy was making progress toward unification, important developments were taking place in the south. In the spring of 1860, a thousand red-shirted Italian patriots sailed from Genoa and landed on the island of Sicily. They were determined to free the Kingdom of the Two Sicilies from its Bourbon king. The commander of the "red-shirts" was Giuseppe Garibaldi, an extraordinary leader who had fought in the revolution of 1848 (page 473). Garibaldi's bravery, patriotism, and love of liberty made him a hero to all Italy.

Thousands of Sicilian patriots joined Garibaldi in 1860. In a little more than two months,

his troops had freed the island of Sicily and crossed over to the Italian mainland. Garibaldi's forces then occupied Naples, and the Bourbon king fled.

Victor Emmanuel completes the unification of Italy. Garibaldi planned to march on Rome next. This alarmed Cavour, who feared such a move would force Napoleon III to defend the Pope's lands. Cavour knew that war with France would be a disaster for Italy. He also felt that Garibaldi was too emotional, rash, and stubborn to lead the drive for unification. For these reasons, Cavour sent Sardinian troops to join Garibaldi and to persuade him not to attack Rome.

Even without Rome, the union of states headed by Sardinia continued to grow. The papal provinces of Umbria and the Marches soon voted for union with Sardinia. Shortly thereafter, the people of Naples and Sicily voted to join the lands ruled by Sardinia. On March 17, 1861, Victor Emmanuel was proclaimed king of Italy.

Two important regions, papal Rome and Austrian-held Venetia, remained outside Italian control. The chance to make Venetia part of Italy came in 1866 during the Seven Weeks' War between Austria and Prussia (page 482). Italy became Prussia's ally and received Venetia when Austria was defeated. Four years later, Prussia and France were at war. When the French troops left Rome, King Victor Emmanuel's army marched into that city and Rome's citizens voted by an overwhelming margin to join the kingdom of Italy. The goal of unification for all the Italian states had at last been achieved.

CHECK-UP

1. (a) How did French rule encourage Italian nationalism? (b) What states existed in Italy in 1815?
2. How did each of these leaders contribute to the cause of Italian unification: (a) Mazzini, (b) Cavour, (c) Garibaldi?
3. (a) Why did Cavour want to prevent Garibaldi from marching on Rome? (b) What did Cavour do to halt Garibaldi?
4. How did Italy under Victor Emmanuel add Rome and Venetia to its territory?

2 Bismarck Leads German Unification

When the Congress of Vienna divided up Napoleon's empire in 1815, it created the German Confederation — a loosely knit alliance of 39 states, with separate rulers, laws, and armies. *Tariffs,* or taxes on imported goods, and differing currency systems hampered trade within the Confederation. The weakness and disunity of the Confederation allowed it to be dominated by Austria.[1]

Many Germans wanted to see their country strong and united. Liberals had tried unsuccessfully in 1848 to unify Germany (page 473), but hopes for unification continued.

Landowners promote economic unity. Before Cavour could work toward unifying Italy, he had to build a strong economic base in Sardinia (page 479). Similarly, the first step toward German unity was an economic one. In the 1830's, a group of aristocratic Prussian landowners — the Junkers (YUHNG-kerz) — wanted to make trade easier throughout the German states. They persuaded Prussia's leaders to abolish all tariffs.

In 1834, under the leadership of Prussia, German states formed the *Zollverein* (TSAWL-fuhr-ine), a customs union that reduced tariff barriers among its members. The *Zollverein* also established a uniform currency system. By the mid-1840's the *Zollverein* included most of the German states. (Austria was not a member of the customs union.)

The economy improved under the *Zollverein,* and industry grew. Seeing the advantages of economic unity, many Germans came to support political unity also. The movement for political unity was led by Prussia, which was becoming the region's political and economic leader.

Bismarck makes plans for unifying Germany. German unification came about largely

---

[1]Only part of the Austrian Empire — its German states — belonged to the German Confederation.

TIMETABLE

The Unification of Italy and Germany

1815	The German Confederation is formed.
1834	German states form the *Zollverein.*
1848	Revolutions fail in Italy and Germany.
1859	Sardinia wins a war with Austria and gains Lombardy.
1860	Garibaldi frees Sicily and Naples.
1861	Victor Emmanuel becomes king of Italy.
1866	Prussia defeats Austria in the Seven Weeks' War.
1867	Prussia organizes the North German Confederation.
1870	Prussia is victorious in the Franco-Prussian War.
1871	William I becomes the ruler of a unified Germany.

through the efforts of Otto von Bismarck, who became Prussia's prime minister and foreign minister in 1862 under King William I. Bismarck opposed liberalism, mistrusted parliaments, and sought to strengthen the power of the king. When Bismarck talked of a united Germany, he really meant that Prussia should dominate the other German states. Shrewd and practical, Bismarck was convinced that Germany could be united only through war. "Not through speeches and majority decisions are the questions of the day decided," he said, "but by blood and iron." Austria was Prussia's major rival for power in the confederation. Bismarck's plan was to drive Austria from the German Confederation and bring the other German states under Prussian domination.

Prussia becomes the dominant German state. Bismarck's first move was against Denmark. When Denmark claimed two coastal regions, Schleswig and Holstein (map, next page), both Prussia and Austria disputed the claim. The two nations declared war on Denmark, and their combined forces quickly defeated the

Bismarck, known as the "Iron Chancellor," masterminded the drive to unify Germany under Prussian leadership.

Danes. Once Prussia and Austria occupied Schleswig and Holstein, they disagreed over what should be done with their new territories. Bismarck used this quarrel to goad Austria into war.

To the surprise of military experts, Prussian troops crushed the Austrian army in the Seven Weeks' War of 1866. Careful planning, an efficient railway system, and superior weapons gave Prussia the advantage despite Austria's greater size and larger population. Austria agreed to allow Prussia to annex Schleswig and Holstein and a number of smaller German states.

After the war, Prussia organized a new union of states called the North German Confederation, with a constitution based upon that of the Frankfurt Parliament of 1848 (page 473). Austria was not included in the new confederation, thereby removing it from German affairs. Bismarck's goal of making Prussia the dominant German power had been achieved. Only the South German states now remained outside Prussia's control, but the Catholic population of these states had little desire to be dominated by Protestant Prussia.

Bismarck seeks war with France. Once again, Bismarck decided to use war as his strategy for unifying Germany. France, fearful of a united Germany, opposed Prussian control of the South German states. If, however, Prussia were to become involved in a war with France, Bismarck was confident that the South German states would join Prussia. He was convinced that the nationalist feelings of the South Germans would cause them to overlook any hostility they felt toward Prussia.

The Franco-Prussian War begins. A cause for conflict with France developed quite unexpectedly in 1870, when the Spanish throne was offered to a prince of the Hohenzollern family, the ruling family in Prussia. As Bismarck well knew, the thought of Hohenzollern Prussia to the east and a Hohenzollern king of Spain to the south alarmed France. Tensions eased when the prince declined the throne, but France demanded that King William I of Prussia promise that the Hohenzollerns would also reject any future offers of the Spanish throne.

Unification of Germany, 1871

German unity came about through a series of annexations and unions. The German Empire was formed in 1871 after a stunning victory in a short war with France.

King William I sent a telegram reporting the incident to Bismarck, who seized the chance to make trouble. By shortening the telegram, Bismarck changed its meaning slightly. Then, he gave it to the newspapers to publish. When the French read the revised telegram, it seemed as if their ambassador had been humiliated. The Prussians interpreted it to mean that their king had been insulted. Soon people in both countries were demanding war.

In July of 1870 France declared war, thus touching off what became known as the Franco-Prussian War. The French believed that their army would sweep across Germany just as Napoleon's troops had done in the early 1800's. But France needed more than the memory of Napoleon to defeat Prussia. The French forces were outnumbered, poorly prepared, and armed with inferior weapons. They were no match for Prussia's powerful military machine. Moreover, as Bismarck had anticipated, the South German states came to the aid of Prussia.

In only six weeks the French armies were defeated, and Paris was under siege by the Germans. Late in January, 1871, when food and coal ran out, Paris surrendered. With the defeat, French emperor Napoleon III gave up his throne, and the French proclaimed their nation a republic once again.

In February, 1871, peace negotiations began at Versailles. According to the treaty that was agreed upon, France had to pay Germany huge sums of money and was also forced to surrender the two border provinces of Alsace and Lorraine to Germany.

Germany is unified. The Franco-Prussian War had been the last step in Bismarck's plan for unifying Germany under strong Prussian leadership. On January 18, 1871, William I was crowned as Germany's kaiser (KY-zer), or emperor. Soon after, Bismarck became the nation's chancellor — its highest official below the kaiser. Germany was ruled by a powerful emperor and chancellor, both of whom were hostile to the ideals of democracy. Even the new legislature was dominated by the kaiser and the aristocratic Prussian Junkers.

The unification of Germany had great significance for Europe. A powerful, aggressive new state had emerged in Central Europe. Its people were intensely nationalistic; its army was the best in Europe and its navy second only to Britain's; its population was growing and its industries were expanding. The new Germany threatened the balance of power in Europe and helped to create fears, tensions, and rivalries that would eventually lead to war.

CHECK-UP

1. Vocabulary: *tariff.*
2. (a) What was the purpose of the *Zollverein*? (b) How did it affect feelings about German unity?
3. (a) What was Bismarck's plan for the unification of Germany? (b) What was his strategy for accomplishing this goal?
4. What was the result of the Seven Weeks' War of 1866?
5. (a) What were the causes of the Franco-Prussian War? (b) What was the outcome? (c) How did the war bring about German unification?
6. What impact did German unification have on the rest of Europe?

3 Nationalism Weakens Empires in Eastern Europe

During most of the nineteenth century Eastern Europe was made up of three large empires: the Austrian Empire of the Hapsburgs, the Ottoman Empire, and imperial Russia. Compared to Western Europe, these Eastern European empires were poor, with inadequate educational systems, high illiteracy, and little industry. Ruled by autocrats, these empires lacked representative forms of government.

NATIONALISM IN EASTERN EUROPE

Eastern Europeans are influenced by the West. As Western influences filtered into these societies, townspeople and villagers began to learn how much better off people were in Western Europe. They became aware of the ideals of liberalism, democracy, and nationalism and heard about the overthrow of the king of France and the reforms that the French people had made in their government. All this made Eastern Europeans look more closely at their own situations.

Among the new influences to reach Eastern Europe, nationalism was the most powerful. It threatened the very existence of the three empires. In each empire, one nationality dominated dozens, if not hundreds, of others. Nationalism encouraged the subject peoples in all three empires to take pride in their heritage and to seek independence. The rise of nationalism among these groups served to increase disunity in Eastern Europe.

Ottomans rule subjects on three continents. Turks dominated the Ottoman Empire. The European part of the empire, however, included Greeks, Bulgarians, Macedonians, Serbs, and Rumanians. Most of these groups belonged to the Eastern Orthodox Church, but some were Protestants or Muslims. The Ottoman Turks also ruled over Arabs and Egyptians in Asia and North Africa.

Austria and Russia rule a variety of peoples. The Hapsburg empire was ruled by German-speaking people in Austria, but the empire included Hungarians, Rumanians, and various Slavic groups — Czechs, Poles, Slovenes, Croats, and Slovaks.

Imperial Russia was even more fragmented. Dominated by Russians, it had acquired most of Poland with its sizable Jewish population. Russia had also gained the lands of the Finns, the Baltic peoples, and the peoples living north of the Black Sea. Farther east, Russia had absorbed the descendants of the Mongols as well as Georgians and Armenians.

AUSTRIA-HUNGARY

Nationalism causes discord in Austria-Hungary. The unification of Italy and of Germany had weakened the Austrian Empire. The empire had lost two wars and had given up control of important territories. Nationalism further weakened the empire.

In Hungary, the Magyars had long been demanding independence (page 472). When defeat by Prussia in 1866 weakened the empire, Emperor Francis Joseph decided that it would be wise to make concessions to the Magyars. In 1867 the empire became the Dual Monarchy of Austria-Hungary. The emperor kept his title in Austria and was also crowned King of Hungary. The Magyar nation of Hungary gained its own constitution and parliament, and was granted complete control over its internal affairs. Foreign and military affairs and common financial concerns were handled by the two governments together. Some Magyar nationalists rejected this arrangement, however, seeking complete independence for Hungary.

Czechs and Germans clash in Bohemia. The formation of the Dual Monarchy did not eliminate nationalist tensions in Austria-Hungary. As nationalism spread among the Czechs in Austria, resistance grew against German cultural and political domination of Bohemia, the Czech region. The Czechs were proud of their past, when Bohemia had been a medieval kingdom. Czech nationalists wanted their language put on an equal basis with German. They sought a status similar to that which had been granted to the Magyars in Hungary.

> ## TIMETABLE
> # Eastern European Empires
>
> | | |
> |---|---|
> | 1825 | Nicholas I comes to power and puts down the Decembrist revolt. |
> | 1830 | Nicholas I adopts a Russification policy after a revolt in Poland. |
> | 1853–1856 | Russia is defeated by Britain, France, and the Ottoman Empire in the Crimean War. |
> | 1867 | The Hapsburg Empire becomes the Dual Monarchy of Austria-Hungary. |
> | 1878 | Serbia, Montenegro, and Rumania gain independence from Ottoman rule. |
> | 1881 | Alexander III tightens czarist rule in Russia. |
> | 1908 | Bulgaria gains independence from Ottoman rule. |
> | 1912–1913 | The Balkan Wars: Ottoman rule in the Balkans comes to an end. |

Nationalism becomes important to the South Slavs. Perhaps the most crucial nationality problem in Austria-Hungary involved the South Slavs, who included Serbs, Bosnians, Croats, and Slovenes. The nation of Serbia became independent of Ottoman control in 1878, and its leaders dreamed of uniting with the other South Slavs in Austria-Hungary. Serbia therefore encouraged nationalist movements among the South Slavs in the Dual Monarchy. The Austrians viewed Serbian agitation as a threat to the empire. The conflict between Austria-Hungary and Serbia was to be the spark that would light the fires of World War I in 1914 (Chapter 29).

THE OTTOMAN EMPIRE

A powerful empire declines. By the nineteenth century, the once-powerful Ottoman Empire was in decline. Ruled by corrupt autocrats, the empire was losing control of its territories. In 1805, Mohammed Ali made Egypt virtually independent within the empire. In 1829 Greece won its independence, and Serbia gained self-rule. A year later, France took over Algeria (in North Africa) and made it a colony.

Called "the sick man of Europe," the empire became the target for the ambitions of its

The Balkans in 1913

By 1913 the Balkan states of Greece, Serbia, Albania, Bulgaria, and Rumania had become independent. Which of these states had coasts on the Black Sea?

neighbors. Imperial Russia sought to expand its influence at Ottoman expense and to gain access to the Mediterranean Sea from its own port on the Black Sea. (The Ottoman Empire held the straits — the Bosporus and the Dardanelles — that linked the two seas.) Austria saw the empire as a possible source of new territory, particularly in the Balkans.

Britain and France did all they could to stall the final collapse of the Ottoman Empire, hoping to keep the "sick man" alive to counter the growing strength of Russia. They delayed independence for Balkan nationalities, urged Ottoman reforms, and intervened whenever they saw trouble. The empire, however, continued to crumble.

The Crimean War threatens the Ottomans. In the early 1850's imperial Russia sent forces into Ottoman territory in hopes of gaining control of the Bosporus and Dardanelles. This led to war in 1853 (officially declared in 1854) in the area known as the Crimea (map, next page). Fearing Russian expansion, Britain and France sent troops to aid the Turks, and these allied forces defeated the Russians in 1856.

At the end of the Crimean War, Britain and France insisted that the Turks make reforms in their autocratic government. Imposed by the Western powers in 1856, the reforms promised a more liberal regime, guaranteed religious freedom, opened government offices to all subjects, abolished torture, and reformed prisons. Britain and France thought that such reforms would prevent rebellion and maintain stability in the empire, but events proved them wrong.

Minorities revolt against Ottoman rule. Internal conflicts had long plagued the Ottomans, and unrest was particularly strong in the Balkans, the mountainous peninsula in southeastern Europe. In the 1870's there were uprisings by the Serbs, Montenegrins, and Bulgarians. Russia entered the conflict on the side of the Balkan rebels, still hoping to gain access to the Mediterranean.

These combined Balkan and Russian forces defeated the Ottoman Turks, and the Treaty of San Stefano forced the Turks to grant independence to Serbia, Montenegro, and Rumania in 1878. According to the treaty, Bulgaria's boundary would be extended to the Aegean Sea, and that country would be occupied by Russian troops. For the time, Russia had a route to the Mediterranean.

Later in 1878, however, a group of European powers, including Russia, met at the Congress of Berlin to alter the San Stefano agreements. Fearing increased Russian influence, the other powers (led by Britain) forced Russia to accept an agreement that took away Bulgaria's Aegean seaport.

Ottoman control of North Africa weakens. There were also clashes in the Ottoman Empire's North African lands. In the 1830's Mohammed Ali, the pasha, or governor, of Egypt, had invaded Syria and conquered territory all the way to the Persian Gulf. It took intervention by Britain for the Ottomans to regain the lost territories. Ottoman control of North Africa, however, grew steadily weaker, and in 1881 France occupied Tunisia and made it a *protectorate.* (In a protectorate the local rulers remain in office, but their power is severely limited by the protecting nation.)

486

The decline continues. By 1900, it was clear that the collapse of the Ottoman Empire was inevitable. A 1908 revolt by the ambitious "Young Turks," who wanted to rebuild the empire, failed to halt the decline. In that same year, Bulgaria declared its independence, and Austria took over Bosnia and Herzegovina.

In 1912, Greece, Bulgaria, Montenegro, and Serbia declared war on Turkey. In the first of two Balkan Wars, the allied Balkan forces succeeded in driving the Turks from Europe, except for the area around Constantinople. The victors, however, could not agree upon the division of the newly won territories, and in 1913 the second Balkan War was fought. The Ottoman Turks joined Greece, Serbia, and Rumania in defeating Bulgaria. The Ottomans thus regained a small part of their lost lands.

As the Turks were driven from Europe, Albania made itself an independent state. In 1912, Italy had taken over Tripoli in North Africa (which became Libya) and some Aegean islands, and in 1913 Greece took Crete. The collapse of the Ottoman Empire seemed near.

The Turks try to destroy the Armenians. Of all the Ottomans' conflicts with minorities, their treatment of Armenians stands out. Justifying their actions by charging treason, the Turks carried out massacres and mass deportations of the Armenian population. Their campaign amounted to *genocide* — the systematic destruction of an entire people. Between 1894 and 1922, more than 1,500,000 Armenians lost their lives. Thousands more fled to other countries, including the United States.

IMPERIAL RUSSIA

Russia remains a backward empire. In the nineteenth century, Russia's huge empire had serious weaknesses, both economic and political. Industrially, Russia remained backward, and its outmoded agricultural system kept tens of millions of serfs tied to the land. In addition,

Russia, 1725–1914

The territorial growth that was begun by the early czars continued for several centuries. Why was the Trans-Siberian Railroad important for Russia?

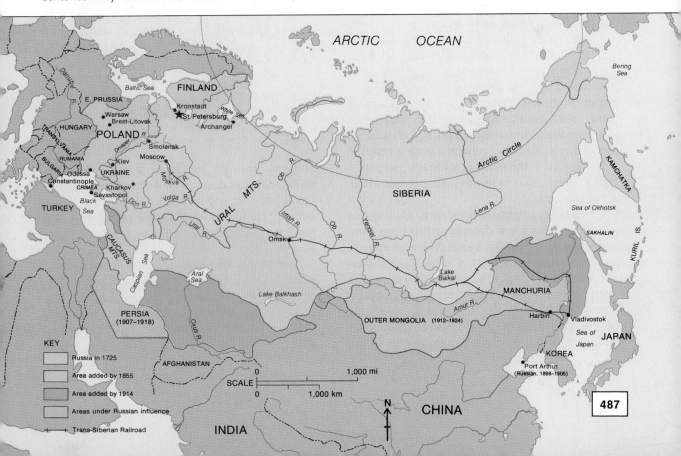

RUSSIAN PEOPLE

A wide gulf separated the landowning nobility and the common people in czarist Russia. In the scene above, Russian peasants pull their carts aside to make way for a landowner's carriage. The woman in the photo at right sold scarves for a living in late nineteenth-century Moscow.

the authoritarian rule of the czars increased political tensions, particularly among minorities such as Poles, Finns, and Ukrainians.

The czars followed the foreign policy of expansion that had begun under Ivan III (page 394). They moved eastward across Siberia and southward beyond the Caspian Sea. The Crimean War had blocked Russia's attempt to gain access to the Mediterranean Sea (page 486). Russia's continued support of Balkan independence, however, reflected both a belief in Pan-Slavism — the unity of all Slavic peoples — and a determination to win access to the Mediterranean Sea.

Nicholas I tightens autocracy. Like earlier czars, Nicholas I was determined to keep complete power in his own hands. He used censorship to control the spread of ideas, kept universities under his watchful eye, and organized a secret police force to keep track of any opposition to his rule. He began his reign in 1825 by suppressing the Decembrist revolt (page 466). Five years later, a revolution among his Polish

subjects brought on more repression (page 467). Nicholas decided that Polish nationalism could only be wiped out by destroying Polish culture. He forced on Poland a policy of Russification — a deliberate attempt to impose Russian culture.

Nicholas also hoped to turn Russia into a powerful state like the nations of Western Europe, yet he was aware that his empire had serious weaknesses. Serfdom held back the modernization of agriculture, but he did not dare free the serfs. His bureaucracy was corrupt, but he could not do without it. He needed educated subjects, but education seemed to prompt disloyalty. His attempts to expand in the Black Sea area led to the Crimean War, which greatly weakened the empire. When Nicholas died in 1855, Russia was still weaker than the Western powers.

Alexander II promotes reforms. The new czar, Alexander II, believed that, in order to grow strong, Russia had to follow the model of the Western countries. Alexander, who ruled from 1855 to 1881, began an era of reform in which the "gates" to the West were thrown open. Because of the changes he sponsored, he became known as the czar-liberator.

Alexander initiated a wide-ranging program of reform. He encouraged economic development through the building of railroads and factories. One of Alexander's most notable actions was the abolition of serfdom in 1861. This reform provided workers for the new industries, since most freed serfs were unable to buy their own farms. Alexander also permitted local self-government, allowing *zemstvos*, local councils made up of nobles, townspeople, and peasants, to be established. More schools were opened, the court system was modernized, and the army was reformed.

Poland rebels again. Alexander's reforms, however, created visions of political freedom and constitutional government, ideas that challenged traditional Russian autocracy. A rising tide of discontent swept over Russia, and in 1863 the czar had to crush another revolt in Poland. After the revolt, Alexander decided to strengthen the policy of Russification in Poland. Polish soldiers and political leaders were exiled and Polish universities were closed. The Russian language replaced Polish in the government and the courts. These measures only served to strengthen the spirit of nationalism in Poland, although the Poles were not yet strong enough to overthrow Russian rule.

Protest grows. Within Russia, also, the czarist government tried to repress opposition. As the czar's police carried out repressive measures, secret societies sprang up. In the late 1870's one revolutionary movement gave birth to a terrorist organization known as "The Will

of the People." A wave of killings swept the country as the government and terrorists clashed. Assassinations took the lives of prominent officials and finally, in 1881, Alexander himself was killed when terrorists threw a bomb into his carriage.

Reform comes to an end. Repression of dissent was intensified under the new czar, Alexander III. His attempts to end revolutionary activity turned Russia into a police state, teeming with spies and informers. Programs of Russification were once again imposed on minorities such as Poles and Finns, and the czar pursued a policy of persecution against the Jews in Russia. Despite the repression, however, dissent and terrorism continued, and tensions ran high.

Russia lags behind the West. Hopes of building a strong Russia on the model of the West seemed destined to fail. The dictatorship remained harsh and repressive, and modernization progressed slowly. While Alexander III did promote a policy of industrialization and railroad-building, at the time of his death in 1894 Russia — and all of Eastern Europe — still lagged far behind Western Europe.

CHECK-UP

1. Vocabulary: *protectorate, genocide.*
2. (a) What three empires ruled Eastern Europe in the late nineteenth century? (b) How did they differ from Western nations? (c) Why was nationalism a threat to the Eastern European empires?
3. (a) How did the Austrian Empire become the Dual Monarchy of Austria-Hungary? (b) Which national groups created tensions within Austria-Hungary?
4. (a) What was the cause of the Crimean War? (b) What powers fought in that war? (c) What was the outcome?
5. (a) Why did Britain and France work to prevent the collapse of the Ottoman Empire? (b) How did the Turks lose control of the Balkans?
6. (a) In what ways did Nicholas I try to strengthen Russia? (b) What reforms were undertaken by Alexander II? (c) What measures were taken by Alexander III to repress dissent in Russia?

Chapter 22 Review

Summary

French rule during the Napoleonic era had promoted Italian unity. This experience sparked Italian hopes for unity free of foreign rule. The Congress of Vienna, however, divided Italy into many small kingdoms, states, and duchies. Giuseppe Mazzini kept Italian nationalism alive, but revolts in 1848 had only short-lived success. Camillo di Cavour used shrewd political moves and strategic wars to unify Italy, with important help from the colorful leader Giuseppe Garibaldi.

Otto von Bismarck steered a strong, nationalistic Prussian state toward dominance of a unified Germany. Aggressively expanding its territories and weakening its rivals through warfare, Prussia succeeded in uniting Germany.

Nationalism had a different effect in Eastern Europe. The Austrian Empire, already weakened by Italian and German expansion, became the Dual Monarchy of Austria-Hungary as a concession to dissenting Magyars. The empire continued to weaken as Czechs and Slavs began to demand their independence.

The crumbling Ottoman Empire fell prey to expansionist ambitions of neighboring nations. Even the support of Britain and France could not halt the Ottoman decline, and the Balkan Wars all but ended the Empire.

Nationalism in the Russian Empire, among such groups as Poles and Finns, came into conflict with the autocratic rule of the czars. As repression increased, tensions heightened, bringing Russia to the brink of revolution.

Vocabulary Review

1. Write the sentences listed below on a sheet of paper. In each sentence, fill in the blank with one of these terms: *balance of power, limited monarchy, nationalism, protectorate, tariff.*
(a) The sense of pride in one's country that comes from sharing traditions, history, and language is ___?___ .
(b) A country in which local leaders are directed by a foreign nation is a ___?___ .
(c) A government in which the powers of the king or queen are checked by a legislative assembly is a ___?___ .
(d) A ___?___ is a tax on imported goods.
(e) A ___?___ prevents any one nation from becoming stronger than others in a given region.
2. Distinguish between the terms in each of the following pairs:
(a) Kingdom of the Two Sicilies; Kingdom of Sardinia.
(b) Seven Weeks' War; Franco-Prussian War.
(c) German Confederation; North German Confederation.
(d) kaiser; czar.
(e) Dual Monarchy of Austria-Hungary; Austrian Empire.
(f) Balkan Wars; Crimean War.
(g) Russification; Pan-Slavism.

People to Identify

Identify the following people. Name the country with which each was connected and tell why that person was important.
1. William I
2. Nicholas I
3. Alexander II
4. Otto von Bismarck
5. Giuseppe Mazzini
6. Camillo di Cavour
7. Giuseppe Garibaldi
8. Francis Joseph

Relating Geography and History

1. **Locating places.** Locate each of the following on a map in this chapter:
(a) Balkans
(b) Sardinia
(c) Crimea
(d) Prussia
(e) Serbia
(f) Siberia
(g) Bosporus
(h) Bulgaria
(i) Austrian Empire
(j) Kingdom of the Two Sicilies
(k) Schleswig-Holstein
(l) Alsace-Lorraine
2. **Reports.** Plan a tour of Italy, for which you will act as tour guide. Include in your tour places that were important in the unification of Italy. Prepare a short speech telling why each town or area is important. Include a map to use with your speech.

Discussion Questions

1. (a) Why was Cavour more successful than Mazzini in bringing about the unification of Italy? (b) What outlook did Mazzini and Garibaldi have in common as leaders?

2. What did Bismarck achieve through war (a) against Austria? (b) against France?

3. Why did the unification of Italy and Germany come so much later than the unification of other European countries?

4. In what ways were the actions of each of the following groups motivated by nationalism: (a) Magyars, (b) Czechs, (c) Serbs?

5. (a) How did the reforms started by Alexander II encourage the development of revolutionary groups in Russia? (b) What was the response of Alexander III to their actions?

6. How was the balance of power in Europe affected by (a) the rise of Germany, (b) the decline of the Ottoman Empire, (c) the attempts of Russia to gain access to the Mediterranean?

Reading Primary Sources

Giuseppe Garibaldi, the leader of the forces that freed Sicily from Bourbon rule, has been called "the sword" of the Italian revolution. His ability to rally fighters to his cause is shown in this excerpt from one of his speeches. Read the passage. Then answer the questions that follow.

> Italians! The Sicilians are fighting against the enemies of Italy and for Italy. To help them with money, arms, and especially men, is the duty of every Italian. . . .
>
> Hearken not to the voice of those who cram themselves at well-served tables. Let us arm. Let us fight for our brothers; tomorrow we can fight for ourselves.
>
> A handful of brave men, who have followed me in battles for our country, are advancing with me to the rescue. Italy knows them; they always appear at the hour of danger. Brave and generous companions, they have devoted their lives to their country; they will shed their last drop of blood for it, seeking no other reward than that of a pure conscience.
>
> "Italy and Victor Emmanuel!" — that [is] our battle-cry. . . . As this prophetic battle-cry re-echoes from the hills of Italy, . . . the tottering thrones of tyranny will fall to pieces, and the whole country will rise like one man.

(a) Who is Garibaldi asking Italians to fight for? (b) How does he want Italians to help? (c) According to Garibaldi, what is the only reward asked by the patriots who are fighting with him? (d) How does the passage show that Garibaldi was not trying to establish a republic? (e) What does he say will happen when his battle-cry is sounded?

Skill Activities

1. Word research. In the nineteenth century many Slavs called for *Pan-Slavism,* a union of all Slavic peoples. *Pan* comes from a Greek word meaning "all." Look up the following words in a dictionary and tell how each is related in meaning to *pan:* (a) panacea, (b) Pan-American, (c) pandemic, (d) panorama. Use each word in a sentence.

2. Identifying cause and effect. Each of the following sentences describes an *effect.* Read the sentence. Then reread the page or pages indicated in parentheses and decide what you think were the most important *causes* of each effect. On a separate sheet of paper, list these causes in your own words and explain why you chose them. (You may select causes other than those discussed on the pages indicated.)

(a) *Effect:* Austria declares war on the Kingdom of Sardinia in 1859 (page 479).
(b) *Effect:* Victor Emmanuel II is proclaimed King of Italy in 1861 (pages 480–481).
(c) *Effect:* Prussia forms the North German Confederation, excluding Austria from membership (page 482).
(d) *Effect:* France and Britain enter the Crimean War against Russia (page 486).
(e) *Effect:* The czars enforce a policy of Russification in Poland (page 489).

3. Comparing. Make a chart comparing the unification of Italy with that of Germany. Include information that answers the following questions: (a) Who were the most important leaders? (b) What were their specific goals? (c) Where and how was unification finally achieved?

4. Reports. The Crimean War marked the beginning of the modern nursing profession. Concerned over the lack of supplies and clothing for soldiers, the British War Office sent Florence Nightingale and a group of nurses to the Crimea. Prepare a report on Florence Nightingale's work in the Crimea and her contributions to the nursing profession.

The city of St. Louis in 1846, during a period when Americans were moving west in increasing numbers, is the subject of this painting by Henry Lewis. Note the wagon train and steamboat.

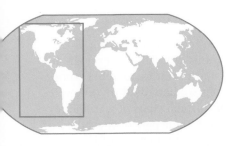

23

Nation-Building in the Americas

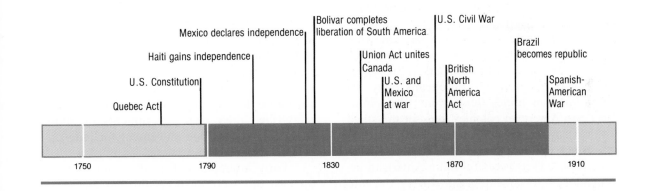

Quebec Act
U.S. Constitution
Haiti gains independence
Mexico declares independence
Bolivar completes liberation of South America
Union Act unites Canada
U.S. and Mexico at war
U.S. Civil War
British North America Act
Brazil becomes republic
Spanish-American War

1750   1790   1830   1870   1910

While nationalism was shaping modern Europe during the nineteenth century, the Americas were also undergoing a period of nation-building. The American and French revolutions inspired Latin Americans to seek self-rule, and by 1824 most of Latin America had gained its independence. In the new republics power often fell into the hands of dictators. Some of these dictators were corrupt, but others worked to make their nations strong.

In the United States, the Constitution protected individual freedoms and guarded against the abuse of power. War with Britain in 1812 and the acquisition of new lands promoted a feeling of unity and increased national pride. The nation survived a terrible Civil War, and in the postwar period the economy expanded and the population grew.

The nation of Canada also developed during this period, although rivalry between British and French settlers often strained national unity.

This chapter discusses the nation-building process in different countries in the Americas.

CHAPTER OUTLINE

1 Latin Americans Gain Their Independence

2 National Unity Develops Slowly in Latin America

3 The United States Expands

4 The United States Survives the Civil War and Grows Stronger

5 Canada Becomes a Nation

1 Latin Americans Gain Their Independence

By the end of the eighteenth century, many Latin American colonists wanted to govern their own countries. These Latin Americans were responding to some of the same problems that had caused people in the British colonies to seek independence. For example, the colonists had to pay high taxes and they could trade only with the home country. In addition, the Latin American colonies had other reasons for wanting independence. Wealthy, educated colonists of creole and mestizo descent were barred from high positions in the government, Church, and army. Blacks and Indians led harsh lives, laboring for Europeans on plantations and in mines. Discontent throughout the Latin American colonies thus set the stage for the struggles for independence.

Black slaves and mulattos revolt on Hispaniola. The first successful Latin American independence movement began during the late 1700's in the West Indies. The French colony of St. Domingue (doh-MANG), located on the island of Hispaniola (map, page 496), was one of the most profitable of the European colonies in the Americas. About 400,000 black slaves worked on St. Domingue's sugar plantations. In addition, about 22,000 mulattos, people of mixed black and European descent, lived in the colony. Most of these mulattos were free and many of them were landowners. They were barred, however, from practicing law, medicine, and other professions. When the revolutionaries in France issued the Declaration of Rights of Man and Citizen in 1789 (page 446), a mulatto named Vincent Ogé (oh-ZHAY) called for similar rights of citizenship for the free mulattos of St. Domingue. Outraged by his demands, the French government had him publicly tortured to death.

This action angered the colony's mulattos, and when the slaves rebelled in 1791, the mulattos joined them. Under the skillful military leadership of an ex-slave named Pierre Toussaint L'Ouverture (too-SAN loo-vur-TOOR), the rebels drove the French from St. Domingue.

Toussaint had barely established a new government when Napoleon came to power in

France and sent troops to regain the colony. The French were unsuccessful, however. In addition to losing many battles to rebel troops, most of the French soldiers died of yellow fever. In 1804, after thirteen years of war, the revolutionaries declared their part of the island of Hispaniola the independent nation of Haiti.[1]

Bolívar liberates northern South America. Events in Europe also contributed to a movement for independence in northern South America. In 1808 Napoleon invaded Spain and put his brother on the throne. Many people in Spain's Latin American colonies refused to be ruled by a French king. They proclaimed their allegiance to the deposed Spanish king and established their own governments in major cities. Soon a genuine movement for independence developed.

Early attempts to free the colonies from Spanish rule were unsuccessful, but they gave colonial leaders experience and taught them how to plan effectively. A Venezuelan, Francisco de Miranda (mih-RAN-duh), tried twice without success to free his country from Spanish rule. Simón Bolívar (bo-LEE-vahr), an idealistic creole who had fought alongside Miranda, was also defeated in several early battles. Bolívar never gave up, however, and he became the most important figure in South America's fight for independence.

Born in Venezuela to a wealthy family, Bolívar was educated in Spain and traveled widely. The ideals of the French and American revolutions had a strong influence on him. In his native land, Bolívar put together a Latin American army. By promising to free the South American slaves when he won independence — a promise he eventually kept — Bolívar gained help from Haiti in 1816. Many British soldiers who were left unemployed after Napoleon's defeat at Waterloo also joined Bolívar's forces.

In 1819, after six years of battling against Spanish forces, Bolívar led thousands of soldiers from the tropical valley of the Orinoco

---

[1]The rest of Hispaniola was the Spanish colony of Santo Domingo.

HEROES OF INDEPENDENCE
Determined patriots like Toussaint L'Ouverture of Haiti (above) and Simón Bolívar of Venezuela (right) led the movements that freed Latin American lands from European control.

River to an icy mountain pass through the Andes. More than one hundred of his followers died in the mountain crossing, but he won a decisive victory against the Spaniards at Boyacá. Soon after, Bolívar captured the city of Bogotá. (Both Boyacá and Bogotá are today in the nation of Colombia.) In 1822 the city of Quito was captured by Antonio José de Sucre (SOO-kray), Bolívar's ablest general. (Quito is in present-day Ecuador.) Bolívar then became president of the newly independent nation, known as Great Colombia.[2]

San Martín frees southern South America. While Bolívar was liberating the northern part of South America, another important leader, José de San Martín (SAHN mar-TEEN) was leading a military force north from Argentina. Argentina had been independent since 1806 when British troops captured the city of Buenos Aires (BWAY-nohs EY-rays) from the Spaniards and were in turn driven out by the people of the city. San Martín realized, however, that Argentina could remain independent only if the Spaniards were also driven from Chile and Peru.

In 1817, San Martín's well-trained troops crossed the Andes and captured Santiago, Chile. In 1821, they captured Lima, the capital of Peru and the stronghold of Spanish power in South America, but the Spanish forces in the countryside remained strong. The following year, San Martín sailed north from Peru to Guayaquil (gwy-uh-KEEL), which Bolívar had just taken. The two leaders met secretly, and while no one knows exactly what decisions were reached, Bolívar's forces took over the fight for Peru's independence.[3]

The final battle lasted for just an hour on December 9, 1824. In the thin, cold Andean air, at an altitude of 9,000 feet, Bolívar's troops, led by Sucre, crushed the Spanish army near the village of Ayacucho (ah-yah-KOO-choh). This battle marked the triumph of the independence movement in South America.

The independence movement in New Spain creates the nation of Mexico. As in South America, the independence movement in New Spain began as a reaction to the invasion of

---

[2]Great Colombia included the present-day countries of Panama, Colombia, Venezuela, and Ecuador (map, page 496).

[3]When San Martín withdrew from the battle, some people in Latin America accused him of abandoning his troops. Disillusioned by this, and unwilling to engage in the political struggles that would follow independence, San Martín sailed to France, where he spent the rest of his life.

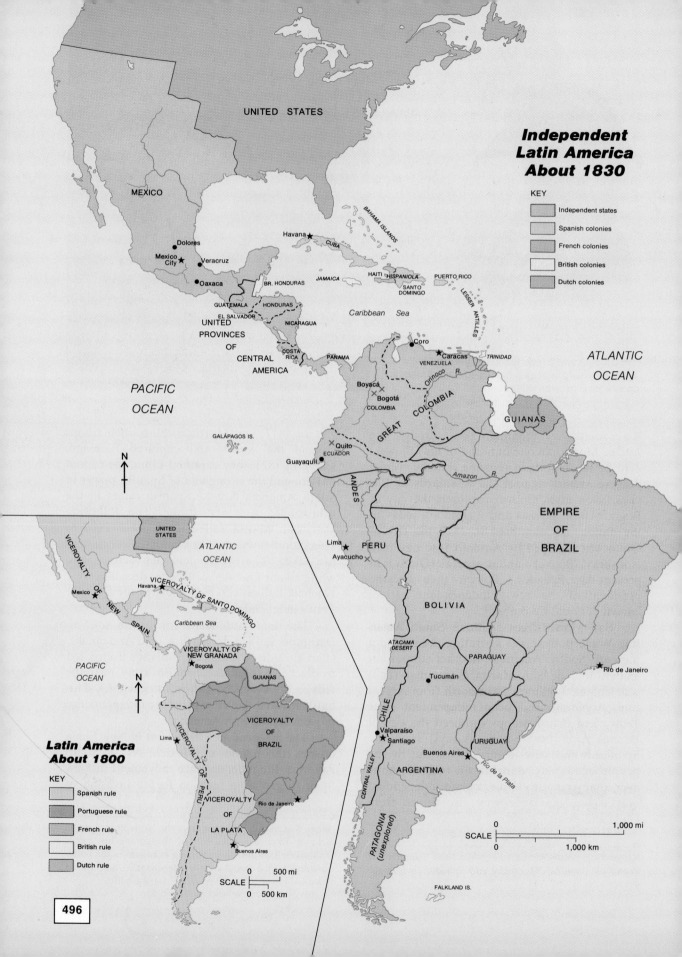

Independent Latin America About 1830

UNITED STATES

MEXICO

Dolores
Mexico City ★
Veracruz ●
Oaxaca ●

Havana ★
CUBA

BAHAMA ISLANDS

BR. HONDURAS

JAMAICA

HAITI HISPANIOLA
SANTO DOMINGO

PUERTO RICO

LESSER ANTILLES

GUATEMALA HONDURAS
EL SALVADOR
NICARAGUA

Caribbean Sea

UNITED PROVINCES OF CENTRAL AMERICA

COSTA RICA
PANAMA

Coro ●
Caracas ★
VENEZUELA

TRINIDAD

ATLANTIC OCEAN

PACIFIC OCEAN

Orinoco R.

Boyacá ×
Bogotá ●
COLOMBIA

GREAT COLOMBIA

GUIANAS

Quito ×
ECUADOR

GALÁPAGOS IS.

Guayaquil ●

ANDES

Amazon R.

EMPIRE OF BRAZIL

N

Lima ★
Ayacucho ×
PERU

BOLIVIA

ATACAMA DESERT

PARAGUAY

Río de Janeiro ★

CHILE

Tucumán ●

Valparaíso ●
Santiago ★

Buenos Aires ★
URUGUAY

Río de la Plata

CENTRAL VALLEY

ARGENTINA

PATAGONIA (unexplored)

FALKLAND IS.

KEY

	Independent states
	Spanish colonies
	French colonies
	British colonies
	Dutch colonies

SCALE
0 _____ 1,000 mi
0 _____ 1,000 km

Latin America About 1800

UNITED STATES

VICEROYALTY OF NEW SPAIN

Mexico ★

ATLANTIC OCEAN

Havana ★

VICEROYALTY OF SANTO DOMINGO

Caribbean Sea

PACIFIC OCEAN

VICEROYALTY OF NEW GRANADA
Bogotá ★

GUIANAS

N

Lima ★

VICEROYALTY OF PERU

VICEROYALTY OF BRAZIL

Río de Janeiro ★

VICEROYALTY OF LA PLATA

Buenos Aires ★

KEY

	Spanish rule
	Portuguese rule
	French rule
	British rule
	Dutch rule

SCALE
0 _____ 500 mi
0 _____ 500 km

496

Spain by Napoleon in 1808. (Mexico was called New Spain before it gained its independence.) Events in New Spain, however, took a different course.

In 1810 creole leaders in New Spain were planning a rebellion against the Spanish authorities. Hearing that the Spaniards knew of this conspiracy, one of its leaders, a creole priest named Miguel Hidalgo (ee-DAL-goh), decided to act quickly. On September 16, he summoned the people of his area by ringing the church bell in the town of Dolores. Hidalgo called for independence, the return of lands that had been taken from Indians, and an end to tribute payments to Spain. Untrained and armed only with knives and slings, Hidalgo's army of Indians and mestizos began to march south, attacking large estates.

By the time they neared Mexico City, Hidalgo headed an army of more than 50,000. Afraid to let this undisciplined force loose in the capital, Hidalgo turned back. The Spaniards pursued and defeated the rebels and executed Hidalgo.

A mestizo priest named José María Morelos (moh-RAY-lohs) next took over leadership of the Mexican revolution. Unlike Hidalgo, Morelos patiently set out to train a Mexican army. By 1813 his small army controlled much of southern Mexico. Then, from an outpost in the hills, Morelos and his group of rebels declared independence from Spain. They began writing a new constitution guaranteeing equality for all people, the end of special privileges for Church and army, and the breakup of the large estates. The prospect of such changes lost Morelos the support of many creoles. After a series of defeats at the hands of the Spanish army, Morelos was captured and executed in 1815.

With the death of Morelos, hopes of independence for Mexico seemed to vanish. Guerrilla fighting continued off and on until 1820, however, when events in Europe again had an important impact on Latin America. In that year soldiers in Spain revolted and forced the king to restore the liberal constitution of 1812, which favored social reform. When the constitution was proclaimed in Mexico, many creoles who had opposed such ideas joined together and drove out the Spanish leaders. Thus, in 1821 Mexicans declared their independence.

Brazil follows a peaceful road to independence. In the eastern part of South America, Portugal's colony of Brazil gained independence peacefully. By 1800 Brazil had much more land, greater resources, and many more people than Portugal. When Napoleon's armies invaded Portugal in 1807, Portugal's King John VI and his family escaped to Brazil. Moving the monarchy across the Atlantic transformed Rio de Janeiro (REE-oh dih zhun-AIR-oh) from a colonial town to a busy capital city.

In 1821 the king returned to Portugal and left his son Pedro to rule Brazil. A year later, on his father's advice, Pedro declared Brazil's independence and became Emperor Pedro I.[4]

Europe's dominance of Latin America ends. In the twenty years from Haiti's independence in 1804 to the battle of Ayacucho in 1824, Europe's dominance of Latin America was ended. Latin Americans overthrew foreign rule and gained their independence. France lost Haiti and Portugal lost Brazil. Spain's great empire in the Americas was dismantled, as only Cuba, Santo Domingo, and Puerto Rico remained in Spanish hands.

Independent Latin America About 1830

Between Haiti's winning of independence in 1804 and the Battle of Ayacucho in 1824, most of Latin America gained independence. Which colonies did Spain still hold after 1830? What other European colonies remained at that time?

CHECK-UP

1. Describe the developments that led to the founding of Haiti.
2. (a) How did Bolívar win independence for northern South America? (b) How did San Martín help to win independence for southern South America?
3. (a) Describe the roles played by Hidalgo and Morelos in the Mexican independence movement. (b) Why did many creoles oppose Mexico's independence movement before 1820?
4. What made Brazil's route to independence different from that of the other countries of Latin America?

---

[4] Brazil did not become a republic until 1889 when Pedro II was overthrown by military leaders.

2 National Unity Develops Slowly in Latin America

Nation-building took place slowly in Latin America. Geographical barriers, social inequality, weak economies, and political disagreements hampered movements to unify countries. Moreover, dictators took control of many governments. These dictators often concentrated on economic development at the expense of political freedom. By 1900, however, several Latin American nations had achieved a measure of political and economic stability.

The new republics face severe barriers to unity. In the decades after independence, there was little spirit of unity in the Latin American nations. Vast distances, lofty mountain ranges, and dense forests made communication within a country difficult. Social barriers also created wide divisions. The rigid social structure of colonial times remained. Indians, mestizos, and blacks still had few rights and were not allowed full participation in the new nations. They felt deep resentment toward the new governments.

Creole landowners dominate Latin American economies. Creoles gained the most by independence. They took over positions of leadership in the government, Church, and army. They also took over the plantations that had been owned by the Spaniards. Few creoles were willing to share their political or economic power with the other groups in Latin American society.

Years of revolution had weakened Latin American economies. Trade and farming had been severely disrupted. The task of rebuilding the economies was in the hands of the wealthy creole landowners. Most of these landowners realized that they themselves could prosper by exporting plantation crops or minerals to European countries. They showed little interest in developing industry or banking. Economies thus became tied to Europe and depended upon the world price of one or two crops or minerals. Independence had given Latin Americans little control of the economic development of their own countries.

Dictators control the governments of the new nations. Unlike the British colonists to the north, Latin Americans had gained little experience in governing themselves during the colonial period. Thus, the early years of Latin American independence were filled with chaos and instability. Leaders drew up constitutions but were unable to put into practice such ideas as regular elections or representative government. Instead, stable central government in Latin American nations was established slowly under leaders known as caudillos (cow-DEE-yohs), a Spanish word meaning "chiefs."

A caudillo was a dictator who came to power by gaining the support of the army and the wealthy landowners. To stay in power, the caudillo gave out land and government positions. Many of the caudillos' appointees were unqualified and corrupt. While some caudillos did work for the good of their countries, each was a dictator who stayed in power through force. Rule by caudillos became so common in nineteenth-century Latin America that the period is often called the Age of Caudillos.

Caudillos unify both Chile and Argentina. Chile was the first Latin American country to develop a stable central government. It accomplished this under the leadership of the caudillo Diego Portales (por-TAH-lehs), a creole businessman. Portales controlled Chile from 1830 to 1837, although he never actually became its president. Portales had the support of the large landowners, and he fought for their interests. He stressed the importance of economic growth and used funds from foreign investors to build railroads, ships, and telegraph lines. In a war against Peru and Bolivia, Chile gained control of the Atacama Desert, which was rich in valuable nitrates.

A firm belief in the need for strong leadership underlay Portales' plans for Chile. The constitution he drew up in 1833 reflected his beliefs, giving the president veto power over laws passed by the legislature, control of elections, and the right to appoint his own successor. In addition, Portales eliminated opposing viewpoints through censorship and exile.

An even more tyrannical ruler brought unity to Argentina. Juan Manuel de Rosas, a creole landowner and businessman, ruled the country from 1835 to 1852. With the help of the militia, spies, and secret police, Rosas ruled harshly, eliminating all opposition. Like Portales, Rosas favored the interests of the wealthy landowners. His policies did strengthen Argentina's central government, however, enabling his successors to begin programs of economic development.

Political disagreements block the road to unity. All of the new Latin American nations were torn by political disagreements. As in Europe during the rise of nationalism, much of the conflict in Latin America was between liberals and conservatives. Liberals were those who generally supported political and social reform.

Among the liberals in Latin America were merchants who opposed limits on trade and lawyers who wanted to do away with the privileges of the Church and of military leaders. Conservatives supported existing traditions. The conservatives in Latin America included large landowners and high-ranking Latin American clergy. Military officers were generally more concerned with promotions than with principles. They supported whoever helped them get ahead.

Throughout Latin America the clash between conservatives and liberals was the most bitter over the question of the Church's place in government matters. During colonial times, the

LINKING PAST AND PRESENT
Cowboys of the Americas

Raising livestock — especially cattle — has been important in the Americas ever since the Spaniards introduced horses, cattle, and sheep in their colonies. Throughout the Americas, cowboys developed methods for managing large herds of cattle on unfenced prairies and rangeland. In Argentina, these cowboys are called *gauchos;* elsewhere in Latin America they are *llaneros* (yah-NEH-rohs). In Hawaii, cowboys are *paniolos,* probably from *Español,* which means "Spanish."

In North America, the original cowboys of the Southwest were the Mexican *vaqueros* (vah-KAIR-ohs). They learned to herd cattle from horseback, roping them with a lariat or lasso. The *vaqueros* wore practical working clothes — a wide-brimmed sombrero to keep off the sun and rain, high-heeled riding boots with spurs, and leather chaps to protect their legs. Easterners who moved to the frontier adopted the customs of the *vaqueros,* creating the traditional picture of the American cowboy.

Benito Juárez, Mexico's first president of Indian descent, had two main goals: to carry out reforms that would benefit the Mexican people and to drive out the French forces that occupied Mexico in 1862.

arms and overthrew the liberal government. The liberals fled to Veracruz, where they set up a government and named Juárez president.

The bloody War of the Reform (1858–1860) that followed was marked by atrocities, betrayals, and massive loss of life. The liberals emerged victorious, regaining Mexico City and electing Juárez president.

France tries to take over Mexico. The cost of the civil war increased the huge debts Mexico owed to foreign nations, especially France and Britain. In 1862, when Juárez declared that Mexico would have to delay payment on its debts, Napoleon III (page 471) sent French troops to Mexico. The Mexican army, weakened by years of civil war, had little chance against modern European weapons. Mexican conservatives, hoping to overthrow the Juárez government, asked Archduke Maximilian of Austria to become Mexico's ruler. With the support of Napoleon III, Maximilian accepted this invitation and in 1864 was installed as the emperor of Mexico.

Juárez refused to acknowledge Maximilian as the ruler of Mexico and raised an army to wage guerrilla war against the French forces. The United States opposed the French presence in Mexico, but could do nothing because its own civil war was raging at the same time. In 1866, however, the tide turned in Juárez's favor when the United States, its civil war over, pressured France to leave Mexico. Faced with troubles at home, Napoleon III withdrew his

Roman Catholic Church had held vast lands and had been a powerful influence on public opinion. After independence, conservatives wanted to keep education, social welfare, marriage, and burial under Church control. Liberals wanted change. They looked on the special status of the Church as a major obstacle to forming strong nations. They believed that gaining control of Church lands would allow their governments to collect money to build public schools and hospitals.

Reforms lead to war in Mexico. The longest and most savage struggle between Church and state took place in Mexico. In 1855 a liberal government set out to reduce the power and privileges of both the clergy and the army. An important figure behind this move toward reform was an Indian lawyer, Benito Juárez (HWAH-rez), the Minister of Justice. Juárez wrote many reforms into the Constitution of 1857. These reforms separated Church and state, ended Church ownership of land, and declared freedom of speech, press, and assembly. They also brought military privileges to an end. This angered conservatives, who then took up

---

TIMETABLE

Nation-Building in Latin America

1804 Haiti gains independence from France.
1821 Mexico declares its independence from Spain.
1822 Emperor Pedro I declares Brazil independent from Portugal.
1824 Bolívar completes the liberation of South America.
1858 Juárez becomes president of Mexico.
1862 France sends forces to Mexico.
1867 Emperor Maximilian is executed. Juárez is re-elected as Mexico's president.
1876 Díaz becomes Mexico's president.

troops. Juárez returned to power, and Maximilian was executed.

Juárez served as Mexico's president until his death in 1872. His attempts to enforce the Constitution of 1857 turned the later years of his presidency into a dictatorship. Although he is a national hero to many, Juárez remains one of the most controversial of Mexico's caudillos.

Mexico's economy develops under Díaz. Mexico's next caudillo, Porfirio Díaz (DEE-ahs), came to power in 1876. Díaz was a general who had been successful against the French. A ruthless dictator, he ruled Mexico almost continuously until 1910.

Díaz pursued economic development as vigorously as Juárez had pursued reform. Under Díaz, foreign businesses invested heavily in Mexican industry and agriculture. Aided by foreign funds and advisers, Mexico built railroads and developed mines and oil fields. The treasury soon produced the first surplus in the history of the Mexican republic.

Today many Mexicans look upon the Díaz dictatorship as a necessary step in the development of the Mexican nation. However, the period did create some critical problems. The major share of the profits in the new industries and mines went to investors in Europe and the United States. The newly rich creoles adopted European ways and looked down on Mexican culture and traditions. This hurt Mexican national pride. Thus, while Mexico appeared to benefit from the economic policies of Díaz, beneath the surface there was a rumbling of discontent that was to erupt in the twentieth century.

CHECK-UP

1. What difficulties did the Latin American republics face in trying to build national unity?
2. (a) Which group gained most from the overthrow of Spanish rule in Latin America? (b) What economic problems did the new Latin American nations face?
3. (a) Who were the caudillos? (b) How did a caudillo usually come to power?
4. (a) What steps did Portales take to strengthen the government of Chile? (b) How did he strengthen Chile's economy? (c) How did Rosas maintain his rule in Argentina?
5. (a) What reforms did the supporters of Juárez write into the Mexican constitution of 1857? (b) Why did Napoleon III send French troops to Mexico? (c) What caused him to withdraw his troops?
6. (a) What steps did Díaz take to strengthen Mexico's economy? (b) What problems did his policies create?

3 The United States Expands

During the nineteenth century the United States expanded and grew more powerful while establishing a strong central government under the Constitution, which had been ratified in 1788 (page 437). In the first half of the 1800's, territorial expansion tested the ability of the new government to maintain unity in a rapidly growing nation.

Several factors strengthen central government. The wise leadership of George Washington helped strengthen the new nation's central government. A hero of the American Revolution, Washington became the first President of the United States in 1789. Washington was popular and greatly respected throughout the new republic. A firm supporter of national unity, he proved to be as able a leader in peacetime as he had been in war.

The new nation was further strengthened by the constitutional provision that gave Congress the powers needed to make the central government function effectively. Elected officials in the Senate and the House of Representatives had the power to make laws that would serve the common good and assure the development of a strong nation. Congress could declare war and make peace and also had the authority to organize an army and navy. It could regulate trade between states and with foreign nations, borrow funds, and pass tax laws. It could coin money and regulate its value. Congress also had the power to set up a court system, which it did in 1789.

The Supreme Court's power of judicial review was another factor strengthening the central government. Established by John Marshall, the Court's Chief Justice from 1801 to 1835, this power allowed the Supreme Court to declare acts passed by Congress or by state legislatures to be unconstitutional.

The new nation doubles in size. In 1783 the lands of the United States stretched to the Mississippi River. To the west was the vast Louisiana Territory, a possession of Spain. In 1800, Spain ceded the area to France. Two years later, American traders were barred from using the port of New Orleans. These traders had been transporting their goods down the Mississippi and then to ocean-going ships at New Orleans.

President Thomas Jefferson feared that Napoleon, the French leader, planned to establish an empire in the Americas. Seeking to prevent French control of the Mississippi River,

The Constitution (page 437) set forth the plan for a strong national government, based on the principle of separation of powers. That principle is carried out by means of the system of checks and balances (diagramed below). Note that the Supreme Court can declare executive acts unconstitutional.

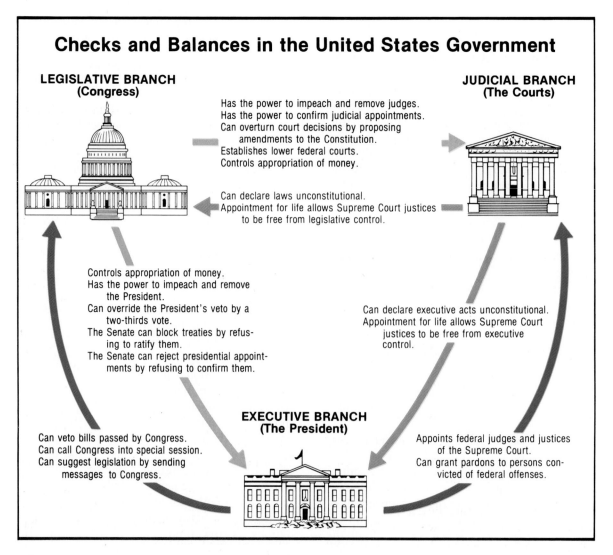

Checks and Balances in the United States Government

**LEGISLATIVE BRANCH
(Congress)**

**JUDICIAL BRANCH
(The Courts)**

Has the power to impeach and remove judges.
Has the power to confirm judicial appointments.
Can overturn court decisions by proposing
    amendments to the Constitution.
Establishes lower federal courts.
Controls appropriation of money.

Can declare laws unconstitutional.
Appointment for life allows Supreme Court justices
    to be free from legislative control.

Controls appropriation of money.
Has the power to impeach and remove
    the President.
Can override the President's veto by a
    two-thirds vote.
The Senate can block treaties by refus-
    ing to ratify them.
The Senate can reject presidential appoint-
    ments by refusing to confirm them.

Can declare executive acts unconstitutional.
Appointment for life allows Supreme Court
    justices to be free from executive
    control.

**EXECUTIVE BRANCH
(The President)**

Can veto bills passed by Congress.
Can call Congress into special session.
Can suggest legislation by sending
    messages to Congress.

Appoints federal judges and justices
    of the Supreme Court.
Can grant pardons to persons con-
    victed of federal offenses.

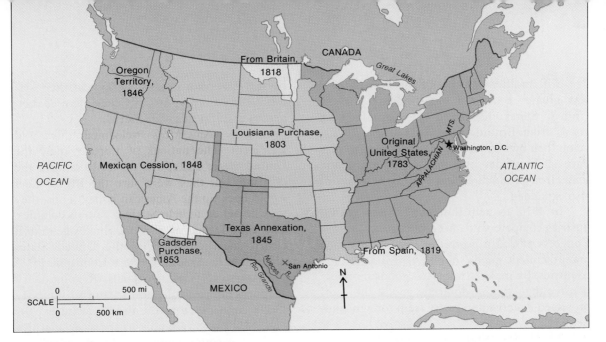

The United States, 1783–1853

The United States gained vast territories in the first half of the nineteenth century. The nation acquired lands from Spain, Britain, France, and Mexico. In what year did the lands of the Mexican Cession become part of the United States?

Jefferson offered to buy New Orleans. He made his offer at a good time, since Napoleon was about to embark upon another war in Europe and needed money to finance it. In addition, the slave revolt on Hispaniola (page 494) had discouraged France's plans for an empire in the Americas. In 1803 the United States was able to buy not only New Orleans but the entire Louisiana Territory. The nation thus doubled in size and, moreover, gained control of the Mississippi River, an important transportation route.

The United States and Britain fight another war. With the addition of the Louisiana Territory, some Americans argued for even further expansion. Eager to broaden their nation's borders, they urged taking Canada from Great Britain.

When Britain and France were at war in the early 1800's, President Jefferson hoped that the United States could remain **neutral,** or avoid taking sides. The actions of the European powers made neutrality difficult, however. Britain seized American ships headed for French ports, while France seized American ships that traded with Britain.

Many people in the United States pressed for war with Britain. Those who favored expansion believed that such a war could give the United States a chance to win Canada from Britain and, possibly, even Florida from Spain (which was Britain's ally). Some Americans also favored war because they believed that the British were supplying guns to hostile Indians on the American frontier. Moreover, Americans were angry because officers of British ships had been forcibly taking sailors from American ships, claiming that they were British subjects.

In 1812 the United States declared war on Britain. The war lasted until late in 1814, with neither side gaining a clear victory. The Treaty of Ghent ended the war, and no lands changed hands.

The War of 1812 strengthens the United States. Despite the fact that the United States gained no new lands, some historians think of the War of 1812 as a "second war of independence." After the war other nations came to recognize the United States as a fully independent nation deserving of respect. The war strengthened national unity by giving Americans greater pride in their country. People of different states, who had thought of themselves as Virginians or Pennsylvanians or New Englanders, began to think of themselves as Americans. They gloried in the victories that the American forces had won.

Still another outcome of the War of 1812 was greater economic independence for the United States. Deprived of manufactured goods from Britain, Americans began to develop their own industries. They learned to produce such articles as guns, paper, glass, and soap. Iron production and the textile industry also expanded.

In 1816, to help the young American industries compete with those of other countries, Congress passed a *protective tariff* — a tax on manufactured goods imported from foreign countries. By making imported goods more expensive than similar domestic goods, the tariff protected American industry from foreign competition.

The United States gains Florida. As the United States grew stronger, it became more forceful in international relations. Indians from Florida, an area held by Spain, were raiding United States territory. In 1818 President James Monroe ordered General Andrew Jackson to stop the Indian raids. Jackson went beyond his orders and invaded Indian lands in Florida. President Monroe did not want a war, but he demanded that Spain either prevent future raids on United States territory or cede Florida to the United States. Burdened with the Latin American wars of independence, Spain gave up Florida in 1819.

The United States declares the Americas closed to colonization. In 1823 the United States took a forceful stand on European involvement in Latin America. Rumors were spreading that the Concert of Europe (page 465) was planning to help Spain regain its colonies in Latin America. Economically and politically weak, the new Latin American republics would not have been able to hold off a European invasion. The United States was sympathetic to the Latin American nations and wanted to see them remain independent. Britain also wanted the Latin American countries to stay independent, for it carried on a profitable trade with them.

In 1823 President Monroe declared that the American continents were "henceforth not to be considered as subjects for future colonization by any European powers." The new policy, known as the Monroe Doctrine, made it clear that the United States looked on any attempts by the European powers "to extend their system to any portion of this hemisphere as dangerous to our peace and safety."

Many Americans welcomed this bold statement. The nations of Europe knew the United States lacked the power to enforce the doctrine, but they were sure the British fleet would back up the American policy. Thus, they took no action to help Spain regain its colonies. The significance of the doctrine was that it clearly marked the stand the United States planned to take in the Western Hemisphere.

Americans seek new lands. Revolutionary advances in the textile industry during the early 1800's contributed to the drive toward expansion. Machines were able to speed up the production of cotton cloth, and Eli Whitney's invention of the cotton gin provided a faster way to remove seeds from the cotton fiber. These advances created a change in agriculture in the South, as plantation owners turned from crops of tobacco, rice, and indigo to cotton, which was much more profitable. Eager for quick profits, farmers planted one crop of cotton after another. Since this quickly wore out the soil, plantation owners continually looked for new lands.

Settlers take over Indian lands. Some of the best soil for cotton included lands that had been farmed for centuries by Indian groups in the Southeast — the Cherokee, Choctaw, Chickasaw, Creek, and Seminole. President Andrew Jackson believed that these Indians should be moved westward to make room for the white settlers. Most Indian groups left regretfully but peacefully, accepting payment for their lands. Some groups held out and battled United States troops. By the 1840's, however, most of the Indians from the Southeast had been resettled west of the Mississippi.

Americans gain a sense of destiny. Even after the relocation of the Indians of the Southeast, Americans sought more land. Population was growing in the lands east of the Mississippi. Many Americans began to look farther west, toward Texas and beyond the Rocky Mountains. The term *manifest destiny* expressed their belief that the country had an unquestionable right to expand to the Pacific Ocean. Events in the mid-1800's helped the United States fulfill this destiny.

504

American settlers had begun moving into Texas even before Mexico gained independence. Joining the American settlers were people from Germany and other European countries. This farm was built by a German family near La Grange, Texas.

Texas wins independence. Southern cotton planters began to look toward Texas as a source of more land. Texas was part of the huge area of Mexico, which had gained independence from Spain in 1821 (page 497). The Mexican government had allowed foreigners to settle in Texas, and by 1830, some 20,000 people from the United States, many of them slave owners, lived there. (Mexico had abolished slavery in 1824.) When it seemed that the Mexican population might soon be outnumbered, Mexico decided to halt immigration from the United States. Angered by the immigration ban and by the harsh rule of Mexico's new leader, General Santa Anna, Texans declared their independence on March 2, 1836, and soon after captured the city of San Antonio.

A few days later 5,000 Mexican soldiers, led by Santa Anna, attacked the Alamo, a fortified mission in San Antonio. Fewer than 200 Texans defended the mission, holding off wave after wave of Mexican troops. The Alamo fell, but only after the last defender was killed. "Remember the Alamo!" became the rallying cry of the Texans.

In April, Texas forces led by Sam Houston defeated the Mexicans and captured Santa Anna. The Mexican dictator signed a treaty granting Texas its independence.

War with Mexico expands the borders of the United States. The Mexican government refused to recognize the treaty signed by Santa Anna. It also insisted that the southern boundary of Texas was the Nueces (noo-AY-sus) River. The Texans, however, insisted that the boundary was the Rio Grande (map, page 503).

In 1845 the United States Congress voted to annex, or add to the nation's lands, the Republic of Texas. Mexico refused to negotiate with the United States over the disputed region between the two rivers. The following year President James Polk ordered United States troops into that region. When the Mexicans attacked a United States patrol near the Rio Grande, Polk told Congress that Mexican forces had "invaded our territory and shed American blood . . . upon American soil." In May, 1846, Congress declared war on Mexico.

The Mexican War lasted for almost two years. Mexico's forces were poorly trained and led, and its government was unstable. United States troops soon took over both New Mexico and California, possessions of Mexico. Santa Anna retreated as United States troops pushed south into Mexico by land and by water. One group of United States soldiers landed at Veracruz and fought their way inland to Mexico City, which they captured after a bitter fight.

The Treaty of Guadalupe Hidalgo (gwah-dah-LOO-pay ee-DAL-goh), signed in February, 1848, ended the war. More than half of Mexico's territory was transferred to the United States (map, page 503). With this additional territory, the United States had extended to the Pacific Ocean.

More land is added peacefully. The United States soon acquired two other areas — one by treaty and one by purchase. In June, 1846, a treaty between the United States and Britain settled a long-standing dispute. The treaty established the boundary between Canada and the Oregon Territory.

In 1853, Mexico sold the United States about 30,000 square miles of land in what are now the states of Arizona and New Mexico. With this acquisition, known as the Gadsden Purchase (map, page 503), the United States filled out its southern boundary.

The years of expansion see important social changes. By the mid-1800's the United States had expanded westward across the North American continent. This era of expansion brought with it other profound changes in American society.

Between 1820 and 1860, thousands came to the United States from Europe. The potato famine in Ireland (page 470), the failure of the revolutions of 1848 (page 473), and the availability of jobs and farmland in the United States were important reasons for the surge of immigration. Immigrants from England, Scotland, and Wales joined the thousands of Irish. From northern Europe came Germans seeking political freedom, and from Scandinavia came farmers who hoped to purchase western lands. American industry and agriculture prospered through the skill and hard work of these many immigrants.

With new territory and a growing population, the nation needed better transportation systems. In the early 1800's workers built hundreds of miles of canals to link the valleys of the Ohio and Mississippi rivers with the Great Lakes and the Atlantic coast. Along these water routes, canal boats carried manufactured goods to the West and raw materials and agricultural products to the East. Railroads also developed during this period. Thousands of miles of track were built between 1820 and 1850.

Political and educational changes accompany expansion. Territories that became states in the early 1800's generally allowed all white men to vote, unlike the older states which had property requirements for voting. The trend to end property requirements spread, and by 1840 almost all white men in the United States could vote.

The growing number of voters increased concern about education. Educators argued that a representative government needed well-informed voters and that tax money should be used to establish public schools. By 1860, public elementary schools were common in the North and West, and a few public high schools had also been started.

Thus, with new lands and people, better transportation, wider voting rights, and a public education system, the United States was a very different country in 1850 from what it had been in 1800.

CHECK-UP

1. Vocabulary: *neutral, protective tariff, manifest destiny.*
2. What factors helped to strengthen central government in the United States?
3. (a) Why did Jefferson offer to buy New Orleans from Napoleon? (b) Why did Napoleon sell Louisiana?
4. (a) What were the causes of the War of 1812? (b) How did the war help to strengthen national pride and economic independence?
5. (a) What was the Monroe Doctrine? (b) How did the European nations respond to it?
6. (a) How was Texas settled? (b) How did Texas become part of the United States? (c) What other territories did the United States acquire between 1846 and 1853?
7. (a) From which European countries did many people immigrate to the United States between 1820 and 1860? (b) What were some of the reasons these people came to the United States? (c) How did voting rights and educational opportunities expand during the first half of the nineteenth century?

4 The United States Survives the Civil War and Grows Stronger

Since 1789 the United States had been growing larger and stronger as a nation. By 1853 its lands reached from the Atlantic Ocean to the Pacific. The North was the nation's manufacturing region, its cities bustling centers of industry and trade. The South was largely an agricultural region, with rich farmlands. Beneath the prosperity, however, were severe problems. Disputes over the extension of slavery into new territories fueled a strong sense of sectionalism — extreme loyalty to one's own region of a nation. Eventually sectionalism erupted in a war that threatened to destroy the nation.

THE CIVIL WAR AND RECONSTRUCTION

Differences between North and South increase. There had been differences between the North and the South even before independence was gained. As the nation grew, these differences increased. Conflicts arising from these differences centered on three main issues — tariffs, states' rights, and the extension of slavery into new territories.

The North welcomed tariffs that protected its industries from foreign competition (page 504). The agricultural South opposed tariffs because they increased the prices of the manufactured goods it imported from Europe.

Another issue was states' rights — the principle that all powers not specifically given to the federal government by the Constitution belong to the individual states. By the mid-1800's, supporters of states' rights were mostly southerners, who saw states' rights as a way to stay in the union and still protect southern interests. These southerners argued that if the people of a state regarded a law passed by Congress as unconstitutional, the state could take steps to change the law. Those who believed in a strong Union, however, argued that the United States would break apart if every state had the right to decide whether a law passed by Congress was constitutional.

The debate over slavery leads to war. Another bitter problem was slavery. As well as being a moral issue, slavery presented important economic considerations. Some Americans insisted on **abolition** — the ending of slavery throughout the country. Most white southerners were enraged at this possibility. They believed that abolition would destroy their economy and their way of life.

Moreover, many white southerners insisted that slaves were property and that citizens had the right to take their property with them wherever they went. Southerners wanted to be able to take their slaves into the new territories. They insisted that when these territories entered the Union, it should be as slave states. This issue intensified the debate over slavery.

As the nation expanded westward and admitted new states, bitter struggles arose over whether or not these new states would allow slavery. The industrial North did not want to be outnumbered in Congress by the slave states, while the South wanted its interests to be supported in Congress by the new states. In addition, southern plantation owners sought new lands in the West as their own soil became exhausted by continued planting (page 504). From the 1820's through the 1850's, Congress tried to balance the interests of the North and the South through a series of compromises, but the debate continued.

In the midst of this debate, the Republican Party was formed on the pledge to end the spread of slavery. When its candidate, Abraham Lincoln, was elected President in 1860, southern states began to **secede** — that is, they formally withdrew from the Union. Soon seven states formed the Confederate States of America, with Jefferson Davis as their president.

President Lincoln did not want war, but he promised to "preserve, protect and defend" the Union. In April, 1861, Confederate forces fired on Fort Sumter, a federal fort in South Carolina. Recognizing that war had become inevitable, Lincoln called for 75,000 volunteers to defend the Union. The Civil War had begun.

A bitter war divides the nation. After war broke out, four more southern slave states

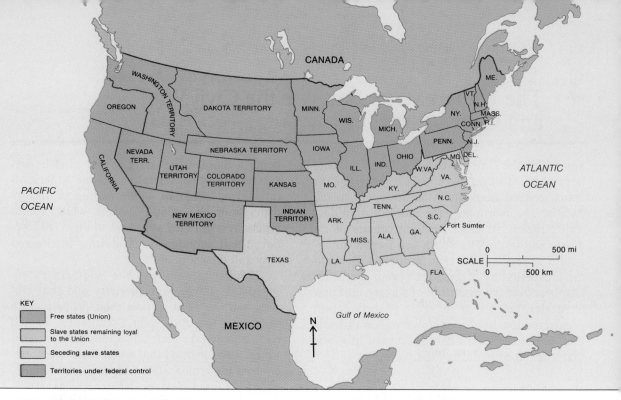

The United States Divided

Soon after Lincoln was elected President, seven states left the Union — South Carolina, Florida, Mississippi, Alabama, Georgia, Louisiana, and Texas. Later, Virginia, Arkansas, Tennessee, and North Carolina also joined the Confederacy. What slave states remained in the Union?

joined the seven states that made up the Confederacy. Twenty-three states remained loyal to the Union.

Each side had certain important advantages. With more people, factories, and railroads, the North was much better equipped for war than the South. The South's advantages, however, lay in its experienced and able officers and its high morale. Its soldiers felt they were defending their section's way of life.

Brilliantly commanded by General Robert E. Lee, the southern forces were victorious in several major battles early in the war, as northern troops tried without success to move through Virginia and capture the Confederate capital. In the long run, however, the Union followed a more successful strategy, blockading southern ports and keeping supplies from reaching Confederate troops. This crippled the South's war effort. In a series of battles Union troops gained control of the Mississippi River, dividing the Confederacy in two. Union forces then marched through Georgia and the Caro-

linas, devastating the land by tearing up railroads, destroying crops, and burning farms and towns. On April 9, 1865, after four years of bitter and costly struggle, the Confederacy surrendered.

The slaves are freed. One major effect of the war had been the freeing of large numbers of slaves. In 1863, President Lincoln had issued the Emancipation Proclamation, declaring the freedom of slaves in those parts of the country that were still fighting the United States. As northern troops occupied Confederate territory, many slaves left their owners. Some followed the Union armies; others set out on their own. Early in 1865, Congress proposed the Thirteenth Amendment, which was to abolish slavery. By the end of the year, the amendment had been ratified by the states and became part of the Constitution.

The South rebuilds. At the end of the Civil War, the South was in ruins. Four years of war had destroyed land and buildings. Most banks and insurance companies had been closed.

Stores had few goods to sell, and people had no money with which to buy goods. The money that had been issued by the Confederacy was worthless. Millions of dollars that had been invested in slaves were lost when they were freed.

Congress wanted to help the South rebuild. Members of Congress decided, however, that the southern states must show a changed attitude toward blacks in order to be readmitted to the Union. To ensure this, two additional constitutional amendments were approved in the years after the war. The Fourteenth Amendment granted full citizenship to black Americans, and the Fifteenth Amendment gave voting rights to black men.

From the beginning of the postwar period, known as Reconstruction, a debate had raged in Congress about how the southern states were to re-enter the Union. A group called the "radical Republicans," who favored harsh treatment of the South, won the debate. The Republican-controlled Congress divided the South into military districts and stationed troops throughout the South to protect state governments organized under the new system. Another purpose was to make sure that southerners complied with the three new amendments to the Constitution.

White southerners resented the Reconstruction period. Some formed secret groups and used violent methods to keep black men from voting and holding office.

The results of Reconstruction were mixed. By 1870 all of the former Confederate states had re-entered the Union. Reconstruction governments had improved education and had built housing, schools, roads, and railways. Such improvements helped revitalize the South's economy.

White southerners soon regained control of the state governments. Troops were withdrawn from the South by 1877, and northern leaders seemed to lose interest in Reconstruction. Some southerners had used violence to keep blacks from voting and holding office. Now southern states were able to pass laws aimed at depriving blacks of their newly won rights. Thus, while important rebuilding had been done, the old system of white dominance had not yet been ended.

POSTWAR EXPANSION

Farmers and ranchers benefit from expansion. The lands west of the Mississippi experienced a period of growth between 1865 and 1914. The discovery of gold in California in 1848 had spurred a great westward migration. Following the hopeful miners were ranchers who built a thriving cattle industry using equipment and methods first developed in Mexico. Another group of western settlers was made up of farmers lured by the Homestead Act. This act granted ownership of up to 160 acres after the settler had lived on the land and cultivated it for five years. The building of railroad lines to the Pacific, accomplished largely by Irish and Chinese immigrants, encouraged the westward movement.

Indians are moved to reservations. Farmers and ranchers came into conflict with the Indians and pushed them out of their traditional lands. White settlers were also slaughtering the herds of buffalo that supplied the Indians of the Great Plains with food, clothing, and shelter. In 1850 an estimated twelve million buffalo roamed the plains. By 1889 probably less than a thousand remained.

Faced with starvation and the loss of their lands, many Indians resisted white settlement. The United States army eventually ended the resistance of many Indian groups. By 1890 the United States government had moved most Indians to reservations — land that was set aside for them by the government — where they were expected to settle down and give up their hunting traditions.

Immigrants contribute labor and skills to the growing nation. Many of the immigrants who came to the United States at this time were from Southern and Eastern Europe — Italy, Austria-Hungary, Russia, and the Ottoman Empire. In 1870, immigrants from these areas had made up 5 percent of the immigration to the United States. By the early 1900's, 75 percent of the immigrants were from Southern and Eastern Europe. In addition to seeking a better life, many immigrants wanted to escape from discrimination. Russian Jews, victims of anti-Jewish policies, looked for freedom in the United States. Many Ukrainians, Lithuanians,

EXPANSION AFTER THE CIVIL WAR

Once the war ended, the nation resumed its expansion. Immigrants helped build railroads to carry settlers west. The crew in the photograph (above, right) worked on tracks that stretched from Lake Superior to the Pacific. Railroad posters (above, left) helped attract settlers to the West. Using new kinds of agricultural machinery, the settlers brought vast stretches of land under cultivation.

Poles, and Finns also came, seeking greater freedom and opportunity.

Most of the immigrants settled in the cities, where they took jobs in the expanding industries. The immigrants built communities that often preserved the atmosphere of their homelands. American cities came to include such areas as Little Italy or Germantown, where people could buy newspapers in their native language, obtain foods of their homeland, and participate in familiar religious services. At the same time, however, immigrants, and particularly their children, acquired American customs. They attended school, learned English, and made friends with people of many different backgrounds.

Standards of living improve. Gradually Americans, both immigrant and native-born, began to achieve a better standard of living. They saved their money, bought homes, and gave their children an education. Thousands became part of a growing middle class that the expanding economy had helped create. Middle-class communities arose in the suburbs outside the cities.

As population increased, school attendance also soared. By 1900, children in thirty states were required to attend public schools. The number of high schools jumped from 800 in 1880 to 5,500 in 1900, and increasing numbers of men and women attended college.

The rising standard of living and new laws limiting hours of work encouraged Americans to participate in many leisure activities. Cities took pride in their symphony orchestras, many of whose musicians were immigrants who had been trained in Europe. People in towns across America enjoyed band concerts, plays, and musical comedies. From the musical traditions of blacks came the beginnings of jazz.

Interest in sports also grew. People became avid fans of local baseball and football teams. Swimming and boating grew in popularity, and the invention of the bicycle turned people of all ages into cyclists.

Reformers' efforts are successful. During the late 1800's and early 1900's, organizations were established to help various groups improve their lives. The expanding economy had opened up jobs for women, for example, and increasing economic independence helped fuel a movement for women's rights. The National American Woman Suffrage Association was organized in 1869 (although it was not until 1920 that women throughout the nation were allowed to vote). In 1909, black leaders formed the National Association for the Advancement of Colored People (NAACP) in an effort to ensure the rights of black Americans.

Reformers were also able to win passage of a number of important laws. Many state and local laws, for example, tried to improve housing, education, and working conditions.

Further expansion is urged. As the United States grew stronger economically, its leaders continued to favor a policy of expansion. The rapid growth of industry created a need for markets for American manufactured goods and a need for raw materials. Moreover, several prominent Americans believed that expansion would demonstrate American power and greatness. It was the destiny of the United States, they argued, to become a great power, and this meant extending American influence to other lands and raising the American flag on distant shores.

The United States gains Alaska and Hawaii. In 1867, Secretary of State William H. Seward bought Alaska from Alexander II of Russia (page 489). Laughingly referred to as "Seward's Folly," Alaska added about 600,000 square miles to the United States. Far from being the "walrus-covered icebergs" that the critics claimed, it turned out to have immensely valuable resources of gold, coal, oil, timber, fish, and furs.

In the same year that Alaska was bought, the United States government took control of the Midway Islands. Located in the middle of the Pacific Ocean, the islands gave American ships a stopping place on the way to Asia. Another Pacific territory that interested Americans was the group of islands known as Hawaii. The United States established a naval base at Pearl Harbor in 1887.

A revolution in 1893, led by Americans living on the island, overthrew Hawaii's Queen Liliuokalani (lee-LEE-oo-oh-kah-LAH-nee) and set up a republic in 1894. President Grover Cleveland did not support the revolution, but five years later, when war broke out with Spain, the United States recognized Hawaii's strategic value and annexed the islands. The annexation met with little resistance, since American businessmen and sugar-plantation owners controlled the Hawaiian government.

The United States fights a war with Spain. War with Spain grew out of the American response to a revolt in Cuba (map, page 496). When Cuba declared its independence from Spain in 1895, the Spanish government used brutal methods to crush the revolution. Many people in the United States were sympathetic to the Cuban rebels and urged the United States to go to war with Spain. The American press also stirred up anti-Spanish feelings.

In February, 1898, the United States battleship *Maine,* which had been sent by the government to Cuba to protect American citizens and their property, blew up in Havana's har-

Theodore Roosevelt fought in Cuba during the Spanish-American War. As President, he followed a policy of active interest in Latin American affairs.

The United States acquires the Panama Canal Zone. United States influence in Latin America increased during the presidency of Theodore Roosevelt (1901–1908). The United States had long recognized the need for a canal to shorten the voyage between the Atlantic and the Pacific oceans. In 1902 the United States wanted to build a canal through the Isthmus (ISS-MUS) of Panama (map, page 496). However, the Isthmus belonged to Colombia, which would not agree to the plan. Soon a revolution, encouraged by President Roosevelt, broke out in Panama. Roosevelt sent American warships to Panama's coast to prevent Colombian troops from stopping the revolution. The United States quickly recognized the independence of the Republic of Panama, and the new nation granted the United States the land on which to build a canal. A zone ten miles wide across the country was given to the United States "in perpetuity," or forever.

Roosevelt's actions in obtaining the Panama Canal Zone were severely criticized both in the United States and in Latin America. He defended his move by saying that an interocean canal was in the interest of all the world's nations. Completed in 1914, the Panama Canal cut 8,000 miles from the trip between the Atlantic and Pacific oceans.

The United States strengthens its power in the Western Hemisphere. To protect the canal, the United States took an increasingly active role in the Caribbean. Roosevelt expanded the meaning of the Monroe Doctrine (page 504) to justify United States leadership in the Americas. The Roosevelt Corollary, as it was called, declared that the United States would intervene and manage the affairs of any Latin American country that could not keep order or pay its foreign debts. In 1907 the United States made the Dominican Republic a protectorate after European nations threatened to send warships to collect debts owed them by that Caribbean nation. Five years later the United States government sent marines into Nicaragua to prevent a revolution that threatened the property of United States citizens.

Many Latin Americans resented the growing influence and power of the United States. They felt their neighbor to the north had turned from a protector to an aggressor. By its

bor. The cause of the explosion was never discovered, but American newspapers were quick to blame Spain. Expansionists clamored for action. Congress decided that United States forces should help Cuba win its freedom. The United States declared war in April, 1898. The Spanish-American War lasted only four months. After important American victories in Cuba, Puerto Rico, and faraway Manila in the Philippines, Spain surrendered.

The United States used its victory to put an end to Spain's colonial rule in the Americas. Cuba won its independence but was ruled by United States military governments until 1909. In addition, the United States annexed Puerto Rico in the Caribbean and Guam (GWAHM) and the Philippines in the Pacific.

Many people in the United States opposed the acquisition of these new overseas territories. They argued that Americans themselves had fought for independence and should not rule other peoples. They pointed to an uprising against American troops in the Philippines as a sign that the people of those islands did not want American rule.

role in the Caribbean, however, the United States revealed its strength as a nation. In only a little more than a century it had grown from an infant republic to a major power in international affairs.

CHECK-UP

1. Vocabulary: *abolition, secede.*
2. (a) Why did the South secede from the Union? (b) What advantages did each side have at the beginning of the Civil War? (c) What military strategy helped the North win the war?
3. (a) What three amendments to the Constitution were adopted to protect the rights of black Americans? (b) Why did the policies of the "radical Republicans" arouse resentment among white southerners?
4. (a) From what countries did many people immigrate to the United States after the Civil War? (b) What were some of their reasons for coming to the United States? (c) What kinds of jobs did most of these immigrants take?
5. How did the United States acquire Alaska and Hawaii?
6. (a) What were the causes of the Spanish-American War? (b) What new territory did the United States acquire as a result of the war?
7. (a) How did the United States gain the territory through which the Panama Canal was built? (b) What was the purpose of building the canal? (c) What role did the United States take in Latin America after the Panama Canal was built?

---

5 Canada Becomes a Nation

The first settlers of the country known today as Canada were Indians and Eskimos (Chapter 14). Starting in the Age of Exploration, however, people of two European cultures, British and French, settled in Canada. The British set up trading posts around Hudson Bay. The French settled the valley of the St. Lawrence River and pushed inland to the Great Lakes and the Mississippi Valley to carry on a thriving fur trade (page 361). Despite a history of conflict between these two peoples, Canada gradually developed as a nation.

Britain takes over New France. The Treaty of Paris, signed in 1763, ended the French and Indian War between Britain and France (page 428). With the treaty, France ceded its North American colony of New France to the victorious British. Most of eastern North America was now in the hands of Britain, which already controlled Hudson Bay, Nova Scotia, and Newfoundland, in addition to the Thirteen Colonies to the south.[5] The treaty reduced France's North American possessions to two small islands off the coast of Newfoundland.

Early plans for self-government offer no voice to French-speaking colonists. At first, the British hoped to rule their new colony, renamed the Province of Quebec, just as they did their other North American possessions. They planned for local laws to be made by colonists in a representative legislature while overall policies would be set by the British Parliament. Catholics, however, could not vote or hold government offices under British law. About 70,000 French-speaking Catholics lived in the colony. Self-government in Quebec would have placed these French-speaking colonists under the political control of a few British merchants. Even the first two British military governors of Quebec opposed this plan. They believed it would intensify conflicts between French-speaking and English-speaking colonists.

The Quebec Act grants rights to the French. Plans to lure English-speaking colonists to Quebec from the Thirteen Colonies were unsuccessful. The colonists to the south were simply not attracted to Quebec's long, harsh winters. By 1774 the British had given up plans to absorb Quebec's French people into a larger English-speaking population.

With the colonies to the south nearing rebellion, peace in Quebec was increasingly

---

[5]Spain, at that time, claimed much of the land west of the Mississippi River, while Russia claimed Alaska.

The Growth of Canada

In 1791 the British Parliament divided Canada into Upper Canada and Lower Canada, as shown in the inset map. Through the years Canada has grown to include ten provinces and two territories. (Years in parentheses show the dates of formation.)

desirable. Parliament therefore passed the Quebec Act of 1774 to establish a permanent government that would guarantee the rights of the French.

The Quebec Act was an effort to treat the French-speaking colonists with fairness and justice. It guaranteed freedom of religion for Catholics and maintained the French pattern of landowning. The act recognized that the French settlers had a history and traditions of their own. The Quebec Act also set up rule by a governor and a council that included both French and English members. These officials were appointed by the British Crown. Though criminals were tried according to English law, French law was used to settle civil disputes. The government, moreover, was required to aid the Catholic Church in collecting taxes.

The American Revolution drives many English-speaking settlers northward. After the

American Revolution broke out (page 431), the Americans failed to get the support of the colonists in Quebec. British merchants in Quebec thought they would be better off if they kept their trade ties with Britain. The French feared that the rights granted by the Quebec Act would not be recognized by the Americans. When the rebelling colonists tried unsuccessfully to capture the city of Quebec, anti-American feelings grew stronger.

Thousands of Loyalists — colonists who remained loyal to the British Crown — sought refuge in Quebec. Some 30,000 Loyalists settled in Nova Scotia and other British territories along the Atlantic coast, a region where few French lived. An additional 10,000 Loyalists entered Quebec, although they were not welcomed by the French.

The British adopt a "divide and rule" policy. After the loss of the Thirteen Colonies, the

British were determined to hold on to what was left of their North American empire. In 1791 Parliament decided to divide the Province of Quebec into two new colonies. The region west of the Ottawa River, which included land along the Great Lakes and the upper St. Lawrence River, was named Upper Canada. In this area (later called Ontario) the population was largely English-speaking. The French settlements northeast of the Ottawa River were called Lower Canada (later renamed Quebec). Each colony was given its own governor, sent from Britain, who chose the executive and legislative councils. The colonists were allowed to elect members of the provincial assembly, but the assembly had only limited powers.

Both French and British Canadians were content to live in peace under a government that provided law and order. The French in Lower Canada soon learned to use their representatives to safeguard their own way of life. The English-speaking people of Upper Canada, alarmed when the United States began to push westward, saw loyalty to Britain as their key to survival.

Ties with Britain are tested. Canadian loyalty to Britain was tested in the War of 1812. The Canadians supported the British and successfully fought off American efforts to seize Canada. This helped strengthen Canadian unity and ties with Britain.

Though loyalty to the British continued after the War of 1812, Canadians began to question the manner in which they were ruled. Settlers, many of them immigrants, were moving into the Canadian west. Population in the older parts of Canada was increasing. Between 1815 and 1850 one-half million immigrants, mainly from the British Isles, arrived in Canada. Many sought political freedom as well as economic opportunity. Canadians began doubting the wisdom of being ruled by distant London.

Lord Durham recommends self-government. In 1837 and 1838, two rebellions took place — one in Upper Canada, the other in Lower Canada. Rebel leaders in both colonies demanded self-government. Though the rebellions were easily put down, lawmakers in Great Britain decided to take a closer look at conditions in Canada. They sent a statesman, Lord Durham, to investigate conditions there.

Durham's report, issued in 1839, recommended two major reforms. Durham suggested uniting Upper and Lower Canada and encouraging British immigration so that the English-speaking population would absorb the French. Despite the failure of a similar plan in the past, Durham believed that the French-Canadian language and customs could be made to disappear.

Durham's second recommendation reflected Britain's experiences in trying to govern the Thirteen Colonies. It was foolish, he argued, for officials in London to involve themselves in matters that had importance only for the colonists. In local affairs, the colonists ought to govern themselves. London officials

TIMETABLE

Nation-Building in North America

1763	The Treaty of Paris gives New France to Britain.
1783	The United States becomes independent.
1788	The Constitution of the United States is ratified.
1791	The British Parliament establishes Upper Canada and Lower Canada.
1803	The United States purchases the Louisiana Territory from France.
1812–1814	The United States and Britain fight the War of 1812.
1823	The Monroe Doctrine closes the Americas to European colonization.
1836	Texas declares its independence from Mexico.
1840	The Union Act of Parliament reunites Upper and Lower Canada.
1845	The United States annexes the Republic of Texas.
1848	The Treaty of Guadalupe Hidalgo ends the Mexican War.
1861–1865	The Civil War divides the United States.
1867	Canada becomes a Dominion.
1898	The United States annexes the Hawaiian Islands. The Spanish-American War ends Spanish colonial rule in the Americas. The United States annexes Puerto Rico, Guam, and the Philippines.

need be concerned, he said, only with Canada's foreign affairs, its trade with other countries, and the disposal of land belonging to the Crown.

Lord Durham's second recommendation shocked leaders in Britain. They could not see how a colony could be governed properly if its governor was responsible to a local assembly rather than to the authorities in Great Britain. They were willing, however, to try out Durham's first recommendation. The Union Act of 1840 reunited Upper and Lower Canada under a single legislature. French was no longer recognized as an official language. The British soon realized, though, that the Union Act was a failure. Increased conflict between French-speaking and English-speaking Canadians made governing the country impossible.

Self-government and union gain support. The British government gradually moved toward accepting Lord Durham's second recommendation. Starting in 1846, Parliament began to allow the colonists more self-government. Lord Durham's prediction that self-government would ensure Canadian loyalty to Britain proved correct.

Even with self-government, however, problems remained. In the legislature, French-Canadians and English-Canadians continued to argue bitterly, each in defense of their own group's interests. In addition, the increasing power of their neighbor to the south made both groups uneasy. Expansionists in the United States once again were calling for the takeover of Britain's North American empire.

It seemed clear that Canada needed a stronger government to maintain its national unity. Some Canadians suggested that they adopt a federal system of government like that of the United States. In a federal system, power is shared between the central government and the state governments (page 436). Canada, however, had problems not faced by the United States, in particular the strong economic and cultural differences between the French-Canadians and English-Canadians. Also, distances between settled areas in Canada were great and, compared with the United States, the population was small. For a union to succeed, then, it had to allow considerable local government. The best solution for Canada seemed to be a confederation, a union of self-governing provinces. This would provide a central government to handle problems that were truly national in scope. At the same time, confederation would permit each province to have a major voice in its own affairs.

A nation is born. In 1864, representatives from all over Canada held a series of conferences to draw up plans for a confederation. Under the leadership of John A. Macdonald, a brilliant politician who was to become the new nation's first leader, the "Fathers of Confederation" worked out the framework of a new national government. The proposed constitution, called the British North America Act, was approved by Britain's Parliament early in 1867 and went into effect on July 1 — the day Canada has celebrated ever since as its national birthday.

The British North America Act made Canada a Dominion — a self-governing nation of what was then the British Empire.[6] The name Canada, an Iroquois word meaning "village," was given to the entire country. The British monarch was the head of state and was represented in Canada by a governor-general. At first this official had considerable authority, but the office declined in importance as Canada's House of Commons gained power. The prime minister, who was the leader of the majority party in the Canadian House of Commons, was to be the nation's chief executive. Both French and English were the nation's official languages. The city of Ottawa became Canada's capital.

The Dominion of Canada originally included the provinces of Ontario, Quebec, Nova Scotia, and New Brunswick; but soon new territories were added. Between 1870 and 1873 the provinces of Manitoba, British Columbia, and Prince Edward Island entered the Dominion. Alberta and Saskatchewan became part of Canada in 1905. After Newfoundland entered the confederation in 1949, Canada had ten self-governing provinces. The nation also possessed two northern territories (the Yukon and the Northwest Territories) which were under the control of Canada's central government.

---

[6] Britain retained control of Canada's foreign affairs and trade until 1931 (Chapter 31).

Lumbering has long been important to Canada's economy. The above water-color painting shows a Vancouver logging camp in the late 1800's.

The struggle for unity continues. The leaders of the new nation realized that a good transportation system was necessary to unite the different parts of their vast nation. Thus, they supported the building of a transcontinental railroad. The completion of the Canadian Pacific Railway in 1885 tied together the provinces, encouraging settlement and development of their resources.

There were still obstacles to unity, however. Economic development was slow, and hard times in the early 1890's caused many people to leave Canada. Mutual distrust continued to divide English- and French-speaking Canadians. The *metis* (may-TEE) were a French-speaking people of mixed French and Indian descent. Twice the *metis* rebelled over disputed western land claims. After the second rebellion, Louis Riel (ree-EL), the *metis* leader, was hanged for treason in 1885. This created deep resentment among French Canadians who saw Riel as a national hero.

Despite such problems, Canada experienced considerable growth. In 1896 the election of Wilfred Laurier (LAW-ree-ay), the first French Canadian prime minister, helped unite the nation. After 1896 immigration from Europe and the United States increased Canada's population. Drawn by free land, many of the newcomers settled on the Canadian prairies,

where they grew wheat and other grains. Other immigrants found work in lumbering, railroad construction, mining, and manufacturing. British and American investments stimulated the growth of Canada's industries. It was apparent that Canada had rich resources that had only begun to be developed. By the early 1900's, the nation's future seemed bright.

CHECK-UP

1. (a) How did the British first hope to rule Quebec? (b) Why did the governors of Quebec resist the early proposals for self-government?
2. (a) Why did the British hope to attract settlers from the Thirteen Colonies to Quebec? (b) Why did their plan fail?
3. (a) Why did Parliament pass the Quebec Act? (b) What were its provisions? (c) Why did the people of Quebec refuse to join the Thirteen Colonies in fighting for independence?
4. (a) Why did the War of 1812 strengthen British-Canadian ties? (b) How did Canadian attitudes toward British rule change after the war?
5. (a) What recommendations were made in the Durham report? (b) How did Parliament respond?
6. (a) Why did Canada choose to become a confederation? (b) What were the provisions of the British North America Act? (c) What obstacles to unity remained?

Chapter 23 Review

Summary

Independence movements spread rapidly through Latin America. Between 1804 and 1824, revolutions overthrew European-controlled governments in virtually all Latin American countries. Nation-building, however, progressed slowly in Latin America, as harsh dictators known as caudillos took control of most countries. Successful caudillos were able to maintain order and strengthen their nations' economies.

The United States, under a strong national government, expanded and grew more powerful in the nineteenth century. National unity and economic independence increased after the United States fought the War of 1812. The new nation's strength was affirmed, moreover, by the Monroe Doctrine — a policy which declared the Western Hemisphere closed to colonization. By midcentury the nation's territory had extended to the Pacific. Growth was accompanied by increased immigration, improved transportation, and expanded voting rights and education.

The Civil War (1861–1865) was a critical challenge to national unity. With the North's victory, slavery was ended and former slaves became citizens. The war's end also signaled a new period of expansion, as farmers and ranchers moved west of the Mississippi, and immigrants arrived in growing numbers. During this period, the United States established itself as the dominant power in the Western Hemisphere.

North of the United States, Britain tried various methods of governing the French-speaking colonists of New France. The American Revolution sent an influx of English-speaking Loyalists to the region. Thus, two colonies took shape — one French-speaking, the other English-speaking. The colonists remained loyal to Britain during the War of 1812, but soon began to seek independence. Limited self-rule did not satisfy the colonists' needs for a strong government. In 1867, Canada was granted self-government.

Vocabulary Review

1. Match the following words with the listed definitions: *abolition, manifest destiny, neutral, protective tariff, secede.*

(a) To withdraw formally from an alliance, organization, or association.
(b) A tax on goods imported from a foreign country.
(c) The nineteenth-century belief that the United States had the right and duty to expand westward to the Pacific Ocean.
(d) The termination of slavery.
(e) Not supporting or assisting either side in a war or dispute.

2. In the items below, explain the importance of each term listed to the history of the region or country named.

(a) *Latin America:* Great Colombia, caudillo, Monroe Doctrine, Roosevelt Corollary.
(b) *United States:* Louisiana Territory, Treaty of Guadalupe Hidalgo, Homestead Act, the Alaska purchase.
(c) *Canada:* Union Act of 1840, British North America Act, Canadian Pacific Railway.

People to Identify

Match the following people with the numbered phrases that describe them: *José de San Martín, John Marshall, Santa Anna, Miguel Hidalgo, Thomas Jefferson, Benito Juárez, Diego Portales, Lord Durham.*

1. The leader of the fight for independence in Argentina.
2. The British statesman who recommended that Canada be given self-government.
3. The priest who started the Mexican independence movement in 1810.
4. The President who bought the Louisiana Territory for the United States from the French emperor Napoleon.
5. The Mexican general who led the battle against the Texans at the Alamo.
6. The caudillo who made Chile strong.
7. The American who established the Supreme Court's power of judicial review.
8. The president of Mexico in the 1860's.

Relating Geography and History

1. Locating places. Locate each of the items in the next column on a map in this chapter:

(a) Boyacá
(b) Santiago
(c) Ayacucho
(d) Dolores
(e) Lima
(f) Quebec
(g) Ottawa
(h) Ontario
(i) Fort Sumter
(j) Mexico City
(k) Rio de Janeiro
(l) Atacama Desert
(m) Buenos Aires
(n) Haiti

2. Making maps. Make a map showing the territories acquired by the United States between 1803 and 1867. Include with your map a key indicating how each gain in territory was made. Use the map on page 503 as a reference. (Also see page 511.)

Discussion Questions

1. What similarities and differences were there in the experiences of Toussaint L'Ouverture, Bolívar, and San Martín in bringing independence to Latin American countries?

2. (a) Why did the revolutions led by Hidalgo and Morelos in Mexico fail? (b) How was independence finally achieved in Mexico? (c) How was France able to take over Mexico in the 1860's? (d) What factors contributed to France's withdrawal?

3. (a) Why was national unity slow to develop in Latin American nations? (b) What factors contributed to the development of strong central government in the United States?

4. What were the positive and negative effects of rule by each of the following caudillos: (a) Diego Portales of Chile? (b) Juan Manuel de Rosas of Argentina? (c) Porfirio Díaz of Mexico?

5. What was the significance of each of the following conflicts for the development of the United States: (a) the War of 1812? (b) the Mexican War? (c) the Civil War? (d) the Spanish-American War?

6. How did the views of northerners and southerners differ on each of the following issues in the years before the American Civil War: (a) tariffs? (b) states' rights? (c) slavery?

7. (a) Why was it necessary for Britain to govern Quebec differently from its other North American possessions? (b) What provisions of the Quebec Act of 1774 represented a change in policy for the British government? (c) Why were settlers in Quebec loyal to Britain after war broke out in the Thirteen Colonies?

8. (a) What obstacles to national unity did Canada face in the first half of the nineteenth century? (b) How did the British North America Act attempt to solve some of these problems?

Reading Primary Sources

The following passage is from a speech made by Simón Bolívar to a congress that met to prepare a new constitution for Venezuela in 1819. Read the passage. Then answer the questions that follow.

> The most perfect system of government is that which produces the greatest possible sum of happiness, social security, and political stability. . . . [It] must be republican, based on the sovereignty of the people, [including] the division of power, civil liberty, the outlawing of slavery, and the abolition of monarchy and privilege. . . .
>
> In order to form a stable government, you must have the foundation of a national spirit. . . . We [must] mold all the people into one whole, . . . [our laws] into one whole, and [the] national spirit into one whole. Unity . . . must be our motto.

(a) According to Bolívar, what should be the goals of a good system of government? (b) What does Bolívar mean when he says that government should be "based on the sovereignty of the people"? (c) What policy does Bolívar recommend on slavery? (d) What does he think is the most important factor for stable government?

Skill Activities

1. Supporting main ideas. For each of the main ideas below, find two or three supporting statements in the chapter you have just read:
(a) The creoles played an important part in the fight for Latin American independence.
(b) The United States' influence in Latin America increased during the administration of Theodore Roosevelt.
(c) Canada's form of government was different from that of the United States.

2. Reports. Find information about one of the following topics and prepare a report: (a) Toussaint L'Ouverture; (b) Simón Bolívar; (c) the Louisiana Purchase; (d) the gold rush of 1849; (e) the United States' purchase of Alaska; (f) the Panama Canal; (g) Dominion Day (Canada's national holiday); (h) the acquisition of Hawaii.

Factories in Clichy, a town near Paris, were the subject of this picture painted in 1887 by the Dutch artist Vincent van Gogh.

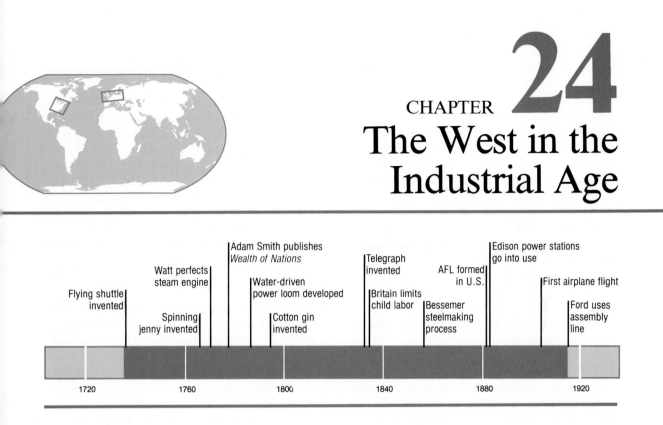

The West in the Industrial Age

Timeline entries:

- Flying shuttle invented
- Watt perfects steam engine
- Spinning jenny invented
- Adam Smith publishes *Wealth of Nations*
- Water-driven power loom developed
- Cotton gin invented
- Telegraph invented
- Britain limits child labor
- Bessemer steelmaking process
- AFL formed in U.S.
- Edison power stations go into use
- First airplane flight
- Ford uses assembly line

Timeline scale: 1720 · 1760 · 1800 · 1840 · 1880 · 1920

In the last part of the eighteenth century, a wave of political and social revolutions began in France and swept across Europe. During this same period, an economic revolution — a revolution in industry — was transforming life in Great Britain. In the nineteenth century these changes in industry spread to other parts of Europe and to the United States. Once started, the process of industrialization moved faster and faster and dramatically altered the way people lived.

Despite the problems created by rapid industrialization, the Industrial Revolution was a triumph. It allowed people to alter their physical environment, made possible the highest standard of living yet known, and speeded up social and political reforms.

This chapter traces the spread of industrialization and describes the social, political, and economic changes that came about in response to the Industrial Revolution.

CHAPTER OUTLINE

1 The Industrial Revolution Takes Shape

2 Industrialization Changes Working and Living Conditions

3 New Economic Theories Develop

4 Reformers Respond to Economic and Social Problems

5 Industrialization Brings Political Change

1　The Industrial Revolution Takes Shape

During the eighteenth century, the way goods were produced and the way labor was organized changed radically in Western nations. Machines were invented to do the work formerly done by men and women. New forms of power, particularly steam, replaced animal strength and human muscle. Better ways were found to obtain and use raw materials. A new production system — the making of goods in factories — came into use. All these changes together made it possible to produce more goods at lower cost. Because society was so completely transformed, these changes are referred to as the Industrial Revolution.

Changes begin in Great Britain. The Industrial Revolution began in Great Britain about 1750 because of a combination of conditions that existed in that country.

1. Labor supply. Britain had an abundant supply of labor. Workers were available as a result of changes that had taken place in agriculture.

2. Natural resources. Britain had large resources of coal and iron ore. From its colonies Britain obtained other resources, particularly cotton to use in the textile industry.

3. Investment capital. Britain had capital available for investing in new industries. Funds came from wealthy landowners and from merchants who had grown rich through trade. Interest rates on loans fell in the eighteenth century, thus encouraging investment.

4. Entrepreneurs. Britain had energetic and daring *entrepreneurs* (ahn-truh-preh-NURZ) — people who organized and managed businesses. These entrepreneurs built factories, found effective ways to organize the production of goods, and located new markets.

5. Transportation. Britain had many fine harbors as well as an extensive canal system. It was far cheaper to transport heavy goods by water than by land. This efficient system of transportation made it easy to carry raw materials to factories and goods to markets.

6. Markets. Great Britain and its colonies overseas provided a good market for the sale of manufactured goods. The nation had a long tradition of trade by sea, and it also had a fleet of merchant ships that could transport goods to other countries and bring back raw materials.

The British government was also a factor in creating conditions favorable to industrialization. It aided commercial interests and factory owners by passing laws that protected businesses and helped them to expand.

Advances are made in agriculture. A revolution in agriculture had paved the way for the Industrial Revolution. Increased farm production made it possible to feed a growing population, and money that had formerly been used to import food could be invested in British industries or in imports of needed raw materials.

New farming methods were devised in the eighteenth century, resulting in larger and better harvests. About 1701, Jethro Tull invented a mechanical drill that made holes in the soil and dropped seeds into them. He also invented a horse-drawn hoe, which broke up and loosened the soil so that plants could grow better. Robert Bakewell set up scientific breeding programs that produced cattle with more meat, sheep with finer wool, and cows with better milk.

In the early 1700's, Charles Townshend, an English statesman, experimented with crop rotation — the practice of alternating crops grown in a field from year to year. Townshend found that clover was effective in restoring soil fertility. He also taught farmers to grow turnips, which could be stored to feed livestock during the winter. Before this time, much livestock had to be slaughtered in the fall because not enough food was available for the animals during the winter.

Lands are enclosed. Knowledge of these new farming methods spread slowly at first. Most farmers had neither the money nor the desire to experiment with them. During the eighteenth century, however, owners of large estates were adding to their lands by buying out small farmers. They were also "enclosing," or fencing in, lands that all people in a village had previously been allowed to use. After 1760,

Parliament encouraged the enclosure movement, as it was called. Wealthy landowners used the new agricultural methods on these additional acres, and farm production soared. On the other hand, poor villagers who had depended upon village lands for raising crops or for pasture lost their means of making a living. Forced out of their cottages, they became beggars or farm laborers or moved to towns and cities.

Inventions change the textile industry. New textile factories provided jobs for some displaced farm workers. Textile-making was the first British industry to be drastically changed by the Industrial Revolution. Before this time, textile workers labored in their own homes and owned or rented the tools they used. Merchants purchased raw materials and distributed them among workers who lived in cottages on farms or in villages. Some workers spun fibers into yarn, and others wove yarn into cloth. This method of production was called the ***domestic system,*** or cottage industry.

In the eighteenth century a number of inventions increased the speed of spinning yarn and weaving cloth. In 1733 John Kay invented a flying shuttle that speeded up the weaving of cloth. One weaver could now use all the thread several spinners could produce. An invention that James Hargreaves perfected in the 1760's then made it possible for spinners to turn out thread more quickly. Hargreaves' "spinning jenny" contained a series of spindles that were turned by a single spinning wheel.

Both the flying shuttle and the spinning jenny were operated with human power, but inventors soon found ways to use water power to run textile machines. Richard Arkwright's water frame, invented in 1769, used water power to run a spinning machine. In 1785 Edmund Cartwright invented a loom that was run by water power.

The new textile machines could turn out such quantities of thread and cloth that manufacturers needed greater supplies of raw materials, particularly cotton fiber. The problem was solved by an American named Eli Whitney. In 1793 he invented a device called the cotton gin. It provided cotton growers with an efficient way of removing seeds from the fibers.

The factory system develops. The new machines not only speeded up the output of thread and cloth but also changed the basic system of production. The machines were too expensive to be owned by individual workers and too large to be set up in farmhouses and cottages. Water power was also needed to operate the machines. For these reasons, the ***factory system*** developed. Machines were set up in buildings located near rivers that could supply water power. Large numbers of workers were brought together to operate the machines. Managers began to use division of labor — that is, each worker performed a single set task or a single step in making a product. All these changes allowed the factory system to produce more goods more quickly, efficiently, and cheaply than the domestic system.

Iron-making processes change. As more machines were used in factories, more iron was needed to build them. Eli Whitney, in manufacturing guns, had devised a way to use standard interchangeable parts in the assembling of machines and tools. This speeded up the making of machinery and increased still more the demand for iron. In the first half of the eighteenth century, however, the British iron-making industry was facing serious problems. The iron ore mined in Britain had many impurities that marred the quality of the finished product. The furnaces that smelted the ore were fueled by charcoal, which was obtained by burning wood. This resource was limited because Britain lacked vast forests.

New methods of production soon revolutionized the iron industry. A breakthrough came in 1744 when Henry Cort devised the puddling process. Cort's method used coal, which was cheaper and more plentiful than charcoal. The puddling process produced iron of better quality. Also, it produced iron fifteen times faster than the older system.

In the 1850's, a quick and inexpensive process was devised for changing iron into steel. Working independently, both William Kelly, an American ironmaster, and Sir Henry Bessemer, an English engineer, discovered this process. Because steel was more durable than iron, it soon came to be used in most heavy equipment.

Landmarks in Technology

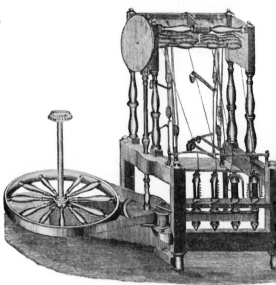

ADVANCES IN THE TEXTILE INDUSTRY

The technological innovations that brought about the Industrial Revolution were first used in English textile factories. During the late 1700's, new machines increased the output of thread and yarn, wove cloth at a rapid rate, printed colored patterns on the cloth, and improved the overall quality of fabrics. The textile manufacturers installed the new machines in large buildings located near sources of water power and hired workers to operate them. Textile mills soon appeared throughout Britain and eventually in the United States, and other industries quickly adopted the factory system.

The water frame (above right) was a water-powered machine that spun cotton thread much faster than traditional spinning wheels. Textile printing machines (below) could print up to six colors on fabrics. Dyes were applied as the cloth passed between rollers onto which patterns had been engraved.

Textile machinery underwent constant improvement. In the English factory shown at right, each machine, controlled by a single worker, twisted cotton fibers into thread on 900 spindles. The British tried to keep knowledge of the new textile technology from spreading to other countries. The label below, showing machinery in a Lowell, Massachusetts, textile mill, makes clear, however, that the British effort to monopolize the new machines failed.

A huge increase in output created the need for better ways to transport raw materials to factories and finished textiles to markets. This 1828 engraving of the Regent's Canal in England (below) shows barges loaded with cargoes of cloth.

Steam engines revolutionize industry and transportation. As the Industrial Revolution gained speed, new sources of power were needed. In 1769 James Watt, a Scottish engineer, developed a practical steam engine. Steam had been used as a source of power since the early 1700's, but Watt's engine was the first to use steam efficiently. In time, all industries came to depend on steam engines. The new engines provided cheap power for coal mines, ironworks, textile plants, and, later, railways and steamships.

As machines speeded up factory production, methods of transporting raw materials and finished products also improved. In 1830 the first railway line was built, connecting the English cities of Manchester and Liverpool. This triggered an age of railway building throughout the world. Railways provided fast, cheap transportation. As transportation costs fell, manufacturers were able to reduce the prices of their goods, and more people were able to buy them.

Science and technology continue to bring changes. Technology in the nineteenth century moved from triumph to triumph. Many of its advances came from the findings of scientists working in research laboratories. Their curiosity resulted in discoveries that had widespread practical uses.

Scientists in many countries were exploring the mysterious force called electricity. About 1800, Alessandro Volta, an Italian professor of physics, invented the first electric battery. This enabled scientists to make electricity and study it under laboratory conditions. In 1831, Michael Faraday, an English physicist and chemist, produced electricity by moving a magnet through a coil of copper wire. Faraday's discovery led to the invention of the electric generator, or dynamo, which produces a current that can run machines. With the use of generators, a new source of power became available for factories. Another English physicist, James Clerk Maxwell, predicted the existence of invisible electromagnetic waves. In 1887 Heinrich Hertz of Germany discovered a way to send, receive, and measure these waves.

The discoveries about electricity were used in remarkable new ways of communication. In the 1830's Samuel F. B. Morse, an American, invented the telegraph. Messages spelled in a code of "dots" and "dashes" could be sent by electricity carried through wires. Within a few decades telegraph lines crossed lands and seas, making communication among countries much faster and easier. In 1876, Alexander Graham Bell, a British-born American professor, patented the telephone, which also used electricity. In 1895, Guglielmo Marconi, an Italian inventor, sent the first "wireless" message. His instrument used the electromagnetic, or radio, waves discovered by Maxwell and Hertz.

The harnessing of electricity not only speeded up communication but also revolutionized people's daily lives. The American inventor Thomas Alva Edison found hundreds of practical uses for electricity, among them the light bulb and the phonograph. In 1882, power stations designed by Edison were put into operation in London and New York. Electric light soon replaced gas globes and kerosene lanterns on city streets and in buildings.

Striking advances also occurred in transportation. In the 1880's the German engineers Karl Benz and Gottlieb Daimler pioneered in the development of the internal-combustion engine. They produced engines small enough to use in early automobiles. An engine designed in the 1890's by Rudolf Diesel, a German engineer, improved railroad and ship transportation. In the United States, about 1914, Henry Ford devised a moving assembly line on which automobiles could be put together by workers using interchangeable parts. Inventors also applied the internal-combustion engine to flying machines. In 1903, two Ohio brothers, Orville and Wilbur Wright, made the first successful motor-powered airplane flight over the sand dunes of a North Carolina beach.

The Industrial Revolution spreads to other countries. In the early years of the Industrial Revolution, Great Britain had attempted to keep other nations from learning about the new inventions and processes. This effort failed. The Industrial Revolution soon spread throughout the Western world. By the late 1800's the United States and Germany rivaled Great Britain as leading industrial nations.

Advances in technology, combined with abundant natural resources of coal, iron ore,

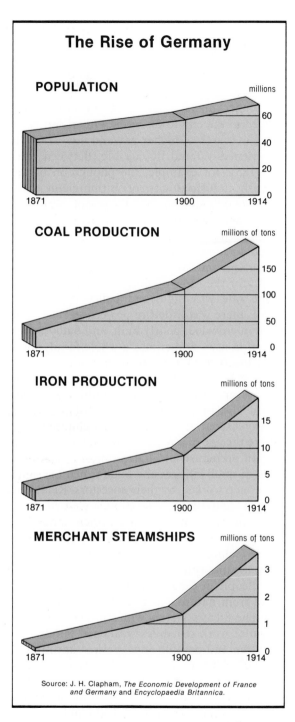

The Rise of Germany

POPULATION

millions

1871   1900   1914

60
40
20
0

COAL PRODUCTION

millions of tons

1871   1900   1914

150
100
50
0

IRON PRODUCTION

millions of tons

1871   1900   1914

15
10
5
0

MERCHANT STEAMSHIPS

millions of tons

1871   1900   1914

3
2
1
0

Source: J. H. Clapham, *The Economic Development of France and Germany* and *Encyclopaedia Britannica.*

Following its unification in 1871 (page 484), Germany began a period of rapid growth, soon becoming a major European power both economically and politically. The graphs show four of the factors that contributed to the rise of Germany. Why was each factor important? What relationships can you see among these factors?

oil, and lumber, spurred industrial growth in the United States (page 511). Tens of thousands of miles of railway tracks were built, mainly by Irish and Asian immigrants. Railroads carried raw materials to factories and manufactured goods to markets. Population growth was another factor in the industrial growth of the United States. From 1860 to 1900 the population increased from 31 million to 76 million.

Late in the nineteenth century, Germany was transformed from a basically agricultural nation into one of the world's industrial powers. The population grew from about 41 million to 56 million in 1900 and close to 70 million by 1914. Coal and iron production meanwhile increased at a remarkable rate. (See the graphs.) By the turn of the century Germany was producing more steel than Britain. Aided by the skill of its scientists and inventors, Germany became a leader in the chemical and electrical industries. It built an extensive and efficient network of railroads, a merchant marine that rivaled Britain's, and an armaments industry second to none. A tremendous increase in Germany's foreign trade accompanied this industrial expansion.

CHECK-UP

1. Vocabulary: *entrepreneur, domestic system, factory system.*
2. What conditions paved the way for industrialization in Britain?
3. (a) What advances in agriculture were made in England during the eighteenth century? (b) What was the enclosure movement? (c) What were the consequences of that movement for village populations?
4. (a) What inventions brought great changes in the British textile industry? (b) Why did the factory system develop?
5. What technological advances were made during the Industrial Revolution in each of the following fields: (a) iron and steel production? (b) communications? (c) the use of steam power?
6. (a) What changes resulted from discoveries about electricity? (b) from the invention of the internal-combustion engine?
7. (a) What factors spurred industrialization in the United States? (b) How did industrialization affect Germany?

2 Industrialization Changes Working and Living Conditions

The Industrial Revolution ultimately improved standards of living and created many opportunities for more and more people. Particularly in the early years, however, rapid industrialization and urbanization caused severe problems. These were most serious for workers in the new factories and for the growing numbers of poor city dwellers.

Factory workers face hardships. The factory system produced goods efficiently but was a hard way of life for most workers. Wages were generally low, and employment was never secure. Sick workers received no pay and were often fired. Elderly workers had their pay cut or lost their jobs. During business slumps employers lowered wages and laid off workers. Sometimes they replaced men workers with women and children, who were paid lower wages.

Because many factory owners did not consider safety an important concern, there were frequent accidents. Poor lighting, dirt, noise from machinery, and smoke and fumes further endangered the workers' health.

Factory work was often dull and repetitive. Workers were subject to the strict discipline of the clock, the machine, and the production schedule. They could not work at their own pace or rest when tired. If they did not keep up, they were fined or fired.

Before the rise of the factory system, children had labored long hours on farms and in cottage workshops. During the Industrial Revolution, parents and employers accepted the idea of children working in factories. There were no laws to prevent or restrict child labor. Factories and mines employed children under the age of ten and paid them very low wages. Supervisors sometimes beat child workers to keep them awake and alert.

City living presents problems. The Industrial Revolution led to rapid *urbanization,* the growth of urban areas that results from the movement of more people to cities. Because of technological advances, fewer workers were needed in agriculture. Farm families that could

no longer make a living in the countryside moved to the city to find jobs. Others left rural areas in search of higher pay and the variety of experiences offered by city life. Between 1801 and 1851, for example, the population of the English industrial city of Birmingham grew from 73,000 to 250,000. Liverpool, England, grew from 77,000 to 400,000.

Nineteenth-century cities were not prepared to handle such rapid growth. Housing, sanitation, and hospital facilities were not adequate for the growing numbers of people. The crime rate was high, and police forces were small; there was little fire protection. The poor lived in crowded, poorly built, and badly maintained houses. Sometimes a whole family huddled together in one room or even shared a room with another family. Open sewers, polluted rivers, factory smoke, and filthy streets allowed disease to spread. In Britain, about twenty-six out of every hundred children died before the age of five.

In preindustrial England most people had lived in small villages and had farmed the same land once worked by their ancestors. Relatives, friends, and the village church gave them a sense of belonging. Working their land also gave farmers a sense of pride and fulfillment. These feelings began to disappear as the movement to cities spread.

People in the industrial centers were separated from nature and from their place of origin. The factory system with its long hours and irregular work schedules weakened family life. Children and parents often worked in different parts of a factory and on different shifts. Family members spent little time together, and it was difficult for parents to supervise their children. Runaways and abandoned children wandered the streets of every city in Britain. To escape from their dreary lives, men and women frequently turned to alcohol. Church attendance declined in urban areas.

The status of older people also changed. In rural areas, older people had an opportunity to

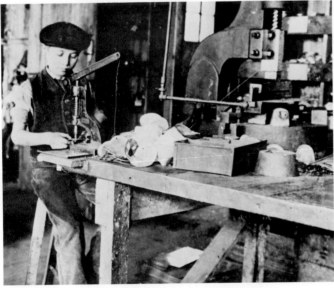

PROBLEMS OF INDUSTRIALIZATION

Workers who moved from the countryside to English towns and cities lived in crowded row houses, as seen in the above engraving of a London scene by the French artist Gustave Doré. Conditions were unhealthful both in housing and in the factories. Children worked long hours and operated machinery that could injure hands (left). Few children stayed in school beyond the age of twelve.

use their knowledge and experience. They taught young people about nature and farming; they showed them how to build and repair. In the industrial cities some of the authority and importance the older people had enjoyed was lost. Their knowledge and experience did not apply to city life.

Industrialization brings long-range benefits. While the Industrial Revolution brought problems for many people, it also created new opportunities and held out promise for improvement in people's lives. Among its significant effects, the Industrial Revolution made it possible to provide for a rapidly expanding population. Factory-made goods were plentiful and priced within the reach of most people. The growing cities offered many varied opportunities for advancement, and workers who acquired special skills and education had hopes of entering the middle class. In time, the worst abuses of industrialization were corrected, and the standard of living of working-class people rose sharply.

CHECK-UP

1. Vocabulary: *urbanization*.
2. What hardships and problems were faced by factory workers in the early decades of the Industrial Revolution?
3. (a) What factors led to the growth of cities in industrializing nations? (b) What problems did rapid urbanization cause for cities?
4. How did urban life affect (a) people's sense of belonging to a community? (b) family life? (c) attitudes toward older people?
5. What were some of the long-range benefits of industrialization?

3 New Economic Theories Develop

Nineteenth-century thinkers spent a great deal of time analyzing the Industrial Revolution and seeking solutions to the problems it created. The solutions they offered often were based on theories that attempted to explain the roles of workers, factory owners, and government in an industrialized society.

Some thinkers oppose government interference. Some thinkers held that government should not interfere with business. They based their views on the doctrine of *laissez faire* (LES-ay FAIR). This doctrine was first stated by a Scottish philosopher and economist, Adam Smith. In his book *The Wealth of Nations,* published in 1776, Smith set forth the principles of a laissez-faire economy. (1) Entrepreneurs should be free to operate their businesses in the way that will bring them the most profits. (2) What is good for the entrepreneur is good for everyone, since profits mean more jobs and more goods. The individual's profits contribute to the nation's profits and, therefore, to a healthy economy. (3) The duty of government is to keep peace and maintain order within the community. (4) Government should not meddle in business. When government interferes, it harms the economy, causing suffering for everyone.

An English stockbroker and writer, David Ricardo, applied the principles of laissez faire to wages. In his book *The Principles of Political Economy and Taxation,* published in 1817, Ricardo stated that supply and demand determine wages. That is, when labor is scarce, wages are high; wages go down when the number of workers increases.

Malthus ties poverty to population growth. A new theory about population supported the doctrine of laissez faire. In *An Essay*

Adam Smith started writing *The Wealth of Nations* after a trip to France, where he met and talked with Voltaire and other Enlightenment thinkers.

on the Principle of Population (1798), the English minister and economist Thomas R. Malthus declared that population always increases at a faster rate than the food supply. As a result, humanity is never far from starvation. Arguing against government relief for the poor, Malthus said that such help would only encourage larger families and increase population. One effect of the growth of population, continued Malthus, is that the supply of workers becomes greater than the demand. This results, said Malthus, in unemployment, low wages, and unending poverty. Malthus concluded that lowering the birth rate was the only effective way of combating poverty.

Reform legislation is urged. Some thinkers found the doctrine of laissez faire unacceptable. It seemed to them that the problems created by the Industrial Revolution could be solved only with the help of government. Early in the nineteenth century, these thinkers urged the passage of laws that would improve working conditions, permit the growth of labor unions, expand voting rights, and increase educational opportunities for the poor.

Socialists offer solutions to economic problems. Many people who tried to analyze the changes brought about by the Industrial Revolution were disturbed by the fact that a few people had become very rich as a result of industrialization, while most had remained poor. Some reformers concluded that better distribution of the wealth produced by the Industrial Revolution could not be attained under a system of private ownership of the principal means of production — factories, mines, railroads, and the like. These reformers advocated socialism. Under socialism, the means of production would be publicly owned and operated for the welfare of the people (page 470).

Cooperative communities are tried. One socialist idea was to create workers' cooperatives owned by those who worked in them. Among the early socialist thinkers who wanted to create such cooperative communities were Charles Fourier (foo-RYAY) and Robert Owen. Since both sought to establish an ideal society, or utopia,[1] they are called utopian socialists.

---

[1]The word *utopia* comes from the title of the book written in the sixteenth century by Sir Thomas More (page 330).

Fourier, a French philosopher, proposed small communities that would be organized to give people enjoyment in their work and pleasant living conditions. Fourier called his communities *phalanxes* (FAY-langks-ez). Each phalanx was to have about a thousand people living on 400 acres of land. To avoid monotony, people would learn a variety of trades and change jobs during the day. All members of the phalanx would share in everything that was produced. Fourier did not, however, call for an equal distribution of money and goods. People with special skills and responsibilities would be better rewarded, although measures would be taken to prevent them from growing too rich.

Fourier's ideas were popular for a few years. A number of communities based on his ideas were started, some in the United States, but all eventually failed.

Owen creates a model town. A Welsh-born manufacturer named Robert Owen had more practical plans for solving some of the problems created by the Industrial Revolution. Born in poverty, Owen was managing a cotton mill in Manchester, England, by the age of 19. In 1799 he became manager and part owner of the New Lanark mills in Scotland.

Distressed by the poverty of the workers, Owen sought to turn New Lanark into a model town. Since virtually everything in the town, including the stores and the homes, belonged to the owners of the factory, Owen was able to put his ideas into practice. He raised wages, improved working conditions, and reduced hours of work. Children under the age of ten did not work in the mills but attended free schools. Classes were provided for older children who worked. Owen saw that his workers had neat homes and supplied food and clothing at reasonable prices. Owen also sought to control drinking and to reduce crime. By 1815, his model town was drawing thousands of visitors from other parts of Britain and from the European continent.

Owen believed that the cause of evil was a bad social environment. He maintained that improved working and living conditions would help people realize the good within themselves, be kind to their families and neighbors, and live satisfying lives. Children who were properly educated and protected from the miseries

Karl Marx, shown here with his wife Jenny, settled in London after having to leave both Cologne and Paris because of his revolutionary views. The first volume of his book *Das Kapital* was published in 1862.

of extreme poverty, argued Owen, would become fine adults.

Owen later urged the formation of socialist communities where profits would be shared by all and members would cooperate with one another for the good of the community. In 1825 he set up such a community in the United States, at New Harmony, Indiana. The residents of New Harmony could not agree on government or religion, however, and the experiment ended in failure.

Marx advocates a new kind of socialism. Another socialist thinker of the nineteenth century was Karl Marx (1818–1883). The son of a German lawyer, Marx spent many years in England. Dismissing the utopian socialists as misguided dreamers, he analyzed the new industrial society and developed a philosophy of history and society. His books and other works, written in association with Friedrich Engels, laid the philosophical foundations for modern communism.

Marx did not believe that the problems of industrialization could be solved by reforming capitalist society. He insisted that capitalism had to be replaced by a different economic and social system.

Marx claimed that his theories (unlike those of the utopians) were based on a "scientific analysis" of history. He held that history follows scientific law just as does the world of nature. To understand the inner meaning of history, said Marx, one must realize that people's first concern has always been to obtain food and possessions. Therefore, he said, it is economic forces — such as the way goods are produced and distributed — that shape history.

Marx describes a "class struggle." All through history, said Marx, there have been two classes in society — the "haves" and the "have nots." The "haves" control the production of goods and possess most of the wealth. The "have nots" do the labor but reap no rewards for their work. Marx claimed that the exploitation of the "have nots" by the "haves" has caused a class struggle throughout history. In modern industrial society, said Marx, economic power is held by the bourgeois (boor-ZHWAH), the middle-class capitalists who own the factories, mines, banks, and businesses. These capitalists, Marx claimed, dominate and exploit the *proletariat* (proh-luh-TAIR-ee-ut), who are the wage-earning laborers.

Marx's political theory was based on his economic thought. He maintained that the class that holds economic power also controls the government for its own advantage. For example, in capitalist society, said Marx, lawmakers pass laws to help capitalists increase their profits. Similarly, the police protect the property of capitalists.

Marx predicts the destruction of capitalism. According to Marx, owners and managers in a capitalist system are not concerned with workers as human beings. While the capitalists reap large profits, said Marx, workers slave in factories under miserable working conditions and for low wages. Once workers are no longer needed, Marx maintained, they are fired, regardless of the misery unemployment brings. In addition, said Marx, capitalism fails to use advances in technology to benefit the masses.

The heart of Marx's doctrine was the conclusion that the capitalist system will disappear. A new economic system — socialism — will be built on its ruins, said Marx. He concluded that the ranks of the working class would steadily grow larger because shopkeepers and the owners of small businesses, unable to compete with powerful capitalists, also would become workers. Soon, he said, there would be only a few rich people and the great proletarian masses.

The result, Marx predicted, would be a great upheaval in society. Made desperate by their poverty, he claimed, the workers would seize control of the government, take over the means of production, and destroy the capitalist system and the capitalist class. Marx believed violent revolution was necessary. *The Communist Manifesto,* written by Marx and Engels in the year 1847, sounded the call for a working-class revolution:

> The Communists . . . openly declare that their ends can be attained only by the forcible overthrow of all existing social conditions. Let the ruling classes tremble at a communistic revolution. The proletarians have nothing to lose but their chains. They have a world to win.
> Workingmen of all countries, unite!

With the destruction of capitalism, Marx said, the class struggle would end and a "classless society" would emerge. All would share fairly in the wealth of the new society, said Marx. With the exploiters gone, Marx maintained, there would no longer be a need for a state, and it would eventually "wither away."

Marx's followers disagree. Marx gained considerable support for his theories. By the end of the nineteenth century, his followers had split into two main camps — orthodox Marxists and revisionists. Orthodox Marxists looked on Marx's basic principles as unquestionably true. They argued that all the energies of the working class should be directed toward a revolution against capitalism. While changing their interpretation of some of Marx's teachings, leading Marxists of the twentieth century clung to the idea that revolution was necessary.

Revisionists accepted parts of Marx's theories but disagreed with him on major points. They agreed that workers should gain control of the government and establish a socialist society, but they rejected Marx's belief that revolution was sure to come. They felt that a socialist society could be achieved through gradual reform and legislation. The Socialist parties that exist in many countries today are products of this reformist tradition.

Marx's predictions fail. Despite Marx's influence on economic thought, scholars point out fundamental flaws in his philosophy of history. Marx greatly underestimated the role of noneconomic forces in history. Economic causes alone cannot explain important historical developments. Political, religious, and psychological influences are also valid explanations for events.

Scholars also point out that several of Marx's predictions were wrong. Marx did not foresee the enormous gains workers have made — higher wages, shorter hours, and better working conditions.

Marx's prediction that the middle class would be pushed down into the ranks of the lower class was also wrong. Instead, the middle class has greatly increased in all industrialized countries.

According to Marx, capitalists control the state and use it to preserve and enhance their own power. In democratic industrialized nations, however, the state represents both workers and capitalists. Measures such as social security, unemployment insurance, and minimum-wage laws indicate that governments are not run solely to keep the "capitalist oppressors" in power, as Marx claimed.

Marx expected the workers of all nations to join forces against "capitalist oppressors." That did not happen. The great wars of the twentieth century were waged between nations, not classes. Marx also predicted that working-class revolutions would break out in the industrialized nations. These revolutions never occurred. Rather, it was in predominantly agricultural nations that Communist revolutions took place. Where Marxist revolutions did occur — Russia, China, and Cuba — the Communists failed to create the kind of socialist society that Karl Marx had envisioned. Instead of the state withering away in those countries, it grew stronger.

4 Reformers Respond to Economic and Social Problems

The problems created by industrialization led to specific demands for reform as well as to new economic theories. In Britain, the United States, and other industrialized countries, reformers fought to improve conditions for the poor and to curb unfair business practices.

REFORMS IN BRITAIN

Parliament passes factory-reform laws. Because the Industrial Revolution had begun in Britain, many of the problems it created became apparent there first. Distressed by the plight of children who worked in mines and factories, humanitarians in Britain held meetings, wrote pamphlets, and drew up petitions calling for factory reforms. As a result of this pressure, Parliament in 1833 passed the Factory Act. It forbade the employment of children under the age of nine. Children aged nine to thirteen could not work more than eight hours a day, and young people aged thirteen to eighteen could not work more than twelve hours a day. Factory inspectors were appointed to make certain that the law was enforced.

The Factory Act set an important precedent. It established the idea that the state could act to protect workers. Later factory acts further reduced the hours children and young people could work and also regulated hours for women. By the early twentieth century the ten-hour day was established in England for all workers over the age of fourteen.

Improvements are made in health and education. The problems created by rapid urbanization were also carefully examined. About the middle of the nineteenth century, doctors and scientists began to understand the relationship between disease and dirt. Cities took steps to improve public health. They paved streets, set safety and health standards for buildings, built sewer systems, provided for regular collections of garbage, and piped water into homes. Improved sanitation and health care in the cities greatly reduced the number of deaths caused by disease.

In the early 1800's elementary education in Britain was managed by private individuals and church organizations. Schools were financed by contributions, grants, and fees paid by students. Few poor children were able to attend school.

Many people in Britain favored educational reforms. They believed that education would help to do away with poverty, crime, and superstition. Starting in 1833, Parliament began to vote small sums of money for elementary education, and by 1869 about half of all British children of school age were in school. The Education Act of 1870 increased this percentage by giving local governments the power to establish elementary schools. By 1891 these schools were free, and attendance was required.

Labor unions emerge. Some reformers focused their efforts on the problems faced by workers in the new industries. Workers in factories depended upon their wages for survival. A cut in pay or the loss of a job meant poverty for them and their families. Because an individual worker could not stand up to a large company, workers in some crafts came together to form trade unions. One method used by organized workers was to call strikes, refusing to work until management agreed to improve conditions.

At first, Parliament resisted the unions. In 1799 and 1800 it passed the Combination Acts, which made unions illegal. Any worker who participated in a strike faced the risk of prison. The Combination Acts were repealed in 1824, and trade unions became legal in Britain. Robert Owen (page 531) was a leader in this movement for union organization. An outbreak of strikes frightened the government, however, and in 1825 Parliament passed a law that allowed workers to unionize but forbade them to strike. Not until 1871 were restrictions on trade unions removed, allowing workers to organize, picket, and strike.

Unions demand political and social change. As the British trade union movement grew stronger and more aggressive, unions became involved in politics. In 1900, representatives of the various trade unions voted to establish a political party to represent workers' interests. In 1906, twenty-nine members of the new Labour Party were elected to Parliament.

Another party, the Liberal Party, won control of Parliament in the 1906 elections. Nevertheless, it understood the significance of the Labour Party victories. Unless the distress of the poor was relieved, more and more workers would support the Labour Party. To prevent this from happening, Parliament passed a number of reform laws between 1906 and 1914. These laws created a variety of social services for British citizens. Meals were provided for needy school children, and medical clinics were set up in the schools. Parents who neglected their children's health could be punished. The government provided pensions for people over the age of seventy. Other laws protected workers and required factories to make working conditions safer. Employees won the right to payment for injuries received on the job. Unskilled

LINKING PAST AND PRESENT

Pottery in Industrial England

Three hundred years ago, "setting the table" did not mean putting out plates and dishes. Except for the very rich, most people ate from "trenchers" made from wood or even used a thick slice of bread as a plate. The secret of making smooth porcelain was known only in Asia, and porcelain dishes (or "china") were a valuable part of international trade. In Europe, however, only the nobility and the wealthy could afford to eat from imported "china."

In the 1600's the Dutch began to make blue-and-white Delftware dishes that imitated "china." Soon pottery makers in Germany, France, and England were making dishes, too. English manufacturers were the first to produce dishes inexpensive enough for ordinary people to buy. The most famous pottery maker was Josiah Wedgwood (1730–1795). He tried new materials and installed steam-powered machines in his factory. (At right, a Wedgwood willow pattern plate.) By about 1850, inexpensive chinaware was used throughout Europe and the

United States. One surprising side effect was improved health, for porcelain and pottery could be washed much cleaner than wooden ware.

Limiting the workday to eight hours was one of the demands made by leaders active in the British trade union movement.

workers in certain industries gained the right to a minimum wage. Employment centers were set up to help workers find jobs. The National Insurance Act of 1911 provided unemployment insurance and free medical treatment for workers.

REFORMS IN THE UNITED STATES

Unions are formed in the United States. In the United States, as in Britain, industrialization and urbanization produced serious problems. Labor union movements began to develop at the same time as American businesses were growing larger. The most successful and lasting of the early unions was the American Federation of Labor (AFL), founded in 1881. The AFL organized skilled workers according to their craft or trade; that is, plumbers, electricians, and carpenters each had a union. Under the leadership of Samuel Gom-

pers, AFL membership grew to about one and a half million by 1904. Unskilled workers, however, who were the vast majority, did not have a strong union until the 1930's.

Unions were formed to help workers gain higher wages and better working conditions. When management failed to respond to workers' demands, unions sometimes called strikes. At times, strikes led to violence by both sides. Strikers smashed machines or attacked non-union workers who were hired as replacements. Private detectives or police hired to guard company property sometimes used force against strikers. State and federal government officials generally sided with employers in labor disputes. Occasionally state governors or the President of the United States sent troops to break up a strike.

Businesses grow larger and more powerful. Business grew rapidly in the United States after the Civil War. Nineteenth-century capitalists held to the laissez-faire principle (page 530). They believed that the government should not set limits on the prices at which businesses sold goods, on the wages they paid workers, or on the profits they made. Prices, wages, and profits, they felt, should be determined by the free play of supply and demand.

By the late nineteenth century, some business organizations were growing extremely powerful. As business leaders found ways of bringing most of the companies in one industry under the control of one management, they were able to establish monopolies. By 1898, for example, Standard Oil refined more than 80 percent of all the oil produced in the United States. It also controlled most of the pipelines that transported the oil. Similar business combinations controlled sugar refining and several other industries. Smaller firms could not compete. The company controlling the industry could push up its prices or lower them as it wished. Many Americans feared that these huge companies would destroy competition in business.

Reforms are introduced. As in Britain, the problems brought by industrialization and urbanization in the United States attracted the attention of reformers. Among those calling for reforms were several writers who became known as "muckrakers." They investigated conditions in slums and in factories, and their books and articles revealed the unfair practices of some business leaders. Ida Tarbell disclosed the business tactics of the oil industry, while Ray Stannard Baker took on the railroads. Lincoln Steffens condemned corruption in city politics. The novelist Upton Sinclair, most famous of the muckrakers, vividly described unsanitary and dangerous conditions in the meat-packing industry in his book *The Jungle* (1906).

Other reformers dedicated their lives to helping the poor in the cities, particularly immigrants. They called for better housing and improved health care. Jacob Riis, a Danish-born reporter in New York City, wrote articles describing slum conditions. In Chicago, Jane Addams founded Hull House in 1889. In this social settlement house, immigrants could take part in adult education classes, recreational activities, and health clinics. In addition to the services that were provided, they gained a sense of belonging. Addams also worked for other social reforms, including voting rights for women, juvenile courts, factory inspection laws, payments for injured workers, and laws regulating working hours for women.

Because of the efforts of such people, many reforms were introduced in the United States during the early 1900's. City governments passed laws regulating housing conditions. Public parks, beaches, and playgrounds were set up. State governments limited the number of hours that women could work each week (generally no more than sixty) and prohibited child labor. Laws protected the right of workers injured on the job to continue to receive pay from their employers while recovering from their injuries.

During the same period, the federal government began to regulate big business. It took legal action against companies that engaged in unfair business practices and broke up some monopolies. It also supervised railroads to prevent them from charging unfair rates.

CHANGES ON THE EUROPEAN CONTINENT

Workers organize. A large urban working class with special problems also developed on the European continent. As in Britain and the United States, workers organized labor unions to secure higher wages, shorter hours, and better working conditions. Most European trade unions were concerned mainly with gaining economic benefits and did not become active in politics.

Some European labor leaders and reformers wanted sweeping changes. Among them were the socialists, who believed that the government should take over the banks, railroads, factories, and natural resources. They argued that only in this way could workers share in the benefits of industrialization. Socialists organized political parties that sought to gain working-class support. Some of these parties supported gradual and peaceful reform, while others claimed that only revolution would bring the changes they desired.

In response to the demands of workers, some European governments introduced social reforms. By 1914 Germany had taken the lead in enacting social legislation. The German chancellor, Otto von Bismarck (page 482), provided workers with sickness and accident insurance and old-age benefits. Laws were passed to improve working conditions and to eliminate child labor in mines and factories. In time, other European countries followed Germany's example.

CHECK-UP

1. (a) What was the importance of Britain's Factory Act of 1833? (b) What steps did city governments in Britain take to improve public health? (c) What steps did the British government take to expand educational opportunities?

2. (a) Why did British workers form trade unions? (b) How did the legal status of unions in Britain change between 1800 and 1871? (c) Why was the Labour Party formed? (d) What reform legislation did Parliament pass in the early twentieth century?

3. (a) What was the first successful large union in the United States? (b) Why did some Americans fear the uncontrolled growth of big business? (c) Who were the "muckrakers"? (d) What reforms were undertaken by Americans in the late 1800's and early 1900's?

4. Which nation in continental Europe took the lead in establishing social-welfare legislation for the benefit of workers?

5 Industrialization Brings Political Change

Urbanization and industrialization had brought sweeping social and economic reforms to the Western nations. Political reforms were another result of these developments. In most of the industrial nations, these reforms made it possible for more people to participate in government.

Parliamentary rule grows in Britain. Unlike the United States, Britain has no written constitution. Its system of government is based on a collection of documents such as the Magna Charta, legal traditions such as the common law, and on laws such as the Petition of Right (page 388).

Although Britain has a monarch, the governing body is Parliament. Parliament's supremacy was established in 1688 by the Glorious Revolution. The British monarch kept the right to veto, or reject, an act of Parliament, but no British monarch has exercised this right since 1707. In Great Britain, the monarch reigns but does not rule.

The British Parliament consists of a House of Lords and a House of Commons. Members of the House of Lords either inherit their seats or are appointed. Members of the House of Commons are elected by the British people. For several centuries the House of Lords dominated Parliament, but during the 1700's power shifted to the House of Commons.

The office of prime minister also gained importance during the eighteenth century. Today the prime minister is usually the leader of the political party that holds the most seats in the House of Commons. The prime minister and other high-ranking government officials determine Britain's foreign and domestic policies. In addition, they propose laws that are then submitted to Parliament. If the House of Commons votes against an important proposal, the prime minister can dissolve Parliament and call for new elections.

Democracy at first is limited. In the early nineteenth century, political democracy in Britain was limited in a number of ways. Women could not vote at all, and property requirements barred many men from voting or holding most public offices. Religious restrictions prevented Catholics, Jews, and other non-Anglicans from being elected to the House of Commons.

Representation in the House of Commons was grossly unequal and did not reflect the great changes in population. Some towns had grown into large cities, while others had been reduced to small villages. Manchester, for example, had become a city of over 100,000 but had no representatives in the House of Commons.

Religious restrictions are removed. The removal of legal restrictions based on religion was an important step toward political democracy in Britain. In 1829 Parliament passed the Catholic Emancipation Act, which opened nearly all government positions to Catholics. Jews and others still lacked full rights, since government officials, lawyers, university students, and others were required to swear by "the true faith of a Christian." Gradually restrictions were lifted so that Jews could hold office in local government, serve on juries, and be admitted to the bar as lawyers. In 1858 Parliament finally abandoned the oath, and Jews could serve in the House of Commons.

Democratic reforms are demanded. In 1830 Parliament was still dominated by aristocratic landowners. The middle class — industrialists, bankers, merchants — pressed for a greater voice in British political life. The Revolution of 1830 in France (page 466) frightened parliamentary leaders, who feared that revolutionary violence would spread to Britain. Parliament soon passed the Reform Bill of 1832, giving the new industrial cities more representation in Parliament. A change in property requirements extended *suffrage* — the right to vote — to well-to-do men in the middle class.

Many workers, however, were still denied suffrage. The Reform Bill spurred them to organize the Chartist movement. Their People's Charter demanded the right to vote for all men, a secret ballot, abolition of property requirements for serving in Parliament, pay for members of Parliament, and annual elections. The Chartists failed to win these demands. Nevertheless, their protests convinced thoughtful

One outcome of industrialization was the establishment of city transportation systems. A London bus around 1900 was the setting for this painting by George Joy.

people that workers had valid complaints. (Eventually all the demands of the Chartists, except for annual elections, became law.)

The right to vote is extended. Over the years workers in industry continued to advocate political reform. They wanted the right to vote. The Reform Bill of 1867 gave the vote to working-class men, thus doubling the number of voters in Britain. Benjamin Disraeli (diz-RAY-lee), a novelist and politician (and a future prime minister), played the leading role in achieving this reform. Disraeli understood that allowing workingmen to vote was inevitable. Some of his fellow Conservative Party members feared that it would ruin Britain, but Disraeli maintained that this democratic advance would strengthen the bonds between the people and the state.

The work of electoral reform was continued by the Liberal Party under the leadership of William Gladstone, who served four terms as prime minister (between 1868 and 1894). The Ballot Act of 1872 provided for the secret ballot. This protected working-class voters from being forced by their employers to support certain candidates. In 1873 the Corrupt Practices Act decreed strict penalties for attempts to bribe voters. The Reform Bill of 1884 doubled the number of voters by giving suffrage to male farm workers. Virtually all men in Britain now had the right to vote.

Women lack political rights. While working-class men in Britain were gaining more rights, women of all classes faced political and social inequality. Most members of the middle class believed that woman's place was in the home. Women should be concerned with their husbands and children, they said, not with politics or business.

As more men gained the right to vote, more women began to demand equal rights. They demanded the right to vote, to hold office, and to inherit, buy, and sell property. In 1837 the English novelist and economist Harriet Martineau commented: "One of the fundamental principles announced in the [American] Declaration of Independence is that governments derive their just power from the consent of the governed. How can the political condition of women be reconciled with this?"

In 1867 John Stuart Mill, a philosopher, economist, and member of Parliament, made the proposal that the vote be extended to women. Parliament rejected his proposal, but 74 members voted in favor (194 opposed it). The following year Lydia Becker, a leading feminist, became the first English woman to speak in public for women's suffrage.

As women became more vocal, however, resistance to their demands grew. Many people, both men and women, felt that women's suffrage was too radical a break with tradition. Some believed that women were represented in government by their husbands or male relatives. Others claimed that women lacked the ability to participate capably in political life. Queen Victoria, who supported many other reforms, called women's suffrage "that mad, wicked folly."

British women organize to gain rights. Many thoughtful British women realized that gaining suffrage was basic to other reforms. They organized reform societies, drew up petitions, and protested unfair treatment.

When these protests were ignored, some women turned to militant tactics. In 1903 Emmeline Pankhurst organized the Women's Social and Political Union (WSPU). Pankhurst was assisted by her daughters Christabel and Sylvia. The WSPU campaigned against political candidates who opposed women's suffrage. To call attention to their cause, WSPU members disrupted the speeches of politicians, marched on Parliament, bombed buildings, burned railway stations, and broke windows. Many citizens were outraged by these tactics. The police reacted with uncharacteristic harshness. Feminists were arrested and given jail sentences.

While the WSPU turned to militant tactics, the National Union of Woman Suffrage and other feminist groups relied on peaceful persuasion. Their appeals gained increasing support in Parliament.

Women work for equality in the United States. The 1830's and 1840's saw a quickening of the pace of reform in America. Some reformers, such as Carry Nation, wanted to prohibit the drinking of alcohol. Some called for better treatment of prisoners, orphans, the blind, and the mentally ill. One group demanded the abolition of slavery. Women participated actively in these reforms, and some of their reformist

British feminist groups published inexpensive papers in their effort to enlist popular support for the cause of woman suffrage.

spirit carried over into the feminist movement. This movement eventually resulted in the formation of the National American Woman Suffrage Association (page 511).

During the 1890's four western states — Wyoming, Colorado, Utah, and Idaho — became the first to extend the vote to women. The courage and determination demanded of pioneer men and women in the West had demonstrated the falseness of the traditional view that women lacked character and strength.

France establishes the Third Republic. Political changes were also under way on the European continent. After the 1848 revolutions in France, Louis Napoleon was elected president of the French republic and four years later became Emperor Napoleon III (page 471). When Napoleon III was captured by the Prussians during the Franco-Prussian War (1870–1871), republicans took over the leadership of France and established the Third Republic.

France found it hard to make its democratic institutions work. Angered by the Prussian defeat and by severe economic conditions, people in Paris formed a government called the Commune. After bloody street fighting, the uprising was crushed.

The Third Republic meets challenges within France. During the 1880's and 1890's the Third Republic was threatened by royalists, aristocrats, nationalists, clergy, and army leaders. These groups wanted to return France to a monarchy or to have military rule.

One of the most serious threats to the stability of the French republic grew out of the Dreyfus Affair. In 1894 Alfred Dreyfus (DRAY-foos), a Jewish army captain, was accused by the French government of being a spy for Germany. Found guilty, Dreyfus was sentenced to life in prison. Within a few years, new evidence showed that he had been framed by other army officers.

Many army leaders, nationalists, leaders in the clergy, and anti-Jewish groups refused to let the case be reopened. They claimed this action would cast doubt on the honor of the army. The defenders of Dreyfus insisted that justice was more important. If Dreyfus was innocent, they said, he should be freed no matter whom it might embarrass. Not until 1906 was Dreyfus's name cleared. The conflict caused by the case continued for years, weakening the republic.

In addition, the Third French Republic suffered from a basic political weakness. Unlike Britain and the United States, France had many political parties. No one party had enough support within the national assembly to provide strong leadership. French premiers (prime ministers) were unable to win support within the assembly and so resigned in rapid succession. France appeared to have a government that lacked direction. Nevertheless, the Third Republic endured as a democratic state until World War II.

Germany remains an authoritarian state. German unity had been brought about by Bismarck (page 484), and Germany remained an authoritarian state. After the Franco-Prussian War, the German Reich (RYK, meaning "empire") was formed. The Reich consisted of several states united under a strong central government.

Adult male citizens elected members of the Reichstag (RYK-shtahg), the lower house of parliament. Members of the Bundestag (BOON-duh-shtahg), the upper house, were appointed by the different states. The Bundestag had more power than the lower house, and its members generally opposed attempts to make Germany more democratic.

Real power in the German Reich rested with the Prussian king, the Prussian generals, the Prussian aristocracy, and a growing number of wealthy bankers and industrialists. The king of Prussia was the kaiser, or emperor, of all Germany; the prime minister of Prussia was also the chancellor of the German Reich. The German kaiser, unlike the British monarch, had considerable control over lawmaking. Through his chancellor he also controlled foreign affairs. He appointed and dismissed the chancellor and commanded the army and navy.

The rulers of Germany opposed democratic ideas and Western-style parliamentary government. The failure of democratic attitudes and procedures to take root in Germany had important consequences for the future.

CHECK-UP

1. Vocabulary: *suffrage.*
2. (a) Describe the British system of government. (b) By what steps were religious restrictions on voting removed by 1858? (c) What were the provisions of the Reform Bill of 1832? (d) What demands were made by the Chartists? (e) What were the provisions of the reform bills of 1867 and 1884?
3. (a) What rights did British feminists demand? (b) What arguments were put forth by those who opposed voting rights for women?
4. (a) How did the reform movements of the 1830's and 1840's lead to the growth of an American feminist movement? (b) In what states did women first gain the right to vote?
5. (a) What kind of government did France have after 1871? (b) What was the Dreyfus Affair? (c) What political weaknesses threatened French democracy?
6. (a) What kind of government did Germany have in the late nineteenth century? (b) Who held most power in the German government?

Chapter 24 Review

Summary

The Industrial Revolution, which began in Great Britain about 1750, was the result of many factors, especially changes in agriculture and advances in technology. Machines began to replace human labor; factories replaced the domestic system of producing goods; and improved methods of transportation and communication were invented. The Industrial Revolution transformed Western society.

From Britain, the Industrial Revolution spread rapidly, particularly in Germany and the United States. Rapid industrialization and urbanization brought both opportunities and problems. In response to the problems, nineteenth-century thinkers proposed changes in society and in economic life. Some advocated a laissez-faire economy, free of government interference. Others urged different forms of government action, including socialism. Utopian socialists founded cooperative communities, but the most influential of the socialist thinkers was Karl Marx. His writings became the basis of modern communism. Marx predicted a struggle between workers and owners that, he said, would eventually end capitalist society.

Other reformers worked for legislation to improve factory conditions, public health, and education. Some workers organized labor unions that also sought reforms in politics and society. More men gained the right to vote, while women in several countries were active in the effort to win political equality.

1. Write the sentences listed below on a sheet of paper. Fill in the blank in each sentence with one of these words: *domestic system, entrepreneur, factory system, laissez faire, proletariat, suffrage, urbanization.*

(a) A person who organizes and manages a business is called an ___?___ .

(b) Marx's word for wage-earning laborers was ___?___ .

(c) The doctrine that government should not interfere with business is called ___?___ .

(d) Workers who made cloth in farmhouses were part of the production method known as the ___?___ .

(e) The movement of people from rural areas to cities is called ___?___ .

(f) A word meaning the right to vote is ___?___ .

(g) The production method that is based on large numbers of people working together in one place is the ___?___ .

2. Distinguish between the terms in each of the following pairs:

(a) *The Wealth of Nations; An Essay on the Principle of Population.*

(b) Factory Act of 1833; Education Act of 1878.

(c) interchangeable parts; assembly line.

(d) Reform Bill of 1832; Chartist Movement.

(e) Paris Commune; Third Republic.

(f) Reich; Reichstag.

People to Identify

Identify the following people and tell why each was important:

1. Jethro Tull
2. James Watt
3. Adam Smith
4. Karl Marx
5. Robert Owen
6. Henry Bessemer
7. Samuel Morse
8. Alfred Dreyfus
9. Emmeline Pankhurst
10. Thomas Malthus

Relating Geography and History

1. Map making and interpretation. Great Britain's natural resources and efficient transportation systems encouraged industrialization after 1750. (a) Use an encyclopedia to locate the canals and railroads that were built as Britain industrialized. Draw a map, using symbols to show these canals and railroads. Include a key. (b) Explain how transportation played a part in Britain's industrialization.

2. Interpretation. (a) What changes did the enclosure movement (pages 522–523) bring about in English agriculture? In your answer, consider both landowners and villagers. (b) How were the changes in agriculture tied to industrialization?

Discussion Questions

1. (a) Why did industrialization lead to the growth of cities? (b) What problems did rapid urbanization create? (c) How did changes resulting from the Industrial Revolution improve life for most workers?

2. (a) How did the laissez-faire economists and the socialists differ in their views on the role of government in business? (b) How did they disagree on the subject of poverty?

3. (a) What major criticisms do scholars have of Marx's theories? (b) Which of Marx's predictions have not come true?

4. What effect did muckrakers and other reformers have on American life in the early 1900's?

5. (a) What part does the prime minister play in the British government? (b) How is the role of the prime minister different from the role of the President in the United States government?

6. (a) What factors contributed to political instability in France's Third Republic? (b) In what ways did Germany continue to be an authoritarian state after its unification?

Reading Primary Sources

The following selection is taken from testimony given by Patience Kershaw, seventeen years old, before a British parliamentary committee in 1842. The committee was investigating conditions in the coal mines. Read the passage. Then answer the questions that follow.

I never went to day-school. I go to Sunday School, but I cannot read or write. I go to [the mine] at five o'clock in the morning and come out at five in the evening. I get my breakfast of porridge and milk first. I take my dinner with me, a cake, and eat it as I go. I do not stop or rest any time for the purpose. I get nothing else until I get home, and then have potatoes and meat, but not meat every day. I [wear] the clothes I have now got on, trousers and ragged jacket. The bald place upon my head was made by [pushing] the corves [baskets used to carry coal to the mouth of a coal mine]. My legs have never swelled, but my sisters' did. . . . I push the corves a mile and more under ground and back . . . eleven times a day. I wear a belt and chain to get the corves out. . . . [The men I work for] beat me if I am not quick enough.

(a) How many hours a day did Patience work in the mine? (b) What kind of job did she do? (c) What physical effect did it have on her and apparently on others? (d) Describe her meals. (e) What happened if she did not work fast enough? (f) What impression might testimony such as this have made on the British public?

Skill Activities

1. Building vocabulary. The Industrial Revolution changed the kinds of tools people used in their work. To control the quantity and quality of goods, owners brought workers together in factories. The word *factory* comes from the Latin verb *facere,* meaning "to make, to do." What is the meaning of each of the following words? How is each word related to the same root as *factory?*

(a) fact   (d) facsimile
(b) faction   (e) artifact
(c) manufacture

2. Making charts. Make a chart with the following headings: *Inventor, Invention, Significance.* In addition to the inventors mentioned in this chapter, find out how each of the following individuals contributed to the Industrial Revolution and include that information in your chart: Samuel Crompton, Thomas Newcomen, John McAdam, Robert Fulton, Alexander Darby, Richard Trevithick, and George Stephenson.

3. Placing events in time. In each of the following groups, arrange the three events or developments in the correct time sequence.
(a)   John Kay invented the flying shuttle.
      Richard Arkwright invented a water-powered spinning machine.
      Eli Whitney invented the cotton gin.
(b)   Samuel F. B. Morse invented the telegraph.
      The first railway line was built in England.
      James Watt invented a practical steam engine.

4. Biographies. Prepare a report about one of the following figures of the Victorian Age: (a) Queen Victoria; (b) Prince Albert; (c) William Gladstone; (d) William Morris; (e) Sir Robert Peel; (f) Benjamin Disraeli.

5. Book reports. Read a novel by one of the following English writers of the 1800's: Charles Dickens, George Eliot, Thomas Hardy, Elizabeth Gaskell. In your report, tell how events of the Industrial Revolution play a part in the story.

Unit Five Review

Review Questions

1. (a) Why did the American colonists seek independence from Britain? (b) In what ways did the goals of the revolutionaries in France differ from the goals of the Americans?

2. Compare what the bourgeoisie hoped to gain from the French Revolution with the reasons for the creoles' participation in the struggle for liberation in Latin America.

3. For what reasons were the following revolutions unsuccessful: (a) the Decembrist uprising in Russia? (b) the workers' revolution of 1848 in France? (c) the 1848 Hungarian revolt against the Austrian Empire?

4. How did extreme nationalism threaten the stability of Europe in the late 1800's and early 1900's?

5. (a) What factors hindered nation-building in Latin America? (b) Why did caudillo rule develop in many Latin American countries?

6. (a) Why were the Articles of Confederation replaced with a federal system of government in the United States? (b) Why did the Canadians decide to adopt a confederation form of government?

7. (a) According to Marx, why would the capitalist system disappear? (b) What changes in industrialized societies did Marx fail to predict?

8. How did the British and German governments differ in their attitudes toward political reform in the nineteenth century?

Projects

1. Making time lines. Prepare a time line for one of the following countries: France, Canada, the United States, Britain, or Germany. Include on the time line important events that occurred in that country from 1750 to 1900. Then choose three of the events you listed and write a short essay explaining why those events were important in shaping the history of the country.

2. Making maps. Prepare a series of three maps. In the first, show Europe before the French Revolution. In the second, show Europe in 1807 when Napoleon's empire was at its height. In the third, show Europe after 1815.

3. Making charts. In this unit you read about many battles. Make a chart with the following headings: *Battle, Participants, Date, Results.* List the following battles in the first column: Saratoga, Waterloo, Trafalgar, Austerlitz, and Ayacucho. Complete the chart by filling in the information for each battle.

Books to Read

Baker, Nina B. *Garibaldi.* Vanguard.

Crankshaw, Edward. *Bismarck.* Viking.

Dickens, Charles. *A Tale of Two Cities.* Macmillan. A classic novel about the French Revolution.

Drabble, Margaret. *For Queen and Country: Britain in the Victorian Age.* Clarion.

Herold, J. Christopher. *The Horizon Book of the Age of Napoleon.* Harper.

Hibbert, Christopher. *Days of the French Revolution.* Morrow.

Lancaster, Bruce, and John H. Plumb. *The American Heritage Book of the Revolution.* American Heritage.

Lawson, Don. *The United States in the Civil War.* Abelard.

Mackenzie, Midge, ed. *Shoulder to Shoulder.* Knopf. The women's suffrage movement in England.

Meigs, Cornelia. *Jane Addams: Pioneer for Social Justice.* Little, Brown.

Meltzer, Milton. *World of Our Fathers: The Jews of Eastern Europe.* Farrar, Straus and Giroux.

Parkinson, Wanda. *The Gilded African: Toussaint L'Ouverture.* Quartet Books.

Schechter, Betty. *The Dreyfus Affair: A National Scandal.* Houghton Mifflin.

Snodin, David. *A Mighty Ferment: Britain in the Age of Revolution 1750–1850.* Clarion.

Turner, Wesley B. *Life in Upper Canada.* Franklin Watts. The settlement of Canada from 1791 to 1841.

Worcester, Donald E. *Bolívar.* Little, Brown.

How to Study World History

Taking Notes

Note-taking is one of the most important study skills you can master. Taking notes will force you to concentrate on finding and writing down the main ideas in a reading assignment. This will help you better remember what you read. Note-taking has another important advantage. If you have made careful, readable, and thorough notes, you can use them to study for tests.

The following suggestions will help you take better notes on your reading assignments.

Finish reading each passage before taking notes. Before writing anything down, read through a paragraph or passage to make sure you understand what it is about. What seems important in the first sentence may simply introduce the topic of the passage. For example, on page 523 of Chapter 24, the paragraph following the subhead **Inventions change the textile industry** describes the domestic system of textile production. The first sentence of the paragraph, "New textile factories provided jobs for some displaced farm workers," is an introductory sentence, not the topic of the paragraph.

Write down only the main ideas and the most important information. Note-taking is a process of picking out the main ideas from the supporting details. Ask yourself what the main ideas are. Watch for words and phrases that signal main points. Examples are: *first, finally, most important,* and *the causes of.* Also pay attention to words in boldface and italic type.

Most people prefer to use words or phrases for note-taking. Important words and phrases are usually nouns and verbs. Articles like *a, an,* and *the* can be left out, and adjectives and adverbs should be used sparingly. Since penciled notes will fade or blur, write your notes in ink. Also write in your own words, words that are understandable to you. Notes on the paragraph following the subhead **Inventions change the textile industry** on page 523 might look like this:

> Domestic system of textile-making (before Industrial Revolution) — merchants buy raw materials and distribute to workers in their homes. Some workers spin yarn; others weave cloth.

Use abbreviations and symbols. Symbols and abbreviations can help you take notes more rapidly. Keep your abbreviations simple so that they will make sense when you reread your notes. The following ideas can help you to use abbreviations effectively: (1) Write only the first syllable or just enough of the beginning of a well-known word to form an easily recognizable unit (*pol* for politics, *dem* for democracy). (2) Use an apostrophe in place of certain letters in a word (*gov't* for government). (3) Write long terms only once and then substitute initials (*IR* for Industrial Revolution).

Symbols can also simplify note-taking. Some commonly used symbols for connective words are & (and), *w/* (with), and *w/o* (without).

Review your notes. Reread your notes within a few days to make sure that you understand your symbols and abbreviations and that you have used them consistently.

Check Your Skill

Use the following questions to check your understanding of what you have read.

1. Note-taking helps you to (a) read more quickly, (b) concentrate on what you are reading, (c) memorize facts.

2. Before taking notes, you should (a) outline the chapter, (b) summarize the chapter, (c) read a complete paragraph.

3. Your notes should consist mostly of (a) main ideas, (b) details, (c) titles and subheads.

4. Once you have developed a system of abbreviations, it is important to (a) write it in your notebook, (b) use it consistently, (c) expand it.

Apply Your Skill

Using the steps outlined above, prepare a set of notes on the first section of Chapter 25, "European Nations Build New Empires" (pages 550–551). Be sure to summarize main ideas, include symbols and abbreviations, and use your own words.

梁承禧

Kingqua

The Age of Imperialism

By the mid-1800's, after more than a half century of revolution and change, strong centralized governments had been established in most of the Western nations. The reforms sought by revolutionaries had given political rights to more people, while the power of most monarchs had decreased. A sense of national pride and nationhood had grown up not only in Europe but also in the Western Hemisphere, where new nations had been built out of former colonial empires. Meanwhile, industrialization and urbanization had radically changed economic, political, and social life in the West.

Several European nations had built overseas empires during the Age of Exploration, but many of these empires nearly disappeared as new nations were established in the Americas. By the middle of the nineteenth century, European nations once again entered a period of empire-building. They sought natural resources for their expanding industries and markets for their industrial products. As populations grew, European nations also sought more land to supply food and allow their people to settle overseas. The Europeans now tried to acquire territory and influence on the continents of Asia and Africa, which had not yet felt the impact of nationalism and industrial development.

The Indian peninsula, or South Asia, had been acquired for Britain by merchant traders in the 1700's. In the 1800's India became a vital part of the growing British Empire. Elsewhere in Asia, European expansion brought chaos in China but spurred moves toward modernization and industrialization in Japan. Africa, whose traditional institutions and society had been weakened by the slave trade, became the main focus of European empire-building.

The following chapters describe the wave of empire-building undertaken in the late 1800's by European nations.

In the new wave of empire-building in the 1800's, European and American traders set up warehouses and offices throughout the world. Canton, China, was an important port for tea merchants, whose businesses lined the busy waterfront. A Cantonese merchant's business card showed his name in both Chinese characters and an English translation.

As representatives of imperial authority, high-ranking officials of the East India Company and the British government had lofty status in eighteenth-century India. Traveling by elephant with an armed escort was one mark of that high position.

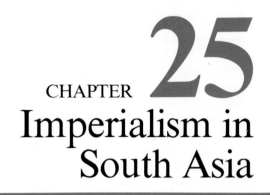

Imperialism in South Asia

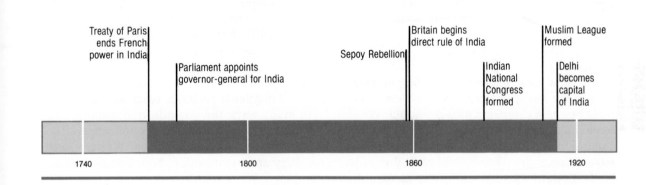

Treaty of Paris ends French power in India	Parliament appoints governor-general for India	Sepoy Rebellion	Britain begins direct rule of India / Indian National Congress formed	Muslim League formed / Delhi becomes capital of India

1740　　　　　　　　　1800　　　　　　　　　1860　　　　　　　　　1920

During the Age of Exploration, in the sixteenth and seventeenth centuries, several European nations gained vast colonial empires in Asia and the Americas (Chapter 16). By the mid-1800's most of these empires had been lost, and in 1870 a new wave of empire-building began.

The empire established by Britain was one that survived and grew steadily into the nineteenth century. In the 1600's merchants of the English East India Company established trading posts on the coasts of South Asia. The East India Company gradually gained control over much of the Indian peninsula and assumed many of the powers of a government in India, introducing British customs, ideas, technology, and education. The British government, however, reduced the East India Company's powers and eventually brought India into the British Empire. By the late 1800's, India was called "the brightest jewel" in the British imperial crown.

Trained in British ideas of law and justice, many educated Indians began to protest British control over the country and to seek more independence and responsibility for their own government.

This chapter describes the changing nature of British rule in India and its place in the context of world imperialism.

CHAPTER OUTLINE

1   European Nations Build New Empires

2   Trade Brings British Rule in India

3   Changes Take Place in British India

1 European Nations Build New Empires

In the worldwide surge of expansion and colonization that accompanied the Age of Exploration, the major European nations established vast overseas empires. By the middle of the nineteenth century, however, nearly all of the European empires in the Americas had been lost as colonies demanded and won their independence. Several nations had retained scattered territories in Africa, Asia, and the Americas, but only Britain and the Netherlands had kept a substantial part of their empires built on overseas trade. In about 1870, the major Western nations began a new wave of empire-building.

A new kind of empire-building develops. Late in the nineteenth century, the Western nations began to compete intensely in their efforts to gain and control overseas possessions. Trade expansion was no longer the main reason for *imperialism* — the takeover and control of other lands. Countries had given up the mercantilist ideas of the Age of Exploration (page 364). The new imperialist period, however, was one of intense nationalism and rivalry in Europe. Countries now sought colonies to acquire territory and prestige, to make up for losses in war, or to stay ahead in the struggle for power. Rapidly expanding populations in Europe also made new territory and overseas settlements desirable. The period from 1870 to the outbreak of World War I in 1914, therefore, is commonly called the Age of Imperialism.

Industrialization contributes to the growth of empires. Another factor in the development of imperialism was the Industrial Revolution, which was well under way in Europe and the United States by the mid-1800's. New factories and machines produced great surpluses of manufactured goods. New sources of labor and raw materials were needed to continue making these products, and new markets in which to sell them were also needed.

In addition, the Industrial Revolution produced new inventions that gave Europe and the United States a technology far ahead of that in nonindustrial nations. The Western nations had military superiority, better transportation and communication, and machines that could replace traditional ways of farming and producing goods. Consequently, it was possible for these nations to gain control of countries that lacked these technological skills.

Some of the motivations for empire-building in the nineteenth century were similar to those in the Age of Exploration. People still sought adventure and excitement in exploring and conquering faraway lands. Some still hoped to convert people of other faiths to Christianity. Some Europeans and Americans also believed it was their responsibility to bring the educational and political ideas of Western civilization to the rest of the world.

Traditional societies react to imperialism. In many ways, the nonindustrial countries and peoples were unprepared for the imperialists. Some were overwhelmed by Western technology and organization, both commercial and military. Those countries that had strong traditional governments and institutions (such as China, Japan, and Persia) could resist outright colonization, but they still faced threats from imperialist nations. The continent of Africa, most of which was divided among many local rulers, was almost entirely taken over by European powers (Chapter 27). Everywhere traditional social and political institutions changed; some broke down altogether.

Imperialism takes different forms. In general, the Western nations built their new empires by taking control of other lands in one of the following ways.

1. Colony: An imperialist nation sometimes formally established its own institutions — law, government, education — in another land, making that region a colony. The colony was ruled as if it were part of the home country.

2. Protectorate: In some lands, a protectorate was established. Local rulers were allowed to keep their titles and perhaps some limited powers, but the imperialist nation actually ran the state. It also "protected" the state against rival states or foreign invasion. Some Indian states had this kind of arrangement within the British Empire.

The Western colonizing powers allowed rulers in some countries to retain their positions and titles. This painting shows the Mogul emperor and Robert Clive, who represented British power in India in the 1760's (page 556), negotiating an agreement.

3. Concession: Sometimes foreign nations or their business interests were given *concessions* by a weaker country — special trading privileges, rights to certain territory (such as a harbor), or access to natural resources. The stronger nation might use its concessions to gain a foothold for a political takeover or the establishment of a sphere of influence.

4. Sphere of influence: Nations that were granted certain privileges or concessions within another country often tried to create a *sphere of influence* — a limited area in which they controlled politics and government. For instance, several European countries established separate spheres of influence in China in the 1890's.

The British Empire leads in expansion. Although some of Britain's American possessions were lost in the 1700's (Chapter 19), the British Empire continued to grow while other empires declined. The British gained control over the Indian subcontinent during the first surge of expansion and colonization. British rule was established by the traders and soldiers of the East India Company, not by the British government. India later became part of the British Empire in the second great wave of European imperialism, which began during the late nineteenth century.

CHECK-UP

1. Vocabulary: *imperialism, concession, sphere of influence.*
2. (a) When did the first wave of European imperialism occur? (b) Why had this ''old'' imperialism declined by the middle of the nineteenth century?
3. (a) When did the second wave of European imperialism occur? (b) What factors contributed to this second wave of imperialism?
4. Name and describe the four basic types of imperialist control.

Landmarks in Technology

THE SPREAD OF MODERN TRANSPORTATION SYSTEMS

The breakthroughs in transportation that accompanied the Industrial Revolution soon spread to far-flung parts of the world as European nations acquired colonies in Africa and Asia. Steamships and railroads tightened the links between the colonizing nations and their possessions. Meanwhile, improved transportation also benefited the colonial areas as railways and paved roads were built. The new means of travel expanded trade, allowed people to move more freely from place to place, and speeded up the exchange of ideas and information.

The first convoy of ships passed through the Suez Canal in 1869 (above). By joining the Mediterranean and Red seas, the Canal shortened the route between Britain and India by 6,000 miles.

The British exported the new transportation technology to their colony of India, helping to unite the huge country, open new areas to trade, and provide jobs. The railway in the drawing was built about 1870 and run by the Sikhs (shown in traditional turbans). Notice that one carriage is reserved for women and children.

The new means of travel were depicted in illustrations of the period. A Chinese artist painted an airplane that looked like a kite (right). Elephants transporting railroad engines on India's Himalayan frontier were the subject of the engraving below.

2 Trade Brings British Rule in India

When the Portuguese established the first European trading posts in India in the early 1500's (page 350), the Indian peninsula, or South Asia, was not a single nation. Though Indian civilization was ancient and its cultural traditions strong (Chapter 11), India had never been completely unified politically. This political disunity, combined with the religious division between Hindus and Muslims, left India unable to resist European traders and adventurers. In the 1700's the British government gradually took over the concessions and territories of the East India Company, thus maintaining British control in India while colonies in other parts of the world were gaining independence.

The Mogul Empire fails to unite India. The European traders who arrived in India in the early 1500's dealt mainly with southern India, which was divided among rival local rulers,

both Hindu and Muslim. In the north, the Mogul Empire was established in 1526 and conquered much of the peninsula. Many local rulers, especially in the Deccan and the south, continued to resist the Moguls, however, and some parts of India never became part of the empire. As Mogul rule weakened in the early 1700's, European traders became deeply involved in the rivalries among Indian rulers.

European nations compete for Asian trade. The Portuguese had established European trade with India. By the early 1600's, however, most major European nations were following mercantilist ideas in trying to increase their wealth and power. The governments of England and the Netherlands (and later France) each chartered a private joint-stock company to finance voyages to Asia and seek profits for their backers (which included the government).

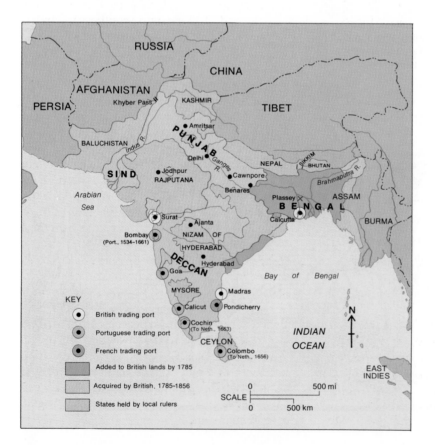

European Rule in South Asia

Lands taken over by the British in India from 1785 to 1856 are shown on this map. What other European nations held colonial outposts in India?

Large sailing ships, such as the one shown moored at Calcutta in the 1790's, carried the East India Company's profitable cargoes between India and the British Isles.

These companies were given monopolies, the exclusive right to represent the country in trade with Asia. The Dutch East India Company effectively broke Portuguese control of the Asian trade, but the Dutch were more interested in trade with the Spice Islands (which later became the Dutch East Indies) than with India.

The English set up trading posts in India. On the last day of the year 1600, Queen Elizabeth I chartered the English East India Company, which was backed by eighty London merchants. In 1613 the Mogul emperor Jahangir granted the East India Company permission to establish a trading post at Surat, and by 1647 there were twenty-seven English trading posts in India, mainly along the coast. By the late 1600's, the East India Company's most important settlements were at Bombay on the northwest coast and Madras and Calcutta on the east (map, page 554).

Agents of the English East India Company soon established a thriving trade. They traveled throughout India, setting up contracts with local weavers of cotton cloth. Some Indian cloth was traded to the Dutch for spices. The rest was sent back to England, where it became England's favorite textile. Calico (named after the port city of Calicut) was widely used for tablecloths and, later, for clothing. By 1625 England was importing some three million yards of calico a year. The East India Company also traded in Persian silks, jewels, and tea. In return, Mogul India imported tin, lead, tapestries, and ivory.

Britain and France clash in India. Just as the European wars of the mid-1700's led to war between French and British settlers in the Americas (page 362), they also brought the French and British into conflict in India. Though France had fewer outposts in India, it held a major fortified trading post at Pondicherry, near the fortified British post at Madras.

India was already in turmoil. The Mogul emperor Aurangzeb, who ruled from 1658 until 1707, had weakened the empire with his harsh policies and wars of conquest. The Marathas in the Deccan and the Rajputs in the north were constantly in rebellion against the Mogul Empire, and the many local rulers in south India had never been conquered. With the death of Aurangzeb, Mogul power declined and internal wars increased.

Both the British and French trading companies had been given fairly broad powers to defend their settlements, negotiate treaties with local rulers, and otherwise promote trade. Soldiers from trading-post garrisons fought in the wars that were waged between rival Indian rulers. These rulers could grant trading privileges to whichever country helped them. The Indian rulers in turn used the long-standing rivalry between the French and British to gain help in their wars.

The outbreak of war in Europe in 1740[1] led to open war between the French and British in India. French troops from the fort at Pondicherry captured Madras and gained control of much of the Deccan and the southern coast. For a time France was the leading European power in India.

Clive begins to build British power. During these battles with the French, Robert Clive, an East India Company clerk, joined the fighting and proved to be a brilliant military leader. In the early 1750's, he led British troops in several daring captures of French forts. Clive then moved north to defend the British trading post at Calcutta in Bengal (map, page 554). The ruler of Bengal, helped by the French, had captured Calcutta in June, 1756. About 150 British residents had been imprisoned in a small room without adequate food, water, or air. All but 23 prisoners had died from suffocation, the heat, or their wounds, making the prison notorious as the "Black Hole" of Calcutta.

The British in India were shocked and angry over this incident. Moreover, Britain and France were once again at war in Europe (the Seven Years' War, 1756–1763). Clive and his army of 3,000 British and Indian soldiers recaptured Calcutta, took other French posts, and defeated an Indian army of more than 50,000 at Plassey in June, 1757. The heroic victory put a pro-British ruler on the throne of Bengal and made this prosperous state a base for East India Company expansion.

French influence in India weakens. Four years later British and Indian forces took the main French outpost at Pondicherry. While the fort was returned to the French by the Treaty of Paris (1763), which ended the Seven Years' War, France lost its other claims in India except for a few trading posts.

The British gain control of northeast India. Robert Clive's administration of the rich territory of Bengal firmly established the British in India, but it made him a controversial figure. From his Indian allies Clive accepted a fortune in jewels and money, rich estates, and a Mogul title. In 1760 he returned to England a wealthy man and was given numerous honors. Other Company officials also accepted (and encouraged) bribes and rich gifts from local rulers; such practices were common in the Mogul court and other Indian states. Many officials accumulated huge private fortunes.

When Clive returned to India in 1765 as governor of Bengal, he had decided to reform the Company's administration, even though this threatened the fortunes of many officials. In the same year, Clive made an important agreement with the Mogul emperor. In return for a yearly payment of 260,000 British pounds to maintain the imperial court, the emperor granted the Company all the tax revenues from Bengal and two neighboring provinces, the richest lands in the Indian peninsula. These taxes amounted to about four million pounds a year, in addition to what the Company earned in trading.

Despite Clive's reforms and the Bengal agreement, members of the English Parliament decided to investigate his administration and the fortune he had made. Two years later he was recalled to England. Feeling that his efforts in India were unappreciated, and upset by the investigation, Clive committed suicide.

Parliament places controls on the Company. Even after Clive was recalled, Parliament continued to question the East India Company's actions in India. Officials were accused of raising the price of grain during the famine of 1770 so that the Company made great profits while many Indians starved. Company money was being spent on wars between local Indian rulers. Moreover, the Company's three important centers — Bengal, Madras, and Bombay — were so far apart that efficient administration was difficult.

In 1773 Parliament passed the first of several laws that limited the Company's power and brought about British government control in India. The Regulating Act gave Parliament the power to appoint a governor-general and council to oversee the East India Company. Warren Hastings, a Company official and

---

[1] The War of the Austrian Succession (1740–1748) involved the major European nations — Prussia, Austria, France, and Britain — in a struggle over the balance of power. The war was triggered by the succession of Maria Theresa, daughter of the Holy Roman Emperor, to the Austrian throne.

strong-willed administrator, was appointed governor of Bengal and general over the other British posts. In the next ten years, Hastings made British control throughout India more secure, using both diplomacy and warfare. Although he had almost no help from the British government, Hastings used Company forces to protect British interests.

India becomes important to Britain. Britain had few funds to spend in India because its treasury had been drained by the Seven Years' War and the fighting in North America. Britain's economy, in fact, now depended on income from the East India Company and on the personal fortunes that its officials brought home from India. In 1784 Prime Minister William Pitt drafted the India Act. Instead of the powers it had assumed as a "government within a government," the East India Company was now limited to trading activities. The British government took charge of military and government actions in India. The Company, however, kept its vast territories and its income from taxes.

Cornwallis establishes the Indian Civil Service. The first governor-general appointed under the India Act was Lord Cornwallis, the general who had surrendered to the Americans at Yorktown in 1781 (page 434). Cornwallis was a strict administrator who made reforms in taxation, landholding, and, most importantly, government service. Under the old system, East India Company employees had acted as merchants, soldiers, and government administrators all at once. With Cornwallis's reforms, government workers were carefully chosen, professionally trained, and well paid. These reforms marked the beginning of the Indian Civil Service, which produced many able and efficient administrators.

High-level civil service jobs, however, were not open to Indians. Cornwallis, his successors as governor-general, and most Britons who came to India brought with them an overwhelming feeling of British superiority. This attitude remained typical of British rule in India. Another governor-general, Richard Wellesley, stated: "No greater blessing can be conferred on the native inhabitants of India than the extension of British rule."

The British make changes in Indian ways. As the British remained in India, they gradually moved away from policies of outright conquest and profit-making toward more thoughtful and humane government. Land reform, agricultural help, and education were emphasized. Educating the people of India in the British way, however, often meant abolishing or ignoring Indian traditions that offended Europeans. In 1829 the governor-general abolished suttee, the Hindu practice in which a widow committed suicide on her husband's funeral pyre. Many Hindus were outraged that the British had abolished a Hindu custom, even though some agreed that suttee had no place in a modern society.

Parliament passed other legislation that ignored Indian customs and traditions. Indian soldiers in British service, called sepoys (SEE-poyz), could be required to serve in other parts of Asia. According to Hindu tradition, however, a caste member would lose status by leaving the country. As Britain was at war in Burma and Afghanistan, reassignment appeared to high-caste sepoys as a very real threat. In 1856, the new governor-general passed a law that abolished still another age-old tradition. It allowed Hindu widows to remarry.

Violence comes in the Sepoy Rebellion. The following year, the British introduced a new kind of rifle into the Indian army. In order to load the rifles, the sepoys had to bite off the tops of the greased cartridges. Rumor spread that the cartridges were smeared with a mixture of beef and pork grease. Hindus hold cows sacred, and the Koran forbids Muslims to eat pork. Indians of both religions were enraged at what appeared to be British insensitivity to their beliefs. The sepoys refused to load their rifles, and some were dismissed or sent to prison. This proved to be the final act of humiliation for the Indian soldiers.

On a Sunday morning in May, 1857, three sepoy divisions near Delhi rose in revolt. They freed their fellow soldiers who had been jailed and then marched to Delhi, where they declared the Mogul ruler to be emperor of India. Fighting was fierce for the first few months of the rebellion. Some sepoys, particularly the battalions formed by the Sikhs (page 243),

News of the rebellion of the sepoys near Delhi quickly spread to other parts of India under British rule, thus triggering further revolt. This old engraving shows Indian cavalry attacking British footsoldiers.

fought on the side of the British, while some independent rulers in northern India joined the rebels. British communities were besieged. At Cawnpore, the rebelling troops promised safe passage to some 400 British civilians, mostly women and children, but these people were massacred before they could escape to safety. Violence continued in northern India for more than a year.

The 1857 rebellion was a turning point in Indian history. Bitterness and resentment lingered for many years on both sides. The British called the event the Indian Mutiny. Indian nationalists called it the first war for independence. Its immediate results were changes in British government policies toward India, the end of the East India Company's power, and the exile (in 1858) of the last Mogul emperor.

CHECK-UP

1. (a) How did England gain a foothold in India? (b) Which nation was Britain's chief rival in India during the first half of the eighteenth century? (c) What was the significance of the Battle of Plassey?
2. (a) Why did Parliament decide to investigate the administration of the East India Company? (b) What were the provisions of the Regulating Act (1773)?
3. (a) How did the India Act of 1784 change the role of the East India Company in India? (b) What powers were assumed by the British government? (c) What reforms were undertaken by Cornwallis?
4. (a) What British policies came into conflict with Indian traditions? (b) What caused the Sepoy Rebellion? (c) What were the results of the rebellion?

3   Changes Take Place in British India

After the Sepoy Rebellion, the British government ruled India directly, bringing changes to the country that would make it even more valuable to the British Empire. Though the policies of the government were in general more understanding of Indian ways than those of the East India Company, the dissatisfaction of Indian nationalists — those who wanted self-government for India — continued to increase. They came to feel that British rule exploited India more than it helped the country.

INDIA IN THE BRITISH EMPIRE

Britain changes ruling policies in India. India's products, markets, and natural resources were coming to be essential to the British economy. In 1858, the year in which the Sepoy Rebellion finally came to an end, Parliament passed the Government of India Act. This law abolished the East India Company and transferred rule over its territories to the British government. The queen's representative in India was the viceroy, who had far less power than the governor-general had had and was directly responsible to the secretary of state for India, a British cabinet officer. Many more British soldiers were sent to India.

Queen Victoria announced other new policies. She promised that the government would not interfere with Indian religious beliefs or expand the territories it held. The East India Company had frequently taken over Indian states or kingdoms, either by deliberately encouraging wars or by seizing lands where rulers had no direct heirs. Under the new policy, the government would interfere only if a ruler mismanaged the state.

The British now ruled directly over about three fifths of the Indian subcontinent (map, page 554). More than 560 states remained under Indian rule. Some, such as Hyderabad and Rajputana, were larger than England itself. The Indian-ruled states, however, were by no means independent. Their leaders controlled local government and education but could not make treaties with foreign countries or other states. British officials handled the military and financial affairs for those states.

In 1876 Parliament declared Queen Victoria "Empress of India," making the people of India subjects of the British monarch and India itself part of the British Empire. The British took several other steps to ensure their control over this valuable possession.

British technology unites India. To govern efficiently a country as large as India, British officials needed better transportation and

PRIMARY SOURCES IN WORLD HISTORY
Proclamation by Queen Victoria

In reaction to the Sepoy Rebellion, Queen Victoria issued a proclamation on November 1, 1858. The document placed India under the control of the British government. It also made some promises to Britain's Indian subjects, as indicated in the following passage:

> . . . We have resolved to take upon ourselves the government of the territories in India, heretofore administered in trust for us by the honorable East India Company. . . .
>
> . . . We disclaim alike the right and the desire to impose our convictions on any of our subjects. . . . None [shall be] molested or [disturbed], by reason of their religious faith or observances, but . . . all shall alike enjoy the equal and impartial protection of the law. . . .
>
> And it is our further will that . . . our subjects, of whatever race or creed, be freely and impartially admitted to offices in our service, the duties of which they may be qualified, by their education, ability, or integrity, duly to discharge. . . .
>
> . . . It is our earnest desire to stimulate the peaceful industry of India, to promote works of public utility and improvement, and to administer its government for the benefit of all our subjects resident therein.

How did the proclamation protect the religious and legal rights of Indians? What provision was made for Indians to take part in their government? What indication was there that Britain wanted to promote the development of India?

communication. Between 1850 and 1870 the British established an Indian telegraph system and postal service, and in 1870 India and Britain were linked by telegraph. Networks of roads and railroads were built, which would ultimately give India the best road system in all Asia. Trains carried troops, hauled cotton and other goods to seaports, delivered food to famine-stricken areas, and provided passenger service for Indians. By this means, millions who had spent their entire lives in local villages came into contact with people in other parts of the country. Indian villagers who traveled to large cities such as Bombay and Calcutta often found that they preferred urban life and never returned home.

The telegraph and the postal service, while less dramatic than the coming of the railroad, produced similar results. They made Indians more aware of the rest of the world and allowed people from different regions to meet and share experiences, news, and ideas. In an accidental way, British technology was helping to unite the people of India.

Britain protects India's frontiers. Another vital link in communication and trade with India was the Suez Canal linking the Red Sea and the Mediterranean. Opened in 1869, the canal provided the quickest sea route between Britain and India. To ensure the safety of this route, Britain bought partial control of the canal and became involved in the politics of Egypt and Africa.

Its efforts to safeguard India also involved Britain in Central Asia. At the time when the East India Company was establishing British rule in the eastern state of Bengal, Persia and Afghanistan were fighting for lands in northwest India. In the mid-1700's the Afghans held Sind, Kashmir, and much of the Punjab (map, page 554). The Sikhs and other Indians later retook these lands.

By the early 1800's three major European powers — France (under Napoleon), Britain, and Russia — were involved in disputes over territory in Persia and Afghanistan. Napoleon abandoned his campaign in this region, but Britain and Russia continued to maneuver Persian and Afghan politics to support their own interests. Britain's main concern was protecting the mountain passes on India's northwest frontier. Russia sought to move south into the lands around the Caspian Sea and perhaps to gain a port on the Indian Ocean.

Trying to keep Afghanistan free from both Russia and Persia, British soldiers and sepoys fought a series of border wars on the northwest frontier. In 1879 Britain gained control of the vital Khyber Pass, but British-Russian rivalry over Afghanistan continued, coming near war several times.

Technology hurts home industries. India was especially valuable to Britain as a source of raw materials and a market for products made by British factories. Cotton from India was quickly and cheaply woven into cloth in British textile mills. The machine-made cloth was shipped back to India, where it was sold at a lower price than domestic homespun cloth.

The British cloth had a devastating effect on India's textile industry. Home spinning had for centuries been an important source of income for peasant families in India. By the late 1800's, however, the Indian textile industry had been nearly destroyed by British imports.

Some Indians accepted the collapse of this traditional handicraft economy as the price of modernization. They argued that European technology was necessary for India to move into the modern era. In the 1870's and 1880's Indian industrialists established mills and factories to produce textiles, iron, and steel. Indian nationalists, however, took the destruction of the home spinning industry as an example of British exploitation. (In the 1920's the traditional spinning wheel became the symbol for the independence movement.)

THE NATIONALIST MOVEMENT

Education introduces European ideas. Many Indian leaders were educated in the British-style universities established in India in the 1850's, and some also studied in England. Since the 1830's, English had been the official language in most Indian schools and in the law courts. Speaking English soon became a sign of education in India. The aim of the schools was to train a loyal group of Indians who would devote their lives to the Civil Service.

As Indian students studied modern science and Western civilization, they also read the

LINKING PAST AND PRESENT
Words Imported from India

The British who lived in India during the centuries of colonial rule began to use words from Hindi and other Indian languages. Because textiles were such an important part of British-Indian trade, many of these words are names for fabrics — *calico* and *madras* from the cities of Calicut and Madras, *chintz* from a word meaning "brightly colored." (The two-piece dress shown in the picture was made of Indian calico exported to Europe about 1770.)

Colonial settlers found it comfortable to wear the loose-fitting Indian garment called *pajamas,* the square scarf called a *shawl,* or the riding breeches known as *jodhpurs* (the name of a state in northern India). They lived in one-story houses called *bungalows* — a style of architecture popular in Bengal. They might eat the spicy Indian dish called *curry* or drink *punch,* originally a drink made from five ingredients. (The Hindu word *pancha,* or "five," also is part of the name of the Punjab, which is crossed by five rivers.) When they returned home, the British took these parts of Indian culture with them.

works of English philosophers who wrote about nationalism and independence. With a new awareness of these Western ideas, educated Indians began to criticize British policies in India. Some British officials feared that educated Indians would become the leaders of an independence movement in India.

Indian resentment increases. All of India's early nationalist leaders were British-trained. In learning to be civil servants, they were taught the high standards of the British system of justice. They soon found, however, that the British did not always live up to these standards, especially in dealing with colonial peoples. Indians who came to expect fair and equal treatment from the British were repeatedly disappointed.

Another serious complaint was that British officials and their families remained separate from Indian society. Signs reading "For Europeans Only" were posted at cultural events and in social clubs, on trains, and in other places where British and Indians met. Even British-educated Indians were denied high-level positions in the Indian Civil Service.

The bitter rejection these Indian leaders experienced led them to take new pride in India's heritage and traditions. Their confidence grew in their ability to govern themselves. Cherishing democratic ideals, they sought to bring about change through peaceful and legal methods.

Nationalists take action. One of India's earliest nationalist leaders was Surendranath Banerjea (soo-RAYN-drah-naht BAH-ner-jee), a Bengali Brahmin and the son of a doctor. Educated at Calcutta University, he went to work in the Indian Civil Service after protesting against its discriminatory policies in hiring Indians. He soon lost his job for breaking a minor rule and traveled to London to plead his case. His appeal was denied, but Banerjea maintained his belief in British principles of law and justice. He returned to India determined to spend the rest of his life seeking self-government for his country. His persistence earned him the nickname "Surrender-not" Banerjea.

In 1876, at the age of 28, he became a teacher and editor of a nationalist paper, which he ran for the next forty years. He also started Bengal's first nationalist party. When he was jailed for his newspaper's criticism of a British judge, Banerjea welcomed imprisonment as a public display of British injustice. This was a tactic that later leaders would also use.

Like other moderate Indian nationalists, Banerjea believed that India would be granted self-government when Parliament thought the country was ready. These leaders believed that India must develop national unity and become politically educated, or else it would slip back into the religious and caste divisions that had made unification impossible in the past.

Other nationalist leaders, however, were most concerned about India's economic future.

TIMETABLE

Imperialism In India

1600   Queen Elizabeth I charters the East India Company.

1613   The East India Company wins a trading post at Surat.

1757   A victory at Plassey gives the British control of Bengal.

1763   The Treaty of Paris ends French power in India.

1773   Parliament appoints a governor-general and council to regulate the East India Company.

1857   The Sepoy Rebellion begins.

1858   The British crush the Sepoy Rebellion, abolish the East India Company, and begin direct rule of India.

1876   India is declared a British possession, and its people become British subjects.

1885   The Indian National Congress is formed.

1905   The partition of Bengal spurs nationalist action.

1906   The Muslim League is formed.

1912   The Indian capital is moved from Calcutta to Delhi.

If Britain continued to drain India of its economic resources, they pointed out, the country would have little left when independence was achieved. Dadabhai Naoroji (now-ROH-jee), a business leader who represented India in Parliament, pointed out another kind of drain on India's resources: "Europeans occupy almost all the high places in every department of government. . . . While in India they acquire India's money, experience, and wisdom, and when they go, they carry both away with them, leaving India so much poorer in material and moral wealth."

The Indian National Congress is formed. In 1885, nationalist leaders formed the Indian National Congress (later called the Congress party) to call public attention to their views. The group was organized by Allan O. Hume, an Englishman who had retired from the Indian Civil Service and remained in India. Hume's dedication to self-government for India equaled that of any Indian leader. Seventy delegates attended the first meeting of the Congress, held in Bombay. Representing every province in British India, they were mostly English-speaking Hindu professionals. The delegates to the Congress did not at first call for self-rule or independence. Trying to work within the system, they asked instead that Indians be given better and more responsible government positions. The Congress also asked for lower military spending, since Indians were being heavily taxed to support British campaigns in Burma and Afghanistan.

Not all educated Indians supported the Congress's program. The few radical members of the Congress wanted much more rapid changes, and they eventually left the group. Also, Indian Muslims hesitated to join the Congress, feeling that it was dominated by British-educated Hindus.

Bengal is divided. In 1905, the viceroy, Lord Curzon, made a decision that he believed would help his office govern India more efficiently. He divided the densely populated state of Bengal into West Bengal and East Bengal (which was united with once-independent Assam). This action ignored the religious and ethnic loyalties of the more than 80 million people of Bengal and made the Hindus a minority in both regions. Though the partition of

Bengal lasted only seven years, it spurred both Muslim and Hindu nationalists to action and drew many more Indians into the nationalist movement.

Indians protest the division of Bengal. Reacting to the partition in 1905, leaders of the Congress called on people to *boycott* British imports, that is, to stop buying or using such goods. To show their support, millions of Indians filled the streets of Calcutta, Bengal's largest city. Bonfires of piles of British cloth lit up the city. The boycott, which began in Bengal, rapidly spread throughout India. The wearing of homespun cotton, handwoven on Indian looms, became an emblem of defiance toward British rule. Boycotts of British sugar, glass, and shoes soon followed. In addition to showing the Indians' anger, the boycott stimulated India's own handicraft industries.

Next, Indians extended the boycott to British-run schools. Congress leaders worked to create an educational system that emphasized India's own history and cultural achievements. A major role in this effort was played by a British journalist and reformer named Annie Besant (BEZ-unt), who adopted Hinduism, moved to India, and became active in the nationalist movement. Besant wrote that the movement "brought with it a new self-respect, a pride in the past, a belief in the future, . . . [and] a great wave of patriotic life, the beginning of the rebuilding of a nation."

Some nationalists began to use terrorist methods, setting off bombs and attacking British officials. The British cracked down. Terrorists were imprisoned and their leaders were deported.

The Muslim minority organizes. The division of Bengal gave Muslims a majority in East Bengal, but their leaders worried that they would not be well represented in country-wide elections. In 1906, they organized the All-India Muslim League. One of its main principles was "communal representation" — the assurance that different religious and ethnic groups would hold a certain number of political offices.

Indians gain representation. English political leaders as well as many Indian leaders continued to believe that the best route to independence was through the democratic process. In 1909 Parliament passed the Indian Councils Act, which gave the local legislative councils more power and opened more government positions to Indians. Muslims and other minorities were granted separate representation on the councils. Parliament also passed an elementary education act. It allowed local school districts in India to make education compulsory for children aged six to ten.

A new king visits India. When George V came to the British throne in 1910, he visited India for his coronation as Emperor of India. After appointing a new viceroy, Lord Hardinge, the king also announced that Bengal would be reunited and that the capital of India would be moved from Calcutta to Delhi. Both decisions pleased Indian nationalists. The new capital, near the center of India, had centuries of tradition. The change of capitals, which took place in 1912, appeared to symbolize a move toward unification.

The times seemed hopeful, but in August, 1914, war broke out in Europe. The war years involved India, as part of the British Empire, and delayed further moves toward Indian independence. Forced to wait, the nationalists grew more impatient to be free of British rule.

CHECK-UP

1. Vocabulary: *boycott.*
2. (a) What changes in British rule were introduced by the Government of India Act? (b) What further changes were announced by Queen Victoria?
3. (a) How did British technology help to unite India? (b) How did it affect India's textile industry?
4. Why did education in British-run schools lead many Indians to resent British rule in India?
5. (a) How did Banerjea and other moderate nationalists believe that Indians should work toward self-government for their country? (b) What changes in British policy were requested by the Indian National Congress in 1885?
6. (a) Why did Lord Curzon decide to partition the state of Bengal? (b) How did Indians respond to the partition?
7. (a) What were the provisions of the Indian Councils Act? (b) What other British actions gave hope for independence to Indian nationalists in the early 1900's?

Chapter 25 Review

Summary

Merchants of the English East India Company arrived in South Asia in the early 1600's. The Indian peninsula was divided politically and religiously, allowing the Company to gain large amounts of territory and become the dominant European power. Robert Clive and Warren Hastings established the foundation for British rule in India, ending French influence there.

India became valuable economically to Britain, and the British government gradually limited the East India Company's powers to commercial activities. British law and educational systems were established in India. British technology brought better transportation and communication but harmed traditional industries. The British disregard of Indian traditions and customs aroused resentment that sometimes led to violence, as in the Sepoy Rebellion (1857–1858).

The Government of India Act (1858) placed India under direct British rule; the country became part of the British Empire in 1876. At the same time, Indian nationalists actively began to seek a greater role in their own government. The Indian National Congress, founded in 1885, led the nationalist movement. The Muslim League, founded in 1906, represented the Muslim minority. The outbreak of World War I delayed further moves toward Indian independence.

Vocabulary Review

1. Write the sentences listed below on a sheet of paper. In each sentence, fill in the blank with one of these words: *boycott, concession, imperialism, sphere of influence.*
(a) __?__ is the policy of extending a nation's dominance over other nations for economic and political advantages.
(b) In some cases an imperialist nation was able to establish a __?__, in which it controlled the politics or government of limited areas of another country.
(c) When the Indians decided to __?__ British imports, they stopped buying or using them.
(d) A __?__ is a grant by one country to another of special trading privileges, facilities, or access to resources.

2. Distinguish between the terms in each of the following pairs:
(a) governor-general; viceroy.
(b) India Act; Indian Councils Act.
(c) Indian National Congress; Muslim League.
(d) Battle of Plassey; Sepoy Rebellion.

People to Identify

Match the following people with the numbered phrases that describe them: *Robert Clive, Warren Hastings, Queen Victoria, Surendranath Banerjea, Allan O. Hume, Lord Curzon.*
1. The British monarch at the time India was declared part of the British Empire.
2. A member of the Indian Civil Service who became one of India's earliest nationalist leaders; earned the nickname "Surrender-not."
3. An East India Company official who led British military forces to victory in the Battle of Plassey.
4. An East India Company official who was appointed governor-general in 1773 and who secured British control in India.
5. The organizer of the Indian National Congress.
6. The British viceroy who divided the state of Bengal.

Relating Geography and History

1. **Locating places.** Locate each of the following on a map in this chapter:
(a) Bombay   (f) Bengal
(b) Madras   (g) Plassey
(c) Calcutta   (h) Surat
(d) Calicut   (i) Afghanistan
(e) Delhi   (j) Pondicherry

2. **Map study and interpretation.** As had been the case with its American colonies, Britain ruled India from a great distance. In 1869, the opening of the Suez Canal (page 560) provided a much quicker sea route between Britain and India. Find the Suez Canal on the map on page 591. (a) What two bodies of water does it link? (b) Suggest a sea route the British could have used to reach India before the Suez Canal opened. (c) How did the distance from Britain to India — even

after the opening of the canal — affect relations between the British and their Indian subjects? Compare and contrast the situation in India with the earlier situation in the American colonies.

Discussion Questions

1. (a) Why did British and French trading companies take part in the wars between rival Indian rulers? (b) What were the results of the open warfare between the French and British in India during the 1740's and 1750's? (c) How did the British East India Company benefit from the British victory at the Battle of Plassey?

2. (a) How was the Sepoy Rebellion viewed by Indian nationalists? (b) How was this event viewed by British officials in India? (c) What changes in British policy resulted from the Sepoy Rebellion?

3. In what ways did each of these acts affect British rule in India: (a) the Regulatory Act of 1773, (b) the India Act of 1784, (c) the Government of India Act of 1858?

4. How did British interest in India lead to its involvement in Egypt and Central Asia?

5. (a) In what ways did British technology help India? (b) What British policies weakened the Indian economy?

6. (a) How did Surendranath Banerjea protest British injustices? (b) Name the early goals of the Indian National Congress. (c) What were the results of the Indian boycotts of British goods?

7. (a) What was the Muslim League? (b) Why was it organized?

8. Explain which of the four forms of imperialism were found in India under British domination. Use examples from the chapter.

Reading Primary Sources

Called the "Father of Indian Unrest," Gangadhar Tilak urged the Indian National Congress to take action to work for Indian independence. The following passage is from a speech Tilak gave in 1907. Read the passage. Then answer the questions that follow.

> This government does not suit us. . . . [British rule] . . . has been established [here] in order that a foreign government may exploit the country. . . . English education, growing poverty, and . . . familiarity with our rulers opened our eyes. . . .
>
> We have come forward with a scheme which, if you accept, shall . . . enable you to remedy this state of things. . . . Your industries are ruined utterly, ruined by foreign rule; your wealth is going out of the country; and you are reduced to the lowest level which [a] human being can occupy. In this state of things, is there [a] . . . remedy by which you can help yourself? The remedy is . . . boycott. We say prepare your forces, organize your power, and then go to work so that they cannot refuse you what you demand. . . .
>
> We are not armed, and there is no necessity for arms either. We have a stronger weapon, a political weapon, in boycott. . . . The whole of this . . . [government], which is carried on by a handful of Englishmen, is carried on with our assistance. . . . They try to keep us in ignorance of our power of cooperation [which would give us the strength to rule ourselves]. . . . The point is to have the entire control in our hands.

(a) What does Tilak claim to be the reason for the imposing of British rule on India? (b) How did the Indians come to realize their dissatisfaction with British rule? (c) According to Tilak, what were the results of foreign rule in India? (d) What does he propose as a remedy? (e) What does he say would be the result if Indians joined in a boycott against the British?

Skill Activities

1. Stating both sides of an issue. British officials and Indian nationalists viewed the Sepoy Rebellion differently. The British called it the "Indian Mutiny," while Indian nationalists referred to it as the "first war for independence." Write two accounts of this occurrence, describing causes and events from (1) the British point of view and (2) the Indian nationalist viewpoint.

2. Reports. Find more information about one of the following topics and prepare a report: (a) the history of the city of Delhi (including its Red Fort); (b) British imperial policies during the reign of Queen Victoria; (c) the Sepoy Rebellion; (d) Robert Clive; (e) Annie Besant.

3. Making charts. Prepare a chart showing the advantages and disadvantages of British rule in India. In one column list the drawbacks of British government in India. In the other column list changes that improved life for Indians under British rule. Then write a short essay, giving your own answer to the question "Did British rule in India hurt or help the people of India?"

The modernization of Japan had its beginnings in the mid-nineteenth century when trade was opened up with Western nations. The Japanese painting below depicts the departure in 1871 from Yokohama of the first Japanese diplomatic party to visit the United States and Europe.

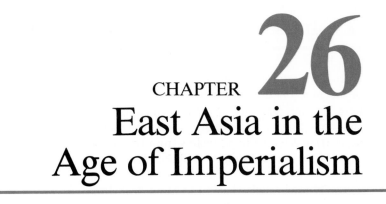

26
East Asia in the
Age of Imperialism

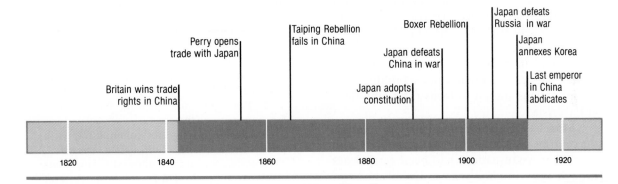

Britain wins trade rights in China

Perry opens trade with Japan

Taiping Rebellion fails in China

Japan adopts constitution

Japan defeats China in war

Boxer Rebellion

Japan defeats Russia in war

Japan annexes Korea

Last emperor in China abdicates

1820   1840   1860   1880   1900   1920

In the late 1700's, both China and Japan were following policies of isolation imposed by their rulers. European nations attempted to break through this isolation and extend their trade and influence in Asia. Contacts with the West affected China and Japan in very different ways.

The Chinese Empire clung to its ancient Confucian traditions. Believing themselves superior to other peoples, the Chinese resisted ideas and practices brought by the Westerners. Soon the imperialist nations established spheres of influence in China. Unable to resist superior European weapons and technology, China was forced to take steps toward modernization.

In Japan, however, leaders quickly came to realize they could not resist the new ideas coming from the West. In a startlingly short period, Japan moved from feudalism to modern industrialism. By the outbreak of World War I, Japan had become a major world power.

This chapter describes the expansion of European imperialist nations into East Asia and the effects of this expansion in China and in Japan.

CHAPTER OUTLINE

1   Imperialist Nations Bring Change to China

2   Revolution Ends the Chinese Empire

3   Japan Becomes a Modern Nation

1 Imperialist Nations Bring Change to China

During the long isolation begun by Ming rulers in the 1400's and 1500's (Chapter 12), the Chinese Empire remained a great civilization. In 1644 the Ming rulers were overthrown by rebellious armies. Nomadic Manchus from the north seized power, establishing the Ch'ing dynasty.

Manchu emperors had long and stable reigns but eventually faced the same problems as earlier dynasties — peasant rebellions, heavy expenditures for defense, corruption and inefficiency in government. The Manchu rulers — whom the Chinese considered foreigners — grew increasingly unpopular. Their power was beginning to weaken when empire-building European nations started to focus their ambitions on East Asia.

Manchus maintain the tributary system. For centuries, China's diplomatic dealings with most other Asian nations had been carried out through the tributary system. Established under the Ming rulers, the system reflected the Confucian principle of relationships between "superiors" and "inferiors." Because China considered all foreign countries inferior, those countries were expected to send lavish gifts, or tribute, to the emperor as a sign of respect. These gifts were presented in elaborate ceremonies at the imperial court, where the emperor returned even more lavish presents. Of all China's neighbors, only Japan refused to take part in the tributary system.

An important aspect of the tributary system was the ceremony that went with it. The person paying tribute was required to *kowtow* — to kneel on both knees and bow three times, touching his nose to the floor. This ritual acknowledged the emperor's superiority over foreign nations.

Foreign trade is controlled. Although the European nations that traded with China were not part of the tributary system, they had to abide by Chinese rules. The Chinese viewed trade as a privilege given to foreigners, not as a right. Chinese officials selected a few commercial firms, known as *hongs,* to act as agents for the government. All *hongs* were situated in Canton, the only port open to foreigners. After about 1700 the *hongs* held a monopoly on all trade between China and the West. Foreign merchants had to follow strict rules:

1. No foreign warships may sail inside the inlet to the river.
2. Neither foreign women nor firearms may be brought into factories [warehouses].
3. Foreign factories shall employ no maids and no more than eight Chinese male servants.
4. Foreign trade must be conducted through the *hong* merchants. Foreigners living in the factories must not move in and out too frequently, although they may walk freely within a hundred yards of their factories.
5. Foreigners may neither buy Chinese books nor learn Chinese.
6. Foreigners may not communicate with Chinese officials except through the *hong.*
7. Foreigners are not allowed to row boats freely in the river. They may, however, visit the flower gardens and the temple opposite the river in groups of ten or less three times a month, on the 8th, 18th, and 28th. They shall not visit other places.
8. Foreign traders must not remain in Canton after the trading season; even during the trading season when the ship is laden, they should return home or go to Macao [a Portuguese colony].

The British demand changes. European traders had accepted the Chinese rules and regulations since the 1600's. The trade in Chinese tea and silk was so profitable that they would abide by any restrictions. By the late 1700's, however, the situation changed. Trade in Asia was expanding, and British officials came to resent the Chinese rules. In 1793 Lord Macartney went to Peking representing King George III of England. His instructions were to establish normal trading relations between Britain and China. He asked that more ports be opened to trading. He also requested a local residence for traders and permission to preach Christianity.

At Macartney's audience with the emperor Ch'ien Lung, it was immediately clear that British and Chinese ideas differed. Instead of

Horses and other valuable gifts were presented as tribute to the Manchu emperors by respectful ambassadors from neighboring Asian lands.

kneeling on both knees when presenting lavish gifts to the emperor, Macartney knelt on one knee only. Since that show of respect was appropriate for the king of England, Macartney considered it appropriate for the emperor of China. There was also a difference of opinion about Macartney's gifts, which included some of the most sophisticated European scientific inventions of the age. Among the gifts were telescopes, plate glass, and mathematical instruments. Because the meeting happened to coincide with the emperor's birthday, Macartney offered these technological marvels as gifts. The emperor, however, saw them as tribute.

After Macartney's visit, the emperor Ch'ien Lung sent a letter to George III. He took note of the king's "respectful obedience" in sending tribute but pointed out that as the "Celestial Empire" possessed an abundance of all things, he had "no need for the products of foreign barbarians." China's trade in tea, silk, and porcelain, the emperor continued, was carried on so that other nations could share in his country's abundance. He then denied all the British requests. The letter concluded with a warning:

> The requests submitted by your envoys not only violate the laws of the Celestial Empire, but are vain, impracticable, and not even in your own best interests. . . . We trust that you will share Our views and forever be obedient. . . . The laws of the Celestial Empire are very strict. . . . Do not say that you were not warned. Tremble and obey!

Trade in opium begins. As the emperor had stated, the Chinese had little desire for Western goods, though Europeans were eager for Chinese tea and silks. The British and other European traders had to buy these goods with silver. To increase their supply of silver, the British began to import opium from India to sell to the Chinese.

Opium, a narcotic drug made from poppies, had been used for centuries in China as medicine. By the 1700's, however, opium smoking was widespread. The Chinese government forbade the sale and import of opium, but many Chinese officials took bribes from the British traders, and large quantities of opium continued to be smuggled into Canton with their help. By the 1830's millions of Chinese were addicts.

The opium trade brings war. Concern about opium addiction, combined with an economic crisis, finally prompted the Chinese government to act decisively against the trade. Silver had once flowed into Chinese banks from British traders to pay for tea and silk. Now silver was leaving China as payment for opium.

In 1839 the Chinese government began a serious campaign against opium use. Opium dealers were arrested and executed, but smuggling continued to increase. The emperor sent an official to Canton to enforce the laws. The official imprisoned British traders and government authorities in their own warehouses and confiscated the traders' stock of opium.

From the British point of view, this treatment of British citizens was cause for war. After several more clashes between the British and the Chinese, the British moved from Canton and occupied the island of Hong Kong. From this base, British warships and troops attacked

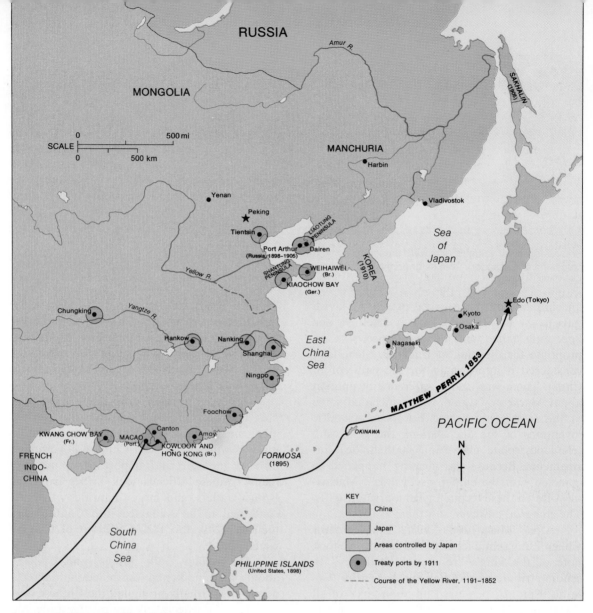

Imperialism in East Asia

The treaty ports whose names are shown in capital letters were like city-states, independent of China's government. What European nations established treaty ports? What area on the continent of Asia was taken over by Japan in 1910?

Chinese coastal cities. The British called their actions the Trade War, arguing that the right to trade freely was the main issue. The Chinese called the conflict the Opium War, claiming that the real issue was the illegal opium trade.

The Chinese forces were badly organized and equipped with old-fashioned weapons. British ships, soldiers, and weapons easily defeated them in battle after battle. Finally, after three years, the Chinese government asked for peace and gave in to British demands.

The West wins trade rights. The Treaty of Nanking (1842) ended the war between Britain and China and established a new pattern for European trade with Asia: the "unequal treaty" system. The Chinese no longer made the rules, as they had done under the tributary system. Instead, conditions for trade were established by treaty. The Treaty of Nanking gave the British the right to trade in five port cities, or *treaty ports,* where traders would be allowed to live. Foreigners accused of crimes would be tried under their own country's laws, not Chinese law. Britain also gained possession of the island of Hong Kong and a cash settlement for the value of the destroyed opium.

In the next few years, additional Western nations concluded similar treaties with China. Under the terms of these agreements, China was to give all countries equal trading rights and privileges.

Unrest grows in China. Encounters with Western nations were not the only problems facing China and its Manchu rulers in the early nineteenth century. In 1800 the people of the Middle Kingdom still thought of themselves as an untroubled, superior civilization. Beneath the surface, however, China was in the midst of crisis. Between 1750 and 1850, China's population increased from 180 million to over 430 million. The demand for food soon outstripped the supply. As had happened frequently in the past, China faced famine.

To make the situation worse, the government had neglected the flood-control system. The Yellow River flooded disastrously. Food prices in cities soared. Starving peasants fled their lands in hopes of finding food. They were often forced to sell their land to speculators at prices far below normal. China's peasants, the backbone of the economy, were driven deeper into poverty. At the same time, landholding public officials and merchants were growing wealthy from bribes, taxes, and high prices. Government administration became corrupt and inefficient.

Secret societies are formed. As in earlier times of unrest, peasant rebellions broke out in many parts of China. Discontented young men and women in the villages began to band together in secret antigovernment societies. Throughout Chinese history, such societies had commonly emerged in troubled times. Some had a religious basis; others were political. Se-

---

LINKING PAST AND PRESENT

"Made in Hong Kong"

The chances are good that some product you often wear or carry is labeled "Made in Hong Kong." This small, bustling British colony is the world's largest exporter of clothing — especially blue jeans. Toys, plastics, electronic goods, and computer parts are also made in Hong Kong's factories and shipped from its busy port. The British first occupied rocky Hong Kong Island because of its excellent harbor, and it officially became a colony in 1842. Britain later gained the Kowloon ("Nine Dragons") Peninsula and a 99-year lease on the mountainous New Territories, both on the Chinese mainland.

The island and the Kowloon district make up one of the world's most crowded cities. In parts of Hong Kong, there are more than 380,000 people per square mile. One large community of people live on sampans, or flat-bottomed houseboats, in the harbor. While most of the people of Hong Kong are Chinese, trade has given the city a lively international atmosphere.

cret societies also often controlled illegal or underground activities such as smuggling. Society members shared secret signs and rituals and pledged absolute loyalty. In return, they could call on the society for help or protection.

One of the oldest secret societies, the White Lotus, led an uprising in northern China about 1800. In the south, the Triad Society was a continuing source of trouble and rebellion against the government of the Manchus.

The Taipings lead a rebellion. In the 1840's a young religious fanatic named Hung Hsiu-ch'uan (HOONG SHOO-choo-AHN) started a new secret society. Hung was a village teacher and had read some Christian missionary writings as well as the Chinese classics. After failing the civil service examination several times, he suffered a breakdown. In his illness he became convinced that he was the "Heavenly Younger Brother" of Jesus and was meant to be the savior of China.

Hung's teachings soon attracted thousands of discontented people in southeastern China. One of his followers organized them into fighting units. The rebels then began to march north toward the Yangtze River, capturing villages and cities. In 1851 Hung declared himself ruler of the "Heavenly Kingdom of Great Peace." His rebel movement took its name from Chinese words that meant "great peace": *t'ai-p'ing* (tie-PING).

The Taiping rebels urge reforms. Hung and his followers called for many changes. As one sign of rebellion, Taiping men cut off their queues, which the Manchu rulers had forced the Chinese to wear. Hung proposed dividing land equally among all peasants. He also urged equal rights for women, including the right to take civil service examinations and become government officials. About a quarter of the rebel soldiers were women, including some officers. Among the Taiping rebels, foot-binding, arranged marriages, and other practices that degraded women were abolished. Violations of these bans were punishable by death. The use of liquor, opium, and tobacco carried the same penalty.

The Taipings established a well-disciplined army of fervent believers in their cause. In four years their numbers increased to over one million men and women. Easily defeating imperial troops, they continued northward. By the spring of 1853 they had established their capital in Nanking and controlled a large part of China.

The rebellion is broken. In 1856, the Taiping Rebellion was seriously weakened by a bloody power struggle that took the lives of important Taiping leaders and 30,000 of their followers. In addition, many people who felt threatened by the Taiping reforms began to aid the imperial forces by organizing private armies. Merchants, officials, and wealthy scholar-gentry (page 255) feared losing their special privileges and their land. Many ordinary people could not accept such drastic changes from Chinese traditions. The Taipings also began to lose peasant support as they adopted some of the practices they had condemned.

For the rebels, the most critical loss was their failure to gain foreign support. The Taiping reforms called for treating Westerners as equals, but to protect their trade treaties, Europeans chose to back the decaying and corrupt Manchu dynasty. Western military men helped train Chinese soldiers to fight the rebels. Finally, in 1864, the Taiping capital of Nanking fell to the imperial armies. About 20 million people had died in the rebellion, and parts of China had been devastated by the fighting.

TIMETABLE

The Decline of Imperial China

1842	The Treaty of Nanking gives Britain Hong Kong and special trading rights in China.
1849–1864	The Taiping Rebellion fails to bring about change in China.
1860	Britain and France win spheres of influence.
1895	Defeat in the Sino-Japanese War awakens China to the need for modernization.
1898	K'uang-hsu's Hundred Days' Reform fails.
1900	An international army ends the Boxer Rebellion.
1911	The Nationalist Revolution begins.
1912	The last Manchu emperor abdicates.

An American cartoon, printed in 1900, showed the "carving up" of China by other nations.

Western nations demand new privileges in China. While the Taiping Rebellion was the most widespread, it was not the only anti-government revolt. The imperial government at the same time was resisting revolts by the Muslims in northwest China and by other peasants near the Yellow River.

Taking advantage of the confusion, the French and British made new trade demands. A minor incident involving an "insult" to the British flag gave Britain a reason to send troops into China. Similarly, Napoleon III's government claimed that Chinese authorities had tortured and executed a French missionary. With these excuses, Britain and France sent an armed expedition in 1856 to invade China. The war went slowly, because many British troops were called away by the Sepoy Rebellion in India (page 557). Nevertheless, French and British forces captured the imperial capital at Peking in 1860, forcing the emperor to flee.

As in the Opium War, the imperial government gave in to foreign demands for more trade. This time the Chinese also had to accept the presence within China of British missionaries who were eager to make converts to Christianity. Other Western nations claimed the same privileges.

Each of the European powers now carved out a portion of Chinese territory as its sphere of influence (page 551). Each area was dominated by the country that claimed special privileges within it. These privileges included the right to trade, to dig for minerals such as coal, to build railroads, and to construct military bases. The British owned Hong Kong and had several treaty ports. The French were dominant in the south, the Germans controlled the Shantung Peninsula, and the Russians were supreme in the north (map, page 570). The Chinese also gave up some land in the north to Russia. Japan took over the island of Okinawa.

CHECK-UP

1. Vocabulary: *treaty port.*
2. (a) How did the tributary system reflect Confucian principles? (b) What rules did Western merchants have to follow in China? (c) What Chinese goods did Europeans want?
3. (a) Why did the British smuggle opium into China? (b) How did this illegal trade lead to war in 1839? (c) Why did the Chinese and the British call the war by different names? (d) What was the outcome of the war? (e) What were the provisions of the Treaty of Nanking?
4. (a) What problems arose in China between 1750 and 1850? (b) What reforms were proposed by the leader of the Taiping rebels? (c) Why did the rebellion fail?
5. (a) How did Britain and France take advantage of China's internal problems in the late 1850's? (b) What privileges did Western nations claim in China as a result?

2 Revolution Ends the Chinese Empire

The Taiping Rebellion failed to overthrow the Manchus, yet it marked a turning point in Chinese history. The rebellion had drained the energy of the Manchu dynasty that had ruled for over 200 years. The government never regained its strength. Moreover, the ideas behind the various peasant rebellions survived and inspired later revolutionaries. Outside influences also weakened the government. Two wars had made it clear that China could not compete militarily with Western weapons and technology. Foreign powers had firmly established themselves in and around China.

New rulers try to strengthen China. In the turmoil of the 1860's, the imperial court was taken over by new Manchu rulers determined to regain control. The new emperor was a young boy. Real power was held by his mother, the Dowager (DOW-uh-jer) Empress, who was known as Tz'u-hsi (TSOO-shee). Tz'u-hsi was clever and crafty and managed to retain control for many years. At the height of her power, she wrote:

> Do you know, I have often thought that I am the cleverest woman who ever lived and that others cannot compare with me. Although I have heard much about Queen Victoria and read a part of her life . . . still I don't think her life is half as interesting and eventful as mine. Now look at me, I have 400 million people all dependent on me.

Neither Tz'u-hsi nor her advisers really understood China's need to modernize. They were willing to adopt just enough Western ways to try to make China strong. These attempted reforms were called the "self-strengthening" movement. The government set up a foreign affairs office, reformed China's tax system, built shipyards and railroads, and had Western science and mathematics textbooks translated into Chinese.

Chinese leaders disagree over modernization. Although they respected Western technology, many Chinese officials still rejected Western ideas. A few saw China's situation differently. Li Hung-chang (1823–1901), a respected Chinese scholar-official, was a leader in westernizing:

> To live today and still say "reject the barbarians" [foreigners] and "drive them out of our territory" is certainly superficial and absurd talk. . . . The method of self-strengthening lies in learning what they can do, and in taking over what they rely upon. Moreover, their possession of guns, cannon, and steamships began only within the last hundred years or so, and their progress has been so fast that their influence has spread into China. If we can really and thoroughly understand [and promote] their methods, . . . can we not expect that after a century or so we can reject the barbarians and stand on our own feet?

During the Taiping Rebellion, Li Hung-chang had gained power and personal wealth by building up an army to fight the rebels. To equip the army, he began to build Western-style weapons and steamships. Although his ideas were unacceptable to many, Li was powerful enough to stay in favor with the imperial court. Holding several profitable government posts, he remained influential for some thirty years. Beginning in the 1870's Li also built up his own industrial enterprises, including a steamship line, coal mines, and a telegraph system. To bring more Western knowledge to China, he sent a number of outstanding students to study at American universities.

Li's attitude, however, was not shared by some Chinese officials, who predicted disastrous results from modernizing:

> With the coming of the railways, big cities will become more congested; great mercantile houses will reap a disproportionate amount of profits; small merchants will find it increasingly difficult to continue in their business; . . . hundreds of thousands of transport workers . . . will be thrown out of work. With no land to farm, and no skill to sell, the unemployed will be forced to become criminals in order to survive.

Traditional ideas slow attempts at modernizing. Most of China's leaders continued to believe that it was possible to modernize without making sweeping changes or abandoning traditions. China's political, economic, and social organization did not fit, however, with the needs of a modern industrial society. Traditional ways slowed down attempts to develop industry, transportation, and government. As long as China's traditional society remained unchanged, only surface reforms could be made.

War brings the Hundred Days' Reform. China's disadvantages were made even clearer by its defeat in the Sino-Japanese[1] War of 1894–1895. In a struggle for control of Korea, China was quickly and decisively defeated by Japan. Chinese officials realized that Japan's victory was due mainly to its swift adoption of Western technology and ideas. The defeat also showed how weak the government was, and foreign nations again began to demand privileges in China. Many Chinese were alarmed and frightened.

A radical reformer named K'ang Yu-wei (KAHNG yoo-WAY) led a protest movement backed by many young scholar-officials. In 1895 they sent the emperor a proposal for reform. Most of K'ang's ideas involved changes in basic institutions: law, government, education, the examination system.

The son of Tz'u-hsi had died, and the emperor was now her nephew, the 24-year-old K'uang-hsu (GWAHNG-SHOO). Only a few years earlier, he had taken the ruling power away from his aunt, the Dowager Empress, and forced her to retire. Now the emperor gave K'ang's ideas his support. "Westerners are all pursuing useful studies," the emperor said, "while we Chinese pursue useless studies."

On June 11, 1898, the emperor began to issue imperial orders for changes and reforms. Few actually went into effect, for they threatened almost everyone in a position of power. The educational reforms endangered those who had studied the classics for the civil service examination. The political reforms upset those in office, who prospered from the system of bribes and favors. Religious reforms, which called for converting Buddhist temples into schools, alarmed the monks. On September 21 — a hundred days after he issued the call for far-reach-

"Boxers," like many other Chinese, blamed foreigners for their country's problems.

ing reforms — K'uang-hsu was dethroned by the Dowager Empress.

Some of the reformers were executed. K'ang fled to Japan, and the young emperor was imprisoned for life. Tz'u-hsi returned China to a pattern of slow change. The failure of the Hundred Days' Reform seemed to show that changes would have to come from the Chinese people, not from the rulers.

Western nations make new demands. The weakness and confusion in the Manchu government encouraged European nations to make still more demands for concessions and spheres of influence. Many were granted, and China's unity seemed threatened. To prevent the breakup of the Chinese Empire, in 1899 the American government called on other countries to agree to an "open door" policy that would give all countries equal trading rights.

The Boxers attack foreign influence. China's leaders tried to blame the country's problems on the growing influence of foreign nations. Popular discontent was still high. Flood and famine were widespread. Another secret society emerged to lead a rebellion. Known in English as the "Righteous and Harmonious Fists," or simply "Boxers," they practiced an ancient martial art. Their secret rituals were supposed to give them special powers.

---

[1]*Sino* (SYE-noh), referring to China, comes from the Latin name for the country.

Like the Taiping rebels, the Boxers originally aimed their frustrations at the scholar-gentry and the Manchu rulers. After the Sino-Japanese War, they became dedicated to driving all foreigners out of China. The Boxers were particularly hostile toward missionaries and Chinese Christian converts.

Late in 1899, revolts led by the Boxers broke out in many parts of China. Missionaries were attacked, and thousands of Chinese Christians were killed. At first opposed by imperial troops, the Boxers were nevertheless supported by many provincial officials and court nobles who also deeply resented foreign influences. Some officials simply looked the other way, while others actively helped the Boxers' actions. Finally the Empress herself came to believe that the Boxers might succeed in driving foreigners out of China.

The climax of the Boxer Rebellion came in June–July, 1900, with the siege of the foreign legations in Peking. Nearly a thousand foreigners, as well as about 3,000 Chinese Christians, had taken refuge in the legations, located in one small area of the city. After 55 days, an international army of 20,000 British, American, Japanese, German, and Russian troops broke through the city walls and rescued them.

Some reforms follow rebellion. The foreign nations demanded compensation for the Boxers' actions against their citizens. A huge cash settlement and more concessions further weakened the Chinese government.

The need for change was now even clearer. Reforms were made in the army, with the help of Western advisers. The ancient civil service examinations were ended in 1905. Students were sent abroad to study in Europe, the United States, and Japan. As reformers demanded more changes in the government, Chinese officials studied other governments, especially the new constitutional monarchy in Japan. In 1908 the Dowager Empress agreed to the gradual establishment of a constitutional parliamentary government in China.

These attempts to modernize were unavoidable, but they further weakened the Manchu dynasty. They encouraged feelings of Chinese nationalism against Manchu rule. In 1908 the Dowager Empress died at the age of 73. The imprisoned emperor had died the day before, and rumors spread that he had been poisoned. The only heir to the imperial throne was three years old. Another struggle began for control of China.

Sun Yat-sen organizes a revolution. Since the 1800's, many revolutionary movements in China had been aimed against the Manchu dynasty. The changes proposed in the Hundred Days' Reform had been far-reaching, but they were still within the framework of an imperial system. The first Chinese revolutionary to call for a complete change in government was a doctor educated in Western ideas.

Sun Yat-sen (SOON YAT-SEN) was born in China but grew up and was educated in mission schools in Hawaii. He went to medical school in the British colony at Hong Kong and in Canton. Working with secret societies, he led an anti-Manchu uprising in 1895 but soon had to flee to Japan. Sun then began to travel to overseas Chinese settlements, gathering followers and raising funds for a revolution. He organized student groups throughout the world and wrote and spoke to promote his ideas.

Sun was embarrassed by China's lowly position in the world of nations. In one of his lectures, he stated:

> . . . the Chinese people have only family and clan solidarity; they do not have national spirit. Therefore, even though we have four hundred million people gathered together in one China, in reality they are just a heap of loose sand. Today we are the poorest and weakest nation in the world and occupy the lowest position in international affairs. Other men are the carving knife and serving dish; we are the fish and the meat.

Sun proposes "Three Principles." Sun called for fundamental changes in Chinese society. He developed a program for a republican revolution and established an organization later called the Kuomintang (gwoh-min-DAHNG), roughly meaning "Nationalist Party." In 1905 he expressed his political, economic, and social goals as the "Three Principles of the People." These three principles are generally translated as nationalism, democracy, and "people's livelihood."

1. Nationalism. Sun hoped the Chinese people could develop a feeling of national

Sun Yat-sen, shown here with his wife Soong Ch'ing-ling, succeeded in establishing a nationalist republican government in China.

unity. This meant not only the overthrow of the Manchu dynasty but also the removal of all foreign powers from Chinese soil.

2. Democracy, or "people's rights." Sun's second principle opposed the Confucian class system and called for equality. He wanted a constitutional government combining Western and Chinese traditions to replace rule by an absolute monarch.

3. "People's livelihood." Sun's third principle emphasized a fairer distribution of land and of the profits made by large landowners, to be accomplished mainly through taxation. Sun also believed that the government should help in the development of industries that would make China less dependent on western nations.

The Nationalist Revolution erupts. Although Sun was the most prominent revolutionary leader, he was not the only one. The Nationalist Revolution came about through a sudden rebellion of soldiers and students on the morning of October 10, 1911. The Manchu government offered little resistance. Four thousand years of unbroken dynastic rule suddenly came to an end. China's imperial government, which had lasted forty centuries because of strong cultural unity and tradition, could not survive modernization and change. The last

Manchu emperor (only five years old) left the throne in February, 1912. A statement was issued saying that the rulers had lost the "mandate of heaven" (page 248).

The republic faces confusion. The end of the Chinese Empire came without much violence. The new republic, however, lacked clear direction and a strong leader. Sun Yat-sen was in the United States, gathering funds for the revolution. Returning to China, Sun was named temporary president of the new republic. But Sun and other revolutionary leaders agreed that the republic must have a solid foundation and military support. Their choice as president was a strange one — the Manchus' most powerful general, Yuan Shih-kai (yoo-AHN SHIR-kye). The Manchu rulers had called on Yuan for help against the revolutionaries. Now he agreed to support the republic.

It quickly became clear that Yuan was loyal to neither side and used power mainly for his personal benefit. Yuan's supporters and Sun's followers soon clashed. In 1913, Sun challenged Yuan and lost. Sun again fled to Japan. Yuan disbanded the new parliament and became a dictator. His aim now was to restore the empire with himself as emperor.

Despite his treachery, Yuan Shih-kai kept the country together. In 1915 his government, backed by the United States and other Western nations, resisted Japanese demands that would have established a protectorate over China. After Yuan's death in 1916, however, China fell into chaos. Warlords began to carve up sections of the country for themselves, while Japan continued its attempts to gain power and territory.

The majority of Chinese people had not yet begun to understand or want a democratic government. Now any pretense of democracy or nationalism disappeared. As in the past, it was China's peasants who suffered most. Warlords forced them into regional armies to fight against other warlords. Taxed beyond their ability to pay, the peasants lost their land.

Warlords struggled for control of China for more than a decade. Sun Yat-sen tried in vain to bring order to an increasingly fragmented society. By the time of his death in 1925, his hopes and dreams seemed further out of reach than they had been before the republican revolution.

1. (a) What was the goal of the "self-strengthening" movement? (b) What reforms did it include? (c) What was Li Hung-chang's attitude toward the modernization of China?
2. (a) What brought about the Hundred Days' Reform? (b) Why did these reforms fail?
3. (a) Who were the Boxers? (b) On whom did they blame China's difficulties? (c) What were the consequences of the Boxer Rebellion?
4. (a) Explain Sun Yat-sen's "Three Principles of the People." (b) What were the consequences of the Nationalist Revolution of 1911?
5. (a) What role did Yuan Shih-kai play in the Chinese government between 1911 and 1916? (b) What problems arose in China after Yuan's death?

3 Japan Becomes a Modern Nation

In the 1630's, the Tokugawa shoguns had adopted a policy of isolation from the West (page 267). They stopped trade and travel by the Japanese and refused to allow foreign ships to enter Japanese ports. The only Europeans allowed in Japan were the Dutch, who kept a small trading port at Nagasaki. By 1850, however, European nations dominated much of Asia. The Japanese realized that it was only a matter of time before one of the Western powers would successfully enter Japan.

The United States fleet reaches Japan. Throughout its history, the United States had taken a keen interest in trade with Pacific lands. In 1851, President Millard Fillmore dispatched a naval squadron to Japan, carrying a letter to the emperor. On July 8, 1853, Commodore Matthew C. Perry sailed unhindered into Tokyo Bay. His ships were new steam-powered vessels, trailing black smoke as they cruised past the Japanese ships in the harbor.

Perry presented the shogun (the feudal leader who ruled Japan) with the President's message. It asked for fair treatment for shipwrecked sailors (who had sometimes been refused help or mistreated), the establishment of a refueling station, and a statement of friendship from the government of Japan. The American fleet left, but Perry said he would return in a year for the Japanese reply. Viewing the situation realistically, Japanese officials acknowledged, " . . . we are not the equals of foreigners in the mechanical arts." Rather than fight an uneven war that would cost Japan dearly, the shogun signed the Treaty of Kanagawa with the United States in March, 1854. This treaty gave foreign traders only limited rights. Nevertheless, it was the first step toward allowing foreign influence in Japan, and it weakened the Tokugawa government. Treaties with the British, Dutch, French, and Russians followed.

Four years later, an American diplomat, Townsend Harris, worked out the treaty that established trade relations. Americans in Japanese port cities would be protected by their own army and their own laws. Low tariffs were set on imports and exports. Foreigners would be allowed to live in some inland cities. Within two years of the treaty, ships of fifteen foreign nations were sailing in and out of Tokyo Bay under similar treaties.

Japan reacts to the "barbarians." The Japanese recognized the strength of the West's technological and military accomplishments, but most resented the foreigners and their demands. Some argued that a strong sense of national purpose could easily defeat foreigners. Through the Dutch, many educated Japanese had kept in touch with world affairs and with some of the scientific advances of the time. Some of those who had studied Western learning argued that it would be wiser to develop a blend of "Western science and Eastern ethics." They maintained that by learning Western ways and adapting them to Japanese culture, the Japanese could become superior to the West.

Powerful lords oppose the shogun. The Tokugawa shoguns had retained power partly by keeping the feudal lords, or daimyo, in competition with one another. Now the unpopularity of the foreign treaties gave these lords a

The arrival of Matthew C. Perry in Tokyo Bay in 1853 marked the end of Japan's isolation and the opening of a new era in relations between Asia and the West.

chance to work together against the shogun. As a symbol of national unity, they wanted to give leadership back to the emperor. Japanese emperors had not had political power for several hundred years, but they were still respected by the people. Now two slogans became popular: *"Sonno!"* ("Honor the emperor") and *"Joi!"* ("Expel the barbarian").

Choshu (CHO-SHOO) and Satsuma (SAH-tsuh-mah) were large, wealthy feudal domains in southwestern Japan. Their lords were hostile both to the shogunate and to the Westerners. They were also rivals for national leadership. Choshu and Satsuma samurai attacked foreign ships and seamen, but these attempts to "expel the barbarian" were met with overwhelming force. American and French warships destroyed the Choshu forts. British warships destroyed the Satsuma capital city and sank the ships in its harbor.

The leaders of Choshu and Satsuma realized that their military forces were useless against the foreigners. They therefore began to adopt Western fighting methods and weapons. In 1866, they joined together to overthrow the shogun and restore imperial government.

The shogun's rule is ended. On January 3, 1868, the forces of the rebel lords seized control of the imperial court in the name of the emperor. By May, 1868, the rule of the Tokugawa shoguns had ended. The emperor was the fifteen-year-old Mutsuhito (muh-tsuh-HEE-toh).

As the name of his reign, the young emperor chose *Meiji* (MAY-JEE), meaning "enlightened government." During his long reign (1868–1912) the Meiji emperor took little part in politics but was an important symbol of loyalty and national unity. The Meiji era saw the transformation of Japan from a feudal society into a modern state.

Meiji rule begins. The actual rule of Japan during the Meiji era was in the hands of the group of young samurai who had led the rebellion against the shogun. Most were well-educated samurai from Choshu or Satsuma. As military men they recognized the gap between Japan's military power and that of the West. They felt that industrialization was Japan's only hope of competing. Once that decision was made, they went to work quickly. One of their earliest decisions was to move the imperial government to Edo (the shogun's capital). The city was renamed Tokyo, which means "eastern capital."

The Charter Oath makes changes in government and society. In April, 1868, the Meiji emperor issued the Charter Oath. The document was written by the ruling group and proclaimed its aims for Japan. The oath called for an assembly that would decide important matters by public debate. It also ended feudalism and opened many new occupations to commoners. The direction that Japan would take in the future was clearly stated in the last of the oath's five points: "Knowledge shall be sought from all over the world so as to strengthen the foundations of imperial rule."

To centralize authority, the daimyo had to give up direct control of their lands to the imperial government. Most did so voluntarily. In return for their land, the daimyo were given large cash settlements.

The samurai class, which included nearly two million people, was abolished. The samurai were ordered to discard their two swords, the centuries-old symbol of their position. The final blow to samurai pride came when the Meiji government issued Japan's first draft law in 1873. All men were subject to the draft and so could carry weapons (once the exclusive right of the samurai). Meanwhile, Japan's military forces were being reorganized. The army followed the French pattern; the navy was modeled after the British navy. All these changes, plus a serious loss of income, seemed to signal the end of the samurai tradition.

Discontented samurai rebel. Even though the leaders of the Meiji government were samurai, their early reforms were hardest on the samurai class. The most serious threat to Meiji rule came from unhappy samurai in Satsuma. In 1877, General Saigo (SAH-EE-GO), who had been one of the leaders in establishing the Meiji government, led an army of some 40,000 discontented samurai toward Tokyo. The government forces crushed the rebellion, ending any threat to the new way of life in Japan.

TIMETABLE

Modernization in Japan

1853 Commodore Perry enters Tokyo Bay.
1854 Japan grants limited trade rights to foreigners.
1868 Rebel samurai seize power for the emperor and end the rule of the Tokugawa shoguns. The Meiji emperor begins his reign.
1889 Japan adopts a constitution.
1895 Japan defeats China in the Sino-Japanese War.
1902 A Japanese-British alliance is formed.
1905 Japan defeats Russia in Manchuria.
1910 Japan annexes Korea.

Modernization moves quickly. Such protests against drastic changes in traditional ways of life were not surprising. Other factors, though, made Japan ready to modernize quickly and successfully.

One of those factors was a strong national feeling. Unlike many other countries in Asia, Japan had a long-standing sense of its identity as a separate nation. National loyalties were more important than loyalties to one's family or to the feudal lord.

Still another factor was the absence of poverty on a large scale in Japan. When the Americans and Europeans first arrived, the Japanese people had a generally high standard of living. Probably about 40 percent of the Japanese people were literate (a high percentage for the time). During the years of Japan's isolation from the Western world, trade and agriculture had prospered, and the country had become urbanized.

A willingness to see value in new ways of doing things was also important. There was little resistance among the Japanese to borrowing ideas that seemed useful or practical. Although the social class lines of feudalism still existed, some samurai had already become merchants or business owners.

The government sponsors modernization. Rapid modernization enabled Japan to avoid being taken over by Western powers. Unlike the Chinese, who could not decide whether or not to modernize, the Japanese were eager to learn the secrets of Western industrialization. Western advisers in industry, agriculture, and education were sought out. Government leaders traveled widely in Western countries. The Meiji government sent Japan's outstanding students to universities in Europe and the United States to study modern banking methods, communications, military organization, government, and education.

The Japanese government also modernized the economy. To avoid borrowing from foreign nations, it changed the system of collecting taxes. Instead of paying taxes on their crops, peasants paid an annual tax based on the value of their land. This ensured the government a steady source of income even when harvests were poor, but it meant that peasant farmers paid many of the costs of modernizing.

Meiji advisers soon realized that the government itself would have to provide much of the capital needed to create an industrial state. The government particularly supported industries that helped to build military strength, such as shipyards and ironworks. It also built ships and ports for foreign trade and developed the textile industry to make silk and cotton cloth for export. A government-financed factory turned out weapons and munitions for Japan's growing army and navy. Before long, private companies began to build factories. Some industrialist families, the *zaibatsu* (ZY-bah-TSOO), became wealthy and powerful.

To speed up communications and transportation, the Meiji government introduced the telegraph and built a railroad linking Tokyo and a coastal port. In Japan's hilly terrain the railroad was an efficient and inexpensive method of transportation. By 1900, Japan had over 15,000 miles of track.

The Meiji leaders also emphasized education as essential to modernizing. They set up a system of compulsory education for men and women as well as for children. In addition to reading and writing, all students were taught patriotism and loyalty to the emperor.

Japan's constitution follows European models. Ito (EE-TOH) Hirobumi, a leader of the ruling group who advised the emperor, led a delegation to Europe in 1882 to study the various forms of government on that continent. Their task was to recommend the form of government that would fit best with Japanese society. A military man, Ito conferred with Bismarck in Germany and took many ideas from the organization of the German state. He headed the committee that wrote a new constitution for Japan. It was completed in 1889 and handed down to the people as a gift from the emperor.

Under the new constitution, the emperor remained hereditary head of state and the highest source of power in the country. A prime minister was appointed to take charge of the day-to-day running of the government. (Ito was the first person to hold that office.) The emperor's main advisers were basically the same Choshu and Satsuma leaders who had brought him to power in 1868. Now twenty years older and more experienced, they had become Ja-

pan's elder statesmen, called *genro*. Their dedication to their country was a model for Japan's youth.

Japan's new constitution provided for a parliament, called the Diet, to make the laws and advise the emperor on government policy. The Diet had an upper house that included nobles or men appointed by the emperor. Members of the lower house were elected by the people. Voting, however, was limited to men over twenty-five years old who paid a certain amount in taxes each year.

The constitution gave the Japanese people specified civil rights. Among them were freedom of speech and religion and freedom from search and seizure. Every freedom, however, was qualified by the clause "except in cases provided in law." Nevertheless, the constitution of 1889 was a step toward democracy.

Western nations were impressed by Japan's adoption of a constitution less than twenty-five years after the end of feudalism. They finally agreed to end the treaties that gave foreigners special privileges. By 1894, the West began to see Japan more as an equal than as a potential colony or sphere of influence. The Japanese, however, still mistrusted the presence of Western nations in Asia.

Japan expands in Asia. Obtaining enough food had always been a problem in Japan. New scientific and medical advances brought a sudden population increase that made this problem acute. By 1890 fifty million people lived on Japan's four main islands. Japan had to import much of its food supply as well as most of the raw materials needed for industrialization. Japanese leaders adopted the same solution as the Western nations — building an empire. Overseas possessions would provide land, food supplies, and raw materials for industry.

By the 1890's Japan's modernized army and navy had become the equal of some of the armed forces in the West. With this advantage, Japan defeated China in the brief Sino-Japanese War fought in 1894–1895 for control of Korea (page 575). China's army failed to win a single battle; its navy was almost destroyed. The peace treaty gave Japan the island of Formosa (present-day Taiwan) and some small neighboring islands, as well as the Liaotung (LYOW-DOONG) Peninsula in the southern part

MODERNIZING JAPAN

The Meiji government's promotion of the exchange of ideas with the West was encouraged by the Japanese emperor. Above, the emperor attended a demonstration of European metal-working processes in a Japanese arsenal. Western-style education was also adopted. University students, like those below, could expect to play a part in the new Japan. Interest in science was reflected in the painting at left, showing women in traditional dress using a telescope.

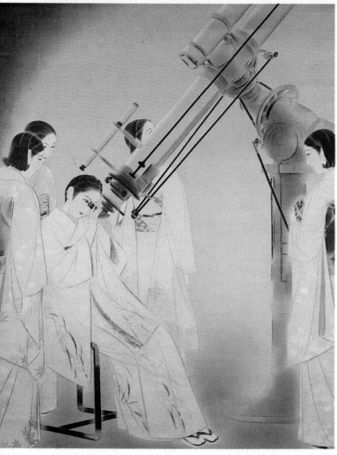

of Manchuria (map, page 570). In addition, China recognized Korea's independence.

Western reaction to Japan's victory was mixed. Some European nations were concerned that their spheres of influence in Asia might be endangered. Port Arthur, a naval base on the Liaotung Peninsula, was a major concern. Germany, France, and Russia were so uneasy that they pressured Japan into giving up its rights in Manchuria in exchange for a large cash settlement in gold. Three years later, however, the Chinese granted the Russians a lease for Port Arthur. Russia also extended the Trans-Siberian railroad across Manchuria to its port at Vladivostok.

Japan makes an alliance with Britain. The Russian moves into Manchuria appeared threatening to both Japanese and Western interests. The British believed that Japan's military strength, shown in its surprising victory over China, would curb Russia's plans for expansion in East Asia. In 1902 delegates from Great Britain and Japan signed a ten-year Anglo-Japanese alliance. In addition to the obvious military advantages, the pact had an important psychological benefit for the Japanese. It restored the Japanese pride lost when Western ships first entered Tokyo Bay.

Japan and Russia clash over Manchuria. The Japanese tried to negotiate with Russia's Czar Nicholas II about his troops in Manchuria. Convinced that Japan was still a weak country, Russia delayed the discussions.

On February 8, 1904, without warning, the Japanese navy attacked the Russian fleet of battleships and cruisers anchored at Port Arthur. This was the opening action of what came to be called the Russo-Japanese War. Nearly a year later, after a long and bloody siege, Port Arthur fell to Japan. On land, Japanese troops steadily forced the Russians out of Manchuria.

In a desperate effort to hold Manchuria, the czar dispatched Russia's Baltic fleet to Japan. Because of the Anglo-Japanese alliance, the British would not allow the Russian fleet to use the Suez Canal. Circling all the way around Africa, the fleet tried to reach Vladivostok in May, 1905, by slipping through the straits that separate Korea and Japan. The Japanese navy destroyed forty of the forty-two Russian ships.

Negotiations end the war. Thoroughly beaten and humiliated, and troubled by rebellion at home, Czar Nicholas sought to hold peace negotiations. Japan, too, was running short of resources and troops. President Theodore Roosevelt of the United States offered to find a diplomatic solution to end the Russo-Japanese War. The treaty signed in 1905 confirmed Japan's claim to the Liaotung Peninsula (including Port Arthur), the South Manchurian Railway, and Russia's mines and industry in Manchuria. Russia also agreed to recognize Japan's interest in Korea, while Japan took over the southern half of Sakhalin Island.

Japan becomes the leading power in Asia. The ending of the Russo-Japanese War forced Western nations to acknowledge that Japan was now an imperialist power and the leading country in Asia. Still expanding its Asian empire, the Meiji government annexed Korea in 1910, with no interference from the West. Elsewhere in Asia, Japan's rapid growth inspired nationalist movements in countries that were still controlled by European imperialist powers.

In 1912, the Meiji emperor died, bringing to a close an era of dynamic progress. Two years later, World War I broke out in Europe. During that war, Japanese trade and industry prospered as the Japanese supplied military equipment and other goods to the Allies. Japan's empire also grew. In 1915 Japan tried to establish a protectorate over China but was blocked by public disapproval at home and protests by several Western nations. As a British ally, Japan declared war on Germany and seized German territories in China, including bases at Kiaochow Bay and on the Shantung Peninsula. Japan also took over the German-held Pacific islands. In secret treaties, the Allies promised to support the Japanese claims later.

After the war, Japanese delegates attended the peace conference as one of the "Big Five" nations, and Japan became a permanent member of the League of Nations Council. With both China and Russia in turmoil, Japan had clearly become the strongest nation in Asia.

CHECK-UP

1. (a) What message did Matthew Perry bring to the government of Japan in 1851? (b) How did the Japanese respond? (c) What were the provisions of the treaty signed by the United States and Japan in 1858?
2. (a) What changes came about in Japan's leadership in the 1860's? (b) What reforms were undertaken by the Meiji government? (c) Which class was hit hardest by the early Meiji reforms?
3. (a) What features of Japanese society enabled that nation to modernize quickly? (b) What steps did the Japanese government take to speed modernization?
4. What were the provisions of the Japanese constitution of 1889 regarding (a) form of government, (b) suffrage, (c) civil rights?
5. (a) What problems did Japan attempt to solve by building an empire? (b) What did Japan gain from its war with China in 1894–1895?
6. (a) What led to the outbreak of the Russo-Japanese War? (b) What did Japan gain from that war?

Chapter 26 Review

Summary

The isolation chosen by China and Japan was forcibly ended in the nineteenth century by empire-building Western nations. Seeking new markets and resources, the United States and several European nations demanded trade rights in China and Japan, and some countries also succeeded in establishing spheres of influence in Chinese territory. These actions by Western countries led to the downfall of the Manchu dynasty in China and of the Tokugawa shogunate in Japan.

In China neither the leaders nor the people were willing to accept change or Western ideas. Humiliating defeats in several wars forced China to begin to modernize. Within the country, rebellions erupted against both the Manchu rulers and the foreigners. A revolution led by Sun Yat-sen finally ended the empire in 1912, but the republican government could not unite the country or end the chaos.

The Japanese, on the other hand, adopted many ideas from the West. Samurai leaders overthrew the ruling shogun, restored imperial rule, and replaced the feudal system with a constitutional parliamentary government. A small and determined ruling group led the Meiji government in quickly establishing industry and modernizing Japanese society. By the early twentieth century, Japan had begun to build its own empire in Asia.

Vocabulary Review

1. Match the following terms with the listed definitions: *concession, monopoly, sphere of influence, treaty port, tribute.*
(a) A part of a country in which a foreign nation holds political and economic power.
(b) A coastal center of trade where the Chinese government allowed Westerners to carry on business.
(c) A special trade privilege, such as the right to use a certain harbor.
(d) A payment made by a country or ruler to a more powerful country or ruler.
(e) The exclusive right to carry on trade in a certain commodity or within a certain area.

2. Distinguish between the terms in each of the following pairs:
(a) Taiping Rebellion; Boxer Rebellion.
(b) Treaty of Nanking; Treaty of Kanagawa.
(c) tributary system; unequal treaty system.

People to Identify

Match the following people with the numbered terms. In each case, explain the relationship. *Sun Yat-sen, Matthew Perry, K'uang-hsu, Hung Hsiu-ch'uan, Ito Hirobumi.*
1. Taiping Rebellion
2. Hundred Days' Reform
3. Constitution of 1889
4. Three Principles of the People
5. Treaty of Kanagawa

Relating Geography and History

1. **Locating places.** Locate each of the following on a map in this chapter:
(a) Canton   (f) Hong Kong
(b) Tokyo   (g) Nanking
(c) Korea   (h) Port Arthur
(d) Peking   (i) Manchuria
(e) Nagasaki   (j) Vladivostok

2. **Making a chart.** By 1911 China had suffered imperialistic advances from many European nations. Look at the map on page 570 showing Chinese treaty ports. Make a chart listing the treaty ports independent of the Chinese government. In the first column, list the treaty ports. In the second column, list the non-Chinese government that controlled each port.

3. **Interpretation.** (a) How did the geography of Japan contribute to that country's decision to build an overseas empire? Consider land available for farming, population growth, and natural resources. (b) What products did Japan hope to gain from overseas possessions?

Discussion Questions

1. (a) What trading privileges in China did Lord Macartney request for Great Britain? (b) Why did China's emperor reject that request?
2. (a) What reasons did the Chinese have for opposing the opium trade? (b) How did the Chinese and the British differ in their view of the

conflict over the opium trade? (c) What effect did the Treaty of Nanking have on the trading privileges given foreigners by the Chinese?

3. (a) What reforms did the Taiping rebels favor? (b) Why did the Taiping Rebellion fail? (c) What effect did the rebellion have on China's relations with European countries?

4. (a) How did the Sino-Japanese War affect the attitude of many Chinese toward modernization? (b) Why did the Hundred Days' Reform fail? (c) What reforms were made following the Boxer Rebellion?

5. (a) What changes in traditional Chinese society did Sun Yat-sen want to make? (b) What happened to the Manchu dynasty as a result of the 1911 revolution? (c) Why did China face political instability after the death of Yuan Shih-kai?

6. (a) How did the response of the Japanese to the demands of foreigners for trading privileges differ from the reactions of the Chinese? (b) Why did the Tokugawa shoguns' decision to accept foreign treaties weaken the shogunate?

7. (a) Why did the rulers of Japan during the Meiji era decide to modernize that country? (b) What aspects of Japanese society contributed to their willingness to modernize?

8. How did Meiji reforms affect (a) the daimyo and (b) the samurai? (c) By the late 1800's, how did the Western powers view Japan?

9. Why did Japan and Russia go to war over Manchuria?

Reading Primary Sources

The passage below is from a statement sent by the Chinese minister in Britain to Queen Victoria. It concerns the attitude of the English toward the opium trade. Read the passage. Then answer the questions that follow.

> Where is your conscience? I have heard that the smoking of opium is very strictly forbidden by your country. That is because the harm caused by opium is clearly understood. Since it is not permitted to do harm to your own country, then even less should you let it be passed on to the harm of other countries. . . .
>
> Of all that China exports to foreign countries, there is not a single thing which is not beneficial to people. . . . Take tea and rhubarb, for example. Foreign countries cannot get along for a single day without [Chinese products]. If China cuts off these benefits, . . . then what can the barbarians rely upon to keep themselves alive? Moreover, the [textiles] of foreign countries cannot be woven unless they obtain Chinese silk. If China, again, cuts off this beneficial export, what profit can the barbarians expect to make? . . .
>
> On the other hand, articles coming from the outside to China can only be used as toys. We can take them or get along without them. Since they are not needed by China, what difficulty would there be if we . . . stopped the trade?

(a) What does the Chinese minister say he has heard about the attitude toward opium in England? (b) What reasons does he give for saying the English should oppose the opium trade? (c) On what products imported from China does the Chinese minister say foreign countries depend? (d) How does he describe the products imported by China from other countries? (e) Who does he think would suffer most from an end to trade between China and other countries? (f) How convincing to Queen Victoria were these arguments likely to be? Explain your answer.

Skill Activities

1. Paraphrasing. Rewrite in your own words each of the following statements. You may use more than one sentence. (Find each statement in the chapter and read it in context before you paraphrase it.)

(a) "To live today and still say 'reject the barbarians' and 'drive them out of our territory' is certainly superficial and absurd talk" (page 574).

(b) "Other men are the carving knife and serving dish; we are the fish and the meat" (page 576).

2. Analyzing cartoons. Examine the cartoon on page 573, and answer these questions: (a) What kind of animal is used to symbolize China? (b) How is the United States symbolized? (c) What animal represents Great Britain? (d) What appears to be happening to China in the cartoon? (e) How might this cartoon reflect the "sphere of influence" concept? (f) What view of the treatment of China by other nations did the cartoonist apparently hold?

3. Relating past to present. The Diet in the Japanese government today is quite different from the Diet established by the Constitution of 1889. Use reference books to find out how the Diet functions in modern Japan.

Mining companies, traders, inventors, explorers, missionaries, and empire-builders — all developed a new interest in Africa during the late 1800's. Below, an expedition sets out from a South African town to explore for gold.

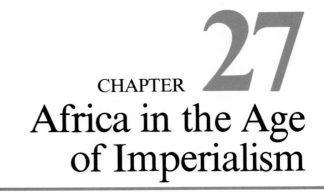

CHAPTER 27
Africa in the Age of Imperialism

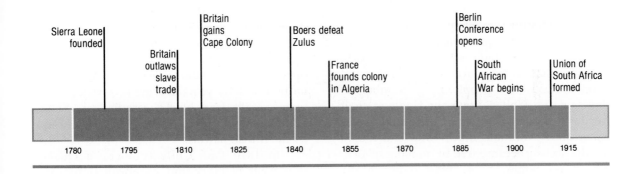

Sierra Leone founded

Britain outlaws slave trade

Britain gains Cape Colony

Boers defeat Zulus

France founds colony in Algeria

Berlin Conference opens

South African War begins

Union of South Africa formed

1780 1795 1810 1825 1840 1855 1870 1885 1900 1915

From the sixteenth century on, European interest in the African continent had centered mainly on the brutal but profitable trade in slaves. By the beginning of the nineteenth century, however, antislavery feelings and economic changes brought about international laws against slave trading. Europeans developed new interests in Africa, and there was a new wave of claims and colonization in African lands.

Explorers and missionaries paved the way for traders and investors in Africa. Settlers soon followed. European nations seeking to build empires claimed territory on the vast continent. Though their claims sometimes conflicted, the European nations generally cooperated in dividing up African lands among themselves. Africans resisted the European takeover, but European weapons and military tactics were superior. By 1914, almost all of Africa was under European control.

This chapter describes the growing European interest in Africa, the conquest of African lands by colonial powers, and the effects of colonial rule on Africa's people.

CHAPTER OUTLINE

1 Africa Draws European Interest

Europeans first took an interest in Africa because of its gold, then because of the land available for plantation agriculture (Chapter 13). Later the slave trade became the main focus of Western interest in the continent. After slave trading was outlawed internationally in the early 1800's, many Europeans developed new kinds of interest in Africa and the African people. Missionaries and explorers traveled to Africa, as did other Europeans seeking opportunities for investment and trade.

The idea of repatriation develops. Even before the slave trade was officially ended, some people became concerned about the situation of freed black people. Large numbers of slaves in the United States had gained their freedom through state laws passed after the American Revolution. Blacks who had fought for the British became free by moving to Britain or its colonies in the West Indies. Many freed blacks, however, were unable to find work, and all were denied equal rights with whites. In both England and the United States, a number of prominent people (including Thomas Jefferson) suggested that the freed blacks return to Africa as colonists.

The idea of repatriation — the move back to Africa — met with differing reactions from black people in the United States and the British territories. Most felt that emigration to Africa would mean resettlement in a foreign land. Their ancestors had not lived in Africa for several generations, and most blacks no longer thought of that continent as their home. For others, however, the move back to Africa was an appealing idea.

Black colonists settle in Sierra Leone. In 1787 antislavery humanitarians in Britain financed the founding of the colony of Sierra Leone in western Africa (map, page 591). One of the organizers was Olaudah Equiano (ek-wee-AHN-oh), a former slave who had become a prominent speaker and writer in the antislavery movement in Britain. Kidnapped at age 11 in what is now Nigeria, Equiano had been sold to a British naval officer in the West Indies. Later he was resold to a Pennsylvania Quaker who helped him earn money to buy his freedom and return to England. When a British ship sailed for Sierra Leone in 1787, carrying the first 500 colonists, Equiano was in charge of their food and supplies. (Two years later, he published his autobiography, which increased the British public's opposition to slave trading.)

The colonists settled near Freetown and soon were joined by freed blacks from Canada. After 1807, when Britain outlawed the slave trade, the new colony became the base for British warships trying to halt slave trading. British operations against the slave trade continued for more than sixty years. During this period more than 50,000 free blacks resettled in Sierra Leone, many of them rescued from slave ships by the British patrols.

In 1810 Paul Cuffe (KUF-ee), a Quaker shipowner of black and American Indian descent, sailed to Sierra Leone to open trade. Impressed by the schools, churches, and organization of the British settlement, Cuffe decided to encourage black Americans to emigrate. In December, 1815, his ship *Traveller* sailed from Massachusetts with 38 freed blacks on board. Cuffe financed the trip and supported the families while they established themselves in Sierra Leone.

Liberia is founded. Cuffe died in 1817, but the idea of emigration to Africa still had supporters. The American Colonization Society, founded in 1816, purchased land in western Africa from local rulers. The first group of 88 settlers from the United States landed in 1820. The colonists found it hard to adjust to the tropical climate, and the Africans in the region were hostile to the newcomers. Soon the colony was abandoned, and many of its settlers moved to neighboring Sierra Leone.

In 1822 a second group of American settlers sailed to Sierra Leone, picked up the earlier colonists, and began a settlement at Monrovia (named after James Monroe, then President of the United States). Though the settlers faced the same problems, this colony pros-

MISSIONARIES IN AFRICA

European and American church organizations established a number of missions in Africa during the late 1800's and early 1900's. While seeking converts to Christianity, they also ran schools and medical centers (above, a British medical mission). Best-known of the British missionaries was David Livingstone (left).

pered and other settlements were started. In 1847, they combined to form Liberia, the first independent republic in Africa. Liberia's government was modeled after that of the United States, and members of families descended from the American colonists kept political and economic power in the country.

Explorers map the African interior. The early European contacts with Africa had been limited to the coastal areas, and little was known about the interior of the continent. Around the beginning of the nineteenth century, the new interest in Africa encouraged explorers from European countries to travel into the interior, mapping and describing what they found. In 1768 the Scotsman James Bruce located the headwaters of the Blue Nile. The Niger River was charted by several British explorers — Mungo Park in 1796 and 1805–1806 and John and Richard Lander in the 1830's. René Caillié (ky-YAY) of France traveled through western Africa and also explored the Niger River in 1827–1828. In the 1850's east-central Africa was crisscrossed by the Englishmen Richard Burton and John Speke, who were the first Europeans to discover the huge lakes that are the source of the Nile.

Missionaries travel to Africa. Church organizations and clergy who worked in the antislavery movement in Britain and the United States also began to take a deep interest in Africa. In eastern Africa, British missionaries worked to break the Arab slave trade. Most of the settlers in Sierra Leone and Liberia were Christians; some worked as missionaries in those countries and in other parts of the continent. Christian churches, both Protestant and Catholic, began to set up mission stations in western Africa in the 1800's. These were self-sufficient communities headed by Americans or Europeans, offering education and medical treatment to Africans who accepted the Christian religion. Mission workers often worked closely with Africans and learned their languages, but they usually lived apart from the African community.

Seeking to spread the Christian religion, missionaries traveled far into the interior of Africa to set up mission stations. Many kept detailed diaries and wrote accounts of their experiences for people at home. The writings of these missionaries aroused great curiosity about Africa among people throughout Europe and the United States.

Livingstone becomes a popular hero. Popular interest in Africa reached a high point during the travels of a Scottish medical missionary and explorer named David Livingstone (1813–1873). In 1841, Livingstone went to the region of Bechuanaland (bech-oo-AH-nuh-land) in southern Africa. There he married Mary Moffat, whose mother and father led mission work in the area. Working together, the Livingstones set up several mission stations along the southern edge of the Kalahari Desert (map, page 275). In 1849, Livingstone accepted an offer to be the translator for a party of explorers. His description of the trip caught the attention of readers in England and made him famous. For the next seven years, Livingstone explored the interior, finding the source of the Zambezi River and traveling all the way to Africa's western coast. He wrote careful descriptions of plants and animals and made maps of natural features, including the great waterfall called by the Africans "The Smoke that Thunders." Livingstone named it Victoria Falls in honor of Queen Victoria. He learned the languages of the people he met and took notes on their customs. Readers in England eagerly awaited his books and newspaper reports.

In 1858, Livingstone began a series of expeditions sponsored by the British government and scientific groups. While exploring the lakes region of the Great Rift Valley on one of these trips, he disappeared. Nothing was heard of him for about five years. In 1871 an American journalist and adventurer, Henry M. Stanley, set out with an expedition to look for Livingstone. After nearly eight months of travel, Stanley found him at a village called Ujiji, near Lake Tanganyika in present-day Tanzania (map, page 591). Livingstone was seriously ill but continued his explorations until his death two years later. His reports, carried to the outside world by Stanley, brought vast new areas of Africa to the attention of people in Europe and the United States.

Stanley explores the Congo. Fascinated by Africa and hoping to become famous, Stanley undertook to carry out the work Livingstone had not completed. In 1877 Stanley finished a three-year exploration of the Congo River. He then went to work for King Leopold II of Bel-

gium. Stanley's expeditions gave Leopold claim to a huge area in the Congo Basin.

European investors become interested in Africa. Explorers and missionaries had given European nations a foothold in Africa. They were followed by traders and investors seeking markets and raw materials. The British had already begun to change their trading pattern in Africa, and the slave trade was less important economically. Palm oil, produced in the Niger River delta and used in the making of soap, was becoming an important raw material for British industries. As the Industrial Revolution transformed Europe, the demand grew for other African products, such as rubber, cotton, and minerals. At the same time, manufacturers wanted a larger market for the increasing amounts of goods turned out by their factories. Africa was seen as both a source of raw materials and a market.

Europeans concentrated their African investments in the production of profitable cash crops such as cotton, coffee, tea, palm oil, or cloves. They laid out plantations and brought together large numbers of African workers to tend and harvest the crops. The products were then shipped to European markets and factories. As in India, some manufactured goods were shipped back to Africa and sold to Africans. To increase their profits still more, investors sought a way to control the cash crop at its source. They took possession of African lands and established settlements.

Europeans settle in southern Africa. Except for missionaries, few Europeans settled permanently in tropical Africa. Southern Africa, however, was a different story. Its climate is more temperate, like that of the countries around the Mediterranean Sea, and the land is good for farming. In 1652 the Dutch East India Company had set up a supply post at the Cape of Good Hope (map, page 352). Dutch ships on their way to Asia stopped at the post for water and other supplies. Dutch farmers, called Boers (BOHRZ), began to settle there in 1657, and the post soon grew into the settlement called Cape Colony. After the repeal in 1685 of the Edict of Nantes that had given French Protestants religious toleration, thousands of Huguenots joined the Dutch settlers.

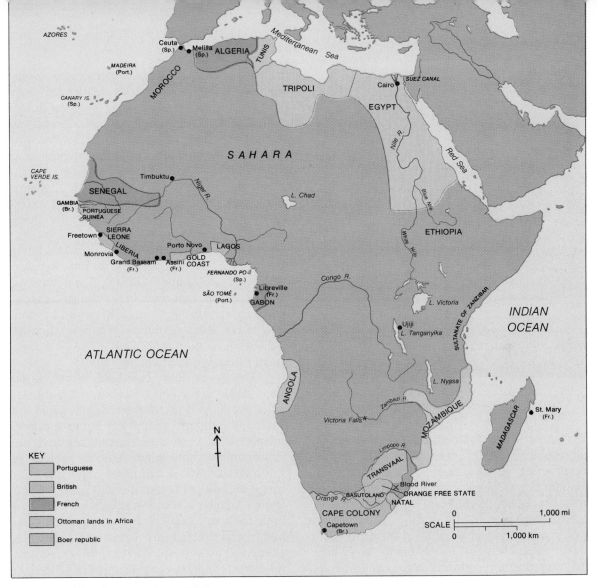

Imperialism in Africa, 1880

By 1880 most of the African continent had been mapped by Europeans, and a number of European nations had established colonial claims. Which nation controlled the Suez Canal?

The Europeans who settled in southern Africa sought large areas of land for farming and cattle herding and so came into conflict with the traditional values of the Africans. According to African tradition, land was owned by the community, and individuals had only the right to use it. The Boers, on the other hand, claimed ownership of thousands of acres of land, whether or not they were actually farming it or using it for pasture. This difference between African and European cultures quickly led to trouble.

Boer settlers take over African lands. The Cape region had been the home of the Khoisan (KWOI-san) people, who were herders. When the migrating Bantu-speaking peoples arrived there (page 281), some of the Khoisan had been absorbed into the Bantu way of life, while others had been pushed into the desert regions. Now the Dutch settlers demanded land and labor from the Khoisan, and by 1658 Khoisan and Dutch peoples were at war. The Khoisan could not withstand Dutch weapons and fighting tactics. Those who survived migrated into

The Zulu drive for power was led first by Shaka and then by his nephew Cetewayo (shown above).

the hostile Kalahari Desert or became laborers for the Boers. The Dutch also raided other neighboring peoples and claimed additional land for Cape Colony.

The Boers discriminate against Africans. Like European colonists in other parts of the world, the Boers had a feeling of superiority toward peoples of non-European ancestry. They believed that the Africans' role was to serve them as laborers. Far outnumbered by the Africans, the Boers also felt that their security depended on a policy of control over the black people in Cape Colony. They enslaved the Africans and set up a system of "pass laws" to control them. No African was allowed to travel without a pass from a Boer official. An African who did not have a fixed address could be sent to prison, and the only way blacks could get a fixed address was to work for the Boers.

The British take Cape Colony. The situation in Cape Colony began to change early in the 1800's. At the Congress of Vienna in 1815, following the Napoleonic Wars, the Dutch lost Cape Colony to Britain. It was a strategic spot for protecting the route to India, Britain's most valuable colony. The British soon arrived in the colony, and from the start their values clashed with those of the Boers.

Preaching freedom, equality, and brotherhood, British missionaries challenged Boer policies toward the Africans. In 1828 the British canceled the Boer pass laws and allowed the Khoisan to buy and own land. A limit was placed on the amount of land an individual European could claim. An even more important step came in 1834 when the British abolished slavery in their possessions. By this act 35,000 Africans who had been slaves of the Boers gained their freedom.

Unable to tolerate British rule, the Boers decided they must leave Cape Colony. Between 1835 and 1837, about 10,000 Boers traveled northeast, on foot and in ox-drawn covered wagons, across the Orange River into Natal. The move, led by Andreas Pretorius, came to be known as the Great Trek. (*Trek* is a Boer word meaning "a difficult journey.")

The Boers claim Zulu land. North of the Orange River, the Boers encountered many African peoples who were migrating to avoid the Zulus, a militant group of Bantu-speaking people. Late in the eighteenth century, the Zulus and several other African peoples in southwestern Africa had come under the control of the Mtetwe (em-TEH-twuh) people. Their leader, Dingiswayo (dee-n'gee-SWAH-yoh), had organized his soldiers by age grades[1] into highly trained fighting units called *impi.* A young Zulu commander named Shaka became ruler when Dingiswayo was killed in 1818. Under Shaka's leadership the powerful Zulu armies swept through neighboring territories, and other Bantu-speaking groups fled before their advance. Although Shaka was assassinated in 1828, the Zulus continued their drive northward into Natal.

As the Boers also moved north into Natal, they settled in lands emptied by people fleeing the Zulu impi. In 1838 they encountered the Zulu forces led by Dingaan, Shaka's half-brother. As neither the Zulus nor the Boers would settle for less than total control of the land, war was inevitable. On December 16, 1838, the Boers, led by Pretorius, defeated the Zulus at the Battle of Blood River. Southern-

---

[1]In traditional African society, each child was a member of a certain "age grade." With this group, he or she passed through the stages of learning adult responsibilities.

most Africa was now entirely under European control, though it was split between the British and the Boers.

The French claim land in North Africa. Europeans were also claiming lands along the Mediterranean coast of northern Africa. Officially part of the Ottoman Empire, these lands had for centuries been occupied by the Muslim Berbers and Arabs. The region, called the Barbary Coast (from the name "Berber"), was divided into the states of Morocco, Algiers, Tunis, and Tripoli.[2] Barbary pirates were a constant threat to ships in the Mediterranean.

France, which lay directly across the sea from the Barbary Coast, sought both to halt the pirates and to claim the land as a natural extension of France. Attempts to establish a French colony in Algeria in the 1830's met with strong local resistance, but in 1848 Algeria was organized as a French colony. Many European settlers arrived, and the colony became an important source of food for France. By the 1880's France had also acquired a protectorate over Tunisia. Several European nations sought to acquire Morocco, but it also later became a French protectorate.

———

By the late 1800's, the interior of Africa had been explored. European missionaries had converted thousands of Africans to Christianity and introduced European ideas. The Boers and British were well entrenched in southern Africa, and the French colony in Algeria was prospering. European nations had gained a foothold throughout the continent. In the next thirty years most of the rest of Africa came under their control.

———

CHECK-UP

1. (a) Why did some blacks return to Africa in the late 1700's and early 1800's? (b) What part did Sierra Leone and Liberia have in the return to Africa?
2. (a) What activities did explorers and missionaries undertake in Africa? (b) How did David Livingstone's work bring Africa to the attention of Europeans and Americans?
3. (a) What kinds of goods interested European investors in Africa? (b) How did they view African colonies?
4. (a) What attitudes and beliefs led to conflict between Boers and Africans in southern Africa? (b) How did the British acquire Cape Colony? (c) How did the British treatment of Africans differ from that of the Boers? (d) What was the Boers' reaction?
5. (a) What was the Great Trek? (b) Who challenged the Boers' move into Natal? (c) What was the result?
6. How did European colonization in North Africa come about?

2 Africa Is Brought Under European Control

As European nations began to compete for overseas possessions during the Age of Imperialism, they turned to the African continent. Explorers, traders, and missionaries had paved the way for European settlement and acquisition of territory. Several European nations already had established outposts and colonies along the coast, and they now claimed lands in the interior. In the mid-1800's, 90 percent of Africa was still ruled by Africans. By 1914, only two African nations — Ethiopia and Liberia — remained independent of European rule.

European nations agree to divide Africa. By the 1870's, British, French, Portuguese and Belgian claims in Africa were in conflict, and other European nations also wanted African colonies. Germany in particular was seeking control of lands in both eastern and western Africa. Its claims in Kamerun and on the east coast created tension with Great Britain. To avoid wars over colonial claims, several international conferences were held to settle such claims through diplomacy. The most significant

---

[2]They are the modern nations of Morocco, Algeria, Tunisia, and Libya.

593

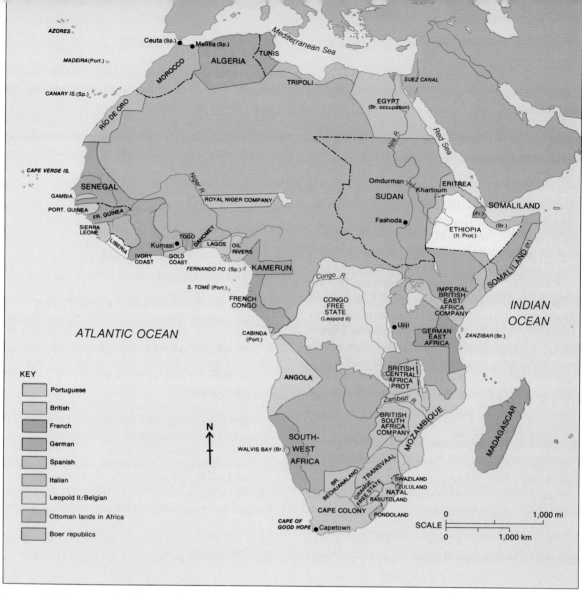

Imperialism in Africa, 1891

Between 1880 and 1891, European control of Africa greatly expanded. (Compare this map with the one on page 591.) How had the situation in Egypt changed?

KEY

- Portuguese
- British
- French
- German
- Spanish
- Italian
- Leopold II/Belgian
- Ottoman lands in Africa
- Boer republics

meeting was organized in Berlin in 1884 by Otto von Bismarck, the German chancellor. Fourteen European nations were represented, along with the United States. There were no representatives from Africa.

The main problem discussed at the Berlin conference was the Congo Basin. King Leopold II of Belgium had already claimed the area for himself, based on treaties made for him by Henry M. Stanley (page 590). Other nations based their claims on trade agreements with African rulers, on settlements made by missionaries, and on explorers' discoveries. At the end of the Berlin Conference, in 1885, the nations agreed that there would be free trade and travel on both the Congo and Niger rivers. More importantly, this agreement, along with others made over the next few years, divided nearly all of Africa among various European nations.

African lands are claimed. In general, the European nations agreed to respect each other's claims and to help each other if African peoples resisted. African reactions to the European takeover, however, varied greatly from region to region. Some rulers agreed to treaties

By the early 1800's southern Africa was dotted with isolated Boer farmhouses. The British takeover changed Boer life.

to secure peace, protection, or trade. Some responded with warfare, but their weapons were no match for the guns and cannon of the European powers.

Britain takes control of the Suez. British interest in Africa had focused mainly on lands in the south. The opening of the Suez Canal in 1869 made Egypt and eastern Africa more important to Great Britain. The new waterway between the Red Sea and the Mediterranean had been built by a French company directed by Ferdinand de Lesseps, but it was run by Egyptians. The British saw the canal as part of a sea route to their colony of India.

Civil wars following Napoleon's campaign in Egypt had made the country relatively independent of the Ottoman Empire. Mohammed Ali, who ruled from 1805 to 1847, encouraged modernization. Railroads and factories were built, schools were established, and health care and agriculture improved. To pay for these changes, Mohammed Ali and his successors borrowed large amounts of money from foreign nations at high interest rates. The cost of the Suez Canal alone added greatly to Egypt's national debt.

By 1875, the Egyptian government was near financial collapse. It accepted Britain's offer to buy nearly half the shares of stock in the Suez Canal Company. Egyptian nationalists objected to European interference, and unrest grew. To protect their economic interests, the British took control of the waterway. By 1882 Egypt had become a British protectorate.

Egypt and Britain share power in the Sudan. Mohammed Ali had brought the Sudan under Egyptian rule in the 1820's. In the early 1880's a Muslim religious leader known as the Mahdi led his followers in a revolt against British and Egyptian forces in the Sudan. The British fort at Khartoum was besieged, and its defenders were massacred by the Mahdi's followers in 1885. They kept control of the region for about ten years. In 1896, concerned about French and Belgian moves into the Sudan, the British began to reconquer the region. A British-Egyptian army led by General Herbert Kitchener defeated the Sudanese decisively at Omdurman in 1898, and the Sudan was placed under joint Egyptian and British rule.

British and Boers clash in southern Africa. The British holdings in southern Africa

Cecil Rhodes' goal was to establish British rule in Africa from the Cape to Egypt.

were on the other major sea route to India. To protect them, Britain took over the Boer settlement of Natal in 1843 and also set up the African state of Basutoland under British protection (map, page 597). Anti-British feelings grew stronger among the Boers, who had trekked north from Cape Colony to get away from the British government. In the 1850's the Boers established two independent republics — Orange Free State and Transvaal.

The British recognized the Boer states, but friction continued. In 1867 diamonds were discovered along the Orange River, and British settlers swarmed into the area. Soon after, the governor of Cape Colony took over the diamond region, though the Boers resisted. Then, in 1886, gold was discovered in Transvaal. The British South Africa Company, led by a financier named Cecil Rhodes, took control of this area and its rich gold mines.

The long hostility between the British and the Boers erupted in 1899 in the South African War (also called the Boer War). The Boers used guerrilla warfare, and the British set up concentration camps in which many Boer civilians died. The bitter war continued for three years; finally the Boers surrendered in 1902.

The Union of South Africa is created. In 1910 the British government combined the British and Boer states in a new country, called the Union of South Africa. The Boers were the majority among the white settlers, and the new government reflected their attitudes. Only white men could vote; whites, blacks, and people of mixed ancestry were to live separately. Because many Boers held bitter memories of the war with Britain, there was political and social tension even among the Europeans in the Union of South Africa.

Cecil Rhodes expands the British Empire. Cecil Rhodes, who headed the gold-mining interests, believed in imperialism and dreamed of British power stretching from "the Cape to Cairo" (that is, from Capetown in South Africa to Cairo in Egypt). He talked of a Cape-to-Cairo railway and communications network. While this goal was not achieved, Rhodes did encourage British settlers to move north into the fertile highlands later named the Rhodesias (map, page 597).

The takeover of these lands was not peaceful. The king of the Matabele people granted mining rights to Rhodes's South Africa Company, but he did not expect white settlers to claim the land. By 1893, the troops of Rhodes's company and the Matabele warriors were at war. Armed with machine guns, the Europeans broke the fierce resistance. Taking over the land, the settlers began to govern themselves as a colony. The mild climate and fertile soil of the Rhodesias continued to attract more white settlers from Europe.

The French meet resistance in western Africa. The French also hoped to acquire an African empire stretching from coast to coast. They intended to expand eastward from Senegal to the Red Sea and control central Africa. Citing Caillié's expedition along the Niger (page 589), the French government claimed all the land between Senegal and Algeria. The Fulani peoples in Senegal, however, continued to resist French penetration of the interior from 1827 until 1890.

The French movement into the interior brought them into the vast territory controlled by the Mandingo leader Samori Touré (too-RAY). Samori had begun to build an army in the 1850's, hoping to revive the ancient Mali empire (page 278). He bought arms and munitions from Europeans on the coast, employed blacksmiths to develop his own arms industry, and efficiently organized his army. By 1880 Samori ruled much of the area between the Niger

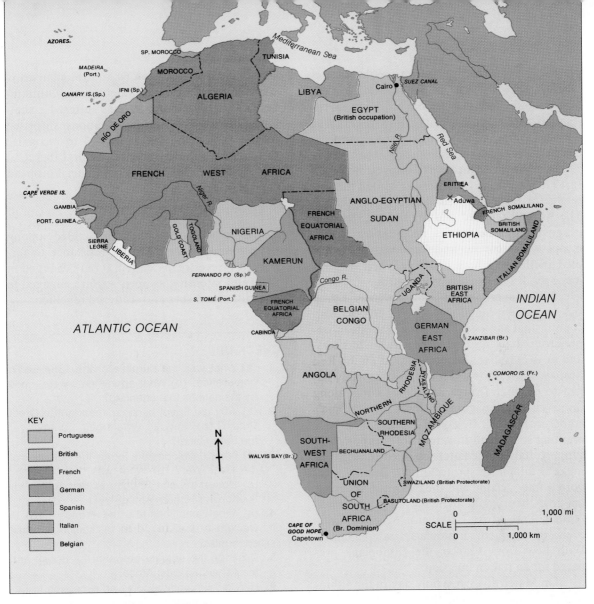

Imperialism in Africa, 1914

European nations claimed most of Africa by 1914. Only Liberia and Ethiopia remained independent. What nation controlled most of West Africa?

River and the coast. Samori's forces resisted the French for nearly twenty years, until he was captured in 1898. The defeat of Samori gave the French effective control over most of the interior of West Africa.

Colonial claims conflict in the Sudan. In 1898 the French dream of a coast-to-coast empire clashed with British ambitions for a Cape-to-Cairo railway. Kitchener's forces in the Sudan (page 595) were building a railroad as they moved southward along the Nile. Meanwhile, a French expedition had moved eastward to claim possession of land along the Nile.

A few weeks after the Battle of Omdurman, the two groups met at Fashoda (map, page 594). For a time, war between France and Britain seemed a serious threat, but the Fashoda incident was settled by diplomacy. The French government, already troubled at home by the Dreyfus affair (page 541), gave up its claims to lands along the Nile.

The Ashanti resist Britain in western Africa. The British also tried to move inland from their Gold Coast settlement in western Africa, but they were constantly challenged by the powerful Ashanti Union (page 286). From 1824 on, the Ashanti and the British fought a series of wars. The Ashanti raided coastal trading posts, and the British twice burned Kumasi, the Ashanti capital. In 1896, the British captured Kumasi again, took the king prisoner, and declared the region a protectorate.

Ashanti resistance was not over, however. In 1900 the British governor demanded the surrender of the golden stool, the royal symbol. The Ashanti rebelled and imprisoned the British governor, missionaries, and soldiers. British troops were sent in, and hundreds of people died in the year-long conflict. When the war was over, Britain was in firm control.

Ethiopia retains its independence. Ethiopia, an ancient kingdom, was the only African country that successfully resisted European imperialism. Italy also wanted African territory, and in 1873 Italians acquired a port on the Red Sea coast of Ethiopia. From this base, Italy began to colonize Eritrea and other lands along the coast (map, page 594). In 1889, Ethiopia's emperor, Menelik II, signed a treaty with Italy granting some land in return for weapons and support. Italy immediately claimed the right to make Ethiopia a protectorate. Britain supported Italy's claim, and the two nations agreed on how they would divide what was termed "Italian East Africa." Emperor Menelik, however, proclaimed Ethiopia's independence. With help from France, the Ethiopians prepared for an Italian invasion.

On March 1, 1896, a holy day in the Ethiopian Christian Church, the Italians attacked. They were met at Aduwa by an Ethiopian army carrying arms equal to their own. Outnumbered four to one, the Italians suffered a shattering defeat. The European nations, surprised by the Ethiopian victory, agreed to recognize the country's independence. With Liberia, it was the only part of Africa not under European control (map, page 597).

Even with the continent divided among the colonial powers, African resistance to foreign rule never really ended. It only changed in form and intensity, as open warfare changed to guerrilla skirmishes and scattered rebellion.

CHECK-UP

1. (a) What was the purpose of the 1884 Berlin conference? (b) What agreements were made by the nations that attended?
2. (a) Why did Egypt become important to Great Britain? (b) How did Britain gain control over the Suez Canal?
3. (a) What developments led to the outbreak of the Boer War? (b) What was the outcome? (c) How did Cecil Rhodes extend British influence in southern Africa?
4. (a) What ambitions did the French have in western Africa? (b) What resistance did they encounter?
5. Describe the conflict between the British and the Ashanti in West Africa.
6. How did Ethiopia become an exception to European colonialism in Africa?

3 European Powers Rule Africa

By 1900 nearly all the African continent was in European hands. As in other parts of the world, different colonial powers followed different policies. All, however, expected their African colonies to provide the home country with wealth from labor and natural resources and at the same time to pay the costs of running the colony.

Colonial powers follow different policies. The colonial policies of the European powers differed more in theory than in practice, but they varied in their effects on traditional African society and culture. Most of the European nations in Africa — France, Belgium, Germany, Portugal — established "direct rule" over their colonies. European government officials replaced African leaders, and European laws and other institutions were established.

"Indirect rule," on the other hand, gave Africans some chance to take part in the colonial system. It was a common policy in British territories, particularly in large colonies where there were few European settlers. Great Britain's official policy was that Africans would eventually be given self-rule but needed to be prepared to govern themselves. Therefore, the local chief or king remained the figure of authority and continued to handle community affairs in traditional ways. The resident, as the top British official was called, enforced British law and directed the chief to collect taxes and provide workers. The local ruler's power was limited, however, and the resident had the final authority.

French colonial rule follows a policy of assimilation. While they established direct rule in their colonies, the French also believed that Africans could in time be assimilated, or absorbed, into French culture. They would become full-fledged citizens, and their African culture would be replaced by French schooling, laws, language, and politics. Their lands would become overseas provinces of France, and not colonies.

In Senegal, for instance, where there had been centuries of contact with France, some coastal peoples were considered members of French society at birth. Other Africans became French citizens by fulfilling such requirements as learning the French language and showing their loyalty by working in the colonial civil service.

Colonial rule reveals European attitudes. European colonial officials, explorers, and missionaries generally were paternalistic toward Africans. That is, they incorrectly regarded Africans as childlike and incapable of managing their own lands or their own lives. This was a result of the European attitude of cultural and ethnic superiority. One justification given for imperialism was the bringing of Western civilization to other parts of the world. White Europeans in Africa also associated darker skin with people they regarded as social and cultural inferiors. Slavery had intensified these prejudices, but the banning of the slave trade did not end them.

Policies of social inequality were enforced more strictly in some colonies than in others. In South Africa, for instance, laws tried to maintain the complete separation of darker-skinned peoples from Europeans. Africans could enter Boer homes only as servants. In other areas, Africans worked in colonial government offices, though only in low-level jobs. Some Africans received higher education or military training, however. Colonial administrators needed black professional workers to enforce colonial policies. African clerks handled the massive amounts of administrative paperwork needed to run a colony. African professional soldiers were assigned to the standing armies that maintained control in the colonies.

Colonial governments tax Africans. European powers in Africa, as in other parts of the world, expected economic advantages from their colonies. Africans were expected to pay taxes in the currency issued by the colonial government. Africans who did not pay their taxes could be fined, arrested, or imprisoned. Because Europeans controlled all the business and government jobs, the Africans had to work for them as farmhands, servants, miners, construction workers, and clerks in order to earn cash.

TIMETABLE

Imperialism in Africa

1787	Sierra Leone is founded.
1807	Britain outlaws the slave trade.
1815	Britain takes possession of Cape Colony.
1834	Britain outlaws slavery in its possessions.
1838	The Boers defeat the Zulus.
1847	Liberia becomes the first independent African republic.
1848	France establishes a colony in Algeria.
1875	Britain gains control of the Suez Canal.
1884–1885	The Berlin Conference arranges the division of Africa among European nations.
1896	Ethiopia defeats Italy and remains independent.
1898	France defeats Samori Touré and gains control in West Africa.
1899–1902	Britain defeats the Boers in the South African War.
1908	Belgium takes over the Congo from King Leopold.
1910	The Union of South Africa is formed.

Some Africans openly protested the tax laws. For instance, the people of Sierra Leone resisted in 1898 when the British government imposed a tax on their houses. Many Africans felt that they should not have to pay a tax on their own homes. They also were concerned because the traditional chief lacked power, and they were angered by insults and mistreatment from the police. Many Africans and Europeans were killed in the Sierra Leone rebellion.

Colonial powers profit from their African colonies. One aim of imperialism was to develop colonial economies so that they would benefit European investors. The colonial powers followed the pattern set by the first Portuguese traders and planters: white ownership of the land and black labor to work it. The colonial powers built communication systems and railroads, linking ports, mines, and plantations. The needs of the Africans were seldom considered. Coastal areas benefited most from economic growth and the beginnings of modernization. Interior regions with no cash crops were often ignored, and traditional ways of life continued there.

Europeans demand labor from Africans. As greater amounts of raw materials and export crops were sent to Europe, more workers were needed. There were large rubber plantations in Portuguese-held Angola and in the Congo. Mines stretched from the Katanga copper belt in the Congo into the gold and diamond deposits in southern Africa. Great expanses of farmland were devoted to such cash crops as cotton and cacao. Because there often were not enough local workers for the plantations, recruiting stations were set up to bring in workers from all over Africa.

African workers in the colonies were often badly treated. For example, to increase cotton production in German East Africa (present-day Tanzania), overseers forced Africans to work the fields in labor gangs. The highest wage was thirty-five cents a month. In 1905 many African plantation workers in the German colony rebelled in the Maji Maji uprising, named after a secret religious cult. Believing that drinking a mixture of grain and water *(maji)* would protect them from European bullets, they bravely faced German machine guns. More than 100,000 Africans were killed in the fighting and the famine that followed it.

Probably the worst treatment of African workers existed in the region known as the

Going on Safari

Early European explorers and travelers in Africa were amazed at the variety of wildlife they found there. Huge flocks of birds lived around the African lakes, while herds of elephants, giraffes, zebras, wildebeest, leopards, and lions roamed the savanna. At first the Europeans exploited these animals as they did other African resources. Both African and European hunters killed many animals, either for sport or for valuable products such as ivory from elephant tusks. Wealthy Europeans went on safaris — trips through the jungle or grasslands to hunt animals and bring home trophies.

By the mid-twentieth century, however, people became concerned that hunting might wipe out some kinds of animals altogether. Many

African nations set aside large parks or reserves where animals were protected. Some of the largest wildlife parks are in the East African countries of Kenya and Tanzania. Though thousands of tourist still go on safari in Africa, many now carry cameras instead of rifles.

Congo Free State. This huge territory became the private colony of King Leopold II of Belgium after the Berlin Conference (page 594). The king granted private mining companies and rubber planters total control over certain areas. Local rulers paid a "labor tax" by sending their people to work as forced laborers in mines and on rubber plantations. The amount of work expected of each laborer was impossibly high, and the Africans were beaten, mutilated, or killed if they failed to produce enough. Thousands of Africans died; thousands more fled to nearby French colonies.

Eventually the brutal conditions in the Congo were revealed. The international outrage that followed forced the Belgian government to take over the colony from the king in 1908. Conditions in the Belgian Congo (present-day Zaire) improved only slightly, however, and the Belgian government continued to follow a paternalistic policy. The people of the Congo were allowed almost no part in governing themselves.

Traditional lifestyles change. The patterns of work made necessary by colonial policies changed traditional African village and family life. African men often were sent to work far from their villages. Women often had to work for Europeans to help meet tax payments. Africans no longer had time to make their own clothing, kitchenware, and furniture, as they had in the past. They turned to manufactured goods bought on credit at stores owned by Europeans or European companies. Trying to keep up with taxes, interest payments, and the cost of living, whole families found themselves deeply in debt to their European employers.

In many areas, African workers who had left their villages lived in crowded towns hastily built close to work centers. Houses were poorly constructed, and poor sanitation made life unhealthful. Few Europeans ventured into these towns. Funds for community development went into the fast-growing European sections, while African communities were ignored.

Some Africans gain education. In some colonies, Africans had an opportunity for education. Missionaries taught elementary reading and writing as well as medical knowledge and technical skills. A small number of Africans were trained to be ministers or teachers. The

Missionary schools, like this one in French-ruled Madagascar, provided Western-style education.

French and the British colonial administrations in particular gave Africans an opportunity to learn European-style government and law.

Traditional village education had always taught children their roles and duties in life. The education brought by the Europeans set the stage for modernization. As in India, educated people began to question why the ideals the Europeans taught were not put into practice in their colonies. Africans saw that to win freedom, they had to meet the European colonials on equal terms. Education became a tool for Africans to regain independence.

CHECK-UP

1. (a) What were the differences between direct rule and indirect rule of European colonies in Africa? (b) Explain the French colonial policy of assimilation.
2. (a) What economic policies did colonial governments in Africa follow? (b) What aims did European powers have in developing the economies of African colonies? (c) How did this affect different parts of a colony?
3. (a) Who was the ruler of the Congo Free State? (b) What conditions in the Congo led to a takeover by the Belgian government?
4. (a) How did new work patterns affect African lifestyles? (b) How did the kind of education provided by Europeans influence Africans?

Chapter 27 Review

Summary

When the international slave trade ended in the early 1800's, Europeans and Americans found new interests in Africa. Concern for the future of freed black slaves brought proposals for their repatriation to Africa, and the colonies of Sierra Leone and Liberia were founded. Explorers and missionaries spread Christianity and western ways in Africa; they also brought information about the continent to people in Europe and the United States. Africa's resources attracted investors, and soon the European nations claimed African lands as part of their empires.

Conquest and colonization followed. The leading imperialist powers in Africa were France, Britain, and Belgium. Germany, Spain, Portugal, and Italy also had colonies. African rulers resisted the takeover but could not withstand superior European armies and weapons.

Styles of colonial rule varied. All colonial powers imposed their own laws and institutions, however, and Africans had limited opportunities to participate in their own governments. Colonialism brought the Africans mainly hard work and few rewards, although some benefited from education and economic development. Wealth and power remained in European hands.

Vocabulary Review

1. Write the sentences listed below on a sheet of paper. In each sentence, fill in the blank with one of the following words: *capitalism, guerrilla warfare, protectorate.*
(a) A weak country that is taken over by a stronger power is called a __?__ .
(b) __?__ is an economic system based on the buying and selling of goods and services.
(c) __?__ uses hit-and-run tactics.
2. Explain the importance of each of the following terms in the history of Africa during the Age of Imperialism: (a) Great Trek, (b) Battle of Blood River, (c) South African War, (d) Cape-to-Cairo Railway, (e) Ashanti Union.

People to Identify

Match the following people with the numbered phrases that describe them: *Paul Cuffe, Andreas Pretorius, Samori Touré, Olaudah Equiano, David Livingstone, Shaka, Henry Stanley, Cecil Rhodes.*
1. An ex-slave whose autobiography helped arouse British opposition to slavery.
2. A Quaker shipowner who took freed blacks to Sierra Leone.
3. A Scottish missionary who explored much of the interior of Africa.
4. An American journalist who explored the Congo River.
5. A Boer leader who led his people on a long migration north from Cape Colony.
6. A Zulu commander who led his people on a campaign into neighboring territories.
7. A financier who sought to extend British holdings in southern Africa.
8. A Mandingo leader who resisted the French campaign to take control of West Africa.

Relating Geography and History

1. **Locating places.** Locate each of the following on a map in this chapter:
(a) Sierra Leone
(b) Liberia
(c) Ethiopia
(d) Natal
(e) Cape Colony
(f) Rhodesia
(g) Senegal
(h) Transvaal
(i) Congo River
(j) Algeria
(k) Sudan
(l) Khartoum
2. **Reports; making maps.** Many Europeans explored Africa in the 1800's. Choose two of the explorers from the list that follows, find out what parts of Africa they explored, and write a report: (a) James Bruce; (b) Richard Burton; (c) Mungo Park; (d) John Speke; (e) Samuel and Florence Baker. Draw a map of Africa to accompany your report. On the map, trace the route of the explorers you have chosen.

Discussion Questions

1. (a) What was the goal of the repatriation movement? (b) How did the American Colonization Society try to carry out that goal?
2. (a) What part did European explorers play in the colonization of Africa? (b) What were the goals of American and European missionaries

working in Africa? (c) What were the goals of Europeans who invested in the African colonies?

3. (a) How did the Boers and the Africans differ in their views of land ownership? (b) What was the result of the clash between the Khoisan and the Boers?

4. (a) What did the Boers hope to achieve by the Great Trek? (b) How was the conflict between the Boers and the British settled?

5. (a) Why did European nations decide to meet at the Berlin Conference (1884)? (b) What agreements were made at that conference?

6. How did each of the following areas come under European control: (a) Algeria? (b) Egypt? (c) Rhodesia?

7. (a) How did "direct rule" differ from "indirect rule" in the governing of African colonies? (b) What did colonial governments consider to be the goals of African economic development?

8. What were the effects of colonial rule on (a) traditional economic practices? (b) living conditions for African workers? (c) education?

Reading Primary Sources

The following primary source is taken from the journal of A. E. Scrivener, a British missionary who toured the Congo Free State when it was still the personal possession of the king of Belgium. Reports by Scrivener and other missionaries led eventually to the takeover of the colony by the Belgian government. Read the account. Then answer the questions that follow.

> [The people of a Congo village had been] living in peace and quietness when the white men came . . . with all sorts of requests to do this and to do that, and they thought it meant slavery. . . . They attempted to keep the white men out of their country, but . . . the rifles were too much for them. So they submitted, and made up their minds to do the best they could under the altered circumstances. First came the command to build houses for the soldiers, and this was done without a murmur. Then they had to feed [the soldiers]. Then they were told to bring in rubber.
>
> This was quite a new thing for them to do. There was rubber in the forest several days away from their home, but that it was worth anything was news to them. A small reward was offered, and a rush was made for the rubber. . . . They rejoiced in what they thought was their good fortune.

> But soon the reward was reduced until they were told to bring in the rubber for nothing. To this they tried to demur, but . . . several were shot by the soldiers, and the rest were told, with many curses and blows, to go at once or more would be killed.
>
> Terrified, they began to prepare their food for the fortnight's absence from the village, which the collection of the rubber entailed. The soldiers discovered them sitting about. "What, not gone yet!" Bang! bang! bang! And down fell one and another dead, in the midst of wives and companions. There is a terrible wail, and an attempt made to prepare the dead for burial, but this is not allowed. All must go at once to the forest. And [they] had to go without even their tinder-boxes to make fires. Many died in the forests from exposure and hunger, and still more from the rifles of the ferocious soldiers. . . .

(a) Why did the Africans want to keep white men out of their country? (b) What made it impossible for them to resist effectively? (c) What did the soldiers order the villagers to do? (d) What punishment did the villagers receive for failing to obey? (e) What happened to the villagers after they went into the forest? (f) How might readers in Europe have reacted to a report such as this?

Skill Activities

1. Word research. Two words used in this chapter have related origins. Both *repatriation* (page 588) and *paternalistic* (page 599) can be traced back to the Latin word for "father." Look back and reread the passages in which those words are used; then look them up in a dictionary. Explain how each word is related to the root word. Also look up the following words and explain their meaning: *patriot, patron, patrimony.*

2. Reading time lines. Time lines are an aid to remembering the correct order of events. Look at the time line on page 587. It shows events in Africa in the Age of Imperialism. (a) What is the first year shown? (b) What is the last year? (c) What is the span, or total number of years? (d) How many years are included in each interval? (e) Why might this period of time have been chosen for the time line rather than, for example, the years from 1550 to 1950?

Unit Six Review

Review Questions

1. (a) How did conditions in India enable European nations to gain a foothold there? (b) How did European nations win trading rights in China? (c) How did they win trading rights in Japan? (d) How did Europeans first gain a foothold in Africa?

2. How did industrialization play a part in the establishment of colonial empires by European nations?

3. (a) What is the difference between a colony and a sphere of influence? (b) Which of those terms best fits the pattern that European control followed in India? (c) in China?

4. Compare the attitude of the European powers toward Japan and toward China.

5. (a) What factors contributed to the resistance of the Manchu leaders to modernization efforts in China? (b) What factors contributed to the rapid and successful modernization of Japan? (c) What effect did efforts to modernize have on the independence of Egypt?

6. Explain how each of the following marked a turning point in history: (a) the Sepoy Rebellion; (b) the Taiping Rebellion; (c) the Battle of Blood River.

7. In which of the countries discussed in Chapters 25–27 were efforts to oppose Western imperialism most successful? Explain your answer.

8. (a) What reasons did British-educated Indians have for resenting their colonial rulers? (b) What positions did black Africans occupy in colonial governments in Africa? (c) How did greater educational opportunities affect the attitudes of black Africans toward colonial rule?

Projects

1. Making maps. Make a world map showing the colonies held by European nations in Asia and Africa in 1900. Use different colors to show the colonies held by Britain, France, Portugal, Germany, Spain, Belgium, and Italy. Add place names to the map, and give the map a key. Use the maps in Chapters 25–27 as a reference.

2. Making time lines. Make a time line showing events in Asia and Africa during the Age of Imperialism. Then review the time lines and time-tables in Chapters 20–22 and 24, and add events that show what was happening in Europe while European nations were expanding in Asia and Africa.

3. Recreating history. Write a script for a panel discussion in which the following people present their ideas on European expansion and its effects on the peoples of Asia and Africa: Robert Clive, Surendranath Banerjea, Sun Yatsen, Matthew Perry, Ito Hirobumi, King Leopold, Cecil Rhodes, and Samori Touré. Do research to find information about these individuals. Use what you learn in writing their speeches.

Books to Read

Buck, Pearl S. *The Good Earth.* John Day. A classic novel about rural life in China in the early 1900's.

Cotterell, Yong Yap, and Arthur Cotterell. *Chinese Civilization from the Ming Revival to Chairman Mao.* Weidenfeld and Nicolson.

Fish, Robert L. *Rough Diamond.* Doubleday. A fictional account of the life of Cecil Rhodes.

Fitzgerald, Charles Patrick. *The Horizon History of China.* American Heritage.

Hirschfeld, Burt. *Fifty-five Days of Terror: The Story of the Boxer Rebellion.* Julian Messner.

McKown, Robin. *The Colonial Conquest of Africa.* Franklin Watts.

Mitchison, Naomi. *African Heroes.* Farrar, Straus and Giroux. The lives of eleven African leaders, from the Middle Ages to the nineteenth century.

Moorehead, Alan. *The Blue Nile* and *The White Nile.* Harper. Accounts of European exploration and expansion along the Nile River.

Reischauer, Edwin O. *Japan: The Story of a Nation.* Knopf.

Reynolds, Robert L., and Douglas MacArthur II. *Commodore Perry in Japan.* American Heritage.

Schiffrin, Harold Z. *Sun Yat-sen: Reluctant Revolutionary.* Little, Brown.

Schirokauer, Conrad. *A Brief History of Chinese and Japanese Civilizations.* Harcourt.

How to Study World History

Writing Outlines and Summaries

An efficient way to take notes on a reading assignment is to outline what you read. An outline is also an important step in preparing a report. The process of making the outline helps you to organize your thoughts. The outline then becomes a guide to follow when you write your report.

Another way to take notes is to summarize what you read. A summary is a brief statement of the important ideas. Both an outline and a summary identify main ideas, but an outline, written as a list, shows the structure of the article or chapter and the relationship of the ideas. A summary, written in paragraph form, records the main ideas as concisely as possible. Summarizing is especially useful for taking notes as you prepare to write a report.

The following paragraphs provide suggestions for efficient outlining and summarizing.

Outlining. The first and most important step in making an outline is to identify the main ideas in the material you are reading and to distinguish these ideas from the supporting details. The main ideas will become main headings in your outline and the supporting details will become subheadings. For example, on page 598 of Chapter 27, the paragraphs under the heading **Colonial powers follow different policies** might be outlined as follows:

I.   Direct rule
 A. Practiced by France, Belgium, Germany, Portugal
 B. Europeans replace African leaders
 C. European laws and institutions established
II. Indirect rule
 A. Practiced by Great Britain
 B. Official policy — Africans were to be prepared for self-rule
 C. Local chiefs remained in charge of community affairs
 D. ''Resident,'' top British official
   1. Enforced British law
   2. Directed chief to collect taxes and provide workers
   3. Had final authority

Notice that in the outline on this page, main headings start with a Roman numeral. Subheadings start with a capital letter, and additional supporting details start with an Arabic numeral. Remember that a main heading should always have at least two subheadings.

Summarizing. The following guidelines will help you improve your ability to write a summary: (a) Look for key words and use them in your summary. (b) Use as few words as possible but avoid changing the meaning of the passage you are summarizing. (c) Write the summary in paragraph form. Remember that a summary should be shorter than the original passage. The purpose is to restate the important points of that passage.

Check Your Skill

Use the following questions to check your understanding of what you have read.

1. A brief statement of the important ideas in a reading selection is (a) an outline, (b) a summary, (c) a preface.

2. In an outline, the main ideas are labeled with (a) Roman numerals, (b) Arabic numerals, (c) capital letters.

3. Outlining helps you to (a) distinguish main ideas from supporting details, (b) underline important passages, (c) distinguish between cause and effect.

4. A summary should (a) use abbreviations, (b) be shorter than the original passage, (c) be written in outline form.

5. In writing a summary, it is useful to look for (a) details, (b) proper names, (c) key words.

Apply Your Skill

On a sheet of paper write an outline for the material under the subheading **Industrialization advances rapidly** in Section 1 of Chapter 28 (pages 618–622). Set off main headings with Roman numerals and subheadings with capital letters. Then write a summary of the material following the next subheading, **Europeans move to cities.**

The Shaping of the Modern World

A Short Survey from the Renaissance to the Twentieth Century

TRANSITION TO MODERN TIMES

The Renaissance and Reformation

In the three centuries following the end of the Middle Ages, European society, politics, and intellectual life underwent many changes. Two momentous movements — the Renaissance and the Reformation — began the transition from the medieval period to the modern era.

Renaissance scholars rediscover classical learning. The word *renaissance* in French means "rebirth." The period known as the Renaissance began with a revival of interest in the literature and civilization of ancient Greece and Rome. Scholars who studied classical works — the humanities — came to be called humanists. Renaissance scholars took an interest in worldly matters and in the development of varied human talents. Their emphasis on human achievements differed from the medieval viewpoint that earthly existence was a preparation for life after death.

The Renaissance began about 1350 in the city-states of northern Italy. Wealthy noblemen and noblewomen became patrons of the arts, encouraging brilliant literature and the creation of artistic masterpieces. Some of the greatest Italian Renaissance artists were Raphael, Michelangelo, and Leonardo da Vinci. The development of printing encouraged the spread of Renaissance ideas to France, England, Germany, and the Netherlands. Cervantes in Spain and Shakespeare in England were among the greatest writers of the time.

Reformers call for changes in Church practice. The Church had been powerful in the Middle Ages, but a number of its practices and traditions drew criticism as early as the fourteenth century. Many people demanded reforms. One critic was a German monk, Martin Luther. In 1517 he made public his differences with the Church and soon had a large number of followers — called Lutherans — in Germany. Both Church officials and the Holy Roman Emperor opposed Luther, but he was protected by the German Lutheran princes.

The Reformation spreads to northern Europe. The movement for reform, which came to be called the Protestant Reformation, found supporters in other countries. In Switzerland the theologian John Calvin developed the form of Protestant belief known as Calvinism. In the 1550's John Knox carried many of Calvin's ideas to Scotland and laid the foundations for the Presbyterian Church.

In England the Reformation became part of a struggle for political power. Wishing a male heir, King Henry VIII sought divorce and remarriage. When the Catholic Church opposed his plans, the king began to withdraw England from the Pope's authority. In 1534 Parliament created the Church of England, headed by the monarch, not the Pope.

In response to the spread of Protestantism, the Roman Catholic Church began the Counter-Reformation, or Catholic Reformation. The Church reformed Church administration and made new efforts to spread Catholic beliefs and suppress opposing ideas. Nonetheless, the Reformation had brought the end of religious unity in most of Europe.

The Age of Exploration

Europeans of the early fifteenth century knew little of the world beyond their borders. The many changes that had been taking place, however, inspired an era of exploration and expansion into other parts of the world.

Explorers seek new routes to Asia. One reason for the sudden burst of exploration was the desire for a sea route to Asia, the source of gold, silver, and spices. Merchants hoped to break the control of the overland routes held by Muslim traders and the Italian city-states. In addition, some European explorers sought land and adventures overseas; some also hoped to spread Christianity.

Encouraged by Prince Henry ("the Navigator"), Portugal took the lead in exploration. In 1498 Vasco da Gama found a sea route around Africa to India. Portuguese traders soon established trading posts and plantations on the coasts of Africa and Asia. While Portugal explored to the east, Spain searched for a westward passage to Asia. On his voyages across the Atlantic between 1492 and 1502, Christopher Columbus failed to reach Asia but landed on the islands of the Caribbean. Ferdinand Magellan's expedition (1519–1522) was the first to circle the world, discovering a westward route from Europe to Asia.

Europeans conquer and colonize the Americas. Seeking gold, the Spanish moved from the Caribbean islands onto the mainland of the Americas, where they conquered vast stretches of territory. The Aztec state in Mexico fell to Hernán Cortés between 1519 and 1521; Francisco Pizarro conquered the Inca empire in Peru between 1531 and 1538. Eventually, nearly all of Central and South America became part of the Spanish colonial empire. Brazil was ruled by the Portuguese.

The English, French, and Dutch sent explorers across the Atlantic and claimed much of eastern North America. All three countries also claimed islands in the Caribbean.

Trade and commerce change. The Age of Exploration brought changes in European political and economic life. Following the theory known as mercantilism, the European powers regarded their empires as existing solely to provide wealth for the home countries. Colonial rivalry led to armed conflicts between nations. The trade and wealth resulting from exploration changed business practices drastically, leading to the rise of capitalism.

The Growth of Modern European States

Politically, the expansion of Europe brought monarchs greater power at the expense of the Church and the nobility. The foundations of several modern nations were established.

Spain comes to dominate Europe. Ferdinand and Isabella, the rulers of Spain in the Age of Exploration, unified their Catholic nation by conquering the last Muslim territory and forcing non-Christians to leave Spain. Enriched by its empire in the Americas, Spain for a brief period became the strongest state in Europe. Its greatest glory came during the sixteenth century, with the reigns of Charles V and Philip II. Spanish power began to weaken after a revolt in the Spanish Netherlands and the shattering defeat in 1588 of the Armada in its attempt to invade England.

The Thirty Years' War disrupts Europe. The Thirty Years' War (1618–1648) began as a civil war between Catholics and Protestants in the Hapsburg lands, but eventually involved most of the European powers. Protestant states, including Denmark and Sweden, opposed the Catholic forces of Hapsburg Austria, Spain, and the Holy Roman Empire.

In 1635 the war became a battle to maintain the balance of power rather than a religious war. To oppose the Hapsburgs, Catholic France joined the war on the side of the Protestants. The war finally ended in 1648, leaving much of Germany in ruins and severely weakening the Holy Roman Empire.

Strong rulers establish France's power. France had been growing in unity and strength since the first Bourbon king, Henry IV, came to the throne in 1589, ending years of religious warfare between French Protestants and Catholics. Henry's son, Louis XIII, delegated great authority to a remarkable statesman, Cardinal Richelieu, who consolidated the authority of the monarchy and maneuvered to increase French influence during the Thirty Years' War. During the long reign of Louis XIV (1643–1715), absolute monarchy triumphed in France, which set the style for all Europe.

The power of English monarchs is limited. The reign of Queen Elizabeth I (1558–1603) was an era of remarkable progress for England. Commanding the unwavering loyalty of her subjects, the queen encouraged England's sea power and made her nation the leading Protestant state. The years following her reign, however, were troubled by struggles between the monarch and Parliament, for the Stuart kings claimed to rule by divine right.

In 1628 Parliament forced King Charles I to agree to the Petition of Right, which set forth certain civil liberties and limited the power of the king. By 1642 civil war broke out between the king's forces and the supporters of Parliament. Parliamentary leaders were mainly Puritans, English Protestants who wished to "purify" the Church of England by eliminating what they considered to be Catholic practices. Oliver Cromwell led the Puritan army to victory over the supporters of the king, and in 1649 Charles was tried for treason and beheaded. Ruling England as a Commonwealth, Cromwell eventually governed as a dictator.

In 1660 Parliament restored the monarchy, but religious and political conflicts persisted. In the "Glorious Revolution" of 1688, Parliament offered the throne to the Protestant rulers William and Mary. The new rulers agreed to the Bill of Rights, which assured the people basic civil rights and established Parliament's power over the English monarch.

Russia is unified and strengthened. In late medieval times, a number of strong states grew up in Eastern Europe — Hungary, founded by the Magyars, and the Slavic kingdoms of Bohemia and Poland. The strongest was Russia, unified by Ivan the Great in the late fifteenth century. Russia first began to develop into a modern state in the reign of Peter the Great (1682–1725). Urging change on the country, Peter introduced influences from Western Europe, reorganized the army, and built the first Russian navy. The most notable of Peter's successors was Catherine II, or Catherine the Great. In her reign (1762–1796), she introduced reforms that benefited the nobles and middle class. Russia acquired more territory and became one of the great powers in Europe.

The Scientific Revolution and the Enlightenment

During the sixteenth and seventeenth centuries, scientists used observation, reason, and mathematics to explain the natural universe. The discoveries and methods of this Scientific Revolution laid the foundations for modern science. During the eighteenth century, philosophers tried to apply scientific reasoning to all areas of human interest. This period became known as the Enlightenment, or Age of Reason.

New theories about the universe are proposed. In the early sixteenth century the Polish astronomer Nicolaus Copernicus challenged the ancient belief that the moon, sun, and planets revolved around the earth. He proposed instead that the earth revolved around the sun. Copernicus' theory received powerful support from the Italian scientist Galileo, who used mathematics to prove his observations of nature. In England, Isaac Newton built upon the discoveries of Copernicus and Galileo and developed the first modern concept of the universe. Newton's work demonstrated that all bodies, whether on the earth or in the skies, behaved according to unchanging natural laws.

Enlightenment philosophers study human society. The leaders of the Enlightenment in France and England — called philosophes — accepted Newton's concept of natural law and searched for the natural laws governing human activity. The most influential political philosopher of the Enlightenment was John Locke. He believed that the purpose of government was to protect people's "natural rights" to life, liberty, and property. In France, the writer Voltaire favored the free expression of ideas.

REVOLUTION AND NATIONALISM

New ways of thinking — an outgrowth of the Renaissance, the Reformation, and the Enlightenment — had brought many changes to the Western world. Concern for individual freedoms led to revolutions in many lands. The spirit of nationalism — a deep feeling for one's country — was also strong.

The American Revolution

The North American colonists win independence from British rule. By 1760 more than 1,500,000 settlers lived in Britain's thirteen North American colonies, which stretched from Georgia in the south to Massachusetts and New Hampshire in the north. When Britain attempted to exercise greater political and economic control over the colonies, the Americans protested against "taxation without representation" and defied British authority. Clashes between the colonial militia and British troops followed, and many patriots urged breaking away from Britain. On July 4, 1776, the colonies declared their independence.

Although the colonists had declared their independence, they had to fight to win it. In 1781, with French assistance, the troops of General George Washington forced the surrender of a large British army at Yorktown in Virginia, ending the Revolutionary War.

For the eight years following independence the United States was governed under the Articles of Confederation, which provided a weak central government. Facing problems in both domestic and foreign affairs, the states in 1787 adopted a new Constitution, which established a federal government that divided power between national and state governments.

The French Revolution and Napoleonic Era

The French rebel against the Old Regime. Long-standing inequalities in French society led to revolution in France in 1789. The nobility and the clergy retained feudal political and economic privileges that left out both the middle classes (the bourgeoisie) and the peasantry, the majority of the French population.

The first phase of the Revolution was dominated by the middle class and was committed to gradual reform and change. In 1789 King Louis XVI, seeking funds, called a meeting of the States-General, an elected legislature that had not met since 1614. Representatives of the bourgeoisie demanded a greater voice for the people and soon were supported by popular revolts. On July 14, 1789, the people of Paris stormed the Bastille, a fortress prison; and in October, a mob led by the women of Paris invaded the royal palace at Versailles. At the same time, peasants in various parts of France rose against their feudal lords.

During the next two years the National Assembly passed laws that wiped out many of the abuses of the Old Regime and drew up a constitution that made France a constitutional monarchy. The Declaration of the Rights of Man, issued in 1789, asserted the ideals of liberty and equality. The king reluctantly agreed to these changes.

The Revolution enters a second stage. In April, 1792, Prussia and Austria went to war against France in an effort to stop the revolution. Fear of invasion led the French to elect delegates with radical views to the National Convention. The Convention abolished the monarchy, declared France a republic, and executed the king. In 1793 the Committee of Public Safety, led by the Jacobins, took over actual rule of France. For several months, in what came to be known as the Reign of Terror, the Committee sent thousands of people to be executed on the guillotine. The execution of the Jacobin leader Robespierre ended the Terror. From 1795 until 1799 France was ruled by the Directory, an ineffective constitutional regime.

Napoleon establishes a European empire. The Directory was easily overthrown in 1799 by Napoleon Bonaparte, a successful military commander. An ambitious and skillful politician, Napoleon brought order and gained the French people's support for his one-man rule. In 1804 he assumed the title of emperor.

Because of his brilliant organizational ability and military skill, Napoleon nearly succeeded in his goal of ruling all Europe. In 1805 his forces won a smashing victory over the Austrians and Russians at the Battle of Austerlitz, and he soon was the master of Western Europe. Only Britain, a great sea power, resisted.

European nations unite to defeat Napoleon. Napoleon's control of the continent began to weaken when rebels in Spain, with British help, fought a long, bloody conflict known as the Peninsular War (1808–1813). In 1812 Napoleon invaded Russia and captured Moscow. The severe Russian winter, however, forced his huge army to retreat with staggering losses. Following this disaster, the major powers of Europe formed a coalition against Napoleon. After several defeats, he abdicated his throne and went into exile on the Mediterranean island of Elba. In 1815, however, Napoleon returned to France, reassembled his army, and entered Paris in triumph. Shortly afterward, British and Prussian forces decisively defeated him at the Battle of Waterloo.

Nationalism in Nineteenth-Century Europe

Despite its violence, the French Revolution inspired ideas of freedom, equality, and nationalism in many parts of Europe. Napoleon's rule had not only spread these ideas but upset the balance of power in Europe. Following Napoleon's downfall, the European monarchies tried to counteract these forces.

The Congress of Vienna tries to restore a balance of power. In 1815, monarchs and diplomats from the nations of Europe met at the Congress of Vienna to work out a peace settlement. The Congress was dominated by the Austrian diplomat Prince Klemens von Metternich, and the peace settlements reflected a reaction against the ideas of the French Revolution. The monarchies that had been toppled by the Revolution and the Napoleonic Wars were restored. To preserve the peace, Russia, Austria, Prussia, and Britain formed the Quadruple Alliance to settle future problems by diplomacy.

Rebellions continue in Europe. Continuing demands for liberty, equality, and political change led to rebellions in the 1820's and 1830's. Encouraged by Metternich, the established monarchs united to suppress uprisings in Spain, Italy, Russia, and Poland. In 1830 the Parisians again rose in revolt against the French king. Radical revolutionaries hoped to establish a republic, but the middle class gained control and named a new king, Louis Philippe.

Revolutions sweep Europe in 1848. Another wave of revolutions broke out in Western Europe in 1848. As before, the revolts began in France, where Louis Philippe was forced to abdicate and a republic was established.

Inspired by the revolution in France, workers and middle-class liberals in Germany hoped to unite the many independent states into one nation. They formed a national assembly, but the movement failed because Prussia refused to join.

In the lands of the Austrian Empire many groups sought freedom from Hapsburg rule. Czech nationalists in Bohemia, patriots in Hungary, and students and peasants in Austria all rebelled in 1848. Nationalist revolts also broke out against rulers in several parts of Italy. All the rebellions were eventually suppressed.

Sardinia leads the unification of Italy. In 1815 the Congress of Vienna had left the Italian peninsula divided into a number of separate states, held mainly by foreign rulers. Only the Kingdom of Sardinia (which included Piedmont on the mainland) was ruled by an Italian family, the House of Savoy. Sardinia took the lead in the movement for unification.

During the 1850's Sardinia's prime minister, Count Camillo di Cavour, gained foreign support in an effort to drive the Austrians from northern Italy. In southern Italy, the patriot forces of Giuseppe Garibaldi occupied the Kingdom of the Two Sicilies (Sicily and Naples). In 1860 these states joined Sardinia under the rule of its king, Victor Emmanuel, who was proclaimed king of Italy in 1861. By 1870 Italy's unification was complete.

Bismarck works to unify the German states. The unification of Germany was the work of the powerful state of Prussia and its chancellor, Otto von Bismarck. Since the Congress of Vienna, 39 German states had been linked in a loose union called the German Confederation, which was dominated by Austria.

Bismarck was determined to unite Germany under Prussian leadership.

Bismarck first maneuvered Austria into war over territory taken from Denmark and crushed the Austrian army in the Seven Weeks' War of 1866. He next organized the North German Confederation, which excluded Austria. To win over the remaining southern German states, Bismarck provoked a war with France in 1870. The Franco-Prussian War ended quickly with France's surrender in January, 1871. The other German states agreed to join with Prussia in a German empire, and the Prussian king was crowned Kaiser (Emperor) William I of a unified Germany.

The Austrian Empire weakens. Defeated by Prussia, Austria faced problems at home. The Austrian Empire in central Europe was the home of many non-German nationalities. In 1867 the largest group, the Hungarians, won a measure of self-rule. The Empire became the Dual Monarchy of Austria-Hungary.

The Ottoman Turks lose European territories. Throughout the nineteenth century the Ottoman Empire lost power and territory. Nationalist movements succeeded in Greece and Egypt, while Russia sought Ottoman Turkish lands. To prevent Russian expansion, Britain and France aided Turkey in the Crimean War (1853–1856), but the empire continued to decline. Uprisings in the Balkans eventually forced the Turks to recognize the independence of Serbia, Montenegro, and Rumania in 1878.

Russian rulers maintain autocracy. A succession of autocratic czars exercised absolute rule over Russia during the nineteenth century. Czar Alexander II abolished serfdom in 1861, but he refused to consider other reforms. Polish nationalist movements were suppressed. Some rulers tried to modernize the Russian economy, but the country lagged behind Western Europe.

Nation-Building in the Americas

Revolutions bring Latin American independence. During the first part of the nineteenth century, the nations in Latin America won independence from European colonial rule. The first successful revolution took place in the wealthy French island colony of St. Do-mingue. Inspired by the Revolution in France, black slaves led by Pierre Toussaint L'Ouverture rebelled against the French and established the nation of Haiti in 1804.

In the Spanish colonies (map, page 496), Simón Bolívar took up the struggle for independence and assembled a powerful army. By 1822 a new nation, Great Colombia — present-day Panama, Colombia, Venezuela, and Ecuador — was established in northwest South America, with Bolívar as its president. In 1822, Bolívar joined forces with José de San Martín, who had driven the Spanish out of Argentina and Chile and captured Lima, Spain's stronghold in Peru. In 1824 Bolívar's army broke Spain's remaining power with a victory over a Spanish army in the rugged Peruvian Andes.

In Mexico, a creole priest, Miguel Hidalgo, began the movement for independence in 1810. The Spanish captured and executed Hidalgo and suppressed his followers. By 1821, however, Spain was forced to recognize Mexico's independence. In 1822 Brazil broke away from Portugal and set up an independent monarchy.

National unity develops slowly. Following independence, dictators known as caudillos (cow-DEE-yohs) frequently gained control in the Latin American republics. Despite harsh policies, the caudillos centralized and stabilized the new governments, with the backing of the army and wealthy landowners.

In Mexico, an Indian lawyer, Benito Juárez, became caudillo and introduced many reforms in the Constitution of 1857. He resisted the French attempt to take over Mexico in 1862, but his rule remained controversial.

The United States expands and prospers. At the time of independence, the territory of the United States stretched only to the Mississippi River, but the country grew steadily. In 1803, President Thomas Jefferson doubled the size of the nation with the purchase of the Louisiana Territory from Napoleon. Settlers flocked into this huge tract of land west of the Mississippi. Florida was purchased in 1819. Texas was annexed in 1845, and California and the Southwest became part of the United States in 1848 at the end of the Mexican War.

Civil war threatens American unity. The stability and growth of the United States were threatened by regional differences over tariffs, states' rights, and slavery. As the country expanded, southerners demanded that slavery be permitted in the new territories, while northerners argued against the extension of slavery. A series of compromises failed to settle the dispute. In 1860 Abraham Lincoln, who was pledged to preventing the spread of slavery in the territories, won the presidency. The southern states seceded from the Union and formed the Confederate States of America. From 1861 to 1865 the nation was torn apart by a savage civil war that cost the lives of over 600,000 Americans. Fighting to preserve the Union, the North was victorious in 1865.

The Industrial Revolution

The Industrial Revolution of the eighteenth and nineteenth centuries transformed the economy and society of Western Europe and the United States. Machines replaced human labor, new sources of energy were found, and manufacturing replaced agriculture as the primary economic activity.

Industrialization transforms Western nations. The Industrial Revolution began in Great Britain, which had a large labor supply, plentiful natural resources, an efficient transportation system, and overseas markets for manufactured goods. The textile industry was the first to adopt the new factory system, in which large numbers of people worked together running machines in factories. Factories used division of labor, with each worker doing only one step in the making of a product. The new system produced goods faster and more cheaply than the domestic system, in which workers produced goods at home.

The steam engine revolutionized transportation as well as industry, and the first railway lines were built during the 1830's. Agriculture also turned to the use of machines.

Other nations followed Britain's lead in industrialization, and the United States and Germany soon became leading industrial powers. Cities grew rapidly as rural people sought factory jobs. Millions of immigrants from Europe moved to the United States in search of employment and opportunity.

Social changes follow industrialization. Rapid industrialization and urbanization brought problems, and these brought demands for reform. Despite opposition by employers, workers formed labor unions to bargain for higher wages and better working conditions. Some governments also took action to protect the rights of workers. The German government was the first to enact social welfare legislation providing sickness, accident, and old age benefits. Other reform movements of the nineteenth century sought to extend the right to vote, to protect child workers, and to limit the misuse of power by large businesses.

Some economists and political philosophers explored the problems of industrialization. In *The Wealth of Nations* (1776), Adam Smith argued for a laissez-faire approach — no government interference in business matters. In the mid-nineteenth century, Karl Marx predicted that the working class, or proletariat, would revolt against capitalism and establish a classless society. Marx's ideas contributed to both modern socialism and communism.

THE AGE OF IMPERIALISM

By the nineteenth century, industrialization was creating a need for overseas markets and raw materials. The great powers of Europe scrambled to gain territory in Africa and land or economic influence in Asia. Colonial empires were also important for national prestige and strategic advantages. A worldwide Age of Imperialism began.

British control of India is established. When European traders arrived in India during the 1500's, they took advantage of the existing religious and cultural rivalries to establish their influence. In the mid-1700's the British and French struggled for dominance. British forces led by Robert Clive defeated the French and drove them from India.

The British East India Company had established British power in India and, in effect, governed the colony until the mid-1800's. Indian discontent, however, erupted in the Sepoy Rebellion of 1857, and the British government assumed direct control. The colony was Britain's most valuable colonial possession, particularly as a source of cotton and a market for textiles made in British factories.

A movement toward Indian independence began to grow in strength in the late 1800's. The Hindu-dominated Indian National Congress, founded in 1885, sought reforms in British rule and more self-government. In 1906, the Muslim minority sought separate goals and formed the Muslim League.

Foreign nations seek influence in China. Since 1644, China had been under the rule of the Manchus, a dynasty whom the Chinese considered foreigners. The Manchus kept China isolated and tried to forbid trade with foreign nations. The Europeans, however, were eager for Chinese trade. Led by Great Britain, they persuaded the Manchu rulers to open the port city of Canton to foreign trade in 1834.

The Europeans steadily expanded their activities and influence in China. The Chinese government's attempt to halt British trade in opium led to the Opium War (1839–1842). China was defeated and had to sign "unequal" trade treaties not only with Britain but with other European nations.

The Chinese Empire comes to an end. Internal struggles also weakened the Manchu dynasty. The Taiping Rebellion (1850–1864), a peasant revolt, was suppressed by the Manchus with the aid of the Western powers. Defeat in the Sino-Japanese War of 1894–1895 further weakened China. The Boxer Rebellion of 1899 was a final attempt by the Chinese to rid the country of Western influence, and its failure allowed the Europeans still more control. Finally, in 1912 a carefully planned revolution by Sun Yat-sen overthrew the Manchu dynasty and established a Chinese republic.

Japan becomes dominant in Asia. Although European traders and missionaries first reached Japan in the sixteenth century, Japan restricted foreign contacts severely. In 1854, however, a show of American naval power forced Japan to open trade with the West. Like China, Japan was compelled to admit foreign merchants and to agree to unequal terms of trade.

The end of Japanese isolation led to dramatic changes. Unlike China, Japanese leaders set out to strengthen the country by taking advantage of Western methods. Rapid change took place during the era of the Meiji emperor, which began in 1868. Feudalism ended, a modern industrial economy emerged, and a powerful army and navy were built. In 1889 the emperor granted a constitution that established a Diet, or parliament.

Japan took advantage of its new-found power, revised its trade treaties, and began to build an empire in Asia. By 1910 Japan had defeated Russia and China in wars, taken control of Korea, and become a major power in Asia.

Imperialist nations divide Africa. As the European powers competed for empires in the Age of Imperialism, the continent of Africa became a primary target for expansion. In the early 1800's, 90 percent of Africa was ruled by Africans, but by 1914 only two African nations — Ethiopia and Liberia — remained independent (map, page 597).

The broad outlines of European colonization in Africa were agreed to by the major powers at the Conference of Berlin in 1884 and 1885. Britain's African empire eventually stretched from South Africa to Egypt. The French moved inland from territories on the coast of West Africa. Belgium controlled the Congo in the heart of the continent, while Germany and Portugal ruled rich colonies in southern Africa. Although their methods of rule varied, European colonial powers used the human and natural resources of Africa to develop economies that would profit the home country.

———

Imperialism frequently meant exploitation and the disruption of the traditional ways of life of the people of a colony. It also often brought opportunities for economic development and education and contributed to the spread of Western ideas.

Civilization in Crisis

By the late nineteenth century, Western civilization dominated much of the world. Many nations of Europe were establishing new empires in Africa and Asia. In some places, Western influence spurred other nations to move toward industrialization, modernization, and Western-style constitutional government.

In Europe and the United States, many earlier trends continued as the nineteenth century drew to a close. The pace of industrialization and urbanization grew quicker. More people gained the right to vote, the chance for an education, and the opportunity to achieve a higher standard of living. A burst of discovery in the sciences introduced the modern scientific era. New developments also began in art, music, and literature.

Civilization was threatened, however, by other continuing trends. Nationalism became extreme in some countries, intensifying political rivalries and bringing a build-up of military strength. By 1914 long-standing hostilities among the European nations exploded into a war that soon involved much of the rest of the world. Partly as a result of the war, several empires collapsed. In Russia, czarist rule was replaced by a political system whose aim was world revolution and the overthrow of capitalist society. Fear of this movement, combined with resentments remaining from World War I, gave rise to other extreme political movements in Europe. National ambitions also disrupted Asia. By the 1930's a second world war seemed inevitable. Beginning in Europe, World War II eventually involved the globe in the costliest war yet known.

The following chapters describe the changes that occurred as the twentieth century began and the world was plunged into two disastrous wars.

Life in Europe around the beginning of the twentieth century seemed to promise a bright and prosperous future, filled with exciting discoveries and inventions. People marveled at the early flights of airships, such as the Zeppelin advertised in this 1913 poster from Germany.

Lives of comfort, leisure, and security were enjoyed by many Europeans in the late 1800's, as reflected in this painting of diners at a fashionable Paris restaurant.

Europe in the Late Nineteenth Century

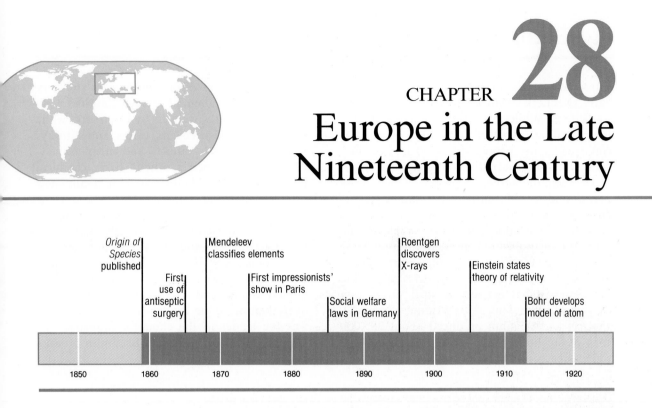

1850	1860	1870	1880	1890	1900	1910	1920	

Origin of Species published

First use of antiseptic surgery

Mendeleev classifies elements

First impressionists' show in Paris

Social welfare laws in Germany

Roentgen discovers X-rays

Einstein states theory of relativity

Bohr develops model of atom

European society in the late nineteenth century was peaceful, prosperous, and secure. For the middle and upper classes, it was a golden age of comfort and luxury. Although many of the problems of industrialization and urbanization continued to make life difficult for working-class people, their opportunities also expanded. More people gained the right to vote and the chance for an education. In general, Europeans lived better and healthier lives than ever before.

New discoveries and ideas caused revolutionary changes in the sciences, and scientific approaches were applied to the study of society and human behavior. Writers, painters, and musicians explored new forms of artistic expression. These changes reflected the vitality of the period, but they also created questions and a mood of uncertainty. Moreover, political forces were at work that threatened Europe's security.

This chapter explores the progress and discoveries made in late nineteenth-century Europe as well as the dangerous forces that were steadily developing.

CHAPTER OUTLINE

1 European Society Has Many Contrasts

2 The Modern Age of Science Begins

3 Artists Seek New Ways of Expression

4 Political Forces Threaten Europe's Stability

1 European Society Has Many Contrasts

European society in the late nineteenth and early twentieth centuries was filled with contradictions. While industrialization had raised the overall standard of living in a number of countries, many people still lived in wretched conditions, and sharp divisions separated social classes. On the surface, Europe seemed prosperous and secure, but many problems threatened this stability.

Industrialization advances rapidly. The rate of industrialization speeded up in the closing decades of the nineteenth century. Steel, electrical, and chemical industries were the pacesetters. The increase in steel production was spectacular. In 1870, Britain, Germany, France, and Belgium produced about 385,000 tons of steel; by 1913 output was 32,000,000 tons — nearly ninety times as great.

Practical uses of electricity were still very new, but their potential seemed limitless. City streets and houses were lit by electricity, while electric-powered streetcars, trains, and subways transported people quickly and inexpensively. Chemists developed synthetic dyes, chemical fertilizers, and medicines, making many new products available.

Great Britain, the earliest country to industrialize, still led in textile production, international finance, and merchant shipping. Its position as the world's leading industrial country, however, was being challenged by the United States and Germany. Germany had overtaken Britain in the production of steel and was the leader in the chemical industry. The United States had surpassed Britain in producing steel, iron, and coal.

A street scene in London during the 1890's reveals details of city life of that period. Note that horse-drawn vehicles were the major form of transportation.

Europeans move to cities. Along with the rapid growth of industry went increased urbanization. While eastern and southern Europe were still largely agricultural, in northwestern Europe the urban revolution moved ahead. All the great European capitals grew rapidly. In 1880 the population of Greater London was five million; in 1914 it was more than seven million. The population of Paris increased from two million to three million in the same period. In 1866, Berlin had 500,000 inhabitants; in 1914 it had more than two million. Large cities grew up in the coal-mining districts of northern France and in the Ruhr region of Germany. As Russia began to industrialize in the late nineteenth century, it became less rural. In 1863 only three Russian cities had a population of more than 100,000; forty years later Russia had some fifteen cities of this size.

Cities were centers of manufacturing, commerce, finance, and culture. They had great universities, museums, concert halls, and theaters. Many had wide boulevards, beautiful parks, and handsome homes. Yet the early problems that had developed as a result of urbanization (page 528) had not vanished. Most European cities also had overcrowded, crime-ridden slums that housed many of the new city dwellers.

Technological and medical advances bring population growth. Though living conditions in urban slums were grim, a number of scientific discoveries in the nineteenth century helped people in general live better, healthier lives. In 1800 the total population of Europe was about 190 million. By 1914 it had soared to 480 million. This population explosion was due in part to an increase in the amount and availability of food. Railways and steamships transported large quantities of grain from the United States and Russia. New methods of refrigeration and canning, moreover, permitted beef to be shipped to Europe from Argentina and the United States.

In addition, fewer infants died of disease, and people lived longer because of advances in medicine and new knowledge about the causes of disease. Sanitation was improved, reducing the danger of epidemics of such age-old diseases as cholera.

New treatments developed by Louis Pasteur greatly advanced medical science. Pasteur developed a method of vaccinating against rabies, a disease that had always been fatal before his time.

Scientists work to prevent disease. In the late 1700's, an English country doctor named Edward Jenner had found the first method for preventing smallpox, a disease that killed many people and left others with badly scarred skin. Jenner observed that dairy workers who had had a mild illness called cowpox seemed not to get smallpox. Making a solution, or vaccine (vak-SEEN), that contained cowpox germs, he injected it into the arm of a young boy. A few weeks later, in a risky experiment, the boy was exposed to smallpox and did not catch it. Jenner's method of vaccination was soon widely used in England and continental Europe.

Though vaccination worked, Jenner did not know the cause of smallpox. Not until about fifty years later did a French chemist, Louis Pasteur (pass-TOOR), discover the tiny organisms, called bacteria, that were the cause of many diseases. In his experiments, Pasteur found helpful as well as harmful bacteria. Realizing that bacteria could be killed by heat, he devised a method of treating milk to make it safer to drink. This process came to be called pasteurization. At about the same time, a German physician, Robert Koch, also began to experiment with bacteria, and in 1882 he found the cause of tuberculosis, a common illness. By finding the causes of disease, both Koch and Pasteur made it possible to prevent or cure many diseases harmful to human beings and animals.

Having gained the knowledge that bacteria were the cause of many diseases, scientists were better able to fight them. In the 1860's Joseph Lister, an English surgeon, began to use antiseptics to kill bacteria in hospital rooms and on surgical instruments. Patients who underwent surgery under antiseptic conditions were in far less danger of contracting fatal infections.

Standards of living improve. In a number of other ways, the lives of ordinary people improved. The standard of living for miners and urban workers rose substantially between 1880 and 1914. Many workers could afford to buy meat and eggs more regularly and to purchase clothes, shoes, and other mass-produced goods. The work week had been reduced to 55 or 60 hours. For the first time, workers had leisure time to spend at sports, music halls, and other popular recreations.

Workers' lives improved in other ways too. Factory inspection laws reduced the number of accidents, although thousands of workers still were killed or injured each year. In the 1880's the German government began to provide benefits for sick, injured, and elderly workers. By 1914, Austria, Italy, Denmark, Switzerland, France, and Britain had started similar social programs.

Public education becomes widespread. The general level of education was raised significantly in the closing decades of the nineteenth century. By 1900 most European countries required children to attend elementary school. Illiteracy had been virtually eliminated in most countries of northern Europe. In other parts of Europe, however, many people still could not read or write.

Even with the spread of compulsory schooling, opportunities for education remained severely limited. Formal education for most youngsters ended at age eleven or twelve, when they went to work. Usually, only children in the middle and upper classes had the necessary preparation and money to attend secondary school or university. In Germany, for example, 92 percent of the youth attended primary school, but only 8 percent entered secondary school. Even fewer people — and almost no women — had the chance for a university education.

Divisions between social classes are great. In every area of life, Europeans were very

Photography advanced rapidly in the late 1800's, making possible a permanent visual record of everyday life. Here weekend strollers in a London park have their pictures taken.

Factory work in the late 1800's meant higher wages for many people but also brought risks to safety and health. The painting shows a German ironworks.

aware of social class differences. The world of workers and peasants was sharply divided from that of the upper classes — landowning aristocrats and wealthy bourgeois bankers, industrialists, and merchants. Members of aristocratic families still dominated the upper ranks of the army, staffed the diplomatic service, and held leading positions in government. They mixed with the prosperous bankers and merchants but often treated them with disdain. (At gala balls in Prussia, a velvet rope separated the nobles from other guests.) Except in England, aristocrats were contemptuous of moneymaking and tried to have nothing to do with industry, commerce, and finance. Nevertheless, to maintain their luxurious lifestyle, they often married members of wealthy middle-class families.

The European middle class itself was divided. The wealthy business and professional families of the upper middle class owned banks, stores, and factories or worked as managers, lawyers, or engineers. Below them socially were small shopkeepers, government workers, and clerks, who worked hard to maintain their position in the middle class.

Peasants and workers face difficult conditions. Workers and peasants — the great bulk of the population — made up the lower class in European society. Although there had been improvements in ordinary people's lives, European working-class living conditions were still difficult.

Among European peasants, the standard of living varied from one region to another. In parts of France, western Germany, and Austria, some peasants owned enough land to allow them to live comfortably. Most peasant families, however, had small holdings from which they could make only a skimpy living. In other parts of Europe, few peasants owned land of their own but worked as farm laborers for the owners of large estates.

As in the early years of industrialization, many urban working-class families were engaged in a constant struggle against poverty. They lived in bleak, overcrowded tenements, usually without central heating or running water. Tuberculosis, still a major cause of death, spread rapidly in these unhealthful surroundings. Working-class parents worried that their children would go hungry. The loss of a job or the death or illness of a wage earner left a family destitute.

Working hours had been reduced since the early days of the Industrial Revolution, but the workday was still very long. Factory working hours in England were limited by government legislation, but other workers regularly toiled 72 or more hours a week. In the Netherlands, for example, sales clerks worked 82 hours a week and were not permitted to sit down during the working day.

Safety in factories had improved to some degree. Yet toiling long hours in damp, airless buildings caused workers' health to deteriorate. So too did daily contact with toxic substances such as lead, arsenic, mercury, and zinc. Accidents were still frequent in coal mines and on the docks. In 1906, for instance, more than a third of the 10,000 longshoremen working on the docks in Rotterdam (in the Netherlands) were killed or injured on the job.

Political parties gain working-class support. Despite the difficulties of their lives, European workers had gained more political power as the right to vote was broadened. By 1912 virtually all adult males could vote in France, Britain, Belgium, Spain, Norway, Sweden, Italy, and Austria (but not Hungary). New political parties sought and gained support among workers. In 1912 the German Social Democratic Party received one third of the votes cast and held more seats in the Reichstag than any other party. Socialist and Socialist Democratic candidates won seats in parliament in France and Austria. In 1906 the newly formed British Labour Party won 29 seats in Parliament.

CHECK-UP

1. (a) In what European industries was growth most rapid in the late nineteenth century? (b) How was Britain's position as the leading industrial nation being challenged?
2. (a) What population changes were taking place in Europe during the late nineteenth century? (b) What scientific advances encouraged population growth?
3. What contributions to the improvement of health were made (a) by Jenner? (b) by Pasteur? (c) by Lister?
4. (a) How did the lives of working-class people improve during this period? (b) What serious problems remained? (c) What developments reflected the increased political power of European workers?

2 The Modern Age of Science Begins

Scientific knowledge increased tremendously in late nineteenth-century Europe. With this new knowledge came better health and improved living conditions as well as expanded understanding of the world.

At the same time, a new surge of scientific curiosity led to startling new theories about the physical universe. The findings in science had a great influence on other fields as well, and scientific ideas were applied to human society and behavior.

THE PHYSICAL SCIENCES

Basic discoveries lead to modern chemistry. The Scientific Revolution (page 402) brought about the beginnings of modern physics and astronomy. Modern chemistry began to emerge in the last part of the eighteenth century as scientists learned more about the structure of matter.

Since ancient times, people had believed that all matter was made of four "elements" —

fire, air, water, and earth. In the 1700's, scientists conducted many experiments to find out more about these "elements." Joseph Priestley, a teacher and amateur scientist in England, began to experiment with air. He found that air was not a single substance but a mixture of gases, and in 1774 he isolated one of those gases, oxygen. Priestley shared his discovery with a French chemist, Antoine Lavoisier (lah-vwah-ZYAY). Lavoisier made many more experiments. He named the gases in air "nitrogen" and "oxygen" and showed that fire is not a substance but a chemical reaction. From his experiments, Lavoisier and his co-workers named many other elements and made the first table of chemical elements. He is considered the founder of modern chemistry. (Lavoisier also was active in French revolutionary politics and was sent to the guillotine in 1794, during the Reign of Terror.)

Marie Curie was one of the first scientists to discover that certain elements are radioactive.

In the early 1800's, John Dalton, an English chemist and mathematics teacher, worked out a theory about the basic structure of matter. Dalton said that each element consists of tiny, indestructible particles of matter, or atoms. According to his theory, all the atoms of one element are alike, and they are different from the atoms of other elements. Furthermore, the atoms of the various elements combine in certain ways to create different substances. For example, one atom of carbon and two of oxygen always combine to form carbon dioxide. Though parts of Dalton's atomic theory were later shown to be wrong, his ideas were basic to the development of both modern chemistry and modern physics.

Dmitri Mendeleev (men-duh-LAY-uf), a Russian chemist, helped make chemistry more systematic and mathematical. In 1868 he devised a table that classified elements according to their atomic structure. Where there were gaps in the list of elements, Mendeleev predicted that elements would be discovered to fill them in. All the elements found since Mendeleev's time have fit into those gaps.

Physicists explore matter and energy. Nineteenth-century chemists had begun to learn about the basic elements and atoms of which all matter is made. In the 1890's and early 1900's, scientists looked further into how these behave. In 1895 Wilhelm Roentgen (RENT-gehn), a German physicist, discovered a new form of electromagnetic waves (page 526). These very short waves penetrated seemingly solid substances. Not sure what the waves were, Roentgen named them X-rays — X meaning "unknown." X-rays soon began to be used both in medicine and in a variety of experiments by other scientists.

In 1897, the French scientist A. H. Becquerel (bek-uh-RELL) found that the mineral uranium gives off high-speed rays, or radiation, similar to X-rays. He shared his discovery with a Polish-born chemist, Marie Sklodowska Curie, and her husband, Pierre Curie, a physicist. In their work, the Curies found that certain other minerals also give off radiation. Such minerals are said to be radioactive. The Curies theorized that the atoms in minerals such as radium were constantly breaking down and giving off energy in the form of radiation.

These ideas contradicted Dalton's theory that atoms were the smallest unit of matter and could not be split. In 1897 a British scientist, J. J. Thomson, discovered a smaller particle within the atom. It was given the name *electron*. Physicists now began to investigate the inner structure of the atom.

Scientists describe the atom. In 1911, Ernest Rutherford, once a student of J. J. Thomson, suggested a model for the structure of the atom. In this model, the atom looked something like the solar system. A heavy central core, or nucleus (NOO-klee-us), was surrounded by electrons moving quickly around it in orbits. Rutherford's model was later changed as scientists found other particles within the atom. His idea about the heavy nucleus, however, was of great importance in nuclear physics.

A young Danish physicist named Niels Bohr came to Britain to work with Thomson and Rutherford. Bohr combined Rutherford's ideas about the atom with an earlier theory about energy. About 1900, Max Planck in Germany had shown that energy was released in short bursts, or quanta (KWAN-tah). In 1913, Bohr worked out a new model of atomic structure, which modern physics still uses. In Bohr's model, electrons spin around the nucleus in certain orbits, or shells. When an electron jumps from one shell to another, a burst of light or other form of energy is given off.

A revolution occurs in physics. Not all scientists in the early 1900's agreed with these findings. Some refused to accept the existence of the atom. Even those scientists working in the new physics and chemistry found many things puzzling. Traditional (or classical) physics was based primarily on the theories of Isaac Newton (page 404). In the universe as Newton saw it, all the parts followed strict mathematical laws and worked in perfect harmony and precision, like a smooth-running machine. The new discoveries in science, however, caused many scientists to question accepted ideas about matter, energy, motion, space, and time.

The greatest challenge to Newtonian physics came from Albert Einstein (1879–1955), a brilliant German-born scientist. In 1905, while working as a clerk in the Swiss patent office, Einstein published a scientific theory that forced people to reconsider the orderly universe described by Newton. Einstein's "special theory of relativity" stated that, while Newton's laws apply in the ordinary world, they do not work for objects moving at speeds near the speed of light. Over many years, Einstein continued to develop the theory of relativity. He sought to unify and bring together all that scientists knew about the workings of the universe.

For Einstein, the final "yardstick" for measuring anything in the universe was the speed of light. As things travel faster — approaching the speed of light — the everyday rules for time, space, and motion change. According to Einstein's theory, the only way to describe the motion of a moving object is to compare it with another moving object. Therefore, all motion is relative to some other motion and to the observer. The theory also affected thinking about time and space; these too were seen as relative, not absolute.

Einstein relates matter and energy. Einstein's 1905 paper also contained his formula for showing the relationship between matter and energy. This question had puzzled scientists like Marie Curie, who studied substances that gave off energy in the form of radiation. Einstein's formula $E = mc^2$, stated simply, means that mass and energy can be converted into each other.[1] The research that grew out of this idea led to modern achievements in atomic energy. The tiny amount of matter in an atom is converted into staggering amounts of energy that can be used in many ways.

THE NATURAL SCIENCES

Just as new discoveries and ideas revolutionized physics and chemistry in the nineteenth century, new theories and explanations also were proposed in the natural sciences. While living organisms had not been studied in the same objective way as physics, chemistry, or astronomy, many naturalists had carefully observed and classified different species of plants and animals. Many people believed that each of these species had been created separately just as it now appeared on earth. Others, however, believed that living things had changed

---

[1] That is, energy (E) is equal to mass (m, the quantity of matter in a body) times the speed of light (c) squared.

The Nobel Prizes

One of the many advances in technology in the late 1800's was a useful, controllable explosive called dynamite. Its inventor was a Swedish chemist named Alfred Nobel (noh-BELL). Although his invention soon made Nobel one of the richest men in the world, he was haunted by guilt about the destructive uses of dynamite in war. When Nobel died in 1896, he left his $9 million fortune to be used for prizes honoring people who had worked for the good of humanity. Each year, on Nobel's birthday, the prizes are given to men and women who have done outstanding work in science, in literature, and in promoting world peace (right, the medal awarded to winners).

Some of the early Nobel Prizes went to the scientists who investigated radioactivity and the atom — Roentgen in 1901 (the first Nobel Prize), Becquerel and the Curies in 1903, and later J. J. Thomson, Max Planck, Ernest Rutherford, Niels Bohr, and Albert Einstein. Marie Curie later won

a second Nobel Prize. The first Nobel Peace Prize went to Henri Dunant, founder of the Red Cross (page 480).

over time. They sought explanations of how this might have happened.

Lamarck suggests a theory of evolution. Early in the 1800's, J. B. Lamarck, a distinguished French scientist, made a careful study of plants and animals. He studied fossils (page 26) and noticed differences between ancient organisms and the living creatures he observed. To explain the differences he noted, Lamarck developed a theory that living things change in ways that allow them to live more successfully in their environment. These changes, he believed, were then passed on to their descendants, and, after many generations, a new type of organism would develop, or evolve.

Geologists study earth history. While naturalists were trying to explain the history of living things, other scientists were looking for evidence about the history of the earth itself. In the late 1700's, a Scottish geologist named James Hutton suggested that the earth's surface was the result of gradual changes occurring

over vast periods of time. The same processes of change, he said, were still going on. Other scientists also were studying rocks, oceans, and mountains. An influential book was *Principles of Geology* (1830–1833) by Charles Lyell, a British scientist. Lyell's work became the basis of modern geology, the study of the structure and history of the earth.

The new ideas about the earth's structure influenced many people, including a young English naturalist named Charles Darwin. Darwin came from a family of scientists, and his grandfather had done work like that of Lamarck. He studied natural events and tried to explain them by means of processes that he could observe going on.

Darwin develops a new theory. From 1831 to 1836, Darwin served as a naturalist on a ship called the *Beagle,* which was on a scientific voyage to South America. Darwin carefully observed the unusual species of plants and animals living on the coast of South America and the Galapagos (gah-LAH-pah-gus) Islands. From his observations, he concluded that many species of animals had perished, that distinct new species had emerged in isolated places (such as the Galapagos), and that there were links between past and present species.

After he returned from the voyage, Darwin continued to observe and draw conclusions from his findings. He was encouraged in his work by Lyell and by the similar theories of another naturalist, Alfred Russel Wallace. Darwin came to believe that all living forms, including human beings, evolved from earlier forms of life that had first existed millions of years ago. Finally, in 1859, Darwin published a book called *On the Origin of Species by Means of Natural Selection,* which became an influential work in the history of science.

Darwin suggests the principle of natural selection. Darwin partly based his theory on Malthus's idea (page 531) that living organisms tend to reproduce faster than the food supply. Consequently, many more individuals of each species are born than can possibly survive the competition for limited food and living space. Therefore, said Darwin, something must determine which individual living things will survive and which will die before they have offspring. The advantage, he suggested, is with those members of a species that are smarter, faster, stronger, or in other ways better fitted to survive than other members of the same species. Darwin called this idea the principle of natural selection.

Darwin also said that some offspring inherit these advantages and so are somewhat different from their ancestors and from other members of the species. Very gradually, some members of the species become so different that a new species evolves.

The theory of evolution had a great impact on many fields of science, bringing about what is sometimes called the Darwinian Revolution. While it provided an explanation for the development and diversity of living organisms, it also aroused questions and controversy among both scientists and the public. *The Origin of Species* was opposed by some religious thinkers, who viewed the theory as a rejection of the account of the creation of life given in the Bible.

Mendel begins work on inherited traits. Darwin's theory did not explain how differences develop between one generation and the next. Gregor Mendel, an Austrian monk, began to work out such an explanation in the 1860's, but his achievement did not become known until about 1900. Mendel performed many experiments with pea plants, crossing yellow peas with green ones, tall plants with short ones, and so on. He found that the new generation of pea plants was not a blending of parental traits; for instance, crossing tall plants and short ones did not produce medium-size plants. Instead, individual plants inherited certain traits of each "parent" plant — some were short, some tall.

Later work by many biologists led to the discovery of *genes,* which carry such hereditary traits from parent to offspring. Mendel's work, however, was the beginning of the science of genetics, the study of inherited traits.

THE SOCIAL SCIENCES

The new scientific ideas and findings had an influence beyond the physical and natural sciences. They stimulated an interest in studying human society and behavior in a scientific way. The modern social sciences developed as thinkers examined society, politics, history, and economic life.

Sociology develops as a field of research. The term *sociology* — the scientific study of human society — was invented by a French philosopher, Auguste Comte (KOHNT), about 1840. This approach to studying society was adopted later by Émile Durkheim in France and Max Weber (VAY-ber) in Germany, who were pioneer thinkers in sociology in the early 1900's. They did careful research, gathered information, and analyzed their findings in attempts to find out what factors affect the ways people behave in groups.

Historians apply the scientific method. Nineteenth-century historians, particularly in Germany, also began to use the methods of science to make the study of history more accurate and objective. Leopold von Ranke (RAHNG-kuh) insisted that historical writers should study primary sources and "tell what actually happened."

The theories of Sigmund Freud, the founder of psychoanalysis, had a far-reaching impact on the social sciences, literature, and art.

mals. He found that an animal's involuntary actions — its reflexes — could be changed, or conditioned, through training.

At about the same time, other students of psychology were trying to understand the influence of emotions on human behavior. The most important thinker in this area was Sigmund Freud (FROID), a doctor who began his work in Vienna in the early 1900's. Freud sought to understand the workings of the unconscious mind, which he felt was the source of human actions. While treating patients suffering from mental disorders, Freud concluded that dreams were an important expression of people's desires and feelings, including those that their conscious mind repressed because they would cause uneasiness or guilt. "The interpretation of dreams," he said, "is the royal road to a knowledge of the unconscious activities of the mind." In his work as a psychiatrist, Freud developed the method known as psychoanalysis, in which mental and emotional problems and disorders are treated by trying to discover their sources in the unconscious mind.

Curiosity about the human past also encouraged thinkers and writers to look deeper into folklore, primitive society, and ancient civilizations. The fields of archeology and anthropology developed, using both historical research and scientific methods of investigation. Many expeditions were sent to explore ancient sites in Egypt and the Near East. Exciting discoveries were made. Heinrich Schliemann (SHLEE-mahn), a German businessman, found the ruins of Troy in 1876. In the 1890's Sir Arthur Evans of Britain began to explore ruins from Minoan civilization.

Psychology seeks the causes of behavior. The new field of psychology, the study of human behavior, also adopted some of the methods and ideas of science. Some psychologists began systematic research and experiments. The first laboratory for psychological experiments was set up in Germany in 1879 by Wilhelm Wundt (VOONT). A few years later, Ivan Pavlov, a Russian experimental scientist, studied the behavior and nervous systems of ani-

CHECK-UP

1. Describe the contributions to modern chemistry made by (a) Priestley, (b) Lavoisier, (c) Dalton, (d) Mendeleev.
2. (a) How did the Curies explain the behavior of minerals such as radium? (b) What discoveries were made in the early 1900's about the structure of the atom?
3. (a) In what way did Einstein disagree with Newton's view of the universe? (b) What did Einstein say was the relationship between matter and energy?
4. (a) What theory did Lamarck offer to explain differences between ancient and modern life forms? (b)) What new ideas did Lyell propose in the study of the earth?
5. (a) According to Darwin, what part did natural selection play in the evolution of a species? (b) What did Mendel discover about inherited traits?
6. (a) What are the social sciences? (b) What part did the scientific approach play in the fields of sociology and history? (c) What approach did Pavlov take to psychology? (d) What was the chief aim of Freud's work?

3 Artists Seek New Ways of Expression

The arts in Europe during the late nineteenth century reflected the discoveries and changes of the times. Painting was influenced by social changes and by scientific discoveries in the fields of physics and psychology. Literature also reflected changes in society — for example, the impact of urbanization and industrialization and the growing awareness of ordinary people. By the early 1900's the arts, like the sciences, were entering the modern age.

Painters experiment with light and color. Until the middle of the nineteenth century, the aim of most painters was to represent exactly what something or someone looked like. About 1860 a group of painters in Paris began to experiment with showing their *impression* of an object, not a realistic representation. They looked at objects outdoors in bright sunlight and tried to capture how movement, color, and light appeared to the eye in a fleeting instant. The leaders of this group were Édouard Manet (mah-NAY), Claude Monet (moh-NAY), Camille Pissarro, Edgar Degas (deh-GAH), and Pierre-Auguste Renoir (rehn-WAHR), and two Americans, Mary Cassatt and J. A. M. Whistler. When these artists gave their first group show in 1874, they were called impressionists.

The impressionists found new subject matter as well as a new way of painting. They painted landscapes in sun and shadow, but they also showed the life of ordinary people in an urban, industrialized world. They showed shop clerks and dock workers in dance halls and cafes and performers in theaters and circuses. They also painted city scenes — bridges, railroad stations, streets filled with traffic.

In the 1880's painting took a new turn with the work of Paul Cézanne (say-ZAHN), a French artist who worked at first with the impressionists. Cézanne moved even farther from realistic painting, showing objects as patterns of forms and flat surfaces. The intent was still the same — to paint the artist's personal view. This movement came to be called post-impressionism. Post-impressionist painters experimented with vivid color and distorted patterns. Paul Gauguin (goh-GAN), a Parisian stockbroker, abandoned his career to paint the landscape and people of the Pacific island of Tahiti. The paintings of Vincent Van Gogh (van GOH), a Dutch-born artist, transformed everyday scenes into patterns of swirling color and movement.

Post-impressionism influenced other developments in art. The expressionists, working

NEW WAYS OF PAINTING

Note the different styles of these three impressionist works of art: (this page) *The Ballet Class* by Degas; (next page) *Drawbridge at Arles* by Van Gogh (top); *Monet Working in His Garden* by Renoir.

628

mainly in Germany, used these techniques to convey intense emotion. Other artists, such as Henri Matisse (mah-TEES) in France, experimented with patterns and line in brilliant colors. About 1907 in Paris, Pablo Picasso (born in Spain) and Georges Braque (BRAHK) began the movement that came to be called cubism. The cubists looked at abstract shapes, trying to show several different views of a three-dimensional object at once.

All these developments were making art more abstract and less related to real objects. By the early 1900's it was not necessary for a painting to be a painting of *something*. It could be pure color, shape, or pattern. Picasso, the most influential twentieth-century artist, expressed the viewpoint of the modern artist: "I paint forms as I think them, not as I see them."

Music follows traditional forms. Unlike painting, music in the nineteenth century continued to develop mainly along the lines set by the Romantics and the nationalistic composers (page 469). The most influential composer was Johannes Brahms, who carried on the German Classical tradition in orchestral music. Outstanding late Romantic composers in Russia included Peter Ilyich Tchaikovsky (chy-KOF-skee) and Sergei Rachmaninoff, both known for beautiful melodies and rich orchestral sounds. Composers in almost every country in Europe continued to use folk melodies and nationalistic themes. They included Edvard Grieg in Norway, Antonín Dvořák (dvor-ZHAHK) in Bohemia, and Modest Mussorgsky in Russia.

Throughout Europe, audiences flocked to opera performances, particularly those of Giuseppe Verdi. Active in Italy's nationalist movement, Verdi became internationally famous for such operas as *Rigoletto, La Traviata,* and *Aida.* Light opera, or operetta, was also popular. Johann Strauss the younger, called "the waltz king," created the popular Viennese style of dance music in the 1870's and 1880's.

It was in opera that the first signs of changes in music appeared in the 1850's, with the "music dramas" of Richard Wagner (page 469). Audiences, critics, and other musicians disagreed violently about Wagner's music, but his approach to harmony and his way of using the orchestra influenced all those who followed him. He particularly influenced the symphonies of Gustav Mahler and the operas and other works of Richard Strauss in Vienna.

Composers experiment with harmony. In the early twentieth century a number of composers began to try out harmonies that sounded strange to their listeners. In France, Claude Debussy (deh-byoo-SEE) tried to create in music what the impressionist painters were attempting on canvas. A Viennese composer, Arnold Schönberg, experimented with a totally new

structure for music. Perhaps the most influential composer of the early 1900's was Igor Stravinsky in Russia, who used some of Schönberg's ideas along with rhythms and ideas from jazz. Audiences found the new music hard to accept. When Stravinsky's ballet *The Rite of Spring* opened in Paris in 1913, the audience was so upset that a riot broke out in the theater.

European literature strives for realism. Writers in the latter part of the nineteenth century rejected some of the stress placed on personal emotions by the Romantics (page 468). They concentrated instead on portraying characters with depth and honesty. The writers known as realists (and later naturalists) wanted literature to be true to life. Their stories reflected social problems and dealt with the everyday lives of ordinary people — factory workers, shopkeepers, peasants. Novels, plays, and stories were set in the slums of cities, in middle-class homes, in villages, and even in prisons. The modern novel and the modern drama developed, reaching their greatest height in Britain, France, and Russia.

In England particularly, there was a new audience for popular fiction. Because of improvements in education, more people were able to read and so could follow their favorite stories, which appeared in installments in weekly magazines. Many of the best-known novels of Charles Dickens were published in this way. Dickens's books, rich in both humor and tragedy, showed conditions in the factories and cities of industrial England. In contrast, the novels of Mary Ann Evans (known by her pen name, George Eliot) and Thomas Hardy pictured life in rural England. These writers explored complex psychological relationships between people.

In France, Gustave Flaubert (floh-BAIR) described the life of a middle-class French woman in his novel *Madame Bovary.* Émile Zola, a supporter of modern trends in both painting and literature, drew grim portraits of middle-class and working-class life.

Some of the greatest masters of realistic fiction were Russian. Ivan Turgenev (toor-GAY-nyef) wrote of the dignity and earthy wisdom of Russian peasants, while Anton Chekhov (CHEH-kof) portrayed middle-class country life in plays and short stories. Fyodor Dostoyevsky (dos-toh-YEF-skee) probed the inner feelings and motives of the characters he created. Count Leo Tolstoy showed the rich background of Russian society in his *War and Peace* (1866).

Modern drama develops. The realists' emphasis on character, realistic settings, and social problems created a new kind of play. The characters in the modern drama were ordinary people who spoke in everyday language, not poetry. The plays of the Norwegian dramatist Henrik Ibsen shocked audiences with their honest pictures of family tensions and social problems. The Irish playwright and poet William Butler Yeats (YAYTS) led a new school of Irish drama, while George Bernard Shaw, born in Ireland, became Britain's leading playwright with his witty plays and criticism of society. Drama in Russia flourished at the Moscow Art Theater led by Konstantin Stanislavsky (stah-

nih-SLAHV-skee), which opened in 1898 with Chekhov's play *The Sea Gull.*

CHECK-UP

1. (a) What did impressionist painters attempt to show in their work? (b) What new subjects did they paint? (c) What artistic movement was begun by Braque and Picasso? (d) What did impressionism and other new developments in art have in common?
2. What earlier trends in music continued into the late nineteenth century?
3. For what kind of music was each of the following composers best known? (a) Brahms, (b) Verdi, (c) Johann Strauss, (d) Wagner.
4. (a) What are some characteristics of realist literature? (b) How did this literature reflect trends of the late nineteenth century?

4 Political Forces Threaten Europe's Stability

For many Europeans, especially the prosperous middle class, the late nineteenth and early twentieth centuries seemed a time of peace and security. Europeans were certain that they possessed a superior civilization. Everywhere they saw signs of progress — creativity in the arts, advances in medicine, science, and technology, improvements in the standard of living. Nevertheless, the growing strength of several forces within European society presented a grave threat to the continent.

National power becomes an overriding goal. In the first half of the nineteenth century, nationalism had been identified with movements for freedom. It led oppressed people to seek independence from foreign rule and gave people who shared similar traditions a feeling of community. National pride inspired achievements in art, music, and literature. In the second half of the nineteenth century, however, nationalism was carried to such an extreme in some countries that it became a dangerous force. Extreme nationalists came to view the power and prestige of their nation as more important than democratic rights, individual freedoms, or traditional values.

In Germany and Austria, particularly, some students and intellectuals regarded democracy and concern for individual rights as signs of weakness and decay. They adopted some of the ideas of the German philosopher Friedrich Nietzsche (NEE-cheh). In writings published in the 1880's, Nietzsche had declared that a leader must be a "superman," a hero who followed no rules but his own. These intellectuals enthusiastically adopted Nietzsche's ideas and saw themselves and those who were like them as "superior."

Extreme nationalists seek to dominate others. Extreme nationalists often glorified war and military might. War, they thought, brought out qualities of heroism and greatness in an individual and in a nation. Extreme nationalists also often claimed the right to rule over all lands and peoples that, they said, "rightfully belonged" to their nation. They called for restoring borders that had existed in the past, sometimes distorting history to support their claims. They believed it was their duty to acquire more land and rule other peoples. Pan-Germans, for instance, wanted to unite all the German-speaking peoples in Central Europe.

Some spoke of uniting the Germans with the Dutch, Swiss, and Scandinavians, who also had Germanic ancestors.

Extreme nationalists embrace racist doctrines. One of the greatest dangers of extreme nationalism was its adoption of *racism,* the doctrine that one's own racial or national group is superior to all others. Extreme nationalists in a number of countries began to attack minority groups, claiming that those peoples were not only inferior but also enemies of national unity.

Racist ideas could not be backed up by science or history, yet they were widely believed. Some of the new fields of study, such as science and sociology, were used in attempts to support racist thinking.

Darwin's ideas are applied to society. Darwin (page 626) had set forth a theory offering explanations in the field of biology. Herbert Spencer, an English philosopher, tried to apply Darwin's theory of evolution to all fields of knowledge, including sociology and economics. Spencer's philosophy, called Social Darwinism, attracted many followers in Britain and the United States in the late 1800's. Social Darwinists held that the concept of natural selection operated in the world of social and economic relations just as it did in nature. They claimed that those who were better fitted for the struggle for survival would become rich and successful. The poor were seen as those who were unable to compete.

Some Social Darwinists extended these ideas into racist thinking. They claimed that certain groups of people were "fitter" — brighter, stronger, and more advanced — than others. These "superior races," they said, were intended by nature to dominate "lesser peoples." Extreme nationalists took these claims to justify aggression, war, and the persecution of minorities. They insisted that nations and races were engaged in a struggle that only the fittest deserved to survive.

Racist thinking becomes widespread. Racist thinking became an increasingly powerful force in the late nineteenth century. Imperialist powers often used it to justify their actions in Africa and Asia.

In Germany, racists claimed that the German people were descended from an ancient "superior race," the Aryans. (The Aryans, who settled in India about 1500 B.C., were part of the people now called Indo-Europeans. Their language was the ancestor of most modern languages of Europe and India.) Houston Stewart Chamberlain, an English writer who became a German citizen, claimed in the 1890's that Germans were physically, morally, and intellectually superior to other peoples. German superiority, Chamberlain declared, was revealed in such characteristics as blond hair, blue eyes, and fair skin.

As these ideas became popular in Germany, some German nationalists insisted that they had the right to dominate "inferior races." German racist feelings were directed particularly toward the Slavic peoples to the east and toward the Jews in Germany itself.

European Jews face long-standing prejudices. Anti-Semitism, or hatred of Jews, was a racist attitude with a long history in many parts of Europe. During the Middle Ages, many people had believed and spread incredible tales about Jews. At the time of the Black Death in 1348, Jews were accused of poisoning wells to kill Christians. Periodically, mobs humiliated, tortured, and massacred Jews. Jews were forcibly converted to Christianity or expelled from certain lands. Often barred from owning land and from belonging to the craft guilds, medieval Jews became merchants and moneylenders. Jews were also required to identify themselves by wearing a badge.

Eventually, in some countries, Jews were forced by law to live in a *ghetto,* a section of town set aside for them. The Jewish quarter was separated from the other parts of the town by walls and gates. At night and during Christian celebrations, Jews were forbidden to leave the ghetto.

In the nineteenth century, the ideals of the Enlightenment and the French Revolution resulted in legal equality for Jews in most of Western Europe. They could leave the ghettos and participate in many activities that had been closed to them. Taking advantage of this new freedom and opportunity, Jews achieved success in business, the professions, science, the arts, and, in some countries, government. Yet most Jews remained poor.

Anti-Semitism takes new forms. Despite legal changes, anti-Semitism remained widespread in nineteenth-century Europe, and Jews were blamed for a variety of social and economic ills. Small shopkeepers and artisans resented competition from Jewish merchants. Peasants did not like dealing with Jewish creditors. Anti-Semitic writers spread the myth that Jews were concerned only with money.

In some countries extreme nationalists took advantage of the prevalent anti-Semitism to charge that Jews were a threat to the nation. Open expressions of anti-Semitism were common in newspapers, magazines, and books. Anti-Semitic organizations and political parties sprang up. The Dreyfus affair in France (page 541) was one example of anti-Semitic feelings.

Persecution of the Jews was most severe in Eastern Europe. Rumania barred most Jews from voting and holding office. Russia restricted their admission into universities and secondary schools. Russian officials permitted and even encouraged *pogroms* (POH-grums), acts of violence against Jewish communities. Hundreds of villages were burned and their people murdered. From the 1880's on, thousands of Russian Jews fled, many to the United States.

The idea of a separate homeland where Jews would be safe from persecution was suggested in 1896 by Theodor Herzl (HAIR-tsul). This movement, known as Zionism, attracted considerable support. It was many years, however, before the idea was carried out with the founding of the state of Israel (Chapter 37).

German anti-Semitism includes nationalist ideas. The small Jewish population of Germany had made many contributions to German economic and cultural life, and German Jews felt they were far better off than the Jews of Russia. Nevertheless, German racists believed and spread the myth that Jews were engaged in a worldwide plot to dominate Germany by gaining control over political parties, governments, banks, and the press. At the same time, they claimed to offer "scientific proof" that Jews were physically and spiritually different from and inferior to Germans. German racists tried to get the government to pass anti-Jewish laws but failed.

By the early 1900's actively anti-Semitic organizations had declined in political power and importance. Much harm had been done,

DR. JEKYLL AND MR. HYDE.

An English cartoonist accused the czar of two-faced behavior in this drawing, charging him with persecution of Jews while seeming to favor peaceful policies.

however, for many Europeans still kept the image of the Jews as a threat to the nation in which they lived.

As the twentieth century began, European society seemed strong and stable. Rapid changes, however, had brought uncertainties and a questioning of traditional outlooks. Dangerous undercurrents were at work. Extreme nationalism and racism were creating bitter hostilities among nations and peoples.

CHECK-UP

1. Vocabulary: *racism, ghetto, pogrom.*
2. (a) How did extreme nationalism differ from the nationalism of the early nineteenth century? (b) How did attacks on minorities relate to the goals of extreme nationalism? (c) Why did racist ideas become part of nationalistic thinking?
3. (a) What was Social Darwinism? (b) How did it tie in with racist ideas? (c) What racist ideas became common in Germany?
4. (a) How was anti-Semitism expressed in Europe during the late nineteenth century? (b) What was Zionism?

Chapter 28 Review

Summary

The late nineteenth century in Europe was a time of rapid industrial growth and urbanization, along with improvements in health, education, and standards of living. Even though peasants' and workers' lives had improved, sharp social and economic divisions still existed between classes. More workers had gained the right to vote, however, which contributed to the growing strength of the working class in European politics.

Startling new discoveries in chemistry and physics marked the beginning of the modern age of science. Scientists investigated the structure of the atom, the nature of radioactivity, and the laws of physics. In biology, the theory of evolution offered an explanation for the development of living things. Human society and behavior also began to be studied in a scientific way.

Painting in the late nineteenth century was marked by experimentation with light, form, and color, leading to movements such as impressionism and cubism. Music generally continued the Romantic style, though it too moved toward modern styles in the early 1900's. Writers abandoned some Romantic ideas in favor of portraying contemporary life in a realistic way.

Meanwhile, Europe was troubled by dangerous political forces. Extreme nationalism rejected ideas of freedom and called for the domination of other lands and peoples. Some nationalists adopted racist ideas; anti-Semitism in particular was widespread.

Vocabulary Review

1. Write the sentences listed below on a sheet of paper. In each sentence, fill in the blank with one of the following words: *ghetto, pogrom, racism, urbanization.*
(a) ___?___ is the notion that one racial or national group is superior to others.
(b) A result of the large-scale movement of people from rural areas to cities was ___?___ .
(c) A section of a town or city where Jews were forced to live was called a ___?___ .
(d) A ___?___ was an organized campaign of persecution aimed against Jews.

2. Distinguish between the terms in each of the following pairs:
(a) atoms; electrons.
(b) pasteurization; radiation.
(c) vaccine; antiseptic.
(d) natural sciences; social sciences.
(e) impressionists; expressionists.

People to Identify

Match the following people with the numbered phrases that describe them: *Albert Einstein, Marie Curie, Joseph Lister, Igor Stravinsky, Gregor Mendel, Dmitri Mendeleev, Sigmund Freud, Johannes Brahms, Antoine Lavoisier, Paul Cézanne.*
1. The English doctor who developed antiseptic surgery.
2. The French chemist who discovered the true nature of fire.
3. The Russian chemist who organized elements in a systematic classification.
4. The Polish-born scientist who discovered radioactivity.
5. The German scientist who developed the theory of relativity.
6. The Austrian doctor who sought to understand how dreams express people's feelings.
7. The Austrian monk whose work marked the beginning of the science of genetics.
8. An influential Russian composer of the early 1900's.
9. A French post-impressionist painter.
10. A nineteenth-century German composer.

Relating Geography and History

1. **Interpretation.** In the late 1800's and early 1900's Europe became increasingly urbanized. (a) What factors contributed to a rapid growth in the overall population of Europe? (b) What attracted people to the cities?
2. **Research.** Charles Darwin observed plant and animal life on his voyage to South America from 1831 to 1836 (pages 625–626). Find the Galapagos Islands on the map on page 496. Read more about Darwin's voyage in an encyclopedia. How, in his view, did the location of

this island group encourage the development of new species?

Discussion Questions

1. (a) How did the lives of working-class Europeans improve in the late 1800's? (b) What problems did they continue to face?

2. How did each of the following add to scientific understanding of atomic structure: (a) John Dalton? (b) Marie and Pierre Curie? (c) J. J. Thomson? (d) Ernest Rutherford? (e) Niels Bohr?

3. How did the application of scientific methods and outlooks affect (a) the study of history? (b) the study of human behavior?

4. (a) In what ways did the aims and subject matter of the impressionists and post-impressionists differ from those of earlier painters? (b) How did developments in music of the late nineteenth century differ from those in painting during the same period?

5. (a) What were the major characteristics of realistic literature in nineteenth-century Europe? (b) In what ways were the aims of naturalist writers of the late nineteenth century different from those of the Romantic writers?

6. (a) Explain how the extreme nationalists viewed individual freedoms and rights. (b) How did the beliefs and goals of the extreme nationalists lead to aggressive behavior?

7. How were (a) racist ideas and (b) Social Darwinism used to support the goals of the extreme nationalists?

8. (a) How had Enlightenment ideas resulted in a freer way of life for many European Jews by the nineteenth century? (b) What new forms did anti-Semitism take?

Reading Primary Sources

In Germany extreme nationalism was often expressed by calls for more territory. The following passage, in which such views are presented, comes from a book published in 1904. Read the passage. Then answer the questions that follow.

A people needs land for its activities, land for its nourishment. No people needs it as much as the German people, which is increasing so rapidly and whose old boundaries have become dangerously narrow. If we do not soon acquire new territories, we are moving towards a frightful catastrophe. It matters little whether it be in Brazil, in Siberia, . . . or in South Africa, as long as we can once again move full of freedom and fresh energy, as long as we can once more offer our children wholesome light and air in plenty. Once more, as 2000 years ago when the [Germanic people] were hammering at the gates of Rome, sounds the cry, now full of anguish and unappeased desires, now arrogant and full of confidence—sounds more and more strongly the cry "We must have lands, new lands!"

(a) What reasons does the writer give for his claim that the German people need more land? (b) What does he say will happen if Germany does not get new land? (c) What opinion does he express on the location of the hoped for new land? (d) To what historical event does the writer refer? (e) To what groups would this message probably have appealed most?

Skill Activities

1. Reports. During the 1800's there were many significant advances in the field of medicine. Prepare a report on one of the following: (a) the stethoscope; (b) X-ray photography; (c) the use of ether as an anesthetic; (d) the work of Louis Pasteur and Robert Koch; (e) the development of smallpox and rabies vaccines; (f) Joseph Lister's improvements in surgery.

2. Making bulletin boards. Locate prints or postcards of impressionist and post-impressionist paintings and use them to make a bulletin-board display. (To review the major artists in each of these art movements, see pages 628–629.) Group the paintings of each movement together, and label each print with the name of the artist. Try to include the work of at least three or four artists. A local art museum or your school or town library may be able to help you.

3. Exploring the arts. Among the composers who used elements of folk songs and dances in their works were Edvard Grieg of Norway; Béla Bartók of Hungary; Bedřich Smetana and Antonín Dvořák of Czechoslovakia; and Alexander Borodin, Modest Mussorgsky, and Nikolai Rimsky-Korsakov of Russia. Select several examples with nationalist themes from the works of these composers. Prepare an oral report about them, explaining the nationalist elements in each piece. If possible, use a tape or record of the pieces to accompany your report.

A new kind of warfare devastated large areas of northern
France as opposing armies battled each other in World War I.
Below, the starkness of the war's destruction is clear in this
painting of French soldiers in the trenches.

CHAPTER 29

World War I

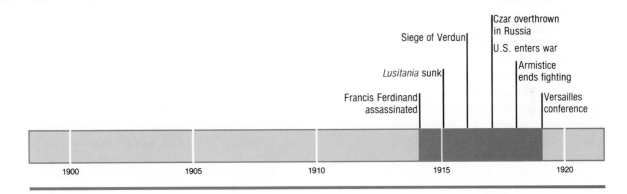

Czar overthrown in Russia

U.S. enters war

Siege of Verdun

Armistice ends fighting

Lusitania sunk

Versailles conference

Francis Ferdinand assassinated

1900   1905   1910   1915   1920

The late nineteenth century brought Europe prosperity, economic growth, and remarkable scientific discoveries and artistic creativity. Representative government became more widespread, and more people gained opportunities for education and a better, healthier way of life. In the peace and stability of the early 1900's, many Europeans felt that this golden age would continue.

Many problems that had gone unnoticed, however, grew more serious as the twentieth century began. The goals of extreme nationalist groups brought conflicts between peoples and states, leading to a build-up of military forces and a system of defensive alliances among European nations. Tensions among the nations of Europe gradually increased until a single incident triggered a war that involved not only that continent but also many other parts of the world. The four years of brutal conflict of this first "world war" were to be a turning point in history.

This chapter describes the conditions that led to war in 1914, the course of the war, and the peace settlements that followed it.

CHAPTER OUTLINE

1 European Nations Are Drawn into War

2 The War Involves Many Nations

3 The Peace Treaties Create Problems

1 European Nations Are Drawn into War

While Europe seemingly was reaching new heights of civilization, the continent was being drawn toward disaster by deep rivalries, intense nationalistic feelings, and the appeal of war. By 1914, the situation in Europe had become so tense that a single incident could serve as the cause for a war involving many nations.

Germany begins a system of alliances. One important cause of tension was the division of the continent into two hostile alliance systems. This approach to conducting foreign affairs had been started by the German chancellor Otto von Bismarck (page 482). After its victory in the Franco-Prussian War (1870–1871), Germany took over the French border provinces of Alsace and Lorraine. To keep France isolated and deprive it of allies that might help it regain those provinces, Bismarck began to make alliances with other European powers. The first, with Austria-Hungary and Italy (1882), became known as the Triple Alliance. The other alliance, with Russia (1887), was weak, however, for Russia and Austria were potential enemies.

When a new kaiser, William II, came to the German throne in 1888, Bismarck was forced out of office. The new leaders of Germany adopted a more aggressive foreign policy, built up the navy, and sought more possessions. Germany abandoned its treaty with Russia and drew closer to Austria-Hungary, which it considered a more reliable ally.

France and Britain agree to oppose German power. The French had been humiliated by their defeat in 1871 and realized that France by itself was no match for Germany. Fearful of Germany's increasing military strength, expanding industries, and growing population, the French Third Republic began to seek allies of its own. After the split between Germany and Russia, France entered into an alliance with Russia in 1894.

Great Britain also was alarmed by the growing might of Germany, which had become a serious rival for sea power and for colonies in Africa. France was eager to have Britain as an ally and so moved to end their long colonial rivalry. In 1904 the two countries formed the *Entente Cordiale* (ahn-TAHNT cor-DYAHL), which means "friendly understanding."

France next sought to ease the tension between its allies. Although Russia and Britain were colonial rivals in western Asia, Czar Nicholas II of Russia also feared Germany and recognized his own nation's weaknesses. In 1904–1905, Russia had lost a war with Japan (page 583), and workers' revolutions were brewing within the country. In 1907, out of their mutual fear of Germany, Britain and Russia signed an agreement. This created the Triple Entente — an understanding among France, Britain, and Russia. It was a treaty of friendship, not a firm military alliance. The Germans, however, regarded the Triple Entente as a hostile alliance that threatened Germany from both the east and the west.

The alliance system increases tensions. By 1914 an armed and uneasy peace existed in Europe. What Bismarck had said in 1879 was still true: "The great powers of our time are like travelers, unknown to one another, whom chance has brought together in a carriage. They watch each other, and when one of them puts his hand into his pocket, his neighbor gets ready his own revolver in order to be able to fire the first shot."

The alliance system was one cause of this tense situation. A country that knew it had allies was more likely to take chances in a crisis and act aggressively. In addition, the alliance system held the danger of a "chain reaction." A conflict between any two nations was likely to expand and involve those countries' allies.

European nations compete in an arms race. Another cause of the increasing tension in Europe was *militarism.* This term describes the attitude of a powerful class of military leaders who had great influence on the policies of their countries. Militarists glorified war and urged a constant build-up of weapons and armed forces. They agreed with the Austrian historian who wrote that quarrels between nations "must be settled not at the [conference] table, but on the battlefield; not with the pen, but with the sword; not with ink, but with blood."

For some years the great powers of Europe had spent huge sums for armaments and, except for Britain (which relied on its navy), had maintained large armies during peacetime. If one country increased the size of its army or built new and mightier battleships, other countries did the same. Generals worked out detailed defense plans that depended on their country's ability to attack first in time of war. The strong support for these policies made it difficult for a nation's civilian leaders to use diplomacy in times of crisis and resist the demands of military officers for war.

Nationalist feelings conflict. Extreme nationalism also increased tensions between several European states. Governments did not always act on their nationalist ambitions, but such feelings made people quick to anger and less likely to use reason. French nationalists wanted to regain Alsace and Lorraine, but German nationalists wanted to extend German power and territory. Russian Pan-Slavists (page 488) wanted Russia to rule over the Slavs of Eastern Europe.

Austria sees Serbia as a threat. Another Slavic nationalist movement was centered in the Balkan kingdom of Serbia. Serbia and other Balkan states had gained their independence from the Ottoman Empire in 1878 (page 486), but the Slavs in Bosnia and Herzegovina had come under Austrian rule. The Serbs now sought to create a "Greater Serbia" by uniting with other Slavic states and with the millions of South Slavs who lived in Austrian-controlled lands. The dream of a "Greater Serbia" caused nightmares in Austria, where minority nationalities were a long-standing problem (page 485). Austrian leaders feared a revolt by the South Slavs, believing that it could break up the empire. Regarding Serbia as a grave threat, some Austrian leaders urged the destruction of the small kingdom.

A shooting triggers a world war. On June 28, 1914, in the Bosnian city of Sarajevo (sahr-ah-YAY-voh), a Serbian nationalist named Gavrilo Princip assassinated Archduke Francis Ferdinand, heir to the throne of Austria-Hungary. By killing the archduke and his wife, the Serbian nationalists hoped to increase the tensions within the Hapsburg lands and prepare the way for a Slavic revolution. The Austrian author-

ities, however, used the assassination as an excuse for an attack against Serbia.

Austria calls on its ally. To carry out its plan against Serbia, Austria turned for support to its ally, Germany. Their alliance held firm, and German leaders promised to back Austria. Both countries wanted a quick attack that would defeat Serbia before other nations could come to its aid.

Confident of German backing, on July 23, 1914, Austria sent Serbia an ultimatum — a list of demands that Serbia had to answer within forty-eight hours. If Serbia did not accept the ultimatum, Austria would declare war. Because militarists in the Austrian government now wanted war, some of the demands were deliberately made too harsh for Serbia to accept.

The Austrian ultimatum alarmed Russia. Although Russia had long considered itself the protector of the Slavs in the Balkans, it had failed to keep Austria from taking Bosnia. If Austria took over Serbia, the Austrians would be well on the way to gaining firm control of the Balkans, which lay on the Russian empire's borders.

To many people's surprise, the Serbs accepted all but one of Austria's demands. They refused only to let Austrian officials take over the investigation of the shooting at Sarajevo. The Austrians, however, had already decided that there could not be a peaceful settlement.

The assassination of Francis Ferdinand, shown here with his wife, touched off a war that engulfed Europe.

World War I Divides Europe

By 1916 most of the nations of Europe had joined one of the two opposing sides — the Central Powers and the Allies. Which European nations remained neutral? Note the line that shows how far the Germans advanced into Russia.

They declared that this refusal meant that Serbia had rejected the entire ultimatum.

German leaders knew that an Austrian attack on Serbia could bring Russia — and perhaps France — into the conflict. Nevertheless, they insisted that Germany must support Austria, since the Austrian alliance was important to German security. Confident German generals believed their armies could defeat Russia and France and make Germany the world's greatest power. German leaders were not overly concerned about Britain, the ally of Rus-

sia and France. Britain's strength was its navy; its army seemed too small to be important in a land war. Moreover, some believed that Britain would remain neutral.

War breaks out. On July 28, 1914 (five days after the ultimatum was issued), Austria declared war on Serbia. Two days later Russia ordered full mobilization of its forces, for its military plans called for war against both Austria and Germany. Similarly, German military planners wanted the advantage of attacking first. When Russia ignored a German warning to stop war preparations, Germany declared war on August 1. Two days later Germany declared war on France, since it was Russia's ally.

More nations join the war. The war in Europe escalated quickly. The system of alliances and military plans trapped the nations one by one in a chain reaction from which they could not escape. To attack France, the German government requested Belgium's permission to march through Belgian lands. When Belgium refused, Germany invaded that country on August 3. The British were now involved, for Britain was pledged to guarantee Belgium's neutrality.[1] Moreover, the British realized that if Belgium and France fell, Germany would be master of Western Europe. On August 4, Britain joined the war on the side of its allies, Russia and France. Two days later, Austria declared war on Russia.

Less than six weeks after the shooting at Sarajevo, all the great powers of Europe — and several smaller nations — were involved in war. Still more countries would become involved until it was a truly "world war," though fought mainly in Europe.

2 The War Involves Many Nations

When war broke out in Europe in August, 1914, most generals and statesmen were confident that the conflict would be short. The public shared this belief, and crowds gathered in the streets of European cities to show their loyalty to their homelands and their readiness to fight. Filled with dreams of adventure and glory, few people thought of the horrors of war. They expected their soldiers to return home in a few months.

Only a few leaders suspected that Europe was stumbling into a world war — four years of bloodshed that would drastically change the world. "The lamps are going out all over Europe," said Britain's foreign secretary, Edward Grey, in 1914. "We shall not see them lit again in our lifetime."

The Central Powers confront the Allies. The opposing sides reflected the alliance system. The Triple Entente countries — France, Britain, and Russia — came to be called the Allies. Germany and Austria-Hungary, members of the Triple Alliance, were now called the Central Powers. Italy, the other member of the Triple Alliance, objected to Austria's aggression and eventually joined the Allies. The Ottoman Empire (Turkey) and Bulgaria joined the Central Powers. In 1917 the United States joined the war alongside the Allies. Other nations in Europe, Asia, and Latin America also allied themselves with one side or another, though most did not send troops into battle.

The war is fought on two fronts. The German army invaded Belgium in August, 1914, confident of a quick victory in Western Europe (map, page 640). According to the German war plan, the bulk of the German army would swing through Belgium into France, capture Paris, and so defeat France. A small army would hold off Russia in the east until this victory. German trains would then rush the victorious troops to the eastern front, where they would drive back the Russian forces. Everything depended on speed.

Germany's carefully laid plan failed, however. The Russians moved faster than expected

---

[1]Shortly after Belgium gained independence in 1830, the great powers of Europe had agreed to respect its neutrality (page 467).

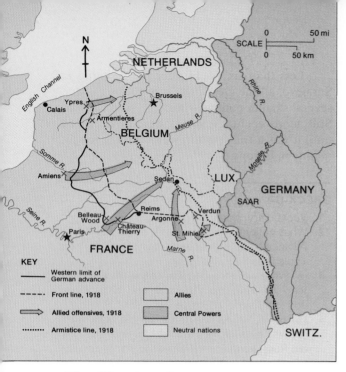

The Western Front

In 1914, the German forces almost reached Paris in their western advance. Describe the location of the front line in 1918.

and invaded East Prussia late in August. Germany had to withdraw some troops from France and rush them eastward.

The remaining Germans on the western front advanced to within forty miles of Paris. Then a French counterattack drove a wedge between the advancing German armies. Instead of winning a quick victory, German troops now faced stubborn British and French resistance along the Marne River, which stopped their push westward. The Germans then tried to reach the coast of the English Channel, capture the port cities, and then swing back toward Paris. Again they were stopped, in battles near Ypres (EE-pruh), Belgium, that took nearly 250,000 lives — French, British, Canadian, Belgian, and German.

Trench warfare is fought on the western front. In the first four months of the war (August-November, 1914), more than one and a half million soldiers were killed or wounded. As the winter of 1914–1915 began, the troops of both armies prepared for a long war. A vast network of trenches was dug for hundreds of miles across France, marking the western front. Between the opposing lines lay "no man's land," a wasteland of barbed wire, mud, torn

earth, and shattered trees. Attacking soldiers had to climb out of their trenches and race across no man's land. An observer described the horrors of trench warfare:

> The Germans sent down an enormous [barrage] of concentrated machine-gun fire. It hummed and whirred through the air around the lines of steadily advancing [British] troops. It thudded home into their sweating bodies, through equipment straps and khaki cloth. In a few minutes the first waves were annihilated. But wave upon wave came pouring out of the trenches to take the place of the fallen. . . . As they got entangled in [the German barbed wire], the Germans used rifle fire to kill them off one by one. . . . Most, however, never got as far as the wire. They lay in no man's land as shells exploded among them, and bullets scythed through the deadly air above their heads.

New weapons add to war casualties. The frightful loss of life in trench warfare was due partly to the use of new kinds of weapons. The rapid fire of machine guns was deadly to soldiers trying to cross no man's land. Huge long-range guns sent heavy barrages of explosive shells into the trenches. Many soldiers were blinded or had their lungs scarred by poison gas. Tanks were first used in the war in 1916, and aerial battles between daring pilots took place for the first time late in the war.

The war enters a period of stalemate. Despite the heavy losses, little territory changed hands. Neither side could advance more than a few miles. In February, 1916, the German army began a major offensive aimed at the French town of Verdun (vehr-DUN), which was protected by a ring of forts. In five months of siege, the Germans gained a little territory but failed to capture Verdun, and by December the French had regained their losses. More than 700,000 French and German soldiers were killed in the long, inconclusive siege of Verdun, and thousands more were wounded.

The stalemate continued throughout 1916 and 1917. Gains of land were measured in yards; lives were lost by the hundreds of thousands. More troops were sent to the front, and the generals continued to order massive attacks.

War continues on the eastern front. There was more movement in the fighting on the eastern front than in the trench warfare of the western front. While the Germans were attacking France in 1914, the Russians won some early victories in eastern Germany. They were badly beaten at Tannenberg, however, by the armies of the German commander, Field Marshal Paul von Hindenburg. In the spring of 1915, another Austro-German offensive forced the Russians into a retreat.

By late 1916 the Russian war effort was near collapse. The Russian army was poorly trained, inadequately equipped, and incompetently led. It had suffered staggering losses —

more than two million men were killed, wounded, or captured in 1915 alone. Moreover, Russia's allies could not ship supplies into its ports. German naval forces blocked the Baltic Sea, while Ottoman Turkey still controlled the straits leading from the Mediterranean to the Black Sea.

Russia is forced out of the war. The Russian army also suffered from poor morale. The heavy casualties at the front and food shortages at home increased the Russians' long-standing discontent with the czar's rule. In March, 1917, a revolution overthrew the czar, and civil war

LINKING PAST AND PRESENT
Travelers in the Sky

Modern travel by air owes a great deal to advances made in aviation during wartime. As early as the 1790's, French officers observed battles from hot-air balloons in the sky. The first true military aircraft, however, were German-made airships, designed about 1900 and called *Graf Zeppelins* after their inventor, a German count (*graf* is German for "count"). Zeppelins like the one shown below provided the first passenger air service, carrying travelers between German cities from 1910 on and making transatlantic flights after World War I.

In the early 1900's, flying in airplanes was only a sport for the adventurous. World War I, however, tremendously speeded up the growth of aviation. Daring pilots in small, open-cockpit planes fought sky battles known as "dogfights." After the war, many former military pilots began their own airline companies, carrying cargo at first and then passengers. In 1919, one passenger was flown from London to Paris — the first scheduled international flight. Today, of course, many millions of people travel by air each year.

spread through Russia (Chapter 30). Leaders of the new government, realizing that Russia could not continue the war, signed a humiliating treaty with Germany in March, 1918. In the Treaty of Brest-Litovsk, Russia had to give up great amounts of valuable land, resources, and population. Germany thus was victorious in Eastern Europe.

The war involves many parts of the world. The major battles of World War I were fought on the western and eastern fronts in Europe. As more nations became involved, fighting broke out elsewhere in Europe as well as in other parts of the world.

1. Italy. Although it remained neutral at first, in 1915 Italy made a secret agreement with France and Britain and was promised territory in Austria and Africa. Italy then joined the war on the Allied side, and fighting broke out on the Austrian-Italian border. In the fall of 1917, combined German and Austrian forces broke through the Italian lines at Caporetto, taking some 275,000 prisoners and forcing the Italian army to retreat.

2. Asia and the Pacific. Japan, which had become an ally of Britain, moved to take over the German spheres of influence on China's Shantung Peninsula, as well as German-held islands in the Pacific Ocean. In return for help from the Japanese navy, the Allies promised to support Japan's claim to these territories after the war. The British dominions of Australia and New Zealand took possession of other German islands in the Pacific.

3. The Ottoman Empire (Turkey). Some of the hardest fighting of the war took place along the coast of Turkey. Ottoman Turkey had put mines in the Dardanelles and heavy artillery on the shore of the straits. These fortifications not only prevented Allied aid from reaching Russian ports but also kept the Russian fleet bottled up in the Black Sea. A combined force of British, French, New Zealand, and Australian troops landed at Gallipoli (guh-LIP-uh-lee) in 1915, trying to reach Constantinople by land and gain control of the Dardanelles. With German help, the Turks resisted strongly, and the Allied forces finally had to withdraw after heavy losses.

In the Arab countries of the Middle East, World War I was largely a series of raids on towns and supply lines. Eager to topple their Ottoman rulers, Arab nationalists supported British forces. Driven out of one area after another, the Turks finally withdrew from the war at the end of October, 1918.

4. Africa. In West Africa, British and French troops seized the German coastal colonies of Togoland and Kamerun (later the Cameroons), while troops from the Union of South Africa took over the neighboring German colony of South-West Africa (map, page 597). In German East Africa (later Tanganyika), a small German army was never decisively defeated. Retreating into the African interior, the German soldiers did not surrender until they received news of the war's end.

The United States tries to remain neutral. When war broke out in 1914, President Woodrow Wilson had announced a policy of neutrality for the United States. This policy was hard to maintain for a number of reasons. Most Americans sympathized with Britain and France because they were democratic countries. A victory by Germany and Austria would be a triumph for authoritarian government. Support for Britain and France was strengthened by effective ***propaganda,*** news and information designed to win support for the Allies by convincing people of the rightness of the Allied cause. War news that came to the United States from Britain pictured the Germans as arrogant and cruel.

Economic reasons also worked against neutrality. Both Britain and Germany interfered with shipping by neutral nations, including the United States. To keep war supplies from reaching Germany, Britain stopped merchant ships and seized their cargoes. The Germans, however, turned their submarine fleet, called U-boats,[2] into a fearsome new weapon of war. U-boats attacked neutral merchant ships carrying food and supplies to Britain, and many sailors and passengers were killed. In May, 1915, nearly 1,200 people were lost when a U-boat sank the British ship *Lusitania.* Among the *Lusitania* casualties were more than a hundred Americans, and anti-German feeling in the United States grew stronger.

---

[2]"U-boat" was short for *Untersee,* the German for "undersea."

NEW WEAPONS

The opposing forces used new weapons of war in their determination to crush each other. Tanks (above, left) were a British secret weapon in 1914 but soon were adopted by other armies. Airplanes (above) were first used for scouting enemy lines and then for "dogfights." German submarines (left, four U-boats in port) were especially feared by the crews of Allied merchant ships.

The United States government was officially neutral, but individual American banks and businesses had loaned one and a half billion dollars to Allied governments. Much of this money was used to buy needed supplies from the United States. American bankers and manufacturers realized that they would probably lose their money if the Allies lost the war.

The United States enters the war. Early in 1917, Americans were pushed closer to war by another threatening German action. In a secret telegram in code, German foreign secretary Arthur Zimmermann had tried to make an alliance with Mexico. He promised that a German victory would return Texas and other parts of the American Southwest to Mexico. The British broke the code, and Zimmermann's offer was made public. Although Mexico remained neutral, the "Zimmermann telegram" angered Americans.

In April, 1917, the United States declared war on Germany, with President Wilson stating that his aim was to "make the world safe for democracy." Germany now tried to end the war quickly, before large numbers of American troops could be trained for combat and sent to France. The treaty with Russia in the spring of 1918 released German troops from the eastern front. Rushed west, they joined the German troops in France in a massive attack along 60 miles of the western front, aiming for Paris. British and French lines reeled before the German advance.

By early summer, troops of the American Expeditionary Force, under the command of General John J. Pershing, began to arrive in France. They joined with Allied forces, which were led by a French general, Marshal Ferdinand Foch (FOHSH). In June, 1918, the German offensive was halted at Chateau-Thierry (shah-TOH-TYEH-ree), on the Marne River.

The Central Powers collapse. The German leaders had thrown all their resources into this last, but unsuccessful, attack. Now Germany faced acute shortages of food, medicine, oil, and munitions. Allied troops swept eastward in a massive counterattack. It was now clear to the German generals that the war was lost. In late September they urged the government to ask for an *armistice* — a halt to the fighting.

Germany's position worsened steadily. In October and November, 1918, Austria and Turkey surrendered, and rebellions in Germany forced the kaiser to give up the throne. The government of the newly established German republic quickly signed the armistice terms drawn up by Marshal Foch.

On November 11, 1918, the armistice was signed. Soldiers on both sides came out of the trenches and cheered. Enemies embraced in the midst of no man's land, rejoicing that the fighting was over. A newspaper correspondent with the British army in France wrote: "Last night for the first time since August in the first year of the war, there was no light of gunfire in the sky, no spreading glow above black trees where for four years of nights human beings were smashed to death. The fires of hell had been put out."

CHECK-UP

1. Vocabulary: *propaganda, armistice.*
2. What nations were the original members of (a) the Central Powers? (b) the Allies?
3. (a) What was the German military plan at the beginning of the war? (b) What went wrong with the plan? (c) Describe battle conditions on the western front.
4. (a) What effect did Ottoman Turkey have on the Russian war effort? (b) What led to Russia's surrender?
5. (a) What part did Italy play in the war? (b) How did the war affect German possessions in Asia, Africa, and the Pacific? (c) Why did the Arabs side with the British?
6. What factors brought the United States into the war?
7. What led Germany to ask for an armistice?

3 The Peace Treaties Create Problems

The most terrible war the world had yet experienced ended in November, 1918. There remained the problem of drawing up a peace settlement. In January, 1919, representatives of the victorious powers assembled in Paris to make decisions that would dramatically change the political map of the world. Twenty-seven European and Asian nations were represented. Most decisions were made by the leaders of four Allied nations: David Lloyd George, prime minister of Great Britain; Georges Clemenceau (cleh-mahn-SOH), premier of France; Woodrow Wilson, President of the United States; and Vittorio Orlando, premier of Italy.

THE PEACE SETTLEMENT

President Wilson sets forth a plan for peace. Even before the armistice, President Wilson had offered a plan for peace in his "Fourteen Points" speech to Congress (January 8, 1918). The points covered several principles that Wilson thought basic to world peace, as well as specific provisions for certain nations.

1. Self-determination. One of Wilson's principles was self-determination — the right of national groups to determine their own political status. This meant, for example, that Austrian lands inhabited by Italians would belong to Italy. The South Slavs and the Czechs in Austria-Hungary would be free to form their own states, while the Poles would once again have a country of their own.

2. "Peace without victory." Wilson declared that the end of the war should bring "a peace without victory." He urged fair treatment for Germany, believing that harsh punishment would cause Germany to seek revenge. Wilson hoped that a just settlement would encourage the defeated nations to work with the victorious Allies for a new and better world. He envisioned free trade and freedom of the seas for all nations.

3. Disarmament. Wilson believed that there could be no hope for peace until militarism had been eliminated. He wanted the nations of the world to disarm so that no country would fear its neighbors or seek to invade them. He also felt that secret treaties were dangerous and that nations should negotiate openly.

4. Fair treatment of colonial peoples. Wilson wanted fair treatment for colonial peoples, calling for "a free, open-minded, and absolutely impartial adjustment of all colonial claims." He hoped that the imperialist nations would eventually apply the principle of self-determination to their colonies, considering the interests of the people as well as their own concerns.

5. League of Nations. To preserve peace, Wilson urged the formation of an international organization, to be called the League of Nations. It was his hope that the League would help both large and small nations settle their quarrels and would discourage aggressors from taking up arms.

Wilson's idealism clashes with European realities. Wilson wanted to get his views written into the peace treaties negotiated in 1919. His idealism, however, clashed with the outlooks of the victorious European Allies. The war had caused great losses and great bitterness. Hatred between nations and peoples had not died when the guns were silenced.

Wilson's idealism clashed especially with French demands. France had suffered greatly during the war, for most of the battles on the western front had been fought on French soil. Almost one and a half million French soldiers had died, and more than three million had been wounded. The French deeply feared a future German attack and were skeptical of Wilson's ideals. They wanted to punish Germany and destroy its capacity to wage war. The French also wanted payment for their industries and farms that had been ruined.

The idea of self-determination meets obstacles. The intermingling of nationalities in European countries complicated attempts to apply the principle of self-determination. No matter how the peacemakers juggled boundary lines, they could not create a Europe free of minority problems. Self-determination for one nationality was likely to violate the rights of another. For example, self-determination called for an independent Poland, which needed access to the sea. The land between the new Poland and the Baltic Sea was inhabited mainly by Germans, however. Giving this land to Poland would violate the principle of self-determination for these people.

Secret treaties drawn up during the war acted as another barrier to self-determination. The European Allies had already agreed on how to share the spoils of war. Italy, for example, had been promised Austrian lands inhabited by Slavs, Germans, and Italians. In the Middle East, Arab lands freed from Ottoman rule had been promised independence during the war. The Allies, however, had agreed among themselves that these lands would come under British and French control through the League of Nations.

Separate peace treaties are signed. The peace settlement made in Paris consisted of five separate treaties, one with each of the defeated states — Germany, Austria, Hungary, Bulgaria, and the Ottoman Empire. (The Dual Monarchy of Austria-Hungary had broken apart in the last weeks of the war.) The settlement with Germany, the Treaty of Versailles (June, 1919), was the most important of the treaties.

The Versailles Treaty reduces German land and power. France was granted many of

Assembled at the Paris peace conference were the Allied heads of state. Seated from left to right: Orlando, Lloyd George, Clemenceau, and Wilson.

its demands by the Treaty of Versailles. Germany had to return Alsace-Lorraine and give France control of the coal mines of the Saar region for fifteen years (to make up for the destruction of French coal mines by the Germans). Germany also lost land to Poland. To give Poland access to the Baltic Sea, the "Polish Corridor" was created, a strip of land that separated East Prussia from the rest of Germany. The Baltic Sea port of Danzig was turned into a free trading city, controlled by neither Poland nor Germany. The Treaty of Brest-Litovsk that Germany had signed with Russia (page 644) also was repealed.

German territory on both sides of the Rhine River was demilitarized. That is, it was to remain free of German troops and fortifications. To prevent Germany from again becoming a military threat, the German army was reduced to only 100,000 men, with no heavy artillery, tanks, or war planes. The draft was abolished; the new German army could consist only of volunteers. The navy was limited to a small fleet, and no submarines were permitted.

Germany also lost its overseas territories in Africa, Asia, and the Pacific Ocean. Its African colonies were given to France and Britain as *mandates,* to be administered by those countries under the League of Nations. Japan gained a

mandate over some of the Pacific islands but its claims on the Shantung Peninsula were not settled. They were left to be worked out between Japan and China, creating another area of friction in Asia.

The Versailles Treaty blamed the war on "the aggression of Germany and her allies." It therefore required Germany to pay **reparations** to other nations. That is, Germany had to pay them for property, factories, farms, ships, and other things destroyed in the war. The exact amount, $33 billion, was not determined until 1921, two years after Germany had signed the treaty. The demand for reparations caused great bitterness among the German people. Many thought the amount was greater than Germany's capacity to pay. They also said that all the warring powers, not just Germany, had been responsible for the war.

New nations are formed. The German losses were not the only territorial changes resulting from the war. After the collapse of the Austro-Hungarian empire, the various nationalities in the empire carved out their own states. The peacemakers recognized these as independent nations (map, next page). Czechs and Slovaks formed the new nation of Czechoslovakia (chek-uh-sloh-VAH-kee-uh). The Croats, Slovenes, and Serbs of Austria-Hungary joined with Serbia to form Yugoslavia. Italy and Rumania also gained land from the old empire. Finally, Austria and Hungary became separate nations. The new Austria, greatly reduced in size and power, was forbidden to unite with Germany.

Territorial changes were also made in the Middle East. The Ottoman Empire was stripped of all its lands outside Turkey. Some parts became independent, while others came under the control of Britain, France, and Greece. Within Turkey, nationalists took advantage of the government's weakness. The Ottoman sultan was overthrown, and in 1923 Turkey became a republic.

The League of Nations is established. The Versailles Treaty included provisions for the establishment of a League of Nations, President Wilson's great hope for avoiding another world war. Members of the League agreed to respect and to preserve the borders of fellow members

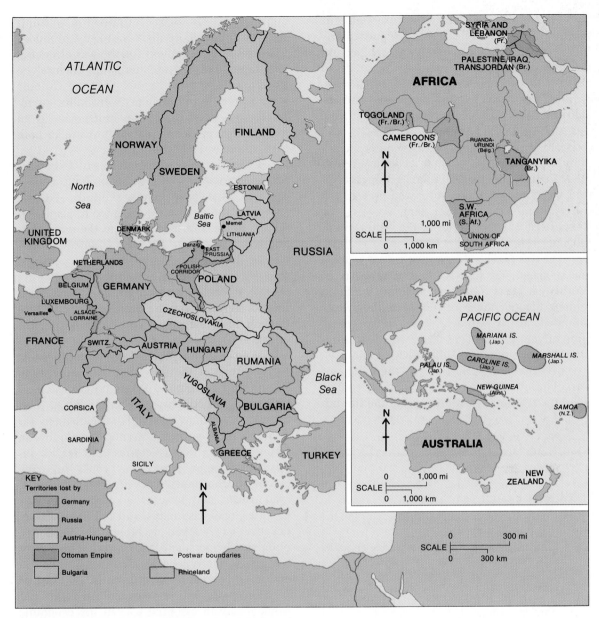

Territorial Changes After World War I

Territorial changes took place on several continents and in the Pacific as a result of World War I settlements. What lands did Germany lose? How was Austria-Hungary split up?

and to submit all disputes to the League. Eventually more than sixty nations joined the League of Nations. The United States Senate, however, refused to ratify the Versailles Treaty, and the United States never became a League member, thereby weakening the organization's efforts.

THE AFTERMATH OF WAR

World War I, called by many "the Great War," was a crucial turning point in world history. The changes that it brought about and the problems that it created continued long after the fighting ended.

The Versailles Treaty is controversial. The fairness of the Versailles Treaty — particularly the treatment of Germany — was debated for many years. Critics of the treaty pointed out that by 1919 a new democratic German government had replaced the leaders who had encouraged war. The peace treaty made it very difficult for this government to survive. Defenders of the treaty, on the other hand, pointed out that the German economy recovered quickly and that German production of iron, steel, and coal soon surpassed prewar levels. The real mistake, they said, was not the treaty itself but the failure of the Allies to enforce it.

The war takes a devastating toll of soldiers and civilians. The loss of life and property in World War I was enormous. At least 10 million soldiers died in the war and 21 million were wounded, nearly wiping out an entire generation of young men. Tens of thousands who returned home were disabled in body or mind.

Civilians also suffered from the effects of war. The French Revolution had started a trend toward the involvement of all the human and material resources of a nation in wartime. In World War I, civilians not only produced weapons and equipment for the war effort but also faced dangers and hardships themselves. Food shortages were severe; fuel and clothing were scarce. Many civilians were killed or injured, and others died from hunger and from an influenza epidemic that swept through both neutral and warring countries.

Countries at war depended on civilian effort and morale. Governments on both sides of the war used propaganda skillfully. Posters, speeches, and news were designed to inspire civilians to contribute their all to the war effort and to unite in love for their country and hatred of the enemy. Newspapers were censored to avoid news of defeats and thereby keep up morale at home. Increasingly governments extended control over the entire economy. Production had one goal — to support the war effort.

Women gain rights and responsibilities. At the outbreak of the war, women suffragists in Britain and the United States postponed their efforts to gain equality and responded to their countries' wartime needs. To release men for military service, many women took jobs on farms and in offices, factories, and service industries. Women worked as cooks in army camps and hospitals. They drove ambulances, mail trucks, and buses, worked in munitions factories, read gas meters, and collected railway tickets. They worked as laboratory assistants, plumbers' helpers, and bank clerks. There were few jobs formerly held by men that women did not take on and perform efficiently.

Their wartime service made it clear that women had an essential role in the economic life of a nation. Many now also sought better educations and careers in professions that had earlier been closed to them. During the war, a number of political leaders, including President Wilson, argued that extending the right to vote to women would aid the war effort. By the end of the war, little opposition remained to granting women political rights.

In 1918, British women over the age of thirty gained the vote. By 1928, parliament lowered the voting age for British women to twenty-one, the same as for men. Also in 1918,

---

TIMETABLE
World War I

1914   Austrian Archduke Francis Ferdinand is assassinated (June).
Austria declares war on Serbia (July).
Germany declares war on Russia and France and invades Belgium. Britain declares war on Germany (August).
The German advance on Paris is halted; trench warfare begins (September).

1915   The *Lusitania* is sunk (May).
Turkey defeats the Allied attempt to open the Dardanelles.

1916   The Germans fail in the siege of Verdun (February–December).

1917   The czar of Russia is overthrown (March).
The United States declares war on Germany (April).

1918   Germany forces Russia to sign the Treaty of Brest-Litovsk (March).
An armistice ends the fighting on the western front (November).

1919   The Treaty of Versailles is signed (June).

the United States Congress approved a constitutional amendment extending the right to vote to women. The Nineteenth Amendment became law in the United States in 1920. It was not only in Britain and the United States that the war brought acceptance of women's political equality. By 1920 women had the right to vote in most northern European countries and in Russia.

The war brings great political changes. World War I brought the downfall of four empires. Revolution put an end to the rule of the czar in Russia and the kaiser in Germany. New nations emerged from the ruins of Austria-Hungary. The war brought the Ottoman Empire, "the sick man of Europe," nearer its final collapse.

World War I and the peace settlements intensified nationalist rivalries. The Germans swore to tear up the Versailles Treaty and to regain lost lands. Italy, though on the winning side, felt that it should have received more Austrian territory as well as a share of Germany's African colonies. Hungary could not accept its loss of land to Rumania. The Japanese were disappointed by the territorial settlements in Asia. Intense nationalism and resentment helped to fuel the fires for another war.

Militarist ideas also persisted, especially in those countries that felt cheated by the peace settlements. Some veterans were reluctant to put away their uniforms and weapons and missed the excitement of battle. In the decade after the war, some of these men joined extremist political parties that glorified war and violence. The philosophies of these extremist parties and the discontent they stirred up paved the way for their leaders to take power in some countries.

The United States avoids involvements in Europe. When the United States had entered the war, the American people had been told that they were fighting "a war to end wars." They too were disappointed with the outcome of the war and began to feel that American soldiers had died in vain. In the period after World War I, many Americans adopted an attitude of *isolationism* — the feeling that their country should avoid involvement in foreign affairs. One reason why the Senate never ap-

As men went off to war, women in a number of countries took on new roles and responsibilities. Like this French factory worker, women in Britain and the United States contributed to the war effort.

proved the Treaty of Versailles was the belief that membership in the League of Nations would bring the United States into more wars.

CHECK-UP

1. Vocabulary: *reparations, mandate, isolationism.*
2. (a) Which countries' leaders made the major decisions at the Paris peace conference? (b) What were the main points of President Wilson's plan for peace?
3. (a) What problems were raised by the principle of self-determination? (b) How did Wilson's aims and those of the European Allies differ? (c) Why?
4. (a) How was Germany "punished" for its part in the war? (b) What new nations were established in Europe by the Versailles peace settlement? (c) What empires were brought to an end by World War I?
5. What were the long-lasting effects of World War I?

Chapter 29 Review

Summary

The forces that led to the outbreak of World War I had existed in Europe for decades. National rivalries and militarism brought about an armaments race and the formation of opposing alliance systems. The Triple Alliance included Germany, Austria-Hungary, and Italy. The Triple Entente was made up of Britain, France, and Russia. A nationalist movement among the Slavs of Serbia led to the assassination of the heir to the Austrian throne in June, 1914. With this excuse, Austria began the war. Within weeks, Austria and Germany were at war against Britain, France, and Russia.

The German military plan assumed a quick victory in France, but by the winter of 1914–1915, it was clear that the war would be lengthy. Trench warfare on the western front in France was made more brutal by new weaponry such as machine guns, poison gas, and tanks. As other nations took sides, the conflict became truly a "world war." In April, 1917, the United States entered the war on the Allied side. Combined Allied forces stopped the final German offensive in France, and the war came to an end in November, 1918.

In the aftermath of the war and the peace settlements, there were widespread political and territorial changes. Idealistic plans for peace were advanced, but bitter feelings and resentment in many nations worked against a permanent peace.

Vocabulary Review

1. Match the following words with the listed definitions: *armistice, isolationism, mandate, militarism, propaganda, reparations.*
(a) An outlook that glorifies war and favors the build-up of military power.
(b) News and information designed to persuade people to accept a particular point of view.
(c) A halt to fighting.
(d) Payments made by one nation to another as compensation for property destroyed in a war.
(e) Administrative control over another country or territory.
(f) The desire to avoid involvement in the affairs of other nations.
2. Distinguish between the terms in each of the following pairs:
(a) Triple Alliance; Triple Entente.
(b) Central Powers; Allies.
(c) western front; eastern front.
(d) Treaty of Brest-Litovsk; Treaty of Versailles.

People to Identify

Identify the following people. Name the country with which each was connected, and tell why he was important.
1. Gavrilo Princip
2. Archduke Francis Ferdinand
3. Woodrow Wilson
4. Arthur Zimmermann
5. William II
6. Ferdinand Foch

Relating Geography and History

1. **Locating places.** Locate each of the following on a map in this chapter:

(a) Serbia	(g) Polish Corridor
(b) Saar	(h) Danzig
(c) Ypres	(i) Czechoslovakia
(d) Verdun	(j) Yugoslavia
(e) Dardanelles	(k) Alsace-Lorraine
(f) Gallipoli	(l) Hungary

2. **Review.** How did the Paris peace settlement affect the boundaries of (a) the Ottoman Empire? (b) Austria-Hungary? (c) What new nations did the settlement create?

Discussion Questions

1. What reasons did the following countries have for seeking alliances with other European powers: (a) Germany, (b) France, (c) Britain, (d) Russia?
2. Explain why each of these factors was an underlying cause of World War I: (a) nationalism, (b) alliance systems, (c) militarism.
3. (a) Why did the United States decide to enter the war on the Allied side? (b) What effect did the American entry into the war have on the fighting in Europe?

4. (a) What were the major goals established by Woodrow Wilson's Fourteen Points? (b) How did French aims for the peace settlement conflict with the Fourteen Points?

5. Why was Wilson's goal of self-determination for nationalist groups difficult to achieve?

6. (a) What requirements were imposed on Germany by the Treaty of Versailles? (b) What was the German reaction?

7. What were some of the long-range consequences of World War I?

Reading Primary Sources

The Versailles Treaty was the most controversial of the Paris peace settlements. Read the following articles from the treaty and answer the questions that follow.

Article 42. Germany is forbidden to maintain or construct any fortifications either on the left bank of the Rhine or on the right bank to the west of a line drawn 50 kilometers to the east of the Rhine.

Article 45. As compensation for the destruction of the coal mines in the north of France and as part payment towards the total reparation due from Germany for the damage resulting from the war, Germany cedes to France in full . . . the coal mines situated in the Saar Basin. . . .

Article 116. Germany acknowledges and agrees to respect as permanent . . . the independence of all the territories which were part of the former Russian Empire on August 1, 1914.

Germany accepts definitely the [cancellation] of the Brest-Litovsk Treaties and of all other treaties . . . entered into by her with the [revolutionary] government in Russia.

Article 160. By . . . March 31, 1920, the German army must not comprise more than seven divisions of infantry and three divisions of cavalry.

After that date the total number of [men] in the [German] army must not exceed 100,000, including officers. . . . The army shall be devoted exclusively to the maintenance of order within the territory and to the control of the frontiers.

Article 231. The Allied . . . governments affirm, and Germany accepts, the responsibility of Germany and her allies for causing all the loss and damage to which the Allied . . . governments and their [citizens] have been subjected as a consequence of the war imposed upon them by the aggression of Germany and her allies.

(a) Which article was intended to prevent the build-up of German forces along Germany's borders with France? (b) According to Article 45, what was France to receive from Germany in compensation for damages? (c) What changes did the treaty make in Russia's agreements with Germany? (d) Which article was intended to destroy Germany's capacity to wage war? (e) How did the treaty force Germany to take the blame for World War I?

Skill Activities

1. Writing newspaper accounts. Write a newspaper article, such as might have appeared at the time, about one of the following: (a) the Battle of Jutland; (b) the war in Africa; (c) the Italian front; (d) the sinking of the *Lusitania;* (e) the signing of the Treaty of Brest-Litovsk; (f) the Battle of the Somme; (g) the arrival of the American Expeditionary Force in France; (h) the first use of airplanes in the fighting in France.

2. Paraphrasing. Rewrite in your own words each of the following statements quoted in this chapter. You may use more than one sentence.
(a) "The lamps are going out all over Europe. We shall not see them lit again in our lifetime" (page 641).
(b) "When one of them puts his hand into his pocket, his neighbor gets ready his own revolver in order . . . to fire the first shot" (page 638).
(c) "[Quarrels between nations] . . . must be settled not at the [conference] table, but on the battlefield; not with the pen, but with the sword" (page 638).

3. Stating both sides of an issue. Disagreement over the Versailles Treaty continued long after it was signed. Write a script for a debate on the treatment of Germany under the Versailles Treaty. Present the arguments of both supporters and opponents of the treaty.

4. Biographies. Georges Clemenceau, David Lloyd George, Vittorio Orlando, Woodrow Wilson, William II, and Nicholas II were national leaders or monarchs during World War I. Choose one of these persons and prepare a report describing the part he played in the war years or in the peace negotiations.

In November, 1917, soon after the end of czarist rule, Lenin proclaimed that Russia was to be ruled by the people. This painting, done years after the event, is a Soviet artist's conception of Lenin's calling Russian soldiers, sailors, and peasants into action.

CHAPTER 30
Russia in Upheaval

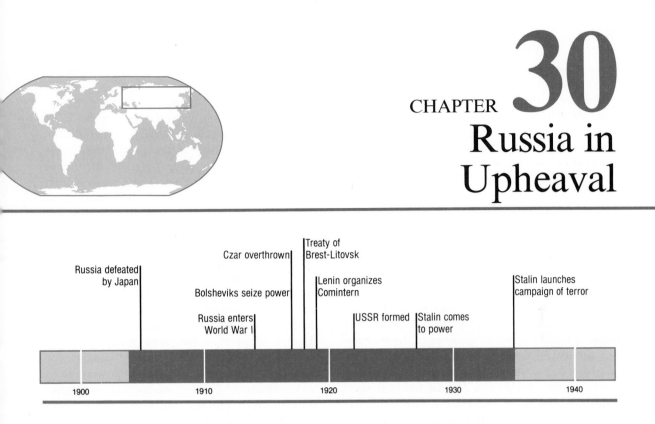

Russia defeated by Japan

Bolsheviks seize power

Czar overthrown

Treaty of Brest-Litovsk

Lenin organizes Comintern

Russia enters World War I

USSR formed

Stalin comes to power

Stalin launches campaign of terror

1900 — 1910 — 1920 — 1930 — 1940

By the outbreak of World War I, czarist Russia lagged far behind the West in industrial development and political progress. The czars' autocratic rule could not unify the country, and revolutionary movements developed. Czarist rule was finally overthrown in 1917, and several factions competed for leadership in Russia.

A radical revolutionary group, which advocated Marxist goals of world revolution and proletariat rule, gained control of Russia's government in 1917. The new rulers, however, faced serious problems of unrest, economic collapse, and a continuing war with Germany. Led by Lenin, the new state became a dictatorship that tried to strengthen and unify Russia by making sweeping changes in the nation's economy and in its traditional society. Lenin's successor, Stalin, used even more ruthless methods to bring change quickly. During this period, the foundations were laid for the rise of the Soviet Union as a world power.

This chapter describes the fall of imperial Russia and the steps taken to establish the Soviet Union.

CHAPTER OUTLINE

1 Czarist Rule Is Overthrown

2 Lenin Builds a Soviet State

3 Stalin Enforces Ruthless Dictatorship

1 Czarist Rule Is Overthrown

For centuries the czars of Russia had sought to make their backward country into a unified nation and world power. Many rulers introduced changes and reforms but found that these undermined their authority. Any lessening of autocratic control brought demands for more reforms, which the czars answered with more repression. At the end of the nineteenth century, czarist Russia remained one of the most firmly autocratic states in the world. Despite the splendor of its court, it was also one of the least developed nations, internally divided and badly ruled.

Russia's leaders fail to understand change. Nicholas II became czar in 1894, at a critical point in world history. A member of the Romanov family, Nicholas had the same goal as his ancestors — to make Russia strong and respected in the world. The 26-year-old czar was a devoted family man who led a simple, pious life. He might have made a good constitutional monarch had he not considered it his duty to continue autocratic rule. Nicholas was unable to lead effectively or to understand the forces at work in Russia and the world.

Western Europe had been transformed in the 1800's by industrialization, urbanization, and the spread of democratic government. European imperialist nations had gained control of large areas of the world and were competing for power in Asia and Africa. Tensions were mounting in Europe itself, as the major European countries built up their armies and navies and formed defensive alliances. Viewing the world from the splendor of Russia's imperial court, Nicholas was blind to the significance of the changes that were taking place.

Some attempts are made to industrialize. Compared with the industrial nations of Western Europe, Russia was weak and undeveloped. In 1900, Sergei Witte (VEET-tyeh), the czar's ablest minister, urged that a program of industrialization be planned. Unlike the czar, Witte realized that the Russian economy had to be modernized. He warned Nicholas II that Russia's "economic weakness may lead to political and cultural backwardness as well."

Under Witte's direction, taxes were increased, and foreign capital was brought in to help develop Russian industries. Witte encouraged the completion of the great Trans-Siberian Railroad (map, page 487) and the extension of other railway lines. These steps helped the growth of heavy industry, particularly iron and steel. To speed development, foreign experts were hired, and many Russians studied abroad. For a while the Russian economy boomed.

Industrialization brings problems. Rapid industrialization, however, led to resentment and disunity among the people of Russia. Agriculture had always been the mainstay of the Russian economy, but now many peasants worked in factories. The workers' standard of living was low, and they were powerless to make changes. Discontent among industrial workers grew. The Russian upper classes were unhappy over the presence in Russia of foreign companies with large investments. In addition, ideas introduced from the West caused people to question Russia's traditions.

Among the Russians who talked of reform were people in business and the professions and some landowners. Although they were well-intentioned and often highly educated, they could not agree on their goals. Some proposed a democratic republic like that in France; others wanted a constitutional monarchy like that in Britain. All worried about the low level of education among most of the Russian people. Some even feared that extending political freedom to workers and peasants might lead to chaos and the collapse of the empire.

Early revolutionary movements fail. From the czar's perspective, the most threatening political reformers were the young Marxist revolutionaries, who took advantage of changing conditions within Russia. Earlier revolutionary movements had failed for lack of support from the mass of the Russian people. In the reign of Alexander II (page 489), radical social reformers had tried to focus their reforms on the situation of the peasants. The peasants, however, distrusted agitators and intellectuals from the cities, and they did not join the movement for reform.

Later revolutionaries adopted the view of history set forth by Karl Marx (page 532). They believed that industrialization and the growth of an industrial working class in Russia made a socialist victory inevitable. To the workers, they promised to end exploitation and the country's economic backwardness. Unable to escape the czar's police, however, most of these revolutionaries ended their lives in prison or exile.

Lenin becomes leader of the Bolsheviks. In the 1890's the Marxist revolutionaries found a leader in Vladimir Ilyich Ulyanov (ool-YAH-nof), better known as Lenin. A brilliant lawyer whose parents were loyal to the czar, Lenin became a revolutionary while still in his teens. Because the czars had always repressed freedom in Russia, Lenin believed that force was necessary to end czarist rule. He argued that only a tight-knit, secret organization of professional

revolutionaries could succeed. This brought a split among the Marxists. Those whom Lenin trained called themselves Bolsheviks (BOHL-shuh-viks), which means "majority" — although they were not the largest faction. They were opposed by other Marxists, known as Mensheviks ("minority"), who hoped that revolutionary goals could be achieved by less violent actions.

Lenin was dedicated to overthrowing the czarist regime and the capitalist system as well. In pursuit of this goal, he went to prison, lived in exile in Siberia,[1] and spent many years abroad as a political refugee. His wife, Nadezhda Krupskaya (KROOPS-kuh-yuh), a

---

[1]Siberia is the vast northeastern region of Russia that stretches from the Ural Mountains to the Pacific Ocean. Starting in the seventeenth century, the czars sent prisoners to labor in its mines. After the fall of czarism, the Russian government continued the policy of sending political prisoners to Siberia.

LINKING PAST AND PRESENT

The Russian Ballet

Although czarist rule in Russia came to an end in 1917, people throughout the world still enjoy one inheritance from the imperial Russian court. As early as 1728, the Russian czars were supporting a school for ballet dancers in St. Petersburg. While the art of ballet did not begin in Russia, it developed a distinctive and familiar style there. The Russian influence on ballet continued into the twentieth century.

In 1862, Marius Petipa became head of the imperial ballet school. With the composer Peter Ilyich Tchaikovsky (page 630), he created some of the world's best-loved ballets, including *The Nutcracker* and *Swan Lake.* In the early 1900's a Russian ballet troupe began to tour Europe and the United States.

Even after the fall of the czar, Russian choreographers, dancers, and stage designers dominated the international ballet world. Ballet has not been forgotten in the modern Soviet Union, where the state supports such internationally famous dance groups as the Bolshoi and Kirov ballets.

woman from an upper-class family, was equally dedicated. Krupskaya and Lenin were married during his exile in Siberia and devoted the rest of their lives to the revolutionary cause.

Revolts follow defeat by Japan. Czarist autocracy came to an end after a series of events that weakened imperial rule. In 1904–1905, Russia was humiliatingly defeated in a brief war with Japan (page 583). Following this defeat, a series of uprisings broke out throughout Russia, involving peasants, workers, sailors in the imperial navy, non-Russian nationality groups, and intellectuals. Each group had its own complaints against czarist rule. The workers of St. Petersburg marched on the imperial palace with their demands, and the palace guards reacted by firing into the crowd. The incident set off strikes and further unrest. Leading the strikers was the *soviet*, or representative council, of workers in St. Petersburg.

After months of disorder, the czar agreed in October, 1905, to the formation of Russia's first parliament, the imperial Duma (DOO-mah). He promised that it would represent all elements of the population and guarantee their civil liberties.

The czarist government undertakes minor reforms. When the imperial troops returned from the war with Japan, the czar regained control and the Revolution of 1905 was stopped short. While meetings of the Duma were called, its power was limited. Nevertheless, between 1907 and 1914, the Duma managed to increase participation in the government somewhat.

The threat of revolution brought other efforts to satisfy the people without weakening the czar's authority. Peter Stolypin (stuh-LIH-pyin) succeeded Witte as chief minister in 1906. Stolypin's main aim was to make the peasants firm supporters of czarist rule. He put through reforms that gave land to more peasants and greater freedom to the most successful peasant farmers, the *kulaks* (meaning "fists"). He weakened the Duma, however, by dismissing it whenever it failed to support his plans.

The reforms undertaken after 1905 did not satisfy people's complaints or weaken the resolve of the revolutionaries. Little progress in strengthening the czarist regime had been made by 1914, when Russia was caught up in World War I.

World War I speeds the end of czarist rule. Its interest in the Balkans involved Russia in World War I even though the country was unprepared. Russia was no match for imperial Germany, the most powerful country in Europe. Neither its industry, its government, nor its military forces were ready. The war was the final blow to the czar's control.

In the summer of 1915, Nicholas II joined his troops at the front, leaving his wife Alexandra to run the government. Alexandra, a German-born princess and the granddaughter of Britain's Queen Victoria, had no experience in ruling. Her decisions were influenced greatly by the knowledge that her son, the heir to the throne, suffered from hemophilia (a disease that prevents blood from clotting). In her despair, Alexandra fell under the spell of Rasputin (ras-PYOO-tin), a monk who convinced her he could cure her son. Trusted advisers warned the czar about Rasputin's scandalous life and the harm he might do to the imperial family, but Alexandra dismissed these critics. By 1915 the leading government officials were men whom Rasputin had recommended. Alarmed, a group of noblemen murdered Rasputin in 1916.

Meanwhile, the war was destroying the morale of the poorly trained, badly equipped, and incompetently led Russian armies. By 1917, after two and a half years of defeats and staggering numbers of casualties, the soldiers had little respect left for either their officers or the czar.

In March, 1917, czarist rule was overthrown. A strike of women textile workers in Petrograd[2] became city-wide and soon erupted into riots over food shortages. When soldiers were ordered to shoot the rioters, they shot their officers instead and joined the open rebellion. Like the 1905 revolution, the March Revolution, as it came to be called, was unplanned. The war had aggravated the tensions that had been building up within the country, and czarist autocracy crumbled from its own weaknesses. A week after rioting began, the czar ab-

---

[2]St. Petersburg was renamed Petrograd at the beginning of the war in 1914, to eliminate the Germanic sound of the name. Its workers had been in the forefront of revolutionary movements from the early 1800's on. After Lenin's death in 1924, the city was again renamed, this time as Leningrad.

Czar Nicholas II and his family appear here in a photograph taken before the czar was overthrown in 1917. Symbolic of imperial Russia were the richly enameled Easter eggs (below) created for the royal family by the jeweler Peter Carl Fabergé.

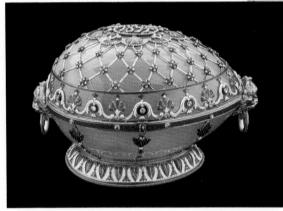

dicated in favor of a Provisional Government set up by the Duma.

Disunity follows the fall of czarist rule. The March Revolution set off a chain reaction of disasters. The many different groups composing the empire were soon at each other's throats. There was disunity even among the new leaders. On one side stood the Provisional Government — called "provisional" because its decisions were subject to eventual approval by a constitutional convention. It represented those educated Russians who had adopted liberal, democratic ideas from the West. Their leader after July, 1917, was Alexander Kerensky (kuh-REN-skee). He and his fellow ministers wanted to protect the rights of individuals and to establish a Western-style parliamentary government. They also wanted to continue the war against Germany.

Opposing the Provisional Government was the Petrograd Soviet. It was an influential but unwieldy group composed of soldiers and workers, and it excluded all members of the upper classes. (In the months that followed, many other soviets sprang up throughout the country, representing both workers and peasants.) The Petrograd Soviet favored social reforms to aid workers and peasants. It did not urge immediate withdrawal from the war but called for an early peace. Unsure of its own readiness for leadership, however, the Soviet reluctantly tolerated the Provisional Government.

By the summer of 1917, the Russian people had lost confidence in both the Provisional Government and the moderate leaders of the Petrograd Soviet. They wanted land reforms, an end to hunger and disorder, and self-determination for non-Russian minorities. Above all, the people were eager to end the war.

The situation provided an opportunity for the radical revolutionaries. At the time of the czar's overthrow, the Bolshevik leaders had been either in jail or in exile. A month later, a German military train brought Lenin and his companions back to Petrograd from their exile in Western Europe. German leaders, planning Russia's defeat, hoped that aid to the Bolsheviks would keep the Russian war effort disorganized and ineffectual.

Political factions compete for leadership. By the end of the summer of 1917, three different forms of government were being offered to

The period between March and November, 1917, was marked by violence as Kerensky's government and the Bolsheviks struggled for power. Workers' demonstrations organized by the Bolsheviks were dispersed by forces of the Provisional Government.

the bewildered and divided peoples of Russia. The first was a parliamentary government dedicated to restoring internal unity and power through democratic methods. This was the course offered by Kerensky's Provisional Government and its supporters. Some members of the old ruling classes backed a military dictatorship that would end disorder and hold the country together by armed force. In August, General Lavr Kornilov (kor-NEE-lof), the army commander in chief, attempted to establish this kind of rule. The movement failed because the Petrograd Soviet won over most of Kornilov's troops.

The third possibility was rule by the workers' and soldiers' soviets, led by the Petrograd Soviet, now under the control of the Bolsheviks led by Lenin. Alone among the political leaders, Lenin understood the demands of the various groups among the Russian people. To the peasants he offered land that would be taken away from the landowners. To the workers he

offered bread and control of the factories. To the soldiers he offered peace. To the national minorities he offered self-determination.

Along with popular support, Lenin also had a reliable organization, with able and energetic aides and a party of roughly 200,000 followers. The Bolsheviks were disciplined and could act as a tightly organized unit.

Another revolution brings Bolshevik control. The Bolsheviks soon gained a majority in the soviets of major cities. By the fall of 1917, people in the cities were rallying to the call "All power to the soviets!" On November 7, 1917, Lenin's supporters, led by Leon Trotsky, seized government buildings in Petrograd and arrested the members of the Provisional Government.[3] The Bolsheviks declared a Soviet Re-

---

[3]The Bolshevik Revolution is often called the October Revolution because prerevolutionary Russia continued to use the "Old Style," or Julian, calendar. By this calendar, the overthrow took place on October 25.

public, dedicated to creating a Marxist society. Lenin now saw himself as both the heir to the nation-building czars and the intellectual leader of a socialist Russia that, he believed, could serve as a model to the world. On the other hand, his new government had inherited all the problems the czars had faced, made worse by Russia's defeats in the war.

CHECK-UP

1. Vocabulary: *soviet*.
2. (a) What steps did Witte take to carry out Russian industrialization? (b) What effects did industrialization have on czarist rule?
3. (a) How did Lenin plan to end czarist rule? (b) Over what major issue did he and his fellow Bolsheviks disagree with the Mensheviks?
4. (a) What were the causes of the Revolution of 1905? (b) What was its outcome?
5. (a) How did World War I help to bring about the end of czarist rule? (b) What kind of government was set up after the March Revolution?
6. (a) Why did the Russian people lose confidence in the new government? (b) What group gained power as a result of the October Revolution?

2 Lenin Builds a Soviet State

The breakdown of order in Russia grew worse after the Bolshevik takeover. A huge gap separated the Bolsheviks' plans for the future from the grim realities of Russian life. The miseries that had brought down the Provisional Government — hunger, fear, disunity, war — multiplied. People fled from the cities to the country, only to encounter war or famine there. Different nationalities — the Finns, the Ukrainians, and others — threatened to form their own states. There was no effective government or army. The chaos left Russia with no industry, no railway transport, and no commerce. Often there was no food.

Soviet Russia accepts German terms for peace. In the winter of 1917–1918, Russia was defenseless before the German invaders. The Bolshevik leaders decided to accept the German terms for peace. In March, 1918, they signed a humiliating peace treaty at the town of Brest-Litovsk (page 644). The Polish lands, the Baltic provinces, and Finland were given up. So too was the Ukraine, the region north of the Black Sea, which had the richest and most fertile farmland in the empire. The Allied defeat of Germany in November, 1918, canceled the Treaty of Brest-Litovsk. Nevertheless, many borderlands were not returned to the Russians. The Bolsheviks recognized the independence of Finland and the Baltic states of Latvia, Lithuania, and Estonia.

The Bolsheviks, who now called themselves Communists, had learned a lesson from the war. Realizing that the price of backwardness was national humiliation and disintegration, they decided that Russia had to be made strong.

Civil war rages. Communist leaders still faced opposition and civil war in many parts of the country. The forces opposing the Communists were called "Whites." They included moderate socialists and supporters of parliamentary government on one hand and defenders of the czarist cause on the other. Though unable to unite or cooperate, they still offered strong resistance to the Communist "Reds." (The Communist forces took their name from the Red Army organized by Leon Trotsky.) In the Ukraine, peasants called "Greens" fought both Whites and Reds.

Meanwhile, foreign armies were also involved in Russia's civil war. Lenin's call for world revolution had so alarmed the governments of the Western countries that they intervened. Forces from France, Britain, the United States, and Japan moved into parts of Russian territory and helped the forces of the Whites. The newly independent nation of Poland declared war on Soviet Russia and took over territory in western Russia.

Lenin establishes a dictatorship. To deal with the rising anarchy and violence, Lenin proclaimed the "dictatorship of the proletariat." As chaos increased, ruthless violence was used to suppress opposition. The Russian secret police (successively called Cheka, GPU, NKVD, and KGB) became more feared than its czarist forerunners. Amid the brutalities of the civil war, the revolutionaries who had been victims of czarist persecution now became the persecuters. Prisoner-of-war camps were changed into concentration camps for political enemies of the Bolsheviks. The secret police seized hostages from the former ruling classes and executed many of them. Czar Nicholas, Czarina Alexandra, and all their children were imprisoned and killed in July, 1918. Counter-revolutionaries — those suspected of opposition to the revolution — were tortured and killed.

The government makes economic changes. During these bloodstained years the Communist dictatorship made some moves to bring about a Marxist society. The first goal was control of economic activity. Industry, banks, and foreign trade came under government control. All men under fifty were drafted for labor or for the armed services. Women were mobilized to work in factories and on construction projects. Strikes were forbidden. To feed the people in the cities and the army, soldiers seized food from the peasants. These emergency measures, termed War Communism, failed to revive the economy. Commerce was at a standstill. Production fell disastrously, and hundreds of thousands of people died from hunger, cold, and disease.

The New Economic Policy is established. By the end of the civil war in 1920, even some Bolsheviks felt the Communist dictatorship was too repressive. Peasants rebelled, and factory workers rioted. In March, 1921, sailors at the Kronstadt (KROHN-shtaht) naval base near Petrograd rose in protest. It took weeks of bloody fighting to crush their revolt. Faced with such opposition, Lenin dropped the harsh tactics of War Communism and introduced the New Economic Policy, usually called NEP.

Under NEP, Lenin put aside the socialist goal of a rigidly planned economy. Realizing the difficulties of building socialism in an undeveloped country like Russia, he allowed some small-scale manufacturing, trade, and agriculture to return to private ownership. The government kept control of major industries, banks, and means of communication.

Russian society undergoes changes. The Bolshevik Revolution had destroyed the ruling class of czarist Russia. Society was no longer led by military officers, bureaucrats, landowners, or educated business and professional people. Many of these Russians had been killed; some had fled the country. Members of the upper classes who remained in Russia were barred from Communist Party membership. The leaders of the new Russia depended on the support of barely literate workers and peasants.

Russia's Communist leaders sought to strengthen their control. They presented their *ideology* — their political philosophy — to the people in a few popular, easy-to-understand slogans and used a swift revolutionary justice that encouraged fear of government power. They promised extensive social services but firmly insisted that everyone had a duty to work. At the same time they abolished or limited employment in private industry, with the aim of creating a socialist state of "workers and

---

TIMETABLE

Russia in Upheaval

1905	Japan defeats Russia. A revolution forces Nicholas to allow formation of the Duma.
1914	Russia enters World War I.
1917	A revolution ends czarist rule (March). The Bolsheviks seize power (November).
1918	Russia is forced to accept the Treaty of Brest-Litovsk.
1918–1920	Civil war brings foreign intervention and loss of territory.
1919	Lenin organizes the Comintern.
1920	The New Economic Policy (NEP) begins.
1922	The Union of Soviet Socialist Republics is formed.
1924	Lenin dies.
1927	Stalin becomes the unchallenged leader of the Soviet Union.
1928	The first Five-Year Plan begins.
1935–1939	Stalin's purges bring terror to the Soviet people.

EARLY SOVIET RUSSIA

The new Soviet leaders initiated a campaign to rid their nation of illiteracy. In the picture above, Russian peasants learn to read and write. Soviet leaders also placed great emphasis on agriculture, as the 1924 Russian coin demonstrates (right).

toilers." People thus became dependent on the state for jobs. Another goal announced by the leaders proclaimed the equality of the sexes, which earned them the support of many women. Party leadership was dominated by men, however. National minorities were granted the right to use their own languages and preserve their cultures, as long as they followed Communist leadership.

Political opposition is suppressed. In March, 1918, the center of government had been moved from the czarist capital, Petrograd, to Moscow. From his headquarters in the Kremlin, an old palace-fortress in Moscow, Lenin directed the Soviet state. Like the czars, he was concerned with overcoming his country's slowness to modernize. The key to success, Lenin argued, lay in unifying the many different peoples of Soviet Russia. He insisted that this could be accomplished only by suppressing all opposition. The only political party permitted in the new Russia was the Communist Party.

Communist Party leaders dominate the government. The new government was led by tough and energetic members of the Party's Politburo (POHL-it-byoo-roh), or "political office." All these men had risen to power working in the revolutionary movement. Believing that Russia's survival depended on their unity, they took drastic steps to prevent conflict within the Party. Those who disagreed with Party policies were thrown out of the Party or imprisoned.

The Politburo depended on about half a million loyal Communist Party members, all trained to strict obedience. Almost all had been industrial workers. Once admitted, Party members were subject to constant checks and expected to show selfless, energetic devotion to the Party.

In theory, the members of the Party elected and controlled their leaders. In practice, however, all decisions were made at the top, just as they had been under the czar. Moreover, the Party leaders not only controlled the government but also supervised trade unions, cooperatives, youth leagues, women's groups, and professional and cultural organizations.

The Soviet government and the Party are linked. Lenin made the workers' and peasants' soviets part of the government structure. Local government was run by soviets that were elected locally but guided by the Party. Above them were district, regional, and republic soviets. The highest government authority in the country was called the all-Russian Congress of

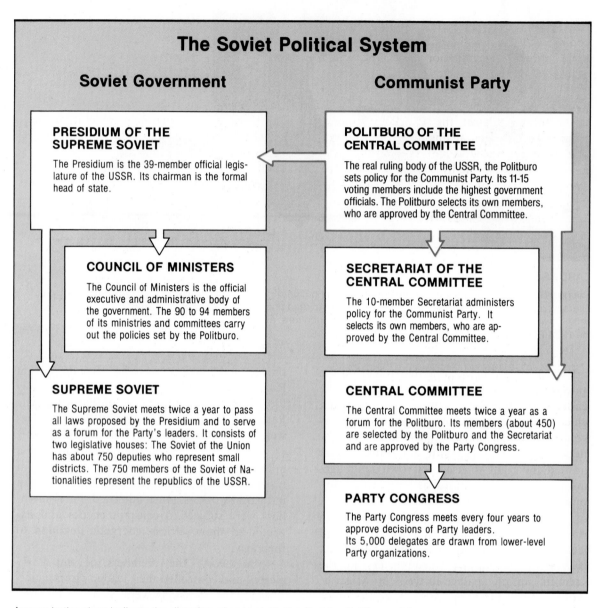

The Soviet Political System

Soviet Government

Communist Party

PRESIDIUM OF THE SUPREME SOVIET

The Presidium is the 39-member official legislature of the USSR. Its chairman is the formal head of state.

POLITBURO OF THE CENTRAL COMMITTEE

The real ruling body of the USSR, the Politburo sets policy for the Communist Party. Its 11-15 voting members include the highest government officials. The Politburo selects its own members, who are approved by the Central Committee.

COUNCIL OF MINISTERS

The Council of Ministers is the official executive and administrative body of the government. The 90 to 94 members of its ministries and committees carry out the policies set by the Politburo.

SECRETARIAT OF THE CENTRAL COMMITTEE

The 10-member Secretariat administers policy for the Communist Party. It selects its own members, who are approved by the Central Committee.

SUPREME SOVIET

The Supreme Soviet meets twice a year to pass all laws proposed by the Presidium and to serve as a forum for the Party's leaders. It consists of two legislative houses: The Soviet of the Union has about 750 deputies who represent small districts. The 750 members of the Soviet of Nationalities represent the republics of the USSR.

CENTRAL COMMITTEE

The Central Committee meets twice a year as a forum for the Politburo. Its members (about 450) are selected by the Politburo and the Secretariat and are approved by the Party Congress.

PARTY CONGRESS

The Party Congress meets every four years to approve decisions of Party leaders.
Its 5,000 delegates are drawn from lower-level Party organizations.

Arrows in the chart indicate the direction of control. Notice that the Politburo of the Central Committee of the Communist Party is the body that actually governs the Soviet Union.

Soviets, later renamed the Supreme Soviet. Its Council of Ministers, staffed with the highest-ranking Party members, formed the executive branch of the government. Though separate in organization, the state and the Communist Party were intimately linked. (See the chart on this page.)

The Soviet Union unites many republics. The many different nationalities within Russia had always been a barrier to unity, and the czars had tried to impose Russian culture on these peoples. A new approach was the Union of Soviet Socialist Republics (called the USSR or Soviet Union, for short), formed in 1922. Each member republic represented a different major nationality, such as the Georgians, Ukrainians, Kazakhs, and Uzbeks (map, page 667). The republics had identical constitutions, all controlled by the Communist Party. Smaller nationality groups were granted limited self-rule within the republics. The Communists thus could claim that they were honoring the principle of self-determination, without endangering the unity of their multinational country.

The Soviet government is hostile to religion. In its pursuit of unity the Communist Party turned against the Russian Orthodox Church and, in fact, against all organized religion. The Eastern Orthodox religion had been a deep influence in the lives of most of the Russian people. One of the first acts of the Bolsheviks had been to seize Church land and property. Under Lenin, the Soviet Union continued the Communist goal of reducing the Church's role in people's lives. Marxist doctrine viewed religion as "opium for the people," a tool by which the traditional ruling class was able to exploit the workers. The Communists also saw the Russian Orthodox Church as a rival for people's loyalties. As a result, the Church and other religious groups suffered much persecution under Communist rule.

The state makes plans for the economy. Under NEP, Lenin had permitted private ownership only as an emergency measure. He never abandoned his goal of transforming Soviet society into "one huge office, one huge workshop," with all workers striving toward one set of goals. Only in that way, he thought, could Russia's enormous resources be utilized for rapid economic development.

In 1921 the State Planning Agency, or Gosplan, was introduced and given the main responsibility for promoting electrification throughout the country. Gosplan was the first step in giving the state complete control over all factors involved in production and distribution. Lenin argued that such control, backed by force and terror, was the only way to make economic planning effective.

Lenin proclaims the superiority of the Soviet system. Control by the state went beyond economic planning. To avoid unfavorable comparison with Western countries, Lenin deepened the isolation that had cut off Russia from the outside world since 1914. He tried to give the peoples of the Soviet state a belief in their nation, proclaiming the superiority of the Soviet regime over Western capitalism and picturing Soviet Russia as leading the world to a socialist future. He offered the ideology known as Marxism-Leninism, a mixture of Marxism with Lenin's own interpretation of Russian conditions. Lenin's hope was that a common set of beliefs might unite the Soviet peoples as they had never been under the czars.

Communism becomes international. Hoping to spread the doctrine of revolution, Lenin looked beyond the Soviet Union. He sent out an appeal for revolution to all who blamed their governments or employers for poverty, suffering, or injustice. Bewildered and angered by war and the confusion of the unsettled times, many people listened to Lenin's plea. Communist parties sprang up in many Western countries as well as in India, China, Egypt, and Turkey.

In 1919 Lenin formed an organization designed to bring together these world-wide revolutionary forces and to use them as an instrument of Soviet foreign policy. This organization was the Communist Third International, often called the Comintern for short. (Earlier attempts at international organization had failed.) The goal of world revolution, however, soon became secondary to that of strengthening Soviet Russia.

CHECK-UP

1. Vocabulary: *ideology.*
2. (a) What was the Treaty of Brest-Litovsk? (b) Why was it canceled? (c) What lands did Russia lose after World War I?
3. (a) Why did a civil war follow the Russian Revolution? (b) Who were the "Whites" and "Reds"? (c) Why did foreign armies move into Russian territories?
4. (a) How did Lenin establish a dictatorship? (b) What were the goals of War Communism? (c) Why did it fail? (d) What changes did the New Economic Policy bring?
5. (a) What moves did Communist leaders make to strengthen their control of Russia? (b) Describe the structure of the government set up by the Politburo.
6. (a) How did Lenin handle the problem of Soviet Russia's many national groups? (b) What was the Communists' attitude toward religion? (c) What was Lenin's ultimate goal for the Soviet economy?
7. (a) What was the Comintern? (b) What were the aims of the Comintern?

3 Stalin Enforces Ruthless Dictatorship

Among those associated with Lenin in creating the Soviet state, Leon Trotsky and Joseph Stalin stood out as leaders. When Lenin died in January, 1924, after a series of strokes, these two men became rivals for command of the Communist Party. The outcome of the power struggle determined the future course of the Soviet Union.

Stalin and Trotsky become rivals. Leon Trotsky[4] was a widely traveled journalist, a forceful orator, and a skilled organizer. Trotsky's planning was behind both the Bolshevik seizure of power in November, 1917, and the strict discipline of the Red Army. Joseph Stalin was of a rougher mold. A shoemaker's son, he was a Georgian from the region south of the Caucasus Mountains. Stalin turned rebel while still at school and, while Lenin and Trotsky were living safely abroad, he stayed in Russia. Working as a revolutionary, he spent much time in prison and in a long exile in Siberia.

In 1922, Stalin was appointed general secretary of the Communist Party. Lenin soon came to distrust Stalin and hoped that Trotsky would succeed him as head of the Party. About a year before his death, Lenin wrote: "Comrade Stalin . . . has concentrated boundless power in his hands, and I am not certain he can always use this power with sufficient caution. On the other hand, Comrade Trotsky . . . is distinguished not only by his remarkable abilities. Personally he is, I think, the most able person in the present central committee. . . . "

Stalin used his position as general secretary to gain control of the Party. Ruthlessly eliminating anyone who opposed him or his goals, Stalin drove Trotsky and his supporters out of the Party and, eventually, out of the Soviet Union. He built a network of obedient officials at all levels of Party organization.

---

[4]Because they were frequently on the run from the czar's police, early revolutionaries used aliases. On his escape to London from Siberia in 1902, Lev Davidovich Bronstein took the name "Leon Trotsky" from a prison official. Stalin was born Iosif Vissarionovich Dzhugashvili; his adopted last name means "like steel."

Stalin gains absolute power. In 1929, on his fiftieth birthday, Stalin was officially hailed as Lenin's successor and as the "great wise father" of the peoples of Soviet Russia. Stalin encouraged the growth of "the cult of personality," a glorification of himself as almost superhuman. Those who were not loyal to Stalin or who disagreed with him were condemned as traitors or heretics. Stalin's rivals either gave in to his plans or were eliminated.

Stalin calls for forced industrialization. Stalin introduced a grim era in Russian history. In place of the slow changes of the New Economic Policy, he imposed a policy of rapid industrialization. In 1931, remembering his country's powerlessness at the end of World War I, Stalin declared: "We are fifty or a hundred years behind the advanced countries. We must make good this distance in ten years or they will crush us."

A series of Five-Year Plans was set up for the deliberate, forced growth of industry. These plans established goals for the production of steel, coal, oil, transportation, and hydroelectric power, as well as for consumer goods. The planners determined all the necessary supplies and raw materials. They set up specific production and distribution schedules for materials, machines, and the workers to run them.

The first and most drastic Five-Year Plan began in 1928 with total state control. All private businesses came to an end. All economic activity, including agriculture, came under state management. The state was responsible for producing all goods, buying and selling these products, and hiring and firing workers. For consumers, the changes meant shortages, delays, and poor service. Consumer demands were not an important consideration in the plan designed to strengthen the Soviet state.

Planning faces difficulties. Economic reorganization on such a large scale created enormous problems. The emphasis on quantity led to the production of shoddy or even unusable goods. Working conditions were grim. Against their will, large numbers of men and women were forced to work in factories and

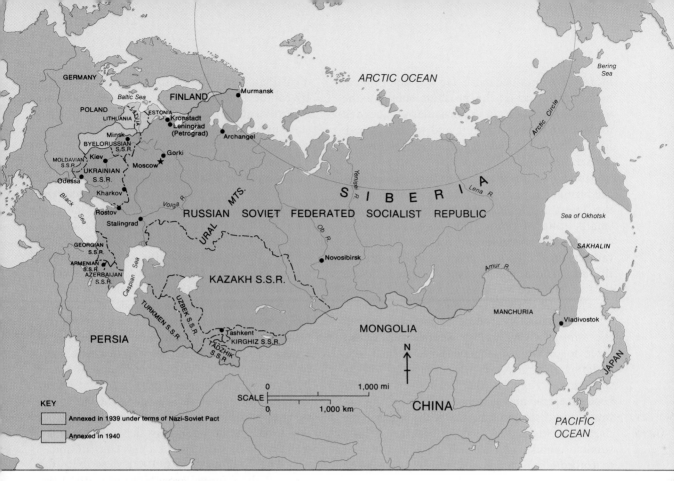

The Soviet Union in 1939

Under the Soviet system, the nation became a union of "republics," each named for its major nationality. What was the largest of the Soviet republics?

workshops, where they were paid low wages based on what they produced. Workers were poorly fed and lived in overcrowded housing. The system was intended to mold workers to obey "the single will of the leaders of the labor process," as Lenin had said in 1918.

The Communist Party tried to raise production through "socialist competition." It rewarded workers who produced more than their fellow workers and held victory celebrations when production goals were surpassed. Young people were encouraged to believe that they were building a beautiful new world. Everyone was expected to practice heroic sacrifice, much as in wartime.

Art is used to serve the state. Even literature and the arts were mobilized to boost Soviet industrial production. Writers, painters, and musicians were expected to produce only works that followed the guidelines of "socialist realism." Their job was to inspire the Soviet

people to dedicate themselves completely to building the nation's future. Much of the art produced was crude propaganda. Novelists described the joys of working for the state in simple tales: Boy meets girl, and their love raises the output of their workshop or factory to new heights. Painters, using a bold and direct style, portrayed people working joyfully in fields or factories.

Stalin plans to reorganize agriculture. Life in the years of rapid industrial expansion was harsh and bitter for the Soviet people. It was made doubly grim by the sweeping changes that took place in agriculture after 1929. Lenin had given the Russian peasants relative freedom, but he had continued to hope that some day agriculture would be as strictly controlled as industry. Stalin found that the peasants would not voluntarily produce the harvests required under the first Five-Year Plan. With shops empty of goods to buy, peasants had no incentive to produce more. He was determined, however, not to let the peasants stand in the way of his plan. Grain in particular was needed to feed the factory workers and to sell abroad. Stalin decided to bring agriculture forcibly under state control.

Stalin's plan called for **collective farming** — the bringing together on large tracts of land all the livestock, tools, and buildings of many small, scattered farms. The larger farms were expected to use machinery, introduce scientific farming methods, and produce food more efficiently. The Soviet peasants, however, had a long memory of serfdom and bitterly resisted giving up the lands they owned.

Peasants defy forced collectivization. In the winter of 1929–1930, Stalin used armed force to collectivize the peasants' farms. Proclaiming that anyone "who is against collectivization is against the Soviet regime," he brought terror and violence to most of the nation. Stalin's prime target was the kulaks, the more prosperous and successful farmers. Thousands of kulaks who resisted were shot or sent to forced-labor camps, known as *gulags*. The remaining peasants slaughtered their horses, cows, and pigs rather than turn them over to the collective.

Forced collectivization had frightful consequences for years to come. The loss of livestock — perhaps 100 million animals — caused severe shortages of meat, dairy products, leather goods, and fertilizer. There were no draft animals for agriculture or transportation. In 1932–1933 a severe famine struck many sections of the Soviet Union at a time when Stalin had planned to sell large amounts of food abroad in order to buy urgently needed industrial equipment. Grain was seized for export, and millions of people starved to death.

Stalin showed no concern for the starving peasants and never considered abandoning his plan. One of his aims was to "liquidate the kulaks as a class." By sending the most resourceful farmers to work in forced-labor camps and on construction projects, he wiped out the most efficient producers in Soviet agriculture.

By the mid-1930's collective farms, each composed of hundreds of households, were the rule in the Soviet Union. The collectives were given production quotas by the current Five-Year Plan. They were also controlled indirectly by Motor Tractor Stations, another part of the collectivization plan. Peasants had to pay these stations in order to have farm machinery for seeding, plowing, and harvesting. The Motor Tractor Stations thus controlled farm operations and the nation's food supply.

Stalin made one concession in collectivizing agriculture. He allowed the peasants to keep small plots of household land for their private use. Food grown on these plots could be sold on the open market for whatever price it would bring. (Much of the food on Soviet tables still comes from these small private plots.)

A new constitution is issued. By the early 1930's much of the world was in a serious depression (page 687). In the Soviet Union, the modest recovery achieved by the New Economic Policy had been wiped out. Food and housing were so scarce that they had to be rationed. Stalin, however, claimed that the Soviet peoples had been raised to a superior stage of development and had at last achieved "true socialism." In 1936 he issued a new constitution.

The Stalinist constitution described the goals of the Communist Party rather than defining the powers of the government. Its section on the rights and duties of Soviet citizens, for example, stated that rights such as free speech

Stalin ignored the well-being of the Russian people during his reorganization of the Soviet economy.

and free assembly must meet "the interests of the working class and . . . strengthen the socialist system." Because it was the Communist Party that defined the interests of the working class, the rights of Soviet citizens could be severely restricted under the constitution.

Opposition to Stalin grows. The characteristics of Stalinism were nation-building by force and modernization through total planning. A silent tide of criticism of these tactics developed by 1930, threatening Stalin's power. Stalin was held responsible for the people's resistance to government policies and for the millions of lives lost in rapid industrialization and collectivization. Soon the criticisms reached into his own family. His wife, Nadezhda Alliluyeva (ah-lee-loo-YEH-vuh), gave some support to her husband's opponents. In 1932 she died, an apparent suicide.

Grumbling within the Communist Party was clearly expressed at the Party Congress of 1934. Stalin, it was said, had gone too far. Some members even suggested that he step down in favor of the Party secretary in Leningrad, Sergei Kirov (KEE-rohf).

Stalin's purge brings terror. Stalin struck back at his critics with a campaign of terror. In December, 1934, Kirov was murdered. Stalin was suspected of planning the killing but claimed to have discovered a plot against the Soviet leadership. Soon after, he launched a purge — that is, an intensive effort to remove all enemies and possible enemies in the Party and in the population at large.

The purge lasted from 1935 into 1939 and claimed the lives of millions of Soviet citizens. Whenever a new wave of arrests was due, the streets of Moscow and other cities emptied as men and women fearfully awaited the midnight call of the secret police. Those arrested were subjected to days and nights of questioning, often under torture. The interrogations lasted until the prisoners signed their "confessions."

To increase people's awe of Stalin's power, public trials were staged for some of the most prominent Bolsheviks. The world was stunned by the spectacle of hardened Communist leaders denouncing their own actions. In this fashion Stalin got rid of both the high-ranking party members who had tried to promote Kirov and the "old Bolsheviks" who had joined the party before 1917. In 1940 he sent an assassin to murder Trotsky, who was in exile in Mexico. The Party members who survived the purge were obedient bureaucrats who would not challenge Stalin.

Stalin's methods achieve unity. Stalin used similar methods to intimidate the Soviet people as a whole. He launched attacks against the leaders of non-Russian nationalist movements, intellectuals, workers, and collective farmers, whether or not they criticized his programs. Even scientists and engineers were sent to labor camps or executed, despite the fact that they were essential to industrialization. The campaign of terror killed more non-Party members than Communists. According to Stalin, the rapid mobilization of Soviet power required every person's total submission to the new order. That is, he demanded that the Soviet Union become a *totalitarian* state under his complete control.

Stalin's terror was seen by some as the horrifying price that the peoples of the Soviet Union had to pay to overcome the weaknesses and backwardness revealed by their country's defeat in World War I. Nonetheless, individual liberties and millions of lives were sacrificed to the goals of economic modernization and the consolidation of Communist power.

CHECK-UP

1. Vocabulary: *collective farming, totalitarian.*
2. (a) Who were the rivals for Soviet leadership when Lenin died? (b) Who won the struggle? (c) What was "the cult of personality"?
3. (a) What was the purpose of the series of Five-Year Plans begun in 1928? (b) How did the Five-Year Plans affect private business, consumers, and workers? (c) How was art made to serve the Soviet state?
4. (a) Why did Stalin collectivize Soviet agriculture? (b) What group of people did he want to destroy? (c) Why did the peasants resist collectivization? (d) What effects did collectivization have on the economy?
5. (a) What criticisms of Stalin were being voiced by the early 1930's? (b) What was Stalin's response? (c) What was the purpose of holding public trials of Soviet officials?
6. How did Stalin's rule lead to a totalitarian state?

Chapter 30 Review

Summary

World War I revealed the weaknesses of the czars' autocratic rule as well as Russia's backwardness in industrialization. Czar Nicholas II, like his predecessors, failed to understand his own country or the changing world. Revolutionary movements against the czars had long existed in Russia. Czarist rule finally was overthrown in March, 1917.

Attempts to establish a democratic government and a military dictatorship both failed. By late 1918, the Bolsheviks, or Communists, led by Lenin, emerged as the leaders of a new state. They formed the Union of Soviet Socialist Republics, a federation based on nationality groups. More civil war had followed the Bolshevik Revolution, and Lenin finally established a dictatorship that attempted to create a state with a planned economy. He offered the people Marxism-Leninism, an interpretation of Marxism that gave the Russian people a set of common goals.

Stalin came to power after Lenin's death in 1924. Stalin ruthlessly enforced policies of industrial growth and the collectivization of agriculture. Years of purges killed millions and made Stalin the all-powerful ruler of the Soviet Union.

Vocabulary Review

1. Write the sentences below on a sheet of paper. In each sentence, fill in the blank with one of these terms: *collective farming, ideology, soviet, totalitarian.*
(a) The ___?___ is a representative council of workers in Russia.
(b) In a ___?___ state, the leader holds complete authority.
(c) Lenin put forth the ___?___ called Marxism-Leninism.
(d) Under Stalin's ___?___ policy, the livestock and equipment of many small farms were brought together on large farms.
2. Distinguish between the terms in each of the following pairs:
(a) Bolsheviks; Mensheviks.
(b) March Revolution; October Revolution.
(c) Petrograd Soviet; Provisional Government.
(d) New Economic Policy; War Communism.
(e) Comintern; Politburo.

People to Identify

Match the following people with the numbered phrases that describe them: *Kerensky, Stalin, Lenin, Nicholas II, Witte, Trotsky, Rasputin.*
1. Last czar of Russia.
2. Adviser to the czar, who favored industrialization and economic reorganization for Russia.
3. Communist Russia's first ruler.
4. Monk who influenced the czar and czarina.
5. Moderate leader and head of the Provisional Government.
6. Organizer of the Red Army, assassinated on Stalin's order.
7. Lenin's successor as dictator of the Soviet Union.

Relating Geography and History

1. **Locating places.** Locate each of the following on a map in this chapter:
(a) Moscow   (d) Kronstadt
(b) Siberia   (e) Petrograd
(c) Black Sea   (f) Ukrainian S.S.R.
2. **Making a chart.** The Soviet Union was formed in 1922 in an effort to unite the different nationalities living within Russian-dominated territory (pages 664–665). On a map in an atlas, locate each of the fifteen republics now in the Soviet Union. Find out the capital city and area (in square miles) of each republic. Make a chart of this information, showing in separate columns the name of the republic, the capital, and the area.

Discussion Questions

1. How did czarist Russia's attempts to industrialize increase disunity within the empire?
2. Give reasons for each of the following revolutions and explain its effect on Russian politics: (a) Revolution of 1905, (b) March Revolution of 1917, (c) Bolshevik Revolution of 1917.
3. (a) What changes in Russian society were brought about by Communist leaders during the civil war? (b) What changes in policy did Lenin make in launching the New Economic Policy?

4. (a) In what ways did the Communist Party appear to be democratic? (b) In practice, who controlled the Soviet government? (c) How were disagreements with Party policy resolved by the Politburo? (d) What organizations in Russian society were controlled by the Communist Party?

5. How did Stalin attempt to bring about (a) more rapid industrialization and (b) reorganization of agriculture? (c) What problems did Stalin's economic reorganization of industry and agriculture create?

6. (a) What groups were affected by Stalin's campaign of terror? (b) What was the effect of this program?

Reading Primary Sources

Czar Nicholas's most capable minister was Sergei Witte. In his daily work Witte had close contact with the czar. In this excerpt from *The Memoirs of Count Witte,* he describes the ruler's weaknesses. Read the passage. Then answer the questions that follow.

His Majesty . . . is afflicted with a strange nearsightedness, as far as time and space are concerned. He experiences fear only when the storm is actually upon him, but as soon as the immediate danger is over, his fear vanishes. Thus, even after the granting of the constitution, Nicholas considered himself an autocratic sovereign in a sense which might be [expressed] as follows: "I do what I wish, and what I wish is good; if people do not see it, it is because they are plain mortals, while I am God's anointed."

When, in the course of my official conferences with His Majesty, I referred to public opinion, [he] oftentimes snapped angrily: "What have I got to do with public opinion?" He considered, and justly, that public opinion was the opinion of the "intellectuals." . . .

The [czar] was made to believe that the people as a whole, exclusive of the intellectuals, stood firmly with him. That was also Her Majesty's conviction. On one occasion, discussing the political situation with the [czarina], Prince Mirski remarked that in Russia everybody was against the existing regime. To this [she] sharply replied that only the intellectuals were against the czar and his government, but that the people always had been and always would be for the czar.

(a) Why did Count Witte call Nicholas "nearsighted"? (b) What can you infer from the account about the czar's usual reaction to crisis? (c) To what event in Russian history does the phrase "the granting of the constitution" probably refer? (d) Describe the czar's views on the right of monarchs to rule. (e) Who did the czar think controlled "public opinion"? (f) Did Witte agree with him? How can you tell? (g) Why did the czar and czarina think public opinion could be disregarded?

Skill Activities

1. Placing events in time. On a separate sheet of paper, arrange the three events in each of the following sets in the correct time sequence.
(a) Defeat by the Japanese triggers an uprising in Russia.
World War I ends a brief period of economic growth.
Nicholas II establishes the Duma.
(b) Russia enters World War I.
The Bolshevik Revolution sets up a Soviet government.
The March Revolution ends czarist rule.
(c) Lenin introduces War Communism.
The New Economic Policy allows for some private enterprise.
Russia is forced to sign the Treaty of Brest-Litovsk.
(d) Stalin begins the forced collectivization of agriculture.
The first Five-Year Plan puts an end to private business.
Stalin launches a purge of his enemies.

2. Writing newspaper accounts. Write a newspaper account, such as might have appeared at the time, about one of the following: (a) the visit of Nicholas II to the troops at the front in 1915; (b) the Bolsheviks' seizure of the government in Petrograd in November, 1917; (c) the death of Lenin in 1924; (d) the public trials of prominent Soviet officials in the 1930's.

3. Relating past and present. The persecution of the Eastern Orthodox Church and other organized religious groups which began under Lenin has continued into recent times. Consult the *Readers' Guide to Periodical Literature* for articles describing the treatment of Eastern Orthodox Christians, Muslims, Jews, and other religious groups in the Soviet Union today. Prepare a short oral report summarizing your findings.

Amid economic troubles, fear of communism, and social unrest, fascist dictators came to power in Europe after World War I. The major fascist nation was Germany, where parades, like this one in Nuremberg in 1933, rallied support for Adolf Hitler's Nazi policies and programs.

31

The World
Between the Wars

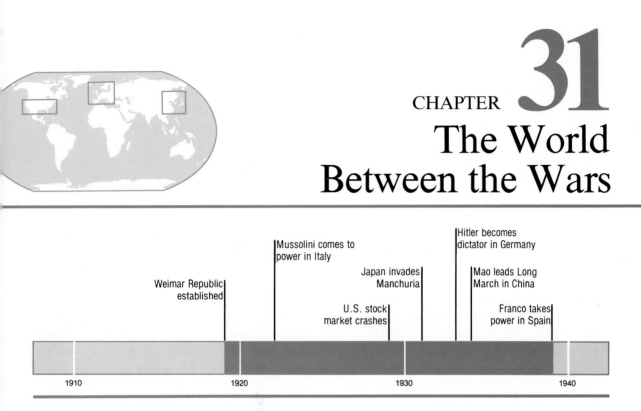

Weimar Republic
established

Mussolini comes to
power in Italy

U.S. stock
market crashes

Japan invades
Manchuria

Hitler becomes
dictator in Germany

Mao leads Long
March in China

Franco takes
power in Spain

1910   1920   1930   1940

Many people had hoped that World War I would make the world safe for democracy. At the war's end, new parliamentary governments were established in Europe. In Asia, the young Chinese Republic was struggling to unite the country. The postwar years brought serious challenges for all these new governments as well as for the more established Western democracies. In addition, many provisions of the peace settlements caused lasting bitterness and resentment, creating tensions in both Europe and Asia. The worldwide depression that began in late 1929 added economic problems to these difficulties.

People in some countries began to doubt that democratic governments could solve these problems. Because of these doubts, as well as an intense fear of the spread of communism from the Soviet Union, some people turned to authoritarian leaders. These leaders promised to restore national power and solve their nations' problems through strong state control. By the 1930's authoritarian governments controlled a number of nations.

This chapter describes the postwar years of the 1920's and 1930's and the political developments that took place in Europe and Asia.

CHAPTER OUTLINE

1   Fascism Emerges in Italy and Germany

2   Authoritarian Rule Spreads in Europe

3   The World Faces Postwar Crises

1   Fascism Emerges in Italy and Germany

In the years following World War I, Italy and Germany faced many social and economic problems. Both nations were troubled by unemployment, inflation, and social unrest. Resentment over the peace settlements lingered, and fear of the spread of Russian communism was widespread. These feelings, combined with the postwar economic problems, created a climate in which dictators could gain control in both these countries.

FASCIST ITALY

Fascism arises in Italy. Though Italy had been on the winning side in World War I, it did not seem like a victorious nation. Half a million Italian soldiers had died and a million more had been wounded. After the war, there were food shortages, rising prices, unemployment, and business failures. Few people in Italy were satisfied with the government that was in power. Workers and peasants, who had been promised social reforms, seized lands from large estates and staged violent strikes. Italian nationalists, moreover, felt that the Versailles Treaty had cheated their country of its share of German and Austrian territories.

An ideology called *fascism* (FASH-iz-um) appeared to some people to offer solutions to these problems. Fascists stressed nationalism and placed the well-being of the state above the welfare of individuals. To strengthen the nation, they insisted, authority must rest with a single strong leader and a small group of devoted party members. Rival political opinions divided and weakened a nation, they said.

Fascism was also in part a reaction to the Communist takeover in Russia. Violently opposed to Marxism, the fascists charged that Marxism divided a nation by promoting conflicts and directing people's loyalties to an international working-class movement.

Mussolini founds the Fascist Party. The leading spokesman for fascism in Italy was Benito Mussolini. Born in 1883, Mussolini taught school for a short time and then became a political journalist. In 1912 he was made editor of the Italian Socialist Party newspaper *Avanti!*. Mussolini broke with the Socialists, however, when they opposed Italy's entry into World War I. He had become a fervent nationalist and joined the army when Italy went to war in 1915.

In 1919, after the war, Mussolini and his followers organized the Fascist Party.[1] Hoping to gain control of the government, he sought support from Italian industrialists, large landowners, military leaders, and high government officials.

Fascism has a broad appeal in Italy. Fascism appealed in different ways to each of these groups. Business owners, government officials, and landowners feared the spread of communism. They wanted a strong government that would end strikes and curb working-class political power. They gave financial support to Mussolini's Fascists. Mussolini often spoke about restoring the glory and military strength of ancient Rome. This dream of a new Italian empire attracted army officers and nationalists.

The new party also had a great appeal for Italy's thousands of war veterans. Unemployed and poor, they felt as if no one cared about their wartime sacrifices. When the government failed to help them, they too became active members of the Fascist Party. The military-style discipline and organization of fascism appealed to many former soldiers. The Fascists wore black-shirted uniforms, carried weapons, paraded in the streets, and fought battles with Socialists and union members.

Fascism also proved attractive to the middle class, including university students, shopkeepers, and professional people. The Italian middle class feared the growing political power of industrial workers and the Socialist Party. They saw labor unions and socialism as threats to private property and admired the

---

[1] The word *fascist* comes from the *fasces* (FASS-eez), an ancient Roman symbol of power and authority. The *fasces* was a bundle of sticks or rods bound together around an ax.

Fascists' attacks against them. By early 1922, the Fascist Party had over 300,000 members and controlled the governments of several major Italian cities.

Mussolini gains national leadership. In October, 1922, Mussolini made his bid for national power. Speaking at a giant rally of his followers, Mussolini said, "Either they will give us the government, or we shall take it by descending on Rome." A few days later thousands of Fascists began a march on Rome.

Leaders in the Italian parliament demanded that the army be used to defend the government against the marchers, but King Victor Emmanuel III refused to act. When key officials in the government, the army, and the police sided with the Fascists, the king appointed Mussolini as prime minister, head of the Italian government.

Mussolini had often criticized democracy as a weak and ineffective system. He set to work to establish a dictatorship in which the Fascist government would have supreme control. He suppressed all other political parties, created a secret police to spy on possible enemies, and imprisoned or deported anyone who threatened his power. The government controlled the radio, the press, and the movies.

In the schools, children and teenagers were taught to admire Mussolini as *Il Duce* (eel DOO-chay), meaning "the Leader," and to accept his ideas without question. University professors had to swear an oath of loyalty to the Fascist state. "Believe! Obey! Fight!" was the Fascist slogan.

The Fascists seek to control society and the economy. As part of the Fascist program to strengthen the nation, the government made changes in social and economic life. To ensure a steady supply of soldiers, Mussolini made it difficult for Italians to leave the country. He taxed single men, limited the number of jobs open to women, and encouraged Italian families to have more children. Heads of large families received cash bonuses and government jobs.

FASCISM IN ITALY

Italy's Fascist dictator, Benito Mussolini, leads a militia parade (above). The poster (left) depicts the Fascist goal of increasing wheat production to help make Italy self-sufficient. Notice the Fascist symbol — the bundle of sticks bound around an ax.

The Fascists tried to make Italy self-sufficient economically, so that it would not have to import food and manufactured goods from other nations. To win the "battle of wheat," marshes were drained and farmers were encouraged to use modern methods of cultivation.

To control industrial production and weaken working-class political power, Mussolini attempted to reorganize the economy. All areas of production — farms, industries, transportation — were divided into 22 nationwide "syndicates," each organized like a corporation. Labor unions were abolished, and each syndicate controlled wages, prices, and working hours in its own area.

Fascist control is limited. The government-controlled Italian press, radio, and movies tried to give the impression that the Fascist government had eliminated crime, poverty, and labor problems and that the Italian economy was prospering. Mussolini proclaimed that his new Roman Empire would control the Mediterranean world. Despite this propaganda, Mussolini and the Fascists had only limited power in Italy. Industrialists, landowners, the Catholic Church, and the army retained much of their old influence and control.

FASCISM IN GERMANY

Although it faced many of the same problems, postwar Germany was in a different position than postwar Italy. The German people were puzzled by their defeat in World War I and resentful of the provisions of the Versailles Treaty. Despite its war losses, Germany was strong industrially and still had the capacity to be a great military power. When a leader emerged who promised to restore Germany's greatness, he won enthusiastic support for his totalitarian state.

Germany becomes a republic. Almost until the end of World War I, the German people had been sure that their armies would be victorious. Defeat left Germany in a state of unrest and confusion. Early in November, 1918, war-weary soldiers, sailors, and workers seized control in several German cities. A republic was proclaimed, and Kaiser William II abdicated and fled to the Netherlands. On the following day German delegates to the peace talks accepted the armistice (page 646).

An elected national assembly met in the city of Weimar (VY-mar) in February, 1919. It adopted a republican constitution and elected Friedrich Ebert (AY-behrt) as president of the republic. The new Germany, known as the Weimar Republic, was led by members of the Social Democratic Party. They were eager for democracy to succeed.

The German people, however, had little experience with parliamentary democracy. Ruled by a kaiser since Germany had been unified (page 484), the Germans were accustomed to authoritarian rule. Some considered democracy a weak form of government unsuited to the German nation.

The Weimar Republic has many critics. The Weimar Republic had many political enemies. The Communists opposed the Social Democrats and socialists who worked with the Weimar government. They wanted to set up a workers' state patterned after the new government in Soviet Russia (page 663). In 1919 Communist uprisings broke out in several German cities. These uprisings failed, but they alarmed many Germans who were already frightened by events in Russia.

At the other political extreme, the Weimar Republic was criticized by German nationalists, military leaders, industrialists, large landowners, and judges. These groups favored authoritarian rule and regarded the Social Democrats as little better than Communists. They feared that the government would take over industry and break up large estates. Militarists and nationalists spread the rumor that Germany had not truly been defeated in the war. They claimed that the leaders of the Weimar Republic had betrayed Germany by urging peace. (It had, in fact, been German army generals who had sought the armistice.) German nationalists and militarists wanted to reject the Treaty of Versailles, rebuild the German army (which the treaty forbade), and restore Germany to a position of power in world affairs. They believed that the Weimar Republic had to be destroyed if these goals were to be met.

Hitler seeks power for the Nazi Party. One of the most vigorous critics of the Weimar Republic was Adolf Hitler. Born in 1889 in a small town in Austria, Hitler quit school at sixteen and went to Vienna, hoping to become an artist. The Academy of Fine Arts rejected him for lack of talent, and Hitler spent five years drifting from job to job. He welcomed the outbreak of World War I and volunteered to serve in the German army, where he was twice decorated for bravery.

During the years in Vienna, Hitler adopted the extreme nationalistic and racist ideas that were widespread in the late nineteenth century (page 632). After the war, he joined a small nationalist political party in Munich. Its name was the National Socialist German Workers Party, but it was commonly called the Nazi Party. Demonstrating an extraordinary talent as a public speaker and organizer, Hitler quickly became the party's leader.

The Nazis gain support. With Hitler as its leader, the Nazi Party began to grow. Parades and mass rallies drew excited crowds who cheered Hitler's speeches attacking the Versailles Treaty and the Weimar government. In 1923 the Nazis tried unsuccessfully to overthrow the government of Bavaria. Hitler was sentenced to five years in jail but was released after nine months. While in jail he wrote down his political views in a book entitled *Mein Kampf* (MINE KAHMPF), or "My Struggle."

Hitler dreamed of a great German empire that would stretch across Europe and deep into the Soviet Union. His personal views and ambitions, expressed in his book, became part of Nazi thinking. He wrote in *Mein Kampf*:

History shows that the right as such does not mean a thing, unless it is backed up by great power. . . . The whole of nature is a continuous struggle between strength and weakness, an eternal victory of the strong over the weak. . . .

One is either the hammer or the anvil. We confess that it is our purpose to prepare the German people for the role of the hammer. . . .

Racism is basic to Nazi thinking. Hitler made racist thinking a basic doctrine of the Nazi ideology. Like earlier racist thinkers, he claimed that the Germans were a "master race" descended from the "Aryan" or "Nordic" people. He considered Jews, Slavs, and other peoples to be "inferior races" who weakened the nation.

Hitler's hatred for "non-Aryans" focused particularly on the Jews. Taking advantage of the anti-Semitism that already existed, Hitler accused the Jews in Germany of being responsible for all the nation's problems. The Nazis blamed the Jews for Germany's defeat in the war, for high unemployment, and for the spread of communism.

Economic problems weaken the Weimar Republic. Movements like Nazism (and leaders like Hitler) often succeed when times are hard and people are unemployed, hungry, insecure, and restless. From 1919 to 1924 the Weimar Republic faced one crisis after another. Germany came near economic collapse in 1923, when inflation made currency almost worthless. German shoppers had to carry large sacks of paper money to buy even a few groceries. The Nazis gained many followers in these years. Between 1924 and 1929, however, conditions were relatively good and the party's growth slowed.

In the fall of 1929, the world was hit by a serious economic depression. In nearly every country, trade declined, banks collapsed, and factories closed down. Prices of stocks and bonds fell drastically and businesses went bankrupt. Unemployment soared. Germany was particularly hard hit by the depression. By 1932 there were over six million people unemployed, nearly half the labor force.

Hitler gains mass support. To win popular support, Hitler issued propaganda that gave simple explanations for Germany's misfortunes. It showed him as *Der Führer* (FYOO-rur), "the Leader" who would bring Germany out of chaos. Hitler's political strategy was simple but effective. Over and over he repeated what he wanted people to believe. He gave them an enemy to hate, a cause to fight for, and a leader to obey. He played on their emotions with his spellbinding speeches and used violence to impress them with the power of the Nazi Party.

As in Italy, many people in Germany were convinced that democratic government was a failure and welcomed the idea of strong leadership. Nazism had particular appeal for the less wealthy people of the middle class — shopkeepers, small farmers, office workers, teachers, and artisans. These people felt threatened both by big business and by working-class political power. They believed Hitler would protect them both from the competition of the large industrialists and from those who might turn Germany into a Marxist state.

Young men without jobs joined the "storm troopers" (or "Brown Shirts"), Hitler's private army. There they gained a feeling of close fellowship and intense dedication to a cause — the greatness of Germany. "For us National Socialism is an idea, a faith, a religion," wrote one of them. Bands of storm troopers broke up meetings of political opponents, attacked Jews, and fought street battles with Communists.

Hitler becomes chancellor of Germany. By the end of 1932 the National Socialists had become the strongest political party in Germany, though they were still far from having a majority in the Reichstag. Viewing the Weimar Re-

Hitler's emotional speeches won him the support of many Germans who wanted a strong leader. Yet his rule was based on violence and terror.

public as inefficient and weak, a small group of influential industrialists, large landowners, bankers, and politicians conspired to put Hitler into power. Even though many disliked his views, they believed he could establish a government that would suit their interests and restore prosperity. In January, 1933, these influential Germans persuaded Paul von Hindenburg, the 86-year-old war hero who had become president of the Weimar Republic, to make Hitler chancellor.

Elections to the Reichstag were set for March, 1933. Shortly before the voting, fire swept through the Reichstag building. Hitler claimed that the fire was the beginning of a Communist takeover plot, and German voters were frightened into supporting Nazi candidates. In response to the Reichstag fire, the government also limited freedom of speech and of the press and outlawed the Communist Party.

The newly elected Reichstag gave Hitler the powers of an absolute dictator and turned Germany into a totalitarian state. Hitler proclaimed the Third Reich (RYK) as the third great empire in German history.[2] New laws banned all political parties except the Nazis, dissolved the trade unions, and set up courts for secret trials. Hitler also took control of the army. While military leaders looked on him as a troublemaker, they did nothing to prevent the Nazi takeover. Like those who had conspired to make him chancellor, the generals believed they could control Hitler.

Hitler, however, took orders from no one. He had real and imaginary enemies killed or sent to concentration camps where they were beaten and tortured. In 1934, he ordered a purge of his own storm troopers, whose rough tactics appeared threatening to army and business leaders. Led by Heinrich Himmler, Hitler's personal guards (the SS) arrested and shot about 1,000 officers. The Nazi secret police, or Gestapo, also ensured that everyone obeyed the Führer.

---

[2]The Holy Roman Empire (page 169) was considered the First Reich; Germany under the kaisers (1871–1919) was the Second Reich.

Nazism takes over in Germany. Many Germans were unaware that anything unusual was taking place in their country. Nazi terror touched only a small percentage of the people. To most Germans, life in the first few years of the Nazi regime seemed normal. The Nazis represented the legal government that they felt it was their duty to obey. Moreover, it appeared to many Germans that the Nazi government was solving the country's problems. The government aided business, started a program of public works, and secretly built armaments on a large scale. In 1937, after four years of Nazi rule, unemployment had fallen from six million to less than one million. The following year, unemployment nearly vanished, and workers' standards of living were rising. Prosperity brought Hitler the loyalty of both the common people and the industrialists.

German Jews are persecuted. The persecution of Germany's Jews grew worse, however. Anti-Semitism became official government policy. Jews lost their citizenship and were forbidden to hold government jobs, own businesses, or carry on their professions. Stores refused to sell to them; landlords refused to rent them houses or apartments. Signs reading "Jews strictly forbidden in this town" or "Jews enter this place at their own risk" were posted in many places. Many Jews fled Germany, though they were forced to leave behind most of their money and property.

When a young Jew killed a German diplomat in Paris, the Nazis used the incident as an excuse for widespread terror. On November 10, 1938, gangs of Nazis set fire to synagogues throughout Germany and vandalized Jewish homes and stores. Many Jews were killed or wounded, and thousands were arrested during this *Kristallnacht* (kris-TAHL-nahkt), "the night of broken glass."

Some Germans oppose Hitler. Some Germans objected to Hitler's policies and were horrified by the Nazi persecutions. For instance, Martin Niemöller, a Lutheran pastor, organized a group of clergy to openly resist the Nazi regime. He and some other members of the group eventually were sent to concentration camps for their views. Many others were frightened into silence like their fellow Germans.

Jewish shop owners inspect the damage done by Nazi raiders on *Kristallnacht,* November 10, 1938. This anti-Jewish violence came in response to the killing of the German diplomat Ernst von Rath.

The Nazis use propaganda to retain control. The Nazis had used propaganda to come to power. Once they were in control, they used propaganda to strengthen their hold on the German people. The radio, newspapers and magazines, films, books, art, and the schools were all used to impress Nazi beliefs on the German people. Children and young people were made to feel proud of joining the Hitler Youth, the Nazi training group for young people. The Nazis burned books that praised democracy or denounced war, as well as those by Jewish authors. History was rewritten to fit Nazi views. Science books described the "superiority" of the "Nordic race."

By 1938, many German people saw things in Nazi Germany that pleased them. Businesses were thriving, workers were employed, and the

German armed forces had been rebuilt. Hitler had made the world take note of the new Germany. Few Germans, however, envisioned the long-range effect that Nazi rule would have on their country.

CHECK-UP

1. Vocabulary: *fascism.*
2. (a) What postwar conditions caused unrest in Italy? (b) Which groups were particularly discontented with the government?
3. How did Mussolini win the support of (a) business owners? (b) war veterans? (c) the middle class? (d) How did the Fascists try to reorganize the economy?
4. (a) How was the Weimar Republic established? (b) What groups were critical of it?
5. (a) What were Hitler's goals? (b) How did anti-Semitism become part of his thinking?
6. (a) What made Nazism appealing to many Germans? (b) What methods did Hitler use to gain popular support and political control? (c) How did most Germans view the Nazi government? (d) What kinds of persecution did Jews undergo in Germany in the 1930's?

2 Authoritarian Rule Spreads in Europe

The lingering problems left by World War I were made worse by a worldwide economic crisis in the early 1930's. One response to these conditions was the rise of fascist dictatorships in Italy and Germany. This marked the beginning of a return to authoritarian rule in much of Europe and a critical challenge to the new democracies.

New democracies fail in Eastern Europe. The peace treaties ending World War I set up new governments in parts of Eastern and Central Europe. Most of them were organized on parliamentary principles like governments in Western Europe. Eastern Europe, however, did not have a tradition of political democracy. Most of the new states had agricultural economies and little industry. Except for Czechoslovakia, they also lacked a sizable population of business and professional people, who were supporters of liberal, democratic ideas in Western Europe. When the new governments were unable to solve postwar problems quickly, people viewed democracy itself as a failure and accepted a return to authoritarian rule.

In the first fifteen years after the war, nearly all the new parliamentary democracies in Eastern Europe were replaced by authoritarian regimes. In Hungary, a republic was replaced by the Leninist dictator Béla Kun after only a few months. In 1919, Admiral Miklos Horthy (HOHR-tee) established another authoritarian government dominated by military leaders and landowners. In Poland, Joseph Pilsudski (pil-SOOT-skee), a popular war hero, seized power in 1926 and set up a similar regime. In 1931 Rumania's King Carol set up a dictatorship. In 1933 and 1934, Chancellor Engelbert Dollfuss dissolved the Austrian parliament, arrested socialists and trade union officials, and bombarded the workers' districts in Vienna. Military officers overthrew Bulgaria's government and outlawed political parties in 1934. The Greeks established a republic in 1924 but by the mid-1930's were ruled by the military dictatorship of Joannes Metaxas.

Only Czechoslovakia preserved the democratic government set up in 1918 under the leadership of Thomas Masaryk and Eduard Beneš (BEH-nesh). The new republic's stability, however, was threatened by the many nationality groups within Czechoslovakia. Nazi activities also caused unrest along the Czech-German border.

Communist parties grew up in many European countries after the Russian Revolution, but no other successful Communist governments were established. Fascism, however, continued to gain supporters in both Eastern and Western Europe, and other fascist dictatorships were established.

The Spanish monarchy is challenged. Since the Spanish-American War in 1898, the Spanish government, a constitutional monarchy, had been under attack by various groups within the country. Some wanted Spain to be a republic. Others were angered at the government's restrictions on the Catholic Church.

Because Spain remained neutral, its industry expanded during World War I, and an industrial working class grew up. After the war, workers in the northeast, around the city of Barcelona, began to demand independence for that region. Widespread industrial strikes led to violence in which hundreds of people were killed or wounded. In 1923, fearing a revolution, King Alfonso XIII allowed General Miguel Primo de Rivera (PREE-moh day ree-VAY-rah) to take power as a military dictator. Primo de Rivera dismissed the parliament, suppressed freedom of speech, and censored the press. Unrest continued, however. Discouraged by ill health and lack of support from the army, Primo de Rivera resigned in 1930.

In 1931 the king restored the constitution. In the elections that followed, supporters of a republic won overwhelmingly and demanded that King Alfonso abdicate. Alfonso fled to France, and a republic was declared in Spain. The new republican government immediately passed laws to limit the power and privileges of the Catholic Church, the landlords, and the army. The republican government tried to reduce the influence of the Catholic Church by taking over its property, closing Catholic schools, and permitting divorce. It cut back the number of army officers, confiscated large estates, and gave land to needy peasants. Workers were given an eight-hour working day and a program of social insurance.

The Popular Front opposes conservative rule. These reforms intensified the opposition of those who had previously been most influential — army officers, landowners, and the Catholic Church. Many joined a fascist-type party called the Falange (fuh-LANJ). In 1933 these conservatives won the elections and repealed many of the reforms. Supporters of the republic feared that the new leaders would restore the monarchy and turn Spain into a fascist state. Strikes broke out as workers pro-

tested, and several regions of Spain declared their independence.

To preserve the republic, all the anti-fascist groups joined in an alliance called the Popular Front. It included liberals, Socialists, Communists, and radical labor groups. In the elections of February, 1936, the Popular Front won an impressive victory.

Civil war breaks out. In July, 1936, Falangist army officers in Spanish Morocco rebelled, and revolts quickly broke out all over Spain. By October, the rebel soldiers had proclaimed General Francisco Franco head of a fascist Spanish state. Bitter civil war raged in Spain for three years between Franco's Falangists and the supporters of the Spanish republic. Hundreds of thousands of people were killed or wounded, and atrocities were committed by both sides during the war.

The Spanish Civil War was made more intense by the intervention of foreign nations. To encourage the spread of fascism, both Hitler and Mussolini sent aid to Franco. Italy sent troops, while ships and planes from Germany bombarded Spanish cities. The Soviet Union

Civil war left Spanish cities and villages in ruins. To aid Spain's fascists, Nazi Germany sent planes and ships to bombard republican forces.

sent help to the republic, and Communists formed a strong group within the republican forces. While their governments stayed out of the war, thousands of volunteers from Britain, France, and the United States flocked to Spain to join a republican force known as the International Brigade.

The supporters of the republic were no match for the fascist forces, however. In 1939 Madrid fell to Franco. Spain came under a fascist dictatorship that lasted until Franco's death in 1975.

CHECK-UP

1. (a) What conditions in Eastern Europe made it difficult for democracy to succeed? (b) How did the situation in Czechoslovakia differ?
2. (a) What were the goals of the Spanish republican leaders? (b) What three groups made up the conservative opposition to the republic? (c) What groups formed the Popular Front?
3. (a) Why did Hitler and Mussolini support Franco? (b) What nation officially aided the republican forces? (c) What was the International Brigade?

3 The World Faces Postwar Crises

Most of the nations of the world faced social problems and economic difficulties in the years after World War I. In response, many nations in Europe and in Asia turned to various forms of authoritarian rule. Fascism spread in Europe, communism gained a foothold in China, and military leaders assumed control in Japan. The well-established democratic nations — the United States, Britain, and France — found other ways to deal with difficulties growing out of a worldwide depression.

THE WESTERN DEMOCRACIES

People in the United States seek peace and prosperity. After World War I, people in the

United States turned their backs on President Wilson's plan for a lasting peace. The Senate did not ratify the Treaty of Versailles, and the United States did not join the League of Nations. Americans wanted to "return to normalcy," to enjoy prosperity at home and avoid involvement in European affairs.

In the 1920's the United States was prospering. Just before the war, assembly-line methods for producing cars had been devised by Henry Ford. Now these methods were used in the production of other goods for consumers. Americans bought great quantities of the new products coming off assembly lines. Between 1919 and 1929, the number of cars on American roads almost quadrupled. Vacuum cleaners, electric toasters, telephones, refrigerators, washing machines, and a popular new invention — the radio — became common in American homes. Profits of American businesses soared, and the standard of living increased for many people.

Signs of economic trouble appear. Not all Americans had a share in the success and prosperity of the 1920's. The nation's farmers in particular faced severe hardships. Although improved seeds and machinery enabled farmers to produce more on the same amount of land, they were already producing more food than people could buy. As the food supply rose, food prices fell. Farm incomes declined, thus causing many farms to fail.

Other Americans were unemployed or earned too little to buy the products of industry. Although profits in industry were high, this prosperity was not reflected in higher wages for workers. Eventually factories were producing more goods than Americans could buy, and they had to cut production and lay off workers.

Another weakness in the economy of the 1920's was the tremendous increase in installment buying. Advertisements persuaded Americans to "buy now, pay later." That is, they

Selling Success in the 1920's

The booming prosperity of the 1920's brought a flood of new products for consumers to buy — and an intense effort to find new ways to sell them. Manufacturers looked for methods to persuade buyers to choose their brand of cars, radios, toothpaste, electric refrigerators, or books on self-improvement. Advertising writers and artists devised techniques still used today — colorful photographs, catchy slogans, testimonials by famous and glamorous people. Advertising dollars supported the fast-growing new medium of radio. Soap manufacturers sponsored daytime dramas (later called "soap operas"), while grocery stores paid for broadcasts of dance music.

The most phenomenal success story of the 1920's was in the automobile industry. Car makers spent millions of dollars on magazine and newspaper advertising to introduce new models of sleekly styled, rainbow-colored cars.

The advertisements were so successful that, by the end of the decade, the number of cars on American roads had nearly quadrupled.

Landmarks in Technology

TWENTIETH-CENTURY COMMUNICATIONS

From discoveries made by scientists and inventors in the late nineteenth century came a flood of new developments that radically changed life in the decades after World War I. A major change was the development of mass communications — ways of sending news, entertainment, and information to millions of people at once, by means of the radio, motion pictures, and the stories and photographs in popular magazines and newspapers. Communications became faster also, through both the telephone and the radio, which came to be widely used in the United States for the first time in the 1920's and 1930's. Advances in technology made all these devices inexpensive and readily available, bringing people closer together and speeding up transactions in business and everyday life.

Motion-picture photography made great advances in the early 1900's, and "moviemaking" soon became commercially successful. At left, Charlie Chaplin — famous as both an actor and a director — films a scene from *The Gold Rush,* made in 1925. Photographers also began to use their cameras to tell a story and record events in everyday life. Popular picture magazines such as *Life* and *Look* published the work of photojournalists like Dorothea Lange (above), whose photographs vividly showed rural American life during the Depression years.

Inventor Thomas Alva Edison (page 526) contributed greatly to the changes in people's lives. His phonograph, patented in 1877, became a popular form of home entertainment by the early 1900's.

Fast communication made possible by the telephone contributed to the business prosperity of the 1920's. At left, an executive in the flourishing motion-picture industry uses the "candlestick" phone typical of that era.

The first commercial radio station went on the air in 1920, and within two years radio had become a national pastime, offering music, news, adventure series (like "The Lone Ranger"), and daytime dramas known as "soap operas" (because their sponsors were soap manufacturers). The first American President to make extensive use of radio to speak to the public was Franklin D. Roosevelt (right), shown making a broadcast speech in 1934.

could buy goods by paying a small amount and promising to pay the remaining cost in small installments. Americans bought cars, furniture, and household appliances on credit. In time many people owed thousands of dollars in installments. When they could not pay their debts, they stopped buying. Factories again had to cut back production, and unemployment once again rose.

Unemployment rose sharply from 1929 to 1932 and leveled off during 1933. Steel production declined from 1929 to 1932 but increased in 1933.

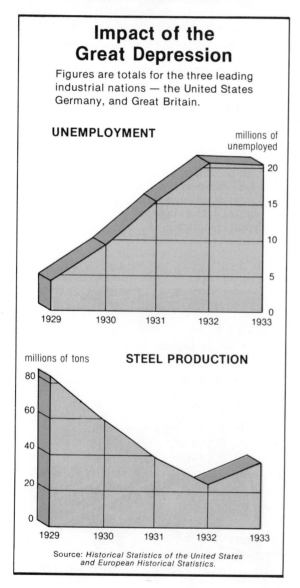

Impact of the Great Depression

Figures are totals for the three leading industrial nations — the United States Germany, and Great Britain.

UNEMPLOYMENT

millions of unemployed

STEEL PRODUCTION

millions of tons

Source: *Historical Statistics of the United States and European Historical Statistics.*

The stock market crashes. A great many Americans were also buying stocks — that is, shares in the ownership of corporations — on credit. An investor could pay only a fraction of the cost of the stock and use credit for the rest. If the stock rose in price quickly, the investor could sell it and make a handsome profit even after paying back the borrowed money. People in all income groups invested in the stock market. As more money was invested, stock prices soared.

This economic "boom" sent prices of stocks higher and higher. In October, 1929, however, stock prices began to fall sharply. Panicky investors hurried to get rid of their stock while it was still worth something. The "crash" came on October 29, and stock prices continued to fall. By the middle of November, stocks were selling for half (or less) of their September prices. Thousands of investors, particularly those who had bought stock on credit, were wiped out financially.

The Depression has a great impact. The collapse of the stock market set off a chain of events that affected all Americans. Those who had lost their money in the stock market crash could no longer afford to buy new goods. Already producing more than they could sell, factories cut production and laid off more and more workers. Unemployed workers could not meet installment payments. Banks had also been caught in the economic "boom" of the 1920's and had made many bad investments. To stay in business, they began to demand that people repay loans. Few banks could collect anywhere near the amount that they had loaned. By 1933 nearly a third of the nation's banks had closed down, at least temporarily. The United States economy moved into the worst depression in its history. The period is still known as the Great Depression.

The Great Depression in the United States added to the world's economic troubles. Badly in need of money, American investors withdrew the capital they had invested in Europe. European banks and businesses also failed. International trade declined. A number of countries raised tariffs on imports in order to protect their own industries, hurting trade still more.

The desperation of this unemployed British office worker was typical of the feeling among those who could not find jobs during the 1930's.

Deprived of foreign customers, American industries were forced to cut production even further and to lay off more workers. Unemployment increased around the world, especially in industrial nations.

Roosevelt introduces a new program for the economy. When President Franklin D. Roosevelt took office in 1933, over thirteen million Americans — 25 percent of the labor force — were out of work. Many people were hungry and homeless, and the nation's mood was one of despair. Roosevelt began a vigorous experimental program of economic reform known as the New Deal. It sought to solve the problems of the Depression through democratic processes and institutions.

President Roosevelt believed that the government had a responsibility to protect the well-being of its citizens. Under the New Deal the federal government played a larger part in the economic life of the country than it ever had before. To restore confidence in the financial community, the government established rules for banking and for the sale of stocks. Such regulations would help protect investors' funds and would ensure against future bank

failures or stock market crashes. The government provided help for the unemployed and set up programs that created jobs. It encouraged farmers to cut back food production so that farm prices would rise. The New Deal also aided organized labor. Laws were passed to protect workers' rights to join unions. The Social Security Act assured an income for the elderly and the unemployed.

Britain also faces economic problems. In the years after World War I, Britain faced staggering economic problems. Britain was dependent on foreign trade, but many of its merchant ships had been lost in the war and it was losing markets to other trading nations. As exports dropped, British industry, mining, and shipbuilding declined, and unemployment soared. Outdated machinery and equipment also slowed production and made costs greater.

Britain's coal industry was particularly hard hit, as the rapid development of water power and oil reduced other countries' demand for British coal. To reduce their costs, mineowners called for wage cuts for the miners. To protest wage cuts, the miners' union went on strike in 1926. The protest soon grew into a nationwide general strike as workers in transportation and other unions struck in sympathy with the miners. The general strike involved nearly three million workers, almost half the British labor force.

While the general strike demonstrated the unity of the British working class, the rest of the population had little sympathy for the striking workers. Many feared that the strikers represented Communist revolutionaries trying to overthrow the government. Union leaders ended the strike after nine days, but the miners stayed on strike for another six months, undergoing great hardships. The general strike brought violence and upheaval in Britain, but its ending reassured people that the basic government structure was not in danger. British workers did not benefit from the general strike, however. The miners had to settle for longer hours and lower wages. In addition, some antilabor laws were passed.

British economic problems grew even worse during the depression. Britain did not adopt a broad program like the New Deal, however. The government provided unemployment insurance and relief payments for the poor, but it did little to stimulate industry or reduce unemployment.

None of Britain's political parties could find effective ways of solving all the country's problems at home and abroad. In 1931, therefore, they formed a *coalition* government, in which the ministers represented all major parties: Liberal, Labour, and Conservative. Rival political leaders in the coalition government attempted to forget their differences and unite behind the prime minister, Ramsay Mac-Donald.

The Empire becomes a Commonwealth of Nations. The British government also had to make major decisions about the widespread territories of the British Empire. By the time of World War I, several former British colonies had become self-governing dominions within the Empire. They had their own tax systems, military forces, and currencies. In 1931, Parliament enacted the Statute of Westminster, which defined a new relationship between Britain and these dominions. Canada, Newfoundland, Australia, New Zealand, and the Union of South Africa became part of a Commonwealth of Nations. The British Parliament had no authority over the Commonwealth nations. These nations were equal members with Great Britain, sharing a common loyalty to the British monarch.

The Irish seek self-government. Another member of the new Commonwealth was the Irish Free State, or Eire (AYR-uh). It had become a dominion only in 1922, amid violence and controversy. The question of Irish "home rule," or independence, had troubled Ireland and England for centuries. Irish nationalists, mainly Roman Catholic, sought independence. Many Protestant Irish in the north, who were a minority in the country, wanted to remain a part of Britain.

The Irish nationalist movement grew stronger, and rebellion broke out in Dublin in Easter week, 1916. British troops suppressed the Easter Rebellion, and its leaders were executed. Bitterness and violence between the Irish and the British continued. In 1921, Ireland was divided. Northern Ireland, or Ulster, remained a part of Great Britain and was represented in the British Parliament. The rest of the country became the Irish Free State. Many Irish nationalists, however, opposed Ireland's becoming a dominion. Led by Eamon De Valera (deh-vah-LAIR-uh), they continued to seek complete independence from Britain.

France seeks repayment for war damage. Like Britain, postwar France faced economic problems, which were made worse by the devastation caused by four years of warfare on French soil. Villages, farms, and railroads had been destroyed. Retreating Germans had wrecked mines, factories, forests, and orchards. In addition, millions of young Frenchmen had been killed or wounded.

To help them rebuild, the French had counted on Germany's payment of reparations (page 648). In 1922, however, the Weimar government announced it could pay no more. Angry, the French sent an army to take possession of the German coal mines and steel mills along the Ruhr River. The occupation increased national tensions in Europe and caused great economic hardship in Germany. Finally, in 1924, an international commission worked out a compromise, the Dawes Plan. Germany agreed to make payments based on its economic prosperity.

The French government took other steps to rebuild its economy quickly. Industrial and agricultural production increased, and growing numbers of tourists contributed to France's economic recovery in the 1920's. The Depression, however, ended this prosperity.

The French government is unstable. In addition to economic troubles, the Third Republic had been politically unstable since its establishment (page 483). France's many political parties could not work together to find remedies for the country's problems. Disenchanted with the government, many French voters turned either to the Communists or to one of the fascist groups that were gaining political strength.

Fear of a fascist takeover led a number of leftist political parties to unite in the Popular

Front.[3] The coalition pledged to defend the French republic against aristocrats, the military, and the clergy. In the election of 1936 the Popular Front, led by Socialist Léon Blum, won a majority in the French assembly.

Blum's government took some ideas from the New Deal program in the United States. To end a wave of strikes that had tied up production, workers' complaints were answered. They were given a forty-hour week, paid holidays, and the right to collective bargaining. To reduce the influence of the wealthiest families, Blum put the Bank of France under government control. He also prepared the way for partial government control of France's armaments industry.

While Blum's government passed notable social reforms, it could not revitalize the French economy and remained in office only a short time. Its reforms angered industrialists and the upper classes. Moreover, the civil war in neighboring Spain caused more political disagreement between factions. By the late 1930's, France was a divided nation, beset by strikes and economic problems and threatened by the growing power of fascist Germany and Italy.

POSTWAR UNREST IN ASIA

China and Japan clash over the Shantung Peninsula. While both China and Japan had joined the Allies in World War I, they had done so for conflicting reasons. Japan, a British ally, had made secret treaties with the West regarding its claims to German territories in China and the Pacific. At the peace conference after the war, Japan counted on the Western nations to support its claims to former German bases in China's Shantung Peninsula. The new republican government in China, on the other hand, hoped for Western support against Japanese aggression. Already weakened by civil war among rival warlords, China was expecting American help in particular.

Unwilling to become involved, the European Allies made no decision about Shantung and left the question to be settled between Japan and China.[4] The angry Chinese left the peace conference and refused to sign the Versailles Treaty. Although the Japanese also resented the decision, they signed the treaty and, in addition, they strongly supported the new League of Nations.

Chinese nationalists seek to strengthen the country. Chinese leaders felt that, in the peace settlements, the West had once again taken advantage of their country's weaknesses. On May 4, 1919, university students and teachers in Peking began demonstrations. They demanded an end to foreign interference, Japanese aggression, and the power of the warlords, and called for nationalism and democracy. In some places, protesters boycotted Japanese products. The May Fourth Movement grew as other students, professionals, workers, manufacturers, and shopkeepers joined the protests.

Reform movements of other kinds also were started in China in the postwar years. The growth of industry created a working class that began to organize unions. Workers' protests often were aimed at foreign owners, both European and Japanese. Movements were also started to encourage literacy, broaden the system of education, and simplify the Chinese written language.

Sun Yat-sen accepts Communist help. Sun Yat-sen and his Kuomintang, or Nationalist, party, had been unable to set up a central government because of the power of the warlords (page 577). Sun had hoped for aid from the Western nations after the war. Only the Comintern, however, representing the Communist government of the Soviet Union, offered China military and political help. In 1923, Sun made

---

[3]The Popular Fronts in both France and Spain were coalitions of several "leftist" groups. The terms *left* and *right* in politics come from the seating arrangements in many European parliaments, where those with liberal or radical views sit on the left side of the assembly hall and conservative members sit on the right. Both terms are used very broadly today.

[4]In 1922, Japan, China, and the Western nations met in Washington to discuss Asia. They agreed to limit their navies and reaffirmed the "open door" policy for China (page 575). At that time, Japan agreed to return the German bases to China.

an agreement with the Comintern. In return for that help, he allowed Chinese Communists to join the Kuomintang.

The Nationalists establish a government. When Sun died in 1925, Chiang Kai-shek (JYAHNG ky-SHEK), his hand-picked successor, became head of the Kuomintang. Chiang and other Nationalists distrusted the Chinese Communists and the Soviet advisers. Their first goal, however, was to establish one government in China. Chiang led the army northward, defeated the warlords, and moved the capital to Nanking. By 1928, his troops had taken Peking and controlled much of eastern China. Other nations recognized Chiang's organization as the official government of China.

At the same time, Chiang was taking action against the Communists. In 1927 the Soviet advisers were expelled from China. Chiang also carried out a purge of the Chinese Communists in the Kuomintang, killing many of them and driving the rest into hiding.

The government works to make changes. The Nationalist government tried to strengthen and modernize China. It reorganized the banking system to attract foreign and local investment. The old "unequal treaties" with the West were abolished. Communication and transportation were improved, and by the 1930's, China's coastal cities were bustling centers of business and manufacturing.

Much of China, however, was unchanged and disunited. Warlords still held power in remote regions. In the agricultural interior, tenant farmers still worked the fields of large landowners. Chiang and his followers had support from the landlords, industrialists, and other wealthy Chinese and Westerners. Their plans did not include reforms for the workers and peasants, and they ignored Sun's promise to distribute land among the peasants.

Chinese Communists plan a new revolution. During the early 1930's many who had supported Chiang became disillusioned with his government's policies and lack of social reforms. Many left the Kuomintang and joined the Communists who had survived Chiang's purge in 1927. Driven into hiding in the hills of Hunan (in south-central China), the Communists were establishing a base for revolution.

Nationalist leader Chiang Kai-shek waged a vigorous campaign against Communists in China.

Their leader was a young Communist named Mao Tse-tung (MAH-oh dzuh-DOONG). While Marxism and Soviet Communism had depended on urban industrial workers, Mao looked for support from the discontented Chinese peasants. Despite the peasants' distrust of outsiders, Mao drew many of them into his Red Army, which was trained in methods of guerrilla warfare.

Chiang forces the Communists into the Long March. Chiang continued his attempts to destroy the Communists, using the warlords' armies as well as government troops. In 1934, Nationalist troops armed with heavy artillery surrounded the Communist base — a settlement of about 100,000 men, women, and children in mountainous Kiangsi province. Those who managed to escape began a journey under Mao's leadership that became famous as the Long March.

The Long March began in October, 1934, in the southern part of Kiangsi province. It ended one year and nearly 6,000 miles later in Yenan (Shensi province) in the hills of northwestern China. The route led through rugged mountains and deserts. Nationalist planes bombed the marchers, and thousands starved or died from disease. Fewer than 20,000 people are thought to have completed the Long March.

Changes in Japan increase its aggression against China. The strength and endurance of the Chinese Communist movement was only one of the serious threats to Chiang's government. Japan had already begun to build an empire in Asia. In the years after World War I, economic problems and political changes made Japan's leaders even more determined to gain Chinese territory.

In the 1920's, many people in Japan began to question their country's traditional society and values. Industrialization and contact with Europe had encouraged many Japanese to welcome new ways and Western political ideas. All Japanese men gained the right to vote in 1925, political parties grew in power, workers and farmers formed unions, and young women sought more freedom. The government tolerated the reform movements, feeling sure it could control them.

The worldwide depression that began in 1929 was disastrous for Japan. The island nation depended heavily on international trade for both markets and raw materials. Now trade declined, and many nations established high tariffs. Japan's lucrative silk market in the United States decreased by almost 70 percent and its rice market was cut in half. This caused severe unemployment among Japanese textile workers and farmers. The country was already using every available plot of land to produce food. Moreover, it simply did not have the coal, oil and iron ore needed for heavy industry.

All of these problems played into the hands of Japan's military leaders, who had always advocated expansion. Japan had already gained territory in China and the Pacific and had annexed Korea. The establishment of the Nationalist government in China, however, seemed to threaten Japan's interests there. Moreover, the Japanese resented Western nations' attempts to limit Japan's power in Asia. Their resentment of the United States was made worse by the passage in 1924 of the "Oriental Exclusion Act," a law that limited the immigration of Asians to the United States.

Military leaders take control. A group of militaristic officers in the Japanese army determined to take control. In September, 1931, Japanese officers stationed in Manchuria staged an explosion on a railway line near Mukden. Blaming the incident on the Chinese, these troops defeated the local warlord's army and quickly occupied Manchuria. Rich in coal and iron ore, this large province supplied Japan with some of the raw materials needed by its industries. The Japanese set up a state they called Manchukuo and built industries and military bases there.

In Japan itself, military leaders were taking more and more control over the government and its policies during the 1930's. Like leaders in Germany and Italy, they charged that moderate policies weakened the nation. They also used threats, terror, and assassination to silence any political leaders who sought to oppose them.

CHECK-UP

1. Vocabulary: *coalition.*
2. (a) Why did many people in the United States enjoy a high standard of living during the 1920's? (b) What were the weaknesses in this prosperity?
3. (a) What caused the stock market crash of 1929? (b) How did this affect other nations?
4. (a) What was the aim of the New Deal programs? (b) How did the New Deal help the unemployed?
5. (a) What economic problems faced Great Britain after World War I? (b) What were the results of the general strike? (c) What problems arose between Britain and Ireland?
6. (a) What was the purpose of the Popular Front in France? (b) What steps did Blum take to solve the nation's problems? (c) What problems did France face by the late 1930's?
7. (a) What issue from World War I caused conflict between Japan and China? (b) What problems did the Kuomintang face in establishing a government? (c) How did Chiang deal with the Chinese Communists? (d) What group did Mao appeal to?
8. (a) Why did the depression hit Japan so severely? (b) What was the Mukden incident? (c) What were its results?

Chapter 31 Review

Summary

In the years after World War I, nations in Europe and Asia faced economic problems and the resentments left by the peace settlements. Fascism, a political ideology based on ideas of extreme nationalism and militarism, gained popularity. Fascism as a political force emerged first in Italy in 1919, when Benito Mussolini founded the Fascist Party. Mussolini set up a dictatorship that attempted to control social and economic life. Germany's anger over the Versailles Treaty gave Adolf Hitler the opportunity to gain power for the National Socialist, or Nazi, Party. Using violence and terror, the Nazis established a totalitarian dictatorship in Germany. Fascist ideas also spread elsewhere in Europe in the 1920's and 1930's. New democracies established after the war collapsed, and authoritarian rulers returned to power. Civil war in Spain ended with victory for the fascists led by Franco.

Economic problems, particularly the worldwide depression of the 1930's, troubled the older Western democracies. The United States, Britain, and France made social and economic changes, and their democratic institutions survived the crises.

Postwar crises affected Asia as well. The Chinese Nationalists, or Kuomintang, established a government that unified part of China. The Chinese Communists, however, drew on peasant support to remain a constant challenge. In Japan, militarists gained control of the government in the 1930's and concentrated on building an empire in Asia.

Vocabulary Review

1. Write the following sentences on a sheet of paper. In each sentence, fill in the blank with one of these words: *coalition, fascism, guerrilla warfare, propaganda, totalitarian.*
(a) __?__ is a political ideology that promotes extreme nationalism and militarism and places the well-being of the state above the welfare of individuals.
(b) Hitler created a __?__ state in which he held complete control and mobilized the German people to support his goals.

(c) Mao Tse-tung trained his Red Army in the tactics of __?__ — sudden surprise attacks by small groups of soldiers.
(d) Leaders of several political parties cooperate in forming a __?__ government.
(e) The __?__ distributed by Mussolini tried to give the impression that his Fascist government had solved Italy's problems.
2. Distinguish between the terms in each of the following pairs:
(a) Weimar Republic; Third Reich.
(b) *Il Duce; Der Führer.*
(c) Falange; Popular Front.
3. Explain the relationship between the terms in each of the following pairs:
(a) Great Depression; New Deal.
(b) Statute of Westminster; Commonwealth of Nations.
(c) Manchukuo; Manchuria.

People to Identify

Match the following people with the numbered phrases that describe them: *Léon Blum, Chiang Kai-shek, Eamon De Valera, Engelbert Dollfuss, Francisco Franco, Paul von Hindenburg, Joseph Pilsudski, Franklin D. Roosevelt.*
1. The Austrian chancellor who dissolved the parliament in 1933.
2. The socialist leader of France's Popular Front in 1936.
3. The German president who appointed Hitler chancellor.
4. The Polish war hero who seized power in 1926.
5. The American President who began reforms to end the Great Depression of the 1930's.
6. A leader of the Irish nationalist movement.
7. Leader of the victorious fascist forces in the Spanish Civil War.
8. The leader of the Kuomintang Party in China in the 1930's.

Relating Geography and History

1. **Using maps.** (a) On the world map at the back of this book (pages 858–859), locate the following original members of the Commonwealth of Nations: Britain, Canada, Australia,

New Zealand, Ireland, South Africa. (b) Another original member was Newfoundland. Why is Newfoundland no longer a member? (Look for the answer in an almanac or encyclopedia.)

2. Map research. Follow the route of Mao Tsetung's Long March (pages 690–691) on the map on page 760. (a) In what province did the journey start? (b) In what province did it end? (c) Using the scale on the map, estimate how far the marchers traveled. (d) Use the library to find an encyclopedia or atlas map that shows the physical features of China. Write a paragraph describing the terrain the marchers covered.

Discussion Questions

1. What conditions in (a) Italy and (b) Germany made fascism attractive to many people after World War I?

2. (a) What criticisms were made of the government of the Weimar Republic? (b) How did Hitler make use of the effects of the worldwide depression to gain political advantage? (c) What groups supported Hitler's drive for power?

3. (a) What attitudes did many Europeans hold toward Jews in the early 1900's? (b) How did Hitler take advantage of these attitudes? (c) What rights were taken from German Jews once Hitler came to power?

4. In what ways were the failures of the new democratic governments in Eastern Europe similar to events in Italy and Germany?

5. (a) How did World War I increase demands for the end of monarchy in Spain? (b) Why did the Falange oppose the republican government? (c) What part did foreign countries play in the Spanish Civil War?

6. (a) What conditions caused the Great Depression in the United States? (b) What steps were taken to solve the problems brought by the Depression?

7. Compare the efforts made by Great Britain and France to overcome the economic problems of the years after World War I.

8. (a) How did Britain's relationship with its former colonies change in 1931? (b) What factors complicated Ireland's becoming a dominion?

9. (a) How did Mao and the Communists gain followers in China during the 1930's? (b) What other problems faced the Chinese government?

10. How did postwar conditions and international events help military leaders come to power in Japan in the 1930's?

Reading Primary Sources

In 1932, Benito Mussolini wrote an article for an encyclopedia explaining his concept of fascism. Read the excerpt from that article reprinted below. Then answer the questions that follow.

> . . . Above all, fascism . . . believes neither in the possibility of nor the . . . [usefulness] of perpetual peace. It thus [rejects] the doctrine of pacifism. [Pacifism is] born of a . . . [rejection] of struggle and [is] an act of cowardice in the face of sacrifice. War alone brings up to its highest tension all human energy and puts the stamp of nobility upon the people who have the courage to meet it. . . . The fascist accepts life and loves it [and] . . . conceives of life as a duty [of] struggle and conquest. Life . . . should be high and full, lived for oneself, but above all for others. . . .

(a) According to Mussolini, how do fascists regard peace? (b) What phrases does Mussolini use to make war sound more honorable than peace? (c) What other phrases in the passage were probably intended to make the reader think favorably of fascism?

Skill Activities

1. Analyzing statistics. The statistics in the table below show the percentage of German workers who were unemployed during the period from 1927 to 1937.

Year	Percentage	Year	Percentage
1927	8.8	1933	26.3
1929	13.1	1935	11.6
1931	23.3	1937	4.6

Use these figures to answer the following questions: (a) What percentage of the German work force was unemployed in 1927? (b) In what year did unemployment reach its highest level? (c) How much did unemployment decline from the year Hitler came to power (1933) to 1937? (d) How might Hitler have used these figures?

2. Word research. Both in France and in Spain a number of political parties joined forces in a "Popular Front." *Popular* is from the Latin word *populus,* meaning "people." Using a dictionary, find five other words that come from this root word. How is each word related to the idea of "people"?

The great British fighting ship *Prince of Wales,* along with the *Repulse,* was sunk in the Pacific by Japanese planes in December, 1941. The battle, shown in this painting by a Japanese artist, demonstrated the new importance of aircraft in naval warfare.

CHAPTER **32**

World War II

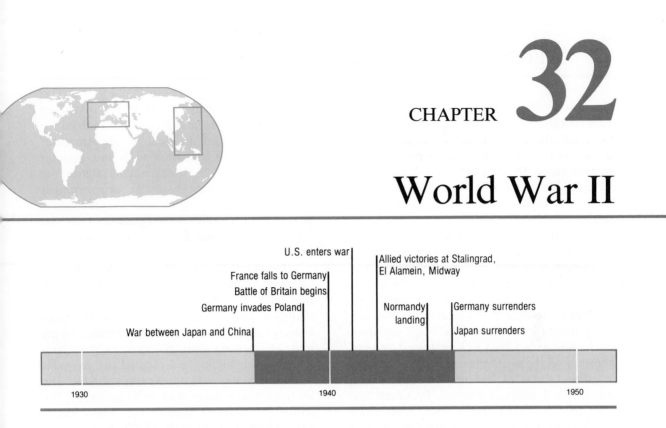

Although international efforts were made to keep peace in the decades after World War I, the world was soon caught up in another widespread and destructive conflict. World War II involved far more of the world's peoples than the earlier war, causing major changes around the globe.

In Europe World War II grew out of Hitler's determination to create a new German empire that would dominate the continent. Britain and France at first did little to halt German aggression, but they reluctantly went to war in 1939. In Asia the expansionist aims of Japan's military leaders led to conquests in the eastern Pacific and brought the United States into the war in 1941. The Axis powers — Germany, Japan, and Italy — won many battles in the early years of the war, but the tide turned in 1942 to bring victory to the Allied nations.

This chapter describes the events in Europe leading to World War II, the early Axis successes in the war, the outbreak of the war in the Pacific, and the eventual Allied victory.

CHAPTER OUTLINE

1   Aggression Leads to War in Europe and Asia

2   Europe Falls to Axis Forces

3   War Breaks Out in the Pacific

4   The Allies Are Victorious

1 Aggression Leads to War in Europe and Asia

The destruction caused by World War I made most countries of the world eager to prevent future wars. In the first decade after the war, many efforts were made to achieve a permanent peace. In the 1930's, however, the rise of fascist dictators in Europe and militaristic leaders in Japan worked against efforts for peace.

Fascist Italy lacked the unity and strength to dominate Europe, but Nazi Germany was a totalitarian state with growing military and industrial power. When other European nations resisted German aggression, the continent was plunged into war. Japan's leaders were seeking to expand their empire in Asia. Their ambitions led to war with China and increased the tensions among the world powers.

The League of Nations attempts to keep peace. The League of Nations, President Wilson's plan for world peace, had been established under the Treaty of Versailles. Its goals were to promote peace and encourage cooperation among nations. Its members promised to bring their quarrels to the League for settlement, rather than going to war. The League also set up the mandate system to provide colonies with a stable transition period to independence. Although more than sixty nations joined the League, the organization was severely weakened by the United States' refusal to join (page 649). Moreover, the League lacked the power to enforce its decisions.

International conferences are held. Still other efforts to maintain peace were made in the 1920's by diplomats from the world's great powers, including the United States. At conferences in London and in Washington, D.C., they discussed disarmament and agreed to limit the size and strength of their navies. In 1925, following the settlement of the German reparations questions (page 688), the European nations met at Locarno, Switzerland. They promised to seek peaceful ways to settle disputes, paying specific attention to trouble spots such as the French-German border. The "spirit of Locarno" prevailed in Europe during the late 1920's.

The most idealistic effort toward peace was the Kellogg-Briand Peace Pact (named for its sponsors, Frank B. Kellogg, the American secretary of state, and Aristide Briand, premier of France). In 1928 fifteen nations signed the agreement renouncing war "as an instrument of national policy," and within a few years nearly every country had signed it. The pact was only a promise, however, and it soon was broken.

Germany violates the Versailles Treaty. Germany joined the League of Nations and took part in some of the postwar efforts to maintain peace. Nevertheless, most Germans bitterly resented the Treaty of Versailles, which had disarmed the country, taken away its conquests and colonies, and ordered the payment of huge sums for war damages (page 648). The Weimar government had tried to revise the treaty by peaceful diplomacy. When Hitler gained power in the early 1930's, he vowed to destroy the treaty altogether.

Hitler's first step in restoring Germany's power was to rebuild its military forces, which the Versailles Treaty forbade. Under the Weimar Republic, Germany had begun secretly to rearm on a small scale. In 1935 Hitler openly declared that Germany would build a peacetime army of 550,000 men. This was a clear violation of the treaty provision that limited the army to 100,000. Britain and France denounced German rearmament, but neither nation took action. Both wanted to preserve peace. Britain was not prepared for war, and France was not ready to fight alone.

Fascist aggression goes unchecked. Beginning with this violation of the Versailles Treaty, Europe's two fascist dictators made other aggressive moves that were only weakly opposed. In 1935 Mussolini's Italy invaded Ethiopia, the independent African kingdom that had resisted earlier Italian invasions (page 598). Haile Selassie (HY-lee suh-LASS-ee), Ethiopia's emperor, appealed to the League of Nations, which condemned Italy for committing an act of aggression. The League also urged its members not to sell arms or strategic raw materials to Italy.

Aggression in Europe and Africa, 1935–1940

Attacks by Germany and Italy on weaker countries plunged Europe into war. What lands did the Soviet Union take over?

Only a few nations cooperated, and the boycott failed. Ethiopia was defeated and became a part of an Italian colony.

In March, 1936, Hitler sent troops into the Rhineland, the region between the Rhine River and the French border. This too violated the Versailles Treaty, which had demilitarized the region. German generals warned Hitler that this move was dangerous, for the German army was still weak. Hitler, however, felt certain that French and British leaders would take no action that might lead to war.

Both the fascist powers displayed their growing military strength in the course of the

GERMAN AND JAPANESE AGGRESSION

Expansionist policies set the stage for World War II. German motorized forces invaded Poland in 1939 (left). Two days later, Britain and France declared war on Germany. In 1937, Japan waged war on China and took over Nanking (above), at that time the Chinese capital.

Spanish Civil War (page 681). Hitler and Mussolini backed Franco's forces with troops and equipment. Although Germany was not supposed to have any military aircraft, Hitler sent in his powerful new air force, the Luftwaffe (LOOFT-vahf-uh). Franco's victory established another fascist government in Western Europe.

Japan launches a war against China. Europe was not the only spot where military aggressors were threatening world peace. The Japanese takeover of Manchuria in 1931 (page 691) had brought international protests. The League of Nations condemned the move but took no action, and in 1933 Japan resigned from the League. Japan's attacks on the Asian mainland continued.

In July, 1937, Japanese and Nationalist Chinese troops clashed near Peiping (Peking). This incident led to the outbreak of the Sino-Japanese War, which is often considered the real beginning of World War II. Japanese troops began an all-out invasion and soon overran much of eastern China. Chiang Kai-shek's Nationalist government was forced to retreat westward, establishing new headquarters at Chungking in western China. By 1938, Japan held Canton, Shanghai, and other coastal cities, and its navy blockaded the China coast.

Austria is brought into the Third Reich. Nazi Germany, meanwhile, continued its steady expansion in Europe. Using the principle of self-determination for nationalities to justify his actions, Hitler now sought to bring together all the German-speaking peoples. These included large populations in Czechoslovakia and in Poland, as well as the people of Austria, Hitler's homeland. A union, or *Anschluss* (AHN-shloos), between Austria and Germany was specifically prohibited by the Versailles Treaty. Hitler nevertheless proposed a plan by which the two "German" states would cooperate. Some Austrians tried to preserve the country's independence, but in March, 1938, Hitler's troops entered Austria and declared it a province of the German Third Reich.

Hitler moves on Czechoslovakia. Hitler again used the principle of self-determination to justify a move into Czechoslovakia. While most of Czechoslovakia's 15 million people were Slavs (Czechs and Slovaks), three million were German. Most lived in the Sudetenland (soo-DAYT-un-land), the western region along the German border. Hostility had existed for centuries between Sudeten Germans and Slavic Czechs. With encouragement from Germany, the Nazis among the Sudeten Germans now began to denounce the Czechoslovakian government for "persecuting" the German minority and depriving it of the right of self-determination. While their demands were for self-rule, the real goal was annexation by Germany.

The young Czech republic had alliances with France and Russia, a large armaments industry, and strong border defenses. As Hitler began to threaten Czechoslovakia, Prime Minister Neville Chamberlain of Britain asked for a conference among the great powers.

France and Britain are reluctant to oppose Hitler. Despite the increasing aggression of Hitler and Mussolini in the 1930's, the Western democracies had continued to give in to their demands. Such a policy is called *appeasement.* Britain and France were following this policy because, after the horrors of World War I, both desired peace at almost any price. In addition, neither Britain nor France felt prepared to go to war against Germany. Britain had drastically reduced spending for armaments. France had a large army but relied mainly on the defenses of the Maginot (MAZH-ih-noh) Line, its huge border fortifications. Built in the 1930's, the line was a series of massive forts and underground shelters, protected by minefields. It stretched the length of France's border with Germany (map, page 697).

Help from the United States in case of war seemed unlikely because of the American people's wish to stay out of European wars. Britain and France also were unsure of the position of the Soviet Union and its unpredictable leader, Stalin. To many people in Western Europe, fascism seemed a more stable and trustworthy form of government than communism. (On their side, the Soviet leaders distrusted the West. Stalin suspected that Britain and France were allowing Germany to grow strong enough to attack the Soviet Union.)

Germany's violations of the Versailles Treaty also went unopposed because many people, especially in Britain, had always felt that the treaty was unjustifiably harsh. They were willing to have some provisions changed, even though they objected to Hitler's methods.

The Munich conference offers "appeasement." In September, 1938, Chamberlain, Hitler, Mussolini, and Premier Edouard Daladier (dah-lah-DYAY) of France met in Munich, Germany, to decide Czechoslovakia's fate. Czechoslovakia was not invited to attend, nor was its ally, the Soviet Union. Continuing the policy of appeasement, Chamberlain and Daladier agreed to Hitler's claim to the Sudetenland.

One reason for the Munich decision was that the people of the Sudetenland were, in fact, German. As before, Britain was not willing to go to war. France, although it had made an alliance with the Czechs, would not risk defending its ally without British help. With no support, Czechoslovakia surrendered the Sudetenland without a fight. Hitler promised to seek no more European territory, and the French and British leaders accepted his assurances.

Chamberlain returned to Britain saying that the Munich agreement had bought "peace with honor . . . peace for our time." Although some statesmen in both France and Britain opposed appeasement, popular opinion approved the decision at the time.

Hitler takes over Czechoslovakia. Despite his promise at Munich, Hitler did not stop with the Sudetenland. In March, 1939, German troops took Prague, the Czech capital, and Czechoslovakia ceased to exist as an independent nation.

The destruction of Czechoslovakia appeared quite different from the German takeovers in the Rhineland, Austria, and the Sudetenland. Czechoslovakia was not a German-speaking state. Moreover, Hitler's promise not to take more territory had clearly been meaningless. It was now apparent that his goal was to dominate Europe.

Hitler's claims in Poland bring a crisis. Hitler's next move, in Poland, also began with a limited demand. The Polish Corridor, created after World War I, was a strip of land that separated East Prussia from the rest of Germany and gave Poland access to the sea (map, page 649). The city of Danzig, predominantly German, had been made a free port tied economically to Poland. In March, 1939, Hitler demanded that Danzig return to German rule and that Germany be granted a railroad and a highway through the Corridor.

The Polish government refused this demand, and Britain and France declared that they would help defend Poland's independence. They tried to persuade the Soviet Union to join them, but Stalin demanded bases in Poland in order to be ready for a German attack. Poland, only recently freed after more than a century of Russian rule, refused to allow Russian troops on its soil.

The Nazi-Soviet Pact brings war. France and Britain needed Soviet help to defend Poland, but negotiations were long and difficult because of mutual distrust. Never sure of Stalin's policies, the Western nations were nevertheless stunned when he and Hitler announced the signing of a pact of friendship and nonaggression in late August, 1939. In this Nazi-Soviet Pact, the Soviet Union agreed, in return for half of Poland, not to interfere with Hitler's invasion.

Early on the morning of September 1, German troops marched into Poland, and German planes bombed railroads and cities. For a day, British and French diplomats persisted in their efforts to prevent war. Nazi aggression could not be stopped, however, and on September 3, 1939, the British and French declared war against Germany.

CHECK-UP

1. Vocabulary: *appeasement.*
2. (a) Why was the League of Nations not an effective organization? (b) What were the aims of the Locarno pact and the Kellogg-Briand pact?
3. (a) What was Hitler's first violation of the Versailles Treaty? (b) What reason did Hitler give for his moves in the Rhineland, Austria, and Czechoslovakia?
4. What aggressive actions were taken (a) by Fascist Italy? (b) by Japan?
5. (a) What decision was made at Munich in 1938? (b) What were the terms of the Nazi-Soviet Pact? (c) Why did France and Britain finally take action in the case of Poland?

2   Europe Falls to Axis Forces

At the time of the invasion of Poland, Germany was far better prepared for war than Britain or France. Country after country fell to Germany and Italy, the Axis powers. After the fall of France, Britain stood alone until 1941, when first the Soviet Union and then the United States entered the war as its allies. By late 1942, the war began to turn in the Allies' favor.

HITLER'S CONQUESTS

Poland falls to the Nazi blitzkrieg. Hitler devised a style of warfare that used quick, massive attacks on land and in the air. It was called the *blitzkrieg* (BLITS-kreeg), or "lightning war." In less than a week after the September 1 invasion of Poland, a blitzkrieg by German tanks, bombers, and paratroopers opened the way to Warsaw. Soviet troops then invaded Poland from the east. On September 27, 1939, after days of heavy bombing, Warsaw surrendered. As they had agreed in the Nazi-Soviet Pact, Hitler and Stalin divided Poland, giving Hitler possession of the disputed city of Danzig.

The Soviet Union claims lands on the Baltic. To be sure of access to the Baltic Sea, the Soviet government established military bases in the countries of Latvia, Lithuania, and Estonia. It then demanded bases in Finland as well as a large piece of territory on the border. When the Finns refused, Soviet troops invaded the country. Throughout the "winter war" of 1939, Finnish troops on skis resisted the Soviet army. In March, though, Finland was forced to make peace and give up the disputed territory.

The blitzkrieg overwhelms Western Europe. Elsewhere there was little action through the winter, and people began to speak of the "phony war." The French hoped to fight a defensive war and were depending on the fortifications of the Maginot Line. The Germans also stayed behind their newly built defenses, the West Wall (or Siegfried Line).

Suddenly in April, 1940, Germany struck with lightning speed at Denmark and Norway. The two Scandinavian countries fell quickly to invading German forces. In the next month Belgium, the Netherlands, and Luxembourg

Churchill's Speech after Dunkirk

The heroic evacuation of Dunkirk marked a British defeat, but its effect was to inspire the British people to resist Hitler with great courage and determination. In this spirit, Prime Minister Winston Churchill — a leader known for his skill as a speaker — made the following speech to the House of Commons on June 4, 1940:

> Even though . . . many old and famous states have fallen into the grip of the Gestapo and . . . Nazi rule, we shall not flag or fail. We shall go on to the end. We shall fight in France, we shall fight on the seas and oceans, we shall fight with growing confidence and growing strength in the air, we shall defend our island, whatever the cost may be. We shall fight on the beaches, we shall fight on the landing grounds, we shall fight in the fields and in the streets, we shall fight in the hills. We shall never surrender. And even if . . . this island or a large part of it were subjugated and starving, then our Empire beyond the seas, armed and guarded by the British Fleet, would carry on the struggle, until . . . the new world, with all its power and might, steps forth to the rescue and the liberation of the old.

Does Churchill seem to think that the Nazis plan to invade Britain? Who does he say would carry

"LET US GO FORWARD TOGETHER"

on the struggle if Britain fell? To what country is Churchill referring in the phrase "the new world"?

also surrendered to Hitler, after heavy bombing had devastated cities and terrorized the civilian population.

Allied forces are rescued at Dunkirk. The fall of Belgium allowed the German army to move around the end of the Maginot Line. Tanks and motorized infantry burst through the French defenses near Sedan (map, page 702) and raced toward the English Channel. This German advance drove a wedge between the French army defending Paris and the Allied (British, Belgian, and French) forces on the coast. Some 330,000 Allied troops retreated to Dunkirk on the English Channel (map, page 702). To rescue the trapped soldiers, every available vessel set sail from England — fishing boats, tugboats, and private yachts, as well as merchant ships and navy destroyers. In about a week, ending on June 4, 1940, most of the soldiers were taken to England, though great amounts of valuable and badly needed equipment were left behind on the beaches. The "miracle of Dunkirk" inspired and united the British people in their resistance to Hitler.

France falls. The German armies advanced steadily across northern France. Millions of French civilians fled south, by train or car, on foot or bicycle. On June 10 Mussolini also declared war, and Italian troops invaded France from the south. The French declared Paris an "open city" to save it from destruction, and the German troops marched in on June 14. A few days later the French government asked for an armistice. Hitler arranged for it to be

World War II in Europe and Africa

Within three years of the invasion of Poland, Axis forces had conquered most of
Europe. Allied advances, however, ended Axis domination of the continent.

signed in the same railway car where Germany
had agreed to the armistice in 1918.

Under the terms of the armistice, Ger-
many occupied northern France (including
Paris) and the coast. In the south a "puppet"
French government was set up at Vichy (VEE-

shee). It was headed by Marshal Henri Philippe
Pétain, a hero of World War I.

The Battle of Britain begins. With the fall
of France, Britain now stood alone. Hitler had
made plans for an invasion, but he hoped the
British would agree to a surrender beforehand.

Radar in War and Peace

One advantage that RAF fighter pilots had in defending Britain against the Nazi blitz was a new device that helped them detect and locate enemy planes. From this system's full name — *radio detection and ranging* — came the term *radar*. Radar depended on radio waves that were beamed into the sky. The radar operators could see on a screen when the waves bounced (or "echoed") off an aircraft. The photograph on the right shows an early radar installation.

Many scientific advances were made after the war to improve radar systems, and they soon became an essential part of flying. Air-traffic controllers at airports use radar to guide planes in and out. Pilots use their radar screens to detect clouds and storms as well as other aircraft in the sky. More recently, radar has been used in many other ways. Weather forecasters use radar to detect approaching storms. Radar equipment in satellites reveals information about the earth's surface. Radar has even been used in studying the behavior of birds and insects.

When Britain refused, Hitler ordered the Luftwaffe to start massive bombings of British factories, airfields, seaports, and cities. On August 8, 1940, hundreds of bombers and fighter planes attacked, beginning months of terrifying air raids. Day and night, German bombers unleashed destruction on British cities, concentrating on London and industrial centers.

The British — both civilians and military forces — stubbornly resisted. Many children and others were evacuated from London to safer areas, but most Londoners remained calm and determined during the "blitz." Courageous British pilots of the Royal Air Force inflicted heavy losses on German aircraft and on ports across the Channel. They were aided by radar, a new device developed by British scientists to detect enemy planes.

By late fall, it seemed that Hitler had abandoned his invasion plans. The "blitz" continued till spring, however. Large areas in Brit-

ish cities were destroyed, and thousands of civilians killed. A German naval blockade prevented the shipment of food and supplies to the British, and people faced severe shortages. Britain could no longer afford to buy supplies or military equipment, and the United States' neutrality prevented it from lending money to a country at war. In March, 1941, therefore, Congress passed the Lend-Lease Act. It allowed President Roosevelt to sell, lease, or lend military equipment to nations whose defense was vital to American security.[1]

Hitler invades the Soviet Union. While British resistance continued, Hitler was planning to open a second front and attack the Soviet Union. Even though Hitler and Stalin had made a nonaggression pact, one of Hitler's aims had always been to destroy communism

---

[1] The Lend-Lease agreement applied not only to Britain but also to China.

and seize Soviet territory. He wanted land for German settlers, rich grain fields to feed the German nation, and oil, coal, and iron ore to supply the German war machine.

To prepare the way for the invasion of the Soviet Union, Hitler's forces occupied Bulgaria and overran Greece and Yugoslavia. By June, 1941, Germany had 3,300 tanks, 5,000 planes, and nearly four million soldiers (including many from Italy, Rumania, Finland, and Hungary) massed along the Soviet border. On June 22 these armies swept into the Soviet Union along a front that extended from the Baltic to the Black Sea.

Hitler's attack brought the Soviet Union immediate offers of help and support from Britain and the United States. Promises of mutual aid were made, and the Lend-Lease agreement was extended to include the Soviet Union.

Germans drive deep into the Soviet Union. Soviet armies suffered enormous losses in the first months of the German offensive, holding back the invaders while slowly retreating. By the first week in October, 1941, German troops were only fifty miles from Moscow. The people of the Soviet Union also suffered great hardship. In September, German forces surrounded the city of Leningrad, trapping some three million people there with only enough food and supplies for a short time. The siege was not completely ended for more than two years. Nearly a million people died from starvation and disease. The Black Sea port of Sevastopol also endured a long siege.

Winter aids the Soviet defense. As the Soviet troops withdrew, they burned crops in the fields and destroyed equipment. These "scorched-earth" tactics left no food or supplies for the advancing Germans. The arrival of autumn rains and winter snow also slowed the German offensive, for blitzkrieg tactics were not effective on muddy, snowy roads. Fresh Soviet troops arrived from Siberia with winter equipment, while the Germans shivered in summer uniforms as the temperature dropped to 30° below zero. German tanks and trucks would not start in the cold. The Russian winter stopped the German army much as it had defeated Napoleon's Grand Army over a century earlier (page 456).

Hitler dominates Europe. Even though their advance into Russia had been stopped, German forces held large areas of the Soviet Union. Early in 1942 Hitler's empire included virtually all of Europe, from the Atlantic Ocean to the Black Sea, as well as some of the colonial possessions of the conquered nations (map, page 697). Only Sweden, Switzerland, Ireland, Portugal, and Spain remained neutral; and fascist Spain was in sympathy with the Axis. By the end of the year, however, crucial battles in the Soviet Union and North Africa marked the turning points in the course of the war.

Stalingrad resists the German attack. Despite the setbacks of the winter of 1941–1942, the next spring and summer brought a new German offensive in the Soviet Union. The

---

TIMETABLE

World War II

1925	European nations agree to the Locarno pact.
1935	Hitler announces German rearmament. Fascist Italy invades Ethiopia.
1936	German troops occupy the Rhineland.
1937	War breaks out between Japan and China.
1938	The *Anschluss* brings Austria into the Third Reich. The Munich agreement allows Hitler to take the Sudetenland.
1939	The Nazi-Soviet Pact is signed. Germany invades Poland. Britain and France declare war on Germany.
1940	Denmark, Norway, Belgium, the Netherlands, Luxembourg, and France fall to Hitler. The Battle of Britain begins.
1941	Germany invades the Soviet Union. The United States enters the war after a Japanese attack on Pearl Harbor.
1942	Stalingrad, El Alamein, and Midway mark turning points in the war.
1943	Italy surrenders following an Allied invasion.
1944	Allied forces invade Normandy (D-Day, June 6)
1945	The war ends in Europe (May 8). Japan surrenders (August 15).

main target of the German attack was Stalingrad[2] on the Volga River (map, page 702). The city was a vital center for north-south transportation by river, railroad, and canal.

In late August, German troops reached the Volga. Six hundred German planes bombarded Stalingrad, enveloping it in flames and killing 40,000 civilians. By September 1, German soldiers were in the suburbs, but people would not abandon their city. Soviet soldiers and civilians fought house to house and street to street. In the words of a Soviet general, the defenders fought "for every brick and stone, for every yard of Stalingrad earth." A German officer wrote in his diary:

> Stalingrad is no longer a town. By day it is an enormous cloud of burning, blinding smoke. It is a vast furnace lit by the reflection of the flames. And when night arrives . . . the dogs plunge into the Volga and swim desperately to gain the other bank. The nights of Stalingrad are a terror for them. Animals flee this hell; the hardest stones cannot bear it for long; only men endure.

In late November, Soviet Marshal Georgi Zhukov brought in new troops. They began a "pincer" movement, closing in from two sides and threatening to trap the German Sixth Army in the city. Exhausted and short of food, medical supplies, weapons, and ammunition, the German commander begged Hitler to order a withdrawal. Instead, Hitler's Luftwaffe commander, Hermann Goering, tried unsuccessfully to send in supplies by plane. Finally, in February, 1943, the remnants of the German troops in Stalingrad surrendered.

The Soviet victory marked the turning point in the war in Eastern Europe. Soviet troops had begun to move westward. The Russian offensive would eventually take them to Berlin.

Victory in North Africa frees the Mediterranean Sea. In the first year of the war, while Hitler was expanding westward in Europe, Mussolini began a campaign to establish Italian control over the Mediterranean. In the fall of 1940, Italian forces from Libya invaded

---

[2]Stalingrad was renamed Volgograd in 1961.

Soviet street fighters (above) fiercely defended the city of Stalingrad against a German siege that lasted from August, 1942, to February, 1943.

Egypt (map, page 702). Their aims were to capture the Suez Canal, which was vital to Allied shipping, and to open the way to the oil fields of the Middle East. Soldiers from Britain and the Commonwealth nations forced an Italian retreat. By early in 1941 the British had taken more than 100,000 Italians prisoner and captured the important city of Tobruk. To keep the British from taking Libya, Germany sent help to the Italians — the trained desert fighters of the Afrika Corps led by Field Marshal Erwin Rommel.

Rommel's troops and the British fought back and forth in the North African desert for over a year. Rommel's skill and clever tactics earned him the nickname "The Desert Fox." In 1942 the British sent Field Marshal Bernard Montgomery to block Rommel's advance toward Egypt and the Suez Canal. The armies of these two brilliant generals clashed at El Alamein (ell ah-lah-MAYN), where the retreating British had taken a stand. Montgomery's forces turned and began a counterattack, and by November, 1942, they had driven Rommel out of Egypt. El Alamein, the first major British victory of the war, made Montgomery a hero.

Late in 1941, a Japanese attack in the Pacific had brought the United States into the war. The combined Allied strategy called for a major effort against Hitler. Early in November,

1942, Allied troops commanded by General Dwight D. Eisenhower began "Operation Torch" in French Morocco and Algeria. Although the French colonies were under the Vichy government, the French commander aided the Allies, and Rommel's army was trapped between the two Allied armies. By May, 1943, the Allies held North Africa. These victories ended the threat to the Suez Canal, made the Mediterranean safe for Allied ships, and gave the Allies a base to invade southern Europe.

EUROPE UNDER HITLER

Hitler imposes a New Order. Despite the Allied victories in Africa and Eastern Europe, most of Europe was firmly under Nazi control. Over this vast empire, Hitler planned to extend a New Order in which all Europe would serve the German "master race." Nazi racial policies were administered by Hitler's police chief, Heinrich Himmler, who was a fanatical believer in Hitler and in "Aryan superiority." The policies called for the enslavement or extermination of all "non-Aryan" or "inferior" peoples. To the Nazis, that meant not only the Jews of Europe but also millions of Slavs (mostly Poles and Russians), Gypsies, and others.

The Nazis regarded peoples of Germanic descent, such as the Norwegians and Dutch, as racial "cousins." They were to undergo re-education to make them valued citizens of a "Greater Germany." Ukrainian, Polish, and Czech children who "looked German" — blond and blue-eyed — were taken from their parents and sent to Germany to be brought up by German parents and trained in German schools.

Persecution begins in Poland. When Poland fell in 1939 (page 700), the Germans and Soviets both carried out sweeping programs of murder and terror against the Poles. Soviet trains transported more than a million Poles from eastern Poland to labor camps and concentration camps in the USSR. Among those marked for deportation were religious leaders, student political leaders, business owners, government officials, and anyone else considered dangerous to Stalinist rule. Some 15,000 offi-

cers in the Polish army also were imprisoned. Four years later the bodies of 4,000 executed officers were found in the Katyn forest near the Dnieper River. The Nazis and Soviets accused each other of the massacre, but Soviet guilt was later well established.

In western Poland, the Nazis began to build concentration camps where university professors, government workers, and others were sent. Under Hitler's resettlement program, thousands of farm families from western Poland were moved to make room for German settlers.

Germany exploits conquered lands. Hitler used the resources of Europe to enrich Germany. German soldiers ate food harvested in occupied France and the Soviet Union and fought with weapons produced in Czech factories. German tanks ran on Rumanian oil. Nazi officials decorated their quarters with paintings and other works of art stolen from museums and private collections all over Europe.

The Nazis also demanded labor from the conquered peoples. Some seven million men and women were sent to forced labor camps in Germany. Hundreds of thousands died there of disease, hunger, mistreatment, and exhaustion. Prisoners of war and political prisoners also were sent to the camps. Of more than five million Russians taken prisoner by the Nazis, about three and a half million died in the camps.

European Jews face the Holocaust. Himmler's deputy, Reinhard Heydrich (HY-drick) was the chief planner of the Nazi program to wipe out the Jews of Europe — still one of Hitler's main goals. Heydrich's plan was entitled the "Final Solution to the Jewish Problem." For the Nazis the "final solution" was *genocide* (JEN-uh-side), the murder of an entire people. This systematic murder has come to be called the Holocaust. From all over Europe, Jews were rounded up, loaded into sealed cattle cars, and shipped to death camps. Many were herded into gas chambers devised for mass murder. Others were beaten, starved, and tortured to death by their guards. Some prisoners — Jews and others — were the victims of cruel medical experiments. Some six million Jews perished in the Holocaust, about one and a half million of them children.

The most notorious of the death camps was Auschwitz (OUSH-vitz), in Poland, where between three and four million died. After the war, Rudolf Hoess, the commandant at Auschwitz, was tried for crimes against humanity and executed. At his trial, he described what happened to prisoners:

> The "final solution" of the Jewish question meant the complete extermination of all Jews in Europe. I was ordered to establish extermination facilities at Auschwitz in June, 1941. . . .
>
> The way we selected our victims was as follows: . . . Those who were fit for work were sent into the camp. Others were sent immediately to the extermination plants. Children of tender years were invariably exterminated since by reason of their youth they were unable to work. . . . We endeavored to fool the victims into thinking that they were to go through a delousing process. Of course, frequently they realized our true intentions, and we sometimes had riots and difficulties due to that fact. Very frequently women would hide their children under [their] clothes, but of course when we found them we would send the children in to be exterminated.

Resistance movements grow up. Nazi rule and Nazi atrocities did not go unopposed in those countries Hitler had overrun. In each occupied country a resistance movement emerged. In France, the resistance aided the Allies when they invaded German-occupied France in 1944. The Danish resistance protected almost all of Denmark's 8,000 Jews by smuggling them into neutral Sweden. Greek and Yugoslav resistance fighters, called partisans, waged guerrilla war against the Germans. At its height the Polish resistance numbered 300,000. Even in Italy and Germany, many people opposed the Fascists and the Nazis. Italian partisans helped the British and Americans liberate Italy.

Resistance fighters ambushed German patrols, led strikes, and sabotaged plants making German war equipment. They printed underground newspapers, and relayed important information to the Allies over hidden radios.

They rescued crews of crashed planes, hid escaped prisoners, and helped them get away to Allied territory. Early in the war, the symbol of the resistance became the "V for Victory" sign, with the Morse code signal "dot-dot-dot-dash."

Resistance fighters — men, women, and children — took great risks. The prison cell, the concentration camp, the torture room, and the firing squad discouraged resistance to Nazi rule. For every German soldier killed by a resistance fighter, many civilian hostages were executed. For instance, when Reinhard Heydrich was assassinated in 1942 by Czech resistance fighters, the Czech village of Lidice was wiped out in revenge. The men of the village were killed, the women shipped to labor camps, and the children sent to Germany.

Resistance took another form as government officials and rulers fled occupied countries and set up "governments in exile." Ordinary citizens who could escape to Britain organized army units that fought with the Allied troops. The Free French, led by General Charles de Gaulle (de GOHL), included survivors of Dunkirk as well as others who escaped later. Poles, Czechs, Norwegians, Belgians, and Dutch also had fighting units.

CHECK-UP

1. Vocabulary: *genocide.*
2. (a) What were the first moves made in central and northern Europe by the USSR and Germany? (b) What part of Europe did Hitler invade next? (c) What happened at Dunkirk?
3. (a) What was the Battle of Britain? (b) How did it end?
4. (a) What were Hitler's aims in invading the Soviet Union? (b) What kind of aid did the USSR get from the West? (c) What slowed the German invasion?
5. (a) What was the turning point of the war in Eastern Europe? (b) Why was victory in North Africa important to the Allies?
6. (a) What were the main aims of Hitler's "New Order" for Europe? (b) What was the Holocaust? (c) What forms did resistance movements take?

3 War Breaks Out in the Pacific

The militarist leaders who came to power in Japan in the 1930's had already increased Japan's holdings in Asia and the Pacific. Attracted by the aggressiveness of Nazi Germany and Mussolini's Italy, Japan joined the two European nations in a pact against world communism. In 1940, Japan became the third member of what was called the Rome-Berlin-Tokyo Axis. Japan's plans and policies for expansion, as well as its aggression in China, brought opposition from the West, especially the United States. The build-up of tensions soon led to war.

Japan expands in southeastern Asia. In 1940, the war in Europe left undefended the British, French, and Dutch colonial possessions in Asia and the Pacific Ocean. Japan sought to incorporate these lands into what it termed the "Greater East Asia Co-Prosperity Sphere" (which already included Korea, Manchuria, and parts of China). These possessions would supply markets for Japanese products; oil, rubber, and tin needed by Japanese industry; and enough rice to feed the nation.

Only the United States was in a position to try to stop Japanese expansion. It began by limiting trade and banning the export of war material. Then, throughout 1941, American and Japanese diplomats carried on discussions. Meanwhile, however, Japanese military leaders had decided to cripple American naval bases in the Pacific, thus making it impossible for the United States to interfere in Asia.

Japanese planes bomb Pearl Harbor. In December, 1941, the diplomatic talks were still going on when the Japanese struck suddenly at the American fleet in the Pacific. Early in the morning of December 7, 1941, Japanese planes took off from aircraft carriers to attack Pearl Harbor, the United States naval base in the Hawaiian Islands. American radar picked up the movement of the planes, but officers in the military information center thought that they were American. No alert was sounded.

At 7:55 A.M. Japanese torpedo planes and dive bombers roared out of the sky, catching the Americans by surprise. The warships in Pearl Harbor and the planes standing in neat rows on the airfields were easy targets for the low-flying Japanese planes. The attack destroyed much of the United States' Pacific fleet and air force (though the aircraft carriers, an important target, were not in port).

At almost the same time, Japanese planes attacked other American island bases, as well as British holdings in Malaya and Hong Kong. Enraged, the United States and Britain declared war on Japan on December 8. A few days later, Germany and Italy declared war on the United States.

Japan continues its conquests in Asia. The year following the attack on Pearl Harbor brought many Japanese victories. By early 1942, they had taken the Philippines (an American possession); Burma and Singapore (both British); the Dutch East Indies; French Indochina, and other territories in southeastern Asia and the Pacific (map, next page). As it captured these former colonial possessions, Japan claimed that it was creating an Asia for Asians. Leaders in Southeast Asia, however, soon found the Japanese occupation intolerable.

Under Japanese rule thousands of Asian laborers and Dutch, Australian, and British prisoners of war were forced to build railways and roads through steep mountains and dense jungle. From the conquered lands Japan took vital rubber, tin, oil, and tons of food. Embittered by Japanese exploitation, the conquered peoples began to organize resistance movements that carried on guerrilla warfare against the occupying Japanese troops.

Local peoples also cooperated with the Allied troops in Asia. British commandos and soldiers from India fought in the jungles of Burma and Malaya. The United States' major interest on the Asian mainland was sending supplies to the Chinese government forces of Chiang Kai-shek. The Japanese occupation of eastern China had forced the Nationalists into the southwest. In 1942, however, the Japanese closed the Burma Road, the only land route into western China (map, page 709). Daring

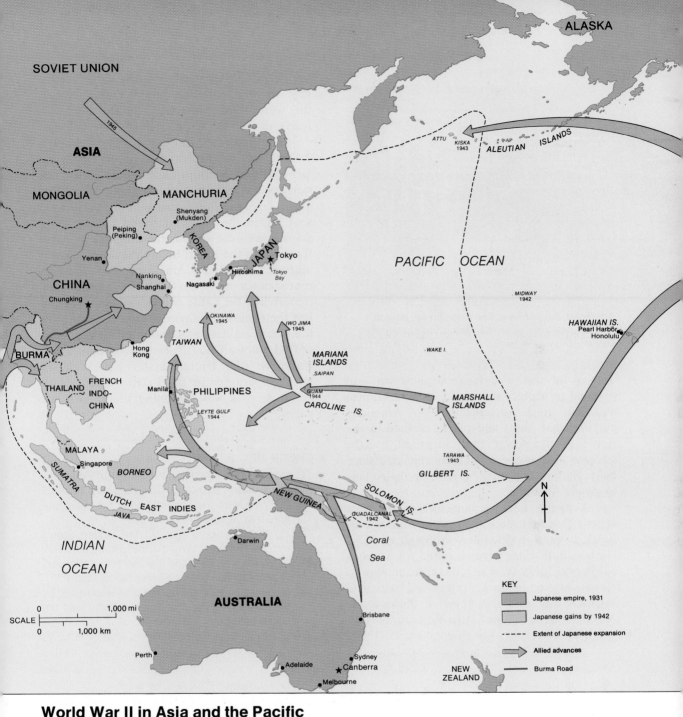

World War II in Asia and the Pacific

Japan had conquered vast areas in Asia and the Pacific by 1942. Beginning in August
of that year, Allied forces won strategic, island-by-island victories.

American pilots had to fly supplies in over the
steep western mountains.

American planes halt the Japanese advances. The attack on Pearl Harbor had
crippled the Pacific fleet, but by the spring of

1942, the United States forces had begun to
rebuild and were ready to fight back. Planes
from American aircraft carriers attacked Pacific
islands and the Japanese capital of Tokyo, putting the Japanese on the defensive for the first

American dive bombers, like these on the aircraft carrier *Enterprise,* sank Japanese ships during the Battle of Midway in 1942.

drawing it into an all-out surprise battle. American naval intelligence, however, had broken the secret Japanese code, and the fleet was ready, though still outnumbered.

The Battle of Midway, on June 4 through 7, 1942, was a naval battle waged mostly in the air. None of the ships fired its big guns. Carrier-based American torpedo planes dived low at the Japanese ships. Although nearly all were shot down, the attack scattered the Japanese ships and forced the Japanese fighter pilots to fly low over the water. Before they could regain altitude, high-flying American dive bombers roared down out of the sky at the Japanese carriers. When the battle ended, the Japanese had lost their four best aircraft carriers, along with the planes on deck and many well-trained and skillful pilots. Despite its loss of the carrier *Yorktown,* the United States had regained naval superiority in the Pacific. The tide of battle in Asia was beginning to turn for the Allies.

time in the war. The Japanese, however, still planned to capture the island of New Guinea and then attack Australia. In May, American and Japanese ships and planes clashed in the Battle of the Coral Sea. Surprised by the strength the American fleet had regained since Pearl Harbor, the Japanese gave up their plans to invade Australia.

A month later, Japan suffered its most serious defeat of the war so far at Midway, an isolated island 1,135 miles northwest of Pearl Harbor. Both sides were prepared for a major battle over Midway, which was near enough to Hawaii to give Japan a strategic air base. The Japanese admirals also hoped to destroy the American fleet (not yet at its full strength) by

CHECK-UP

1. (a) Why did Japan join the Axis? (b) What was the Greater East Asia Co-Prosperity Sphere? (c) Why was the United States the main obstacle to Japanese expansion?
2. (a) What incident brought the United States into the war? (b) Why did the Japanese easily achieve victories in the first months of the war? (c) Which countries' colonies fell to Japan?
3. (a) What Japanese invasion plan was halted by the Battle of the Coral Sea? (b) Why was the Battle of Midway important?

4 The Allies Are Victorious

By the end of 1942, the victories at Stalingrad, El Alamein, and Midway had given the Allies the advantage in Eastern Europe, the Mediterranean, and the Pacific. In Western Europe, massive Allied invasions concentrated on ending Hitler's control there. In the Pacific, the war moved from island to island until the United States' use of the atomic bomb suddenly brought Japan's surrender.

Italy surrenders. The occupation of North Africa gave the Allies a base for the invasion of Italy. In July, 1943, British and American troops landed on the island of Sicily. That same month Mussolini was overthrown, and the new Italian government surrendered to the Allies on September 3. To drive the remaining German armies out of Italy, Allied troops landed on the Italian mainland. With the help of Italian partisans, they fought their way north against stiff German resistance. The Allies took Rome in June, 1944, but fighting did not end completely until the following year.

The Allies invade France. The Allies were also planning a still larger invasion of Western Europe, known by the code name "Operation Overlord." After months of preparation, a huge Allied invasion force commanded by General Eisenhower prepared to cross the English Channel and invade Nazi-occupied France. D-Day, as the day of the landing in Normandy was called, came on June 6, 1944. The success of the invasion depended on coordinating thousands of ships and planes. The landing troops had to secure beachheads within the first few hours, before German guns and tanks could stop their efforts to push inland.

D-Day caught the Germans by surprise. They had expected an invasion but had no way of knowing exactly when or where it would come. Some 120,000 Allied assault forces — mostly American, British, Canadian, and Free French — landed on five beaches on the coast of Normandy. On some beaches the soldiers struggled ashore through four-foot waves in the face of fierce German gunfire.

Allied control of the air was crucial to the success of D-Day. Allied planes supported the assault troops by bombing enemy positions and supply lines. Beachheads were established and more soldiers and supplies were rushed into battle. Less than a month after D-Day, there were a million Allied soldiers in France. By the end of August, Paris was liberated, and the Allies were pushing toward Germany.

By autumn, 1944, the German cause seemed hopeless. Soviet armies were nearing Germany from the east. In the west, American and British forces had reached the German frontier. Allied bombers were destroying German factories, railways, bridges, and military installations. Heavy bombing was devastating German cities, causing many civilian casualties. Early in the year, some high German army officers had even plotted to kill Hitler by planting a bomb in his offices.

The last German attack is stopped. Desperate, Hitler made one last attempt to stop the Allied advance into Germany. In mid-December, 1944, German troops and tanks attacked the American troops in the hilly forests near Germany's border with Belgium and Luxembourg. The attack took the Americans by surprise, and the Germans broke through their lines. Outnumbered five to one, the Americans stubbornly held key towns and roads in what is called the Battle of the Bulge. Unable to crush this resistance, and short of gasoline for tanks and trucks, the German offensive halted. At the beginning of January, the Allies launched a counteroffensive that soon wiped out the German gains.

Germany surrenders. The Allies now could advance into Germany from both east and west. Marshal Zhukov's Soviet troops, pushing through Poland, reached the outskirts of Berlin on April 21. American and Soviet troops met a few days later in eastern Germany. On April 30, 1945, with Soviet troops only blocks away from his underground headquarters in Berlin, Hitler committed suicide. Two days earlier, Mussolini had been captured and executed by Italian partisans. A demoralized and devastated Germany surrendered unconditionally; the end of war in Europe was announced on May 8, 1945 — V-E Day.

The Pacific war moves from island to island. Though the war in Europe was over, the war with Japan continued in the Pacific and on the Asian mainland. In the Pacific, the United States took the offensive against Japan after the Battle of Midway. The plan was to "island-hop," seizing only those islands that were in strategic positions on the sea route to Japan (map, page 709). In August, 1942, American marines and soldiers attacked the Japanese base at Guadalcanal in the Solomon Islands, while Australians and other Allied troops fought in New Guinea. Although jungle warfare was slow and casualties were high, the Allies moved from island to island, ever closer to Japan. Strategic victories came at Tarawa in the Gilbert Islands, and in the Marshalls and Marianas. In the fall of 1944, the Japanese fleet was shatteringly beaten in the air-sea Battle of Leyte Gulf, and American troops began to reclaim the Philippines. By 1944, American planes were firebombing Tokyo almost daily.

Casualties ran high in the Pacific because of the Japanese feeling that surrender meant dishonor. Infantry soldiers fought to the death

THE ALLIED VICTORY

During the successful D-Day invasion in June, 1944 (above), Allied forces landed on five beaches at Normandy, in German-occupied France. The invasion was an essential step toward the victory over Germany. At the end of the war in the Pacific, Japanese leaders surrendered aboard the American battleship *Missouri* in September, 1945 (right).

rather than be taken prisoner. "Kamikaze" pilots in planes loaded with bombs deliberately crashed into American ships. In the battle for the island of Iwo Jima (EE-woh JEE-muh), American planes and ships bombarded the Japanese forces for two and a half months before marines were sent ashore. Yet it took the marines three days to gain only 700 yards. In a month of fighting, almost 5,000 Americans were killed and another 15,000 were wounded. Casualties were even higher at Okinawa, the last battle in the Pacific war: 12,500 Americans, 120,000 Japanese, and 42,000 Okinawans were killed, and another 35,500 Americans were wounded.

Allied leaders plan for war and peace. Wartime meetings between the leaders of the Allied countries coordinated their military plans and established agreements about the future of Europe. The first conference of the "Big Three" —

Roosevelt, Churchill, and Stalin — was at Tehran, Iran, in November, 1943, before the Normandy invasion. Another meeting occurred shortly before the end of the war in Europe. At this conference, at Yalta on the Black Sea, Soviet help in the war against Japan was promised in return for territory in Asia.

In July, 1945, after Germany's surrender, Stalin, Churchill, and the new American President, Harry Truman, met at Potsdam, Germany. (Churchill's government lost the election midway through the conference, and he was replaced by Clement Attlee, the new prime minister.) One subject discussed at the meeting was the use of a powerful new weapon that the United States had been testing. Throughout the war, scientists had been working to make a weapon that would use the immense amounts of energy within the atom (page 624). The United States now had this weapon, an atomic bomb. At the Potsdam meeting, the three leaders demanded Japan's surrender.

A new weapon ends the war. A few days after the Potsdam meeting, President Truman made the decision to drop the first atomic bomb. An invasion of Japan from Okinawa had been planned, but Truman hoped to end the war quickly and avoid further battle casualties. On August 6, 1945, an atomic bomb was dropped on the Japanese city of Hiroshima (hee-roh-SHEE-muh).

The world was horrified by the destructiveness of the new weapon. The single atomic bomb completely demolished about 60 percent of the city of Hiroshima. For four miles around the target point, virtually no buildings were left standing. More than 80,000 people were killed, and 37,000 more suffered severe injuries. Others later died from the effects of the radiation released by the explosion.

On August 8, 1945, the Soviet Union carried out the promise made at Yalta, declaring war on Japan and invading Manchuria (Manchukuo). The next day, because Japan's government had not replied to the demand for unconditional surrender, a second atomic bomb was dropped. The target was Nagasaki, an important shipbuilding city. Shortly afterwards Japanese officials asked for peace. On August 15 — V-J Day — Emperor Hirohito announced the defeat to the people of Japan.

On September 2, officials of the Japanese government signed the document of surrender on board the battleship *Missouri* in Tokyo Bay. There General Douglas MacArthur expressed the hopes of a war-weary world:

> It is my earnest hope and indeed the hope of all mankind that from this solemn occasion a better world shall emerge out of the blood and carnage of the past — a world dedicated to the dignity of man and the fulfillment of his most cherished wish — for freedom, tolerance, and justice.

The Allies occupy Germany and Japan. The victorious Allied forces took control in both Japan and Germany. The United States formed an army of occupation in Japan, but the Japanese imperial government was allowed to continue to run the country. In conquered Germany, however, separate American, British, French, and Soviet occupation zones were established.

Worldwide destruction is great. World War II had been the most dreadful war in history. Perhaps fifty million people died, both soldiers and civilians. Of those, about twenty million were in the Soviet Union, whose losses were the most severe. Civilians suffered greatly everywhere. Millions were killed as the war raged on their farmlands and in their cities; millions more were killed in bombing raids. At least ten million died in the Nazi death camps, including six million Jews. Millions of others, made homeless, became refugees.

The war left vast areas of destruction, particularly in Europe and Asia. Cities, farms, and factories were in ruins. Bridges, railway systems, waterways, and harbors were destroyed; farmlands laid waste; livestock killed; coal mines wrecked. The world faced a gigantic task of rebuilding.

War criminals are tried. The feeling was strong that those who had led the world into this destruction should be punished. Many of the surviving Nazi leaders were arrested and put on trial for "crimes against humanity." The trials, held in Nuremberg, Germany, began in November, 1945. For most of the world, they brought the first knowledge of the horrors of the Holocaust and the Nazi death camps. About half of those tried at Nuremberg were sentenced to death; others were imprisoned. Several Japanese commanders who had ordered the cruel treatment of prisoners of war also were put on trial by a military court.

CHECK-UP

1. (a) What was the Allied strategy in Western Europe after 1942? (b) How were the Allies able to invade Italy? (c) What was D-Day?
2. Describe the American and Soviet advances in Germany in the last weeks of the war in Europe.
3. (a) What was the American battle plan in the Pacific? (b) Why were casualties high? (c) Where were the first two atomic bombs dropped? (d) What was the result?
4. (a) How did the occupations of Japan and Germany differ? (b) What was the purpose of the Nuremberg Trials?

Chapter 32 Review

Summary

In the decade after World War I, many nations took part in efforts to preserve peace. The rise of dictators in Germany and Italy, however, as well as the influence of military leaders in Japan, led to aggression in Europe and Asia. The leaders of France and Britain at first did little to halt Germany's violations of the Versailles Treaty or Hitler's takeover of the Rhineland, Austria, and the Sudetenland (Czechoslovakia). At Munich in 1938 they continued the policy of appeasement. Hitler seized Czechoslovakia and moved to take Polish territory.

The question of Poland, plus a surprise alliance between Germany and the Soviet Union, led Britain and France to declare war in September, 1939. In the meantime, Japanese aggressions against China led to war in Asia. Japan soon occupied much of eastern China, while German forces rapidly overran Western Europe. By 1940 Britain alone faced Hitler in Europe. The German invasion of the Soviet Union, however, brought the USSR into the war. In December, 1941, a surprise Japanese attack on Pearl Harbor, Hawaii, involved the United States in the war as well.

The Axis powers — Germany, Italy, Japan — were all successful in the early years of the war. By late 1942, however, three Allied victories — Stalingrad, El Alamein, and Midway — had turned the tide. The Allied victory in Europe came in May, 1945. War continued in Asia, but the dropping of atomic bombs on two Japanese cities brought Japan's surrender in August, 1945.

Vocabulary Review

1. Match the following words with the listed definitions: *appeasement, dictator, genocide, neutral, racism.*

(a) Not supporting or assisting either side in a war or dispute.
(b) The systematic murder of an entire people.
(c) A ruler with absolute power.
(d) The policy of giving in to the demands of an aggressor in order to maintain peace.
(e) The notion that one's own racial or national group is superior to others.

2. Explain the importance of each of the following in the history of World War II: (a) *Anschluss,* (b) Maginot Line, (c) Nazi-Soviet Pact, (d) blitzkrieg, (e) Battle of Britain, (f) Lend-Lease Act, (g) resistance movements, (h) D-Day, (i) Greater East Asia Co-Prosperity Sphere, (j) Rome-Berlin-Tokyo Axis.

People to Identify

Match the following people with the numbered phrases that describe them: *Charles de Gaulle, Henri Philippe Pétain, Bernard Montgomery, Dwight D. Eisenhower, Heinrich Himmler, Winston Churchill, Neville Chamberlain, Erwin Rommel.*

1. The British prime minister who followed a policy of appeasement.
2. The German field marshal who was known as the "Desert Fox."
3. The British field marshal who led his army to victory in North Africa.
4. Britain's prime minister from 1940 to 1945.
5. The head of France's Vichy government.
6. Hitler's police chief.
7. The leader of the Free French forces.
8. The American general who commanded the Allied troops on D-Day.

Relating Geography and History

1. Locating places. Locate each of the following on a map in this chapter:

(a) Dunkirk
(b) Warsaw
(c) Moscow
(d) Sudetenland
(e) Stalingrad
(f) Pearl Harbor
(g) Manchuria
(h) Guadalcanal
(i) Coral Sea
(j) Hiroshima

2. Research. During World War II, battles were fought not only in Europe but also in Africa and the islands of the Pacific. Use an encyclopedia or atlas to find the location of the following battles: Stalingrad, El Alamein, Midway, the Coral Sea, the Battle of the Bulge, Leyte Gulf. Then mark each battle site on an outline map of the world. Make a chart giving information about the battles (name, date, location, forces involved, and outcome). Write a sentence telling how each battle affected the course of the war.

Discussion Questions

1. (a) How did Hitler justify German occupation of the Rhineland, Austria, and the Sudetenland? (b) In what way was Hitler's takeover of Czechoslovakia different from his earlier moves? (c) Why was Czechoslovakia particularly important to France and Britain?

2. (a) Why did British and French leaders let fascist aggression go unchallenged in the mid-1930's? (b) At what point did Britain and France realize that they would have to go to war to stop Hitler? (c) How was the Soviet Union involved in the events leading to the outbreak of war?

3. (a) What role did the United States take in the war in Europe before December, 1941? (b) How did Japan become allied with Italy and Germany? (c) What did Japan hope to gain by attacking the American fleet at Pearl Harbor?

4. How did the war come to an end in (a) Italy? (b) Germany? (c) Japan?

Reading Primary Sources

The following selection describes an uprising against the Nazis by the Jews in the Warsaw ghetto. Of the 400,000 people forced into the ghetto in 1940, only 60,000 remained alive in April, 1943, when this uprising occurred. Read the selection. Then answer the questions that follow.

> Every night scouts stood at their posts listening for the faintest sound . . . ready to sound the alarm . . . if the enemy should come. . . .
>
> At six o'clock . . . the black Nazi death-battalions marched [boldly] into the ghetto in full battle array, with [armored] cars, machine guns, tanks. . . . The proud German column . . . was met with fire from three sides. . . . Grenades and incendiary bottles cascaded down on them. . . . Such strong resistance apparently surprised the Germans. They quickly left the ghetto.
>
> The next morning, after cutting off the electricity and the water supply, they were back. This time they did not parade down the center of the street. They came singly or in small groups, moving close to the walls. They [moved] under a hail of hand grenades, dynamite bombs, and incendiary bottles thrown from windows, roofs, and attics. . . . [Our fighters] battled for every building and for every floor of every building. . . . The Germans usually set fire to the buildings. Our fighters would dash through prepared openings in the attic walls to begin the fight in the adjoining building. . . .
>
> [After] the wave of fire receded, . . . small groups still held out without water, without food, without ammunition. All hope of striking back at the enemy was gone. There was nothing left to do but try to escape.

(a) What actions indicate that the Jews were preparing for an attack? (b) How did the Nazis change tactics for their second attack? (c) What was the Jews' strategy of fighting? (d) What was the Nazi strategy? (e) What did the Jews finally decide to do?

Skill Activities

1. Placing events in time. On a separate sheet of paper, list the events in each of the following groups in the proper sequence, giving the correct date for each event.
(a) Germany invades Poland.
   The Battle of Britain begins.
   France surrenders.
(b) Hitler and Stalin sign a nonaggression pact.
   Germany invades the Soviet Union.
   The Nazi siege of Stalingrad fails.
(c) Japan invades China.
   The Battle of Midway is fought.
   Japan bombs Pearl Harbor.
(d) Allied troops invade Italy.
   The British win a victory at El Alamein.
   American and Japanese forces clash in the Battle of the Coral Sea.

2. Reports. Write a report on the role in World War II of one of the following individuals or of a person mentioned in the chapter: (a) Isoroku Yamamoto, (b) Tomoyuki Yamashita, (c) Hideki Tojo, (d) Vidkun Quisling, (e) George C. Patton, (f) Chester W. Nimitz, (g) Lord Louis Mountbatten, (h) William F. Halsey, (i) George C. Marshall, (j) Karl Doenitz, (k) Hermann Goering, (l) Omar N. Bradley, (m) James Doolittle. Use encyclopedias and other books from your library to find information.

3. Making political cartoons. Prepare a political cartoon on one of the following topics: (a) Fascist Italy invades Ethiopia; (b) the Munich conference; (c) the Nazi takeover of Czechoslovakia; or (d) the Nazi-Soviet Pact.

Unit Seven Review

Review Questions

1. (a) What part did nationalist feelings play in the events that led to World War I? (b) How did the fascist leaders of Italy and Germany view nationalism?

2. (a) Why did the United States decide to enter the First World War? (b) What was the attitude of most Americans toward European affairs in the period between the two world wars? (c) What events led to a gradual change in American attitudes by the early 1940's?

3. (a) What were Germany's objections to the Versailles Treaty? (b) How did German feeling about the Versailles Treaty play a part in the events that led to World War II?

4. (a) What developments in the late 1800's and early 1900's weakened the government of Czar Nicholas II in Russia? (b) How did the Bolsheviks under Lenin succeed in gaining control of the Russian government?

5. How did the economic depression of the 1930's affect the growth of fascist parties in Italy and Germany?

6. (a) Why did fascists oppose communism? (b) In what ways were these political systems similar?

7. (a) What led to the growth of militarism in Japan? (b) Why did the Japanese join the Axis powers in World War II?

8. Identify the war with which each of these battles was connected and explain why each was significant: (a) Midway; (b) Stalingrad; (c) Verdun; (d) El Alamein.

Projects

1. Ranking. Before World War I, Austria-Hungary, France, Germany, Great Britain, Italy, Japan, Russia, and the United States were all powerful nations. Try to rank these powers in order of strength (1) in 1914 and (2) today. Consider factors such as population, armed forces, value of imports and exports, miles of railroad, and size of annual national budget. Use an almanac or an encyclopedia to obtain this information. What other factors might be taken into account?

2. Making maps. Prepare a series of maps showing Europe (1) before 1914, (2) after the Paris peace settlements of World War I, and (3) after World War II. Write a short essay to accompany the maps, in which you identify the countries whose territorial boundaries were most greatly affected by the wars and explain the reasons for the boundary changes.

Books to Read

Barnett, Corelli. *The Great War.* Putnam. A history of World War I.

Bethell, Nicholas. *Russia Besieged (World War II Series).* Time-Life.

Bowen, Ezra. *Knights of the Air.* Time-Life. The story of air battles in World War I.

Butler, David. *Lusitania.* Random. A fictional account of the sinking of the *Lusitania.*

Frank, Anne. *The Diary of a Young Girl.* Doubleday. The diary of a Dutch-Jewish teenager who hid from the Nazis.

Graff, Stewart. *The Story of World War II.* Dutton.

Hersey, John. *Hiroshima.* Knopf.

Marrin, Albert. *The Airman's War: World War II in the Sky.* Atheneum.

Meltzer, Milton. *Never to Forget; the Jews of the Holocaust.* Harper.

Mosley, Leonard. *The Battle of Britain (World War II Series).* Time-Life.

Remarque, Erich Maria. *All Quiet on the Western Front.* Buccaneer Books. A famous novel about World War I.

Sim, Kevin. *Women at War; Five Women Who Defied the Nazis and Survived.* Morrow.

Snyder, Louis L. *World War II.* Franklin Watts.

Toland, John. *Adolf Hitler.* Doubleday.

Tuchman, Barbara W. *The Guns of August.* Macmillan. The beginning of World War I.

World at War Series. Children's Press. A series of easy-to-read books on World War II. Titles include *Submarines in the Pacific; D-Day; Battle of the Coral Sea; Mussolini: A Dictator Dies;* and *Fall of the Fox: Rommel.*

Young, Peter, ed. *The World Almanac Book of World War II.* Prentice-Hall.

Writing Reports

In studying world history, you will sometimes write reports. The following suggestions will help you divide the task into simple steps.

Choosing a topic. Choose a subject that you are interested in, one you will enjoy reading about. Once you have selected a general subject, narrow your topic. To limit a broad subject, you might choose an important person, a single country, or one event or development.

Finding information. When you have chosen and limited your subject, look for sources of information. In the library, look up the subject in the card catalogue. Also check the "Books to Read" section in the appropriate Unit Review of this book. You can find recent magazine articles on your subject by looking it up in the *Readers' Guide to Periodical Literature.* From these sources, compile a list of possible sources.

Write each reference on a separate note card. For books, include the author's name, the title, the publisher, and the city and year of publication on the card. For articles, list the author's name, the title, the name and date of the magazine, and the page numbers. When you have a list of sources, you are ready to read each reference and take notes for your paper.

Collecting information. As you read each source, take notes. Write your notes on note cards, and on each card write about only one subject. Continue to read various sources and take notes until you feel that you have enough information.

Organizing your information. Reread all of your note cards and separate them into stacks that contain similar ideas. Then read through the notes in each stack and decide on a phrase or sentence that presents the topic of that group of notes. This phrase or sentence will become a major heading in the outline of your report.

When you have chosen a heading for each stack of note cards, you will have the major headings for the outline of your paper. Arrange the headings in a logical order and assign a Roman numeral to each main heading.

The next step is to determine the subheadings under each main heading. Arrange the note cards of each stack in a logical order. Use these cards to decide on the subheadings for each main heading. Now complete your outline by writing each major heading and its subheadings in the order you have selected. (Review procedures for outlining, page 605.)

Writing the report. Follow your outline and use the information on your note cards to write the first draft of your report. Do not worry about making your first try perfect. Simply write the thoughts as they come to you. After you have finished the first draft, you should revise your report. First, check your draft against your outline to make sure that you covered what you intended to include. Then read the draft and revise sentences that are not clear. Finally, check your report for correct grammar, spelling, and punctuation. Copy or retype your report in its final form.

Check Your Skill

Use the following questions to check your understanding of what you have read:

1. An important factor to consider in choosing a topic is (a) finding a subject you have written about before, (b) your interest in the topic, (c) the teacher's interests.

2. Once you have chosen a general subject, you should (a) narrow your topic, (b) take notes, (c) consult the card catalogue.

3. Titles of books that might be helpful for a report can be found in (a) an atlas, (b) the library's card catalogue, (c) a dictionary.

4. Before you begin taking notes for your report, you should (a) write a rough draft, (b) prepare a list of sources, (c) decide on the headings for your outline.

Apply Your Skill

Choose a topic from Chapter 32 for a short research report. After a trip to the school library, list five sources of information for your report.

$$\mathcal{L} = -\frac{1}{4} \mathcal{F}^{\mu\nu}_a \mathcal{F}_{a\mu\nu} + \bar{q}(i\not{D} - M)q$$

The Contemporary Age

The first half of the twentieth century had been a time of crisis and turmoil, marked by two devastating world wars. The era after World War II was a time of searching for ways to maintain peace despite the growing power and fearsomeness of the world's weapons. Competition between the United States and the Soviet Union created a climate of tension that became known as the cold war.

World War II had involved all parts of the world, and the postwar years brought great changes everywhere. Most of the Western European nations recovered quickly, and many underwent remarkable economic growth. Recovery was somewhat slower in Eastern Europe, where people continued to challenge Soviet domination in their countries. The war speeded up the rise of nationalist movements in Asia, and many former colonial possessions gained their independence. Civil war in several Asian countries brought Communist governments to power. In Africa, nearly all the colonial territories sought and gained their independence from European nations in the postwar years.

Changes in the Middle East came partly from moves for independence but were also affected by the wealth and political influence that oil brought many nations in the region. The establishment of the Jewish state of Israel in a predominantly Muslim area created continuing conflicts. In Latin America, many nations still struggled with economic problems, while the United States and Canada — both strong economically — faced other challenges both at home and abroad.

The following chapters describe the challenges of the years after World War II and tell how these challenges were met in different regions of the world.

The late twentieth century was a time of exploration for humankind — both on Earth and in space. These roads to the future are suggested in the painting "Highways (No. 2)" by Ingo Swann. People still sought to understand the universe better, using mathematics in their efforts to describe the structure of matter.

- CHAPTER 33   The Cold War
- CHAPTER 34   Changing Europe
- CHAPTER 35   Changing Asia
- CHAPTER 36   Changing Africa
- CHAPTER 37   The Changing Middle East
- CHAPTER 38   The Changing Americas
- CHAPTER 39   The World Today

Cold war tensions in postwar Europe are symbolized by the barbed wire that blocks access to the Brandenburg Gate, an entry point into East Berlin.

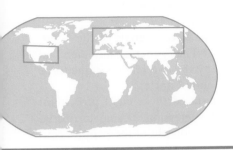

CHAPTER

The Cold War

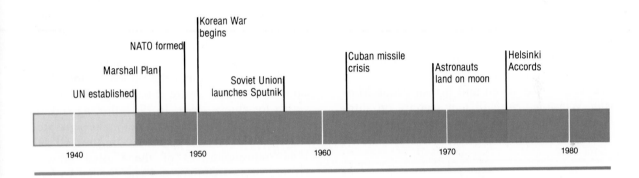

Even before World War II ended, leaders of the Allied nations began to make plans for the postwar world. One of their goals was the creation of a peacekeeping organization, and by 1945 the United Nations had been established.

At the war's end, the United States and the Soviet Union emerged as the world's most powerful nations. Rivalries between these two superpowers created an atmosphere of crises and tension that became known as the cold war. One source of tension was the establishment of a number of Soviet-backed Communist governments in Eastern Europe after World War II. In response, the United States government adopted policies designed to control the spread of communism both in Europe and elsewhere. Each of the superpowers formed defensive alliances and began to build up a store of weapons. At the same time, however, American and Soviet leaders sought ways to lessen the risk of actual war.

This chapter describes the formation of the United Nations and tells how the cold war affected the postwar world.

CHAPTER OUTLINE

1 The United Nations Is Formed

2 Cold War Tensions Develop

3 World Leaders Work to Lessen Tensions

1 The United Nations Is Formed

When Allied leaders met during World War II to confer on wartime strategy, they also made plans for the postwar years. Some of the discussions concerned ways of dealing with Germany, Italy, and Japan after the war was won. Others took up the question of establishing an organization that would help maintain world peace and prevent a third world war. Plans for such an organization were put into effect even before the war ended in Europe and Asia.

The Atlantic Charter states peace aims. By the summer of 1941, nearly all of Western Europe had fallen to the Axis powers. Although the United States was not yet at war, President Franklin D. Roosevelt and British Prime Minister Winston Churchill met secretly on shipboard off the coast of Newfoundland to discuss the wartime and peacetime goals of the Western democracies. The general statement of principles issued by the two leaders came to be known as the Atlantic Charter.

The Charter stated these eight principles: (1) No territorial aggression; (2) no territorial changes without the consent of the peoples concerned; (3) restoration of self-government to all peoples; (4) equal access to raw materials for all countries; (5) world economic cooperation; (6) freedom from fear and want; (7) freedom of the seas; (8) worldwide disarmament.

The United Nations Charter is drawn up. As the war continued, the Allied nations became increasingly aware of the need to work together to achieve peace. In 1942, they agreed to act as "United Nations" and not make separate treaties with any Axis power. In the fall of 1944, representatives of the United States, Great Britain, China, and the Soviet Union gathered at Dumbarton Oaks, an estate in Washington, D.C. There they made plans for an international organization to maintain peace and security after the war.

To put these plans into effect, delegates from 50 nations gathered in San Francisco in April, 1945. They drew up and signed a charter for an organization to be known as the United Nations (or UN). Its primary purpose was to preserve peace and "save succeeding generations from the scourge of war." Other goals stated in the Charter were the promotion of self-determination, respect for the rights and freedoms of all human beings, and cooperation among nations in solving social, cultural, and economic problems.

The organization set up by the Charter had six main divisions within the United Nations — the General Assembly, the Security Council, the International Court of Justice, the Trusteeship Council, the Secretariat, and the Economic and Social Council.

Every UN member nation was to be represented in the General Assembly. The Assembly was given the authority to discuss any matter within the scope of the UN Charter and recommend solutions. Other important duties were to

---

TIMETABLE
The Cold War

1945	The United Nations is established. Soviet forces occupy Eastern Europe.
1947	Truman pledges aid to countries threatened by communism. The Marshall Plan is launched.
1949	The German Federal Republic (West Germany) and German Democratic Republic (East Germany) are established. NATO is formed.
1950–1953	UN forces fight the Korean War.
1956	Khrushchev announces a policy of "peaceful coexistence."
1957	The Soviet Union launches *Sputnik.*
1961	The Berlin Wall is built. The Bay of Pigs landing in Cuba fails.
1962	The Cuban missile crisis threatens war.
1963	The Nuclear Test Ban Treaty is signed.
1969	American astronauts land on the moon.
1972	A Strategic Arms Limitation Treaty is signed.
1975	The Helsinki Accords recognize postwar boundaries in Europe.

choose the people or nations that would serve in other divisions of the organization and to vote on new member nations. Each member nation was given one vote in the Assembly.

The Security Council had responsibility for investigating international disputes and working for their peaceful settlement. To halt an aggressor nation, the Council might refuse to grant it diplomatic recognition, boycott its exports, or send troops to maintain peace.

The Security Council originally had five permanent members — the United States, Great Britain, France, the Soviet Union, and China.[1] Six (later ten) other members were elected by the General Assembly for two-year terms. Security Council actions required the approval of all permanent members. Each had veto power to block action by the Council.

The Secretariat was set up to run the everyday business of the UN, such as making surveys of populations and resources, translating documents, and setting up international conferences. At the head of the Secretariat was the Secretary-General. The first person to hold this office was Trygve Lie (LEE) of Norway.

Other UN organizations were to handle specific areas of interest. The International Court of Justice was established primarily to deal with questions of international law. The Trusteeship Council was established to oversee territories that had been mandates under the League of Nations (page 648) as well as some of the lands taken from the Axis powers. Member nations were given the responsibility to oversee the trust territories and help them move toward independence. The Economic and Social Council, working under the General Assembly, was to help coordinate the work of UN agencies working in such fields as world trade, economic development, and human rights.

Many specialized agencies also were attached to the UN. They dealt with a variety of fields, including meteorology, health, tariffs, and postal services.

The United Nations Charter is ratified. By the fall of 1945, the Charter of the United

John Foster Dulles, Adlai Stevenson, and Eleanor Roosevelt were United States delegates to the United Nations in the years after World War II.

Nations had been ratified by the Big Five — the United States, Britain, China, the Soviet Union, and France — and by a majority of the member nations. The UN eventually established its main headquarters in New York City, though other branches of the organization also worked elsewhere.

CHECK-UP

1. (a) When and why was the Atlantic Charter issued? (b) What four nations met to make plans for the United Nations?
2. (a) What was the major goal in establishing the United Nations? (b) Name the six main divisions of the United Nations and tell what responsibilities each was given.
3. (a) What nations are permanent members of the Security Council? (b) What is the voting procedure in the Council?

---

[1]China was originally represented in the UN by the Nationalist government. In 1971 the UN recognized the People's Republic of China and gave it China's place in the Security Council.

2 Cold War Tensions Develop

When World War II ended in the summer of 1945, the center of world power was no longer Western Europe. The United States and the Soviet Union emerged as the two strongest nations in the postwar world. Relations between these two nations had never been friendly, but they had been wartime allies against Germany. In the postwar years the rivalry and suspicion between the United States and the Soviet Union intensified. The resultant atmosphere of tension, in which the two superpowers competed with money, aid, and military strategy, is known as the cold war.

The United States is the leader of the West. Unlike the European Allies, the United States had escaped the destruction of the war. A prosperous nation with plentiful resources, it led the world in industrial and agricultural production. By 1945, therefore, the United States was the acknowledged leader — politically and economically — of the Western nations. Militarily, the United States was at that time the only nation that had atomic weapons.

The USSR dominates Eastern Europe. Of all the nations involved in the war, the Soviet Union had suffered the greatest losses. The death toll of Soviet soldiers and civilians was estimated at 20 million, and the Nazi occupation had destroyed cities, farms, and factories. On the other hand, in 1945 the USSR had the largest army in the world, hardened by nearly four years of combat. Stalin, the dictator of the USSR, feared another war. To protect its political and economic system, the Soviet Union used its military strength to establish control over Eastern Europe.

At the Yalta conference (page 712), Stalin had been promised Eastern Europe as a Soviet sphere of influence but had assured the other leaders that elections would be held there. As the Red Army moved toward Germany, it freed Bulgaria, Hungary, Poland, and Rumania from the Nazis and occupied those areas.

Communist governments are established. With the backing of the Soviet Union and its military forces, Communist parties played a leading role in the postwar political reorganiza-tion of these Eastern European countries. By the late 1940's Communists controlled the governments in Bulgaria, Hungary, and Rumania. A Communist government also had been set up in Poland, though its authority was disputed by the Polish government in exile in London.

In two other Eastern European nations, Communists also came to power. In Yugoslavia, the partisans led by Marshal Tito (TEE-toh) had been helped by the Allies in their resistance to the Nazis. The Allies supported Tito's formation of a Communist government in 1945. In neighboring Albania, local Communists also gained power at the end of the war.

The Communist Eastern European countries became part of the Soviet *bloc* (map, next page). Those nations dominated by the Soviet Union were considered Soviet "satellites."

The "iron curtain" separates Eastern Europe from the West. The Soviet Union soon set about stopping contacts between its satellites and the Western nations. Trade with the West was halted, and travel in either direction was limited. Western newspapers, magazines, books, and radio programs were banned in the satellite nations.

The United States and the Western European countries viewed these developments with growing uneasiness. Their fears were expressed in 1946 by Winston Churchill, speaking at Westminster College near St. Louis, Missouri. Churchill described his view of postwar Europe:

> From Stettin in the Baltic to Trieste in the Adriatic, an iron curtain has descended across the Continent. Behind that line lie all the capitals of the ancient states of Central and Eastern Europe. Warsaw, Berlin, Prague, Vienna, Budapest, Belgrade, Bucharest, and Sofia —all these famous cities and the populations around them lie in what I must call the Soviet sphere. . . . this is certainly not the liberated Europe we [the Allies] fought to build up. Nor is [the new Europe] one which contains the essentials of permanent peace.

Churchill's words so aptly described the situation that "Iron Curtain" became the term

Postwar Europe

The postwar period saw new boundaries and alliances in Europe. European members of NATO and of the Soviet bloc are shown on the map.

KEY

- Soviet Union
- Soviet territorial gains since 1939
- Other Communist countries
- NATO members, 1955
- Nonaligned nations
- Prewar boundary

SCALE
0 — 300 mi
0 — 300 km

used for the sharp division between the Soviet bloc and the West.

Western leaders fear the spread of communism. Fearing still more Soviet expansion in Europe, the West reacted strongly to Communist activity in Turkey and Greece. In 1945 Stalin demanded that Turkey allow the Soviet Union to set up military bases along the straits between the Black Sea and the Aegean. In neighboring Greece, which was torn by civil war, Communist-backed forces were gaining the upper hand.

Britain supplied military and economic aid to both Greece and Turkey, but by early 1947,

Marshall Plan aid included farm equipment, as shown in this photo of French farmers.

the British government realized it could no longer afford such aid. Britain, like much of Western Europe, was on the verge of economic collapse. The British appealed to the United States to take the lead in halting the spread of communism in Europe.

Truman establishes a new American policy. In response to the British appeal, President Harry Truman announced a new American foreign policy, which came to be known as the Truman Doctrine. Speaking to Congress in March, 1947, he asked that military and economic aid be sent to Greece and Turkey. He also called for the United States to supply economic and military aid to any country that requested help in resisting communism. Truman stated his policy in these words:

> Our way of life is based on the will of the majority, and is distinguished by free institutions, representative government, free elections. . . . The . . . [Soviet] way of life is based upon the will of a minority forcibly imposed upon the majority. It relies upon terror and oppression. . . . The free peoples of the world look to us for support in maintaining their freedom. . . . If we falter in our leadership, we may endanger the peace of the world — and we shall surely endanger the welfare of our nation.

The Truman Doctrine became the basis of the cold war policy known as *containment.* Its aim was to "contain," or limit, Communist governments to those countries where they already existed, and to prevent communism from being imposed by force in other nations.

American aid speeds European recovery. All the European nations needed aid to survive the postwar period without political upheaval or economic collapse. The United States, therefore, offered its help in the rebuilding of Europe. In June, 1947, Secretary of State George C. Marshall proposed a generous program of economic assistance for Europe. "Our policy," said Marshall, "is directed not against any country or doctrine but against hunger, poverty, desperation, and chaos."

Marshall's proposal was put into effect as the European Recovery Program, commonly called the Marshall Plan. Between 1948 and 1952 the United States provided Western Europe with aid valued at more than $12 billion. The results were striking. By 1952 industrial production in the Marshall Plan countries had risen above prewar levels, and a new era of prosperity had come to Western Europe.

Stalin tries to spur recovery in Eastern Europe. The Marshall Plan had been offered to all the European countries. Stalin would not let the Soviet satellites participate, however, and economic recovery in Eastern Europe was slow compared to that in the countries receiving Marshall Plan aid. To counter the resentment this caused, Stalin set up the Cominform (Bureau of Information of the Communist and Workers Parties) in October, 1947. The purpose of the Cominform was to spread Communist propaganda within the Soviet bloc. Calling for loyalty to world communism, it directed the work of the Communist parties in Eastern Europe and had ties with the Communist parties in France and Italy.

In 1949 the Soviet Union set up a plan of economic aid and cooperation among the Iron Curtain countries. It was called Comecon (Council for Mutual Economic Assistance). The Soviet satellites, however, were unable to achieve economic growth comparable to that in Western Europe.

Czechoslovakia falls to Communist control. Soviet domination in Eastern Europe continued to grow. Czechoslovakia, which Hitler had seized in 1939 (page 699), was re-established as an independent democratic nation in 1945. Eduard Beneš was re-elected president, but Soviet pressure on the country was strong.

Over the next two years, the Communists moved to take over Czechoslovakia. The Czech Communist Party, well organized and backed by the Soviet Union, won about a third of the votes when elections were held in 1946. A coalition government was formed in which Communists held key government positions, including the office of prime minister. Gaining power in the labor unions as well as in government, the Communists took control and eliminated all opposition. Foreign minister Jan Masaryk, who had close ties with the West, died mysteriously. Beneš was pressured into resigning, and the Communists established a Soviet-style government. By June, 1948, Czechoslovakia was firmly under Soviet control.

Yugoslavia resists Soviet domination. Yugoslavia's Communist government, which had been established by Tito and his partisans (page 724), was the only Eastern European nation to resist Soviet control successfully. When it came to choosing between Yugoslav or Soviet interests, Tito chose to strengthen his own country. During 1948, relations between the Soviet Union and Yugoslavia grew steadily worse. The Soviet Union withdrew military and technical help, the Cominform expelled Yugoslavia, and the Soviet Union finally broke off economic relations and abandoned its treaty of friendship. One by one, the satellite nations followed the Soviet lead.

Yugoslavia's isolation from the other Communist countries, however, did not force the country back into the Soviet orbit. Instead, Tito strengthened the country's ties with the West and with the new nations of Asia and Africa.

The Western European nations agree to a defense treaty. The Soviet actions in Eastern Europe convinced leaders in Western Europe to strengthen and unify their defenses. On March 17, 1948, Britain, France, Belgium, Luxembourg, and the Netherlands signed the Brussels Treaty. The treaty was a mutual-defense pact, a fifty-year agreement that if one of the member countries were attacked, the others would come to its aid.

The cold war brings a crisis in Germany. Cold war tensions increased steadily in 1948, and East and West came into direct conflict in occupied Germany. As they had agreed at the Potsdam conference, each of the wartime Allies occupied one area of Germany (map, page 728). Delays in signing a peace treaty and other disagreements soon made this joint control difficult. The Western nations realized that Germany had to be included in long-range plans for Europe. Giving up hope of Soviet cooperation, France, Britain, and the United States agreed in the spring of 1948 to combine their occupation zones to form a West German state. This decision was bitterly opposed by the Soviet Union, which feared a strong, reunited Germany.

The Soviet response to the plan for a German state was a sudden blockade of Berlin in June, 1948. Although the city lay in Soviet-occupied territory, it was also divided into four occupation zones. The Western nations regarded West Berlin (their combined zones) as a free city within Communist-ruled Eastern Europe (map, page 728).

On June 24, 1948, Soviet troops blocked all roads, railroads, and waterways linking West Berlin to the Western zones, cutting off food and other supplies from the two million West Berliners. Within two days of the beginning of the Berlin blockade, however, American and British cargo planes were flying in supplies to West Berlin and carrying children and others to safety in the Western zones. Operating around the clock, regardless of weather, the Berlin airlift flew over two million tons of goods — food, fuel, medical supplies, machinery — into West Berlin. Realizing that the blockade would not change Western policy, Stalin ended it in May, 1949.

Governments are set up in a divided Germany. Germany remained a center of cold war tensions. Shortly after the Berlin blockade was lifted, the Western allies carried out their plan for a German state made up of the territory that had been the French, British, and American zones of occupation. The Federal Republic of Germany (or West Germany) was to be a parliamentary democracy. A few months later, the Soviets installed a Communist regime in

Divided Germany and Berlin

France, Britain, the United States, and the Soviet Union occupied Germany after World War II. Which of these powers occupied West Berlin? East Berlin?

their zone, creating the German Democratic Republic (or East Germany).

The Western nations form NATO. The crisis in Berlin helped bring about military cooperation among the Western powers. In April, 1949, they formed a mutual-defense pact, the North Atlantic Treaty Organization, or NATO. The original NATO members were Norway, Denmark, Iceland, the Netherlands, Belgium, Luxembourg, Britain, France, Portugal, Italy, the United States, and Canada.[2]

Like the Brussels Treaty (page 727), the NATO agreement provided that "an armed attack against one or more of [its members] in Europe or America shall be considered an attack against them all." As part of NATO's security system, American troops, planes, and nuclear weapons were to be stationed in Western Europe. This aspect of the NATO alliance took on greater importance when, in the fall of 1949, it was announced that the Soviet Union had successfully tested an atomic bomb.

Communism makes gains in Asia. Since 1945, the West's attempts to contain communism had focused on the Soviet Union's grow-

---

[2]In 1952 Greece and Turkey also became members, and in 1955 West Germany joined the alliance.

ing power in Europe. In 1949, however, the long battle between Nationalist and Communist forces in China (page 690) ended with a Communist victory. The People's Republic of China was proclaimed on October 1, 1949. At the time, this appeared to strengthen the position of the Soviet Union. The two huge Communist nations signed agreements on defense and economic aid.

War breaks out in Korea. Communist China soon became involved in the war over control of its neighbor Korea (map, page 709). Korea had been under Japanese rule at the beginning of World War II. Like postwar Germany, it had then been occupied by the Allies. Soviet forces occupied the country north of the 38th parallel of latitude; American troops were in the south. In 1947 the United Nations passed a resolution to reunite Korea and hold elections. The Soviet Union, however, would not permit UN observers to enter the north. Elections were held only in American-occupied South Korea, where the Republic of Korea was established in August, 1948. A month later, a Communist-controlled government, the Democratic People's Republic of Korea, was set up in the north. Both claimed to be the government for the entire Korean peninsula.

On June 25, 1950, some 80,000 North Korean troops crossed the 38th parallel and invaded South Korea. The UN Security Council condemned the aggression by North Korea and requested member nations to help South Korea.[3] American troops, planes, and ships made up much of the United Nations forces that were rushed to South Korea. Australian, Canadian, British, and Turkish troops also played a large part in the fighting, as did the South Koreans themselves. The UN forces were commanded by General Douglas MacArthur.

By October, 1950, the UN forces had driven the North Koreans back across the 38th parallel. The decision was then made to take the UN forces into North Korea, even though some people feared this would bring China into the war. When the UN troops approached the

Yalu River, the boundary with Manchuria, they encountered thousands of Chinese Communist soldiers who had crossed the border to reinforce the North Koreans. The UN forces were pushed south across the 38th parallel.

As the UN troops fought to regain the ground they had lost, General MacArthur demanded an all-out attack on China, including the bombing of bases in Manchuria. UN officials, however, wanted to limit the war. When MacArthur persisted in his efforts to broaden the war, President Truman removed him from command in Korea. Peace talks began, and an armistice was signed on July 27, 1953. Even then, the 38th parallel remained the boundary of a divided Korea.

The Korean conflict increases cold war tensions. Casualties, both civilian and military, were high in the Korean war. The Koreans themselves suffered the most, because their industry, farms, and homes were destroyed. For the United States, the struggle in Korea made relations with Communist China more difficult. John Foster Dulles (DUH-luss), secretary of state under President Eisenhower, continued an active containment policy in the 1950's. Not only did the United States aid countries resisting communism; it also made defensive alliances, in Asia and elsewhere.

CHECK-UP

1. Vocabulary: *bloc, containment.*
2. (a) How did the Eastern European countries become part of the Soviet bloc? (b) What did Churchill mean by the term "Iron Curtain"?
3. (a) What did Truman propose to do to stop the spread of communism? (b) What was the purpose of the Marshall Plan?
4. (a) Why did tensions develop between the occupying powers in Germany? (b) What was the Western nations' plan for Germany? (c) How did Stalin react to this plan?
5. (a) What territories were combined to form West Germany? (b) How was East Germany created? (c) What Western defense alliance grew out of the crisis in Germany?
6. (a) What happened to Korea in the peace settlements after World War II? (b) How were governments established in North and South Korean? (c) Why were UN forces sent to Korea? (d) How did China become involved in the Korean conflict?

---

[3]The Soviet Union did not use its veto to block the Council's resolution because it was at the time boycotting the Council for its refusal to admit the People's Republic of China to the UN.

3 World Leaders Work to Lessen Tensions

The cold war entered a new stage after Stalin died in 1953, and tensions eased for a time. An uneasy balance continued between the superpowers, however. New crises threatened peace, and certain areas continued to be trouble spots. Nevertheless, efforts toward lessening tensions went on with some success.

The Soviet bloc agrees to a defense pact. The question of a united Germany remained critical during the 1950's, as both East and West Germany were recognized as independent nations. West Germany was admitted to NATO in 1955 and allowed to rearm. As a countermeasure to the NATO alliance, the Soviet Union immediately signed a mutual-defense pact with seven of the Eastern European countries. (Yugoslavia did not join.) This agreement, the Warsaw Treaty Organization, or Warsaw Pact, provided for Soviet troops to be stationed in each satellite country. These armies were under the leadership of a Soviet commander in Moscow.

The Americans and Soviets enter an "arms race." During the 1950's, the stockpiling of nuclear weapons began to be an important element in the tensions between the USSR and the United States. Each nation tried to develop weapons so powerful that the other would not dare to attack. This policy of discouraging an attack by making one's opponent fear a counterattack is called *deterrence*.

New types of weapons were developed by the superpowers as the arms race went on. In 1952, the United States exploded the first hydrogen bomb; the following year, the Soviet Union also tested a hydrogen bomb. Both developed rockets that carried nuclear warheads. In 1954 the United States launched the first nuclear submarine, armed with atomic missiles. By 1957 the Soviets had developed intercontinental ballistic missiles (ICBM's), rockets that could reach targets in any part of the world.

American and Soviet leaders meet at Geneva. The tensions of the cold war led world leaders to look for ways to avoid actual war. In the summer of 1955, Western and Soviet officials held the first "summit" conference, a meeting between the top officials of each government. At the first summit conference, held in Geneva, Switzerland, these leaders discussed disarmament, German reunification, and chances of wider contacts between the West and the Communist nations. They also agreed that nuclear war would be a disaster for all nations. Although no specific treaties were made, the first summit conference was a sign that the superpowers were willing to meet and talk over their differences.

Soviet policies undergo change. The "spirit of Geneva" helped to set the tone of Soviet-American relations after 1955. By 1956 Nikita Khrushchev (kroosh-CHOF) had come to power in the Soviet Union. He denounced Stalin and his cult of personality (page 666) and began a program of "de-Stalinization" in the Soviet bloc. Stalinist policies were harshly criticized, and pictures of Stalin were removed from factories, businesses, and schools. The role of the secret police was downgraded, and people who had survived the hardships of forced labor camps began to reappear in Soviet society.

In dealing with the West, Khrushchev proclaimed a new Soviet policy, which he called "peaceful coexistence." He urged the United States and the Soviet Union to compete peacefully in producing more goods, providing a better standard of living for their people, making scientific and technical advances, and giving more aid to developing nations.

Rebellions take place in the satellite nations. Attitudes in the Eastern European nations also changed in the period of de-Stalinization. Open protests against Soviet policies came from farmers who disliked collectivization, workers who wanted better pay, and intellectuals who opposed censorship. In Poland and Hungary, discontent erupted into open rebellions in 1956 (page 751).

The space race begins. The rivalries between East and West went beyond a struggle for political power to competition for prestige and leadership in such fields as science and technology. On October 4, 1957, the Soviet Union sent the first artificial satellite, called

Rockets into Space

In the 1200's, Chinese warriors fired flaming rockets — known as "Chinese arrows" — at invading Mongol horsemen. During the War of 1812, Francis Scott Key described the "rockets' red glare" as he wrote "The Star-Spangled Banner." The principles used in these early rockets made it possible to launch Sputnik in 1957, take astronauts to the moon, and send spaceships to distant planets.

Early rockets were powered by solid fuels such as gunpowder and traveled only a short distance. In 1903 a Russian scientist, Konstantin Tsiolkovsky (tsee-ohl-KAHV-skee), suggested two ideas — that rockets could work in space and that liquid fuels would be a better propellant. An American physicist, Robert H. Goddard, experimented with these ideas. On March 16, 1926, Goddard launched a rocket propelled by gasoline and liquid oxygen. The rocket traveled only 184 feet, but its flight marked the beginning

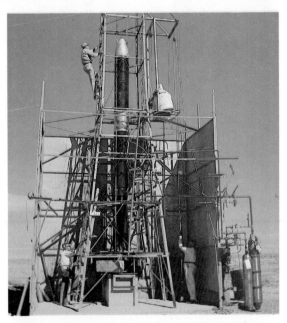

of the space age. Descendants of Goddard's rocket not only carry powerful nuclear weapons but also lift satellites into orbit and travel to Jupiter and beyond.

Sputnik, into orbit around Earth. Three months later, the first American satellite was launched, and the two nations began a "race in space."

Soviet engineers had been concentrating on rocketry for some time, but an intensive American space program in the 1960's enabled the United States to catch up. The first satellite to land on the moon was Soviet (1959), and the first person to orbit the earth was Soviet cosmonaut Yuri Gagarin (1961). Less than a month after Gagarin's flight, however, Alan Shepard became the first American astronaut to go into space. By the end of the decade — July 20, 1969 — American astronauts Neil Armstrong and Edwin Aldrin became the first persons to land on the moon.

Tensions increase after the U-2 incident. "Peaceful coexistence" brought some easing of tensions between the superpowers. Soviet and American leaders, along with other nations, signed the Antarctic Treaty, prohibiting military activity in the southernmost continent. They also joined in a resolution calling for the

peaceful uses of outer space. In 1959 Vice President Richard M. Nixon met with Khrushchev in Moscow, and later that year Khrushchev became the first Soviet leader to visit the United States. Plans were made for a summit conference between Khrushchev and Eisenhower in Paris in 1960.

Accusations of spying, however, undermined the Paris meeting. In May, 1960, an angry Khrushchev announced that, a few days earlier, Soviet missiles had shot down an American plane of a type called U-2. Equipped with a variety of cameras and recording devices, the plane had been taking photographs near a major industrial area in the Ural Mountains. The Paris summit meeting was canceled.

A wall divides Berlin. Another crisis in Germany soon increased tensions still more. Since 1945, thousands of discontented East Germans had entered West Berlin, using the city as an escape route from Communist rule. In August, 1961, the East German government built a wall closing off East Berlin from the

731

Soviet leader Nikita Khrushchev visited an Iowa farm during his 1959 visit to the United States.

western part of the city. Made of barbed wire and later reinforced with massive concrete slabs, the wall was twelve feet high and stretched for 28 miles. At "checkpoints" along the wall, guards limited traffic in and out. Explosive mines were planted near the base of the wall. The Berlin Wall soon came to symbolize the contrasts between the freedom in West Berlin and the repression in the East.

The Cuban missile crisis threatens world peace. The development and spread of nuclear weapons had introduced a new element of risk in the cold war. This led to a tense confrontation over Cuba, an island nation in the Caribbean Sea. In January, 1959, guerrilla forces headed by Fidel Castro overthrew the ruling dictatorship. Castro's revolutionary government took over large landholdings (some belonging to American businesses) and set up an economic system much like those in Communist countries.

Although Castro had considerable popular support, particularly among workers, his regime threatened middle-class property owners and professional people. Many Cubans from these groups had fled to the United States when Castro gained power. These anti-Castro Cubans hoped to invade Cuba, believing it would be easy to overthrow Castro. Distrustful

of Castro's policies, some United States officials supported the plan, and about 1,500 Cuban exiles began to train and arm for an invasion.

In April, 1961, the anti-Castro forces landed in southern Cuba at the Bay of Pigs. The Cubans did not rise to support the anti-Castro forces, and the invasion failed. Most of the invaders were captured within two days.

Soon after the Bay of Pigs landing, Castro asked the Soviet Union to help protect Cuba from other invasion attempts. By October, 1962, American intelligence flights over Cuba had found evidence of launching sites for nuclear missiles. Alarmed at the presence of Soviet rockets only 90 miles from the United States, President John F. Kennedy went on television and demanded that the Soviet Union remove them immediately. He announced that American ships were heading toward Cuba to stop Soviet ships from delivering any more missiles. After a tense few hours, Khrushchev agreed to remove the weapons from Cuba.

Efforts are made to lessen the risks of war. The Cuban missile crisis had alerted leaders to the possibility that cold war tensions could trigger armed conflict. Western and Soviet leaders began to look for ways to lessen this risk. A major step was taken in 1963, when Britain, the United States, and the Soviet Union signed the Nuclear Test Ban Treaty. The three powers agreed to stop testing nuclear weapons in the air, in space, and under water. Underground testing was permitted.

To keep nuclear weapons from spreading to more nations, the United States, Britain, the Soviet Union, and many other nations signed the Nuclear Nonproliferation Treaty in 1968. Under its terms, the countries that did not have nuclear weapons agreed not to develop them. The nations that already had nuclear capacity promised that they would promote research to find peaceful uses of nuclear energy.

The superpowers also sought to lessen the threat of war by providing for direct communication between the Soviet and American leaders. A "hot line" telephone link was set up between Moscow and Washington.

Shifts occur in the alignment of nations. By the 1970's the superpowers' position in world affairs had changed, partly because of shifts in attitude among their allies. A split between

China and the Soviet Union in 1961 had divided the Communist nations' loyalties. Yugoslavia continued to follow an independent course. Albania left the Warsaw Pact and turned to China. Rumania refused to allow Warsaw Pact troops within its borders.

There were shifts in the Western alliances also. In 1966 France pulled its troops out of NATO and demanded that NATO troops leave French soil. Other NATO members expressed concern about the alliance's heavy dependence on nuclear weapons. Some were worried that Western Europe might become the battleground for a nuclear war. Others were uneasy because the nuclear weapons in Western Europe could be used only with American approval. They were not sure Americans would be willing to defend Western Europe at the risk of a Soviet attack on the United States.

Many new nations are nonaligned. Early in the postwar period, most nations had been allied with either the West or the Soviet bloc. In the 1950's, dozens of new nations gained independence in Africa and Asia. These new nations, along with some established but still developing nations such as Egypt and India, were spoken of as the Third World. Most had ties to neither the Soviet Union nor the United States and therefore were considered nonaligned — not committed to the policies and goals of either side in the cold war. The nonaligned nations became an important factor in the balance of power between the Soviet bloc on one hand and the West and Japan on the other. By the 1970's, Third World countries had gained considerable influence in the UN.

Other Western nations take a larger role. As the Western European nations recovered from the war and grew stronger economically, they also took a greater role in world affairs. Willy Brandt (BRAHNT), the chancellor of West Germany from 1969 to 1974, worked for a new approach to East-West relations, particularly as they affected Germany. Brandt urged the NATO nations and the Soviet bloc to follow principles that would promote *détente* (day-TAHNT), meaning "a relaxing of tensions."

Following these principles, Brandt tried to end the long-standing problem over Germany's status. In 1970 West Germany agreed to accept the Polish-German boundaries set up at Yalta and Potsdam. In 1972 a treaty between West Germany and East Germany made the division into two nations an accepted fact.

That same year the United States, Britain, France, and the Soviet Union — the countries that had occupied Germany since 1945 — agreed that West Berlin was not part of West Germany. In recognition of the city's ties with West Germany, however, they ruled that traffic should move freely between the two places.

Treaties between the West and the Soviet Union encourage détente. American and Soviet leaders made gestures to show they were working toward détente. President Nixon visited Moscow and Peking in 1972, and Leonid Brezhnev (BREZH-nef), leader of the Soviet Union after 1964, visited Washington. The Soviet and American leaders also signed the first Strategic Arms Limitation Treaty (SALT) in 1972. SALT I limited the number of sites from which missiles could be launched and froze stockpiles of nuclear arms at existing levels.

Hopeful moves toward détente also resulted from meetings held at Helsinki, Finland, and Stockholm, Sweden. At the Finnish city, representatives of the United States, Canada, the Soviet Union, and over 30 European nations met in 1975 and signed the Helsinki Accords, accepting the European borders drawn in 1945. The nations promised to settle disputes peacefully, respect one another's internal affairs, and protect human rights. In 1986, delegates of 35 European nations, including both NATO and Warsaw Pact members, signed the Stockholm Pact. This agreement called for on-site inspections of military activities by designated observer nations and was expected to reduce the risk of accidental war in Europe.

CHECK-UP

1. Vocabulary: *deterrence, détente.*
2. (a) What was the Warsaw Pact? (b) What action prompted the pact?
3. What was the policy of (a) de-Stalinization? (b) peaceful coexistence? (c) What effects did these policies have in the Soviet satellites?
4. How did the Cuban missile crisis affect relations between the superpowers?
5. (a) What was SALT I? (b) What agreements were reached in the Helsinki Accords? (c) What was the Stockholm Pact?

Chapter 33 Review

Summary

Allied leaders' hopes for a permanent peace after World War II led to the founding of the United Nations in 1945. Postwar politics were dominated by the United States and the Soviet Union, and rivalry between the superpowers created an atmosphere of tension known as the cold war. After the Eastern European nations became Soviet satellites, the United States tried to "contain" the spread of communism, a policy expressed in the Truman Doctrine. The Marshall Plan aided European economic recovery.

Rival defensive pacts — NATO and the Warsaw Pact — reflected cold war tensions in Europe. The status of Germany, which was occupied by the Western powers and the Soviet Union, was a continuing problem in the postwar years. The Soviet Union used pressure on West Berlin, first imposing a blockade and later building the Berlin Wall, in an attempt to force the Western powers out.

In 1949 Communists gained control of China. The spread of communism to Korea led to war between UN forces and Communist troops. In the Western Hemisphere, Cuba came under Communist rule, and the Cuban missile crisis brought the United States and the Soviet Union close to war.

As part of the rivalry that characterized the cold war, the United States and the Soviet Union competed in space and in a nuclear arms race. In time, faced by the dangers of nuclear war, the superpowers tried to ease tensions through summit meetings and test-ban treaties. The Helsinki Accords of 1975 marked the high point of this period of détente.

Vocabulary Review

1. Write the following sentences on a sheet of paper. Fill in the blank in each sentence with one of these words: *bloc, containment, détente, deterrence.*
(a) Through a policy of __?__, the United States hoped to prevent the spread of communism.
(b) The policy of __?__ is intended to discourage a hostile power from attacking by making it fear a counterattack.
(c) __?__ is an easing of tensions between nations.
(d) The Soviet __?__ included the Soviet Union and the satellite nations of Eastern Europe.
2. Distinguish between the terms in each of the following pairs:
(a) European Recovery Program; Council for Mutual Economic Assistance.
(b) North Atlantic Treaty Organization; Warsaw Pact.
(c) Federal Republic of Germany; German Democratic Republic.

People to Identify

Match the following people with the numbered phrases that describe them: *Willy Brandt, Leonid Brezhnev, Nikita Khrushchev, Trygve Lie, George C. Marshall, Marshal Tito.*
1. First UN Secretary-General.
2. American secretary of state who started a program of economic assistance for Europe after World War II.
3. Leader of postwar Yugoslavia.
4. Soviet leader who began the policy of "peaceful coexistence."
5. West German chancellor who began a new policy toward Eastern Europe.
6. The head of the Soviet government after 1964.

Relating Geography and History

1. **Locating places.** Locate each of the following on a map in this chapter:
(a) Berlin
(b) East Germany
(c) West Germany
(d) Hungary
(e) Rumania
(f) Czechoslovakia
(g) Yugoslavia
(h) Poland
(i) Bulgaria
2. **Making maps.** On an outline map of Europe, use three different colors to show the members of NATO (as of 1955); the nations bound by the Warsaw Pact; and nonaligned nations. Include a key indicating what each color represents. (a) What Communist nation did not join the Warsaw Pact? (b) What non-European nations also belong to NATO? (c) Find Finland on the map. Why might Finland have chosen to remain neutral?

Discussion Questions

1. Describe how Communist-led governments were established after World War II in (a) Bulgaria and Hungary, (b) Yugoslavia, (c) Albania, and (d) Czechoslovakia.

2. How did the aid given by the Marshall Plan affect postwar recovery in both Western and Eastern Europe?

3. What was the purpose of each of the following agreements: (a) the Brussels Treaty? (b) the NATO pact? (c) the Warsaw Pact? (d) SALT I?

4. (a) Why did Stalin oppose a strong Germany? (b) What was the purpose of the Berlin blockade, and why did it fail?

5. (a) How did the United Nations become involved in the dispute between North and South Korea? (b) How did the Korean conflict affect cold war tensions?

6. What effect did Khrushchev's de-Stalinization policy have on the satellite countries of Eastern Europe?

7. How did each of the following events affect cold war tensions: (a) the Geneva summit conference? (b) the U-2 incident? (c) the Berlin Wall? (d) the Cuban missile crisis? (e) Brandt's policy of détente?

Reading Primary Sources

Nikita Khrushchev began his de-Stalinization program with a speech before the Twentieth Communist Party Congress in February, 1956, denouncing the "crimes" of Stalin's rule. Read the excerpts from that address reprinted below. Then answer the questions that follow.

> Lenin used severe methods only in the most necessary cases, when the exploiting classes were still in existence and were vigorously opposing the revolution. ... Stalin, on the other hand, used extreme methods and mass repression at a time when the revolution was already victorious, when the Soviet state was strengthened, [and] when the exploiting classes were already eliminated. ... It is clear that here Stalin showed ... his intolerance, his brutality, and his abuse of power. ...
>
> Stalin was a very distrustful man, sickly and suspicious; we knew this from our work with him. He could look at a man and say: "Why are your eyes so shifty today?" or "Why are you turning so much today

and avoiding looking me directly in the eyes?" [This] suspicion created in him a general distrust even toward eminent Party workers whom he had known for years. Everywhere and in everything he saw "enemies, two-facers, and spies. . . ."

(a) According to Khrushchev, what was the difference between Lenin's and Stalin's use of harsh methods in repressing opposition? (b) What does Khrushchev say about Stalin's attitude toward long-time associates? (c) How did these statements fit in with Khrushchev's new policy?

Skill Activities

1. Outlining and writing summaries. Using pages 722–723 of this chapter, prepare an outline showing the organization of the United Nations and its divisions. In your outline, list each of the six United Nations divisions as a major heading. List the responsibilities of the division as subheadings. Then choose one division and find out more about its current activities. Write a summary of what you learn from your research. (To review how to prepare outlines and write summaries, see page 605.)

2. Word research. Many acronyms — words formed from the initial letters of a name or series of words — have come into use since the 1930's. For example, NATO stands for "North Atlantic Treaty Organization." Find each of the following acronyms in a dictionary or encyclopedia. Make up sentences that show you understand the meaning of these acronyms: (a) SALT, (b) radar, (c) NASA, (d) SEATO, (e) Comecon, (f) Comintern, (g) sonar.

3. Reports. Find information about one of the following topics and prepare a report: (a) the role of General Douglas MacArthur in the Korean War; (b) current activities of the North Atlantic Treaty Organization; (c) American space achievements in Projects Mercury, Gemini, and Apollo; (d) Berlin since the end of World War II; (e) Khrushchev's visit to the United States in 1959.

4. Writing an essay. Reread Winston Churchill's speech on page 724. Then write an essay explaining what Churchill might have meant by the last line of this quotation: "Nor is [the new Europe] one which contains the essentials of permanent peace."

Flags of several nations decorate a shopping arcade in downtown London. Because of the free flow of goods between Common Market countries, European shoppers were able to choose among products from many nations.

Changing Europe

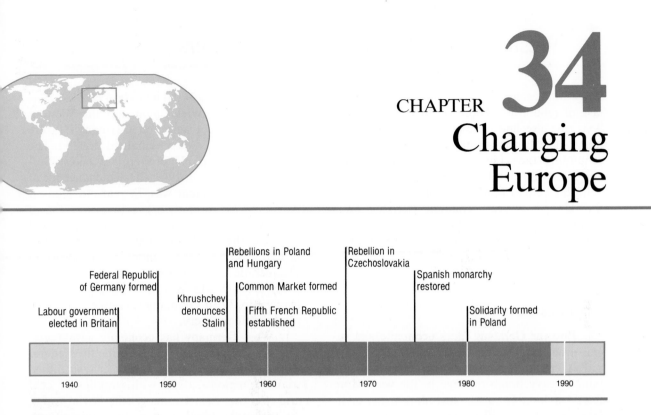

The nations of Europe had to undertake the difficult task of rebuilding after the devastation of World War II. Western Europe, with the help of Marshall Plan aid from the United States, recovered quickly, and several nations achieved remarkable economic growth. The Western European countries also had to deal with a variety of political, social, and economic problems in the postwar period. These problems slowed development but did not stop it. In the later 1950's, many European nations began to cooperate economically, helping their trade and economies to flourish.

In the Soviet Union and Eastern Europe, recovery and growth were slower, but the Soviet Union still became one of the world's major economic powers. New attitudes in the leadership of the USSR brought some relaxations in control, leading the people of the satellite nations to demand more freedom.

This chapter describes how the nations of Western Europe and the Soviet bloc recovered from World War II and how they changed in the postwar period.

CHAPTER OUTLINE

1 Western Europe Recovers and Prospers

2 Cooperation Encourages Economic Growth

3 Changes Take Place in the Soviet Bloc

1 Western Europe Recovers and Prospers

Postwar Western Europe faced a formidable task of rebuilding. Those countries freed from Axis rule also had to re-establish their governments. The European nations concentrated on rebuilding the cities, transportation systems, and industries that had been damaged by war. With the help of Marshall Plan aid supplied by the United States, economic recovery was rapid. Except for a slowdown in the 1970's, industrial growth continued and brought prosperity to most of the nations of Western Europe.

WEST GERMANY

Postwar Germany faces economic and social problems. As the center of the Nazi empire, Germany's industries and cities had sustained heavy bomb damage in the war. More than 4 million Germans, including many civilians, had been killed. Germany needed to rebuild its cities, find housing, food, and clothing for its people, and establish new leadership for the country.

Germany also had to absorb some 12 million refugees who had been displaced by the boundary changes made at the end of the war (page 713). The German populations were expelled from the lands that had been given to Poland and the Soviet Union. Germans who had lived in Poland and in the Sudetenland of Czechoslovakia before the war also were forced to leave those countries.

Germany also needed new leaders. A number of Nazi leaders had been tried for war crimes at Nuremberg (page 713), and the occupying Allied powers set up a program of "denazification" as well. Hundreds of ex-Nazis were prosecuted for the crimes they had committed in the concentration camps, while local courts tried thousands of other German officials. Although the intention was to remove all Nazi supporters from government offices and the schools, some former Nazis later held official posts because of the country's need for trained leaders and educators.

Adenauer leads the new state of West Germany. As the Soviet Union and the Western powers could not agree on Germany's future (page 727), the country remained divided. The new Federal Republic of Germany (West Germany) was set up in 1949. Elected chancellor of the new government was 73-year-old Konrad Adenauer (AH-dun-ow-ur), a long-time foe of both Nazism and communism. Adenauer had served in the legislature of the Weimar Republic and was one of the founders of the Christian Democratic Union, Germany's leading political party after World War II. Under Adenauer's leadership, West Germany was able to make a remarkable recovery.

West Germany has economic advantages. The parts of Germany that became the Federal Republic included the country's heavily industrialized regions, along with supplies of coal and iron ore. East Germany (the Soviet zone), on the other hand, was mainly agricultural. West Germany still had many skilled workers and trained managers available. It also benefited from the knowledge and skills of thousands of East German refugees and from the labor of over three million workers from southern and southeastern Europe, who were attracted to Germany by the opportunity to earn higher wages.

Because so much German industry had been destroyed in the war, factories, mines, and transportation networks had to be completely rebuilt. The West Germans took advantage of this opportunity and installed modern equipment and up-to-date techniques. Germany's new industries were among the most efficient in the world.

In Adenauer's first year in office, West German exports increased by 75 percent. The economic growth rate, the highest in the West, continued to climb steadily through the 1950's, and people's standard of living improved. In 1949 the average income in Germany was $320. By 1973, it had soared to $4,943. From a defeated nation, West Germany had been turned into the economic leader of Europe.

Germany adopts more flexible policies toward the East. Although Adenauer's economic policies won wide support, his tight control of the government aroused political opposition. After Adenauer retired in 1963, the Social Democratic Party gained strength against the Christian Democrats.

In 1969, the Social Democrats gained control of the government. The new chancellor was Willy Brandt, the former mayor of West Berlin, who during the war had been in the resistance movement in Norway. Brandt continued policies that promoted West German prosperity, but the Social Democrats made changes in foreign policy. Brandt's approach to "Ostpolitik" ("eastern policy") improved relations between West Germany and the nations of Eastern Europe and lessened postwar tensions in Europe (page 733).

Brandt resigned in 1974 after a member of his staff was found to be an East German spy. His successor, Helmut Schmidt, emphasized the economy, increasing trade and German participation in the Common Market (page 745). By the 1980's, however, the German economy was troubled by inflation and unemployment. In 1982 a coalition headed by the Christian Democrats defeated the Social Democrats. Elections were influenced by a new force in German politics, the Green Party, a group working for disarmament and environmental issues. Nuclear weapons as well as the economy were issues faced by Chancellor Helmut Kohl.

FRANCE

The Fourth Republic begins to rebuild France. Unlike divided and occupied Germany, France could begin to rebuild as soon as it was liberated from Nazi rule. As before the war, however, the many French political parties disagreed among themselves. By 1946, a coalition government representing sharply differing political views established the Fourth Republic.

Although France had suffered less from wartime bombing than Germany, the Nazis had stripped the country of machinery, motor vehicles, and agricultural goods that were useful to the German war effort. To rebuild quickly and efficiently, the Fourth Republic

Scientific instruments are important products in West Germany's high-technology industries. Above, West German workers help build a space satellite.

nationalized major banks, insurance companies, the coal and steel industries, and electrical companies. Jean Monnet (moh-NAY), a banker and diplomat, was named to head a planning agency that set production goals, made economic forecasts, and encouraged investments. Marshall Plan funds (page 726) also were used. In the first five years of Monnet's plan, France's *gross national product* (GNP) — that is, the total value of all goods and services produced in the nation — increased by 14 percent over what it had been in 1938. Social reforms also were made, including the extending of the right to vote to women.

Political divisions split France. As the economic crises passed, the different political parties in the French government found it increasingly difficult to work together. Opposition came from the Communists on one hand and a

Charles de Gaulle formed the Fifth Republic in 1958 to give France a stronger government. He led the country until his resignation in 1969.

Communist-led nationalist movement in Vietnam (one part of Indochina), was at war with the French colonial forces. The United States aided France, while the Chinese Communists backed the Vietminh in years of guerrilla warfare. After a disastrous defeat at Dien Bien Phu in 1954, the French troops withdrew from Indochina, and Vietnam was divided.

Rebellion in Algeria brings de Gaulle to power. Soon after France's defeat in Vietnam, a revolt broke out in Algeria. Although Algeria was governed as part of France rather than as a colony, many Algerian Muslims wanted complete independence. About a million French settlers, or *colons* (kuh-LOHNZ), however, wanted to remain a part of France. Late in 1954 an Algerian nationalist group known as the FLN (National Liberation Front) began to attack French military posts and French settlers' property.

The French government sent soldiers to restore order, but by 1957 it appeared that the rebels would succeed. To counter the Muslim-led rebellion, the *colons* and some army units took over the Algerian government. Fearful of outright civil war, the French government called on General de Gaulle to form a new government.

De Gaulle uses his powers to strengthen France. De Gaulle took steps to make his government, the Fifth Republic, stronger and more unified than the Fourth Republic. A new constitution strengthened his powers as the French president and took authority away from the Assembly. To end the crisis in Algeria, he gave Muslim Algerians more land and a greater voice in the government. Fearing independence, however, some *colons* formed the terrorist group known as the Secret Army Organization. Others left Algeria. De Gaulle negotiated with the FLN, and Algeria gained its independence in 1962. Other French colonies became part of the French Community, gaining self-government but cooperating in economic, social, and defense matters.

Wanting France to be a world leader again, de Gaulle concentrated on strengthening the country politically and economically. He increased France's economic ties with other European nations and signed trade agreements

new party, led by wartime hero Charles de Gaulle, on the other.

The French were also divided over European political issues. In 1949 France had joined other Western nations in the North Atlantic Treaty Organization (page 728). The admission of West Germany to the NATO pact in 1955, however, aroused controversy in France because of the nation's experience with German aggression in three wars.

Colonial wars weaken the Fourth Republic. Weakened by political disputes, the government of the Fourth Republic was not able to handle problems that arose in the French colonies in Asia and Africa. France's colonies in Indochina had been occupied by Japan in World War II. By the mid-1940's the Vietminh, a

with former French colonies. By offering jobs in French industries to people from Algeria, southern Italy, and other less industrialized countries, France greatly increased its work force. France's GNP grew at a steady rate of about 4 percent a year.

De Gaulle fervently believed in France's national sovereignty and often blocked efforts toward European unity. He opposed Britain's entry in the Common Market in 1961, and in 1966 he withdrew France's forces from NATO. He particularly sought to show France's independence of American influence. During de Gaulle's term of office, France exploded its first atomic bomb and became one of the first Western nations to establish diplomatic relations with Communist China.

De Gaulle's leadership survived a widespread student rebellion and general strike in 1968, a year in which unrest occurred in many parts of the world. The following year, however, mounting opposition to his policies led him to retire.

French policies change. De Gaulle's successors, Georges Pompidou and Valéry Giscard d'Estaing (zhees-KAHR des-TAN), continued similar policies for about ten years. France moved toward more economic and military cooperation with the other European nations but built up its own independent nuclear defenses. By the 1970's, France was troubled by inflation and unemployment, however, and in 1981 French voters chose a Socialist president and gave the Socialists a majority in the French Assembly. The new president, François Mitterrand, nationalized several banks and some large industries and looked for ways to increase the benefits the French government provided for its citizens. The programs did not, however, solve all France's economic problems. Mitterrand also put less emphasis on French independence and reaffirmed France's commitment to NATO.

THE UNITED KINGDOM

Britain makes sweeping economic changes. Great Britain, unlike most of the nations on the continent, had remained unconquered during World War II. Nonetheless, the country's cities and industries had been severely damaged and many merchant ships had been sunk, reducing foreign trade. There were severe shortages of food and other goods. In the first elections after the war ended in Europe, the Labour Party campaigned with a platform calling for extensive government assistance to citizens — popularly known as the "welfare state." Labour won a resounding victory in the 1945 elections, bringing to office a Labour government headed by Clement Attlee.

The Labour Party program intended the government to assume responsibility for its citizens' well-being "from the cradle to the grave." In 1946 Parliament passed the National Insurance Act and the National Health Service Act. These acts greatly expanded earlier programs of unemployment insurance, health care, allowances for housing, assistance for the elderly, and benefits for dependents. In the following year, Britain also nationalized the Bank of England and certain basic industries — civil airlines, coal mining, public transportation, electricity, and gas. Corporations were set up to manage these industries.

Britain still had serious problems with rebuilding its trade so that it could sell enough goods abroad to pay for products it had to buy from other countries. In an effort to decrease imports, wartime rationing restrictions on foods such as sugar and meat were continued. In 1949 the Labour government decided also to devalue the pound sterling, the British unit of currency. They decreased the value of the pound from $4.03 to $2.80. This lowered the prices of British exports so that Britain could sell more goods abroad. On the other hand, imports now cost the British people more.

Britain's colonial empire begins to disappear. Both demands for independence and the costs of running its colonies brought changes in the British Empire. From 1946 onward, many colonies and other territories gained self-rule. In 1947 Britain agreed to Indian demands for self-rule, creating independent India and Pakistan (Chapter 35). Ceylon (now Sri Lanka) and Burma became self-governing in 1948. Most of the former colonies joined the Commonwealth of Nations (page 688), although some later withdrew. These changes in the Empire reduced Britain's costs but in some cases lost valuable colonial markets for British goods.

Economic problems continue. Discontented with economic problems, British voters in 1951 returned the Conservatives to office. Conservative leaders kept the social programs of the welfare state, although they reduced taxes and returned some industries to private ownership. After a period of prosperity, the economy again slowed down in the 1960's. Britain seemed unable to keep pace with the fast-growing economies of other Western European nations. Outdated machines and methods kept British industry less productive. The nation faced labor troubles and rising unemployment, as well as racial unrest because of the large numbers of blacks emigrating to Britain from Commonwealth nations.

Government leadership changed several times in the 1960's and 1970's, but neither Labour nor the Conservatives could solve the country's economic difficulties. Cutbacks in military spending and welfare programs, limits on prices and wages, and increased taxes were among the solutions attempted. The country did make advances in energy production. In the 1960's and 1970's, natural gas and oil began to be pumped from wells in the North Sea off the coast of Scotland. In 1973 Britain joined the Common Market, but the benefits of this move were uncertain.

Thatcher deals with aggression. The Conservative government elected in 1979 was headed by Margaret Thatcher, the first woman to become British prime minister. Thatcher tried to decrease government spending drastically, but inflation and unemployment continued to grow in the 1980's.

Thatcher received strong public support in Britain for her policies in the Falklands, an island group located in the South Atlantic, east of Argentina. Great Britain had colonized the Falklands in 1833, and while Argentina later claimed the islands, no attempt had ever been made to dislodge the British colony. Then, on

---

LINKING PAST AND PRESENT

Riches from the Sea

The oil reserves found in the floor of the North Sea are not the first riches that Europeans have taken from the cold northern oceans. Since ancient times, fishing boats from northern Europe and the British Isles have traveled out into the stormy seas to bring back shiploads of silvery herring, cod, and haddock. Explorers followed the fishermen, traveling farther and farther westward. Fishermen built villages in Iceland and Greenland and eventually on the coast of North America. In 1498 English explorer John Cabot (page 360) discovered the Grand Banks, a shallow ocean area off Canada that is perhaps the world's richest fishing grounds.

For centuries, rivalry for the rich harvests of the North Sea and the North Atlantic brought conflicts between the French, English, and Dutch. As recently as 1975, Britain and Iceland clashed over fishing rights. The rich fish catch

from the northern oceans still amounts to some 10 billion pounds of fish a year for European and North American fisheries.

April 2, 1982, the Argentine government suddenly sent an invasion force to the Falklands. The action was condemned by the UN Security Council, and Thatcher immediately sent the British fleet to the Falklands. British forces quickly took over Argentine military positions and the Argentine troops surrendered.

Civil war breaks out in Northern Ireland. In addition to its severe economic problems, Britain had to deal with a worsening of the tense situation in Northern Ireland. This region, mainly Protestant, had remained a part of Britain when Ireland was divided in 1921. (The southern part, Eire, or the Irish Free State, had been a Commonwealth dominion but left the Commonwealth in 1948 to become the Republic of Ireland.) The government of Northern Ireland was dominated by the Protestants, and the large Catholic minority had little voice in the country. Many nationalists among them hoped that all Ireland would be reunited. In 1968 the Catholics began to hold demonstrations to demand more political and economic rights. The Protestants attacked the demonstrators, and rioting broke out. As violence spread, the British government sent troops to Northern Ireland to keep order.

A radical wing of the Irish Republican Army (IRA) became involved in the fighting. The IRA had been in existence as a nationalist group since the Easter Rebellion of 1916. Its "provisional" wing now used terrorism and guerrilla tactics against British forces and the Protestant community. The provisional IRA accused the British of sympathy with the Protestants; several Protestant volunteer military groups fought back with equal violence. Bombings and gun battles in the streets of Irish cities killed both soldiers and civilians.

Finally, in 1972, the British government assumed control of the government of Northern Ireland and attempted to bring Protestants and Catholics together in a coalition. The attempts failed, however, for the extremists in both groups persisted in carrying out acts of violence.

In 1985 the British and Irish governments signed an agreement that gave the republic of Ireland a voice in the affairs of Northern Ireland. The two governments hoped that this

In 1979 Conservative party leader Margaret Thatcher of Britain became the first woman prime minister in Europe's history.

Anglo-Irish Pact would help bring peace by reassuring the Catholic minority that their interests would be protected. The pact was denounced by extremists on both sides, however, and Protestant groups swore never to accept it. Civil strife continued to tear Northern Ireland apart.

SOUTHERN EUROPE

Italy lacks political unity. Rather than restore the monarchy after the fall of Mussolini, the Italian people in 1946 voted to establish a republic. A coalition government was formed by the Christian Democrats, Communists, and Socialists. As in France, political disagreements led to instability, and Italy's leadership changed frequently in the postwar years. Nevertheless, the country made a rapid recovery from the war, in part because of Marshall Plan aid. The government concentrated on building up industry in the triangle formed by the cities of Milan, Turin, and Genoa, and Italy's economy grew faster than that of any other European country except West Germany. The breakup of large estates in southern Italy redistributed land and helped agricultural growth. Many southern Italians, however, migrated to the north or took jobs in other European countries to improve their standard of living.

In the 1980's, Italy faced labor problems and unrest. Some extreme Communist groups turned to political terrorism, weakening the government of the Christian Democrats, who were allied with the Socialists.

Dictatorship ends in Portugal and Spain. Portugal and Spain, both neutral in World War II, had been ruled by dictators since the 1930's. In the 1960's, the Portuguese colonies in Africa rebelled, and the reign of Antonio Salazar was weakened even before his death in 1970. In 1974 the army overthrew Salazar's successor. Though the government remained unstable, it moved toward democracy. In 1986 the Portuguese people elected their first civilian president in more than half a century.

After World War II, both the Western Allies and the Soviet Union had few dealings with Spain because of the fascist rule of Francisco Franco. By the 1950's, however, the Western nations sought to improve defenses against the Soviet bloc. In exchange for military bases on Spanish soil, the United States extended a billion dollars in loans and grants to Spain. The Spanish government used those funds to expand industry and modernize agriculture. Between 1949 and 1959, Spain had one of the highest growth rates in Europe.

Spain had re-established the monarchy in 1947, though Franco ruled as dictator till his death in 1975. Juan Carlos I then took the throne as a constitutional monarch and began a move toward democracy and economic development. Many of Spain's industries, however, were small factories with outmoded equipment and inefficient management. Spain also had to import most raw materials for its industry.

Rebellions by minorities caused unrest in Spain, as two groups within the Spanish population sought independence, sometimes using violence. In the Pyrenees region were small groups of Basques (BASKS), who spoke a language unrelated to any other in Europe. Another distinct group were the Catalans, who lived along the eastern coast, the most industrialized area of the country. Both groups had sought independence for centuries. In 1980 they were granted home rule within the Spanish state, but many continued to demand complete independence.

Military dictatorship ends in Greece. Civil war had broken out in Greece at the end of World War II. Disputes between supporters of monarchy and those who sought a republic ended in 1967 when a group of military officers known as "the colonels" seized the government. Announcing that they were protecting Greece from communism, they forced out King Constantine II, suspended the constitution, imposed censorship, and jailed many opponents. Many prominent Greeks went into exile.

The rule of "the colonels" ended in 1974; constitutional government was restored and a republic proclaimed. Led by former premier Constantine Karamanlis, Greece joined NATO and the Common Market. New policies for Greece were announced, however, when the Socialists won the 1981 elections. Socialist Premier Andreas Papandreou (pah-pahn-DRAY-oo) questioned Greece's involvement with NATO military plans and began new social and economic changes.

CHECK-UP

1. Vocabulary: *gross national product.*
2. (a) What caused a refugee problem in West Germany after World War II? (b) What factors helped to make West Germany an economic power in Europe?
3. (a) What events in Asia and Africa weakened the Fourth Republic in France? (b) How did de Gaulle strengthen the French presidency? (c) Why did he withdraw from NATO?
4. (a) What was the aim of the Labour Party's postwar program for Britain? (b) What contributed to Britain's economic troubles? (c) How did events in the Falkland Islands affect British politics?
5. (a) What demands were made by the Catholics in Northern Ireland? (b) What brought on violence in the 1960's? (c) Why did the British government take control of the government of Northern Ireland in 1972?
6. (a) What economic changes took place in postwar Italy? (b) What changes in government occurred in Spain and Portugal in the 1970's? (c) Who were "the colonels" in Greece?

2 Cooperation Encourages Economic Growth

An important factor in Western Europe's post-war economic growth was a new effort toward cooperation among the nations of the region. European nations devised plans to share resources and make trade easier. By the early 1980's Western Europe had become the world's largest trading bloc. European nations also shared concerns about defense and weapons.

European nations form an economic union. The aid received from the United States as part of the Marshall Plan (page 726) was crucial to postwar rebuilding in Western Europe. Yet more than foreign aid was needed for Europe's long-range development. To stretch their limited resources of money, raw materials, and people, some Western European nations decided to work together in certain economic areas.

The idea of an economic union was first suggested by French planner Jean Monnet (page 739), who is often called the "Architect of United Europe." Acting on Monnet's idea, Robert Schuman, France's foreign minister, proposed in 1950 that six countries — France, West Germany, Italy, Belgium, Luxembourg, and the Netherlands — pool their supplies of important resources. Tariffs were to be eliminated on coal, iron, and steel — all essential goods for industrial development, construction, and transportation. The Schuman plan was adopted in 1951 as the European Coal and Steel Community (ECSC).

The ECSC also made it possible for workers from one country in the group to take jobs in any other member nation. This helped make efficient use of the labor forces of six nations.

The Common Market is formed. Iron and steel production rose rapidly under the ECSC, and ECSC members soon planned organizations with wider goals. In 1957, under the Treaty of Rome, these nations formed the European Atomic Energy Community (Euratom) and the European Economic Community (EEC).

Euratom was set up to coordinate development of nuclear power for economic growth. The European Economic Community, usually called the Common Market, had broader goals. It sought to encourage the flow of goods within Europe by eliminating tariffs on all products traded between member nations. The Common Market countries also agreed to charge the same import duties on goods bought from other countries, and they worked toward a common agricultural policy. Transportation agreements helped people and goods move easily between member nations, and the free flow of technology and capital promoted growth.

The Common Market brought an economic boom in Europe in the 1960's. Laborers and farm workers, known as "guestworkers," migrated from less developed countries in southern and southeastern Europe and from the former French and Italian colonies in North Africa. An estimated 30 million guestworkers traveled to the industrial heartland of Europe, contributing to its economic growth and to their own nations' prosperity.

In 1967 the Coal and Steel Community, the Common Market, and Euratom were combined in a single governing structure known as the European Community. The Community expanded in the 1970's and 1980's when the United Kingdom, Denmark, Ireland, Greece, Portugal, and Spain were accepted as members.[1] The European Community further increased its influence when it allowed nations that had once been European colonies to become associated members. Goods from these overseas associated members were imported at lower tariffs than goods of nonmembers. This helped increase the flow of raw materials to European industries from the former colonies.

A second trading group is formed. A number of nations outside the central Common Market group created a separate economic union, the European Free Trade Association (EFTA), in 1959. By the 1980's its members included Austria, Norway, Sweden, Switzerland,

---

[1]The United Kingdom had applied for Common Market membership in 1961, but de Gaulle (page 741) had opposed its inclusion because of the strong ties between Britain and the United States.

and Iceland. Finland was an associate member. (The United Kingdom, Portugal, and Denmark, three of the original members, left EFTA when they joined the Common Market.) Like the Common Market, EFTA sought to get rid of trade barriers among members. EFTA, however, allowed each member to set its own tariffs on imports from other countries.

In 1973 EFTA and the European Community agreed to eliminate tariffs on industrial goods traded between members of either organization. In effect, this made all of Western Europe a single free market zone for manufactured goods.

The energy crisis brings about an economic setback. Economic cooperation and outside aid

THE COMMON MARKET

Hamburg, in West Germany, is a major Common Market port (left). A stamp from the British territory of Gibraltar (below) commemorated Britain's entry into the Common Market. Millions of "guestworkers" (page 745), like the Italian bricklayers in the bottom photograph, contributed to the prosperity of the European Community.

BRITISH ENTRY: JANUARY 1973
5p.
E.E.C.
GIBRALTAR

brought steady growth in the Western European economies from the 1950's on. Rising oil prices in the 1970's, however, hurt nearly all the industrial nations. Most of the Western European nations depended on imported oil to run their factories and transportation systems and heat their homes. The main source for this oil was the Arab nations, which had the largest oil reserves in the world.

In 1973 the Arab nations cut back oil production, and OPEC (the Organization of Petroleum Exporting Countries) raised prices for crude oil. As Europe's supplies of petroleum were used up, the cost of imported oil rose. This drove up the prices of goods and services and forced industries and consumers to spend more of their income for oil and less on other goods. To conserve energy, the oil-importing nations also encouraged a business slowdown. As production slowed, unemployment rose.

By the late 1970's, however, many governments were working to develop alternative sources of energy — coal, hydroelectric, and nuclear power. Countries along the North Sea, particularly Britain, began off-shore drilling for the large reserves of oil and natural gas that had recently been discovered in the sea floor. These changes helped the Western nations decrease the amount of oil they imported. The demand for oil dropped, and prices fell, further encouraging recovery.

Europeans question mutual defense plans. In addition to their cooperation in economic affairs, the Western European nations were also joined by the North Atlantic Treaty Organization (page 728). The NATO agreement was originally set up to protect Western Europe from Soviet aggression and allowed for the placement of American nuclear missile stations in Europe. In the 1980's, many Western Europeans objected to the installation of American short-range missiles. They feared that their countries would be the first target of a Soviet attack. In West Germany, large-scale public protests were held, led by a new political party, the Green Party (page 739). Protesters tried to halt the installation of the missiles and called for a freeze on nuclear weapons. Similarly in Britain, there were large demonstrations late in 1983, when American cruise missiles were delivered to sites in Britain. The British and West German governments, however, continued their plans to place NATO nuclear weapons in Europe.

CHECK-UP

1. (a) What plan for European recovery did Robert Schuman propose in 1950? (b) What was the name of the organization that grew out of his plan?
2. (a) What was the purpose of Euratom? (b) of the European Economic Community?
3. (a) What name was given to foreign workers who took jobs in the industrialized European countries? (b) How did they contribute to the European economy?
4. (a) What organizations were included in the European Community? (b) How did the European Free Trade Association differ from the Common Market? (c) How did European nations react to the oil crisis in 1973?

3 Changes Take Place in the Soviet Bloc

The Soviet Union and the nations of the Soviet bloc recovered from World War II more slowly than the West. Centralized planning and a lack of investment funds hindered attempts to increase production and economic growth. Slow economic recovery and the lack of freedoms brought protests in the satellite nations and in the Soviet Union itself. Such protests often were met with repressive measures.

THE SOVIET UNION

The Soviet economy is rebuilt. Soviet losses in World War II were the greatest of any European nation (page 724). Industry and agriculture had been devastated. Some 70,000 Soviet villages had been destroyed, and over 30,000 factories had become only piles of rubble. In some areas every house had been burned, every tree cut, every stretch of railroad torn up, every mineshaft flooded and dynamited, every factory demolished.

To speed recovery, Stalin instituted a new Five-Year Plan and returned to rigid party discipline and terror. As had been agreed at Potsdam (page 712), the USSR also claimed reparations from the nations of Eastern Europe. After the war ended, the Soviet Union began to rebuild its own industrial sites with resources taken from Eastern Europe — industrial machinery, raw materials, railroads, entire factories, and even skilled workers. The greatest Soviet production efforts were put into heavy industry and defense, while consumer needs for food, housing, and clothing were often neglected. Housing shortages in Soviet cities were severe.

Khrushchev introduces changes. Factories and transportation systems were rebuilt under Stalin's program, but agricultural production was hampered by outmoded machinery and poor planning. After Stalin's death in 1953, there was a struggle for leadership in the Soviet Union. By 1958, Nikita Khrushchev had become both premier and Party secretary — the two most important posts in the Soviet Union. Khrushchev attacked the USSR's problems with energy and imagination. He tried to increase industrial efficiency by replacing the central planning board with regional councils whose members understood local conditions.

As an agricultural expert, he tried innovative approaches. His most ambitious project was the attempt to bring part of the steppe into cultivation. This area stretched over 230,000 square miles, from Stalingrad to Novosibirsk (map, page 667). To transform grassland into fields of wheat, the Soviet leader recruited thousands of Soviet students and soldiers to plow the land and plant it. Large harvests in the 1950's helped the overall economy.

Khrushchev loses power. Khrushchev's other policies also marked a break with Stalinist approaches and a relaxation of cold war tensions (page 731). By the early 1960's, problems were apparent, however. Although industrial production increased steadily, Khrushchev's boast that the Soviet Union would "bury" the United States never came close to being realized. Factory managers, chosen mainly for their Party loyalty, lacked the necessary technical skills and knowledge. Khrushchev's agricultural innovations also ran into problems. The steppe region was too dry for reliable farming, and crop failures became common after 1963.

In foreign policy, his approach of "peaceful coexistence" led to a break with China and to increasing opposition by other Soviet leaders. Two years after Khrushchev was forced to retreat over the Cuban missile crisis (page 732), his associates in the Politburo bluntly dismissed him for what they called "hare-brained schemes."

Brezhnev's policies encourage economic growth. Two men replaced Khruschev —Aleksei Kosygin (koh-SEE-ghin) and Leonid Brezhnev. By the 1970's, however, Brezhnev had emerged as the undisputed head of the Soviet Union. He reversed some of Khrushchev's policies, although he continued to seek détente with the West (page 733).

The icy northern rim of the Soviet Union includes vast areas of permafrost, a layer of permanently frozen ground hundreds of feet thick. Underground research helps the Soviet government plan mines, industry, and transportation in the permafrost region.

Under Brezhnev, industrial production increased by 75 percent with the use of Western technical assistance, capital, and production methods. Industrial planning was placed in the hands of the factory managers.

Brezhnev, like Khrushchev, tried to use the resources of Siberia. Huge sums were spent to open up mines, build industries, and extend transportation systems. By 1971 the Soviet Union, with 30 percent of the world's iron ore, had become the world's leading steel producer. As it tapped its vast reserves of coal and oil, the Soviet Union became the world's largest producer of both these energy sources. Trade increased nine times over its level in the 1950's.

Soviet consumers also began to fare better. Many workers' wages were substantially increased, and millions of apartments were built, greatly easing the housing shortage.

Major economic problems continue. Despite this growth, the Soviet economy continued to have problems. An emphasis on military supplies and equipment created shortages of clothing, food, and other consumer items. Transportation remained slow and inefficient because of the vast distances and severe climates in the Soviet Union.

Agriculture also remained a problem. Bad weather caused crop failures, while poor management and lack of transportation facilities resulted in food shortages. By 1980 the Soviet Union was the world's largest importer of wheat, much of it from the United States. These imports used up funds needed for home industry and investment. At the time of Brezhnev's death in 1982, the Soviet growth rate had dropped to its lowest level since World War II.

Even at its most productive, the Soviet economy failed to provide the standard of living enjoyed in the West or even in the satellite nations. Although the average Soviet citizen was better housed, fed, and clothed than before the Bolshevik Revolution, the estimated gross national product remained about half that of the United States.

Disaster strikes at Chernobyl. One way that Soviet economic planners tried to boost the low standard of living was through the use of inexpensive nuclear energy. In 1986, however, the worst nuclear accident in history happened at a Soviet power plant. An explosion at the Chernobyl (chair-NOH-bil) power station in the Ukraine killed 31 people, injured hundreds, and spread radioactive fallout over much of the world. Exposure to high levels of radiation was expected to cause many more deaths over the next decade.

The Soviet government was widely criticized for withholding information throughout the crisis. For Europeans, the lack of accurate information in the days immediately following the accident was especially worrisome because they lay directly in the path of the spreading radiation.

Within weeks after the accident, Soviet workers sealed off the damaged nuclear reactor with concrete and began the long task of "decontaminating" the area around Chernobyl. A panel of Soviet scientists and officials reported four months later that technical errors and violations of safety procedures had caused the accident. The panel also declared that the lesson of Chernobyl would "not go unheeded." But the human and economic costs of the accident would surely be felt for years to come.

Soviet leaders emphasize security. After Khrushchev's fall from power (page 748), the Soviet Union returned to a more militant foreign policy. The size of the army and navy was increased and the government began to spend more money on armaments. Soviet military and economic aid was sent to pro-Soviet governments and guerrilla movements in Asia, Africa, the Middle East, and Latin America. The Soviet Union also tried to retain tighter control of its satellite nations. The "Brezhnev Doctrine" asserted the USSR's determination to intervene in the affairs of any Socialist state where the government seemed in danger of being overthrown.

The Soviet Union invades Afghanistan. The Brezhnev Doctrine was used in 1979 to justify the Soviet invasion of Afghanistan, where a newly installed Communist government was meeting widespread resistance.[2] Soviet troops gained control of Kabul (map, page 863), the Afghan capital, but they were unable to subdue

---

[2]In response to the Soviet invasion of Afghanistan, the United States and many other nations boycotted the 1980 Olympic Games, which were held in Moscow.

anti-Communist guerrillas in the countryside. The fighting dragged on through the 1980's. Thousands of Soviet troops and hundreds of thousands of Afghans were killed. More than five million Afghans fled the country, going mostly to Pakistan and Iran.

The Soviets, meanwhile, launched a program to reshape Afghanistan in the Soviet image. Soviet advisers even took over the educational system, seeking to eliminate all Western influence. Moreover, Afghanistan became economically dependent on the Soviet Union.

Soviet leadership changes hands. Brezhnev's successor, Yuri Andropov, continued efforts to strengthen the Soviet Union's economy and defenses. Andropov's death in 1984, after only fifteen months in office, raised questions about whether Soviet leadership would remain in the hands of older Politburo members or pass to younger men. One of the older leaders, Konstantin Chernenko, was chosen. When Chernenko died after thirteen months in office, the Central Committee chose as his successor a much younger man, Mikhail Gorbachev (gor-buh-CHAWF).

Unlike previous Soviet leaders, Gorbachev had not fought in the Second World War and had not risen to power under Stalin's brutal regime. Although he pledged to continue the policies of his predecessors, many observers wondered whether Gorbachev's selection might prove to be a turning point in Soviet relations with the West. In November, 1985, Gorbachev became the first Soviet leader to meet with an American President since 1979.

In domestic affairs, Gorbachev called for economic, social, and political reforms and pledged to follow a policy of *glasnost* (GLAHS-nuhst) or "openness" about the nation's problems. Although none of his proposals threatened fundamental change in the Soviet Union, Gorbachev faced opposition from Party traditionalists who feared that reform might undermine their power. They also resented his charges of laziness and corruption in the official hierarchy. Meanwhile, Gorbachev sought to consolidate his control of the Party and the Soviet bureaucracy, replacing many officials with people loyal to him. The Chernobyl accident was a setback for Gorbachev, exposing him to criticism both at home and abroad. The

Mikhail Gorbachev became leader of the Soviet Union in 1985. He is seen here with his wife Raisa during attendance at a Warsaw Pact meeting in Budapest, Hungary.

Another well-known dissident was Alexander Solzhenitsyn (sol-zhuh-NEET-sin), a mathematician who spent years in a forced-labor camp for making anti-Stalin remarks. In a short novel, *One Day in the Life of Ivan Denisovich,* he described life in these camps. The book was published in the Soviet Union, where it caused a sensation. (Solzhenitsyn was awarded the Nobel Prize for Literature in 1970.) Solzhenitsyn wrote further about the camps in *The Gulag Archipelago,* but this work and his protests against censorship angered Soviet authorities. Exiled in 1974, he eventually settled in the United States.

Andrei Sakharov, one of the physicists who helped develop the hydrogen bomb, later became critical of the Soviet build-up of nuclear weapons. His campaign for nuclear disarmament won him great admiration in the West, and he was given the Nobel Peace Prize in 1975. The Soviet government grew increasingly critical of Sakharov and finally exiled him to Gorki, a city closed to Westerners. In 1986, Sakharov was released from exile and returned to Moscow. Soviet dissidents still faced great risks, however, in expressing their views.

EASTERN EUROPE

Eastern Europe experiences economic growth. Except for Czechoslovakia, the Eastern European nations in the Soviet bloc were largely agricultural before World War II. After the war, the satellite nations concentrated on developing industry and mining. They were not allowed to accept Marshall Plan aid, and Comecon (page 726) was not effective. Nevertheless, economic growth took place in the Soviet bloc. By the late 1960's East Germany had the tenth highest industrial production in the world. The other countries in Eastern Europe also became industrialized. Only Albania still had large numbers of people working in agriculture by 1980, and even that country received more income from mining and manufacturing than from farming.

As production grew in Eastern Europe, trade in the Soviet bloc expanded. In time Eastern Europe developed trade with other countries, and Eastern European products began to appear on the shelves of Western stores. In the 1970's Eastern European standards of living

long Soviet silence on the disaster for a time had also cast doubt on Gorbachev's commitment to *glasnost.*

Soviet leaders and policies are criticized. Despite the controls and censorship exercised by the Soviet government through the postwar decades, people within the USSR dared to voice dissent. Some Soviet ciizens chose to go into exile, although leaving the country was in many cases limited by government regulations. Other Soviet citizens criticized the government, risking the threat of imprisonment or forced-labor camps.

Khrushchev's policy of de-Stalinization in the late 1950's was accompanied by less rigid censorship and more open criticism of the Soviet system. Nonetheless, the *dissidents,* those who disagreed with Soviet policy, often were persecuted. Boris Pasternak, a poet and novelist, was for many years forced to publish his books abroad. In 1958, the Soviet government banned the publication of *Doctor Zhivago,* his novel about the Russian Revolution. Pasternak won the Nobel Prize for Literature in 1958 but was forced to reject the prize.

In 1981 Lech Walesa led Polish workers in strikes, marches, and demonstrations for greater freedom.

more equality in its dealings with the Soviet Union.

The protests in Poland inspired a more serious revolt in Hungary. In October, 1956, Hungarian students in Budapest held a rally in support of the Poles. Police ordered the students to disperse and then fired on the crowd, bringing on a widespread revolt. Hungarian workers, writers, and some army officers joined the students, and protests began in other parts of Hungary. The rebels in Budapest toppled the huge statue of Stalin, the symbol of Soviet control, took over radio stations and key industrial centers, and demanded that Soviet troops leave Hungary. Imre Nagy (NAJH), the former Hungarian prime minister, was restored to power. On October 30, the Soviet forces began to leave Budapest, and Nagy promised the Hungarians free elections and an end to one-party government. He also withdrew Hungary from the Warsaw Pact and asked for UN help.

The Soviet Union reacted quickly to these changes. On November 4, over 2,000 Soviet tanks turned back and began to cross the Hungarian plain toward Budapest. Nagy was replaced by Communist Party leader János Kádár. For two weeks Hungarian "freedom fighters," armed with small weapons, held off the Soviet forces. The UN denounced the Soviet moves, but the Hungarians had no hope of victory. At least 3,000 Hungarians were killed in the revolution[3] and over 200,000 fled their country. Soviet troops remained.

Although the revolution did not free the Hungarians from Soviet control, political repression in Hungary was reduced under the Kádár regime. By the 1980's Hungary seemed to have more freedom than any other satellite country.

Rebellion in Czechoslovakia is suppressed. As the Soviet government tried to strengthen the unity of the Soviet bloc, the people of the satellites continued to seek more freedoms. In the spring of 1968, student protests were widespread in Western Europe, causing Czechoslovakian protesters to demand more freedom of expression. A new Czech Communist leader, Alexander Dubček (DOOB-chek), loosened con-

gradually rose. Although they did not reach the same level as those in Western Europe, they did overtake that in the Soviet Union.

Poland and Hungary protest Soviet control. As conditions improved in Eastern Europe, people grew more resentful of Soviet domination. After the death of Stalin in 1953, Khrushchev denounced Stalinist programs and attitudes. Sensing some easing of Soviet control, the people of Poland and Hungary immediately began to express their dissatisfactions.

Late in June, 1956, workers in the city of Poznan, Poland, rioted to demand "bread and liberty." To restore order, the Soviet leaders removed Stalinist officials and reinstated Wladislav Gomulka (goh-MOOL-kuh), who had previously been forced out of the Polish Communist Party for opposing Stalin. Gomulka ended the collectivization of Polish agriculture, loosened government controls over industry, and gave more freedom to the Roman Catholic Church, which had remained important in Polish life. The Polish government also demanded

---

[3]This is the official government estimate. Other sources say as many as 20,000 Hungarians died in the revolt.

trols and made reforms. He promised the Czechoslovakians "communism with a human face." The new policy, called the "Czech spring," worried Soviet leaders. As part of the Brezhnev Doctrine (page 750), the Warsaw Pact nations sent troops into Czechoslovakia to restore control.

An economic crisis leads to strikes in Poland. The next outbreak of protests came from Poland, where Gomulka's rule had become increasingly repressive. In December, 1970, he was replaced when workers at a shipyard in Gdansk (guh-DANSK)[4] protested against sharp increases in food prices. The new government, however, was no more successful than Gomulka in increasing production. By 1980 Poland's foreign debt was $20 billion. The GNP was so low that the government found it hard to pay even the yearly interest on its debts.

Shortages of food and clothing led to rationing and food riots. Polish workers took over the shipyard in Gdansk, and strikes spread through the nation. The government finally agreed to wage increases, granted workers the right to strike, and allowed the formation of independent unions.

An independent union voices Polish complaints. The Polish workers formed Solidarity, the first labor union in the Soviet bloc not under government control. Lech Walesa (wah-LEN-sah), the leader of the strike at Gdansk, became head of the new union.[5] Solidarity demanded more rights for workers, an end to censorship, more freedom for the Catholic Church, and the release of political prisoners. To underline their demands, Polish workers held strikes, hunger marches, and protest demonstrations throughout 1981. Western reaction to Solidarity was warmly supportive and included open encouragement from Pope John Paul II.[6]

Meanwhile, Poland's economic problems mounted. Wheat, flour, rice, and cereal were added to the list of rationed goods, and the government repeatedly increased prices for these basic foods. Each increase brought renewed protests from Solidarity. As the unrest grew, there were fears that the Soviet Union might step in to stop the protests as it had done in Czechoslovakia in 1968. These fears increased when Warsaw Pact troops held maneuvers in East Germany, just 60 miles from the Polish border.

Strict control is restored in Poland. In October, 1981, General Wojciech Jaruzelski (yah-roo-SEL-skee) became head of the Polish Communist Party, and in December he declared *martial law* — that is, strict controls maintained by military forces. Jaruzelski set up censorship, imposed a curfew, and banned most travel. Solidarity leaders throughout Poland were taken into custody.

In 1982, Solidarity was banned, and Jaruzelski proclaimed that future unions would be subject to Communist Party control. Although martial law was ended in 1984, government repression remained strict. At the 1986 meeting of the Polish Communist Party, Jaruzelski claimed victory over the banned labor movement, but determination persisted among Polish workers. Aided by sympathetic members of the Roman Catholic clergy, they continued to meet in small groups and to demonstrate against government policies.

CHECK-UP

1. Vocabulary: *dissident, martial law.*

2. (a) How did reparations help the Soviet Union rebuild after World War II? (b) What changes did Khrushchev make in Soviet agriculture? (c) What caused his fall from power?

3. (a) What problems did Brezhnev fail to solve? (b) What was the Brezhnev Doctrine?

4. (a) Explain Gorbachev's *glasnost* policy. (b) Why was the Chernobyl accident a setback for Gorbachev?

5. (a) What criticisms of the Soviet government were made by Solzhenitsyn and Sakharov? (b) How did the government react?

6. What were the causes of (a) the 1956 rebellions in Poland and Hungary? (b) the 1968 changes in Czechoslovakia? (c) the Polish revolts in the 1980's? (d) How did the Soviet Union react in each case?

---

[4]Gdansk is the Polish name for the city of Danzig.

[5]In recognition of the sacrifices he made to improve conditions for people in Poland, Lech Walesa was awarded the Nobel Peace Prize in 1983.

[6]John Paul II, who became Pope in 1978, was not only the first Polish Pope but also the first from a Communist nation.

Chapter 34 Review

Summary

Western Europe made a remarkable recovery after World War II, due partly to the aid received from the United States under the Marshall Plan. West Germany's economic growth was the fastest, making it one of the world's leading industrial powers. French recovery was hampered by colonial wars in Indochina and Algeria, but the economy improved under the strong rule of Charles de Gaulle. The postwar Labour government in Britain established a welfare state, but the economy failed to thrive under a succession of governments. Britain's problems were increased by violence in Northern Ireland and the war with Argentina over the Falkland Islands.

In the countries of southern Europe, the rule of dictators in Spain, Portugal, and Greece was replaced by more democratic governments. Italy established a republic, and its northern regions became more industrialized.

Western European nations began economic cooperation with the formation of several effective organizations such as the Common Market, which allowed shared use of resources and ended many trade barriers.

The Soviet Union faced a huge task of rebuilding, and economic recovery was slow. Khrushchev's innovations in industry and agriculture brought temporary gains, and a lessening of controls under Brezhnev brought more improvement. The economies in the satellite nations of Eastern Europe improved more quickly, and the people of these nations sought greater freedom from Soviet domination. Revolts in Poland, Hungary, and Czechoslovakia were repressed but did win more freedom for the people of those countries. Dissidents within the Soviet Union also worked to end repression and gain the right to freedom of expression.

Vocabulary Review

1. Match the following terms with the listed definitions: *bloc, dissident, gross national product, martial law.*
(a) The total value of all goods and services produced in a nation during a specified time period.

(b) An individual who openly disagrees with government policies in his or her country.
(c) A group of nations or people united for a common purpose.
(d) Rule by the military, usually involving such measures as censorship of the press and the imposition of a curfew.

2. Distinguish between the terms in each of the following pairs:
(a) European Community; European Free Trade Association.
(b) Fourth Republic; Fifth Republic.
(c) Northern Ireland; Republic of Ireland.
(d) Soviet bloc; French Community.
(e) Solidarity; freedom fighters.
(f) *Doctor Zhivago; Gulag Archipelago.*

People to Identify

Identify the following people. Name the country with which each is associated and tell why he or she is important:
1. Konrad Adenauer
2. Willy Brandt
3. Charles de Gaulle
4. Nikita Khrushchev
5. Alexander Solzhenitsyn
6. Clement Attlee
7. Juan Carlos I
8. Margaret Thatcher
9. Jean Monnet
10. Lech Walesa
11. Imre Nagy
12. Wladislaw Gomulka

Relating Geography and History

1. **Locating places.** Locate each of the following on a map in the Atlas section of this book (pages 858–864):

(a) Vietnam	(e) Sri Lanka
(b) Algeria	(f) Burma
(c) India	(g) Falkland Islands
(d) Pakistan	(h) Argentina

2. **Making charts.** Make a chart of the nations in the European Community. In separate columns, list the name of the country; the year in which it joined the Community; its major exports; and its major imports. Use an encyclopedia or almanac and this book to find the information.

Discussion Questions

1. Compare postwar economic development in West Germany and in Britain. List several factors that helped or hindered the growth of industry in each nation.

2. How did colonial demands for independence following World War II affect (a) Great Britain? (b) France? (c) Portugal?

3. What were the causes of civil strife in each of the following countries: (a) Algeria? (b) Northern Ireland? (c) Spain? (d) Greece?

4. (a) How did the plan for a European Coal and Steel Community lead to the European Community? (b) How has the European Community aided Western Europe's economic growth?

5. (a) What were some general differences between the nations of Eastern and Western Europe in 1945? (b) How did these affect the speed of economic recovery after World War II?

6. (a) In what ways did Khrushchev and Brezhnev follow similar policies? (b) In what ways did Brezhnev change Soviet policies?

7. Why did (a) Boris Pasternak, (b) Alexander Solzhenitsyn, and (c) Andrei Sakharov meet with disfavor from Soviet leaders?

Reading Primary Sources

During the Hungarian revolution against Soviet control in October, 1956, a committee of writers, artists, scientists, and students composed a declaration listing the changes desired by the Hungarian people. Read the following excerpts from that declaration. Then answer the questions that follow.

> 1. Immediate settlement of our relations with the Soviet Union. Withdrawal of Soviet troops from Hungarian territory. . . .
> 3. General elections with secret ballot. The candidates must be named by the people.
> 4. Factories and mines must really belong to the workers. The factories and the land must remain the property of the people and nothing must be returned to the capitalists or the big landowners. The factories must be managed by freely elected Workers' Councils. . . . The government must protect the right of artisans and small shopkeepers to exercise their trade. . . .

> 6. The unions must truly defend the interests of the working class, and their leaders must be freely elected. The peasants will be able to set up their own unions.
> 7. The government must guarantee the freedom of agricultural production and help the small farmers and the voluntary cooperatives. The hateful system of compulsory [grain] deliveries must be abolished.
> 8. The peasants, frustrated by enforced collectivization, must be restored to their rights and compensated.
> 9. The government must guarantee the full freedom of the press and freedom of assembly.

(a) What demands do the Hungarian protesters make of the Soviets? (b) According to the declaration, how would government leaders be chosen? (c) How would factories be organized and run? (d) What does the excerpt imply to be the problems of the peasants and small farmers? (e) What freedoms are specifically called for?

Skill Activities

1. Identifying cause and effect. Each of the following sentences describes a development that had far-reaching effects in modern Europe. For each development, reread the page or pages indicated in parentheses and decide what you think were its most important *effects.* On a separate sheet of paper, list these effects and explain why you chose them. (You may select effects other than those discussed in this book.)
(a) German factories, mines, and transportation networks were destroyed during World War II (page 738).
(b) The British Labour government devalued the pound sterling (pages 741–743).
(c) Imre Nagy withdrew Hungary from the Warsaw Pact (pages 751–752).

2. Reports. Use the *Readers' Guide to Periodical Literature* to find information for a report about one of the following anti-Soviet uprisings: (a) Poland in 1956, (b) Hungary in 1956, (c) Czechoslovakia in 1968, (d) Poland in 1981.

3. Biographies. Several people discussed in this chapter won the Nobel Peace Prize, including Willy Brandt, Andrei Sakharov, and Lech Walesa. Write a biography of one of them or of another recent winner, describing his or her early life and prize-winning achievements.

Against a background of ruined temples and pagodas, modern buses rumble down the dusty streets of a village in Burma. Built in the ninth century, the village of Pagan was once a royal city and an important Buddhist religious center.

CHAPTER

35

Changing Asia

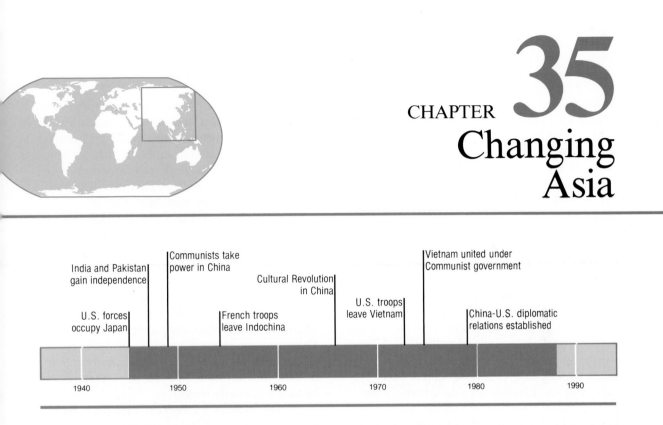

Before World War II, much of Asia was under the control of the Western imperialist nations. China was weak and divided. Of all the countries in Asia and the Pacific, only Japan was a world power.

World War II brought independence for the Asian colonies and new directions in China and Japan. Political independence, however, did not solve the underlying problems that faced many countries of Asia. Rapid population growth, combined with a slow rate of economic growth, kept standards of living low. At the same time, people's expectations for a better life continued to rise.

In China, the Communist government was able to raise living standards, but not as much as the nation's leaders had hoped. India continued to struggle with poverty and religious divisions. Poverty, rebellion, and war plagued much of Southeast Asia. Japan, however, created an "economic miracle" and became a world economic leader.

This chapter focuses on developments since 1945 in China and Japan and in the nations of the Indian subcontinent and Southeast Asia.

CHAPTER OUTLINE

1 Communist Rule Brings Change in China

2 Japan Becomes an Economic Leader

3 New Nations Are Created in South Asia

4 Conflicts Disrupt Southeast Asia

1 Communist Rule Brings Change in China

The struggle between Nationalist and Communist forces in China began in the 1920's and continued during the conflicts with Japan that led into World War II. Despite American support, Chiang Kai-shek's Nationalists lost the battle for mainland China. The new Communist regime brought great changes in the Chinese way of life.

The United States aids Nationalist China. World War II in China was a three-way struggle among the Chinese Nationalists, the Chinese Communists, and the Japanese. As before the war, the United States and other Western powers continued to support Chiang Kai-shek's Nationalist government. The United States in particular supplied millions of dollars' worth of military aid, medical supplies, and food. Chiang, however, considered Mao Tse-tung and the Communists the greater enemy. Chiang therefore depended on the Allies to oppose the Japanese, while he kept his best troops to fight Mao's Red Army.

The Communists win control. The Communists harassed the Japanese forces with skillful guerrilla tactics during the war, gaining needed supplies and weapons. Mao, however, also kept in mind the coming struggle with the Nationalists. Many Chinese were impressed by the successes of Mao's Red Army, and popular support for the Communists continued to grow. With the end of the war against Japan, civil war broke out again between Mao's Communist troops and the forces of the Nationalist government. By 1949, the Communists had gained control of mainland China. Chiang Kai-shek and the Kuomintang (Nationalist) loyalists fled to the island of Taiwan (map, page 760), where they claimed to be China's legitimate government. On the mainland, Mao Tse-tung proclaimed the birth of the People's Republic of China on October 1, 1949.

COMMUNIST RULE IN CHINA

The People's Republic faces great difficulties. As Mao established his authority, he also set up a new form of government for the People's Republic. A popular assembly, the National People's Congress, was made up of several thousand members elected by provincial congresses and the army. It met seldom, however, and its real work was carried on by a Standing Committee whose chairman was president of the People's Republic. The other government body was the State Council, whose leader was China's premier. Actual power in China rested with the Communist Party, which was under Mao's firm control. He also held the post of president until 1959.

The problems facing China's new government after twenty years of war were colossal. Industries were producing at less than half of their prewar level. Railroads, bridges, ports, and roads were in disrepair. Trade had come to a halt, and inflation was so high that paper money was nearly worthless.

Mao initiates a Five-Year Plan for industry and agriculture. China's economy began to recover slowly in the early years of Communist rule. The government took over large factories and began land reforms. By 1953, Mao was able to impose a strict economic program on the nation — the first of a number of Five-Year Plans aimed at increasing industrial and agricultural production. Industry began to grow — particularly steel production, which tripled during the first Five-Year Plan.

The first Five-Year Plan also continued reforms in agriculture. Starting in 1950, the government had taken land from the landlords and distributed it among the peasants. The Communists then set up a system of mutual-aid teams, made up of four or five peasant families who worked the land together. The peasants on these teams kept their own land but cooperated in using their tools and labor. Eventually groups of teams were combined into larger units called cooperatives. Each cooperative produced and sold its own crops and divided the profits among its members.

Cooperatives soon gave way to collective farms — large state-owned farms similar to those Stalin had instituted in Russia (page 668). Collectivization in China was more gradual

CHINA UNDER MAO

During his twenty-seven-year rule, Mao Tse-tung (right) exerted a profound influence on China. Above, workers on an agricultural commune studied Mao's writings.

than in the USSR, but by 1957 all of China's farms were collectivized. Although China still was not producing enough to feed all its people, rationing and price controls brought a fairer distribution of food.

China attempts a Great Leap Forward. Communist leaders were not satisfied with the modest gains of the first Five-Year Plan. In 1958 they initiated an ambitious second Five-Year Plan, called the Great Leap Forward. Its goal was to increase both industrial and agricultural production rapidly. One part of the plan called for the establishment of many small industries in the countryside. Mao hoped that this program would double industrial production and lessen the gap in living standards between urban and rural China. With great effort, the Chinese built hydroelectric plants, bridges, and irrigation projects. The small rural factories, however, could not meet the goals of the Great Leap Forward. Much of the iron produced, for example, was of such poor quality that it could not be used.

The agricultural goals of the Great Leap Forward also were difficult to achieve. In hopes of making agriculture more efficient, the agricultural collectives were combined into even larger units called *communes* (KOM-yoonz). Centrally run, each commune included about 5,000 households working on 10,000 acres of land. The communes were not a success, however, for many peasants were unhappy with living conditions on the huge farms. In addition, farm machinery was scarce, and natural disasters led to poor harvests. To avoid famine, China had to buy grain from abroad.

Before the five years of the Great Leap Forward had ended, Communist leaders realized that the plan had not succeeded in rapidly making China a modern, self-sufficient nation. They turned instead to slower and more long-range plans for economic development.

The Cultural Revolution rejects Chinese traditions. By the mid-1960's, Communist rule had brought massive social change, greatly expanding education, increasing women's rights, and according greater respect to workers and peasants. In traditional China, learning had been the privilege of the scholar class, but now young people from worker and peasant families were encouraged to attend school. The course of study became more practical, including the Chinese language, mathematics, applied science, agriculture, English, and Russian. When students were not attending classes, they worked on farms or in factories.

Mao, however, feared that the original enthusiasm and spirit of the revolution were being lost. Certain groups still had special privileges, which worked against the ideal of a

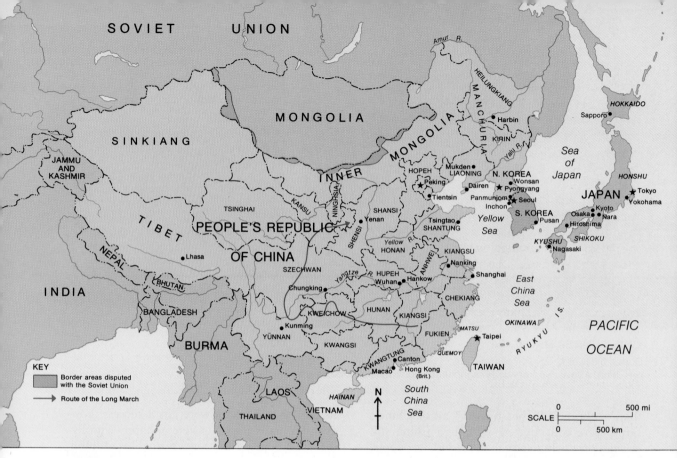

East Asia

The People's Republic of China lies on the Asian mainland, while the Republic of China is based on the island of Taiwan. What do the darker green areas on the map indicate?

society in which all were equal. In 1966, therefore, Mao launched the Cultural Revolution to purge China of "The Four Olds" — old thoughts, old culture, old customs, and old habits.

The Cultural Revolution caused great upheavals. Privileged people such as government officials and students were sent to work on the communes or in factories. Traditional Chinese art and literature were also major targets of the Cultural Revolution. Mao and his followers believed that writers and artists should glorify the accomplishments of the common people. Opera, long a favorite form of entertainment in China, remained popular, but the cast and plot changed considerably. Heroes of the revolution — farmers and tractor drivers — replaced princes, scholars, and noblewomen.

The Red Guard creates disorder. The most eager supporters of the Cultural Revolution were the millions of young followers of Mao who were organized in military-style units as the Red Guard. These young people, some of whom were still in junior high school, journeyed throughout China campaigning against anyone who exhibited traditional ideas.

The Red Guard created chaos in China's cities. Its members used violence to oust officials, managers, or teachers who did not show enough revolutionary enthusiasm. They battled against the army and against less radical government and Party officials. Red Guard groups even fought each other. Realizing that his youthful army was creating disorder, Mao called an end to the Cultural Revolution in 1968.

China turns away from Mao's ideas. The chaos of the Cultural Revolution weakened Mao's influence, and other leaders gained control of China's government and its Communist Party. Without losing sight of their revolutionary principles, the new leaders looked toward the issues of economic and technological development and put less emphasis on revolution. Premier Chou En-lai (JOH EN-LIE) became the symbol of China's new spirit.

Mao's leadership changes China. The revolution in China had cost millions of lives. By the time of Chairman Mao's death in September, 1976, however, China had moved into the modern world. The country had made important advances under Mao's leadership. Famine was wiped out, health care was dramatically improved, and illiteracy was almost eliminated. Agricultural reforms were successful enough to supply people's basic needs for food and clothing. Women were treated as the equals of men for the first time in China's 4,000-year history. Moreover, Mao was the first ruler in 150 years to unite the country. His version of Marxism emphasized social change and influenced millions of followers who read his "Little Red Book," *The Sayings of Chairman Mao.*

CHINA AND THE WORLD

In the years immediately after the Communist victory in 1949, the People's Republic of China concentrated on rebuilding the war-torn country. Relations with most other nations were limited, and the Western nations and Japan viewed the new regime with suspicion.

China and the United States conflict. The United States in particular had long supported Chiang Kai-shek, and the idea of a Communist-controlled China was alarming to most Americans. Many feared a Communist takeover in Asia comparable to the Soviet moves in Eastern Europe.

Another source of conflict between the two nations was the status of Taiwan (tie-WAHN). The United States and the United Nations continued to recognize Chiang's government on Taiwan as the only government of China. The defense of Taiwan also became an issue in the early 1950's, when the Communists attacked nearby Quemoy and Matsu. The United States signed a mutual-defense treaty with Chiang and gave Taiwan economic and military aid.

The Korean War (page 729) increased the hostility between the United States and China. While Americans wanted to halt the spread of Communist rule, the Chinese leaders feared that the United States, as the leader of the UN forces, was preparing to invade China. American concern over communism in Southeast Asia led to involvement in Vietnam (page 775).

Relations with the Soviet Union deteriorate. Although Mao and Stalin had long disagreed over how the revolution in China should be carried out, the People's Republic and the Soviet Union for a time appeared to present a solid Communist front. The Soviet Union supplied millions of dollars in aid and technical assistance. Nevertheless, by 1956, Soviet Premier Khrushchev's policies of de-Stalinization disturbed Chinese Communists. They also disagreed with the policy of peaceful coexistence with the West.

At the 22nd Party Congress held in Moscow in 1961, Khrushchev denounced the Communist nation of Albania for allying itself with China. China's representative walked out of the meeting, making official the split between the Soviet Union and China. After that incident, Soviet and Chinese leaders frequently made speeches attacking each other's viewpoints.

In 1966, the war of words intensified over a border dispute. The Chinese claimed that 750,000 square miles of fertile and underpopulated Soviet territory along the Amur River (map, page 760) rightfully belonged to China. In March, 1969, fighting broke out along the disputed border. The fighting did not grow into full-scale war, but the two Communist giants continued to fortify the border along the Amur River, and relations remained tense.

Chinese-American relations improve. While Sino-Soviet relations worsened, the climate between China and the United States improved. With the end of the Cultural Revolution, the new leadership in China adopted a more flexible foreign policy. China's leaders realized that American technology would help efforts to modernize. Moreover, they feared Soviet aggression. The United States, for its part, hoped to end the Vietnam War and establish détente with both Communist powers.

In 1971 President Richard M. Nixon announced that he had accepted an invitation to visit mainland China the following year. With this shift in American policy, the General Assembly of the United Nations voted in November, 1971, to oust Taiwan as the representative of China and admit the People's Republic. On Nixon's visit to China, he and Chou En-lai discussed the establishment of better relations between their two nations.

New leaders look to the West. Relations with the United States continued to improve in the late 1970's. The new leaders moved away from some of Mao's doctrines of Chinese self-reliance and isolation. Many leaders who had been closely associated with Mao were removed from power. Emphasis was placed on rapid development in agriculture, industry, defense, and science. China's new approach recognized the need for industrialization and for technical assistance from other nations. Teng Hsiao-p'ing (DUHNG shee-ow PING), a senior Party official and a veteran of the Long March (page 690), emerged as the most powerful person in China.

On January 1, 1979, the People's Republic of China and the United States formally established diplomatic relations. Within a month, Teng Hsiao-p'ing made an official state visit to Washington. The warmer relationship between the two nations that had been nurtured by Presidents Nixon and Carter continued under President Reagan, who visited China in 1984.

CHECK-UP

1. Vocabulary: *commune.*
2. (a) What did Mao hope to accomplish with the Cultural Revolution? (b) Who carried out Mao's ideas? (c) What were the results?
3. (a) Describe the relations between Communist China and the United States during the two decades following the Communist Revolution. (b) What led to the split between China and the Soviet Union? (c) How did a change in American policy affect the UN status of China and Taiwan?
4. What policies were followed by the leaders who succeeded Mao?

2 Japan Becomes an Economic Leader

After the Allied victory in World War II, the United States army occupied Japan from 1945 to 1952. Under American influence, Japan made changes in its government without completely abandoning its own traditions. A remarkable economic recovery made Japan a leader among world nations.

The American occupation brings changes in government. The long-range objective of the American occupation was to make Japan a democratic country. Rather than impose a new form of government, however, the United States decided to work in partnership with the existing Japanese government structure. To carry out these goals, President Harry Truman appointed General Douglas MacArthur to direct the Allied occupation forces.

The first step of the occupation was to demilitarize Japan. Military leaders were removed from official posts and forbidden to hold government positions; trials for war crimes were held. Occupation officials then moved to make basic political reforms.

A new constitution establishes a democracy. In 1947 the authoritarian Japanese constitution of the Meiji era (page 579) was replaced by a democratic constitution. The constitution established a two-house Diet (legislature) elected by the people, with a prime minister and cabinet government responsible to the Diet. Japanese emperors had always been considered divine, but the Emperor Hirohito was to serve only as the "symbol of the state."

The new constitution showed considerable American influence. A bill of rights guaranteed education, freedom of speech and religion, and other rights. The constitution also stated that the Japanese would "forever renounce war" and would not maintain military forces. A supreme court was set up with the authority to declare laws unconstitutional. Workers gained the right to bargain with employers. Women won equal political and economic rights, as well as legal equality in marriage and family affairs. Long-standing Japanese custom and traditions, however, often stood in the way of these new freedoms.

Reforms help the spread of democracy. For centuries, much of the land in Japan had been in the hands of large landowners. Most small farmers had rented the land they cultivated. After World War II, the government limited

Japan's Living National Treasures

Many nations of the world have ancient arts and crafts that people treasure, but only in Japan has the government made a special effort to preserve and cherish the skills of traditional artisans. Each year since 1955 the Japanese government has chosen certain artists who work in fields of art that date back hundreds of years. These artists are given the title of Living National Treasure, or *Ningen Kokuho* (nee-gen koh-koo-HO). Their works include pottery and ceramics, textile weaving, lacquerwork, and swordmaking.

The artisans who have been named Living National Treasures preserve traditional methods and teach them to younger artists. This master swordmaker, for instance, uses methods like those that have been used since about A.D. 800. The swords he makes would have been

treasured by the samurai of feudal Japan; today they are valued and admired for their beauty and the skill that goes into making them.

---

the amount of land each farmer could own, purchased the surplus, and sold it at low prices to landless peasants. This reform created a prosperous class of small landowning farmers.

The occupation encouraged other reforms that led to greater equality. The *zaibatsu* — great industrial firms owned by a handful of powerful families — were ordered to disband and sell their stock on the open market. Industrial workers were encouraged to form unions.

The Japanese also reformed the system of education. Prewar education in Japan had emphasized the virtues of loyalty and obedience to the emperor and the nation. Postwar educational reforms focused on introducing democratic values, establishing more colleges, and using modern methods of teaching.

Japan and the United States become allies. One reason for the success of the occupation was MacArthur's leadership in carrying out the American decision not to seek revenge on Japan. Another was the Japanese people's own skill in changing the system that had involved their country in a disastrous war.

In April, 1952, Japan regained its full independence when a peace treaty, signed by Ja-

pan, the United States, and 47 other nations, went into effect. Another treaty allowed American forces to use Japanese bases and gave the United States a firm ally in Asia. The United States, in turn, guaranteed Japan's security against attack, while Japan itself re-established some military "self-defense" forces.

Japan's economy flourishes. While postwar Japan underwent great political changes, its economic recovery was even more remarkable. Between 1946 and 1967, Japan's gross national product grew at a rate of 10 percent a year — higher even than the growth rate in West Germany, the fastest growing European economy. Japan led the world in shipbuilding; its automobile industry became second only to that of the United States. Japanese automobiles, ships, steel, cameras, and electronic equipment were exported in record quantities. Less than 25 years after its defeat, Japan had become the third largest economic power in the world.

The economic miracle in Japan was due to many factors. Prewar Japan had had a thriving industrial and business community, providing the nation with a basis for rebuilding and mod-

The Japanese Constitution of 1947

One of the major goals of the new Japanese constitution of 1947 was to bring a democratic system of government to the nation. The constitution gave legislative power to the National Diet (Japan's parliament). Like the U.S. Constitution, it also provided a "Bill of Rights." Among those rights are the following:

15. The people have the inalienable right to choose their public officials and to dismiss them.

20. Freedom of religion is guaranteed to all. . . .

21. Freedom of assembly and association as well as speech, press, and other forms of expression are guaranteed. . . .

24. Marriage shall be based only on the mutual consent of both sexes, and it shall be maintained through mutual cooperation with the equal rights of husband and wife as a basis. . . .

25. All people shall have the right to maintain the minimum standards of wholesome and cultured living. . . .

26. All people shall have the right to receive an equal education corresponding to their ability, as provided by law.

31. No person shall be deprived of life or liberty, nor shall any other criminal penalty be imposed, except according to procedure established by law.

Who has the right to choose Japanese public officials? What provisions does the constitution make for education? What freedoms are guaranteed in Articles 20 and 21?

---

ernizing. The Japanese government had a uniquely cooperative relationship with this business community. In other countries, corporations raised money through the sale of stocks and bonds. In Japan the government loaned money to businesses indirectly through the government-owned Bank of Japan. Because of the small military budget and tax policies that encouraged savings, more capital was available for investment. Businesses could spend large sums of money on research and development, particularly in high-technology fields such as electronics. In addition, during Japan's economic recovery, Western nations allowed the country to protect its growing industries with high tariffs on imports.

Friction develops with trading partners. At a time when most nations had huge trade deficits, Japan enjoyed a trade surplus — that is, it exported a greater value of goods than it imported. By the 1980's, other countries were demanding that Japan reduce its exports and buy more foreign goods. This pressure came especially from the United States, where automobile makers and other industries faced heavy competition from Japanese imports. In 1986, Prime Minister Nakasone (nah-kah-SOH-nee) pledged to take steps that would reduce friction with Japan's trading partners.

Japan faces the problems of industrialization. Despite Japan's economic success, problems remained. Always short of land and natural resources, Japan was dependent on foreign sources for food and raw materials. Agricultural production increased after the war, but Japan still had to import almost all of its crude oil, cotton, iron ore, soybeans, wheat, and sugar and about half of its lumber.

In addition, the emphasis on rapid economic growth led to neglect of people's needs in other areas. More and more Japanese moved to the already overcrowded cities, creating problems with public transportation, roads, sewage systems, and housing. Like other industrialized nations, Japan also suffered from severe environmental pollution.

International relations affect Japanese defense policies. Close ties with the United States had played a part in Japan's economic success since World War II. As relations between the United States and the People's Republic of China began to improve in the early 1970's, the Japanese became uneasy. They felt America's commitment to Japan as its ally in Asia might be weakening. As provided in the antiwar clause of the constitution, Japan had only a small self-defense force and depended on the United States for military security. Some Japanese became increasingly fearful that their pact with the United States might not be enough to guarantee Japan's security. These fears were reflected in Japan's growing military budget. Still small by American standards, it rose sharply in the 1980's. This development brought controversy between those Japanese who wanted Japan to take a greater part in its own defenses and those who opposed any military build-up.

Japanese relations with China improve. Like the United States, Japan did not recognize the new Communist leadership in China for many years, even though many Japanese businesses hoped to expand trade with the Chinese mainland. After the death of Mao, however, Japan was encouraged by the less revolutionary attitudes in China's leadership. Diplomatic relations were established in 1972, and in 1978 China and Japan signed a ten-year Treaty of Peace and Friendship. China's efforts toward modernization provided a new market for Japan's industries, and the two nations established better trade relations.

———

Japan's treaty with China demonstrated the dramatic changes in conditions in Asia since World War II. Japan, highly dependent on international trade for its raw materials and energy needs, sought greater world prestige not through war but through its unique ability to modernize and strengthen its economy.

CHECK-UP

1. (a) What were the immediate objectives of the American occupation of Japan? (b) What were the provisions of the new constitution?
2. (a) Why was Japan able to make such a rapid economic recovery from World War II? (b) What problems did industrialization cause?
3. (a) What was Japan's relationship with China in the 1950's and 1960's? (b) How and why did this change in the 1970's?

3 New Nations Are Created in South Asia

A movement for independence was under way in India in the late 1800's, but Indian nationalists postponed their demands at the outbreak of World War I. India contributed raw materials, money, and troops to the war effort. In return, Britain promised greater self-rule for India. After the war, in 1919, the British Parliament passed a new Government of India Act, which increased India's self-rule in domestic affairs but left Britain in control of India's foreign policy and national security. Many Indians were not satisfied with these changes, and demands for independence grew stronger.

THE INDEPENDENCE MOVEMENT

The Amritsar massacre strengthens the independence movement. Disappointed by the British response to their demands for greater participation in government, some nationalists began using acts of violence. The British Parliament's response was the passage of several restrictive laws, including a ban on all political meetings.

As strikes and riots broke out all over India to protest the repressive laws, British troops responded harshly. The most serious incident occurred at the town of Amritsar (in the Punjab) on April 13, 1919, when a British general ordered his troops to fire at hundreds of Indians who were attending a political meeting. Four hundred Indians were killed, and twelve hundred were wounded. Although the British government made a formal apology for the massacre, India's leaders were now convinced that the only solution to their country's problems was *Hind Swaraj*, Indian home rule.

Gandhi calls for nonviolent resistance. The most respected and admired of the protest leaders, Mohandas K. Gandhi (GAHN-dee), sought

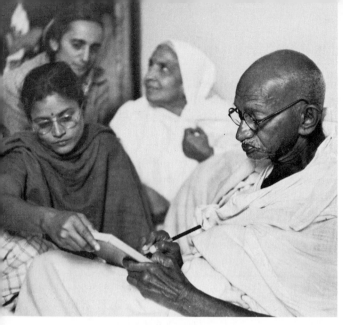

Mohandas Gandhi's policy of nonviolent resistance set the pattern for India's struggle toward independence.

an end to repression but rejected violence in any form. A small, frail man who showed no interest in worldly possessions, Gandhi attracted millions of followers, who called him the Mahatma (mah-HAHT-mah), or "Great Soul." For thirty years he dominated India's independence movement.

Between 1893 and 1915 Gandhi had lived in South Africa, where he led a series of boycotts forcing white officials to repeal laws that discriminated against the Indians who lived there. He developed the tactic of using *civil disobedience* — nonviolent resistance to laws and acts that are thought unjust.

Indians participate in boycotts. Nonviolent protests in India usually took the form of boycotts in which Indians halted all work and dedicated the day to prayer and fasting. To protest the Amritsar massacre, Gandhi called for a nationwide boycott. Protesters boycotted offices, disrupted elections, and refused to pay their taxes. When British troops and policemen tried to disperse the crowds with clubs and rifles, the advocates of nonviolence did little more than protect their own bodies.

Gandhi calls for a return to traditional industries. Gandhi's methods were simple but effective. In defiance of the law he encouraged Indians to restore such traditional industries as spinning cotton, rather than buying finished cloth from the British. He also led nonviolent demonstrations, such as a march to the sea in protest of the tax on salt. The British arrested and jailed Gandhi a number of times, but they could not stop the acts of civil disobedience. These nonviolent acts gained worldwide publicity, and Gandhi won much sympathy and support.

Gandhi attacks the caste system. Gandhi's struggle for India's freedom and dignity was not limited to defying British laws. He also attacked the age-old tradition of Untouchability (page 231), pledging to gain equality for India's millions of outcastes, whom he called *Harijans* (hah-REE-junz), or "God's children." Gandhi believed that India could not be truly independent as long as its people remained divided.

The independence movement has divided goals. In the 1930's Gandhi began to share leadership with Jawaharlal Nehru (jah-WAH-har-lal NAY-roo), a British-educated political leader whose family had long been active in the nationalist movement. Gandhi and Nehru had somewhat different dreams for India's future. Gandhi hoped for a self-sufficient India that would return to a simple peasant life, while Nehru's vision of India's future was patterned on the industrialized nations of the West. Gandhi and Nehru did agree, however, that their major goal should be an independent, united India in which Hindus and Muslims could live together in harmony. Events in the 1930's undermined that hope, as Muslim leaders began to call for the formation of a separate state in northwestern India, to be named Pakistan, from words meaning "Land of the Pure."

Britain enacts new reforms. The British Parliament rejected the Muslims' proposal, passing instead another Government of India Act in 1935. The new act created an elected legislature for India that had control over all domestic affairs. The act also increased the number of eligible voters and attempted to strengthen the representation of minorities, an important concession to the Muslims. Six million women became eligible to vote in provincial elections. Parliament also pledged that India would soon be granted independence.

In the first election for India's legislature, the Hindu-led Indian National Congress (page 562), was voted into power throughout most of India. Indian Muslims were disturbed by the idea of being a minority in a Hindu state. Their spokesman, Mohammed Ali Jinnah, asked the Congress party to endorse his group, known as the Muslim League (page 563), as the single representative for India's Muslims. Nehru, the leader of the Congress party, rejected Jinnah's proposal, however, setting the stage for a later violent confrontation.

World War II prompts resistance. During World War II, many Indians supported the war effort. India provided the Allies with troops, supplies, and military bases. Nevertheless, leaders of the powerful Congress party declared a policy of noncooperation unless Britain would agree to immediate independence for India. They remembered that cooperation in World War I had not brought the independence that had been promised. Britain was not willing to meet the nationalists' demands, however. As campaigns for independence disrupted the war effort, the British jailed Gandhi, Nehru, and tens of thousands of other nationalists.

Disagreement delays independence. After the war, independence riots broke out in India. In response, Britain offered to grant India its independence. The original plan was for a united India, but an outraged Jinnah called for a Direct Action Day to protest Britain's decision. The protests were peaceful in most parts of the country. In Calcutta, however, rioting took the lives of 5,000 Muslims and Hindus.

Convinced by these protests that a united India was impossible, the British Parliament and Indian leaders agreed in 1947 that the British would leave India and the subcontinent would be divided into two nations — a Hindu India and a Muslim Pakistan. Partition was set for mid-August of 1947.

Partition brings unrest and violence. The boundaries for partition were hastily drawn along religious lines, based on the predominance of Hindus or Muslims in certain regions of the country. Muslim Pakistan was formed of two parts — West Pakistan in the Punjab and East Pakistan in what had been part of Bengal (map, page 554). Within the new boundaries of India and Pakistan, however, lived millions of Hindus and Muslims who suddenly found themselves in the "wrong" country. Many chose to remain where they lived, but millions of others fled to the safety of a new homeland. On both sides fanatics committed atrocities. Between 300,000 and one million refugees lost their lives during the partition.

Distressed at the violence, Gandhi decided to fast in protest against the inhumane actions by the members of both religions. This concern for all Indian people eventually cost Gandhi his life. In January, 1948, a fanatical Hindu, believing Gandhi to be a traitor to his own religion, assassinated him.

INDEPENDENT INDIA

Many Indians gain new rights after independence. Despite the violence surrounding partition, Indians celebrated their independence on August 15, 1947. Within three years, the nation had drafted its first constitution, which was modeled on the democratic institutions of the United States and Britain. Nehru became India's first prime minister and served in that office until his death in 1964. Under his leadership, the nation followed a democratic course and was viewed as a model for other newly independent countries.

The new constitution outlawed the limitations imposed by Untouchability. Jobs, education, political offices, and public buildings were legally opened up to India's 60 million outcastes. Enforcing this order was difficult, however, particularly in rural areas where people clung to their Hindu traditions. The constitution also removed many restrictions on the women of India. Women had been active in the independence movement and continued to participate in politics. The constitution granted them greater voting and property rights.

One of Nehru's hardest tasks as prime minister was to give the new nation a sense of unity. Never in India's long history had the subcontinent been united; the different regions had been separated from one another by different religions, languages, and customs. After independence, India remained culturally divided. Although Hinduism was the dominant religion, it had many subdivisions. Moreover, in some areas there were significant Muslim minorities.

India becomes concerned with defense. Because hostility between India and Pakistan continued after independence, the new nation quickly became concerned with national defense. In 1947, India clashed with its neighbor over Kashmir (map, page 554), a region that both countries coveted for its water and other resources. Although Kashmir's population was predominantly Muslim, its former ruler, a Hindu prince, had given the state to India at the time of partition. Pakistan demanded that the people of Kashmir be allowed to vote to determine their status, but India refused. Indian and Pakistani troops fought in Kashmir until a UN truce was arranged in 1949. The territory was divided but was still a cause of conflict.

The People's Republic of China, India's neighbor, posed a later threat to Indian security. In 1962 Chinese troops moved into Indian territory during a border dispute. Although China quickly withdrew its troops, the invasion embarrassed the ruling Congress party and frightened India. Nehru reluctantly set aside large sums for national defense.

The Congress party declines in power. The Indian National Congress had led the independence movement in India, and it remained in control of the government after independence. In the 1960's, however, the Congress party began to lose votes when it attempted to introduce cooperative and collective farming along the lines followed in China (page 759). This cost the government the valued support of landlords. The Chinese invasion also lost votes for the Congress party. The death of Nehru further undermined the party's prestige.

Indira Gandhi leads India. In 1966 the Congress party elected Indira Gandhi, Nehru's daughter, to the office of prime minister. During her first five years in office, Gandhi won admiration for her effective leadership, administrative abilities, and encouragement of economic development. The government took some control of India's economy, nationalizing banks, coal mining, and other industries.

The next few years, however, brought serious problems and renewed unrest. Severe drought cut food production, and hunger, already a serious problem, became even more widespread. In addition, the rising price of oil on the world market hampered both industrial and agricultural development. Adding to India's problems were thousands of refugees who were fleeing from civil war in East Pakistan (page 770). The United States and other wheat-growing countries sent millions of tons of grain to India. Nevertheless, food riots, strikes, and violent demonstrations erupted.

Indira Gandhi is charged with abuse of power. During this troubled period, some Congress leaders blamed Indira Gandhi for corruption and mismanagement in government. In June, 1975, a court found her guilty of election campaign fraud and barred her from holding office for a period of six years. Two weeks later, however, the prime minister declared a state of emergency. Over the next two years, Indira Gandhi had thousands of her political opponents jailed, censored the press, limited civil liberties, and barred India's supreme court from reviewing her decisions.

Indira Gandhi's opponents were increasingly disturbed by her authoritarian rule. In March, 1977, she and the Congress party were voted out of office. She regained popular support, however, and was re-elected in 1980.

Indira Gandhi is assassinated. Indira Gandhi's primary goal was to maintain a united India. When she believed unity was threatened, she did not hesitate to use strong measures to meet the threat. Critics charged that her methods severely weakened India's democratic institutions. During the 1980's, for example, she repeatedly suspended state governments in order to implement her own policies. Nor did she draw the line at the use of force. In 1984, Gandhi sent military forces to crush a Sikh rebellion in the Punjab, where Sikh extremists had been using violence in waging a campaign for greater political independence. (To review the Sikhs, see page 243.) Hundreds of people were killed in the fighting, and Sikhs throughout India were outraged when government forces stormed the Golden Temple in Amritsar (map, page 554), the Sikhs' holiest shrine.

Four months later, Indira Gandhi was assassinated by three of her own Sikh bodyguards. Her son, Rajiv (rah-JEEV) Gandhi, was immediately chosen as her successor. The new prime minister vowed to continue his mother's policies. In elections held in December, 1984, India's voters gave Rajiv Gandhi's party a record number of seats in the Indian parliament. The Sikh-Hindu conflict remained one of his more difficult problems.

INDUSTRY IN INDIA
Greater industrial production is a goal in present-day India. Indian industries include the making of fine rugs (above) and scientific instruments (right).

India remains a land of contradictions. Between the 1960's and the 1980's India's agricultural output doubled because of a combination of modern technology, improved agricultural techniques, and an absence of natural disasters. By the 1980's, India also was the tenth largest industrial producer in the world. While it continued to produce and sell the traditional staples of sugar and textiles, iron, steel, and engineering products made up a greater share of its exports. Economic plans in the 1980's were intended to increase the number of jobs by improving agricultural and industrial production.

Serious problems continued to plague India, however. Unemployment remained high, and many people lived in crushing poverty, undernourished and often ill. Well over half of India's people remained illiterate. The overcrowded cities faced problems of inadequate health care, housing, and sanitation facilities.

Nonetheless, in its first decades of independence, India overcame many social, political, and technological problems. India's women, especially in the cities, began to break out of their traditional roles. They worked as doctors and scientists and served as members of parliament. Conflicts between Hindus and Muslims occurred less often and with less severity. Finally, India's government remained stable through several decades of economic crisis and political unrest.

PAKISTAN AND BANGLADESH

Pakistan is a divided nation. The partition of the Indian subcontinent created a Pakistan that was divided geographically and culturally. A thousand miles of India's territory separated East and West Pakistan. Other factors also separated the people of the two regions. West Pakistan was a dry, hilly, and moderately populated region. Its main language was Urdu (OOR-doo), and its people were better educated and had a higher standard of living than people in East Pakistan. East Pakistan was hot, rainy, and densely populated. Floods and famine were common. The East Pakistanis spoke Bengali (ben-GAH-lee) and in their customs and traditions were closer to the Hindus than to the West Pakistanis.

For the first twenty years of Pakistan's existence, West Pakistanis dominated the government. East Pakistan, overcrowded and impoverished, looked with envy at the other half of the country. Political problems also beset the new nation from the beginning. Mohammed

Ali Jinnah died in 1948, a year after Pakistan was founded. For the next decade the nation suffered through short-lived governments that cared little for the people's needs.

Then, in 1958, General Mohammed Ayub Khan seized power. Imposing martial law and ruling as a military dictator, he rid Pakistan of corrupt officials and of markets where goods were sold at inflated prices. He also granted peasants increased responsibilities in local politics. Pakistan under Ayub Khan's rule began to make progress in land redistribution and industrial development. By 1965 the national income had increased by 25 percent.

Ayub Khan's political fortunes began to decline, however. In 1969, faced with protests and riots, he resigned and turned over the government to army leaders. His place as president was taken by another general, Mohammed Yahya Khan.

East Pakistanis revolt. Relations between East and West Pakistan grew worse. In the 1970 elections, the East Pakistanis won enough votes to gain control of the National Assembly. This meant that Mujibur Rahman, leader of the Bengali party, would become prime minister of Pakistan. Yahya Khan, however, refused to accept the election results and had Rahman and other opposition leaders arrested. The arrests turned into a massacre as hundreds of thousands of East Pakistanis were slaughtered by the army. Millions of refugees fled to India, and terror and civil war swept the region.

Bangladesh becomes independent. In March, 1971, East Pakistan declared its independence as the new nation of Bangladesh (meaning "the Bengal nation"). The army of the Pakistani government invaded, but India intervened on the side of the rebelling Bengalis and the invasion was halted. Mujibur Rahman became the new country's first prime minister and then its president.

Independent Bangladesh, one of the world's most overcrowded nations, faced severe problems. Its economy was mainly agricultural but could not produce enough food for its growing population. Much of the country, including its few industries, had been devastated in the civil war. Floods, famine, and plague caused widespread suffering and death. Mil-

lions of tons of grain were imported to help feed the more than 90 million people.

Bangladesh was also troubled by political instability. After a series of coups and assassinations, military leaders took over the country in 1982 and declared martial law.

Pakistan emphasizes Islamic ways. Pakistan (former West Pakistan) faced serious problems also. In 1970, Zulfikar Ali Bhutto (BOO-toh) became prime minister. In an attempt to stabilize the country's economy, Bhutto nationalized Pakistan's agricultural and textile industry. This action, along with Pakistan's shaky economic status, discouraged foreign investors. In addition, Bhutto made many enemies and was accused of corruption.

In 1977, for the third time in thirty years, the army seized control of the government. Bhutto was imprisoned and later executed. The new regime, headed by General Zia ul-Haq (ZEE-uh ool-HAK), replaced Pakistani civil law with traditional Islamic law (page 210). Islamic laws and traditions were also given greater emphasis in Pakistan's schools. Although elections for a new national legislature were held in 1985, leaders of opposition parties were barred from taking part. In 1986 Benazir Bhutto, daughter of the executed prime minister, returned to Pakistan from exile to lead an opposition movement.

CHECK-UP

1. Vocabulary: *civil disobedience.*
2. (a) What were the provisions of the 1919 Government of India Act? (b) Why did it disappoint most Indians? (c) How was the independence movement affected by the Amritsar massacre?
3. (a) How did Gandhi and Nehru differ in their hopes for India's future? (b) On what issues did they agree?
4. (a) Why was India partitioned before it gained independence? (b) On what basis was the partition made? (c) What problems resulted?
5. (a) What achievements were made in India's first decades of independence? (b) What problems remained?
6. (a) Why did the Bengalis of East Pakistan want independence? (b) How did East Pakistan become Bangladesh?
7. How were Islamic ways emphasized in Pakistan in the 1970's and 1980's?

Southeast Asia

Name the eight nations of Southeast Asia. Note that the island of New Guinea is divided between the nations of Indonesia and Papua New Guinea.

4 Conflicts Disrupt Southeast Asia

The region known today as Southeast Asia includes the mainland nations of Burma, Thailand, Kampuchea (Cambodia), Laos, and Vietnam, as well as the island nations of Indonesia, Malaysia, the Philippines, and Singapore (map, above). Among the millions of people living in the region are many distinct racial, cultural, linguistic, and religious groups, each with its own history.

Ancient kingdoms become colonial possessions. Since ancient times, Southeast Asia has been an important crossroads for world trade. Great kingdoms, such as those of the Khmer and Thai (TIE) peoples, developed as early as the sixth to tenth centuries A.D. Once Vasco da

Gama found his way around Africa to India (page 350), Europeans became rivals for control of the resources and trade of Southeast Asia.

By the end of the 1800's, foreign powers controlled much of the region. Siam (modern Thailand), once the most powerful kingdom in Southeast Asia, signed trade treaties with Britain and France in 1855 to keep them from taking over the country. In 1863 troops sent by Napoleon III (page 471) made Cambodia a French protectorate. Four years later the French began to expand into what is now Vietnam and created a federation of states called Indochina. Earlier in the century, Britain had

771

bought the island of Singapore, and by 1886 Burma came under British rule. In 1898 the United States acquired the Philippines in the Spanish-American War.

The colonial powers developed Southeast Asia's natural resources, establishing prosperous plantations that grew rubber, rice, sugar, and coffee. Tin mines and oil wells produced mineral wealth for European investors. As in other colonies, little manufacturing was established by the colonial powers, and the Western nations sold their own manufactured goods to the Southeast Asians.

World War II leads to independence. From the beginning, the Southeast Asians resented foreign rule. As dissatisfaction with colonial rule grew, nationalist movements emerged. When World War II broke out in Europe, Great Britain, France, and the Netherlands were forced to leave their colonies unprotected while they defended their homelands against Nazi aggression. Once the European powers had left, the Japanese overran and occupied most of Southeast Asia.

Nationalist movements opposed to colonial rule already existed in some areas. The Japanese occupation increased the people's desire for independence. Lacking the manpower to govern the conquered territories, the Japanese delegated political authority to local leaders. Many of these leaders became the focus of national liberation movements against both Japan and the Western colonial powers. When Japan lost the war in 1945, nationalists gained control of the governments in many Southeast Asian countries and proclaimed their independence. Throughout Southeast Asia, however, independence and national unity were achieved only after violent struggles.

THE ISLAND NATIONS

Power changes hands in the Philippines. In 1946 the Philippines gained independence from the United States. The new nation faced many serious problems. The capital city, Manila, had been reduced to rubble during the last days of the Japanese retreat, and the economy was badly disrupted. Filipinos were torn between their desire for economic independence and their desperate need for American aid. More-

over, the government of the new republic was riddled with corruption and had to deal with armed rebellion. Communist-led anti-Japanese guerrillas had refused to stop fighting at the end of the war. They now fought Philippine government forces for control of remote areas. The fighting did not subside until 1954.

During the late 1960's and early 1970's, warfare again broke out in the countryside. At the same time, revolts started up among the nation's Muslim minority (most Filipinos are Roman Catholics), and students demonstrated against government policies. In response to these actions, President Ferdinand Marcos declared martial law and jailed many of his opponents. Although martial law ended in 1981, the Philippine nation was still far from being able to call itself a democracy.

Corruption, rebellion, and poverty had been continuing problems through the 1970's and into the 1980's. Many Filipinos were unhappy with Marcos's leadership, but they had no effective organization to voice their dissatisfaction. The event that created effective opposition to Marcos was the assassination of Benigno Aquino (ah-KEEN-oh) in August 1983.

Aquino, one of Marcos's most outspoken critics, was returning to the Philippines after three years of exile in the United States. As he stepped off the plane at the Manila airport, he was shot and killed. Many Filipinos believed that the Marcos government had ordered the assassination. Demonstrations calling for an investigation of the killing led to the growth of an organized, powerful opposition movement. Over the next two and a half years, antigovernment leaders demanded economic, political, and military reforms.

Finally, under pressure both at home and from the United States, Marcos agreed to hold an election. His chief opponent was Corazon Aquino, widow of the slain politician. Though new to politics, Mrs. Aquino won the support of a coalition of anti-Marcos parties. In February 1986, the presidential election was held and President Marcos claimed victory. Fraud and violence marked the voting, however, and observers generally held Marcos loyalists responsible. The opposition also claimed victory, and Aquino's followers began a campaign of nonviolent resistance to the Marcos government.

Cadets at the Philippine Military Academy stand at attention for review by President Corazon Aquino during a graduation ceremony in 1986.

They were soon joined by key members of the armed forces.

Faced with a choice between civil war and exile, Marcos and his family flew from the Philippines to Hawaii. Aquino immediately formed a government and called for national reconciliation. An early challenge came from military leaders who hoped to take power. In response, Mrs. Aquino fired her defense minister and sought to strengthen her position as national leader. Outbreaks of violence, however, were a reminder of the difficulty of establishing democracy and stability in a country that had a long history of poverty and turmoil.

Indonesia suffers economic problems. The Netherlands tried to regain control of the East Indies after the war, but nationalist forces bitterly resisted Dutch control. Pressure from the United States persuaded the Netherlands to give the area its independence, and in 1949 it became the Republic of Indonesia. The country's first president was a nationalist leader named Sukarno (soo-KAHR-noh).

Sukarno ruled for fifteen years but was unable to manage the economy successfully. Massive funds went toward projects such as stadiums and monuments, while agriculture and development of the country's resources were neglected. Because so much food had to be imported, rising prices in the world food market caused rapid inflation in Indonesia.

Sukarno had considerable Communist support, and in 1965 Communists tried to take over the government. In a bloody civil war, the army suppressed the revolt. Its leader, General Suharto, became president.

Suharto's government was able to reduce inflation and increase production, but severe problems continued. Because many of Indonesia's businesses were foreign-owned, profits seldom remained in the country. In 1970 students and workers rioted against foreign ownership. In response to this protest, the government restricted investment from abroad and required foreign companies to establish partnerships with Indonesians. The nation still had a huge foreign debt, however, with high unemployment and little capital for investment.

In an attempt to solve these economic problems, Indonesia began to exploit its vast resources of petroleum, natural gas, and minerals. Like India, Indonesia emphasized industries that depended on the use of natural resources and human labor.

Malaysia is plagued by ethnic conflicts. When World War II ended, Malaya became a British protectorate. After years of rebellion, it gained independence in 1957, and in 1963 it united with Sabah, Sarawak, and the former crown colony of Singapore to form the Federation of Malaysia (map, page 771), which became part of the British Commonwealth.

Problems soon arose between the Federation's two dominant cultures. Most of the people in the islands were Malays, but in Singapore most were Chinese. Fearing that the Chinese would gain control of their government, leaders forced Singapore to withdraw from the Federation in 1965. Many Chinese, and many Indians as well, remained in Malaysia, however. These groups were generally better educated and more prosperous than the Malay farmers, and they controlled much of Malaysia's commerce. In 1969, Malays rioted against the dominance of Chinese and Indians in their country. To keep the nation together, the government began programs to improve the standard of living among the Malays.

Malaysia is the leading rubber-producing nation, providing about half of the world's total supply. Below, a woman works on a Malaysian rubber plantation.

Despite the nation's internal strife, Malaysia's economy remained one of the soundest in Southeast Asia. The country was the world's leading exporter of rubber.

Singapore has a strong economy. Singapore's economy prospered after it left the Federation of Malaysia in 1965. Led by an anti-Communist government that controlled all aspects of political life, Singapore had one of the strongest economies in Asia. Manufacturing, shipping, oil refining, and banking were its important economic activities.

MAINLAND SOUTHEAST ASIA

The French withdraw from Indochina. The French returned to Indochina after World War II to find much of it under the control of the Vietminh, a nationalist movement founded in 1941 by Ho Chi Minh. Ho, a Communist, had set up a government in the northern part of Vietnam. Unwilling to part with its colonies in Indochina, France sent troops to fight against the nationalist army. Vietnamese peasants, who looked on the French as imperialists, gave help and supplies to Ho's guerrilla forces. Communist China also aided the Vietminh, while the United States helped France. In March, 1954, the Vietminh severely defeated the French troops at Dien Bien Phu (DYEN-BYEN-FOO), and the French left Indochina.

The 1954 peace talks, held at Geneva, Switzerland, included representatives from North and South Vietnam, Cambodia. Laos, France, China, Great Britain, the United States, and the Soviet Union. In the settlement, known as the Geneva Accords, France granted independence to Laos and Cambodia, and Vietnam was temporarily divided at the 17th parallel of latitude. Elections to unite the country were scheduled for 1956. Until then, it was agreed, Ho Chi Minh's Communist government would control the north, and a non-Communist government would lead the south.

Vietnam is engulfed in war. South Vietnam's leaders refused to sign the Geneva Accords. They would not accept a divided nation, particularly one in which the Communist north was so much richer in industry, minerals, and farmland. In addition, South Vietnam's leaders feared that since the division put a majority of Vietnamese under Communist rule, the Communists would win the 1956 elections.

Ho Chi Minh and his Communist forces were nonetheless determined to reunite the nation under their leadership. North Vietnamese soldiers crossed the 17th parallel to recruit and train South Vietnamese who were sympathetic to the north's cause. These southerners became known as the Vietcong. By 1957, Vietcong forces were attacking villages in the south, and by 1960 they were strong enough to attack South Vietnamese army units.

Meanwhile, South Vietnamese President Ngo Dinh Diem tried to restore order. Diem resorted to harsh methods, jailing his opponents and ignoring the needs of his people. His support dwindling, Diem was overthrown by a military coup and murdered late in 1963.

The United States sends troops. The successes of the Vietcong and the instability of South Vietnam worried United States leaders. Determined to prevent the spread of communism, the United States had set up the Southeast Asia Treaty Organization (SEATO) in 1954. SEATO members pledged aid against aggression in the region.[1] In addition, as Vietcong strength increased, the United States added military advisers to the economic and military aid it had been giving to South Vietnam.

South Vietnam's dependence on United States support grew greater. In 1964, North Vietnamese patrol boats attacked American destroyers in the Gulf of Tonkin. As a result, the United States Senate passed the Gulf of Tonkin Resolution, giving President Lyndon B. Johnson the power to send United States forces to Vietnam. From 1965 through 1967, Johnson continued to increase the number of troops and the frequency of bombing raids.

The Communists launch a major offensive. In January of 1968, during a Vietnamese religious holiday, Vietcong and North Vietnamese forces struck at virtually all the important cities and towns in the south. (The attack became known as the *Tet* offensive, after the

---

[1]The treaty, which remained in effect until 1977, was signed by the United States, Great Britain, France, Australia, New Zealand, the Philippines, Pakistan, and Thailand.

TIMETABLE

Changing Asia

1919	The Amritsar massacre brings demands for Indian independence.
1945	United States forces occupy defeated Japan.
1947	India and Pakistan gain independence. Japan adopts a democratic constitution.
1948	Mohandas Gandhi is assassinated.
1949	The People's Republic of China is established; the Chinese Nationalist government flees to Taiwan. The Republic of Indonesia gains independence.
1954	French troops leave Indochina.
1965	American fighting forces are sent to Vietnam.
1966	Mao Tse-tung launches the Cultural Revolution.
1971	Bangladesh declares its independence from Pakistan.
1973	A truce is signed in Vietnam.
1975	Vietnam is united under Communist North Vietnam. Communist rebels gain power in Laos and Cambodia.
1978	Japan and China sign a treaty of friendship.
1979	China and the U.S. establish diplomatic relations.
1984	Indira Gandhi is assassinated.
1986	A nonviolent revolution brings a new government to power in the Philippines.

---

holiday.) South Vietnam staggered under the attack. After the Tet offensive, people in the United States began to question whether South Vietnam had a chance of winning the war. The war was becoming increasingly unpopular in the United States, and American leaders now considered withdrawing from Vietnam.

United States forces slowly leave Vietnam. Peace talks began in Paris in 1968, but American troops remained in Vietnam for another five years. In 1969 President Richard M. Nixon ordered the withdrawal of troops but continued bombing raids and ground fighting. In an attempt to destroy Vietcong supply lines and sanctuaries, United States forces invaded Cambodia in 1970 and gave support to a South Vietnamese attack on Laos in 1971. A 1972 North Vietnamese offensive was answered by a major United States bombing campaign.

The war, however, was draining the energy and morale of all sides. Early in 1973 a peace agreement was signed, and soon all United States forces had left Vietnam.

North Vietnam takes control. The war continued for two years after the American withdrawal, but without United States support the South Vietnamese army suffered many setbacks. In April, 1975, when their capital city of Saigon fell to the North Vietnamese, South Vietnam surrendered. (Saigon was then renamed Ho Chi Minh City.)

By 1976, Vietnam was a united country, ruled by the former North Vietnamese leaders. These leaders instituted a massive program of reorganization, taking control of factories and businesses, "re-educating" teachers, revising textbooks, and sending many city dwellers to rural areas in hopes of increasing agricultural production. Thousands of anti-Communists began to flee from Vietnam during this period of change. Crowding into small boats to seek refuge, they became known as "boat people."

Cambodia becomes the Communist nation of Kampuchea. The turmoil of the Vietnam war spread to neighboring nations. Cambodia (also once part of French Indochina) had been independent since 1953 under its ruler Prince Norodom Sihanouk (SEE-uh-nuhk). Sihanouk's government had hoped to remain neutral during the war in Vietnam, but North Vietnamese and Vietcong troops used Cambodian territory as an escape route and for supply bases. In 1969 United States planes began to bomb these bases in Cambodia. A year later, the United States supported the overthrow of Sihanouk by Lon Nol, a strong anti-Communist. Vietnamese Communists, however, penetrated even farther into Cambodia as they fled from American and South Vietnamese forces.

With Vietnamese help, a group of Communists in Cambodia, the Khmer Rouge (KMEHR ROOZH), planned the overthrow of Lon Nol. The Khmer Rouge were successful, taking over the country in 1975. Under their leader, Pol Pot, they declared Cambodia a Communist nation and renamed it Kampuchea (kam-puh-CHEE-uh). The new regime proved to be one of the most brutal of the twentieth century. The nation's cities were evacuated by force as part of the government's plan to wipe out all traces of prerevolutionary ways of life. Former city dwellers of all ages were made to do hard agricultural labor and had to submit to political indoctrination at the hands of fanatic revolutionaries. Mass executions became common. As many as one million people, about a sixth of the total population, were killed outright by the new government. A million or more people died of disease and starvation as a direct result of government actions and policies.

Vietnam invades Kampuchea. Pol Pot's government was hostile to the newly united Vietnam, and forces of the two countries clashed in fighting along the border. Finally in 1978, Vietnamese troops, with the help of Kampuchean rebels, invaded Kampuchea. In support of Pol Pot, China then briefly invaded parts of Vietnam. In 1979, Pol Pot was overthrown and replaced by Heng Samrin, a Communist leader friendly to Vietnam.

Civil war in Kampuchea followed the invasions. The Vietnamese Communists and their Kampuchean supporters fought a coalition of forces organized in 1982 for the purpose of expelling the Vietnamese from Kampuchea. These forces included backers of Pol Pot, backers of Prince Sihanouk, and a staunchly anti-Communist group led by Son Sann, another former head of state. The resistance forces were plagued, however, by conflicts among themselves and a severe shortage of funds. They received some support from China and the United States, both of which had an interest in keeping Kampuchea from becoming dominated by Soviet-supported Vietnam.

Communists take control in Laos. Laos won its independence in 1954 and had hoped to remain neutral among Communist and non-Communist neighbors. Civil war beset the nation, however, involving three factions — pro-Western forces, neutralists, and the Communists (called the Pathet Lao). In the early 1960's, a fourteen-nation conference met and installed a neutralist leader called Souvanna Phouma, but the new ruler failed to end the fighting. The Pathet Lao gained control of more and more of the country, finally taking complete control of the government in 1975. When anti-Communist forces continued to fight, Laos asked Vietnam for help. Thousands of Vietnamese troops moved into Laos to support the Communist government.

Critics of the Laotian regime charged that it was dominated by the thousands of Vietnamese advisers who had taken important places in all government agencies and offices. A decade after the Communist takeover, however, internal opposition to the regime was no longer a serious threat, and 60,000 Vietnamese troops remained in Laos.

Laos also added to the stream of Indochinese refugees. When the Communists gained control of the country, people of the well-to-do class began to leave by the thousands. Others soon followed. By 1985, more than a quarter of a million people had fled from Laos, seeking to escape poor economic conditions and lack of individual freedom.

Thailand tries to maintain peace with its neighbors. Thailand (which had been called Siam before 1939) was never colonized by Europeans. Occupied by Japan during World War II, the kingdom regained its independence after Japan's defeat. Pro-Western in its outlook, Thailand sent troops to fight in the Korean and Vietnam wars and also helped to organize SEATO. During the Vietnam War, Thailand allowed the United States to set up military bases within its borders.

Beginning in the 1960's, the Thai government had to deal with two different armed rebellions. Malay Muslims in the south fought to establish a separate state, while Communist guerrillas fought government forces in both the south and the northeast. These revolts continued into the 1980's.

The upheaval throughout the Indochinese peninsula was a matter of serious concern to Thailand, which shares borders with both Laos and Kampuchea (map, page 771). After 1975, when Communists took over the governments of both of those nations, the Thai government sought to maintain good relations with its neighbors. Thailand, whose economy was one of the strongest in the region, hoped to cooperate with Laos, Kampuchea, and Vietnam on economic development. It also hoped to obtain promises from those governments not to interfere in Thailand's internal affairs.

Vietnam's invasion of Kampuchea in 1978 made the situation difficult. Refugees flooded into Thailand, severely straining its resources. Vietnamese leaders then accused Thailand of supporting Pol Pot and of harboring Khmer Rouge rebels. Vietnamese and Kampuchean troops repeatedly clashed with Kampuchean rebels in the refugee camps that straddled the border between Thailand and Kampuchea. The Thai government, fearful of further Vietnamese expansionism, channeled aid to anti-Vietnamese rebels in Kampuchea.

Dislocation continues in Southeast Asia. Among those most affected by the turmoil in Southeast Asia were the hundreds of thousands of refugees who fled their homes in Laos, Kampuchea, and Vietnam. As many as 200,000 refugees sought shelter in Thailand. Other displaced persons, the "boat people," simply sailed their small craft into the ocean, hoping to be rescued and relocated. While some managed to find new homes, many died at sea. By the late 1980's, probably a million and a half boat people had fled their homelands, victims of the upheaval that had plagued Southeast Asia since the end of World War II.

CHECK-UP

1. (a) How did the issue of land reform create conflict in the Philippines? (b) What were Indonesia's major problems under Sukarno? (c) Why did Singapore leave the Federation of Malaysia?

2. (a) What event caused the French to withdraw from Vietnam? (b) Why did the United States become interested in events in Vietnam?

3. (a) Who were the Vietcong? (b) Why did Ngo Dinh Diem lose support in South Vietnam? (c) What incident led President Johnson to send United States troops to Vietnam and increase the amount of bombing?

4. (a) What was the Tet offensive? (b) How did it affect United States involvement in the Vietnam War? (c) When did the American forces leave Vietnam? (d) What was the outcome of the struggle between North and South Vietnam?

5. (a) What happened to Cambodia under the rule of Pol Pot? (b) What led to civil war in Kampuchea?

6. (a) Who were the Pathet Lao? (b) What caused tension between Thailand and Vietnam?

Chapter 35 Review

Summary

In China, war with Japan was followed by a civil war in which Mao Tse-tung's Communists expelled the Kuomintang in 1949. Mao's new government, known as the People's Republic of China, reformed agriculture, but industry progressed slowly. The excesses of the Cultural Revolution led to a move away from extremism among China's leaders, resulting in friendlier relations with nations of the West.

In Japan, defeat in World War II led to occupation by the United States and an attempt to rebuild Japan as a democratic nation. After the war, Japan's "economic miracle" made its economy one of the strongest in the world.

India won its independence from Britain in 1947. Muslims insisted on having their own nation, however, and Pakistan was also formed in 1947 amid violence and bloodshed. Though India remained culturally divided and poor, its economy began to improve and its government remained stable. Civil war split Pakistan in two, creating the poverty-stricken nation of Bangladesh from former East Pakistan. Pakistan itself remained under military rule.

Long controlled by foreign powers, most of Southeast Asia became independent during or just after World War II. Violence, conflict, and authoritarian rule plagued the region after independence. Vietnam was engulfed in war until 1975, when Communist forces took over the nation. Communist rebels also came to power in Cambodia and Laos in 1975.

Vocabulary Review

1. Match the following terms with the listed definitions: *civil disobedience, commune, gross national product, martial law.*
(a) An agricultural unit in China made up of a number of large state-owned farms.
(b) Strict controls maintained over a nation by military forces, usually including censorship and limits on people's movements.
(c) The use of nonviolent resistance to defy laws thought to be unjust.
(d) The total value of all goods and services produced in a country in a specific time period.

2. Distinguish between the terms in each of the following pairs:
(a) Kuomintang; Taiwan.
(b) Great Leap Forward; Cultural Revolution.
(c) commune; *zaibatsu*.
(d) West Pakistan; Bangladesh.
(e) Indochina; Vietnam.
(f) Vietcong; Vietminh.
(g) Cambodia; Kampuchea.
(h) Dutch East Indies; Indonesia.

People to Identify

Match the following people with the numbered phrases that describe them: *Douglas MacArthur, Mao Tse-tung, Mohandas Gandhi, Jawaharlal Nehru, Mohammed Ali Jinnah, Indira Gandhi, Mohammed Ayub Khan, Sukarno, Ho Chi Minh, Pol Pot.*

1. Communist founder of the movement for Vietnamese independence.
2. Spiritual leader of India's independence movement.
3. Leader of the Red Army and the first president of the People's Republic of China.
4. American general who led the occupation forces in Japan.
5. Nationalist leader who became India's first prime minister.
6. Founder of the Muslim League.
7. Military dictator of Pakistan from 1958 to 1969.
8. First president of the Republic of Indonesia.
9. Khmer Rouge leader who changed his country's name to Kampuchea.
10. Congress party politician who became India's prime minister in 1966.

Relating Geography and History

1. Locating places. Locate each of the following on a map in this chapter:
(a) Taiwan
(b) Dien Bien Phu
(c) Amur River
(d) Tokyo
(e) Philippines
(f) Vietnam
(g) Laos
(h) Thailand
(i) Malaysia
(j) Singapore
(k) Bangladesh
(l) Gulf of Tonkin

2. Map study. Use the map of Southeast Asia on page 771 to help you answer the following questions. (a) Which countries of Southeast Asia are entirely on the mainland? (b) What country includes both mainland and island territory? (c) Which countries share a border with China? (d) What is the capital of Indonesia? (e) On what island is this city located? (f) What are the two main islands of the Philippines?

3. Making charts. Many nations in Asia gained independence from colonial rule after World War II. Use information in the chapter, and from an almanac or encyclopedia, to make a chart of these nations. Use the following headings: Name of Country; Date of Independence; Former Name (as a colony); Colonial Ruler; Leaders of Nationalist Movement; Population.

Discussion Questions

1. (a) What actions did the Chinese Nationalists and the Chinese Communists take during World War II? (b) How might these actions have helped Mao Tse-tung and the Communists gain victory in 1949?

2. Describe the new political systems established after World War II (a) in China and (b) in Japan.

3. What major problems did these new nations face: (a) the People's Republic of China? (b) India? (c) Pakistan? (d) Malaysia?

4. (a) How did the economies of China and Japan differ before World War II in terms of industrialization and foreign trade? (b) How did these differences affect the two countries' postwar recovery?

5. (a) Describe some of the tactics of civil disobedience used by Gandhi. (b) Why did violence break out at the time of partition despite Gandhi's influence? (c) What economic changes had occurred in India by the 1980's?

6. What circumstances led to war (a) between India and Pakistan? (b) between East and West Pakistan?

7. (a) Why had colonial rule in Southeast Asia become weak by 1945? (b) How was Ho Chi Minh's success in Vietnam similar to Mao Tse-tung's victory in China? (c) How did the Vietnamese government influence events in Laos and Kampuchea? (d) What was Thailand's position in the conflict among the other Southeast Asian nations?

Reading Primary Sources

Independent India became an important nonaligned nation, and in 1956 Prime Minister Jawaharlal Nehru explained his country's position in a speech on American radio and television. Read the excerpts from Nehru's speech. Then answer the questions that follow.

> The preservation of peace forms the central aim of India's policy. It is in the pursuit of this policy that we have chosen the path of nonalignment in any military . . . alliance. Nonalignment does not mean passivity of mind or action, lack of faith or conviction. . . . It is a positive and dynamic approach to such problems that confront us. We believe that each country has not only the right to freedom but also [the right] to decide its own policy and way of life. . . .
>
> We believe, therefore, in nonaggression and noninterference by one country in the affairs of another and the growth of tolerance between them. . . .
>
> We therefore endeavor to maintain friendly relations with all countries, even though we may disagree with them in their policies or structure of government. We think that by this approach we can serve not only our country but also the larger causes of peace and good fellowship in the world.

(a) According to Nehru, what is the main goal of India's foreign policy? (b) Reread the description of the nonaligned nations on page 733. Which sentences in Nehru's speech describe India's nonalignment policy? (c) What reasons does Nehru give for this policy?

Skill Activities

1. Reports. Find information on one of the following topics and prepare a report: (a) the island of Taiwan; (b) the status of women in present-day China, India, or Japan; (c) working conditions in Japanese factories; (d) education in the People's Republic of China; (e) the state of Kashmir; (f) Singapore.

2. Drawing political cartoons. Prepare a political cartoon on one of the following topics: (a) the founding of the People's Republic of China; (b) China's Great Leap Forward; (c) Japan's postwar "economic miracle"; (d) the use of civil disobedience in India.

On the island of Madagascar off East Africa, the giant
"saucer" of a tracking station follows the paths of satellites
across the sky. In the foreground, a team of oxen pulls the
covered cart of a Malagasy farmer.

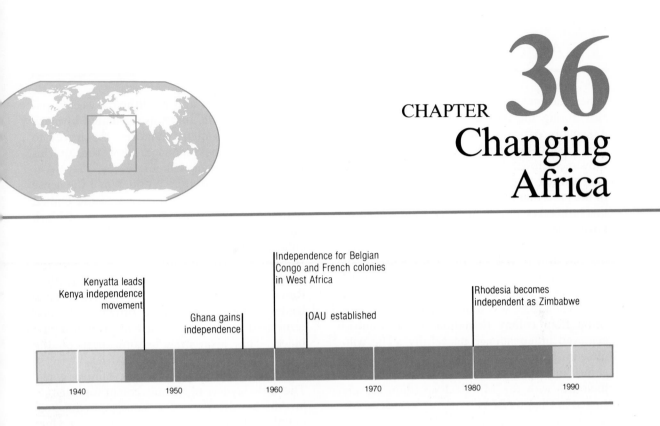

In 1945 there were only four independent nations in Africa — Egypt, Ethiopia, Liberia, and South Africa. Thirty years later, nearly all of the countries on the continent had gained self-government. Circumstances both in Europe and in Africa contributed to the movements for independence.

Some African nations made steady progress toward majority rule and freedom. In others, independence came abruptly, and there was little time for people to prepare for self-government and separation from the colonizing power. Although the transition from colony to independent nation was peaceful in much of Africa, there was violence in some areas. Few changes occurred in independent South Africa, where the white minority maintained an official policy of segregation.

After independence, the new nations of Africa began the process of modernization. They sought ways to bring about a sense of national unity, build strong, stable governments, develop their economies, and educate their people.

This chapter describes how the African colonies became independent countries and how these developing nations have dealt with their new freedom.

CHAPTER OUTLINE
1 African Nations Gain Independence
2 New African Nations Face Challenges

1 African Nations Gain Independence

When European nations took over most of Africa during the Age of Imperialism (Chapter 27), many Africans fought to keep their freedom from colonial rule. After World War I, a movement toward nationalism and independence started to gain momentum. Early leaders of the movement in black Africa sought ways to increase black representation in the colonial governments. After World War II, demands for complete independence grew. Ghana, once under the British, was the first nation to become independent in the postwar years. Over the next twenty years, other countries gained self-rule. While there was some violence in the transition from colony to nation, most countries achieved independence peacefully. (The colonies in North Africa, mostly Muslim, also gained independence in this period. Because of their ties with the Middle East, they are discussed in Chapter 37.)

EARLY MOVEMENTS FOR INDEPENDENCE

Early nationalists appeal to African pride. The independence movement in modern Africa had its roots in a growing respect for the African past. During the era of the slave trade (Chapter 13) and colonialism, Europeans had tended to undervalue African culture. In the late nineteenth century, black leaders began to encourage Africans to view their own heritage with pride. One of the first was James Johnson, a teacher in Sierra Leone, who called for a nationalist movement in Africa. While Johnson thought in terms of a single African state, his ideas were an early sign of the movement that would later transform Africa.

Other moves to restore a sense of black pride developed early in the twentieth century. In 1914 a young Jamaican named Marcus Garvey founded the Universal Negro Improvement Association (UNIA). Garvey called for the independence of blacks everywhere and, like those who had urged "repatriation" (page 588), tried to encourage American blacks to settle in Liberia. Garvey set up a number of black-owned businesses and published a weekly paper, *Negro World,* that was circulated in black communities in many countries. He proved to be a poor business manager, however, and his ideas were never carried out.

In the period after World War I the sense of black pride grew, particularly in the United States. The 1920's saw an outpouring of black literature, art, drama, music, and dance. This cultural reawakening, which was centered in Harlem, a predominantly black neighborhood in New York City, was known as the Harlem Renaissance. At the same time in Africa, black leaders were talking of "negritude," a French term used to describe a sense of pride in being black. This awareness became part of the movement for independence in Africa.

Early African leaders seek limited goals. The early leaders of the movement for self-rule in Africa were part of a European-educated, mainly urban, black upper class. Their chief concern was broadening opportunities for this group, who tended to be concentrated in urban centers like Lagos, Accra, or Freetown. For example, the African National Congress, a nationalist group founded in 1912, called for greater black representation in the colonial assemblies, a regional university, and an end to discrimination in the civil service. These goals had little meaning for the majority of black African people.

Black leaders begin to develop modern political parties. In the 1930's some African leaders developed a broader outlook. They wanted full independence and sought to develop a sense of nationalism among their people. Foremost among these new leaders was Nnamdi Azikiwe (ah-ZIK-uh-wee) of Nigeria. The son of an Ibo (EE-boh) clerk, Azikiwe — commonly known as "Zik" — was educated in America. When he returned to Africa in 1934, he edited a newspaper in the Gold Coast. In 1937 he moved to Nigeria and began to publish the *West African Pilot,* which helped spread ideas of self-determination throughout the colony. In this way he hoped to unite both urban and rural black Africans in an independence movement.

A leader of the movement for independence in Ghana, Kwame Nkrumah became that nation's prime minister in 1957 and then president in 1960. Six years later he was overthrown by military leaders.

World War II influences the movement for African independence. Although Azikiwe's methods were adopted by other black leaders, the independence movement in Africa made little progress until after World War II. The war not only weakened many of the nations that had colonies in Africa but also made black Africans more aware of what they were being denied. Those who served in the armed forces of the European nations had the opportunity to see black soldiers doing jobs that would have been reserved for whites in Africa. They also had the chance to exchange ideas with other Africans and with Asians who also sought self-rule. The principles of self-determination expressed in the Atlantic Charter (page 722) further inspired hopes for self-government in Africa.

Ghana gains its independence. Soon after the end of the war in 1945, Britain began to prepare its colonies in West Africa for independence. Most British officials assumed that preparation for self-rule, modeled after the processes followed in Canada and India, would take at least fifty years. Only twelve years later, however, the British colony of the Gold Coast gained independence, taking the name of Ghana.

Ghana was in a favorable position to make the transition to self-government relatively smoothly. The Gold Coast had a prospering economy and a well-developed educational system. Furthermore, there was little rivalry between the different peoples within the Gold Coast.

The leader of Ghana's independence movement was Kwame Nkrumah (en-KROO-muh). The son of a goldsmith, Nkrumah had been educated in the United States and learned political organization there. He also adopted Azikiwe's methods. Nkrumah founded the Convention People's Party, which won an election victory in 1951 that made him prime minister. Under Nkrumah, black representation in the government increased steadily. On March 6, 1957, the Gold Coast combined with other British territories to become the first colony south of the Sahara to gain its independence in the postwar period.

Over the next few years many other British colonies in Africa became independent through the same gradual process of gaining representation in the existing government — Nigeria and Cameroon in 1960, Sierra Leone and Tanganyika in 1961, Uganda in 1962, and Gambia in 1965.[1]

---

[1]Cameroon, once a German colony, was divided into British and French mandates, which later became UN trust territories. The French area gained independence in 1960 and was joined by the British zone the following year. Tanganyika united with Zanzibar in 1964 to form Tanzania.

France's colonies vote for self-rule. France also had a colonial empire in West Africa. The independence of these colonies came about largely through the efforts of Charles de Gaulle (page 740). Under de Gaulle, France and its colonies (known as Overseas Territories) became the French Community. The territories were given a choice: they could become members of the Community or they could choose complete independence and lose French economic aid. Only Guinea, under the leadership of Sekou Touré (too-RAY), chose independence in 1958. The following year, however, the constitution of the Community was amended to allow the French colonies to achieve self-government without losing aid. In 1960 all of the territories in French West Africa became independent nations.

France's other colonies in Africa south of the Sahara — French Equatorial Africa, Somaliland, and Madagascar (map, page 597) — were offered the same choice as the states in West Africa. Most voted for independence and were divided into self-governing states in 1960. Only French Somaliland chose to remain under French rule.[2]

Violence accompanies independence in the Congo. The Belgian Congo gained its independence in 1960, the same year as the French territories, but self-government was achieved in a very different atmosphere. Belgium's government had followed a paternalistic policy for

---

[2]At the time it was named the French Territory of the Afars and Issas. When it became independent in 1977, it took the name of its capital city — Djibouti.

Names from Africa's Past

A sense of pride and awareness of Africa's past influenced many newly independent nations as they chose names for their countries. Gold Coast, the first colony to gain independence, chose the name of the ancient Sudanic empire of Ghana, famous for its gold (page 277). According to legend, the people of ancient Ghana later migrated to the coastal region of present-day Ghana. The central African nation of Mali, which became independent from France in 1960, likewise took the name of an ancient kingdom. On the coast, Dahomey returned to the old name Benin.

Many of the new names in southern Africa reflected the widespread migrations of Bantu-speaking peoples. Southern Rhodesia took the name Zimbabwe, the great cultural center of a tenth-century Bantu civilization (page 281). Malawi (formerly known as Nyasaland) called itself after early Bantu migrants into the region. In this way, the move to independence changed the map of Africa to reflect Africa's own history and languages.

REPUBLIQUE DU MALI

250F

POSTES

Kpelié Sénoufo

many years (page 601). Although colonial officials had planned a gradual movement toward self-rule, blacks in the Congo had never held high government positions. Until 1952, blacks were not even allowed to attend universities in Belgium. White settlers in the Congo opposed independence, for they feared they would lose all their investments in agriculture and mining. Rivalries also existed among different groups of Africans in the colony.

In the late 1950's riots broke out among black Congolese protesting unemployment and the lack of political involvement. As violence spread, white settlers fled the Congo, taking with them their capital and technical skills and their experience in government and business administration.

The Belgian government decided to set a date for independence as soon as possible. In May, 1960, elections were held in an atmosphere of unrest. There had been no time to educate voters, and the different political parties disagreed over the form of government to be established. Representatives of copper-rich Katanga province sought a federal system of government. Other groups wanted government to be centralized.

Independence for the Congo[3] was proclaimed in June, but within two weeks the army had mutinied against its white officers. Katanga province, under the leadership of Moise Tshombe (SHOM-beh), seceded. Faced with civil war, Patrice Lumumba, prime minister of the new Congo government, asked the United Nations and then the Soviet Union for help. Alarmed at this move, President Joseph Kasavubu dismissed Lumumba, who was killed soon afterward under mysterious circumstances. UN troops intervened in Katanga, and several years of unrest followed. In 1965 the army, led by Joseph Mobutu, took control of the government. Under a new constitution, Mobutu acquired considerable power as president. The new nation eliminated Belgian names for cities and natural features and changed the name of the country to Zaire (zah-EER).

---

[3]The new nation was known at the time as Congo (Kinshasa) to distinguish it from Congo (Brazzaville), a former French colony.

TENSION OVER RACIAL POLICIES

The black nationalists' moves for self-rule were made more complex by the presence of a sizable white population in parts of Africa. This was true not only in the Congo but also in other colonies — especially the British-controlled lands of Kenya, the Rhodesias, and South Africa, and the Portuguese territories of Angola and Mozambique. Many of the white families had lived in Africa for generations. They thought of themselves as Rhodesians or Angolans, not as Europeans, and they had no desire to leave their homelands.

Africa's white population increases. After World War II, large numbers of Europeans migrated to Africa. In Northern and Southern Rhodesia the white population almost tripled between 1946 and 1960 — from 22,000 to 76,000 in Northern Rhodesia and from 82,000 to 223,000 in Southern Rhodesia. Angola and Mozambique experienced similar increases. Angola's white population grew from 44,000 to 250,000 and Mozambique's from 27,000 to 130,000. Investments by these white settlers were bringing in growing profits. In Southern Rhodesia, for example, the 1956 value of the products from white-owned farms was ten times the prewar value. Copper from white-owned mines in Northern Rhodesia brought in twelve times more in the 1950's than it had in 1940.

Most white settlers, who were a minority in these colonies, opposed rule by the black Africans. They feared the loss of their lands and investments if the black majority gained political power.

Kenyatta leads Kenya to independence. In Kenya, white settlers not only ran the government but in 1938 were granted permanent and exclusive use of the fertile highlands region. Movements for self-rule developed among the blacks in the colony, particularly among the Kikuyu (kee-KOO-yoo), a Bantu-speaking people who were the largest population group. In 1947 Jomo Kenyatta, a Kikuyu, was elected leader of the black independence movement, the Kenya African Union. Like most other black leaders in Africa, Kenyatta had been educated abroad. The author of *Facing Mount*

JOMO KENYATTA

Jomo Kenyatta served as the president of Kenya during its early years as an independent republic. In the capital city of Nairobi stands the modern Kenyatta Conference Center, named for this revered leader.

Kenya, an anthropological study of the Kikuyu, he gained great popularity among the black Kenyans.

When the colonial government failed to increase black representation in the assembly, the Mau Mau, a secret organization, began attacks on white-owned plantations in 1952. The Mau Mau also used force to make blacks declare their loyalty to the nationalist cause. Convinced that Kenyatta was the head of the organization, the British government imprisoned him from 1953 to 1961. Mau Mau attacks resulted in the deaths of thousands of people — many more blacks than whites — before the government regained control in 1960.

Despite the upheaval, Kenya moved steadily toward self-government. In 1963 it became independent, and Kenyatta was elected prime minister. The following year he became the president of Kenya and remained its head of state until his death in 1978.

Northern Rhodesia and Nyasaland gain self-rule. White settlers in southern Africa, particularly Southern Rhodesia, were as opposed to self-government as the whites in Kenya. Nevertheless, the British government began to prepare its colonies in southern Africa for independence. As a first step, in 1953 Britain combined Northern and Southern Rhodesia and Nyasaland in the Central African Federation, which Southern Rhodesia dominated.

Black leaders in Nyasaland and Northern Rhodesia therefore began to work for independence from the federation as well as for self-government. In Nyasaland the independence movement was led by Hastings Banda. The independence leader in Northern Rhodesia was Kenneth Kaunda (KOWN-duh), a former schoolteacher and one of the few black leaders who had not been educated abroad. To gain support, Kaunda rode from village to village on his bicycle and made up his own political songs. As his popularity grew, demands for self-government spread. In 1964 Northern Rhodesia became independent Zambia, and Nyasaland was renamed Malawi, from the name of an ancient Bantu people who had settled in the region.

White settlers in Southern Rhodesia resist majority rule. While Nyasaland and Northern Rhodesia made steady progress toward independence, the blacks in Southern Rhodesia faced a bitter struggle with the white settlers, who were less than 5 percent of the population. Besides fearing economic loss, most white Rhodesians apparently doubted that the blacks were capable of governing themselves.

Discontent grew among the black Rhodesians as the government placed restrictions on their rights. When communal lands were taken and turned into private farms, unrest broke out among the black population. To end the violence, the government of Southern Rhodesia in 1959 made it legal to arrest and hold a person for trial for an unlimited period.

The British government opposed the colonial government's actions and continued to press for majority rule in the colony. Some dissatisfied white settlers therefore formed a political party, the Rhodesian Front. This party, led by Ian Smith, won the 1962 elections in Southern Rhodesia. Rhodesian Front leaders agreed to set up a government in which black and white Rhodesians had equal representation, but they rejected the idea of majority rule.

Rhodesia declares its independence. Britain refused to consider Rhodesian demands for independence without guarantees of fair representation for blacks. Defying this ruling, in 1965 Prime Minister Ian Smith proclaimed the country independent. Among world nations, only South Africa recognized this independence. The United Nations called for a boycott of oil shipments to Rhodesia but could not enforce its ruling.

Black leaders in Rhodesia continued the struggle for majority rule. By the 1970's the black population in Rhodesia numbered over 6,600,000. The white minority — 260,000 people — still controlled the government. Convinced that the government had to be overthrown by force, some black leaders began guerrilla warfare against the white government. As unrest spread, many white settlers left the country.

Smith's government in Southern Rhodesia received aid from South Africa and Mozambique. Although the black nationalists were aided by other African nations, the Rhodesian government was too powerful to overthrow. The situation in Rhodesia was suddenly altered, though, by changes in nearby Portuguese territories.

Unrest develops in Portuguese colonies. Angola and Mozambique, the first European colonies in Africa, were governed as overseas territories of Portugal. The Portuguese government officially followed a policy of assimilation (page 599), but only 35,000 of the ten million blacks in the territories had been granted the status of citizen by 1960.

Widespread violence erupted in 1961 when the Angolan government forced blacks to grow cotton for export instead of food for their own needs. When rioting broke out, government planes fired on African villages, and rioters attacked Portuguese plantations, killing some 750 Portuguese settlers. Government troops, however, crushed the revolt, killing about 20,000 blacks.

The black leaders of Angola escaped to neighboring Zaire and Zambia and made attacks on Angola from there. Guerrilla forces with bases in Zambia and Tanzania attacked white settlers' lands in Mozambique. By the late 1960's Portugal was involved in wars in both Angola and Mozambique.

Events in Portugal bring colonial independence. The sudden overthrow of the Portuguese dictator in 1974 quickly decided the issue of independence for Portugal's colonies in Africa and elsewhere. All the colonies except Macao, off the eastern coast of China, were granted independence by the new government.

Self-rule failed to bring peace in Angola, however, as rival groups struggled for power. Finally the Soviet-backed group, aided by troops from Cuba, defeated the forces supported by the West. In 1976 a Marxist government, backed by the Cuban forces, was established in Angola. Anti-Communist guerrillas, calling themselves the Union for the Total Independence of Angola (UNITA), fought throughout the 1980's to free the nation from Soviet domination and one-party rule. During the same period, Angola was the scene of clashes between South African troops and guerrilla fighters in areas bordering on Namibia (nuh-MIB-ee-ah, see page 789).

Like Angola, independent Mozambique became a one-party Marxist state. Most Portuguese settlers left the country, leaving Mozambique with acute shortages of capital and tech-

South Africa's policy of *apartheid* was reflected in signs at the Johannesburg airport, which pointed out the services limited to "nonwhites" only.

nical experts. Beginning in the late 1970's, the government faced an anti-Communist guerrilla movement backed by Rhodesia (until 1980) and South Africa. The guerrillas were successful in using sabotage to disrupt Mozambique's already shaky economy. By the mid-1980's there were signs that the government was trying to form closer ties with the West and was somewhat relaxing state control of economic activity in order to increase productivity.

Majority rule is established in Rhodesia. The Portuguese withdrawal from Angola and Mozambique had an immediate impact on Rhodesia. Both South Africa and Portugal, through its colonies, had supported Ian Smith's government. After independence, however, Mozambique became a refuge for those who opposed the Rhodesian government. Surrounded by hostile countries, Smith's government finally agreed to majority rule.

When elections were held in Rhodesia in 1979, all the adults in the country were, for the first time, allowed to vote. In the following year Rhodesia became independent. As a tie to the past, it took the name Zimbabwe (page 281). With the independence of Zimbabwe, nearly all of Africa had gained self-government.

Problems arose in Zimbabwe between the two black groups that had fought for majority rule. The new nation was a parliamentary democracy, but its prime minister, Robert Mugabe (moo-GAH-bay), soon announced his intention of creating a one-party Socialist state. Joshua Nkomo (en-KOH-moh), leader of an opposition group called Zimbabwe African People's Union (ZAPU), struggled to maintain his organization's power, but during the mid-1980's ZAPU faced increasing hostility and harassment from the ruling party. Some ZAPU supporters resorted to guerrilla warfare against Mugabe's government.

South Africa adopts a segregation policy. South Africa became an independent dominion in 1910 (page 596), and it remained a nation completely dominated by people of European descent. The country's population was 17 percent white, the highest in Africa. The majority of whites were speakers of Afrikaans, a language derived from the Dutch spoken by the original Boer settlers (page 590). South Africa's economy was the most developed in Africa, leading the world in gold and diamond production. The economy, like the political and social life of the country, had always been controlled by whites.

The majority of South Africans — 71 percent — were blacks. In South African terms, the rest were classified by law as "Coloureds" (people of mixed ancestry) and Asians. These groups were segregated from the white population by an official policy that was put into practice after World War II.

In the 1948 elections the National Party, dominated by the Afrikaans-speaking population, gained control of the government. The new government immediately instituted a policy called *apartheid* (uh-PART-hite), an Afrikaans word meaning "apartness." Although this policy was later renamed "separate development" and "plural democracy," what it meant was that blacks. Coloureds, and Asians would be segregated from the white population.

Many South African laws restricted the rights of nonwhites and spelled out policies for segregation. Neither blacks nor Coloureds were allowed to vote in South Africa. Marriage between whites and nonwhites was illegal, and separate areas were set aside for the different populations. Nonwhites were not allowed to live in white areas or even to enter them except as employees. The government kept track of the movement of blacks by requiring them to carry passes that had to be presented at numerous checkpoints. Nonwhites were allowed to live only on the fringes of the towns or were sent to reserves, regions set aside by the government as so-called "homelands." The government also discouraged nonwhites from gaining an education.

Bantustans are established. About 13 percent of the land in South Africa had been set aside for the black "homelands." or Bantustans. Eventually the idea developed of making the Bantustans into semi-independent states within the South African federation. Because most of the land in these areas was arid and suitable for only limited farming, many of the Bantustans became little more than rural slums. To survive economically, the blacks who lived there traveled into South Africa to work. The South African government declared some of the reserves to be independent, but no other nation in the world recognized this status.

South Africa extends its policies to Namibia. South Africa also defied world opinion when it extended its policy of segregation into neighboring Namibia (page 787). The former German colony of South-West Africa, Namibia had been made a mandate of South Africa after World War I. Arid and thinly populated, with a forbidding coastal desert region, Namibia was important for its minerals, grazing lands, and fishing. The intention of the League of Nations was that South Africa would prepare the mandate for eventual independence. Instead of granting the colony independence, however, South Africa extended its policies of *apartheid* to Namibia after World War II. In 1966 the United Nations voted to end South African control of Namibia and ordered South African officials to leave that territory.

The South African government ignored the United Nations, however. Black nationalist activity grew steadily in Namibia, and a guerrilla movement was begun by the South-West Africa People's Organization (SWAPO), a Marxist-led group. SWAPO fighters attacked targets in Namibia from bases in Angola, across Namibia's northern border.

International efforts to negotiate independence for Namibia brought no final settlement. The major barrier to agreement was South Africa's insistence, backed by the United States, that a Namibian settlement be linked to the withdrawal of Cuban troops from Angola.

Both blacks and whites oppose government policies. Most English-speaking South Africans and many Afrikaners opposed some aspects of the segregation policies, although they supported the idea of white leadership. Some white South Africans developed political parties that worked toward allowing nonwhites representation in the government. The clergy, intellectuals, writers, artists, and students also protested the policy of *apartheid*. In 1955 a group of 3,000 South Africans spoke out for majority rule, declaring: "South Africa belongs to all who live in it, black and white.... No

---

TIMETABLE

Changing Africa

1912	The African National Congress is founded.
1914	Marcus Garvey founds the Universal Negro Improvement Association.
1937	Azikiwe begins publishing the pro-independence *West African Pilot.*
1947	Jomo Kenyatta becomes leader of the Kenya independence movement.
1957	The British colony of Gold Coast becomes the independent nation of Ghana.
1960	The French colonies in West Africa gain their independence. The Belgian Congo becomes independent.
1963	The Organization of African Unity is founded.
1964	Jomo Kenyatta becomes president of Kenya.
1965	Ian Smith proclaims Rhodesia's independence.
1970	The UN declares South Africa's occupation of Namibia to be illegal.
1976	A Marxist government is established in Angola. Riots break out in Soweto, South Africa.
1980	Rhodesia becomes the independent nation of Zimbabwe.
1984	South Africa adopts new constitution.
1986	South Africa declares state of emergency.

government can justly claim authority unless it is based on the will of all the people."

Government repression of protests eventually led to violence. In 1960 a protest march against pass laws was held in Sharpeville, a town near Johannesburg. Police fired on the protesters, killing 69 blacks. In response, some blacks formed an organization called "The Spear of the Nation" and began to carry out acts of sabotage. The government in turn outlawed black nationalist groups, including the Pan-African Congress, a militant group founded in 1958, and the older African National Congress (page 782). Protests became more violent. In 1976, rioting in Soweto (an area of Johannesburg) led the government to imprison critics and to increase repression and intimidation. Government crackdowns, however, failed to halt the protests. During the late 1970's and early 1980's, criticism of the National Party's policies became both more widespread and more vocal.

South Africa adopts a new constitution. In response to calls for reform, the National Party proposed a new constitution during the early 1980's. It called for the establishment of a parliament that would have separate chambers for whites, Coloureds, and Asians (but with no representation for blacks). The members of each chamber or house would be elected by the racial group they were to represent and would decide on policies for that group. Matters of national concern would be decided by all three houses. The method of electing the president ensured that the white chamber would control the outcome of the election. The new constitution was approved by more than 65 percent of South Africa's white voters and went into effect in 1984.

Within the Coloured and Asian populations, the new constitution produced deep divisions. Some members of these groups supported the new constitution as a step in the direction of peaceful reform in South Africa. They emphasized the significance of the constitution's recognition of the political rights of nonwhites and argued that gradual change was best for all South Africans. Others opposed the new constitution and urged a boycott of the upcoming elections. They criticized the constitution because it gave the black majority no representation and because it guaranteed that whites would remain in control of the nation's affairs. Some Coloureds and Asians accused the government of using the reform proposal to divide them politically from black South Afri-

Desmond Tutu, Anglican Archbishop of southern Africa, received the Nobel Peace Prize in 1984 for his work in the campaign to end *apartheid* in South Africa.

cans. Elections for the new members of parliament were boycotted by 70 to 80 percent of the Coloured and Asian populations.

Some reforms are undertaken. In addition to the new constitution, the South African government passed a number of reforms during the 1980's. Interracial marriage was legalized, the hated pass laws were abolished, citizenship was granted to urban blacks, and the government even committed itself to an eventual elimination of the entire system of *apartheid*. These reforms, however, fell far short of black demands for full political rights.

One reason for the slow pace of reform was fear that major changes, if made abruptly, would result in social and economic upheaval in South Africa. In addition, the National Party faced challenges from right-wing parties that opposed even gradual reform. Supporters of the President of South Africa — P. W. Botha (BOH-tuh) — argued that he had to move cautiously to avoid a white blacklash that might bring those parties to power.

Critics of the government, on the other hand, charged that it was not seriously committed to reform. They pointed out that South Africa remained a segregated society, with separate schools and residential areas set aside by law for different racial groups. Many critics called for immediate change, warning the government and the world that South Africa was headed for full-scale civil war unless black demands for representation were quickly met.

Violence erupts. In the fall of 1984, soon after the first elections under the new constitution were held, violence broke out in South Africa's black townships. Some of the violence was directed by black militants against other blacks whom they regarded as "collaborators" with the white government. There were also attacks on government installations and many instances of street fighting between blacks and government security forces. In addition, there were nonviolent protests by black groups, including rent strikes, work stoppages, and mass boycotts of classes in the public schools.

In response to the rising tide of unrest in the black townships, the South African government declared a state of emergency in 1986 and undertook harsh repressive measures. The police were given broad powers to deal with people arrested for political violence. These included the power to detain suspects without trial, to search houses and other buildings without warrants at any time, to ban meetings, and to set curfews. Increasingly during this period, police were backed up by military units whose training had not prepared them to deal with civilians. Their rough methods and disregard for citizens' rights drew widespread criticism. In addition to these measures, Botha's government began a strict program of political censorship against the foreign press, whose coverage of South African affairs the government regarded as biased and inflammatory.

South Africa is criticized abroad. South Africa's racial policies had long been condemned by most other nations. After much criticism from other states in the British Commonwealth, South Africa withdrew in 1961 and declared itself an independent republic. Its athletes were banned from participation in many sporting events, including the Olympic Games.

During the 1980's, South Africa's isolation steadily increased. Many Western countries imposed sanctions on investment and trade with South Africa and even withdrew their ambassadors to express their disapproval of the government's policies. The United Nations passed strongly worded condemnations of *apartheid*. Anti-*apartheid* demonstrations were held in many cities of the Western world, where feeling against South Africa was intense. Some private institutions, such as churches, universities, and unions, sold the stock they had held in companies that did business in South Africa.

The South African economy suffers. Economic sanctions and the withdrawal of investments from South Africa contributed to the nation's economic problems. Foreign banks, moreover, began to question South Africa's long-term political stability. Fearing that the South African government might one day be overthrown and its debts repudiated, bankers began to reduce the number and size of loans they made to South Africa. Coming at a time when the government was spending unusually large sums on internal security, these factors combined to plague South Africa's economy with inflation, unemployment, and declining productivity. As nationwide unrest continued, the country's future seemed very uncertain.

1. (a) What were the goals of early black leaders in Africa? (b) How did World War II affect the movement for independence in Africa?
2. (a) By what process did the British colonies in West Africa gain independence? (b) Which was the first to become self-governing after World War II? (c) What led to independence for France's colonies?
3. How did Belgian policies make independence difficult in the Congo (Zaire)?
4. How did the presence of white settlers affect independence movements (a) in the Congo?

(b) in Southern Rhodesia? (c) in Kenya? (d) in Angola?
5. (a) What does *apartheid* mean? (b) How did this policy affect the rights of nonwhites in South Africa?
6. (a) How did Namibia come under the control of South Africa? (b) What was the United Nations' attitude toward South African attempts to keep control of Namibia?
7. (a) What changes were made by South Africa's new constitution? (b) Why was there much criticism of the new constitution? (c) How did other nations show their opposition to South Africa's racial policies?

2 New African Nations Face Challenges

The leaders of the newly independent African nations were faced with a number of challenges. In many countries, especially those where independence had come suddenly, there had been little preparation for self-government. Rivalries existed between different African peoples, and many Africans' loyalties were to their local rulers, not to a national government. The need to develop strong economies created other problems. While conflict broke out between some states, most of the new nations looked for ways to work together to solve their common problems.

Cultural differences cause unrest. One source of disunity in the new nations was rivalry among the different African peoples. Few Africans at the time of independence had a sense of national unity. In most cases, the colonial boundaries became the boundaries of the new nations, frequently bringing together population groups that were bitter rivals. Before strong nations could be built, the African governments had to overcome these rivalries as well as differences in language and traditions.

The peoples of Kenya, for example, included Bantu-speaking Kikuyu and Luo, Masai who spoke languages from the Nile region, and several smaller groups. These people had different ways of living as well as different languages. The Kikuyu were farmers, whereas the Masai were herders. Their differences spilled over into politics. Fear that the Kikuyu would dominate the country created unrest when Kenya became independent. Kenyatta (page 785) lessened the potential conflict by including all the groups in Kenya's government.

Perhaps the bitterest clash between different African peoples took place in Nigeria, where the Ibo and Yoruba people had always been rivals. In January, 1966, aiming to end widespread corruption, a group of Ibo army officers murdered leading politicians and military officers, many of whom were Yoruba. Yoruba soldiers next attacked the Ibo people in the north. Some 10,000 Ibo were massacred in September, and the remainder fled to eastern Nigeria. In May, 1967, the Ibo proclaimed the independent Republic of Biafra. Civil war between Biafra and the Nigerian government lasted until the Ibo were defeated in 1970. Besides those killed in the fighting, nearly a million civilians died of famine.

African nations look for political stability. Conflicts among African peoples added to the problems of political instability that many new nations faced. Most black Africans had never taken part in politics, and few had been able to gain experience in upper-level government positions before independence. Although the nationalist leaders were effective political organizers, many turned out to be poor administrators. Once in office, some used dictatorial methods, imprisoning or exiling opponents and forbidding opposition political parties. There was also corruption in many new governments. Some newly appointed government officials took advantage of their positions to amass personal fortunes instead of working for the development of their country.

Many of the new African leaders found, however, that the political machinery they had used to gain independence was effective for developing a government organization. Among the leaders who used their experience to create strong governments were Jomo Kenyatta of Kenya, Félix Houphouët-Boigny (oof-WAY-BWAHN-yuh) of Ivory Coast, and Julius Nyerere of Tanzania.

The African nations urge technological development. As a first step in uniting their countries some African governments looked for ways to improve transportation systems. Many of the roads and railroads constructed during colonial rule were built to connect ports and plantations. Transportation between different parts of a country remained difficult. In Mozambique, for example, roads and railroads ran east to west, from inland plantations to coastal ports. Most of the people, on the other hand, lived along the coast. A north-south road uniting the people of the country was an important goal of the government. New transportation links between countries were also important for trade and communication.

Many African nations also tried to develop industry based on their resources. Mining operations in Zaire and Zambia were expanded, while Nigeria developed a prosperous oil industry. Other countries emphasized industries that processed the food raised on plantations in the countryside.

To provide energy for their industrial needs, many nations had to import expensive oil. Some, however, were able to make use of coal deposits or to build dams to supply hydroelectric power. The Kariba dam in Zimbabwe, one of the earliest, supplied enough power for the country as well as an excess that could be sold to South Africa. The Cabora Bassa reservoir in Mozambique and the Akosombo dam in Ghana provide water for irrigation as well as electric power.

Emphasis on industry hurts agriculture. The drive to industrialize, however, often caused neglect of agriculture in Africa. Moreover, to pay back the funds borrowed for industrial development most African nations had to depend on income from their agricultural products. This put an emphasis on export crops — peanuts in Senegal, cacao in Ghana — at the expense of food crops for domestic use. At the same time, more people were moving from

COPPER MINING IN ZAIRE
Copper, Zaire's major export, is mined in open-pit areas, as shown above. After smelting, the metal is stored and transported in the form of ingots (left).

EDUCATION IN AFRICA

The newly independent African nations needed educated people to work in government, schools, hospitals, and industries. Leaders emphasized modern education at all levels, from elementary to college, and also in the professions and in technical fields. Shown here are medical graduates (above) and a student at a technical college (left) in Kenya.

rural areas to the cities, and the declining farm population was unable to produce enough food for the nations' needs.

To improve agricultural production, African nations began to train farmers in modern farming methods, introducing the use of machinery and improved seed and livestock. Irrigation of dry areas and the use of fertilizer also increased production. Yet most African nations still faced the dilemma of needing both more food and more capital for investment.

Famine devastates parts of Africa. During the 1980's, the worst drought in a hundred years struck Africa. In the sub-Saharan part of the continent, tens of millions of people faced starvation. Unable to sustain life on their lands, many people who still followed traditional ways left their homes and wandered in search

of food. Western nations donated huge shipments of food and medical supplies. The Red Cross and other relief organizations set up emergency camps where the donated goods were distributed to people who were able to reach those locations.

Despite these efforts, poor distribution systems and political upheavals kept food from reaching large numbers of people. The situation was probably worst in Ethiopia, where civil war raged in certain regions. Ethiopia's Communist-dominated government often diverted food relief supplies away from rebel areas. Still another complication was this government's plan to relocate huge numbers of rural people from drought areas to more fertile lands. Food assistance was sometimes denied to people who resisted the relocation program.

Many African nations seek a greater variety in export products. Under colonial rule, emphasis usually was placed on one profitable product for export, and some African nations continued this pattern. Such one-crop economies, however, are vulnerable to changes in price on the world market. To avoid this problem, many African nations sought to develop a greater variety of products, with the help of foreign capital and technical advice.

Houphouët-Boigny of Ivory Coast, for example, maintained close ties with France after independence. He welcomed foreign investment and the advice of French technicians and administrators. With their aid, Ivory Coast developed one of the most varied economies in Africa. In addition to producing the third largest amount of coffee and cacao in the world, the country exported lumber, food products, and diamonds. It also developed deposits of iron ore and oil, becoming one of the most prosperous nations in Africa.

African leaders promote education. To provide the teachers, trained administrators, business managers, scientists, and technicians their countries needed for development, many African leaders made education a major goal. As most African languages are unwritten, the literacy rate at the time of independence was very low in many countries. In some, fewer than 10 percent of the people could read and write.

An all-out drive to expand educational opportunities was quickly put into effect in the new African nations. Elementary and secondary schools and colleges were established. Although it was often difficult to find enough trained teachers in the years immediately after independence, school enrollment steadily increased. In Zaire, for example, the number of secondary students rose from 30,000 to 270,000 between 1958 and 1970.

The African governments also set up programs of on-the-job training. These programs developed skills in a variety of fields ranging from public health to industrial management and helped to provide the workers needed by the developing economies.

Africa gains importance in international politics. The new African countries acquired political influence as part of the Third World (page 733). Furthermore. Africa's geography and resources — the factors that had attracted imperialist powers in the nineteenth century — continued to be important. For example, the "horn" of Africa — Ethiopia, Djibouti, and Somalia — commands the sea route connecting the Indian Ocean, the Red Sea, and (by way of the Suez Canal) the Mediterranean Sea (map, page 597).

The strategic importance of East Africa became evident in 1974 when Emperor Haile Selassie of Ethiopia was overthrown by the pro-Marxist army. The army next used Soviet arms and soldiers from Cuba and East Germany to take over land in Somalia. In 1977 Somalia used the Soviet arms it had acquired to invade Ethiopia. When the Soviet Union sided with Ethiopia, Somalia turned to the United States for aid. Foreign interests thus interfered with the development of both Ethiopia and Somalia. Similar rivalry for influence brought conflicts in a number of African states.

African nations seek cooperation. Despite such conflicts, many countries in Africa developed cooperative projects. Most of the independent nations belonged to the Organization of African Unity (OAU), founded in 1963 at Addis Ababa, Ethiopia. Members of the OAU pledged to respect each other's territory and to settle boundary disputes by negotiation. They set up commissions to deal with social, economic, educational, and health problems that concerned all of Africa. Echoing the sentiments of early independence leaders, they reaffirmed their pride in their African heritage.

CHECK-UP

1. What factors worked against a sense of national unity in many new nations of Africa?
2. (a) What were the main economic goals of the new nations? (b) What patterns from colonial times hindered economic development? (c) What problems did industrial development cause? (d) What changes were made in agriculture?
3. (a) Why did foreign nations continue to seek influence in Africa? (b) How did their policies affect African nations?

Chapter 36 Review

Summary

Except for Egypt, Ethiopia, Liberia, and South Africa, most of Africa was ruled by foreign powers in 1945. After World War II, independence movements swept through Africa. Inspired by a new awareness of their heritage and by ideals of self-government learned in their studies abroad, black leaders in Africa began to develop political parties that put pressure on the European powers to grant their colonies independence. In 1957 Ghana was the first such colony to gain self-rule. In the next decade other British and French colonies also became independent.

In colonies with large numbers of white settlers there was often resistance to majority rule. Before these colonies gained their independence, most endured periods of violence.

By 1975, however, nearly all of Africa was independent, and the African leaders turned their attention to building strong nations. Besides the problem of developing national unity, they had to find ways to encourage political stability, promote economic development, and educate their people.

South Africa remained a problem to the rest of Africa. Other nations, in Africa and elsewhere, denounced its official policy of *apartheid* — the segregation of whites and nonwhites. They urged majority rule both in South Africa and Namibia, a country that South Africa had ruled since World War I.

Vocabulary Review

1. Write the sentences below on a sheet of paper. Fill in the blank in each sentence with one of these terms: *federal system, mandate, nationalism, plantation.*
   (a) South Africa's __?__ over Namibia was intended to prepare the country for independence.
   (b) The movement toward __?__ and independence in Africa gained strength after World War II.
   (c) Crops such as cacao are grown on a __?__ occupying large areas of land.
   (d) Some people in the Congo wanted a __?__ of government rather than a strong central government.

2. Distinguish between the terms in each of the following pairs:
   (a) *Negro World; West African Pilot.*
   (b) Harlem Renaissance; negritude.
   (c) Kikuyu; Mau Mau.
   (d) Southern Rhodesia; Northern Rhodesia.
   (e) African National Congress; Organization of African Unity.
   (f) Bantustan; *apartheid.*
   (g) Biafra; Nigeria.

People to Identify

Match the following people with the numbered phrases that describe them: *Nnamdi Azikiwe, Marcus Garvey, Félix Houphouët-Boigny, Kenneth Kaunda, Jomo Kenyatta, Patrice Lumumba, Kwame Nkrumah, Moise Tshombe, Ian Smith.*

1. Leader of Katanga province in the Congo.
2. Independence leader among the Kikuyu.
3. Prime minister who declared the independence of Southern Rhodesia.
4. First prime minister of independent Congo.
5. Independence leader in Northern Rhodesia.
6. Early twentieth-century leader who encouraged American blacks to move to Africa.
7. Nigerian leader whose newspaper spread ideas of independence in Africa.
8. Ivory Coast leader who drew on French aid to modernize his nation's economy.
9. Leader of first British colony to gain independence after World War II.

Relating Geography and History

1. **Comparing maps.** Compare the map of colonial Africa on page 597 with the one in the Atlas at the back of the book. List the names of the countries of modern Africa along with the names each one had as a colony. Then make a second list grouping together the countries according to colonial ruler: Britain, France, Germany, Belgium, or Portugal.

2. **Research.** Use an encyclopedia or atlas to get information about Africa's mineral resources. (a) On an outline map, draw in symbols to show where major deposits of resources, such as copper or oil, are located. Include a key explaining your use of symbols. (b) Which of these resources once attracted European impe-

rialists? (c) What African countries have developed industries based on these resources?

Discussion Questions

1. (a) Describe some of the early twentieth-century moves toward restoring black pride and building a sense of nationalism. (b) How did growing up under colonial rule affect the early African nationalist leaders' goals? (c) Why did these goals have only limited appeal?

2. (a) Why was Ghana able to make a smooth transition to independence? (b) Compare the ways in which the former British and French colonies gained their independence. (c) Why was the Congo's transition to nationhood difficult?

3. (a) Why did the presence of white settlers complicate the drive for independence in southern Africa? (b) Why did Nyasaland (Malawi) and Northern Rhodesia (Zambia) make the transition to independence more easily than Southern Rhodesia? (c) What factors led to Rhodesia's gaining independence as Zimbabwe?

4. How did South African laws restrict the freedoms (a) of nonwhites? (b) of all South Africans? (c) What were the objections to the establishment of Bantustans? (d) Why did the UN declare South African control of Namibia illegal?

5. What problems did most African nations face in the areas of (a) transportation? (b) industrial development? (c) agricultural development? (d) education? (e) How did these reflect the practices of colonial rule?

Reading Primary Sources

Julius K. Nyerere was a former schoolteacher who led the movement for *uhuru* (the Swahili word for "freedom") in Tanzania and became the country's president. Nyerere's plan for Tanzania's development focused on traditional culture, agricultural improvement, and the development of self-reliance. In a speech in 1968, he described an important part of his plan — the creation of *ujamaa* villages, cooperative rural settlements based on socialist principles. Read the excerpts from the speech. Then answer the questions that follow.

> *Ujamaa* villages are intended to be ... created by the people and governed by those who live and work in them. ... No one can be forced into an *ujamaa* village. No official of the government or party can go to an *ujamaa* village and tell the members what they must grow, what they should do together, and what they should continue to do as individual farmers. ... [The people] and no one else, will decide how much of their land they will cultivate together from the beginning and how much they will cultivate individually. They, and no one else will decide how to use the money they earn jointly — whether to buy an ox-plow, install water, or do something else.
>
> ... To get *ujamaa* villages established, and to help them to succeed, education and leadership are required. ... It is [the political leaders'] job to explain what an *ujamaa* village is, and to keep explaining it until the people understand. But the decision to start must be made by the people themselves — and it must be made by each individual.
>
> In fact, once an *ujamaa* village is created, it is a democracy at work. For it provides an example of free discussion among equals, leading to their own decision-making. ...

(a) How were *ujamaa* villages intended to be formed and governed? (b) According to this speech, what part would the government play in the villages? (c) What decisions would the villagers make? (d) In what way, according to Nyerere, would such villages be examples of democracy?

Skill Activities

1. Word research. Leopold Sédar Senghor, a poet and statesman from Senegal, referred to African cultural pride as *negritude*. The suffix *-tude* comes from the Latin *-tudo*, "a condition or state of being." What do the following words mean? (a) exactitude; (b) fortitude; (c) gratitude; (d) magnitude; (e) solitude.

2. Bulletin boards. Each new nation of Africa chose a flag design when it gained independence. Choose one country and use an encyclopedia or a reference book on flags to find out what the colors and symbols on its flag represent. Make a drawing of the flag and write a short paragraph telling what it stands for.

3. Biographies. Leaders from Africa gained prominence in world affairs as their nations gained independence. Write a short biography describing the background and accomplishments of one of the following: (a) Leopold Sédar Senghor; (b) Albert John Luthuli; (c) Haile Selassie; (d) Tom Mboya; (e) Angie Brooks; (f) Robert Mugabe.

The island nation of Bahrain, in the Persian Gulf, has grown wealthy from both its oil resources and its strategic location as a center for trade and shipping. The new riches helped Bahrain build modern towns and industries.

37

The Changing Middle East

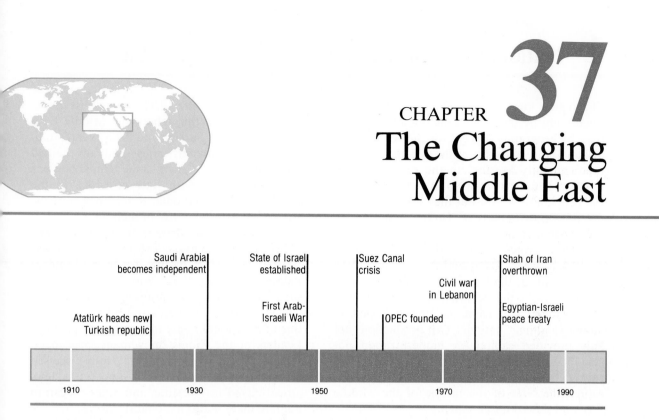

	Saudi Arabia becomes independent	State of Israel established	Suez Canal crisis	Shah of Iran overthrown
			Civil war in Lebanon	
Atatürk heads new Turkish republic		First Arab-Israeli War	OPEC founded	Egyptian-Israeli peace treaty

1910   1930   1950   1970   1990

World War I brought the collapse of the Ottoman Empire and freed the Middle East from Turkish rule. Much of the region, however, was under European control in the years after the war. As nationalist movements developed, the countries of the Middle East began to win their independence and struggled to build strong, modern economies.

Profits from rich oil deposits greatly aided some Middle Eastern nations on their road to modernization. Oil also gave political power to the Middle East and, in addition, led to competition between the superpowers for influence in the region.

Jewish immigration and the creation of the state of Israel in 1948 produced tensions in the Middle East. Arabs felt that their lands were being taken from them, and the destruction of Israel became a goal of Arab nationalism. The bitter Arab-Israeli conflict dragged on and drained the economies of all nations involved.

This chapter describes the important events and developments in the Middle East since the end of World War I, as well as the conflicts that have led to continuing unrest in these nations.

CHAPTER OUTLINE
1 Nationalists Come to Power in the Middle East
2 Conflicts Disrupt the Middle East

1 Nationalists Come to Power in the Middle East

The region known as the Middle East is defined more by language, religion, and customs than by geography. Except for the Jewish state of Israel, the countries of the Middle East are predominantly Muslim. In the nations of the Arabian Peninsula and North Africa, most of the people are Arabs, but they are linked with the non-Arab nations of Turkey and Iran by their Islamic faith.

Three issues — nationalism, oil, and the conflict between Arabs and Jews — provide a background for the history of the Middle Eastern nations in the twentieth century. Nationalist leaders who came to power hoped to modernize their nations. Oil production not only provided capital for modernization but also focused world attention on the region. The conflict between Arabs and Jews, however, disrupted the lives of the people of the Middle East and slowed development.

THE RISE OF NATIONALISM

Much of the Middle East was once part of the vast Ottoman Empire, which, at its height, stretched from the Danube River to the Persian Gulf (map, page 221). Ottoman power began to crumble in the nineteenth century. After the empire's defeat in World War I, it lost all of its Middle Eastern lands except Turkey. Nationalism became a powerful force in the former Ottoman lands.

Nationalist movements gain strength. Nationalism had gained strength among the Arab peoples of the Middle East during World War I. Arabs had fought on the Allied side against the Ottomans, hoping that victory would bring them independence. At the war's end, however, the League of Nations divided most of the Arab lands into mandates ruled by Britain or France (page 647). Britain controlled Iraq and Palestine (including Trans-Jordan), while France ruled Syria and Lebanon. Egypt and the Arabian kingdoms remained under British influence, as they had been since the late 1800's. Arab nationalists felt betrayed; they demanded independence from foreign control.

Beginning in the 1920's, nationalist movements succeeded throughout the Middle East. The nations of Turkey and Iran were established, and Arab territories gradually gained their independence. In 1948 the United Nations established the Jewish state of Israel. In the 1950's Egyptian nationalists set up a republic and ended British control in their nation.

Arabs oppose Jewish immigration. The growth of Arab nationalism in the 1920's was spurred by events in the British mandate of Palestine. During World War I, Britain had issued the Balfour Declaration, stating that it "viewed with favor the establishment in Palestine of a national home for the Jewish people." Leaders of the Zionist movement (page 633), such as Chaim Weizmann (VYTZ-mun), pressed for action to set up a Jewish state. Some Jews already lived in Palestine, and others began to migrate there. Arab nationalists, however, were enraged at the thought of a Jewish homeland in what they considered to be Arab territories. Opposition to Zionism thus became another issue in the growth of Arab nationalism.

Oil brings political power. Foreign control of oil industries also became an important issue to the new leaders of some Middle Eastern nations. Throughout most of the twentieth century, the Middle East has been a major producer of oil, a fuel essential to industrialized societies. By 1945, oil was the region's most important export. For many years, however, the profits from oil went to foreign companies and investors, often with little resistance from the Middle Eastern nations, which had unstable governments and weak economies.

As nationalist movements gained strength, leaders began to demand a greater share of oil profits for their nations. In 1960 the world's thirteen major oil-producing nations formed the Organization of Petroleum Exporting Countries (OPEC). Through this organization, these countries could act together in setting oil prices and dealing with the industrial nations. The group included the eight largest oil producers of the Middle East — Algeria, Iran, Iraq, Kuwait (koo-WAYT), Libya, Qatar (KAY-

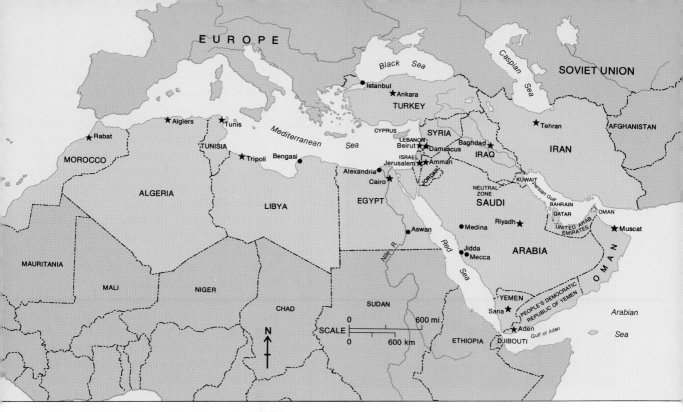

The Middle East and North Africa

The histories and cultures of the nations of the Middle East and North Africa are closely linked. Which of these countries have coasts on the Mediterranean Sea?

tahr), Saudi Arabia, and the United Arab Emirates.[1]

While OPEC controlled world oil production, the profits and power of its member nations soared. During the 1970's, OPEC tried to use its power to influence the foreign policies of oil-consuming countries (page 812). In response, industrialized nations cut their consumption and increased their own production of oil. World oil prices fell sharply during the mid-1980's as a result, and competition for markets caused dissension among the OPEC countries.

TURKEY AND IRAN

Kemal modernizes Turkey. One of the earliest nationalist movements in the Middle East was the "Young Turks" who sought to take control in the Ottoman Empire. By the end of World War I (page 648), the crumbling empire held only Asia Minor and a strip of territory around Constantinople (renamed Istan-

bul in 1930). An attempt by the Allies to end the empire altogether brought a Greek invasion of Turkey in 1919. As Ottoman forces could not resist the Greeks, Mustafa Kemal, a Turkish military hero and member of the Young Turks, formed a nationalist army. By 1923 the nationalists had defeated the invaders, overthrown the last Ottoman sultan, and declared Turkey a republic. As Turkey's first president, Kemal took the name Atatürk — "Father of the Turks."

Turkey was a backward, tradition-bound country where ways of living had changed little since the 1500's. It was clear to Atatürk that his nation had to modernize, and he believed that strong authoritarian rule was the road to reform. Atatürk's first move was to separate the government from the Islamic religion and its traditions. He began by eliminating the official government position held by the caliph (page 210) as leader of the Muslim world. Atatürk's government next took control of the educational and legal systems from religious leaders.

Atatürk enacted other reforms that broke with Islamic traditions. He replaced the Arabic script with the Roman alphabet and began a

---

[1] The other members of OPEC were Ecuador, Gabon, Indonesia, Nigeria, and Venezuela.

A hero of the Gallipoli campaign in World War I, Mustafa Kemal organized the Turks to create a new nation, gaining the title "Father of the Turks."

full-scale attack on illiteracy. In a nation where women had long been placed in a lesser position, Atatürk granted them equal rights with men, including the right to vote and to hold office. He abolished the Islamic practice of permitting a man to have more than one wife. Atatürk even demanded that Turks abandon traditional dress and adopt Western styles.

Besides trying to transform Turkish society, Atatürk was determined to eliminate Western control of industry and trade. He set up state banks, agricultural training stations, and cooperatives. His programs were hampered, however, by poor industrial planning and resistance to change. Many of Atatürk's reforms were just starting to take hold when the dictator died in 1938.

Political and economic problems plague Turkey. Turkey remained neutral during most of World War II, joining the Allies early in 1945, when victory seemed certain. Turkey remained friendly with the United States after the war, and in 1947, President Harry Truman sent aid to Turkey to keep it from falling under Communist control (page 726).

During the 1950's, new Turkish leaders favored foreign investment and less government control over the economy. These policies greatly increased the national debt, and a military coup in 1960 returned the country to the more nationalistic programs of Atatürk.

Severe inflation, high unemployment, and political unrest continued in Turkey. Hundreds of people were killed each year in clashes between political factions. Military leaders once again seized power in 1980 and managed to reduce inflation and end the violence. With aid from Western nations, Turkey's economy began to show signs of improvement.

Strong leadership modernizes Iran. Another strong, authoritarian leader directed the revolution that created Iran. Persia (as the nation was called until 1935) was dominated by Great Britain and Russia during the Age of Imperialism. The two nations shared control of Persia's government and commerce, and Britain controlled Persia's oil fields.

In 1921 Riza Khan, an army commander, overthrew Persia's weak government. Four years later he deposed the shah — Persia's traditional ruler — and took the crown and the name Riza Shah Pahlavi (PAH-luh-vee). An admirer of Atatürk, Riza Shah launched a program of modernization. His goal was to strengthen the nation and free it from foreign control. Aided by growing oil profits, Riza Shah promoted the building of roads and railroads, improved the postal system, and developed programs to bring about industrial and agricultural growth. In addition, he improved medical care, promoted public education, and, like Atatürk, encouraged Western styles of dress. In 1935, the country returned to its older name, Iran, meaning "land of the Aryans."

A new shah continues modernization. When he refused to side with the Allies in World War II, Riza Shah was forced from his throne by British and Russian troops. He was succeeded by his son, Mohammed Riza Pahlavi, who allowed the Allies to station troops in Iran and to use the nation's railways.

The new shah continued the work of modernizing Iran after the war. In the 1950's, however, his power was challenged by nationalists. Led by Iran's powerful prime minister, Mohammed Mossadegh, the nationalists overthrew the shah and took over foreign-owned oil facilities. The nationalists were soon thrown out themselves, however, and the shah returned to leadership with strong Western support.

The shah enacted many reforms that rejected ancient traditions. Large estates were broken up and land was distributed to peasants. The government encouraged greater use of modern agricultural methods. In 1963 women were given both the right to vote and the right to serve as members of the Iranian parliament. The shah also sought to strengthen Iran's military power. Using Iran's huge oil revenues, he built a formidable military force armed with modern weapons.

The shah faces opposition. Critics increasingly charged that the shah was a dictator. He was denounced for spending billions on defense while Iran's standard of living remained low, for maintaining close ties with the United States, and for allowing the secret police to use brutal methods. Conservative Muslims condemned his modernization programs and adoption of Western ways. They demanded a return to traditional Islamic laws and customs.

Ayatollah Khomeini, head of Iran's Shi'ite Muslims, regained the political power that religious leaders had traditionally held in Islamic societies.

Islamic leaders take control. Increasing political violence forced the shah to leave Iran in 1979. The new government, headed by the Shi'ite religious leader, Ayatollah[2] Ruhollah Khomeini (koh-MAY-nee), abolished most of the shah's reforms and ruled the nation according to Islamic law. All dissent was suppressed, and thousands of Iranians were imprisoned and executed. Many educated Iranians fled the country. In November, 1979, a mob seized the American embassy in Iran's capital city, Tehran. For over a year, the Khomeini government refused to return the Americans who were held hostage in the embassy (page 832).

The Islamic revolution spread. The Islamic revolution in Iran stirred religious passions throughout the Middle East. Rapid social change and years of Western domination had produced dislocations and resentments that made fertile ground for the growth of revolutionary religious fanaticism. Fundamentalist movements demanding a return to ancient ways of life sprang up in many countries during the next decade, threatening governments as different from each other as Socialist Iraq and monarchist Saudi Arabia.

Iran goes to war with Iraq. As unrest swept Iran, Saddam Hussein (hoo-SAYN), the ruler of neighboring Iraq, ordered an invasion of Iran in 1980. Hussein hoped to seize disputed border regions and islands in the Persian Gulf. He also hoped that the invasion would bring down the Khomeini government, shatter the Iranian army, and make Iraq the dominant power in the Persian Gulf region. The Iraqis failed to follow up their early victories, however. Moreover, Iranian leaders used the invasion to arouse the nationalist feelings of their people, who rallied behind the Khomeini government.

Most of the Arab states backed Iraq and provided money and arms. Iran was openly supported only by Libya and Syria. The costs of the Gulf War, as the conflict was called, were tremendous. By the mid-1980's, a million and a half people may have died and valuable oil

[2]An ayatollah (eye-uh-TOH-luh) is an Islamic religious leader. To review the Shi'ites, see pages 210–211.

OIL WEALTH

Wealth from oil revenues brought tremendous changes in the lives of people in Middle Eastern nations. Saudi Arabia in particular used the billions of dollars from oil production (right) to modernize. Although some Middle Eastern nations rejected Western ideas, most adopted Western technology such as television (above).

facilities in both countries had been destroyed. Neither side appeared anywhere near victory; yet both sides determined to fight on in this bitterly fought conflict.

THE ARAB STATES

Oil changes Saudi Arabia. Unlike the other Arab territories in the Ottoman Empire, Saudi Arabia did not become a mandate after World War I. It became an independent kingdom in 1932, after the conquests of Abdul Aziz Ibn Saud (IB-en sah-OOD) had united the region. Most of the people of Arabia, however, were impoverished bedouin whose loyalty was to their tribe (page 208). They had little interest in political matters or national unity.

With the discovery of vast oil reserves in the 1930's, Saudi Arabia suddenly moved into the twentieth century. Bedouin whose parents had been herders started driving trucks and working on oil rigs. They became familiar with Western technology and ways of living.

Saudi leaders — nearly all of them members of the powerful Saud family — worked to build a prosperous and literate nation. They brought modern technology into their highly traditional Islamic society. In the 1950's Prince Faisal (FYE-sal), the nation's prime minister, used oil profits to begin a modernization program, building hospitals, schools, and extensive irrigation works. By the time Faisal became king in 1964, modern urban centers had grown up in Saudi Arabia. The modernization program begun by Faisal provided free education for all children. The government invested heavily in projects to bring water to its arid lands and to improve agricultural production. It used the knowledge and skill of technical advisers from the West and of Western-educated Saudis to develop industry.

By the 1970's Saudi Arabia was one of the wealthiest nations in the world. The government's yearly income from oil added up to billions of dollars. Large amounts were invested in real estate, banks, and companies in industrialized nations around the world. In the 1980's, however, Saudi oil exports began to decline as industrialized nations conserved oil and searched for other energy sources.

Much Saudi wealth also went toward the conflict with Israel, for billions of dollars were spent on arms purchases. Saudi troops battled the Israelis in 1948 and 1973, and the Saudi government provided financial aid to its Arab allies.

In 1975 King Faisal was assassinated, but his policies were continued by Prince Khalid, who succeeded him as king and prime minister. Prince Fahd, the deputy prime minister, became king when Khalid died in 1982.

Small Arab states thrive on oil weatlh. Seven small Arab nations lie on Saudi Arabia's border along the coasts of the Arabian Sea and the Persian Gulf (map, page 801). The two easternmost of these nations share the name *Yemen* (YEH-mun). The Yemen Arab Republic (North Yemen) and the People's Democratic Republic of Yemen (South Yemen) both remained poor and underdeveloped nations. Oil profits, however, created riches for the other five small nations — Oman (oh-MAHN), the United Arab Emirates, Bahrain (bah-RAYN), Qatar, and Kuwait.

Egypt's modernization begins in the 1800's. Egypt was able to begin its modernization programs early in the 1800's. Under Mohammed Ali (page 595), Egypt modernized industry and agriculture, improved its transportation system, and expanded education. Mohammed Ali's successors continued modernization programs, including the building of the Suez Canal. Britain's financial and strategic interests in the canal gave it a foothold in Egyptian affairs, and British troops remained in Egypt from the 1880's on.

Made a British mandate after World War I, Egypt was granted partial independence as a constitutional monarchy in 1922, but Britain continued to supervise the nation's foreign affairs. In 1936 Britain recognized Egypt's independence and agreed to withdraw its troops from Egypt except for the region around the Suez Canal. During World War II, however, British forces returned in the campaign to drive Italian and German troops from Egypt (page 705), preventing Axis control of the oil fields of the Middle East and the Red Sea route to the Indian Ocean.

A new Egyptian government claims the Suez Canal. Many Egyptians had long resented British control of their country. Many also resented the corrupt rule of King Farouk and the serious economic inequalities in Egyptian society. In 1952 Egyptian army officers overthrew the king and took over the government. A year later they declared Egypt a republic. A leading figure in the revolt was Colonel Gamal Abdel Nasser (NAH-sur), who by 1954 gained sole authority in Egypt.

Nasser's first goal was to end foreign interference in Egypt, and in 1956 the Egyptian government took control of the Suez Canal from the British and French investment company. Hoping to regain the canal and remove Nasser from power, Britain and France combined with Israel to seize the waterway. The United States sharply criticized Britain and France for this action, and the Soviet Union threatened to step in and help Egypt. Under pressure from the United Nations, Britain, France, and Israel withdrew their forces from Egyptian territory. A UN Emergency Force was stationed on the Egypt-Israel border to prevent further hostilities. The UN force remained until 1967, when Nasser demanded it be withdrawn.

Nasser strengthens Egypt's economy. Nasser's next goal was to make Egypt economically strong. To help the peasants, he limited the amount of land one person could own, reduced rents, and set up cooperatives where farmers could get tools and seeds at low prices.

In 1956 Nasser began the building of the Aswan High Dam on the Nile River, with the help of technical and financial aid from the Soviet Union. The dam stored water to irrigate new farmlands and provided hydroelectric power. Despite its benefits, however, the dam created problems.[3] Since ancient times, the yearly flooding of the Nile had carried mineral-rich silt to fertilize farmlands (page 45). Because the dam ended the floods, farmers had to buy chemical fertilizers.

---

[3]The building of the dam threatened valuable relics and monuments of Egypt's past. The Great Temple of Rameses II at Abu Simbel (page 48), for example, was raised to higher ground to prevent its being damaged by the new lake that the dam created.

Water for Desert Lands

In the dry lands that extend through much of the Middle East, water has always been scarce and precious. Nomadic herders traveled from oasis to oasis to find water for themselves and their animals, and towns and trading centers grew up around these wells and springs. Middle Eastern towns centered on the community well, while homes often were built around a courtyard fountain. Modern Middle Eastern nations have had to devise new ways to produce enough water for their growing populations and expanding industry and agriculture.

The great wealth that oil has brought to many of these nations has been used to finance huge water projects. Desalination — taking the salt out of sea water — has been the most common method. In Kuwait, for instance, large plants distill sea water and produce some six million gallons of fresh water a day. Another idea that has been considered is towing icebergs from the Antarctic and melting them to supply more fresh water for these desert lands.

Nasser also tried to strengthen Egypt's economy by decreasing its dependence on the export of cotton, its major crop. He put large businesses under government control and encouraged the development of industry. Although Egypt's income increased, development was not fast enough to meet the needs of the nation's rapidly growing population. Land reform and the Aswan High Dam, viewed as the solutions to agricultural problems, failed to bring the success Nasser hoped. In addition, a major obstacle to economic development was conflict with Israel (page 811), for which Egypt set aside huge sums for military spending.

Nasser calls for Pan-Arabism. Despite Egypt's continuing problems, Nasser gave Arabs a new sense of pride. He rapidly became the most prominent and popular figure in the Arab world. Arabs in many lands viewed Nasser as a leader who would restore honor to the Arab peoples, who had suffered centuries of foreign rule.

Nasser became the leader in the movement for Pan-Arabism, or Arab unity. He expressed the goals of the movement as the following: (1) elimination of all foreign control over Arab affairs, (2) unification of the Arab world, and (3) the destruction of Israel. Nasser eventually recognized, however, that Arab unity was at best a distant goal that had to overcome national self-interest and distrust among Arab nations. In 1958 Syria and Egypt joined together to form the United Arab Republic, but three years later, military leaders took over in Syria and withdrew it from the union.

After Nasser's death in 1970, no Arab leader commanded sufficient power and respect to unite the Arab world. Nasser's successor, Anwar el-Sadat (sah-DAT), was more interested in Egypt itself than in Arab unity. Unlike Nasser, Sadat reduced government controls on business and on individual freedoms and set Egypt on a new course.

At first, Sadat continued the policy of hostility toward Israel. In the late 1970's, however, he surprised the world by seeking Arab-Israeli peace (page 812). Many Arabs opposed Sadat's outlook, and in 1981 he was assassinated. His successor, Hosni Mubarak (moo-BAHR-ahk), promised to continue Sadat's policies.

Unrest troubles Iraq. Oil wealth helped the nation of Iraq avoid the economic weaknesses that Egypt suffered. The development of its oil resources allowed Iraq (a British mandate until 1932) to make considerable economic progress after World War I. Faisal, the first king under the British mandate, became one of the leaders who encouraged Arab nationalist feelings. Later a strong prime minister, Nuri Pasha es-Said (NOO-ree PAH-shah es-sa-EED) led Iraq and encouraged modernization during the 1940's and 1950's. With British help, roads and railroads were built, an irrigation system was constructed, and a pipeline was laid to carry oil to the coast. Nuri and the young king, Faisal, however, were regarded as favoring the Western powers, and they were murdered by pro-Communist army officers in 1958. After 1958, Iraq underwent increasing political violence. Not until 1968 did a stable government emerge, led by Ahmed Hasan al-Bakr. General Saddam Hussein succeeded al-Bakr in 1979.

A continuing problem for the government of Iraq was a rebellion among the Kurds, a non-Arab Muslim group who for many years had sought self-government. By 1980, however, the Kurds were largely subdued.

In foreign affairs, Iraq maintained ties with the Soviet Union, from whom it obtained advanced weapons. Iraq denounced Egypt for seeking peace with Israel and continued to maintain a policy of hostility toward the Jewish state. The invasion of Iran in 1980 was expected to bring a quick victory, but instead, Iraq was caught in a costly war (page 803).

Palestinian Arabs immigrate to Jordan. The nation of Jordan (called Trans-Jordan until 1950) was poorer than most of its Arab neighbors. Lacking the wealth of the oil-rich nations and the industrial resources of Egypt, Jordan was a largely agricultural nation.

Jordan was carved out of Britain's mandate in Palestine in 1921 and was ruled by an Arab prince, Abdullah. After World War II it became independent as the Hashemite Kingdom of Jordan.[4] Two years later war broke out between the Arab states and the new Jewish nation of Israel. Although Israel was victorious, Jordan gained part of the West Bank of the Jordan River (map, page 810).

The war created an additional problem when hundreds of thousands of Palestinians fled to Jordan from Israeli territories. Eager for their own state, most Palestinians felt no loyalty to King Hussein (hoo-SAYN) of Jordan. Increasingly, they acted as a state within a state. Their raids on Israel brought reprisals and threatened the security of Jordan. Eventually Hussein ordered the Jordanian army to drive out the Palestinian guerrillas.

The West Bank of the Jordan was the economic heartland of Jordan. When Israel took it over in a 1967 war (page 811), Jordan's economy suffered. In 1979, a treaty between Israel and Egypt made provisions for negotiations concerning control of the West Bank. Jordan however, remaining hostile to Israel, condemned the treaty.

Political turmoil drains Syria's economy. Jordan's neighbor Syria became a French mandate after World War I and gained its independence after World War II. Conflicting groups within Syria made it politically unstable, however, until Hafez al-Assad became president in 1971. President Assad encouraged oil production and the building of a vast dam on the Euphrates River to irrigate Syria's rich farmlands and provide hydroelectric power.

Economic development was hampered by involvement in the turbulent politics of the Middle East. Syria was determined to regain lands taken by Israel in the Six-Day War in 1967. In a 1973 war with Israel, however, Syria lost even more territory. In 1979, Syria condemned the Egyptian-Israeli peace treaty. Syria's economy was further drained when Syrian troops were sent into the conflict that raged in its neighbor, Lebanon.

Civil war shatters Lebanon. Also a French mandate after World War I, Lebanon was granted its independence in 1943, and three

---

[4]The Hashemite dynasty is a family of Arab rulers considered to be descendants of Mohammed. Members of this dynasty became rulers in both Iraq and Jordan.

years later all French troops left. The newly independent nation prospered but was troubled by political unrest that led to civil war.

While there were many factions, or conflicting groups, in Lebanon, the civil war involved three major groups — Christians, Muslims, and Palestinian Arabs. Lebanon's Christians were the nation's dominant group, economically and politically, after independence. The Muslims sought greater power and higher living standards. The more than 300,000 Palestinian Arabs in Lebanon (most of whom were Muslims) had migrated there after Israel was established in 1948.

In 1975 a bitter civil war broke out as Christians fought Muslims and Palestinians. By the 1980's, tens of thousands had died in the war. Tensions were heightened as Syria and Israel both entered the conflict (page 813).

North African nations modernize. Politically and culturally the North African nations of Libya, Tunisia, Algeria, and Morocco are considered a part of the Middle East. North Africa shares the religion, language, and culture of the Arab nations; these ties to the Middle East began with the early expansion of Islam and were strengthened under Ottoman rule.

When Ottoman power declined in the 1800's, North Africa came under European control. European influence, however, was largely restricted to the cities and the coastal area. After World War II, the peoples of North Africa finally gained independence.

The independent countries introduced programs of modernization but differed in their approaches. Tunisia and Morocco gained capital for modernization through close trade ties with Western Europe and the United States and through tourist income. Algeria adopted some features of socialism in seeking to modernize. Most of its industry was taken over by the state. It benefited from rich deposits of natural gas. Algeria often took the role of a leader in fighting for Third World interests.

Libya came under the rule of an army officer, Muammar al Qaddafi (kuh-DAHF-ee), in 1969. Qaddafi ruled according to what he called "Islamic Socialism." He nationalized much of Libya's economy and required its people to live in strict accordance with Islamic law. Aiming to eliminate all Western influences from his country, Qaddafi forged ties with the Soviet Union and the Arab states. His hatred of Israel and the West led him to give support to terrorist organizations (page 813) not only in the Middle East but apparently even in Northern Ireland and the Philippines.

CHECK-UP

1. (a) What was the Balfour Declaration? (b) How did Arabs respond to it?
2. (a) What is OPEC? (b) What Middle Eastern nations are members of OPEC?
3. (a) How did Saudi Arabia finance its modernization programs? (b) What changes did modernization bring to Saudi Arabia?
4. (a) When did Egypt begin its modernization programs? (b) Why did British troops occupy Egypt? (c) How did Nasser try to end foreign interference in Egypt? (d) How did Nasser try to strengthen Egypt's economy?
5. (a) What was Pan-Arabism? (b) What were its goals?
6. What independent nations emerged from the British and French mandates in the Middle East?
7. What has been the approach to modernization taken in (a) Tunisia and Morocco? (b) Algeria? (c) Libya?

2 Conflicts Disrupt the Middle East

One of the bitterest conflicts of modern times has been the dispute between Arabs and Israelis. The roots of this conflict reach back many centuries. Much of the Arab world suffered domination by foreign powers well into the twentieth century, and sentiments of Arab nationalism and solidarity grew. The Jews, on the other hand, believed that they had a historical right to reclaim their ancient homeland in the Middle East (page 55). Those who migrated to Palestine, however, encountered hostility and resentment from the Arabs, who consid-

Thousands of European Jews who had survived the Holocaust emigrated to new homes in Palestine. The flags show the Star of David, traditional symbol of Judaism.

ered Palestine their land. After the nation of Israel was created in 1948, open conflicts broke out between the Arabs and Israelis, and tensions in the region endangered world peace.

THE FOUNDING OF ISRAEL

Jews flee Nazi persecution. The Zionist movement of the late 1890's (page 633) proposed the creation of a state where Jews could escape the anti-Semitism that was common in Europe. Jews who sought a homeland in the Middle East were encouraged by Britain's Balfour Declaration (page 800). Jews did not begin to migrate to Palestine in large numbers, however, until the 1930's when Hitler came to power in Germany. Nazi persecution of the Jews caused growing numbers to seek refuge in Palestine. Soon resentment of the increasing Jewish population sprang up among the Arabs, who saw the European Jews as foreign intruders. Violence often erupted.

The Arab reaction caused Britain to abandon its plans to create a Jewish state out of its mandate in Palestine. In the British view, one friendly, westernized state in the Middle East could not make up for the loss of good will among the Arab nations. The Arab population totaled 40 million, and Arabian oil was vital to Britain's economy. Prominent among the Jewish nationalist leaders were Chaim Weizmann and David Ben-Gurion.

World War II, however, made the Zionists more determined than ever to build a Jewish state in Palestine. After the nightmare of the Holocaust (page 706), Jewish survivors, scattered in refugee camps, wanted to emigrate to Palestine.

Palestine is divided. By 1946 Jews made up over a third of the population of Palestine. Unable to quiet the mounting hostility between Arabs and Jews, Britain turned the problem over to the United Nations in 1947.

The Jews presented several arguments to the UN in support of their case for a Jewish state. Palestine, they insisted, had been their land until the Romans drove them out during the first and second centuries A.D. The Jews had never given up hope of returning to Palestine. Moreover, they had suffered persecution for centuries and would not be safe until they had a country of their own. The Jewish advocates also pointed out that the Arabs had several nations of their own but had never established a government in Palestine. Jewish pioneers in Palestine, they continued, had made the desert bloom, built cities, established industries and schools, and introduced modern medicine to help both Arabs and Jews.

The Arabs, on the other hand, argued that Palestine had been an Arab land for centuries, and that its population was predominantly Arab. While they sympathized with Jewish suffering, they pointed out that it was not the

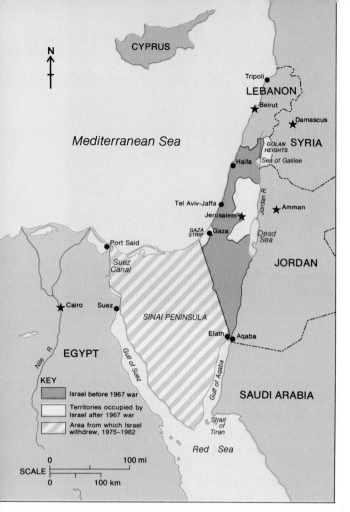

Middle East Trouble Spots

The area at the eastern end of the Mediterranean Sea became a focal point for conflicts. From what territory did Israel withdraw in the late 1970's?

Israelis build a modern state. The new Jewish state of Israel made impressive economic achievements. Israeli scientists made valuable contributions to the improvement of agriculture and to the removing of salt from sea water. Extensive irrigation and land reclamation projects enabled Israel to convert arid lands into rich fields of grain and groves of oranges. The young nation built modern industries and increased its exports, and Israelis attained a high standard of living.

Conflicts with the Arab nations, however, disrupted Israel's economic successes. Defense costs were staggering, amounting to as much as a third of the gross national product. The nation had to import fuel, wheat, and meat products; and rising inflation around the world made these imports increasingly costly. More and more, Israel had to depend on aid from private individuals and foreign governments.

THE ARAB-ISRAELI CONFLICT

The 1948 war has lasting effects. As soon as the creation of the Jewish state of Israel was announced in 1948, the armies of six Arab nations attacked Israel. Israeli forces were able to resist the attack and win the war, and UN diplomats arranged a truce. No final peace settlement followed the truce, however. The Arab states refused to recognize the existence of Israel. They continued to talk of the day when Arab arms would drive the Israelis into the sea and restore Palestine to the Arabs.

The 1948 war had important consequences for the future. It did not bring about an Arab state in Palestine, for Israel had occupied much of the territory that the United Nations had assigned to the Palestinian Arabs, while Jordan took nearly all the rest. Egypt occupied the Gaza Strip along the coast.

The war also produced an enormous refugee problem in the Middle East. Hundreds of thousands of Palestinian Arabs fled into the Arab states to escape the fighting and the rule of the Israeli government.

Israel is involved in the Suez Canal crisis. The 1948 war was only the beginning of armed hostilities between Israel and the Arab nations. In 1956 Israel joined with Britain and France to

Arabs who had persecuted the Jews. Arab representatives said that it would be an act of great injustice to solve the Jewish problem at the expense of the Arabs in Palestine.

After these arguments were presented, a UN committee decided: "The claims to Palestine of the Arabs and Jews, both possessing validity [worth], are irreconcilable. . . . Among all the solutions advanced, partition [of Palestine] will provide the most realistic and practicable settlement." By a vote of 33 to 13, with 10 nations abstaining, the General Assembly divided Palestine into two states — one Arab, the other Jewish. In 1948, the Jewish state of Israel was created. Weizmann became its first president, and Ben-Gurion, as prime minister, led the new state for 15 years.

attack Egypt after Nasser had taken over the Suez Canal (page 805). United Nations pressure, however, forced Israel to withdraw from Egyptian territory, and the UN forces patrolled the border.

During the years after the Suez Canal crisis, an uneasy peace existed between Israel and Egypt. Gradually, however, Egypt grew more aggressive. It increased its forces in the Sinai Peninsula (map, page 810), which bordered on Israel. In 1967 Nasser ordered United Nations forces to leave Egyptian territory. Egypt made a military pact with Jordan, supported Syrian attacks along Israel's border, and repeatedly threatened to destroy Israel.

Israel wins the Six-Day War. Egypt's next move was to blockade the mouth of the Gulf of Aqaba, by which Israeli ships reached the Red Sea. At this action, Israel decided to attack. In June, 1967, Israeli forces struck quickly. Within a few hours they had destroyed the Arab nations' air forces, catching hundreds of planes on the ground. Within six days Israeli forces had shattered the Egyptian army in the Sinai, destroying and capturing large quantities of Soviet equipment. Israel took over the Sinai Peninsula, the Golan Heights of Syria, and the West Bank of the Jordan River, including Jordan's half of Jerusalem.

The Six-Day War worsened Arab-Israeli relations. Israel insisted no territory would be returned until Arabs recognized the Jewish state's right to exist and ended acts of hostility. Arab leaders, however, regarded the plight of the Palestinian refugees as a crime against the Arab people and had little desire to meet any terms set by Israel.

Egypt begins the October War. After the Six-Day War, the Soviet Union, seeking Arab friendship, supplied Egypt and Syria with additional military aid. Thousands of Soviet advisers trained the troops of the two Arab nations. Within a few years the Egyptian army was better trained, better led, and better equipped than it had been before the Six-Day War. Anwar el-Sadat, Nasser's successor, planned for Egyptian troops to attack Israeli positions in the Sinai Peninsula. He reasoned that a successful operation would restore Arab honor, demonstrate that Israel could be beaten, and

strengthen Egypt's bargaining position over its losses in the 1967 war.

In October, 1973, Egyptian forces crossed the Suez Canal and overwhelmed the lightly defended Israeli fortifications. At the same time strong Syrian forces penetrated the Israeli-occupied Golan Heights.

Syria and Egypt made impressive gains in the opening days of what became known as the October War. Their missiles reduced the advantage held by the Israeli air force and proved costly to Israeli tanks. The battle turned in Israel's favor, however, when Israeli reserve units reached the front. When the fighting stopped, the Israelis held more Syrian territory than before the war and had crossed to the west bank of the Suez Canal.

Palestinian Arabs remain hostile to Israel. One major continuing issue throughout the conflicts in the Middle East was the fate of the Palestinian Arabs. Made homeless by the war, many of them were forced to live in refugee

TIMETABLE

The Middle East

1919	Ottoman territories in the Middle East are divided into French and British mandates.
1923	Kemal Atatürk heads the new Turkish republic.
1932	Saudi Arabia becomes independent.
1936	Britain recognizes Egyptian independence.
1948	The state of Israel is established, leading to the first Arab-Israeli war.
1956	A crisis develops over control of the Suez Canal.
1960	OPEC is founded by the oil-producing nations.
1964	The Palestine Liberation Organization (PLO) begins.
1967	Israel defeats Egypt in the Six-Day War.
1973	Arabs and Israelis fight the October War. Arab nations halt oil shipments to U.S.
1975	Civil war breaks out in Lebanon.
1979	The shah of Iran is deposed; the Khomeini government supports the seizure of American hostages. Egypt and Israel sign a peace treaty.
1980	Iran and Iraq go to war.
1983	Terrorism escalates.

camps, suffering great poverty and dreadful conditions. The Middle Eastern countries provided little aid, and the refugees were supported largely by the United Nations.

In 1964 Palestinian Arabs formed the Palestine Liberation Organization (PLO) to represent their people and to work toward establishing a nation for them. Headed by Yasir Arafat (AHR-uh-faht), the PLO engaged in terrorist activities such as hijacking airplanes and bombing buildings in Israel. PLO members attacked and killed Israeli athletes at the 1972 Olympic Games. In response to PLO terrorism, Israel attacked the organization's bases in Lebanon and elsewhere. Resolution of the Palestinian issue was blocked by the PLO's refusal to recognize Israel's right to exist. Israel, for its part, refused to negotiate with an organization that used terrorist methods.

The superpowers are involved. The Arab-Israeli problem was complicated by the involvement of the United States and the Soviet Union in the Middle East. Both as a source of oil and as a strategic location, the region was critically important in the rivalry between the two superpowers. Adopting a pro-Arab stand, the Soviet Union supplied some Arab nations with weapons, military training, technical assistance and financial aid. The United States,

American President Jimmy Carter (center) helped to negotiate the historic "Camp David agreements," signed in 1978 by President Sadat of Egypt (left) and Prime Minister Begin of Israel.

which had continued to back Israel, also sought to combat Soviet influence in the Arab world. It strengthened ties with Egypt, Jordan, and Saudi Arabia and pressed for a negotiated solution to the Arab-Israeli conflict.

Arab nations create an oil crisis. The Arab members of OPEC, the Organization of Petroleum Exporting Countries (page 800), discovered a new tactic to use in the competition between the superpowers. To make it clear that they regarded support for Israel as an act of hostility, the oil-producing Arab states turned to economic tactics. During the 1973 war with Israel, they raised the price of oil, decreased production, and cut off supplies to the United States and the Netherlands — two nations that openly supported Israel.

As its need for oil grew, the United States widened contacts with the Arab nations. It sought to maintain a delicately balanced policy in the Middle East. While maintaining its ties with Israel, the United States also tried to remain friendly with the Arab nations. It supplied Israel with modern weapons and shipped arms to some Arab lands. It also gave Egypt considerable economic aid.

Egypt and Israel seek peace. By the late 1970's, Egypt — alone among the Arab countries — and Israel showed some willingness to end the cycle of fear, military build-up, and war. Both countries were gravely aware that they could not keep spending huge sums on weapons if they wished to have strong economies. In 1977 President Sadat of Egypt made a dramatic visit to Israel, and a long process of negotiating began. President Jimmy Carter of the United States played a crucial role. Meeting in the United States at Camp David, the presidential retreat, Sadat and Prime Minister Menachem Begin (BAY-gihn) of Israel reached an agreement in 1978.[5] The next year Egypt and Israel concluded a peace treaty in which Israel agreed to return all of the Sinai Peninsula to Egypt. While much of the Arab world opposed the pact, it seemed to hold out the promise of a new era in the Middle East.

Conflicts shift to Lebanon. Hopes for peace in the Middle East declined in 1981

---

[5]Sadat and Begin were jointly awarded the Nobel Peace Prize in 1978 for their efforts.

when Sadat was assassinated by Muslim fundamentalists who opposed peace with Israel and cooperation with the West. Sadat's successor, Hosni Mubarak, promised to honor the treaty.

A greater threat to the peace settlement came in 1982 when Israel invaded Lebanon, a nation already torn by civil war (page 808). Israel feared the presence in Lebanon of the PLO forces that had fled to that country. Supplied with Soviet tanks and heavy artillery and aided by Syrian troops, the PLO forces were raiding Israel's northern border. Israel hoped that the invasion would destroy the PLO as an effective organization and drive it from Lebanon. Israeli leaders believed they could then work out a compromise with more moderate Palestinians on the West Bank. Israeli leaders also hoped to sign a peace treaty with Lebanon once the PLO was driven from that nation.

The 1982 invasion did not succeed completely, although Israel captured huge quantities of PLO arms, destroyed Syria's missile sites in Lebanon, and shot down scores of Syrian planes. Late in 1983 Arafat and the PLO were forced to leave Beirut (bay-ROOT), Lebanon's capital city, and southern Lebanon. The PLO was not destroyed, however. Moreover, Syria refused to withdraw its forces from Lebanon after the 1982 invasion.

A multinational peace-keeping force of United States, French, and Italian troops supervised the evacuation of the PLO, and troops remained in Lebanon after the evacuation. In October 1983, a terrorist bomb destroyed the United States Marine headquarters in Beirut killing 241 Americans. A second attack killed 58 French soldiers. The Lebanese government grew steadily weaker, and in 1984 the multinational forces withdrew from Lebanese territory, but rival factions continued to battle each other in this troubled country.

Terrorism grows in the Middle East. The attacks on the French and American forces in Beirut were part of a growing pattern of terrorism in the Middle East. Terrorism is the use of violence against persons or property for the purpose of creating fear and influencing the policies of a government. Terrorists hope that their actions will draw attention to their cause. In the long run, they hope to break down society's will to resist their demands.

Motivated by hatred and envy of the West, frustration over Israel's repeated military successes, religious fanaticism, and power struggles within the Arab world, Mideast terrorists killed hundreds of innocent people during the 1980's. Terrorist incidents included kidnappings, assassinations, plane and ship hijackings, and bombings of airports, stores, and other crowded places. The main victims of terrorism were citizens of Israel, of the United States (page 832), and of the more moderate Arab countries.

Some terrorists worked alone or in small groups. Those whose actions caused the worst harm, however, were usually trained and financed by national governments. The governments of Iran, Libya, and Syria were known in the 1980's to be major sponsors of state-supported terrorism. Only rarely was it possible to arrest and prosecute individual terrorists for their crimes. Moreover, since it was difficult to retaliate against terrorist groups or the governments that sponsored them without harming innocent people, finding an effective way of coping with this deadly trend often seemed an impossible task.

———

Throughout the Middle East, old conflicts spurred new ones as hostile relations persisted. The superpowers, with vital interests in the region, carefully monitored all developments and at times intervened. Despite hopes for peaceful negotiation, the Middle East often seemed on the brink of war.

CHECK-UP

1. (a) What arguments did Jews present in 1947 to support the establishment of a Jewish state in Palestine? (b) What arguments did Arabs present against the establishment of a Jewish state? (c) What did the UN decide?
2. What were the results of the 1948 war?
3. What caused fighting to break out (a) in 1956? (b) in 1967? (c) in 1973?
4. (a) What leaders took part in the negotiations between Egypt and Israel in 1978? (b) What was the Arab world's reaction to the treaty?
5. (a) Why did Israel invade Lebanon in 1982? (b) What were the results?
6. (a) What is terrorism? (b) Why has it been difficult for governments to find a way of dealing with terrorist attacks?

Chapter 37 Review

Summary

Nationalism became a powerful force in the Middle East as the region emerged from foreign domination after World War I. Nationalist leaders came to power and worked to modernize their nations. Wealth from oil helped modernization and gave the region political power.

The nations of Turkey and Iran were both modernized under authoritarian rulers. In Iran, the shah's harsh rule was later overthrown by anti-Western religious leaders. Oil wealth brought Saudi Arabia quickly into the modern world. A popular Arab leader, Gamal Abdel Nasser, worked to improve Egypt's economy and struggled for Arab unity. Iraq experienced much unrest after its modernization in the 1940's and 1950's, and a long lasting war with Iran drained Iraq's economy. The West Bank, once Jordan's economic center, was in Israeli hands after the 1967 Arab-Israeli war. Syria's economic development was hampered by its involvement in the civil war that engulfed Lebanon. Oil profits made Oman, the United Arab Emirates, Bahrain, Qatar, and Kuwait rich states. North and South Yemen remained backward, however.

Of the North African states, Tunisia and Morocco maintained close trade relations with the West, while Algeria took a socialist path to modernization. Libya, a leading oil producer, was ruled by a fervent Arab nationalist.

After it became a nation in 1948, Israel's modernization was rapid and impressive. Its success was disrupted, however, by bitter conflict with the Arab nations.

Vocabulary Review

1. Write the sentences below on a sheet of paper. Fill in the blank in each sentence with one of these words or phrases: *caliph, dictator, gross national product, mandate.*
(a) Palestine became a British __?__ under the League of Nations after World War I.
(b) Some critics of the shah of Iran accused him of being a __?__.
(c) Military spending took large portions of the __?__ of nations involved in the Arab-Israeli conflicts.
(d) The ancient Islamic position of __?__ was abolished by the Turkish republic.
2. Distinguish between the terms in each of the following pairs:
(a) Aswan High Dam; Suez Canal.
(b) Pan-Arabism; Zionism.
(c) Ottoman Empire; Turkish republic.
(d) Palestine Liberation Organization; Organization of Petroleum Exporting Countries.
(e) Six-Day War; October War.

People to Identify

Match the following people with the numbered phrases that describe them: *Yasir Arafat, David Ben-Gurion, Faisal, Mustafa Kemal, Ayatollah Khomeini, Gamal Abdel Nasser, Riza Shah, Ibn Saud, Anwar el-Sadat.*
1. Turkish independence leader known as "Father of the Turks."
2. Army commander who took control of Persia in 1921 and began modernization.
3. Islamic religious leader who led Iran after the overthrow of the shah in 1979.
4. First ruler of independent Saudi Arabia.
5. Prime minister, later king, of Saudi Arabia who began a modernization program in the 1950's.
6. Egyptian army colonel who became leader of the movement for Arab unity.
7. First prime minister of the state of Israel.
8. Head of the Palestine Liberation Organization.
9. Egyptian leader who worked for peace with Israel.

Relating Geography and History

1. **Locating places.** Locate each of the following on a map in this chapter:

(a) Turkey	(g) Israel
(b) Lebanon	(h) Golan Heights
(c) Saudi Arabia	(i) Sinai Peninsula
(d) Iran	(j) Suez Canal
(e) Iraq	(k) Jerusalem
(f) Syria	(l) Gaza Strip

2. **Research.** Water has always been a scarce resource in the Middle East. How have modern nations in this part of the world tried to increase the amount of water available to their peoples?

Use encyclopedias and the *Readers' Guide to Periodical Literature* to find information, and see pages 805–806 of this book.

Discussion Questions

1. What steps to modernize their countries were taken by (a) Atatürk? (b) Riza Shah? (c) Nasser?

2. (a) Why did some Iranians oppose the modernization efforts of Shah Riza Pahlavi? (b) What changes were made under the rule of the Ayatollah Khomeini? (c) What was the popular reaction to these changes?

3. What views were shared by the governments of Qaddafi in Libya and Khomeini in Iran?

4. What were Iraq's goals in going to war with Iran in 1980?

5. How did the discovery of oil change life in Saudi Arabia?

6. (a) Why was Nasser such a popular figure in the Arab world? (b) What is Pan-Arabism, and why have its goals not been achieved?

7. (a) How did the problem of Palestinian refugees come about? (b) Why was the Palestine Liberation Organization founded?

8. (a) What economic and scientific achievements helped Israel to modernize? (b) How did the Arab-Israeli conflict affect Israel's economic growth? (c) What was the significance of the peace negotiations between Israel and Egypt in 1978–1979?

9. (a) What circumstances in late nineteenth-century Europe led many Jews to become Zionists? (b) What effect did World War II and Nazi persecutions have on the Jewish nationalist movement?

10. (a) What were the original causes of the Lebanese civil war? (b) Why did foreign countries become involved in the Lebanese conflict? (c) What effect did their intervention have?

Reading Primary Sources

In November, 1917, the British foreign secretary, Arthur Balfour, wrote to Baron Edmond de Rothschild, the Zionist leader in Britain. Read his letter and answer the questions that follow.

Dear Lord Rothschild,
I have much pleasure in conveying to you, on behalf of His Majesty's Government, the following declaration of sympathy with Jewish Zionist aspirations . . . :

"His Majesty's Government view with favor the establishment in Palestine of a National Home for the Jewish people, and will use their best endeavors to facilitate the achievement of this object, it being clearly understood that nothing shall be done which may prejudice the civil and religious rights of existing non-Jewish communities in Palestine, or the rights and political status enjoyed by Jews in any other country." I should be grateful if you would bring this declaration to the knowledge of the Zionist Federation.
Yours sincerely,
[Signed] Arthur James Balfour

(a) For whom was Balfour speaking in this letter? (b) On what part of this letter did Zionists base their claim of British support? (c) What does the declaration say about Palestinian Arabs' rights?

Skill Activities

1. Placing events in time. From the information in the chapter, find the year in which each of the following events occurred. On a separate sheet of paper, arrange these events in chronological order, putting the date next to each:
(a) Egyptian President Sadat is assassinated.
(b) The United Nations divides Palestine.
(c) Iranian women gain the right to vote.
(d) Egypt loses the Sinai Peninsula in the Six-Day War.
(e) The nation of Israel is created.
(f) Civil war breaks out in Lebanon.
(g) The Egyptian army crosses the Suez Canal into Israel as the October War begins.
(h) Arab OPEC members restrict oil shipments.

2. Word research. The plight of Palestinian refugees has been one of the major problems in the Middle East. *Refugee* comes from the Latin *fugere,* "flee." What does each of these words mean? (a) fugitive; (b) refuge; (c) centrifugal; (d) subterfuge.

3. Reports. Find information about one of the following topics and write a report: (a) present-day conflicts between Shi'ite and Sunni Muslims in the Middle East (see pages 210–211); (b) Israeli agriculture; (c) the career of Golda Meir; (d) the moving of ancient Egyptian monuments threatened by the building of the Aswan Dam; (e) the history of the Sinai Peninsula; (g) the status of women in Middle Eastern nations.

Trucks, cars, and buses that travel on the modern Pan-American Highway pass by an ancient fortress built by the Chimu people of Peru. The Chimu ruled coastal Peru about A.D. 1000 and were conquered by the Incas in 1460.

CHAPTER 38
The Changing
Americas

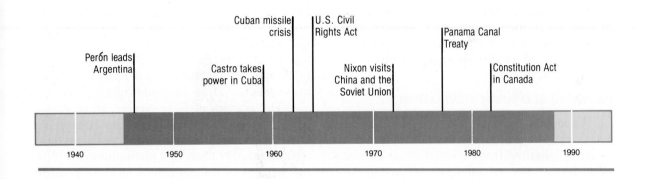

Perón leads
Argentina

Castro takes
power in Cuba

Cuban missile
crisis

U.S. Civil
Rights Act

Nixon visits
China and the
Soviet Union

Panama Canal
Treaty

Constitution Act
in Canada

1940   1950   1960   1970   1980   1990

The twentieth century brought challenges to the nations of the Western Hemisphere. The countries of Latin America faced the need to develop stronger economies and more stable governments. Their successes were limited, however, and political tensions often resulted as groups chose different ways of achieving these goals.

The United States emerged as a world superpower after World War II, and the nation prospered. While its economy remained strong, American Presidents sought solutions to problems such as inflation and recession. A central social issue became the drive for equal rights, which expanded greatly in the postwar years. In foreign affairs, both cold war tensions and efforts to achieve peace affected United States policies.

Canada became a strong industrial nation after World War II. Its leaders sought to maintain national unity and to reduce the nation's dependence on the United States.

This chapter presents the recent history of the nations of the Western Hemisphere.

CHAPTER OUTLINE

1   Latin American Nations Seek Stability
2   The United States Faces the Postwar Era
3   Canada Strives to Maintain Unity

1 Latin American Nations Seek Stability

The heritage of Latin America's colonial past continued to influence the region's development during the nineteenth and twentieth centuries. Although most of Latin America became independent by 1824, its leaders faced the challenge of unifying their nations and rebuilding economies ravaged by revolution (Chapter 23). Wealthy creole landowners dominated the new nations. As in colonial times, economies were dependent on the sale of plantation crops or minerals in the world market. Because little industry developed, Latin America's economic problems lasted into the twentieth century.

PATHS TO ECONOMIC DEVELOPMENT

Economic problems block modernization. The weak, dependent economies that Latin America inherited from colonial times created obstacles, as the region tried to modernize. Economies that depended on a single export product — agricultural or mineral — made the nations of Latin America highly vulnerable to changes in world prices. A drop in the price of a crop such as sugar, cacao, bananas, or coffee could devastate a nation's economy. Mining in Latin America also fit the one-product pattern. The region's prosperity depended on demand for raw materials in the industrialized nations.

Foreign control creates problems. Foreign investors added to the problems of the Latin American economies. After Latin America gained its independence, investors from the United States and Europe provided most of the capital and technical knowledge needed to develop mines and plantations. Many of these investors were more concerned with profits than with the region's economic development. Often they supported government by caudillos (page 498) because a stable government was necessary for business to run smoothly.

Foreign investors also supported the traditional system of land ownership. In colonial times, land had been held by a few wealthy families, while the majority of the people were poor and landless. Independence did not change this pattern. On the contrary, to meet growing demand, landowners and mining companies expanded their holdings. Landless Indians and peons thus had nowhere to work but in the mines or on large plantations.

Díaz encourages foreign investment in Mexico. The situation in Mexico at the beginning of the twentieth century was typical of the economic, political, and social patterns in Latin America at that time. The caudillo Porfirio Díaz came to power in 1876 (page 501). Díaz was a harsh dictator, but his rule brought order and stability to Mexico. This encouraged foreign investment, and capital flowed into the nation's mines, plantations, and railroads. Mexico's economic future seemed bright.

The policies of Díaz created grave problems, however. He had allowed his supporters and foreign investors to take over peasant lands and incorporate them into plantations. By 1910 one percent of the population held 85 percent of Mexico's land. As more and more land was used to grow export crops, there was less land available to grow food. Many landless peasants had no place to work; some faced starvation.

Rebellion turns to revolution. After more than thirty years in power, Díaz decided to allow free elections in 1910. As the election approached, sentiment against Díaz ran high. The powerful caudillo was surprised to find his rule challenged by Francisco Madero (mah-DAY-roh), a wealthy creole. Díaz had his opponent arrested and jailed and won the election through fraud, but Madero escaped and called for revolution.

Violent revolt soon broke out among peasants demanding land reform. The peasants' leader, Emiliano Zapata (sah-PAH-tah), gave his support to Madero, and Díaz was overthrown. As president, Madero failed to keep the support of either the peasants or the landowners. After his overthrow in 1913, civil war swept the country. Peasants led by Zapata and Pancho Villa (VEE-yah) fought a guerrilla war against government troops.

A new constitution provides a pattern for the future. Although fighting continued till 1920, a government established in 1917 drew up a new constitution. Combining nationalist and socialist ideas, the constitution served as a blueprint for reform. It gave the government power to organize agricultural collectives and to put petroleum and mineral resources under national control. It allowed the formation of labor unions, established an eight-hour work day, and provided for free, compulsory education. Limits were set on the political power and wealth of the Catholic Church.

The 1917 constitution provided a basis for modern Mexico. Stable government was established by 1920, under the presidency of General Alvaro Obregón (oh-vray-GOHN). It was Lázaro Cárdenas (KAHR-day-nahs), president from 1934 to 1940, who did the most to carry out the aims of the constitution. Cárdenas distributed huge tracts of land to peasant villages and expanded the building of rural schools. In 1938 he ordered the national government to take over the oil holdings of foreign companies.

Mexico's economy expands. During the next thirty years, new factories were constructed, agriculture and tourism grew, and the government built highways and railroads. Mexico also widened the base of its economy beyond mining and plantation agriculture.

Amid this progress, however, many Mexicans continued to live in poverty. They ate poorly and received little education or medical care. As in most of Latin America, Mexico's population grew rapidly, putting severe strain on the economy. Millions of people migrated from the countryside to the cities, hoping for jobs. The fast-growing urban populations brought problems of housing, overcrowding, and pollution. As population soared, thousands of Mexicans crossed the United States border illegally, searching for work.

An economic boom creates difficulties. By the 1970's Mexico faced the problems of high inflation and unemployment and insufficient agricultural production. The nation was importing more goods than it was exporting. Under President José Lopez Portillo (por-TEE-yoh), the country began an intensive search for oil reserves within its own borders. Valuable oil reserves were found and put under the control of

LINKING PAST AND PRESENT

From Mayan Walls to Modern Murals

The Mexican revolution in 1910 marked the beginning of the modern nation and a surge of national pride in Mexico's past. After the revolution, many Mexican artists began to look away from Spanish colonial styles and back to the themes of ancient Mayan art. Three great Mexican artists of the time became famous for their mural painting — painting on walls. Over a thousand years earlier, Mayan artists also had decorated temple walls with bold murals in strong colors.

The modern mural painters — Diego Rivera, José Clemente Orozco, and David Siqueiros — adopted ancient painting techniques, styles, and colors. They placed their paintings on the walls of public buildings so that all people could see and understand them. While they used symbols from Mexico's past, they used ideas from the present — portraying workers, peasants,

revolutionaries, and scenes from history. On the modern steel-and-concrete buildings of the new Mexico City, these artists recaptured the spirit of the Mexican past.

PEMEX (Pétroleos Mexicanos), the government-owned oil monopoly. Mexico soon became one of the world's major oil exporters.

The oil boom created unexpected problems, however. The government channeled huge amounts of money into oil production and allowed other exports to decline in importance. As agriculture was neglected, not enough was produced to feed Mexico's rapidly growing population. Food had to be imported, with millions of dollars going toward grain imports. Prices of food and other goods rose. Hoping that economic growth would improve social conditions, the government cut spending for social programs. The oil boom thus widened the gap between rich and poor in Mexico, as most of its benefits went to the wealthy.

The drop in world oil prices during the 1980's, moreover, crippled Mexico's economy. Inflation soared, and the government seemed on the brink of defaulting on its enormous foreign debt (that is, failing to pay the interest on that debt). A severe earthquake hit Mexico City in 1985, adding to the nation's difficulties. Up to 20,000 persons were killed, and tens of thousands were left homeless and destitute.

The depression brings new leadership in Latin America. While revolution was transforming Mexico in the early twentieth century, the rest of Latin America experienced little change. During the worldwide depression of the 1930's (page 680), however, world prices for Latin America's exports declined sharply. As exports decreased, unemployment rose rapidly and discontent became widespread. Latin American leaders were forced to think about ways to overcome the sharp reduction in trade and encourage economic development.

The different Latin American nations chose a variety of approaches to economic development. In some countries, military leaders emerged who returned to the methods of caudillos and used dictatorial power to control the economy. Other leaders attempted political and social changes through nationalizing the economy, protecting domestic industry, and creating programs of education and social welfare.

Dictators try to modernize Brazil and Argentina. One of the new Latin American leaders was Brazil's Getulio Vargas (VAHR-gus),

who took over his nation's government in 1930 with the help of the army. Until 1945 he ruled Brazil with dictatorial powers. While Vargas called himself the "Father of the Poor" and made many social reforms, he also imposed censorship and restricted constitutional rights. Vargas strengthened the government's control over resources and transportation and made Brazil's economy less dependent on the export of coffee. United States investors helped Brazil build a steel mill and set up the first automobile plant in Latin America.

Vargas was driven from office by military leaders. After a series of civilian presidents, the army took over the nation in 1964, and military leaders ruled for two decades.

Brazil's great rival in military and economic power was Argentina. The crisis and unrest of the depression had led to a military takeover in Argentina. By 1946, one of the leaders of the takeover, Juan Perón (pay-ROHN), was elected president. Perón's wife Evita became virtually co-president of Argentina. She began reforms in education, gained the right to vote for Argentine women, and won immense popularity among the workers and the poor. Perón nationalized transportation and communication systems, but the economy continued to depend on exports of wheat and beef. When demand for these products declined, prosperity faded. Perón's support diminished, particularly after the death of Evita Perón in 1952, and he was ousted by a military coup in 1955.

A series of unstable and repressive governments followed. Unemployment and inflation rose and the country faced strikes and protests. In 1973, Perón returned and was again elected president. He died the next year and was succeeded by his third wife, Isabel Perón.

Argentina's problems continued, and by 1976, military leaders again took control of the government. In 1982, Argentine troops invaded the Falkland Islands, a British colony several hundred miles off the coast. The Argentines were defeated in a brief war (page 743) but continued to claim the Falklands. In 1983 the military leaders of Argentina gave up their rule to an elected civilian president.

As a way of dealing with their economic problems, Brazil and Argentina agreed in 1986 to a plan that would take an important step toward unifying their economies. The first action taken under this agreement aimed at doubling trade between the two countries and in other ways stimulating the growth of local industries.

Concern mounts over human rights. While leaders such as Perón brought some reforms and made economic gains, their methods often were repressive. As inflation, unemployment, and poverty continued, signs of discontent increased — riots, guerrilla activity, and labor unrest. In an attempt to keep order, governments in several Latin American nations limited freedom of speech and the press and other rights. Opponents of the ruling party were often jailed and executed without a trial.

Before civilian rule was restored during the 1980's, the governments of both Brazil and Argentina had been widely criticized as violators of human rights. In Argentina the civilian government elected in 1983 ordered trials for the nine officers who had ruled the country between 1976 and 1982. During that period, the military government had operated hundreds of secret prisons and torture centers. About 9,000 Argentinians, who came to be called "the disappeared ones," had apparently been killed by death squads acting for the government. In the trials, which ended in 1985, five of the nine former officials received prison sentences. Hundreds of lower-ranking military officers also faced criminal charges. In Brazil the military feared a similar fate. In order to ease the transition to civilian rule, however, the Brazilian government said that it would not prosecute army officers believed to have violated human rights.

Some nations seek other approaches to development. Unlike the military rulers of Brazil and Argentina, some Latin American leaders tried to bring about economic development through social and economic reform. In 1969, for example, the military leaders of Peru nationalized plantations and oil fields. They distributed land to peasants and set up farming cooperatives. Problems of inflation and unemployment remained, however.

Another nation that sought development through social change and economic reform was Chile. In 1970, Chileans elected a Marxist president, Salvador Allende (ah-YEN-day), as

Juan and Evita Perón enjoyed great popularity at the height of their power. After Evita's death, economic and social problems led to Perón's overthrow.

head of a coalition government. Allende nationalized mines and banks, initiated land reform, and raised wages. The economy began to improve, but foreign investors, fearing their property would be seized by the Marxist government, began to withdraw their capital from Chile. Economic problems threw the country into turmoil and, in 1973, Allende was killed in a coup by military forces.

The new Chilean military government, led by General Augusto Pinochet (peen-oh-CHET), immediately began to suppress opposition. Pledging to wipe out communism in Chile, the government declared a state of emergency, suspended the legislature, imposed severe censorship, and used violence against political opponents. Many Chileans left the country, and the government was criticized by the United Nations for its violations of human rights.

Revolution brings changes in Cuba. Cuba had gained its independence from Spain in the Spanish-American War of 1898 (page 511), but its freedom was not complete. The Platt Amendment of 1901 permitted the United States to keep naval bases in Cuba and intervene in Cuban affairs to maintain peace. In addition, as United States investment in Cuba grew, the island nation became increasingly dependent upon its powerful neighbor. In 1952,

ECONOMIC DEVELOPMENT IN LATIN AMERICA

Economies in most Latin American countries depend on a few basic activities. Venezuelan oil (above) has strengthened the economy of that country. Fish processing (above, right) is important in Argentina. Farm workers (below, right) harvest cotton, a major Peruvian export. Terraced farming (below) increases the amount of productive land in Costa Rica, where half the people work in agriculture.

Fulgencio Batista (bah-TEES-tah) took control of the Cuban government. Batista's dictatorship aroused fear and resentment. In 1956 Fidel Castro began a guerrilla war against Batista. In January of 1959, after three years of bitter warfare, Batista was ousted, and Castro took power.

In the first hundred days of his regime, Castro nationalized foreign holdings, replaced the professional army and navy with volunteer forces, launched a campaign against illiteracy, and began a long-range program to root out racial discrimination.

Castro allied himself with the Soviet Union, set up a one-party Marxist state, and executed or imprisoned those of his opponents who did not flee the country. In 1961 the United States broke diplomatic ties with Cuba and backed an unsuccessful invasion of the island by Cuban exiles (page 732). The next year, tensions between Cuba and the United States grew worse when Soviet missile bases were found in Cuba. The crisis was resolved when the Soviet Union agreed to remove its missiles from Cuba.

In 1977, Cuba and the United States agreed to establish informal diplomatic ties, but relations remained uneasy. The United States criticized the presence of Cuban troops supporting Communist forces in the African nations of Ethiopia and Angola (page 787). Cuba's arming and training of leftist forces in Central America became an issue in the 1980's.

Haitians rebel against tyranny. The poorest nation in the Western Hemisphere, Haiti had a long history of political instability and harsh rule. In 1957, François Duvalier (doo-val-YAY) came to power. Emphasizing black pride and national sovereignty, Duvalier brought stability to Haiti but only by using terror to silence his opponents. In 1971 he was succeeded by his son, Jean Claude. Under this new ruler, who accumulated immense wealth, Haiti remained grindingly poor. Early in 1986, Jean Claude Duvalier was ousted from power after three months of violent protests over economic conditions, corruption, and police brutality. He was succeeded by a governing council that promised to hold elections, but economic problems and dissatisfaction over the slow pace of reform continued to keep Haiti in a state of unrest.

Latin American nations battle the drug trade. During the 1980's, concern over the illegal drug trade increased throughout the Western Hemisphere. Growing demand for drugs had led to the rise of a flourishing underground industry in many Latin American nations, including Mexico, Bolivia, Peru, Colombia, Brazil, and Ecuador. This activity was of special concern to the United States, where large amounts of the illegal drugs were sold.

International efforts to halt the drug traffic were stepped up, but law enforcement agencies faced serious obstacles. These obstacles included official corruption and the difficulty of policing the remote areas where the drugs were grown and processed. The major problem, however, was the economic dependence of many Latin American nations on the drug trade. Bolivia, for example, earned more from drug exports than from all other exports combined. Burdened with enormous national debts, the governments of these impoverished nations feared the economic and political consequences of enforcing anti-drug laws.

CONFLICT IN CENTRAL AMERICA

The small nations of Central America (map, page 824) shared many problems with the rest of Latin America — one-product economies, limited local industry, dependence on foreign capital, and extremes of poverty and wealth. A small number of wealthy families owned much of each country's land and wealth. Many groups sought ways to change this situation, and in the 1970's and 1980's Central America became a battleground for conflicting outlooks.

Rebels overthrow Nicaragua's dictator. During the 1930's, General Anastasio Somoza (soh-MOH-sah) came to power in Nicaragua and set up a dictatorship. He was succeeded by his son Luis in 1956 and by his other son, Anastasio Somoza Debayle, in 1967. The Somoza regime improved Nicaragua's economy, but there was widespread repression and corruption. Protest against the regime became violent as in the late 1970's terrorist groups carried out kidnappings and bombings. In response, the government imposed martial law.

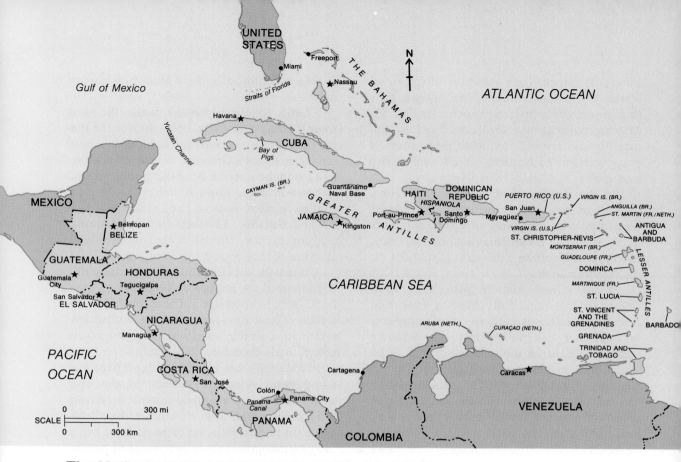

The Nations of Central America and the Caribbean

The nations of Central America lie on a strip of land linking North and South America. In recent years political turmoil has focused attention on the region.

In 1979 rebel guerrillas known as the Sandinistas (sahn-dih-NEE-stahs) were victorious in a civil war against government forces.[1] Somoza resigned and went into exile. The new Marxist regime started programs to redistribute land, to improve housing, and to provide health care and education to more people. It also severely restricted civil liberties, limited the activities of the Roman Catholic Church, and imposed compulsory military service. The Sandinistas were soon challenged by anti-Communist guerrillas known as contras. The contras attacked targets in Nicaragua from bases in Honduras and Costa Rica.

The Sandinista government faced opposition from the United States, and tension between the two countries heightened during the 1980's. Accusing Nicaragua of training and arming leftist guerrillas in El Salvador, the United States sent aid to the contras. The Nicaraguan government, in turn, accused the United States of sponsoring "state terrorism" and of looking for an excuse to invade Nicaragua.

Civil war rages in El Salvador. A military dictator also came to power in El Salvador in the early 1930's. General Maximiliano Hernández Martínez firmly established his rule in 1932, with harsh repression of all opposition. Martínez remained in power until 1944 and was succeeded by a series of military dictators.

During the late 1970's, demands for land and jobs for the nation's poor again became widespread. In 1979 army leaders overthrew El Salvador's dictator and formed a junta (HOON-tah), a small ruling group. The new leaders took over many large farms and began to distribute land, but the protesters were not satisfied. In 1980 a bitter civil war began between government forces and anti-government rebels.

---

[1]The name *Sandinista* comes from General Cesar Augusto Sandino, who fought against the United States forces occupying Nicaragua during the 1920's.

As in Nicaragua, the outcome of the civil war in El Salvador was a matter of concern to the superpowers. The Soviet bloc aided the Marxist rebels; the United States aided government forces. In 1984, American-sponsored elections were held in El Salvador. The winner was a moderate candidate, José Napoleón Duarte (DWAR-tay). It remained to be seen whether Duarte could find a way to end El Salvador's long civil war and maintain civilian authority in a nation where the army had long dominated the government.

Honduras becomes involved in conflict. Honduras, which borders both El Salvador and Nicaragua, developed in much the same pattern as its neighbors. Its economy was dependent on large banana plantations set up by American fruit companies in the 1890's. Through the years government leadership changed often as a result of revolts and coups.

In 1969, a new law redistributed farmlands among Hondurans, taking land away from many Salvadorians who lived in the country. The Salvadorians migrated back to their own country, intensifying shortages of land and jobs there. The resulting tensions brought on a brief war between El Salvador and Honduras.

Its location gave Honduras strategic importance in the battle of conflicting viewpoints in Central America. United States aid and advisers helped Honduras block possible arms shipments from Nicaragua to Salvadorian rebels. In addition, contra forces opposing the Sandinista government raided Nicaragua from bases in Honduras.

Guatemala battles rebels. Until 1944, Guatemala also was ruled by a series of dictators who favored foreign investment as the way to economic development. Popular protest, however, brought on a ten-year period of reform. President Juan José Arévalo (ah-REV-ah-loh) instituted a democratic constitution and made important reforms in health, education, and labor. Arévalo was succeeded by Colonel Jacobo Arbenz. Under Arbenz, the Guatemalan government took over many large landholdings, including the American-owned fruit plantations, and redistributed the land among farmers. Arbenz was overthrown in 1954 and was followed by military leaders who ruled harshly, reversing most of the earlier reforms.

In the late 1970's, political violence became widespread in Guatemala, coming from rebel guerrilla forces and various terrorist groups, both pro-Communist and anti-Communist. The government waged a ruthless campaign against opposition and succeeded in reducing open violence. But Guatemala had also lost American aid because of its corruption and human rights violations, including at least 5,000 political murders. Moreover, the army had killed thousands of Indian peasants and had driven additional thousands from their villages into southern Mexico, straining relations between Guatemala and Mexico.

In 1983 an army general took control of the Guatemalan government. Two years later, under pressure from the United States, the government called for national elections. In 1985 the people of Guatemala elected their first civilian president in more than 25 years.

Guatemala also faced tension along its border. The small nation of Belize (buh-LEEZ), formerly British Honduras, was granted independence from Britain in 1981. Because Guatemala claimed Belize's territory, British troops remained there to protect the former colony.

Panama acquires rights to the canal. A central issue in Panama was the controversy over the Panama Canal. After winning its independence from Colombia in 1903 with American help, the new Panamanian government granted the United States the right to build the Panama Canal, completed in 1914 (page 512). The Canal Zone, which bordered both sides of the Canal, remained American property and prospered while the rest of the country remained poor. During the 1950's and 1960's, people in Panama began to demand control of the Canal Zone and the canal.

In 1968 a strong leader emerged — General Omar Torrijos (toh-REE-hohs). Torrijos supported the movement for Panamanian control of the canal and sought a new Panama Canal treaty with the United States. In 1977 the new treaty was approved; it provided for returning the Canal Zone and transferring control of the canal to Panama by 1999.

Democratic leaders head Costa Rica. Unlike its neighbors, Costa Rica became a democracy early in the twentieth century and achieved a relatively high standard of living.

President Julio Acosta (ah-COHS-tah) set up a democracy in 1919. Acosta and his successors distributed land, raised wages, expanded education, and taxed imports to protect local industry. Economic problems grew, however, with inflation rising in the 1980's.

Long a neutral country with no armed forces, Costa Rica was affected by the turmoil in the region in the 1980's. Fear of Nicaragua's Sandinista government caused Costa Rica's leaders to accept United States aid and to begin to re-establish an army.

CHECK-UP

1. How were Latin America's economies hurt (a) by dependence on one or two products? (b) by dependence on foreign investment? (c) by patterns of land ownership?

2. (a) How did Díaz's policies both help and harm Mexico? (b) How was constitutional government established in 1917? (c) How did Cárdenas carry out the aims of the constitution? (d) What problems did Mexico's oil boom cause?

3. (a) How did Vargas strengthen Brazil's economy? (b) Why did Argentina's prosperity fade under Perón? (c) How did Peru seek economic development? (d) What kind of government did Pinochet impose in Chile? (e) What path toward development did Cuba take?

4. (a) Who were the Sandinistas? (b) Which side did the United States government support in El Salvador's civil war? (c) How was Honduras involved in the conflicts in Nicaragua and El Salvador? (d) How did political violence affect Guatemala in the 1970's and 1980's? (e) What Central American country was able to maintain democracy through much of the 1900's?

2 The United States Faces the Postwar Era

At the end of World War II the United States was economically prosperous, politically stable, and militarily secure. Eager for peace, Americans quickly brought their troops home from overseas and turned to "winning the peace." The future looked promising as Americans prepared to enter the last half of the twentieth century. Nevertheless, United States leaders were challenged in the postwar years by crucial problems in both foreign and domestic affairs.

DOMESTIC ISSUES

The postwar years bring prosperity. For the United States, the period after World War II was one of affluence, growth, and confidence. As the war ended, consumers went on a buying spree, spending wartime savings on goods and services that had not been available during the war years. An expected postwar depression never came, and millions of people found new jobs. Spending, however, increased more rapidly than the production of goods and services, leading to inflation.

Prosperity continued throughout the 1950's and 1960's, in spite of inflation and brief *recessions,* or slowdowns in business activity. A record-breaking number of Americans had full-time jobs, earnings were higher than ever before, and the nation enjoyed the highest standard of living in the world.

The postwar years bring changes in life styles. Peace and prosperity created changes in Americans' ways of living. With their increased purchasing power, many people bought new homes, particularly in suburban areas around major cities. As the number of cars in the nation increased, Congress approved the building of thousands of miles of new highways. With easier transportation, suburban shopping centers became popular. Americans continued to buy consumer goods such as televisions, washers, dryers, dishwashers, and cameras.

Changes in ways of living reflected changes occurring in the nation's population. The population grew because of a high birth rate, immigration, and medical advances that increased the average life span. More people began moving to the West, especially to California. The shift of population continued into the 1980's as Americans were attracted to the warm weather and expanding job opportunities of the sunbelt — the states stretching from the southeast Atlantic coast to southern California.

Prosperity inspires programs of aid. Although prosperity also led to higher standards of living, not all Americans benefited. Every major city had slum areas that housed the poor and unemployed, and declining farm incomes created rural poverty.

Amid the growth and confidence of the postwar years, United States leaders initiated programs of aid to help people at home and abroad improve their way of life. Programs of domestic aid included funds for education, medical care for the elderly and the poor, and urban renewal programs. International aid programs begun soon after the war, such as the Marshall Plan (page 726), sought to help European nations maintain economic and political stability. Other innovative programs of international aid were the Peace Corps and the Alliance for Progress, instituted during the Kennedy administration. Through the Peace Corps, for example, Americans lived in developing countries where they gave educational and technical aid. The Alliance for Progress, begun in 1961, provided aid to Latin America. The successes of the Alliance were limited, however, and the United States ended the program in 1974.

Civil rights becomes a major issue. Another issue of increasing concern in the postwar years was civil rights — the movement to gain equality for black Americans. Blacks had benefited from the nation's growing prosperity, and urban blacks in particular had greater earning power and a wider choice of jobs. Social and economic discrimination because of race continued, however.

In the 1940's, civil rights leaders began a struggle against discrimination and segregation. Leaders of the movement turned to the federal courts, and, in a series of cases beginning in 1941, the Supreme Court ruled against various forms of segregation. A Supreme Court decision in 1954 — *Brown* v. *Board of Education of Topeka* — overturned an 1896 Court decision that allowed "separate but equal" schools for black students. The court ordered schools to end segregation with "all deliberate speed." Resistance to this decision forced President Eisenhower to send federal troops to Arkansas in

Martin Luther King, Jr., won international respect for his leadership of the civil rights movement. Note the picture of Mohandas Gandhi on the wall.

1957 to protect black students. In the early 1960's, President Kennedy used federal marshals in Mississippi and National Guard units in Alabama to ensure that black students were allowed to enter state universities.

Civil rights leaders used other means besides the federal courts to achieve their goals. Following the example set by Gandhi in India (page 766), blacks began to seek justice through nonviolent direct action. In 1955, blacks in Alabama boycotted a bus system for its discriminatory policies. The leader of the boycott was a Baptist minister named Martin Luther King, Jr.,[2] who soon emerged as a national leader in the drive for civil rights. Boycotts and "sit-ins" throughout the South forced businesses to desegregate their facilities.

---

[2] For his leadership and courage, King was awarded the Nobel Peace Prize in 1964. In 1968 he was assassinated. Beginning in 1986, the day of his birth (January 15) was celebrated as a national holiday.

Civil rights demonstrations continued and spread to the North. In 1963, more than 200,000 Americans took part in a march on Washington, D.C., in support of the civil rights movement. While most protests were peaceful, devastating riots did break out in black areas of major cities between 1965 and 1967.

President Kennedy had proposed a new civil rights law but was assassinated in November, 1963, before the bill was passed. His successor, Lyndon Johnson, persuaded Congress to pass the Civil Rights Act of 1964, banning discrimination in employment, in access to public accommodations, and in the use of federal funds. A year later Congress passed the Voting Rights Act, which allowed federal workers to register voters who had been denied registration by the states. The Civil Rights Act of 1968 banned housing discrimination.

The struggle for equality widens. During the late 1960's and early 1970's, the struggle for black equality led other groups to raise their voices against injustice. Hispanics sought release from generations of poverty and discrimination. American Indians criticized government policies that ignored treaties and destroyed tribal ties and customs.

Women constituted the largest group struggling for equality. After the founding in 1966 of the National Organization for Women (NOW), women conducted campaigns seeking job opportunities and equal pay. Some reforms were made, which gave women equal rights in areas such as obtaining credit or borrowing money. Jobs in nontraditional fields became more accessible to women, and significant numbers of women reached high-level positions in government and business for the first time.

American women continued, however, to face obstacles to advancement. Some supported a constitutional amendment known as the Equal Rights Amendment (ERA), which forbade discrimination based on sex. The amendment had many opponents and failed to win approval by the necessary number of state legislatures.

Patterns of immigration shift. The proportion of ethnic groups in the nation's population was affected by legislation passed by Congress in 1965. This legislation amended the United States' immigration laws, doing away with the old system of nation-by-nation quotas that had favored Europeans. The new system set one overall quota for the Western Hemisphere and another for the Eastern Hemisphere. The result was an enormous wave of new immigrants, especially from Asia and Latin America. Between 1920 and 1940, for example, the top three nations from which immigrants had come were Canada, Germany, and Italy. In 1984, however, Mexico, the Philippines, and Vietnam led all other nations in numbers of people entering the United States. Other nations from which large numbers of immigrants came in the 1970's and 1980's were Korea, China, India, Jamaica, the Dominican Republic, and Cuba.

Watergate brings Nixon's resignation. From 1972 to 1975, much of the nation's attention was concentrated on the issue and controversy that became popularly known as "Watergate." In June, 1972, five men were arrested for breaking into the Democratic Party's national headquarters at the Watergate, an apartment-and-office complex in Washington, D.C. The men, found to be connected to President Nixon's re-election committee, were convicted of burglary and wiretapping.

Evidence was soon uncovered, first by newspaper reporters and then by a Senate investigating committee, that high-ranking presidential aides had planned the burglary and concealed evidence about it. In addition, they had engaged in a series of other illegal activities. Several of the President's top aides were eventually tried and convicted of crimes in connection with the Watergate burglary and the cover-up that followed it.

President Nixon disputed evidence that connected him with the cover-up. The Judiciary Committee of the House of Representatives recommended that Nixon be impeached, however. Nixon resigned on August 9, 1974, and was succeeded by Vice President Gerald Ford, who later pardoned Nixon for any federal crimes he might have committed. Though Watergate had shocked the nation, the smooth transfer of power to a new President had demonstrated the strength of America's constitutional government.

A tragedy forces reconsideration of the space program. A source of pride for the American people since the early 1960's had been the nation's impressive achievements in the exploration of space (page 842). On January 28, 1986, however, the space program suffered a stunning blow. The space shuttle *Challenger,* setting out on a routine mission, exploded shortly after launch. All seven crew members, including teacher-astronaut Christa McAuliffe, lost their lives.

A presidential commission was appointed to investigate the causes of the disaster. It found that the National Aeronautics and Space Administration (NASA) had tried to launch more missions than it was capable of handling. The commission urged that the shuttle program continue but recommended a series of major changes aimed at improving safety standards.

The shuttle tragedy drew Americans' attention to the space program as a whole and led to much rethinking of the nation's long-range goals in space. "This has been a difficult passage for America," said President Ronald Reagan, "but we will go on, just as the crew of the *Challenger* would have wanted us to."

Leaders work to keep the economy strong. The nation's economy remained strong, but growth was interrupted as heightened inflation during the late 1960's was combined with recession and unemployment in the early 1970's. Presidents instituted various programs to solve economic problems. Nixon lowered taxes and interest rates to stimulate business and, in 1971, imposed three-month controls on wages, prices, and rents to increase consumer buying. Inflation continued under President Jimmy Carter, and was made worse by rising world prices for oil.

To stimulate production and curb inflation, President Ronald Reagan called for a reduction in taxes and cutbacks in government spending. Inflation rates declined and business activity increased. Reagan's economic policies were controversial, however. A major issue on which Americans disagreed was *how* government spending should be reduced. In general,

Reagan's supporters favored cuts in domestic programs, while his critics favored reductions in military spending. Since the Democratic-controlled House of Representatives had to approve annual budgets, compromises were made on both sides.

Another criticism of Reagan's economic policies concerned the rapid growth of the national debt. Many Americans believed that taxes should be raised to reduce the deficit. Others feared that a tax increase would lead to a recession, which would only make the problem worse. Although the unemployment rate declined gradually after 1983, unemployment, especially among minority groups, remained a concern throughout the 1980's.

Debate over economic issues during the Reagan presidency raised questions about the nation's complex tax laws. In an attempt to simplify the tax system and make it more fair, Congress passed a sweeping tax reform law in 1986. The new law eliminated many "loopholes" that had allowed some Americans to avoid paying their fair share of taxes. It also increased the taxes paid by corporations and reduced the percentage of their incomes that many Americans had to pay in income tax.

TIMETABLE

U.S. Presidents Since 1945

1945   Harry S. Truman (Democrat) becomes President at the death of Franklin D. Roosevelt.

1948   Truman is returned to office.

1952   Dwight D. Eisenhower (Republican) elected.

1956   Eisenhower is re-elected.

1960   John F. Kennedy (Democrat) elected.

1963   Lyndon B. Johnson (Democrat) becomes President after Kennedy's assassination and wins election in 1964.

1968   Richard M. Nixon (Republican) elected.

1972   Nixon is re-elected.

1974   Gerald Ford (Republican) sworn in after Nixon's resignation.

1976   Jimmy Carter (Democrat) elected.

1980   Ronald Reagan (Republican) elected.

1984   Reagan is re-elected.

FOREIGN AFFAIRS

The cold war tensions between the United States and the Soviet Union (Chapter 33) dominated United States foreign affairs from the end of World War II through the 1980's. The two superpowers competed for power and prestige, in both military and nonmilitary ways. The United States became militarily involved in Asia and sought new alliances.

The spread of communism brings charges of disloyalty. Soviet postwar expansion in Europe, as well as the mood of the cold war, intensified fears of communism, and some Americans began to worry about the presence of Communist spies and agents in the United States itself. In 1947, President Truman created the Loyalty Review Board to investigate government employees. The House of Representatives Un-American Activities Committee (HUAC) also began an investigation of the entertainment industry, and in 1950 a little-known senator from Wisconsin, Joseph McCarthy, began his own search for Communist spies. McCarthy accused hundreds of officials of disloyalty, destroying many people's reputations and livelihood on the basis of little or no evidence. McCarthy was finally censured by the Senate in 1954 after he failed to back up his charges of Communist activity in the army.

The United States becomes involved in the Vietnam War. Fear of the spread of communism in Asia as well as in Europe involved the United States in war in Southeast Asia. As France lost control over its colonies in Indochina in the early 1950's (page 740), United States military advisers were sent to help anti-Communist forces in Southeast Asia. In 1965, American troops were sent to Vietnam following a reported Communist attack on a United States torpedo boat in the Gulf of Tonkin, off the Vietnamese coast (map, page 771).

The Vietnam War dragged on, involving hundreds of thousands of United States troops (page 775). By 1968, American involvement in Southeast Asia was becoming more and more unpopular in the United States. Some Americans rejected the view that the war was vital to national security and that the United States had the responsibility to preserve order around the world. These dissenting Americans expressed their opinions in antiwar demonstrations in the late 1960's and early 1970's. In 1968 President Lyndon Johnson decided not to seek re-election but concentrated his efforts on achieving a cease-fire. At the end of March, 1968, he halted much of the bombing of North Vietnam. Peace talks began in Paris shortly afterwards.

A truce in Vietnam is negotiated. In his campaign for the presidency in 1968, Richard Nixon pledged to end the war honorably. Henry Kissinger, who served first as a national security adviser and then as Nixon's Secretary of State, became a dominant figure in foreign policy decisions in the Nixon era. In October, 1972, Kissinger and Le Duc Tho of North Vietnam worked out an agreement, and in 1973 a peace settlement was signed. Within a few months, American troops left Vietnam. The costs of the war to the United States had been great — more than 56,000 Americans killed and about 300,000 wounded. In addition, many American soldiers remained "missing in action."

The United States takes steps toward détente. The end of American involvement in Vietnam allowed United States leaders to concentrate on improving relations with China and the Soviet Union. Negotiating behind the scenes, Kissinger established a new understanding with officials in the People's Republic of China, leading to the announcement in 1971 that President Nixon would visit China the following year. This visit signaled a change in American policy and the beginning of scientific, cultural, and commercial exchanges between the two nations.

Later in 1972, Nixon became the first American President to visit Moscow since World War II. During the visit President Nixon and Soviet leader Brezhnev signed the first Strategic Arms Limitation Treaty (SALT) (page 733). The agreement limited the numbers and types of missiles each nation could have. Plans for commercial and scientific cooperation were also made. The American people hoped that presidential visits to China and the Soviet Union would be steps toward a lasting détente (page 733).

The visit of President Nixon to China signaled a drastic change in relations between the United States and China. Here the President and Mrs. Nixon are seen with Chinese leaders during their historic visit in 1972.

War in the Middle East brings an oil crisis. In 1973, the October War broke out in the Middle East (page 811). Because the United States supported Israel in the war, the oil-rich Arab countries placed an *embargo* on oil. That is, they forbade the shipment of oil to the United States. With about 25 percent of the nation's oil imports stopped, fuel prices rose, causing sharp increases in the cost of living. Even though imports were resumed in 1974, Nixon resolved to curb dependence on Arab oil, and new efforts were made to find alternative energy sources.

Carter stresses human rights. The election of Jimmy Carter as President in 1976 brought a new focus to foreign policy — the active promotion of human rights around the world. During his first years in office, Carter spoke out against *apartheid* in South Africa and Rhodesia. He also pressed Soviet leaders to release imprisoned dissidents and to allow Soviet Jews to emigrate.

Carter's administration brought other developments in foreign affairs. In 1977, a long-lasting dispute with Panama over the Canal Zone was settled (page 825). In 1979 full diplomatic relations were established with the People's Republic of China. Carter's greatest diplomatic triumph was achieved in 1978 as he mediated peace talks between President Sadat of Egypt and Prime Minister Begin of Israel. As a result of the "Camp David agreements," the two Middle Eastern leaders signed a peace treaty in 1979 (page 812).

Americans confront terrorism. While Egypt and Israel were involved in peace talks, a crisis developed in Iran. In November, 1979, a mob invaded the United States embassy in Tehran and seized staff members as hostages (page 803). The Ayatollah Khomeini, Iran's new leader, declared that the hostages would be released only when the United States returned the shah to Iran for trial. President Carter refused to turn over the shah. He tried to gain the release of the hostages by means of negotiations, a trade embargo, and a military rescue mission, but these efforts failed. Finally, Carter agreed to return Iranian funds in the United States and cancel Iran's debts. After almost fifteen months in captivity, the American hostages were released in January, 1981.

Over the next decade, Americans increasingly became the targets of terrorist attacks (page 813). In 1983 and 1984, for example, there were about 400 attacks on Americans abroad. These attacks included bombings, kidnappings, murders, and hijackings. Many of them were traced to groups secretly aided by Muammar al Qaddafi, the Libyan ruler (page 808). The United States responded with an economic boycott of Libya, but the boycott was ineffective because other Western nations refused to join in.

In April, 1986, President Reagan ordered American bombers to strike at terrorist-related targets in Libya. The attack was in retaliation for a bombing in Berlin that had killed one American and wounded many more. U.S. offi-

831

American President Ronald Reagan (left) met with Prime Minister Nakasone of Japan, President Mitterand of France, and Prime Minister Thatcher of Great Britain at the Economic Summit of Industrial Nations, held in Tokyo in 1986.

cials reported they had "indisputable evidence" linking the Berlin bombing to a Libyan terrorist network. Reagan made clear that the purpose of the air strike was to bring pressure on Qaddafi to halt the anti-American terrorist campaign.

The nation's antiterrorist policy was caught up in the flood of questions that followed a disclosure of secret arms shipments to Iran. It was revealed in late 1986 that officials of the Reagan administration had arranged for the sale of weapons to Iran. The transaction was handled in a way that sidestepped legal restrictions and government policy. President Reagan reported to the nation that he had known of the action. He had hoped to improve relations with Iran and get that country's help in securing the release of American hostages held by terrorists in Lebanon. It was soon revealed that some of the money received for the weapons had been secretly channeled to anti-government forces in Nicaragua, against the wishes of Congress.

In official investigations, under way in 1987, questions were raised about the extent of White House knowledge of the undercover operations and whether laws had been broken. Many Americans worried that the contradiction between stated policy and secret activities might affect the government's ability to conduct foreign relations.

Central American policy becomes an issue. After the Vietnam experience, many Americans were reluctant to concern themselves with Third World conflicts, but United States involvement in Central America became a major foreign policy issue during the Reagan years. The administration charged that the Nicaraguan Sandinistas (page 824) were not only oppressing their own people but were committed to spreading Communist revolution throughout Central America. A Communist-controlled Central America, warned administration officials, would pose a grave threat to the security of the United States. For this reason, President Reagan backed both the Nicaraguan guerrillas (called contras) who were trying to overthrow the Sandinistas, and the government of El Salvador, which was fighting a Communist guerrilla movement (page 825) in that country.

The Reagan policy was heatedly debated in Washington and throughout the United States. Some critics said that the United States should not intervene in the internal affairs of Latin American nations. It was also argued that the anti-Communists supported by the United States government were not deserving of American support because of their human rights abuses. Critics warned, moreover, that Reagan's policies might lead to American military involvement in an unwinnable war — "another Vietnam." Administration critics agreed that the United States should seek a negotiated settlement with the Nicaraguan government rather than send military aid to the contras. Administration supporters argued that the Sandinistas would not negotiate a fair settlement unless they faced a serious military threat. In

1986, Congress voted by a narrow margin to send military aid to the contras, but the debate over Central American policy seemed far from over.

Meanwhile, the United States had been drawn into military action in another part of Latin America. In 1983, the Marxist government of the small Caribbean island of Grenada (gruh-NAY-duh) was overthrown by more extreme Marxists. United States troops invaded the island, expelled the Marxist government, and restored democratic institutions to the former British colony. American soldiers, who had been welcomed by the majority of Grenadians, left the island in 1985.

Americans debate national policy toward South Africa. What the nation's stand on South Africa should be was another urgent topic of debate in the late 1980's. South Africa had long been an ally of the United States; its strategic location and valuable mineral deposits made it an important country. When black unrest called world attention to South Africa's repressive racial policies (page 791), Americans disagreed about the best way to respond. The Reagan administration favored a policy of "constructive engagement," meaning that the United States would continue to do business with South Africa and use its status as an ally to press for change. Critics, however, charged that constructive engagement was ineffective. They called on the United States government to adopt strict economic sanctions against South Africa in order to force that country's government to step up the pace of reform. In 1986, Congress took such a step by passing, over President Reagan's veto, legislation that would impose sanctions on South Africa.

Soviet actions draw criticism. Soviet-American relations continued to be the major concern in foreign policy debates through the 1980's. While Presidents Ford and Carter continued the policy of détente begun by Richard Nixon (page 733), events late in Carter's presidency began to raise doubts about the Soviet Union's intentions. In 1979, Soviet troops invaded Afghanistan (page 750). Fearing a possible thrust of Soviet forces into Pakistan or Iran, Carter placed an embargo on sales of American grain to the Soviet Union, called for a boycott of the upcoming Moscow Olympic Games, and asked the Senate to postpone consideration of the arms limitation treaty he had signed earlier that year (SALT II).

Soviet policies drew even sharper criticism from President Reagan. The United States reacted strongly to repression of the Polish workers' movement, Solidarity, and to the threat of a Soviet invasion of Poland in 1981 (page 753). The Soviet Union was also condemned by most of the non-Communist world in 1983, when a Soviet fighter plane shot down a South Korean commercial airliner that had accidentally entered Soviet air space. All 269 persons on board were killed. In defense of this action, the Soviet Union declared that the airliner had ignored warning signals and that the Soviet air defense officials who ordered the attack had no way of knowing the target was a civilian airplane.

Efforts to reduce armaments continue. Although relations between the United States and the Soviet Union were considerably cooler after 1979, negotiations on arms limitation continued. The SALT II treaty had never been ratified by the Senate, but arms control talks resumed in Geneva in 1982. The talks reflected the heightened tension between the two nations. Though the negotiators were unable to reach agreement on significant issues, President Reagan and the new Soviet leader, Gorbachev, did meet at a summit conference held in Geneva, Switzerland, in late 1985, and signed a series of agreements on scientific, cultural, and trade matters.

Less than a year later, Reagan and Gorbachev again met, this time in Reykjavik (RAY-kyuh-veek), the capital of Iceland (map, page 862). The two leaders came close to reaching an agreement that would have drastically reduced the nuclear arsenals of both superpowers. But one major issue stood in the way. This was President Reagan's Strategic Defense Initiative (SDI), a plan to develop an antimissile system based in space. The Soviet leader asked for a ten-year delay in development of the SDI system. President Reagan said, however, that the plan was essential for America's future defense. Despite the failure of the Iceland summit meeting, arms-control negotiators continued their regular meetings in Geneva.

CHECK-UP

1. Vocabulary: *embargo, recession.*
2. What changes in ways of living and population followed World War II?
3. (a) Why was the *Brown* v. *Board of Education* decision (1954) important? (b) What civil rights legislation was passed during the 1960's? (c) What groups, in addition to black Americans, demanded equal rights?
4. What changes have there been in immigration since 1965?
5. How did the Watergate affair bring about the resignation of a President?
6. What major economic issues have faced the United States in recent years?
7. (a) How did U.S. troops become involved in Vietnam? (b) When and how did that involvement come to an end?
8. What steps did U.S. leaders take during the 1970's to improve relations (a) with China? (b) with the Soviet Union?
9. (a) What were important diplomatic events of the Carter administration? (b) How did terrorism become a major concern in U.S. foreign relations?
10. What issues have been debated in U.S. policy on (a) Central America? (b) Africa?

3 Canada Strives To Maintain Unity

By the end of World War II, despite a relatively small population and a short history as an independent nation, Canada had become one of the world's leading industrial nations. In the period of growth and prosperity that followed the war, the young country had to face a number of serious challenges to its unity.

Laurier lays the foundations for growth. Canada's economic success, though stimulated by World War II, was the result of earlier developments. Prime Minister Wilfrid Laurier (LAW-ree-ay), who led Canada from 1896 to 1911, encouraged immigration, the building of new railroads, and more trade with the United States. Canada entered a period of economic growth that was interrupted only by the Great Depression of the 1930's. Rich mineral deposits were discovered, while lumbering and manufacturing made rapid gains. Capital for investment in Canada's expansion poured in from Great Britain and the United States.

War spurs Canada's economy. As a Commonwealth nation, Canada not only sent troops into World War II but also produced vast quantities of food, materials, and munitions for the Allies. To meet the demand for food, Canadian farmers stepped up their use of machinery and brought new lands under cultivation. Canada's most dramatic wartime growth, though, was in industry. The nation's abundant natural resources, as well as its labor force, factories, and transportation systems, were directed toward the war effort. Canadian-built ships, tanks, and aircraft played an important part in the Allied victory.

Prosperity continues after the war. The postwar years brought continuing prosperity to Canada. Production increased greatly, population grew, and unemployment remained low. Established industries expanded and new ones developed. Oil was discovered in Alberta in 1947, making Canada an important oil-producing nation. Giant hydroelectric projects in nearly every province produced electricity. The discovery of vast deposits of uranium in Saskatchewan and Ontario in the 1950's led to the building of nuclear power stations to generate electricity.

Canada's postwar growth also was stimulated by the completion in 1959 of the St. Lawrence Seaway, a joint project with the United States that opened the Great Lakes to ocean shipping from the Atlantic. The seaway helped the economy on both sides of the border and provided some states and provinces with hydroelectric power. Except during winter months, freighters from distant countries could serve the heartland of North America. The seaway carried more shipping each year than the Suez and Panama canals combined.

Problems accompany growth. By the 1980's, Canada was among the world's leading manufacturing and trading nations, but it had some major economic problems. Its prosperity

834

Many Canadian exports are shipped to international markets by way of the St. Lawrence Seaway (above, near Montreal).

was based largely on the export of raw materials and semi-manufactured goods, such as pulp (a mixture of materials used to make paper) and lumber. On the other hand, Canada imported more manufactured goods per person than any other country in the world. Many Canadians wanted more of their raw materials to be used by their own industries, to decrease dependence on imports and to provide jobs for the nation's unemployed.

The United States plays a major role in Canada's economy. Canadians also expressed concern over their country's relations with the United States, Canada's most important trading partner. Almost three quarters of Canada's exports were sold in the United States, while well over half of Canada's imports came from its neighbor to the south. American stockholders and companies owned or controlled more than half of Canada's major industries.

American involvement in the Canadian economy strained relations between the two countries. Some Canadians saw their reliance on American markets and capital as a threat to their independence and economic growth. They argued that profits from the sale of their raw materials and manufactured goods did not fully benefit Canadians, and they feared the effects of American business recessions. On the other hand, friction resulted from heavy exports of Canadian lumber to the United States. American lumber interests charged that low-priced

Canadian forest products had an unfair advantage in competition with American products.

Canadian provinces seek more influence. The war effort had demanded national unity among Canadians. In the postwar years, however, disagreements arose over the division of power between the federal government and the provinces, particularly in economic matters. Canada's provincial governments were considered the owners of resources, but the central government regulated all trade. This led to disputes between the federal government and some provinces. For example, the province of Alberta wanted to use American investment capital to open up new oil fields, but the federal government wanted to reduce such investments. In Saskatchewan, the provincial government began buying out American-owned potash mines in spite of the opposition of federal leaders, who believed that profits from mining should benefit the entire country.

The debate between the federal government and the provinces also moved into other areas. For instance, Canada's national leaders wished to improve health care, unemployment

TIMETABLE

The Changing Americas

1910	Revolution in Mexico overthrows Díaz.
1914	The Panama Canal is completed.
1917	A new constitution sets goals for Mexico.
1930	Getulio Vargas comes to power in Brazil.
1946	Juan and Evita Perón lead Argentina.
1952	Batista becomes dictator in Cuba.
1954	U.S. Supreme Court rules against "separate but equal" schools for black students.
1959	Canada and the United States open the St. Lawrence Seaway. Fidel Castro overthrows Batista in Cuba.
1961	The United States cuts ties with Cuba.
1964	Congress passes the Civil Rights Act.
1968	A new political party urges Quebec's separation from Canada.
1973	Allende's government is overthrown in Chile.
1974	Nixon resigns the presidency.
1977	The United States and Panama agree to transfer control of the Panama Canal.
1979	Sandinista rebels take control of Nicaragua's government.
1982	The Constitution Act gives Canada full self-rule.

benefits, pensions for the elderly, and education — even though these involved powers usually delegated to the provinces. Some provincial leaders charged that there was already too much federal interference in their affairs. All the provinces sought a larger share of tax money to improve local government services and to stimulate the economy.

French Canadians seek influence in Quebec. The most serious threat to national unity stemmed from the situation of the French-speaking majority in the province of Quebec. Eighty percent of Quebec's people were French-speaking or bilingual, yet most of its businesses were run by English-speaking Canadians. The language used in business and government, moreover, was English, creating hardships for those who spoke only French. In addition, living standards in Quebec were below the national average. As a result, political leaders in the province began demanding major reforms in the 1960's.

Soon a "quiet revolution" was under way in Quebec. The provincial government, dominated by French Canadians, began to establish more self-government for Quebec. Their goal was expressed in the slogan "Masters in our own house." In 1962, for example, the province purchased the privately owned electric companies and took control of that industry. In an attempt to strengthen Quebec's educational and cultural life, the province took over the schools from the Catholic Church. In addition, provincial leaders initiated cultural exchanges with French-speaking nations.

Some French-Canadian leaders wanted more than reform — they sought Quebec's separation from Canada. Quebec, they argued, was not a province but a nation within the nation, with its own culture and history. They believed that Quebec's French-speaking people were different from other Canadians and should have the right to govern themselves.

The federal government opposed these attempts to separate Quebec from Canada. After the election in 1968 of Pierre Elliott Trudeau, a French Canadian, as prime minister, the federal government moved to improve relations with Quebec. English-speaking federal officials were encouraged to learn French. Provinces were asked to make both English and French

Canada has two official languages, French and English. In most provinces, signs like the one above are in both languages. In French-speaking Quebec, however, many signs are only in French.

their official languages and to establish schools for French-speaking children. Moreover, English-Canadian schools were urged to teach French as a second language. Firms doing business in Quebec sought talented French Canadians as executives. More federal funds were given to the province, and the two levels of government tried to find ways of cooperating. In 1969, Canada enacted the Official Languages Act, which recognized both English and French as national languages.

Separatists call for independence. Despite these reforms, several separatist groups in Quebec joined together in 1968 to form a new political party the *Parti Québécois* (par-TEE kay-bek-WAH). Its leader, René Lévesque (lay-VEK), sought political independence from Canada. Lévesque realized, however, that Quebec could not survive without economic ties to the rest of the country. He called for political sovereignty for Quebec but economic association with the rest of Canada. In the provincial elections of 1970, Lévesque won much support but was defeated by Robert Bourassa (boo-rah-SAH).

Many separatists found it difficult to accept Lévesque's defeat. Impatient for change, a small group resorted to violence, planting bombs and engaging in kidnappings and robberies. At the request of Quebec's government, Prime Minister Trudeau placed Montreal under martial law until order was restored. In 1971 the crisis ended after some of the terrorists were arrested and tried for their crimes.

In 1976, Lévesque was elected premier of Quebec on a platform of political independence for the province. A referendum, or popular vote, in 1980, however, showed that a substantial majority of people in Quebec opposed separation from Canada.

Canada becomes involved in world affairs. World War II not only brought prosperity to Canada but also ended the country's traditional policy of isolationism. Geography, trade, and cultural interests all compelled Canada to take a more active role in international affairs. With the United States on its southern border and the Soviet Union lying across the polar ice cap, Canada would surely be involved in any confrontation between the two superpowers. Moreover, Canada's trade routes crisscrossed the Atlantic and Pacific oceans, and the country also had cultural ties with both French- and English-speaking countries in Europe and the Third World. All these factors shaped Canada's foreign policies during the postwar period.

Canada supports peace-keeping efforts. Canada helped create the United Nations in 1945 and remained a major supporter of that organization. Canada contributed funds and troops to almost every peace-keeping operation undertaken by the United Nations.

From the beginning of the cold war in 1946, Canada stood firmly with the nations of the West in opposing Soviet expansion. In 1949 Canada played a major role in the creation of NATO (page 728) and contributed troops, funds, and materials. Canadians also gave economic aid to developing nations.

Canada and the United States cooperate for defense. As in trade and economic matters, Canada's closest ties in foreign affairs and defense were with the United States. When World War II began in Europe in 1939, Prime Minister Mackenzie King and President Franklin D. Roosevelt had agreed to cooperate closely to protect the North American continent. This cooperation continued during the postwar era.

The two countries together planned, built, and operated the radar installations defending the continent. In 1957 the North American Air Defense Command (NORAD) was established to ward off a possible air attack on North America. Both nations agreed to pool information and staff a single headquarters.

Canada seeks its own path. Despite its close relations with the United States, Canada often chose a separate path in foreign affairs. While Canada provided the United States with supplies for the war in Vietnam, for example, it also admitted those Americans who were unwilling to be drafted into the armed forces for service in Vietnam. Moreover, Canada continued its trade with Cuba after the United States had cut off commerce with that nation, and it granted recognition to the People's Republic of China before the United States did.

Canada ends its legal ties to Britain. In 1982, Canada also gained increased independence from Britain. While it remained a member of the Commonwealth of Nations, its last legal ties to Britain were ended when Queen Elizabeth II approved the Constitution Act of 1982. Under this act, Canada gained control over its own constitution and was able to add a charter of rights guaranteeing basic rights and liberties. (Previously, the British Parliament had to approve any changes in the constitution established by the British North America Act.)

CHECK-UP

1. (a) How did World War II affect Canada's economy? (b) What important resources were discovered in the postwar years?
2. Why did many Canadians express concern over United States involvement in the Canadian economy?
3. (a) What problems of Quebec's French-speaking people came to national attention in the 1960's? (b) What changes did the Quebec government make?
4. (a) How did Canada and the United States cooperate for defense? (b) In what ways did the two nations choose different paths in foreign affairs?
5. How did Canada's ties with Britain change in the 1980's?

Chapter 38 Review

Summary

Throughout the twentieth century, Latin Americans sought various paths toward economic development. Poverty, inflation, unemployment, and dependence on foreign capital persisted, however. The presence of a Communist government in Cuba created political tensions, and Central America became a major battleground for conflicting economic and political outlooks.

The United States prospered in the postwar years, and affluence spurred programs of aid at home and abroad. Postwar leaders worked to keep the economy strong, initiating programs to face economic challenges such as inflation. Other important domestic issues also faced the United States. These included the growing movement for equal rights, the protests of the Vietnam era, and the transfer of power after the Watergate scandal.

The United States emerged from World War II as a superpower. Cold war tensions influenced foreign policy from the end of the war into the 1980's, and United States leaders exerted influence in world trouble spots such as the Middle East and Central America. While the 1970's was a period of détente and arms negotiations with the Soviet Union, relations became strained once again in the 1980's.

In Canada, increased production during World War II spurred the economy, and prosperity continued after the war. Economic and military dependence on the United States created concern, however. Conflicts between the provinces and the federal government endangered national unity, as western provinces sought to control their own resources and French Canadians in Quebec threatened to separate from Canada.

Vocabulary Review

1. Match the following terms with the listed definitions: *détente, embargo, martial law, recession.*
(a) A temporary slowdown in business activity.
(b) The relaxing of tensions between nations.
(c) A decision by one country to stop the sale and shipment of certain goods to another.
(d) Control maintained by military forces.

2. In the items below, explain the importance of each term listed to the history of the region or country named.
(a) *Latin America:* caudillos, juntas, Sandinistas, Canal Zone, PEMEX.
(b) *United States:* Peace Corps, House Un-American Activities Committee, SALT II, *Brown v. Board of Education,* Civil Rights Act of 1964.
(c) *Canada:* Official Languages Act, *Parti Québecois,* Constitution Act of 1982.

People to Identify

Match the following people with the numbered phrases that describe them: *Salvador Allende, Jimmy Carter, Fidel Castro, Porfirio Díaz, Martin Luther King, Jr., Henry Kissinger, Wilfrid Laurier, Evita Perón, Omar Torrijos, Pierre Trudeau, Emiliano Zapata.*
1. Caudillo who brought order to Mexico in the later 1800's.
2. Leader of Cuban revolution in 1956.
3. Argentine political leader who gained support from the poor.
4. Marxist president of Chile, 1970 to 1973.
5. Leader of the Mexican peasants in a guerrilla war against government troops.
6. Canadian prime minister who worked for national unity in the 1970's.
7. Secretary of State who guided U.S. foreign policy decisions in the early 1970's.
8. American President who mediated peace talks between Egypt and Israel.
9. Minister who led the civil rights movement in the United States in the 1960's.
10. Prime minister of Canada from 1896 to 1911.
11. General who led the movement for Panamanian control of the Canal.

Relating Geography and History

1. **Locating places.** Locate each of the following on a map in this chapter:
(a) Nicaragua   (d) Cuba
(b) El Salvador   (e) Guatemala
(c) Honduras   (f) Panama Canal

2. Interpretation. Since World War II, Canada has increased production of many raw materials and semi-manufactured goods. (a) What natural resources has Canada developed for export to other nations? (b) Find the St. Lawrence Seaway on a map in an atlas or encyclopedia. What bodies of water does it connect? (c) How has the St. Lawrence Seaway contributed to Canada's economic growth?

Discussion Questions

1. (a) How did the economic problems of Latin American nations in the twentieth century reflect colonial policies? (b) What political patterns emerged from these economic problems?

2. (a) How did the economic policies of Porfirio Díaz create problems for Mexico? (b) What major reforms were made by the Constitution of 1917 and the Cárdenas government? (c) What economic problems continued in Mexico, and why?

3. (a) Compare the changes made by the Perón government in Argentina and the Vargas government in Brazil. (b) What brought the overthrow of the Allende government in Chile? (c) Why have recent governments in Brazil, Argentina, and Chile been criticized for human rights violations?

4. (a) How did the United States become involved in Cuban politics about 1900? (b) How did this affect U.S. reactions to the changes made by Castro? (c) What incidents increased tensions between the United States and Cuba?

5. (a) What actions of the Somoza government in Nicaragua led to its overthrow? (b) What changes were made by the Sandinista government? (c) What caused civil war to begin in El Salvador? (d) How was Honduras involved in the conflicts in El Salvador and Nicaragua?

6. How did cold war tensions influence United States policy regarding (a) loyalty investigations? (b) involvement in Vietnam? (c) détente? (d) What other foreign policy questions arose after World War II?

7. (a) List the goals of the civil rights movement of the 1960's and 1970's. (b) How successful was the movement in achieving them? (c) How did this movement relate to other groups' protests against inequalities in American society?

8. (a) What twentieth-century developments led to Canada's postwar economic prosperity? (b) What factors in U.S.-Canadian relations caused concern in Canada? (c) What issues were a threat to Canadian unity?

Reading Primary Sources

One of the leading advocates of Quebec separatism was René Lévesque. In his book *An Option for Quebec,* Lévesque explained the French Canadians' deep commitment to maintaining their own language and culture. Read the selection and answer the questions that follow.

> We are Québecois.
> What that means first and foremost — and if need be, all that it means — is that we are attached to this one corner of the earth where we can be completely ourselves: this Quebec, the only place where we have the unmistakable feeling that "here we can really be at home." Being ourselves is essentially a matter of keeping and developing a personality that has survived for three and a half centuries.

(a) How does the separatists' slogan "Masters in our own house" relate to the feelings Lévesque describes? (b) Keeping in mind that Canada's first European settlers were French, explain the final sentence in the quotation. (c) The Official Languages Act (page 836) was passed the year after this was written. How did this act relate to Lévesque's statements?

Skill Activities

1. Making a time line. To see the relationship in time of events in the Americas, make a time line showing the following developments. Use the chapter to find the specific date for each event.

> The St. Lawrence Seaway is opened.
> Mexican government takes over oil companies.
> Juan and Evita Perón become leaders in Argentina.
> Fidel Castro leads a revolution against the Batista government.
> The *Parti Québecois* is formed.
> Argentine troops invade the Falklands.
> Arbenz is overthrown in Guatemala.
> President Nixon resigns after Watergate.
> Sandinistas take control in Nicaragua.
> A cease-fire agreement is made in Vietnam.
> President Nixon visits China.
> Panama Canal Treaty is signed.
> "Separate but equal" schools are declared illegal by U.S. Supreme Court.

As people left their home planet for the first time, they could see the earth from a new point of view. Through the swirling clouds of the atmosphere, this picture shows the Indian Ocean, with Africa to the left and the Arabian Peninsula above.

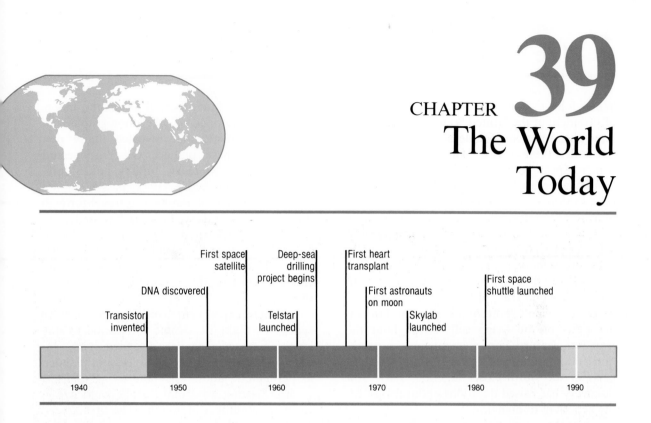

The world in the last decades of the twentieth century was a place of rapid change in many areas, affecting people in every nation. As they had long dreamed of doing, humans left their own planet for the first time, sending spaceships into the galaxy and traveling to the moon. They also explored new areas of knowledge on Earth, making discoveries in science and medicine. The development of computers was basic to many of the advances of this period.

Change also occurred in the way many of the world's people lived, as industrialization and urbanization continued to increase. Hunger and poverty remained problems in many parts of the world, however, and some nations struggled for economic growth. Better and faster systems of transportation and communication increased contacts among the nations of the world, bringing greater understanding of the variety of peoples and cultures on the earth.

This chapter describes some of the scientific and technological changes that were taking place late in the twentieth century and also discusses new patterns of living that were developing in this period.

CHAPTER OUTLINE
1 The World Explores New Frontiers
2 Patterns of Living Change

1 The World Explores New Frontiers

When John F. Kennedy was seeking the office of President of the United States in 1960, he offered the American people a "New Frontier," but added these words: "The New Frontier of which I speak is not a set of promises — it is a set of challenges." People throughout the world have explored many new frontiers since the end of World War II, and these have proved to be *both* promises and challenges. Startling new discoveries have been made in science, medicine, and technology. Humans have walked on the moon and sent spacecraft into the distant regions beyond the planets. They have explored the deep regions of the ocean and the inner parts of the living cell. Throughout the twentieth century, improvements in transportation and communication have brought distant parts of the world closer together. Each new discovery has raised questions about its use for the benefit of humankind.

The space age opens up a new frontier. The launching of the satellite *Sputnik* in October, 1957, began the space age and opened a new frontier for human adventure, exploration, and dreams. The United States and the Soviet Union began to compete in space. Both nations worked toward sending up piloted spacecraft, and both were successful in the spring of 1961 (page 731). The United States successfully landed the first humans on the moon in 1969, while the Russians made the first "spacewalk" and exchanged crews between two spacecraft.

Space programs had tremendous scientific value. They revealed much new information about the earth and all the parts of the solar system. These discoveries had practical uses in communications, weather forecasting, agriculture, navigation, and countless other areas that affected people's everyday lives.

Space probes explore the solar system. Efforts to send humans into space were paralleled by those to create better and more versatile spacecraft run by instruments only. These space probes could undertake longer, more hazardous journeys than piloted flights. By the early 1980's, spacecraft from earth had landed on Venus and Mars as well as on the moon. They were equipped to take photographs and make experiments that revealed many new facts about these planets. Other spacecraft made flybys of Mercury, Jupiter, and Saturn. *Pioneer 10,* launched in 1972, passed Jupiter and then left the solar system to travel through the Milky Way galaxy. *Voyager 2* passed Jupiter in 1979, Saturn in 1981, and Uranus in 1986, and continued on into the outer reaches of the solar system. The interplanetary probes carried recorded information about the human race and world cultures.

People experiment with ways of living in space. To make it possible for people to stay longer in space, scientists designed space stations and shuttles. Space stations were planned as permanent laboratories and living quarters in orbit, testing ways that people could live in space for a number of months. The first American station, *Skylab,* was lifted into orbit by a rocket in 1973. Several Soviet *Salyut* space stations were launched from 1971 onward. One *Salyut* crew remained on board a space station for six months.

Also in the 1970's, the United States began to build a fleet of space shuttles, which were to be used for carrying cargo to space stations, placing satellites in orbit, making experiments, and launching spacecraft. Shuttles were designed to orbit the earth at up to 17,000 miles an hour. The shuttle *Columbia* made its first orbital flight in 1981. The explosion of *Challenger* (page 829) temporarily halted the schedule of shuttle flights.

Satellites create a worldwide communications network. The space age had begun with the launching of *Sputnik,* and scientists continued to launch other artificial satellites with a variety of uses. The United States and the Soviet Union remained leaders in the space program, but by 1970, France, Italy, Japan, and China had placed satellites of their own in orbit, mainly for weather and scientific observations. A number of other nations used American or Soviet launch facilities.

LINKING PAST AND PRESENT
The Red Planet

The planet Mars, Earth's nearest neighbor, was one of the first objects in the sky to capture the attention and imagination of ancient sky-watchers. Its reddish color reminded them of war and bloodshed, and from the Babylonians onward, astronomers named the planet after their people's god of war. The Greeks called it Ares; the Romans, Mars.

Of all the planets, Mars is most like Earth, and people long believed that it was — or had been — inhabited by intelligent beings. Observing long streaks on its surface, some astronomers in the late 1800's were sure these were canals built to carry water from the planet's polar ice cap. Science fiction writers populated the Mars of their imagination with a variety of creatures, including huge spidery monsters, four-armed green giants, and red-skinned humans.

The *Viking* and *Mariner* space probes in the 1970's found no Martians. Their photographs did show a dusty red landscape marked by huge volcanoes several miles high and deep canyons thousands of miles long.

Worldwide communication advanced greatly with communications satellites, first put to practical use in the early 1960's. Placed in orbit high above the earth, these satellites received and relayed telephone and television signals. On July 10, 1962, *Telstar 1* sent the first TV picture from the United States to Europe. An aluminum sphere about 35 inches in diameter, *Telstar 1* could relay one television channel or several hundred telephone voice messages. (*Telstar 2,* launched in 1963, sent the first transatlantic color TV program.) By the 1980's, communications satellites could carry 24 television channels and 18,000 two-way telephone conversations, and satellites with even greater capacities were planned.

Communications satellites eventually were formed into the Intelsat[1] system, which included more than a hundred nations in the 1980's. The basic system depended on three satellites positioned in orbit over the Atlantic, Pacific, and Indian oceans, reaching nearly every place on earth. The USSR also operated a satellite system known as Intersputnik, connecting Eastern European countries and Cuba. A number of countries had their own satellite systems.

In addition to carrying news and entertainment programs, communications satellites were used by many countries to broaden programs of public education. In Third World nations, televised instruction allowed education specialists to train teachers and teach students in far regions of the country. In the late 1970's India and Indonesia, for example, experimented with sending TV programs to rural villages by means of satellite transmissions.

Nations cooperate in space programs. As the Intelsat system showed, space exploration provided opportunities for cooperation among nations. The International Geophysical Year (July, 1957–December, 1958) marked a period of worldwide scientific efforts in the field of earth and space science. In 1975, American astronauts and Soviet cosmonauts met in space, docking their Soyuz and Apollo spacecraft in orbit together, sharing a meal, and carrying out joint experiments.

---

[1]*International Telecommunications Satellite Consortium.*

Landmarks in Technology

THE COMPUTER REVOLUTION

The course of history has been marked by several periods of change so great that they were termed "revolutions." The Commercial Revolution, the Scientific Revolution, and the Industrial Revolution all brought radical changes in the ways people lived and worked. The computer revolution of the late twentieth century rested on a tiny chip of silicon about the size of a fingernail. This "microchip" was part of a chain of developments that began in the 1940's and 1950's, when computers were huge machines run by vacuum tubes and filling an entire room. As first the transistor and then the silicon chip allowed the design of miniaturized circuits, computers became smaller, faster, and more useful in different applications. From slim pocket calculators to huge interplanetary rockets, computers brought a revolution in technology.

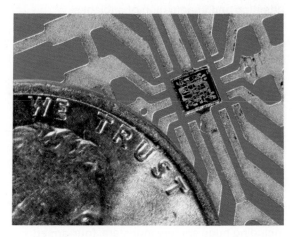

Many times smaller than the penny in the corner of the picture, the microchip (above) led to remarkable developments in the world of computers.

Computers were used for many purposes in the field of medicine. At left, a hospital staff worker looks up records stored in the hospital's computer. Computers also help nurses and physicians in making diagnoses, monitoring patients' conditions, and many other medical procedures.

Automation in many industries came to depend on computer-operated machines programmed to make repairs and perform certain routine or hazardous jobs. The robot at left is a welder at an industrial plant in Illinois.

Computers made it possible to combine and analyze large amounts of data quickly, generating graphics like this map (right) of areas in Richmond, Virginia. Many companies began special programs to retrain employees to work with computers. Below, workers at the Tokyo newspaper *Asahi Shimbun* discuss a new computer installation.

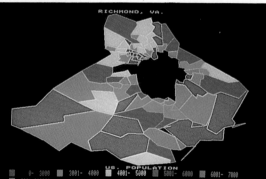

American astronauts on the flights of the space shuttle *Columbia* in 1984 tested new equipment to be used for making repairs outside the shuttle. One of the shuttle crew's tasks was to make repairs to a damaged satellite in orbit.

Because of the high costs of space programs, the European nations in 1975 formed the European Space Agency to coordinate their work. The agency's projects included scientific and communications satellites as well as an orbiting workshop-laboratory called the Spacelab. Designed to be carried on board the space shuttle, the Spacelab was equipped for experiments in space medicine, physics, and chemistry.

The earth's oceans are another frontier. International scientific cooperation was also a part of programs to explore another frontier — the unknown depths of the oceans. One large-scale international program, the Deep-Sea Drilling Project, was orginally begun by the United States but by the 1970's involved scientists from Britain, Japan, West Germany, France, and the USSR. From the ship *Glomar Challenger,* scientists took sample cores of the materials that make up the ocean floor. By analyzing these samples, they learned more about the crust of the earth, the geology of the sea floor, and the history of the earth.

Biologists explore the mysteries of the living cell. While some scientists were probing the depths of sea and space, others were investigating the tiny cells of which living things are made. In the mid-1800's Mendel (page 626) had found that certain traits were inherited. Later work showed that genes carried these traits from parent to offspring. No one, however, knew how this took place. In the 1950's James D. Watson, an American, and Francis H. Crick, a Briton, figured out the chemical processes that go on inside the gene.[2] In 1953 Watson and Crick described the structure of a large molecule known as DNA, which is present in the nucleus of living cells. It was, they found, made up of thousands of atoms, arranged like building blocks in a twisted double strand. The different arrangements of "building blocks" in each DNA molecule spelled out a "genetic code" that determined the biological traits of living things.

Medical science seeks new cures for diseases. The new knowledge of molecular biology — the chemistry of living things — helped medical researchers discover causes and cures for many illnesses. Advances in technology and in other areas of science also produced new drugs and new equipment.

One large group of new drugs, the antibiotics, were used to kill disease-causing bacteria. The first of these "wonder drugs," penicillin, had been discovered accidentally in 1928 by Alexander Fleming, a British bacteriologist, but it was not widely used until World War II. Another powerful antibiotic, streptomycin, also began to be used in the 1940's against tuberculosis, common in many parts of the world.

---

[2]Watson and Crick, along with British biophysicist Maurice Wilkins, were given the 1962 Nobel Prize for Medicine.

International health groups and individual countries used new methods in programs to wipe out other diseases that afflicted people in many nations. The World Health Organization (WHO) began a campaign in the 1950's to eliminate malaria, which affected about 50 million people a year in tropical countries. The program involved both better synthetic versions of quinine (page 359) and the destruction of mosquitoes that carry malaria. WHO later began a campaign to vaccinate people against smallpox (page 619), and by 1979 it was thought that this age-old epidemic disease had been wiped out throughout the world.

Advanced medical knowledge and technology helped doctors seek cures for heart disease, cancer, and other serious health problems. "Open heart" surgery was perfected in the United States and used in hospitals throughout the world. The first successful human heart-transplant operation was done in 1967 by a South African surgeon, Dr. Christiaan Barnard. Later, doctors transplanted other organs and tried to devise artificial organs that could replace diseased or damaged parts of the body.

Lasers concentrate the energy of light. Some startling new medical procedures depended on the laser (LAY-zur), a concentrated, high-energy beam of light. Laser surgery was used for delicate operations such as repairing tissue in the eye. Lasers also were applied in industry, engineering, space technology, communications, and scientific research. One specialized use was holography, a process for making three-dimensional photographs of objects.

Computers are the new frontier of high technology. Playing a vital part in all these advances in space exploration, communications, biology, and medicine was the computer — the invention that revolutionized the mid-twentieth-century world. By the 1980's, computers touched the lives of people in every nation. Their impact was felt first in the industrialized nations, where they were widely used to store and retrieve information in banks, libraries, stores, factories, offices, hospitals, and government. Computers guided spacecraft and were essential in controls for military equipment and weapons. Personal computers for home use were also becoming widespread by

Medical specialists at a clinic in Costa Rica were part of a worldwide effort to prevent illnesses and improve people's health.

the mid-1980's. (Pages 844–845 trace the development of computer technology.)

Two inventions that played major roles in the development of computers also had an impact on many other fields. The transistor, invented in 1947, replaced large vacuum tubes in many kinds of electronic equipment. It was the first step in making smaller and smaller circuits and controls. The microchip (or integrated circuit), which combined thousands of transistors on a tiny silicon chip, was another step. It made possible the development of smaller and faster computers and could also be used for the miniature circuits in products such as digital watches and pocket calculators.

CHECK-UP

1. What were the purposes of (a) space probes? (b) space stations? (c) space shuttles?

2. (a) What kinds of signals do communications satellites relay? (b) What did scientists discover by analyzing material from the sea floor?

3. (a) What discovery explained how biological traits are inherited? (b) What is a laser?

4. What effect did the transistor and the microchip have on the development of computers?

2 Patterns of Living Change

Revolutionary changes in science and technology in the mid-twentieth century had an impact on the lives of people throughout the world. This was a time of great social and economic change. Industrialization increased rapidly, and many people's standards of living rose. Nonetheless, there remained a great gap between the rich and poor nations of the world. Economic growth in many developing nations was slowed by lack of capital to develop sufficient industry and agriculture to support their growing populations. Changing patterns of work and lifestyle caused overcrowding in urban areas. These problems all interacted with a worldwide concern for the earth itself — the state of the environment and the availability of natural resources. At the same time, communication brought new understanding among the peoples of the world.

The world's cities grow larger. In the industrialized nations, rapid urbanization had begun along with the growth of industry (page 528). The great cities of these nations continued to grow, while people in less developed nations also began to flock to the cities in search of jobs and a new way of living.

Rapid urbanization created overcrowded conditions in many of the world's cities. As a result, architects began to look for new ways of providing adequate housing and work space for the millions of city dwellers. Many cities began to give new attention to their older downtown areas and to seek ways of making city life more interesting and pleasant.

In some places a new kind of "city" developed, made up of many neighboring large cities connected by good highways or high-speed mass transportation systems. Such a huge built-up urban area was called a ***megalopolis.*** These areas existed in many industrial nations — around Paris and London and in Germany's Ruhr Valley; in the Tokyo-Osaka region in Japan; and in the northeastern United States.

Population pressures affect many nations. Population growth in the cities was part of an overall increase in world population. From 2.5 billion in 1950, world population reached 5 billion in 1986. This was due in part to new medical discoveries that prevented epidemics, cut down the number of infant deaths, and increased people's life spans.

In the poorer developing countries, however, growing populations caused severe problems. The economic gains these nations made often were wiped out by the need to divide food and goods among more and more people every year. As a result, hunger, poverty, and disease remained a part of everyday life for millions of people throughout the world. A few nations, such as China and India, instituted programs for limiting population growth.

A gap separates rich and poor nations. Because of the difficulties they faced, many nations of the Third World remained desperately poor. The per capita GNP in such countries as Mali, Chad, Afghanistan, and Ethiopia was $170 or less a year. (In Switzerland, the wealthiest European nation, it was more than $14,000.) In many countries, also, a tiny fraction of the population held most of the nation's land and weatlh.

Japan has been a world leader in modern, high-speed mass transportation. Here the *Shinkansen,* or "bullet train," rushes past Mount Fuji.

CONTEMPORARY ARCHITECTURE

Twentieth-century architects explored new methods and materials in their designs, but the dominant style in city buildings was the angular International Style (right). The glass-walled twin towers house the Brazilian Congress in the new capital at Brasilia, planned in the 1950's by Oscar Niemeyer. Different approaches to urban spaces were used in Habitat (below), an apartment complex in Montreal, Canada (built in 1967 by Israeli architect Moshe Safdie), and in the Opera House in Sydney, Australia (above right), by Danish architect Joern Utzon. American architect Frank Lloyd Wright designed homes such as "Fallingwater" (above) to follow the forms of the natural landscape.

Rice, grown on flooded terraces or paddies like these in the Philippines, is the basic food crop for millions of people in many parts of the world.

In the 1960's a serious effort was made to use new seeds and farming methods to increase world food production. The resulting changes came to be known as the "Green Revolution."

Scientific efforts concentrated on basic crops such as rice, wheat and corn, and crop yields increased dramatically in India, Pakistan, Malaysia, and Turkey. The new methods had some drawbacks, however, because of the need to buy and use chemical fertilizers. In some places, too, the increased crops still did not keep pace with population growth.

Natural resources and the environment cause concern. Not only the food supply but the overall "quality of life" for the people of the world depended greatly on using natural resources wisely. Both farming and industry contributed to various kinds of pollution of the air and water. Chemicals from fields and factories, exhaust fumes from automobiles, smoke from industry, and radioactive materials were concerns in many nations, and various approaches to these environmental problems were tried. In the 1970's and 1980's people in northern Europe and North America also worried about "acid rain" — rainfall polluted by chemicals in the air — which affected lakes and streams far from industrial areas.

Protecting farmland, pasture land, and wildlife was a concern in many nations. Changing patterns of weather, plus overgrazing by herds of animals, destroyed once-fertile lands in the Middle East and Africa. As in ancient times, however, some countries found ways to irrigate land and "make the deserts bloom." Several African nations set aside huge parks to protect their wildlife (page 600), and international concern focused on programs to safeguard endangered animals.

The search for sources of energy sometimes conflicted with concerns for the environment. Mining coal or drilling for oil, for instance, could be harmful to wilderness or coastal areas. Nuclear plants to generate electricity were built in a number of nations; many people, however, had doubts about their efficiency and safety. The need for energy sources that would not harm the environment led to research into hydroelectric power, solar power, and the energy of wind and waves.

The plight of people in the poor nations was made worse by their awareness of the affluent lives of people elsewhere. World War II had introduced modern communications — especially radio — to millions of people in remote places. For the first time, isolated rural and village populations came into contact with the outside world, learning from the community radio about ways of life that were new and amazing to them. Their new knowledge about the rest of the world made people of the poorer nations hope for — and expect to have — better and more comfortable lives.

Improvements are made in agriculture. A crucial issue for poor and densely populated nations was producing enough food for their people. Many could neither grow enough food nor afford to buy it from abroad. Food shortages were sometimes also a problem even in the industrialized countries. The Soviet Union, for instance, often experienced shortages of grain.

CULTURAL EXCHANGE

Better communications gave people throughout the world opportunities to enjoy the art treasures and cultural heritage of their neighbors in other countries. Above, banners outside the Metropolitan Museum of Art in New York City announce exhibits of art treasures from three different nations and periods in history — seventeenth-century Dutch art, Renaissance Italy, and contemporary France. At right, brilliantly costumed performers from China bring the centuries-old style of the classic Peking Opera to the stage of an American theater.

World cultures interact. By the mid-twentieth century, urbanization, modern communications, and better transportation had brought more contact among people whose ways of life were very different. People in nearly every country now had opportunities to become acquainted with the different ways of life in their own and other nations. Television and radio could bring the same events and experiences to millions of people simultaneously. A family in Japan could watch a soccer match being played in Buenos Aires or in Hamburg. Audiences throughout the world could watch Olympic athletes compete in Yugoslavia or southern California. They could see televised performances of rock, opera, dance, or jazz from Vienna, Tokyo, London, or New York.

In music, art, dance, and literature, different cultures interacted and influenced one another. American jazz influenced both popular and classical music in other countries. British rock groups, led by the Beatles, influenced music worldwide in the 1960's, while the Beatles in turn incorporated elements of Indian music and American country-and-western in their songs. Films by directors such as Sweden's Ingmar Bergman, Italy's Federico Fellini, India's Satyajit Ray, and Japan's Akira Kurosawa drew international audiences.

Many nations set up "cultural exchanges" in which troupes of performers visited one another's countries. Nations also sent touring exhibits of paintings, sculptures, and archeological treasures that represented their heritage. With greater knowledge and understanding of other traditions and ways of life, people began to appreciate more deeply the diversity and richness of the modern world.

CHECK-UP

1. Vocabulary: *megalopolis.*
2. (a) What were the effects of urbanization in the twentieth century? (b) What were some factors in the rapid growth of world population after 1950? (c) What problems did population growth cause in the developing nations?
3. (a) What was the "Green Revolution"? (b) What environmental problems were concerns in the 1980's?
4. How did communications affect the exchange of cultural ideas among nations?

Chapter 39 Review

Summary

Important developments in science, technology, and ways of living shaped the world in the last decades of the twentieth century. Space programs brought scientific and technological advances, including probes to other planets, the space shuttle, and communications satellites. Discoveries were also made in such varied fields as oceanography and medicine — the structure of the ocean floor, the genetic code of living things, new kinds of antibiotics, and the development of lasers. Vital to all the new developments in science and technology — and to many other fields — was the computer.

Ways of living also changed, often in response to scientific and technological change. The growth of industry crowded more and more people into urban areas. This was part of an overall increase in world population, which was partly due to medical advances. Population growth intensified the burden of poverty and hunger on Third World nations in particular, and scientists searched for methods to increase world food production.

Many people became concerned about the environment, for farming, industry, and urbanization all affected the quality of the earth's air and water. The advances of the era also brought people of different nations closer together. New forms of communication and transportation helped people learn more about the other peoples and societies of the world.

Vocabulary Review

1. Use the following terms to fill in the blanks in this sentence: *megalopolis, urbanization.*

   As industry grew in many nations, __?__ became more rapid and sometimes brought about the growth of a huge "super-city," or __?__ .

2. Explain the importance of each of the following in recent scientific and technological advances: (a) *Sputnik,* (b) *Voyager 2,* (c) *Telstar,* (d) *Skylab,* (e) *Columbia,* (f) Intelsat system, (g) European Space Agency, (h) Deep-Sea Drilling Project, (i) microchip, (j) laser, (k) Green Revolution.

Relating Geography and History

1. **Making charts.** Using an encyclopedia or almanac, make a chart of the literacy rates and per capita incomes of the following six nations in East Asia: Japan, mainland China, China (Taiwan), North Korea, South Korea, the Philippines. (a) Which of these countries has the highest per capita income? (b) Which has the highest literacy rate? (c) What factors might affect the range of literacy rates and per capita incomes among nations in the same part of the world?

2. **Reports.** Use the *Readers' Guide to Periodical Literature* to find articles about the "Green Revolution" (page 850). Write a short report based on the information in the articles you find. In your report, include a discussion of the goals of the "Green Revolution," some of the new agricultural methods used, the results achieved, and the areas of the world in which the greatest increases in production were achieved.

Discussion Questions

1. (a) How have advances in the space program affected people's daily lives? (b) What were the goals of the space shuttle and space station programs?

2. (a) In what ways have communications satellites improved communication and education? (b) How have they helped the exchange of ideas among different peoples of the world?

3. (a) Describe how the discoveries related to DNA added to knowledge about human beings. (b) How did other discoveries in biology and medicine affect people's everyday lives?

4. How did computers change following the discovery of the transistor in 1947?

5. (a) What changes in society and economic life were happening throughout the world in the last decades of the twentieth century? (b) What problems particularly affected the developing nations? (c) How did better communications make people more aware of the economic gap between rich and poor nations?

Reading Primary Sources

The plans of NASA (National Aeronautics and Space Administration) included the building of more space stations in the future. Some of those plans are described in the following excerpts from an article in *Science Digest*. Read the excerpts and answer the questions that follow.

In one plan under consideration, a space shuttle will carry metal beams that will form the basic structure of the station. Working from . . . [the shuttle], astronauts will use the beams to build . . . the station's frame. Work and habitation modules, measuring not more than 55 feet long and 12 feet in diameter, will be built on the ground and boosted into orbit. One could serve as quarters for a crew of four to eight people; another could be a command center housing computers, utilities, and avionics [aviation electronics] equipment; a third might be a warehouse for storage of supplies.

Sensitive scientific equipment, such as space telescopes, are likely to orbit as free-flying satellites or on platforms many miles from the station to avoid contamination by propellant gases or jostling by human activity. Unmanned robotic craft, called tele-operators will retrieve the free-fliers for servicing.

With construction and operation of a space station, science fiction will become reality. But even this will eventually become routine. And once again the frontier will be pushed farther out, as far out, perhaps, as the moon. The time will then be ripe for the establishment of a lunar base.

(a) According to this article, what part does the space shuttle play in the construction of a new space station? (b) How many people might live and work in a space station? (c) How would space telescopes and other sensitive scientific equipment be kept separate from the space station? Why would this be necessary? (d) What might be the next frontier after the orbiting space station?

Skill Activities

1. Word research. American men and women in the space program are called *astronauts,* a word that comes from two Greek words: *astron,* meaning "star," and *nautes,* meaning "sailor." What do the related words in this list mean? (a) astronomy; (b) aster; (c) disaster; (d) nautical; (e) cosmonaut.

2. Making graphs. Use the following statistics to make a line graph showing world population growth since the fifteenth century — about the time the Age of Exploration began. When the graph is finished, answer these questions:

(a) When did world population begin to grow very rapidly?
(b) What major historical development was taking place about the same time?
(c) What relationship can you see between these two events?
(d) In terms of percentages, about how much did the population of the world grow between 1900 and 1990?

1400: 150 million	1850: 1.13 billion*
1520: 300 million	1900: 1.6 billion
1650: 510 million	1950: 2.5 billion
1700: 625 million	1970: 3.6 billion
1750: 710 million	1980: 4.5 billion
1800: 910 million	1990: 5.25 billion (est.)

*the same as 1,130 million

3. Research and reports. Choose a subject from the chapter or from the following list of suggestions. Use the library to find information and then write a report: (a) weather satellites used for forecasting; (b) space medicine; (c) information yielded by space probes about Venus, Jupiter, or Saturn; (d) the ship *Glomar Challenger;* (e) holography; (f) attempts to protect wildlife in Africa or another region; (g) acid rain; (h) the Sahel region of Africa; (i) international health programs; (j) new developments in city architecture (see page 849).

4. Taking a survey. In 1965 a Gallup Poll survey of Americans showed they were most concerned about the Vietnam War, civil rights, and the threat of war. Ten years later, major worries were unemployment and the high cost of living. A 1985 poll revealed that international tension and the possibility of war had again become a leading national concern, while unemployment and the high cost of living continued to cause anxiety. Decide on a sample group and take a similar survey of your own, asking people the question "What present-day problem are you most concerned about?"

5. Exploring the arts. In the last decades of the twentieth century, changes affected the arts as well as the sciences. Prepare a report on either (a) the influence of technological advances on modern music (such as electronic music), painting, or sculpture; or (b) cultural exchanges and influences among performing artists from different parts of the world.

Unit Eight Review

Review Questions

1. (a) Why did the United States assume leadership of the Western world after World War II? (b) What led to the "East-West split" between the United States and the Soviet Union after the war? (c) In what ways was Japan part of the "Western world"? (d) Why did Third World nations gain more importance by the 1970's?

2. What part did each of the following policies play in the politics of the postwar era: (a) containment? (b) deterrence? (c) détente?

3. Explain the causes of each of the following events and describe its effects on Soviet-American relations: (a) the division of occupied Germany; (b) the first summit conference (1955); (c) the U-2 incident; (d) the Cuban missile crisis; (e) SALT I.

4. Explain how each of the following became two nations in the period after 1945: (a) Germany; (b) Korea; (c) India; (d) Pakistan.

5. Because of their rapid economic recovery after World War II, West Germany and Japan have been described as "economic miracles." What factors contributed to their growth?

6. (a) How did the European Economic Community contribute to postwar economic growth in Western Europe? (b) Compare this growth with that of nations in the Soviet bloc.

7. How did each of the following affect the relationship between the United States and China in the postwar period? (a) Taiwan; (b) the Korean War; (c) the Sino-Soviet split; (d) Nixon's visit to China; (e) the death of Mao Tse-tung.

8. (a) What led to nationalist movements in Southeast Asia in the 1940's and 1950's? (b) Why did the United States become involved in the war in Vietnam? (c) How did Vietnam become a united country again? (d) What effects did the Vietnam War have on Kampuchea and Laos?

9. (a) What were some reasons for the increased importance of Africa and the Middle East in international affairs? (b) What is OPEC, and how did its Arab members use the organization as a weapon in the 1973 Arab-Israeli war?

10. (a) What economic problems did African and Latin American nations share? (b) How were these problems related to their former position as colonies?

Projects.

1. Research and report. Leaders who have tried to modernize their nations include Atatürk, Mao, Nehru, Nasser, Riza Shah, Faisal, Kenyatta, Nyerere, Castro, Cárdenas, Arbenz, and Ben-Gurion. Choose two of these leaders and compare their goals, the methods they used, and the effects of change on their nations.

2. Writing an essay. In this book you have studied historical periods known by names such as the Age of Exploration, the Age of Reason (or the Enlightenment), and the Age of Imperialism. Some historians have called the modern period the "Age of Anxiety." Create your own name for the period from 1945 to the present. Write an essay telling the reasons for your choice.

Books to Read

Bernstein, Carl, and Bob Woodward. *All the President's Men.* Warner. The cracking of the Watergate conspiracy by two young journalists.

Branley, Franklyn M. *Energy for the Twenty-First Century.* Harper and Row.

Collins, Larry, and Dominique Lapierre. *Freedom at Midnight.* Avon. The gaining of India's independence.

Earl, Sylvia, and Al Giddings. *Exploring the Deep Frontier.* National Geographic Society.

Eban, Abba. *My People: The Story of the Jews.* Behrman.

Ferguson, Linda. *Canada.* Scribner.

Gandhi, Mohandas. *Autobiography.* Heineman.

Isenberg, Irwin, ed. *South America: Problems and Prospects.* Wilson.

Laskey, Melvin, ed. *The Hungarian Revolution.* Ayer.

Oliver, Roland, and Michael Crowder. *The Cambridge Encyclopedia of Africa.* Cambridge.

Roberson, John. *China from Manchu to Mao.* Atheneum.

Salisbury, Harrison. *China: One Hundred Years of Revolution.* Holt, Rinehart and Winston.

Smith, Hedrick. *The Russians.* Times Books.

Preparing for Tests

Throughout your school career, you will need to know the skills used in taking tests. Successful test-takers are almost always people with good study habits. They have learned to review what they already know about a subject, to write down or think about questions that might be asked, and then to practice answering those questions from memory after reviewing. Successful test-taking is also a matter of knowing how to deal with different types of test questions.

Answering multiple-choice questions. Multiple-choice questions are frequently used in tests in the social sciences. In such questions, you are asked to choose the correct answer from several (usually three or four) possible answers. For example, this multiple-choice question might be asked about Chapter 39: "For missions to distant planets, the space programs use unpiloted craft called (a) space shuttles, (b) space probes, (c) space stations, (d) lasers."

First, read the question carefully and try to answer it before looking at the choices. Then read all the choices. If you are not certain of the right answer, eliminate those that you know are wrong. Then pick the best remaining answer.

Look again at the question for Chapter 39. You may know that (d) can be eliminated because a laser is not a spacecraft. Choice (c) can be ruled out because people can live in a space station, and so it is not "unpiloted." This will narrow your choices to only two.

Answering matching questions. Matching questions are another common type. (An example of a matching exercise is "People to Identify" in the Chapter 35 Review on page 778.) In answering matching questions, match first those items that you know with certainty. Look for clues in the remaining items. For example, if the question calls for the name of a Latin American leader, you might look first at Spanish-sounding names.

Answering essay questions. An essay question requires you to write a short composition in a limited time. Essay questions can be more complex than other types of questions. Read the question and the directions with care so that you will know exactly what is asked of you: listing, discussing, comparing, etc. If you are given a choice of questions to answer, read all of them before you choose. Be sure to allot the time that you will spend on each question according to the number of points it is worth. That is, spend more time on a question worth 25 points than on one worth 15. Start with the question that you feel you know best. On scratch paper jot down the names, dates, facts, or terms required in your answer and arrange them in appropriate order or in outline form.

Be specific in your essay, but do not pad it with unrelated details. An answer that is brief, detailed, and well organized will receive more points than a long rambling essay. Reread the question after you have finished your answer to be certain that you have done all that you were asked to do. Finally, reread your answer to be certain that you have made no errors in grammar, usage, spelling, or punctuation.

Check Your Skill

Use the following questions to check your understanding of test-taking skills.

1. In studying for a test, a good way to start is to (a) reread your book, (b) take notes on the test material, (c) review what you already know about a subject.

2. If you are unsure of the answer to a multiple-choice question, you should (a) guess, (b) skip the question, (c) eliminate the answers you know are wrong.

3. The best answer to an essay question is one that is (a) well organized and to the point, (b) long and detailed, (c) a short summary of all you know.

Apply Your Skill

For practice in answering essay questions, select one of the discussion questions from the Unit Review on the facing page. Answer all parts of the question without using your textbook, following the guidelines for essay questions.

Atlas and Reference Section

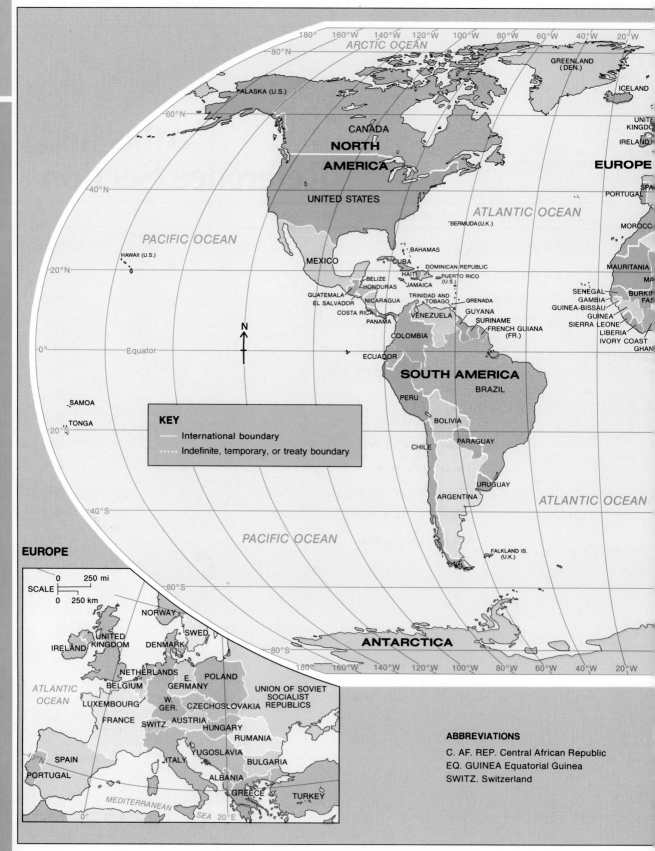

ATLAS

180° 160°W 140°W 120°W 100°W 80°W 60°W 40°W 20°W

ARCTIC OCEAN

80°N

GREENLAND
(DEN.)

ICELAND

ALASKA (U.S.)

60°N

UNITED
KINGDOM

IRELAND

CANADA

NORTH
AMERICA

EUROPE

40°N

UNITED STATES

PORTUGAL   SPA

ATLANTIC OCEAN

*BERMUDA (U.K.)

MOROCC

PACIFIC OCEAN

20°N

HAWAII (U.S.)

MEXICO

BAHAMAS

CUBA

DOMINICAN REPUBLIC

MAURITANIA

MA

BELIZE
HONDURAS

HAITI
JAMAICA

PUERTO RICO
(U.S.)

SENEGAL
GAMBIA

BURKIN
FAS

GUATEMALA
EL SALVADOR   NICARAGUA

TRINIDAD AND
TOBAGO   GRENADA

GUINEA-BISSAU
GUINEA

COSTA RICA
PANAMA

VENEZUELA

GUYANA
SURINAME
FRENCH GUIANA
(FR.)

SIERRA LEONE
LIBERIA
IVORY COAST   GHAN

N

0°

Equator

COLOMBIA

ECUADOR

SOUTH AMERICA

BRAZIL

SAMOA

PERU

20°S

TONGA

BOLIVIA

KEY

International boundary

Indefinite, temporary, or treaty boundary

CHILE

PARAGUAY

URUGUAY

40°S

ARGENTINA

ATLANTIC OCEAN

PACIFIC OCEAN

60°S

FALKLAND IS.
(U.K.)

80°S

ANTARCTICA

180° 160°W 140°W 120°W 100°W 80°W 60°W 40°W 20°W

EUROPE

SCALE
0   250 mi
0   250 km

60°S

NORWAY

SWED

IRELAND

UNITED
KINGDOM

DENMARK

80°S

ATLANTIC
OCEAN

NETHERLANDS
BELGIUM

E.
GERMANY

POLAND

UNION OF SOVIET
SOCIALIST
REPUBLICS

LUXEMBOURG

W.
GER.   CZECHOSLOVAKIA

FRANCE   SWITZ.   AUSTRIA
HUNGARY

RUMANIA

40°N   SPAIN

ITALY

YUGOSLAVIA

BULGARIA

PORTUGAL

ALBANIA

GREECE

TURKEY

MEDITERRANEAN   SEA   20°E

0°

ABBREVIATIONS

C. AF. REP. Central African Republic
EQ. GUINEA Equatorial Guinea
SWITZ. Switzerland

858

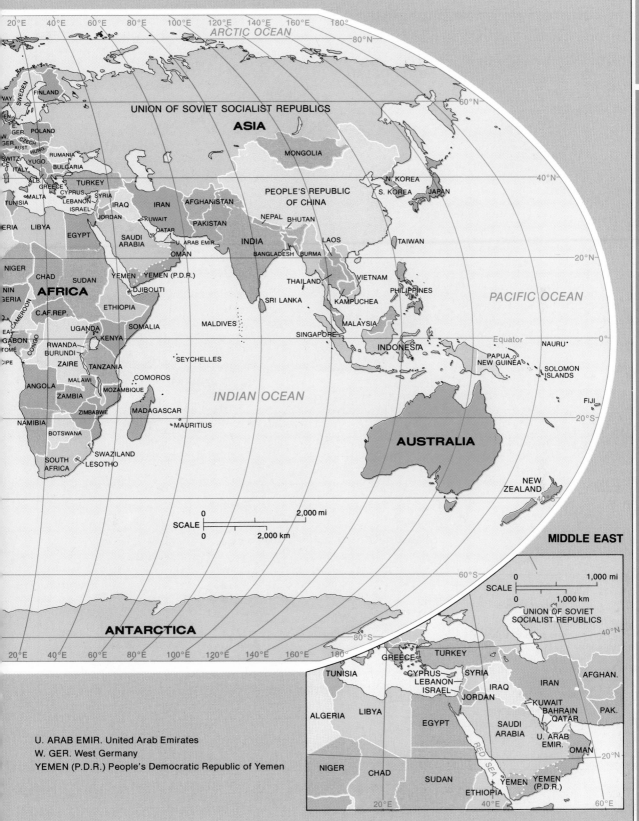

20°E 40°E 60°E 80°E 100°E 120°E 140°E 160°E 180°

ARCTIC OCEAN

80°N

SWEDEN
FINLAND
VAY
N. GER.
POLAND
W. GER.
AUST.
CZECH
HUNG.
SWITZ.
CE
ITALY
YUGO.
ALB.
GREECE
MALTA
CYPRUS
TUNISIA
LEBANON
ISRAEL
JORDAN

60°N

UNION OF SOVIET SOCIALIST REPUBLICS

ASIA

MONGOLIA

40°N

N. KOREA
S. KOREA
JAPAN

TURKEY
SYRIA
IRAQ
IRAN
AFGHANISTAN

PEOPLE'S REPUBLIC
OF CHINA

KUWAIT
QATAR
PAKISTAN
NEPAL
BHUTAN

ERIA
LIBYA
EGYPT
SAUDI
ARABIA
U. ARAB EMIR.
OMAN

INDIA

LAOS

TAIWAN

20°N

BANGLADESH
BURMA

NIGER
CHAD
SUDAN
YEMEN
YEMEN (P.D.R.)
DJIBOUTI

THAILAND

VIETNAM

PACIFIC OCEAN

AFRICA

SRI LANKA

PHILIPPINES

KAMPUCHEA

NIN
ERIA
C.AF.REP.
ETHIOPIA
UGANDA
SOMALIA

MALDIVES

MALAYSIA

EA
GABON
CONGO
TOMÉ
CIPE
RWANDA
BURUNDI
KENYA

SINGAPORE

Equator

NAURU

0°

ZAIRE
TANZANIA

SEYCHELLES

INDONESIA

PAPUA
NEW GUINEA
SOLOMON
ISLANDS

MALAWI
COMOROS
ANGOLA
MOZAMBIQUE
ZAMBIA
ZIMBABWE
MADAGASCAR

INDIAN OCEAN

FIJI

NAMIBIA
MAURITIUS

20°S

BOTSWANA

AUSTRALIA

SOUTH
AFRICA
SWAZILAND
LESOTHO

NEW
ZEALAND

SCALE
0 — 2,000 mi
0 — 2,000 km

MIDDLE EAST

60°S

0 — 1,000 mi
SCALE
0 — 1,000 km

UNION OF SOVIET
SOCIALIST REPUBLICS

40°N

80°S

20°E 40°E 60°E 80°E 100°E 120°E 140°E 160°E 180°

ANTARCTICA

GREECE
TURKEY

TUNISIA
CYPRUS
LEBANON
ISRAEL
SYRIA
IRAQ
JORDAN
IRAN
AFGHAN.

KUWAIT
BAHRAIN
QATAR
PAK.

ALGERIA
LIBYA
EGYPT
SAUDI
ARABIA
U. ARAB
EMIR.
OMAN

U. ARAB EMIR. United Arab Emirates
W. GER. West Germany
YEMEN (P.D.R.) People's Democratic Republic of Yemen

NIGER
CHAD
SUDAN
RED SEA
YEMEN
YEMEN
(P.D.R.)
ETHIOPIA

20°N

20°E 40°E 60°E

859

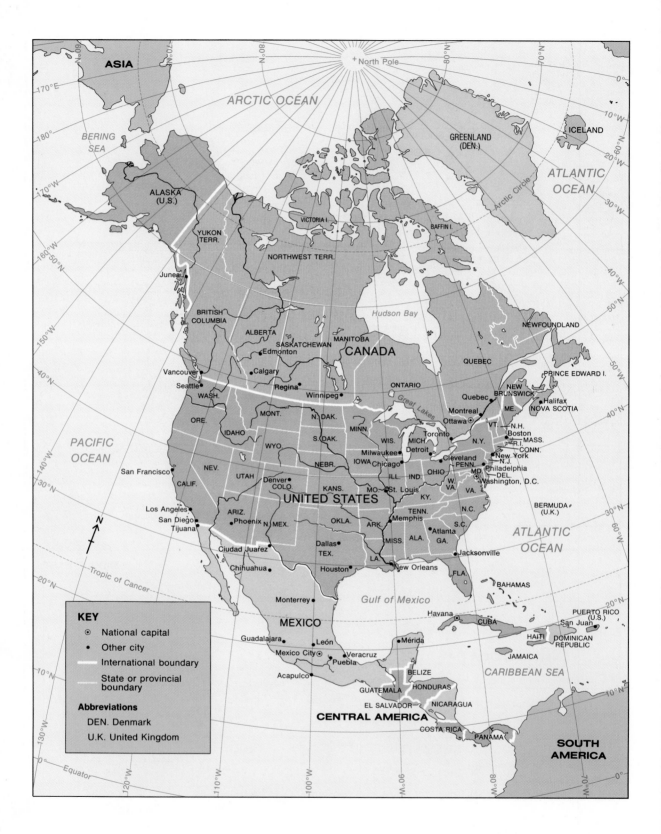

ASIA

ARCTIC OCEAN

North Pole

GREENLAND
(DEN.)

ICELAND

ATLANTIC
OCEAN

BERING
SEA

170°E
180°
170°W
160°W
150°W
140°W
130°W
120°W

ALASKA
(U.S.)

Arctic Circle

YUKON
TERR.

VICTORIA I.

BAFFIN I.

Juneau

NORTHWEST TERR.

BRITISH
COLUMBIA

ALBERTA

SASKATCHEWAN

MANITOBA

CANADA

Hudson Bay

NEWFOUNDLAND

Edmonton

QUEBEC

Vancouver

Calgary

Regina

Winnipeg

ONTARIO

PRINCE EDWARD I.

Seattle

WASH.

Quebec

NEW
BRUNSWICK

Halifax
NOVA SCOTIA

ME.

Montreal

ORE.

MONT.

N. DAK.

MINN.

Ottawa

Toronto

VT.
N.H.
Boston
MASS.
R.I.
CONN.

IDAHO

WYO.

S. DAK.

WIS.

MICH.

N.Y.

Milwaukee

Detroit

Cleveland

PACIFIC
OCEAN

NEV.

UTAH

NEBR.

IOWA

Chicago

OHIO

PENN.

New York
N.J.
Philadelphia
DEL.
MD.
Washington, D.C.

San Francisco

CALIF.

Denver
COLO.

KANS.

MO.
St. Louis

ILL.
IND.

KY.

W.
VA.

VA.

BERMUDA
(U.K.)

Los Angeles

ARIZ.

Phoenix

N. MEX.

OKLA.

ARK.

TENN.
Memphis

N.C.

San Diego
Tijuana

Ciudad Juarez

Dallas
TEX.

MISS.

ALA.

S.C.

Atlanta
GA.

ATLANTIC
OCEAN

Tropic of Cancer

Chihuahua

Houston

LA.
New Orleans

Jacksonville

FLA.

BAHAMAS

Monterrey

Gulf of Mexico

Havana

PUERTO RICO
(U.S.)

MEXICO

CUBA

San Juan

Guadalajara

León

Mérida

HAITI

DOMINICAN
REPUBLIC

Mexico City

Veracruz
Puebla

JAMAICA

CARIBBEAN SEA

Acapulco

BELIZE

HONDURAS

GUATEMALA

NICARAGUA

EL SALVADOR

CENTRAL AMERICA

COSTA RICA

PANAMA

SOUTH
AMERICA

Equator

60°N
50°N
40°N
30°N
20°N
10°N
0°

0°
10°W
20°W
30°W
40°W
50°W
60°W
70°W

KEY

⊙ National capital

• Other city

International boundary

State or provincial
boundary

Abbreviations

DEN. Denmark

U.K. United Kingdom

0   800 mi
SCALE
0   800 km

CENTRAL
AMERICA

CARIBBEAN SEA

GRENADA

Barranquilla
Maracaibo
Caracas
TRINIDAD AND TOBAGO

ATLANTIC OCEAN

10°N

VENEZUELA

Medellín
Georgetown
GUYANA
Paramaribo
Cayenne
SURINAME
FRENCH GUIANA (FR.)

Bogotá
Cali
COLOMBIA

Equator
0°

Quito
ECUADOR
Guayaquil

Belém

Fortaleza

BRAZIL

PERU
10°S

Lima
Recife

Cuzco

L. Titicaca
La Paz
Salvador

BOLIVIA
Brasília

Sucre

PACIFIC OCEAN
20°S

Belo Horizonte

PARAGUAY
20°S

Tropic of Capricorn
Asunción
São Paulo
Rio de Janeiro

CHILE

30°S

Córdoba
Pôrto Alegre

Rosario
URUGUAY
ATLANTIC OCEAN
30°S

Santiago
ARGENTINA
Buenos Aires
Montevideo
La Plata

40°S

KEY
⊙ National capital
• Other city
— International boundary

40°S

Abbreviation
U.K. United Kingdom

50°S

FALKLAND IS.
(U.K.)

N

0   600 mi
SCALE
0   600 km

South America   861

Reykjavik · ICELAND

Arctic Circle

NORWEGIAN SEA

FAEROE IS.
(DEN.)

ATLANTIC
OCEAN

SHETLAND IS.

Murmansk

SWEDEN

FINLAND

Helsinki

NORWAY

Bergen

Oslo

Stockholm

Leningrad

ORKNEY IS.

HEBRIDES

NORTH
SEA

BALTIC SEA

Moscow

UNION OF SOVIET
SOCIALIST REPUBLICS

Glasgow

Edinburgh

Belfast

IRELAND

UNITED KINGDOM

DENMARK

Copenhagen

Minsk

Dublin

Cork

Birmingham

Cardiff

London

NETHERLANDS
The
Hague

Amsterdam

Hamburg

Berlin

E.
GERMANY

POLAND

Warsaw

Kiev

Antwerp

Brussels

BELGIUM

Bonn

Frankfurt

Kraków

CHANNEL IS. (U.K.)

Le Havre

W. GERMANY

Prague

CZECHOSLOVAKIA

Odessa

Paris

LUXEMBOURG

Munich

LIECHTENSTEIN

Vienna

FRANCE

Bern

SWITZERLAND

AUSTRIA

HUNGARY

Budapest

RUMANIA

Geneva

Lyon

Bordeaux

Milan

Trieste

Belgrade

Bucharest

BLACK
SEA

MONACO

SAN
MARINO

YUGOSLAVIA

BULGARIA

Marseilles

ANDORRA

ITALY

Sofia

Istanbul

CORSICA
(FR.)

Rome

ALBANIA

Tirana

PORTUGAL

Madrid

Barcelona

Naples

GREECE

TURKEY

Lisbon

SPAIN

SARDINIA
(IT.)

Athens

Seville

BALEARIC IS.
(SP.)

SICILY

RHODES
(GR.)

GIBRALTAR (U.K.)

CRETE

MALTA

MEDITERRANEAN SEA

AFRICA

KEY

⊙ National capital

• Other city

— International boundary

Abbreviations

DEN. Denmark   IT. Italy

FR. France   SP. Spain

GR. Greece   U.K. United Kingdom

0   400 mi
SCALE
0   400 km

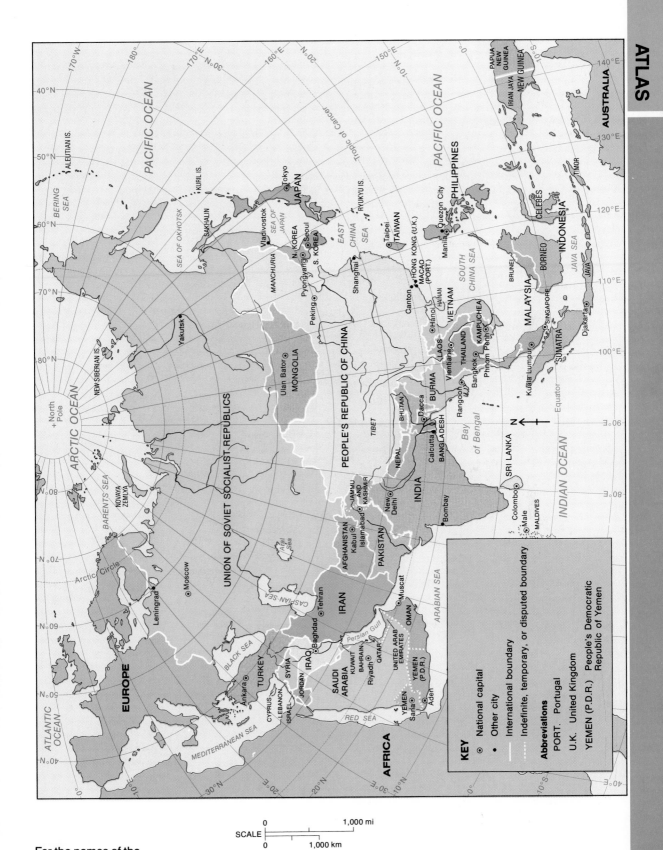

PACIFIC OCEAN

PACIFIC OCEAN

AUSTRALIA

PAPUA NEW GUINEA

IRIAN JAYA NEW GUINEA

ALEUTIAN IS.

BERING SEA

SEA OF OKHOTSK

KURIL IS.

SAKHALIN

Vladivostok

SEA OF JAPAN

Tokyo

JAPAN

N. KOREA

Seoul S. KOREA

Pyongyang

MANCHURIA

Peking

EAST CHINA SEA

RYUKYU IS.

Taipei TAIWAN

Shanghai

HONG KONG (U.K.)

MACAO (PORT.)

Canton

HAINAN

PHILIPPINES

Quezon City

Manila

SOUTH CHINA SEA

BRUNEI

MALAYSIA

BORNEO

SINGAPORE

CELEBES

INDONESIA

JAVA SEA

SUMATRA

JAVA

Djakarta

TIMOR

Yakutsk

NEW SIBERIAN IS.

North Pole

ARCTIC OCEAN

NOVAYA ZEMLYA

BARENTS SEA

UNION OF SOVIET SOCIALIST REPUBLICS

Ulan Bator

MONGOLIA

PEOPLE'S REPUBLIC OF CHINA

TIBET

Hanoi

VIETNAM

LAOS

Vientiane

BURMA

Rangoon

THAILAND

Bangkok

KAMPUCHEA

Phnom Penh

Kuala Lumpur

Moscow

Arctic Circle

Leningrad

CASPIAN SEA

Aral Sea

Tehran

IRAN

Baghdad

IRAQ

Kabul

AFGHANISTAN

Islamabad

PAKISTAN

JAMMU AND KASHMIR

NEPAL

New Delhi

BHUTAN

Dacca

BANGLADESH

Calcutta

INDIA

Bombay

Bay of Bengal

Rangoon

SRI LANKA

Colombo

Male

MALDIVES

INDIAN OCEAN

Equator

N

EUROPE

ATLANTIC OCEAN

BLACK SEA

TURKEY

Ankara

CYPRUS

LEBANON

ISRAEL

SYRIA

JORDAN

Baghdad

IRAQ

KUWAIT

SAUDI ARABIA

Riyadh

BAHRAIN

QATAR

UNITED ARAB EMIRATES

Persian Gulf

Muscat

OMAN

ARABIAN SEA

YEMEN (P.D.R.)

YEMEN

Sana

Aden

RED SEA

MEDITERRANEAN SEA

AFRICA

KEY

⊙ National capital

• Other city

— International boundary

····· Indefinite, temporary, or disputed boundary

Abbreviations

PORT. Portugal

U.K. United Kingdom

YEMEN (P.D.R.) People's Democratic Republic of Yemen

0   1,000 mi

SCALE

0   1,000 km

For the names of the republics of the USSR, see the map on page 667.

Asia and the USSR   863

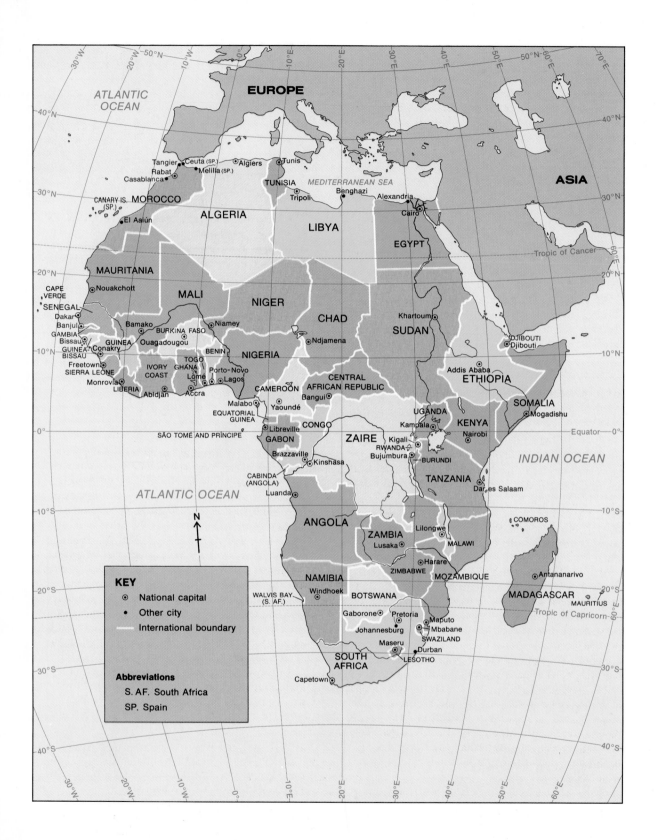

ATLANTIC OCEAN

EUROPE

ASIA

MEDITERRANEAN SEA

Tangier Ceuta (SP.)
Rabat Melilla (SP.) ⊙Algiers ⊙Tunis
Casablanca
TUNISIA
CANARY IS. **MOROCCO** Benghazi Alexandria
(SP.) ⊙Tripoli ⊙Cairo
El Aalún **ALGERIA**
LIBYA *Tropic of Cancer*
EGYPT

MAURITANIA
CAPE ⊙Nouakchott **MALI**
VERDE **NIGER**
SENEGAL Khartoum⊙
Dakar⊙ Bamako **CHAD** **SUDAN**
Banjul⊙ BURKINA FASO ⊙Niamey
GAMBIA Ouagadougou DJIBOUTI⊙
Bissau⊙ ⊙Ndjamena Djibouti
GUINEA **GUINEA** ⊙Conakry BENIN
BISSAU **NIGERIA**
Freetown⊙ TOGO Addis Ababa⊙
SIERRA LEONE IVORY GHANA⊙ Porto-Novo **ETHIOPIA**
Monrovia⊙ COAST Lomé⊙ ⊙Lagos
LIBERIA Abidjan Accra **CENTRAL**
CAMEROON AFRICAN REPUBLIC **SOMALIA**
Malabo⊙ ⊙Mogadishu
EQUATORIAL Yaoundé⊙ Bangui⊙ **UGANDA**
GUINEA Kampala⊙ **KENYA**
SÃO TOMÉ AND PRÍNCIPE Libreville⊙ **CONGO** Nairobi⊙
GABON Kigali⊙ *Equator*
ZAIRE RWANDA
Brazzaville⊙ Bujumbura⊙ **INDIAN OCEAN**
⊙Kinshasa BURUNDI
CABINDA
(ANGOLA) **TANZANIA**
Luanda⊙ Dar es Salaam⊙
ATLANTIC OCEAN
COMOROS
ANGOLA
ZAMBIA Lilongwe⊙
Lusaka⊙ **MALAWI**
Antananarivo⊙
Harare⊙
NAMIBIA ZIMBABWE **MOZAMBIQUE**
WALVIS BAY Windhoek⊙ **MADAGASCAR**
(S. AF.) **BOTSWANA** MAURITIUS
Tropic of Capricorn
Gaborone⊙ Pretoria⊙ Maputo⊙
Johannesburg⊙ Mbabane⊙
Maseru⊙ SWAZILAND
SOUTH ⊙Durban
AFRICA LESOTHO
Capetown⊙

KEY

⊙ National capital

• Other city

— International boundary

Abbreviations

S. AF. South Africa

SP. Spain

N

SCALE

0   900 mi

0   900 km

Using the Atlas

Every event that you will read about in this book (except for space flights) happened somewhere on the face of the earth. That is why maps are so useful in the study of world history. Throughout this book, you will find maps that will help you follow the story of important happenings.

Besides the maps in the main part of the book, you will find Atlas maps on pages 858–864. These Atlas maps include a map of the world, followed by maps of North America, South America, Europe, Asia and the Soviet Union, and Africa. Notice that on the world map you can see where all the countries of the present age are located, while the regional maps give you a closer view of different parts of the world. On page 417 you will find valuable suggestions for using maps as you study world history.

MAP PROJECTIONS

All maps are drawings that show the placement and arrangement of features on the earth's surface — not only visible things (roads, cities, seas, for example) but also invisible things (such as international boundaries, trade routes, and areas where ancient civilizations once flourished). Because the earth is round, the best way to show its surface is on globes. In fact, globes are the only fully accurate way of representing the earth's surface, but globes cannot fit into a world history textbook. Moreover, when you look at a globe, you see only half the world at one time. Centuries ago, therefore, maps were invented as a way of showing the earth's surface and the placement on it of various kinds of features.

Since the world is round and maps are flat, there is always some distortion in a map's representation of the earth's surface. To deal with this problem, mapmakers have devised a number of systems called **projections.** A projection is a way of showing how the curved surface of the earth would look if *projected* onto a flat surface. The various projections have different advantages and disadvantages. The best way to see what distortions are present in any projection is to compare a map using that projection with a globe.

USING MAPS IN WORLD HISTORY

Maps are essential tools in studying world history. Most important, they help you find the places where historical events occurred. By looking at the map on page 176 as you read the account of the Crusades, for example (pages 174–177), you will be better able to visualize the expeditions of the Europeans who tried to take control of the Holy Land from the Muslim Turks during the Middle Ages. You can also use maps to identify the present-day location of historical places such as battle sites and early centers of civilization. Comparing the maps on pages 299 and 861 will show you what modern countries now exist in what was once the Inca Empire.

Maps also show how countries or regions have changed over the years. To see how Germany has changed through time, for example, you can look at the maps on pages 640, 649, and 862. See how many different kinds of historical information you can find on the maps in this book. To begin, you might look at the maps on pages 234, 281, 305, 339, and 554.

USING THE GRID SYSTEM

As you look at the Atlas maps, notice that each one has numbered blue lines. These lines are part of a giant imaginary grid system that covers the earth's surface. The grid system is made up of criss-cross lines of **latitude** and **longitude,** which are ways of measuring distance on the earth. Latitude is measured in degrees north and south of the equator (which is shown as 0° and is called "zero degrees"). Longitude measures distance east or west of the prime meridian, an imaginary line that passes through Greenwich, a town just outside London, England (page 405). Longitude is measured from the prime meridian (0°) halfway around the world to 180°, a line stretching from pole to pole through the Pacific Ocean.

Since every place in the world has one and only one grid location (that is, one set of latitude and longitude readings), that location is the same for any given place on any map. Thus, you will always find London at 51° north latitude and 1° west longitude. Similarly, Los Angeles is always at 34° north latitude and 118° west longitude. That is why the grid system has become the standard way, the world over, of referring to locations on maps.

As you study world history, develop a habit of locating on maps the places mentioned in the text. Maps will help you understand much better the events and developments that you read about.

Time Chart of World History

	to 3500 B.C.	3100	2700	2300	1900	1500
Europe	The chart on pages 866–871 shows events that were happening at the same time in six different parts of the world. Notice that events in the ancient world are grouped by 400-year intervals; happenings in the Middle Ages are shown in 100-year spans; and those in the modern era are broken down into periods of 50 years each.		Artisans on Crete work with bronze and gold, 2600.	Aryan migrations begin, 2000.	Aryans invade Greece, 1900. Minoan civilization at its height in Crete, 1700.	
Western Asia	Hunting peoples become herders and farmers. Villages are built: Jericho, 7000, Çatal Hüyük, 6000. Metalworking begins.	City-states grow up along the Tigris and Euphrates rivers. Sumerians develop cuneiform writing.	Phoenicians trade with Egypt. Sargon of Akkad conquers Sumer, 2350. Trade between Sumer and Indus Valley, 2300.	City-state of Ur dominates Sumer, 2100. Laws of Ur are written.	Hammurabi of Babylon unites Mesopotamia, 1792. Hittites invade Mesopotamia, 1600. Thutmose of Egypt conquers Near East, 1512.	
South and East Asia		Cities of Harappa and Mohenjo-Daro are built in the valley of the Indus River.	Indus Valley culture develops trade and a writing system, 2500.	Hsia dynasty are legendary rulers in Yellow River Valley (China), 2000.	Shang dynasty in China, 1600–1500. Shang artisans work in bronze. Aryans invade Indian peninsula, 1500.	
Africa	Villages are built along the Nile River.	Menes unites Upper and Lower Egypt, 3100.	Old Kingdom (Egypt), 2686–2181. Great Pyramid at Giza is built, 2600.	Rulers from Thebes establish Egypt's Middle Kingdom, 2040–1786. Kushite culture grows up along Nile, 2000.	Hyksos from Asia rule Egypt, 1670.	
The Americas		Corn is grown in Valley of Mexico.			Farming villages in Mesoamerica, 1500.	

The Ancient World

00	1100	700	300 B.C.	A.D. 100	A.D. 500
Mycenaean culture spreads to Greece, 1400. Palace at Knossos is destroyed, 1400. Achaeans dominate Aegean region, 1300. Trojan War, 1300.	Dark Age in Greece, 1100–800. Hellenic civilization develops, 800. Greeks adopt alphabet, 800. Homer writes the *Iliad* and *Odyssey*. Archons rule Athens.	Greeks defeat Persians at Marathon, 490. Socrates dies, 399. Peloponnesian War, 431–404. Golden Age of Athens, 400's. Roman Republic, 509.	Rome and Carthage begin Punic Wars, 264 B.C. Hannibal invades Italy, 218 B.C. Julius Caesar rules Rome, 46 B.C. Roman Empire begins under Augustus, 27 B.C.	Pax Romana ends, A.D. 180. The Roman Empire is divided. Germanic invasions begin, A.D. 376. Western Roman Empire falls, A.D. 476.	
Hittite Empire, 1450. Hittites learn to work with iron. Hebrew Exodus from Egypt, 1290.	Assyrian Empire at its height, 660. Assyrian capital of Nineveh destroyed, 612. Saul is first Israelite king, 1020. Solomon rules Israel, 972–922.	Nebuchadnezzar conquers Hebrews, 586. Cyrus builds Persian Empire, 547. Lydians mint coins, 560. Alexander the Great builds an empire, 334–323.	Jesus is crucified, A.D. 30. Rome crushes Jewish revolt in Judaea, A.D. 70.	New capital of Roman Empire built at Constantinople, A.D. 330.	
Vedic Age in India, 1500–500.	Upanishads record Hindu beliefs, 800–600. Chou dynasty rules China, 1100–771. Chinese culture spreads under Eastern Chou, 770–256.	Persians conquer north India, 518. Confucius teaches, 500. Yamato dynasty begins in Japan, 500. The Buddha teaches in India until 483. Alexander invades India, 327.	Asoka rules Mauryan Empire, 269–232 B.C. Ch'in establish empire, 221 B.C. Great Wall of China is built. Yayoi era, Japan. Han begin 400-year rule, 220 B.C.	Chinese invent paper-making. "Tomb culture" in Japan, A.D. 200. Han empire is divided, A.D. 220. Gupta Empire unites north India, A.D. 320–500.	
New Kingdom (Egypt), 1570–1090. Hatshepsut is first great woman ruler. Akhenaton changes religion, 1300's. Tutankhamen is pharaoh, 1358. Rameses (1304–1237) wars with Hittites.	Phoenician traders found Carthage, 814. Kushites control Egypt, 700's.	City-states grow up in East Africa, 600–500. Kushites move to Meroë, 540. Ironworking develops. Bantu migrations begin, 500.	Euclid and others work at library in Alexandria, Egypt. Kushite empire at its height, 200 B.C. Romans destroy Carthage, 146 B.C.	Ptolemy describes an earth-centered universe, A.D. 300. Axum conquers Kush, A.D. 350. Gold-salt trade in Ghana, A.D. 300. Christianity spreads to Axum, A.D. 395.	
Olmecs develop parent culture in Mesoamerica, 1200. Northwest Coast culture, 1000. Farming begins in the Andes. Mesoamerican culture spreads northward.	Villages in central Andes become religious centers.	"Mound Builders" farm in the Ohio Valley, 400–300.	Olmec culture vanishes. Anasazi build farming culture in the Southwest.	Teotihuacán is built, A.D. 100. Mayan culture develops in Yucatan, A.D. 300. Hopewell peoples trade widely, A.D. 400.	

Time Chart of World History

	A.D. 500	600	700	800	900	1000
Europe	Theodoric rules Italy, 493–526 Gregory the Great is Pope, 590–604. St. Benedict founds a monastery, 529. Clovis makes conquests in Gaul, about 500.	Slavic peoples invade the Balkans. Visigoths conquer Spain, 631. Pepin rules the Franks, 687–714.	Venerable Bede writes history of England, 731. Franks halt Muslim invasion, Tours, 732. Spain comes under Muslim rule, 756. Charlemagne crowned, 800.	Viking invasions of Europe. Rus set up forts at Kiev and Novgorod. Treaty of Verdun divides Charlemagne's empire, 843.	Otto the Great begins Holy Roman Empire, 962. Kievan Russia forms ties with Byzantine Empire, about 990.	
Western Asia	Justinian rules Byzantine Empire, 527–565.	Persians attack Byzantine lands in the Near East. Mohammed makes the Hegira, 622. Muslim conquests begin, 632. Umayyads claim the caliphate, 661.	Muslims besiege Constantinople, 717–18. Abbasid rulers move Muslim capital to Baghdad, 763.	Harun al-Rashid is caliph of Baghdad, 786–809.		
South and East Asia	Sui dynasty emperors build Grand Canal, 589–618. Shotoku gains power in Japan, 592. Buddhism is established at Japanese court.	Harsha rules in India, 606–646. China flourishes in T'ang dynasty, 618–907. 17-Article Constitution in Japan, 604. Taika Reforms, 646.	Age of T'ang poets in China. Rajputs stop Muslim invasion of India, 712. Japanese capital moves to Heian, 784.		Disorder follows fall of T'ang dynasty, 907. Sung dynasty begins, 960.	
Africa		Arab merchants begin settling in East Africa.		Luba establish agricultural economy.	Ghana reaches height of power, 1000.	
The Americas	Height of Mayan civilization, 500. Teotihuacán is destroyed, 600.		Anasazi begin to build pueblos in the Southwest.	Mayan civilization collapses, 850–950.		

The Middle Ages

1000	1100	1200	1300	1400	1500
High Middle Ages begin, 1050. Christian Church is divided, 1054. Norman Conquest of England, 1066. First Crusade, 1096.	Gothic cathedrals are built. Concordat of Worms, 1122. Henry II establishes English common law. Richard the Lion-Hearted leads Third Crusade, 1190.	Magna Charta, 1215. Inquisition begins, 1232. Mongols under Genghis Khan overrun Eastern Europe, 1237–41. "Model Parliament" in England, 1295.	Dante writes the *Divine Comedy,* 1307. Hundred Years' War begins, 1337. Black Death reaches Europe, 1347–48. Chaucer's *Canterbury Tales,* 1390.	Age of Exploration begins, 1415. Gutenberg develops printing press, 1450's. Renaissance flourishes in Italy. Ferdinand and Isabella reunite Spain, 1492.
Seljuk Turks defeat Byzantines at Manzikert, 1061. Crusader states established.	Saladin recaptures Jerusalem, 1187.	Crusaders capture Constantinople, 1204. Mongols destroy Baghdad, 1258. Death of Genghis Khan divides Mongol Empire, 1260.	Tamerlane conquers western Asia, 1390's. Ottoman Turks invade Europe, 1390's.	Constantinople falls to Ottoman Turks, 1453.
Feudalism develops in Japan. Muslims invade India, 1000. Lady Murasaki writes *Tale of Genji,* 1000. Chinese print books from wooden blocks.	Southern Sung dynasty at its height, 1127–1279. Minamoto establishes first shogunate, 1185. Samurai dominate society in Japan.	Delhi sultanate established, 1206. Mongols invade China, 1215. Kublai Khan rules China, 1260–94. Marco Polo arrives in China, 1275. Mongol invasion of Japan fails, 1281.	Ming dynasty founded in China, 1368. Mongols under Tamerlane destroy Delhi, 1398. Ashikaga shogunate is established, 1338.	Portuguese under da Gama reach India, 1498. Cheng Ho leads voyages of exploration for Ming rulers, 1405-33. Zen Buddhism influences arts in Japan.
Muslims from North Africa invade Ghana, 1054. Rulers of Mali convert to Islam.		Sundiata expands Mali empire, 1230. Trading states develop on East African coast.	Mansa Musa rules Mali, 1312-32. Great Zimbabwe is completed, 1400. Kongo kingdom begins.	Dias sails around tip of Africa, 1488. Portuguese set up sugar plantations in West Africa. Songhai capture Timbuktu, 1468.
Anasazi complete Pueblo Bonito, 1085.	Drought destroys the Anasazi culture, 1150. Mississippian culture builds cities, 1200.		Aztecs arrive in Mexico and build Tenochtitlán, 1325.	Inca empire at its height, 1438. Aztecs rule empire in Mesoamerica. Columbus reaches Caribbean, 1492. Treaty of Tordesillas, 1494. Cabot explores North America coast, 1497.

Time Chart of World History

	1500	1550	1600	1650	1700	1750
Europe	Luther criticizes Catholic Church, 1517. Charles V rules Hapsburg empire, 1519. Turks defeat Hungary at Mohács, 1526. Copernicus' theory published, 1543.	Elizabeth I rules England, 1558–1603. Turks are defeated at Lepanto, 1571. St. Bartholomew's Day massacre, 1572. English defeat Spanish Armada, 1588. Edict of Nantes, 1598.	Galileo and Kepler study the moon and planets, early 1600's. Thirty Years' War, 1618–48. English Civil War, 1642. Louis XIV rules France, 1643–1713.	Stuarts restored to English throne, 1660. Louis XIV repeals Edict of Nantes, 1685. Peter the Great rules Russia, 1682–1725. Newton publishes the *Principia*, 1687. Glorious Revolution in England, 1688.	War of the Spanish Succession, 1701–13. The Enlightenment. Philosophes begin work on *Encyclopedia,* 1750. Baroque period in art and music.	
Western Asia	Suleiman leads Ottoman Empire, 1520–66.	Defeat of Turks at Lepanto limits westward expansion of Ottoman Empire, 1571.				
South and East Asia	Baber establishes Mogul Empire, 1526. Portuguese arrive in Japan, 1542.	Hideyoshi reunites Japan, 1580's. Tokugawa shogunate is established, 1600.	English East India Company is chartered, 1600. Dutch East India Co. (1602) controls Asian trade. Shah Jahan builds Taj Mahal, c. 1630. Japan limits foreign contacts, 1630's.	Marathas rebel against Mogul rule.	Mogul emperor Aurangzeb dies, 1707.	
Africa	Slave trade with the Americas licensed by Spain, 1518. Timbuktu is a center of Islam, 1520's. Portuguese conquer East African cities, 1511.	Moroccans destroy Songhai empire, 1590.	Yoruba kingdom of Oyo flourishes. Ashanti Union formed.	Kingdom of Benin declines. Boers settle in Cape Colony, 1657.	Kingdom of Dahomey conquers coastal states.	
The Americas	Aztecs conquered by Cortés, 1521. Incas defeated by Pizarro, 1532. Cartier claims land for France, 1534. Zuñi pueblos conquered by Coronado, 1549.	Spain claims American Southwest. Powhatan confederacy organized, late 1500's. Iroquois League unites Five Nations, 1580.	English colonists settle Virginia, 1607. New England colonies begin, 1620–30. First black settlers arrive, 1619. Quebec founded, 1608.	English settlers arrive in middle and southern colonies.	Tuscarora join Iroquois League, 1722. Georgia is the last British colony, 1733.	

The Modern Era

50	1800	1850	1900	1950
Seven Years' War, 1756–63. Catherine II rules Russia, 1762–96. French Revolution, 1789–95. Linnaeus classifies plants, 1750's. Classical period.	Napoleon becomes emperor, 1804. Battle of Waterloo, 1815. Congress of Vienna, 1815. Revolutions sweep Europe, 1830 and 1848. Romantic period.	Italy unified, 1861. Franco-Prussian War, 1870–71. German Empire formed, 1871. Darwin's *Origin of Species*, 1859. Impressionists hold first show, 1874. X-rays named, 1895.	Einstein's theory of relativity, 1905. World War I, 1914–18. Russian Revolution, 1917. Hitler gains power, 1933. World War II in Europe, 1939–1945. Germany divided, 1949.	Revolutions in Hungary and Poland, 1956. Common Market, 1957. *Sputnik*, 1957. DeGaulle leads France, 1958–69. Helsinki Accords, 1975. Chernobyl nuclear accident, 1986.
Ottoman Turkey loses territory in Russo-Turkish Wars, 1768–74, 1787–92.	Mohammed Ali becomes pasha of Egypt, 1805, and conquers Ottoman lands.	Britain and Russia clash over Afghanistan.	Ataturk leads Turkish republic, 1923. Saudi Arabia gains independence, 1932. Israel founded, 1948.	Six-Day War, 1967. Arab oil embargo, 1973. Civil war begins in Lebanon, 1975. USSR invades Afghanistan, 1979. Israel and Egypt sign peace treaty, 1979. Terrorism increases, 1980's.
British defeat French at Plassey, 1757. France loses outposts in India, 1763. Arts and commerce thrive in Tokugawa Japan.	Opium War between Britain and China, 1839–1842.	Japan is opened to trade with the West, 1854. Sepoy Rebellion, 1857. Taiping Rebellion in China, 1864. Meiji era begins in Japan, 1868. Boxer Rebellion, 1900.	Chinese Empire ends, 1912. Long March, 1934. India and Pakistan independent, 1947. People's Republic of China, 1949. World War II, 1941–45. First atomic bomb is dropped, 1945.	Korean War, 1950–53. War begins in Indochina, 1954. Vietnam truce, 1973. Cultural Revolution in China, 1966. Bangladesh declares independence, 1971. Philippines revolution, 1986.
Colonists settle in Sierra Leone, 1787.	Britain outlaws slave trade, 1807. European explorers map Africa. Liberia begun, 1847. Britain acquires Cape Colony, 1815. Great Trek, 1835–37. Zulu wars end, 1838.	Livingstone explores Africa, 1850's on. Suez Canal opened, 1869. Berlin Conference divides Africa, 1885. South African (Boer) War, 1899–1902. Ashanti wars, 1900.	Union of South Africa is formed, 1910. African National Congress begins, 1912. Kenyatta leads move for independence, 1947.	Ghana gains independence, 1957. 28 African nations gain independence, 1958–1967. Famine in sub-Saharan region, 1980's. Opposition to South African racial policies escalates, mid-1980's.
French and Indian War ends, 1763. Quebec Act, 1774. Declaration of Independence, 1776. Battle of Yorktown, 1781. U.S. Constitution is ratified, 1788.	Louisiana Purchase, 1803. Monroe Doctrine, 1823. Mexico declares its independence, 1821. Bolívar liberates South America, 1824. Canada united, 1840.	U.S. Civil War, 1861–65. France claims empire in Mexico, 1862. Canada becomes a dominion, 1867. Spanish-American War, 1898.	Mexican Revolution, 1910. Panama Canal completed, 1914. Stock market crash in U.S., 1929. U.S. enters World War II, 1941. V-E and V-J Day, 1945.	Cuban revolution, 1959. Moon landing, 1969. Watergate hearings, 1973. Constitution Act in Canada, 1982. Civilian rule restored in Argentina, 1983, and Brazil, 1985.

Table of Nations

The table below lists the nations of the world in alphabetical order with-in major geographical regions (identified by the headings in color). For each nation, the capital city, land area, and population are given.

Africa

Nation	Capital	Area (sq. mi.)	Population
Algeria	Algiers	919,595	22,817,000
Angola	Luanda	481,350	8,164,000
Benin	Porto-Novo	43,483	4,141,000
Botswana	Gaborone	222,000	1,104,000
Burkina Faso	Ouagadougou	105,870	7,094,000
Burundi	Bujumbura	10,747	4,807,000
Cameroon	Yaoundé	183,569	10,009,000
Cape Verde	Praia	1,557	318,000
Central African Republic	Bangui	241,313	2,744,000
Chad	Ndjamena	495,752	5,231,000
Comoros	Moroni	719	420,000
Congo	Brazzaville	132,046	1,853,000
Djibouti	Djibouti	8,996	304,000
Egypt	Cairo	386,900	50,525,000
Equatorial Guinea	Malabo	10,830	359,000
Ethiopia	Addis Ababa	472,432	43,882,000
Gabon	Libreville	103,346	1,017,000
Gambia	Banjul	4,093	774,000
Ghana	Accra	92,100	13,552,000
Guinea	Conakry	94,925	5,734,000
Guinea-Bissau	Bissau	13,948	875,000
Ivory Coast	Abidjan	124,502	10,500,000
Kenya	Nairobi	224,960	21,044,000
Lesotho	Maseru	11,720	1,552,000
Liberia	Monrovia	43,000	2,307,000
Libya	Tripoli	679,536	3,876,000

Africa (continued)

Nation	Capital	Area (sq. mi.)	Population
Madagascar	Antananarivo	230,035	10,227,000
Malawi	Lilongwe	45,747	7,292,000
Mali	Bamako	478,819	7,898,000
Mauritania	Nouakchott	397,953	1,691,000
Mauritius	Port Louis	787	1,020,000
Morocco	Rabat	177,116	23,667,000
Mozambique	Maputo	303,073	14,022,000
Namibia[1]	Windhoek	318,261	1,142,000
Niger	Niamey	489,206	6,715,000
Nigeria	Lagos	356,700	105,448,000
Rwanda	Kigali	10,169	6,489,000
São Tomé and Príncipe	São Tomé	372	108,000
Senegal	Dakar	75,954	6,980,000
Seychelles	Victoria	150	67,000
Sierra Leone	Freetown	27,925	3,987,000
Somalia	Mogadishu	246,199	7,825,000
South Africa	Pretoria, Cape Town	437,876	33,241,000
Sudan	Khartoum	967,491	22,932,000
Swaziland	Mbabane	6,704	692,000
Tanzania	Dar es Salaam	364,900	22,415,000
Togo	Lomé	21,925	3,118,000
Tunisia	Tunis	63,379	7,424,000
Uganda	Kampala	91,343	15,158,000
Zaire	Kinshasa	905,365	31,333,000
Zambia	Lusaka	290,586	7,054,000
Zimbabwe	Harare	150,699	8,984,000

[1]Status disputed. See page 789.

TABLE OF NATIONS

The Americas

Nation	Capital	Area (sq. mi.)	Population
Antigua and Barbuda	St. John's	171	82,000
Argentina	Buenos Aires	1,072,067	31,186,000
Bahamas	Nassau	5,380	235,000
Barbados	Bridgetown	166	253,000
Belize	Belmopan	8,867	168,000
Bolivia	La Paz, Sucre	424,162	6,358,000
Brazil	Brasilia	3,286,470	143,277,000
Canada	Ottawa	3,851,809	25,644,000
Chile	Santiago	292,132	12,261,000
Colombia	Bogotá	455,355	29,956,000
Costa Rica	San José	19,652	2,714,000
Cuba	Havana	44,218	10,221,000
Dominica	Roseau	290	74,000
Dominican Republic	Santo Domingo	18,704	6,785,000
Ecuador	Quito	109,484	9,647,000
El Salvador	San Salvador	8,260	5,105,000
Grenada	St. George's	133	86,000
Guatemala	Guatemala City	42,042	8,600,000
Guyana	Georgetown	83,000	771,000
Haiti	Port-au-Prince	10,714	5,870,000
Honduras	Tegucigalpa	43,277	4,648,000
Jamaica	Kingston	4,411	2,288,000
Mexico	Mexico City	761,600	81,709,000
Nicaragua	Managua	50,180	3,342,000
Panama	Panama City	29,761	2,227,000
Paraguay	Asuncion	157,047	4,119,000
Peru	Lima	496,222	20,207,000
St. Christopher and Nevis	Basseterre	100	40,000
St. Lucia	Castries	238	123,000
St. Vincent and the Grenadines	Kingstown	150	103,000
Suriname	Paramaribo	63,251	381,000

The Americas (continued)

Nation	Capital	Area (sq. mi.)	Population
Trinidad and Tobago	Port-of-Spain	1,980	1,204,000
United States	Washington, D.C.	3,540,939	240,856,000
Uruguay	Montevideo	72,172	2,947,000
Venezuela	Caracas	352,143	17,791,000

Asia

Nation	Capital	Area (sq. mi.)	Population
Afghanistan	Kabul	251,000	15,425,000
Bangladesh	Dacca	55,598	104,205,000
Bhutan	Thimphu	18,000	1,446,000
Brunei	Bandar Seri Begawan	2,226	240,000
Burma	Rangoon	261,789	37,651,000
China	Peking	3,691,521	1,045,537,000
India	New Delhi	1,229,737	783,940,000
Indonesia	Djakarta	735,268	176,764,000
Japan	Tokyo	143,574	121,402,000
Kampuchea (Cambodia)	Phnom Penh	69,884	6,388,000
Korea, North	Pyongyang	46,768	20,543,000
Korea, South	Seoul	38,031	43,285,000
Laos	Vientiane	91,429	3,679,000
Malaysia	Kuala Lumpur	128,328	15,820,000
Maldives	Male	115	184,000
Mongolia	Ulan Bator	604,250	1,942,000
Nepal	Katmandu	54,463	17,422,000
Pakistan	Islamabad	310,400	101,855,000
Philippines	Manila	115,830	58,091,000
Singapore	Singapore	238	2,584,000
Sri Lanka	Colombo	25,332	16,638,000
Taiwan	Taipei	13,895	19,601,000
Thailand	Bangkok	198,455	52,438,000
Vietnam	Hanoi	127,246	61,994,000

TABLE OF NATIONS

Nation	Capital	Area (sq. mi.)	Population
Europe (and the Soviet Union)			
Albania	Tirana	11,100	3,020,000
Andorra	Andorra la Vella	175	49,000
Austria	Vienna	32,375	7,546,000
Belgium	Brussels	11,781	9,868,000
Bulgaria	Sofia	42,823	8,990,000
Cyprus	Nicosia	3,572	673,000
Czechoslovakia	Prague	49,374	15,542,000
Denmark	Copenhagen	16,631	5,097,000
Finland	Helsinki	130,119	4,931,000
France	Paris	211,208	55,239,000
Germany, East	Berlin	41,767	16,692,000
Germany, West	Bonn	96,010	60,734,000
Greece	Athens	50,961	9,954,000
Hungary	Budapest	35,919	10,624,000
Iceland	Reykjavik	39,709	244,000
Ireland	Dublin	26,600	3,624,000
Italy	Rome	116,500	57,226,000
Liechtenstein	Vaduz	61	28,000
Luxembourg	Luxembourg	999	367,000
Malta	Valletta	122	354,000
Monaco	Monaco-Ville	0.73	28,000
Netherlands	Amsterdam, The Hague	16,041	14,536,000
Norway	Oslo	125,056	4,165,000
Poland	Warsaw	120,727	37,546,000
Portugal	Lisbon	34,340	10,095,000
Rumania	Bucharest	91,700	22,830,000
San Marino	San Marino	24	23,000
Soviet Union	Moscow	8,649,489	279,904,000
Spain	Madrid	194,885	39,075,000
Sweden	Stockholm	173,800	8,357,000
Switzerland	Bern	15,941	6,466,000
United Kingdom	London	94,247	56,458,000
Vatican City	Vatican City	0.17	737
Yugoslavia	Belgrade	98,766	23,284,000
Middle East (except North Africa)			
Bahrain	Manama	254	422,000
Iran	Tehran	636,293	46,604,000
Iraq	Baghdad	169,284	16,019,000
Israel	Jerusalem	7,992	4,208,000
Jordan	Amman	37,297	2,756,000
Kuwait	Kuwait	7,780	1,771,000
Lebanon	Beirut	4,015	2,675,000
Oman	Muscat	105,000	1,271,000
Qatar	Doha	4,000	305,000
Saudi Arabia	Riyadh	865,000	11,519,000
Syria	Damascus	71,498	10,931,000
Turkey	Ankara	300,947	51,819,000
United Arab Emirates	Abu Dhabi	32,000	1,326,000
Yemen Arab Republic	Sana	75,290	6,339,000
Yemen, People's Democratic Republic of	Aden	111,000	2,275,000
Oceania			
Australia	Canberra	2,966,150	15,793,000
Fiji	Suva	7,078	715,000
Kiribati	Bairiki	264	63,000
Nauru	Yaren	8	8,000
New Zealand	Wellington	103,884	3,305,000
Papua New Guinea	Port Moresby	178,704	3,395,000
Solomon Islands	Honiara	11,500	283,000
Tonga	Nuku'alofa	290	104,000
Tuvalu	Funafuti	10	8,000
Vanuatu	Port-Vila	5,700	136,000
Western Samoa	Apia	1,093	165,000

Sources: *Information Please Almanac and World Factbook.*

Glossary

This glossary includes many of the important words and terms used in this book. Remember that many words have more than one meaning. The definitions given here are the ones that will be most helpful to you in reading world history.

A

abdicate: to give up a powerful position, especially a throne (*page 456*).

abolition: the legal ending of slavery (*page 507*).

absolute monarchy: a government in which a monarch has complete power (*page 169*).

Age of Disunity: the period (A.D. 220 to 589) when China was beset by constant warfare and lack of unified government (*page 255*).

Age of Exploration: the period (1415–1620) when European sea captains made ambitious voyages of exploration and set the stage for an expansion of European power around the world (*page 347*).

Age of Imperialism: the period (1870–1914) when major European nations acquired or expanded overseas empires for the purposes of (1) gaining prestige, new territory, new markets, and new sources of raw materials and (2) competing in international rivalries (*page 550*).

Age of Pericles: the period (about 460 B.C. to 429 B.C.) when, under the leadership of Pericles, Athens reached the height of its achievement (*page 73*).

Age of Reason: *see* Enlightenment.

ahimsa (uh-HIM-sah): nonviolence, the central belief of Jainism (*page 235*).

alchemy (AL-kuh-mee): an ancient field of study that was based on searching for ways to turn common metals into gold (*page 185*).

alliance: an agreement between two or more states for their mutual benefit (*page 73*).

anarchy (AN-ur-kee): the absence of any governmental authority (*page 661*).

anthropologist: a scientist who uses various kinds of evidence in studying the physical and cultural characteristics of human societies (*page 26*).

antibiotic: a drug that kills disease-causing bacteria (*page 846*).

antiseptic: a substance capable of killing bacteria (*page 620*).

apartheid (uh-PART-hite): in South Africa, the government policy of racial segregation and white supremacy (*page 788*).

appeasement: the policy of giving in to the demands of an aggressor in order to maintain peace (*page 699*).

apprentice: a young person bound by agreement to a master artisan for a specific amount of time in return for instruction in a craft (*page 160*).

aqueduct (AK-wih-dukt): a bridgelike structure supporting a channel through which water is transported over a distance (*page 115*).

archeologist (ar-kee-AHL-uh-jist): a scientist who studies the remains of ancient homes, graves, and towns and the artifacts found at those sites (*page 26*).

archon (AR-kon): one of a group of officials, chosen from the nobility, who ruled Athens before Solon's political reforms (*page 70*).

armistice: a halt to fighting; a truce (*page 646*).

artifact: an object, shaped or made by a human being in the past, that has survived to the present (*page 26*).

artisan: a person skilled in a craft (*page 31*).

Asia Minor: the peninsula where Europe and Asia meet, at the eastern end of the Mediterranean Sea (*pages 48, 53*).

assembly: a group of persons who have the authority to meet and pass laws (*page 70*).

assembly line: a manufacturing system in which a product advances on a moving line from one worker to another, each of whom adds a part or performs some other task (*page 526*).

assess: to estimate the value of property for taxation (*page 165*).

astrolabe (AHS-truh-layb): an instrument that helped sea captains of the 1400's and 1500's find their latitude (*page 346*).

atheist (AY-thee-ist): a person who denies the existence of God (*page 408*).

atom: the smallest unit of an element (*page 623*).

atomic theory: a theory about the role of atoms in the structure of material things (*page 87*).

autocrat: a ruler with unlimited power (*page 394*).

B

balance of power: the distribution of power among nations so that no one state dominates (*page 380*).

barter: trade in which people exchange goods without using money (*page 31*).

basin: a low-lying land region from which a river and its tributaries collect water (*page 274*).

bedouin (BED-oo-in): a nomadic Arab (*page 208*).

biology: the scientific study of living things (*page 89*).

blitzkrieg (BLITS-kreeg): a sudden, rapid military attack; from a German word meaning "lightning war" (*page 700*).

bloc: a group of nations, parties, or people united for a common purpose (*page 724*).

bourgeois (boor-ZHWAH): in Marxist terminology, the middle-class capitalists who own the means of production, such as factories, mines, banks, and businesses (*page 532*).

bourgeoisie (boor-zhwah-ZEE): the middle class, especially in France (*page 443*).

boyar: a noble in czarist Russia (*page 394*).

boycott: to refuse to buy or use a product (*page 563*).

Bronze Age: a period (beginning in different regions at different times) when bronze replaced copper and stone as the main material in tools and weapons. In the Near East, this age began about 3000 B.C. (*page 32*).

bullion (BULL-yun): gold or silver measured in large quantities (*page 351*).

bureaucrat (BYOO-ruh-krat): a trained public official who is appointed rather than elected (*page 249*).

Bushido **(BOO-SHEE-DOH):** the code of behavior followed by samurai (warriors) in traditional Japanese society (*page 264*).

C

caliph (KAY-lif): a Muslim political and religious leader (*page 210*).

capital: wealth or property that is used to produce more wealth (*page 366*).

capitalism: the economic system that is based on a free market and open competition (*page 366*).

caravel (KAIR-uh-vel): a type of sailing ship used by the Portuguese during the 1400's (*page 347*).

cardinal: a high-ranking official of the Roman Catholic Church (*page 170*).

caste (KAST) system: the Hindu system of rigid social groups based on class, occupation, and tradition (*page 230*).

caudillo (kow-DEE-yoh): in Latin America, a dictator who came to power by gaining the support of the army and of wealthy landowners (*page 498*).

censorship: the policy of stopping the publication and distribution of works that government or other authorities find objectionable (*page 409*).

Central America: the part of North America that lies between Mexico and South America (*page 293; maps, pages 293, 824*).

Central Asia: a large region of Asia, located to the northwest of India; today, the western part of China (*page 205; map, page 219*).

charter: a document granting a group of people certain rights and privileges (*page 161*).

chivalry (SHIV-ul-ree): the code of behavior followed by feudal nobles and knights (*page 146*).

circumference (sur-KUM-fur-uns): the boundary of a round thing, such as the planet earth; also the measurement of that boundary (*page 90*).

circumnavigation: sailing completely around something, for example, the earth (*page 354*).

city-state: an independent state consisting of a city and the surrounding territory (*page 40*).

civil disobedience: the use of nonviolent resistance to defy laws thought to be unjust (*page 766*).

civil service system: a system basing government employment on competitive tests (*page 255*).

civil war: a war fought between groups in the same country or region (*page 138*).

clan: a group of families or a small tribal community (*page 260*).

climate: the general weather conditions of a place including the usual temperature range and rain- and snowfall over long periods (*page 29*).

coalition (koh-uh-LISH-un): an alliance of different factions, parties, or nations (*page 688*).

code of laws: a systematically organized collection of laws (*page 43*).

collective farming: the bringing together of the livestock, equipment, and buildings of many small farms on one large piece of land under government control (*page 668*).

colony: a settlement of people in a territory outside their homeland, but still bound to the parent country by government, trade, or culture (*page 68*).

Commercial Revolution: the period of Western history (1450–1700) when new resources and new business practices resulted in great changes in all economic aspects of life (*page 362*).

common law: a system of law that developed in England, based on earlier royal court decisions and on established customs (*page 166*).

commune (KOM-yoon): an agricultural unit in China made up of a number of large, state-owned farms (*page 759*).

concession: a grant by one country to another of special trading privileges, facilities, or access to resources (*page 551*).

confederacy: a loose alliance of several states, communities, or cultural groups (*page 307*).

confederation: a union of self-governing provinces (*page 516*).

conquistador (kon-KEE-stah-dohr): one of the Spanish conquerors of American Indian civilizations (*page 355*).

conservatism: a political philosophy that emphasizes the preservation of traditions and established institutions (*page 462*).

constitution: a plan of government (*page 434*).

consul: the title given to the two officials who governed the Roman Republic (*page 96*).

containment: the policy of limiting Communist governments to those countries where they already exist (*page 726*).

continent: one of the seven large land masses of the earth (Africa, Antarctica, Asia, Australia, Europe, North America, South America) (*page 29*).

contract: a legal agreement (*page 41*).

council: a group of persons elected or appointed to serve some governmental purpose (*page 71*).

Counter-Reformation: the reform movement that began within the Roman Catholic Church in the 1500's as a reaction to the Reformation (*page 340*).

counterrevolution: a movement that opposes a revolution and attempts to restore the government that was previously in power (*page 449*).

coup d'état (**KOO day-TAH**): the sudden overthrow of a government (*page 452, footnote*).

creole (KREE-ohl): a descendant of Spanish or Portuguese colonists in the Americas (*page 357*).

crop rotation: the practice of alternating crops grown in a field from year to year (*page 522*).

cuneiform (KYOO-nee-uh-form): a system of writing devised by ancient Near Eastern peoples, using wedge-shaped characters inscribed on clay tablets (*page 41*).

customs union: an international organization formed for the purpose of reducing tariff barriers among its members (*page 481*).

czar (ZAR): the title of the emperors of Russia from the late 1400's to 1918 (*page 394*).

czarina (zah-REE-nuh): a Russian empress (*page 396*).

D

daimyo (DYE-MYOH): a local lord in traditional Japanese society (*page 265*).

decree: an order issued by some official authority (*page 193*).

deist (DEE-ist): a person who believes in God but rejects the authority of organized religion (*page 408*).

deity (DEE-ih-tee): a god or goddess (*page 31*).

delta: the land area (often triangular) formed by soil deposited at the mouth of a river (*page 45*).

democracy: a form of government based on rule by the people (*page 70*).

denazification: a process of eliminating the practices and influence of Nazism (*page 738*).

depression: a period of drastic decline in economic activity, marked by widespread unemployment and hardship (*page 677*).

desert: a dry region that has little vegetation (*page 45*).

détente (day-TAHNT): a relaxing of tensions between nations (*page 733*).

deterrence: the policy of discouraging an attack by making one's enemy fear a counterattack (*page 730*).

dharma (**DAR-muh**): the rights and duties of members of various classes in Indian society (*page 229*).

dialect: the form of a language spoken in a certain region (*page 188*).

dialogue: a discussion in the form of a conversation; also a literary work written in such a form (*page 88*).

dictator: a ruler with absolute power (*page 102*).

diplomacy: relations between governments, especially in respect to making agreements, treaties, and alliances (*page 98*).

dissident: one who openly disagrees with his or her nation's policies (*page 751*).

divine right: the theory that monarchs receive their power from God and consequently should not be questioned or disobeyed (*page 383*).

doctrine: a rule, principle, or belief that is accepted as part of the basis for a philosophy or religion (*page 128*).

domain: a territory over which a ruler holds power (*page 144*).

domestication: the taming of wild animals to make them useful to human beings (*page 30*).

domestic system: a method of production in which raw materials are distributed to employees who work in their homes to produce goods (*page 523*).

dominion: one of certain self-governing nations within the Commonwealth of Nations (*page 688*).

duchy (DUCH-ee): the land ruled by a duke or duchess (*page 169*).

dynastic cycle: the rise and fall of dynasties in a regular pattern (*page 252*).

dynasty: a series of rulers from the same family (*page 46*).

E

economy: the system by which a society produces and distributes its goods and services (*page 47*).

edict: an official order or decree (*page 378*).

electron: a certain kind of particle contained within an atom (*page 624*).

embargo: the suspension of foreign trade, often limited to certain products and directed at specific nations (*page 831*).

émigré (**ay-mih-GRAY**): one of the nobles who fled France during the French Revolution (*page 445*).

empire: a state and the conquered lands that it rules (*page 41*).

GLOSSARY

enclosure movement: a widespread trend in England during the 1700's, involving (1) the buying up of small landholdings by large landowners and (2) the fencing in of lands previously open for use by all people in a village (*page 522*).

enlightened despot: a European ruler who introduced reforms that seemed to reflect the spirit of the Enlightenment (*page 412*).

Enlightenment: the period of Western history (in the 1700's) when thinkers, especially in Britain and France, tried to use reason to understand and improve society, government, and humanity. Also called the Age of Reason (*page 407*).

entente (ahn-TAHNT): a French word meaning "understanding" (*page 638*).

entrepreneur (ahn-truh-pruh-NUR): a person who starts up and operates his or her own business (*page 522*).

epic: a long poem that tells the adventures of a hero or heroes (*page 66*).

equator: the line of latitude (0°) that divides the earth into the northern and southern hemispheres (*page 274; map, pages 858–859*).

erosion (ih-ROH-zhun): the wearing away of features of the earth's surface, usually by the action of natural forces, such as wind or water (*page 377*).

excommunicate: to expel a person from the Roman Catholic Church (*page 171*).

executive: the branch of government that has the responsibility for leadership and for carrying out laws (*page 409*).

expressionist: one of the group of painters, active in the late 1800's, who used new techniques to convey intense emotion (*page 628*).

F

factory system: a method of production in which workers are brought together to produce goods by machines in factories (*page 523*).

fallow: referring to farmland that is not planted (*page 150*).

famine: a severe shortage of food (*page 43*).

fascism (FASH-iz-um): an ideology stressing dictatorship and nationalism and placing the strength of the state above the welfare of individual citizens (*page 674*).

federal system: a two-level system of government made up of a supreme national government and states retaining strong local powers (*page 436*).

Fertile Crescent: a crescent-shaped area of land stretching from the Persian Gulf to the eastern shore of the Mediterranean Sea (*page 40*).

feudalism: the political system of medieval Europe, under which lords granted land to other nobles in return for loyalty, military assistance, and services (*page 145*).

fief (FEEF): land granted by a feudal lord to another noble (*page 145*).

filial piety: respect for and obedience to one's parents (*page 250*).

fossil: human or animal bones or teeth and other traces left in rocks by ancient plants or animals (*page 26*).

fresco: the art of painting on wet plaster, or a picture painted in this way (*page 332*).

G

galley: a ship of the ancient Roman navy (*page 111*).

gene: one of the tiny units that carry hereditary traits from parents to offspring (*page 626*).

genocide (JEN-uh-side): the systematic murder of an entire people (*page 706*).

geocentric theory: the belief that the earth is the center of the universe (*page 402*).

geologist: a scientist who analyzes fossils and the rocks in which they are found (*page 26*).

ghetto: a section of a European town or city where Jews were required to live (*page 632*).

glacier: a large, slow-moving sheet of ice, often formed in mountain ranges (*page 29*).

gladiator: a person, usually a slave or condemned criminal, who fought other gladiators or wild animals as public entertainment in ancient Rome (*page 112*).

Glorious Revolution: the change in monarchs in England in 1688; James II was removed from power and Parliament offered the throne to William of Orange and Mary, the daughter of James II; the new monarchs became William III and Mary II (*page 390*).

grand jury: a jury that determines whether evidence justifies charging a person with a crime (*page 166*).

gravity: the attraction that masses of matter exert on each other (*page 404*).

Greco-Roman culture: the eastern Mediterranean culture that developed from the blending of Greek and Roman cultures (*page 113*).

gross national product (GNP): the total value of all goods and services produced in a nation over a specific period of time (*page 739*).

guerrilla warfare: a type of warfare in which small groups of fighters make surprise attacks (*page 456*).

guild: a medieval organization formed by merchants of the same trade or by artisans of the same craft; it protected its members and set business policies (*page 160*).

gulag (GOO-lahg): a forced-labor camp in the Soviet Union (*page 668*).

H

heliocentric (hee-lee-oh-SEN-trik) theory: the belief that the sun is at the center of the universe (*page 402*).

Hellenic (huh-LEN-ik) Age: the period (about 800 B.C.–323 B.C.) when the civilization of the ancient Greeks took shape and reached its height (*page 64*).

Hellenistic (hel-uh-NIS-tik) Age: the period following Alexander's conquests (from about 323 B.C. to about 100 B.C.) when Greek culture spread through the lands he had conquered (*page 77*).

helot (HEL-ut): a person forced to work as a farm laborer in ancient Sparta (*page 69*).

heresy (HEHR-uh-see): the holding of beliefs considered wrong by the Church (*page 172*).

hieroglyphics (hy-ruh-GLIF-iks): the ancient Egyptian writing system that used pictures to symbolize words or sounds (*page 49*).

humanist: a Renaissance scholar of ancient Greek and Roman literature and philosophy (*page 326*).

humanities: subjects such as language, literature, history, and philosophy, that are concerned with human beings and their cultures (*page 326*).

I

Iberia (eye-BIR-ee-uh): the peninsula where Spain and Portugal are located (*page 173*).

Ice Age: one of the extremely long periods during which temperatures in large parts of the Northern Hemisphere were cold enough to produce huge sheets of ice over much of the land area (*page 29*).

icon (EYE-kon): a religious image painted on wood (*page 206*).

ideology (eye-dee-AHL-uh-jee): a set of often rigid or inflexible political beliefs (*page 662*).

imperial: relating to an empire or emperor (*page 106*).

imperialism: the policy of empire-building, or extending a nation's control over other lands to gain economic and political advantages (*page 550*).

impressionist: one of the group of painters, active in the late 1800's, who sought to show how movement, color, and light appeared to the eye in a fleeting instant (*page 628*).

incentive: something that makes a person want to undertake a certain action (*page 156*).

indentured servant: an individual who agrees to work a certain number of years in exchange for passage by ship to a new land (*page 426*).

indulgence: a pardon for sinning, given by the Catholic Church, at first as a reward for some special service and later in return for a contribution of money (*page 336*).

inertia (in-ER-shuh): the tendency of a physical body to remain at rest or, if moving, to continue to move (*page 404*).

inflation: rising prices caused by a scarcity of goods and an abundance of available money and credit (*page 365*).

inscription: something that is written, especially on an object, such as a stone foundation, tomb, wall, or tablet (*page 44*).

irrigation: supplying farmlands with water by means of canals or ditches (*page 34*).

isolationism: the policy of avoiding involvement in the affairs of other nations (*page 651*).

isthmus (ISS-mus): a narrow strip of land connecting two larger land masses (*page 353*).

J

jihad (jih-HAHD): Arab term meaning "holy war" (*page 210*).

joint-stock company: a company financed by the selling of shares of stock that give the purchasers part ownership (*page 364*).

journeyman: one who has completed an apprenticeship and works for a master craftsman for daily wages (*page 160*).

judiciary: the branch of government responsible for interpreting laws, judging lawbreakers, and dealing with disputes between individuals (*page 409*).

junta (HOON-tah): a small ruling group, especially in a Latin American country (*page 824*).

jury: a group of citizens whose purpose is to give a judgment on some legal matter (*page 70*).

K

kaiser (KY-zer): the title of the German emperor in the late 1800's and early 1900's (*page 484*).

karma: in Hindu belief, the accumulated good and bad acts of all one's previous lives (*page 230*).

kulak (koo-LAK): a peasant farmer in Russia (*page 658*).

L

laissez faire (LES-ay FAIR): the doctrine that government should not interfere with business (*page 530*).

land bridge: a long stretch of land that connects two large land areas and serves as a crossing point between these two areas (*page 29*).

laser (LAY-zur): a high-energy beam of light (*page 841*).

latifundia: the great landed estates of the ancient Romans (*page 100*).

latitude: distance north or south of the equator (*page 865*).

layman: a person who is not a member of the clergy (*page 173*).

legislature: a governmental body that has the responsibility for making laws (*page 409*).

liberalism: a political philosophy that emphasizes progress and reform (*page 462*).

limited monarchy: a government in which the powers of the monarch are limited by law or by a governing body such as a parliament (*page 167*).

longitude: distance east or west of the prime meridian (*page 865*).

M

mandate: a country or region that is assigned by some official authority to be administered by another nation (*page 648*).

mandate of heaven: the approval of the gods, according to the early Chinese, for rulers to stay in power as long as they ruled well (*page 248*).

manifest destiny: the nineteenth-century doctrine that the United States had the right and duty to expand westward to the Pacific Ocean (*page 504*).

manor: the self-sufficient estate of a medieval lord (*page 149*).

manorialism (muh-NAWR-ee-ul-iz-um): the economic system of Europe during the Middle Ages, based on large estates owned by nobles and worked by serfs (*page 149*).

market economy: an economic system that depends on the buying and selling of goods and services with little or no government intervention (*page 367*).

martial law: strict controls maintained over a nation by military forces (*page 753*).

martyr (MAR-tur): a person who endures persecution even to the point of death rather than give up his or her religious beliefs (*page 129*).

medieval (mee-dee-EE-vul, meed-EE-vul): belonging or related to the Middle Ages (*pages 137, 139*). *Also see* Middle Ages.

megalopolis (meg-uh-LAHP-uh-lis): a densely populated urban area comprising several cities linked by good transportation routes (*page 848*).

mercantile: relating to merchants or trade (*page 366*).

mercantilism: an economic policy that stressed the accumulation of gold and silver, the founding of colonies and the regulation of their trade, and the making of profit from foreign trade (*page 364*).

mercenary: a soldier of foreign background, hired for pay (*page 364*).

Mesoamerica (meh-zoh-uh-MEHR-ih-kuh): the region that stretches from central Mexico into Central America (*page 293*).

Middle Ages: the period of Western history that followed the end of ancient civilization. The Middle Ages are subdivided by some historians into the early Middle Ages (500–1050), the High Middle Ages (1050–1270), and the late Middle Ages (1270–1500) (*page 125*).

middle class: in the Middle Ages, a social class that emerged in the towns, including merchants, artisans, their families, and others who did not have feudal obligations; later, those who were socially and economically between the working class and the nobility or very wealthy upper class (*page 163*).

migrate: to move from one region or country and settle in another (*page 53*).

militarism: the policy of glorifying war and promoting the build-up of military power (*page 638*).

militia (muh-LISH-uh): an organized, trained army of citizens (*page 431*).

missionary: someone who travels with the goal of making converts to a particular religion (*page 127*).

monopoly: the control of all (or nearly all) trade and production in a certain product (*page 346*).

monotheism: the belief in one God (*page 56*).

mosaic (moh-ZAY-ik): a picture or design formed by fitting together small pieces of colored stone or glass (*page 206*).

mosque (MOSK): a Muslim place of worship (*page 215*).

muezzin (myoo-EZ-in): a Muslim prayer leader (*page 215*).

multicultural: characterized by the presence of people of different cultural backgrounds (*page 369*).

myth: a traditional story or legend told about supernatural beings and heroes (*page 66*).

N

nationalism: a feeling of devotion to and pride in one's country (*page 452*).

nationalize: to bring under government control a resource or economic operation that previously was privately owned and operated (*page 739*).

national state: an independent state consisting of a certain area and a unified group or groups of people (*page 164*).

natural law: the name given by ancient Greeks to the general laws followed by nature (*page 87*).

natural rights: rights that all human beings are entitled to (*page 408*).

Nazism (NAHT-siz-um): the ideology of the National Socialist German Workers' Party, based on state control of the economy, racist nationalism, and national expansion (*page 677*).

Near East: the area from Egypt to Mesopotamia (*page 29*).

Neolithic Age: the period of prehistory, beginning about 8000 B.C., when people began to apply improved techniques for shaping and polishing stone tools. Also called the New Stone Age (*page 29*).

neutral: not supporting or assisting either side in a war or dispute (*page 503*).

New Stone Age: *see* Neolithic Age.

nomad: one of a group of people who have no fixed home and wander from place to place in search of food and water (*page 27*).

nonaligned: not committed to the goals and policies of either side in a competitive situation (*page 733*).

nonconformist: someone who does not belong to a national or established church; for example, an English Protestant who does not belong to the Church of England (*page 390*).

North Africa: the region of Africa along the Mediterranean coast (*page 68*).

GLOSSARY

O

oasis (oh-AY-sis): a place in a desert where water is available from a spring or well (*page 208*).

Old Stone Age: *see* Paleolithic Age.

optics: the scientific study of light and vision (*page 184*).

oracle: a temple where priests and priestesses in ancient Greece gave prophecies, or the priest or priestess who made the prophecy (*page 66*).

organism: a living thing — plant or animal (*page 27*).

ostracism (AHS-truh-siz-um): in ancient Athens, the practice of forcing a person believed to be dangerous to leave the city-state for ten years (*page 71*).

outcaste: an Untouchable; a person excluded from all castes in Hindu society (*page 231*).

P

paddies: wetlands in which rice is grown (*page 30*).

pagan: a person who does not follow or accept one of the great world religions (*page 213*).

Paleolithic (pay-lee-oh-LITH-ik) Age: the longest part of the prehistoric period; ended approximately 8000 B.C. Also called the Old Stone Age (*pages 27, 29*).

Pan-Arabism: a movement calling for a strong sense of unity among Arab peoples and nations (*page 802*).

papacy (PAY-puh-see): the office or authority of the Pope (*page 169*).

papyrus (puh-PY-rus): a reedlike plant from which the ancient Egyptians made paper scrolls (*page 49*).

parent culture: a culture from which other, later cultures derived their ways of living (*page 294*).

parliament: an assembly of representatives who make the laws of a nation (*page 167*).

partisan (PAR-tih-zun): a member of a fighting group that attacks the conquering forces in an occupied region or country (*pages 710–711*).

partition: the division of something into parts (*page 393*).

pasha: the governor of a part of the Ottoman Empire (*page 486*).

pass laws: South African laws that, by requiring blacks to carry passes at all times, enabled officials to control the movements of nonwhites (*page 592*).

pasteurization: a treatment that kills bacteria in milk (*page 620*).

paterfamilias (pah-tur-fah-MIL-ee-us): the father of a family and head of a household in ancient Rome (*page 111*).

patriarch (PAY-tree-ark): in the Byzantine Empire, the head of the Church in Constantinople (today, a title held by high-ranking bishops in certain churches) (*page 202*).

patrician (puh-TRISH-un): one of the class of wealthy landowners to which the leaders of the Roman Republic belonged (*page 96*).

patron (PAY-trun): someone who supports the arts (*page 328*).

***Pax Romana* (PAKS roh-MAH-nuh):** the period (27 B.C. to A.D. 180) when ancient Rome and the empire it ruled enjoyed long stretches of peace and prosperity (*page 105*).

peaceful coexistence: relations between nations that are peaceful rather than hostile or warlike (*page 730*).

penance: an action undertaken to show regret and sorrow for wrongdoing (*page 336*).

peninsula: a piece of land nearly surrounded by water (*page 53*).

peon: a peasant, especially in the American lands conquered by Spain (*page 357*).

persecution: systematic, continual mistreatment (*page 129*).

perspective: the impression of depth and distance on the flat surface of a painting (*page 332*).

pharaoh (FAIR-oh): a ruler of ancient Egypt (*page 46*).

philosophe (FIL-oh-sof): any of the leading social critics and writers of the Enlightenment (*page 408*).

philosophy: the study by logical reasoning of basic truths and ideas (*page 86*).

pilgrim: a traveler to a sacred place (*page 174*).

plague: a widespread outbreak of a serious disease (*page 124*).

plain: a low-lying, level stretch of land (*page 40*).

plantation: a large farm on which crops are grown and harvested by human labor (*page 283*).

plateau: a high level area (*page 208*).

plebeian (plih-BEE-un): a member of the class of common people in ancient Rome (*page 97*).

pogrom (POH-grum): an organized campaign of persecution carried out against Jews, especially in Russia (*page 633*).

polis (POH-lis): a city-state of ancient Greece (*page 69*).

polytheism (PAHL-ee-thee-iz-um): the belief in many gods (*page 40*).

Pope: the bishop of Rome and head of the Roman Catholic Church (*page 139*).

potlatch: a traditional celebration of special occasions, featuring lavish gifts, among the Northwest Coast Indians of North America (*page 304*).

potter's wheel: a spinning disk or turntable on which clay is shaped by hand or with hand tools (*page 35*).

predestination: the belief that certain people are chosen by God for salvation (*page 338*).

prehistory: the period of time before writing and record-keeping systems were developed (*page 26*).

privateer: a ship that is privately owned but which is authorized by a government to attack and capture enemy ships (*page 361*).

private ownership: the right of individuals to own and control capital (money and property); a major characteristic of capitalism (*page 367*).

profit motive: the desire to make a profit; one of the major characteristics of capitalism (*page 367*).

projection: a way of drawing the curved surface of the earth as a flat map (*page 865*).

proletariat (proh-luh-TAIR-ee-ut): wage-earning laborers (*page 532*).

propaganda: news and information designed to persuade people to adopt a particular point of view (*page 644*).

prophet: a person who is believed to be able to communicate messages from God (*page 56*).

proprietary colony: a colony established on land granted to a noble (the "proprietor") by a monarch (*page 426*).

protective tariff: a tax on imported goods, intended to protect a country's own industries (*page 504*).

protectorate: a country protected and partially controlled by a stronger country (*page 486*).

province: a territory governed as an administrative or political unit of a country or empire (*page 98*).

psychology: the study of human behavior (*page 627*).

pueblo (PWEB-loh): "town" in Spanish; one of the large community dwellings used by certain Indian peoples of the Southwest (*page 303*).

Q

quipu (KEE-poo): an Inca system of record-keeping using colored cords knotted at intervals to indicate different sums (*page 302*).

R

racism: the belief that one's own racial or national group is superior to others (*page 632*).

radiation: high-speed rays of energy given off by certain elements (*page 623*).

radical: extreme; a term often applied to someone who demands revolutionary changes in government (*page 448*).

rain forest: a thick forest in a region that has heavy rainfall and warm humid air (*page 274*).

rajah: a chief in the early Aryan society of India; later, a ruler of a state in India (*page 229*).

rani (RAH-nee): a queen in Hindu society (*page 232*).

realist: a writer who aims at depicting reality and whose work usually reflects social problems and the lives of ordinary people (*page 630*).

recession: a moderate, temporary slowdown in business activity (*page 826*).

Reformation: in Europe in the 1500's, the movement that rebelled against the authority of the Roman Catholic Church (*page 338*).

Reich (RYK): the German word for "empire"; specifically the German nation formed in 1871 by the uniting of several states under a strong central government (*page 541*).

Renaissance (reh-nuh-SAHNS): the period of Western history, beginning in the 1300's, when far-reaching changes occurred in the arts, intellectual life, and ways of viewing the world (*page 326*).

reparations (rep-uh-RAY-shunz): payments made by one nation to another in compensation for property destroyed in war (*page 648*).

repatriation: a move back to one's ancestral land (*page 588*).

republic: in ancient Rome, a form of government that was not a monarchy (*page 96*); in modern times, a democratic government in which citizens choose representatives to govern them (*page 448*).

reservation: a section of land set aside by a government for a certain purpose; in the United States, for example, land reserved for the use of an Indian tribe (*page 509*).

reservoir: a body of water built or created to store water (*page 45*).

Restoration: the period (1660–1685) when Charles II, who represented the "restoring" of the monarchy, reigned in England (*page 390*).

revolution: (1) an extreme and long-lasting change in ways of living (*page 156*); (2) a sudden change from one ruler or government to another (*page 390*).

romanticism: a nineteenth-century movement that stressed emotion and imagination over order and reason, and which influenced European social and political thinking, art, and literature (*page 467*).

ronin (ROH-NIN): in Japanese society, a samurai or warrior who had no lord to serve (*page 268*).

royal colony: a colony owned directly by a monarch (*page 426*).

S

sacraments: special Christian ceremonies, such as baptism, communion, and marriage (*page 139*).

samurai (SAH-MOO-RYE): a class of noble-warriors in feudal Japan (*page 263*).

satellite: (1) a nation that is dominated politically by another nation (*page 724*); (2) an object placed in orbit around the earth (*page 730*).

savanna: a flat, open grassland with scattered clumps of trees and shrubs (*page 274*).

schism (SIZ-um): a division within a religious organization (*page 193*).

scientific method: the use of experimentation and observation in the study of the natural world (*page 403*).

Scientific Revolution: the great change in ways of thinking about the physical world that came about in the late 1500's and the 1600's, when the foundations of modern science were laid (*page 402*).

scribe: in ancient societies, a person who was trained to make documents and records (*page 41*).

script: a type of writing (*page 44*).

secede: to withdraw formally from an alliance, organization, or association (*page 507*).

sectionalism: extreme loyalty to one's region (*page 507*).

self-sufficient: able to produce everything that is needed (*page 149*).

separation of powers: the division of a government into several branches, each having its own powers (*page 409*).

sepoy (SEE-poy): a soldier in Britain's Indian army (*page 557*).

serf: a medieval peasant who was legally bound to remain on the estate of a lord (*page 149*).

shire: a county in England (*page 165*).

shogun (SHO-gun): one of the military leaders who ruled Japan in the name of the emperor from the twelfth to the nineteenth centuries (*page 263*).

shrine: a sacred place (*page 40*).

silt: particles of sand and clay (*page 45*).

socialism: a political and economic philosophy that calls for government or worker ownership and operation of business and industry for the benefit of society (*page 470*).

sociology: the scientific study of human society (*page 626*).

Southeast Asia: the region of Asia that includes such nations as Burma, Thailand, Laos, Vietnam, Malaysia, and Indonesia (*page 254; maps, pages 254, 863*).

soviet: a representative council of workers, peasants, or soldiers in the Soviet Union (*page 658*).

sphere of influence: a limited area of a country in which another country gains the right to control politics or government (*page 551*).

steppe: a vast plain in Central Asia (*page 207*).

stockholder: a person who owns shares of stock in a joint-stock company or corporation (*page 364*).

straits or **strait:** a narrow passage of water connecting two larger bodies of water (*page 202*).

subcontinent: a large land mass, such as India, that is geographically and culturally distinct from the rest of a continent (*page 226*).

succession: the order in which one person after another becomes ruler of an empire or kingdom (*page 106*).

suffrage: the right to vote (*page 538*).

sultan: the ruler of a Muslim country (*page 175*).

summit conference: a meeting of top officials of two or more nations (*page 730*).

surplus: a greater supply than is needed (*page 50*).

T

tariff: a tax on imported or exported goods (*page 481*).

technology: the development of methods, materials, and tools used in doing work (*page 31*).

terrace: a wide, steplike bank of soil (*page 300*).

terrorism: the use of violence, especially against random victims, to win demands or influence the policies of a government (*page 813*).

theology: the study of religious thought (*page 182*).

totalitarian: designating a government in which unified action is achieved through the complete authority of the leader (*page 669*).

totem (TOH-tum): a clan or family symbol among the Northwest Coast Indians of North America (*page 304, footnote*).

tract: a stretch of land (*page 156*).

treaty port: a coastal center of trade in China where Westerners were allowed to carry on business (*page 570*).

trek: a Boer word meaning "difficult journey" (*page 592*).

tribune: in ancient Rome, an official who was responsible for protecting the rights of the common people (*page 97*).

tributary: a river or stream that flows into a larger river or stream (*page 226*).

tributary system: the system by which foreign countries were expected to send lavish gifts (tribute) to the Chinese emperor as a sign of respect and inferior status (*pages 260, 568*).

tribute: payment demanded from a conquered people as evidence of their submission to the conquerors (*page 48*).

triumvirate (try-UM-vih-rut): in ancient Rome, a group of three leaders who shared supreme power in a government (*page 102*).

trust territory: a territory assigned by the United Nations to be administered by a particular country (*page 723*).

tyrant: a ruler who held complete power in a Greek city-state; a dictator (*page 70*).

U

ultimatum (ul-tuh-MAY-tum): a statement that threatens some serious action if certain demands are not met (*page 639*).

urbanization: the movement of people from rural areas to cities, resulting in the growth of the cities (*page 528*).

utopia (yoo-TOH-pih-uh): an ideal society (*page 531*).

V

vassal: a medieval noble who pledged loyalty and services to a feudal lord in exchange for a grant of land and serfs (*page 145*).

vernacular (vur-NAK-yuh-lur): a language, such as French or Italian, that developed from Latin and became the language of everyday life (*page 185*).

viceroy (VYS-roy): a representative of the Spanish king in Spain's American colonies (*page 356*).

Z

ziggurat (ZIG-uh-rat): one of the large brick temples built by the people of Mesopotamia (*page 40*).

Index

Southern Sung, Chinese dynasty, 258
South German states, 482, 483, *m483*
South Korea, 729, *m760*
South Manchurian Railway, 583
South Slavs, 391, 485, 639, 647
South Vietnam, 774–776. *See also* Vietnam
South-West Africa (Namibia), *m594,* 644, *m649. See also* Namibia
South-West Africa People's Organization (SWAPO), 789
South Yemen. *See* People's Democratic Republic of Yemen
Souvanna Phouma, 776
Soviet bloc nations, 724, *m725,* 726, 730, 733, 744, 751–753
soviets, workers', 658, 663; Congress of, 663–664
Soviet Union, government of, 659–660, *c664;* communism in, 661–665, 666, 667, 669, 690; republics of, 664–665, *m667;* under Stalin, 666–669; collectivization in, 668, 730; constitution of, 668–669; and Spanish Civil War, 681–682; and China, 689, 748, 761; Nazi-Soviet pact, 700, 703; in World War II, 703–705, 711, 712, 713, 747–748; persecution of Poles by, 706; war losses of, 713; and occupation of Germany, 713, 733; and UN, 722, 723; Eastern Europe dominated by, 724, 726–727; and cold war, 724–726, 730, 731; after World War II, *m725,* 747–751; and Berlin blockade, 727; atomic bomb tested by, 728; in Korea, 729; and summit conferences, 730, 731; and "peaceful coexistence," 730, 731, 748; and space race, 730–731; and Nuclear Test Ban Treaty, 732; and Cuban missile crisis, 732, 748, 819; and SALT I, 733, 830; and SALT II, 833; and détente, 748, 830; and Chernobyl incident, 749–750, 751; invades Afghanistan, 750, 833; dissidents in, 751, 831; and *glasnost,* 751; and Africa, 795; and Middle East, 805, 807, 811, 812, 813; in El Salvador, 825; and South Korean airliner, 833. *See also* Russia
Soweto, 790
Soyuz spacecraft, 843
space programs, 730–731,

p731, 829, 842, 843, 846, *p846,* 853
Spain, and Roman Empire, *m98;* Germanic tribes in, 120, 122, *m122,* 138; taken by Charlemagne, *m142,* 143; Muslims in, 173, 182, 211, *m211,* 212, 213, 214; Reconquest of, 173, *m174,* 219; as center of learning, 182; Byzantine forces in, 203; African colonies of, 283; in America, 299, 351–354, *m352–353,* 355–360, 361, 497, 513n.; Renaissance in, 331; revolts in, 346, 465, 744; and growth of trade, 365, 368; dominates Europe, 374–376; defeat of Invincible Armada, 376, 387; declining power of, 376–378; independence of Netherlands from, 382; and War of the Spanish Succession, 385–386; alliances of, 450; Napoleon in, 456; American colonies independent of, 494–497, *m496;* cedes Florida, 504; Civil War in, 681–682, *m697,* 698; fascism in, 681–682, 704, 744; monarchy restored in, 744; and European Community, 745
Spanish-American War, 511–512, 772
Spanish Armada, 376
Spanish Civil War, 681–682, *m697,* 698
Sparta, *m67,* 68, 69, 72, *m72,* 73, 75–76, *m76*
Spartacus, 102
Speke, John, 589
Spencer, Herbert, 632
sphere of influence, definition of, 551
Spice Islands, *m352–353,* 555
spice trade, 212, 239, 346, 350, 351, 361
Sputnik satellite, 731, 842
Sri Lanka (Ceylon), 235, 741, *m863*
Stalin, Joseph, 666, 667–668, *p668,* 699, 700, 712, 724, 726, 727, 730, 748, 761; quoted, 666, 668; purges by, 669
Stalingrad, Battle of, *m702,* 704–705, *p705,* 710
Stamp Act, 429
Stanislavsky, Konstantin, 631
Stanley, Henry M., 590, 594
Star Chamber, 388
states' rights, 507
steam power, 522, 526
Steele, Richard, 413
steel production, 523, 527, 618, 666, 749, 758
Steffens, Lincoln, 537
Stephen (Saint), king of Hungary, 391

steppe, 207
Steuben, Baron von, 434
stockholder, 364
Stockholm Pact, 733
stock market crash, 686
Stoicism, 91, 115
Stolypin, Peter, 658
Stone Age. *See* Neolithic; Paleolithic
Stonehenge, *p24*
Strait, 202; of Magellan, *m352–353,* 354
Strategic Arms Limitation Treaty, SALT I, 733, 830; SALT II, 833
Strategic Defense Initiative (SDI), 833
Strauss, Johann and Richard, 630
Stravinsky, Igor, 630
Stuart kings (England), 387–388
Stuart Restoration, 389–390
Stupas, *p233*
subcontinent, 226
submarines, 644, *p645,* 730
succession, 106
Sucre, Antonio José de, 495
Sudan, 274, *m275,* 276–279, *m277,* 283, 595, 597
Sudetenland, *m697,* 698, 699, 738
Sudras, 229, 232
Suez Canal, 560, 583, *m591,* *m594,* 595, *m702,* 705, 706, 805, *m810;* in 1869, *p552;* conflict over, 810–811
suffrage, 538–539. *See also* Voting
suffragists, 650
sugar, 283, 284, 350, 368, 494
Sugar Act, 429
Suharto, 773
Sui dynasty, 255–256
Suiko (empress), 261
Sukarno, 773
Suleiman "the Magnificent," 221
Sulla, Lucius Cornelius, 102
Sully, Duc de, 379
sultans, 175, 221, 241, 279
Sumer, *m33, m40,* 40–43, 227
summit conferences, 730, 731
sunbelt, 826–827
Sundiata, 278
Sung dynasty, 258, 259
Sunni Ali, 279
Sunni Muslims, 211
Sun Yat-sen, 576–577, *p577,* 689–690; quoted, 576
Sun Zhong-shan. *See* Sun Yat-sen
Supremacy, Act of, 340
Supreme Court, U.S., 502, 827
Supreme Soviet, 664, *c664*
Surat, *m241, m554,* 555
surplus, 50; trade, 764
Susa, 58 *m59*
suttee, 557
Swahili, 281–282

SWAPO. *See* South-West Africa People's Organization
Sweden, 207, 338, 393; in Thirty Years' War, 381, 382; in Great Northern War, 395; colonies of, 424; in Napoleonic Wars, 454, *m455,* 457; and Congress of Vienna, 464, *m464;* in World War II, 704, 707; in EFTA, 745
Switzerland, 338, 339, 382, *m385,* 464, *m464,* 620, 704, *m725,* 746, 848
Syria, 48, 53, *m59,* 203, 486, *m801,* 807, *m810,* 811; Muslims in, 175, 204, 210, 211, 214; Turks in, 219, 221; Mongols in, 220; controlled by France, 800; in United Arab Republic, 806; in Six-Day War, 807; in October War, 811

T

Taika Reforms, 261–262
Taiping Rebellion, 572, 574
T'ai-tsung, 256
Taiwan, 581, 758, *m760,* 761
Taj Mahal, *p242,* 243
Tale of Genji, The (Murasaki), 262
Talleyrand, Prince, 463
Tamerlane, 220, 221, 241
Tamil language; Tamils, 239
Tanganyika, 644, *m649,* 783
T'ang dynasty, 256–258, *m257,* 259, 261
Tannenberg, Battle of, *m640,* 643
Tanzania, 590, 600, 783n., 787, 793, *m864*
Taoism, 250, 258, 264
Tarawa, *m709,* 711
Tarbell, Ida, 537
tariffs, 481, 504, 507, 746, 764
Tarim Basin, 254, *m254*
Tarsus, 127, *m128*
taxes, in ancient Egypt, 50; Roman, 120; medieval, 164; in Norman England, 165, 166, 167; in France, 192, 386, 443, 444; Byzantine, 205; in India, 243, 556; in China, 249; in Japan, 267, 268, 580; in Africa, 278, 599–600, 601; in Mesoamerica, 297; in English colonies, 428; without representation, 429; reform in U.S., 829
Tchaikovsky, Peter Ilyich, 630
tea; tea trade, 256, 258, 361, 368, 568, 569, 590
Tea Act, 430
technology, Neolithic, 31, 33; in Egypt, 46; Roman engineering, *p108–109,* 110, 115; in medieval farming, 156, *p158–159;* Muslim

Acknowledgments

Text Credits and Sources

Grateful acknowledgment is made to authors, publishers, and other copyright holders for permission to reprint (and in some selections to adapt slightly) copyright material listed below.

Page 37: From *Cro-Magnon Man* (*The Emergence of Man* series) by Tom Prideaux and the Editors of Time-Life Books, Inc. Time-Life Books, Inc., Publisher. Copyright © 1973, Time, Inc. **Page 44:** From *Ancient Near Eastern Texts Relating to the Old Testament* (third edition with Supplement), edited by James B. Prichard. Copyright © 1969 by Princeton University Press. Excerpts from "The Code of Hammurabi" adapted by permission of Princeton University Press. **Page 46:** Excerpts from *The Ancient Egyptians* by Adolph Ehrman, ed., Copyright © 1966. Reprinted by permission of Methuen and Co. **Page 61:** Herodotus: *History (Book 1)* translated by George Rawlinson. John Murray, 1880. **Page 67:** One short extract from Homer: *The Iliad* translated by E. V. Rieu (Penguin Classics 1950), pp. 128–129. Copyright © the Estate of E. V. Rieu, 1950. Reprinted by permission of Penguin Books, Ltd. **Page 79:** From *Greek Literature in Translation*, edited by George Howe and Gustave Harrer. Copyright 1924, Harper and Brothers Publishers. **Page 82:** A poem by Sappho from *Ancient Greek Literature in its Living Context* by H. C. Baldry. Copyright © 1968, Thames and Hudson, Ltd. **Page 83:** Excerpts from *Oedipus the King* by Sophocles. Translated by Bernard M. W. Knox. Copyright © 1959. Reprinted by permission of Washington Square Press, Inc. **Page 83:** Six lines from *The Women of Troy* by Euripides, from Euripides: *The Bacchae and Other Plays*, translated by Philip Vellacott (Penguin Classics Revised Edition 1972), pp. 93, 94. Copyright © Philip Vellacott 1954, 1972. Reprinted by permission of Penguin Books, Ltd. **Page 93:** One short extract from Thucydides: *The Peloponnesian War*, translated by Rex Warner (Penguin Classics Revised Edition 1972), p. 48. Translation Copyright © Rex Warner, 1954. Reprinted by permission of Penguin Books, Ltd. **Page 114:** Adapted from *The Satires of Juvenal*, translated by Hubert Creekmore. Copyright © 1963, Hubert Creekmore. Reprinted by arrangement with The New American Library, New York, N.Y. **Page 117:** From *Roman Civilization: Selected Readings*, excerpt from "Roman Law" from Volume II: *The Empire* edited by Napthali Lewis and Meyer Reinhold, pp. 535, 539, 540, 547–548, 550, 551. Copyright © 1951, 1955, Columbia University Press. Reprinted by permission. **Page 131:** From *The Agricola and the Germania*, revised translation by S. A. Hanford (Penguin Classics 1970), pp. 105–106. Copyright © 1948, 1970, the Estate of H. Mattingly. Copyright © 1970 S. A. Hanford. Reprinted by permission of Penguin Books, Ltd. **Page 141:** From *The Rule of St. Benedict*, edited and translated by Abbot Justin McCann. Copyright © 1952. Reprinted by permission of Paulist Press. **Page 153:** Excerpt from *Medieval Village, Manor, and Monastery* by G. G. Coulton. Copyright 1925, Cambridge University Press. Reprinted by permission of Cambridge University Press. **Page 179:** From *Translations and Reprints from the Original Sources of European History*, edited by the Department of History of the University of Pennsylvania. University of Pennsylvania Press, 1895. **Page 188:** Thirteen lines from the "Prologue" from Chaucer: *The Canterbury Tales*, translated by Nevill Coghill (Penguin Classics Revised Edition 1977), pp. 23, 24, 31. Copyright © 1951 by Nevill Coghill, Copyright © Nevill Coghill 1958, 1960, 1975, 1977. Reprinted by permission of Penguin Books, Ltd. **Page 195:** Excerpts from *The Decameron* by Giovanni Boccaccio translated by Richard Aldington. Doubleday and Company, Inc., 1930. Copyright © Madame Catherine Guillaume. Reprinted by permission of Rosica Colin, Ltd. **Page 223:** Excerpt from *The Alexiad of the Princess Anna Comnena*, translated by Elizabeth A. S. Dawes. Copyright © 1967. Reprinted by permission of Routledge & Kegan Paul, Ltd. **Page 245:** Adapted from *The Laws of Manu with Extracts from the Seven Commentaries*, translated by Johann Georg Buhler. The Clarendon Press, 1886. **Page 250:** From traditional Confucian writings. **Page 258:** From *Translations from the Chinese*, translated by Arthur Waley. Copyright 1919 and renewed 1947 by Arthur Waley. Reprinted by permission of Alfred A. Knopf, Inc. and George Allen and Unwin (Publishers), Ltd. **Page 268:** "The World Upside Down," from *An Introduction to Haiku* by Harold G. Henderson. Copyright © 1958 by Harold G. Henderson. Reprinted by permission of Doubleday and Co., Inc. **Page 271:** Adapted from W. G. Aston, "Nihongi: Chronicles of Japan from the Earliest Times to A.D. 697" in *The Transactions and Proceedings of the Japan Society of London* (Supplement I), Kegan Paul, Trench, Trubner and Co., Ltd., 1896. **Pages 284, 289:** From *The African Past* by Basil Davidson. Copyright © 1964. Little, Brown and Co. and Penguin Books Ltd. **Page 289:** From Ibn Battúta: *Travels in Asia and Africa*, translated and selected by H. A. R. Gibb. Routledge and Kegan Paul, Ltd., 1929. **Page 299:** From *Firefly in the Night* by Irene Nicholson. Copyright © 1959. Reprinted by permission of Faber and Faber, Ltd. **Page 307:** "Songs of the Tewa," from *American Indian Prose and Poetry* by Herbert J. Spinden, 1933. **Page 309:** Excerpts from *The Book of the Jaguar Priest*, translated by Maud Worcester Makemson. Copyright © 1951, Henry Schuman, Inc. Published by Harper and Row Publishers. **Page 343:** From Baldassare Castiglione: *The Book of the Courtier*, translated by Leonard Eckstein Opdycke. Charles Scribner's Sons, 1903. **Page 354:** Excerpts from *The European Renaissance* by J. H. Parry. Copyright © 1968. Reprinted by permission of Harper and Row. **Page 371:** Excerpts adapted from *The Bernal Diaz Chronicles*, translated by Albert Idell. Copyright © 1956, Albert Idell. Reprinted by permission of Doubleday and Co., Inc. and Barthold Fles, Literary Agent. **Page 390:** From the English Bill of Rights, 1689. **Page 399:** Excerpt from *A King's Lessons in Statecraft: Louis XIV: Letters to his Heirs* translated by Herbert Wilson. T. Fisher Unwin, Ltd. Copyright 1924. Reprinted by permission of Ernest Benn, Ltd. **Page 415:** From

Antony Van Leeuwenhoek and His "Little Animals," translated and edited by Clifford Dobell. Copyright 1932, Harcourt, Brace and Company. **Page 436:** From the Preamble to the Constitution of the United States. **Page 439:** From *Writings of Benjamin Franklin,* edited by Albert H. Smyth. **Page 447:** From *The Declaration of the Rights of Man and Citizen,* 1789. **Page 459:** From John Frederick Sackville: *Dispatches from Paris: 1784–1790* (2 vols.) selected and edited from the Foreign Office Correspondence by Oscar Browning. London, Office of the Society, 1910. **Page 475:** From *The Reminiscences of Carl Schurz.* The McClure Company, 1907. **Page 491:** From a speech by Giuseppe Garibaldi, 1860. **Page 519:** From a speech by Simón Bolívar, 1819. **Page 543:** From testimony before a British parliamentary committee, 1842. **Page 559:** From a proclamation by Queen Victoria, 1858. **Page 565:** From *Bal Gangadhar Tilak, His Writings and Speeches.* Ganesh and Co., 1918. **Page 585:** Excerpt from *China's Response to the West* by Ssu-yu Teng and J. K. Fairbank. Copyright © 1954. Reprinted by permission of Harvard University Press. **Page 603:** From *King Leopold's Rule in Africa* by Edmund D. Morel. Heineman, Ltd., 1904. **Page 635:** *The Race and World Power* by A. Wirth, 1904. **Page 642:** From *The Big Push* by Brian Gardner. Copyright © 1961. Reprinted by permission of Macmillan Publishing Co., Inc. **Page 653:** From the Versailles Treaty, 1919. **Page 671:** Excerpts from *The Memoirs of Count Witte* by Count Serge Witte, translated by Abraham Yarmolinsky. Copyright 1920, 1921 by Doubleday and Company, Inc. Reprinted by permission of the publisher. **Page 693:** From *Pageant of Europe* by Raymond Stearns. Harcourt, Brace, and World, 1961. **Page 701:** From a speech by Winston Churchill, 1940. **Page 715:** From *The Stars Bear Witness* by Bernard Goldstein. Translated by Leonard Shatzkin. The Viking Press, 1949. **Page 735:** From a speech by Nikita Khrushchev, 1956. **Page 755:** From the *Resolution of the Central Committee of the Hungarian Workers' Party,* 1956. **Page 764:** From the Japanese Constitution of 1947. **Page 779:** From a speech by Jawaharlal Nehru, 1956. **Page 797:** From a speech by Julius K. Nyerere, 1968. **Page 815:** From the Balfour Declaration, reprinted in *The Times,* London, Nov. 9, 1917. **Page 839:** From *An Option for Quebec* by Rene Lévesque. Copyright © 1968. Used by permission of The Canadian Publishers, McClelland and Stewart Limited, Toronto. **Page 842:** From a speech by John F. Kennedy, 1960. **Page 853:** From "First Base in Space" by Stephen Solomon, in *Science Digest,* October, 1983.

Art Credits

Cover: Concept by Richard C. Bartlett. Front image: Coll: Norbert Schimmel. Back image: Ekdotike Athenon S. A.
Frontispiece: © 1978 William Hubbell/WC.
Time lines: Paul Foti, Boston Graphics, Inc.
Maps: Donnelley Cartographic Services (pages 352–353, 366–367 and 858–859, Robinson Projection)
Charts on pages 150, 502, 527, 664, and 686: Richard Pusey, Charthouse.

The following abbreviations are used for sources from which several illustrations were obtained:

AH — American Heritage. **AI** — After Image. **AL/AR** — Alinari/Art Resources. **AR** — Art Resources. **ASI** — Archives Snark International. **BA** — Bettmann Archive. **BBC/BA** —BBC Hulton Picture Library/Bettmann Archive. **BL** — British Library. **BLO** — Bodleian Library, Oxford. **BM** — British Museum. **BN** — Bibliothèque Nationale, Paris. **BS** — Black Star. **CI** — Milt & Joan Mann/Cameramann International. **ETP** — Editions Tallandier Photothèque. **FGTO** — French Government Tourist Office. **GC** — The Granger Collection. **GI/AR** — Giraudon/Art Resources. **HF** — Hirmer Fotoarchive. **HPS** — Historical Pictures Service, Chicago. **LB** — Lee Boltin. **LOC** — Library of Congress. **MC** — Mansell Collection. **MFA** — Museum of Fine Arts, Boston. **MH** — Michael Holford. **MMA** — Metropolitan Museum of Art. **MP** — Magnum Photos. **NASA** — National Aeronautics and Space Administration. **NASM/SI** — National Air & Space Museum, Smithsonian Institution.

NMM — National Maritime Museum, Greenwich, London. **NYHS** — Courtesy of New-York Historical Society, New York. **NYPL** —New York Public Library. **PA** — Peter Arnold. **PML** — Pierpont Morgan Library. **PR** —Photo Researchers. **RMN** — Service de Documentation Photographique de la Réunion des Musées Nationaux. **RV** — Roger-Viollet. **SC/AR** — Scala/Art Resources. **SI** — Smithsonian Institution. **SM** — Staatliche Museen Preussischer Kulturbesitz, Berlin. **TL** — Time-Life Books, Inc. **UPI/BA** — United Press International/Bettmann Archive. **VAM** — Victoria and Albert Museum. **WC** — Woodfin Camp. **WW** — Wide World.

22 *(right)* Phoenician inscribed gold plate (detail), dedicated to shrine of goddess Astarte, Pyrgi, Italy. SC/AR. *(bottom)* Stephanie Stokes/The Stock Market. **24** © 1982 Michael Furman/The Stock Market. **27** Tomb of Emperor Q'in Shi Huang. An Keren/Rapho. **28** *(left)* Lascaux Cave (detail), France. FGTO. *(right)* "Laurel Leaf" Solutrean flint spear. MH. **30** *(left)* "Frescoes of Tassili" (detail). Coll: Musée de l'Homme, Paris. Coll: Henri Lhote. Photo: © Erich Lessing/MP. *(right)* Coll: SI. **32** Funerary jar, Kansu Province, *c.* 2000 B.C. VAM. Photo: MH. **34** *(top)* © Paolo Koch/PR. *(middle)* © Arch. Photo/Vaga, New York/S.P.A.D.E.M. *(bottom)* "The Fields of the Blest" (detail), copy in tempera of wall painting, *c.* 1200 B.C. Coll: MMA. **38** (detail). Coll: Cairo Museum. Photo: LB. **42** *(top)* From Ur, early Dynastic II Period, 2600–2400 B.C. Coll: © Bagdad, Iraq Museum. Photo: HF. *(middle)* *c.* 2350–2150 B.C. Coll: © Baghdad, Iraq Museum. Photo: HF. *(bottom left)* Mesopotamian bas relief. Coll: © Musée de Louvre. Photo: RMN. *(bottom right)* © BM. **47** © Malcom S. Kirk/PA. **51** *(top)* (detail) from tomb of Rekhmira, temple at Karnak, copy of wall painting, Egyptian, *c.* 1475 B.C. Coll: © MMA. *(middle)* "The Fields of the Blest" (detail), copy in tempera of wall painting, *c.* 1200 B.C. Coll: © MMA. *(bottom left)* Harpist from Egyptian fresco of festival scene from the Tomb of the Vizier (detail). HF. *(bottom right)* Egyptian statue of Ranofer, high priest of Memphis, painted limestone, from Saqqara, Dynasty V. Coll: Cairo Museum. Photo: HF. **52** Relief from the tomb of Vizier Ramose, 18th Dynasty, Thebes. MH. **54** Syracusan. Coll: BM. **55** Coll: Louvre. Photo: GI/AR. **56** Coll: Israel Museum, Reifenberg Collection. Photo: © David Harris. **57** King Assurbanipal's Lion Hunt, Assyrian, alabaster relief from Nineveh, *c.* 650 B.C. Coll: BM. **58** George Holton/PR. **62** (detail). Dan J. McCoy/Rainbow. **65** *(top left)* Lion hunt on ceremonial dagger. Coll: National Archaeological Museum, Athens. Photo: HF. *(top right)* Coll: Archaeological Museum, Athens. Photo: Erich Lessing/MP, Paris. *(middle)* Coll: Seattle Art Museum, The Norman and Amelia Davis Classic Collection. *(bottom)* Mycenaean vase, stirrup jar, *c.* 1200–1125 B.C. Coll: MMA, Louisa Eldridge McBurney Gift Fund, 1953. **71** Coll: BM. **74** *(left)* "Attic Red Figured Lekythos" (detail), by the Brygos painter. Coll: © 1983 MFA, Francis Bartlett Fund. *(right)* School cup (detail), clay, 480 B.C. Coll: Antikenmuseum, SM. **77** *(left)* by Lysippus, marble, *c.* 6th–4th century B.C. Coll: Louvre. Photo: © Erich Lessing/MP. *(right)* Grave Stele of a Warrior, Hymettian marble, *c.* 535–525 B.C. Coll: MMA, Fletcher Fund, 1938. **80** Tholas, Delphi. Gerry Clyde/MH. **83** *(left)* © Gary Cralle/IB. *(right)* Terra cotta, from Smyrna. Coll: Louvre. Photo: © Erich Lessing/MP. **84** "Mask of Tragic Hero," marble, Italy, late 1st or 2nd century A.D. Coll: MFA, Otis Norcross Fund. **85** *(top)* Found at Satala (now Sadagh), Eastern Turkey. MH. *(middle)* "The Boxer," bronze. Coll: Museo Nazionale delle Terme, Rome. Photo: AR. *(bottom)* Relief of Artemis, east frieze of the Parthenon. © Erich Lessing/MP. **89** Coll: Palazzo Spada-Galleria, Rome. Photo: AL/AR. **90** "The Art of Eudoxe, Treatise on Astronomy" (detail), written in Greek, Egyptian, 2nd century B.C. Coll: Louvre. **94** Relief of Roman officers (detail), Coll: Louvre. **99** *(right)* Bronze, 2nd century A.D. Coll: BM. Photo: MH. *(bottom)* (detail). German Archeological Institute, Rome. **101** *(top)* Roman bas relief (detail), 1st century B.C. Coll: Staatliche Antikensammlungen und Glyptothek, Munich. *(middle left)* (detail). Coll: Museo

Torlonia, Rome. Photo: AL/AR. *(middle right)* (detail), 4th century A.D. Coll: BM. Photo: MH. *(bottom)* Coll: Musée d'Avignon. Photo: French Government Tourist Office. **102** Coll: Museo Nazionale, Napoli. Photo: AL/AR. **105** *(top left)* Rome. Photo: MH. *(top right)* Blue gem on glass paste, by gem cutter Herophilos. Coll: Kunsthistorische Museum, Vienna. Photo: © Erich Lessing/MP. *(bottom)* Coll: Vatican Museum. **108** *(bottom left)* Coll: Museo della Civiltá Romana, Rome. Photo: David Lees from *Great Ages of Man/ Imperial Rome,* © 1965 Time, Inc. Time-Life Books Inc., Publisher. *(bottom right)* © 1983 Erich Lessing. **108–9** *(top)* Pont du Gard, France. Ethel Hurwicz/MH. **109** *(top right)* © Chris K. Walter/The Picture Cube. *(bottom)* GC. **111** *(left)* (detail), Mosaic, 1st century B.C. Coll: Museo Prenestino, Palestrina. Photo: MH. *(right)* Picture Point, London. **112** "Mother and Child," 3rd century A.D. Coll: MMA, Gift of J. Pierpont Morgan, 1917. **114** Coll: Museo Nazionale, Naples. Photo: SC/AR. **118** © K. Kerth/Zentrale Farbbild Agemtur GmbH. **121** *(left)* Sutton Hoo helmet. Coll: BM. *(right)* Saxony horseman. Coll: Landesmuseum fur Vorgeschichte, Halle/Saale. **124** 1st century A.D. FGTO. **125** German Archeological Institute, Rome. **127** *(top)* Pavement mosaic (detail), from et-Tagbah (Heptapegon), Israel, in the Church of the Multiplication of the Loaves and Fishes, mid-5th century. Israel Ministry of Tourism. *(middle)* Mid-Byzantine from Ephesos. Coll: Selcuk Museum, Turkey. Photo: © Erich Lessing/MP. *(bottom)* Coll: Mausoleo Galla Placidia, Ravenna. Photo: SC/AR. **134** *Chroniques de Froissart* (detail), Ms. Fr 2643, fol. **1.** Coll: BN. **136** *Très Riches Heures du Duc de Berry,* "June" (detail). Coll: Musée Condé, Chantilly. Photo: GI/AR. **140** *(top)* GI/ AR. *(bottom left)* (detail). Ms. 170, fol. 75v. Coll: Bibliothèque Publique de Dijon. *(bottom right)* Moralized Bible (detail), Paris, Ms. 240, fol. 8, 1235. Coll: PML. **141** AR. **143** Statue of Charlemagne (detail) in the converted church of St. Johann de Mustair, Switzerland. © Ann Munchow. **144** Coll: Statens Historiske Museum, Stockholm. Photo: Werner Forman Archive. **147** *Lancelot du Lac* (detail), Ms. 806, fol. 239, France, 14th century. Coll: PML. **148** *(left)* *Histoire d'Olivier de Castille* (detail), Ms. Fr 12574, fol. 181v, Flemish, 15th century. Coll: BN. *(right)* Coll: MMA, funds from various donors, The Bashford Dean Memorial Collection. **151** *(left)* *Hours of the Virgin* (detail), Ms. 399, fol. 12v. Coll: PML. *(right)* French illuminated Ms. (detail), 15th century. GC. **154** *Chroniques de Hainout* (detail), Ms. 9242, fol. 274v. Coll: Bibliothèque Royale Albert Ier, Brussels. **158** *(bottom)* French illuminated Ms. (detail), 15th century. GC. **158–9** *(top)* (detail) Ms. Fr. 2092, fol. 37 v. Coll: BN. **159** *(top right)* *Hours of the Virgin,* "July" (detail), Ms. 399, fol. 8v. Coll: PML. *(bottom)* (detail), Ms. Douce 88, fol. 51. Coll: BLO. **161** *Political and Economic Ethics of Aristotle* (detail), Ms. 927, fol. 145. Coll: Bibliothèque Municipale, Rouen. Photo: Lauros/GI/AR. **162** *(left)* (detail), Ms. Roy 15E III, fol. 269. Coll: BM. *(right)* French illuminated Ms. (detail), 14th century. GC. **165** (detail). MH. **166** (detail) Wriothesley Manuscript. Coll: Royal Library, reproduced by Gracious Permission of H. M. Queen Elizabeth II. **170** "Vita della Contessa Matilda di Canossa" (detail), A.D. 1115 Coll: Biblioteca Vaticana, Madeline Grimoldi Archives. **175** *(top)* A. F. Kersting, London. *(bottom)* From Les Histoires d'Outremer, 13th century. Coll: BN. **180** Ms. Bodley 264, fol. 218r. Coll: BLO. **184** *(left)* Laurentius da Voltalina Kolleg des Henricus D'Allemania (detail), Min 1233. Coll: Kupfersitch Kabinett, SM. *(right)* *Optics* (detail), by Roger Bacon, Ms. Royal 7, Fviii, fol. 54v. Coll: BL. **186** *(left)* From set of tapestries depicting the Nine Heroes (detail), French, *c.* 1385. Coll: MMA, The Cloisters Collections, Munsey Fund, 1932. *(right)* Manesse Codex, Cod. Pal. Germ. 848, fol. 251r. Coll: Universitats Bibliothek, Heidelberg. **187** Miniature (detail), 13th–14th century. Coll: Ajuda Library, Lisbon. Photo: Horacio De Sousa Novais. **188** Church of S. Paulo a Ripa d'Arno, Pisa. AL/AR. **189** *(left)* Bayeux Cathedral of Notre Dame. FGTO. *(right)* By Filippo de Memmo, tempera on wood, *c.* 1317–1347. Coll: MMA, gift of Irma N. Straus, 1964. **190**

(detail). Coll: BL. **191** (detail), French-Flemish School, 15th century. Coll: Archives Nationales. Photo: GI/AR. **192** *Chroniques de Froissart* (detail), Ms. Fr. 2643, fol. 207, *c.* 1460. Coll: BN. **198** *(left)* AH. *(right)* "Emperor Kuang Wu Fording a River" by Ch'iu Ying, Ming Dynasty, 16th century. Coll: National Gallery of Canada, Ottawa. **200** F.B. Grunzweig/PR. **206** *(left)* Russian icon of the Madonna (detail). MH. *(right)* (detail), Hagia Sophia, Turkey. Photo: Courtesy of Dumbarton Oaks, Washington, D.C. **209** *(left)* Scene from Sirar-i Nabi (detail), Constantinople, 1594. Coll: NYPL, Spencer Collection. *(right)* Kaaba at Mecca, Islamic tile. MH. **212** Coll: MMA, Rogers Fund, 1944. **214** Ceramic wall tile panel (detail), from pavilion of Shah Abbas the First, Isfahan, Islamic, late 16th or early 17th century. Coll: VAM. **216** *(top)* Fotomas Index, London. *(bottom)* World map by El-Idrisi, 1533. Ms. Pococke 375, fol. 5 3v–4r. Coll: BLO. **217** *(top left)* © 1980 Roland and Sabrina Michaud/WC. *(top right and bottom)* Coll: Majies Library, Teheran. **218** Coll: Arthur T. Gregorian. **220** Scene from the Sulayman-Name (detail), Constaninople, 1579. Coll: Chester Beatty Library, Dublin. **224** (detail), Kula, Punjab Hills, early 18th century. © 1983, MFA, Ross-Coomaraswamy Collection. **228** *(left)* Harappa culture from Chanhu-Daro, clay. Coll: © 1983, MFA. *(right)* Prehistoric square seal amulet, white steatite, Indian, Harappa culture from Chanhu-Daro, Sind. Joint expedition of the American School of Indic and Iranian Studies and MFA, 1935–1936 season. Coll: MFA. **231** *(left)* *c.* 13th century. Coll: The Asia Society, New York, Mr. & Mrs. John D. Rockefeller 3rd Collection, 1979.30. Photo: Otto E. Nelson. *(right)* Coll: MMA. Photo: © LB. **233** *(left)* © Bruno Barbey/MP. *(right)* Bodhidhame, porcelain, late Ming Dynasty. Coll: Lawrence Rockefeller. Photo: © LB. **236** Coll: Nelson-Atkins Museum of Art, Kansas City, Missouri. **238** Coll: Sarnath Museum. Photo: UNESCO. **242** *(top)* © Pete Turner/IB. *(bottom left)* by Khem Karan, gouache on paper. Coll: MMA, Rogers Fund, 1925. *(bottom right)* "Tadi Ragini" (detail), Rajasthan, Bundi *c.* 1725. Coll: © 1983 MFA, gift of John Goelet. **246** Robe, (detail) Ching Dynasty. Coll: MMA, gift of Robert E. Tod, 1929. **249** Coll: MMA, Department of Far Eastern Art, "Great Bronze Age of China" exhibit, from Historical Museum, Beijing, People's Republic of China. **251** "Ladies Preparing Newly Woven Silk" (detail), ink, colors, and gold on silk, by Emperor Hui Tsung, Northern Sung Dynasty, early 12th century. Coll: MFA, Chinese and Japanese Special Fund. **252** © 1983 Michal Heron. **259** *(left)* Covered water jar, Ming Dynasty, *c.* 1522–1566. Coll: The Asia Society, New York, Mr. and Mrs. John D. Rockefeller 3rd Collection, 1979. Photo: Otto E. Nelson. *(top right)* "Two Birds on a Blossoming Branch," *c.* 12th–13th century. Coll: Asian Art Museum of San Francisco, The Avery Brundage Collection. *(bottom right)* "Recumbent Water Buffalo," Chinese jade, possibly Yuan Dynasty, A.D. 1280–1368 or Early Ming Dynasty, A.D. 1368–1644. Photo: MH. **263** Ceremonial coverlet in kimono shape, cotton, resist dyed and painted with dyes and gouache, Japanese 19th century. Coll: MMA, Seymour Fund, 1966. **264** By Mitsuaki. Coll: BM. **269** *(left)* Ivory okinome. Coll: American Museum of Natural History. Photo: LB. *(right)* Japanese color print by Torii Kiyonobu. Coll: BM. **272** An Oba (king) in center with two attendants (detail), Benin bronze. Coll: Museum of Mankind, BM. Photo: MH. **276** Bas relief at Naga's 2,000-year-old Lion Temple depicts the Black Kushite Ram-God. Photo: © Marc & Evelyne Bernheim/WC. **279** Map of Catalane of 1375. Coll: BL. **280** Mask of the Zaire Souge Tribe, wood. Coll: MMA, Rockefeller Collection. Photo: LB. **282** *(left)* Zimbabwe stone statue. Coll: Paul and Ruth Tishman. *(right)* Great Zimbabwe Ruins. Photo: Zimbabwe Tourist Board, Chicago Office. **285** *(left)* Belt mask, ivory, Benin Tribe, Nigeria, *c.* A.D. 1550. Coll: MMA, Rockefeller Collection. Photo: LB. *(right)* Bronze Ashanti weight. Coll: Museum of Mankind, BM. Photo: MH. **286** Miango Tribe Compound, North Nigeria. © 1981 Marc and Evelyne Bernheim/WC. **287** "Slave deck of Albany Prize to HMS Albatros." Coll: NMM. **290** Orange pottery, Jaina Island Style, late Classic Period, Campeche, Mexico, A.D. 600–900. Coll: Munson-Williams-Proctor Institute Museum of Art. **294** Pre-Columbian sculpture, Guerrero Province, Mexico, 10 B.C. Coll: MMA, The Michael C. Rockefeller Memorial Collection, Gift of Nelson Rockefeller, 1965. **296** *(left)* Tikal Temple I. Coll: © University Museum, University of Penn. *(right)* Mayan lintel, F. Yaxchilan, Chichén Itzá Pyramid, A.D. 726. Coll: Anthropological Museum of Mexico City. Photo: MH. *(bottom)* Mayan frieze, Toltec. Coll: Museum of Anthropology, Mexico City. Photo: © Robert Frerck/Odyssey Productions. **298** 15th century. Coll: BM. Photo: © LB. **300** Paracas textile, a mythological demon carrying a trophy head. Necropolic embroidery, Paracas Peninsula, Peru. Coll: National Museum of Anthropology and Archeology, Lima, Peru. Photo: © LB. **301** *(top)* © John Henebry Jr. *(bottom left)* Mochica vase, 6th or 7th century A.D. Coll: Museum of Mankind, BRM. Photo: MH. *(bottom right)* Mochica, Peru. Coll: MMA, Rockefeller Collection. Photo: © LB. **306** *(top)* Bella Coola mask representing the sun, British Columbia. Coll: Courtesy of American Museum of Natural History. *(middle left)* Coll: National Park Service. Photo: Courtesy of *Reader's Digest,* from *America's Fascinating Indian Heritage.* *(middle right)* Membres bowl with grasshopper design, Swarts Ranch, Grant County, New Mexico. Coll: © President and Fellows of Harvard College, Peabody Museum, Harvard University. Photo: F. P. Orchard. *(bottom)* © 1979 Michal Heron.

322 *(top)* An autographed portion of the first sonata for violin by Mozart, 1782. Coll: Bibliothèque du Conservatoire de Musique, Paris. Photo: GI/AR. *(bottom)* "The Port of Marseille" (detail), by Joseph Vernet, 1754. Coll: Louvre. Photo: RMN. **324** "School of Athens" (detail), by Raphael. Coll: Vatican. Photo: SC/AR. **327** "Venice" (detail), by Canaletto. Coll: Columbia Museums of Art and Science, Samuel H. Kress Collection, Columbia, S.C. Photo: Hunter Clarkson. **329** *(top)* "Copy of Map of Catena" (detail), Florence, 1490. Coll: Museum of Florence. Photo: SC/AR. *(bottom)* Coll: Biblioteca Riccardiana. Photo: SC/AR. **330** (detail) by Hans Holbein the Younger. Coll: MMA, Robert Lehman Collection, 1975. **333** Cross section of Old St. Peter's as published by Giovanni Battista Costegati (the Younger) in *Architettura della Basilica di S. Pietro in Vaticano,* engraving, Rome, 1684. Coll: MMA, Rogers Fund, 1952. **334** *(left)* (detail). Coll: Galleria dell'Accademia, Florence. Photo: AL/AR. **334–5** *(middle)* (detail). Coll: Kunsthistorische Museum, Vienna. Photo: Erich Lessing/MP. **335** *(left)* (detail), Tuscan School, 15th century. Coll: R. Museo Nazionale Collezione Carrand. Photo: AL/AR. *(right)* (detail). Coll: National Gallery of Art, Washington, Ailsa Mellon Bruce Fund. **337** *(left)* Coll: Galleria degli Uffizi, Florence. Photo: AL/AR. *(right)* (detail). Coll: BM. **340** (detail) by Hans Holbein the Younger. Coll: Barberini Gallery, Rome. Photo: SC/AR. **341** (detail), Church of Jesus, Rome. Photo: SC/AR. **344** Martines map of India (detail), Ms. Harley 3450 no. **6.** Coll: BL. **348** *(top)* by Abd Al-Kharim. Coll: BM. Photo: MH. *(middle)* © NMM. *(bottom)* Map of Magellan, Battista Agnese's Portolan Atlas, Venice, 1544. Coll: LOC, Geography and Map Division. **349** *(top)* "Caravel with Four Masts." Coll: Osterreichische Nationalbibliothek. *(bottom left)* Coll: © NMM. *(bottom middle)* Coll: © NMM. *(bottom right)* Coll: © NMM. Photo: MH. **351** Photo: AL-Brogli/AR. **356** Coll: NYHS. **357** Navajo pictograph of Spanish army/priest (detail), Canyon De Chelly. Photo: © Robert Frerck/Odyssey Productions. **358** "The Old West" (detail). Coll: Benson Latin American Collection, The General Libraries, The University of Texas at Austin. From *The Spanish West,* Publisher, © 1976 Time Inc. Photo: Frank Lerner/TL. **359** *Cinchona Officinalis,* uncolored copper engraving, from *Medical Botany,* William Woodville, London, 1790–95. Photo: Courtesy of the Hunt Institute for Botanical Documentation, Carnegie-Mellon University, Pittsburgh, PA. **369** *(left)* Parrot by Jacopo Ligozzi. Coll: Galleria degli Uffizi, Florence, Gabinetto Disegni. Photo: SC/AR. *(right)* "Geographer" (detail), by Jan Ver-

meer van Delft. Coll: Stadelsches Kunstinstitut, Frankfurt-am-Main. Photo: Jurgen Hinrichs. **372** (detail). Coll: William Tyrwhitt-Drake, Bereleigh House, Peresfield, England. **374** "Emperor Charles V at the Battle of Muhlberg" (detail). Coll: Museum del Prado, Madrid. Photo: SC/AR. **381** "Tilly's Siege of Magdeburg, 1631" (detail). GC. **384** *(left)* (detail). Coll: Museum of Versailles. Photo: RMN. *(right)* Leo de Wys Inc. **387** Cecil Beaton/Camera Press. **388** Terracotta by Joseph Wilton, *c.* 1760. Coll: VAM. **389** "Great Fire of London" (detail), from the Dutch School, 1666. Photo: GC. **392** Medallion by David d'Angers, 1845–46. Coll: MMA, Gift of S. P. Avery, 1898. **394** "Ambassadors and Boyars" (detail), 1576. Coll: NYPL. **395** George Holton/PR. **396** (detail) by Torrelli. Photo: GC. **400** "Mozart as a Child with his Father and his Sister" (detail), by Louis Carmotelle. Coll: Musée Carnavalet, Paris. Photo: GI/AR. **403** Photo: D.E. Smith Collection, Columbia University. **405** © 1978 Lowell Observatory and National Optical Astronomy Observatories/Kitt Peak. **406** (detail). Photo: Royal Society of Medicine. **410** "First Reading of L'Orphelin de Chine' at the home of Mme Geoffrin" (detail), by Lemonnier, 1725. Coll: Musée de Beaux-Arts, Rouen. Photo: GI/AR. **412** (detail) by Antoine Pesne. Coll: Staatliche Museen Preussischer Kulturbesitz, Gemaldegalerie, Berlin. Photo: Robert Harding Picture Library.

418 *(top)* "Inauguration by Queen Victoria and Albert, Crystal Palace Exhibition" (detail), by H. Selons. Coll: VAM. Photo: Snark/Edimedia. *(bottom)* (detail). Photo: HPS. **420** "George Washington at Verplanck's Point, N.Y., 1782, after Victory at Yorktown" (detail), 1790. Coll: The Henry Francis du Pont Winterthur Museum. **425** *(top)* "Pilgrims going to Church" (detail), by George Henry Boughton, 1867. Coll: NYHS. *(middle)* by Francis Place. Coll: The Historical Society of Pennsylvania. *(bottom)* "Jamesfort" (detail), by Sidney King. Coll: Colonial Williamsburg. **427** "Tobacco Plantation" (detail). Coll: Astor, Lenox and Tilden Foundations, NYPL, Rare Book Division. **430** "Colonists Toppling Statue of King George III in N.Y." (detail), by William Wolcutt. Coll: Private. **431** (detail) by Rembrandt Peale, 1805. Coll: NYHS. **433** (detail) by Joseph Siffred Duplessis. Coll: MMA, Bequest of Michail Friedsam, 1931, The Friedsam Collection. **434** "The Camp of the American Army at Valley Forge, February, 1778" (detail), by Edwin Austin Abbey, 1910. Coll: Pennsylvania Capitol Preservation Committee. **435** U.S. Salem Custom House, 1805. Coll: Index of American Design, National Gallery of Art, Washington. **440** "Napoleon Crossing the Alps" (detail). Coll: Malmaison Chateau. Photo: GI/AR. **443** (detail), by Marie Louise Élisabeth Vigée-Lebrun, 1788. Coll: Museum of Versailles. Photo: RMN. **446** MC. **451** MC. **453** Head of an unknown Egyptian, donated to Louvre after the French Revolution by Henry Salt, British Consul to Egypt, known as the "Salt Head." Coll: Louvre. **456** (detail). Coll: Museum of Versailles. Photo: RMN. **460** "Vienna Congress" (detail), after painting by Johann Baptist Isabey. Photo: BA. **463** Coll: Royal Library, © reserved to H. M. Queen Elizabeth II. **466** "Greek War of Independence" (detail), by Peter Heinrich von Hess, 1828. Photo: Archives Photographiques Larousse. **468** *(top)* (detail), 1823. Coll: Nationalgalerie Staatliche Museen Preussischer Kulturbesitz, West Berlin. *(bottom left)* "An Afternoon at the Home of Liszt" (detail), by Josef Kriehuber, 1846. Coll: Albertina Collection, Vienna. *(bottom right)* 1828. Coll: Marburger Universitatsmuseum für Kunst und Kulturgeschichte. **470** *(bottom)* BA. **471** "Reading Dispatches Received by Pigeon Post During Siege of Paris," 1870. BBC/BA. **476** "Arrival of Farini in Piazza S. Carlo, Turin, March 18, 1860" (detail), by Carlo Bossoli. Coll: Museo Nazionale del Risorgimento, Turin. **479** *(left)* Coll: Museo Nazionale del Risorgimento, Turin. Photo: AR. *(right)* H. Armstrong Roberts/E.P. Jones. **480** Coll: The Illustrated London News Picture Library. **482** HPS. **488** *(top)* (detail) by P. G. Kovaleoski. Coll: State Tretyakov Gallery, Moscow. Photo: ASI/AR. *(bottom)* Coll: Museum of History and Reconstruction, Moscow, courtesy of Robert Gohstand. **492** "St. Louis in

1846" (detail), by Henry Lewis. Coll: St. Louis Art Museum. **495** *(left)* by Dominique. HPS. *(right)* Photo: Courtesy of GeoMundo, monthly magazine © Editorial America, S. A. **499** "Gauchos in a Horse Corral" by James Walker. Coll: Thomas Gilcrease Institute of American History and Art, Tulsa, Oklahoma. **500** Vintage albumen print, *c.* 1860. Coll: Bancroft Library, University of California, Berkeley. **505** "Louis Hoppe Meyenberg's Farm, Williams Creek, Settlement by La Grange, Fayette County, Texas." Coll: Courtesy of San Antonio Museum Assn., San Antonio, Texas. **510** *(top)* Horse team harvesting in Walla Walla, Washington, 1902. Coll: Mrs. L. Dexter, Wicklow Farm, South Woodstock, VT. *(bottom left)* NYHS. *(bottom right)* Coll: University of Washington. **512** Painted tray. Coll: SI, National Museum of American History, Michael DiSalle Collection. **517** "A Loggers' Camp" by Edwin Sandys. Coll: Public Archives of Canada, No. c-11040 417-I-32. **520** "Huth Factories at Clichy" (detail), by Vincent van Gogh, 1887. Coll: The St. Louis Art Museum, gift of Mrs. Mark C. Steinberg. **524** *(top)* Arkwright's First Spinning Machine, 1769, from Evan Leigh's *The Science of Modern Cotton Spinning*, London: 1875. Coll: Merrimack Valley Textile Museum. *(bottom)* Photo: BA. **525** *(top)* (detail). Coll: Deutsches Museum, Munich. *(middle)* Engraving by J. Carter after T. Allom, from Baine's *History of the Cotton Manufacture of Great Britain*, London, 1835. Coll: Merrimack Valley Textile Museum. *(bottom)* Engraving of the City Basin, Regents Canal by Thomas H. Shepherd, 1828. Photo: MC. **529** *(top)* "Over London by Rail," by Doré. Photo: MC. *(bottom)* Factory interior, Britain, *c.* 1900. Photo: BBC/BA. **530** Photo: BA. **532** Photo: HPS. **535** Wedgewood Willow pattern plate. Coll: VAM. Photo: MH. **536** (detail). MC. **539** "Bayswater Omnibus," by G. W. Joy, 1894. Coll: The Museum of London. **540** Grace Chappelow selling Votes for Women.' Coll: The Museum of London.

546 *(top)* Canton Factories (detail), Chinese artist, oil on glass. Coll: Peabody Museum of Salem. Photo: Mark Sexton. *(bottom and right)* Massachusetts Historical Society. **548** "An English Dignitary being Transported by Elephant with an Armed Escort" (detail), 18th century. Coll: VAM. Photo: MH. **551** "The Late Lord Clive Receiving the Duanney from the Great Mughal Emperor Shah Alam" (detail), by Benjamin West, 1765. Coll: BL. **552-3** *(top)* "Passage of El-Guisr," by Edouard Rion from the book *Inauguration of the Suez Canal* by G. Nicloe, 1869. Coll: BL. **552** *(bottom)* Lahore or Amritsar woodcut, *c.* 1870. Coll: VAM. **553** *(right)* Chinese painting, 1910. Coll: Musée de L'Air et de L'Espace, Paris-Le Bourget, France. *(bottom)* Editions Robert Laffont, Paris. **555** "British East Indiaman at Calcutta" (detail), by Frans Balthezar Solvyens, 1794. Coll: Peabody Museum of Salem. Photo: Mark Sexton. **558** From *History of the Indian Mutiny* by Charles Ball, London, 1858–59. Coll: BL. **559** Portrait of Queen Victoria (detail), by F. Winterhalter, 1859. BBC/BA. **561** Two-piece dress of painted and dyed cotton probably from Coromandel Coast, Northern Madras. Dress probably made in France *c.* 1770. Coll: VAM. Photo: MH. **566** "Departure of Iwakura Mission from Yokohama in 1871" (detail), by Yamaguchi Hoshun. Coll: Seitoku Kinen Egakkan, Tokyo. Photo: Prof. Marius B. Jansen. **569** "Kazakh Khirghis envoys presenting horses to Ch'ien-Lung" (detail), Ch'ing Dynasty. Coll: Musée Guimet, Paris. Photo: RMN. **571** J. Messerschmidt/ Bruce Coleman. **573** "The Real Trouble Will Come with the Wake," *Puck*, August 15, 1900. **575** National Archives, No. 111-SC-83087. **577** BBC/BA. **579** Milt & Joan Mann/ Gartman Agency. **582** *(top)* Mikado (Meiji) visiting the arsenal of Yokosuka: the foundry. After a sketch by M. Koenig. Editions Robert Laffont, Paris. *(bottom left)* "Women Watching Stars," by Ota Chou, 1936. Coll: National Museum of Modern Art, Tokyo. Photo: Bradley Smith. *(bottom right)* "Japanese Graduates of University of Tokyo," by Fuzoku Gwago, 1900. Coll: BM. **586** "Encampment at the Mangwe River, South Africa, 1870" (detail), by T. Baines. Coll: Private. Photo: MH. **589** *(left)* BBC/BA. *(right)* Dispensary at Msalabani, present-day Tanzania, *c.* 1890. Photo: The United

Society for the Propagation of the Gospel. **592** By Carl Sohn (detail), 1882. Coll: © reserved to H. M. Queen Elizabeth II. **595** Print by Samuel Daniel. Coll: BM. Photo: Fotomas Index, London. **596** MC. **600** Peter Davey/Bruce Coleman. **601** Normal School at Antananarivo, Madagascar, established by London Missionary Society, 1879. Photo: HPS.

614 Zeppelin demonstration organized by the Reichenberger Zeitung, poster by Heinrich Honich, 1913. Coll: Kaiser Wilhelm Museum, Krefeld. **616** "Pre-Catalan Restaurant in Bois de Boulogne, Paris, 1909" (detail), by Henri Gervex. Coll: Comte de Hamal, Paris. **618** "St. Martin-in-the-Fields" (detail), by William Logsdail, 1888. Coll: The Tate Gallery. **619** "Pasteur in His Laboratory" (detail), by Albert Edelfelt, 1885. Coll: Versailles Museum. Photo: Lauros-GI/AR. **620** "Street Photographer, Clapham Common" (detail), by J. Thomson, 1877. Coll: The Royal Photographic Society. **621** "Ironworkers" (detail), by Adolph von Menzel, *c.* 1875. Coll: National Galerie, East Berlin. **623** Coll: Suddeutscher Verlag. **625** HPS. **627** Photo: National Library of Medicine. **628** "The Dancing Class," by Hilaire Germaine Edgar Degas. Coll: MMA, bequest of Mrs. H. O. Havemeyer, 1929, The Havemeyer Collection. **629** *(top)* "Drawbridge at Arles with a Group of Washerwomen," by Vincent van Gogh. Coll: Rijksmuseum Kroller-Muller, Otterlo, Netherlands. Photo: Erich Lessing/MP. *(bottom)* "Monet Working in His Garden at Argenteuil," by Auguste Renoir, 1873. Coll: Wadsworth Atheneum, Hartford, Conn., bequest of Anne Parrish Titzell. **633** Photo: HPS. **636** "Trenches in Winter, 1915–16, Souchez (Artois)" (detail), by F. Flameng. ETP. **639** Archives Photographiques Larousse. All rights reserved. **643** NASM/SI. **645** *(top)* Lauros GI/AR. *(middle)* "Aerial warfare — enemy plane in flames, hit by shrapnel," by F. Flameng, 1918. ETP. *(bottom)* Four German subs (U-Boats) and despatch vessel *Sleipner* at left. Photo: U.S. Naval Historical Center. **648** GC. **651** French women working in a factory. RV. **654** "Lenin Exhorting a Crowd" (detail), by V. Serov. Coll: State Tretyakov Gallery, Moscow. **657** © Pete Turner/IB. **659** *(left)* Renaissance Egg, gold, jewels, enamels, by Peter Carl Fabergé, 1894. Coll: The Forbes Collection, New York. Photo: H. Peter Curran. *(right)* A La Vieille Russie Inc. **660** Sovfoto/Eastfoto. **663** *(left)* Sovfoto/Eastfoto. *(right)* Silver ruble of 1924. RV. **668** Sovfoto/Eastfoto. **672** ETP. **675** *(left)* by Adolfo Busi, 1928. Civiche Raccolte D'Arte Applicata Ed Incisioni. *(right)* WW. **678** RV. **679** WW. **682** David Seymour/MP. **683** HPS. **684** *(top right)* Coll: The Dorothea Lange Collection, The Oakland Museum, Oakland, CA. Photo: Paul Taylor. *(bottom)* Coll: Museum of Modern Art, Film Stills Archive. **685** *(top left)* Culver Pictures, Inc. *(top right)* Coll: SI, Collection of Business Americana. *(bottom)* UPI/BA. **687** BBC/BA. **690** WW. **694** "The Sinking of the *HMS Repulse* and *Prince of Wales*" off Singapore, 1941. Artist: Nakamura. Captured WW II art. Coll: United States Air Force. **698** *(left)* WW. *(right)* UPI/BA. **701** Coll: Imperial War Museum. **703** Assembling 45° antenna sail section of V beam at Bedford Airport. MIT Museum. **705** Pictorial Parade, Inc. **710** National Archives, No. 80-A-7878. **712** *(left)* U. S. Coast Guard. *(right)* U. S. Army.

718 *(top)* "Highways (No. 2)," by Ingo Swann, 1976. Coll: NASM/SI. *(bottom)* Formula for the Lagrangian function. **720** Fritz Henle/PR. **723** Franklin D.Roosevelt Library. **726** UPI/BA. **731** Dr. Robert H. Goddard's rocket ready for flight testing near Roswell, N. M., March 21, 1940. NASA. **732** Elliott Erwitt/MP. **736** Burlington Arcade, London. Tom & Michelle Grimm/AI. **739** Thomas Hopker/WC. **740** Henri Cartier-Bresson/MP. **742** A. Carp/IB. **743** Homer Sykes/WC. **746** *(top)* Lothar Reupert/IB. *(middle)* SI. *(bottom)* German Information Center. **749** Howard Sochurek/ WC. **751** Alain Nogues/Sygma **752** Chris Niedenthal/BS. **756** David Burnett/Contact Press Images. **759** *(left)* China Pictorial. *(right)* Hou Bo/New China Pictures Co. HPS. **763** Masamine Sumitani, Living National Treasure. Stern/BS. **766** Henri Cartier-Bresson/MP. **769** *(both)* Johangir Gazdar/WC.

773 Sygma.   774 David Alan Harvey/WC.   780 Albert Moldvay/AR.   783 UPI/BA.   784 Courtesy of H. E. Harris & Co., Inc.   786 *(left)* David Moore/BS.   *(right)* John Moss/BS.   788 Airport at Johannesburg, South Africa. Keith Gunnar/Bruce Coleman.   790 Steven Ferry/Gamma Liaison.   793 *(both)* Alex Webb/MP.   794 *(left)* Paul Chiasson/Gamma Liaison.   *(right)* Bruno Barbey/MP.   798 Bahrain. Robert Azzi/WC.   802 Pictorial Parade, Inc.   803 Kalari/Sygma.   804 *(top)* Minosa-Scorpio/Sygma.   *(bottom)* Harry Redl/BS.   806 Tor Eigeland/BS.   809 Jewish refugees, survivors of Bergen-Belsen concentration camp, leaving for Palestine under HIAS auspices. Coll: Hebrew Immigrant Aid Society.   812 Owen/BS.   816 Loren McIntyre.   819 Mural by Diego Rivera, El Palacio Nacional, Mexico City. Photo: Harvey Lloyd/PA.   821 UPI/BA.   822 *(top left)* Alain Keler/Sygma. *(top right)* Jim Pickerell.   *(middle)* Mar del Plata, Argentina.

Jacques Jangoux/PA.   *(bottom)* Palmares, Costa Rica. CI.   827 Bob Fitch/BS.   831 MP.   832 Toshi Matsumoto/Sygma.   835 St. Lambert Lock, St. Lawrence Seaway, Montreal. CI.   836 J. P. Laffont/Sygma.   840 NASA.   843 Viking I Lander, landed on Mars 7/20/76. NASA.   844 *(top)* Peter Dreyer/Global Focus.   *(bottom)* Will McIntyre/PR.   845 *(top)* Frank Fisher/AI.   *(middle)* Frank Fisher/AI.   *(bottom)* Ronda Bishop/AI.   846 NASA.   847 Paul Fusco.   848 D. & J. Heaton/AI.   849 *(top left)* © Ezra Stoller/ESTO.   *(top right)* Richard Weiss/PA.   *(bottom left)* CI.   *(bottom right)* Loren McIntyre.   850 Ernesto Bazan/MP.   851 *(left)* Al Mozell/MMA.   *(right)* Angelo Giampicallo/BS.

856 Map of the world (detail), by Pieter van der Keere, 1607 (pirated from Peter Plancius's map of 1594). GC.